The World Trade Organization: Legal, Economic and Political Analysis

Volume II

The World Trade Organization: Legal, Economic and Political Analysis

Volume II

The World Trade Organization: Legal, Economic and Political Analysis

Volume II

Editors

Patrick F. J. Macrory

Director, International Trade Law Center, International Law Institute, Washington, D.C.

Arthur E. Appleton

Counsel, White & Case (Geneva)

Michael G. Plummer

Professor of International Economics, Johns Hopkins University, SAIS-Bologna

 Springer

Library of Congress Cataloging-in-Publication Data

The World Trade Organization : legal, economic and political analysis / editors Patrick
  F.J. Macrory, Arthur E. Appleton, Michael G. Plummer.
       p. cm.
   Includes bibliographical references and index.
   ISBN-10: 0-387-22685-0 (alk. paper)   e-ISBN-10: 0-387-22688-5
   ISBN-13: 0-978-0387-22685-9   e-ISBN-13: 0-978-22688-0
     1. World Trade Organization. 2. Foreign trade regulation. 3. Labor laws and legislation,
International. 4. International trade. I. Macrory, Patrick F. J. II. Appleton, Arthur
Edmond. III. Plummer, Michael G., 1959-

   HF1385.C654 2005
   382'.92—dc22   2004052576

Printed in the United States of America.

9 8 7 6 5 4 3 2

springer.com

CONTENTS

TABLE OF CASES

WTO Decisions

GATT Panel and Working Party Reports

Part III Economic, Political, and Regional Issues

A.   Economic Perspectives

CHAPTER 37

ECONOMIC PRINCIPLES OF INTERNATIONAL TRADE

Mordechai E. Kreinin* and Michael G. Plummer**

TABLE OF CONTENTS

* Michigan State University.
** Johns Hopkins University SAIS-Bologna.

I. Introduction

International trade theory has come a long way since the days of the classical economists. However, the intuition that can be gained from the great theorists such as Adam Smith and David Ricardo still dominates the thinking of modern economists. In particular, Ricardo demonstrated that free trade was a "first-best" policy solution.[1] This holds true today, even though the formal analysis of international trade theory has changed substantially. In fact, many of the opponents of international trade today (from the "anti-globalists" on the left of the political spectrum to the economic nationalists on its right) present arguments that Ricardo himself was able to dismiss over a hundred years ago. While the names and the subjects have changed, the basic principles have not.

This chapter, written for a general audience, serves as a primer to the basic theory of international trade. Its goal is to endow the reader with a sufficient background to understand the underlying framework of the subsequent economics chapters in this book, including basic definitions, conceptual approaches, and analytical results of empirical applications. We start with a review of the modern theory of international trade, beginning with the factor-proportions—or "neoclassical"—theory, which continues to serve as the basic building bloc of most other models, both theoretical and empirical. We also review extensions of the model and alternative approaches, such as the sector-specific model, the "human skills" paradigm, the product life-cycle hypothesis, and models that include different specifications of market structure, such as monopolistic competition. Next, given the importance of regionalism in the international marketplace, and its key role in many of the chapters of this volume, we offer an overview of the theory of preferential trading arrangements, focusing on the economic effects of regionalism. Finally, we use a series of empirical approaches to shed light on which existing and proposed regional trade blocs meet important economic criteria. This empirical exercise also gives the reader an idea of the most common approaches to empirical modelling in international trade, something that will be developed much further in the subsequent economics chapters.

II. Modern International Trade Theory

International trade is often cited as a key engine of growth in the international economy. Indeed, in the post-war period, international trade has grown considerably more rapidly than global output, leading to a significant internationalization of the global economy. In the United States, for example, the share of trade in GDP has doubled over the past two decades. This section considers several theoretical approaches to what underlies international trade flows and their direction.

A. Neoclassical Trade Theory: The Factor Proportions Model[2]

Attempts to explain the reason for, and the direction of, international trade, dates back to the "father of modern economics," Adam Smith. In his book *The Wealth of Nations* he shows that each of two countries would export to the other country the commodity

---

[1] Economists frequently distinguish between "first-best policies," which unambiguously lead to greater efficiency, and "second-best policies," which may or may not, as they inevitably involve some sort of trade-off.

[2] This section borrows from Mordechai E Kreinin, INTERNATIONAL ECONOMICS: A POLICY APPROACH (2002).

that is more efficiently produced in it. That became known as the principle of "absolute advantage." Years later, David Ricardo considered a more general case: what if one country is more efficient (produces at lower cost) than the other in the production of both goods? Mutually beneficial trade can still exist as long as the *degree of advantage* is not the same in both industries. Thus, if Country I has a 3 to 1 advantage over Country II in producing commodity A, and only a 2 to 1 advantage in producing commodity B, Country I would export A to B and Country II would export B to A. The case where one country has a cost advantage over another in producing many commodities is common. What matters is the *degree* of advantage, otherwise known as *comparative* advantage. Each country exports the commodity in which it possesses a comparative advantage (highest degree of advantage) and imports the commodity in which it has a comparative disadvantage (lowest degree of advantage). Through this process, the world could be made better off through a more efficient division of labor.

But what is it that confers upon Country I a comparative advantage in good A, and Country II a comparative advantage in good B? The theory that reigned supreme for many years in answering this question is called "The Factor Proportion Theory." It marries the factor *intensity* of commodities with the factor *endowments* of countries. For the purpose of explanation we assume two countries, the United States and the United Kingdom, producing two commodities, wheat and textiles, with the use of two productive factors, capital and labor.

Each producer of a commodity has a range of available production methods from which one is selected. The basic economic feature that distinguishes various production techniques is the labor/capital ratio. The producer adjusts the factor use ratio to the ratio of factor prices (wages for labor; rent for capital) in the marketplace. The more expensive is labor relative to capital, the less labor and the more capital the producer would use. Each commodity is assumed to be produced under identical production conditions in the two countries, in the sense that *if faced with the same factor prices, producers in both countries would use the two factors in the same ratio.*

On the other hand, the production processes required differ from one commodity to the other within each country in a definite, unique, and consistent manner: For any given pair of factor prices, the production of wheat utilizes a higher capital/labor ratio than the production of textiles. This is expressed by saying that wheat is capital-intensive relative to textiles or, equivalently, that textiles are labor-intensive relative to wheat. The extension of this relationship to a world of more than two commodities involves the *ranking* of all goods by their capital/labor ratio.

How are countries distinguished from one another? They differ in their resource endowment: If the United States possesses a higher capital-to-labor ratio than the United Kingdom, we say that the United States is the relatively capital-abundant country, while the United Kingdom is the relatively labor-abundant country.

If we assume that demand conditions are similar in the two nations, then relative factor prices are determined by their supply as reflected in the resource endowment. Thus, capital becomes relatively cheaper (rent is relatively lower) in the United States and labor relatively cheaper (wages are relatively lower) in the United Kingdom. More precisely, the wage-rental ratio is higher in the United States than in the United Kingdom. Combine this result with the earlier postulates concerning manufacturing in the two countries and the following conclusions emerge: The United States specializes in the production of wheat, the commodity that uses much of its relatively cheap factor (capital)—it exports wheat and imports textiles; the United Kingdom specializes in textiles, the commodity that uses much of its relatively cheap factor (labor)—it exports textiles and imports wheat. Wheat is relatively cheaper in the United States because it is capital intensive, while textiles are relatively cheaper in the United Kingdom because they are labor intensive.

In sum, each country exports the commodities that are relatively intensive in the factor with which it is relatively well endowed. That is how it acquires a comparative advantage in these commodities.

Although extremely simple, this model has considerable explanatory power. One of its implications is that each country exports the "factor services" of its abundant factor, as embodied in the bundle of its export goods, and imports the "factor services" of its abundant factor, as embodied in the bundle of its import goods. (Commodity trade and factor movements, therefore, are substitutes, as a country can either export its factor services or its factors.[3]) Thus, trade raises the demand for, and the price of the abundant factor, and lowers the demand for, and the price of, the scarce factor. The effect of trade on the country's income distribution is at the heart of the controversy over free trade versus protectionism in many countries: The scarce factor lobbies for protectionism, to minimize its losses. Likewise, factors employed in the export industries gain from trade, and those employed in import-competing industries lose. Even though the gains exceed the losses, so that the country as a whole gains from trade, demands for protectionism are often heeded, as is evident, for example, from the 2002 steel case in the United States. It has also important implications for income distribution: through free trade, labor would gain in labor-abundant countries (improving income distribution and lowering poverty rates) and lose in capital-abundant countries (exacerbating income distribution).

B. Alternative Theories

Despite its considerable explanatory power, the factor proportions theory cannot explain all of international trade. In particular this theory cannot adequately explain the vast expansion of trade among the industrial countries whose factor endowment ratios are rather similar. Much of this exchange is intra-industry trade, namely, trade in similar products that are differentiated (or distinguished) from each other by some feature(s); for example, the exchange between the United States and Europe of Boeing for Airbus aircraft. Consequently several alternative explanations emerged in the 1970s and 1980s. A few of them are reviewed below.

First, the sector-specific model is a widely used variant of the factor proportion theory.[4] It assumes a two-sector economy, with agriculture using land and labor, and manufacturing employing capital and labor. Only labor is mobile between the two sectors. Suppose a country is land-abundant so that it has a comparative advantage in agriculture. When free trade is introduced to an otherwise isolated economy, the domestic price of farm products rises. Labor is drawn from manufacturing to agriculture, so that more labor is combined with (specific factor) land, while less labor is combined with capital. The value of the marginal product of land rises and that of capital declines: Owners of land gain and capital-owners lose, whereas the effect on the mobile factor (labor) is ambiguous. These redistributional effects of trade are highlighted by this model. In

---

[3] This result has critical real-world policy implications. For example, during the NAFTA debate in the United States, groups concerned with immigration issues were supportive of NAFTA, as they (in this model, correctly) concluded that either Mexico would send its labor to the United States, leading to potential social problems, or the services of this labor embodied in exports.

[4] *See, e.g.,* R.W. Jones, *A Three-Factor Model in Theory, Trade, and History,* in TRADE, BALANCE OF PAYMENTS, AND GROWTH, ESSAYS IN HONOR OF C. KINDLEBERGER (J. Bhagwati et all eds. 1971).

fact, much of the debate over trade policy is an argument between the losers and the gainers.

Second, there is the "human skills" model. In industrial economies, the training and sophistication of the labor force is the most important characteristic distinguishing one country from another. Therefore, countries that are relatively well endowed with professional personnel and highly-trained labor will specialize in and export skill-intensive goods. Conversely, relative abundance of unskilled labor promotes the export of commodities embodying mostly untrained labor. An extension of this hypothesis can be used to explain comparative advantage in high-technology products. Because they are produced by knowledge-intensive industries, these products are developed in countries endowed with a high proportion of research scientists and engineers in the labor force, and spend considerable amounts (relative to their GDP) on research and development.

Third, the "product life-cycle" hypothesis stresses the standardization process of products.[5] Early manufacture of a new good involves experimentation with both the feature of the product and the manufacturing process. Therefore, in its beginning stages, the good is non-standardized. As markets grow and the various techniques become common knowledge, both the product and the process become standardized and perhaps even subject to international standards and specifications. At that time, production can begin in less-sophisticated nations. According to this hypothesis, highly sophisticated economies are expected to export non-standardized goods, while less sophisticated countries specialize in more standardized goods.

Finally, there are theories that depart from the assumption of perfectly competitive markets. Monopolistic competition is a market structure in which there are many firms, and entry into the industry is easy and unrestricted, ensuring that economic profits will be competed away to zero in the long run.[6] In these aspects the market structure is similar to perfect competition. But unlike perfect competition, consumers do not view the good produced by the various firms as perfect substitutes. Rather, the good produced by each firm is differentiated in some way—such as the service associated with it, packaging, or even brand name—from those produced by other firms in the industry. Such firms can operate under increasing returns to scale: If the firm increases all inputs by a given proportion, its output rises by a *greater* proportion. Put differently, the firm's unit production cost declines as output expands.

Expansion of the market has two beneficial effects for consumers: It results in a larger number of firms producing more varieties of the (differentiated) product; and because each firm *produces a larger output, at lower average cost*, each variety would be available at a lower price.

Perhaps a theoretical example would help illustrate this model. Assume that Switzerland is a relatively capital abundant country while France is relatively labor abundant, and that the watch industry is relatively capital intensive while the pen industry is relatively labor intensive. If watches were a homogeneous product (a perfectly competitive industry) then, when trade opens up, Switzerland would export watches to France and import pens.

---

[5] *See, e.g.,* R. Vernon, *International Investment and Trade in the Product Cycle*, 80 QUARTERLY JOURNAL OF ECONOMICS 190 (May 1966); and L. Wells, *A Product Cycle for International Trade?,* JOURNAL OF MARKETING (July 1968). Note that rapid technological diffusion shortens the product cycle.

[6] The notion of economic profits includes the opportunity cost of capital to mere accounting profits. If they are zero, this means that the firm was able to make the same return on its capital in terms of profits as the going rate in the entire economy.

But the watch industry is monopolistically competitive, with each firm manufacturing a different *variety* of watches. Because of economies of scale in producing each variety, neither of the two countries would produce all the varieties. Switzerland will become a net exporter of watches. But there will be consumers in Switzerland who prefer varieties produced by French firms, and those watches will be imported. So there will be an exchange of watches between the two countries, or *intra-industry trade*.

The overall trade pattern that would emerge in these circumstances would have both inter-industry (between industries) and intra-industry components.[7]

(a) Inter-industry trade would reflect comparative advantage. Switzerland would export watches to France and import pens.

(b) In addition there would develop intra-industry trade that has nothing to do with comparative advantage. Because economies of scale in watch-making prevent one country from producing all the varieties, Switzerland and France would export to each other different varieties of watches. The pattern of intra-industry trade is unpredictable.

Switzerland would export only watches (and no pens) under both types of trade, thus becoming a net exporter of watches. France would export pens under inter-industry trade and watches under intra-industry trade. It would be a net exporter of pens and a net importer of watches. The more similar the countries are in their technologies and factor endowments, the less would be their inter-industry and the greater would be their intra-industry trade. Indeed much of the trade among the industrial countries is of the intra-industry variety, while most North-South trade tends to be of the inter-industry variety.

However, intra-industry examples can be found in North-South trade as well. For instance, General Electric has realized that because American consumers prefer refrigerators with two doors, it is not profitable to manufacture single-door refrigerators within the United States. In contrast, the Mexican preference is for single-door refrigerators. Therefore, G.E. supplies the low-volume, double-door segment of the Mexican market from its U.S. plants, and the low-volume, single-door segment of the U.S. market out of Mexico.[8]

Intra-industry trade introduces an additional gain from international trade. Because trade creates a larger market, a country can reduce the number of varieties it produces, thereby lowering production costs of each variety (economies of scale effect), and at the same time increase the number of varieties available to consumers (via imports). There is a gain from lower prices and a gain from a wider choice. This benefit accrues to all, and no redistributional effects occur. It calls for very little economic adjustment to trade. Indeed European economic integration proceeded with minimal internal disruption in the participating countries because it generated mainly intra-industry trade from which all benefit. Likewise the U.S.—Canada Auto Agreement (1965), which set up free trade in automobiles and parts between the two countries, enabled Canada to reduce the number

[7] For discussion, *see* S. Linder, AN ESSAY ON TRADE AND TRANSFORMATION (1962); E. Helpman, *International Trade in the Presence of Product Differentiation, Economies of Scale, and Monopolistic Competition*, 11 JOURNAL OF INTERNATIONAL ECONOMICS 305 (August 1981); and P. Krugman, *New Theories of Trade among Industrial Countries*, 73 AMERICAN ECONOMIC REVIEW 343 (May 1983).

[8] *See* J. Gannon, *NAFTA Creates Jobs for Joe and José*, WALL STREET JOURNAL, editorial page (March 29, 1993).

of models (varieties) it produces and lower per-unit production costs. At the same time, it increased the number of models available to Canadian consumers.

C. Integrated Approaches

The contemporary view treats separately two components of international trade:

(a) Inter-industry trade is the exchange between countries of totally different commodities, such as trading textiles and shoes for aircraft and computers; or the exchange of primary materials for finished manufactures. Much of this trade is between nations of vastly different factor endowments, such as the developing countries and the industrial countries, and can be explained by the factor endowment model, or its extension into skills and technology.

(b) Intra-industry trade refers to a two-way trade in a similar commodity such as the exchange of automotive products between the United States and Canada or among some of the European countries, and the exchange of commercial aircraft between the United States. and Europe. A growing proportion of international trade falls in this category. Much of it is conducted among the industrial countries, whose factor endowments are very similar.

Two features of the producing firms involved in intra-industry trade are important: (a) they tend to be oligopolies[9] or monopolistically competitive, mainly with differentiated products; and (b) economies of scale in production and distribution play an important role in their behavior.

Under these circumstances, factor endowments determine whether a country will be a net exporter or a net importer within broad commodity classes, but the advantages of long production runs lead each country to produce only a limited range of products within each class. The result is that countries with similar capital-labor endowment ratios and skill levels will still have an incentive to specialize in producing different goods within each industry and to engage in trade—hence the emergence of vast intra-industry trade.

The benefits from such trade are not confined to reallocation of resources. They include the rationalization of industries to take advantage of economies of scale, greater competition among large firms (across national boundaries), and a larger product variety available to consumers. The effects on income distribution and on returns to factors, so prominent in comparative advantage models, are vastly outweighed by these benefits. All productive factors gain from trade.

One reason the United States and Europe find it difficult to adjust to increased imports from developing countries, even when accompanied by increased exports to them, is that these imports represent inter-industry rather than intra-industry trade. Resources within the importing country must shift from one industry to another rather than within segments of the same industry. Such adjustment will take place at a higher cost, particularly in the short run.

III. The Theory of Preferential Trading Agreements

There are two common types of preferential trade agreement: Customs Unions ("CU") and Free Trade Areas ("FTAs"). A CU is a group of countries that abolish trade restrictions among themselves and set up common and uniform restrictions against imports from non-members. The European Community, established in 1957 with the Treaty of Rome,

---

[9] A few large firms make up each industry.

and now encompassing fifteen countries (soon to rise to 25), is a prime example. In an FTA, internal trade restrictions are also eliminated, but each country retains its own restrictions against imports from non-members. There is no common external tariff. The North American Free Trade Agreement ("NAFTA") is a case in point. Both CUs and FTAs discriminate against outside countries, and as such they violate the rule of non-discrimination, embodied in Article I of the GATT/WTO and known as the Most Favored Nation ("MFN") rule. But the GATT provides for these two exceptions to the MFN principle in Article XXIV. Indeed, as will be discussed below, preferential agreements have proliferated in recent years, and dozens of them exist on the five continents.

A. Static Effects of Preferential Trading Groups

It is a standard result of international trade theory that free trade in commodities maximizes global efficiency in a distortion-free world. Through trade, countries are able to specialize in the production of commodities in which they have comparative advantage. As noted above, they export these products, and import those in which the country is relatively non-competitive. Hence, trade allows for a more efficient division of labor. Free trade is the "first-best" policy from a global efficiency perspective.

Prior to the seminal 1950 work by Jacob Viner, *The Customs Union Issue*,[10] it was believed that, if a preferential trade grouping ("PTG') did not raise tariff and non-tariff barriers against non-member countries, it would constitute a movement toward free trade because it would involve a net reduction in (intra-regional) barriers. By reducing trade distortions a PTG would increase the gains from trade.

Viner was the first to demonstrate the shortcomings of this reasoning. He argued that if a PTG were to represent a step in the direction of free trade, then by definition it must be the case that post-PTG commodity purchases should be supplied from lower cost sources than was the pre-union case. Such an effect would occur if and when inefficient domestic (say, Mexican) production, previously protected by tariffs, contracts as a result of a more efficient partner country (say, U.S.) production. In Viner's terminology, this is "trade creation" and represents a movement toward free trade. However, some protected commodities that were previously imported from a non-partner country (say, Japan)– the lowest-cost producer–will now be imported from the partner country (the United States), a higher-cost producer, because of the tariff discrimination against non-members. This is "trade diversion", and represents a movement away from free trade since it diverts imports away from the lowest cost source. Hence, we cannot determine *a priori* the efficiency effect of a PTG; it will represent a movement toward free trade only if trade creation exceeds trade diversion.[11]

This economic approach to the effects of a PTG conflicts with popular thinking. To an economist, trade creation is beneficial to a country because it leads to the contraction of inefficient industries, whose resources can be used more effectively elsewhere in the economy. On the other hand, trade diversion leads to greater inefficiency by spurring production in the partner country in areas in which it has *intra-regional* comparative advantage but comparative disadvantage at the *global* level.[12] Yet, to many non-economists, contraction of domestic production (trade creation) is considered welfare-reducing, for

---

[10] JACOB VINER, THE CUSTOMS UNION ISSUE (1950).

[11] By introducing the distinction between trade creation and trade diversion, Viner established the foundations upon which the General Theory of Second Best would be built, a widely-used concept in microeconomics.

[12] Of course, it is possible for the partner country to have intra-regional and global comparative advantage in a certain product. But if this is the case, the home country would have been importing the product from that country before the union as well, meaning that there would be no trade diversion.

it means a loss of jobs. Trade diversion is viewed positively, as it suggests a gain to the union at the expense of non-partners. These sentiments were expressed forcefully during the NAFTA debate in the United States, in which the emphasis was on job loss to Mexico and on trying to keep the Japanese and the Europeans out of the North American market.

How can these views be reconciled? To the extent that they can be, reconciliation has to relate to basic assumptions. The Viner model and subsequent elaborations of it implicitly or explicitly assume that (*inter alia*): (1) markets are competitive; (2) there is full employment of economic resources at all times; (3) tariff revenues are redistributed to consumers; and (4) there are no externalities in production or consumption. If we lift these assumptions, we could obtain different results. For example, if there exists unemployed labor, then the contraction of domestic industry through the trade creation effect would lead to more unemployment and, hence, reduce welfare; trade diversion may be beneficial by putting resources back to work.

B. Dynamic Effects of Preferential Trading Groups

There have been a number of critiques of and extensions on the Viner paradigm,[13] but the essential intuition behind trade creation and trade diversion resulting from changes in relative prices remains intact. However, these static economic effects of PTGs generally refer to one-time changes in the allocation of resources (allocative efficiency). On the other hand, the "dynamic effects" of PTGs are long-term effects that can conceivably be more important than the static effects. We define (liberally) four possible areas as "dynamic" in nature: economies of scale, X-efficiency improvements, changes in investment flows, and the potential for industrial expansion in a developing-country context.

Economies of Scale. The advantages derived from access to an expanded market have always been an attraction for countries to form PTGs. A main benefit is the possibility of reaping economies of scale in production. The argument is straightforward: In industries where production technology is characterized by decreasing costs, the domestic market alone may be too small to permit production at an optimal level. If there are high tariff walls on these goods in foreign countries, international trade might be of little or no help in allowing these firms to expand output toward the optimum. With the formation of a PTG and the subsequent intra-union free trade, the expanded market could present the domestic decreasing- cost firms with adequate demand to produce at the optimum, a point which is particularly relevant for developing countries where local markets are small.[14] Economies of scale are thus a possible argument in favor of PTGs.[15]

[13] See, for example: James Meade, THE THEORY OF CUSTOMS UNIONS (1955); F. Gehrels, *Customs Unions from a Single Country Viewpoint*, 24 REVIEW OF ECONOMIC STUDIES 61 (1956–57); R. Lipsey, *The Theory of Customs Unions: A General Survey*, 70 THE ECONOMIC JOURNAL 496 (1960); M. Michaely, *On Customs Unions and the Gains from Trade*, 74 ECONOMIC JOURNAL 577 (Sept. 1965); R. Cooper and Massell, *A New Look at Customs Union Theory*, 75 ECONOMIC JOURNAL 742 (December 1965); Wonnacott and Wonnacott, *Is Unilateral Tariff Reduction Preferable to a Customs Union?*, 71 AMERICAN ECONOMIC REVIEW 704 (Sept. 1981); Kemp and Wan, *An Elementary Proposition Concerning the Formation of Customs Unions*, 6(1) JOURNAL OF INTERNATIONAL ECONOMICS 95 (February 1976).

[14] For a more detailed discussion of the microeconomic foundations of the economies-of-scale argument, see F.M. Scherer, INDUSTRIAL MARKET STRUCTURE AND ECONOMIC PERFORMANCE, Ch. 4 (1980).

[15] See W. Cordon, *Economies of Scale and Customs Union Theory*, 73 JOURNAL OF POLITICAL ECONOMY, 465–475 (June 1972) for a theoretical exposition of the effects of regional economic integration on economies of scale.

X-Efficiency. The term X-efficiency relates to the optimal organization of the productive process, e.g., work methods, incentive programs, plant layout, management, and psychological environment at the workplace. These can be separated into three categories: (1) intra-plant motivational efficiency, (2) external motivational efficiency, and (3) non-market input efficiency. Leibenstein[16] shows empirically that the counterpart to X-efficiency, X-inefficiency, is a far more significant cause of failure to achieve the social optimum in production than is allocative inefficiency (e.g., due to monopolistic practices).

It is therefore important for our purposes to include the X-efficiency factor in searching for the economic viability of PTGs. If inefficient practices in the workplace of a protected industry are replaced by efficient methods due to competition from the partner country, a PTG will improve productivity. This is called "forced efficiency"[17] and represents an improvement in welfare. In addition, there may be other benefits, such as improved technology and method sharing, new ideas to stimulate the psychological atmosphere at the workplace, and increased standardization of quality and specification requirements allowing for longer production runs. When a PTG is formed of economic partners at diverse levels of economic development, the less-developed members would stand to gain more from benefits inherent in X-efficiency spillovers.

Investment Effects. A PTG may have several effects on the direction of investment flows. First, after a PTG is formed, domestic capital previously invested in partner countries in order to circumvent tariffs can now flow to where the return to capital is highest. This results in a more efficient allocation of investment funds. In addition, the formation of a PTG reduces the risk and uncertainty of investing in partner countries, as there is no longer risk of changes in foreign commercial policy, and the PTG itself may have investment provisions.

However, there may also be an efficiency reduction associated with investment changes induced by PTG formation. Investment funds that would be more efficiently invested in non-partner countries may be diverted to partner countries in the PTG. This investment diversion is caused by the "non-economic" attraction of investment funds to the FTA in order to evade its discriminatory tariff wall.[18] For example, suppose Kia Motors wished to build an automobile assembly plant off-shore for export to the U.S. market. Further, assume that it deems Indonesia to be the most efficient location. With the creation of NAFTA, Kia could decide to build the plant in Mexico instead.[19] Thus, while this *investment-diversion* effect reduces global efficiency, it constitutes an increased investment flow to North America.[20]

PTGs and Economic Development. In addition to the dynamic factors mentioned above, PTGs can be used as part of an economic development strategy. In developing

---

[16] H. Leibenstein, *Allocative Efficiency vs. X-Efficiency*, 56 AMERICAN ECONOMIC REVIEW 392 (1966)

[17] This term is from R. Lipsey, *The Theory of Customs Unions: A General Survey*, in INTERNATIONAL TRADE: SELECTED READINGS 281 (J. Bhagwati ed. 1981).

[18] Mordechai Kreinin, *On the Dynamic Effects of a Customs Union*, 72 JOURNAL OF POLITICAL ECONOMY 193 (1964)

[19] In making this decision, Kia would have to take into account the extremely-high domestic content requirements of NAFTA, which in automobiles comes to 62.5 percent of value added. Hence, NAFTA creates an additional incentive for Kia to move its operations to Mexico in lieu of Indonesia, thereby increasing the *investment diversion* effect.

[20] In considering investment diversion at the firm level, we need to point out the underlying assumptions that: (1) financing constraints exist; and (2) the investing company only requires one plant. Otherwise, there would be no investment diversion, only investment creation. In the example above, Kia motors would build plants both in Mexico *and* Indonesia.

countries, the nurturing of the industrial base is often considered of paramount importance for a number of reasons, such as self-sufficiency aspirations, work-force and social externalities, and political clout of industrialists. In other words, industrial production "appears as a collective consumption good yielding a flow of satisfaction to the electorate independent of the satisfaction they derive directly from the consumption of industrial products"[21]. Therefore, if the country wishes to protect and expand its domestic industrial production, and forming a PTG is the least expensive way of achieving this goal (because a large market is needed to attain lower-cost production), it follows that PTGs are indeed economically rational.

With the formation of a customs union, the developing country in question experiences a growth in market size for its industrial products. If it specializes in the industry in which it has intra-union comparative advantage and the other country does likewise, then the same level of industrial production can be sustained at a lower marginal cost. Or, alternatively, for the same cost of production, the level of industrial production can be greater.

C. New Theories

Many of the new approaches that have emerged in the international trade literature center around locational advantages and the "natural" development of intra-regional trade before an agreement is reached. Empirically, PTGs in the global economy are mostly geographically based, that is, they all tend to include countries comprising the same geographical area. Also, it would appear that, *ceteris paribus*, the closer are countries to each other, the larger the percentage of trade that takes place between them. Hence, two-thirds of EU trade is intra-regional; Canada and the United States are each other's most important trading partners; and Mexico is heavily reliant on trade with the United States. The larger the volume of trade between countries within a regional bloc, the greater the potential for trade creation and the smaller the potential for trade diversion, making the agreement more likely to be efficiency-enhancing rather than efficiency reducing. The exception might be between geographically-close developing countries whose trade tends to be inter-industry rather than intra-industry.

Thus, according to Krugman and others, "natural" economic integration takes place between geographically-close countries due to lower transportation (and related) costs; hence forming a PTG between such countries would be consistent with the market and, therefore, would increase efficiency.[22] As a rule of thumb, it is suggested that a PTG in which intra-regional trade is greater than, or equal to, 50 percent of trade would increase efficiency.

Moreover, Frankel stresses that it is not enough merely to consider values of intra-regional trade.[23] His "natural" economic bloc would be one in which the "bias" for trade within the region has been growing over time. Using the possible formation of a market-determined "natural" economic bloc in Asia, he suggests that the growth of intra-regional trade in Asia in the 1980s reflects mainly an economic growth effect rather than a "natural" increase in trade between countries of the region. Estimating a gravity

[21] H. Johnson, *An Economic Theory of Protectionism, Tariff Bargaining, and the Formation of Customs Unions*, JOURNAL OF POLITICAL ECONOMY 73, 256, 258 (April 1965)
[22] Paul Krugman, *Is Bilateralism Bad?*, in INTERNATIONAL TRADE AND POLICY (Helpman and Krugman eds. 1991)
[23] Jeffrey A. Frankel, *Is Japan Creating a Yen Block in East Asia and the Pacific?*, NBER WORKING PAPER NO. 4050, (April 1992)

model of the region's trade, he shows that the bias in favor of intra-East Asian trade, though positive, has actually been *falling* over the 1980s if one corrects for the growth bias.

However, these approaches to the "natural" determinants of a trade bloc have several shortcomings. First, few economic blocs meet the 50 percent criterion. While intra-regional trade in the EU exceeds that mark *today*, this occurs only after 36 years of a wide-reaching PTG. At the formation of the EC, the percentage of intra-regional trade was closer to one-third. Also, as will be noted in the next section, intra-regional flows as a percentage of total trade in NAFTA prior to the agreement itself fell short of 50 percent. It is about one-fourth in the case of ASEAN. Does this mean that all these blocs should be considered *a priori* "un-natural"? Moreover, such an approach says nothing about the degree of distortion involved in the other 50 percent of trade. If discrimination against the extra-regional 50 percent is high, can the group still be considered "natural"? If a PTG has only one-third intra-regional trade but its extra-regional trade is such that there would be little diverted trade, is this necessarily an "un-natural" bloc?

Kreinin and Plummer suggest that a "natural" economic bloc might be alternatively defined as a bloc which preserves a country's structure of trade, that is, its rankings of industries according to comparative advantage.[24] For example, if one assumes that the existing global trade of a country is a good proxy for what its free trade pattern of comparative advantage would be, a high correlation between the ranking of industries by a country's comparative advantage within a proposed regional bloc and that of its global trade would indicate a "natural" economic bloc. They undertake this exercise for possible trading arrangements in the Asia-Pacific region and conclude that, while ASEAN's intra-regional trade is not highly correlated with constituent countries' global trading patterns, a more general East Asian Economic Bloc and APEC would be.

More of these themes are taken up in Chapter 51 of this book. Suffice it to conclude that the implications of the theory of PTGs (as is the case with all second-best policies) is that it is difficult to know *a priori* if a given grouping will be economically efficient. In fact, it may just be that PTGs are driven by political rather than economic considerations. Moreover, perhaps the most important economic question is whether a PTG is a "building bloc" or a "stumbling bloc" towards global free trade. Chapter 51 offers some interesting insights into this debate in the case of developing countries in Latin America.

IV. Some Empirical Examples

There is an extensive empirical literature that estimates the economic effects of PTGs in the real world. It varies from simple techniques based on direction of trade flows to complicated economy-wide Computational General Equilibrium (CGE) models, such as the one used in Chapter 38 (by Deardorf, Stern and Brown). These models have been surveyed elsewhere.[25] However, it is useful to consider how economically "rational" existing and emerging PTGs seem to be. We do this by expanding upon the theoretical models developed in the "natural economic bloc" ("NEB") literature.

There are a number of ways in which one might define a NEB, as well as determine whether or not one exists. In this section, we employ three oft-used methodologies to

[24] Mordechai E. Kreinin and Michael G. Plummer, *Natural Economic Blocs: An Alternative Formulation*, 8(2) THE INTERNATIONAL TRADE JOURNAL 193 (Summer 1994)

[25] For an extensive survey of these models, see Mordechai E. Krenin and Michael G. Plummer, ECONOMIC INTEGRATION AND DEVELOPMENT: HAS REGIONALISM DELIVERED FOR DEVELOPING COUNTRIES? (2002).

assess the degree to which various grouping meet the NEB criteria. These empirical approaches include: trade share analysis, double-density calculations, and an econometric gravity model.

It might be useful to note that this type of analysis has not only been used to ascertain whether or not an NEB exists on the real side of the economy (i.e., with respect to trade), but also to what degree monetary union makes sense for a group of countries. Many empirical studies focusing on the economics of monetary union in Europe, dollarization in Latin America and Asia, and so on, use various indicators of economic integration as one means of determining the potential benefits from monetary integration. The basic intuition is that the more integrated the economies are on the real side, the more they have to gain through price stability brought about by monetary union and the less they have to lose by giving up an independent monetary policy. Hence, what is good for real integration is also good for monetary integration. In fact, this has led the European Commission to conclude that, even though it is not clear that the criteria for an "optimal" currency area are met in Europe, the process of integration that will be set in motion through a common currency will ensure that these criteria will eventually be satisfied.

A. Trade-Share Analysis

The simplest approach to evaluating whether or not NEB conditions exist involves measuring shares of trade with partner countries as a percentage of total trade. A 50 percent trade share will be used as a rule of thumb for meeting the criteria by any trade grouping (as discussed above).

Table 1 shows intra- and extra regional trade shares (imports and exports) for several important groupings (APEC, EU-15, NAFTA, ASEAN, the Central European Free Trade Area, MERCOSUR, and the ANDEAN Pact) for three years: 1990, 1995, and 2000. Several important conclusions emerge: First, both APEC and the EU-15 meet the 50 percent rule, with intra-regional trade shares accounting for about three-fourths and two-thirds of total trade, respectively. Second, intra-NAFTA exports as a percentage of the total have risen from 43 percent in 1990 (i.e., prior to the formal free trade area, though the Canada-US Free Trade Area had just begun) to 56 percent of total trade in 2000. Third, intra-ASEAN trade has increased from about one-fifth of total trade in 1990 (i.e., prior to the ASEAN Free trade Area) to about one-fourth of total trade in 2000. Finally, intra-regional trade in the other regional groupings formed in emerging and developing markets constitute but a small percentage of total trade.

Thus, according to the NEB rule-of-thumb, out of these groupings only APEC, the EU-15 and possibly NAFTA would be considered NEBs. Of course, it is important to underscore that the 21 countries forming APEC account for a large percent of global GDP and total world trade. And the EU-15 is not only a large group of developed countries, but intra-regional trade shares reflect over four decades of discrimination against outsiders. Clearly, size matters in trade-share analysis and may confuse the definition of what is "natural". This is why normalization according to size might be justified in identifying NEBs; this is done by the double-density technique.

B. "Double-Density" Measures of Trade Intensities

As noted by Petri, increases in intra-regional trade signify an increase in inter-dependence but do not offer a strong indication of the "bias" toward regionalization, as it may reflect levels and changes in other variables, such as economic size (as noted above) and trends

Table 1: Merchandise trade of selected regional integration arrangements, 2000
(Billion dollars and percentage)

		Value	Share in total exports/imports			Annual percentage change		
		2000	1990	1995	2000	1990–00	1999	2000
APEC (21)								
Total exports		2931	100.0	100.0	100.0	8	7	18
	Intra exports	2127	67.5	73.1	72.6	9	9	20
Total imports[a]		3171	100.0	100.0	100.0	8	10	21
	Intra-imports	2159	65.4	71.7	68.1	9	11	15
EU (15)								
Total exports		2251	100.0	100.0	100.0	4	0	2
	Intra exports	1392	64.9	63.1	61.8	4	1	0
Total imports[b]		2362	100.0	100.0	100.0	4	2	5
	Intra-imports	1396	63.0	63.8	59.1	4	1	0
NAFTA (3)								
Total exports		1224	100.0	100.0	100.0	8	6	14
	Intra exports	686	42.6	46.1	56.0	11	12	18
Total imports		1672	100.0	100.0	100.0	10	11	18
	Intra-imports	674	34.4	37.7	40.3	11	12	18
ASEAN (10)								
Total exports		427	100.0	100.0	100.0	11	9	19
	Intra exports	101	20.1	25.5	23.7	13	10	28
Total imports		367	100.0	100.0	100.0	8	8	23
	Intra-imports	90	16.2	18.9	24.5	13	9	31
CEFTA (6)								
Total exports		117	—	100.0	100.0	—	1	12
	Intra exports	13	—	14.6	11.5	—	−7	9
Total imports		149	—	100.0	100.0	—	−2	12
	Intra-imports	14	—	11.3	9.5	—	−4	12
MERCOSUR (4)								
Total exports		85	100.0	100.0	100.0	6	−9	14
	Intra exports	18	8.9	20.5	20.9	16	−26	17
Total imports		89	100.0	100.0	100.0	12	−16	8
	Intra-imports	18	14.5	18.1	20.1	16	−25	14
ANDEAN (5)								
Total exports		58	100.0	100.0	100.0	6	11	33
	Intra exports	5	4.3	12.2	8.8	14	−28	32
Total imports[c]		40	100.0	100.0	100.0	8	−20	11
	Intra-imports	6	7.7	12.9	13.9	15	−20	32

[a]Imports of Canada, Mexico, Peru and Australia are valued f.o.b.
[b]Imports of Canada and Mexico are valued at f.o.b.
[c]Imports of Peru and Venezuela are valued at f.o.b.
Note: The figures are not fully adjusted for differences in the way members of the arrangements in this table record their merchandise trade.
Source: WTO, International Trade Statistics 2001, B30 Table 1.9.

in income growth.[26] For example, the increase in intra-APEC exports from 68 percent of total trade in 1990 to 73 percent in 2000 may be just a reflection of faster economic growth

[26] Peter A. Petri, *East Asian Trade Integration: An Analytical History,* in REGIONALISM AND RIVALRY: JAPAN AND THE UNITED STATES IN PACIFIC ASIA, CHAPTER ONE (1993).

in APEC than in the rest of the world. Thus the increase in trade shares was induced by income-growth rather than a "natural" tendency to trade. To control for this effect, a "double-density" measure can be used, which normalizes bilateral or intra-regional trade shares by the importance of the country or region in total trade. An example might best illustrate the approach. The share of ASEAN in Singapore's total exports in 2000 came to 30 percent. However, ASEAN imports as a percentage of total world imports was only 5.5 percent in 2000. Hence, normalizing the share of ASEAN in Singapore's exports (0.3) by the importance of ASEAN as a recipient of global imports (0.055) gives us a "double-density" value of 5.5; in other words, Singapore exports 5.5 times as much to ASEAN as one would expect if ASEAN were a random group of countries. Therefore, an alternative definition of a NEB is one in which the double-density measure is greater than 1.

Table 2a-d presents double-density coefficients for four existing trade groups included in Table 1: The EU-15, NAFTA, ASEAN, and MERCUSOR. The results are quite different from those in Table 1. The EU-15 countries do, indeed, have double-density ratios greater than 1 in all cases; however, they are infrequently greater than 2 and, then, only for a few small countries (in particular, Portugal, Belgium, the Netherlands, and Spain). On the other hand, ASEAN and MERCUSOR have much higher ratios than the EU-15. In ASEAN, the double-density ratios ranged from 2.6 (the Philippines) to 5.5 (Singapore) in 2000; moreover, the ratios increased everywhere over the past decade except in Malaysia and Singapore where they were already very high. The double-density ratios are even higher for MERCUSOR, amounting to 11 and 24 for Brazil and Argentina, respectively, and 33 and 49 for the smaller countries of Uruguay and Paraguay, respectively. All have been increasing with the exception of Uruguay. For NAFTA, the double-density ratios are also high, higher than those for ASEAN or the EU countries, with the exception of Canada-Mexico trade, where the double-density measures are less than one. Hence, within NAFTA, an NEB exists (according to this criterion) for Mexico and Canada each *vis-a-vis* the United States, as well as between United States and these two trading partners. NAFTA could have just as well been two bilateral agreements between the United States and Canada and between the U.S. and Mexico, because free trade between Canada and Mexico doesn't make much sense according to this definition.

C. Econometric Gravity Approach

Our final empirical exercise is the estimation of an econometric model of bilateral trade flows that attempts to capture a trade-bias coefficient. In particular, gravity models have been popular in the empirical international trade literature, as they generate strong and robust results and are able to address a number of important questions. However, they have been criticized for having a questionable theoretical basis, although it is possible to generate a gravity-model specification from a standard factor-proportions model.[27]

In short, gravity models attempt to explain bilateral import demand (X_{ij}) by a variety of explanatory variables, such as, income of the importing country (Y_i), income of the exporting country (Y_j), population of the importing and exporting countries (N_i and N_j, respectively), and a variable that accounts for the distance between the importing and exporting countries (D_{ij}). Expressed in logarithmic form, a typical gravity model of

---

[27] Jeffrey Frankel, REGIONAL TRADE GROUPINGS (1998).

Table 2a: EU—Double density measures of trade intensity*
(Billion dollars and percentage)

		Total exports	Exports to EU	EU exports/ Tot. country exports (1)	EU tot. imports/World imports (2)	Double density measure EU (1/2)
Austria	1990	41,265	28,018	67.9	44.0	1.5
	1995	57,533	37,929	65.9	39.0	1.7
	1998	62,584	38,754	61.9	39.0	1.6
	1999	64,292	41,625	64.7	38.2	1.7
	2000	63,903	39,428	61.7	35.4	1.7
Belgium-	1990	117,703	92,284	78.4	44.0	1.8
Luxembourg	1995	171,001	120,809	70.6	39.0	1.8
	1998	178,811	142,985	80.0	39.0	2.1
	1999	179,320	138,806	77.4	38.2	2.0
	2000	186,148	138,229	74.3	35.4	2.1
Denmark	1990	36,870	23,317	63.2	44.0	1.4
	1995	50,594	30,773	60.8	39.0	1.6
	1998	48,173	31,715	65.8	39.0	1.7
	1999	49,705	32,520	65.4	38.2	1.7
	2000	49,631	32,647	65.8	35.4	1.9
Finland	1990	26,571	16,611	62.5	44.0	1.4
	1995	40,310	22,247	55.2	39.0	1.4
	1998	43,145	22,310	51.7	39.0	1.3
	1999	41,867	24,111	57.6	38.2	1.5
	2000	45,635	25,464	55.8	35.4	1.6
France	1990	216,588	137,039	63.3	44.0	1.4
	1995	286,795	180,067	62.8	39.0	1.6
	1998	306,052	189,468	61.9	39.0	1.6
	1999	302,443	196,833	65.1	38.2	1.7
	2000	298,127	186,329	62.5	35.4	1.8
Germany	1990	421,100	256,132	60.8	44.0	1.4
	1995	523,007	290,323	55.5	39.0	1.4
	1998	542,812	304,792	56.2	39.0	1.4
	1999	544,076	304,881	56.0	38.2	1.5
	2000	551,505	309,878	56.2	35.4	1.6
Greece	1990	8,105	5,493	67.8	44.0	1.5
	1995	10,945	6,698	61.2	39.0	1.6
	1998	10,868	5,729	52.7	39.0	1.4
	1999	10,150	4,806	47.3	38.2	1.2
	2000	10,229	5,115	50.0	35.4	1.4
Ireland	1990	23,743	18,539	78.1	44.0	1.8
	1995	44,610	31,514	70.6	39.0	1.8
	1998	64,284	43,938	68.3	39.0	1.8
	1999	71,258	45,208	63.4	38.2	1.7
	2000	79,868	49,279	61.7	35.4	1.7
Italy	1990	170,304	107,154	62.9	44.0	1.4
	1995	234,003	134,280	101.9	39.0	2.6
	1998	245,469	130,262	53.1	39.0	1.4
	1999	235,806	131,986	56.0	38.2	1.5
	2000	237,750	130,525	54.9	35.4	1.6

(*Continued*)

Table 2a: (*Continued*)

		Total exports	Exports to EU	EU exports/ Tot. country exports (1)	EU tot. imports/World imports (2)	Double density measure EU (1/2)
Netherlands	1990	131,775	105,557	80.1	44.0	1.8
	1995	196,902	137,362	69.8	39.0	1.8
	1998	200,769	129,073	64.3	39.0	1.6
	1999	201,197	169,251	84.1	38.2	2.2
	2000	212,507	164,329	77.3	35.4	2.2
Portugal	1990	16,417	13,246	80.7	44.0	1.8
	1995	22,596	18,728	82.9	39.0	2.1
	1998	24,770	19,709	79.6	39.0	2.0
	1999	24,564	19,176	78.1	38.2	2.0
	2000	23,323	18,537	79.5	35.4	2.2
Spain	1990	55,642	39,789	71.5	44.0	1.6
	1995	91,613	66,216	72.3	39.0	1.9
	1998	109,037	76,050	69.7	39.0	1.8
	1999	110,246	74,571	67.6	38.2	1.8
	2000	113,747	80,305	70.6	35.4	2.0
Sweden	1990	57,540	35,495	61.7	44.0	1.4
	1995	79,584	45,273	56.9	39.0	1.5
	1998	84,944	46,799	55.1	39.0	1.4
	1999	84,842	47,650	56.2	38.2	1.5
	2000	86,933	46,596	53.6	35.4	1.5
UK	1990	185,172	106,455	57.5	44.0	1.3
	1995	242,008	129,095	53.3	39.0	1.4
	1998	272,879	142,012	52.0	39.0	1.3
	1999	269,139	140,402	52.2	38.2	1.4
	2000	284,090	162,499	57.2	35.4	1.6

Note: The trade intensity measure (Iij) is defined for country i's exports to country j as the share of i' exports going to j (Xij/Xi) relative to the share of j's imports (Mj) in world imports (Mw). That is (Iij) = (Xij/Xi)/(Mj/Mw).
Source: Computed from WTO statistics, *WTO International Trade Statistics 2000*, IMF *Direction of Trade Statistics Yearbook 1995 and 2000,*
The Economist Intelligence Unit *Country Profiles 2001*, Statistics Finland.

bilateral trade takes on the form of:

$$\ln X_{ij} = A + \delta_1 Y_i + \delta_2 \ln Y_j + \delta_3 \ln N_i + \delta_4 \ln N_j + \delta_5 \ln D_{ij} + \ln e_{ij}$$

where i = importing country; j = exporting country; A = intercept; δ_i = coefficients of the explanatory variables; and log e_{ij} = lognormal error term.[28]

Gravity models can be used in several ways and are flexible with respect to model specification. For example, modern gravity equations tend to exclude population variables and include the product of *per capita* income of the trading countries, on the theoretical

---

[28] Standard trade theory would suggest that the coefficients of the explanatory variables would have the following signs: $\hat{\delta}1 > 0$, $\hat{\delta}2 < 0$, $\delta 3 > 0$, $\hat{\delta}4 < 0$, $\hat{\delta}5 < 0$.

Table 2b: NAFTA—Double density measures of trade intensity*

		Double density measure NAFTA	Double density measure US	Double density measure Canada	Double density measure Mexico
United	1990	1.5	—	6.1	5.8
States	1995	1.5	—	6.7	5.4
	1998	1.5	—	6.2	5.0
	1999	1.5	—	6.3	4.9
	2000	1.4	—	6.1	5.1
Canada	1990	3.9	5.1	—	0.3
	1995	4.1	5.4	—	0.3
	1998	3.8	5.1	—	0.2
	1999	3.6	4.8	—	0.2
	2000	3.4	4.5	—	0.2
Mexico	1990	4.1	5.4	0.1	—
	1995	4.4	5.7	0.8	—
	1998	3.9	5.2	0.4	—
	1999	3.7	4.9	0.5	—
	2000	3.5	4.6	0.5	—

Note: The trade intensity measure (I_{ij}) is defined for country i's exports to country j as the share of i' exports going to j (Xij/Xi) relative to the share of j's imports (Mj) in world imports (Mw). That is (Iij) = (Xij/Xi)/(Mj/Mw).

Source: Computed from WTO statistics, *WTO International Trade Statistics 2001*

Table 2c: ASEAN—Double density measures of trade intensity*
(Billion dollars and percentage)

		Total exports	Exports to ASEAN	ASEAN exports/ Tot. country exports (1)	ASEAN tot. imports/ World imports (2)	Double density measure (1/2)
Indonesia	1990	25.68	2.57	10.0	4.6	2.2
	1995	45.42	6.50	14.3	6.8	2.1
	1999	48.67	8.28	17.0	5.1	3.4
	2000	62.12	10.89	17.5	5.5	3.2
Malaysia	1990	29.42	8.62	29.3	4.6	6.4
	1995	73.91	20.41	27.6	6.8	4.1
	1999	84.46	20.13	23.8	5.1	4.7
	2000	98.24	26.07	26.5	5.5	4.8
Philippines	1990	8.07	0.59	7.3	4.6	1.6
	1995	17.50	2.36	13.5	6.8	2.0
	1999	36.50	4.99	13.7	5.1	2.7
	2000	39.78	5.63	14.2	5.5	2.6
Singapore[a]	1990	52.75	13.57	25.7	4.6	5.6
	1995	118.27	38.24	32.3	6.8	4.8
	1999	114.69	32.15	28.0	5.1	5.5
	2000	137.88	41.50	30.1	5.5	5.5
Thailand	1990	23.07	2.75	11.9	4.6	2.6
	1995	56.44	12.33	21.8	6.8	3.2
	1999	58.44	10.86	18.6	5.1	3.7
	2000	69.06	13.42	19.4	5.5	3.5

[a]includes significant re-exports

Note: The trade intensity measure (I_{ij}) is defined for country i's exports to country j as the share of i' exports going to j (X_{ij}/X_i) relative to the share of j's imports (Mj) in world imports (Mw). That is (Iij) = (Xij/Xi)/(Mj/Mw).

Source: Computed from WTO statistics, *WTO International Trade Statistics 2001*

Table 2d: MERCOSUR—Double density measures of trade intensity*
(Billion dollars and percentage)

		Total exports	Exports to MERCOSUR	Mercosur exports/ Tot. country exports (1)	Mercosur tot. imports/ World imports (2)	Double density measure (1/2)
Argentina	1990	12353	1833	14.8	0.8	17.9
	1995	20967	6780	32.3	1.5	21.1
	1999	23333	7071	30.3	1.4	21.7
	2000	26298	8352	31.8	1.3	23.7
Brazil	1990	31414	1320	4.2	0.8	5.1
	1995	46506	6154	13.2	1.5	8.6
	1999	48011	6778	14.1	1.4	10.1
	2000	55086	7762	14.1	1.3	10.5
Paraguay	1990	959	379	39.5	0.8	47.8
	1995	919	528	57.5	1.5	37.5
	1999	741	307	41.4	1.4	29.6
	2000	852	553	64.9	1.3	48.5
Uruguay	1990	1693	595	35.1	0.8	42.5
	1995	2106	995	47.2	1.5	30.8
	1999	2237	1007	45.0	1.4	32.2
	2000	2295	1023	44.6	1.3	33.3

Note: The trade intensity measure (I_{ij}) is defined for country i's exports to country j as the share of i' exports going to j (X_{ij}/X_i) relative to the share of j's imports (Mj) in world imports (Mw). That is (Iij) = (Xij/Xi)/(Mj/Mw).
Source: Computed from WTO statistics, *WTO International Trade Statistics 2001*

ground that wealthy countries tend to trade more with each other because they have common tastes.

A regional binary variable(s) is then added to estimate whether or not formal economic integration has a statistically-significant effect.[29] The larger the coefficient, the greater the tendency to trade within (or with) that region. We do this for two proposed PTGs, APEC and the FTAA, as well as the EU-15. The motivation is to examine regional integration in a "three-bloc" world, which has been postulated as a logical conclusion to the regionalism trend.

Our sample contains 5404 bilateral trade flows each year over the 1980 to 1999 period and we estimated a gravity model for each such flow. In the overwhelming majority of cases, the estimates are robust (with the exception of the *per capita* income variable), and the regression fits are good. The adjusted R^2 (which tells us how much of the variance of the dependent variable—in this case, bilateral trade—is explained by the explanatory variables) is over 0.40 in the past decade, generally on par with other gravity models.

The estimated coefficients on the APEC and EU-15 binary variables are always statistically significant and high, with the APEC variable rising since 1980 (from 1.70 that year to 2.41 in 1999) and approaching the level of the EU-15. On the other hand, the FTAA is not an NEB using this econometric approach: the estimated coefficient on the FTAA variable is never statistically different from zero, suggesting that it does not add anything to the explanation power of the regressions.

---

[29] Frankel, note 27 *supra*.

Table 3: Gravity model estimations of regional trade blocs
(Dependent variable: Trade between country pairs)

	C	GDP Host	GDP Partner	Distance	Adjacency	APEC	FTAA	EU	Adj. R Squared
1980	11.76**	0.81**	0.47*	−1.87**	0.23*	1.70**	0.05	2.52**	0.35
1981	11.25**	0.82**	0.49*	−1.80**	0.24*	1.65*	−0.04	2.36**	0.36
1982	11.07**	0.84**	0.48*	−1.80**	0.38*	1.68**	−0.19	2.52**	0.37
1983	11.20**	0.82**	0.47*	−1.80*	0.29*	1.68**	−0.36	2.52**	0.37
1984	11.15**	0.84**	0.50*	−1.82**	0.25*	1.55**	−0.25	2.57**	0.37
1985	10.72**	0.85**	0.47*	−1.77**	0.30*	1.61**	−0.21	2.61**	0.37
1986	10.68**	0.87**	0.46*	−1.78**	0.22*	1.77**	−0.08	2.68**	0.38
1987	10.46**	0.89**	0.46*	−1.77**	0.30*	1.90**	0.04	2.72**	0.39
1988	10.78**	0.89**	0.46*	−1.79**	0.22*	2.06*	−0.13	2.70**	0.41
1989	11.06**	0.89**	0.45*	−1.81**	0.41*	2.19**	0.00	2.71**	0.43
1990	10.82**	0.90**	0.46*	−1.79**	0.53*	2.21**	−0.02	2.74**	0.43
1991	11.40**	0.90**	0.48*	−1.86**	0.34*	2.09**	−0.05	2.61**	0.43
1992	11.23**	0.91**	0.46*	−1.82**	0.31*	2.10**	0.02	2.58**	0.43
1993	11.15**	0.90**	0.45*	−1.82**	0.28*	2.21**	0.04	2.56**	0.42
1994	11.92**	0.84**	0.42*	−1.88**	0.16	2.38**	0.18	2.61**	0.42
1995	12.26**	0.82**	0.43*	−1.89**	0.10	2.29**	0.04	2.48**	0.42
1996	12.88**	0.95**	0.47*	−2.07**	0.05	2.53**	0.13	2.62**	0.43
1997	12.03**	1.01**	0.59**	−2.04**	0.16	2.37**	0.11	2.45**	0.44
1998	11.60**	0.98**	0.56**	−1.96**	0.12	2.27**	0.33	2.63**	0.43
1999	10.78**	0.94**	0.59**	−1.84**	0.29*	2.41**	0.10	2.68**	0.45

Statistic significance at 95% and 99% denoted by * and **, respectively

All variables are in logarithmic form, save the binary variables

A joint Per Capita Income variable was also esitmated but in no case was it statistically significant and hence is not included in the tables

Sources: Direction of Trade Yearbooks, IMF, and authors' calculations.

V. Conclusions

This chapter has reviewed the principles of international trade theory and some aspects of empirical modeling. International trade has been an active research field and, hence, it was possible to review only a few of the most important theories. In particular, special attention centered on the factor-proportion theory and its extensions. It is hoped that the theoretical review will endow the reader with sufficient background to understand the basic principles of international trade needed to follow the other economics chapters in this book.

Next, the theory of international trade was applied to models dealing with regionalism. Following a review of the theory of regional integration and its relevant empirical approaches an important conclusion emerges: there are no "magic numbers" to suggest whether a preferential trading arrangement is economically beneficial or not. Rather, one is limited to *relative* conclusions, i.e., whether or not a grouping makes sense relative to another grouping, or has a grouping met the efficiency criteria after integration even if it failed to do so prior to formal integration.

CHAPTER 38

COMPUTATIONAL ANALYSIS OF MULTILATERAL TRADE LIBERALIZATION IN THE URUGUAY ROUND AND DOHA DEVELOPMENT ROUND

Drusilla K. Brown*, Alan V. Deardorff**, and Robert M. Stern***

TABLE OF CONTENTS

* Tufts University
** University of Michigan
*** University of Michigan

I. Introduction

In this chapter, we first use the Michigan Model of World Production and Trade to simulate the economic effects of the Uruguay Round of multilateral trade negotiations completed in 1993–94 on the major industrialized and developing countries/regions. We estimate that the Uruguay Round negotiations increased global economic welfare by $73.0 billion. The developed countries overall have an estimated welfare gain of $53.8 billion, and the developing countries an estimated welfare increase of $19.2 billion.

We have also simulated the effects of assumed 33 percent reductions in trade barriers in the ongoing Doha Development Round. There is an estimated increase in global welfare of $574.0 billion. There is a global welfare decline of $3.1 billion from agricultural liberalization due primarily to the assumed reductions in export subsidies. There are global welfare gains of $163.4 billion from reductions in tariffs on manufactures and $413.7 billion from reductions in services barriers. All of the countries/regions covered in the Michigan Model show overall welfare increases, with the largest absolute gains going to the developed countries.

We present an overview of the Michigan Model in Part II of this chapter, and the detailed computational results of the analysis of the trade negotiations in the Uruguay Round and the detailed Doha Development Round in Parts III and IV. Conclusions and implications are discussed in Part V.

II. Overview of the Michigan CGE Model

The Michigan Model is a computable general equilibrium ("CGE") simulation model designed to assess the potential economic effects of trade liberalization. The distinguishing feature of the Michigan Model is that it incorporates some aspects of the New Trade Theory, including increasing returns to scale, monopolistic competition, and product heterogeneity. A complete description of the formal structure and equations of the model can be found on line at www.spp.umich.edu/rsie/model/.

The version of the model that we will use consists of twenty countries/regions (plus rest-of-world) and eighteen production sectors. The country/region and sectoral coverage are indicated in the tables noted below. Agriculture is modeled as perfectly competitive and all other sectors as monopolistically competitive with free entry and exit of firms. The model is implemented using GEMPACK software, as described by Harrison and Pearson[1].

Needless to say, the data needs of the Michigan model are immense. The main data source is "The GTAP-4 Database" of the Purdue University Center for Global Trade Analysis Project.[2] The reference year for this database is 1995. We have extracted the following data, aggregated to our sectors and regions, from this source:

1. Bilateral trade flows among twenty countries/regions, decomposed into eighteen sectors. Trade with the rest-of-world ("ROW") is included to close the model;
2. Input-output tables for the twenty countries/regions, excluding ROW;
3. Components of final demand along with sectoral contributions for the twenty countries/regions, excluding ROW;

[1] W.J. Harrison and Ken Pearson, *Computing Solutions for Large General Equilibrium Models Using GEMPACK,* 9 COMPUTATIONAL ECONOMICS 83 (1996)

[2] Robert McDougall, et al., GLOBAL TRADE: ASSISTANCE AND PROTECTION: GTAP-4 DATABASE (1998).

4. Gross value of output and value added at the sectoral level for the twenty countries/regions, excluding ROW;
5. Bilateral import tariffs by sector among the twenty countries/regions;
6. Elasticity of substitution between varieties in demand;
7. Bilateral export-tariff equivalents among the twenty countries/regions decomposed into 18 sectors.

The monopolistically competitive market structure in the nonagricultural sectors of the model imposes an additional data requirement of the number of firms at the sectoral level. These data have been drawn from the United Nations, *International Yearbook of Industrial Statistics, 1998*.[3] We also need estimates of sectoral employment for the countries/regions of the model. These data come from: UNIDO, 1995, *International Yearbook of Industrial Statistics*, and the World Bank, 1997, *World Development Report*. The employment data have been aggregated according to our sectoral/regional aggregation to obtain sectoral estimates of workers employed in manufactures. The *World Development Report* was used to obtain data for the other sectors.

We have projected the GTAP-4 1995 database to the year 2005 by extrapolating the labor availability in different countries/regions by an average weighted growth rate of 1.2 per cent per annum. This figure was computed from the growth-rate forecasts for the period 1997–2010 provided for various countries in Table 2.3 of the World Bank's 1999 *World Development Indicators*. All other major variables have been projected, using an average weighted growth rate of GDP of 2.5 per cent per annum, for all of the countries/regions of our model during the period 1990–1997, as per Table 11 of the 1989/99 *World Development Report*.[4]

III. Computational Scenarios of Uruguay Round Liberalization

The projected database provides us with an approximate picture of what the world could be expected to look like in 2005 if the Uruguay Round ("UR") negotiations had not occurred. The UR reductions in trade barriers were implemented beginning in 1995 and will be completed by 2005. Accordingly, we have analyzed the impact of the UR-induced changes that are expected to occur over the course of the ten-year implementation period as a consequence of the negotiated reductions in tariffs and NTBs.[5] The scaled-up database for 2005 is then readjusted to mimic the world as it might look in the post-UR implementation. In Part IV of this chapter, we will report on some liberalization scenarios for the ongoing WTO (Doha) negotiating round, involving possible reductions in tariffs on agricultural products and manufactures and reductions of barriers to services trade.

---

[3] It should be noted that the above source does not provide number-of-firms data for all countries. We have used the number-of-firms data for similar countries in these cases.

[4] *See* Thomas W. Hertel and Will Martin, *Would Developing Countries Gain from Inclusion of Manufactures in the WTO Negotiations?*, paper presented at the CONFERENCE ON THE WTO AND THE MILLENNIUM ROUND (September 1999) and Thomas W. Hertel, *Potential Gains from Reducing Trade Barriers in Manufacturing, Services and Agriculture*, 82 FEDERAL RESERVE BANK OF ST. LOUIS REVIEW 77 (2000) for a more elaborate and detailed procedure for calculating year 2005 projections. *See also* our discussion below on the 2005 projections.

[5] It should be noted that we are not considering the effects of the Agreement on Trade Related Intellectual Property Rights ("TRIPS") and the other agreements on rules and procedures that were encompassed in the Uruguay Round negotiations.

In this section, we report on the following three scenarios:[6]

UR-1 *The Agreement on Textiles and Clothing ("ATC") is analyzed by simulating the effects of the phase-out of the Multifiber Agreement ("MFA") under the Uruguay-Round Agreement. This is done by assuming complete elimination of the MFA export-tax equivalents on textiles and wearing apparel for the developing countries/regions subject to the MFA and other quotas imposed on their exports to the industrialized countries.*

UR-2 *All the countries/regions in the model reduce their bilateral import tariffs as per the UR Agreement on manufactures.[7]*

UR-3 *This combines* ***UR-1*** *and* ***UR-2****.*

A. Computational Results[8]

Table 1 provides aggregate, or economy-wide, results from the scenarios listed above for the countries/regions that have been modeled. Disaggregated sectoral results for the **UR-3** scenario for the United States and for India are reported for illustrative purposes in Tables 2–3.

To help the reader interpret the results, it is useful first to review the features of the model that serve to identify the various economic effects that are being captured in the different scenarios. Although the model includes the aforementioned features of the New Trade Theory, it remains the case that markets respond to trade liberalization in much the same way that they would with perfect competition. That is, when tariffs or other trade barriers are reduced in a sector, domestic buyers (both final and intermediate) substitute toward imports and the domestic competing industry contracts production while foreign exporters expand. With multilateral liberalization reducing tariffs and other trade barriers simultaneously in most sectors and countries, each country's industries share in both of these effects, expanding or contracting depending primarily on whether their protection is reduced more or less than in other sectors and countries. At the same time, countries with larger average tariff reductions than their trading partners tend to experience a real

---

[6] Agricultural liberalization in the Uruguay Round negotiations was supposed to be as follows: agricultural import tariffs were to be reduced by twenty percent for the industrialized countries and by thirteen percent for the developing countries; agricultural export subsidies were to be reduced by 36 percent for the industrialized countries and by 24 percent for the developing countries; and agricultural production subsidies were to be reduced by twenty percent for the industrialized countries and by fourteen percent for the developing countries. However, as noted in JOSEPH FRANCOIS, The next WTO Round: North-south stakes in new market access negotiations 11 (2001): "Basically, in agriculture, we are in a world that allows scope for great policy discretion and uncertainty as a result of the loose commitments made." What this means is that many countries introduced quantitative restrictions on imports in the form of tariff-rate quotas. There is also evidence of considerable leeway in the choice of the reference period from which to measure reductions in export subsidies. Furthermore, the disciplines on domestic subsidies were weakened by changes in the definition of the Aggregate Measure of Support. As a consequence, relatively little agricultural liberalization was accomplished in the Uruguay Round negotiations. In the absence of detailed information on the various agricultural policy changes that have been made, we have chosen therefore not to include agricultural liberalization in the Uruguay Round computational scenarios.

[7] See Joseph Francois and Anna Strutt, *Post-Uruguay Round Tariff Vectors for GTAP Version 4*, FACULTY OF ECONOMICS, ERASMUS UNIVERSITY, ROTTERDAM, THE NETHERLANDS (1999) for details on the post-UR tariff rates.

[8] There have been a substantial number of CGE modeling studies of the Uruguay Round that are summarized and critiqued in Joseph F. Francois, Bradley McDonald, and Hakan Nordstrom, *A User's Guide to Uruguay Round Assessments*, CENTER FOR ECONOMIC POLICY RESEARCH (CEPR) DISCUSSION PAPER SERIES, NO. 1410 (June 1996) and Joseph Francois, *General Equilibrium Studies of Multilateral Trade Negotiations*, in THE POLITICAL ECONOMY OF POLICY REFORM (Douglas Nelson ed. 2001b).

Table 1: Summary results of the Uruguay Round change in imports, exports, terms of trade, welfare and the real return to capital and labor

Country	Imports (Millions)	Exports (Millions)	Terms of Trade (Percent)	Welfare (Percent)	Welfare (Millions)	Real Wage (Percent)	Return to Capital (Percent)
Scenario UR-1: Removal of the Multifiber Arrangement							
Developed Countries							
Australia & New Zealand	144.7	114.0	0.030	0.018	94.5	0.012	0.028
Canada	782.3	719.4	0.065	0.094	683.8	0.066	0.133
European Union and EFTA	2517.7	2275.1	0.055	0.058	6320.8	0.051	0.071
Japan	−121.4	191.0	−0.050	0.004	257.1	−0.002	0.012
United States	6497.4	4482.0	0.148	0.095	8608.2	0.084	0.114
Developing Countries							
Asia							
India	1517.9	1992.1	−0.954	0.231	972.2	0.224	0.238
Sri Lanka	98.7	159.1	−1.101	0.143	23.8	0.032	0.251
Rest of South Asia	449.1	652.8	−1.088	0.263	307.4	0.207	0.319
China	1849.7	2760.4	−0.366	−0.161	−1458.5	−0.120	−0.194
Hong Kong	1544.3	1364.5	0.187	−0.473	−609.2	0.121	−0.988
South Korea	405.0	428.0	−0.015	0.025	142.7	0.045	0.006
Singapore	−510.4	−591.4	0.054	−0.001	−0.8	−0.025	0.020
Indonesia	147.5	207.8	−0.089	−0.005	−13.8	0.030	−0.032
Malaysia	223.0	354.0	−0.121	0.275	328.7	0.735	0.025
Philippines	2080.9	2513.8	−1.316	0.900	794.3	2.057	0.045
Thailand	140.3	259.0	−0.143	0.029	59.4	0.161	−0.019
Other							
Mexico	−45.3	24.8	−0.030	−0.010	−36.6	−0.010	−0.010
Turkey	−157.3	−120.0	−0.094	−0.015	−31.6	−0.031	−0.006
Central Europe	−20.3	−0.6	−0.026	0.037	138.3	0.026	0.054
Central & South America	−162.9	−106.2	−0.050	−0.004	−73.9	−0.002	−0.006
Total	**17380.9**	**17679.5**			**16506.8**		
Scenario UR-2: Tariff Reductions in Manufactures							
Developed Countries							
Australia & New Zealand	2848.0	2527.6	0.347	0.327	1674.8	0.345	0.300
Canada	1071.9	1354.5	−0.086	0.127	926.3	0.137	0.114
European Union and EFTA	16826.6	15358.5	0.145	0.159	17405.6	0.157	0.163
Japan	8680.6	8331.3	0.062	0.102	6608.4	0.092	0.115
United States	12426.0	13459.3	−0.133	0.123	11187.1	0.124	0.122
Developing Countries							
Asia							
India	2585.3	3628.9	−2.099	0.446	1875.4	0.316	0.577
Sri Lanka	98.8	106.3	−0.193	0.558	93.0	0.507	0.608
Rest of South Asia	3454.8	4820.1	−7.541	2.025	2366.5	2.224	1.828
China	3112.6	1917.7	0.456	0.305	2762.2	0.347	0.271
Hong Kong	763.5	480.1	0.254	0.360	464.1	0.346	0.373
South Korea	2858.6	2733.2	0.068	0.422	2403.3	0.409	0.435
Singapore	3539.8	3647.5	−0.078	2.111	1570.3	1.943	2.258
Indonesia	936.5	894.5	0.068	0.247	626.0	0.291	0.215
Malaysia	2790.9	3411.4	−0.563	1.919	2293.9	1.816	1.974
Philippines	2452.6	3102.1	−1.989	1.917	1691.7	1.853	1.964
Thailand	1264.7	1002.3	0.291	0.366	753.9	0.597	0.283
Other							
Mexico	−64.9	1.4	−0.026	0.019	66.3	0.038	0.010
Turkey	319.3	253.9	0.143	0.123	259.1	0.122	0.124
Central Europe	1871.7	1846.1	0.020	0.294	1091.2	0.311	0.270
Central & South America	3778.8	2999.5	0.423	0.022	377.1	0.043	0.004
Total	**71616.2**	**71876.4**			**56496.0**		

(Continued)

Table 1: *(Continued)*

Country	Imports (Millions)	Exports (Millions)	Terms of trade (Percent)	Welfare (Percent)	Welfare (Millions)	Real wage (Percent)	Return to capital (Percent)
Scenario UR-3: Uruguay Round Combined Liberalization							
Developed Countries							
Australia & New Zealand	2992.8	2641.6	0.377	0.345	1769.3	0.357	0.328
Canada	1854.2	2073.9	−0.021	0.221	1610.1	0.202	0.247
European Union and EFTA	19344.2	17633.6	0.200	0.216	23726.4	0.208	0.234
Japan	8559.2	8522.3	0.011	0.106	6865.5	0.090	0.127
United States	18923.4	17941.3	0.014	0.218	19795.3	0.208	0.236
Developing Countries							
Asia							
India	4103.2	5620.9	−3.053	0.677	2847.5	0.540	0.815
Sri Lanka	197.5	265.4	−1.293	0.701	116.8	0.539	0.859
Rest of South Asia	3903.9	5473.0	−8.629	2.288	2673.9	2.430	2.147
China	4962.4	4678.2	0.089	0.144	1303.8	0.227	0.077
Hong Kong	2307.9	1844.7	0.442	−0.113	−145.1	0.467	−0.615
South Korea	3263.6	3161.2	0.053	0.447	2546.1	0.454	0.441
Singapore	3029.4	3056.1	−0.024	2.110	1569.4	1.917	2.278
Indonesia	1084.0	1102.4	−0.021	0.242	612.2	0.321	0.183
Malaysia	3013.9	3765.4	−0.684	2.194	2622.6	2.552	1.999
Philippines	4533.4	5615.9	−3.305	2.817	2486.0	3.910	2.009
Thailand	1405.0	1261.3	0.148	0.395	813.3	0.758	0.264
Other							
Mexico	−110.2	26.1	−0.056	0.008	29.6	0.027	0.000
Turkey	162.0	133.9	0.049	0.108	227.6	0.091	0.117
Central Europe	1851.4	1845.5	−0.006	0.331	1229.4	0.336	0.324
Central & South America	3615.9	2893.3	0.373	0.017	303.2	0.041	−0.002
Total	**88997.2**	**89555.9**			**73002.8**		

depreciation of their currencies in order to maintain a constant trade balance, so that all countries therefore experience mixtures of both expanding and contracting sectors.

Worldwide, these changes tend to cause increased international demand for all sectors, with world prices rising most for those sectors where trade barriers fall the most. This in turn causes changes in countries' terms of trade that can be positive or negative. Those countries that are net exporters of goods with the greatest degree of import-tariff liberalization will experience increases in their terms of trade as the world prices of their exports rise relative to their imports. The reverse occurs for net exporters in industries where liberalization is slight—perhaps because it already happened in previous trade rounds.

The effects on the economic welfare of countries arise from a mixture of these terms-of-trade effects, together with the standard efficiency gains from trade and also from additional effects due to elements of the New Trade Theory, the latter of which are mostly, but not all, beneficial.[9] Thus, we expect on average that the world will gain from multilateral liberalization, as resources are reallocated to those sectors in each country where there is a comparative advantage. In the absence of terms-of-trade effects, these efficiency gains should raise national welfare measured by the equivalent variation for every country, although some factor owners within a country may lose, as will be noted below. However, it is possible for a particular country whose net imports are concentrated

[9] *See* discussion below.

Table 2: Sectoral results of the Uruguay Round: percent change in exports, imports, output, scale and employment for the United States

Product	Exports (Percent)	Imports (Percent)	Supply (Percent)	Scale (Percent)	Employment (Percent)	Employment (000's)
Agriculture	1.24	−0.89	0.37	0.00	0.37	14967.1
Mining	2.53	−0.93	0.77	0.33	0.44	3103.9
Food, Beverages & Tobacco	8.40	12.27	0.24	0.22	0.04	1236.0
Textiles	−0.08	8.38	−2.59	0.01	−2.59	−32076.8
Wearing Apparel	−1.83	26.37	−7.94	0.57	−8.39	−97094.5
Leather Products & Footwear	2.86	0.33	0.20	0.21	0.04	27.0
Wood & Wood Products	2.04	0.18	0.28	0.16	0.17	7512.7
Chemicals	2.13	1.57	0.21	0.22	0.03	931.1
Non-metallic Min. Products	1.74	2.61	0.07	0.16	−0.04	−283.1
Metal Products	2.15	0.39	0.42	0.25	0.21	5823.1
Transportation Equipment	2.12	−0.49	0.65	0.27	0.40	10645.1
Machinery & Equipment	1.61	2.02	0.23	0.21	0.11	2366.5
Other Manufactures	2.24	0.28	0.60	0.21	0.46	8227.8
Elec., Gas & Water	0.25	−0.04	0.16	0.17	0.03	1341.3
Construction	1.54	−1.00	0.15	0.17	0.01	1918.4
Trade and Transport	1.27	−2.63	0.25	0.18	0.11	34642.6
Other Private Services	1.49	−1.39	0.25	0.21	0.08	30102.6
Government Services	1.05	−0.97	0.05	0.06	0.02	6609.4
Average	**1.95**	**1.74**	**0.15**		**0.00**	**0.00**

Table 3: Sectoral results of the Uruguay Round: percent change in exports, imports, output, scale and employment for India

Product	Exports (Percent)	Imports (Percent)	Supply (Percent)	Scale (Percent)	Employment (Percent)	Employment (000's)
Agriculture	0.70	−2.04	−0.09	0.00	−0.05	−143922.3
Mining	3.73	−2.07	1.79	0.67	1.41	46546.0
Food, Beverages & Tobacco	5.18	10.66	0.06	0.35	−0.07	−7841.8
Textiles	18.86	7.43	4.34	1.25	3.34	388153.9
Wearing Apparel	54.34	−9.57	29.23	1.33	28.26	231337.8
Leather Products & Footwear	7.97	34.60	4.61	1.21	3.70	42892.0
Wood & Wood Products	4.81	31.29	−2.68	0.60	−3.09	−226363.1
Chemicals	4.44	12.54	−1.02	0.70	−1.46	−21998.1
Non-metallic Min. Products	6.55	22.26	−0.45	0.66	−0.94	−32502.0
Metal Products	4.37	7.23	−2.34	0.65	−2.76	−96777.2
Transportation Equipment	7.09	25.24	−1.62	0.79	−2.23	−30912.3
Machinery & Equipment	2.65	16.36	−5.65	1.10	−6.56	−156588.3
Other Manufactures	2.60	19.31	−1.55	0.76	−1.98	−106883.9
Elec., Gas & Water	4.37	−2.27	1.21	1.11	0.36	6171.9
Construction	2.86	−2.68	−0.27	−0.03	−0.08	−11520.2
Trade and Transport	2.49	−2.99	0.33	0.28	0.26	124360.2
Other Private Services	2.05	−2.39	−0.24	−0.06	−0.03	−962.6
Government Services	1.57	−2.12	−0.18	−0.03	−0.01	−3189.9
Average	**11.31**	**8.22**	**0.43**		**0.00**	**0.0**

in sectors with the greatest liberalization to lose overall, if the worsening of its terms of trade swamps these efficiency gains.

On the other hand, although the New Trade Theory is perhaps best known for introducing new reasons why countries may lose from trade, in fact its greatest contribution is to expand the list of reasons for gains from trade. It is these that are the dominant contribution of the New Trade Theory in our model. That is, trade liberalization permits all countries to expand their export sectors at the same time that all sectors compete more closely with a larger number of competing varieties from abroad. As a result, countries as a whole tend to gain from lower costs due to increasing returns to scale, lower monopoly distortions due to greater competition, and reduced costs and/or increased utility due to greater product variety. All of these effects make it more likely that countries will gain from liberalization in ways that are shared across the entire population.

In perfectly competitive trade models such as the Heckscher-Ohlin Model, one expects countries as a whole to gain from trade, but the owners of one factor—the "scarce factor"—to lose through the mechanism first explored by Stolper and Samuelson[10]. The additional sources of gain from trade due to increasing returns to scale, competition, and product variety, however, are shared across factors, and we routinely find in our CGE modeling that both labor and capital may gain from liberalization. That is often the case here.

One additional point about our model should be mentioned, related to the modeling and role of nontariff barriers ("NTBs"), such as those applying to textiles and apparel. These are quantitative restrictions, captured in the model by endogenous tariff equivalents that rise and fall with changing supplies and demands for trade. The tariff equivalents generate quota rents that accrue to whatever group is granted the rights to trade under the restriction, which in the case of the MFA are the developing countries that export textiles and wearing apparel. Liberalization of these NTBs reduces or eliminates these quota rents, and this can be costly to those who possessed them disproportionately beforehand. Therefore, it is not the case that exporting countries necessarily benefit from relaxation of these trade barriers, since their loss of quota rents can more than outweigh their gains from increased exports. Indeed, their exports can actually decline, along with their national welfare, if increased exports from other countries displace them in world markets.

In the real world, all of these effects encompassed by the Michigan Model occur over time, some of them more quickly than others. Our model is however static, based upon a single set of equilibrium conditions rather than relationships that vary over time. Our results therefore refer to a time horizon that is somewhat uncertain, depending on the assumptions that have been made about which variables do and do not adjust to changing market conditions, and on the short- or long-run nature of these adjustments. Because our elasticities of supply and demand reflect relatively long-run adjustments, and because we assume that markets for both labor and capital clear within countries, our results are appropriate for a relatively long time horizon of several years—perhaps two or three at a minimum.

On the other hand, our model does not allow for the very long-run adjustments that could occur through capital accumulation, population growth, and technological change. Our results should therefore be thought of as being superimposed upon longer-run growth paths of the economies involved. To the extent that these growth paths themselves may be influenced by trade liberalization, therefore, our model does not capture that.

---

[10] Wolfgang Stolper and Paul A. Samuelson, *Protection and Real Wages*, 9 REVIEW OF ECONOMIC STUDIES, 58–73 (1941)

B. Aggregate Results

In Table 1, we report various economy-wide changes for each of the countries/regions of the model. These include changes in exports and imports in millions of dollars, the changes in terms of trade, real wage rate and real return to capital in percentages, and changes in economic welfare measured by equivalent variation, both in millions of dollars and as percent of country GDP. The terms of trade is the world price of a country's exports relative to its imports. The equivalent variation is the amount of money that, if given to the country's consumers at initial prices, would be equivalent in terms of their level of welfare to the effects of the assumed liberalization. In general, as discussed above, a worsening (fall) in a country's terms of trade has an adverse effect on its consumers' welfare. But this can be outweighed by the other gains from trade due to economic efficiency and the other benefits modeled by the New Trade Theory.

UR-1: Elimination of the MFA Quota Constraints—The results for the Uruguay Round elimination of the MFA quota and other bilateral constraints on developing country exports of textiles and apparel, shown in Scenario **UR-1** of table 1, indicate an increase in global welfare of $16.5 billion. In interpreting the results, it should be noted that, with increased exports of these goods to world markets, their prices will fall and the terms of trade of the MFA exporting countries and their economic welfare may deteriorate. This decline in terms of trade is experienced as a loss of quota rents from the MFA and can be seen in column (3) in table 1 for most of the developing countries/regions. Several of those countries/regions also experience reductions in welfare. The developed countries all gain from MFA elimination. Changes in returns to labor and capital are mostly small.

UR-2: Liberalization of Manufactures—Scenario **UR-2** in table 1 covers the reductions in import tariffs on manufactures that were negotiated in the Uruguay Round. Global economic welfare increases by $56.5 billion and the gains are positive for all countries/regions. The largest welfare increases noted are for EU/EFTA ($17.4 billion), the United States ($11.2 billion), and Japan ($6.6 billion). The effects on returns to labor and capital are uniformly positive.

UR-3: Combined Liberalization Effects (UR-1 + UR-2)—The combined effects of the Uruguay Round (UR) liberalization are indicated in Scenario UR-3 of table 1. As noted, this table is the linear combination of **UR-1** and **UR-2**. Global welfare is increased by $73.0 billion. It is noteworthy that the developed countries all gain, with an increase in welfare of $23.7 billion for the EU/EFTA, $19.8 billion for the United States, and $6.9 billion for Japan. The developing countries in the aggregate show an estimated welfare increase of $19.2 billion from the combined UR liberalization. All the individual developing countries/regions noted, except Hong Kong, show an increase in welfare. Changes in the real wage and the return to capital are positive but relatively small for the developed countries, and relatively sizable in several of the Asian developing countries.

C. Sectoral Results

A major contribution of our CGE modeling is to identify those sectors that will expand and those that will contract as a result of various patterns of trade liberalization, as well as the sizes of these changes. Given our assumption that expenditure adjusts within each country to maintain a constant level of total employment, it is necessarily the case that each country experiences a mixture of expansions and contractions at the industry level. This must be true of employment, and it is likely to be true as well for industry output. To report these sectoral results in any detail is tedious, since there are eighteen sectors in each country/region. We therefore report, in Tables 2–3, the sectoral results only for the combined UR liberalization for the United States and India, for illustrative purposes. The sectoral results for the other scenarios and countries/regions are available from the authors on request.

For the United States, there are increases in employment in all sectors, except for textiles (−32,077) and wearing apparel (−97,094), reflecting especially the effects of elimination of the MFA quota constraints. For India, the largest employment increases are in textiles (388,154), wearing apparel (231,338), trade and transport (124,360), leather products & footwear (42,892), and mining (46,546). India's largest employment declines are in agriculture (−143,922), wood & wood products (−226,363), and the combined sectors including industrial products and machinery. The percentage changes in employment are relatively small for the United States, except in textiles and wearing apparel. The employment changes for India are relatively sizable in several sectors. In interpreting the employment changes, it should be noted that these changes would be mitigated given that the UR liberalization has been phased in over a ten-year period. We may also note, from the changes reported for scale (output per firm), that there is evidence of positive scale effects for most of the sectors.

IV. Computational Analysis of the Doha Development Round

In this part, using the Michigan Model, we report some of the economic effects that may result from the ongoing Doha Development Round of multilateral trade negotiations. The Doha Round was launched officially at the beginning of 2002 and is scheduled for conclusion by the end of 2004.[11] The Doha Round scenarios here assume 33 percent reductions in post-Uruguay Round tariffs and services barriers, as follows:

> **DR-1** *Agricultural liberalization is modeled as a 33 percent reduction in post-Uruguay Round agricultural import tariffs, export subsidies, and domestic production subsidies.*
> **DR-2** *Liberalization of manufactures is modeled as a 33 percent reduction in post-Uruguay Round tariffs on manufactures.*
> **DR-3** *Services liberalization is modeled as a 33 percent reduction in estimated post-Uruguay Round services barriers.*
> **DR-4** *This combines **DR-1**, **DR-2**, and **DR-3**.*

A. Data

As noted in Part II, our basic data source is the GTAP-4 Database, supplemented with employment data, and projected to 2005, which is when the Uruguay Round will have been fully implemented. The projected database has in turn been readjusted to include the results of the Uruguay Round implementation as analyzed above.

The main accomplishment of the Uruguay Round in the area of services was the creation of the General Agreement on Trade in Services ("GATS"), which is an umbrella agreement setting out the rules governing the four modes of providing services transactions. These modes include: (1) cross-border services (e.g., telecommunications); (2) services provided to consumers visiting from abroad (e.g., tourism); (3) services

---

[11] As was the case in our analysis of the Uruguay Round negotiations, we do not consider the effects of the negotiations on the various rules and procedures to be covered in the Doha Round.

requiring a domestic presence in the form of foreign direct investment ("FDI"); and (4) movement of natural persons. In an earlier study, Brown and Stern developed a new version of the Michigan Model for the purpose of analyzing the behavior of multinational firms, which are major providers of services, both intra-firm as well as in the production and sales of foreign affiliates located in host countries.[12] To approximate existing services barriers, Brown and Stern used estimates of barriers to FDI provided by Hoekman[13], based on the gross operating margins of services firms listed on national stock exchanges for the period, 1994–96.[14] We use these estimates here as *ad valorem* equivalent tariffs for the services sectors included in the current version of the Michigan Model. Our simulation **DR-3** assumes then that the services barriers are to be reduced by 33 percent in the Doha Round.

B. Aggregate Results[15]

The aggregate results of the assumed Doha Round scenarios are presented in Table 4, and the sectoral results of the combined scenarios (**DR-4**) for the United States and India are presented in Tables 5 and 6.

DR-1: Agricultural Liberalization—The results for assumed 33 percent reductions in post-Uruguay Round agricultural import tariffs, export subsidies, and production subsidies (taken here as a proxy for the Aggregate Measure of Support) are shown in Table 4. The more detailed results are available from the authors on request. In the model, the reductions in agricultural import tariffs will have the effects of tariff reductions already described. In the case of export subsidies, their effects will be to reduce world prices and raise domestic prices. When export subsidies are reduced, world prices would then rise and domestic prices in the subsidizing countries would fall, with the possible consequences that economic welfare may rise in the countries reducing their export subsidies and fall in net-importing countries now facing higher world prices. Similarly, production

[12] Because of computer-capacity constraints, Dusilla K. Brown and Robert M. Stern, *Measurement and Modeling of the Economic Effects of Trade and Investment Barriers in Services,* 9 REVIEW OF INTERNATIONAL ECONOMICS 262 (2001) used a three-sector aggregation consisting of agriculture, manufactures, and services and a twenty-country/region breakdown. They also made allowance for international flows of FDI and increases in capital stocks in response to the multilateral trade liberalization that they analyzed.

[13] Bernard Hoekman, *The Next Round of Services Negotiations: Identifying Priorities and Options,* 82 FEDERAL RESERVE BANK OF ST. LOUIS REVIEW 31 (2000)

[14] The gross operating margins were calculated as the differences between total revenues and total operating costs for construction, trade and transport, other private services, and government services. Some of the differences between total revenues and costs are presumably attributable to fixed cost. Given that the gross operating margins vary across countries, a portion of the margins can also be attributed to barriers to FDI. For this purpose, we have selected as a benchmark for each sector the country with the smallest gross operating margin, on the assumption that operations in this country can be considered to be freely open to foreign firms. The excess in any other country above the lowest benchmark is then taken to be due to barriers to establishment by foreign firms. That is, the barrier is modeled as the cost increase attributable to an increase in fixed cost borne by multinational corporations attempting to establish an enterprise locally in a host country. We further assume for purposes of our analysis here that we can interpret this cost increase as an ad valorem equivalent tariff on international services transactions generally. Further details are available from the authors on request.

[15] The potential gains from the Doha Round are also analyzed in Hertel, *supra* note 4 and Thomas W. Hertel, Bernard M. Hoekman, and Will Martin, *Developing Countries and a New Round of WTO Negotiations,* 17 THE WORLD BANK RESEARCH OBSERVER 113 (2002). These studies are based on the GTAP CGE model, which is a widely used modeling structure. Perfect competition is assumed in all sectors. National product differentiation (i.e., the Armington assumption) is also assumed, which may tend to exaggerate terms-of-trade effects.

Table 4: Summary results of the Doha Development Round: change in imports, exports, terms of trade, welfare and the real return to capital and labor

Country	Imports (Millions)	Exports (Millions)	Terms of trade (Percent)	Welfare (Percent)	Welfare (Millions)	Real wage (Percent)	Return to capital (Percent)
Scenario DR-1: 33 Percent Reduction in Agricultural Protection							
Developed Countries							
Australia & New Zealand	566.2	−168.1	0.798	−0.063	−320.7	−0.182	−0.224
Canada	−248.6	−768.3	0.168	−0.051	−368.4	−0.218	−0.209
European Union and EFTA	157.1	416.2	−0.041	0.258	28328.0	−0.045	0.023
Japan	564.3	3199.9	−0.470	−0.044	−2826.4	−0.039	−0.003
United States	2690.9	928.3	0.219	−0.122	−11081.1	−0.190	−0.193
Developing Countries							
Asia							
India	324.2	285.3	0.066	0.384	1617.4	−0.109	−0.030
Sri Lanka	−93.9	−67.5	−0.240	−2.734	−455.7	−0.307	−0.480
Rest of South Asia	106.6	157.2	−0.118	0.310	362.1	−0.078	−0.119
China	−522.8	−652.7	−0.013	−0.434	−3932.0	−0.163	−0.320
Hong Kong	−380.7	−256.9	−0.026	−0.294	−379.0	−0.186	−0.180
South Korea	285.4	912.9	−0.333	−0.230	−1311.4	0.132	0.134
Singapore	−153.9	−39.5	−0.067	−0.244	−181.4	−0.038	−0.068
Indonesia	−436.5	−466.7	−0.006	−1.259	−3185.5	−0.113	−0.462
Malaysia	−10.8	49.0	−0.076	−0.264	−315.8	0.189	0.104
Philippines	−344.8	−241.8	−0.199	−1.336	−1179.1	−0.062	−0.076
Thailand	−621.2	−1119.3	0.613	0.045	92.4	−0.703	0.054
Other							
Mexico	−200.7	−193.6	−0.089	−0.121	−425.6	−0.354	−0.185
Turkey	−189.1	−119.0	−0.087	−0.414	−871.4	−0.327	−0.347
Central Europe	−432.7	−428.6	0.025	−0.457	−1695.6	−0.363	−0.391
Central & South America	1500.6	870.3	0.377	−0.285	−4988.0	−0.252	−0.358
Total	**2559.5**	**2297.3**			**−3117.2**		
Scenario DR-1a: 33 Percent Reduction in Agricultural Export Subsidies							
Developed Countries							
Australia & New Zealand	−314.2	−449.3	0.153	−0.020	−102.3	0.047	0.059
Canada	−259.4	−274.2	−0.005	−0.065	−472.1	−0.018	−0.017
European Union and EFTA	−3081.5	−3917.3	0.071	0.011	1193.9	0.035	0.040
Japan	−1251.3	−1008.3	−0.056	−0.067	−4371.6	−0.019	−0.026
United States	−1338.0	−1030.7	−0.018	−0.052	−4697.2	−0.021	−0.020
Developing Countries							
Asia							
India	−91.0	−76.7	−0.028	−0.260	−1094.6	−0.020	−0.070
Sri Lanka	−123.4	−88.0	−0.439	−2.801	−466.8	−0.344	−0.366
Rest of South Asia	−91.4	−58.0	−0.084	−0.360	−420.6	−0.041	−0.052
China	−751.1	−737.1	−0.045	−0.199	−1798.8	−0.060	−0.070
Hong Kong	−346.2	−245.7	−0.035	−0.235	−303.2	−0.173	−0.160
South Korea	−423.3	−367.8	−0.025	−0.275	−1563.4	−0.081	−0.088
Singapore	−247.0	−171.7	−0.043	−0.238	−176.7	−0.207	−0.230
Indonesia	−589.8	−488.6	−0.190	−1.033	−2613.8	−0.108	−0.210
Malaysia	−362.3	−355.6	−0.026	−0.387	−462.9	−0.100	−0.137
Philippines	−494.2	−420.9	−0.140	−1.416	−1249.5	−0.223	−0.191
Thailand	−979.3	−1311.7	0.413	0.229	472.4	−1.420	0.414
Other							
Mexico	−330.7	−270.0	−0.093	−0.339	−1195.1	−0.027	−0.061
Turkey	−497.0	−407.5	−0.151	−0.696	−1463.2	−0.064	−0.262
Central European Assoc.	−681.1	−618.3	−0.035	−0.327	−1214.7	−0.072	−0.074
Central & South American Assoc.	−113.6	−83.9	−0.006	−0.070	−1228.7	−0.013	−0.015
Total	**−12365.5**	**−12381.1**			**−23229.0**		

Table 4: (*Continued*)

Country	Imports (Millions)	Exports (Millions)	Terms of trade (Percent)	Welfare (Percent)	Welfare (Millions)	Real wage (Percent)	Return to capital (Percent)
Scenario DR-1b: 33 Percent Reduction in Agricultural Import Tariffs							
Developed Countries							
Australia & New Zealand	686.9	359.8	0.345	−0.069	−352.3	−0.167	−0.213
Canada	100.7	−86.5	0.066	−0.020	−144.3	−0.055	−0.060
European Union and EFTA	1254.5	1513.4	−0.023	0.024	2590.4	0.022	0.025
Japan	2885.3	4331.8	−0.230	0.079	5157.4	0.127	0.162
United States	4388.7	2930.0	0.149	−0.048	−4340.3	−0.060	−0.068
Developing Countries							
Asia							
India	229.4	243.9	−0.025	0.367	1544.0	0.016	0.036
Sri Lanka	37.2	30.4	0.107	0.397	66.1	0.082	0.040
Rest of South Asia	191.0	210.7	−0.102	0.687	802.7	0.112	0.124
China	572.8	619.4	0.000	0.155	1407.0	0.041	0.040
Hong Kong	166.5	109.8	0.026	0.077	98.5	0.083	0.078
South Korea	1208.9	1728.4	−0.288	0.274	1557.7	0.349	0.378
Singapore	311.4	354.0	−0.030	0.118	88.1	0.253	0.244
Indonesia	141.7	120.7	0.037	0.047	118.3	0.022	−0.009
Malaysia	522.4	671.8	−0.126	0.329	392.9	0.283	0.342
Philippines	291.7	333.8	−0.093	0.422	372.2	0.193	0.240
Thailand	342.8	275.2	0.063	0.030	62.7	0.318	−0.100
Other							
Mexico	−10.4	−49.2	0.024	0.008	26.8	−0.001	−0.035
Turkey	241.1	264.5	−0.056	0.188	395.1	0.037	0.044
Central European Assoc.	262.7	194.1	0.054	−0.019	−72.2	−0.033	−0.069
Central & South American Assoc.	464.6	295.5	0.092	−0.018	−308.4	−0.048	−0.072
Total	**14289.9**	**14451.3**			**9462.5**		
Scenario DR-1c: 33 Percent Reduction in Agricultural Production Subsidies							
Developed Countries							
Australia & New Zealand	193.4	−78.6	0.300	0.026	133.8	−0.062	−0.070
Canada	−89.9	−407.5	0.107	0.034	248.0	−0.146	−0.131
European Union and EFTA	1984.1	2820.1	−0.089	0.224	24543.7	−0.102	−0.042
Japan	−1069.7	−123.6	−0.184	−0.056	−3612.2	−0.147	−0.139
United States	−359.8	−970.9	0.088	−0.023	−2043.6	−0.109	−0.105
Developing Countries							
Asia							
India	185.7	118.1	0.120	0.278	1168.0	−0.105	0.004
Sri Lanka	−7.8	−9.9	0.092	−0.330	−54.9	−0.045	−0.154
Rest of South Asia	7.1	4.6	0.067	−0.017	−20.0	−0.148	−0.191
China	−344.5	−535.0	0.032	−0.391	−3540.2	−0.144	−0.290
Hong Kong	−201.0	−121.0	−0.017	−0.135	−174.3	−0.096	−0.097
South Korea	−500.2	−447.7	−0.021	−0.229	−1305.7	−0.135	−0.155
Singapore	−218.4	−221.8	0.006	−0.125	−92.8	−0.084	−0.082
Indonesia	11.6	−98.9	0.146	−0.273	−690.0	−0.027	−0.243
Malaysia	−170.9	−267.2	0.075	−0.206	−245.7	0.006	−0.100
Philippines	−142.3	−154.6	0.034	−0.342	−301.8	−0.033	−0.125
Thailand	15.4	−82.8	0.137	−0.215	−442.7	0.399	−0.261
Other							
Mexico	140.4	125.6	−0.019	0.211	742.7	−0.327	−0.089
Turkey	66.7	24.0	0.119	0.093	196.7	−0.300	−0.129
Central European Assoc.	−14.3	−4.4	0.006	−0.110	−408.8	−0.257	−0.249
Central & South American Assoc.	1149.6	658.7	0.291	−0.197	−3451.0	−0.191	−0.272
Total	**635.1**	**227.1**			**10649.3**		

(*Continued*)

Table 4: (*Continued*)

Country	Imports (Millions)	Exports (Millions)	Terms of trade (Percent)	Welfare (Percent)	Welfare (Millions)	Real wage (Percent)	Return to capital (Percent)
Scenario DR-2: 33 Percent Reduction in Manufactures Tariffs							
Developed Countries							
Australia & New Zealand	3720.7	3457.2	0.267	0.545	2790.6	0.508	0.515
Canada	1996.0	2097.3	−0.013	0.347	2526.2	0.216	0.251
European Union and EFTA	23184.8	22840.3	0.050	0.358	39273.0	0.190	0.199
Japan	19071.4	15817.0	0.548	0.696	45190.9	0.234	0.304
United States	20454.2	18337.3	0.167	0.260	23634.2	0.198	0.224
Developing Countries							
Asia							
India	3280.4	4054.2	−1.384	0.733	3084.4	0.439	0.592
Sri Lanka	536.8	592.1	−1.025	3.207	534.5	1.565	2.010
Rest of South Asia	1892.0	2018.4	−0.604	1.895	2214.7	0.889	1.025
China	16080.3	19416.3	−1.221	1.199	10859.3	1.470	1.323
Hong Kong	3182.8	1840.3	1.246	1.444	1859.1	0.947	0.647
South Korea	8023.4	8440.7	−0.233	1.515	8622.9	1.158	1.003
Singapore	4382.9	4161.8	0.131	2.276	1692.5	2.481	2.611
Indonesia	2362.7	2336.0	0.053	0.835	2113.3	0.645	0.447
Malaysia	4242.8	4805.2	−0.488	2.555	3055.1	2.896	2.812
Philippines	3984.0	4535.1	−1.192	5.478	4834.4	3.310	2.461
Thailand	3406.1	3970.1	−0.675	0.873	1798.6	1.664	0.972
Other							
Mexico	916.3	1132.6	−0.166	0.364	1283.1	0.195	0.204
Turkey	1421.0	1558.6	−0.335	0.827	1740.3	0.349	0.272
Central Europe	3866.3	4366.4	−0.428	0.734	2724.2	0.816	0.722
Central & South America	5038.9	6103.2	−0.612	0.206	3610.0	0.159	0.108
Total	**131043.7**	**131880.0**			**163441.4**		
Scenario DR-3: 33 Percent Reduction in Services Barriers							
Developed Countries							
Australia & New Zealand	2354.4	1962.3	0.385	1.050	5379.6	0.694	0.657
Canada	2244.0	2136.3	0.083	0.811	5910.4	0.317	0.316
European Union and EFTA	35478.1	35336.8	0.032	1.295	142003.2	0.553	0.546
Japan	14797.7	15501.6	−0.067	0.891	57875.1	0.247	0.277
United States	32467.7	32231.5	−0.033	1.448	131426.8	0.524	0.534
Developing Countries							
Asia							
India	919.2	803.9	0.212	0.552	2321.6	0.170	0.204
Sri Lanka	121.7	99.1	0.335	1.202	200.4	0.881	0.507
Rest of South Asia	374.3	286.7	0.286	0.689	804.9	0.293	0.453
China	5660.3	6210.9	−0.128	1.320	11959.1	0.840	0.603
Hong Kong	7587.2	8058.4	−0.611	4.382	5643.1	5.638	5.927
South Korea	4842.2	5002.5	−0.102	1.339	7619.5	0.913	0.956
Singapore	3325.1	3776.2	−0.297	3.322	2470.8	4.821	3.972
Indonesia	1401.3	1469.4	−0.072	1.256	3177.0	0.327	0.307
Malaysia	1487.6	1466.8	0.049	1.267	1514.5	1.026	0.928
Philippines	1986.7	2195.0	−0.462	2.342	2067.1	1.739	1.622
Thailand	3324.2	3625.3	−0.413	1.401	2886.4	1.088	0.904
Other							
Mexico	863.1	809.1	0.110	0.878	3099.3	0.204	0.195
Turkey	1733.3	1462.9	0.589	1.781	3745.9	0.695	0.884
Central Europe	3841.7	3744.5	0.061	1.409	5227.2	1.067	0.996
Central & South America	4199.9	4442.8	−0.179	1.050	18363.5	0.256	0.272
Total	**129009.6**	**130621.8**			**413695.4**		

Table 4: (*Continued*)

Country	Imports (Millions)	Exports (Millions)	Terms of trade (Percent)	Welfare (Percent)	Welfare (Millions)	Real wage (Percent)	Return to capital (Percent)
Scenario UR-4: 33 Percent Reduction in all Trade Barriers							
Developed Countries							
Australia & New Zealand	6641.2	5251.4	1.449	1.532	7849.3	1.020	0.947
Canada	3991.3	3465.3	0.238	1.107	8068.2	0.315	0.359
European Union and EFTA	58819.3	58592.5	0.041	1.911	209609.8	0.697	0.768
Japan	34433.4	34518.5	0.012	1.544	100239.5	0.442	0.579
United States	55612.4	51496.8	0.353	1.586	143980.5	0.533	0.565
Developing Countries							
Asia							
India	4523.7	5143.3	−1.106	1.669	7023.4	0.500	0.766
Sri Lanka	564.6	623.7	−0.930	1.675	279.2	2.139	2.037
Rest of South Asia	2372.9	2462.3	−0.436	2.894	3381.8	1.104	1.360
China	21217.8	24974.6	−1.361	2.085	18886.9	2.148	1.606
Hong Kong	10389.2	9641.7	0.609	5.532	7123.1	6.399	6.394
South Korea	13151.0	14356.1	−0.668	2.624	14930.8	2.203	2.094
Singapore	7554.0	7898.6	−0.233	5.354	3982.0	7.264	6.516
Indonesia	3327.5	3338.6	−0.025	0.832	2104.8	0.858	0.292
Malaysia	5719.6	6321.0	−0.515	3.558	4253.8	4.111	3.845
Philippines	5625.9	6488.3	−1.854	6.485	5722.5	4.987	4.007
Thailand	6109.1	6476.1	−0.475	2.319	4777.4	2.050	1.930
Other							
Mexico	1578.6	1748.0	−0.145	1.122	3957.0	0.045	0.214
Turkey	2965.1	2902.4	0.167	2.194	4614.5	0.718	0.809
Central Europe	7275.2	7682.1	−0.342	1.686	6255.3	1.521	1.327
Central & South America	10739.4	11416.1	−0.414	0.971	16985.8	0.163	0.021
Total	**262611.2**	**264797.6**			**574025.4**		

subsidies will have the effect of reducing prices both domestically and abroad. When production subsidies are reduced, the cost of agricultural products will rise with consequent terms-of-trade effects similar to those just discussed. In addition, depending on the input-output structure, a rise in the cost of agricultural inputs will push up marginal cost relative to average total cost in some sectors. In order to return to the optimal markup of price relative to marginal cost, firm output in these sectors has to fall, and economic welfare may then decline due to reduced scale economies.

In the underlying results, the reductions in agricultural import tariffs alone increase global economic welfare by $9.5 billion. Welfare increases in the EU/EFTA, Japan, the Asian developing countries, Mexico, and Turkey as resources are shifted away from agriculture. Correspondingly, welfare declines in Australia/New Zealand, Canada, and the United States as resources are shifted to agriculture and away from nonagricultural industries. As noted above, when export subsidies are reduced, world prices would rise and domestic prices would fall. This is borne out in the underlying results insofar as welfare increases in the EU/EFTA and declines in all of the countries/regions in the model, except Thailand. Global welfare falls by an estimated $23.2 billion. When production subsidies are reduced, domestic and foreign prices rise, and depending on input-output structures, the increased cost of agricultural inputs may cause firm output in some sectors to decline for the reasons discussed above. In the underlying results, it turns out that the EU/EFTA region benefits the most when its agricultural production subsidies are reduced, whereas welfare declines for most developing countries/regions. Global welfare rises by $10.6 billion. Agricultural liberalization thus involves a complex of differential changes because both tariffs and subsidies are being reduced. The net effect indicated in Table 4

Table 5: Sectoral results of the Doha Development Round: percent change in exports, imports, output, scale and employment for the United States

Product	Exports (Percent)	Imports (Percent)	Supply (Percent)	Scale (Percent)	Employment (Percent)	Employment (000's)
Agriculture	13.90	4.06	1.86	0.00	1.87	75688.4
Mining	1.26	0.52	0.61	0.65	−0.02	−131.6
Food, Beverages & Tobacco	7.63	−2.83	0.27	−0.44	0.73	23186.0
Textiles	2.18	5.96	−1.29	0.28	−1.53	−18399.5
Wearing Apparel	6.15	11.31	−4.30	0.76	−4.89	−52044.9
Leather Products & Footwear	3.44	6.18	−4.56	0.94	−5.31	−3642.3
Wood & Wood Products	2.23	−0.10	0.50	0.29	0.29	12853.9
Chemicals	3.36	1.94	0.67	0.61	0.12	3424.3
Non-metallic Min. Products	3.06	3.89	0.25	0.48	−0.07	−571.0
Metal Products	2.11	1.87	0.44	0.60	−0.08	−2239.2
Transportation Equipment	1.63	2.33	0.39	0.66	−0.23	−6108.3
Machinery & Equipment	1.88	1.97	0.48	0.48	0.18	4030.0
Other Manufactures	2.50	1.89	0.49	0.53	0.13	2336.8
Elec., Gas & Water	0.70	−0.18	0.42	0.47	0.03	1284.8
Construction	10.25	11.80	0.42	0.47	0.01	1737.6
Trade and Transport	9.79	16.71	0.44	0.64	−0.08	−23770.4
Other Private Services	13.44	22.60	0.59	0.79	−0.09	−32536.9
Government Services	12.47	17.68	0.25	0.32	0.06	14902.1
Average	**5.49**	**4.98**	**0.42**		**0.00**	**0.00**

Table 6: Sectoral results of the Doha Development Round: percent change in exports, imports, output, scale and employment for India

Product	Exports (Percent)	Imports (Percent)	Supply (Percent)	Scale (Percent)	Employment (Percent)	Employment (000's)
Agriculture	11.50	0.71	−0.19	0.00	−0.15	−449827.9
Mining	5.43	−1.84	2.68	1.03	2.07	69399.1
Food, Beverages & Tobacco	7.75	17.83	0.40	0.06	0.52	60679.6
Textiles	8.69	21.56	1.82	0.78	1.23	148188.9
Wearing Apparel	14.06	24.77	9.30	0.86	8.75	95004.0
Leather Products & Footwear	9.30	9.13	6.63	1.10	5.82	69966.9
Wood & Wood Products	5.40	5.53	0.03	0.46	−0.27	−18859.3
Chemicals	5.75	10.53	−0.65	0.92	−1.29	−19167.5
Non-metallic Min. Products	7.61	15.32	0.55	0.92	−0.20	−6811.1
Metal Products	5.23	11.70	−2.15	1.13	−3.01	−102891.1
Transportation Equipment	7.33	12.93	−0.03	1.23	−1.05	−14198.4
Machinery & Equipment	4.53	10.83	−3.04	1.58	−4.44	−99199.1
Other Manufactures	4.93	15.52	−0.51	1.21	−1.32	−70109.0
Elec., Gas & Water	6.33	−4.53	0.71	0.75	0.17	2982.9
Construction	15.90	2.99	0.63	0.72	0.14	20273.2
Trade and Transport	15.06	14.66	0.26	0.64	−0.07	−35549.3
Other Private Services	16.86	10.16	0.58	0.58	0.35	10009.5
Government Services	15.45	−2.91	1.22	0.86	0.81	340108.6
Average	**9.22**	**8.30**	**0.50**		**0.00**	**0.0**

is a reduction in global welfare of $3.1 billion, as the negative welfare effects of lower export subsidies offset the positive welfare gains from reductions in import tariffs and domestic production subsidies.

DR-2: Liberalization of Manufactures—The assumed 33 percent reduction of post-Uruguay Round manufactures tariffs results in an increase in global welfare of $163.4 billion, which is considerably greater than the $56.5 billion welfare gain from the Uruguay Round manufactures liberalization. As was the case in the Uruguay Round results, the assumed liberalization of manufactures in the Doha Round would increase welfare in all of the countries/regions listed and would have positive effects as well on real wages and the return to capital. The largest welfare gains are for Japan ($45.2 billion), the EU/EFTA ($39.3 billion), and the United States ($23.6 billion). While the welfare gains for the developing countries/regions are much smaller in absolute terms, the percentage gains are mostly larger, ranging from 0.2 percent for Central & South America to 5.5 percent for the Philippines.[16] There are also sizable percentage increases in the real factor returns in the Asian developing economies.

DR-3: Services Liberalization —As noted above, the Uruguay Round negotiations on services resulted in creation of the GATS, but no significant liberalization of services barriers occurred. Following the conclusion of the Uruguay Round, there have been successful multilateral negotiations to liberalize telecommunications and financial services. While it would be desirable to assess the economic effects of these sectoral agreements, we cannot do so because of lack of data. What we have done then is to use the estimates of services barriers based on the calculations of gross operating margins for services firms in the countries/regions in our model, as already described. These estimates of services barriers are intended to be indirect approximations of what the actual barriers may in fact be. Assuming that the ad valorem equivalents of these barriers are reduced by 33 percent, it can be seen in table 4 that global economic welfare rises by $413.7 billion, which exceeds the $163.4 billion welfare increase for manufactures liberalization. All of the countries/regions listed experience positive welfare gains as well as increases in real wages and returns to capital. The EU/EFTA region has the largest welfare gain of $142.0 billion for the group of industrialized countries, compared to $131.4 billion for the United States, and $57.9 billion for Japan. For the smaller industrialized and developing countries, the percentage increases in welfare and factor returns are especially noteworthy. It should be borne in mind that these results of services liberalization depend on the size of the services barriers that have been calculated indirectly from financial data and may possibly be overstated. It seems fair to say nonetheless that the welfare effects of reductions in services barriers would tend to be considerably greater than the welfare effects of reduced tariffs on manufactures.

DR-4: Combined Liberalization Effects (DR-1 + DR-2 + DR-3)—The results for **DR4** are a linear combination of the other three scenarios. Overall, in table 4, global welfare rises by $574.0 billion. Among the industrialized countries, the EU/EFTA region has a welfare gain of $209.6 billion, the United States a gain of $144.0 billion, and Japan a gain of $100.2 billion. The percentage welfare gains and increases in returns to factors are sizable in most of the smaller industrialized countries and in the developing countries.

---

[16] Our results differ from those obtained by Hertel, Hoekman, and Martin, *supra* note 15, p. 121, who conclude that: "...the bulk of the gains go to developing countries, which are estimated to receive three quarters of the total gains from liberalizing manufacturing trade." The differences in our results compared to Hertel et al. most likely stem from the assumptions made in projecting the database for the model to 2005. That is, Hertel et al. project significantly greater expansions of the output and trade of the developing countries than in our simpler extrapolations noted above.

C. Sectoral Results

The sectoral results for **DR-4** in the United States and India are presented for illustrative purposes in tables 5 and 6. The sectoral results for other scenarios and countries/regions are available from the authors on request. The largest employment increases for the United States are in agriculture (75,688), food, beverages, and tobacco (23,186), wood & wood products (12,854), and government services (14,902). There are employment declines in textiles ($-18,400$), wearing apparel ($-52,045$), leather products & footwear ($-3,642$), trade and transport ($-23,770$), and other private services ($-32,537$). For India, there are employment increases in mining (69,399), food, beverages, and tobacco (60,680), textiles (148,189), wearing apparel (95,004), leather products & footwear (69,967), construction (20,273), and government services (340,109). The employment declines are in agriculture ($-449,828$), the combined sectors of industrial products and durable manufactures, and trade and transport ($-35,549$). As was the case with the sectoral results for the Uruguay Round trade liberalization noted in Tables 2 and 3, it can expected that the Doha Round trade liberalization will be phased in over a period of several years so that possible sectoral employment dislocations would be mitigated.

V. Conclusions and Implications

The following conclusions can be drawn from our computational analysis of the Uruguay Round trade negotiations:

- The elimination of the MFA quota constraints resulting from the Uruguay Round agreement is beneficial to economic welfare in the developed countries but detrimental to some of the developing countries/regions. The detrimental effects occur because of the decline in world prices and deterioration of the exporting countries' terms of trade, including the loss of quota rents.
- Because there is considerable evidence of backsliding from the formal Uruguay Round commitments to reduce agricultural import tariffs, export subsidies, and production subsidies, we assumed that no significant agricultural liberalization resulted from the Uruguay Round.
- The liberalization of trade in manufactures was beneficial to all the developed and developing countries/regions covered in the model.
- The combined effects of the Uruguay Round trade liberalization were welfare increasing for the developed and developing countries/regions, except for Hong Kong. The largest absolute gains were for the developed countries.
- The sectoral effects of the Uruguay Round trade liberalization varied, depending on the patterns of liberalization for individual countries. Employment dislocations appeared relatively small, considering that the trade liberalization was to be phased in over a ten- year period.

The computational results of assumed 33 percent reductions of trade barriers in the Doha Development Round negotiations can be summarized as follows:

- The assumed reductions in agricultural import tariffs, export subsidies, and production subsidies suggested that the EU/EFTA would be the prime beneficiaries. The net effect on global welfare would be negative, with the overall welfare decline from the reduction in export subsidies offsetting the overall gains from reductions in import tariffs and production subsidies.

- The effects of manufactures liberalization would be uniformly positive for all developed and developing countries/regions. The industrialized countries show the largest absolute welfare increases, while several developing countries/regions show sizable gains as a percentage of their GDP.
- All of the developed and developing countries/regions would have significant increases in welfare due to the assumed liberalization of services barriers. These welfare increases would be substantially greater than the increases due to manufactures liberalization, although that result especially depends, of course, on the estimated sizes of the trade barriers in services and the extent to which they will be reduced.
- The combined effects of the assumed Doha Development Round liberalization would be sizable in both absolute and percentage terms for the developed and developing countries/regions. The largest absolute gains would be for the developed countries.
- Sectoral employment dislocations would be mitigated insofar as the Doha Round liberalization would be phased in over several years time.

Our computational results thus suggest that there are substantial benefits to be realized from the Doha Development Round negotiations, especially for manufactures and services and for both developed and developing countries. This is in contrast to the effects of the Uruguay Round trade liberalization, which may have been tilted against developing countries.[17]

We should note, as discussed above, that our computational model is based on a comparative static approach, meaning that we move from an initial position to a new equilibrium in which all of the liberalization occurs at one time. That is, we abstract from a variety of dynamic and related effects that may occur through time, especially the international mobility of real capital, increases in real investment via capital accumulation, and technological improvements. The economic benefits that we have calculated, especially for the Doha Development Round, may therefore be interpreted as a lower bound for the benefits that may be realized from the multilateral trade negotiations.[18]

BIBLIOGRAPHY

Brown, Drusilla K. and Robert M. Stern. *Measurement and Modeling of the Economic Effects of Trade and Investment Barriers in Services*, 9 REVIEW OF INTERNATIONAL ECONOMICS 262 (2001).

Finger, J. Michael and Julio J. Nogues. *The Unbalanced Uruguay Round Outcome: The New Areas in Future WTO Negotiations*, 25 THE WORLD ECONOMY 321 (2002).

Francois, Joseph F., Bradley McDonald, and Hakan Nordstrom. *A User's Guide to Uruguay Round Assessments*, Centre for Economic Policy Research Discussion Paper Series, No. 1410 (June 1996).

---

[17] See J. Michael Finger and Julio J. Nogues, *The Unbalanced Uruguay Round Outcome: The New Areas in Future WTO Negotiations,*25 THE WORLD ECONOMY 321 (2002) for arguments of how and why many of the aspects of the Uruguay Round negotiations resulted in an outcome that was unbalanced against the developing countries and the implications from the Uruguay Round experience that may be applicable in a new trade round.

[18] See Francois, *supra* note 8, esp. pp. 31–34 for an elaboration of how the usefulness of CGE modeling studies can be improved in applications to the Doha Round negotiations.

Francois, Joseph and Anna Strutt. *Post-Uruguay Round Tariff Vectors for GTAP Version 4, processed*, Faculty of Economics, Erasmus University, Rotterdam, The Netherlands (1999).

Francois, Joseph. *General Equilibrium Studies of Multilateral Trade Negotiations,* in THE POLITICAL ECONOMY OF POLICY REFORM (Douglas Nelson ed.), in preparation.

Francois, Joseph. *The Next WTO Round: North-South Stakes in New Market Access Negotiations*, Centre for International Economic Studies, Adelaide, and Tinbergen Institute, Amsterdam and Rotterdam (2001).

Harrison, W.J. and Ken Pearson. *Computing solutions for large general equilibrium models using GEMPACK*, 9 COMPUTATIONAL ECONOMICS 83 (1996).

Hertel, Thomas W. and Will Martin. *Would Developing Countries Gain from Inclusion of Manufactures in the WTO Negotiations?*, presented at the Conference on the "WTO and the Millennium Round," Geneva, September 20–21, 1999.

Hertel, Thomas W. *Potential Gains from Reducing Trade Barriers in Manufacturing, Services and Agriculture*, 82 FEDERAL RESERVE BANK OF ST. LOUIS REVIEW 77 (2000).

Hertel, Thomas W., Bernard M. Hoekman, and Will Martin. *Developing Countries and a New Round of WTO Negotiations*, 17 THE WORLD BANK RESEARCH OBSERVER 113 (2002).

Hoekman, Bernard. 2000. *The Next Round of Services Negotiations: Identifying Priorities and Options*, 82 FEDERAL RESERVE BANK OF ST. LOUIS REVIEW 31 (2000).

McDougall, Robert et al. 1998. *Global Trade: Assistance and Protection: GTAP-4 Database*, Purdue University, W. Lafayette, IN (1998).

Stolper, Wolfgang and Paul A. Samuelson. 1941. *Protection and Real Wages, 9* REVIEW OF ECONOMIC STUDIES 58–73 (1941).

CHAPTER 39

SAFEGUARDS

Chad P. Bown* and Meredith A. Crowley**

TABLE OF CONTENTS

* Department of Economics and International Business School, Brandeis University
** Department of Economic Research, Federal Reserve Bank of Chicago. The opinions expressed in this paper are those of the authors and do not necessarily reflect those of the Federal Reserve Bank of Chicago or the Federal Reserve System.

I. Introduction

What do Argentine shoes, Indian tire rubber, Korean garlic and American wheat gluten have in common? Although some are final consumer goods while others are intermediate inputs and they differ in terms of their market structures, production technologies, cost structures, and capital intensities, they share a common situation in the WTO trading system. All were temporarily shielded from foreign competitors by measures under the WTO's Agreement on Safeguards. Table 1 describes the countries that have most frequently implemented safeguard measures under the GATT and WTO regimes.

Because safeguard measures have been used only rarely in the past, many policymakers and industry representatives are unfamiliar with them. In the world of temporary trade protection, antidumping duties have stolen the stage, though safeguards could become more prominent in the future. If the WTO's antidumping code is reformed, safeguards are the next logical choice for a country that needs a temporary shield against imports. Moreover, the rules regarding the use of safeguard measures in the GATT are biased towards favoring the same industries that currently seek protection under antidumping laws.

What is a safeguard measure? A safeguard measure is a temporary restriction on trade—either a tariff or a quota—that is used to protect a domestic industry from fair foreign competition. In contrast and as discussed at length in other chapters of this volume, antidumping duties offset what is deemed to be unfair pricing by foreign exporters, while countervailing duties "level the playing field" between a foreign government-subsidized exporter and a domestic producer. In general, a safeguard measure can be used to restrict imports of a particular good as long as imports of that good have increased and the higher

Table 1: Country use of Article XIX and the Agreement on
Safeguards, 1950–2001

Country	Number of *Article XIX* cases resulting in protection 1947–1994	Number of *Agreement on Safeguards* cases resulting in protection 1995–2001
Australia	38	0
EEC	26	0
US	25	5
Canada	22	0
Austria	8	0
South Africa	4	0
Chile	3	2
Finland	2	0
New Zealand	1	0
Norway	1	0
Czech Republic	1	2
India	0	6
Egypt	0	3
Korea	0	2
Latvia	0	1
Argentina	0	2
Brazil	0	1
Other	19	6
Total	**150**	**30**

Source: WTO

level of imports has caused or threatens to cause serious harm to the domestic industry. For example, if several firms in the American shoe industry were about to go bankrupt because Americans started to substitute their purchases toward imported shoes from a new, highly-efficient Argentine shoe company, the American industry would be eligible for a safeguard measure under the WTO rules.

The fact that Article XIX of the General Agreement on Tariffs and Trade, together with the WTO Agreement on Safeguards ("AS"), allows countries to arbitrarily restrict trade may seem surprising. After all, the preamble to the Uruguay Round ("UR") Agreements identifies the WTO's primary objective as "expanding the production of and trade in goods and services" by forming an agreement "directed to the substantial reduction of tariffs and other barriers to trade".[1] Why, therefore, does the WTO allow the use of safeguard measures?

From an economist's point-of-view, there are two ways to approach this question. First, an economist could argue that, somehow, despite our understanding that countries gain from trade and that trade restrictions are costly, temporary trade restrictions can make all countries that belong to the WTO better off. At first glance, this seems to contradict the teachings of every undergraduate course on international trade: freer trade is supposed to improve upon the welfare of all countries that embrace it. However, in the real world, countries interact repeatedly, comparative advantages change as workers acquire skills, and international prices fluctuate unexpectedly in response to everything from scientific discoveries to changes in the weather. When such realities are taken into consideration, it may actually be possible for all countries to benefit from temporary trade restrictions, relative to a scenario in which temporary trade restrictions were explicitly prohibited.

On the other hand, an economist might explain the presence of safeguard measures on a combination of both economic and political-economic grounds. The use of safeguards certainly will have consequences for income distribution, making some countries, industries, and factors of production better off even though they cause harm to others. In this case, safeguards may be permitted under the WTO to provide governments with a means to address their redistributive motives,[2] or to demonstrate favor to politically preferred interest groups if those groups have more power than those that are harmed by the potential use of safeguards.

In this chapter, we will consider both economic and political-economic reasons for policymakers to use safeguard measures. In Part II we start from the evolution of safeguards from the 1947 GATT, before turning in Part III to the Uruguay Round reforms leading to the Agreement on Safeguards. In Part IV we consider the economic effects of safeguards, before turning in Parts V and VI to a discussion of some possible reforms to the Agreement on Safeguards and also suggestions on areas in which further research is needed.

II. Background

Historically, safeguard measures permitted under Article XIX and the Agreement on Safeguards have been distinguished from other GATT-sanctioned trade protection—antidumping duties, countervailing duties and balance of payments

---

[1] *Uruguay Round Agreement Establishing the World Trade Organization.*

[2] This also requires that governments fail to have access to other policy instruments to redistribute income that would be more efficient than trade restrictions, a point that we will return to below.

exceptions—by the trade problems they were used to remedy.[3] Safeguard measures trace their roots to the United States-Mexico trade agreement of 1942. Fearing that the lowering of a tariff on some particular good could result in a larger-than-expected import surge that would hurt domestic firms, the U.S. government insisted that the agreement include a provision permitting it to re-institute tariffs in the face of large import surges.

Foreseeing that the same problem could arise in the multilateral trading system, the framers of the GATT incorporated the use of temporary trade restrictions into the agreement in the form of Article XIX. Article XIX provides that safeguard measures can be used when an increase in imports *resulting from a tariff cut* harms domestic firms producing the same or a similar product. Over time, the GATT stopped enforcing the requirement that the use of safeguards be tied to tariff cuts. Today, under the Uruguay Round's Agreement on Safeguards, safeguard measures can be used whenever a government determines that a domestic industry is suffering serious harm under the burden of increased imports that arise due to "unforeseen developments." They can be applied for an initial four-year period with the possibility for a maximum additional four-year extension.

In keeping with the GATT's guiding principle of nondiscriminatory treatment for all its members, safeguard measures were intended to be applied to all members equally. When an importing country imposes a safeguard tariff, it raises the tariff on imports from all source countries, even those with only a very small presence in the importing country's market. Moreover, while the GATT has traditionally had a strong preference that countries use tariff measures when imports must be restricted, prior to 1994, countries often used quotas and tariff-rate-quotas to protect themselves temporarily from imports. Such quantitative restrictions are undesirable for a variety of reasons,[4] including the fact that though governments may try to allocate quota rights fairly, quantitative restrictions are fundamentally discriminatory and, thus, at odds with the GATT's guiding principle of equal treatment for all countries.

To the GATT framers, a safeguard was the reinstatement of a tariff that had been removed or lowered during a trade negotiation. Thus, the GATT 1947 required countries that imposed safeguards to offer compensation to the exporting countries that lost some of their export market. With the GATT focus on trade liberalization, the preferred form of compensation was that affected exporting countries would be afforded tariff reductions on some other product. However, if countries could not agree on compensation, the GATT could authorize an exporting country to retaliate against the safeguard measure with its own tariff increase as a last resort.

Under the GATT 1947, retaliation against a safeguard measure was explicitly authorized under Article XIX:3(a). While affected countries may not have frequently resorted

---

[3] There are other places under the GATT aside from Article XIX where countries can implement safeguard-type measures such as Article XXVIII for permanent protection, Articles XII or XVIII:b for balance of payments problems, Article XXI or XX for national security or other general exceptions, and Article XXV for the granting of waivers. While we will focus on Article XIX, for a discussion of these other areas see John H. Jackson, *Safeguards and Adjustment Policies*, in THE MULTILATERAL TRADING SYSTEM: ANALYSIS AND OPTIONS FOR CHANGE (R.M. Stern ed. 1993) and J. Michael Finger, *GATT Experience with Safeguards: Making Economic and Political Sense out of the Possibilities that the GATT Allows to Restrict Imports* [*sic*] POLICY RESEARCH WORKING PAPER 2000, DEVELOPMENT RESEARCH GROUP, WORLD BANK, (1998).

[4] With limited exceptions, quantitative restrictions were generally prohibited under GATT Article XI.

to retaliation,[5] perhaps more importantly, many economists believe that the threat of retaliatory tariffs probably led countries to avoid using formal safeguard measures when the conditions otherwise may have been appropriate to do so.

Although compensation for safeguard measures was often negotiated in the 1960s and 1970s, as tariff rates fell and more products came to be freely traded, as a practical matter, it became difficult for countries to agree on compensation packages. This undoubtedly contributed to the rise of voluntary export restraints ("VERs"), export restraint agreements ("ERAs"), and orderly marketing agreements ("OMAs") in the 1980s. The GATT did not explicitly prohibit these measures, but it did not specifically allow their use either. Consequently, they came to be called "grey-area measures."

Under a grey-area measure like a VER, an importing country asks exporting countries to voluntarily accept a quantitative restriction on exports. The restriction causes the price of the good in the importing country to rise. The difference between the price the good would sell at under free trade and the higher price it sells at under the quota is known as the "quota rent." Under a standard quota system that is administered by the importing country, the importing country's government can receive the equivalent monetary value of the quota rents by arranging for a competitive auction for the licenses that give agents the right to import. Under a simple tariff system, the quota rents are equivalent to the tariff revenue received by the import-restricting country's government.

The basic difference between a VER arrangement and a quota or tariff is that in the former case the exporting countries' firms get the quota rents. Because VERs both restrict imports and compensate foreign firms, both domestic firms and foreign firms often prefer such an arrangement to a similar trade-restricting quota or tariff policy. However, VERs distort world-wide trade flows and, consequently, can harm the well-being of other countries. Moreover, consumers in importing countries are forced to pay higher prices on the products in question. One of the most famous examples of a VER was the United States-Japan automobile VER of 1981. This VER raised the price of Japanese cars in the United States 14 percent each year in 1983 and 1984[6].

Procedurally, Article XIX permitted the use of safeguards if there were (1) an increase in imports and (2) serious injury to the domestic firm or industry *caused* by the increase in imports. As a practical problem, under Article XIX there was a high degree of variation across countries as to how they enforced these injury rules. Jackson quotes an unidentified European trade official as saying "we can always find 'injury' whenever we need to for political purposes"[7]. At the other extreme, Baldwin describes how the narrow definition of injury in the US Trade Act of 1962 made it virtually impossible for U.S. domestic producers to receive safeguard protection[8].

Going into the UR, a number of problems with Article XIX were evident. (1) Countries were using quotas and tariff-rate quotas instead of tariffs when they implemented safeguards; (2) discriminatory, non-MFN application of safeguards was distorting world-wide trade flows; (3) compensation and retaliation provisions were leading countries to

[5] Of the 150 formal GATT applications of safeguards provisions between 1947–1994, there were eleven instances in which an affected country either cited Article XIX:3 or made a formal appeal for retaliation. WTO, *Analytical Index: Guide to GATT Law and Practice*, Vol II (1995), at 539–559.

[6] Pinelopi Goldberg, *Product Differentiation and Oligopoly in International Markets: The Case of the U.S. Automobile Industry*, in 63 ECONOMETRICA 929 (1995)

[7] John H. Jackson, THE WORLD TRADING SYSTEM: LAW AND POLICY OF INTERNATIONAL ECONOMIC RELATIONS 9 (1997)

[8] Robert E. Baldwin, THE POLITICAL ECONOMY OF U.S. IMPORT POLICY 85–86 (1985)

use grey-area measures that automatically provided compensation to exporting firms; (4) policymakers feared that "temporary" safeguards might be applied "permanently;" and (5) the injury criteria were vague.

Furthermore, concurrent with the rise of VERs, countries were using unfair trade laws to restrict trade far more frequently than the vast majority of economists thought reasonable. During the 1980s and 1990s it became apparent that importing country governments were using unfair trade remedies not as protection against the anti-competitive practices of foreign firms, but as safeguard measures. Unfair trade remedies were a desirable form of protection because they did not require compensation and they could be targeted against specific foreign exporters and thus were even more discriminatory than the application of a safeguard measure. Given the relationship between safeguard measures and these other forms of protection, reforms of other areas and rules of the GATT outside Article XIX could also have a profound effect on the way countries use safeguards under the WTO.

With these numerous problems in mind, the UR negotiators undertook the important task of reforming the use of safeguards.

III. Uruguay Round Reforms Affecting Safeguards

The Uruguay Round reforms amplified the GATT Article XIX escape clause provisions into the WTO Agreement on Safeguards, and Jackson notes that they were "a substantial achievement, and indeed a heroic statement of principle."[9] In this part we focus on the UR reforms affecting the economic incentives facing countries that consider the implementation of a safeguard measure. To do so, we first address areas of reform of the AS itself. At the end of this part, we turn to other UR reforms and rules that affect a government's incentives to use a safeguard measure.

A. Reforms in the Agreement on Safeguards

1. Available Policy Instruments
The first area of reform is the decision of which policy instruments that countries implementing safeguard measures shall have at their disposal. As suggested in Part II, under the GATT, countries often implemented safeguard measures through use of tariffs, quotas, tariff-rate quotas, and the popular VERs. Under the AS, countries can implement protection through either tariffs, quotas or tariff-rate quotas. Although the lack of reform that might eliminate the use of quantitative restrictions is disappointing, one substantial reform changes the way the WTO treats VERs, OMAs, and ERAs, as they are now expressly prohibited under Article 11:1(b). This decision to permit quotas, tariff rate quotas and similar quantitative restrictions does have an important economic impact that we will further describe in Part IV below.

2. MFN versus Specificity
A second reform of the escape clause involved the question of whether use of safeguard protection can be country-specific, or whether a safeguard-imposing country must follow the non-discrimination rules of the most-favoured-nation ("MFN") clause. The agreement requires safeguard measures to be imposed on an MFN basis, as stated in Article 2:2, "[s]afeguard measures shall be applied to a product being imported irrespective of its

---

[9] Jackson, *supra* note 7, at 210.

source," and in the case of a quantitative restriction, Article 5:2(a) states that the quota shares should be allocated based on the share of the market that exporters had in a prior representative period.

However, there are two situations in which the MFN rule apparently does not have to be followed. First, Article 5:2(b) allows countries to depart from the principle if "clear demonstration is provided to the Committee [on Safeguards] that . . . imports from certain Members have increased in disproportionate percentage in relation to the total increase of imports of the product concerned in the representative period." Second, the Agreement does not allow restriction of imports from developing countries that have less than three percent of total imports, unless the aggregate share of all such countries is more than nine percent (AS, Article 9:1).

3. Compensation and Retaliation

A major reform of the Uruguay Round was the provision that countries facing absolute import surges would not be required to offer compensation for the first three years during which safeguard measures are imposed, as provided in Article 8:3. Although the general rule of the WTO under Article 8:2 is that compensation must be offered to affected countries after a safeguard measure has been implemented, this important exception means that in practical terms, it rarely is.

As we suggested in Part II, compensation for implemented safeguard measures can take the form of additional liberalization by the protection-implementing country. If no agreement on compensation between the safeguard-implementing and the exporting country is reached, Article 8:2 sanctions the withdrawal of "substantially equivalent concessions," or an increase in a foreign tariff based on the rule of reciprocity, as was the case under GATT Article XIX.

One intent of the reform which limits compensation was arguably to make use of safeguards relatively more attractive in "legitimate circumstances," relative to the alternative popular policy instruments whose use had far out-paced the escape clause—such as anti-dumping duties, protection for balance of payment purposes, VERs or other "grey-area" measures. On the other hand, the removal of compensation makes it more likely that a country who might not have imposed safeguard measures at all may be induced into doing so, because now the costs of doing so are less than would otherwise be the case.

As suggested in the last part, a second and popular means of compensation under the escape clause, or the implicit compensation of "quota rents" embodied in the policy of a VER, was also outlawed by the AS. At the least, this serves to eliminate a useful, and arguably efficient compensation mechanism for instances in which a country that implements a safeguard measure does not face an "absolute surge in imports" and thus must compensate affected trading partners in some manner.

4. Procedural Reforms

The last set of reforms accomplished by the UR negotiations were primarily procedural in nature. These included formally defining the injury requirement, establishing a surveillance monitoring body, and specifying the maximum length that a safeguard measure can be in place.

An important procedural improvement over Article XIX was the establishment of a more precise definition of "injury." Under the WTO it is now defined as a "significant overall impairment in the position of the domestic industry." (AS, Article 4:1(a)). The

AS also included a more explicit determination of the data to be used to measure injury: "the rate and the amount of the increase in imports of the product concerned in absolute and relative terms, the share of the domestic market taken by increased imports, changes in the level of sales, production, productivity, capacity utilization, profits and losses, and employment" (AS, Article 4:2(a)).

Second, the new AS also provides for surveillance with the establishment of a Safeguards Committee whose charge it is to monitor and oversee use of the AS provisions by WTO members. For example, Article 12 of the AS states that members must notify or consult with the Committee on Safeguards if they initiate a safeguard investigation and then make any decision on imposing or extending safeguard protection. Under Article 13, the Committee is also charged with overseeing use of the agreement and compliance with its procedural elements.

Finally, Article 7 established the maximum duration that a safeguard measure can remain in place and the conditions necessary for the initial period of the safeguard application to be extended. First, Article 7:1 limits the continued application of a safeguard measure to the length of time necessary to prevent serious injury and facilitate adjustment, and at a maximum, the "period of initial application and any extension thereof, shall not exceed eight years." (AS, Article 7:3) In order to extend a safeguard measure beyond its initial four-year maximum, the WTO member imposing the safeguard must also show evidence that the industry being protected by the measure is adjusting, and in cases in which safeguards have been applied for longer than one year, the Member "shall progressively liberalize [the measure] at regular intervals during the period of application." (AS, Article 7:4).

These procedural reforms could have an economic impact on various stages of a country's safeguard process; for example, both at the petition initiating stage and at the domestic government's accept/reject stage. First, if the safeguard process is bureaucratic (or apolitical) in nature, a clearer definition of what constitutes "injury" would be expected to affect the pattern of petitions that industries initiate. With a well-defined criterion of what would make a "successful" petition, an industry may tend to alter the pattern of initiated petitions to those that fit that criterion. The effect could work in either direction—industries that think they are injured but that do not satisfy the better-defined criteria may be less likely to petition, and industries that did not understand the earlier criteria now with the clarification may be more likely to initiate and put pressure on the domestic government.

Second, at the domestic safeguard authority's decision-making stage, the pattern of accepted versus rejected petitions may change, relative to the pre-UR case. But again the reduced uncertainty could have an economic impact that would go in either direction—leading to either more or fewer acceptances. For example, domestic governments may have been likely to accept a weak safeguard petition under the GATT, but would no longer feel comfortable accepting the same petition given the clearer definition of injury established by the UR reforms. This increased transparency also reduces some of the discretion it may have enjoyed earlier. For the case of the United States, the government may no longer be able to hide behind the argument that a petition does not satisfy the injury requirement (when that requirement was ill-defined), and therefore if it chooses not to protect it will have to come up with other reasons why. Politically, this may be more difficult. On the other hand the United States may now be able to erect credible arguments that other petitions fail to satisfy the injury requirement so that they can now more credibly rely on the WTO for commitment power to not implement protection in other situations.

B. Reforms Captured in Other UR Agreements that Affect the Use of Safeguards

Given that countries can implement trade policy restrictions by substituting between policy instruments, reforms of other areas of the GATT also have an impact—whether intended or unintended—on use of the AS.

One example of an important reform was captured in the WTO's new Dispute Settlement Understanding ("DSU") and relates to the compensation available to affected trading partners should countries fail to bring their policies into conformity with their WTO obligations. In trade disputes where countries are unable to negotiate mutually agreeable compensation, the DSU has established a level of permissible retaliation in recent trade dispute cases (e.g. *EC—Bananas* and *EC—Beef Hormones* [10]) that is similar to the level of retaliation authorized by the AS.

To consider the impact that this has on a country's potential use of the AS, take the extreme case in which a country wishes to offer protection to a domestic industry that was injured by imports, but there was no "absolute surge in imports." Thus, the country will have to offer compensation under the AS. Moreover, suppose there is no evidence of dumping. The country must choose between implementing a safeguard and offering compensation or implementing an illegal antidumping duty ("ADD") and facing possible DSU-authorized retaliation. If the retaliation that can be authorized under both the AS and the DSU is identical, there is little economic incentive for the country to use the legal safeguard provisions. Even if the country were to impose an ADD and the affected trading partner filed a dispute, in the worst-case scenario that the ADD-imposing country lost the dispute, it would only have to yield the same compensation as it would have faced under the safeguard provisions. In this case, if there is even a tiny chance that the ADD-imposing country could win the dispute, then the country is clearly better off "cheating" and using the antidumping ("AD") measure rather than the safeguard provisions, even when there is no evidence of dumping or injury.

Furthermore, we also expect that the procedural reforms that have served to essentially define the minimum length of the dispute settlement process to have an effect on the duration of application of a particular safeguard measure.[11] Under the GATT regime, due to the fact that individual countries (including the defending country) had the power to veto the process at any stage, the length and even conclusion of a trade dispute was uncertain and even indeterminate. However, under reforms to the DSU, maximum time limits for different phases of the process have been adopted—initial consultations will last no more than sixty days, the period from the establishment of a panel to the circulation of its report will take no longer than nine months, etc. Petersmann suggests that the DSU "will be the quickest worldwide system for the settlement of disputes among states."[12]

Recall that the change in compensation requirements under the AS gives a government the right to impose safeguard measures as a response to an "absolute increase in imports" without having to provide compensation for three years. We argued that the likely impact of this reform is that governments will typically design safeguard measures that respond to an "absolute increase" to tend to be no longer than three years in length in order to

[10] Decision by the Arbitrators, *European Communities—Regime for the Importation, Sale and Distribution of Bananas*, WT/DS27/ARB (1999), and Decision by the Arbitrators, *European Communities—Measures Concerning Meat and Meat Products (Hormones)* WT/DS26/ARB (1999) and WT/DS48/ARB (1999).
[11] *See Uruguay Round Understanding on the Rules and Procedures Governing the Settlement of Disputes* for the time limits for each phase of the WTO's dispute settlement process.
[12] Ernst-Ulrich Petersmann, The GATT/WTO Dispute Settlement System: International Law, International Organizations and Dispute Settlement 183 (1997)

avoid the compensation requirement.[13] In a similar manner, once the minimum length of the full dispute settlement process is established, this can also affect the way in which a domestic policymaker designs or chooses to implement a dubious safeguard measure that knowingly does not satisfy the criteria set out in the AS. Given that retaliation (compensation) cannot be applied retroactively and must end once a WTO-illegal policy has been removed, policymakers can implement an illegal safeguard measure for the anticipated length of the dispute settlement process.[14]

A second important reform introduced by the UR Agreements that may be having an impact on the way countries use the AS relates to the issue of VERs. Under the WTO Agreement on Antidumping, price undertakings are explicitly allowed and arguably are even encouraged as a means for countries to resolve an AD case. Price undertakings refer to an explicit agreement between the investigating AD authority and the foreign exporting firm that is the subject of the AD investigation where the foreign firm agrees to raise its price to a level that eliminates the "dumping margin" established by the domestic AD authority. However, such a price increase will typically decrease imports, thus the foreign firm's "voluntary" price increase leads to an outcome (in terms of welfare) quite similar to that generated by a VER.

The economic impact of this reform for the AS, is that if a country seeks to protect a domestic industry by "managing trade", this is explicitly encouraged under the Agreement on Antidumping and explicitly prohibited under the AS. All else equal, this flexibility may lead to more antidumping activity and less safeguard activity.

There are separate safeguards provisions for many of the "new" areas of trade brought into GATT discipline with the establishment of the WTO: agriculture, apparel, textiles and clothing and services. Each of these areas of trade has a distinct UR Agreement which has its own safeguard provision therein, for example, see Article 6 of the Agreement on Textiles and Clothing, and Article 5 of the Agreement on Agriculture. Furthermore, Article X of the General Agreement on Trade in Services calls for negotiations on services safeguards and provided a one-time three year window for modification or withdrawal of commitments.

The final point that we should make is that there was virtually no reform to another Agreement on Safeguards alternative, Article XXVIII. While in practice Article XXVIII has been rarely used, for countries that seek to protect an industry permanently, they are still able to do so just as they were under the GATT regime.

IV. Economic Effects

Because safeguard measures have been rarely used, does this imply that their economic effect is small? Here we argue that such a conclusion is faulty, as in order to accurately

---

[13] The US steel safeguard applied in March 2002 was imposed for three years and one day.

[14] Note, however, that if a government implements a safeguard measure that does not satisfy the "absolute surge in imports" requirement, provided the WTO Council for Trade in Goods does not disapprove, the government may not need to wait until the completion of the panel process of a formal DSU dispute to obtain compensation in the form of authorized retaliation. For an example, see the EU's response to the U.S. steel safeguard measures implemented in March 2002, *Immediate Notification Under Article 12.5 Of The Agreement On Safeguards To The Council For Trade In Goods Of Proposed Suspension Of Concessions And Other Obligations Referred To In Paragraph 2 Of Article 8 Of The Agreement On Safeguards European Communities.* G/SG/43, May 15, 2002, and G/SG/43/Suppl.1, June 20, 2002. Furthermore, there are also DSU "urgency" exceptions that countries may resort to, perhaps in order to help prevent trading partners from drawing out the length of the dispute settlement process in order to keep a temporary protective measure in place.

assess the role of safeguards in the world trading system, we need to compare the economic outcome of a world in which safeguards are permitted to the economic outcome in a world in which they are not allowed. To simply assess them by measuring the costs and benefits on the few occasions in which they have been used captures only a small part of the picture. In this part, we will review two broad categories of economic research, the theoretical research that analyzes the difference between a world with safeguards and a world without safeguards, and the empirical research that measures the costs and benefits of safeguard measures that have been used in the past.

From the perspective of policymakers who must determine the details of how policies are designed and implemented, some of the most important economic research will be focused on the specifics of safeguard measures. Are tariffs better than quotas? For whom? Should protection last three years or eight? If a country faces higher imports of bicycles from China, but not from Mexico, should a safeguard tariff be imposed against China, or both China and Mexico? If French cheesemakers suffer a significant loss when the United States institutes a safeguard measure against cheese, should the United States be made to compensate France? If so, how?

An increasing number of economic researchers have examined safeguard measures from a variety of angles. The theoretical research papers typically address the common question: why does the WTO allow the use of safeguards?

Essentially, there are two categories of answers in the economics literature. The first argument is that safeguard measures can create a net benefit for the world as a whole. The safeguard may make some countries better off and others worse off, but if we add up the gains and losses to everyone in the world, the sum total is positive. In other words, the gains of temporary trade protection outweigh the losses. We pursue this argument in the next two sections. In the third section, we turn to another argument justifying safeguard measures—that its presence is motivated by the interests of importing countries, and in particular, import-competing industries in those countries. In Section D we explore some of the economic arguments that seek to explain why safeguards are used or not-used relative to other policy instruments that have similar features to the safeguard provisions. Finally, in Section E we turn to other related (and future) empirical work on safeguards.

A. Does the Inclusion of Safeguards Result in More or Less Liberalization Overall?

Perhaps the most widely cited argument for safeguards is that they can facilitate greater tariff liberalization by governments during trade negotiations. Because a government has an escape valve if a tariff reduction causes pain to its own producers, it has more freedom to make larger and potentially more risky tariff reductions. Because there are large gains from permanent tariff reductions and relatively small costs from imposing temporary safeguards in a few sectors, the world gains by having safeguards in a trade agreement, even when they are not actually used. Jackson provides an intuitive discussion of this.[15]

Ethier asks: how does the interaction between unilateralism and multilateralism affect the pace of trade liberalization?[16] His central concern is to analyze a trading system like the GATT/WTO which is characterized by the general practice of negotiating tariff reductions to benefit all members and the occasional use of temporary unilateral tariff

---

[15] Jackson, *supra* note 7
[16] Wilfred J. Ethier, *Unilateralism in a Multilateral World*, 112 ECONOMIC JOURNAL 266 (2002).

increases through safeguards or antidumping duties. He develops a multi-country model in which countries grow at different rates. He shows, first, that the pace of trade liberalization is constrained by the slowest-growing countries in the world. He then illustrates how allowing these countries to temporarily raise their tariffs can accelerate the pace of worldwide trade liberalization. The key insight is that when countries negotiate tariff reductions, they do not know if their growth will be fast or slow. In a trade agreement that does not allow temporary tariff increases, countries fear that their growth will be slow and will negotiate only small tariff reductions. When safeguards are added to the trade agreement, countries negotiate larger tariff reductions because they know that if they turn out to have slow growth, they can temporarily increase their tariffs.

Klimenko, Ramey, and Watson arrive at a similar result by examining the question of why the WTO's Dispute Settlement Body ("DSB") exists.[17] In their paper, they show that when countries regularly renegotiate their tariffs, as in the GATT/WTO trade rounds, a DSB is necessary for the trade agreement to survive. A DSB makes it possible for countries to punish each other for violations. Because countries want to avoid punishment, they are less likely to violate a trade agreement that includes a DSB. As an extension to their paper, they also show that if the DSB allows countries to temporarily raise their tariffs (as is the case with safeguard measures) in response to some unexpected change in the economic environment, they will negotiate larger tariff reductions initially.

Although some of the theoretical arguments suggest that safeguards help to facilitate trade liberalization, other economists arrive at the opposite conclusion. Staiger and Tabellini show that allowing for safeguard measures could reduce the credibility of a trade agreement.[18] If governments are not fully committed to liberal trade, the productive factors in their economies may not efficiently reallocate because changing sectors is costly, and they *expect* their government to step in and utilize the safeguard provisions at their disposal. From this perspective, the inclusion of a safeguard measure can weaken the overall agreement.

B. Safeguards as Insurance against Negative Terms of Trade Shocks

Another economic argument in favor of the inclusion of a safeguard clause is that it acts as a form of insurance against changing international prices, or, in economics jargon, fluctuations in the terms of trade. Consider a country that imports a good whose price fluctuates substantially. For example, the price of steel imported by the United States rises with the price of its main inputs—iron and energy—and falls as new factories with low-cost technologies come online. When prices change, the economic environment can become so different that countries want to pull out of a trade agreement that constrains them to set low tariffs.

Bagwell and Staiger explore how price fluctuations affect large players in a trade agreement—countries like the United States, the EU and Japan which have markets that are so large that their safeguard measures can significantly alter world prices.[19] They argue that due to the self-enforcing nature of the trade agreement, in periods of large import volumes, a safeguard measure acts as a pressure valve to enable countries to

[17] Mikhail Klimenko, Garey Ramey, and Joel Watson, *Recurrent Trade Agreements and the Value of External Enforcement*, UC SAN DIEGO MIMEO (2002)

[18] Robert Staiger and Guido Tabellini, *Discretionary Trade Policy and Excessive Protection*, 77 AMERICAN ECONOMIC REVIEW 823 (1987)

[19] Kyle Bagwell and Robert W. Staiger, *A Theory of Managed Trade*, 80 AMERICAN ECONOMIC REVIEW 779 (1990)

sustain cooperation by temporarily raising tariffs. In the absence of a safeguard clause, countries would not be able to sustain cooperation, and the result would be a costly trade war of high levels of tariff retaliation. Fischer and Prusa show that even small countries, which cannnot affect world prices by imposing a safeguard, can use safeguards to insure themselves against international price shocks.[20]

To date, empirical research in economics has not been able to prove or disprove the ideas put forth in the papers mentioned above. In some ways this is an impossible task—how can we prove that countries negotiate lower tariffs when a safeguard is part of a trade agreement when all the trade agreements in existence include safeguards?[21]

C. Safeguards Assist Import-Competing Industries

The starting point for another important area of research is the belief that the WTO allows the use of safeguards because of concerns for the interests of importing countries, and in particular importing countries with firms and industries that compete with foreign firms. This may arise because the agent that benefits from the potential safeguard is politically powerful, and the result is that these papers then investigate how the politically powerful agent gains from the safeguard. If one country pursues a policy that benefits itself but harms other countries, economists want to understand how and why the policy creates a benefit so that they can develop alternative policies that create a similar benefit but reduce or eliminate the harm to others. Here we pursue three potential arguments explaining why governments may seek to assist import-competing industries: to help them catch-up to their foreign competitors, to facilitate their exit from the industry, or to reap the gains from a politically-preferred sector.

1. Technological Catch-Up

Several theoretical papers[22] explore how safeguards benefit import-competing firms that are technologically behind their foreign competitors. These papers examine the consequences of using a temporary safeguard to induce domestic firms to adopt newer, more efficient production technologies. Economists have long understood that a government subsidy is better than a tariff for helping a firm adopt a new technology.[23] A direct subsidy can achieve the same result as a safeguard, but because it does not also increase the

---

[20] Ronald D. Fischer and Thomas J. Prusa, *Contingent Protection as Better Insurance*, NBER WORKING PAPER 6933 (1999)

[21] A related paper is the recent empirical contribution by Robert Staiger and Guido Tabellini, *Do GATT Rules Help Governments Make Domestic Commitments?*, 11 ECONOMICS AND POLITICS 109 (1999), who compare two different policy environments (U.S. escape clause petitions and U.S. Tokyo Round sectoral exclusions) to investigate the question of whether GATT rules help governments make trade policy commitments to its private sector. The fact that they find evidence to support the claim that GATT rules do give governments commitment power also provides support for the theory that the inclusion of an escape clause can have damaging effects that erode a government's ability to commit to liberalization.

[22] Kiminori Matsuyama, *Perfect Equilibria in a Trade Liberalization Game*, 80 AMERICAN ECONOMIC REVIEW 480 (1990); Kaz Miyagiwa and Yuka Ohno, *Closing the Technology Gap Under Protection*, 85 AMERICAN ECONOMIC REVIEW 755 (1995); Kaz Miyagiwa and Yuka Ohno, *Credibility of Protection and Incentives to Innovate*, 40 INTERNATIONAL ECONOMIC REVIEW 143 (1999); Meredith Crowley, *Do Safeguard Tariffs and Antidumping Duties Open or Close Technology Gaps?*, FEDERAL RESERVE BANK OF CHICAGO Working Paper 2002–13 (2002).

[23] Avinash K. Dixit and Victor Norman, THEORY OF INTERNATIONAL TRADE (1980); Richard E. Caves, Jeffrey A. Frankel and Ronald W. Jones, WORLD TRADE AND PAYMENTS: AN INTRODUCTION (2002); and Paul R. Krugman and Maurice Obstfeld, INTERNATIONAL ECONOMICS: THEORY AND POLICY (2000), are a few standard textbooks that make this point.

price facing consumers, it is less costly to society as a whole.[24] Thus, using a safeguard to facilitate technological improvement is a "second-best" policy at best. However, if a government wants to use a trade policy to induce technological improvement, what specific features should this safeguard measure have? How long should it last? Should it be applied against imports from all countries or just a few?

Matsuyama, and Miyagiwa and Ohno, provide theoretical support for the requirement of a strict termination date for safeguard protection and allowing exporting countries to retaliate against safeguard measures that extend beyond the three year "grace period" where an absolute increase in imports is involved.[25] Miyagiwa and Ohno find that safeguards provide an incentive for protected firms to innovate quickly only if the cost of the new technology is falling over time and the termination date for safeguard protection is credibly enforced by foreign retaliation. One implication of their paper is that the exact length of time that a safeguard must be in place in order to induce a domestic firm to acquire a new technology will depend critically on how quickly the cost of the new technology is falling. Thus, the WTO's three-year time limit will provide too much protection in some cases and not enough in others. The cases in which it provides too little protection are particularly troubling. The safeguard will force consumers to pay higher prices but will not yield any benefit to the economy. Crowley finds that a nondiscriminatory safeguard tariff can accelerate technology adoption by a domestic import-competing firm, but will slow down technology adoption by foreign exporting firms.[26] Because an MFN safeguard tariff can delay a foreign firm's adoption of new technology, its worldwide welfare costs may exceed its benefits.

Unfortunately, the little empirical evidence on the effect of safeguards on technology adoption is not very encouraging. A 1982 study by the US government's administrative body that reviews safeguard petitions, the US International Trade Commission ("USITC"), found that most safeguards failed to promote positive adjustment to import competition. Rather than assisting companies in upgrading their facilities, in most cases safeguards merely slowed an industry's inevitable decline. A review of U.S. safeguard cases since 1974 shows that some industries seek and receive protection repeatedly—for example, stainless alloy tool steel was granted safeguard protection in 1976 and again in 1983.

2. Senescent Industries

Another group of theoretical papers shows how firms in declining industries can utilize political support to maintain protection. Hillman, Brainard and Verdier, and Magee all examine the use of tariff protection to allow a dying industry to collapse slowly, rather than quickly.[27] Because these papers all assume that there are high costs to quickly scaling back production, they find that a temporary tariff that can slow an industry's decline

---

[24] More generally, economists have shown that an import tariff has an equivalent economic impact as the simultaneous imposition of a production subsidy and consumption tax. The direct subsidy would thus be more efficient than a safeguard tariff as it would not have the second welfare distortion of the tax effect that raises the price facing consumers.

[25] Matsuyama, *supra* note 22; Miyagiwa and Ohno, *supra* note 22.

[26] Crowley, *supra* note 22.

[27] Arye Hillman, *Declining Industries and Political-Support Protectionist Motives*, 72 AMERICAN ECONOMIC REVIEW 1180 (1982); S. Lael Brainard and Thierry Verdier, *Lobbying and Adjustment in Declining Industries*, 38 EUROPEAN ECONOMIC REVIEW 586 (1994); S. Lael Brainard and Thierry Verdier, *The Political Economy of Declining Industries: Senescent Industry Collapse Revisited*, 42 JOURNAL OF INTERNATIONAL ECONOMICS 221 (1997); Christopher Magee, *Declining Industries and Persistent Protection*, 10(4) REVIEW OF INTERNATIONAL ECONOMICS 749 (2002)

can improve an importing country's welfare. However, this type of policy also slows the reallocation of capital and labor into other industrial sectors in which they would be more productive. This loss of productivity is an indirect welfare cost on the country imposing the safeguard measure.

3. Political-Economy Motives

Both the economist Robert Baldwin and the political scientist Wendy Hansen have found that political factors are important in determining whether or not an American petition for safeguard protection is successful.[28] Evidence that safeguards are politically tainted in a country like the United States that has transparent and well-defined administrative procedures underscores the necessity for the WTO to thoroughly review how safeguard policy is being carried out by its many members.

D. Frequency and Use of Safeguards Relative to Other Trade Policy Instruments

There is some empirical research that addresses the question: why have safeguards been used so rarely? Hansen and Prusa argue that the existence of another policy tool, the antidumping duty, explains the rare use of safeguard measures.[29] Indeed, during the 1987–1994 period, while there were only eighteen safeguard measures implemented worldwide, Miranda et al.[30] report that over seven hundred antidumping measures were used, after 1586 antidumping investigations.[31] In the case of the United States, Baldwin argues that the strict injury criteria of the U.S. law, especially prior to 1974, has led the US ITC to reject many safeguard petitions.[32]

While there is undoubtedly some truth to these ideas, there are other potentially important explanations. For example, economists believe that provisions for compensation and the threat of retaliation may have dissuaded countries from imposing safeguards in numerous instances. However, it is impossible to document all of the potential occasions in which a country chose not to pursue a safeguard, although it may have considered doing so.

Nevertheless, Bown has proposed a theory to explain why countries that have committed to implementing protection will choose to use safeguard measures, as opposed to using GATT/WTO-illegal alternatives that may result in a trade dispute.[33] The explanation is that countries will use safeguards when the trading partners that are affected by the increase in import protection have a substantial capacity to retaliate. By considering

[28] Baldwin, *supra* note 8; Wendy L. Hansen, *The International Trade Commission and the Politics of Protection*, 84 AMERICAN POLITICAL SCIENCE REVIEW 21(1990).
[29] Wendy L. Hansen and Thomas J. Prusa, *The Road Most Taken: the Rise of Title VII Protection*, 18 THE WORLD ECONOMY 295 (1995)
[30] Jorge Miranda, Raul A. Torres and Mario Ruiz, *The International Use of Antidumping: 1987–1997*, 32 JOURNAL OF WORLD TRADE 5 (1998)
[31] A simple comparison of the number of safeguard and antidumping measures that are implemented does not tell the entire story, however, given that AD measures are country-specific and each safeguard measure can affect multiple exporting countries. Suppose we were to compare the number of countries affected instead of measures imposed. If we assumed that that an average of twenty countries were affected by each safeguard measure (e.g., the average number of countries affected in the twenty-one safeguard measures investigated by Chad P. Bown and Rachel McCulloch in *Nondiscrimination and the WTO Agreement on Safeguards*, 2(3) World Trade Review 327 (2003), the relevant comparison would be 360 versus 700 affected countries. This would still indicate a significant bias toward the use of antidumping measures.
[32] Baldwin, *supra* note 8.
[33] Chad P. Bown, *The Economics of Trade Disputes, the GATT's Article XXIII and the WTO's Dispute Settlement Understanding*, 14(3) ECONOMICS AND POLITICS 283 (2002)

the GATT rules of retaliation that take place under safeguards and dispute settlement negotiations, the safeguard provisions can be interpreted as providing cover to countries that must implement protection but who wish to mitigate the retaliatory response and limit the compensation due to affected trading partners. Given that the affected trading partners are large, policymakers find the safeguard measures attractive if retaliation threats under dispute settlement provisions are either unpoliced or excessive, which may have been the case under the GATT regime.

Bown[34] pursues the empirical question of whether the concern for retaliation affects a government's policy decision of how to implement protection: under the GATT's safeguard provisions or through some 'GATT-illegal' provision that results in a viable trade dispute. Using data on 1973–1994 Article XIX safeguard measures[35] and trade disputes that were filed under Article XXIII, the results suggest that countries use the safeguard measures as opposed to GATT-illegal policies when there is a substantial concern for retaliation.

While the threat of retaliation may be important to a government's determination of how to implement protection, this does not address the question of whether the threat of retaliation affects the decision of whether a government will offer safeguard protection, relative to no protection at all. Recent empirical research by Blonigen and Bown[36], however, does find that the threat of retaliation is an important deterrent for firms and governments that are considering trade protection in the form of antidumping duties, a related policy instrument. Using data on U.S. antidumping measures between 1980–1998, they find that the threat of foreign firms retaliating through antidumping duties on U.S. exports affects the decision of which foreign firms are named in a petition, while the threat of a GATT/WTO trade dispute and potential retaliation through that channel affects the U.S. government in its antidumping duty determination decision. Thus, while the Bown result suggests that retaliation threats affect how countries implement protection, the Blonigen and Bown result suggests that retaliation threats also affect the decision of whether a government should implement protection at all. Given that safeguard measures and antidumping duties are potentially substitutable policy instruments, these related empirical results on retaliation threats may also have implications for both how firms (in addition to countries) choose between policy instruments when they seek import protection, and also whether to seek protection through safeguard measures at all.

E. Further Empirical Research on Safeguards

Hansen and Prusa have produced an important paper that explored the available data on U.S. safeguard measures.[37] They examine the trade-restricting effects of five U.S. safeguard measures imposed between 1980 to 1988. They find that trade volumes fell by an average of 34 percent after the government imposed the safeguard measure. On the other hand, over the same time period, they find that trade volumes fall by an average of only eleven percent when the government imposes an antidumping duty. Even though

---

[34] Chad P. Bown, *Trade Disputes and the Implementation of Protection under the GATT: An Empirical Assessment*, 62(2) JOURNAL OF INTERNATIONAL ECONOMICS 263 (2004).

[35] The paper also uses data on countries invoking protection through the GATT's Article XXVIII, which is similar to Article XIX (in terms of how compensation is handled), although it provides for permanent protection

[36] Bruce A. Blonigen and Chad P. Bown, *Antidumping and Retaliation Threats*, 60(2) JOURNAL OF INTERNATIONAL ECONOMICS 249 (2003).

[37] Hansen and Prusa, *supra* note 29

safeguard measures are more effective at restricting imports, U.S. industries file more antidumping than safeguard petitions and the success rate for antidumping (63 percent) is higher than for safeguard (26 percent) petitions. Hansen and Prusa thus conclude that while it may have a less effective impact on overall trade, antidumping protection is most likely more popular because it is easier to obtain. As one of the few empirical papers on safeguards, this is a useful starting point for future research.

The empirical research on safeguards applies almost entirely to the pre-UR regime. One exception is recent work by Bown and McCulloch who use data on WTO safeguard measures implemented under the 1995–2000 period to investigate the differential impact that the form of the safeguard (tariff, tariff rate quota, quota) has on exporting country market shares.[38] They find that exporters' market shares after the application of the safeguard are more closely tied to historical market shares for quantitative measures than tariffs, supporting the idea that quotas have the potential to discriminate in favor of historical suppliers and be biased against new entrants.

Other questions that economic researchers might consider include the following: what has changed since the creation of the WTO? Furthermore, we previously identified five concerns that existed before the UR and discussed the UR reforms intended to address them. Thus, regarding the use of compensation and retaliation, how has the prohibition on retaliation during the first three years of a safeguard measure directed against an absolute increase in imports affected its use?

There is evidence that some countries are increasing their usage of safeguards. From 1980 to 1994, the United States imposed only seven safeguard measures, or fewer than one every two years. In contrast, between 1994 and 1999, the United States imposed five safeguard measures or one per year. On a worldwide basis, it seems that safeguard use has increased. Table 2 documents the number of safeguards reported to the GATT/WTO per year divided by both the number of GATT/WTO members and by the total trade volume of the members. Safeguard use fell fairly steadily from about 1960 to 1994. Interestingly, after the UR reforms were implemented around the world, their use began to grow. It is too early to determine if this is the beginning of a long-term trend or just a temporary increase, but it seems that safeguards have become a little more popular.[39]

Anecdotally, two interesting phenomena can be observed. First, many countries imposing safeguards have chosen to apply them for three years rather than four—presumably to avoid compensation or retaliation. Second, threats of retaliation have become concrete. In the wake of the U.S. safeguard measure on steel, several countries have published lists of U.S. products that would be hit with tariffs if the safeguard remains in place for more than three years or if the measure is otherwise found by the DSU to violate the United States's WTO obligations and the United States refuses to bring it into conformity.[40] For example, the EU claimed that for many of the products there had only been a relative increase in imports so that they did not have to wait three years for compensation.

---

[38] Chad P. Bown and Rachel McCulloch, *Nondiscrimination and the WTO Agreement on Safeguards*, 2(3) WORLD TRADE REVIEW 327 (2003).

[39] There was a substantial increase in the use of safeguards in 2002 after the March U.S. steel safeguard decision resulted in higher U.S. tariffs. Many trading partners responded by also implementing safeguard protection against the likely deflection of exports of steel from the United States.

[40] As of February 2003, nine WTO members (EU, Japan, Korea, China, Switzerland, Norway, New Zealand, Brazil, and Taiwan) had initiated formal cases against the United States under the DSU regarding the March 2002 safeguard measure on steel imports. For the list of the goods the EU had threatened to retaliate over, *see Immediate Notification Under Article 12.5 Of The Agreement On Safeguards To The Council For Trade In Goods Of Proposed Suspension Of Concessions And Other Obligations Referred To In Paragraph 2 Of Article 8 Of The Agreement On Safeguards European Communities.* G/SG/43, May 15, 2002.

Table 2: The relative frequency of Safeguards Use, 1950–2000

Year	Number of members	Value of trade*	Safeguard measures imposed	Safeguards per member	Safeguards per value of trade
1950	28	208.39	1	0.036	0.048
1951	32	289.60	0	0.000	0.000
1952	32	288.78	2	0.063	0.069
1953	33	299.64	0	0.000	0.000
1954	33	313.22	1	0.030	0.032
1955	34	338.80	2	0.059	0.059
1956	34	357.98	2	0.059	0.056
1957	36	376.08	3	0.083	0.080
1958	36	355.80	5	0.139	0.141
1959	36	384.27	3	0.083	0.078
1960	37	431.22	2	0.054	0.046
1961	39	445.47	2	0.051	0.045
1962	43	468.48	7	0.163	0.149
1963	59	496.61	2	0.034	0.040
1964	63	553.03	5	0.079	0.090
1965	64	593.95	2	0.031	0.034
1966	68	637.60	3	0.044	0.047
1967	73	659.83	5	0.068	0.076
1968	74	708.47	5	0.068	0.071
1969	75	783.76	2	0.027	0.026
1970	77	860.29	3	0.039	0.035
1971	79	929.45	3	0.038	0.032
1972	80	1066.46	1	0.013	0.009
1973	82	1410.13	2	0.024	0.014
1974	82	1871.04	3	0.037	0.016
1975	82	1778.71	5	0.061	0.028
1976	82	1892.69	12	0.146	0.063
1977	82	2004.17	7	0.085	0.035
1978	83	2150.96	7	0.084	0.033
1979	84	2473.04	4	0.048	0.016
1980	84	2739.51	7	0.083	0.026
1981	85	2450.58	2	0.024	0.008
1982	87	2143.20	5	0.057	0.023
1983	89	2025.41	5	0.056	0.025
1984	89	2095.21	4	0.045	0.019
1985	89	2055.43	4	0.045	0.019
1986	91	2233.55	4	0.044	0.018
1987	94	2578.34	4	0.043	0.016
1988	95	2867.28	1	0.011	0.003
1989	95	3015.29	1	0.011	0.003
1990	99	3321.87	1	0.010	0.003
1991	102	3296.72	5	0.049	0.015
1992	104	3468.51	3	0.029	0.009
1993	114	3365.46	3	0.026	0.009
1994	128	3755.71	0	0.000	0.000
1995	128	4428.90	0	0.000	0.000
1996	128	4568.03	3	0.023	0.007
1997	130	4667.64	3	0.023	0.006
1998	133	4570.74	5	0.038	0.011
1999	135	4717.20	10	0.074	0.021
2000	140	5241.68	15**	0.107	0.029

*Value of WTO trade in billions of 1996 U.S. dollars.

**15 measures including provisional safeguards of up to 200 days. 10 measures not including provisional measures.

Source: author's calculation based on WTO, International Trade Statistics (2001). Nominal data deflated using the U.S. GDP deflator.

Regarding the type of policy measure, since 1994 countries have imposed both tariffs and quotas. Thus, despite rule changes introduced in the UR, safeguards are still not subject to the basic GATT/WTO principle of equal treatment for all countries. This is compounded by evidence that even when countries are imposing safeguard tariffs, they are regularly applying safeguards in a discriminatory way.[41]

As for the injury criteria, it is difficult to assess their stringency without detailed data on safeguard investigations around the world. However, it is encouraging to observe that countries are turning down some safeguard petitions. Of the 35 safeguard investigations conducted around the world between 1995 and 1999, only 21 resulted in import-restricting measures.[42]

It is also too early to tell at this stage if countries will try to make temporary safeguard protection permanent by extending protection beyond the eight year maximum limit that the AS allows, perhaps through either Article XXVIII or through other WTO provisions, such as the Agreement on Antidumping. The fact that exporting countries have threatened retaliation if measures are not removed after three years suggests that most countries will choose to comply with the AS time limits.

Finally, as the data compiled by Miranda et al. indicate[43], the use of antidumping duties has exploded over this time period, and it is certainly the case that they are being used when a safeguard would be the more appropriate trade policy. In the next section we discuss the interplay between antidumping policy and safeguard policy, and the need for joint reform of both safeguards and antidumping.

In summary, economics research on safeguards points to their many potential benefits—most importantly, the role they play in sustaining trade agreements. Sadly, in practice it appears that safeguards may not be used when they can create benefits for society and may be used when they cannot.

V. Unfinished Business

In this part we provide a discussion of where to go from here. The caveat we note from the outset is that it is difficult to make any policy reform that will target a deficiency in the current system without introducing another problem somewhere else. Thus our goal is to discuss potential reforms and to illustrate as clearly as possible their benefits and costs. Ultimately it is then the role of researchers and policy-reformers to try to estimate the magnitude of the costs and benefits of policy changes, in order to determine which should be pursued. While we propose what are ultimately a set of empirical questions, these questions may admittedly be difficult to answer conclusively because of the rather infrequent resort to safeguard measures and thus limited data availability. Nevertheless, we start from the perspective that safeguards in their current form under the WTO are not being utilized as researchers and policymakers envision, especially given their unpopularity relative to the explosion of implementation and use of national antidumping statutes.

---

[41] Bown and McCulloch, *supra* note 38

[42] Furthermore, the application of many of these safeguards have been determined under the DSU to be inconsistent with WTO obligations. Douglas A. Irwin, *Causing Problems? The WTO Review of Causation and Injury Attribution in U.S. Section 201 Cases*, 2(3) WORLD TRADE REVIEW 297 (2003), investigates the problems of recent U.S. safeguard actions that have been brought before the DSU and that resulted in rulings that USITC decisions had failed to ensure that injury to the domestic industry was not caused by non-import factors (e.g., domestic shocks) and was not mis-attributed to imports.

[43] Miranda et al., *supra* note 30.

The first issue that must be addressed is the question of the frequency of protectionist measures being implemented under the WTO system. Given the substitutability between policy instruments, it may be useful to take a step back and recognize the inevitability and indeed, potential welfare-enhancing feature of GATT/WTO provisions that give domestic governments the ability to temporarily protect domestic industries. From this perspective, perhaps the most important questions to consider when discussing reforms to the WTO that would affect safeguards are: should the measures be applied on an MFN basis? Should the measures be accompanied with compensation? Should the use of safeguards be made more attractive or at least more transparent?

A. MFN Versus Discrimination

An empirical question that reformers need to take into consideration is whether the economic "benefits" from requiring the MFN application of safeguards outweigh the "costs" of an MFN policy. The benefit of a temporary MFN measure is that there is no trade diverted into the protection-implementing country's market from less efficient sources, as could have been the case had the country been permitted to implement a discriminatory policy. Furthermore, if countries are given the ability to discriminate, governments may take advantage of that by allowing their trade policy to be tailored so as to avoid potential retaliation by "large" countries, thus implicitly targeting smaller trading partners that do not have the capacity to retaliate.[44]

On the other hand, there are other practical benefits to not forcing countries to implement safeguard measures on an MFN basis. First, a discriminatory policy may be preferred if the safeguard scheme requires compensation based on the fact that with fewer trading partners affected by the measure, less compensation is required. In a system with a *de facto* inflexible compensation mechanism such as that faced by the WTO currently, this has its benefits as there is the potential for fewer secondary inefficiencies to be generated through retaliation-as-compensation. If safeguards were applicable on a non-MFN basis, this would arguably also improve their attractiveness relative to antidumping measures which are discriminatory by their very nature.

Another open question is what are the full, international trade-diversionary effects of a non-MFN as opposed to an MFN safeguard policy? While a non-MFN policy can generate trade diversion into the protected market, because fewer countries are targeted, there is perhaps less trade that is deflected, from export to the protecting market to export to other international destinations. With a safeguard measure that is applied on an MFN basis, an unanswered empirical question is what is happening to overall world trade? Is it simply being dampened or suppressed, or is more trade being deflected to other international destinations? In the second case, this could lead to surges of imports to other importing countries and hence calls to resort to protection there as well. The implications of this are currently not well understood but should be considered.

B. Compensation Versus No-Compensation

A second empirical question to consider is whether the economic "benefits" from requiring compensation with the application of a safeguard measure outweigh the "costs"

---

[44] *See* the evidence for the case of antidumping duties in the United States, a discriminatory policy, presented by Bruce A. Blonigen and Chad P. Bown, *Antidumping and Retaliation Threats*, 60(20) JOURNAL OF INTERNATIONAL ECONOMICS 249(2003).

of requiring compensation. The costs to requiring compensation in the current system are larger than the monetary costs might indicate—due to the inflexible nature of the *de facto* current system which more and more frequently requires countries to rely on the threat of retaliation and the difficulties inherent in compensation negotiations. Furthermore, requiring compensation makes more attractive the inappropriate use of alternative policy instruments, such as antidumping duties, that are just as easy (or arguably easier) to obtain but which require no compensation.

Given that retaliation imposes costs (through the inefficiencies generated) that are larger than the benefits to the retaliating country (which receives the compensation), one legitimate question is why require compensation at all? Are there explicit benefits to a compensation requirement? Recall that the imposition of a tariff measure by any large country generates a "negative externality"—it imposes a cost on the foreign exporting country. Specifically, the protection drives down the price received by the trading partner's exporters, generating potential welfare gains for itself at the expense of these foreign agents. Because the country does not face all of the costs of its protection, it engages in an excessive level of protection, relative to that which it would invoke if it were to face all the costs of its actions. A compensation requirement, on the other hand, forces the protection-implementing country to internalize more of the externality, imposing fewer costs of the protection onto its trading partners. Because of the internalization, it faces costs closer to the "true" costs of implementing the protection, thus it will tend to implement such protection less frequently, only when the (political, economic) gains are larger than those "true" costs.

What reforms to the compensation requirements might be considered? Recall that while the UR reforms did much to change the *size* of the compensation required (e.g., there is no compensation required for the first three years in AS cases with an absolute surge in imports) the effect on increasing the relative attractiveness of the safeguard provisions appears to have been minimal. Governments still prefer to use antidumping measures, even though in many instances if they were to implement the protection as a safeguard measure, they would also not have to offer compensation. Nevertheless, an important negative effect on the compensation mechanism induced by the UR reforms was actually a restriction to the *means* by which countries were able to compensate each other through resort to safeguards, with the general prohibition of VERs. One reform is thus to try to introduce an additional *explicit* means of compensation that has the efficiency properties of a VER, so that the costs of compensation are not increased simply because of the means through which the compensation is exchanged (retaliation).

Bown, for example, has suggested that compensation might take the form of the protection-implementing country refunding the tariff revenue collected to the foreign government, whose firms have been adversely affected by the domestic government's protection.[45] The benefit to such a mechanism is that the effect on economic welfare across countries in this case can work in a manner similar to a VER, as the exchange of tariff revenue could be equivalent to the exchange of the "quota rents" under a VER. In addition, this would not necessarily have the same discriminatory or anti-competitive

---

[45] Chad P. Bown, *Why are Safeguards under the WTO so Unpopular?*, 1 (1) WORLD TRADE REVIEW 47 (2002). To clarify, this should not be confused with the recent controversial Byrd Amendment which changed U.S. trade law to automatically allocate tariff revenue collected in U.S. antidumping and countervailing duty cases to the *U.S.* industries that supported the petition. The Byrd Amendment has been found by the WTO Appellate Body to violate the WTO Agreements on Antidumping and Subsidies and Countervailing Measures, see Report of the Appellate Body, *United States—Continued Dumping and Subsidy Offset Act of 2000*, WT/DS217/AB/R (2003).

(collusive) side-effects or "costs" of the VERs of the past, as the safeguard tariff could still be applied on an MFN basis and there would be no need for negotiation between foreign and domestic firms or the domestic and foreign governments, and thus no scope for arm-twisting or discriminating on the basis of "power" relationships.[46] Furthermore, the compensation of tariff revenue could be handed directly to the foreign firms which would help overcome the problem of how to effectively compensate the "losers" of a safeguard measure, which is hard to do when the only response available is retaliation.[47]

C. Additional Transparency

Additional useful reforms to the safeguard provisions would include further refinements of the Agreement in order to differentiate between alternative categories of safeguard measures, perhaps along the lines of the different economic reasons that policymakers use to justify their use. If countries also provided a reason why they are resorting to that form of protection, this would add transparency to the system.

Furthermore, a more refined safeguards agreement could potentially have different rules on the applicability of MFN and compensation, based on the (legitimate) justifications behind why countries are resorting to the measures. Much as the AS already does not require compensation during the first three years for an "absolute increase" in imports, compensation might also be eliminated in the instances in which a government implements safeguards in order to facilitate an orderly exit of the declining, domestic industry. On the other hand, more compensation might be required if safeguards were being used for reasons of technological catch-up or because of pure political considerations.

Nevertheless, any increased transparency requirements in the safeguard provisions that were not also included in antidumping provisions, would also be costly as they would act to make the alternatives relatively more attractive.

D. Reforms to other WTO Agreements

As experience after the UR has shown, any reforms that might be designed to make safeguards more attractive will have limited effectiveness if they are not combined with reforms to the Antidumping Agreement and perhaps penalties and compensation under the DSU that makes the use of antidumping measures less attractive.

VI. Conclusion

Safeguards play an important, multi-faceted role in trade regimes such as the GATT and now the WTO. How and when they are used—both relative to the alternative of free trade and also the alternative of policy instruments such as antidumping measures—are affected by a variety of influences in the underlying rules of the system.

---

[46] Bown, *supra* note 45, has also suggested that this is an additional reason why antidumping measures are attractive to protection-implementing countries relative to safeguard measures. As noted above, under the Agreement on Antidumping, managed trade arrangements are encouraged through the resort to "price undertakings," which economists like Michael O. Moore, *VERs and Price Undertakings under the WTO*, GEORGE WASHINGTON UNIVERSITY mimeo (2001), have argued can be equivalent (or even worse) than a VER on welfare grounds.

[47] This would require, however, an additional mechanism to ensure that foreign exporters did not anticipate the refund and further reduce prices in the domestic market, thus eliminating the effectiveness of the safeguard protection from the perspective of the domestic industry, which was benefiting from the higher prices.

In this chapter we have documented the historical and continuing role of safeguard provisions in the GATT and WTO agreements. We have provided a review of the primary economic explanations for the benefits of including safeguard provisions into trade agreements such as the GATT/WTO as well as the costs of doing so. We have also identified some of the important pitfalls that arise and which can lead to misuse of the provisions, once they have been included. We have discussed the relationship of safeguards with other, substitute policy instruments in the system, in particular antidumping duties. Throughout our discussion, we have attempted to highlight the most relevant rules and procedures of the WTO system that affect safeguards in order to illustrate how these rules generate incentives that affect the ways that countries use safeguards. Finally, we have documented some ideas for potential reforms to the safeguards and related agreements and provided a discussion of their costs and benefits, in the attempt that future researchers and reformers play special attention to the full interaction of the safeguards provisions with the overall WTO agreement.

BIBLIOGRAPHY

Bagwell, Kyle and Staiger, Robert W. "A Theory of Managed Trade." 80 *American Economic Review* 779–795 (1990).

Baldwin, Robert E. *The Political Economy of U.S. Import Policy*. (1985) Cambridge: The MIT Press.

Blonigen, Bruce A. and Bown, Chad P. forthcoming. "Antidumping and Retaliation Threats." 60(2) *Journal of International Economics*: 249–273 (2003).

Bown, Chad P. "Trade Disputes and the Implementation of Protection under the GATT: An Empirical Assessment." 62(2) *Journal of International Economics* 263–294 (2004).

Bown, Chad P. "The Economics of Trade Disputes, the GATT's Article XXIII and the WTO's Dispute Settlement Understanding." 14(3) *Economics and Politics* 283–323 (2002).

Bown, Chad P. "Why are Safeguards under the WTO so Unpopular?" 1 *World Trade Review* 47–62 (2002).

Bown, Chad P. and Rachel McCulloch. "Nondiscrimination and the WTO Agreement on Safeguards." 2(3) *World Trade Review* 327–348 (2003).

Brainard, S. Lael and Verdier, Thierry. "Lobbying and Adjustment in Declining Industries." 38 *European Economic Review* 586–595 1994.

Brainard, S. Lael and Verdier, Thierry. "The Political Economy of Declining Industries: Senescent Industry Collapse Revisited." 42 *Journal of International Economics* 221–237 (1997).

Caves, Richard E., Frankel, Jeffrey A. and Ronald W. Jones. *World Trade and Payments: an Introduction* (2002). (Ninth edition). Boston: Addison-Wesley.

Crowley, Meredith. "Do Safeguard Tariffs and Antidumping Duties Open or Close Technology Gaps?" Federal Reserve Bank of Chicago & Working Paper 2002–13 (2002).

Dixit, Avinash K. and Norman, Victor. *Theory of International Trade* (1980).

Ethier, Wilfred J. "Unilateralism in a Multilateral World." 112 *Economic Journal* 266–292 (2002).

Finger, J. Michael. "GATT Experience with Safeguards: Making Economic and Political Sense out of the Possibilities that the GATT Allows to Restrict Imports." Policy Research Working Paper 2000, Development Research Group, World Bank, Washington, DC (1998).

Fischer, Ronald D. and Prusa, Thomas J. "Contingent Protection as Better Insurance." NBER Working Paper #6933 (1999).

Goldberg, Pinelopi. "Product Differentiation and Oligopoly in International Markets: The Case of the U.S. Automobile Industry." 63 *Econometrica* 891–951 (1995).

Hansen, Wendy L. "The International Trade Commission and the Politics of Protection." 84 *American Political Science Review* 21–46 (1990).

Hansen, Wendy L. and Prusa, Thomas J. "The Road Most Taken: the Rise of Title VII Protection." 18 *The World Economy* 295–313 (1995).

Hillman, Arye. "Declining Industries and Political-Support Protectionist Motives." 72 *American Economic Review*, 1180–1187 (1982).

Irwin, Douglas A. "Causing Problems? The WTO Review of Causation and Injury Attribution in U.S. Section 201 Cases." 2(3) *World Trade Review* 297–325 (2003).

Jackson, John H. "Safeguards and Adjustment Policies." in R.M. Stern, (ed.), *The Multilateral Trading System: Analysis and Options for Change*. (1993) Ann Arbor, MI: The University of Michigan Press.

Jackson, John H. *The World Trading System: Law and Policy of International Economic Relations*, (1997) Second Edition. Cambridge: The MIT Press.

Klimenko, Mikhail; Ramey, Garey; and Watson, Joel. "Recurrent Trade Agreements and the Value of External Enforcement." UC San Diego mimeo (2002).

Krugman, Paul R.; and Obstfeld, Maurice. *International Economics: Theory and Policy* 2000 (Fifth edition). Reading, MA: Addison-Wesley.

Magee, Christopher. "Declining Industries and Persistent Protection," 10(4) *Review of International Economics* 749–762 (2002).

Matsuyama, Kiminori. "Perfect Equilibria in a Trade Liberalization Game." 80 *American Economic Review* 480–492 (1990).

Miranda, Jorge.; Torres, Raul A.; and Ruiz, Mario. "The International Use of Antidumping: 1987–1997." 32 *Journal of World Trade* 5–71 (1998).

Miyagiwa, Kaz and Ohno, Yuka. "Closing the Technology Gap Under Protection." 85 *American Economic Review* 755–770 (1995).

Miyagiwa, Kaz and Ohno, Yuka. "Credibility of Protection and Incentives to Innovate." 40 *International Economic Review* 143–163 (1999).

Moore, Michael O. "VERs and Price Undertakings under the WTO." George Washington University mimeo (2001).

Petersmann, Ernst-Ulrich. *The GATT/WTO Dispute Settlement System: International Law, International Organizations and Dispute Settlement* (1997) London: Kluwer Law International.

Staiger, Robert and Tabellini, Guido. "Discretionary Trade Policy and Excessive Protection." 77 *American Economic Review* 823–837 (1987).

Staiger, Robert and Tabellini, Guido. "Do GATT Rules Help Governments Make Domestic Commitments?" 11 *Economics and Politics* 109–144 (1999).

United States International Trade Commission. "The Effectiveness of Escape Clause Relief in Promoting Adjustment to Import Competition." USITC Publication # 1229, Investigation # 332–115 (March 1982).

WTO. *Analytical Index: Guide to GATT Law and Practice*. Vol II (1995).

WTO. *Uruguay Round Agreement Establishing the World Trade Organization*. (1995) Geneva: WTO.

WTO. *Report (2000) of the Committee on Safeguards*, G/L/409 (2000).

WTO. *Report (2001) of the Committee on Safeguards to the Council for Trade in Goods*, G/L/494 (2001).

WTO. *International Trade Statistics* (2001). Geneva: WTO.

WTO. *Immediate Notification Under Article 12.5 Of The Agreement On Safeguards To The Council For Trade In Goods Of Proposed Suspension Of Concessions And Other Obligations Referred To In Paragraph 2 Of Article 8 Of The Agreement On Safeguards European Communities*. G/SG/43, May 15, 2002, and G/SG/43/Suppl.1, June 20, 2002.

WTO. *Immediate Notification Under Article 12.5 Of The Agreement On Safeguards To The Council For Trade In Goods Of Proposed Suspension Of Concessions And Other Obligations Referred To In Paragraph 2 Of Article 8 Of The Agreement On Safeguards European Communities*. G/SG/43/Suppl.1, June 20, 2002.

CHAPTER 40

ANTI-DUMPING AND COMPETITION LAW

P. J. Lloyd*

"Unfair competition is selling cheaper than someone else"

Ralph Harris
Everyman's Guide to Contemporary Economic Jargon,
in GROWTH, ADVERTISING AND THE CONSUMER (1964)

TABLE OF CONTENTS

* The University of Melbourne. I would like to acknowledge the helpful suggestions made by Mary Amiti, Donald MacLaren, Keith Maskus, Michael Plummer and Jose Tavares on an earlier draft.

I. The Problems of Anti-Dumping Action in the WTO

It has often been observed that anti-dumping actions have risen rapidly in number since the conclusion of the Uruguay Round negotiations. The WTO (and before it the GATT) Committee on Antidumping produces semi-annual reports which give data on the number of anti-dumping investigations and measures adopted by members of the organisation. Until the mid-1980s only the United States, Australia, New Zealand and countries that are now members of the EU took anti-dumping action regularly. In 1990 only nine members were reported as taking anti-dumping action during the year. The WTO reported that 27 members had taken anti-dumping actions in the six-month period January 1-June 30, 2002.[1] The main new users have been Mexico, Brazil, South Africa, India and Korea.

More countries are introducing legislation providing for anti-dumping duties, though there is no obligation for them to do so under WTO rules. These include developing and transition economies such as China.[2] As of October 5, 2002, 75 countries had reported to the WTO that they had legislation providing for anti-dumping action.[3] Thus anti-dumping action is becoming a standard tool of international trade policy.

As important as the frequency of action is the magnitude of the implicit tariffs resulting from the action. There is no systematic data on this aspect. Messerlin and Reed calculated that the protective dumping margins in the United States and EU are on average two to three times higher than the rates of regular tariffs.[4] Blonigen and Prusa report that the average dumping margin in the United States over the past decade has been sixty per cent.[5] Calculations of dumping duty rates in Australia provide similar results; for a sample of goods subject to antidumping duties in 1994 the unweighted average antidumping duty was 35 per cent whereas the unweighted average tariff on the same goods was only seven per cent.[6]

Action may take the form of a price undertaking as well as the imposition of a duty. This has an effect on the consumer/buyer that is the same as that resulting from an antidumping duty, but unlike an antidumping duty, a price undertaking also raises the landed price. Exporters or importers may raise the price before a dumping examination. I know of no empirical study in any country of the magnitude of price increases due to price undertakings. Prusa[7] estimates that about 25 per cent of the cases investigated in the United States by the Department of Commerce are withdrawn, often after an agreement to restrict the quantities exported, that is, they induce voluntary export restraints. Because of these "voluntary" price and quantity responses, the statistics of antidumping actions substantially understate the impact of laws.

But the problem is not merely that anti-dumping actions are becoming a major restraint on trade. There is concern with other characteristics of anti-dumping actions. First, the only conditions that must be satisfied relate to proof of dumping and injury and, therefore,

[1] World Trade Organization, REPORT (2003) OF THE COMMITTEE ON ANTI-DUMPING PRACTICES, G/L/653 (October 28, 2003), ("*2003 Report*")¶10. The EU is counted as only one member in this statistic.
[2] For a discussion of the development of anti-dumping actions in the Americas, *see* J. Tavares, C. Macario and K. Steinfatt, *Antidumping in the Americas*, 35 JOURNAL OF WORLD TRADE 555–574 (August 2001)
[3] *2003 Report, supra* note 1, ¶6.
[4] P.A. Messerlin and G. Reed, *The US and EC Antidumping Policies*, 105 THE ECONOMIC JOURNAL 1565, Table 2 (November 1995)
[5] B.A. Blonigen and T.J. Prusa, *Antidumping*, IN HANDBOOK FOR INTERNATIONAL ECONOMICS (Basil Blackwell ed. 2003)
[6] K.M. Vautier and P.J. Lloyd, INTERNATIONAL TRADE AND COMPETITION POLICY: CER, APEC AND THE WTO, Appendix 1 (1997)
[7] T.J. Prusa, *Why are So Many Antidumping Petitions Withdrawn?*, 33 JOURNAL OF INTERNATIONAL ECONOMICS, 1–20 (August 1992)

actions can be taken unilaterally even when the substantive rates of duty are bound at a zero rate. Consequently, they breach the reciprocity involved in past tariff negotiations. Second, again because of the nature of the proof of dumping and injury required under the rules, anti-dumping action discriminates among countries of origin of imports of the goods concerned.[8] In particular, anti-dumping action is taken predominantly by the industrialized countries and the imports that bear the duties are predominantly sourced from developing countries. Hence, it has become another of the issues that divide the developed and the developing countries in the WTO. Third, though this characteristic is not evident from the trade statistics alone, conduct that is actionable when the seller is outside a country is not actionable when the same conduct occurs but the seller is a domestic supplier. This is discriminatory in another way and obviously leads to economic inefficiencies. Fourth, anti-dumping actions have become a major source of conflict among the members of the WTO. The imprecision of the present rules has led to an increasing number of complaints under the Dispute Settlement Procedures in recent years.[9] Altogether, these features mean that anti-dumping action has become a major problem for the organisation.

There are some recent surveys of aspects of anti-dumping actions. The data is surveyed comprehensively by Miranda, Torres and Ruiz[10]. James calculates the national intensities of use (that is, the country share of definitive measures relative to the country share of imports) and the asymmetries of actions taken against and by individual member countries.[11] The former provides a normalized measure of the frequency of use and the latter shows how a country is affected both as a user and as a subject of other countries' actions. Blonigen and Prusa survey the literature on anti-dumping, separating the pre-investigation, investigation and post-investigation phases of the process.[12]

This paper reexamines dumping from the point of view of a form of business conduct that might be subject to competition law. This point of view is relatively new but it is causing a fundamental rethinking of the economics of anti-dumping actions. Part II briefly reviews the history of GATT and WTO law on dumping. Part III considers the central question of whether dumping should be addressed by "fair trading" laws or by competition law. Part IV considers reform proposals that are based on the competition law view of dumping. The conclusions are summarized in Part V.

II. A Brief History of Anti-Dumping Action in the GATT/WTO

Dumping entered the set of international trade policies subject to GATT regulation from the outset in 1947. Article VI differs from other Articles in GATT in that it is concerned with "unfair trade" whereas the other articles are concerned with trade restrictions as an aspect of the objective of efficiency in the world economy. Dumping (and subsidization

[8] Article 9 of the 1994 Agreement states that any duty must be imposed on a non-discriminatory basis on imports from all sources found to be dumped and causing injury, except on imports from sources from which price undertakings have been accepted. Non-discrimination on that portion of the imports of the product liable for anti-dumping action, however, implies discrimination between the dumped and the non-dumped imports of the product in the ordinary sense of trade discrimination.

[9] E. Vermulst and N. Komuro, *Anti-dumping Disputes in the GATT/WTO: Navigating Dire Straits*, 35(1) JOURNAL OF WORLD TRADE LAW 5 (1997). As of October 2003, Seventeen panel and Appellate Body reports involving anti-dumping issues had been adopted by the Dispute Settlement Body.

[10] J.R. Miranda, A. Torres, and M. Ruiz, *The International Use of Anti-dumping*, 32(5) JOURNAL OF WORLD TRADE LAW 5 (1998)

[11] W.E. James, *The Rise of Anti-dumping: Does Regionalism Promote Administered Protection?*, 14 ASIAN-PACIFIC ECONOMIC LITERATURE 14 (November 2000)

[12] Blonigen and Prusa, *supra* note 5.

which is also covered by the Article) was perceived as being "unfair" to domestic competitors and therefore a practice which tends to undermine respect for the rules of the international trading system and the willingness of countries to liberalize international trade.[13]

Article VI of GATT (1947) defined dumping as a situation in which "...the price of the product exported from one country to another is less than the comparable price, in the ordinary course of trade, for the like product when destined for consumption in the exporting country". If there is no such domestic price, a constructed price can be calculated based on the highest comparable price for the like product in a third country or the cost of production. The difference between the "normal value" and the "export price" is called the "margin of dumping". The duty cannot exceed the dumping margin.

The Article allows members to apply anti-dumping duties on imports of a product so long as two conditions are met. The goods must be dumped, and the dumping must cause or threaten material injury to an established domestic industry or materially retard the establishment of a domestic industry. The GATT/WTO law does not seek to regulate dumping—the action of private parties—but instead regulates the use of anti-dumping measures.

From the time the GATT rules were introduced, there have been numerous complaints from the exporting countries subject to anti-dumping actions that the discretion available to the importing countries enables them to overstate the dumping margins and the injury, and most particularly, the existence of dumping in the first place. Exporting countries claim that dumping duties are often applied when they should not be under the letter of the GATT law, and that anti-dumping actions are used to harass and discourage cheap imports.

An attempt was made to tighten the GATT rules in the Anti-dumping Code that was agreed to in 1967 as a part of the Kennedy Round and later revised in the Tokyo Round. The Code gave greater precision to the definitions of Article VI relating to like products, dumping, injury and domestic industry. The Code laid down for the first time procedures and rules of administration; time limits for the period of investigation and retro-activity of anti-dumping duties, the rights of interested parties to be heard, rules of evidence and other administrative rules.

The Code allowed a determination of dumping if the export price is less than the cost of production of the good exported only if there were no sales of the like product in the exporting country or no proper comparison can be made between the export and the domestic price. This was a tighter definition. However, the United States, Canada, Australia and New Zealand agreed in 1978 that pricing below average cost was "not in the ordinary course of trade" and therefore could be determined to be dumping on the basis of a constructed normal value calculated from the cost of production plus a reasonable amount for administrative, selling and any other costs and for profits.

The Code also introduced two new measures. First, it provided a definition of a price undertaking as a "satisfactory voluntary undertaking from any exporter to revise its prices or to cease exports to the area at dumped prices so that authorities are satisfied that the injurious effect of the dumping is eliminated."[14] The Code explicitly permitted a price undertaking that raised prices no more than the margin of dumping, but only allowed it to be entered into after preliminary findings of dumping and injury. This measure resulted from British and Canadian complaints during the Kennedy Round that the U.S. Treasury (which at that time was responsible for dumping investigations) had been slow in its

---

[13] JOHN H. JACKSON, THE WORLD TRADING SYSTEM, Chapter 10 (1989)
[14] Article 7 of the code.

dumping investigations and had encouraged producers to give price undertakings even though the Tariff Commission enquiry might not have resulted in a finding of injury and the imposition of a duty. Second, the Code introduced a provision for preliminary duties. Both became widely used.

The Uruguay Round Agreement on the Implementation of Article VI made a stronger attempt to tighten the regulation of governments' anti-dumping actions. The Agreement sets out yet more detailed rules concerning the determination of dumping and of injury and the establishment of a causal link between them. It also set out more detailed procedures to be followed in initiating and conducting anti-dumping investigations and clarified the role of dispute settlement panels in disputes concerning anti-dumping actions taken by Members. It introduced a "sunset clause", requiring an anti-dumping duty to terminate within five years unless a fresh review determines that the expiry of the duty would be likely to lead to continuation or recurrence of dumping and injury. But the Agreement retained all of the central features of the system.

A new feature of the Agreement, compared to the earlier Article and Code, is that it allowed consideration of the combined effect of dumped imports from several supplying countries. This was called "cumulation". With the experience of six years of application of the Uruguay Round amendments, the change relating to cumulation across countries can now be seen as a change for the worse. Before the Uruguay Round Agreement, the practice was used on a limited scale and it was doubtful that it conformed to the GATT law. The Uruguay Round Agreement made the practice WTO-legal. This has increased the coverage of complaints and their likelihood of success in countries that use this provision.

In the United States, in the ten years following the introduction of the mandatory cumulation amendment, Prusa[15] finds that 75 per cent of anti-dumping cases have involved cumulation. Hansen and Prusa[16] and Prusa[17] verify that cumulation has had an effect on the affirmative finding of injury which is "super-additive", that is, greater than the effect predicted on the basis of the summation of the countries import shares. In the EU, cumulation has made it easier for the Commission to prove injury and has thereby increased the frequency of anti-dumping actions. Tharakan, Greenaway and Tharakan[18] find that 66.3 per cent of all injury determinations over the period 1980–97 were determined on the basis of the cumulation of imported market shares. Following the line of analysis of U.S. anti-dumping actions by Hansen and Prusa[19], they also find a super-additive effect.

Under GATT and WTO rules anti-dumping actions relate solely to trade in goods. No provision for anti-dumping in services was introduced into GATS. Hoekman and Leidy examined the possibility of introducing provision for anti-dumping action in services trade.[20] They concluded that such action would make very little sense because of the different nature of services trade; services often have to be delivered in the country in

---

[15] T.J. Prusa, *Cumulation and Anti-dumping: A Challenge to Competition*, 21 THE WORLD ECONOMY 1021 (November 1998).

[16] W.L. Hansen and T.J. Prusa, *Cumulation and ITC Decision-making: The Sum of the Parts is Greater than the Whole*, 34 ECONOMIC INQUIRY 746 (1996).

[17] Prusa, *supra* note 15.

[18] J. Tharakan, D. Greenaway and J. Tharakan, *Cumulation and Injury Determination of the European Community in Antidumping Cases*, WELTWIRTSCHAFTLICHES ARCHIV 320–39 (1998).

[19] Hansen and Prusa, *supra* note 16.

[20] B. Hoekman and M.P. Leidy, *Antidumping for Services?*, in POLICY IMPLICATIONS OF ANTIDUMPING MEASURES (P.K.M. Tharakan ed. 1991).

which the consumers reside, and the intangibility and the bundling of services make it difficult to establish unit prices.

These rules have maintained the basic features of anti-dumping actions for more than fifty years. In some respects the changes negotiated in agreements in GATT rounds have made the rules less permissive but they have also broadened the measures to include pricing below average cost, price undertakings and preliminary measures and they have become more permissive in terms of cumulation across countries. On balance, these changes to the GATT/WTO rules may have weakened rather than strengthened the discipline on countries taking anti-dumping actions.

III. International Trade or Competition Law?

International trade economists have traditionally taken a very different view of dumping from international trade officials. From the time of the classic study of dumping by Viner[21], international trade economists have regarded dumping as a form of price discrimination. There has been a proliferation of models of dumping which offer new explanations of this behavior; for example, demand uncertainty or strategic dumping to discourage firms in the dumped markets from reaching a scale of output that would make them competitive in the exporting country.[22] Only the cases of predatory and strategic dumping are regarded by economists as harmful to the competition process and to the welfare of the country in which the goods are "dumped".

During the 1990s a number of new models of dumping behavior were developed. Many of these treat dumping as a strategic response to the possibility of anti-dumping action. Anti-dumping law creates incentives for firms in both the importing and exporting countries to act strategically in order to influence the determination of dumping and of injury. These models cover both dumping determinations based on price differences and those based on cost of production in the exporting country. They relate to situations of duopoly and oligopoly and use multi-stage game theory with cooperative and non-cooperative outcomes. Blonigen and Prusa[23] survey these models.

International trade economists have long regarded most anti-dumping action in practice as a form of contingent protection.[24] As voluntary export restraints and other non-tariff barriers have been curtailed by the GATT and WTO, anti-dumping action is being used as a substitute form of non-tariff barrier which is still permissible under the WTO rules. The marked cyclical pattern of new anti-dumping actions and the heavy concentration in certain industries, especially steel and chemical products, support the view that anti-dumping action in practice is contingent protection rather than action against "unfair trade".[25]

---

[21] J. Viner, DUMPING: A PROBLEM IN INTERNATIONAL TRADE (1926).

[22] *See* the entry by W.J. Ethier, *Dumping*, in THE NEW PALGRAVE DICTIONARY OF ECONOMICS (J. Eatwell, M. Milgate and P. Newman eds. 1987) for the literature until the mid-Eighties.

[23] Blonigen and Prusa, *supra* note 5, Section 3.2.

[24] *See*, for example, P.J. Lloyd, ANTI-DUMPING ACTIONS AND THE GATT SYSTEM (1977) and J.M. Finger, ANTI-DUMPING: HOW IT WORKS AND WHO GETS HURT (1993)

[25] Miranda, Torres, and Ruiz, supra note 10, and Tavares, supra, note 2, have argued that new developing country users of anti-dumping action have used this instrument as a form of safeguard action when trade liberalisation lowered tariffs and non-tariff barriers. (See also J.M. Finger, F. Ng and S. Wangchuk, *Antidumping as Safeguard Policy*, manuscript (2000).) Safeguards are applied in a particular set of contingencies associated with an import surge.

Anti-dumping action may be preferred as a safeguard instrument because the standards of injury are lower, no compensation is required as with safeguard action, and it may be applied for a period up to five years. The

As James put it, "Anti-dumping actions are the current weapon of choice of protectionists."[26] As an alternative instrument of protection, anti-dumping has a number of advantages over other instruments. It does not, unlike safeguard action under Article XIX, require compensation. It is subject to weak discipline. In fact, in some countries it essentially provides protection on demand. Over the ten years 1987–1997, the proportion of all completed anti-dumping investigations which resulted in the imposition of definitive measures was 51 per cent for countries reporting to the GATT/WTO. It was 64 per cent for the United States and 62 per cent for the EU.[27] In the United States over the past decade the Department of Commerce has issued only three negative determinations of dumping out of almost four hundred determinations.[28] Anti-dumping action can be used when prices are at the bottom of their distribution and therefore the benefit to local producers who are threatened with insolvency or are downside risk-averse is greatest. It can provide protection against the cheapest source of imports under the guise of "unfair competition" (as noted in the quotation at the head of the article).

Indeed, several economists have argued that national legislators introducing legislation providing for anti-dumping actions and the architects of GATT understood that the action was essentially protectionist but described it as designed to combat "unfair" trade in order to disguise the intent. As Finger graphically put it:

> "Antidumping is the fox put in charge of the henhouse: trade restrictions certified by GATT. The fox is clever enough not only to eat the hens, but also to convince the farmer that it is the ways things ought to be. Antidumping is ordinary protection with a grand public relations program".[29]

If anti-dumping action is to improve the national welfare, it should take account of the interests of buyers. But anti-dumping provisions in the WTO and in the legislation of most nations that take anti-dumping actions ignore these interests. Unless the terms of trade effect is sufficiently large, an anti-dumping duty will harm the importing country. This is the standard analysis of an *ad valorem* tariff, based on equal weighting of the welfare losses and gains to buyers and sellers respectively. This conclusion holds *a fortiori* for a price undertaking as the higher price is received by the foreign supplier rather than the home government or alternatively demand is diverted to higher-cost alternative import sources, both cases resulting in a negative terms of trade effect. For this reason, international trade economists have been widely opposed to government anti-dumping action.

In many cases, buyers are other firms that are buying intermediate goods rather than final consumers. That is, the producer interest of the law is further biased towards the interests of incumbent producers of the competitive goods.

---

history of safeguard actions under the GATT/WTO is, however, not encouraging. Safeguard actions have been subject to abuse too and procedures were tightened in the Uruguay Round.

[26] W.E. James, *The Rise of Anti-dumping: Does Regionalism Promote Administered Protection?*, 14 ASIAN-PACIFIC ECONOMIC LITERATURE 14 (2000).

[27] Miranda, Torres and Ruiz, *supra* note 10, Table 24.

[28] Blonigen and Prusa, *supra* note 5, at 23

[29] J.M. Finger, *The Meaning of "Unfair" in US Import Policy*, WORKING PAPER WPS 745, COUNTRY ECONOMICS DEPARTMENT, WORLD BANK,42 (1991). *See also* J.W. Suomela, FREE TRADE VERSUS FAIR TRADE: THE MAKING OF AMERICAN TRADE POLICY IN A POLITICAL ENVIRONMENT, Chapter 3.1.3 (1993); J.M. Finger, *The Origins and Evolution of Antidumping Regulation*, in ANTIDUMPING: HOW IT WORKS AND WHO GETS HURT, *supra* note 24; and A.O. Sykes, *Antidumping and Antitrust: What Problems Does Each Address?*, in BROOKINGS TRADE FORUM 1998 (R.Z. Lawrence ed. 1998)

As dumping is a matter of international trade law, it should also take account of the interests of the exporting country. Dumping duties harm the exporting nation. Price under-takings also harm the exporting nation because they raise the price and reduce the quantity below the outcome in a market without intervention. However, the cost to the export-ing nation is less with a price undertaking than with an equivalent duty as the exporter receives the higher price. GATT/WTO law ignores the interests of the exporters as it ignores the interests of the buyers in the importing country.

Anti-dumping action derives from a completely outdated view of dumping. Article VI of GATT 1947 states categorically that "The contracting parties recognize that dump-ing . . . is to be condemned if it causes or threatens material injury to an established industry in the territory of a contracting party or materially retards the establishment of a domestic industry." There is no economic theory or model accepted today that finds that this conduct is always harmful. There is nothing "fair" about these provisions as they ignore the interests of buyers and of the foreign sellers.

Since there is no justification for anti-dumping action in economic theory other than to combat harmful predatory or strategic pricing, it is necessary to view dumping explicitly from a competition perspective. Pricing behavior is appropriately examined under the methods of competition analysis and the principles and procedures of competition law.

From a competition perspective, dumping as defined in the GATT/WTO is an act of price discrimination between markets or perhaps, with a liberal interpretation of the provision relating to no comparable price, selling below cost. The theory of price dis-crimination indicates when price discrimination may occur. Price discrimination between buyers in two different markets requires some restraint on trade that segments the mar-kets as well as some monopoly power in the global markets. This segmentation provides an assurance that the product sold in the market with the lower price cannot be resold back to the first market. When the markets are in different countries and the higher price is charged in the exporter's home market, the discrimination is called dumping. High price differences can occur only if there are high tariffs or non-tariff measures or natural protection due to transport costs.

For international price discrimination, the substantial lowering of both government protection measures under the GATT and of transport margins in the 1980s and 1990s must have reduced the scope for international price discrimination. Industrial tariffs averaging around five per cent in the OECD countries, which are the main users of ant-dumping actions, and transport margins of less than ten per cent suggest that much measured "dumping" is spurious. In an age of differentiated products, many "like prod-ucts" are in fact differentiated and the price differences might reflect product differ-entiation rather than dumping. The use of constructed values for the determination of the dumping margin allows a finding of dumping when there is no price discri-mination.

Under national competition laws price discrimination might or might not be judged to be conduct that is anti-competitive. National laws vary considerably in their treatment of price discrimination. For example, in the United States the Robinson-Patman Act prohibits sellers from discriminating in the prices, terms of sale or advertising where competitive injury may result to seller's competitors or to unfavored purchasers. In the EU Article 82 covers price discrimination when this is used by a dominant firm to restrict competition. Some other countries with comprehensive competition laws do not prohibit price discrimination; for example, Australia which is another frequent user of anti-dumping actions, removed from the Trade Practices Act in 1995 a separate provision relating to price discrimination, though price discrimination might still be caught under the more general provision relating to the abuse of dominant power. Several countries prohibit predatory pricing *per se*. For example, in the United States Section 2 of the Sherman Act prohibits predatory pricing and other predatory conduct (however, predation has been difficult to prove in most jurisdictions.) Competition law typically does not prohibit selling below cost *per se* although prohibitions on the abuse of a dominant position might catch some below-cost pricing.

This variation in the prohibition of price discrimination reflects the analysis of competition economists. Standard models of price discrimination show that price discrimination may have a pro-competitive or an anti-competitive effect.[30]

The view that the GATT rules are producer-oriented and protectionist is confirmed by the observation that the rules do not cover the situation in which the price charged by a discriminating monopolist is higher in the importing nation than the exporting nation, the case which truly harms the importing nation.

The opposition of international trade economists to the use of anti-dumping action to counter cross-border price discrimination has been supported by the empirical findings on the pattern of dumping actions. A review by Messerlin and Reed[31] of anti-dumping cases handled by the U.S. and EU authorities revealed that at most ten per cent and more likely only five per cent of cases involve predatory dumping, and that the only country that was in a position to practice strategic dumping was Japan. (cf. the views of the OECD CLP Committee which has found that claims of predatory pricing are often unfounded and recommended that governments apply a market structure test to find if the conduct should be challenged).[32]

Starting around 1990, economists began to observe that some anti-dumping actions are themselves anti-competitive in effect. The EU is one of the countries or blocs of countries with anti-dumping law in which there is evidence that anti-dumping action has itself had anti-competitive effects in some instances by, for example, reinforcing the position of a domestic cartel.[33] Similarly, in Australia and Brazil, it has been found that anti-dumping action has sometimes had anti-competitive effects.[34] Domestic producers sometimes use anti-dumping complaints as a means of restricting foreign competition and thereby reinforcing price-fixing agreements in the domestic markets.

More recently, economists have used a number of the models to see if dumping has a pro-competitive or an anti-competitive effect in markets with imperfect competition. There is a family of models of imperfect competition in which government intervention may change the competitive behavior in the market equilibrium.[35] In several of these models anti-dumping action may induce collusion in a market that was non-collusive before the intervention. These models tend to support the finding that some anti-dumping actions are anti-competitive.

---

[30] *See*, for example, L. PHILIPS, THE ECONOMICS OF PRICE DISCRIMINATION (1983).

[31] Messerlin and Reed, *supra* note 4.

[32] World Trade Organization, ANNUAL REPORT 1997, Volume 1 (1997), Note 171.

[33] EUROPEAN COMPETITION POLICY 79–81 (P. Montagnon ed. 1990); P. Messerlin, *Antidumping Regulation or Procartel Law? The EC Chemical Case,* 13 THE WORLD ECONOMY 465 (1990); Messerlin and Reed, *supra* note 4; R. Veufelers and H. Vandenbussche, *European Anti-dumping Policy and the Profitability of National International Collusion,* 43 EUROPEAN ECONOMIC REVIEW 28 (1999)

[34] *See* the Industry Commission of Australia, ANNUAL REPORT 1995–96, Appendix E (1995); and C.A. Primo Braga and S.D. Silber, *Brazilian Frozen Concentrated Orange Juice: The Folly of Unfair Trade* Cases, in ANTIDUMPING: HOW IT WORKS AND WHO GETS HURT, *supra* note 23, respectively

[35] *See* Blonigen and Prusa, *supra* note 5 and references therein.

In the model of Hartigan[36], the intervention could have the reverse effect of inducing competition in a market that was collusive before the intervention by lowering the costs of renegotiation of collusion. This model relates to a duopoly situation with a single domestic seller and a single foreign seller who is a monopolist in its home market. This is an uncommon occurrence in dumping cases, if indeed it occurs at all. Typically several domestic producers file a complaint jointly, and increasingly, as noted above, the investigation cumulates production across several exporting countries. In any case, if this situation should occur, the preferred intervention is the application of competition law to prohibit collusion outright.

An issue that has not received attention is whether anti-dumping duties or price undertakings will be effective in restoring competition even if it is true that there is predatory or strategic dumping. In general, the answer is no. Anti-dumping action does not bear directly on the firm's or firms' competitive behavior. It only raises the price of the dumped good for the duration of the action. The appropriate action would be a prohibition of the practice with appropriate penalties if the offense continues.

These models indicate that anti-dumping action under international trade law is not the instrument or, to use the language of competition law, the remedy to correct business conduct in the form of harmful price discrimination or selling below average cost. If dumping has no effect on competition or has a pro-competitive effect, no anti-dumping action or other action should be taken. If, on the other hand, price discrimination or selling below average cost does restrict competition, the conduct should be prohibited. And it should be prohibited for sellers operating solely in the national market as well as for sellers selling across national borders. Similarly, non-price forms of predation and entry deterrence by dominant producers should be prohibited along with price predation.

Competition law is the correct means to combat anti-competitive effects across national borders when they occur. The competition law of each country has national economic goals as its objective or objectives. These vary among countries but they are converging to the objective of preserving competition in markets or of protecting consumer interests, which are more suitable than the anti-dumping objective of protecting incumbent producers. Given that dumping may have either a pro-competitive or an anti-competitive effect, the Rule of Reason should apply.

Some studies have shown that many of the anti-dumping actions that are now taken would not be taken if the current definition of dumping were retained but standards of national competition law were substituted for those of international trade law. In the United States, for both price discrimination and predatory pricing, Lipstein compares the standards in relation to the definition of a market and proof of injury.[37] For both forms of pricing and in all respects, the standards under U.S. competition laws are much stricter than those of its anti-dumping law. Tharakan, Vermulst and Tharakan[38] consider as a case study the EU determination in the 'Personal Fax Machines' case. They ask if the pricing of the goods and the injury would have violated competition law standards in the exporting countries and in the EU. They conclude that the outcome might have been very different and less trade-restrictive if competition standards had been applied.

---

[36] J.C. Hartigan, *An Antidumping Law can be Procompetitive*, 5 PACIFIC ECONOMIC REVIEW 5 (February 2000)

[37] R. Lipstein, *Using Antitrust Principles to Reform Antidumping Law*, in GLOBAL COMPETITION POLICY (E. Graham and J.D. Richardson eds. 1997)

[38] M. Tharakan, E. Vermulst and J. Tharakan, *Interface between Anti-dumping Policy and Competition Policy*, 21 THE WORLD ECONOMY 1035 (November 1998)

There is also the question of the definition of dumping compared to the definition of predatory pricing. The definition of predatory pricing is contentious. Sometimes average total cost is used but marginal cost and average variable cost and non-cost rules have been proposed.[39] Some of these are more permissive than average total cost and are likely therefore to allow conduct which could be deemed dumping under international trade law.

Thus, at least in the case of two of the biggest users of anti-dumping actions, the substitution of competition law standards for international trade law standards would lead to a substantial tightening in the regulation of anti-dumping actions. The same outcome is likely to hold in other countries that take anti-dumping actions.

IV. Proposals for the Reform of Anti-Dumping Actions

There are many possible reforms that would reduce the harm done to the welfare of residents of the importing nations that impose the duties and to the exporting nations.

To start with, as anti-dumping duties are discretionary, the individual member nations of the WTO that currently take anti-dumping actions could reform their national laws or administration unilaterally to make them less trade-restrictive. This is unlikely to happen in most countries, however, as the political support for protectionism by means of anti-dumping actions seems to be in the ascendancy, and the appeal of anti-dumping action as a form of protectionism increases as more discipline is applied to the traditional instruments of protection. We need greater discipline on anti-dumping actions in the multilateral system.

The analysis of the previous section indicates clearly that the optimal solution is the most radical one. Logically, it would be best to eliminate anti-dumping regulation altogether. Another attempt to tighten the law with a view to reducing the discretion and arbitrariness under the present system would not address the real problems. As Hoekman and Kostecki concluded after the Uruguay Round

> "AD [anti-dumping] is fundamentally flawed from an economic perspective and cannot be fixed by tinkering with the methodological arcana of investigations. For all practical purposes, there is nothing wrong with dumping, as it is normal business practice. The problem is anti-dumping."[40]

To economists, dumping is not an international trade problem. International pricing may be a competition problem and as such it should, in principle, be addressed exclusively as a part of national competition laws. Lipstein[41], and Lloyd and Vautier,[42] and probably others, have recommended the abolition of anti-dumping provisions in the WTO.

Four regional trading agreements have taken this view for intra-area dumping. They are the EU, the European Economic Area, the CER Agreement between Australia and New Zealand and the Canada-Chile Agreement. All have abolished the possibility of anti-dumping actions against members of the areas.[43] In the first three cases, this step

[39] The definitions are discussed in W.K. Viscusi, J.M. Vernon and J.E. Harrington, ECONOMICS OF REGULATION AND ANTITRUST 283–289 (2000).

[40] B. Hoekman and M. Kostecki, THE POLITICAL ECONOMY OF THE WORLD TRADING SYSTEM: FROM GATT TO WTO 1174 (1995)

[41] R. Lipstein, *It's Time to Dump the Dumping Law*, INTERNATIONAL ECONOMIC INSIGHTS, (November/December 1993)

[42] P.J. Lloyd and K.M. Vautier, PROMOTING COMPETITION IN GLOBAL MARKETS, 168 (1999)

[43] For background on this aspect, see Lloyd and Vautier, *supra* note 42, Chapters 4, 5 and 6; G. Niels and A. ten Kate, *Trusting Antitrust to Dump Antidumping, Abolishing Antidumping in Free Trade Agreements without Replacing it with Competition* Law, 31 JOURNAL OF WORLD TRADE 29 (December 1997); and Tavares *et al., supra* note 2

was taken only after a high degree of integration of the members' economies and the availability of area-wide competition remedies in the event of anti-competitive behavior. A single market would prevent market segmentation and make price discrimination impossible. The Canada-Chile Agreement set a precedent in agreeing to abolish ant-dumping actions within the area without any substitute measures, though the Agreement still permits safeguard actions against imports from member countries.

In fact, in the United States and some other countries, dumping arose as a part of anti-trust legislation. It is only in recent decades that it has again come to be regarded more and more as an international trade rather than a competition problem and standards in the two fields have diverged.

One possible objection to the substitution of action under national competition law for action under international law is that some of the countries that have anti-dumping laws do not have competition laws that cover predatory pricing or price discrimination or other pricing behavior that might produce dumping as measured under international laws. Indeed, few of the new countries that take anti-dumping action have effective national competition laws. However, this absence of competition law can be taken as a lack of concern in these countries over such conduct.

This solution is not going to be adopted in the negotiations under the next Round. The Doha Ministerial Declaration states that:

> ...we agree to negotiations aimed at clarifying and improving the disciplines under the Agreements on Implementation of Article VI of GATT 1994 and on Subsidies and Countervailing measures, while preserving the basic concepts, principles and effectiveness of these Agreements and their instruments and objectives, and taking into account the needs of developing and least-developed participants.[44]

Preserving the basic concepts and principles of the existing WTO law retains the dual tests of dumping and injury. Yet, this still leaves a number of options for reform. Some countries have put forward proposed reforms in the traditional areas of stricter standards and improved administration as well as new issues such as anti-circumvention rules, special and differential treatment for developing countries. Other reforms are also possible. These will be considered in the form of an agenda for reform of WTO law on dumping and anti-dumping actions in the forthcoming Round.

One simple reform would be to require all countries to report to the WTO all dumping margins and the *ad valorem* equivalent of the duties imposed and of the price undertakings. This would make the extent of the protection more transparent.

The negotiations should reconsider the aspect of the definition of dumping dealing with sales below the average cost of production. The rules set out in the Uruguay Round Agreement to determine when the exporter's cost of production may be used in place of the actual home market price and to govern the calculation of the constructed price have proven quite inadequate and allowed a substantial extension of the application of anti-dumping actions.

Similarly, the rules introduced in the Uruguay Round Agreement relating to cumulation across countries need to be tightened considerably. This rule has made it much easier to prove injury to the domestic industry.

Another substantial reform within the present definition of anti-dumping would be the amendment of Article VI to supplement the (producer) injury test by a national economic

---

[44] World Trade Organisation, MINISTERIAL DECLARATION (2001), ¶28, reproduced in the Appendix to this book.

welfare test. As noted above, the interests of consumers are ignored in Article VI and the Uruguay Round Agreement on the Implementation of Article VI and the definition of domestic industry for the purposes of assessing injury is in terms of domestic producers of like products, which does not include the downstream industry users of the products. This additional test would obligate countries investigating alleged dumping to offset gains from dumping to downstream producers and/or consumers against incumbent producer losses. Such a reform could go a long way to reducing the use of anti-dumping action as a form of contingent protection. (An international welfare test would be even less likely to result in anti-dumping action as it would take account of the benefit of dumping to the exporter.)

More radically, a competition law standard could supplement the existing trade law standards in the assessment of harm to the economy in which goods are dumped. About a decade ago, economists began to ask whether competition objectives and standards could be used within the WTO to guide the applications of anti-dumping actions.[45] Canadian anti-dumping law already allows competition considerations to be taken into account in the determination of both the dumping margin and injury.

Several proposals have been put forward. Hoekman and Kostecki suggested that allegations of dumping be investigated by the competition authority of the exporter's home country, assuming it had one, and a finding of anti-competitive behaviour be required before anti-dumping duties are imposed by the importing country.[46] In effect, this would add a competition test to the existing dumping and injury tests. This would make an anti-dumping action consistent with the competition law of the exporting country. Alternatively, the alleged dumping could be investigated by the competition authority of the importing country, assuming it had one. Messerlin and Tharakan suggest a "two-tier" approach in order to weed out complaints that did not involve predation[47]. In the first tier, the investigation would confirm that the seller accused of dumping has sufficient market power to be able to recoup losses.

Under both of these proposals anti-dumping action would vary with the competition standards applied by the competition authority in the exporting country, assuming that one existed. As consistency of standards across importing countries is desirable, there would have to be WTO negotiations to adopt a common competition standard for all members.

Any amendment of the test of injury or the addition of a third test might be considered to breach the undertaking in the Doha Ministerial Declaration that the negotiations preserve the concepts and principles of the Uruguay Round Agreement on the Implementation of Article VI. For example, if it were required that any allegation pass a third test relating to national interest or competition standards, it would mean in some cases that anti-dumping action could not be taken, even though the case satisfied the requirements relating to the proof of dumping and the proof of injury. On the other hand, the Doha Ministerial Declaration also agreed that negotiations will take place on the interaction between trade and competition policy. While this does not provide a mandate for the introduction of a competition standard in anti-dumping actions taken under Article VI, it explicitly "recognizes the case for a multilateral framework to enhance the contribution of competition policy to international trade and development". There is a tension in the

---

[45] For example, *see* Hoekman and Kostecki, *supra* note 40, at 258; B. Hoekman and P.C. Mavroidis, *Dumping, Antidumping and* Antitrust, 30 JOURNAL OF WORLD TRADE LAW (February 1996); and the AMERICAN BAR ASSOCIATION, REPORT OF THE TASK FORCE OF THE ABA SECTION OF ANTITRUST LAW ON THE COMPETITION DIMENSION OF NAFTA, Chapter 6 (1994).

[46] Hoekman and Kostecki, *supra* note 40, at 258.

[47] P.A. Messerlin and P.K.M. Tharakan, *The Question of Contingent Protection*, 22 THE WORLD ECONOMY (December 1999).

Declaration between the desire to improve the discipline on anti-dumping action on the one hand and the intention of preserving the principles and concepts of the existing agreements on the other that will have to be resolved.

V. Conclusion

Anti-dumping action as a remedy for cross-border price discrimination and selling below average cost is a fundamentally mistaken policy. Dumping is not usually harmful to the importing country. Moreover, anti-dumping action itself is normally harmful to both the importing and the exporting country. The rules have led to the use of anti-dumping action as a form of back-door protection that is discriminatory and has become a major source of bilateral and systemic frictions in the world trading system.

The adoption of a competition approach to dumping focuses on the true costs and benefits of this form of business conduct and it suggests possible reforms that will align government interventions more closely to the true costs of harmful predation or price discrimination. The point of view that dumping should be regarded as a competition problem has not yet penetrated the consciousness of the national or WTO negotiators.

Major reform of the WTO rules relating to anti-dumping is limited by the words chosen in the Doha Ministerial Declaration. There is unlikely to be much support among developed countries for changing anti-dumping provisions from the WTO in a substantial way. The U.S. Government in particular remains adamantly opposed to any tightening of the WTO rules relating to anti-dumping action.[48] On the other hand, the Declaration itself recognises the need to improve the discipline on ant-dumping actions. This conflict is the challenge of the next Round.

Some suggestions for an agenda of reform of the discipline on anti-dumping actions have been listed above. Reform is likely to be a difficult process, as it has been in the past, but the much greater importance of anti-dumping action as a form of border trade intervention and restriction today make it imperative that major reforms be achieved.

BIBLIOGRAPHY

American Bar Association *Report of the Task Force of the ABA Section of Antitrust Law on The Competition Dimension of NAFTA*, Chicago: American Bar Association (1994).

Blonigen, B. A. and T. J. Prusa 'Antidumping' , NBER Working Paper No. W8398(July 2001), available at http://papers.nber.org/papers.

Ethier, W.J. 'Dumping' in J. Eatwell, M. Milgate and P. Newman (eds*), The New Palgrave Dictionary of Economics*, London: Macmillan (1987).

Finger, J. M. 'The Meaning of "Unfair" in U.S. Import Policy', Working paper WPS 745, Country Economics Department, World Bank (1991).

Finger, J. M. *Antidumping: How it Works and Who Gets Hurt*, The University of Michigan Press, Ann Arbor (1993).

Finger, J. M. 'The Origins and Evolution of Antidumping Regulations' in J. M. Finger (ed.), *Antidumping: How it Works and Who Gets Hurt*, The University of Michigan Press, Ann Arbor (1993).

Finger, J. M., F. Ng and S.Wangchuk 'Antidumping as Safeguard Policy', manuscript (2000).

---

[48] Lindsey and Ikeson argue that this attitude should and may change as a result of the increasing number of anti-dumping actions being taken against U.S. exporters. B. Lindsey and D. Ikeson, *Coming Home to Roost Proliferating Antidumping Laws and the Growing Threat to U. S. Exports*, Cato Institute (2001).

Hansen, W.L. and T.J. Prusa 'Cumulation and ITC Decision-making: The Sum of the Parts is Greater than the Whole', 34 *Economic Inquiry* 746–769 (1996).

Harris, R. "Everyman's Guide to Contemporary Economic Jargon" in <u>Growth, Advertising and the Consumer</u> (1964).

Hartigan, J. C. 'An Antidumping Law can be Procompetitive', 5 *Pacific Economic Review*, 5, February, 5–14 (2000).

Hoekman, B. and M. Kostecki *The Political Economy of the World Trading System: From GATT to WTO*, Oxford: Oxford University Press (1995).

Hoekman, B. and M. P. Leidy 'Antidumping for Services?', in P. K. M. Tharakan (ed.), *Policy Implications of Antidumping Measures*, Amsterdam: North-Holland (1991).

Hoekman, B. and P.C. Mavroidis 'Dumping, Antidumping and 30 Antitrust', 30 *Journal of World Trade Law*, February (1996).

Industry Commission *Annual Report 1995–96,* Canberra: Australian Government Publishing Service.

Jackson, J.H. *The World Trading System*, Cambridge, Mass.: MIT Press (1989).

James, W. E. 'The Rise of Anti-dumping: Does Regionalism Promote Administered Protection?', 14 *Asian-Pacific Economic Literature*, 14–26 (November 2000).

Lindsey, B and D. Ikeson 'Coming Home to Roost Proliferating Antidumping Laws and the Growing Threat to U. S. Exports', Cato Institute (2001).

Lipstein, R. 'It's Time to Dump the Dumping Law', *International Economic Insights*, November/December (1993).

Lipstein, R. 'Using Antitrust Principles to Reform Antidumping Law', in E. Graham and J. D. Richardson (eds.), *Global Competition Policy*, Institute for International Economics, Washington, D. C. (1997).

Lloyd, P.J. *Anti-dumping Actions and the GATT System*, London: Trade Policy Research Centre (1977).

Lloyd, P. J. and K. M. Vautier *Promoting Competition in Global Markets*, Edward Elgar, Cheltenham (1999).

Messerlin, P. "Antidumping Regulation or Procartel Law? The EC Chemical Case", 13 *The World Economy*, 465–92 (1990).

Messerlin, P.A. and G. Reed 'The US and EC Antidumping Policies', 103 *The Economic Journal*, 1565–1575 (November 1995).

Messerlin, P.A. and P.K.M. Tharakan, *The Question of Contingent Protection, The World Economy* 22 (December 1999).

Miranda, J. R., A. Torres and M. Ruiz 'The International Use of Anti-dumping', 32 (5) *Journal of World Trade Law*, 5–71 (1998).

Montagnon, P. (ed) *European Competition Policy*, London: Royal Institute of International Affairs (1990).

Niels, G and A. ten Kate 'Trusting Antitrust to Dump Antidumping, Abolishing Antidumping in Free Trade Agreements without Replacing it with Competition Law', 31 *Journal of World Trade*, 29–43 (December 1997).

Phlips, L. *The Economics of Price Discrimination*, Cambridge Ujiversity Press, Cambridge (1983).

Primo Braga, C. A. and S. D. Silber 'Brazilian Frozen Concentrated Orange Juice: The Folly of Unfair Trade Cases', in J. M. Finger (ed.), *Antidumping: How it Works and Who Gets Hurt*, The University of Michigan Press, Ann Arbor (1993).

Prusa. T. J. 'Why are So Many Antidumping Petitions Withdrawn?', 33 *Journal of International Economics*, 1–20 (August 1992).

Prusa, T. J. 'Cumulation and Anti-dumping: A Challenge to Competition', 21 *The World Economy*, 1021–1034 (November 1998).

Suomela, J. W. *Free Trade versus Fair Trade: The Making of American Trade Policy in a Political Environment*, Institute of European Studies Publications 7/93 (1993).

Sykes, A. O. 'Antidumping and Antitrust: What Problems Does Each Address?', in R. Z. Lawrence (ed.), *Brookings Trade Forum 1998*, Brookings Institution Press, Washington, D. C (1998).

Tavares, J., C. Macatio and K. Steinfatt 'Antidumping in the Americas', 35(4) *Journal of World Trade*, 555–574, (August 2001).

Tharakan, M., D. Greenaway and J. Tharakan, 'Cumulation and Injury Determination of the European Community in Antidumping Cases', *Weltwirtschaftliches Archiv*, (1998) 320–39.

Tharakan, M., E. Vermulst and J. Tharakan, 'Interface between Anti-dumping Policy and Competition Policy', *The World Economy*, 21, (November 1998), 1035–1060.

Vautier, K.M. and P.J. Lloyd, *International Trade and Competition Policy: CER, APEC and the WTO*, Wellington: Institute of Policy Studies (1997).

Veugelers, R. and H. Vandenbussche, 'European Anti-dumping Policy and the Profitability of National International Collusion', *European Economic Review*, 43, 11–28 (1999).

Vermulst, E. and N. Komuro, 'Anti-dumping Disputes in the GATT/WTO: Navigating Dire Straits', *Journal of World Trade Law*, 31 (1), 5–43 (1997).

Viner, J., *Dumping: A Problem in International Trade*, League of Nations: Geneva (1926).

Viscusi, W. K., J. M. Vernon and J. E. Harrington, *Economics of Regulation and Antitrust*, The MIT Press, Cambridge, Mass (2000).

World Trade Organization (WTO), *Annual Report 1997*, Volume 1, World Trade Organisation, Geneva (1997).

World Trade Organisation, *Annual Report 2001*, World Trade Organisation, Geneva (2001a).

World Trade Organisation, *Ministerial Declaration*, World Trade Organisation, Geneva (2001b).

CHAPTER 41

SUBSIDIES AND COUNTERVAILING MEASURES

Alan O. Sykes*

TABLE OF CONTENTS

* Frank & Bernice Greenberg Professor of Law, University of Chicago. I am grateful to participants in the Law and Economics Workshop at Northwestern University for their thoughtful comments. I thank Jessica Romero for able research assistance.

I. Introduction

Subsidies present thorny problems for the international trading system. The legitimate activities of governments inevitably affect the economic position of firms within their jurisdictions, yet the perception sometimes arises that government programs confer an unacceptable advantage on those firms. The controversial task of determining which sorts of government activities create unacceptable advantages, and what to do about them, has occupied an important place on the agenda of the WTO/GATT system since its inception.

The Uruguay Round of GATT negotiations produced an important new WTO Agreement on Subsidies and Countervailing Measures ("SCM"). It also established separate rules for agricultural subsidies in the WTO Agreement on Agriculture, and took some minimal steps toward addressing subsidies issues in services industries within the General Agreement on Trade in Services ("GATS"). Because the rules on subsidies within GATS are so undeveloped,[1] I will concentrate here on trade in goods, with primary emphasis on the SCM agreement and only a few words to say about agriculture.

In brief, I suggest that *some* of the WTO disciplines on subsidies are useful and sensible from an economic perspective, particularly (a) the nonviolation nullification and impairment doctrine that protects the market access expectations associated with particular trade commitments from frustration due to the introduction of unexpected subsidy programs; and (b) the general prohibition on export subsidies (outside of agriculture). *The treatment of domestic subsidies under WTO law is far more problematic*, in substantial measure because of the conceptual and practical difficulties in determining what constitutes an undesirable "subsidy." Further, *the opportunity for importing nations to employ countervailing duties in the WTO system is likely a source of more harm than good.* From the standpoint of welfare economics, a strong argument can be made that the WTO system should give up on its efforts to discipline domestic subsidies through general rules, and concentrate on the few sectors (such as agriculture) where a consensus arises that pressures for competitive subsidization are a source of economic waste. Likewise, global welfare would likely increase if general authority for the use of countervailing duties were eliminated.

Part II of this chapter provides an introduction to the economic issues that bear on the regulation of subsidies and countervailing measures. Part III then provides some legal background, beginning with the treatment of subsidies and countervailing measures in the GATT system prior to the Uruguay Round, and proceeding to consider the important developments in the law of the WTO. Part IV is an economic discussion of what has been accomplished within the WTO/GATT system and what has not, while Part V provides a brief conclusion.

II. Economic Background

Subsidies are of concern to the members of the WTO/GATT system for three reasons. First, subsidies can undermine market access commitments by importing nations. Promises to reduce or eliminate the use of traditional instruments of protection like tariffs and quotas can prove worthless if other instruments of import protection are substituted for them, and new subsidy programs are one such instrument.

---

[1] For a discussion of how subsidies issues might eventually be addressed within GATS, *see* Gilles Gauthier, Erin O'Brien and Susan Spencer, D*eja Vu, or New Beginning for Safeguards and Subsidies Rules in Services Trade?,* in GATS 2000: NEW DIRECTIONS IN SERVICES TRADE LIBERALIZATION 165 (Pierre Sauve and Robert Stern eds. 2000).

Second, and related, subsidies can divert customers from one exporting nation to another. The benefits to exporters of market access commitments secured through international negotiations are threatened just as much by subsidies to competing exporters in third countries as by subsidies to import-competing industries in the nations that make commitments.

Finally, and somewhat more amorphously, subsidies are said by many observers to "tilt the playing field" in a way that is unfair or otherwise objectionable, quite independently of whether they frustrate the market access expectations associated with WTO/GATT commitments on particular products or services. It is well known among economists, for example, that subsidies can distort resource allocation by diverting resources from higher-valued to lower-valued uses. Put slightly differently, they can distort comparative advantage and produce a less efficient global division of labor, leading to lower economic welfare. In the view of some observers, additional disciplines are required to thwart the use of subsidies that result in unfair or economically inefficient distortions of international trade.

Elements of all three concerns are reflected in the WTO/GATT legal system. Before discussing the law, however, it is useful to set forth some economic background.

A. What Is a "Subsidy?"

Although the term "subsidy" is quite familiar in economics, it is rarely defined precisely. Often it is used synonymously with a government transfer of money to an entity in the private sector. On other occasions, the term "subsidy" may refer to the provision of a good or service at a price below what a private entity would otherwise have to pay for it. On still other occasions, it may refer to various government policies that may favorably affect the competitive position of private entities, such as procurement policies or programs to educate workers. Yet, it is by no means clear that all such measures are "subsidies" in any meaningful sense.[2] Governments engage in a wide range of tax and expenditure policies that impose costs and confer benefits on private entities. The suggestion that a "subsidy" arises anytime a government program benefits private actors ignores the other side of the ledger—the numerous government programs that impose costs on those same actors.

To an economist, perhaps a natural benchmark for identifying subsidization is a hypothetical market equilibrium without the presence of government. The classic economic models of general competitive equilibrium, for example, are entirely decentralized and embody no government sector.[3] When the government enters the picture through tax and expenditure policies, it will alter equilibrium prices and output. Activities for which the net returns are reduced will be discouraged to some degree, and those activities can be said to be "taxed." Activities for which the net returns are enhanced will be encouraged to a degree, and they may be said to be "subsidized."

The difficulty with this concept of subsidization is that it is exceedingly difficult to apply as a practical matter. The hypothetical market equilibrium without government cannot be observed, and indeed it is not clear that the concept is coherent. Implicit in the classic general equilibrium models is a capacity for actors to engage in transactions, yet it is difficult to see how such a capacity can arise in a large economy without a government to create property rights. Further, the deviations from any benchmark equilibrium that

[2] This set of issues is addressed thoughtfully in Richard Snape, *International Regulation of Subsidies*, 14 THE WORLD ECONOMY 139 (1991).
[3] *See, e.g.*, GERARD DEBREU, THE THEORY OF VALUE (1959).

result from government activity are exceedingly complex. Governments engage in a wide variety of taxation practices—income taxes, payroll taxes, capital taxes, value-added taxes, sales and excise taxes, and others. Not only are the number of tax instruments large in number (and often administered by several levels of government), but the incidence of the various taxes (the relative burden of the tax on the demand side versus the supply side of the market that is taxed) is often quite uncertain. Governments also engage in innumerable regulatory programs that impose costs on private entities of various sorts: occupational health and safety programs, environmental quality programs, programs to transfer resources to certain disadvantaged groups, and untold others. Finally, government expenditure programs provide vast benefits to private sector entities in direct and indirect ways, including public education, highways, research and development funding, low cost insurance, fire and security services, a legal system, and on and on. Even national defense services no doubt benefit private firms by reducing risk and lowering the cost of capital.

Against this backdrop, it is surely impossible in practice to ascertain the "net" impact of government on any entity according to the sort of benchmark put forth above. Of necessity, therefore, one must search for other benchmarks to determine when a "subsidy" exists.

The simplest alternative is to look at each government program in isolation, and to ignore the question of whether any benefits that it confers may be offset by costs elsewhere. If a particular program confers benefits on a private entity, a "subsidy" may be declared to exist without further inquiry. Thus, for example, if a firm receives a loan from the government at a below-market rate, one might say that a "subsidy" arises without any regard to the various tax and regulatory burdens imposed on the firm.

A second possible alternative is to assume that *generally applicable* tax, expenditure and regulatory policies affect most enterprises about equally and thus do not confer any net "subsidy." Equivalently, one might assume that any subsidy conferred by generally applicable programs is uniform across industries, and will be counteracted by an offsetting movement in exchange rates. Programs of narrow applicability that target benefits at particular industries, by contrast, might be assumed to confer benefits that encourage production in that industry. To illustrate, a government might make an investment tax credit available to all industries that use durable goods. On the premise that all industries benefit about equally and that any affects on international competitiveness wash out through exchange rates, such a program might be ignored for purposes of identifying "subsidies." By contrast, if the automobile industry is the beneficiary of a special tax credit program for investment in automobile manufacturing, a "subsidy" might be found as to that industry.

A third possible alternative is to focus on the impact of government on private activities *relative to the impact of other governments on similarly situated entities elsewhere.* In the international context, one might look for programs that seem to confer particularly large benefits on particular entities relative to the benefits that governments confer on similar entities in other countries. The presumption would be that most governments tax and regulate in roughly similar fashion, resulting in similar background effects on the competitive position of most private entities—only when a program for a particular group of private entities stands out as especially generous relative to such programs elsewhere would a "subsidy" be present. Thus, for example, if most governments provide a certain range of benefits to their farmers, those programs might be presumed to cancel each other out in international trade more or less, and no "subsidy" would be found. But if a particular country provides industrial assistance to the semiconductor industry in a context where no such aid is provided by other governments, a "subsidy" might be said to exist.

Each of these alternatives has obvious deficiencies. The first has the virtue of simplicity, but its essential failing was noted above—by ignoring the offsetting costs imposed by government on private actors it raises a great danger that "subsidization" will be found where a private entity has not been meaningfully advantaged by government programs. Indeed, because so many government programs are funded out of general revenues, a narrow focus on particular government expenditure programs without any offset for most forms of taxation would lead to the conclusion that there is rampant "subsidization" in virtually any economy.

The second alternative is little more than *deus ex machina*. The insuperable complexities of calculating the net impact of national governments on domestic industries are avoided by assuming that generally applicable programs have a neutral impact while targeted programs do not. But there is no reason to believe that this assumption is correct. Many broadly applicable programs have widely disparate effects on different industries. Consider a simple example like public education—it will lower the cost of labor to industries that use educated workers, but it may *increase* the cost of labor to industries that use lower-skilled workers by lowering the supply of such workers. Many similar examples might be given with respect to tax and regulatory programs. And, of course, the question of what is to be considered "generally applicable" or "targeted" is hardly straightforward.

The third alternative changes the inquiry fundamentally, and treats "subsidization" as an alteration in the competitive position of private entities relative to similar entities elsewhere. This shift in emphasis perhaps captures the notion that subsidization involves "tilting the playing field," and might be defended on that basis. But it too raises difficult practical problems. The presumption that most governments tax and regulate similarly with respect to background factors that affect the competitive position of private entities is highly suspect, and the mere fact that a particular type of program exists in one country and not another, or is more generous in one country than in another, is at best a weak marker for a program that shifts the competitive balance overall.

In sum, it is far easier to conceptualize a "subsidy" in simple economic models than it is to identify a subsidy in practice. Even when a government program viewed myopically might seem to afford uneconomic assistance to an industry, such assistance may in fact offset other tax and regulatory burdens that disadvantage the industry. Any administrable rule for deciding whether a particular government program is a subsidy or not will no doubt result in serious errors of overinclusion and underinclusion for this reason alone. Other complexities will be considered below.

B. The Effects of Subsidies on Producers

For now, let us put to the side the problem of identifying subsidies, and simply assume that they exist. What are their effects?

Subsidies to the producers of goods and services lower the producers' costs of production, other things being equal. This reduction in their costs of production can lead to an expansion of their output in two ways, depending on the nature of the subsidy. First, some subsidies depend directly on output—the subsidy program may provide a producer with $1 for each widget that it produces, for example (or $1 for each widget that it exports, the classic "export subsidy" discussed below). Subsidies that increase with output in this fashion are economically equivalent to a reduction in the short-run marginal costs of production for the producer that receives them. In general, producers will respond to a reduction in short-run marginal costs by lowering price. Of course, when price falls, the quantity demanded by buyers will rise and output will expand to meet the increased demand.

Second, even where the amount of the subsidy is not contingent on output and does not affect short-run marginal costs of production, subsidies can affect long-run marginal costs in a way that causes additional productive capacity to come on line or to remain on line. For example, imagine an unprofitable company that is unable to cover its variable costs of production at any level of output, and would thus shut down its operations under ordinary circumstances. A subsidy to that company that is contingent on it remaining in business can avert a shut-down in operations—it must simply be enough to allow the company to cover its variable costs at some level of output. Likewise, a subsidy can induce a company to build new capacity to enter a market when the expected returns to entry absent the subsidy would not be high enough to induce entry.

It is also possible, to be sure, that a "subsidy" will have no impact on the output of recipients. Imagine, for example, that a government simply sends a company an unexpected check for $1 million. The money is in no way contingent on the company's output, or on it remaining in business. The owners of the company will be pleased to receive this subsidy, of course, but there is no reason for them to change their operations in any way—whatever level of output was most profitable without the subsidy will also be most profitable with the subsidy.

These observations suggest another important issue that must be confronted in conceptualizing subsidies. For a government program to confer a "subsidy," must it encourage an increase in output by the recipient? If it does not, then it cannot "tilt the playing field" in a way that causes detriment to competing producers. But if this question is answered affirmatively, it becomes necessary to inquire whether the government program in question affects marginal costs in the short run, or has an effect on long-run marginal cost that is sufficient to cause capacity to remain in production when it would exit otherwise, or to enter when it would not otherwise. Such issues are not always easily resolved.[4]

C. Distinguishing Good Subsidies from Bad Subsidies

Economic theory offers no general objection to the use of subsidies. As suggested above, a "subsidy" need not have any effect on the behavior of a private actor to the extent that it is offset by other costs that the government imposes on that actor. And even where a "subsidy" program can be deemed to confer a net benefit, any effect that it has on the economic activity of its recipients may well be socially desirable.

Students of microeconomics will be familiar with the proposition that subsidies may be used constructively by governments to remedy "market failures." For example, it may be difficult for individuals who invent socially valuable things to recoup their costs of research and development—depending on the nature of the innovation and the efficacy of any intellectual property protection, inventions may be copied by competing sellers and sold at a price that will not allow inventors an adequate return to their efforts. An appropriately calibrated government subsidy for research and development may then be economically desirable.

Even when obvious market failures are absent, some government programs may confer benefits on private sector entities that are collateral to their central purpose and that are

---

[4] Some commentators have proposed that countermeasures under international law should be limited to cases where the subsidy in question has a "cross-border" effect via an effect on the output of the recipients. *See* Charles Goetz, Lloyd Granet and Warren Schwartz, *The Meaning of "Subsidy" and Injury" in Countervailing Duty Law*, 6 INT'L REV. L. & ECON. 17 (1986). A symposium on this proposal, with a principal paper by Richard Diamond, may be found in 21 L. & POL. INT'L BUS. 503 (1990).

not usually seen as harmful. Public education programs may lower the cost of labor for many firms, as noted, but even if such programs might be deemed "subsidies" to private enterprise in a sense, few observers would regard them as objectionable. The best explanation is perhaps that most observers regard public education as contributing to a reasonable *distribution* of opportunities among citizens. Indeed, in some quarters, education is now viewed as a basic human right.

But it is also well-known that subsidies can distort resource allocation. Many subsidies simply transfer resources to well-organized interest groups without remediating any demonstrable market failure. From the standpoint of an economist, this last group of subsidies can be an appropriate target of legal discipline, while the first two groups are not. It is thus useful to consider in somewhat greater detail some particular types of subsidies that economists tend to deem undesirable.

1. Protective Subsidies
As noted above, depending on the nature of the subsidy program, subsidies may lead recipients to reduce prices and expand output. Such behavior by a subsidized firm will attract customers away from unsubsidized firms. It follows immediately that subsidies can be used to protect domestic firms from foreign competition. A subsidy to domestic firms that compete with imported goods or services can induce them to expand their share of the market relative to the share of imports, in much the same way as a tariff or a quota.

Subsidies for the purpose of protecting domestic firms from import competition, and subsidies that have such an effect without remediating some market failure or promoting some accepted distributional goal, will be termed "protective subsidies." So defined, protective subsidies are economically undesirable for two reasons.

First, as indicated earlier, protective subsidies may upset the expectations associated with particular market access commitments in the WTO/GATT system. If nation A receives a promise from nation B to eliminate the tariff on widgets in return for a reciprocal commitment on gadgets by nation A, and nation B then replaces the tariff on widgets with a subsidy that has the same effect as the tariff, nation A's ability to sell widgets to customers in nation B has not improved and its benefits from the bargain are lost. When bargains are undermined in this fashion, nations will become reluctant to enter them in the first instance. For this reason, protective subsidies can interfere with the negotiation of reciprocal agreements to reduce trade barriers, agreements that generally desirable from an economic standpoint.

Second, even if a protective subsidy does not upset expectations under a trade agreement, it still distorts resource allocation by affording protection. When domestic firms expand output at the expense of imports because of a subsidy, productive resources are diverted into domestic production and away from foreign production (wasteful diversion may occur from unsubsidized domestic firms to subsidized domestic firms as well). Resource allocation is distorted because goods and services are no longer produced at the lowest possible cost—domestic firms produce more and foreign firms produce less only because of the artificial reduction in the costs of domestic firms attributable to subsidization. In addition, subsidy programs must be financed somehow, and virtually all forms of taxation to raise the money necessary for subsidies will cause additional economic distortions.

It is important to note, however, that protective subsidies may be no worse than other devices for protecting domestic firms against foreign competition. Comparing a subsidy to a tariff that achieves the same level of protection (as measured by the market shares of domestic and imported producers), for example, both have the same effect in diverting production from lower cost foreign firms to higher cost domestic firms. The tariff creates a further distortion by increasing prices to consumers, and pricing some consumers out of the market who are willing to pay the marginal cost of production to obtain the good or service in question but are not willing to pay the elevated price after the tariff is put in place.[5] The subsidy avoids the increase in price to consumers and the associated distortion. But the taxation necessary to finance the subsidy likely creates some other distortions, and it is impossible to say in general whether the subsidy is on balance better or worse from an economic standpoint.[6] Thus, in an environment in which some protection is tolerated for political reasons, it is by no means clear that subsidies are a bad way to provide it, as long as they do not upset the market access expectations associated with trade agreements.

The wisdom of subsidies can become even more difficult to assess if one adds a political dimension to the analysis. Imagine a society in which the electorate has a taste for rural, agrarian life and wishes to see it preserved. The electorate enthusiastically supports government programs to preserve family farms. Is a protective subsidy present? Or should one instead view the resulting political equilibrium as an efficient transfer to family farmers based on the electorate's willingness to pay to see them remain in operation? Does the answer turn on the issue of whether the farm program results from preferences of the electorate at large, or from deficiencies in the political process that allow well-organized interest groups (farmers) to exact transfers from poorly organized interest groups (taxpayers)?[7]

2. Subsidies for Export Promotion
Just as subsidies can protect firms in an importing nation from foreign competition, so too can they enhance the position of subsidized exporters relative to unsubsidized exporters in third-country markets. For example, suppose that nations A and B both export to country C. Nation A then introduces a subsidy that lowers the cost of its exports to country C, and its exporters lower their prices on exports to country C as a result. Nation B will then see its share of exports to country C diminish while nation A will see its share expand.

This diversion of exports from one nation to another can result from any subsidy that causes firms engaged in exporting to expand their output. Thus, it may or may not be intended by the government that grants the subsidy, and may or may not result from a subsidy that responds sensibly to market failure.

A particular set of subsidy practices, however, seems clearly aimed at inducing an expansion of exports—namely, subsidies that are contingent in one way or another on the volume of exports. Such "export subsidies" may take the simple form of a fixed payment for every unit of a good or service that is exported, or may take more subtle

---

[5] For an accessible treatment of the basic welfare economics of tariffs, *See*, e.g., Peter B. Kenen, THE INTERNATIONAL ECONOMY 17–19, 175–77 (1985), excerpted in John H. Jackson, William J. Davey and Alan O. Sykes, LEGAL PROBLEMS OF INTERNATIONAL ECONOMIC RELATIONS, 40–44 (2002).

[6] For a discussion of the relative costs and benefits of different policy instruments that afford protection, *See* Alan O. Sykes, *"Efficient Protection" Through WTO Rulemaking*, in EFFICIENCY, EQUITY AND LEGITIMACY: THE MULTILATERAL TRADING SYSTEM AT THE MILLENNIUM 114 (Roger Porter, Pierre Sauve, Arvind Subramanian and Americo Zambetti eds. 2001)

[7] These sorts of issues are considered in detail in Warren F. Schwartz and Eugene Harper, Jr., *The Regulation of Subsidies Affecting International Trade*, 70 MICH. L. REV. 831 (1972).

forms such as below-market export financing or insurance, tax benefits for exportation, and many other measures.

From an economic standpoint, export subsidies are generally undesirable. First, export subsidies diminish market access opportunities for competing exporters, and can upset their expectations pursuant to negotiated trade agreements. Trade agreements then become less valuable to them, other things being equal, and fewer such agreements may be entered. Alternatively, or perhaps in addition, competing exporters may prevail on their governments to establish subsidy programs of their own to restore competitive balance. The resulting battle of competing subsidy programs then dissipates resources on a broader scale for no useful economic purpose.

The other distortions associated with export subsidies are entirely familiar. By inducing the expansion of higher cost exporters at the expense of lower cost exporters, exported goods and services are no longer produced at the lowest possible cost. And the taxes used to finance the subsidy programs create further distortions that depend on the method of taxation.

Against these distortions associated with export subsidies, it is almost impossible to devise any scenario in which they might be economically justified. Although it is possible to imagine several settings in which a nation's exports may be "too low" from an economic standpoint, an export subsidy is most unlikely to be the optimal remedy.

First, exports may be uneconomically low because export subsidies by other nations have diverted business toward their exporters. But the appropriate response to that problem is an agreement among nations to eschew export subsidies, not a policy of competing subsidies that can exacerbate waste while doing nothing to eliminate the distortions of subsidization. Second, exports may be low because of protectionist policies in export markets. Such barriers are a subject of direct negotiation under trade agreements, however, and can be dismantled directly through those negotiations. To the extent that protection must remain in the system for political reasons, attempts by exporting nations to overcome it through export subsidies will likely just result in more protection to counteract them. Third, exports might be said to be low because of some distortion in foreign exchange markets that causes an exporting nations' currency to be overvalued. Even assuming that "overvaluation" can occur by some sensible criterion, however, the proper response to it is currency market intervention or a change in the macroeconomic policies that cause overvaluation, not industry-by-industry export subsidies. Fourth, exports might be too low because of some market imperfection in an industry that causes its output to be too low—perhaps the returns to innovation are hard to capture, for example, so that an industry does too little research and development and loses its share in world markets as a result. But the appropriate subsidy response here is not an export subsidy, but an R&D subsidy. The general point is that while various market imperfections might affect exports and a subsidy may be a proper policy response to some of those imperfections, the proper subsidy will be conditioned not on exports *per se* but on the activity that is undersupplied due to market failure (research in our example). Finally, exports in an industry might be too low because that industry is "overtaxed" by its own government in some sense, raising its costs and reducing its competitiveness uneconomically. But again the optimal remedy is not an export subsidy but a general reduction in the industry's tax burden.

This list of scenarios in which exports are in some sense "too low" may be incomplete, and perhaps the reader can imagine others. Yet, I think it exceedingly unlikely that an important class of cases exists in which export subsidies are the best response to any market imperfection—some other policy instrument, such as a different type of subsidy operating directly on the distorted behavioral margin, or a multilateral agreement to eschew export promotion policies, will almost certainly dominate the export subsidy.

D. Subsidized Imports from the Importing Country's Perspective

The fact that subsidies may distort resource allocation hardly means that everyone will be harmed by them. The direct recipients of subsidies can only benefit from them even if the economy of the subsidizing nation as a whole suffers. Likewise, the consumers of subsidized goods and services will enjoy the lower prices that result from subsidies, even if taxpayers at large and unsubsidized producers suffer. The fact that some groups gain from subsidies and some groups lose, even when the subsidies are economically undesirable considering gains and losses in the aggregate, creates constituencies for subsidization that may prevail politically regardless of economic logic.

Of particular relevance to the WTO/GATT legal system is the perspective of importing nations regarding subsidized imports. In general, nations benefit from a reduction in the prices of goods that they import. It is straightforward to demonstrate in the standard case of a competitive industry that the economic losses to import-competing domestic firms are outweighed by the gains to domestic consumers from the opportunity to purchase goods or services more cheaply. The intuition for this result draws on the fact that domestic firms hurt by lower prices can economize on their losses by shifting productive resources to activities with higher returns, while domestic consumers gain from not only the price reduction on all units purchased at the previously higher price, but reap additional gains from the opportunity to purchase more units at a lower price.[8] The net gain to an importing nation from lower priced imports does not depend in any way on the reason why price declines—a price decline due to foreign subsidies has the same economic consequences in the standard case as an equivalent price decline due to other factors. This observation lies behind a well-known economists' quip to the effect that the proper response of an importing nation to subsidies that lower the price of imports is to "send a thank-you note to the embassy."

To be sure, it is possible to devise scenarios in which subsidies granted by foreign governments to their exporting firms can be harmful to an importing nation. One possibility is that the subsidy may drive out all competitors of the subsidized firm(s) under circumstances where it is difficult for competitors to re-enter the market later, leaving the subsidized firm(s) with monopoly power that results in higher (rather than lower) prices.[9] Related possibilities are explored in the literature on "strategic trade policy," which develops economic models in which subsidies are employed to expand the market share of firms in industries that yield better than competitive returns due to the presence of monopoly profits or positive externalities—it is theoretically possible in such models that subsidies will produce a net loss to nations that import the subsidized goods or services.[10] A thorough examination of this literature would take us far afield, and it is

---

[8] See the diagrammatic exposition in Kenen, *supra* note 4.

[9] See Janusz Ordover, Alan Sykes and Robert Willig, *Unfair International Trade Practices*, 15 N.Y.U. J. INT'L L. & POLITICS 323 (1983).

[10] See, e.g., James Brander and Barbara Spencer, *Export Subsidies and International Market Share Rivalry*, 18 J. INT'L ECON. 83 (1985); Avinash Dixit and Alan Kyle, *The Use of Protection and Subsidies for Entry Promotion and Deterrence*, 75 AM. ECON. REV. 139 (1982); Jonathan Eaton and Gene Grossman, *Optimal Trade and Industrial Policy Under Oligopoly*, 101 Q. J. ECON. 386 (1986); Paul Krugman, *Industrial Organization and International Trade*, in HANDBOOK OF INDUSTRIAL ORGANIZATION, VOL. II, 1179–1223 (Richard Schmalansee and Robert Willig eds. 1989).

enough to note here that these scenarios represent special cases. For the bulk of industries that operate under competitive conditions, subsidies to exporting firms will confer net benefits on nations that import their production.[11]

The proposition that importing nations usually benefit from the opportunity to buy subsidized goods or services from abroad is plainly at odds with the popular notion that subsidized imports are "unfairly traded." Economists have relatively little to say about what is fair or unfair, and I take no position on the question whether a principled fairness argument offers an objection to subsidized imports. I note only that the same political constituency that benefits from any form of trade protection—namely, import-competing domestic firms—will benefit from countermeasures against subsidized imports as well. Many countries have national laws that authorize countermeasures against subsidized imports under specified conditions. These laws are termed "countervailing duty laws," and will be discussed in more detail below.

III. Legal Background

The original drafters of GATT in 1947 paid little heed to the trade issues associated with subsidies. GATT's lack of attention to the matter was quickly perceived to be unsatisfactory; however, the subsequent history of the WTO/GATT system reflects steadily increasing discipline on the use of subsidies by member nations.

A. Subsidies and Countervailing Measures in the GATT System Prior to the Uruguay Round

The original GATT contained limited provisions with respect to subsidies and countervailing measures, which were embodied in Articles XVI, II, VI and III. Like all of the GATT, these provisions applied to trade in goods but not to trade in services.

GATT Article XVI originally consisted of a single paragraph containing a loose reporting requirement with respect to subsidies that operated to reduce imports or increase exports. Article II:2(b) of GATT authorized the use of countervailing duties (and antidumping duties), even if they resulted in tariff rates that exceeded negotiated tariff commitments, as long as they were imposed in accordance with Article VI. Article VI in turn imposed three significant requirements on the use of countervailing duties. First, any such duty could not exceed the estimated amount of the "bounty or subsidy" granted on a product, although no definition of those terms was included. Second, duties could not be imposed unless "the effect of the ... subsidization ... is such as to cause or threaten material injury to an established domestic industry, or is such as to retard materially the establishment of a domestic industry." Finally, to the extent that subsidies might result in lower prices for exportation that could be treated as dumping, no product could be subjected to both antidumping and countervailing duties "to compensate for the same situation."[12] A final provision bearing on the use of subsidies was Article III:8(b). The "national treatment" requirements of Article III broadly required member nations to treat domestic and imported products alike for purposes of domestic tax and regulatory

---

[11] A detailed exploration of the impact of subsidies on the welfare of importing nations, including a discussion of the strategic trade literature, may be found in Alan O. Sykes, *Countervailing Duty Law: An Economic Perspective*, 89 COLUM. L. REV. 199 (1989).

[12] GATT Art. VI: 3,5 and 6.

policies. Paragraph 8(b) created an exception, stating that Article III did not "prevent the payment of subsidies exclusively to domestic producers."

Thus, the original GATT was quite tolerant of subsidies. It did acknowledge the permissibility of countervailing duties when import-competing industries were injured by subsidies, and it undertook to limit those duties to an amount that would offset the subsidy.

These rules were soon perceived to be inadequate. The first development came with respect to subsidy policies that upset market access expectations under tariff commitments. As early as 1950, a working party found that an unexpected change in subsidy policy that disadvantaged imported goods relative to domestic competitors could be found to deny the benefits associated with a tariff concession, and thus to constitute what is termed a "nonviolation nullification or impairment" of GATT benefits that gives rise to a right of redress under the dispute settlement provisions of Article XXIII.[13]

Article XVI was later amended during a 1954–55 review session to add some commitments to reduce the use of export subsidies. With respect to subsidies on "primary products,"[14] the obligation was to avoid the application of subsidies that resulted in a nation obtaining a "more than equitable share of world export trade." For products other than primary products, the obligation was to avoid subsidies that resulted in a price for exportation of a product that was below the price charged for the like product in the domestic market.[15] Of course, "export subsidies" as defined above will indeed tend to lead to export prices that are below home market prices, and thus the amended Article XVI amounted to something close to a prohibition on the use of export subsidies on other than primary products (although a complaining member nation would likely have had to show a price differential to prevail in the event of a complaint). These amendments, however, were not accepted by all GATT signatories.[16]

In 1960, a GATT working party devised an "illustrative list" of practices that would likely result in the two-tier pricing structure that would violate the obligations of Article XVI with respect to other than primary products. The working party report was "adopted" by the GATT membership and thus became an authoritative basis for determining whether a violation of those obligations was present.[17]

The next stage in the evolution of GATT Subsidies law was an agreement popularly known as the "Subsidies Code," negotiated during the Tokyo Round of the late 1970s. Its principal achievements were three: it tightened the restrictions on the use of export subsidies; it elaborated the procedures that must be followed in investigations that may lead to the use of countervailing duties; and it identified some criteria to be examined in determining whether subsidized imports were a cause or threat of material injury. The illustrative list of export subsidies was included in the Code as an annex. Like the amendments to Article XVI, however, the Code was accepted by only a limited number of GATT signatories.

[13] *See* Report of the Working Party, *Australian Subsidy on Ammonium Sulphate*, II BISD 188 (adopted April 3, 1950).

[14] These were defined as any product of farm, forest or fishery, or a mineral, in its natural form or else processed to the point customarily required for it to be marketed in substantial quantities in international trade. *See* GATT Ad Art. XVI.

[15] GATT Art. XVI:3–4.

[16] For a discussion of their legal status within the GATT system, see JOHN H. JACKSON, WORLD TRADE AND THE LAW OF GATT 371–76 (1969).

[17] See GATT, BISD 9th Supp. 185 (1961).

In sum, the legal environment prior to the Uruguay Round had the following essential characteristics:

— subsidies were generally permissible for domestic producers, although a number of GATT signatories had accepted obligations to reduce the use of export subsidies, especially on other than primary products.
— countervailing duties were permissible if calibrated to the amount of subsidization and based on a finding of injury; a number of signatories had also agreed in the Subsidies Code to follow certain procedures in investigating subsidy allegations.
— new subsidy programs that frustrated market access expectations associated with tariff concessions were understood to give rise to a right of action under GATT.

GATT disputes through the years were clustered around these basic principles. Thus, a few cases challenged subsidy practices as impermissible export subsidies.[18] Occasionally, a dispute would arise over whether a countervailing duty had been imposed in excess of the amount of the subsidy bestowed on the product in question.[19] And new subsidy programs might be challenged as upsetting the expectations associated with tariff concessions.[20]

As for the use of countervailing duties in the GATT system, their use was relatively uncommon. The United States employed them far more often than any other nation. Between 1980 and 1991, only 128 definitive countervailing duties were reported to the GATT Secretariat by all members combined. Of that total, 110 were imposed by the United States.[21]

B. The Uruguay Round Agreements

Two new WTO agreements (in addition to the old GATT which survives in the WTO) bear importantly on the issue of subsidies—the Agreement on Subsidies and Countervailing Measures ("SCM Agreement"), and the Agreement on Agriculture. (The General Agreement on Trade in Services essentially defers subsidies issues to future negotiations.). The agreements are extremely detailed, and I will not attempt to survey all of their legal provisions, which are discussed in detail in Chapter 16 of this book. Instead, this section lays out the features that raise the most interesting and important economic issues.

1. Subsidies and Countervailing Measures

The SCM Agreement adds a great deal to the law that existed before it. It applies only to trade in goods, however, and its restrictions on the use of subsidies do not apply to

[18] *See*, e.g., Report of the GATT Panel, *DISC—United States Tax Legislation*, BISD 23rd Supp. 98 (presented to the Council of Representatives on November 12, 1976). This report was not adopted until a compromise arrangement in 1981 produced a declaration that affirmed the principles in footnote 59 of the Tokyo Round Subsidies Code. The United States then replaced DISCs with Foreign Sales Corporations (FSCs), a meaure that has been successfully challenged before the WTO. Report on Appellate Body, *United States-Tax Treatment for Foreign Sales Corporations*, WT/DS/04 AB/R (2001)
[19] *See* Report of the GATT Panel, *United States—Countervailing Duties on Imports of Fresh, Chilled and Frozen Pork from Canada*, BISD 38th Supp. 30 (adopted July 11, 1991).
[20] *See* Report of the GATT Panel, *EEC—Payments and Subsidies Paid to Processors and Producers of Oilseeds and Related Animal-Feed Proteins*, BISD 37th Supp. 86 (adopted January 25, 1990).
[21] *See* JOHN H. JACKSON, WILLIAM J. DAVEY AND ALAN O. SYKES, LEGAL PROBLEMS OF INTERNATIONAL ECONOMIC RELATIONS 768 (1995).

agricultural subsidies that conform to the requirements of the Agreement on Agriculture during the "implementation period" of that Agreement.

The GATT and even the Tokyo Round Subsidies Code contained no definition of the term "subsidy." However, Part I of the SCM agreement defines "subsidy" in some detail. It entails a "financial contribution by a government," in the form of (i) a direct transfer of funds, (ii) a decision to forego revenue that is "otherwise due," (iii) the provision of goods and services, or (iv) an income or price support scheme, *if* the financial contribution confers a "benefit."[22] The requirement that a benefit be conferred makes clear that not all government programs are subsidies—if a government provides goods and services at market prices, for example, no benefit arises and thus no subsidy exists.

The fact that a program is a "subsidy" by this definition is not enough to subject it to WTO constraints. Rather, only subsidies that are "specific" are subject to possible condemnation under WTO law, or to countervailing duties by WTO members. The concept of specificity originated in U.S. law, and relates to the degree of targeting in the government program at issue. Subsidies that are expressly limited to "certain enterprises" are specific, that term left undefined. By contrast, when the program does not "favour certain enterprises over others," but is available on the basis of "objective criteria or conditions" to enterprises at large, it is not specific—an example given of such a criterion would be the number of employees in an enterprise. Subsidies that appear on their face to be non-specific, however, can become specific as applied. Further, subsidies that are limited to a particular geographic region within the jurisdiction of the administering authority are defined to be specific.[23]

A major innovation in the Agreement was the creation of a "red light, yellow light, green light" system to govern subsidies. Two types of "red light" subsidies are completely prohibited—export subsidies, including all subsidies listed in the illustrative list now attached as Annex I, and subsidies contingent on the use of domestic over imported goods. All such subsidies are defined to be "specific" regardless of their details.[24]

The "yellow light" subsidies are termed "actionable" subsidies—they are not prohibited altogether, but may be challenged under certain conditions. A subsidy is actionable if it is specific and if it causes one of three types of hatus to another member: (a) injury to a domestic industry; (b) impairment of the benefits of a tariff concession; or (c) "serious prejudice to the interests of another Member."[25] The first two concepts are familiar from earlier GATT law—injury was required in connection with the use of countervailing duties, and new subsidies were understood to have the potential to impair the benefits of tariff concessions. Previously, however, only the second type of subsidy gave rise to action under GATT law. Subsidies that merely caused injury to an industry in an importing nation were permitted but could be countervailed.

The new conception of harm that did not exist in prior GATT law is "serious prejudice." The types of harm that can justify a finding of serious prejudice include a loss of exports by the complaining member to the home market of the subsidizing member, and a loss of exports by the complaining member to exporters from the subsidizing member in a third country market. Thus, the notion of serious prejudice makes subsidies potentially actionable any time they cause injury to the export industries of other members. Prior law is thereby extended in two ways: an action may be brought when a subsidy displaces

---

[22] SCM Agreement Art. 1.1.

[23] *Id.* Art. 2 & n. 2.

[24] *Id.* Arts. 3 & 2.3.

[25] *Id.* Art. 5.

exports from the complaining member to a third country market, and an action may be brought when a subsidy displaces exports from the complaining member to the market of the subsidizing country, even if the subsidy would not be deemed to impair market access expectations associated with a tariff commitment (as in a case where there was no tariff binding, or where the subsidy already existed at the time of the tariff negotiations). The burden of proof to show serious prejudice is on the complaining member in general, although under a provision which lapsed in 2000 the subsidizing member had the burden of proving the absence of serious prejudice when the subsidies were of a particular magnitude or type (such as *ad valorem* subsidization of a product in excess of five percent of its value, or subsidies to cover operating losses).[26]

The "green light" subsidies were introduced on an experimental basis for a five-year period, which expired in the year 2000. At present, the experiment has not been renewed. While the "green light" provisions were in effect, certain types of subsidies were "non-actionable" even if they were specific and caused one of the harms enumerated above. The three categories of subsidies temporarily insulated from challenge were: (i) certain R&D subsidies; (ii) certain regional development subsidies; and (iii) certain subsidies for environmental compliance costs.[27] Nations that complied with the restrictions in each category could grant the subsidies without fear of challenge or countervailing measures— the green light rules thus created "safe harbors" for the enumerated government programs.

Much of the SCM Agreement pertains to the imposition of countervailing duties, and sets forth a variety of substantive and procedural restrictions on their use. In large part these were also found in the Tokyo Round Subsidies Code. Substantively, the agreement makes clear that market benchmarks should be used in valuing subsidies,[28] and requires that "all relevant factors" be considered in determining whether injury is present.[29]

2. Agriculture

Agricultural subsidies remain widespread in the global economy, and the Agreement on Agriculture undertakes to limit them. It falls far short of the disciplines contained in the SCM Agreement, however, and was envisioned simply as a first step toward addressing a situation that had become quite unsatisfactory under GATT.

In particular, GATT Article XVI contained a "loophole" for subsidies on primary products, which include all basic agricultural commodities. While amended Article XVI generally prohibited export subsidies on other than primary products, the rule for primary products was simply that export subsidies should not result in the subsidizing nation obtaining a "more than equitable share" of world export trade in the subsidized product. After some wrangling, this test was ultimately found to be too vague to be enforceable, with the result that agricultural export subsidies were completely undisciplined. As noted, GATT had little to say about domestic subsidies either, and so agricultural subsidies became rampant (and still are).

During the Uruguay Round, efforts were made to negotiate limits on agricultural subsidies, but it was clear that major players such as the European Union, the United States and Japan were unwilling to accept dramatic reductions in their farm programs. A decision was made to devise an agreement that could facilitate a gradual reduction in such subsidies over time, by treating them in much the same way as the GATT treats tariffs

---

[26] *Id*. Art. 6.
[27] *Id*. Art. 8.2.
[28] *Id*. Art. 14.
[29] *Id*. Arts. 15–16.

on goods. Both export subsidies and domestic subsidies became the subject of specific commitments, and nations agreed to limit certain types of domestic and export support programs in accordance with negotiated ceilings. The permissible level of subsidies is scheduled to decline over time, and it is anticipated that future negotiations will produce further reductions.

Annex 2 of the Agreement exempts certain types of domestic support programs from the negotiated commitments. Generally speaking, the types of programs that are exempt are those which have relatively less impact on output—programs that cushion the incomes of farmers, for example, without encouraging them to increase their production. Article 13 of the Agreement also creates some safe harbor provisions for subsidies that conform to the Agreement, exempting them from countervailing duties and the like under GATT.

The arrangements in the Agriculture Agreement are complex and could readily serve as the basis for an entirely separate academic treatment. I will devote relatively little further attention to them here, and will simply note that aside from the introduction of negotiated ceilings and the exemption for domestic subsidies that have less of a distortive effect on output than others, there is little economically novel about the approach of the Agriculture Agreement to subsidies discipline.

IV. An Economic Perspective on the WTO Rules

There are many subtle economic issues relating to the treatment of subsidies under WTO law. I cannot hope to touch on all of them here, and will simply emphasize the most general and important ones.

A. Protecting the Bargain under GATT and GATS

As noted in Part I of this chapter, part of the concern about subsidies in the WTO system relates to the possibility that they will undermine the market access expectations associated with the commitments that members have made to each other. Not all subsidies do so, of course: only subsidies that are unexpected and that alter the competitive balance between exporters and their domestic competitors in a manner that trade negotiators did not anticipate.

Both GATT and GATS respond sensibly to this issue with the "nonviolation nullification or impairment" doctrine. Any change in policy by member governments, including the introduction of new subsidies, may be shown to deny benefits that members reasonably expected to obtain as a result of negotiated concessions. Once this showing has been made, the complaining member is entitled to redress in the form of a withdrawal of the offending measure, or other trade compensation. This policy protects the value of the bargain for all members and thereby encourages more bargains to be struck.

A nice feature of the nonviolation doctrine is the fact that it does not require subsidies to be carefully defined or measured. A complaining member need simply demonstrate that an unanticipated government program has improved the competitive position of domestic firms at the expense of their foreign competition. The administration of the doctrine is thus reasonably straightforward, and the fighting issue is likely to be whether the government policy in question was foreseen by trade negotiators. On that issue, WTO law has also moved sensibly in the direction of a rebuttable presumption that measures introduced subsequent to a tariff negotiation are unanticipated. For measures extant at the time of the negotiation in question, a rebuttable presumption arises that their effects on the market in question could be anticipated.[30]

The nonviolation doctrine is of no help, however, in addressing the other reasons for concern about subsidies. In particular, it has no bite when a third country introduces new subsidies that result in a shift in business toward its exporters. And it does nothing to address the problem of subsidies that create other economic distortions. These problems bring us to the much more complex (and problematic) rules found in the Agreement on SCM.

B. The Red Light: Export and Domestic Content Subsidies

The GATT system has long viewed export subsidies as particularly problematic, culminating with the prohibited subsidy category in the WTO SCM agreement, which makes it illegal to employ export subsidies in goods markets (save for the agricultural sector). The prohibited category also encompasses, as noted, subsidies that are conditioned on the use by the recipient of domestic over imported goods.

The prohibition on export subsidies has two convincing economic justifications. First, as noted earlier, market access expectations can be upset not only when an importing nation introduces a new subsidy to domestic firms, but also when third countries introduce subsidies that result in a diversion of business to their exporters. A relatively inexpensive way for third countries to divert trade toward their exporters is through the use of export subsidies, and history teaches that nations will employ them in the absence of legal constraint. The prohibition on export subsidies thus eliminates an important policy instrument for export promotion that can erode the benefits of the bargain and thus discourage trade bargains in the first instance. It also ensures that nations will not go down the road of competing with each other to subsidize their exporters.

Second, even if an export subsidy would do nothing to frustrate the market access expectations of other trading nations (as where it is longstanding and fully anticipated), it is almost certainly a source of economic distortion. As noted earlier, economic theory suggests that subsidies can at times serve as a device for remedying market failure. In general, a subsidy to correct a market failure should be made contingent on the activity that is undersupplied because of the market failure.[31] For the reasons given previously, it is exceedingly difficult to imagine a market failure that is best addressed with an export subsidy.

The other "red light" subsidy category, subsidies contingent on the use of domestic over imported goods, presents somewhat more of a puzzle. GATT Article III, a provision now incorporated into WTO law, permits the granting of subsidies exclusively to domestic producers of goods (subject to the possibility that they may be countervailed, and now that they may be "actionable" under certain conditions). Such subsidies, of course, can encourage the production of more domestic goods at lower prices, and result in the purchase of domestic rather than imported goods by buyers. A subsidy to buyers that encourages them to buy domestic rather than imported goods has the same effect. Indeed, a per unit subsidy to all domestic buyers of a good can be completely equivalent in its effects to an equal per unit subsidy to all domestic sellers—net output of domestic producers, net imports, and net price to buyers will be exactly the same under competitive conditions.

[30] *See* Report of the Panel, *Japan—Measures Affecting Consumer Photographic Film and Paper,* WT/DS44/R (1998).
[31] *See*, e.g, HARRY JOHNSON, ASPECTS OF THE THEORY OF TARIFFS, 117–51 (1971).

One is led to wonder, therefore, why the domestic producer subsidy is widely tolerated while the subsidy to domestic purchasers conditioned on the purchase of domestic goods is prohibited. By the same token, the prohibition may have little economic bite—a nation that cannot use a subsidy to domestic purchasers can substitute one to domestic sellers, and probably achieve much the same result.

C. Domestic Subsidies and the Definition of Subsidy in WTO Law

As noted, WTO law identifies domestic "subsidies" as financial contributions that confer a "benefit," and makes them actionable or subject to countermeasures only if they are "specific." As such, WTO rules are seriously deficient in relation to a number of the problems with the identification of undesirable subsidies discussed in Part I of this chapter.

First, the existence of a "financial contribution" that confers a "benefit" cannot be analyzed in isolation if the goal is to ascertain the net impact of government on the competitive position of an industry. Often, such benefits will offset by other tax or regulatory burdens, and nothing in WTO law permits such issues to be considered systematically. Although an effort to sort out these net effects would be extraordinarily complicated and fraught with error, to ignore the problem is to render the system unable to detect true subsidization of an industry except by chance.

One argument that might be advanced to rescue the WTO approach in the face of this objection has already been addressed. It is simply baseless to assume that generally applicable tax, expenditure and regulatory programs collectively have a neutral impact on all industries, and that only targeted or "specific" programs can be a source of net benefits. The folly of such an assumption is well-illustrated by considering the sector that most observers would regard as the most subsidized in the world—agriculture. Under the specificity test as it has evolved, a program aimed at growers of particular agricultural product, such as wheat, would be specific. But a program that gave assistance to all farmers regardless of what they grow would not be specific.[32] Thus, the degree to which agricultural subsidies are "specific" will depend in large measure on form rather than substance—governments that bundle farm subsidies together into generally applicable farm programs may escape a finding of specificity, while those with multiple pieces of legislation that each focus on one or a few farm products may not. Although agricultural subsidies are to a considerable degree exempted from discipline under the SCM agreement during the implementation period for the Agriculture Agreement, the broader point remains.

It has also been suggested that targeted programs are more likely than untargeted programs to be motivated by protectionist considerations—the narrower the group of beneficiaries, the argument runs, the more likely that the program in question is a "special interest deal" rather than a program geared to some high-minded purpose. There may be some merit to this argument, but it seems highly speculative. Agriculture once again provides a good example, where the most powerful special interest lobbies in the subsidies sphere often secure government largesse that is deemed non-specific as a legal matter.

In addition, even when an industry is a net beneficiary of government largesse, those benefits may be socially justifiable. Some industries may be a source of positive external economies (most likely in the high technology area), while others may receive assistance because of the desire of the polity to preserve them (cultural industries, family farms?).

---

[32] This rule is formally embodied in the countervailing duty regulations of the U.S. Department of Commerce. *See* 19 C.F.R. §351.502(d).

Aside from the now expired "green light" subsidy rules, to be discussed below, WTO law does nothing to address the question whether the ostensible "subsidy" addresses some legitimate problem. The specificity test, in particular, bears essentially no relation to this question. Indeed, where a principled justification for a subsidy exists, it will likely arise narrowly and case-by-case, so that the policy response will often appear "specific."

Finally, WTO law to a considerable degree ignores the question whether subsidies have an effect on the output of the beneficiary, and thus the attendant question whether foreign competitors can be harmed by it (and to what extent). There is no requirement that the "benefit" from the subsidy have any effect on production, for example. Likewise, WTO members are arguably permitted to use countervailing duties against measures that confer "specific" "benefits" even if the subsidy program in question has no effect on short run marginal costs or industry capacity.[33] The requirement of injury to a domestic industry prior to the use of countervailing duties might seem to preclude them when no effect of the subsidy on output is present, but that constraint has not materialized in practice given the way that the injury test has been operationalized.[34]

Of course, the requirement that a "benefit" exist imposes some restrictions. A subsidy bestowed long in the past, for example, followed by an arm's-length sale of assets to another party, may have no "benefit" to the owner of those assets presently.[35] Further, in any action predicated on "serious prejudice" under the SCM agreement, the respondent country may be able to rebut the existence of an serious prejudice by showing that the subsidy program in question did not increase output. But on the whole, WTO law does not in general require proof that the subsidy in question has resulted in an expansion of output that has injured the complaining party.

The failure of WTO law to require measurement of the net impact of domestic programs on an allegedly subsidized industries, to assess whether any net benefit to them is justifiable, or to assess the effect of subsidies on output is perhaps unsurprising given the enormous administrative challenges that such inquiries would entail and the difficulties that would attend any effort to achieve consensus on how to undertake them. As a result, however, WTO rules for the identification of problematic domestic subsidy programs are deeply and profoundly flawed from an economic standpoint.

D. The Yellow Light, Green Light Approach

As noted, the SCM agreement goes beyond prior law in making certain domestic subsidies "actionable" (that is, they can be challenged as violations of WTO law and not simply

---

[33] *See* the discussion of the U.S.-Canadian lumber dispute in JACKSON, DAVEY and SYKES, *supra* note 18, pp. 845–51. The suggestion that only output-increasing subsidies should be subject to countervailing duties is discussed in the sources cited in note 3 *supra*.

[34] Agencies that administer the injury test often look at factors such as the correlation between the volume of subsidized imports and the indicia of injury to domestic firms, for example, which does not establish harm due to the subsidy itself. Indeed, there is a long-running controversy over whether WTO law requires injury to be linked to the subsidy, or simply to the presence of the subsidized imports in the importing nation. *See* the discussion of the material injury test in JACKSON, DAVEY and SYKES, *supra* note 18, pp. 737–46.

[35] *See* Report of the Appellate Body, *United States—Imposition of Countervailing Duties on Certain Hot-Rolled Lead and Bismuth Carbon Steel Products originating in the United Kingdom*, WT/DS138/AB/R, (2000), ¶¶52–68. The proposition that a sale of assets at fair market value cleanses those assets of any "subsidy" previously received may, however, be contested in some instances. If the prior subsidy program resulted in the construction of uneconomical capacity, for example, the fact that it is sold at arm's-length and remains in operation thereafter would not change the fact that the subsidy had caused an expansion of output.

countervailed if they injure an import-competing industry) even if they do not impair market access expectations associated with tariff concessions. The basis for such an action can arise whenever a specific subsidy causes injury to an import-competing industry, displaces exports to the subsidizing country, or displaces exports to a third country market. Subsidies with the potential to cause such effects are colloquially termed the "yellow light" subsidies.

On one level, the opportunity to challenge such subsidies as violations of WTO law is an important step forward for two reasons First, under prior law, domestic subsidies that harmed import-competing industries abroad could merely be countervailed by the importing nation, which is an inferior option for reasons that will be addressed below in the discussion of countervailing duties. As a brief preview of the discussion, countervailing duties do not necessarily discourage undesirable subsidization, and may simply divert subsidized goods to other markets. The waste caused by the subsidy then remains and global economic welfare may worsen rather than improve.

Second, prior law afforded no remedy to exporters when a *domestic* subsidy to competitors caused them to lose exports to third country markets. That is, if country A gave a domestic subsidy to some exporting industry, and that industry expanded its exports to country B at the expense of exporters in country C, the exporters in country C had no legal options for redress. A countervailing duty in their home market is of no help when the harm is suffered in a foreign market. The nonviolation nullification or impairment doctrine is of no use (even if the subsidizing country had bound its tariff on the subsidized good) because the loss of market access occurs in a third country market, not the market of the subsidizing nation. The extension of the concept of "serious prejudice" to cover this scenario thus creates a potentially important new remedy.

Yet, the notion that the "yellow light" category adds valuable new remedies to address harmful domestic subsidies must ultimately rest on the ability of WTO law to identify problematic domestic subsidies in the first instance. That proposition, in turn, brings us full circle to the issues discussed above. If WTO law does a poor job at identifying the net impact of government on industries, a poor job of assessing whether government assistance to industry is justified, and a poor job of determining whether it has a significant impact on foreign competitors, it is not clear that adding new remedial options does anything worthwhile.

As for the now expired category of "green light" subsidies relating to research and development, development assistance to disadvantaged regions, and environmental compliance costs, there are two possible views. The more cynical perspective proceeds from the suspicion that the WTO can never do a good job of identifying undesirable domestic subsidies, and hence that such subsidies should generally be ignored by WTO law unless they upset the market access expectations associated with specific concessions. Then, any set of safe harbor provisions appears a step forward.

But one can also argue that the particular safe harbor provisions created by the green light experiment (with the possible exception of the R&D category) are questionable. A general objection to these provisions relates to the fungibility of money, and the attendant possibility that the safe harbor rules will be subject to abuse. If government provides resources to a firm with environmental compliance costs, for example, what is to ensure that the marginal effect on behavior lies in environmental compliance? Quite plausibly instead, the subsidy may be used to expand productive facilities and increase output with no impact on the environment relative to the counterfactual world without the subsidy (where the firm would still have had to meet its environmental obligations). Likewise, when a subsidy is nominally given for research and development, how can trading partners be assured it in fact results in more R&D at the margin rather than some other output expanding behavior?[36] In short, the premise that subsidies can be dedicated to particular purposes and shown to be used in that fashion is shaky.

More particular objections may be addressed to each of the three safe harbor categories. The R&D category presents the best case for a safe harbor, in that research and development affords a paradigm example of an activity that *may* generate positive externalities and that *may* be undersupplied by a private market. Yet, nothing in the WTO rules on the subject required any showing that the particular research in question plausibly required subsidization. The opportunity to subsidize was present to the same degree for all industries regardless of their technological progressivity or the difficulty that private actors have in appropriating the returns to innovation. Perhaps administrative considerations dictate a blanket approach, however, and if so then perhaps a safe harbor for R&D has some logic (subject to the caveat above about the fungibility of money).

The category covering assistance to disadvantaged regions is more problematic. All sizable nations likely contain regions with lower than average per capita income, and there is no economic basis to suppose that subsidies for industrial development in such regions will address any market failure. To the contrary, they may induce businesses to locate inefficiently to take advantage of the subsidy, and simply provide an opportunity for the interest groups in pursuit of wasteful subsidies to obtain them more easily.

Subsidies to cover environmental compliance costs are also questionable on economic grounds. To be sure, pollution is the classic economist's example of a (negative) externality. But the usual economic prescription for negative externalities is to require the party that creates the externality to "internalize" it—in the environmental area, the corollary is the well-known "polluter pays" principle. Thus, standard economic models of optimal environmental policy call for polluting activities to be taxed, not subsidized. A subsidy for environmental compliance costs can abate pollution to be sure, but only at the cost of encouraging a larger than desirable scale of polluting activity. It is by no means clear why the WTO should create a safe harbor for the inferior policy instrument of subsidization.

E. Countervailing Duties

For the reasons given in Part I of this chapter, countervailing duties usually strike economists as peculiar. Subsidies may be wasteful, but even when they are the economic loss is generally borne by the taxpayers in the nation that bestows the subsidy. Nations that import the lower-priced, subsidized merchandise are net economic beneficiaries for the same reasons that any reduction in the price of things they buy from abroad is a benefit. When nations respond to subsidies with countervailing duties, therefore, they tend to reduce their economic well-being, other things being equal. The suspicion thus arises that countervailing duties result when well-organized protectionist interest groups use the fortuity of "subsidization" to secure protection from import competition that they might not secure otherwise.[37] The mere threat to use countervailing duties may also be harmful, as it may become the basis for government-to-government "settlement" negotiations that raise prices and achieve effects similar to a cartel.

---

[36] Other commentators have made similar points. *See*. e.g., William Wilcox, *GATT-Based Protectionism and the Definition of a Subsidy*, 16 B.U. INT'L L.J. 129 (1999).

[37] Studies of the use of countervailing duties in practice suggest that they tend to appear in industries where the forces of protection are active and are pursuing multiple avenues to obtain it. *See* Howard Marvel and Edward Ray, *Countervailing Duties*, 105 ECON. J. 1576 (1995).

Exceptional cases may arise, of course, as suggested by the literature on strategic trade policy and related work. If a foreign government employs a subsidy to shift rents to its firms in an industry that earns better than competitive returns, a countervailing duty of sorts may at times be a rational response (as may other policies, such as competing subsidies).[38] But without dwelling on that rich and complex literature, suffice it to say that the industries which fit the strategic trade framework are limited in number. Moreover, studies of the use of countervailing duties in practice suggest that they are used primarily in established and often declining industries, where technological progress is limited and returns are, if anything, below the competitive level. Such industries do not fit the strategic trade framework.[39] Indeed, nothing in national or WTO law respecting countervailing duties is in any way sensitive to the conditions that strategic trade theory might suggest are relevant to the use of duties for strategic purposes.

Outside of the strategic trade area, the only plausible defense of countervailing duties is the suggestion that they enhance global welfare by discouraging wasteful subsidy practices. Thus, the argument runs, even if the importing nation typically harms itself if one takes a narrow view of countervailing duties, under a broader view all nations are discouraged from wasteful subsidies; global economic welfare increases and all nations on average benefit.[40]

This argument is an empirical claim that cannot be verified or falsified as a practical matter. Nevertheless, there are reasons to doubt that countervailing duties within the WTO system do much to discourage subsidies. As noted earlier, they have been used infrequently and predominantly by only a few nations (most notably the United States). Uncoordinated, unilateral countervailing duties may simply divert subsidized goods to markets that do not employ them rather than discourage wasteful subsidies. The existence of the injury test as a predicate to countervailing duties is a further obstacle to their efficacy in discouraging waste, as it ensures that only a limited number of countries can employ them in response to a wasteful subsidy practice. Of course, nations without an import-competing industry claiming injury and clamoring for protection might have no incentive to employ countervailing duties even if they could use them legally, but this observation simply underscores the reasons why countervailing duties will be used sporadically and in an uncoordinated fashion that greatly reduces their deterrent value. In addition, countervailing duties will never be employed unless the subsidy program becomes known to trading partners, and only then after a lag during which the beneficiaries of the subsidy may derive considerable benefit.[41]

For these reasons, it seems preferable for wasteful subsidy practices to be treated as violations of WTO law, and to be challenged and condemned as such, rather than for importing nations to employ countervailing duties. A successful WTO challenge to a subsidy practice, assuming that the losing nation complies with the ruling, will indeed eliminate the subsidy and the associated economic waste. One could therefore make a strong argument that the provisions of the SCM agreement that authorize and regulate the use of countervailing duties are counterproductive, and that the exclusive remedy for nations adversely affected by a foreign subsidy should be a WTO challenge to the subsidy.

[38] See sources cited *supra* note 9.
[39] See Marvel and Ray, *supra* note 34; Howard Marvel and Edward Ray, *Countervailing Duties*, in NEW PALGRAVE DICTIONARY OF LAW AND ECONOMICS, VOL. I, 538–41 (Peter Newman ed. 1998).
[40] See John H. Jackson, THE WORLD TRADING SYSTEM 282 (1997).
[41] Some of these issues are discussed further in James Hartigan, *Perverse Consequences of the GATT: Export Subsidies and Switching Costs*, 63 ECONOMICA 153 (1996); Larry Qiu, *What Can't Countervailing Duties Deter Export Subsidization?*, 39 J. INT'L ECON. 249 (1995).

Before embracing this position, however, one must be careful to recollect the inherent weaknesses of WTO law regarding the identification and measurement of harmful subsidies. To the degree that WTO law is incapable of determining which domestic subsidy programs are truly harmful, the notion that WTO dispute panels should get seriously involved in telling governments how they can spend their money is highly problematic. On this rather pessimistic view, therefore, the role of countervailing duties may be primarily to defuse political pressures for action against "unfair" practices while doing little violence to the ability of sovereign governments to act as they wish.

F. Agriculture

Conventional wisdom has it that the agricultural sector is heavily subsidized in most developed nations. Whatever difficulties may arise in determining the net impact of government on industries in general, most observers seem to agree that agriculture is a net beneficiary of government largesse.

It is ironic that the one sector considered to be the most subsidized is subject to the least degree of discipline on subsidies (among goods markets). As noted, both export and domestic subsidies are generally permissible under the WTO Agreement on Agriculture, though subject to negotiated ceilings and some reduction over time.

The absence of tight discipline on export subsidies is unfortunate for the reasons discussed at length earlier. Export subsidies are almost certainly a source of economic distortion, and indeed the agricultural sector affords a case study of how pressures for competitive subsidization have led trading nations down the road of mutually wasteful expenditures.

The resistance to the elimination of domestic farm programs is likely a source of economic waste as well, for much the same reason that any form of protectionism is a source of waste. But as indicated in the discussion of protective subsidies, it is hardly clear that protection through subsidization is any worse from an economic standpoint than other forms of protection. Thus, if the political equilibrium is such that agriculture must be protected, domestic farm programs may be no more troublesome than border measures.

One objection that might be tabled to the continued coexistence of domestic farm programs and protective border measures for the same commodities (assuming that protection is inevitable) is that multiple protective measures complicate trade negotiations. If country A wishes to bargain for access to the agricultural markets of country B, it is harder to evaluate the benefits of a tariff concession from country B in the face of a subsidy program that also protects farmers in country B. The added transaction costs of negotiation in the face of multiple instruments of protection can be avoided by channeling all protection into a single, transparent policy instrument—this is the essential rationale for efforts in the WTO/GATT system toward "tariffication" of all trade barriers.

Yet, the prevalence of domestic farm programs suggests that border measures alone are inadequate to the task of achieving the anticompetitive purposes compelled by current politics. One need only look at the United States, which is a net exporter of many agricultural commodities, to realize that import restrictions may do little to ensure politically acceptable prices or rates of return to the producers of certain commodities.

Thus, perhaps the best that can be done is to schedule all the protective policies, both subsidies and tariffs, and bargain over both simultaneously to achieve limits on their magnitude. This is the approach of the Agriculture Agreement, and one might reasonably hope that sequential rounds of negotiations over these protective instruments in the agricultural area will produce gradual liberalization, much as the sequence of negotiating rounds under GATT brought great reductions in the tariffs applicable elsewhere.

There is also something to be said for the effort in Annex 2 of the Agriculture Agreement to favor subsidies that do not encourage output. To the degree that subsidies are being granted for reasons that do not relate to the correction of an externality, programs that confer financial benefits on the intended recipients without inducing an expansion of their output may create fewer distortions. The caveat, of course, relates to the fundamental problem of identifying subsidies in the first instance—an output-expanding subsidy might counteract some distortion associated with other tax and regulatory policies. But in the agriculture sector, where most observers believe that net subsidies are present at the outset, efforts to channel farm aid into programs that do not stimulate agricultural production may make good sense.

V. Conclusion

The WTO legal system does a good job in ensuring that unanticipated subsidy programs do not frustrate the reasonable expectations associated with negotiated trade commitments. It also embodies a sensible prohibition on export subsidies in goods markets outside of agriculture, a prohibition that might usefully be extended to agriculture and services sectors in the years to come.

The system is far less successful in addressing domestic subsidies. Its criteria for determining which government programs are actionable or countervailable are highly imperfect from an economic standpoint, and the challenges associated with efforts to do a better job are vast. It is by no means clear that general principles to sort unacceptable from acceptable domestic subsidy programs can be devised and administered successfully. A better strategy in the end may be to embrace the approach of the Agriculture Agreement, which treats domestic subsidies as a topic of negotiation and allows nations to agree to reduce them product-by-product.

Similarly, it is unlikely that countervailing duties serve an economically useful purpose. They are simply one more arrow in the quiver of import-competing industries that seek protection, and likely have no systematic value in discouraging wasteful subsidy practices. Whatever the rules that determine which domestic subsidies are permissible or impermissible, an argument can be made for eliminating countervailing duties as a remedial measure and substituting an action against the subsidy within the WTO.

BIBLIOGRAPHY

Barcelo, John J., *Subsidies and Countervailing Duties—Analysis and a Proposal*, 9 L & Pol. Int'l Bus. 779 (1977).

Brander, James and Barbara Spencer, *Export Subsidies and International Market Share Rivalry*, 18 J. Int'l Econ. 83 (1985).

Diamond, Richard, *Economic Foundations of Countervailing Duty Law*, 29 Va. J. Int'l L. 767 (1989).

Cass, Ronald, *Trade Subsidy Law: Can a Foolish Inconsistency Be Good Enough for Government Work?*, 21 L. & Pol. Int'l Bus. 609 (1990).

Diamond, Richard, *A Search for Economic and Financial Principles in the Administration of United States Countervailing Duty Law*, 21 L. & Pol. Int'l Bus. 507 (1990).

Dixit, Avinash and Alan Kyle, *The Use of Protection and Subsidies for Entry Promotion and Deterrence*, 75 Am. Econ. Rev. 139 (1982).

Eaton, Jonathan and Gene Grossman, *Optimal Trade and Industrial Policy Under Oligopoly*, 101 Q. J. Econ. 386 (1986).

Gauthier, Gilles, Erin O'Brien and Susan Spencer, Deja Vu, or *New Beginning for Safeguards and Subsidies Rules in Services Trade?, in GATS 2000: New Directions in Services Trade Liberalization* (Pierre Sauve and Robert Stern eds. 2000), pp. 165–83.

Goetz, Charles. Lloyd Granet and Warren Schwartz, *The Meaning of "Subsidy" and "Injury" in Countervailing Duty Law*, 6 Int'l Rev. L. & Econ. 17 (1986).

Hartigan, James *Perverse Consequences of the GATT: Export Subsidies and Switching Costs*, 63 Economica 153 (1996).

Jackson, John H., *The World Trading System* (2d ed. 1997).

Johnson, Harry, *Aspects of the Theory of Tariffs* 117–51 (1971).

Krugman, Paul, *Industrial Organization and International Trade, in Handbook of Industrial Organization, Vol. II* (Richard Schmalansee and Robert Willig eds. 1989), pp. 1179–1223.

Marvel, Howard, and Edward Ray, *Countervailing Duties*, 105 Econ. J. 1576 (1995).

Ordover, Janusz, Alan Sykes and Robert Willig, *Unfair International Trade Practices*, 15 N.Y.U. J. Int'l L. & Politics 323 (1983).

Qiu, Larry, *What Can't Countervailing Duties Deter Export Subsidization?*< 39 J. Int'l Econ. 249 (1995).

Schwartz, Warren F. and Eugene Harper, Jr., *The Regulation of Subsidies Affecting International Trade*, 70 Mich. L. Rev. 831 (1972).

Snape, Richard, *International Regulation of Subsidies*, 14 The World Economy 139 (1991).

Sykes, Alan O., *Countervailing Duty Law: An Economic Perspective*, 89 Colum. L. Rev. 199 (1989).

Sykes, Alan O., *Second-Best Countervailing Duty Policy: A Critique of the Entitlement Approach*, 21 L. & Pol. Int'l Bus. 699 (1990).

Sykes, Alan O., "Efficient Protection" Through WTO Rulemaking, in Roger Porter, Pierre Sauve, Arvind Subramanian and Americo Zampetti eds., *Efficiency, Equity and Legitimacy: The Multilateral Trading System at the Millennium* (Washington: Brookings Institution 2001), pp. 114–41.

Wilcox, William, *GATT-Based Protectionism and the Definition of a Subsidy*, 16 B.U. Int'l L. J. 129 (1999).

CHAPTER 42

AGRICULTURE

Kym Anderson*

TABLE OF CONTENTS

* Professor of Economics and Associate Dean (Research) in the School of Economics and Executive Director of the Centre for International Economic Studies, University of Adelaide (on leave at the Development Research Group of the World Bank since June 2004).

I. Introduction

One of the great achievements of the Uruguay Round of trade negotiations was the bringing of agricultural policies under much greater multilateral discipline through the new World Trade Organization. The Uruguay Round Agreement on Agriculture ("URAA") led to the conversion of non-tariff barriers to agricultural imports into bound tariffs, and those bound tariffs were scheduled for phased reductions, as were farm production and export subsidies, between 1995 and 2000 (or 2004 in the case of developing countries).

This chapter makes several claims. One is that traditional agricultural market access issues remain the main priority for the next round, because agricultural protection rates in OECD countries were still huge at the turn of the century. But 'dirty' tariffication and the introduction of tariff-rate quotas in the URAA mean that large commitments in terms of bound tariff cuts and/or quota expansions will be needed if agricultural protection is to be reduced significantly. Whether that is done in the same way as in the UR (percentage cuts to bound tariffs, export subsidies and domestic support and growth in the share of consumption imported), or whether a more radical approach is needed, is a point for discussion.

Second, for several reasons reforms in other sectors also are important for developing country agriculture, not least because having them on the negotiating agenda can bring to the table groups that can counter farm protectionist lobbies. Adding new issues to the agenda can contribute in a similar way, albeit at the risk of diverting attention away from traditional market access issues.

Third, among the other issues that will be raised in the next WTO round are two of concern to some high-income, food-importing countries. These issues relate to the assertions by these countries that stricter technical barriers to farm trade are necessary for food safety reasons, and that agriculture's so-called 'multifunctional' nature requires that the sector be treated differently from other sectors. If handled badly in the Doha round, both could lead to outcomes detrimental to developing country agriculture.

The chapter begins by making the obvious point that, given the diversity within the group, there is more than one set of developing country interests in agricultural trade issues. Since those interests are not always well understood, an attempt is made to clarify them and identify the extent to which the different sub-groups would benefit from agricultural reform. The chapter then examines the traditional issues as they affect developing country agriculture, before turning to the newer issues including food safety and agriculture's so-called multifunctionality. It concludes by reviewing some of the options facing developing country negotiators.

II. Defining Developing Country Interests

Almost all developing countries have an interest in the agricultural parts of the next round of multilateral trade negotiations, either directly or indirectly. Consider four groups of such countries. First, the exporters of tropical farm products face relatively low tariffs on most of their primary exports, but there are important exceptions such as bananas. Also, they face much higher effective tariffs on many of the processed versions of tropical products, which hinders their capacity to export the processing value-added component.

Second, developing country exporters of farm products grown also in temperate areas (e.g., grains, livestock products, sugar and oilseeds) typically face high import tariffs and restrictive tariff rate quotas when trying to sell into OECD countries' markets. They have a clear interest in seeing those barriers lowered. It is true that among this group is a subset of developing countries whose exports of farm products enjoy preferential access into OECD countries' markets. In the short term at least, they may lose sales revenue on those items if the OECD countries' MFN tariff rates are lowered. Even so, they may gain enough sales of other farm products whose tariffs have been lowered to more than offset the cut in their margin of preference, and/or they may be able to negotiate compensation.

Third, there are the net food-importing developing countries that fear that agricultural subsidy cuts by OECD countries will lead to higher international food prices for their imports (and perhaps fewer concessional imports via food aid or subsidized sales). Yet even those developing countries need not lose from farm support cuts abroad. If, for example, they are close to self-sufficient in food (as so many net food importers are), and reform abroad raises the international price of food, they may switch to become sufficiently export-oriented that their net national economic welfare rises. A second possibility is that the country's own policies are sufficiently biased against food production that the country is a net importer despite having a comparative advantage in food. In that case, it has been shown that the international price rise can improve national economic welfare even if the price change is not sufficient to turn that distorted economy into a net food exporter.[1] That comes about because the higher price of food attracts mobile resources away from more-distorted sectors, thereby improving the efficiency of national resource allocation. Because of these two possibilities, the number of poor countries for whom a rise in international food prices might cause some hardship is much smaller than the number that are currently not net exporters of agricultural products.

Within developing countries, the vast majority of the poor are in farm households that would benefit directly from a food price rise. Most of the rest of the poor would benefit indirectly from farm trade liberalization via a rise in the wage for unskilled labour, which may be sufficient to more than offset the rise in food prices. Since the more affluent people in cities would find it relatively easy to pay a little extra for food, the vulnerable group of under-employed poor would be quite small and could be compensated with food aid programs at low cost.

Fourth, for those developing countries which are rapidly accumulating capital, developing their infrastructure, and industrializing, their comparative advantage is gradually moving from primary products to (initially unskilled) labour-intensive manufactures. While that lowers their direct interest in agricultural trade reform abroad, it heightens their interest in reducing barriers to their exports of textiles and clothing. That interest of theirs in textile trade is shared by agricultural-exporting developing countries, for if newly industrializing countries ("NICs") could export more manufactures, they would tend to become larger net importers of farm products.[2] Conversely, lowered industrial-country barriers to farm trade would reduce the need for the more land-abundant developing countries to move into manufactures in competition with the newly industrialized ones. This suggests scope for the two groups to band together and negotiate as a single voice calling for barriers to both farm and textile trade to be lowered.

---

[1] K. Anderson and R. Tyers, *More on Welfare Gains to Developing Countries from Liberalising World Food Trade*, 44 (2) JOURNAL OF AGRICULTURAL ECONOMICS 189 (May 1993).

[2] That is more so the more their government is constrained by WTO commitments from following the earlier EU, Japanese and Korean examples in raising food import barriers increasingly as industrialization proceeds (K. Anderson and Y. Hayami, THE POLITICAL ECONOMY OF AGRICULTURAL PROTECTION, (1986)). Manufacturing exporters in newly industrializing countries have a direct interest in such constraints to agricultural protection growth at home, because farm supports raise the price and reduce the quantity of mobile resources (especially low-skilled labour) available for factory work.

Even if a country's national economic welfare were to decline following the change in its terms of trade resulting from the next multilateral trade negotiations, that does not mean the economy would be better off not participating in the round. On the contrary, that economy's welfare would fall even more if it did not participate, because it would forego the economic efficiency gains from reforming its own policies.[3] There is also the likelihood in the Doha round—already dubbed a "development round' by the EU and others—that participating poor economies that lose from multilateral liberalization could secure more compensation than in previous rounds, in the form of technical and economic assistance commitments.

It is thus in the national economic interest of such countries to be pressured from abroad to commit to such reform, painful though that may be politically for its government. The political pain tends to be less, and the prospect for a net economic gain greater, the more sectors the country involves in the reform. The economic gain is prospectively greater the more sectors it involves because a wider net reduces the possibility that reform is confined to a sub-set of sectors that are not the most distorted. In the latter case, resources might move from the reformed sector to even more inefficient uses, thereby reducing rather than improving the efficiency of national resource use.

Of course net national economic welfare is not the only criterion that drives governments to act as they do. Indeed until recently, it may not have been even a major one. However it is steadily becoming more dominant, for at least two reasons. One is the rapid globalization of the world that technological and economic policy changes have stimulated over the past decade or so, a major effect of which is that economies will be penalized ever-more rapidly and severely through capital flight for bad economic governance. The other reason is the broader mandate of the WTO, which makes it easier now than before the Uruguay Round for developing countries to engage profitably in cross-sectoral exchange of market access commitments. Both developments add a new liberalizing dimension to the domestic political market for protection policies.[4]

With these points in mind, we turn first to examine developing country interests (a) in the traditional market access issues associated with the next WTO round, and then (b) in some of the newer issues.

III. The Traditional Issues

A. The Legacy of the Uruguay Round Agreement on Agriculture

For most farm products and OECD countries, actual tariffs are providing no less protection now than did the non-tariff import barriers of the late 1980s/early 1990s, according to Ingco[5] and the WTO[6]. This is because in most cases tariffs were bound well above the

---

[3] For empirical support for this proposition, see for example M.D. Ingco, *Has Agricultural Trade Liberalization Improved Welfare in the Least-Developed Countries? Yes*, POLICY RESEARCH WORKING PAPER 1748 (1997) with respect to least-developed countries and K. Anderson and A. Strutt, *Impact of East Asia's Growth Interruption and Policy Responses: The Case of Indonesia*, 13(2) ASIAN ECONOMIC JOURNAL 205–18 (June 1999) with respect to Indonesia. The point is made strongly also in THE URUGUAY ROUND AND THE DEVELOPING COUNTRIES (W. Martin and A.L.Winters eds. 1996).

[4] G.M. Grossman and E. Helpman, *Trade Wars and Trade Talks*, 103(4) JOURNAL OF POLITICAL ECONOMY 675 (August 1995); A.L. Hillman and P. Moser, *Trade Liberalization as Politically Optimal Exchange of Market Access*, in THE NEW TRANSATLANTIC ECONOMY (M. Canzoneri et al., eds. 1995)

[5] M.D. Ingco, *Tariffication in the Uruguay Round: How Much Liberlization?*, 19(4) THE WORLD ECONOMY 425 (July 1996)

[6] WTO, OVERVIEW OF DEVELOPMENTS IN THE INTERNATIONAL TRADING ENVIRONMENT: ANNUAL REPORT OF THE DIRECTOR-GENERAL (15 November 2002), Chart 3.

Table 1: Depth of Uruguay Round tariff cuts and post-UR bound and applied tariffs on imports, by sector and region

	Depth of UR cut in bound tariff rate t (as % of 1 + t)	Post-UR bound tariff rate (%)	Post-UR applied tariff rate (%)	Depth of cut needed in bound tariff rate t (as % of 1 + t) to bring it down to sector's post-UR applied rate	Proportional cut needed in bound tariff rate t (as % of t) to bring it down to region's post-UR average applied rate
AGRICULTURE					
OECD countries	1.5	15	14	0.9	83
Developing economies	4.7	60	18	26.3	78
All WTO members	2.6	24	14	8.1	82
TEXTILES &					
CLOTHING					
OECD countries	1.4	11	8	2.7	76
Developing economies	4.1	24	21	2.4	45
All WTO members	1.6	12	10	1.8	53
OTHER					
MANUFACTURES					
OECD countries	1.0	4	3	1.0	35
Developing economies	2.7	20	13	5.8	34
All WTO members	1.3	6	4	1.9	35

Source: Finger and Schuknecht (1999).

applied rates (or the tariff equivalents of the quantitative restrictions) in place at the end of the Uruguay Round. That is true in other sectors also, but to a much lesser extent. Table 1 suggests that a bound tariff cut just forty per cent greater than in the Uruguay Round would bring the average bound rate down to applied rate average for manufactures, whereas for agriculture the depth of cut would need to be three times greater than in the Uruguay Round to close the gap (compare column 1 and 4). The final column of Table 1 (found at the end of the chapter) shows that a one-third cut in the bound tariffs on 'other manufactures' would bring its average down to each region's applied rate average for all goods, whereas for textiles and clothing a cut of about one-half would be needed and for agriculture (including processed food) the cut would have to be about four-fifths.

Binding agricultural tariffs well above applied rates has also allowed countries to vary applied tariffs below the binding so as to stabilize the domestic market in much the same way as the EU has done in the past with its system of variable import levies and export subsidies. This means there will be little of the reduction in fluctuations in international food markets this decade that tariffication was expected to deliver.[7]

Even getting agricultural (and textile) bound tariffs down to currently applied rates on those products would require big cuts. Yet applied rates for textiles and clothing are 2.5 times, and for agriculture 3.5 times, those for other manufactures. Clearly, action

[7] Francois and Martin demonstrate, however, that since many agricultural tariffs are specific and farm prices fluctuate from year to year for seasonal reasons, binding those tariffs does lower both the mean and variance of their *ad valorem* equivalents over time, even when the bindings are well above the applied rates. J.F Francois and W. Martin, *Commercial Policy Variability, Bindings, and Market Access*, EUROPEAN ECONOMIC REVIEW 48(4): 665–79, June 2004.

is needed on two tariff fronts: getting bound rates down to applied rates, and lowering applied rates on these two outlying industry groups—both of which are of vital interest to developing countries.

As if that were not enough, a third front requires attention. Agricultural-importing countries agreed also to provide minimum market access opportunities, such that the share of imports in domestic consumption for products subject to import restrictions rises to at least five per cent by the year 2000 under a tariff rate quota (less in the case of developing countries). Even though within-quota imports attract a much lower tariff than out-of-quota imports, such tariff rate quotas ("TRQs") have several undesirable features: they legitimize a role for state trading agencies, they generate quota rents, they introduce scope for discriminating between countries, and they can reduce national welfare by much more than similarly protective import tariffs.

More specifically the Appendix to this chapter shows, among other things, that:

- in the presence of TRQs the national welfare cost of agricultural protection can be considerably greater than under a similarly protective tariff-only regime, and that cost tends to rise more when there is (as in the latter 1990s) a fall in international food prices;
- with a TRQ regime, a cut in the out-of-quota bound tariff may have only a fraction of the effect on prices and quantities traded (and possibly none at all) of a cut of the same size under a tariff-only regime, not only when the bound rate exceeds the applied rate but also when the applied rate is above the prohibitive tariff in the presence of a TRQ;
- the effect of a tariff cut on national welfare, by contrast, may be much greater when a TRQ rather than a tariff-only regime is in place, depending on how the quota is being administered before and after that reform; and
- an expansion of the market access (quota) commitment need not expand trade and welfare, for it is always possible for the quota administrator to allocate the quotas so as to ensure under-fill such that no more or even less imports in total flow in.

Models such as GTAP (a global economy-wide model) are in principle capable of handling these complications though careful additional programming, but to generate reliable numbers requires also assimilating a much greater volume of policy data than is required when a simple tariff-only regime exists. Until all those data are collected and added appropriately to the model databases, model results of the effects of a cut in the bound tariff will necessarily over-estimate price and quantity effects but may under-estimate the welfare effects of reform.

A number of these undesirable features of TRQs in food-importing countries—1,366 of which have been notified to the WTO—are illustrated in Elbehri et al.[8]. Table 2 summarizes some of the data from that study. The low in-quota and very high out-of-quota tariffs mean potentially huge benefits are going to those allocated quota licenses. In numerous cases quotas are far from being filled, however, one possible reason being that quotas are allocated (inadvertently or deliberately) to imports from high-cost suppliers incapable of making full use of them. And the fact that the quota often represents a high proportion and sometimes one hundred per cent of actual imports suggests that some out-of-quota tariffs are virtually prohibitive.

[8] A. Elbehri, M. Ingco, T. Hertel and K. Pearson, *Agricultural Liberalization in the New Millennium*, WTO/WORLD BANK CONFERENCE ON AGRICULTURE AND THE NEW TRADE AGENDA FROM A DEVELOPMENT PERSPECTIVE (October 1999)

Table 2: In-quota and out-of-quota tariff rates and estimated maximum TRQ quota rents, selected agricultural products and OECD countries, 1996

	In-quota ad valorem Tariff, %	Out-of-quota ad valorem Tariff, %	Maximum quota rents ($US billion)	Quota fill ratio, %	Quota As a % of total imports
European Union					
Wheat	0	87	0.0	21	2
Grains	35	162	0.4	74	26
Sugar	0	147	2.4	100	87
Dairy	24	91	1.1	99	80
Meats	19	128	2.3	100	73
Fruits & vegetables	11	51	0.0	78	20
United States					
Sugar	2	129	1.0	97	76
Dairy	11	70	0.6	77	95
Meats	5	26	0.0	67	102
Canada					
Wheat	1	49	0.0	27	218
Grains	1	58	0.0	5	2400
Dairy	7	262	0.3	100	75
Meats	2	27	0.0	124	72
Japan					
Wheat	0	234	3.4	109	95
Grains	0	491	10.8	109	84
Dairy	29	344	2.8	93	91
Korea					
Rice	5	89	0.0	100	53
Grain	3	326	1.9	148	61
Oilseeds	8	545	0.0	157	62
Dairy	21	106	0.0	85	106
Meats	40	42	0.4	97	77
Fruits & vegetables	47	305	0.0	99	83

Source: Elbehri, Ingco, Hertel and Pearson (1999).

The aggregate level of domestic support ("AMS") for industrial-country farmers was to be reduced to four-fifths of its 1986–88 level by the turn of the century. That too would require only modest reform in most industrial countries, partly because much of the decline in the AMS had already occurred by the mid-1990s. This has been possible because there are many forms of support that need not be included in the calculation of the AMS, the most important being direct payments under production-limiting programs of the sort adopted by the United States and EU. A risk that needs to be curtailed is that the use of such "blue box" instruments, as with exempt "green box" instruments such as quarantine and environmental provisions, may spread to other countries and other commodities as the use of farm income support via trade and direct domestic price support measures is gradually curtailed through the WTO.

Thus, without underrating the Uruguay Round's achievement of establishing rules for agricultural trade and securing some reform, it has to be recognized that very limited progress has been made over the past five years in reducing agricultural protection and market insulation, and a great deal of reform remains to be undertaken relative even to textiles and clothing let alone other manufactures.

B. The Potential Gains from Further Trade Policy Reform

When the implementation of the Uruguay Round is complete in 2005, what will be the potential for further gains from reforming agricultural markets of OECD countries compared with the gains from protection cuts in other sectors; and how large are those potential gains from OECD liberalization compared with gains from developing country reforms? According to a recent paper using Version 3 of GTAP [9], the gains from removing remaining tariffs and subsidies would be huge.[10] That empirical work is in the process of being updated using Version 4 of GTAP.

The economic significance of the projected distortions in the different sectors by 2005 depends not only on the size of the price wedges but also on the size of each sector's production and the importance of its products in consumption. Table 3 suggests that if all merchandise trade distortions were removed globally, almost half (48 per cent) of the estimated global economic welfare gains (ignoring environmental effects) would come from agricultural and processed food policy reform in OECD countries—even though such products in those countries contribute only four per cent of global GDP and less than one-tenth of world trade. Another one-sixth would come from reform of farm and food policies of developing countries (defined here as in the WTO to include newly industrialized countries such as Korea). Textiles and clothing reforms appear pale by comparison with agricultural reform: their potential global welfare contribution is barely one-tenth that of agriculture's (7 per cent compared with 65 per cent). This big difference reflects two facts: one is that projected distortions to prices for agriculture are more than twice those for textiles and clothing in 2005; the other is that textiles and clothing contributes only 1.5 per cent to the value of world production and five per cent to the value of world trade, half or less the shares for farm products.[11]

However, two assumptions are crucial in generating the results reported in Table 3. One is that China and Taiwan are assumed to join the WTO (as they did at December 2001 and January 2002, respectively) and enjoy the same accelerated access to OECD markets under the UR Agreement on Textiles and Clothing ("ATC") as other developing countries that already are WTO members. The other crucial assumption is that OECD countries fully implement the ATC. The latter is far from certain to happen though, particularly if China were to phase out its 'voluntary' export restraints ("VERs") on textiles and clothing by 2005. Dropping either of those assumptions reduces very substantially the estimated gains from Uruguay Round implementation[12], and therefore would raise the potential gains from textile and clothing reform in the next and subsequent WTO rounds.

Even so, agricultural protection would remain far more costly to the world economy than barriers to textiles and clothing trade—and more than twice as costly as protection to other manufactures, despite the latter having much bigger shares in the value of world production and trade than farm and processed food products.

[9] K. Anderson, B. Hoekman and A. Strutt, *Agriculture and the WTO: Next Steps*, 9 (2) REVIEW OF INTERNATIONAL ECONOMICS 192 (May 2001)
[10] Because that computational exercise involved removing all trade distortions, many of the difficulties raised in the Appendix that relate to measuring the effects of partial reform of a tariff rate quota regime, are absent.
[11] Anderson, *supra* note 9
[12] K. Anderson, B. Dimaranan, T. Hertel and W. Martin, *Economic Growth and Policy Reforms in the APEC Region: Trade and Welfare Implications by 2005*, 3(1) ASIA-PACIFIC ECONOMIC REVIEW 1 (April 1997).

Table 3: Sectoral and regional contributions to the economic welfare gains[a] from completely removing trade barriers globally, post-Uruguay Round, 2005

(a) in 1995 US$ billions

Liberalizing region	Benefitting region	Agriculture and food	Other primary	Textiles & clothing	Other manufactures	Total
High Income						
	High Income	110.5	−0.0	−5.7	−8.1	96.6
	Low Income	11.6	0.1	9.0	22.3	43.1
	Total	**122.1**	**0.0**	**3.3**	**14.2**	**139.7**
Low Income						
	High Income	11.2	0.2	10.5	27.7	49.6
	Low Income	31.4	2.5	3.6	27.6	65.1
	Total	**42.6**	**2.7**	**14.1**	**55.3**	**114.7**
All Countries						
	High Income	121.7	0.1	4.8	19.6	146.2
	Low Income	43.0	2.7	12.6	49.9	108.1
	Total	**164.7**	**2.8**	**17.4**	**69.5**	**254.3**

(b) in per cent of total global gains

Liberalizing region	Benefitting region	Agriculture and food	Other primary	Textiles & clothing	Other manufactures	Total
High Income						
	High Income	43.4	0.0	−2.3	−3.2	38.0
	Low Income	4.6	0.1	3.5	8.8	16.9
	Total	**48.0**	**0.0**	**1.3**	**5.6**	**54.9**
Low Income						
	High Income	4.4	0.1	4.1	10.9	19.5
	Low Income	12.3	1.0	1.4	10.9	25.6
	Total	**16.7**	**1.1**	**5.5**	**21.7**	**45.1**
All Countries						
	High Income	47.9	0.1	1.9	7.7	57.5
	Low Income	16.9	1.0	4.9	19.6	42.5
	Total	**64.8**	**1.1**	**6.8**	**27.3**	**100.0**

[a]No account is taken in these calculations of the welfare effects of environmental changes associated with trade liberalization, which could be positive or negative depending in part on how environmental policies are adjusted following trade reforms.
Source: Anderson, K., J. Francois, T. Hertel, B. Hoekman, and W. Martin, "The Cost of Rich (and Poor) Country Protection to Developing Countries," JOURNAL OF AFRICAN ECONOMIES 10(3): 227–257, September 2001.

Moreover, if OECD governments did renege on the spirit of the ATC, for example by using safeguards and anti-dumping measures to limit their textile imports after 'voluntary' export restraints are abolished at the end of 2004, the industrialization of developing countries as a group would slow down and hence their need to depend on farm products to trade their way out of poverty would be greater.

The distribution of the gains across regions that would result from full trade liberalization is clear from Table 3. As always, most of the gains accrue to the liberalizing region. For example, all but one-tenth (12/122) of the gains from high-income countries removing distortions to their trade in farm and food products accrues to those countries.

Even so, that farm trade reform contributes more than one-quarter of the total welfare gains to developing countries from developed countries liberalizing their merchandise trade (12/43). As for developing countries liberalizing their own farm and food policies, three-quarters of the benefits therefrom stay with the developing countries themselves (31/43), and those policies contribute almost half of the gains from those countries' overall merchandise trade reform (31/65).

WTO members were right, therefore, to insist that agricultural reform must continue into the new century without a pause. In particular, developing countries as a group have a major stake in the process of farm policy reform continuing: according to the model results in Table 3, farm and food policies globally contribute forty per cent (17/43) of the cost to developing economies of global goods trade distortions. Textile and clothing policies also harm them greatly, but nowhere near as much as farm policies.[13]

For reasons explained in the previous section, even many food-importing developing economies would benefit from farm policy reforms of high-income countries. For the subset that would suffer a deterioration in their terms of trade, however, the extent of the rise in their food import prices would be very small. The earlier Anderson, Hoekman and Strutt study found that full liberalization of OECD farm policies would boost global agricultural trade by more than fifty per cent, but would cause real international food prices to rise by only five per cent on average, such is the extent of global farm supply response to liberalization.

C. What Should be Done to Further the Agricultural Reform Process?

In terms of farm export subsidies, nothing less than a ban is needed to bring agriculture into line with non-farm products under the GATT. They are, after all, almost exclusively a Western European phenomenon apart from sporadic U.S. involvement: five-sixths of all export subsidies in the mid-1990s were granted by the EU, and all but two per cent of the rest were accounted for by the United States, Norway and Switzerland.[14]

With respect to domestic subsidies, it was hoped that gradual reform of policies of the United States and the EU, in particular the further de-coupling of farm income support measures from production as with America's FAIR Act of 1996, might allow removal of the 'blue box' in the next round of talks (which was an anomaly introduced into the UR negotiations in 1992 simply to satisfy just two members so the negotiations could proceed). Policy developments during 2001–02 in both Brussels and Washington, however, suggest their domestic supports are not likely to be reduced soon. Efforts to tighten the 'green box' criteria, so as to reduce the loopholes they provide for continuing output-increasing subsidies and to further reduce the Aggregate Measure of Support, also may not be able to bear immediate fruit.

But the most important area requiring attention has to do with import market access. Tariffication appeared to be a great step forward. However, the combination of dirty tariffication by developed economies (setting bound rates well above applied rates) and the adoption of very high ceiling bindings by developing economies allows many countries

[13] It should be recognised that these results ignore the effect of tariff preference erosion. In so far as a developing country receives such preferences at present in OECD markets, the above results slightly overstate the potential gains from their reforms.

[14] S. Tangermann and T. Josling, *The Interests of Developing Countries in the Next Round of WTO Agricultural Negotiations*, paper presented at THE UNCTAD WORKSHOP ON DEVELOPING A PROACTIVE AND COHERENT AGENDA FOR AFRICAN COUNTRIES IN SUPPORT OF THEIR PARTICIPATION IN INTERNATIONAL TRADE NEGOTIATIONS 16 (1999).

still to vary their protection as they wish in response to changes in domestic or international food markets. Reducing bound tariffs from 50–150+ per cent to the 0–15 per cent range of tariff rates for manufactures is one of the major challenges ahead. If the steady rates of reduction of the past are used, it will be several decades before that gap is closed—and some time even before many of those bound tariffs reach current applied rates.

At least three options for reducing bound tariffs present themselves. One is a large across-the-board tariff cut. Even if as much as a fifty per cent cut were to be agreed, however, many very high bound tariffs would still remain. A second option is the "Swiss formula" used for manufactures in the Tokyo Round, whereby the rate of reduction for each item is higher the greater the item's tariff level. This has the additional economic advantage of reducing the dispersion in rates that was introduced or exacerbated during the Uruguay Round. In particular, it would reduce many of the tariff peaks and the extent of tariff escalation that bothers developing countries. And a third option is the one used successfully in the information technology negotiations, namely, the "zero-for-zero" approach whereby, for selected products, tariffs are eliminated altogether. In contrast to the second option, this third option would increase the dispersion of tariffs across products, increasing the risk that resources will be wastefully diverted from low-cost to higher-cost activities. While that might appeal as a way of allowing attention to then focus on the politically difficult items such as dairy and sugar, the manufacturing sector experience with long-delayed reductions in protection of textiles and cars makes it difficult to view this third option optimistically as a quick solution.

The just-mentioned tariff reductions refer to above-quota imports. There is also a pressing need to focus on in-quota imports, that is, those that meet the minimum access requirements in the UR Agreement on Agriculture (generally five per cent of domestic sales by 2000 for developed economies). Those quotas were introduced ostensibly to guarantee traditional exporters a minimum level of market access, equal at least to what was available before tariffication, given that tariffs have been bound at rates greatly above applied rates. As many as 36 WTO member countries listed TRQs in their Uruguay Round schedules, of which at least half actively use them. But as the Appendix makes clear, this system of tariff rate quotas ensures that agricultural trade policies continue to be very complex. In particular, their existence reduces the extent to which future tariff cuts will lead to actual import growth in the medium term, and it is worrying that quotas have on average been barely two-thirds filled according to the count of notifications to the WTO Committee on Agriculture during 1995 and 1996.[15]

Agricultural-exporting countries are understandably reluctant to suggest that TRQs be removed, because TRQs provide at least some market access at low or zero tariffs. Nor would allowing TRQs to be auctioned be seen by all as a solution, because that would be like imposing the out-of-quota tariff on quota-restricted trade that the TRQ was designed to avoid. If banning TRQs is not yet possible, the next-best alternative is to expand them, so as to simultaneously reduce their importance, increase competition, and lessen the impact of high above-quota tariffs.

One can imagine an outcome from TRQ expansion that is either optimistic or pessimistic from a reformer's viewpoint. On the one hand, optimists may say: if the TRQs were to be increased by, say, the equivalent of one per cent of domestic consumption per year, it would not be very long in most cases before the quota became non-binding. Expanding the TRQ could thereby be potentially much more liberalizing in the medium

---

[15] Tangermann and Josling, *supra* note 14

term than reducing the very high above-quota tariffs. Such an approach may require binding within-quota tariffs at a reasonable level (such as that for manufactures).

On the other hand, negotiators familiar with the tortuous efforts to reform the quota arrangements for textiles and clothing trade see the agricultural TRQs as a way of re-cycling the acronym "MFA" before it disappears in 2004 when the last of the textile quotas are scheduled to be removed. In this case it would stand for a 'multilateral food arrangement'.[16] Since the first inception of textile quotas was around 1960, it looks as if it will take fifty years or so before they are finally abolished. Is that the expected lifetime of agricultural TRQs?

Those with this more pessimistic view may wish to put the case for a more radical approach to the next round of agricultural negotiations, namely to bring agriculture much more into line with the treatment of non-agricultural goods in the WTO. For example, they might call for the total elimination of agricultural TRQs (along with export subsidies and export credits) and a major reduction in bound (out-of-quota) tariffs. To soften the blow of that request, their quid pro quo could be to suggest WTO put less emphasis on trying to discipline farm domestic measures other than direct output-increasing subsidies. The almost infinite scope for re-instrumentation of domestic price-support measures makes disciplining them very difficult anyway. And, as Snape[17] has pointed out, tightening constraints on border measures would ensure an increasing proportion of the cost of support programs would be exposed via the budget and thereby subjected to regular domestic political scrutiny.

D. Why Agriculture Needs Other Sectors in the Next WTO Round

Agricultural negotiations and supportive analytical efforts to date have focused primarily on the traditional instruments of agricultural intervention, namely border measures and producer subsidies. Yet much of the distortion to incentives facing internationally competitive farmers stems from their own countries' non-agricultural policies.[18] Since the WTO negotiations focus on reciprocal exchange of market access concessions, export-oriented farmers have a negotiating interest not only in better access to food markets abroad but also in more competition from abroad in their own economies' markets for non-farm products. That applies not only to industrial goods but also to services.

There are at least three reasons why the WTO's non-agricultural negotiations are relevant to agriculture. One is that the government of a WTO member that imports farm products and exports non-farm goods and services will be more interested in lowering its impediments to agricultural imports if agricultural-exporting members lower their impediments to non-farm imports. This is because its loss in political support from farmers will be compensated by political support from non-food exporters.[19] The second reason has to do with the fact that many non-farm goods and services are needed by farmers as intermediate inputs or to get farm products to the final consumer. If because of trade

[16] J.F. Francois, *Approaches to Agricultural Policy Model Construction*, paper presented at the UNCTAD workshop on Agricultural Policy Modeling, Geneva, 24–25 March (1999)

[17] R.H. Snape, *The Importance of Frontier Barriers*, in PROTECTION AND COMPETITION IN INTER-NATIONAL TRADE (H. Kierzkowski ed. 1987)

[18] M. SCHIFF AND A. VALDES, THE POLITICAL ECONOMY OF AGRICULTURAL PRICING POL-ICY: VOL. 4, A SYNTHESIS OF THE ECONOMICS IN DEVELOPING COUNTRIES (1992)

[19] G.M. Grossman and E. Helpman, *Trade Wars and Trade Talks*, 103 (4) JOURNAL OF POLITICAL ECONOMY 675 (August 1995); A.L. Hillman and P. Moser, *Trade Liberalization as Politically Optimal Exchange of Market Access*, in THE NEW TRANSATLANTIC ECONOMY (M. Canzoneri *et al.*, eds. 1995)

impediments those non-farm products are more expensive than they need be, costs are raised so net farm incomes are reduced.[20] The third reason is that farmers compete with non-farm sectors for mobile factors of production, most notably investment funds and labour. To the extent that a country's non-farm sectors are supported by trade impediments, so its farmers can be disadvantaged by having to pay higher prices for those factors.

There is yet another reason why it is important to have other sectors on the negotiating table at the same time as agriculture. It is that many developing country WTO members are unable to engage in market access exchange just with agricultural goods, as they have relatively little intra-sectoral trade in farm products.

For all these reasons, the probability of the next WTO round delivering further agricultural reforms will be significantly greater if negotiations also seek to achieve protection cuts for other sectors, including services.

Fortunately, services are already scheduled to be on the agenda for the next Round. Further liberalization of manufacturing industries is also required, especially in developing countries where industrial tariff rates are still high. Additional textile and clothing reform, which would give a major boost to developing economies as a group, would encourage labour-intensive industrial production in newly industrializing countries. That would be at the expense of agricultural production in those countries in so far as farm household labour is attracted to factories. Hence it would have the flow-on effect of providing new market opportunities for agricultural exporters in other countries. This shows up even in model simulations involving an across-the-board liberalization in all manufacturing globally[21]. Hertel and Martin's unreported simulation results show that when manufacturing tariffs are cut globally by forty per cent, agricultural exports of developing countries *as a group* would hardly change, but the net food imports of the developing East Asia sub-group would rise by $2.8 billion per year (in 1995 U.S. dollars) while Latin America's and Sub-Saharan Africa's net agricultural exports would rise by $2.5 billion per year.

IV. Agriculture and 'New' Trade Issues

Inclusion of new trade agenda issues in the next round is considered by some developing country negotiators as undesirable because it would distract attention from the market access issues that are deemed to be of greater importance to them. However, their inclusion could have the advantage that more OECD non-agricultural groups would take part in the round which, depending on the issue, could counter-balance forces favouring agricultural (and other sectoral) protection. As well, better rules on some of those new issues would reduce the risk of farm trade measures being replaced or made ineffective by domestic agricultural measures and technical barriers to trade that may be almost as trade-distorting—a risk that has grown considerably in the past year or so.

---

[20] The importance of post-farm gate activities to farm income increases rapidly with urbanization. It is not uncommon for the costs (including normal profits) of getting a farm product from the farm gate to the retail consumer to be several times the farmer's cost of production of the unprocessed product. Also important to exporters of bulky farm products are maritime shipping costs. Shipping lines not only tend to be owned by OECD firms, but also tend to be cartelized. A recent study by J.F. Francois and I. Wooton, *Trade and Competition in Shipping Services and the GATS*, 9(2) REVIEW OF INTERNATIONAL ECONOMICS (2001) estimated that, depending on the degree of collusion, shippers could absorb, in the form of higher markups, up to half the gains from trade liberalization.

[21] *See, e.g.,* T.W. Hertel and W. Martin, *Developing Country Interests in Liberalizing Manufactures Trade*, paper presented at the WTO/WORLD BANK'S CONFERENCE ON DEVELOPING COUNTRIES IN A MILLENNIUM ROUND (September 1999)

Such issues as competition policy and investment policy are as relevant for developing country agriculture as for other groups. However, since they may not be included in the Doha round, and their implications for agriculture are in any case discussed well elsewhere,[22] attention in the rest of this section is focused on the interests of developing countries in two emerging issues that very directly affect agriculture. They are the issues surrounding (a) technical standards, including SPS and food safety in the wake of the new biotechnologies, and (b) agriculture's so-called multifunctionality.

A. Technical Standards, Including SPS and Food Safety Measures

The inability of the Standards Code that came out of the Tokyo Round to adequately address sanitary and phytosanitary ("SPS") issues, plus the desire to reduce the risk of re-instrumentation of agricultural support to SPS measures in response to the reforms committed to under the URAA, gave birth to the SPS Agreement during the UR. That agreement defined new criteria that had to be met if a country chose to impose regulations more onerous than those agreed in international standards-setting bodies. It, together with the UR's strengthening of the dispute settlement procedures at the WTO, was bound to raise the profile of SPS matters. That profile has been raised even more dramatically, especially in Europe, with the emergence of several food safety issues: 'mad-cow' disease, beef hormones, and transgenic food products or genetically modified organisms ("GMOs").

Developing countries have a complex set of interests in these developments. One is that the SPS Agreement requires a WTO member to provide scientific justification for any measure that is more trade-restrictive than the appropriate international standard would be, and to assess formally the risks involved. At least some technical assistance to help developing countries meet these requirements has been provided, but more may be needed.

A second interest is in maintaining and increasing access to other members' markets that are protected by SPS measures. Again some technical assistance in meeting those importers' standards is helpful. However, numerous countries use very blunt quarantine instruments that excessively restrict imports well beyond what is necessary for protecting the health of their plants and animals, or their citizens in the case of food safety concerns. For example, there are outright bans on imports of many products, including into agricultural-exporting countries seeking to preserve a disease-free image. The levels of protection involved are in some cases equivalent to tariffs of more than one hundred per cent. Without some form of notification requirement on WTO members that forces members to disclose the degree to which trade is restricted by such measures, reform in this area is likely to be confined to the very small proportion of those cases that are brought before the WTO's dispute settlement body ("DSB"). The resource requirements of such legal proceedings ensures that the pace of reform by that means alone would be glacial, and would be skewed towards concerns of those richer WTO members able to afford to bring such cases to the DSB.

Who gains and who loses from an SPS measure varies from case to case, depending on how widespread are the externalities affecting production and/or consumption. In the straightforward situation where the import restriction is aimed simply to prevent the rise in the cost of disease control for domestic farmers, the latter group gains at the expense of domestic consumers and overseas producers. James and Anderson[23] provide

---

[22] e.g., Tangermann and Josling, *supra* note 14

[23] S. James and K. Anderson, *On the Need for More Economic Assessment of Quarantine Policies*, 41 (4) AUSTRALIAN JOURNAL OF AGRICULTURAL AND RESOURCE ECONOMICS 525 (December 1998)

an example where the cost to consumers is likely to have outweighed any possible benefit to producers, resulting in a net national loss (not to mention the loss to potential overseas suppliers) from apparently excessive protection in that case where broader externalities appeared to be absent.

Those domestic consumers are unlikely to be a source of pressure for liberalization of quarantine barriers, however, and not just for the usual reasons (poor information, high costs of collective action because of free riding, etc.). As well, citizens are often concerned about possible risks to the natural environment from importing exotic diseases and/or about the safety of imported food. And their demands for higher quality, safer food and for environmental protection are going to continue to rise with their per capita incomes.

However, perceptions about the safety of different foods and food production and processing methods, and conformity assessment procedures, differ greatly—even among countries with similar income levels. The WTO Dispute Settlement case, brought by the United States and Canada against the EU over its ban on imports of beef that had been produced with the help of growth hormones, shows that standards differences across countries are difficult to resolve even with a great deal of scientific advice. So too does the controversy over the banning of intra-EU beef trade over the 'mad-cow' disease scare. How much more, then, are trade disputes likely to arise over issues in which the scientific evidence is far less complete? Thus not having consumers' concerns represented in the SPS Agreement has been a two-edged sword: on the one hand it has meant the absence of a voice arguing that domestic consumers should have better access to lower-priced imported food currently excluded by excessive quarantine regulations; but on the other hand it has kept out of the SPS debate such issues as the consumers' 'right to know' via, for example, labeling. That latter concern is not going to disappear though. On the contrary, it is likely to show up in dispute settlement cases under the WTO's Agreement on Technical Barriers to Trade ("TBT").[24]

Whether or not wealthy consumers are irrational and hyper-risk averse when it comes to food safety issues is not really the point. Providing them with more scientific information, and improving the reputation of national, regional and international standards-setting bodies, may be valuable initiatives but they may do little to alter consumer opinions in the medium term, and in any case such information is scarce on new issues.[25]

In the case of policy dialogues surrounding GMOs, far more heat than light has been generated so far. Attempts to promote science-based assessment of the risks involved have met with extreme versions of the precautionary principle, manifest in the form of compete bans on their production, importation and/or sale in numerous markets. Proposed solutions such as segregating GMO products and identifying them via labels on affected food items have been rejected by many consumer groups; they have also been resisted by the major producing countries in North and Latin America, who claim that 'like' products are involved and so no costly GMO labeling is warranted. The fact that the production of some GMO products is less damaging to the environment than is the production of traditional farm products has done little to dissuade civil society groups of their opposition to GMOs.

[24] Indeed one paper has already been posted on the Internet advocating activists to argue under the TBT Agreement for the right of WTO member governments to require compulsory labeling of products containing GMOs sold in their markets (M. Stillwell and B. Van Dyke, *An Activist's Handbook on Genetically Modified Organisms and the WTO*, CENTER FOR INTERNATIONAL ENVIRONMENTAL LAW (1999)).
[25] L.P. Mahe and F. Ortalo-Magne, *International Co-operation in the Regulation of Food Quality and Safety Attributes*, in PROCEEDINGS OF THE OECD WORKSHOP ON EMERGING TRADE ISSUES IN AGRI-CULTURE (October 1998); S. Henson, *Regulating the Trade Effects of National Food Safety Standards*, OECD WORKSHOP ON EMERGING TRADE ISSUES IN AGRICULTURE (October 1998)

How are developing countries affected by this issue? Two ways in particular are worth noting: one is via the impact of the new technology in so far as it is lowering costs of food production; the other is via any food trade barriers that may be erected in response to consumer concerns in (mostly OECD) countries. The former would benefit those food-exporting developing countries able to attract the new technology, which places a premium on them having in place sound intellectual property law and enforcement (because seed companies would otherwise be wary of selling into or producing in such countries). If they cannot make productive use of the new biotechnologies, however, their competitiveness on international markets may be eroded as international food prices come down. Net food importing developing countries could benefit from that price fall (subject to the provisos discussed in the first section of this chapter), and perhaps even more so if OECD countries ban imports of GMO products. The likely impact is clouded, however, by the fact that a premium might be attached to GMO-free products in international trade. This is clearly an area requiring more empirical economic research, ideally taking into account the impact of the new biotechnology on the competitiveness of the often-multinational input-supplying firms (to examine the extent to which such firms, rather than farmers or consumers, may capture the gains from the new technology).

While such agricultural issues will arise increasingly under the Uruguay Round's SPS and TBT agreements, they will also arise in other, non-agricultural-related contexts. As with state-trading, subsidies, and competition policies, there is a strong case for developing common disciplines for all types of products, whether agricultural or not. In the case of TBT, there is nothing special about food as compared with, say, dangerous chemicals or heavy metals involved in the production or disposal of manufactured goods. A key advantage of having a common set of rules for risk analysis and risk management is that inconsistencies in current arrangements, and the problems that will keep causing for dispute settlement, would be reduced.

B. Agriculture's So-Called Multifunctionality

Considerable attention has been given in some OECD countries to the term 'non-trade concerns', which appears in Article 20© of the URAA. WTO members agreed that, in negotiating the continuation of the agricultural policy reform process after 1999, 'non-trade concerns' would be taken into account. While not spelt out in any detail, the preamble to the URAA defines those concerns to include security of food supplies and protection of the environment. A third concern is the viability of rural areas. The governments discussing these three items are characterizing them as positive externalities and in some cases public goods that are jointly produced along with food and fibre. Hence their use of the word 'multifunctionality' to describe these features of agricultural production.

Does agriculture deserve more price support and import protection than other sectors because of the non-marketed externalities/public goods it produces jointly in the process of producing marketable food and fibre? That is, do these unrewarded positive externalities exceed the negative externalities from farming by more than the net positive externalities produced by other sectors? If so, to what extent if any are those farmer-produced externalities under-supplied? And where there is under-provision, what are the most efficient ways to boost their production to the socially optimal levels?

So-called 'non-trade' concerns are becoming an issue in the WTO in numerous areas, not just with respect to agriculture. They are a direct consequence of the lowering or outlawing of trade barriers: with less natural and governmental protection from import competition, domestic policies are becoming relatively more important as determinants of the international competitiveness of certain industries. Despite their 'non-trade' adjective, these concerns need to be dealt with in the WTO because they certainly can affect trade. Ideally they should be handled in the same way for all sectors (for example, under an expanded Agreement on Subsidies and Countervailing Measures), but until that is done they cannot be ignored in the up-coming agricultural negotiations.

These concerns are not really new, but they are being packaged a little differently than in the past. A key question at stake is: do they require exceptional treatment, or are WTO provisions sufficient to cater for them, for example via the URAA's 'green box'? The short answer appears to be that WTO provisions are adequate for dealing with the main cases raised.

Both economic theory and policy practice have taught us at least five lessons of relevance to this issue. First, where there are several policy objectives, an equal number of policy instruments typically is required to deal efficiently with them. Second, the most efficient/lowest cost policy instrument or measure for achieving a particular objective (such as overcoming a market failure) will be that which addresses the concern most directly. Third, trade measures in particular are rarely the most efficient instruments for addressing 'non-trade' concerns. Fourth, trade reform will be welfare-improving so long as optimal domestic interventions are in place to deal with those 'non-trade' concerns. And fifth, whenever governments intervene in a market, even if it is to overcome a market failure, there is the risk of government failure—and that could be more welfare-reducing than the market failure the intervention is trying to offset. The government failure could result simply from there being insufficient information and analysis available to design an appropriate intervention (bureaucratic failure); or it could result from deliberate action at the political level aimed at rewarding particular groups covertly for their political support, even though that intervention may be costly to the community at large.

Every productive sector generates both marketed and non-marketed products. Some of those non-marketed products are considered more desirable than others, and some are considered undesirable. Since tastes and preferences change over time and differ between countries, so too will society's valuation of those non-marketed products. And as technologies, institutions, policy experiences and market sizes change in the process of development, so will the scope for being able to market some of those previously unmarketable products that were jointly produced with each sector's main products.

For a case to be made that farming should receive more assistance from government than other sectors, it needs to be demonstrated that agricultural production not only is a *net* contributor in terms of externalities and public goods, but also is *more* of a net contributor than other sectors and especially the sectors that would expand if agricultural supports were to shrink. Demonstrating that is an almost impossible task, given the difficulties in obtaining estimates of society's ever-changing (a) evaluation of the myriad externalities and public goods generated by the economy's various sectors and (b) marginal costs of their provision. Hence the practice of intervening only in the most obvious situations requiring a correction.

Even if a clear case could be made for an intervention, the appropriate measure is unlikely to be import restrictions or output price supports for a broad range of marketed farm commodities. Rather, it will be a finely tuned measure to encourage the optimal extra amount of just the public-good or external aspect that has been under-supplied (or would be under laissez faire).

The policy task thus involves several steps: to get a sense of *society's willingness to pay* for the non-marketable by-product; to determine the *most efficient policy instrument* for encouraging farmers or others to supply that by-product for society; and then to determine the *optimal level of encouragement* so as to equate the marginal social benefit with the marginal social cost of that intervention, bearing in mind the risks associated with one or both forms of government failure identified above.

Some of the more-specific conclusions from a recent review of these issues[26] are worth stressing. First, several policy instruments will be necessary to address efficiently (which means directly and precisely) the numerous policy objectives encompassed in the 'non-trade' concerns. General agricultural price support programs are not among the efficient measures. This is true even of direct domestic supports, let alone indirect supports via import barriers or export subsidies (which also distort consumer prices), because—to use the surgical analogy—those instruments are far too blunt to efficiently achieve the specific objectives involved.

With respect to food security, the most efficient policy instrument for boosting it above that provided under free markets is probably subsidies to stockholding of staple foods. That is already allowed for in Annex 2 of the URAA. Import restrictions to boost self sufficiency, far from helping, may even diminish food security for vulnerable groups struggling to pay the high price of protected domestic food. And once bound tariffs are lowered to applied rates, greater stability in international food markets will prevail which will boost food security in all parts of the world.

Environmental protection has many facets and so requires a range of policy instruments. Reducing farm output price supports, as under the URAA, probably provides the single biggest potential contribution to the rural environment in agricultural-protectionist OECD countries, through lowering the level and intensity of farm production. While those supports are still in the process of being phased down, there should be additional taxes, charges or other regulations on pollution from farm inputs to offset the extra damage caused by them via output price supports. Such input taxes are of course permitted under WTO rules. In so far as agriculture provides positive externalities or public goods, appropriate policies are de-coupled payments for their specific provision to the optimal level in each location (assuming that optimal level is above the level that would otherwise prevail, bearing in mind the marginal social cost of further provision). Since most of those goods can be provided independently of farming per se, de-coupling is not only possible but also desirable, because non-farmers may be able to provide some of those goods or services at lower cost than farmers. Some provision for such payments is made both in the URAA and in the WTO Agreement on Subsidies and Countervailing Measures.

Ensuring the viability of rural areas also is a laudable goal, but again the blunt instrument of general farm product price supports is far from optimal, particularly since agriculture is not even the dominant source of income in many (particularly near-urban) rural areas. Far more appropriate are WTO-consistent targeted adjustment assistance (including re-training) packages and perhaps subsidies to essential services that would otherwise be withdrawn from strategic left-behind remote areas.

In short, WTO rules and URAA reform commitments are not at all incompatible with the adoption of efficient measures for addressing the so-called 'non-trade' concerns discussed above. There is plenty of synergy and no need for trade-offs between domestic policy objectives and agricultural protection reform objectives as embodied in WTO

---

[26] K. Anderson, *Domestic Agricultural Policy Objectives and Trade Liberalization: Synergies and Trade-offs*, in PROCEEDINGS OF THE OECD WORKSHOP ON EMERGING TRADE ISSUES IN AGRICULTURE (October 1998) and published in revised form as *Agriculture's Multifunctionality and the* WTO, 44 (3) AUSTRALIAN JOURNAL OF AGRICULTURAL AND RESOURCE ECONOMICS 475 (September 2000)

rules. However, it needs to be recognised that some re-instrumentation of farm support measures is inevitable and is already evident as traditional measures (tariffs, export subsidies and domestic price supports) are phased down. Getting a particular measure included on the list of 'green box' measures, in order for it to be excluded when calculating the Aggregate Measure of Support, will be a much sought-after prize by agricultural protectionist forces during the next round of WTO negotiations. Careful scrutiny of the grounds for such inclusions is likely to be a high payoff activity for developing country trade negotiators in the period ahead.

Both exporting and import-competing countries should welcome the call for closer scrutiny of instruments used for addressing 'non-trade' concerns. This is partly because once those superior instruments are identified and adopted at closer to optimal levels, greater food security and environmental protection will result. But perhaps equally importantly, the current blunt instruments of support to farm product prices could then be dismantled more rapidly, as there would be even less reason to maintain them. Consumers, taxpayers and exporters of non-farm products in the countries protecting farmers, together with the world's more-efficient farmers, could then join with those anxious to conserve global resources in celebrating this improvement in the management of our economy and environment.

V. Conclusions and Options for Developing Countries

The next WTO round has already been dubbed a 'development' round by several prominent EU spokespersons. This is partly a response to the disappointment expressed by developing countries in the extent to which they perceive they gained from the Uruguay Round, and partly a reflection of the fact that their weight in the WTO has grown considerably. Developing countries now comprise almost five-sixths of the WTO membership, and that share is to continue rising as the thirty or so developing and transition economies currently in the midst of accession negotiations gradually complete that process, many before the end of the next round.

The Doha round thus offers probably the best prospects ever for developing countries in general—and their rural communities in particular—to secure growth-enhancing reforms. In the mercantilist tradition of multilateral trade negotiations this will necessarily take the form of requests and offers, but it should be recognized that the so-called concessions that are offered are in fact beneficial to the economies making those reform offers: a win-win game in terms of nations' economic welfare.

Traditional agricultural market access liberalization should be the key priority issue in the next WTO round of multilateral trade negotiations, given the enormous potential for global and developing country welfare gains from reducing agricultural protection. Assurances are also needed that the EU and the United States will honour fully the spirit of their commitment to gradually expand market access for textiles and clothing, and not simply replace the remaining quantitative restraints on trade in those products with 'safeguard' measures by the end of the phase-out in 2005. Substantial progress in freeing up more trade in both these sectors is essential if the next round is to be a genuine development round.

Such reform could boost enormously the earnings of the world's poor, the vast majority of whom are in rural households of developing countries. Rural households would benefit even in newly industrializing economies that take advantage of expanding opportunities to export textile products, for example through some of their household members moving to new jobs in nearby clothing factories.

From an agricultural development perspective, attention should focus also on reducing protection granted to other manufacturing and services industries. Protection in those sectors still bestows a significant anti-agricultural bias in many developing countries, making it more difficult for them to benefit from the agricultural and textile trade reforms of OECD countries. Those reforms can be done unilaterally, but the next WTO round offers an opportunity to obtain a quid pro quo, and can be a useful instrument through which to lock in such reforms domestically.

This next round will, however, be conducted in an environment in which globalization forces (including ever-faster development and international transfers of information, ideas, capital, skills and new technologies) will, by having ever-stronger impacts on domestic markets, simultaneously trigger insulationist policy reactions. For example, further reductions in traditional measures of farm protection will meet significant resistance in numerous OECD countries, as farm groups join with food safety and environmental groups to argue for new forms of agricultural protection.

In these circumstances the mercantilist nature of trade negotiations may require that the agenda of the next WTO round include not only other sectors but also some "new trade agenda" items such as investment and competition policies, so as to provide the potential for beneficial issue linkages and tradeoffs. Such new items may cause political and administrative difficulties in some developing countries, but they also create additional opportunities to secure domestic reforms that would boost their economies. Limited analytical and negotiating resources in developing countries make a number of them hesitant about having lots of new issues in the next round, to say the least. But developing countries may need to agree to discuss at least some of the new trade issues if they want to ensure agricultural (and textile) market access remains high on the WTO's agenda.

Given the apparent good will towards making this next WTO round a development round, and given that many developing countries have embraced major reforms unilaterally during the past decade or so,[27] perhaps developing countries should adopt a quite different approach from the past this time. Consideration might be given, for example, to exchanging more MFN market access with OECD countries rather than seeking special and differential treatment ("S&DT") and tariff preferences. S&DT simply allows developing country governments to continue to keep shooting their economies in the foot by delaying beneficial reforms; and tariff preferences tend to divide developing countries into sub-groups, thereby weakening their individual and collective bargaining strength.

A striking example of the latter has been exposed in the prolonged and extremely costly dispute over access to the EU market for bananas. The EU policy regime involves layers of preferences that have divided developing countries into 'we' and 'they' groups and thereby weakened their chances of securing a better deal for all.

Another illustration of how preferential treatment has reduced the resolve of developing countries to push for OECD farm policy reform has to do with their food imports from the protectionist countries. Food export subsidies, export credits and non-emergency food aid all are by-products of OECD farm support programs. Without those programs most developing countries would be better off through expanded trade opportunities, and those that would not could be compensated with expanded access to OECD markets for tropical products and/or direct financial aid (which would be a far more efficient way of transferring resources to developing countries than doing it in kind as a way of disposing of surpluses).

---

[27] C. Michaelopoulos, *The Integration of Developing Countries into the Multilateral Trading System*, MIMEO, WORLD BANK AND WTO SECRETARIAT (1999).

With these examples in mind, would developing countries' interests be served by the new EU proposal for OECD countries to provide preferential access to exports of least-developed countries? If the things that matter (such as agricultural and textile products) were to be effectively excluded from such a deal, little of substance would be gained by the least-developed countries, and yet those countries would then feel less able to join other developing countries in seeking lower MFN tariffs on products of export interest to all developing countries. Meanwhile, OECD countries could use this initiative as an excuse for not reforming as much in the key areas.

All this suggests a potentially high payoff for developing countries acting collectively to push hard for greater market access for farm and textile products, and for technical and economic assistance to aid their reform processes, in return for providing more access to developing country markets for goods and services. The political price of the latter offer is, after all, now much lower than it used to be: the forces of globalization are such that economies are now rewarded more, via inflows of foreign capital, for good domestic economic governance, but they are also penalized more if poor policy choices are not corrected. Two such corrections that would at the same time help the cause of reducing agricultural protection abroad would be for developing countries to commit to not using taxes or other restraints on agricultural exports, and to reduce their (often very high) ceiling bindings on their own import tariffs on farm products.

More specific requests that developing countries might put on their wish-list include the following:

- remove tariffs on tropical (including processed) agricultural products,
- replace specific with ad valorem tariffs on imports of interest to developing country exporters, since the former (which apply to 42 per cent of U.S. and EU agricultural tariffs) discriminate against products of lower quality and ones whose international price is declining through time,
- use the Swiss formula approach in making market access commitments, since that will reduce tariff peaks and escalation most,
- seek a firm phase-out date for agricultural TRQs, as was obtained for textiles and clothing in the Uruguay Round, but with limits on the extent to which safeguards can replace the quantitative restrictions at the end of the phase-out period,
- seek firm commitments, preferably written into OECD countries' schedules, on the extent of economic and technical assistance to cope with adjustment to re-forms, especially for least-developed and net food-importing developing countries, and
- support the liberalization of trade in maritime services, given the potential for the cartelized OECD firms that own most of the liners to extract, via higher markups, much of the exporters' gain from goods trade liberalization.

Finally, what else should developing countries do to help their own reform processes complement those abroad? One obvious thing is to direct new economic and technical assistance funds towards reducing the under-investments in rural infrastructure (human as well as physical), agricultural research and development, and agricultural technology transfer. Liberalizing foreign investment rules and improving intellectual property law enforcement would enhance the prospects for both transfers of new biotechnologies and their further development locally. And removing domestic disincentives to farmers in the form of agricultural export taxes, manufacturing protection, and over-valued exchange rates remain essential.

APPENDIX

EFFECTS OF IMPOSING A TARIFF-RATE QUOTA REGIME ON THE DOMESTIC PRICE, TRADE AND WELFARE OF A FOOD-IMPORTING ECONOMY

Consider an economy that imports an agricultural product imposes a tariff-rate quota ("TRQ") regime under the rules of the Uruguay Round Agreement on Agriculture. That involves setting a bound tariff (typically more than the tariff actually applied) on out-of-quota sales and a lower in-quota tariff for a specified volume of imports. As is clear from Table 1, the extent of the difference between those two tariff rates for various products and OECD countries is considerable.

The initial impact of imposing such a TRQ regime is depicted in Figure 1 where this economy's import demand curve for the product is line D. For simplicity, the economy is assumed to be a sufficiently small player in the global market for this product that its imports do not affect the international price, and its in-quota tariff is assumed to be zero, in which case the quota volume, Q, is imported at the international price P*.

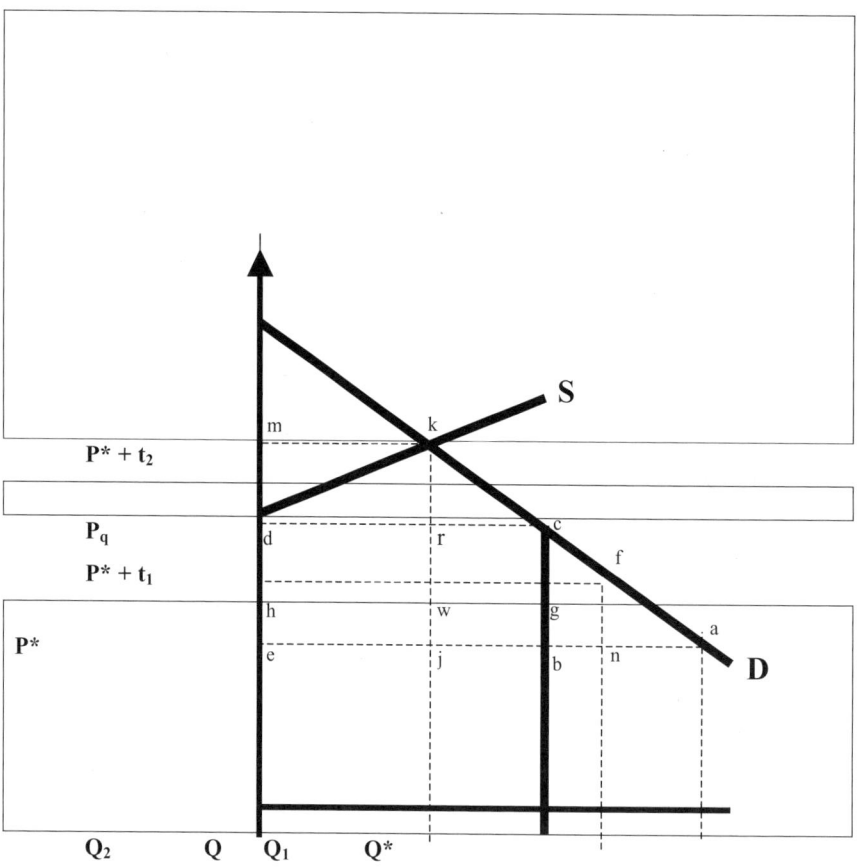

Figure 1: Domestic price, trade and welfare effects of an agricultural tariff rate quota regime on a small economy

If this was an import quota regime (now illegal under WTO), the domestic price would be P_q and the national economic welfare loss from restricting imports to Q, instead of allowing the free-trade volume Q^*, would be area *abc* plus a percentage of the potential quota rent which is area *bcde*. What that latter percentage is depends on how the import licenses are administered: it is zero only if all licenses go to domestic firms and those firms are allowed to import from the lowest-cost suppliers abroad. (By contrast, if say only Q_2 of the Q units were allocated to domestic firms, the national welfare loss would be greater by area *bcrj*.)

It is possible to achieve the same outcome under a TRQ regime as under a traditional import quota. In terms of Figure 1, all that is required is to set the out-of-quota applied tariff (and therefore the bound rate) at $P_q - P^*$ per unit or more.

Only if the out-of-quota applied tariff is set at a value of less than $P_q - P^*$ per unit would there be any out-of-quota imports under a TRQ regime. If the applied rate was set at the specific rate of t_1 per unit, for example, the domestic price would be $P^* + t_1$ and an additional $Q_1 - Q$ units would be imported. Compared with a prohibitive out-of-quota tariff, this would generate less potential quota rent (lower by area *cdhg*) but would cause domestic consumer surplus net of domestic producer surplus to be higher by area *cdhf*, and tariff revenue of area *fgbn* would be collected by the government. Hence net economic welfare would be greater by area *fcbn* as compared with no out-of-quota imports, again assuming all licenses go to domestic firms and those firms are free to source imports from the lowest-cost suppliers abroad.

If some licenses are made valid only for imports from high-cost foreign suppliers (as applies for some products under the European Union's Lome Convention, for example), this importing economy's welfare would be further reduced. It could be reduced by even more than the maximum quota rent for volume Q (area *bcde*). Suppose, for example, the licenses are restricted to imports from a set of countries whose export supply curve measured at cif prices is line S. Even if the out-of-quota applied tariff was more than t_2, those foreign suppliers could afford to export only Q_2 units to this economy, causing the domestic price to be $P^* + t_2$ rather than P_q because of the quota being underfilled by $Q - Q_2$ units. In this case there would be no quota rents, and the net economic welfare cost of imposing such a TRQ regime would be much larger than described in the previous two paragraphs. Specifically, compared with free trade, the welfare cost of this regime would be area *aemk*, regardless of whether the licenses are allocated to domestic or foreign firms, whereas the cost of the regimes described in paragraphs one and two are potentially just areas *abc* and *anf*, respectively. To that needs to be added the cost to government of administering the license allocation system and the lobbying costs of firms seeking a share of those licenses.

Effect of an International Price Fall

If the international price of this product were to fall—as it has during the implementation of the Uruguay Round—the nominal rate of protection (the percentage by which the domestic producer price exceeds the border price) would remain constant under an ad valorem tariff regime but would rise under a specific tariff regime. However, it would rise even more under a TRQ regime if the out-of-quota tariff had been prohibitive (i.e., above $P_q - P^*$ per unit). Indeed if $P^* + t_2$ was above P_q by more than the fall in the international price, the import volume and domestic price would remain unchanged despite that price fall. It is thus possible that even though agricultural producer supports were supposed to decline during the implementation of the Uruguay Round though cuts in bound tariffs (as well as producer and export subsidies) plus growth in TRQ volumes, protection levels may have increased in some cases because of a more-than-offsetting fall in international food prices since 1995.

Effects of a New Commitment to Lower the Bound Tariff

Suppose at the end of the URAA implementation period this economy commits itself to lower its bound tariff on this product. If a tariff-only regime was in place, the impacts of that reform would be somewhere between zero and 100 per cent of the impacts of an equally large cut in the applied tariff, depending on the extent to which the bound rate exceeds that applied rate. (The proportion starts to rise above zero only after the bound rate reaches the applied rate.) In the presence of a TRQ regime, however, the impacts are even smaller if the out-of-quota tariff is still prohibitive. Indeed even if licenses were held by domestic firms and imports were sourced from the most efficient suppliers, there would be no impact at all from that reform commitment if the cut in the bound rate was insufficient to bring the applied tariff down to less than $P_q - P^*$ in Figure 1. The maximum impacts are possible only if the out-of-quota applied tariff is not prohibitive, *and* the bound rate is not above the applied rate.

If there were (a) restrictions on sourcing from lowest-cost suppliers, and/or (b) only some of the quota (say Q_2) was allocated to domestic firms, the welfare gains from bringing the applied tariff down to a non-prohibitive level would be substantially greater than without those features of quota administration. For example, if the tariff was reduced from more than t_2 to t_1, there would be an additional gain of (a) area *bemkc* if the requirement on domestic firms to source from high-cost imports along curve S was removed, and (b) area *gcru* if only Q_2 of the quota licenses were in the hands of domestic firms.

Effects of a New Commitment to Expand the Quota

Even more than a commitment to lower the bound tariff, a commitment to expand the quota could have anything between zero and more than 100 per cent of the standard impact described in textbooks. If the quota had not been administered frictionlessly in the past and had not been fully allocated to domestic firms, and there were changes in favour of domestic importers as part of the new commitment, the economy's actual welfare gain could exceed the maximum gain normally estimated for a quota increase.

Conclusions

The following conclusions can be drawn from the above:

- TRQs add considerable complexity to modeling empirically even the domestic impacts of agricultural trade policies and their reform;
- in the presence of TRQs the national welfare cost of agricultural protection can be considerably greater than what a given domestic-to-borderprice wedge would imply if a tariff-only regime prevailed;
- a fall in the border price of the product causes that cost of protection to rise if a TRQ regime with a prohibitive out-of-quota tariff is in place, and by more than if a specific tariff alone is used;

- modeling an x per cent cut in the bound tariff as if it is a cut of that size in the applied rate can overstate the price and quantity effects of reform not only because the bound rate exceeds the applied rate but also because the applied rate is above the prohibitive tariff in the presence of the quota, such that the actual effects could range (in a non-linear, double-kinked fashion) from anything between zero to 100 per cent of the modeled effects;
- the modeled effects of a tariff cut on national welfare, by contrast, could understate or overstate the gains from further reform, depending on how the quota is being administered before and after the next reform;
- an expansion of the market access (quota) commitment need not ease this measurement problem, for it is always possible for the quota administrator to allocate those quotas so as to ensure under-fill such that no more or even less imports in total flow in; and
- modeling the effects of the TRQ regime, and changes to it, on bilateral trade flows and thereby on the welfare of this economy's trading partners also is more complex than modeling their effects under a tariff-only regime, with in-quota and out-of-quota tariff preferences for some trading partners adding further complications for modelers.

Models such as GTAP are in principle capable of handling these complications though careful additional programming, but to generate reliable numbers requires also assimilating a much greater volume of policy data than is required when a simple tariff-only regime exists. Until all those data are collected and added appropriately to the model's database, modeling the effects of an x per cent cut in the bound tariff will necessarily generate upper-bound estimates of price and quantity effects, the true impacts being somewhere between those from the model and zero. But it is possible that modelers may *under-estimate* rather than over-estimate the *welfare* effects of reform, depending on the way the quotas are administered before and after the next round of commitments.

BIBLIOGRAPHY

Anderson, K., *Domestic Agricultural Policy Objectives and Trade Liberalization: Synergies and Trade-offs*, in Proceedings of the OECD Workshop on Emerging Trade Issues in Agriculture (Paris, 25–26 October 1998), and published in revised form as *Agriculture's Multifunctionality and the WTO*, 44(3) AUSTRALIAN JOURNAL OF AGRICULTURAL AND RESOURCE ECONOMICS 475–94 (September 2000).

Anderson, K., 'Agriculture, Developing Countries, and the WTO Millennium Round', Ch. 6 in *Agriculture and the New Trade Agenda*, edited by M.D. Ingco and L.A. Winters, Cambridge University Press, 2004.

Anderson, K., B. Dimaranan, T. Hertel and W. Martin, *Economic Growth and Policy Reforms in the APEC Region: Trade and Welfare Implications by 2005*, 3(1) Asia-Pacific Economic Review 1 (April 1997).

Anderson, K., J. Francois, T. Hertel, B. Hoekman, and W. Martin, "The Cost of Rich (and Poor) Country Protection to Developing Countries." JOURNAL OF AFRICAN ECONOMIES 10(3): 227–257, September 2001.

ANDERSON, K. AND Y. HAYAM, THE POLITICAL ECONOMY OF AGRICULTURAL PROTECTION (1986)

Anderson, K., B. Hoekman and A. Strutt , *Agriculture and the WTO: Next Steps*, 9(2) REVIEW OF INTERNATIONAL ECONOMICS 192, (May 2001).

Anderson, K. and A. Strutt, Impact of East Asia's Growth Interruption and Policy Responses: The Case of Indonesia, 13(2) ASIAN ECONOMIC JOURNAL 205, (June 1999).

Anderson, K. and R. Tyers, *More on Welfare Gains to Developing Countries from Liberalising World Food Trade*, 44(2) JOURNAL OF AGRICULTURAL ECONOMICS 189 (May 1993).

Cottier, T. and P.C. Mavroidis (eds.), STATE TRADING IN THE TWENTY-FIRST CENTURY (1998).

Elbehri, A., M. Ingco, T. Hertel and K. Pearson, *Agricultural Liberalization in the New Millennium*, paper presented at the WTO/World Bank conference on Agriculture and the New Trade Agenda from a Development Perspective, Geneva, 1–2 October 1999.

Finger, J.M. and L. Schuknecht, *Market Access Advances and Retreats: The Uruguay Round and Beyond*, paper presented at the Annual World Bank Conference on Development Economics, Washington, D.C., April, 1999.

Francois, J.F., *Approaches to Agricultural Policy Model Construction*, paper presented at the UNCTAD workshop on Agricultural Policy Modeling, Geneva, 24–25 March, 1999.

Francois, J.F., *Market Access Liberalization in the WTO 2000 Negotiations*, paper presented at the WTO/World Bank conference on Agriculture and the New Trade Agenda from a Development Perspective, Geneva, 1–2 October, 1999.

Francois, J.F. and W. Martin, *Commercial Policy Uncertainty, Bindings, and Market Access*, EUROPEAN ECONOMIC REVIEW, 48(3): 665–79, (June 2004).

Francois, J.F. and I. Wooten, *Trade in International Transport Services: The Role of Competition*, 9(2) REVIEW OF INTERNATIONAL ECONOMICS 249 (2001)

Grossman, G.M. and E. Helpman *Trade Wars and Trade Talks*, 103(4) JOURNAL OF POLITICAL ECONOMY 675 (August 1995).

Henson, S., *Regulating the Trade Effects of National Food Safety Standards*, OECD Workshop on Emerging Trade Issues in Agriculture, Paris, 25–26 October, 1998, available at http://www.oecd.org/agr/trade/.

Hertel, T.W. (ed.), Global Trade Analysis: Modeling and Applications (1997).

Hertel, T.W., and W. Martin, *Developing Country Interests in Liberalizing Manufactures Trade*, paper presented at the WTO/World Bank's Conference on Developing Countries in a Millennium Round, Geneva, 19–20 September, 1999.

Hillman, A.L. and P. Moser, *Trade Liberalization as Politically Optimal Exchange of Market Access*, in THE NEW TRANSATLANTIC ECONOMY (Canzoneri *et al.* eds. 1995).

Hudec, R.E., *Does the Agreement on Agriculture Work? Agricultural Disputes After the Uruguay Round*, IATRC Working Paper #98-2, Department of Applied Economics, University of Minnesota, April, 1998.

Ingco, M.D., Tariffication in the Uruguay Round: How Much Liberalization?, 19(4) THE WORLD ECONOMY 425, (July 1996).

Ingco, M.D., *Has Agricultural Trade Liberalization Improved Welfare in the Least-Developed Countries? Yes*, Policy Research Working Paper 1748, World Bank, Washington, D.C., April, 1997.

Ingco, M.D. and F. Ng, Distortionary Effects of State Trading in Agriculture: Issues for the Next Round of Multilateral Trade Negotiations, World Bank Policy Research Working Paper 1915 (1998).

James, S. and K. Anderson, *On the Need for More Economic Assessment of Quarantine Policies*, 41(4) AUSTRALIAN JOURNAL OF AGRICULTURAL AND RESOURCE ECONOMICS 525 (December, 1998).

Josling, T., S. Tangermann and T.K. Warley (1996), *Agriculture in the GATT*, London: Macmillan and New York: St Martin's Press.

Mahe, L.P. and F. Ortalo-Magne, *International Co-operation in the Regulation of Food Quality and Safety Attributes*, in Proceedings of the OECD Workshop on Emerging Trade Issues in Agriculture, Paris, 25–26 October, 1998, available at http://www.oecd.org/agr/trade.

Michaelopoulos, C., The Integration of Developing Countries into the Multilateral Trading System, mimeo, World Bank and WTO Secretariat (1999).

Roberts, D., Implementation of the WTO Agreement on the Application of Sanitary and Phytosanitary Measures: The First Two Years, Working Paper #98-4, Department of Applied Economics, University of Minnesota, May 1998.

Roberts, D. and K. DeRemer, *Overview of Foreign Technical Barriers to U.S. Agricultural Exports*, ERS Staff Paper No. 9705, Washington, D.C.: U.S. Department of Agriculture, March, 1997.

Schiff, M. and A. Valdes, The Political Economy of Agricultural Pricing Policy: Vol. 4, A Synthesis of the Economics in Developing Countries (1992).

Skully, D., T*he Economics of TRQ Administration,* IATRC Working Paper #99-6, St Paul: University of Minnesota, May 1999.

Snape, R.H., *The Importance of Frontier Barriers*, in PROTECTION AND COMPETITION IN INTERNATIONAL TRADE (H. Kierzkowski ed. 1987).

Stillwell, M. and B. Van Dyke, *An Activist's Handbook on Genetically Modified Organisms and the WTO* (Center for International Environmental Law, March, 1999), available at (uwww.consumerscouncil/org/ccc/policyhandbk399.htm).

Tangermann, S. and T. Josling, *The Interests of Developing Countries in the Next Round of WTO Agricultural Negotiations*, paper presented at the UNCTAD workshop on Developing a Proactive and Coherent Agenda for African Countries in Support of their Participation in International Trade Negotiations, Pretoria, 29 June to 2 July, 1999.

Tyers, R. and K. Anderson, Disarray in World Food Markets: A Quantitative Assessment (1992).

WTO, OVERVIEW OF DEVELOPMENTS IN THE INTERNATIONAL TRADING ENVIRONMENT: ANNUAL REPORT OF THE DIRECTOR-GENERAL (2002).

CHAPTER 43

ENVIRONMENTAL ISSUES

Chad P. Bown and Rachel McCulloch*

TABLE OF CONTENTS

* Department of Economics and International Business School, Brandeis University. Financial support from the Schulhof Foundation is gratefully acknowledged.

I. Introduction

What role does the World Trade Organization play in efforts to safeguard the environment? What role *should* it play? Environmental groups and green-leaning governments have come to view the WTO, with its large membership and its relative success in achieving a rules-based international regime, as the prime candidate for international arbiter on environmental issues. However, many proponents of expanded global trade, and especially policy makers in developing countries, are skeptical about an expanded role for the WTO in maintaining environmental standards. They fear that WTO-approved trade sanctions may be used to enforce adherence to environmental norms not necessarily shared by or appropriate for all nations, and that environmental protection may in practice translate into a fresh justification for old-fashioned protectionism.

Although the word "environment" itself appears nowhere in the original articles of the General Agreement on Tariffs on Trade, Article XX allows broad exceptions for environmental policies that would otherwise constitute violations of GATT principles:

> [N]othing in this Agreement shall be construed to prevent the adoption or enforcement by any contracting party of measures... necessary to protect human, animal or plant life or health... [or]... relating to the conservation of exhaustible natural resources....

But Article XX also specifies that application of such measures must not constitute "a means of arbitrary or unjustifiable discrimination between countries where the same conditions prevail, or a disguised restriction on international trade...."[1] Much of the recent controversy over the WTO's appropriate role in achieving environmental objectives centers on application of Article XX, and thus at least implicitly on the weight that should be given to efficiency gains from expanding international trade relative to health and welfare benefits from raising environmental quality. This trade-off lies at the very heart of the controversy. Seen from the perspective of the WTO's intended role as champion of open international markets, Article XX offers potential green cover for protectionist-inspired national policies.[2] Yet environmentalists regard the scope of Article XX as unduly narrow, preserving only very limited and circumscribed national sovereignty with respect to environmental initiatives.

This chapter begins by laying out the set of linkages and policy issues now collectively termed "trade and environment," and then examines the role of the GATT and WTO in these areas (Part II). Part III focuses on relevant innovations made in the Uruguay Round. Part IV reviews recent economic analysis and empirical findings on the trade-environment nexus. The remainder of the chapter discusses the most important "unfinished business" in this area (Part V) as well as some policy conclusions (Part VI).

---

[1] As detailed in Part III of this chapter, the Uruguay Round negotiations supplemented Article XX by providing similar exemptions for policies affecting trade in services and in new agreements on agriculture, product standards, intellectual property rights, and subsidies.

[2] Writing from the perspective of international economics, we use *protection* (protectionist/protectionism) in reference to policy measures intended to shield domestic producers from foreign competition. Such policies create benefits for the shielded sector but usually inflict a net loss on the country as a whole. Thus, international economists almost always favor less protection, and this is also the main goal of the GATT/WTO system. But environmentalists want *more* protection—of the environment. As has been observed, this difference in the use of language can itself be a source of confusion in the trade-environment area: "the word 'protection' warms the hearts of environmentalists but sends chills down the spines of free traders." DANIEL C. ESTY, GREENING THE GATT: TRADE, ENVIRONMENT, AND THE FUTURE 36 (1994).

II. Background

In the 1990s, heightened public interest in environmental issues led to a rapid "greening" of regional and multilateral negotiations on trade. Although environmental and conservation lobbies in the United States and most other advanced countries had begun to mobilize at least two decades earlier, their agenda until the 1990s was largely domestic. For the United States, the shift in focus toward trade issues started with the North American Free Trade Agreement ("NAFTA") and the *Tuna-Dolphin* case[3] in the GATT, discussed below.[4]

International economic theory has traditionally been constructed around a single policy objective: maximization of national welfare. In practice, this almost always means maximization of national income as conventionally measured, i.e., without any attempt to include the estimated cost of environmental damage or benefit of environmental cleanup. Trade is accordingly viewed as beneficial largely to the extent that it raises national income. Environmental issues, along with such other politically salient considerations as income distribution and national defense, are seen as only tangentially related to trade. Until the mid-1990s, few texts on international economics even raised the possibility that trade might have significant environment effects or that trade policies might be used to achieve environmental objectives.[5] In his influential treatment of the "scientific" tariff, Harry Johnson refers collectively to these other considerations as *non-economic* objectives of protection, i.e., objectives apart from maximization of national income.[6] Bhagwati and Srinivasan demonstrate that trade policy is rarely if ever the most efficient way—the one entailing least sacrifice of national income—to achieve such goals. Trade policy is thus regarded as a "second-best" means to achieve environmental objectives.[7] A study prepared for the 1999 Seattle WTO ministerial reiterates this conclusion: "Trade barriers are poor environmental policies."[8] In practice, however, it has become increasingly difficult to justify exclusion of environmental issues from negotiations on trade.[9]

For the United States, the environmental side-agreement appended to the North American Free Trade Agreement in 1992 set the precedent for linking environmental safeguards to trade liberalization. At the international level, given the absence of a

[3] Report of the GATT Panel (unadopted), *United States—Restrictions on Imports of Tuna*, BISD 39 S/155 (1991).
[4] I.M. Destler and Peter J. Balint, THE NEW POLITICS OF AMERICAN TRADE: TRADE, LABOR, AND THE ENVIRONMENT, Chapter 3 (1999).
[5] More recently, however, authors have been making up for lost time. The first edition of Charles Kindleberger's classic textbook (Charles P. Kindleberger, INTERNATIONAL ECONOMICS (1953)) omits any mention of environmental concerns; a recent update (Thomas A. Pugel and Peter H. Lindert, INTERNATIONAL ECONOMICS (2000)) includes an entire chapter on the subject.
[6] Harry G. Johnson, *The Cost of Protection and the Scientific Tariff,* 68(4) JOURNAL OF POLITICAL ECONOMY 327 (1960).
[7] Jagdish N. Bhagwati and T. N. Srinivasan, *Domestic Distortions, Tariffs, and the Theory of the Optimum Subsidy,* 71(1) JOURNAL OF POLITICAL ECONOMY 44 (1963).
[8] Håkan Nordström and Scott Vaughan, TRADE AND ENVIRONMENT 3 (1999).
[9] Labor and environmental concerns often appear in tandem as twin threats posed by globalization. Although the International Labor Organization could in principle be the lead forum for labor issues, no comparable general-purpose organization exists in the area of environment. Individual environmental issues ranging from the ozone layer to wildlife have given rise to over two hundred free-standing multilateral environmental agreements, with signatories ranging from a handful to one hundred or more in number.

parallel organization dedicated to environmental protection,[10] the WTO, with its inclusive membership and built-in mechanism for dispute resolution on trade matters, has emerged as an obvious candidate for resolving disputes on environmental issues as well.

Potential conflict between trade expansion and environmental protection became the stuff of headlines in November 1999, when environmental activists and other opponents of globalization combined forces to disrupt the WTO ministerial meeting in Seattle. Subsequent lobbying efforts, together with some rulings perceived as anti-environment emanating from WTO panels, helped to keep the trade-environment issue constantly before the public. Environmental issues have thus gained some legitimacy as an element of global trade diplomacy. Indeed, it has become almost essential from the standpoint of political viability for any new trade agreement to include environmental safeguards. Likewise, environmental non-governmental organizations ("NGOs") have gained official standing in the WTO and other international forums.[11]

Yet many economists and trade officials remain unconvinced of the benefits from systematic linkage of environmental and trade issues or from opening trade negotiations to NGO participation. So far there is no international consensus on environmental goals or on the value to be placed on achieving any specific goal. Some analysts even reject the whole notion of a trade-off, arguing that, especially in the longer run, the goals of trade expansion and environmental protection are largely complementary; the higher per-capita incomes brought about by expanded trade raise both the ability and the willingness to make environmental investments.[12] The free-trade-oriented *Economist* makes this case in an editorial, "Why Greens Should Love Trade" (October 9, 1999), timed to appear a few weeks before the Seattle WTO ministerial. Yet most participants in the debate acknowledge that pollution abatement and similar policies do typically entail a trade-off, the terms of which will necessarily vary across countries because of diversity in ecological conditions, per-capital income, and even social conditions.[13]

Thus, differences in income, climate, population density, preferences, and other relevant conditions are an obvious source of tension in any effort to protect global commons (oceans, ozone layer, biodiversity). However, even in the cases where economic activity has little or no effect outside a single country's borders, nations seeking to maintain the highest environmental standards have strong motives to induce or even require other

---

[10] Some important environmental issues involve global commons and cannot be treated adequately without broad international cooperation. See Esty, *supra* note 2, and Daniel C. Esty, *Greening World Trade,* in THE WORLD TRADING SYSTEM: CHALLENGES AHEAD (Jeffrey J. Schott ed. 1996) on the case for a Global Environmental Organization and John Whalley and Ben Zissimos, *An Internalisation-based World Environmental Organisation,* 25(5) THE WORLD ECONOMY 619 (2002) on an internalization-based World Environmental Organization. In Part VI of this chapter we consider obstacles a global environmental organization would face.

[11] Sylvia Ostry, *The WTO After Seattle,* paper prepared for presentation at the AMERICAN ECONOMIC ASSOCIATION ANNUAL MEETING (January 2001).

[12] A few economists, notably Michael Porter, adhere to the even more optimistic position that stringent environmental policies can actually promote economic growth and international competitiveness by stimulating innovation (Michael E. Porter and Claas van der Linde, *Toward a New Conception of the Environment-Competitiveness Relationship,* 9(4) JOURNAL OF ECONOMIC PERSPECTIVES 97 (1995)). Other empirical researchers remain unconvinced, however. Brian Copeland and M. Scott Taylor, in *Trade, Growth and the Environment,* 42(1) JOURNAL OF ECONOMIC LITERATURE (2004), speculate that the occasional positive relationship between trade competitiveness and pollution abatement expenditures merely reflects that both variables are endogenous.

[13] Moreover, ex-post remediation of the kind that has been carried out in most of the industrialized countries is likely to be far costlier than preventive action. Thus, global efficiency could well be served by measures to encourage early environmental cleanup in developing countries, an issue to which we return in Part V.

nations to do likewise. U.S. measures to protect dolphins in extraterritorial waters are sometimes justified in terms of "psychological spillovers," conveying the idea that U.S. residents can indeed be harmed by events occurring entirely outside their borders. Esty defends trade policy in aid of extraterritorial environmental goals on the ground that "trade, like any realm of human endeavor, cannot exist without baseline rules, defined by community standards and values."[14] As precedent he cites nineteenth-century British qualms about trade with slave-holding American states. Another justification for international action concerns environmental damage in countries without representative democracy. In such cases, there is less basis for assuming that national standards reflect the preferences of domestic residents.

A final obstacle to international consensus on measures to protect the environment is the lack of a well-developed understanding of many key issues at the trade-environment interface. The underlying environmental science itself remains incomplete in some highly contentious areas, notably global warming.[15] Likewise, economic theory and empirical evidence concerning the trade-environment link can so far offer only limited guidance for policy making.[16] Meanwhile, the trade-environment agenda continues to be broadened to include complex new concerns such as bioengineering, where scientific investigation is only in its infancy.

A. Environmental Issues in the GATT and the WTO

Notwithstanding the extraordinary publicity surrounding the Seattle demonstrations, the proposition that environmental concerns should be addressed internationally along with trade policies was far from new in 1999. "Trade and environment" issues first came to prominence almost three decades earlier. In 1971 the GATT established a Group on Environmental Measures and International Trade, intended as "a standby machinery which would be ready to act, at the request of a contracting party, when the need arose."[17] The United Nations Conference on the Human Environment, held in Stockholm in 1972, highlighted the possibility that strong environmental policies could undermine the international competitiveness of a country's industries. While the danger that competitiveness concerns might promote a "race to the bottom" or at least discourage adoption of stronger environmental protection—"regulatory chill"—remains a core issue today, the trade and environment agenda has broadened over the years. In addition to the traditional and still pressing concerns of air and water pollution, negotiations may now include such topics

---

[14] Daniel C. Esty, *Bridging the Trade-Environment Divide,* 15(3) JOURNAL OF ECONOMIC PERSPECTIVES 123 (2001).

[15] Article 5:7 of the Uruguay Round Agreement on Sanitary and Phytosanitary Measures requires a scientific basis for national product standards but also recognizes a "precautionary principle" where relevant scientific research evidence is considered insufficient. However, there is disagreement among members as to the legal status of the precautionary principle. While some, notably the European Union, would like to see the principle strengthened, others are concerned that precaution might be over-used in order to implement otherwise unjustifiable protection.

[16] Copeland and Taylor, *supra* note 12.

[17] Nordström and Vaughan, *supra* note 8. The first activation came nearly twenty years later, just prior to the Uruguay Round, at the request of the countries from the European Free Trade Area. The main environmental issue raised in the intervening years related to trade of domestically prohibited goods. Such goods included pharmaceuticals and pesticides whose sale in the exporting country's domestic market was no longer permitted due to health or environmental concerns, as well as radioactive or other hazardous waste materials.

as depletion of natural resources, use of hormones to promote cattle growth,[18] reduction of biodiversity, and genetic modification of plants and animals. Moreover, these newer aspects of the trade-environment interface have become increasingly contentious, despite—or perhaps because of—the lack of a firm scientific basis for collective action.

Environmental issues had moved into the mainstream of the GATT by April 1994, when ministers from more than one hundred countries met in Marrakesh to conclude the Uruguay Round of multilateral trade negotiations. Negotiators agreed to establish a Committee on Trade and Environment within the new WTO. Moreover, the preamble to the agreement establishing the WTO describes its mandate as "expanding the production and trade in goods and services, while allowing for the optimal use of the world's resources in accordance with the objective of sustainable development . . . in a manner consistent with respective needs and concerns at different levels of economic development."

B. The Content of "Trade and Environment"

Recent conflicts between free traders and environmentalists[19] reflect several types of linkages and associated issues at the interface between trade and environment policies. From the environmentalist perspective, there are at least four distinct concerns. The first is that expansion of trade may produce environmental damage, either directly, if new export opportunities encourage polluting industries to expand their operations and/or increase pollution associated with transport of goods, or indirectly, as conventional gains from trade raise national incomes and consumption. A related second concern is that some countries will use weaker environmental protection as a way of increasing their international competitiveness. A third issue is that individual countries seeking to maintain high environmental standards may be restrained by GATT/WTO rules from using trade policy for this purpose. Finally, GATT/WTO rules may inhibit international cooperation to reduce environmental threats by restricting the use of trade sanctions to enforce multilateral environmental agreements.

For their part, free traders fear that a coalition of environmentalists and protectionists could reverse decades of progress toward open international markets. Such a coalition could block poor nations from pursuing economic development via export expansion. From the perspective of those who wish to promote trade, there are at least two distinct concerns. First, WTO-sanctioned trade barriers designed to achieve environmental goals may become instruments of "eco-imperialism," permitting richer and greener countries to force their own preferred norms on countries with lower incomes and different priorities. Second, allowing trade restrictions in aid of environmental goals provides yet another loophole for garden-variety protectionism. The active participation of U.S. labor unions in anti-WTO protests on environmental grounds adds weight to this concern.

Of these diverse issues, the first (possible environmental damage resulting from expansion of trade) relates directly to the WTO's central objective of achieving and maintaining open global trade, and thus poses a key question in the trade-environment debate: Could trade expansion cause enough environmental damage to offset completely the resulting

[18] European Union restrictions on imports of beef raised using hormones have already given rise to a WTO trade dispute. *See* Report of the Appellate Body, *European Communities—Measures Concerning Meat and Meat Products (Hormones))*, WT/DS26/AB/R and WT/DS48/AB/R (1998).
[19] Following Esty, *supra* note 2, at 3, we simplify the exposition by using these terms to describe the two sides in the ongoing debate. We thus largely ignore differences in goals within each camp and also that many participants in each camp agree at least in principle on the need to balance environmental and narrowly economic objectives.

gains in national incomes? The other issues are linked to current or potential WTO rules specifying environmental exceptions to basic WTO principles. Below we discuss each area in turn. In Part III of this chapter, we highlight relevant changes in GATT/WTO rules negotiated in the Uruguay Round, while in Part IV we look more closely at recent contributions to economic theory and supporting empirical evidence.

1. Trade as a Threat to Environmental Quality

Many environmentalists view expanded trade (globalization) as a threat to environmental quality. The threat is perceived to arise through one or both of two channels. The first and more direct channel is the effect of trade expansion on the composition of output in each country.[20] Specifically, freer trade may increase the ability of dirty industries to expand where environmental regulation—or enforcement of environmental standards—is relatively weak. This relocation of dirty production to less-regulated sites is presumed to increase pollution[21] in exporting countries and worldwide.[22] As discussed in Part IV of this chapter, the relevance of this channel depends on the assumption that environmental regulation is an important component of total production cost, i.e., that countries with the lowest environmental standards are therefore likely to have comparative advantage in dirty industries. To the extent that increased trade means that goods travel longer distances to markets, pollution associated with transport may also rise.

A second and less direct channel through which globalization itself may affect the environment arises through the usually favorable net impact of expanded trade on economic growth and per-capita income. If environmental externalities such as pollution are roughly proportional to output, higher output necessarily translates into higher total pollution.[23] However, other effects work in the opposite direction. First, the social demand for clean air and water tends to rise with per-capita income. In economic terminology, environmental quality has a high income-elasticity; it is a "superior" good. As nations grow more prosperous, their leaders tend to adopt stronger environmental policies.[24] Moreover, globalization improves nations' access to advanced technologies to implement these policies. Both of these changes are expected to have a favorable impact on technique, i.e., to reduce environmental damage per unit of output. Finally, growth

---

[20] As further discussed in Part IV of this chapter, the environmental impact of growth or trade can be partitioned conceptually into three distinct components: effects on the *composition* of output (relatively less or more production by dirty industries), on the *technique* of production (relatively less or more environmental damage per unit of output produced), and on the overall *scale* of production (a proportional increase in associated damage).

[21] For expository concreteness, environmental damage is discussed here and in much of what follows as pollution that results from production. Part V of this chapter briefly discusses other types of environmental damage.

[22] The effect of expanded trade on the environment depends critically on the particular form of pollution controls as well as whether a particular location has high or low standards. When pollution is regulated entirely by quantity restrictions such as emissions permits, and this quantity limit remains unchanged, expansion of dirty industries will result in an increased value of permits, and thus in cost to producers per unit of emissions; total environmental damage will not rise (Copeland and Taylor, *supra* note 12).

[23] Use of power and associated emissions are considered to be roughly proportional to output. On the other hand, poverty can itself contribute to some types of environmental deterioration, such as deforestation and water pollution.

[24] The process is far from automatic, however, and clearly depends on the form of the political system. Steve Charnovitz, *World Trade and the Environment: A Review of the New WTO Report* (2000), available at <http://www.gets.org/pages/steve.charnovitz.cfm> (accessed 29 July 2002), argues that the link is stronger in democratic societies. The environmental record in Eastern Europe and the Soviet Union in the decades prior to transition offers indirect evidence.

usually changes the composition as well as the scale of economic activity. Because the proportion of income spent on services tends to rise with per-capita income, the resulting change in the composition of output would be expected to reduce environmental damage per unit of aggregate output even if each individual good and service continued to be produced with unchanged technique. The observed net effect of all these changes,[25] termed the environmental Kuznets curve ("EKC"), often shows total pollution (of a specific type) rising with income at low per-capita income levels but then falling as income rises further. Theoretical and empirical analysis of the relationship between growth and environmental quality is reviewed below in Part IV.

2. Environmental Policies as a Determinant of International Competitiveness

National environmental policies typically affect production costs. Although the size of the effect is subject to debate, differences in national environmental policies or in the vigor of enforcement efforts at least potentially constitute one determinant of comparative advantage. Absent differences in technology or relative factor abundance, low-standard countries would have comparative advantage in dirty industries. Environmentalists accordingly fear that lower-income countries will become "pollution havens" due to their willingness to put economic growth ahead of environmental safeguards. A separate but related concern is that nations will compete for global markets and foreign direct investment by reducing environmental standards (race to the bottom) or will be reluctant to raise standards unilaterally due to competitiveness concerns (regulatory chill).

Although both situations reflect the potential role of environmental standards as a source of comparative advantage, the two differ in their implications for efficiency and welfare. Trade based on differences in preferred standards, i.e., the existence of pollution havens, does not necessarily imply economic inefficiency.[26] In contrast, competition for markets through strategic lowering of standards may result in a "prisoners' dilemma" situation. In such a case, although every country might prefer a high-standard regime to a low-standard regime, without international cooperation each country expects to gain from choosing a low standard (in the language of game theory, choosing a low standard represents a dominant strategy for each player in a non-cooperative game). The result without cooperation is a global low standard rather than the high standard all nations would prefer. In this case—but not where differences in standards reflect differences in national preferences—international coordination of standards could raise global efficiency.

Available data, mainly for the United States, show that the *average* cost associated with meeting environmental regulations constitutes a small fraction of total production cost, suggesting that concerns about the role of low environmental standards as a determinant of production location may be overstated.[27] Yet average costs do not tell the whole story. Because compliance costs are much higher for certain "dirty" industries, the possibility remains that differences in environmental policies could have a significant effect on trade and FDI in at least a few sectors where abatement costs are especially high.

Many environmentalists, along with their protectionist anti-globalization allies, favor a policy remedy for competing imports that appear to be driven by significant differences

[25] These are respectively the *scale*, *technique*, and *composition* effects of growth on environmental damage as defined in footnote 20, *supra*.
[26] Copeland and Taylor, *supra* note 12. Even in the absence of trade, a country might prefer a low standard. In this case, the concern is clearly not international competitiveness but, rather, that the cost of compliance with a higher standard is perceived to exceed the benefit.
[27] Nordström and Vaughan, *supra*, note 8, at 36–38.

in environmental standards—what they term *environmental dumping* or *eco-dumping*. In the context of the WTO, the remedy could take the form of required harmonization of environmental standards across countries,[28] possibly encouraged or reinforced by allowing high-standard nations to apply anti-dumping and/or countervailing duties to imports whose low cost is due in part to weak environmental protection.[29] Free traders, familiar with the widespread abuse of conventional anti-dumping duties, strongly oppose introducing a major new device that is likely to be captured by protectionist forces.

3. GATT/WTO Restraints on National Environmental Protection

While some countries may opt for lower standards for reasons of income, tastes, or geography, others may reduce, or fail to raise, environmental safeguards in order to enhance trade competitiveness. In either case, any effect on trade is due to a *difference* in standards across countries; if two countries were to simultaneously impose equivalent increases or decreases, the effect on comparative advantage would be minimal.[30] However, if one country desires a higher standard while a second does not, required upward harmonization in effect forces the second country to bear part of the cost of achieving the first country's target. Thus, one element in the debate on harmonization of environmental standards is essentially about who should bear the economic cost of achieving higher national standards.[31] Developing countries with lower per-capita incomes are understandably suspicious that rich countries favoring high environmental standards may seek to shift part of the cost onto their lower-standard trading partners. The "polluter pays" principle, integral to domestic market-based solutions to environmental spillovers, is likely to be problematic among sovereign nations with very different levels of per-capita income, i.e., with significant differences in willingness and *ability* to pay. A central problem for the international community is to find efficient means of improving global environmental performance without inflicting unacceptable costs on poorer nations in the process.[32] We return to this issue in Part V of this chapter.

A closely linked issue is the WTO position on national policies to achieve environmental goals. As noted above, the use of trade policy to achieve environmental objectives is, in economic terminology, almost always second-best. At least in theory, there is a more direct policy that can achieve the same objective at lower cost in terms of foregone national income. For example, suppose that logging in a particular area causes destruction of species habitat (a *negative externality*, in economic terminology). To reduce environmental damage to the socially optimal level, the government could levy a tax on

[28] Jagdish N. Bhagwati and T.N. Srinivasan, *Trade and the Environment: Does Environmental Diversity Detract from the Case for Free Trade?* in FAIR TRADE AND HARMONIZATION—VOLUME 1: ECONOMIC ANALYSIS 161 (Jagdish N. Bhagwati and Robert Hudec eds. 1996), argue that such harmonization is seldom optimal from the perspective of global welfare.

[29] Environmental groups such as the Sierra Club intervened in the most recent battle between the United States and Canada in the longstanding conflict over Canada's alleged low stumpage fees for loggers operating on government-owned land. However, environmental concerns were not at the heart of the legal case. Indeed, these concerns were not even discussed in the U.S. Commerce Department's final decision in 2002, which resulted in the imposition of a substantial countervailing duty. For details, see *Certain Softwood Lumber Products From Canada,* 67 FR 15545 (April 2, 2002). Canada subsequently appealed the U.S. decision to the WTO and to a NAFTA panel.

[30] Even with identical standards and enforcement, industries in the two countries could experience differences in compliance costs for a variety of reasons, such as differences in geography, technology, or cost of capital.

[31] Here we are concerned with purely local environmental issues. In this case the only "spillover" across borders is in costs associated with compliance. As discussed in Part IV, the situation is more complex with transboundary effects.

[32] Bhagwati and Srinivasan, *supra* note 28, at 199.

logs (from a specific source) equal to the dollar value of the negative external effect, i.e., equal to the *additional* cost to the rest of society that logging companies would otherwise disregard in their business decisions. The tax "internalizes the externality," causing loggers to choose on the basis of social rather than private cost of logging. Alternatively, the government could impose quantitative limits on logging in the relevant area (e.g., using transferable logging permits that in equilibrium would increase loggers' cost per log by the same dollar amount as the tax). These policies are both first-best in that they address the problem at its source. In principle they are equivalent, although in practice one is likely to be preferable in terms of cost of implementation and enforcement or political acceptability.

Trade policy offers another way to reduce the damage from logging. Assuming that the country is a log exporter, an export tax or equivalent export quota would lower the net price received by domestic loggers and thus reduce domestic logging, just as with the logging tax or permit requirement. However, an export tax would also lower the price paid by domestic purchasers, thus encouraging inefficiently *high* domestic use of logs in construction or manufacturing.[33] For this reason, the trade approach is considered a second-best means of reducing environmental damage from logging. Like the optimal policy, the second-best policy reduces the negative externality from domestic logging. But at the same time it introduces a new inefficiency from excessive domestic use. Only precise measurement can show whether the net effect on social welfare is positive rather than negative—overall welfare may fall even when the reduced logging and associated reduction in environmental damage is taken into account. The same effects, and the same ambiguity regarding the overall effect on welfare, would occur if trade were restricted by importers rather than exporters.

A special case arises when the relevant activity occurs in an exporting country that is unwilling and/or unable to implement the first-best policy.[34] In this case, other countries may act to reduce the damage (e.g., destruction of fragile rain forest and associated loss of biodiversity) by limiting their own imports of the logs and products made from them, or by requiring eco-labeling to allow consumers to choose goods whose production is less environmentally damaging. In 2001, Brazil banned virtually all mahogany exports after finding that the most of the wood was being harvested illegally on public and Indian land.[35] Brazil claimed that trade restrictions were necessary to reduce profits from illegal logging and thus preserve the Amazon rainforest.

An example of second-best policy carried out by importing countries is the collective action taken since the 1960s by members of the Conference on International Trade in Endangered Species ("CITES").[36] Here the first-best policy would be to restrict killing and/or sale of endangered species. However, this policy can only be applied in the exporting countries, which have largely been unable to enforce such restrictions. CITES members have therefore adopted the second-best approach of prohibiting imports of endangered species.

Article XX of the GATT clearly allows second-best policies to achieve environmental objectives even though they restrict trade, but two high-profile cases have underscored

---

[33] In the longer run, second-best export restrictions on wood and wood products also create an incentive for conversion of forested lands to more profitable uses, usually agriculture (Esty, *supra* note 2, at 189).

[34] Charnovitz, *supra* note 24.

[35] Jonathan Karp and Miriam Jordan, *U.S. Ports Hold On to Brazilian Mahogany,* THE WALL STREET JOURNAL (March 29, 2002).

[36] For details on membership and structure of CITES, see <http://www.cites.org/index.html> (accessed 15 July 2002).

important GATT/WTO limits on their application. The *Tuna-Dolphin* case arose over the incidental drowning of dolphins—large marine mammals—in fishing for tuna with purse-seine nets. Beginning in 1972, the United States applied a number of non-trade-policy measures, including dolphin-safe net requirements for U.S. ships and all ships in U.S. waters, voluntary labeling of dolphin-safe tuna, and government pressure on major U.S. canners to eschew purchases of dolphin-unsafe tuna. Although these measures had already reduced estimated mortality from about 130,000 dolphins in 1986 to just 25,000 by 1991,[37] the United States nonetheless imposed a ban on tuna imports from Mexico and four other countries. Mexico's immediate protest to the GATT was ultimately upheld, mainly over the principle that imports cannot be restricted solely on the basis of exporters' process and production methods ("PPMs").[38]

Ignoring its exact legal basis, environmentalists cite the decision as evidence that GATT/WTO rules and their application are inherently anti-environment.[39] Still, the logic of the *Tuna-Dolphin* decision implies limits on the ability of one country to restrict trade as a means to influence the environmental standards of other countries.[40] To those who see trade mainly as a potential lever for achieving environmental or other types of non-economic objectives rather than as a means to raise allocative efficiency and national incomes, the outcome was surely a disappointment. Activists subsequently began to target the PPM issue, arguing that exclusion of goods based on PPMs is not inconsistent with GATT principles, as is usually claimed.

The *Shrimp-Turtle* case[41] presents issues similar to those in *Tuna-Dolphin*, but with one critical difference: the sea turtles trapped by shrimp fishers are an endangered species. A U.S. prohibition on shrimp imports from countries without adequate (in the eyes of U.S. authorities) sea turtle safeguards was successfully contested in the WTO by four Asian countries. The WTO's Appellate Body ("AB") upheld the initial ruling in 1998 but on much narrower grounds.[42] While the panel decision held that import bans of this type could not be justified, the AB found fault only with U.S. administrative procedures rather than with the import restriction itself. In particular, the four countries that initiated the case were subject to far harsher treatment than certain other countries. The United States won a final appeal in 2001 after changing the way the law was implemented. Changes included U.S. efforts to open international negotiations on protection of the endangered sea turtles, financial assistance for developing countries involved in the negotiations, and technical assistance and training in the installation and use turtle-safe nets for interested governments.[43] The rulings in this case thus confirmed that conservation measures can

[37] Pugel and Lindert, *supra* note 5, at 250.

[38] C. Ford Runge, FREER TRADE, PROTECTED ENVIRONMENT, 72–73 (1994). Dolphins are not an endangered species, distinguishing this case from the *Shrimp-Turtle* case, discussed below. Subsequent agreements among the interested parties reduced dolphin mortality to about 2000 per year after 1998, but controversy continues about the effects of stress experienced by dolphin in tuna-fishing areas. A 2001 report from the U.S. National Oceanic and Atmospheric Administration ("NOAA") describes ongoing research on dolphin populations <http://www.nmfs.noaa.gov/prot_res/PR2/Tuna_Dolphin/chase-recapture.html> (accessed July 15, 2002).

[39] Michael M. Weinstein and Steve Charnovitz, *The Greening of the WTO*, 80(6) FOREIGN AFFAIRS 148 (2001) conjecture that although the environmental movement has achieved most of its initial goals regarding the WTO, "the need to keep their supporters energized makes some groups loath to say so."

[40] To be more precise, an importing nation cannot do this without compensating affected exporters.

[41] *United States—Import Prohibition of Certain Shrimp and Shrimp Products*, WT/DS58/R (1998).

[42] Weinstein and Charnovitz, *supra* note 39, at 152.

[43] United States Trade Representative, *USTR on WTO Decision Supporting U.S. on Shrimp-Turtle Law*, October 22, 2001, <http://usinfo.state.gov/wto/01102201.htm> (accessed 1 January 2002).

be consistent with WTO agreements but must be administered fairly, i.e., in a way that does not constitute disguised protection for favored producers. The final resolution of the dispute also set an interesting precedent for international burden-sharing: the United States assumed much of the cost of implementing its preferred environmental standard through cash transfers and technical assistance to the developing country producers.

4. GATT/WTO Conflicts with Multilateral Environmental Agreements

Although environmental regulation is largely implemented at the national and sub-national level, economies and ecosystems are highly interdependent. Some major environmental goals, ranging from maintaining biodiversity to protecting the ozone layer, are appropriately viewed as global commons. For these goals, actions taken by any one country, and particularly by smaller countries, create diffuse global benefits enjoyed mainly by those *outside* the country. As a result, nations choosing individually on the basis of benefits to their own citizens tend to do too little; environmental protection is undersupplied from the global perspective.[44] An effective approach to regional (e.g., Rhine water quality) or global (biodiversity, ozone layer, global warming) commons issues thus requires international cooperation.

A kind of intellectual benchmark for such cooperation is the action that would be undertaken by a hypothetical inclusive and effective organization, variously termed a "Global Environmental Organization" or "World Environmental Organization." Such an organization would be capable of formulating and enforcing appropriate policies that internalize all environmental externalities, i.e., capable of ensuring that all economic decisions in every country reflect *global* social costs and benefits. However, no such organization is even on the horizon. Instead, the most salient environmental issues have been tackled by narrowly defined agreements and treaties.

Of more than two hundred such multilateral environmental agreements ("MEAs"), almost all are extremely specific in their objectives, far from inclusive in membership, and reliant on voluntary compliance alone. Only six have more than fifty parties.[45] The WTO has identified about twenty MEAs with trade provisions or implications.[46] So far no trade dispute has arisen from conflict between MEA operations and WTO principles. However, environmentalists seek blanket WTO authorization to use trade sanctions as a means of enforcing compliance by members of an MEA and/or in preventing nonmembers from undermining an agreement's effectiveness. To what extent is such use sanctioned under Article XX? Without further advance clarification, this scope will be delineated over time as enforcement actions give rise to trade disputes and their resolution within the WTO. But multilateral agreements typically require years to reach operational status, and ambiguity concerning the relationship between MEAs and the WTO increases the difficulty of achieving the international agreements required to tackle global environmental problems. Nonetheless, free traders in the WTO are unlikely to give environmentalists *carte blanche* with regard to the use of trade sanctions as a means of enforcing MEAs.

5. Trade Sanctions and Eco-Imperialism

Achieving higher environmental standards at the local or national level typically entails higher production costs and thus some sacrifice of national income as conventionally

---

[44] Economists view the situation as an example of the prisoners' dilemma as described above. Only if all affected nations commit credibly in advance can the socially preferable outcome be achieved.

[45] William Krist, *Multilateral Environmental Agreements and the World Trade Organization*, WOODROW WILSON CENTER (March 2001) <http://wwics.si.edu/tef/stoconfpap.htm> (accessed 9 August 2001).

[46] <http://www.wto.org/english/thewto_e/whatis_e/tif_e/bey4_e.htm> (accessed 29 July 2002).

measured. For a country that trades with the rest of the world, higher production costs can also mean a loss of international competitiveness in affected industries to countries that have not matched the higher standards implemented at home. Any resulting increase in imports allows a high-standard country to consume goods whose production is environmentally damaging while incurring only part or sometimes even none of the associated damage. The domestic import–competing industry will typically suffer lower output and profits, however. Competition from less-controlled producers abroad may thus be regarded as "unfair." Injured parties may seek—and may succeed in obtaining— restrictions on imports whose lower cost is due partly to the lower environmental standards of the exporting nation.

Because of differences across countries in incomes, tastes, and environmental conditions, individual nations are unlikely to adopt identical standards with regard to environmental protection. Developing countries in particular are concerned that richer trading partners may seek to impose their preferred standards on all exporters. Like conventional dumping, eco-dumping typically benefits the importing country as a whole but creates losses for importing-competing producers. The *Tuna-Dolphin* and *Shrimp-Turtle* cases discussed above are both instances in which the United States sought, with some success, to impose its own environmental priorities on producers in developing nations.

6. Environmental Concerns as Green Cover for Protectionism

Even when free traders share the same concerns as environmentalists, they remain suspicious—often with some reason—that highlighted environmental objectives simply provide a convenient excuse for old-fashioned protectionism. U.S. fishing fleets as well as would-be dolphin protectors favored the U.S. ban on imports of dolphin-unsafe tuna. In the protests that disrupted the 1999 WTO ministerial meeting in Seattle, environmental NGOs worked in tandem with the same U.S. labor unions that have perennially favored import restrictions. But international economists have been slow to recognize that, for better or for worse, environmental issues are likely to remain a WTO concern. While international economists rightly point out that trade policy is almost never a first-best way to achieve environmental goals, the same is true for virtually *all* uses of trade policy. Moreover, safeguarding the environment may well be a worthier non-economic objective from a social perspective than delaying the demise of an uncompetitive senescent industry.

Free traders also emphasize that economic growth depends on trade and investment. If environmentalists succeed in slowing down or reversing the process of globalization, there is a price to be paid in terms of lower growth and less-efficient use of resources. Many free traders point to the generally favorable association between higher incomes and increased attention to environmental concerns. However, it is important to remember that this process is far from automatic. Although poverty demonstrably contributes to certain types of environmental degradation, increased wealth by itself cannot ensure reductions in harmful practices.

III. The Uruguay Round Agreements

A significant advance in the Uruguay Round was to initiate negotiations on specific areas of concern in the trade-environment nexus. Until the Uruguay Round negotiations, Article XX of GATT (1947) had provided the sole basis for exceptions to trade policy obligations on grounds concerning environmental objectives. Although panel rulings in formal trade disputes such as *Tuna-Dolphin* had established bounds for permissible environmental exceptions to a country's trade policy obligations within the GATT framework,

Article XX itself was the only element of the pre-Uruguay Round GATT treatment of environmental issues that had actually emerged from international negotiations.

The Uruguay Round Agreements ("URAs") did *not* include an explicit "Agreement on Trade and the Environment" to centralize all linkages between international trade and issues relating to the environment. Negotiators took a much more diffuse approach, introducing references to the environment and environmental exceptions to trade policy obligations into many of the newly codified areas. The resulting agreements on technical barriers to trade, sanitary and phytosanitary measures, trade-related intellectual property rights, subsidies and countervailing measures, agriculture, and services all contain specific language that underscores the interaction between trade and environmental objectives. And, while the URAs do not include an agreement on trade and the environment, a WTO directive established a Committee on Trade and Environment to identify, monitor, and assess issues relating to trade and the environment as they arise.

Even with the development of the new areas under the URAs, Article XX of GATT 1947 remains the key underlying component linking trade and the environment within the WTO system. However, the URAs are important because they add new possibilities for countries seeking to defend trade-restricting actions on environmental grounds.[47] Below we examine the newly codified areas in the URAs as they relate to the environment and identify the economic incentives created by the terms of the new agreements.

A. Standards

The Agreements on Technical Barriers to Trade ("TBTs") and Sanitary and Phytosanitary ("SPS") Measures are complementary codes focusing on product standards and food safety. The TBT Agreement is a modified version of a stand-alone Standards Code negotiated during the 1973–79 Tokyo Round; the SPS agreement introduces standards for food safety as well as regulations to promote human, animal, and plant health and safety. These agreements allow countries to adopt explicit product standards that are consistent with underlying WTO principles. In particular, standards must not be designed so as to discriminate between domestic products and imports (a violation of the national-treatment clause of Article III) or between imports from different sources (a violation of the MFN clause of Article I). For example, Article 5:1 of the SPS agreement may allow trade restrictions for environmental purposes in some circumstances. Such restrictions must be based on an appropriate assessment of "risks to human, animal or plant life or health, taking into account risk assessment techniques developed by the relevant international organizations." Restrictions must also be transparent and non-discriminatory in their application.

The initial obscurity of the TBT and SPS agreements evaporated with several high-profile disputes over product standards. While the agreements have been interpreted as allowing for the establishment of standards based on a product's *end-use* or *quality* or *content*, an important unresolved question is whether the WTO also permits standards based on *production method*. This issue is one common thread linking recent cases such as *Tuna-Dolphin, Shrimp-Turtle*, and *Beef Hormones*; in each case production method served as the justification for a ban on imports.

[47] Matthew Stilwell argues, in the context of GMO labeling, that the implied criteria for exceptions in the various agreements may differ in subtle ways. *See Center for Environmental Law, Protecting GMO Labeling from a WTO Challenge,* (2001), available at <http://www.cid.harvard.edu/cidtrade/issues/biotechnologypaper.html> (accessed 19 April 2003).

A central question in each of these standards disputes is whether a country may impose its own national production standard on goods that it consumes but that are produced elsewhere. In the *Tuna-Dolphin* case, the justification for the standard was a concern for the humane treatment of marine mammals; in the *Shrimp-Turtle* case, the standard was intended to bolster conservation efforts on behalf of an endangered species; in the *Beef Hormone* case, the basis was the "precautionary principle" and the lack of persuasive evidence that non-hormone-treated beef and hormone-treated beef have the same end-use effect on humans. The permissibility of such standards within the WTO framework is also likely to become a pivotal issue in the new and highly contentious area of genetically modified organisms ("GMOs").

The first economic concern regarding any product standard relates to the reason that a trade-restricting measure is being imposed. As WTO rules rest on the underlying principle of liberal and non-discriminatory trade, an initial consideration is whether the standard constitutes a genuine response to a perceived threat to health or safety, rather than a disguised effort to protect domestic producers from competing imports or to discriminate between foreign producers. The TBT and SPS agreements specify the use of internationally accepted standards,[48] and thus rely on information provided by international standard-setting bodies. Since the WTO defers to these standard-setting bodies as "experts" in the relevant areas, their transparency and organization becomes an important factor in determining the outcome of actual cases.

A further concern is the effect of standards on production efficiency and the gains from trade. International harmonization of product standards may reduce costs of compliance for a firm serving more than one national market. Agreement on a common standard can lead to efficiency gains via network externalities. However, mandatory harmonization of *production* standards across countries could significantly reduce one of the primary sources of gains from trade, i.e., the gains arising from differences in production conditions across countries and resulting specialization based on comparative advantage.

B. Intellectual Property

Another substantive Uruguay Round agreement that includes an explicit environmental exception is the Agreement on Trade-Related Aspects of Intellectual Property Rights ("TRIPS"). This agreement seeks to strengthen the rules protecting patents, trademarks, copyrights, and trade secrets. One link between intellectual property and the environment is contained in Article 27 of TRIPS, which permits governments to refuse to issue patents "that threaten human, animal or plant life or health, or risk serious damage to the environment."

C. Subsidies

One goal in the Uruguay Round was to limit the use of subsidies in many areas of international trade, thus shifting countries away from government-supported production and towards market-based reforms. While the effort to control subsidies and countervailing

---

[48] For example, the Preamble of the SPS agreement states that its aim is to "further the use of harmonized sanitary and phytosanitary measures between Members, on the basis of international standards and guidelines and recommendations developed by the relevant international organizations, including the Codex Alimentarius Commission, the International Office of Epizootics, and the relevant international and regional organizations operating within the framework of the International Plant Protection Convention. . . ."

duties was not new to the GATT/WTO system,[49] the URAs clarified the rules on permissible and impermissible subsidies.[50] Notably, the Agreement on Subsidies and Countervailing Measures ("SCM") and the Agreement on Agriculture ("AoA") include explicit exceptions for subsidies with environmental objectives. The SCM temporarily allowed for subsidies that helped firms adapt to new environmental laws, as long as those subsidies were less than twenty per cent of the firms' actual compliance costs.[51] Similarly, the AoA specifically exempts environmental programs from mandated cuts in subsidies.[52]

Perhaps as important as the introduction of these exceptions for subsidies with environmental objectives is the increased discipline the WTO system imposes on non-environmental subsidies. Environmental problems are often caused or aggravated by government subsidies, especially subsidies to natural-resource-based industries such as agriculture, fishing, and logging. Farm subsidies and price supports, combined with restrictions on land under cultivation, create incentives for overuse of chemicals to increase crop yields. Likewise, government support of excess capacity in fishing fleets has exacerbated the conservation problems of the world's fisheries. WTO limits on subsidies thus have the potential to reduce environmental damage along with inefficient high-cost production.

D. Services

Article XIV of the General Agreement on Trade in Services ("GATS") contains exceptions analogous to those in Article XX(b) of GATT (1947) covering trade in goods.

IV. Economic Theory and Empirical Evidence

As the liberalization of world trade has become an important concern for the environmental movement, more economists have turned their attention to modeling and estimating the effects of trade and trade policy on the environment. An early examination of many trade-environment issues from an economic perspective[53] arose from a 1991 workshop organized for the GATT Secretariat. Surveys of more recent literature include Nordström and Vaughan[54] and Copeland and Taylor.[55] Here we summarize briefly some important theoretical results concerning the trade-environment nexus, as well as relevant empirical findings. Our review focuses on two fundamental questions: How does international trade affect the environment? What is the appropriate role for a trade agreement such as the WTO with respect to environmental concerns?

[49] Articles VI and XVI of GATT (1947) deal respectively with countervailing duties and export subsidies. The stand-alone Subsidies Code negotiated in the Tokyo Round also addresses these issues.
[50] See Chapters 16 and 41 in this book.
[51] Article 8.2 (c) of the Agreement on Subsidies and Countervailing Measures specifies the conditions under which environmental subsidies are "non-actionable." However, the initial exemption was for a five-year period subject to renewal (SCM Article 31). It has not been renewed so that the exemption no longer applies.
[52] Annex 2: 12(a) of the Agreement on Agriculture indicates which types of subsidies are exempted from the reduction commitment.
[53] Kym Anderson and Richard Blackhurst, THE GREENING OF WORLD TRADE ISSUES (1992).
[54] Nordström and Vaughan, *supra* note 8.
[55] Copeland and Taylor, *supra* note 12.

A. Environmental Externalities and Economic Policy

From the economic perspective, most environmental issues arise from *externalities*, i.e., effects of consumption or production that fall on others. Activities creating air or water pollution thus entail *negative* externalities, while environmental cleanup generates *positive* externalities. The key consideration is the extent to which a consumer or producer's actions and decisions affect others not directly involved. This criterion may be interpreted narrowly, i.e., whether physical effects extend beyond the agent's private property, or more broadly, to include even psychological externalities. In the international context, a further distinction is made between external effects that occur entirely within a single country's borders and "transboundary" effects that spill over to other countries.

Existence of a negative externality implies that the *private* cost of an activity (the cost borne by the consumer or producer who causes the externality) is below its *social* cost. In the absence of corrective government action, market-determined consumption and production of polluting goods will usually be too high from the social point of view because decisions are based on private rather than social costs.[56] Likewise, the level of any activity with a positive externality will tend to be too low. Such situations are called *market failures* because the "invisible hand" is unlikely to achieve a socially desirable resource allocation.[57]

From the economic viewpoint, the socially optimal level of pollution or other environmental damage is not zero unless the damage can be eliminated at no cost. In general, the socially optimal level depends on the social cost in terms of foregone economic output of a further reduction, i.e., the *opportunity cost* of abatement. The level of pollution (or pollution abatement) is socially optimal when the social cost in foregone output of a further reduction just balances the social benefits resulting from that reduction. The use of cost-benefit analysis in designing environmental policies is intended to achieve this kind of balance. However, this approach is far from straightforward in practice, as its implementation requires decision makers to place a dollar value on such intangible benefits as cleaner air or greater biodiversity. Moreover, effects usually extend far into the future and must therefore be discounted accordingly.

Policies to improve environmental outcomes are of two basic types: market-based instruments and direct controls. Appropriately designed taxes attempt to *internalize the externality* and thus ensure that decision makers choose actions based on their full social cost, not the private cost alone. But because of the difficulties entailed in measuring costs and benefits, such policies are unlikely to achieve this goal exactly. Rather than trying to fine-tune the market response, policy makers may opt instead for an approach that limits quantity directly, as with emissions permits,[58] or requires the use of a particular abatement technology. But regardless of which approach is chosen, policy makers are

---

[56] When property rights are fully defined and enforced, and costs of transactions among interested parties sufficiently low, private action alone may be sufficient to assure an efficient outcome (Ronald Coase, *The Problem of Social Costs*, 3 JOURNAL OF LAW AND ECONOMICS 1 (1960)). In such an outcome, the polluter may agree to compensate those affected, but it is also possible that those affected will pay the polluter to abate the pollution.

[57] Policies to address environmental spillovers are used when voluntary action, including Coasian private contracts between the parties responsible for the externality and all those affected by it, is considered insufficient to achieve a satisfactory outcome.

[58] If such permits may be bought or sold freely, their market value will approximate the tax rate required to achieve the same reduction in emissions. However, the fiscal implications will differ unless permits are distributed via competitive auction.

likely to give less consideration to costs or benefits experienced beyond the boundaries of the relevant jurisdiction, while globally efficient outcomes require such transboundary effects to be given equal weight. A reasonable assumption is that internalization via policy is incomplete: policy measures do not fully internalize environmental externalities (social cost remains above private cost), and that the remaining gap is larger in the case of transboundary effects.

Given this starting point, how do trade and economic growth (which may result from trade or other causes) affect environmental conditions and environmental policies? To better explore the complex relationships, recent analysis has relied on a conceptual partition of the environmental impacts of trade or economic growth into three distinct components: effects on the *composition* of output (relatively less or more production by dirty industries), on the *technique* of production (relatively less or more environmental damage per unit of output produced), and on the overall *scale* of production (a proportional increase in associated damage).

B. Economic Growth and the Environment

Conceptually, economic growth is likely to increase environmental damage via the scale effect, but this negative impact of growth may be more than offset by favorable composition and technique effects. Grossman and Krueger[59] were among the first to demonstrate empirically that economic growth does not necessarily imply accompanying deterioration of the environment. Using cross-country data, they estimate the reduced-form relationship between GDP and various measures of national pollutants, such as urban air pollution, oxygen levels in river basins, fecal contamination of river basins, and heavy metal contamination of river basins. Decomposing the overall impact of national income into the scale, technique, and composition effects, they conclude that while higher GDP is related to higher pollution in the very poorest countries, beyond a certain GDP threshold (around $8000 in 1985 U.S. dollars), further increases in GDP are typically associated with an improvement in environmental quality. This is the U-shaped relationship between national income and pollution subsequently labeled the environmental Kuznets curve.[60]

A substantial literature has explored the robustness of the empirical evidence for a U-shaped income-pollution relationship. An important recent contribution is Harbaugh, Levinson, and Wilson.[61] With access to a richer data set and through the use of alternative econometric techniques and additional covariates in the estimation, the authors call into question the finding of a robust U-shaped relationship between a group of important air pollutants and national income. They also conclude that the available empirical evidence does not support broad claims either for an unequivocally positive or an unequivocally negative effect of economic growth on the environment.

[59] Gene M. Grossman and Alan B. Krueger, *Environmental Impacts of a North American Free Trade Agreement,* in THE U.S.-MEXICO FREE TRADE AGREEMENT (Peter Garber ed. 1993); Gene M. Grossman and Alan B. Krueger, *Economic Growth and the Environment,* 110(2) QUARTERLY JOURNAL OF ECONOMICS 353 (1995).

[60] The name is based on its similarity to the U-shaped pattern for the relationship between economic growth and income inequality hypothesized by Simon Kuznets.

[61] William T. Harbaugh, Arik Levinson, and David Molloy Wilson, *Reexamining the Empirical Evidence of the Environmental Kuznets Curve,* 84(3) REVIEW OF ECONOMICS AND STATISTICS 541 (2002). *See* James Andreoni and Arik Levinson, *The Simple Analytics of the Environmental Kuznets Curve,* 80(2) JOURNAL OF PUBLIC ECONOMICS 269, footnote 1 (2002) for a comprehensive list of papers in this literature.

Related theoretical work by Andreoni and Levinson[62] shows that an EKC can be derived from optimizing behavior even in a model with a single consumer and thus no externalities and no possibility of market failure. The result depends on increasing returns in abatement of the pollution generated during production of the consumption good: proportional increases in both pollution and clean-up effort are associated with a more than proportional increase in pollution abatement. This assumption is plausible whenever abatement entails significant fixed costs.

With many consumers optimizing individually, the usual environmental externality is incorporated into the model. The U-shaped relationship now remains, but each individual consumes too much and abates too little, relative to the social optimum. Given the environmental externality and resulting market failure, public policy can raise social welfare by internalizing the externality. As Andreoni and Levinson emphasize, their results do not imply that economic growth alone will solve pollution problems, nor do they offer theoretical support for a laissez-faire approach to environmental problems. On the contrary, they show that although the pollution-income path may have an inverse-U shape even in the absence of environmental regulations, pollution will be inefficiently high at every income level.

C. Trade and the Environment

To assess how international trade affects the environment, it is useful to proceed in two steps. First we examine the impact of international trade on the environment when the environmental concern is local pollutants, i.e., where the source and the effect are in the same political jurisdiction. We then turn to the impact of trade on the environment in the presence of transboundary pollutants.

1. Trade's Impact with Local Pollutants

Copeland and Taylor[63] use a simple model of North-South trade that illustrates each of the possible channels through which trade can affect local pollution. They analyze the impact of trade on pollution when countries differ only in per-capita income (relative endowment of human capital); environmental standards are assumed to rise with income. North therefore applies higher environmental standards. Trade allows South to become a pollution haven, exporting pollution-intensive products to North. In this model, trade does raise pollution for South and for the world as a whole, but trade is nonetheless welfare-improving for both countries. Because environmental impacts are local and standards are adjusted endogenously to maximize national welfare, there is no market failure in this model, either with trade or without.

In terms of the standard decomposition, the *scale* effect implies that pollution will rise in both countries. However, the *technique* effect, here captured by the assumption that environmental standards rise with income, will lead to the adoption of cleaner production methods in both countries, thus reducing pollution per unit of output in each industry. The *composition* effect depends on the comparative advantage of the country. The composition effect reduces the average pollution intensity of production if the marginal industry that leaves the country due to specialization is dirtier than the average industry in the country. If the marginal industry is cleaner than the average national industry, then average pollution

---

[62] Andreoni and Levinson, *supra* note 61.

[63] Brian Copeland and M. Scott Taylor, *North-South Trade and the Environment*, 109(3) QUARTERLY JOURNAL OF ECONOMICS 755(1994).

intensity will rise. Under the assumptions of the model, the composition effect must dominate as industries relocate in order to take advantage of differences in environmental standards. A larger initial North-South gap in per-capita income results in a larger increase in pollution worldwide due to trade.

Differences in environmental protection are the only source of comparative advantage in Copeland and Taylor,[64] so that South necessarily has a comparative advantage in dirty industries. In reality, however, many polluting industries are relatively capital intensive. Without significant differences in environmental standards, such industries would be expected to locate in capital-abundant, i.e., more developed, countries. To capture this second determinant of industry location, Antweiler, Copeland, and Taylor [65] include factor endowments as an additional source of comparative advantage. This theoretical framework introduces the possibility that capital-intensive industries may prefer to locate in the capital-abundant North, where capital is cheaper, even though environmental taxes there are higher due to higher incomes. The authors use this framework to disentangle two competing hypotheses: the pollution-haven hypothesis, i.e., that trade will allow dirty industries to relocate to low-income countries with relatively weak environmental standards, and the factor-endowments hypothesis, i.e., that trade will allow dirty capital-intensive industries to relocate to relatively capital-abundant higher-income countries despite higher environmental standards.

In the empirical part of the analysis, Antweiler *et al.* examine the impact of liberalized trade in manufactured goods on the environment, where "the environment" is measured by sulfur-dioxide (SO_2) emissions. Estimating the sizes of the scale, technique, and composition effects, the authors find that the composition effect is small, so that the factor-endowment motive for trade dominates the pollution-haven hypothesis. The net impact of the trade-induced scale and technique effects is a reduction in pollution from these sources. Overall, liberalized trade is found to be good for the environment: a one per cent increase in GDP created by trade liberalization is associated with a fall of nearly one per cent in pollution concentrations. These empirical results suggest that, at least for sulfur-dioxide emissions, the favorable technique effect associated with higher incomes due to expanded trade is much larger than the composition effect (international relocation of production) and the scale effect (higher production levels). However, there is no basis for concluding that the relative magnitudes of the three effects will be similar for other types of industrial pollution or that expanded trade will necessarily be associated with a net decrease in every type of pollution.

One important implication of these models is that trade *does* affect the environment, even when policy makers set optimal domestic environmental policies and adjust these policies as per-capita income rises. When the net impact is a *cleaner* environment, as found by Antweiler, *et al.*,[66] this outcome arises almost entirely through the technique effect: income gains induced by trade cause governments to respond with more-stringent environmental policies, which in turn create incentives for industry to adopt cleaner production techniques. A favorable net outcome therefore rests critically on the ability and willingness of policy makers to adjust environmental standards optimally as per-capita incomes rise.

---

[64] *Id.*

[65] Werner Antweiler, Brian R. Copeland, and M. Scott Taylor, *Is Free Trade Good for the Environment?* 91 (4) AMERICAN ECONOMIC REVIEW 877(2001).

[66] *Id.*

In addition to trade-induced increases in income that encourage adoption of stronger environmental policies, another potential benefit from trade arises through the spatial separation of "environmentally incompatible" industries such as "dirty" manufacturing and an environmentally sensitive sector such as agriculture or fishing.[67] By allowing incompatible industries to move farther away from each other, trade can reduce or eliminate some negative externalities that depress productivity in the other industry, thereby raising productivity overall.

2. Trade's Impact with Transboundary Pollutants

Although industrial pollution is often a national or local problem, some of the most controversial environmental issues involve transboundary pollutants. Without international coordination, policies designed to maximize *national* welfare are likely to under-correct for this type of externality. Trade may thus reduce efficiency and welfare once environmental consequences are taken into account. Where the number of countries affected is small, regional agreements may suffice to achieve the required coordination. Examples of such cases include acid rain along a shared border and pollution of a river that runs through two or more countries. But for the limiting case in which one country's actions affect all countries equally, global environmental quality can be considered a pure public good, subject to the usual incentive problems associated with the optimal provision of public goods. Without international coordination, each country will "spend" too little, from the global perspective, to reduce emissions that threaten the ozone layer or contribute to global warming. The case of *global* pollution differs importantly from the framework described above because the relocation of dirty industries to lower-income pollution havens can reduce environmental quality everywhere, not just in the new location. This transboundary effect can undercut the standard gains from trade.

Unteroberdoerster[68] revisits the spatial separation of environmentally incompatible industries via trade in the case of pollution with transboundary effects. In this setting, specialization due to trade has repercussions for pollution in a partner country. The relative size of the transboundary component of pollution is key. Under some conditions, free trade may increase pollution and, over time, reduce environmental quality in both countries. In fact, trade can cause the world production possibility frontier to shift inward as transboundary pollution shrinks productivity in the partner country. However, this unfavorable outcome requires both that the emitting industry in one country is more polluting than its counterpart in the other country and that the ratio of transboundary to national pollution is sufficiently high.

Copeland and Taylor analyze the effects of trade among many countries when global environmental quality is a pure public good.[69] As in earlier work,[70] they focus on the role of environmental policy as a determinant of trade by assuming that differences in per-capita income (human capital endowments) and thus in environmental standards are the only source of comparative advantage. Each of many countries in the higher-income North and lower-income South maximizes national welfare with respect to a limit on its

[67] Brian Copeland and M. Scott Taylor, *Trade, Spatial Separation, and the Environment,* 47(1) JOURNAL OF INTERNATIONAL ECONOMICS 137 (1999).

[68] Olaf Unteroberdoerster, *Trade and Transboundary Pollution: Spacial Separation Reconsidered,* 41(2) JOURNAL OF ENVIRONMENTAL ECONOMICS AND MANAGEMENT 269 (2001).

[69] Brian Copeland and M. Scott Taylor, *Trade and Transboundary Pollution,* 85(4) AMERICAN ECONOMIC REVIEW 755 (1995).

[70] Copeland and Taylor, *supra* note 63.

own total emissions; these limits are implemented through the sale of pollution permits. Even in this extreme case of transboundary pollution, poorer countries choose higher limits; in autarky, permits are thus cheaper in these countries.

Trade can then be interpreted as the indirect exchange of two factors of production: human capital and pollution permits. The effects of trade depend on the extent of differences in endowments of human capital between North and South. If differences are not too large, so that trade in goods equalizes factor prices, trade has no net impact on the environment. Although the autarky equilibrium is sub-optimal from a global perspective (too much consumption and too much pollution), trade does not exacerbate that inefficiency. However, if income differences are large and trade in goods alone does not equalize factor prices, the price of pollution permits will remain relatively lower in poorer countries. Trade then allows these countries to become pollution havens, and free trade has a negative impact on the global environment. However, both of these effects are moderated if pollution permits as well as goods can be traded internationally. And, not surprisingly, reductions in pollution by a coalition of countries or through North-South income transfers tied to pollution reduction can achieve Pareto improvements. These results reflect the underlying inefficiency from setting environmental policy at the national level when benefits are global.

3. Avenues for Further Research
Even given the substantial increase over the last decade in formal economic analysis of the impact of international trade on the environment, empirical results concerning the size (and perhaps even the sign) of the impact of trade on the environment should still be regarded as preliminary, and many more pollutants in addition to sulfur dioxide remain to be investigated. Although the initial results appear promising for proponents of liberal trade, they are not yet conclusive. Moreover, there has been little empirical work assessing the effects of trade on transboundary pollution. Finally, despite the attention to these issues in recent trade negotiations, there has been little theoretical or empirical work specifically assessing the environmental impact of liberalized agricultural trade and the reduction of state-sponsored subsidies on the environment, and in particular the effects on runoff, groundwater, and pollutants associated with chemical-intensive farming.[71]

D. Trade Agreements and the Environment
The literature reviewed in the previous sections addresses the environmental impact of increased trade, usually with a focus on the interaction between income levels and endogenous national environmental standards. A related line of research investigates implications of sensitive environmental issues for the role and design of *international trade agreements*. A key issue here is the extent to which current WTO rules curtail the ability of signatories to apply desired environmental safeguards at the national level.

1. Adequacy of WTO Rules to Accommodate Environmental Safeguards
Economists view trade agreements as a means for countries to achieve mutual gains either by coordinating behavior directly or by establishing rules of behavior that are likely to

---

[71] Agricultural support programs often create incentives for adoption of chemical-intensive techniques that increase yield per acre. Thus, a potential benefit of reducing import restrictions, export incentives, and price supports is the reduction of some types of environmental damage.

increase global efficiency.[72] An example of direct coordination is a trade agreement that enables relatively large countries—which have less incentive to remove trade barriers unilaterally because of associated terms-of-trade losses—to benefit from liberalization. Such a trade agreement helps large countries out of the prisoners' dilemma resulting from terms-of-trade effects. By compelling each country to give up sovereignty with respect to its trade policy, the trade agreement can make all trading partners' better off.

Alternatively, a trade agreement may serve as a way for governments that lack commitment power with respect to the actions of their private sector to commit credibly to trade liberalization.[73] Given this frame of reference and that trade agreements generally require governments to give up sovereignty over their trade policies, must countries in a similar fashion cede control over their domestic policies in order to move toward global efficiency with regard to environmental concerns? Bagwell and Staiger address this question for the case of local pollutants and large countries—ones whose unchecked trade and domestic policy choices could generate negative terms-of-trade externalities for trading partners.[74] Perhaps surprisingly, they conclude that it is *not* necessary for countries to cede control over domestic environmental policy in order to achieve global efficiency.

In the case of local pollutants, the international transmission of environmental problems occurs only through the government's desire to manipulate its environmental policy to improve its trade prices and thus generate welfare gains for itself (with corresponding terms-of-trade losses for its trading partners). While one way to deal with this problem would be to negotiate directly over national environmental policies by bringing them into the WTO, this drastic measure is not required; current WTO rules are already adequate to handle most of the problem. With a minor reform that would actually give governments *more* sovereignty, the existing WTO framework could produce a globally efficient outcome.

The Bagwell-Staiger analysis has two elements, both of which focus on WTO rules regarding market-access commitments. First, consider the case in which a domestic industry with competitiveness concerns seeks import relief from its government. Because the country's tariff rates are bound under the WTO, the government cannot respond unilaterally by manipulating its trade policy. It has an incentive to relax its environmental standards as an alternative means to improve the competitiveness of the domestic industry, thereby imposing some costs on its trading partners through the induced change in the terms of trade. However, the WTO already has rules and procedures that address this problem. An affected exporting country can intercede with a *non-violation*[75] complaint

[72] Kyle Bagwell and Robert W. Staiger, 89(1) *An Economic Theory of GATT,* AMERICAN ECONOMIC REVIEW 215 (1999).

[73] Robert W. Staiger and Guido Tabellini, *Discretionary Trade Policy and Excessive Protection, 77(5)* AMERICAN ECONOMIC REVIEW 823(1987).

[74] Kyle Bagwell and Robert W. Staiger, *Domestic Policies, National Sovereignty, and International Economic Institutions,* 116(2) QUARTERLY JOURNAL OF ECONOMICS 519 (2001); Kyle Bagwell and Robert W. Staiger, *The WTO as a Mechanism for Securing Market Access Property Rights: Implications for Global Labor and Environmental Issues,* 15(3) JOURNAL OF ECONOMIC PERSPECTIVES 69 (2001).

[75] A violation complaint alleges a trading partner's violation of one or more specific WTO rules. In contrast, a non-violation complaint may be brought to the WTO when a member undertakes an activity (here, lowering environmental standards) that violates no explicit WTO rule yet nullifies or impairs the market-access benefits expected by its trading partner. *See* Chapter 29 of this book; and Ernst-Ulrich Petersmann, THE GATT/WTO DISPUTE SETTLEMENT SYSTEM: INTERNATIONAL LAW, INTERNATIONAL ORGANIZATIONS AND DISPUTE SETTLEMENT, CHAPTER 4 (1997). In practice, very few non-violation complaints have been brought, and not all of these have been successful.

and initiate a trade dispute. The non-violation complaint would make the WTO-valid argument that, although the domestic policy action reducing the country's environmental standards did not violate any WTO rules, the action did affect the market-access commitments expected by the exporting country. Thus, enforcement of current WTO rules appears to be sufficient to deal with race-to-the-bottom concerns.

The second element of the Bagwell-Staiger analysis relates to the adequacy of current WTO rules to deal with concerns of regulatory chill—governments' hesitation to tighten domestic environmental policies if some of the benefits of those policies accrue to trading partners in the form of expanded market access. Bagwell and Staiger[76] suggest two possible means of addressing this issue, one of which involves giving governments more sovereignty than the WTO rules currently allow. One way for an international trade agreement like the WTO to address the regulatory-chill problem is to grant a government the right to raise its tariffs when it imposes a more-stringent domestic pollution policy, thus neutralizing the net market-access impact of the policy change. Although this approach conforms to the spirit of WTO practice, current rules prohibit members from raising their bound tariffs even if there is no net impact on their market-access commitments. Increasing a bound tariff could give rise to a *violation* complaint, even though the *net* effect of the two changes would be to leave the exporting country's market access unchanged.

Alternatively, the government raising its environmental standards could offer domestic producers a subsidy to offset the financial burden on environmentally regulated industries. Some subsidies of this type were explicitly authorized as non-actionable under the Uruguay Round Subsidies Agreement, although as noted above the exemption is no longer applicable.[77] However, for countries that would find it difficult to generate the tax revenue needed to implement subsidy policies, the tariff-increase approach may be more feasible. Because current WTO rules prohibit uncompensated tariff adjustments, this would require a minor reform of the rules.

2. The WTO as a Self-Enforcing Agreement

Given that the organization has no real enforcement power of its own, the WTO relies primarily on the retaliation threats of its members to sustain cooperative outcomes such as low tariffs and liberalized trade. The threat of retaliation—and of the possible breakdown of the agreement—restrains countries from cheating. But success in achieving and maintaining lower tariff barriers has led countries to use domestic policies as alternative means of achieving the same policy objectives, so that recent negotiations have increasingly focused on the trade impact of domestic policies, including environmental policies.[78] Article III of the GATT stipulates that no domestic policy should be applied in such a way as to "afford protection to domestic production." Because explicit protection in the form of tariffs (up to the bound level) is allowed under the GATT rules, Article III embodies a preference for the use of tariffs rather than domestic policies.

Given that the WTO lacks a centralized means of enforcement and globally efficient outcomes are thus not attainable, an important question is how best to allocate the scarce

---

[76] Bagwell and Staiger, *supra* note 74.

[77] For a discussion, *see* Michael J. Trebilcock and Robert Howse, THE REGULATION OF INTERNATIONAL TRADE 196 (1999).

[78] Josh Ederington and Jenny Minier, *Is Environmental Policy a Secondary Trade Barrier? An Empirical Analysis, 36(1)* CANADIAN JOURNAL OF ECONOMICS 137 (2003), in an empirical analysis, find results consistent with U.S. use of environmental policy as a secondary means to protect import-competing industries. By modeling environmental policy as endogenous, Ederington and Minier also obtain larger estimated effects on trade than those reported by earlier researchers.

enforcement power arising from the self-interest of its members. Should it be used to achieve maximum cooperation on trade policies, maximum cooperation on domestic policies (including environmental measures), or some mix of the two? Ederington's theoretical analysis of international coordination of trade and domestic policies concludes that when enforcement power is limited, countries should cooperate fully over domestic policies, allowing each country to use these optimally to counter domestic distortions such as environmental externalities.[79] Trade policies should then be set so as to maintain the agreement's viability. In particular, this rules out the idea of an environmental "escape clause" allowing members to relax their environmental polices when faced with external shocks. Rather, adjustments necessary to sustain the agreement and to prevent countries from defecting should come through adjustments in trade policies only, as permitted under the WTO's Agreement on Safeguards.[80]

Ederington's result is an application of the theory of economic distortions to trade policy.[81] Here the assumed source of the inefficiency is trade. Specifically, sufficiently large surges in import volumes create a terms-of-trade motive for one country to defect from the agreement (the country's private benefit from defecting exceeds the social benefit, which is negative). Therefore, the efficient means of addressing the distortion is through a trade policy. Use of an environmental policy would be at most second best.

3. Avenues for Further Research

The theoretical literature on the role of trade agreements has so far addressed mainly issues relevant to localized pollution rather than global-commons concerns. One important open question is whether the WTO should be used to negotiate and/or enforce international environmental agreements. Bagwell and Staiger,[82] in assessing the WTO's role as a mechanism for securing market-access property rights, see no basis for expecting that the success of the GATT/WTO in facilitating trade liberalization would carry over to negotiations on global-commons issues. However, their stance on the issue of enforcement is neutral: "At this early stage in the research literature, it is impossible to advance with confidence an answer to whether using WTO trade sanctions as an enforcement mechanism for global labor and environmental standards would end up benefiting either free trade, labor, or the environment." Threats of retaliation via trade policy might lead, *ceteris paribus*, to more international cooperation on environment—and, likewise, threats of retaliation via environmental policy might lead to more international cooperation on trade. However, it is also possible that issue linkage would result in more cooperation in one area and less in the other than if each were dealt with separately.

---

[79] Josh Ederington, *International Coordination of Trade and Domestic Policies,* 91(5) AMERICAN ECONOMIC REVIEW 1581 (2001).

[80] Kyle Bagwell and Robert W. Staiger, *A Theory of Managed Trade,* 80(4) AMERICAN ECONOMIC REVIEW 779 (1990), establish such a motive for including a safeguards clause in an international trade agreement. By allowing countries to increase protection temporarily when facing import surges (and thus strong terms-of-trade incentives to deviate from the cooperative agreement), a safeguards clause helps to maintain viability of the agreement.

[81] Distortions are situations where private costs and/or benefits diverge from social costs and/or benefits. As noted above, these are cases where market failure is likely. A central conclusion from the literature on policy in the presence of distortions is that the best policy is one that addresses the distortion at its source. A "second-best" policy is the best choice available when the optimal policy is ruled out for political or budgetary reasons.

[82] Kyle Bagwell and Robert W. Staiger, *The WTO as a Mechanism for Securing Market Access Property Rights: Implications for Global Labor and Environmental Issues,* 15(3) JOURNAL OF ECONOMIC PERSPECTIVES 69, 85 (2001).

V. Unfinished Business

Some new trade-environment disputes have already emerged during the short history of the WTO, while a number of others brought to the GATT prior to 1995 remain unresolved. This section examines several issues where WTO consideration is currently in progress or likely to begin soon. Perhaps it is not surprising that the most contentious of the current issues (beef hormones, genetically modified organisms, biodiversity) are newer concerns only loosely related to ongoing efforts with regard to air and water pollution. For the latter, decades of experience with policy making at the national level and efforts to establish international cooperative regimes have already borne some fruit: an improved scientific basis for policy formation as well as better performance. While the newer issues are analytically similar to traditional pollution concerns in that they also entail negative production or consumption externalities, policy making is hampered by lack of an adequate scientific base. This is partly because the issues are newer, but also because they usually involve the possibility that today's actions will have negative consequences far in the future. Design of an appropriate policy response, whether at the national or international level, hinges critically both on the accuracy with which future changes can be predicted and the choice of the discount rate used to compare costs and benefits accruing over time.[83]

A. Process and Production Methods

One key issue sure to be raised under the WTO's Dispute Settlement Understanding is the WTO position on rules that distinguish among traded goods on the basis of process and production methods. Specifically, members seek to establish when it is permissible to limit imports from a trading partner based solely on that partner's PPM. In GATT/WTO terminology, to what extent can goods produced by different methods nonetheless be considered "like products"?

Restraint of trade on the basis of PPM was rejected by a GATT panel in the *Tuna-Dolphin* case, discussed above. The panel concluded that the primary goal of the U.S. ban on imports of dolphin-unsafe tuna was to pressure other countries to adopt U.S.-style regulations concerning protection of dolphins.[84] The panel also found that the United States had not exhausted means other than restriction of imports in its efforts to protect dolphins. In fact, subsequent to the panel ruling, nine countries including Mexico and the United States signed a multilateral agreement on protection of dolphins.[85]

A U.S. restriction on imports of shrimp on the basis of PPM was likewise rejected by a WTO panel, as also discussed above. A subsequent ruling by the WTO Appellate Body following an appeal did not reverse the panel decision against the United States. However, the 1998 report of the Appellate Body affirmed the right of members to take actions necessary to protect the environment and also that measures to protect sea turtles

[83] All environmental issues have an intertemporal dimension, but it is notable that the greatest progress has been made in reducing emissions such as sulphur dioxide, whose negative effects can be seen or smelled today. Also, merely documenting longer-term effects, say of GMOs, necessarily requires a longer period of observation and analysis.

[84] This kind of forced harmonization offers two types of potential benefits for the United States. First, it reduces the number of dolphins killed outside U.S. waters by ensuring that all those wishing to serve the U.S. market adopt dolphin-safe methods in tuna fishing. In addition, it restores the initial competitiveness position of U.S. tuna fishers, and thus shifts part of the cost of the U.S. policy onto U.S. trading partners. Of course, any type of import restriction also imposes higher prices on domestic consumers.

[85] Trebilcock and Howse, *supra* note 77, at 406–410.

would be permitted under Article XX. The problem with the U.S. policy was in its implementation, which was found to discriminate among exporting countries—exporters in the western hemisphere received financial and technical assistance and were allowed more time to comply with the policy. Even though the Appellate Body did not rule in favor of the United States, the report can been seen as strengthening the use of Article XX as a basis for the unilateral application of trade measures in some circumstances. Specifically, trade measures to achieve environmental objectives could be used if efforts to achieve a multilateral solution have failed and the measures themselves are not discriminatory in their application.[86] Following improvements in implementation to eliminate discrimination among exporters, the U.S. policy prevailed in a WTO challenge with respect to implementation of the decision in 2001.

The disputes in the *Tuna-Dolphin* and *Shrimp-Turtle* cases both acknowledged environmental concerns. In each case the issue is not the stated goal of the policy but, rather, the trade-restricting method used to achieve it. However, some environmental goals are more controversial. In the *Beef Hormones* case, the European Union banned imports of U.S. beef from cattle treated with hormones, even though decades of scientific research indicate that such beef poses no risk to human health.[87] A WTO panel and the Appellate Body both concluded that the EU ban violated WTO provisions.[88] After the European Union failed to change its policy, the United States exercised its right under the WTO to impose retaliatory restrictions on imports from the European Union.[89]

PPMs would also be a substantial issue in any case concerning trade restrictions of genetically modified organisms brought under the DSU. In recent decades, genetic engineering has produced new varieties of wheat, corn, and other crops, with higher yields and less vulnerability to common pests. By 2001, one hundred million acres worldwide had been planted with these new varieties, with the United States accounting for the lion's share.[90] As in the case of beef hormones, the weight of scientific evidence suggests that GMOs provide no significant risk to human health. Yet many consumers in Europe are reluctant to eat foods containing GMOs, and environmentalists have raised the concern that GM crops might crossbreed with wild plants to produce "super-weeds." EU regulatory authorities have thus placed a *de facto* moratorium on approval needed to market new products in the European Union. A number of countries have passed or are considering mandatory labeling of foods containing GMOs.[91] While U.S. trade and agriculture officials have lodged protests in various forums, some North American farmers are already switching back to traditional varieties to ensure access to important

---

[86] The report gave further support to environmental groups in stating that WTO panels may accept "amicus briefs" (friends of the court submissions) from NGOs or other interested parties <http://www.wto.org/wto/english/tratop_e/envir_e/edis08_e.htm> (accessed 14 August 2001).

[87] Given that the WTO defers to the Codex Alimentarius Commission on matters of food safety, support from the Codex standard played a key element in the ruling against the European Union. While Trebilcock and Howse, *supra* note 77, at 152 point out that the Codex standard on hormones was adopted by a vote of 33 to 29 with seven abstentions, they also note that the Codex has been criticized for a "closed-door policy" and procedures that do not ensure an outcome based on the weight of scientific evidence.

[88] A further complication is evidence that some European farmers use hormones obtained illegally via a black market <http://www.sciencenews.org/20020105/bob13.asp> (accessed 29 July 2002).

[89] The EU offered additional concessions on non-hormone-treated beef as a settlement. However, the U.S. took an inflexible stance in the bargaining, either to underscore a principle or because it did not have sufficient amounts of non-hormone treated beef to benefit from accepting the EU offer.

[90] U.S. General Accounting Office, *International Trade: Concerns Over Biotechnology Challenge U.S. Agricultural Exports* 3, Report to the Ranking Minority Member, Committee on Finance, U.S. Senate (GAO-01-727, June 2001).

[91] *Id.* at 6.

export markets. Ironically, concerns about the possible long-term risk of GMOs may mean increases in environmental damage from the additional chemicals normally required for commercial success with older varieties. Furthermore, the uncertainty regarding market access for GM crops is likely to affect planting decisions of developing countries in Africa that rely on the EU markets for their agricultural exports.

Because the issues at stake—such as when scientific evidence is adequate for use in determining policy and when the precautionary principle justifies restriction of imports—have become so controversial, it may be risky for the future of the WTO system to allow the parameters of acceptable trade restriction on the basis of PPM to be determined entirely by case law. Reliance on DSU case law may be politically palatable when the issues involved are benign and limited to trade. However, when the issues involved in the international debate include politically sensitive questions over the environment, science, trust of regulatory authorities, and even ethics, direct international negotiations over the issues will carry more weight politically than would third-party adjudication by a body like the DSU that is already viewed with substantial distrust and skepticism.

Another important concern raised by the PPM experience is the flexibility of the WTO, in its current form, to respond to the dynamic nature of environmental concerns, given that the scientific information required to make informed policy decisions is evolving as well. Many environmental issues that need to be addressed (global warming, defor-estation, coral reefs, biodiversity, etc.) have uncertain future costs if left untreated. Yet addressing these environmental issues today entails certain costs in terms of foregone national income as resources are moved out of current production and into prevention of environmental degradation. These costs and benefits have a significantly larger intertem-poral dimension than the costs and benefits of market access that the GATT/WTO system has successfully negotiated over its history. Progress in negotiating over the environment will require flexibility, long-term cooperation, and a consensus on both the underlying scientific base and the appropriate discount rate to be used when current costs weighed against future benefits.

There are at least two different concerns over the current structure of the WTO in handling these needs. Because the WTO itself does not have ongoing legislative powers, it is not amenable to flexible, ongoing discussions of the sort needed to respond to envi-ronmental concerns. Occasional negotiating rounds may not be adequate to address such potentially serious concerns. Furthermore, the WTO as currently structured has shown little ability to credibly match intertemporal gains and losses. As shown by its experi-ences with TRIPs, the Agreement on Textiles and Clothing, and other agreements with relatively long phase-in periods, intertemporal trading is difficult to sustain politically.

B. Internalization Versus Polluter Pays

As discussed in Part IV of this chapter, internalization of externalities is central to the market-based approach to achieving environmental goals. The goal of this internaliza-tion approach is to ensure that the optimizing decisions of individuals and firms reflect the full social cost or benefit from their actions. To the extent that the internalization is achieved via a system of taxes and subsidies or an equivalent system of marketable permits—polluters also bear, at least proximately,[92] the cost of the choices they make: the polluter pays an extra amount equal to the value of the negative external effect, and the

---

[92] As with any tax, ultimate incidence (the actual change in net price received or paid) depends on elasticities of producer supply and consumer demand.

abater likewise enjoys a cost reduction equal to the value of the positive external effect. However, even at the regional or national level, such policies may be modified to soften income-distribution effects deemed undesirable and/or politically unacceptable. In the United States, small businesses, though often among the worst polluters, are nonetheless exempted from most policies intended to protect the environment. Older autos, typically owned by those in lower income groups, are usually exempt from environmental regulations that apply to newer vehicles, although some communities have instead adopted incentives to remove these high-emissions vehicles from the road.

It is notable that burden-shifting approaches to internalization are often seen as necessary even within a single country or smaller area, where an elaborate system of taxes and payments is available to modify the distribution of income and consumption. In the global community, where differences between rich and poor are so much larger, there is no overall redistribution mechanism comparable to that applied within most individual countries, whether rich or poor. The international distribution of costs associated with protecting global commons therefore becomes an important consideration in policy design. In the highly improbable event that all can agree on the monetary equivalent of social costs and benefits, poorer countries with more immediate problems are likely to apply much higher discount rates to future benefits. Thus, even disregarding the very real uncertainty about future outcomes, the set of environmental objectives seen as worth pursuing from a social perspective will be nonetheless be smaller for poorer countries than for wealthy ones. For this reason, efforts to reach agreement on environmental objectives and on measures to achieve them will likely fail unless poorer countries are compensated for their participation—or threatened with possible consequences of their non-participation (e.g., trade sanctions or worse). In the *Shrimp-Turtle* case, the country most interested in the relevant environmental issue (the United States) eventually agreed to pay at least part of the cost entailed in addressing the underlying problem.[93] Outside the GATT/WTO system, debt-for-nature swaps are an example of international compensation used to achieve environmental objectives. In recent years, financial assistance from the World Bank has sometimes been conditional on implementation of environmental safeguards.

Unfortunately, the WTO system relies on voluntary exchanges of trade concessions and lacks an explicit compensation scheme to facilitate cross-country bargaining. Except for perhaps the most politically sensitive sectors in developed countries (agriculture, textiles, steel), tariff barriers have been negotiated to very low levels, making it increasingly difficult to find mutually acceptable trade concessions needed to strike bargains between countries over future trade, environmental or any similar issues. The current sole alternative to additional trade liberalization—compensation in the form of tariff retaliation—is both inefficient and a contributor to the perception that the GATT/WTO system is based on "power" relationships. We return to the idea of achieving more internalization of global externalities via international compensation in Part VI.

VI. Conclusions and Future Directions

Many environmentalists see the GATT/WTO system as a significant obstacle to progress on environmental issues. However, our review of recent high-profile cases finds that actual panel and Appellate Body decisions have had the effect of encouraging international

---

[93] Press release, United States Trade Representative, June 15, 2001 <http://www.ustr.gov/releases/2001/06/01-40.pdf> (accessed 7/22/02).

cooperation to achieve environmental goals. It is true that decisions in the *Tuna-Dolphin* and *Shrimp-Turtle* cases limited the ability of the United States to require trading partners to adopt U.S.-style environmental safeguards. These decisions discourage powerful countries with large markets from the use of unilateral trade restrictions to force adoption of a preferred environmental safeguard, rather than pursuing the same objective via negotiation among interested parties. In the *Shrimp-Turtle* case, the Appellate Body report explicitly reaffirmed that WTO rules do not prevent members from taking unilateral trade action to protect the environment if international cooperative efforts fail, but also that unilateral measures may not be applied in a way that discriminates between WTO members. The *Shrimp-Turtle* case is also significant as an example of negotiated compensation (in the form of U.S. technical and financial assistance) to defray the cost to lower-income countries of conforming to the U.S. standard of sea-turtle protection.[94]

The primary goal of the GATT/WTO system is to expand global trade. While economists generally argue that more trade is likely to improve environmental conditions, environmentalists fear that the opposite will be true. Recent contributions to the economic analysis of the trade-environment nexus help to untangle the complex relationship between environmental standards and trade. One clear implication from this literature is that trade expansion *is* likely to affect the environment. Via the scale effect and perhaps also the composition effect, increased trade will—other things equal—lead to additional pollution and a dirtier environment. The upward adjustments in domestic and global environmental policies necessary to offset the scale effect from higher production activity are often a response to rising incomes, but this effect should not be regarded as automatic.

Along with most free traders, WTO officials tend either to minimize the importance of the link between trade and environment or to emphasize the evidence of a favorable net effect. Instead, WTO experts should alert national policy makers to the likely impact of liberalized trade on pollution and other environmental damage in the absence of stronger safeguards, and encourage members to use trade-induced increases in GDP partly to facilitate the upward adjustments in national standards needed to ensure that freer trade will also mean more environmental protection. Under current GATT rules, policy makers may be discouraged from making optimal adjustments in national standards because of their impact on trade competitiveness. However, our review of the literature indicates that a minor modification of current rules would allow individual nations to use trade policy to neutralize such competitive effects.

Although measures implemented at the national or sub-national level are sufficient to produce socially optimal outcomes with regard to localized environmental effects, optimizing solutions to some problems require international coordination. However, it is far from obvious that a global forum is best for tackling all or even most of these problems. Many examples of transboundary environmental impacts involve just a few countries, often only two. For these, direct negotiations, possibly entailing compensation or issue linkage, may be more productive than efforts coordinated by a global environmental organization.[95] Even for a "global" issue such as carbon-dioxide emissions, concerted

---

[94] Providing financial compensation to developing countries in return for action to safeguard global commons is central to the Whalley and Zissimos, *supra* note 10, proposal for a World Environmental Organization, which we discuss below.

[95] A possible danger is that new arrangements in which richer nations compensate poorer ones for improved environmental policies might result in foot-dragging on needed policy improvements or even threats of new environmentally damaging actions in the hope of extracting greater compensation from other nations.

action at the OECD level alone could achieve important benefits. Still, environmentalists and an increasing number of international economists see a role for a specialized international organization dedicated to safeguarding the global environment. Existing institutions, such as the United Nations Environmental Programme ("UNEP") and the newer United Nations Commission on Sustainable Development, are largely advisory bodies with "narrow mandates, small budgets, and limited support."[96] These coexist with hundreds of organizations and treaties that address specific environmental concerns ranging from climate change to coral reefs. But no current organization has the authority to coordinate ongoing efforts at the national level and to develop general principles to guide such efforts.

Esty[97] makes the case for a GATT-inspired Global Environmental Organization ("GEO") that would centralize development and implementation of environmental standards and resolve environment-related disputes.[98] Interestingly, the first candidate for a basic principle to guide such a GEO is "universal acceptance of the polluter pays principle—forcing governments, industry, and individuals alike to bear the full costs of the environmental burdens they impose on society."[99] Above we have discussed the problems likely to arise when the polluter-pays principle is applied in an international context. Without transfers to alleviate the financial burdens imposed when poor countries adopt the higher standards usually preferred by richer ones, such an approach is likely to increase North-South tensions without achieving much cooperation.

Whalley and Zissimos[100] address this problem directly in their proposal for a World Environmental Organization ("WEO"). The WEO would seek internalization of environmental externalities at the international level though Coasian[101] bargaining (and trading) over environmental objectives. They favor a property-rights approach to clarifying and confronting the issue of global externalities and environmental protection. Because the "environmental assets" highly valued by citizens of developed countries are often owned by citizens of developing countries, an internalization-based WEO would entail the exchange of environmental protection commitments for direct cash transfers from developed countries.[102] To avoid problems of time-inconsistency, the WEO would use an escrow account to administer these commitments.

Although the concept of explicit compensation for commitments to protect environmental assets is important, establishment of such a WEO would face formidable obstacles. One initial problem concerns acceptance of existing property rights. Some environmentalists question whether a unique global environmental asset such as the Amazon rainforest should be considered the property only of the countries that contain it. Even granting this, government ownership and control of such land is often contested (legally and/or de facto) by indigenous residents and other groups. Environmental bargains of

---

[96] Esty, *supra* note 2, at 78.

[97] *Id.* at 78–83.

[98] Although the proposal initially attracted little support from international economists, subsequent disruption of the Seattle ministerial and other WTO meetings underlined immediate practical benefits from shifting the locus of environmental debate into another body.

[99] Esty, *supra* note 2, at 80.

[100] Whalley and Zissimos, *supra* note 10.

[101] Coase, *supra* note 56, argues that, under certain conditions, contracting among affected parties can establish a socially efficient allocation of resources in the presence of an externality. In such cases, no government action is needed to "internalize the externality." Required conditions include well-defined property rights and low transactions costs.

[102] They also argue that the agreement could be expanded to allow for the exchange of environmental protection commitments for trade concessions.

the kind proposed by Whalley and Zissimos cannot proceed without agreement on the initial allocation of the relevant property rights.

A separate problem is that, given their experiences with World Bank and International Monetary Fund conditionality, developing countries may be hesitant to participate in such an arrangement if they perceive it as being forced on them by developed countries. To the extent that environmental cash payments are seen as replacing other aid, what Whalley and Zissimos present as a carrot will look like just another stick. Furthermore, Newell[103] foresees strong opposition to the implication that protection of environmental assets is worth only as much to the global community as OECD countries are willing to pay. Finally, the very long time-span suggested by Whalley and Zissimos (twenty to forty years) between commitment and receipt of payment poses special problems. Are the governments representing today's poor amenable to measures that impose costs now and promise financial benefits that will be reaped only by future governments and citizens? Unless countries have a way to take financial commitments to the bank and turn them into cash today, the line of interested southern countries is likely to be a short one.[104] But to the extent that cash is delivered in advance of performance, the problem of time-inconsistency returns. Adherence to commitments could, of course, be monitored on an ongoing basis, but this approach is likely to be costly, intrusive, and controversial.

In the near term, given the absence of a GEO or a WEO, is there a consensus role for the WTO to play with respect to safeguarding the global environment—something that does not interfere with its primary trade-liberalization mandate? As we have suggested above, an important first step—and one closely related to the WTO's core mission—is to improve countries' understanding of trade-induced environmental changes and to emphasize the need to adjust domestic environmental policies accordingly. Economic research has shown that many aspects of globalization can affect both the level and the types of environmental damage experienced by any given country. One possible role for the WTO, perhaps in cooperation with an environmental organization such as UNEP, is in tracking the pattern of trade in specific pollution-intensive industries, identifying how industry production and trade are changing across countries, and thus keeping a special eye on the composition effect discussed in Part IV above.

Ultimately, favorable changes in production technique are what allow trade-induced economic growth to be accompanied by improvements in environmental quality, but these favorable changes do not occur automatically. Governments liberalizing trade may need assistance in determining when and how to adjust environmental policies in response to the resulting changes in production and the environment. The WTO can provide technical assistance on trade-related environmental concerns that would be similar in spirit to assistance offered to developing countries by the recently established Advisory Center on WTO Law to improve their understanding of their WTO rights and obligations.[105]

Finally, what should the WTO *not* do, with respect to the trade-environment nexus? Members' increasingly resort to the use (and abuse) of WTO-legal antidumping and countervailing duties and safeguards measures means that trading countries now face substantial uncertainty as to whether their negotiated market access rights will actually

---

[103] Peter Newell, *A World Environment Organization: The Wrong Solution to the Wrong Problem,* 25(5) THE WORLD ECONOMY 659 (2002).

[104] Newell, *supra* note 103, at 664, points to the very modest results achieved through debt-for-nature swaps, which already offer deals somewhat parallel to what Whalley and Zissimos envision.

[105] Website. <http://www.acwl.ch/> (accessed 29 July 2002).

be realized. The WTO should not add to the problem of discretionary administered protection by allowing members to restrict trade for reasons of alleged eco-dumping.

BIBLIOGRAPHY

Advisory Centre on WTO Law. 2002. Website. <http://www.acwl.ch/> (accessed 29 July 2002).

Anderson, Kym, and Richard Blackhurst. 1992. *The Greening of World Trade Issues.* Ann Arbor: University of Michigan Press.

Andreoni, James and Arik Levinson. 2001. "The Simple Analytics of the Environmental Kuznets Curve," *Journal of Public Economics*, 80(2): 269–286.

Antweiler, Werner, Brian R. Copeland, and M. Scott Taylor. 2001. "Is Free Trade Good for the Environment?" *American Economic Review*, 91(4): 877–908.

Bagwell, Kyle, and Robert W. Staiger. 1990. "A Theory of Managed Trade," *American Economic Review*, 80(4): 779–795.

Bagwell, Kyle, and Robert W. Staiger. 1999. "An Economic Theory of GATT," *American Economic Review*, 89(1): 215–248.

Bagwell, Kyle, and Robert W. Staiger. 2001a. "Domestic Policies, National Sovereignty, and International Economic Institutions," *Quarterly Journal of Economics,* 116(2): 519–62.

Bagwell, Kyle and Robert W. Staiger. 2001b. "The WTO as a Mechanism for Securing Market Access Property Rights: Implications for Global Labor and Environmental Issues," *Journal of Economic Perspectives*, 15(3): 69–88.

Bhagwati, Jagdish N., and T. N. Srinivasan. 1963. "Domestic Distortions, Tariffs, and the Theory of the Optimum Subsidy," *Journal of Political Economy,* 71(1), 44–50.

Bhagwati, Jagdish N., and T. N. Srinivasan. 1996. "Trade and the Environment: Does Environmental Diversity Detract from the Case for Free Trade?" in Jagdish N. Bhagwati and Robert Hudec, eds., *Fair Trade and Harmonization—Volume 1: Economic Analysis.* Cambridge, MA: MIT Press, 161–221.

Charnovitz, Steve. 2000. "World Trade and the Environment: A Review of the New WTO Report." <http://www.gets.org/pages/steve.charnovitz.cfm> (accessed 29 July 2002).

Coase, Ronald. 1960. "The Problem of Social Costs," *Journal of Law and Economics* 3: 1–44.

Copeland, Brian and M. Scott Taylor. 1994. "North-South Trade and the Environment," *Quarterly Journal of Economics*, 109(3): 755–87.

Copeland, Brian and M. Scott Taylor. 1995. "Trade and Transboundary Pollution," *American Economic Review*, 85(4): 716–737

Copeland, Brian and M. Scott Taylor. 1999. "Trade, Spatial Separation, and the Environment," *Journal of International Economics,* 47(1): 137–168.

Copeland, Brian and M. Scott Taylor. 2004. "Trade, Growth and the Environment," *Journal of Economic Literature* 42(1): 7–71.

Destler, I.M., and Peter J. Balint. 1999. *The New Politics of American Trade: Trade, Labor, and the Environment.* Policy Analyses in International Economics 58. Washington, D.C.: Institute for International Economics, October.

Ederington, Josh. 2001. "International Coordination of Trade and Domestic Policies," *American Economic Review*, 91(5): 1580–1593.

Ederington, Josh, and Jenny Minier. 2003. "Is Environmental Policy a Secondary Trade Barrier? An Empirical Analysis," *Canadian Journal of Economics,* 36(1): 137–154.

Esty, Daniel C. 1994. *Greening the GATT: Trade, Environment, and the Future.* Washington, D.C.: Institute for International Economics, July.

Esty, Daniel C. 1996. "Greening World Trade," in Jeffrey J. Schott, ed., *The World Trading System: Challenges Ahead.* Washington, D.C.: Institute for International Economics, December.

Esty, Daniel C. 2001. "Bridging the Trade-Environment Divide," *Journal of Economic Perspectives*, 15(3): 113–130.

GATT (1947). General Agreement on Tariffs and Trade 1947, as amended, including notes and supplementary provisions. Geneva: GATT.

Grossman, Gene M. and Alan B. Krueger. 1993. "Environmental Impacts of a North American Free Trade Agreement," in Peter Garber, ed. *The U.S.—Mexico Free Trade Agreement*. Cambridge, MA: MIT Press.

Grossman, Gene M. and Alan B. Krueger. 1995. "Economic Growth and the Environment," *Quarterly Journal of Economics*, 110(2): 353–377.

Harbaugh, William T., Arik Levinson, and David Molloy Wilson. 2002. "Reexamining the Empirical Evidence of the Environmental Kuznets Curve," *Review of Economics and Statistics*, 84(3): 541–551.

Johnson, Harry G. 1960. "The Cost of Protection and the Scientific Tariff," *Journal of Political Economy*, 68(4): 327–345.

Karp, Jonathan, and Miriam Jordan. 2002. "U.S. Ports Hold On to Brazilian Mahogany," *The Wall Street Journal*, March 29.

Kindleberger, Charles P. 1953. *International Economics*. Homewood, IL: Richard D. Irwin, Inc.

Krist, William. 2001. "Multilateral Environmental Agreements and the World Trade Organization," discussion paper, Woodrow Wilson Center, March <http://wwics.si.edu/tef/wtoconfpap. htm> (accessed 9 August 2001).

Newell, Peter. 2002. "A World Environment Organization: The Wrong Solution to the Wrong Problem." *The World Economy* 25 (5): 659–671.

Nordström, Håkan, and Scott Vaughan. 1999. *Trade and Environment*. Special Studies 4. Geneva: World Trade Organization.

Ostry, Sylvia. 2001. "The WTO After Seattle." Paper prepared for presentation at the American Economic Association annual meeting, New Orleans, January.

Petersmann, Ernst-Ulrich. 1997. *The GATT/WTO Dispute Settlement System: International Law, International Organizations and Dispute Settlement*. London: Kluwer Law International.

Porter, Michael E., and Claas van der Linde, "Toward a New Conception of the Environment-Competitiveness Relationship," *Journal of Economic Perspectives* 9(4): 97–118.

Pugel, Thomas A., and Peter H. Lindert. 2000. *International Economics (eleventh edition)*. Boston: Irwin McGraw-Hill.

Runge, C. Ford. 1994. *Freer Trade, Protected Environment*. New York: Council on Foreign Relations.

Staiger, Robert W., and Guido Tabellini. 1987. "Discretionary Trade Policy and Excessive Protection," *American Economic Review*, 77(5): 823–37.

Stilwell, Matthew. 2001. "Protecting GMO Labeling from a WTO Challenge." Center for International Environmental Law. <http://www.cid.harvard.edu/cidtradeissues/ biotechnologypaper.html> (accessed 19 April 2003).

Trebilcock, Michael J., and Robert Howse. 1999. *The Regulation of International Trade* (second edition). New York: Routledge.

United States Trade Representative. October 22, 2001. "USTR on WTO Decision Supporting U.S. on Shrimp-Turtle Law." <http://usinfo.state.gov/wto/01102201.htm> (accessed 1 January 2002).

Unteroberdoerster, Olaf. 2001. "Trade and Transboundary Pollution: Spacial Separation Reconsidered." *Journal of Environmental Economics and Manangement*, 41(2): 269–285.

U.S. General Accounting Office. 2001. "International Trade: Concerns Over Biotechnology Challenge U.S. Agricultural Exports." Report to the Ranking Minority Member, Committee on Finance, U.S. Senate (GAO-01-727), June.

Weinstein, Michael M., and Steve Charnovitz. 2001. "The Greening of the WTO," *Foreign Affairs*, 80(6): 147–156.

Whalley, John and Ben Zissimos. 2002. "An Internalisation-based World Environmental Organisation," *The World Economy*, 25(5): 619–642.

CHAPTER 44

LABOR STANDARDS

Charles Pearson[*]

TABLE OF CONTENTS

[*] Johns Hopkins University SAIS-Washington.

I. Introduction

The WTO is virtually silent on labor issues. The single exception is article XX (e) of the GATT which permits but does not require countries to exclude goods made by prison labor.[1] Should this silence be broken? In recent years there has been increasing pressure to extend WTO obligations to include minimum labor standards in some form. The idea is extremely controversial, with fault lines between North and South, between business and labor, and between advocates of free trade and groups with humanitarian and human rights interests.[2] This chapter attempts to sort out the issues and analyze the merits of including labor standards in the WTO. To accomplish this Part II provides a brief description of the evolution of the issue and the types of labor standards that might be included. Part III presents five arguments for inclusion. Part IV explores the economics of labor standards should they find their way into the WTO, and Part V elaborates on certain practical difficulties. Part VI draws conclusions. To anticipate, I find the case for inclusion of labor standards in the WTO to be dubious, and suggest that other avenues for labor protection would be more productive.

Before starting, however, I wish to comment on the similarities and differences between labor and environmental standards as they relate to trade. They are often analyzed together under the (ill-defined) rubric of "social dumping". There are many similarities. In both cases enforcement of strict standards is thought likely to increase production costs and to affect international competitive position. Both generate a concern for a "race to the bottom" in regulatory competition. Both labor and environmental standards can be used for covert protectionist purposes. And in both cases proponents of stronger standards often view the trade system as a convenient instrument for promoting their (non-commercial) interests internationally.[3]

But there are also significant differences that need to be kept in mind. First, deficient labor standards do not create transnational pollution. The superficial attraction of using trade measures for managing transnational pollution and international environmental resources adds a complexity to the trade environment debate that is absent in the labor standards trade case[4]. Second, there is no parallel in the labor standards debate to the issue of environmentally-related product standards. Whereas there is a reasonable case for restricting imports of products whose use might damage the health, safety, or environment of the importing country, one cannot argue that imports of products from countries that fail to adhere to minimum labor standards directly damage the importing country. Third, while there is a legitimate concern that trade can lead to environmental degradation in countries with weak standards, it seems less likely that trade will *worsen* labor conditions

---

[1] The original motivation was apparently protection from unfair competition, not ethical concerns. A 1930 law in the United States banned imports made from "forced" labor or "indentured labor under penal sanctions", but exempted items if U.S. production was insufficient to satisfy consumption. Steve Charnovitz, *The Influence of International Labor Standards on the World Trading Regime*, 126 INTERNATIONAL LABOR REVIEW 565, 569–70 (1987).

[2] This is a great generalization with many crossovers and shades of opinion. Virtually all commentators agree, however, that some labor in some countries experience dreadful working conditions.

[3] In technical terms this may be defended as a second-best response to an international market failure. Labor or environmental conditions in country A may enter the utility of country B's residents but they have no effective "market" to buy improvements abroad.

[4] While there are no tangible international externalities, one can argue that for humanitarian reasons the worldwide welfare of workers enters utility functions in industrial countries. In that case deficient labor standards *may* be thought to create "costs" outside the country's borders. Of course it does not follow that trade measures are necessarily the appropriate response.

in countries with weak labor standards.[5] Finally, the institutional setting is different in the two cases. The International Labor Organization ("ILO") is a mature institution with a rich if not totally successful history of establishing and monitoring international labor norms. There is no equivalent International Environment Organization dedicated to setting international environmental standards.[6] The first two differences suggest that the fair labor standards issue, while equally controversial and emotional, may be somewhat more tractable to analyze. The last difference, an institutional alternative to the WTO, is also significant.

II. Evolution of the Labor Standards Issue

The connection between regulations to protect labor and international competitive position can be traced to the first half of the Nineteenth Century and humanitarian efforts in Europe to moderate the harsh working conditions of the early years of the Industrial Revolution.[7] The issue then as now was whether international competition undercut a country's ability to legislate costly labor protections with regard to working hours, child labor, and safety measures. The suggested solution, then as now, was to reach international agreement on common, or at least minimum, labor standards. But in the early years of the debate trade sanctions supporting this objective were not contemplated. Progress in harmonizing labor regulations among industrial countries was slow and spotty but ultimately culminated in the establishment of the ILO immediately following World War I. The ILO's principal approach has been to promote international labor conventions and work for their ratification and implementation. After World War II the ILO moved beyond conventions centering on quite specific working conditions, for example the length of the workweek. Consistent with the emphasis on universal human rights, it took up newer issues—the right of collective bargaining, discrimination in the workplace, and pay equality. Morici and Schulz[8] describe enforcement procedures in the ILO.

The nexus between labor standards and trade was also considered in the aborted International Trade Organization in the immediate post World War II period.[9] The relevant provision recognized the connection between labor standards and trade, called on members to take "appropriate and feasible" actions to eliminate unfair labor conditions within their territory, and acknowledged the role of the ILO should trade-labor disputes arise. These provisions did not survive in what was then considered an interim commercial agreement, the GATT.

---

[5] The common argument is that trade with weak labor standard countries will harm labor interests in importing countries. It is possible of course to construct a model in which labor conditions are especially poor in the export sector and trade will move workers from the (relatively) better-protected sectors to the export sector.

[6] The United Nations Environment Program established in 1972 and the UN Commission on Sustainable Development established two decades later function quite differently from the ILO.

[7] Virginia Leary, *Workers Rights and International Trade: The Social Clause*, in FAIR TRADE AND HARMONIZATION PREREQUISITES FOR FREE TRADE? (Jagdish Bhagwati and Robert Hudec eds. 1996); Charnovitz, *supra* note 1.

[8] Peter Morici and Evan Schulz, *Labor Standards in the Global Trading System*, ECONOMIC STRATEGY INSTITUTE (2001).

[9] The ITO was to have been the third pillar of the triumvirate of international institutions, along with the International Monetary Fund and the World Bank, all designed to remedy the pernicious economic nationalism and beggar-thy-neighbor policies of the inter-war period. The ITO allowed too much interventionism and loss of sovereignty for the U.S. Congress to stomach, and the so-called Havana Charter was withdrawn by President Truman before a ratification vote was taken. *See* WILLIAM DIEBOLD, THE END OF THE ITO (1952).

The issue of labor standards arose in the Uruguay Round negotiations (1986–1994) along with the environment trade issue but nothing concrete concerning labor emerged.[10] At a subsequent WTO ministerial meeting in Singapore (1996) the labor-trade connection was again raised, but rejected with the statement that the ILO was the competent body to deal with labor standards. This treatment was reconfirmed in the Doha Declaration (2001) launching the delayed Millennium Round, "We reaffirm our declaration made at the Singapore Ministerial Conference regarding recognized core labor standards". As background it should be remembered that any serious attempt at inserting labor standards in the WTO was and is strongly opposed by developing countries, who consider it a ploy to limit their comparative advantage in labor intensive products. The support of fair labor standards by organized labor in industrial countries does nothing to allay that suspicion. Developing countries are also sensitive to infringements on their national sovereignty, as indeed are all countries.

United States policy during this period is of some interest. A loose coalition between human rights groups and elements of organized labor was successful in introducing labor conditions into the Caribbean Basin Initiative ("CBI") in 1983, the renewal of the Generalized System of Preferences ("GSP") in 1984, and revisions of Section 301 of the Trade Law in 1988.[11] There was also Congressional pressure, expressed through House resolutions, for consideration of labor standards in the Uruguay Round, but as noted above these were unsuccessful.

The real test for a labor-trade linkage was NAFTA. In the background was a widely held concern that with free trade and a secure investment climate, a significant portion of U.S. industry would migrate southward to Mexico seeking low wage low cost production. Weak enforcement of otherwise adequate labor and environmental standards in Mexico would facilitate the relocation. Thus the interest of environmentalists concerned with the creation of pollution havens, humanitarian groups concerned with abusive exploitation of Mexican labor, and organized labor concerned with protecting jobs, wages, and labor rights, were joined. While old-fashioned protectionism played an important role, there was also a concern that as a result of competition with Mexico, labor and environmental standards in the United States would be eroded, the "race to the bottom" concept discussed below.[12] This was not totally idle speculation. The maquiladora program was firmly established and Mexican wages in manufacturing were less than twenty percent of U.S wages.[13]

Faced with the need to overcome opposition in Congress and a desire to differentiate his approach to NAFTA from his predecessors, President Clinton decided to negotiate two side agreements, one concerning environmental protection and the other labor, the North American Agreement on Labor Cooperation ("NAALC"). Two features of these agreements are significant. First, there was a deliberate effort to hive off the two contentious issues into separate agreements and to keep the basic NAFTA agreement "clean" of labor and environmental strictures. Second, both agreements deliberately avoided any serious

---

[10] The Uruguay Round agreements did call for the establishment of a Committee on Trade and Environment but its accomplishments have been modest.

[11] The CBI and the GSP offer preferential access to the U.S. market. As unilaterally conferred benefits CBI and GSP could contain whatever conditions the U.S. wished to impose. Section 301 of U.S. Trade Act has been the principal instrument for pursuing alleged foreign "unfair" trade practices.

[12] Interestingly, the race to the bottom concern played a significant role in Canada during the debate over the US-Canada FTA. (Brian Alexander Langille, *General Reglections on the Relationships of Trade and Labor*, in FAIR TRADE AND HARMONIZATION: PREREQUESITES FOR FREE TRADE?, Volume 2 (Jagdish Bhagwati and Rober Hudec eds. 1996).

[13] Charles Pearson, U.S. TRADE POLICY: A WORK IN PROGRESS (2003).

attempt to harmonize labor and environmental standards among the three countries, and in the case of labor, there was no attempt to condition trade rights on adherence to internationally recognized labor standards. Instead NAFTA members pledged to promote effective compliance with their own labor (and environmental) laws. NAALC does contain a dispute settlement mechanism for controversies involving worker health and safety, child labor, and minimum wages, but not for disputes involving freedom of association and collective bargaining. The latter are widely considered the heart of internationally-recognized labor rights. The dispute mechanism itself sets out a convoluted and time-consuming procedure. In the end a persistent pattern of labor law violations might result in fines, and if the fines were ignored, limited trade sanctions could be imposed. But the clear intention was to settle or dismiss disputes before they reach the point of sanctions.[14] In any event, fines were limited to .007 percent of total bilateral trade. If trade sanctions are employed they can only raise duties to the lower of the MFN rate or the pre-NAFTA rate, and are further limited to the amount of the (ignored) fine.

The fallout from the bitter NAFTA fight has been extensive and prolonged. One result was that fast track authority (now known by the more upbeat "Trade Promotion Authority" or "TPA") was withheld from President Clinton for the remainder of his terms in office, in large part due to the unresolved labor and environmental standards issues. In December 2001 TPA passed the House by a paper-thin margin of one vote. The bill sets as negotiating objectives: "to promote respect for worker rights and the rights of children consistent with core labor standards of the International Labor Office," and to seek provisions in trade agreements that countries "do not weaken or reduce the protection afforded in domestic environmental and labor laws as an encouragement for trade". Note that 1988 trade legislation also had as a principal negotiating objective respect for workers' rights.[15]

It is perhaps time to be more specific about the labor standards and workers rights that are being proposed for inclusion in the WTO. We do so without speculating as to their prospects in negotiations, but rather to tease out economic implications. We divide them into two groups, the first of which might be considered internationally recognized labor standards.[16] The distinction between the two groups is a bit artificial but essentially rests on the contention that certain rights are universal and should be protected regardless of the level of economic development (the first group), and that another group of labor standards may appropriately vary with the level of income of the country (the second group). There are four elements to the first group:

Group One Standards:

1. Freedom from forced labor.
2. Abolition of child labor, or the less-demanding prohibition of exploitative forms of child labor.
3. Freedom from discrimination in employment.
4. Freedom of association and of collective bargaining.

---

[14] Kimberly Ann Elliot, *Finding Our Way on Trade and Labor Standards?*, INSTITUTE FOR INTERNATIONAL ECONOMICS, INTERNATIONAL ECONOMICS POLICY BRIEFS (2001) has proposed fines rather than trade sanctions to resolve the trade-labor impasse. See also Mary Jane Bolle, *NAFTA Labor Side Agreement: Lessons for the Worker Rights Fast Track Debates*, CONGRESSIONAL RESEARCH REPORT 97-861 (2001).

[15] Bolle, *supra* note 14.

[16] These parallel the ILO's 1998 *Declaration of Fundamental Principles and Rights at Work* Significantly the United States has not ratified ILO conventions dealing with discrimination, forced labor and free association, and collective bargaining (Drusilla Brown, *Labor Standards: Where Do They Belong on the International Trade Agenda?*, 15(3) JOURNAL OF ECONOMIC PERSPECTIVES 89 (2001)).

The first three elements in this group can be thought of as fundamental human rights, and the last as an element of civic rights. The argument has been made that this group of labor standards, in contrast to the group discussed below, is or should be independent of the level of economic development. Three aspects of this group stand out. First, the full implementation of these rights would be felt throughout the economy and not limited to the tradable goods sector or to the export industries. The notion of 'trade-related' labor standards makes little sense. This contrasts with the two WTO agreements on trade-related investment measures ("TRIMs") and trade-related intellectual property ("TRIPS"), where it is conceptually and empirically possible to consider the direct trade aspects of these subjects. While it might be possible to initiate complaints of a violation of these standards in specific export products, the prospect of enforcing labor standards only when they affect exports suggests an undesirable two-tiered labor standard regime. In practical terms, fully enforcing these four labor standards would have impacts throughout the economy, magnifying their economic impact.[17]

Second, in general it would be analytically difficult to quantify in trade or monetary terms the effects of violating one or more of these standards. If such violations were alleged to provide an implicit (and illegal) subsidy to exports, and if traditional WTO/GATT procedures were to be followed, any countervailing duty or sanction by an importing country would have to be commensurate with the implicit subsidy margin, an extremely difficult and contentious calculation. It has proved difficult enough to calculate subsidy margins in simple tax subsidy cases. Of course if the purpose of retaliation is not to restore "fair" competition but to coerce the country into improved labor standards, then there would be no need to calculate implicit margins. Any severe sanctions would do.[18]

Third, as considered below, one can argue that two and possibly three of these labor standards might actually improve the efficiency and competitive position of the offending industry.[19] This view is put forward by Martin and Maskus[20] and is considered in the theory section below.

The second group of labor standards is more specific, and focuses on wages, workplace regulations, and other general conditions of labor. This group of standards includes minimum wages, workplace health and safety regulations, hours of employment, and vacation/retirement rights. These standards are not thought to be universal, and it is appropriate that rich countries aspire to higher standards than poor countries. The economics of these regulations are somewhat easier to analyze and in most cases are likely to increase production costs.[21] At the same time however these more specific labor regulations are

---

[17] It is of course possible that violation of one or more of these standards is concentrated in the export sector. But as cited by Keith Maskus, *Should Core Labor Standards be Imposed Through International Trade Policy?*, WORLD BANK POLICY RESEARCH WORKING PAPER 1817 (1997), Mita Aggarwal, *International Trade, Labor Standards, and Labor Market Conditions: an Evaluation of Linkages*, US INTERNATIONAL TRADE COMMISSION WORKING PAPER 95-06-C (1995), finds labor standards to be lower in less export-oriented and non-tradable goods sectors than in export-oriented industries.

[18] Theodore Moran, BEYOND SWEATSHOPS: FOREIGN DIRECT INVESTMENT AND GLOBALIZATION IN DEVELOPING COUNTRIES (2002) makes the interesting point that retaliation might involve more sophisticated manufacturers that compete directly in industrial country markets. If so it discourages the upgrading of the labor intensive export sector and delays the normal progression to higher labor standards.

[19] Discrimination and forced labor; perhaps collective bargaining.

[20] Will Martin and Keith Maskus, *Core Labor Standards and Competitiveness: Implications for Global Theory*, 9(2) REVIEW OF INTERNATIONAL ECONOMICS 317 (2001).

[21] Some of the regulations may improve productivity and efficiency and lower production costs. A similar argument that strict environmental standards can improve competitiveness has been made (Michael Porter and Claas Van der Linde, *Toward a New Conception of the Environment—Competitiveness Relationship*,

the least likely candidates for inclusion in the WTO, precisely because they can legitimately vary among countries. This point is also made by Burtless,[22] who concludes that the case for enforcing labor standards through trade measures is strongest when such standards involve basic human rights, and weakest when the standards involve specific conditions of employment (e.g., pay, working hours, etc).

III. Arguments for Inclusion

Five arguments of varying quality have been advanced for including labor standards in the WTO. In discussing these we assume it is possible to identify situations in which countries permit or encourage egregious failures to maintain minimum labor protection standards. We call such situations "grossly inadequate labor standards" or GILS. Adequacy in some cases, especially for Group 2 standards, implies measuring standards against the level of economic development of the country. Low wages are not GILS *per se.* Whether in practice GILS can be unambiguously identified is another matter and discussed in Part V below.

Please note that none of the five arguments for inclusion contends that inadequate labor standards creates a trade balance problem for importing countries. In a floating exchange rate world, cost differentials arising from labor standard differentials are accommodated through exchange rate movements, so that effects on the aggregate trade balance are not relevant. The competitiveness concern is only of concern as it affects individual industries.

A. Efficiency in World Production

GILS, and especially discrimination and forced labor, suggest distortions or inefficiencies in labor markets and hence distortions in the pattern of international trade. Just as the WTO restricts two other distorting practices, subsidies (and especially export subsidies) and dumping, this argument asserts it would be logical to work toward the elimination of trade- and production-distorting GILS. Viewed in this light, GILS are an implicit or regulatory subsidy.

B. Grossly Inadequate Labor Standards Promote Unfair Trade

This argument asserts that it is unfair to expect labor and industry in importing countries to compete with products made under GILS. The WTO and the GATT before it is concerned with fairness as well as efficiency. Both the anti-dumping and the countervailing duty provisions of the WTO are grounded in notions of fairness (albeit fairness for producers not consumers) as well as efficiency. Just as these provisions help restore a level playing field, eliminating GILS would contribute to fair trade. Moreover, the group most likely to benefit from eliminating GILS, low-skill, low-wage labor in industrial countries, is perhaps the most deserving. In a larger sense, public support for liberal trade is contingent on a perception of fairness.

9(4) JOURNAL OF ECONOMIC PERSPECTIVES 97 (1995)), but is disputed (Karen Palmer, Wallace Oates, Paul Portney, *Tightening Environmental Standards: The Benefit-Cost or the No-Cost Paradigm?*, 9(4) JOURNAL OF ECONOMIC PERSPECTIVES 114 (1995)).
[22] Gary Burtless, *Workers Rights*, 19(4) BROOKINGS REVIEW 10 (2001).

C. Regulatory Race to the Bottom

A third reason for including labor standards in international trade rules is to prevent a regulatory race to the bottom. The logic of the argument invokes strategic behavior and a variation of the prisoners' dilemma game. It starts by asserting that there is an "inequity of bargaining power" between firms and workers in unregulated labor markets.[23] Government response is twofold—to establish and protect the right to association and collective bargaining, indirectly redressing the inequality, and to intervene in labor markets with substantive regulations concerning child labor, minimum wages, discrimination etc, thus offering more direct protection. The next point is that governments compete to capture productive activity by advancing their trade interests and by attracting foreign investment. The tools for doing so are well known and include favorable tax treatment, subsidized infrastructure, and direct subsidies. Labor policy is part of the tool chest. Thus "regulatory competition" among countries results. Unlike product competition, which generally results in higher quality and lower prices, regulatory competition tends to lower labor (and other) standards. The third part of the argument is now obvious—countries are in a prisoners' dilemma. While it is in the collective interest of all countries to maintain appropriate labor standards, the rational strategy for a single country is to "defect", lower its standards, attract investment, and enhance its competitive position. All countries recognize this dilemma and either for defensive and offensive reasons a regulatory race to the bottom results. If the logic of this argument is accepted it follows that an international regime capable of sanctioning defectors is needed to provide the collective good, appropriate labor standards. The WTO with its ability to authorize trade sanctions becomes an obvious candidate.

D. Humanitarian Concerns

The fourth argument for including labor standards in the WTO is ethical—it is the right thing to do. To the extent possible the international community wishes to reduce or eliminate slave labor, child labor, racial and gender discrimination, dangerous labor, sexual exploitation in the workforce, monopsonistic power, and a host of other practices that offend our sense of equity and justice. Our humanitarian concerns do not stop at our borders. Proponents of this argument often point out that the ILO has had indifferent success in eliminating these practices. The WTO, with its ability to authorize sanctions, becomes the default enforcement institution. This argument does not pretend that trade causes exploitative labor practices or indeed that trade in GILS goods is necessarily extensive. It merely views the trade system as a convenient tool for accomplishing good in the world. In the pure version of this argument there is no need to link trade sanctions to any particular implicit subsidy—the mere existence of GILS would trigger restrictive trade measures sufficient to alter practices in the target country. Viewed in another light and to use an unpleasant term, trade would be an instrument of international coercion.[24]

E. Accelerate Growth in Poor Countries

The final argument for including labor protection obligations in the WTO is that it would accelerate growth in developing countries. The logic is that in many (not all) instances

---

[23] Note that it is logically difficult to simultaneously maintain arguments B and C. If there is in race a race to the bottom the unfair competition is erased, or at least canceled.

[24] Economic sanctions to promote noncommercial objectives are common and increasing. *See* Pearson, *supra* note 13.

GILS work against long-term development. For example child labor stunts educational achievement and may slow the shift to a more sophisticated pattern of production. Gender discrimination reduces the efficient supply of labor. For whatever reason—ignorance, cupidity, government failure—countries need to be nudged into adopting better labor protection, a win-win situation.

There are problems with all of these arguments. The alleged trade-distorting effects of GILS need empirical demonstration. And trade sanctions to remove GILS may simply introduce additional distortions and inefficiency. The antidumping and countervailing duty provisions of the WTO have been much abused, and to pattern a labor standard obligation on current unfair trade rules is problematic. Covert protection through labor standards cannot be dismissed. The race to the bottom argument also has weaknesses. One can question the premise of inequality of bargaining power. Labor has options. If exploited it may move to other employment. And firms have an interest in recruiting, training and maintaining their workforce. Countries also have options. They may choose not to trade off labor standards but to compete for productive activity on the basis of stable macro policies, education policy, clean government, etc. As noted below it is not clear that GILS are a powerful attraction for foreign investment or give a boost to trade. The literature on the efficient wage hypothesis also casts doubt on the ability of GILS to bolster economic activity. The humanitarian argument also raises questions. Would the threat of trade sanctions be a form of labor market imperialism, akin to allegations of eco-imperialism, in which the values of the North are forced on the South? Would the coercive use of trade measures actually improve the lot of labor in poor countries? Is the liberal trade system robust enough to use as a tool for noncommercial humanitarian objectives?

IV. Theory and Evidence

The multiplicity of arguments for melding labor standards in the WTO complicates analysis. But a start can be made. We examine four questions.

A. Do Grossly Inadequate Labor Standards Improve International Competitive Position?

Would trade sanctions reduce "unfair" competition? A surprising number of models suggest that eliminating GILS would either increase competition and work against the interests of low-wage, low-skill labor in industrial countries, or undermine humanitarian objectives of improving the lot of labor in poor countries. We provide intuitive expositions of several of these models.

Consider first a monopsonistic employer in the export sector of a developing country.[25] By controlling labor demand the firm restricts hiring to the point where marginal expenditure on labor equals the marginal revenue product of the last worker. At this point the wage is somewhere below the marginal revenue product of the last worker—a classic example of exploitation. Now assume a complaint is filed with the WTO and a trade sanction (tariff) results. This shifts the labor demand curve in the export industry inwards, depressing the output, employment, and the (exploitative) wage. While this may offer some protection against "unfair" competition in importing countries, it also implies lower employment and lower wages in the export industry.[26]

---

[25] Will Martin and Keith Maskus, *Core labor Standards and Competitiveness: Implications for Global Theory*, 9(2) REVIEW OF INTERNATIONAL ECONOMICS 317 (2001)

[26] The displaced workers will also tend to depress wages elsewhere in the economy.

Suppose instead the threat of sanctions results in granting the right to collective bargaining and an effective union emerges. In that event the monopsonistic market power may be broken and wages rise to their competitive levels. The result would be an increase in employment, output and competitive pressure—an outcome that may please humanitarian interests, but displeases producers and workers in importing countries that had complained of unfair competition from unfairly exploited labor.[27]

Corden and Vosden[28] arrive at a similar conclusion—policy results that may please humanitarians may displease those that seek protection from unfairly produced imports and *visa versa*—but they do so with a somewhat different model. They work with a two-sector model and assume quite reasonably that costly labor protection regulations can only be effectively imposed in one sector (the informal, non-regulated, non-tradable goods and services sector becomes the residual employment sector). If there is a monopsony in the export sector and if costly labor standards are imposed, real wages might increase without decline in employment, pleasing humanitarians but disappointing protectionists as there is no decline of employment, output or competitive pressure (labor to this sector inelastically supplied over the relevant range). In effect the stronger labor regulations represent an increase in the real wage, "paid" for by squeezing the monopsonist's profits (which might be foreign MNCs). In contrast if monopsony in the regulated sector is absent, costs rise and employment, output and competitive pressures fall. This suits protectionist interests, but creates a two-tiered wage structure, with real wages falling in the informal, unregulated sector as it absorbs the displaced workers. The informal, unregulated sector is likely to experience the deepest levels of poverty.

The effects of linking labor standards to trade depends in part on whether the target country changes its policy or absorbs the trade sanctions. Consider for example gender or racial discrimination, which is prevalent in many countries rich and poor, and which is a target for labor standards. Suppose the export sector discriminates against females resulting in lower employment and lower wages. Now suppose this results in a complaint in the WTO and a tariff is levied. The effect of the tariff is to shift down the demand for female labor but will have no effect on employment and wages unless it brings the equilibrium wage below the original, discriminatory wage. Thus the results will either be no improvement in female wages and no relief from "unfair competition" in importing countries or, at the extreme, lower female wages in the export sector.[29] If instead the country responds to the threat of trade sanctions and eliminates discrimination, female wages and employment and output in the export sector will rise, pleasing humanitarian interests but again displeasing producers in importing countries that had complained of unfair competition arriving from exploitation of female workers.

B. What Does the Evidence Concerning Grossly Inadequate Labor Standards and Trade Competitiveness Show?

A comprehensive review by the OECD in 1996 found no evidence that countries with weak core labor standards had better export performance than high standard countries.

---

[27] Other outcomes are possible. A union intent on maximizing (union) wages could restrict output and employment below the original position.

[28] W. Max Corden and Neil Vosden, *Paved with Good Intentions: Social Dumping and Raising Labour Standards in Developing Countries*, in GLOBALIZATION UNDER THREAT, (Zdenek Drabek ed. 2000)

[29] Martin, *supra* note 25.

An update of that study published in 2000 reached the same conclusion.[30] The latter study also concluded that there is "no robust evidence that low standard countries provide a haven for foreign firms", undercutting the notion that exploitation of labor drives foreign direct investment. The failure to find an empirical link between labor standards and export performance cuts two ways. On the one hand it weakens the claim that firms and workers in industrial countries face a flood of unfairly traded products. But it also weakens the argument that stronger labor standards would harm developing countries' export prospects. Also to be fair not everyone accepts the OECD's conclusions. For example Morici and Schulz[31] estimate that manufacturing labor costs per worker are reduced by $6000 per year in economies where freedom of association and child labor are not well protected (after adjusting for national differences in productivity). If correct, the trade-competitiveness affects would be substantial.

The weak link between labor standards and trade competitiveness casts light on another controversy—whether trade is responsible for increasing wage inequality between skilled and unskilled workers in the United States in recent decades. This question has generated a large literature[32]. The two contending explanations for rising inequality are trade, especially trade with low wage countries, and technological changes that biases labor market demand toward skilled workers. We need not review that controversy but simply note that if GILS have minimal effects on competitiveness, it is difficult to implicate them in wage suppression in the United States. This works against the second argument for including labor in the WTO.

C. How Robust is the Regulatory Race to the Bottom Theory?

The answer is ambiguous and depends on how policy is modeled. Bagwell and Staiger present a sophisticated analysis of the links between labor standards and the WTO based on a reinterpretation of role of the WTO in the liberal trade system. Their analysis can be summarized as follows. In their view the WTO (and the GATT before it) exists to facilitate the negotiation of property rights for export market access. Governments are willing to make "concessions" on import barriers to gain secure export market access. The concessions imply an adverse movement in their terms of trade but improved export market access offsets this[33]. Through successive tariff negotiations a balance of market access concessions is achieved (not necessarily equivalent levels of access). Now consider labor (or environmental) standards that increase the cost of production. Bagwell and Staiger argue that *if* property rights over market access are secure (cannot be infringed upon) and *if* the WTO is given the task of preventing a regulatory race to the bottom, then tariff negotiations under WTO auspices will not trigger a race to the bottom or a "regulatory chill".[34] For example if a developed country exporter wishes to tighten its

---

[30] OECD, TRADE, EMPLOYMENT, AND LABOR STANDARDS: A STUDY OF CORE WORKERS' RIGHTS AND INTERNATIONAL TRADE (1996); OECD, INTERNATIONAL TRADE AND CORE LABOR STANDARDS (2000).

[31] Morici and Schulz, *supra* note 8.

[32] *See* for example the collection of articles in the Spring 1997 issue of *The Journal of Economic Perspectives* (Volume 11 (2)), and FEENSTRA, THE IMPACT OF INTERNATIONAL TRADE ON WAGES (2000). By and large Europe has escaped increasing inequality, but trade may have contributed to stubbornly high unemployment rates (PAUL BRENTON AND JACQUES PELKMAN, GLOBAL TRADE AND EUROPEAN WORKERS (1998)).

[33] This implies that countries are "large" and can affect international prices.

[34] The chill is an unwillingness to tighten standards out of concern for adverse trade consequences.

standards without harming its import-competing firms, it would be permitted to raise tariffs. The combination of tighter domestic standard and higher tariff would maintain the same level of foreign access to its market, thus preserving foreigners' secure market access.

Alternatively if a developed country sees its export market access threatened by a reduction in developing country standards, it could initiate a complaint under GATT's nullification and impairment provisions (Article XXIII). The trade partner would then either offer a compensating trade concession on another product or relinquish a previous trade concession that it had gained earlier. This would again restore the balance of market access commitments. In essence tariffs and standards become substitutes in establishing market access.

The race to the bottom and the regulatory chill problems arise when market access commitments are not secure. In that event a country might lower a labor standard, impairing market access opportunities of its trade partners. This would be more likely if the partners were limited by trade rules in their ability to retaliate or if they could not use the nullification and impairment provisions. *Insecure* market access sets the stage for a race to the bottom. While the analysis is undoubtedly clever, the prospect of permitting tariff increases to offset loss of market access due to domestic regulatory changes make one nervous. What regulatory changes would be fair game? Would this new tool for trade restrictions be captured by protectionist interests? Would a developed country carry out its obligation and reduce import barriers if a poor country tightened its labor standards?[35]

Brown, Deardorf, and Stern,[36] and Brown[37] also consider the race to the bottom question. They reach the surprising conclusion that trade may encourage excessively strong labor standards in developing countries, and that coordination (not harmonization) of standards may increase world welfare. This result hinges on the terms of trade effects of standards. If standards are labor using, and if they are tightened in labor-abundant developing countries, the supply of labor for conventional output fall, wages rise, the price of labor intensive goods for export rises, and developing country terms of trade improve. ("labor using" standards means that they are expected to contract world labor supply). As Brown puts it, "developing countries, as a group, have an incentive to *overprotect* labor"[38].

In contrast, in this model labor-scarce rich countries will tend to set unduly low standards, not for race to the bottom reasons, but to improve their own terms of trade. With both sets of countries potentially mis-setting their standards, and with the terms of

---

[35] A practical question in all this is whether the market access consequences of a labor or environmental standard can be measured. Unlike tariffs that are stated in quantitative terms, standards do not easily translate into quantitative measures of market access. But unless they can be measured there is a serious potential for endless squabbling. Recall for example the bitter argument between the United States and the EC over the loss of U.S. market access in agriculture when Spain and Portugal joined the EC and its Common Agriculture Policy. More recently, determining compensation due to the EC as a result of U.S. export subsidies under its Foreign Sales Corporation tax scheme was in dispute. In the end the WTO authorized the EC to impose punitive duties of $4 billion on U.S. exports, although the United States. argued for a $1 billion cap.

[36] Drusilla Brown, Alan Deardorff, and Robert Stern, *International Labor Standards: A Theoretical Analysis*, in FAIR TRADE AND HARMONIZATION PREREQUISITES FOR FREE TRADE?, (Jagdish Bhagwati and Rober Hudec eds. 1996).

[37] Brown, *supra* note 16.

[38] *Id.*, at 102. Whether higher labor standards are labor using or labor saving is not settled. For the most part Maskus, *supra* note 17, and Martin and Maskus, *supra* note 25, view GILS as reducing labor supply, and higher standards as increasing supply. Ingo Walter, *International Trade and Resource Diversion: The Case of Environmental Management*, 110 WELTWIRTSHCAFTLICHES ARCHIVE 482–93 (1974) was the first to examine the factor intensity of environmental regulations and their implications for trade.

trade effects canceling at the global level, some coordination of labor standards would improve world welfare.[39]

D. Can the WTO Protect Child Labor?

The elimination of abusive child labor practices occupies a central place in efforts to extend WTO's scope to labor conditions. What does theory say? By and large theory suggest that the use of coercive trade measures to improve the lot of child labor will not work, and may cause it to worsen. This is not surprising. At a general level the theory of domestic distortions[40] shows that the use of trade measures to solve what are essentially domestic distortions is problematic. At a more specific level one reason is that a tariff on exports produced with child labor reduces price and output in that sector of the poor country, reducing the equilibrium child wage and displacing some child workers to informal sector activities where conditions may be even worse. If the exporting country responds to the threat of a tariff by, say, enforcing a minimum age limit, and the child labor market is initially competitive, wages may rise but some displacement of children to an unregulated informal sector would still result.[41] If the child labor market were monopsonistic the restriction would tend to depress an already exploitative child wage, again with some displacement to an unregulated informal sector.[42]

A second problem stems from the different preferences for child labor in rich and poor countries.[43] Suppose the existence of child labor in poor countries has a negative effect on utility functions in rich countries, a sort of negative international externality or spillover. Suppose the rich country imposes a tariff on the import of products made with child labor sufficient to bring employment of children to a level it, the rich country, considers acceptable. In addition to the normal inefficiencies of a tariff, this would depress the wage of the remaining child workers. In effect they would bear part of the burden of the tariff and part of the cost of satisfying rich country preferences, an inequitable outcome. A lump sum transfer targeted to lowering the cost of education, an alternative for child workers, or for increasing adult incomes, would probably be more efficient at reducing child labor.

Some of the difficulties with policies to reduce child labor are expounded in models presented by Basu and Van.[44] Their analysis accommodates multiple equilibria in the labor market—one equilibrium in which both children and adults work, and one in which adult wages are sufficiently high that children do not work. Starting from the "bad" equilibrium in which children work, a ban on child labor could push adult wages up and bump the economy to a new equilibrium in which only adults work (and the ban becomes redundant). But if the increase in adult wage is insufficiently large, the ban reduces household welfare and the new equilibrium is not attained. Poor families are worse off.

[39] John Krutilla, *Environmental Regulation in an Open Economy*, 20 JOURNAL OF ENVIRONMENTAL ECONOMICS AND MANAGEMENT 127–42 (1991) investigates a parallel situation in which optimal environmental standards interact with terms of trade tariffs.
[40] Max W. Corden, TRADE POLICY AND ECONOMIC WELFARE (1997).
[41] This is an example of the theory of the second best, which states that correcting one distortion while leaving others uncorrected (i.e., conditions in the informal labor market) may or may not improve welfare.
[42] In a more sophisticated version the supply of child labor would be made a negative function of adult wages. Children displaced from an export sector would tend to depress adult wages, shifting out the supply of child labor unless children were withdrawn from the labor market entirely.
[43] Maskus, *supra* note 17.
[44] Kaushik Basu and Pham Hoang Van, *The Economics of Child Labor*, 88(3) AMERICAN ECONOMIC REVIEW 412 (1998).

This conclusion might be modified if, as a result of the ban, school enrollments increase and over time human capital increases. But in practice the result might be unemployed children without funds for school fees or illegal employment of children. Basu and Van also consider a partial ban on child labor, recognizing that governments are often unable to control labor market conditions in all sectors. The results depend on the relative size of the sector in which child labor is banned. If it is relatively small the policy is a failure, and child labor conditions and household welfare falls[45]. If the sector is large the economy may again be bumped up to the new equilibrium in which only adults work. Although Basu and Van do not explicitly model trade sanctions in response to child labor exports the analysis of bans is indirectly useful for those situations in which the *threat* of sanctions results in a partial or full ban on child labor.[46]

Still, as in many second-best situations, theoretical conclusions are sensitive to modeling assumptions. It is possible for example to use a specific factors-type model, with child labor specific to the export sector. In such a model a tariff imposed on the export good would lower export price and by lowering returns to child labor, change the relative returns to child labor vs. continued education in favor of schooling, thereby reducing child participation in the labor market. With these somewhat ambiguous theoretical conclusions it is useful to seek empirical studies relating child labor and international product prices. Edmonds and Pavcnik in their study of Vietnam use variations among regions and over time in the price of rice, a major export crop, and data drawn from household surveys on child labor.[47] In the period considered, 1993–98, the average real price of rice rose 29 percent, in part due to phasing out an earlier rice export quota scheme. They find that a thirty percent increase in rice prices is associated with a ten percentage point decrease in the child labor force participation rate, with the largest decrease for girls of secondary school age. Presumably higher rural incomes reduced the supply of child labor. Interestingly, the much smaller group of child workers living in urban households showed an increase in child labor participation rates. The explanation may be that as consumers, not producers, of rice, the price increase reduced urban household incomes, pushing more children into the workforce. This study did not directly address child labor in factories, but in Vietnam, as in many poor countries, child labor is concentrated in the agricultural sector (for some reason factory sweatshops have captured more attention in the North than farm sweatshops). The tentative conclusion is that if trade restrictions lowering Vietnam's rice export price had been in effect, some or all of the reduction in child labor in the rural sector would not have occurred. In a more positive vein, we may conclude that improved market access for developing country agricultural exports may be a significant force for reducing child labor in poor countries. If so the appropriate role for the WTO would be to strive for trade liberalization and to resist requests for inclusion of "fair" labor standards.

We summarize the answers to the four questions posed in this section as follows. First, many models suggest a conflict between the objective of reducing alleged unfair competition and the humanitarian objective of improving labor conditions in poor

---

[45] This may be important. A 1994 U.S. Department of Labor study estimated that only five percent or fewer of child workers were employed in export industries in manufacturing or mining.

[46] In commenting on this analysis Kenneth Swinnerton and Carol Ann Rogers, *The Economics of Child Labor: Comment*, 89(5) AMERICAN ECONOMIC REVIEW 1382 (1999), show that inequality in income distribution lies behind the multiple equilibria in the Basu-Van analysis, and that under certain conditions redistribution of income and wealth could eliminate child labor.

[47] Eric Edmonds and Nina Pavcnik, *Does Globalization Increase Child Labor? Evidence from Vietnam*, NBER WORKING PAPER 8760 (2002).

countries. Second, the empirical evidence that weak core labor standards improve a country's competitive position is itself weak. Furthermore, if weak standards do not confer a competitive advantage, the race to the bottom argument loses force, and it is unlikely that weak standards *per se* have caused wage suppression in the United States and other industrial countries (note—this does not absolve trade with low wage countries, only GILS). Third, while not conclusive, theory and empirical evidence tends to argue against using or threatening restrictive trade measures to reduce child labor.

It may be useful to close this part with a few broader theoretical considerations. First, it is well established that care for free trade does not require harmonization of labor standards affecting production costs. Indeed if standards accurately reflect social and economic status, harmonization of standards decreases world welfare.[48] Diversity of standards in itself is not a justification for coercive policy. Second the powerful theory of domestic distortions concludes that if distortions exist, the first best policy is directed toward the distortion itself.[49] Using trade tools to correct domestic labor market failures in developing countries is clearly second best policy. Third, international coercion can create a "forced rider" situation in which the benefits of a policy are enjoyed by one group of countries and the costs by another. In the labor standards context this implies that if sensitivities in the North requires assurance that the products they consume are produced under "fair" labor conditions, they should be prepared to compensate countries in the South for the costs of this policy. Fourth, the argument that public support for liberal trade can be shored up by assurances of fair labor standards is suspect. While support in the North may strengthen, support in the South may weaken as they perceive bullying through coercive trade measures.

E. Other More Practical Considerations

Should there be agreement to include labor standards in the WTO a number of practical questions arise. We discuss three very briefly. The first question is where in the WTO/GATT structure should provisions concerning labor standards be lodged. Three candidates are Article XVI dealing with subsidies and the related Agreement on Subsidies and Countervailing Measures; Article XX, the general exceptions clause; and Article XXIII. The logic of the subsidy article is that failure to maintain adequate labor standards can be viewed as an implicit subsidy creating unfair trade conditions. The logic of using Article XX is that it already provides blanket authority to restrict or ban products made by prison labor, and certain labor standards, at least, for example a prohibition on bonded labor or other forms of forced labor, would be a relatively minor extension. On closer inspection neither is attractive.[50] The principal objection is that both Articles XVI and XX allow countries to unilaterally restrict trade based on their own assessment. While it is true that the target country could lodge a complaint with the WTO and, if found valid, could retaliate, the serious potential for abuse and covert protection inherent in labor standards suggest that unilateral initiation of trade restrictions is not desirable. This

[48] Jagdish Bhagwati, *The Demands to Reduce Domestic Diversity among Trading Nations*, FAIR TRADE AND HARMONIZATION PREREQUISITES FOR FREE TRADE (Jagdish Bhagwati and Robert Hudec eds. 1996).
[49] Corden, *supra* note 40.
[50] Article XX (h) contains an exception for normal GATT obligations for certain international commodity agreements. While it may be useful to also make exceptions for international environmental agreements with trade measures, it seems inappropriate for labor standards, as the latter would not rest on explicit trade measures incorporated in a freestanding international agreement.

leaves Article XXIII, the nullification and impairment provision, which at least has the virtue of providing multilateral consideration of violations. If adherence to certain labor standards were made a WTO obligation, and if Article XXIII were invoked, the allegation of violation would be subject to more impartial multilateral scrutiny. As an alternative to expanding one of these three articles, a new multinational accord might be negotiated as was done for intellectual property protection in the TRIPS agreement.

A second question is what in fact constitutes a GILS? Take freedom of association and right to collective bargaining for example. Countries differ in the level at which labor is organized—the firm, the industry and nationally. Are all equally acceptable? Systems also differ with respect to right to work versus closed shop laws. Are both acceptable? Are "lockout" and replacement of striking workers acceptable practices? Most countries forbid strikes in critical or sensitive sectors but the limitations are by no means uniform. At what point does a restriction on strikes in particular sectors move from the acceptable to the unacceptable category? A simple listing of these variations in the right to association and collective bargaining reveals that practice can vary widely, and that international uniformity in a single standard may not be feasible. While it may be possible to identify a few countries that expressly prohibit *any* type of worker association or *any* effort at collective bargaining, the more common situation is likely to involve a disagreement over how a standard is being implemented. Deciding such cases will be problematic.

A third practical question, referred to earlier, will be devising a trade response that is proportional to the subsidy implicit in the violation of the standard. This is an important point. The GATT has never been a coercive system. If a country violates a GATT provision, say a subsidy or through dumping, or by increasing a bound tariff, members may if they wish retaliate by withdrawing prior trade concessions, assuming that the offending country does not provide compensation in the form of tariff concessions on other products. But the retaliation is limited to the amount by which the monetary value of their trade rights were nullified or impaired.[51] As Hudec points out, retaliation in GATT has traditionally been employed to maintain a balance of reciprocity and not to coerce change in trade partners' economic systems.[52] Adherence to this sensible practice would appear to limit the effectiveness of labor standards in the WTO to accomplish sweeping changes in labor practices. Punitive trade sanctions would be a novel and potentially damaging change in GATT practice.

V. Conclusions

The case for including labor standards in WTO obligations is weak. When viewed in the light of theory, empirical evidence, and practical difficulties the most frequently cited arguments for inclusion lose considerable force. At the most fundamental level there is a confusion of purpose as between protecting against "unfair" competition and improving labor conditions in poor countries. Moreover, the potential for subverting labor standards to protectionist purposes in industrial countries, and the real possibility of harming workers in poor countries, argue for caution. Even if the use of trade sanctions were

---

[51] Countries are of course free to ban the import of products whose imports threaten their domestic healthy and safety without calculating the trade value, but this is irrelevant to the labor standards question.
[52] Robert Hudec, *GATT Legal Restraints on the Use of Trade Measures against Foreign Environmental Practices*, in FAIR TRADE AND HARMONIZATION PREREQUISITES FOR FREE TRADE (Jagdish Bhagwati and Robert Hudec eds. 1996).

rare, labor standards could create considerable mischief through harassment of trade. Nevertheless the long history of attempts to link trade and labor standards suggests the issue will not soon disappear. If left unaddressed it will fester and corrode support for a liberal trade system.

Fortunately there are alternatives to trade sanctions enforced through the WTO. These include strengthening the ILO's monitoring and technical assistance programs, expansion of voluntary commitments not to derogate from domestic labor standards for competitiveness purposes (as in NAFTA), a more prominent mechanism to shine light on alleged violations, and carrots for improved performance in the form of trade incentives as are found in the U.S and EU GSP schemes and in the CBI. Private sector initiatives can also help. Labeling and certification schemes, in which consumers with adequate information can demonstrate their humanitarian concerns in the marketplace, and industry level codes of conduct with regard to their overseas operations and those of their suppliers and subcontractors, such as the 1998 Apparel Industry Initiative in the United States, are examples. In the long run of course rapid economic growth in poor countries offers the best prospect for curbing abusive labor practices.

BIBLIOGRAPHY

Aggarwal, Mita. "International Trade, Labor Standards, and Labor Market Conditions: an Evaluation of Linkages" Washington D.C.; US International Trade Commission, Working Paper 95-06-C (1995)

Basu, Kaushik and Pham Hoang Van. "The Economics of Child Labor" *88(3) American Economic Review 412* (1998)

Bhagwati, Jagdish. "The Demands to Reduce Domestic Diversity among trading Nations" in Jagdish Bhagwati and Roben Hudec (eds) *Fair Trade and Harmonization Prerequisites for Free Trade?* Vol. 1, Cambridge Mass, MIT Press (1996)

Bolle, Mary Jane. "NAFTA Labor Side Agreement: :Lessons for the Worker Rights Fast Track Debates" Washington D.C., Congressional Research Report 97–861 (2001)

Breton, Paul and Jacques Pelkmans. *Global Trade and European Workers* 1998. London: MacMillan Press.

Brown, Drusilla. "Labor Standards: Where Do They Belong on the International Trade Agenda?" 15(3) *Journal of Economic Perspectives* 89 (2001)

Brown, Drusilla, Alan Deardorff, Robert Stern. "International Labor Standards: A Theoretical Analysis" in Jagdish Bhagwati and Rober Hudec (eds) *Fair Trade and Harmonization Prerequisites for Free Trade?* Vol 1, Cambridege Mass, MIT Press (1996)

Burtless, Gary. "Workers Rights" 19(4) *Brookings Review* 10 (2001)

Charnovitz, Steve. "The Influence of International Labor Standards on the World Trading Regime" 126 *International Labor Review* 565 (1987)

Corden, W. Max and Neil Vosden. "Paved with Good Intentions: Social Dumping and Raising Labour Standards in Developing Countries" in Zdenek Drabek (ed) *Globalization under Threat* Cheltenham UK; Edward Elgar (2000)

Corden, W. Max. *Trade Policy and Economic Welfare* 2nd ed., London Oxford University Press (1997)

Diebold, William. *The End of the ITO* Princeton Essays in the International Finance No.16 (1952)

Edmonds, Eric and Nina Pavcnik. "Does Globlization Increase Child Labor? Evidence from Vietnam" NBER Working Paper 8760 (2002)

Elliot, Kimberly Ann. "Fin(d)ing Our Way on Trade and Labor Standards?" Washington D.C.; Institute for International Economics, International Economics Policy Briefs (2001)

Feenstra, Robert. (ed.) *The Impact of International Trade on Wages* Chicago: University of Chicago Press (2000)

Hudec, Robert. "GATT Legal Restraints on the Use of Trade Measures against Foreign Environmental Practices" in Jagdish Bhagwati and Rober Hudec (eds) *Fair Trade and Harmonization
Prerequisites for Free Trade?* Vol 2, Cambridge Mass, MIT Press (2006)

Kurtilla, John. "Environmental Regulation in an Open Economy" 20 *Journal of Environmental
Economics and Management*, 127 (1991)

Langille, Brian Alexander. "General Reflections on the Relationships of Trade and Labor" in
Jagdish Bhagwati and Rober Hudec (eds) *Fair Trade and Harmonization Prerequisites for
Free Trade?* Vol 2, Cambridge Mass, MIT Press (1996)

Leary, Virginia. "Workers rights and International Trade: The Socal Caluse" in in Jagdish Bhagwati
and Rober Hudec (eds) *Fair Trade and Harmonization Prerequisites for Free Trade?* Vol 2,
Cambridge Mass, MIT Press (1996)

Martin, Will and Keith Maskus. "Core Labor Standars and Competitiveness: Implications for
Global Theory", 9 (2) *Review of International Economics* 317 (2001)

Maskus, Keith. "Should Core Labor Standards be Imposed Through International Trade Policy?"
Washington D.C.; World Bank Policy Research Working Paper 1817 (1997)

Moran, Theodore. *Beyond Sweatshops: Foreign Direct Investment and Globalization in Developing Countries.* Washington D.C.: Brookings Institution (2002)

Morici, Peter and Evan Schulz. "Labor Standards in the Global Trading System" Washington
D.C.: Economic Strategy Institute (2001)

Organization for Economic Cooperation and Development. *Trade, Employment, and Labor Standards: A Study of Core Workers' Rights and International Trade*, Paris, OECD (1996)

Organization for Economic Cooperation and Development. *International Trade and Core Labor
Standards* Paris: OECD (2000)

Palmer, Karen, Wallace Oates, Paul Portney. "Tightening Environmental Standards: The Benefit-
Cost or the No-Cost Paradigm?" 9 (4) *Journal of Economic Perspectives* 114 (1995)

Pearson, Charles. *U.S. Trade Policy: A Work in Progress* (2003)

Porter, Michael and Claas Van der Linde. "Toward a New Conception of the Environment—
Competitiveness Relationship, 9 (4) *Journal of Economic Perspectives* 97 (1995)

Swinnerton, Kenneth and Carol Ann Rogers. "The Economics of Child Labor: Comment" 89 (5)
American Economic Review 1382 (1999)

U.S. Department of Labor. *The Use of Child Labor in U.S. Manufactured and Mixed Imports* Vol. 1
of *By the Sweat and Toil of Children* Washington D.C.: U.S. Department of Labor (1994)

Walter, Ingo. "International Trade and Resource Diversion: The Case of Environmental Management" 110 *Weltwirtshcaftliches Archive* 482 (1974)

CHAPTER 45

SERVICES: THE CASE OF POSTAL VERSUS EXPRESS DELIVERY SERVICES

Michael G. Plummer*

What is important about these [services] negotiations ... is that they offer vast potential for raising living standards globally but especially in developing countries, many of which stand to benefit the most from further opening of services markets. In fact, 25 developing countries earn more than half of their total export income from services.
Mike Moore, WTO Press Release, 28 June 2002 (www.wto.org).

TABLE OF CONTENTS

* Johns Hopkins University SAIS-Bologna.

I. Introduction

In developed countries, services continue to constitute by far the largest share of national economies. For example, in the EU and the United States, approximately seventy and eighty percent, respectively, of the economy falls under the general rubric of services. Services have also increased in importance in trade: in the year 2000, the share of services in total exports came to approximately 28 percent in the United States and 22 percent in the EU, with an average for the entire OECD coming to about 19 percent.[1]

The same trend is observable in developing countries. During the development process, it is typical that: (1) agriculture falls as a percentage of GDP; (2) manufacturing first rises and then falls as the economy matures; but (3) services continue to grow throughout the development process. As a percentage of trade, services exports of developing countries have risen from nine percent in 1980 (approximately half the share of developed countries) to about eighteen percent in 2000, on a par with that of the developed countries.[2]

While this process has been constant throughout history, services take on a special importance in the 21st Century. This is due to a number of factors, including: (a) consumer tastes have become increasingly sophisticated: a good share of the growth in consumer spending is in the general area of "high tech," including such services areas as computer software, internet-related services, and telecommunications innovations; (b) production processes have become more complicated, sophisticated, and international in scope, with global competition increasing substantially; and (c) inputs under the general area of "services" tend to be essential to industrial and enterprise growth and competitiveness.[3] Indeed, businesspeople, scholars, and policymakers are increasingly appreciating the strong link between the competitiveness and efficiency of the services sectors and that of the economy as a whole. The links between the two are pervasive.

Hence, it was a high priority of member-states to extend the auspices of the GATT to include services during the Uruguay Round, which led to the creation of the General Agreement on Trade in Services ("GATS"). GATS continues to take form, and issues such as market access in various commercial services will no doubt play a critical role in the Doha Trade Agenda.

Given the complicated and diverse nature of trade in services, liberalization at the global level can be more delicate and in many ways more difficult than trade in goods. Services can be high tech or low tech; inputs and/or final products; privately-provided or publicly-provided; and closely related to other areas, such as foreign direct investment ("FDI"). Trade in goods internationally tends to be almost always privately provided, with strong GATT/WTO controls on state intervention, including the technical prohibition against state subsidies and constraints in the form of state-owned enterprises having to abide by market principles (GATT Article XVII). Many services areas, however, still include government involvement, and state prerogatives in certain areas are recognized by the GATS. Moreover, trade in goods tends to be separate from FDI, though clearly there exist indirect links between trade and FDI.[4] In the area of services, however, trade in services can be intricately linked to FDI; in some sectors, trade in services is impossible *without* FDI.

---

[1] OECD, GATS: THE CASE FOR OPEN SERVICES, 20–21 (2002)

[2] OECD, *supra* note 1

[3] OECD, *supra* note 1.

[4] Trade can either cause or be caused by FDI. That is, a firm might set up a plant in country X; intra-firm trade will then show up as international trade. However, it may also be that a company might begin to establish its brand in a foreign market through exports before following up with investment in a plant. In the first case, the data would suggest that FDI causes trade; in the second case, trade "causes" (or at least precedes) FDI.

The OECD (2002) defines four "modes" of trade in services: (1) cross-border supply, in which a company exports the service from home, e.g. by fax or email; (2) consumption abroad, in which the user of the service consumes it outside his/her home country, e.g. tourism; (3) commercial presence, in which a company directly supplies the service to foreign customers (this involves establishment of an affiliate abroad and constitutes over three-fourths of all trade in services); and (4) presence of natural persons, in which the service-exporting country sends personnel abroad to supply services.

In this chapter, we will focus on the need for services liberalization in the global economy, with a focus on developing countries. Moreover, we will use the process and complications associated with the liberalization of express delivery services as a case study. This area is particularly interesting because: (a) it is an industry that has become highly international; (b) it has become an important input to a variety of emerging industries and a key ingredient in the competitiveness of firms and countries; (c) liberalization runs up against various competition policy issues, especially since it potentially affects private and public services[5]; and (d) it is exactly the type of industry where greater international access created through global agreements can produce major benefits to developed and developing countries alike.

Part II of this chapter discusses the main economic issues associated with liberalization of trade in services, and makes the case for reform especially in developing countries. Part III considers the case of express services, including the existing situation and an analysis of what the optimal approach might be. Part IV provides some concluding remarks and recommendations.

II. Services Liberalization and the Stakes for Economic Development

A series of multilateral negotiations under the auspices of the GATT/WTO have been very successful in bringing down barriers to trade in manufactured goods. Once Uruguay Round tariff cuts are fully implemented (generally by the end of 2005), the average tariff on manufactures for the United States, EU, and Japan will be approximately four percent, four percent, and two percent, respectively. While there do exist numerous "spikes" (that is, sectors in which protection continues to remain quite high), by and large trade in manufactures is fairly free in the developed country markets, with the notable exceptions of textiles, clothing and steel. Developing country tariffs are, in general, much higher than in the developed world, but a large majority of developing countries has liberalized substantially trade in manufactures over the past fifteen years. In fact, most of the benefits that would accrue to global free trade would go to developing countries, according to various computational general equilibrium models that have been used to estimate such effects.[6]

Given the political sensitivities associated with trade in agricultural goods, much less has been accomplished under the GATT/WTO framework. Indeed, agricultural trade continues to be highly distorted, and while some positive trends are in evidence (e.g., Japan's

---

[5] A excellent example of unfair competition that potentially exists in this context can be found in the March 2001 European Commission case against the German state postal service provider, Deutsche Post AG. In its ruling, the European Commission agreed that Deutsche Post AG had abused its monopoly position in letter services to cross-subsidize its business parcel services through a system of fidelity rebates and predatory pricing (see: http\\europa.eu.int\comm\competition\citizen\citizen_dominance.html). Deutsche Post was fined €24 million.

[6] See, of example, ROBERT SCOLLAY AND JOHN GILBERT, AN ASIAN TRADE BLOC? (2001).

"tariffying" its rice imports, occasional proposals by the EU Commission to liberalize EU agriculture) problems seem to be emerging elsewhere (e.g., the US Farm Bill passed in 2002, which will increase subsidies to an already heavily subsidized sector by some $170 billion over the next 10 years). In fact, agriculture has often been the most difficult sector for trade negotiations and almost undermined the Uruguay Round itself. Still, while agriculture will no doubt continue to be a difficult sector to liberalize, it is not nearly as important as the manufacturing sector and is dwarfed by the services sector in the developed world (agriculture constitutes less than three percent of GDP in the United States and five percent in the EU).

The developing world is a different story. Agriculture continues to play an important role in the economy in general and in trade in particular in the least-developed countries and in many middle-income countries. In order to be successful, the Doha Round will have to include at least some agricultural liberalization if the developing countries are going to agree to any accord. Still, as the development process unfolds, manufactures and, especially, services will become increasingly important. As noted above, services have been growing rapidly in importance and already constitute eighteen percent of developing-country exports. Some developing countries, like Turkey and India, have shares that are even greater than those of the United States and the EU.[7] According to Dee and Hanslow [8], of the $260 billion increase in global income that would be generated from global free trade, fully half would accrue because of services-related liberalization. Given the spill-over effects of greater efficiency in the services sector (from more efficient infrastructure-related services, including transport, to financial services), the health of any economy, developed or developing, is intricately linked to the development of its services sector.

Chart 1 shows growth in services trade by region and globally over the 1993–2000 period. Growth in Asia, which has been by far the most successful region in terms of economic development in the developing world, is particularly impressive, with the exception of the Asian Crisis years (when output also collapsed). In all regions, services trade has grown faster than the economy as a whole for most years.

Moreover, as can be seen from Table 1, the share of global services trade by country may not have changed much in terms of developing-developed countries (North American and the EU continue to constitute almost two-thirds of global trade in services) but the distribution between countries in the developing world has changed substantially, with the successful countries increasing their shares significantly. For example, Africa and Latin America have seen their shares generally stagnate (or fall) to approximately two percent and four percent, respectively, whereas Asia increased its share from about twelve percent to sixteen percent (excluding developed-country Japan, which actually saw its share drop). China, which achieved the highest real economic growth of major economies over this time-span, saw its share in trade in services expand the most rapidly, actually tripling over this period. It is no coincidence that China also received the most FDI in the developing world.[9]

An association between rapid real economic growth and rapid growth in services trade does not mean that the latter caused the former. Such estimation is much more

---

[7] OECD, *supra* note 1, p. 21.

[8] P. Dee and K. Hanslow, *Multilateral Liberalization of Services Trade,* CANBERRA, AUSTRALIAN PRODUCTIVITY COMMISSION (as cited in OECD, *supra* note 1)

[9] According to preliminary estimates by UNCTAD, China may have actually received more FDI in 2002 than the United States.

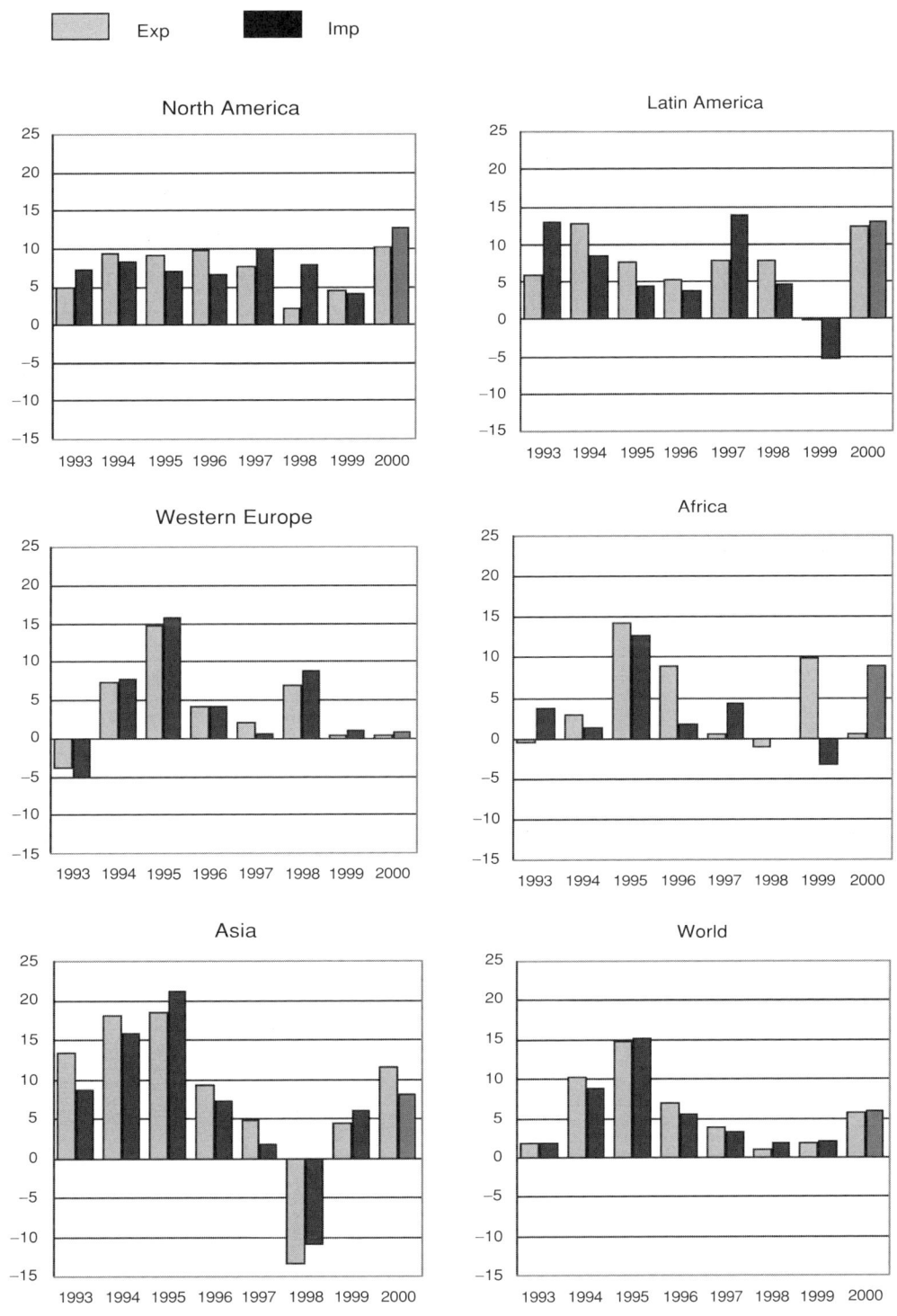

Chart 1: World trade in commercial services by selected region, 1993–00 (Annual percentage change in value)
Source: World Trade Organization, http://www.wto.org, June 2002

Table 1: World exports of services by selected region and economy, 1980–2001 (percentage)

	Share				
	1990	1995	1999	2000	2001
World	100.00	100.00	100.00	100.00	100.00
North America	19.31	18.81	20.63	21.16	20.68
Canada	2.34	2.14	2.47	2.49	2.41
United States	16.97	16.68	18.17	18.67	18.27
Latin America	3.79	3.72	3.92	4.11	4.00
Argentina	0.29	0.30	0.31	0.30	0.28
Brazil	0.47	0.50	0.50	0.61	0.61
Chile	0.23	0.27	0.27	0.26	0.27
Mexico	0.92	0.80	0.84	0.93	0.87
Western Europe	53.06	47.57	47.97	45.95	46.54
France	8.46	6.98	5.94	5.57	5.49
Germany	6.59	6.31	6.00	5.52	5.54
Italy	6.20	5.14	4.22	3.81	4.13
United Kingdom	6.87	6.43	8.16	7.92	7.53
European Union (15)	47.18	42.58	43.27	41.20	41.96
Central and Eastern Europe, the Baltic S	...	...	...	...	...
Czech Rep.	–	0.56	0.49	0.46	0.48
Hungary	0.34	0.43	0.41	0.43	0.53
Poland	0.41	0.89	0.61	0.71	0.83
Russian Fed.	–	0.89	0.66	0.66	0.70
Africa	2.37	2.14	2.24	2.12	2.10
Algeria	0.06	0.06	0.08	...	...
Egypt	0.61	0.69	0.67	0.66	0.66
Kenya	0.10	0.07	0.05	0.05	...
Morocco	0.24	0.17	0.20	0.20	...
Nigeria	0.12	0.05	0.07	...	...
South Africa	0.42	0.37	0.36	0.34	0.33
Tunisia	0.20	0.20	0.20	0.18	0.19
Middle East	...	...	...	...	...
Israel	0.58	0.65	0.79	0.98	0.78
Saudi Arabia	0.39	0.29	0.39	0.33	...
Asia	16.79	22.00	19.75	20.84	20.69
Australia	1.26	1.32	1.24	1.23	1.10
China	0.73	1.55	1.90	2.07	2.15
Hong Kong, China	2.31	2.88	2.70	2.89	2.99
India	0.59	0.57	1.02	1.21	1.39
Indonesia	0.32	0.45	0.32	0.35	...
Japan	5.28	5.37	4.38	4.69	4.40
Korea, Rep. of	1.17	1.86	1.87	1.98	1.97
Malaysia	0.48	0.96	0.86	0.93	0.95
New Zealand	0.31	0.37	0.31	0.29	0.27
Philippines	0.37	0.78	0.35	0.28	0.23
Singapore	1.62	2.48	1.74	1.85	1.83
Taipei, Chinese	0.89	1.25	1.25	1.39	1.45
Thailand	0.80	1.23	1.06	0.95	0.89

Source: World Trade Organization, http\\:www.wto.org, June 2002

complicated; indeed, there exists a chicken-and-egg simultaneity problem here. However, regardless of which causes which, the development of the services sector is clearly an important part of the development process. As noted by the OECD, there is a very close relationship between the share of services in output and *per capita* GDP: the correlation coefficient is 0.80 (where 1.0 would imply a perfect correlation).[10]

Beginning in the 1950s and continuing arguably through the 1970s, there was a strong debate in economics over the usefulness of economic liberalization in developing countries. One school embraced what came to be known as the "import substitution" model, which argued that developing countries would best develop on their own rather than integrating with the developed world; otherwise, they would be marginalized, exploited, and condemned to perpetual economic under-development. Another school, known as "export promotion," argued that economic liberalization, both domestically and in terms of external commercial policies, was not only desirable but actually necessary if countries are to develop.

These schools of thought are developed more thoroughly in Chapter 37 of this book. Suffice it to note here that development experience—as well as the sheer power of the economic logic behind the export-promotion model—essentially settled the debate in the 1980s: countries that were outward-looking, particularly in Asia, did far better than countries espousing an import-substitution strategy. Indeed, in the 1980s, Latin America, which for most of the decade remained fairly closed, actually experienced a "lost decade," in which economic growth was stagnant, while outward-looking Asia grew by leaps and bounds. Some scepticism re-emerged during the Asian Crisis of 1997–1999, but the origins of the crisis were arguably not found in an overly-outward orientation, but rather a range of other issues.[11] In fact, it is possible to argue that countries most affected by the crisis were not liberal enough. For example, there was a strong negative relationship between the openness of the financial-services sector in Asian economies to competition from foreign financial companies and the severity of the financial crisis (Singapore, for example, which was generally quite open to foreign banks, was not severely affected by the financial crisis, despite being closely integrated with heavily-affected economies in Southeast Asia). The response of the Asian economies to these problems has generally been to speed-up their economic liberalization and strengthen their outward-oriented policies, while at the same time making sure that the legal, infrastructural, and corporate-governance context is appropriate. The heavily-affected Asian economies experienced a strong rebound in 1999–2000 and, while 2001 saw a slowdown due to sluggish demand in the developed world, economic growth in 2002 was fairly strong and forecasts for 2003 continue to be bright, though somewhat dimmed due to the effects of the war in Iraq and the SARS outbreak.

Today, there exists an anti-liberalization campaign that, rather than finding its roots in an economic model like import-substitution, ostensibly endeavors merely to critique economic integration. This approach, sometimes referred to as the "No Global" movement,

---

[10] OECD, *supra* note 1.

[11] While the sources of the Asian Crisis are many and complicated (*see, for example*, various publications of the Asian Development Bank at www.adb.org) they include: premature liberalization of financial markets (without sufficient monitoring mechanisms), which led to abuse; corporate governance problems; overly-rigid commitments to fixed exchange rates; "double mismatches" in terms of maturity and denomination of debt (that is, banks increasingly financed activities by borrowing short-term in foreign currency while having long-term domestic loans in home.currency); and excessive current account deficits financed increasingly by foot-loose capital rather than FDI. *See also,* Chapter 71 of this book, discussing Indonesia's experience with the GATT and the WTO, and analysing the reasons for its financial problems in the 1990s.

does not seriously challenge the export-promotion model intellectually, but has criticized the results of liberalization (often out of context) and raised a number of issues that have been embraced by certain policymakers (in developed countries) to further their own political ambitions. The OECD does an excellent job of exposing many of the shortcomings of this approach.[12] But, in reality, the no-global *zeitgeist* has not really affected the liberalization trend in developing countries. The failure, for example, to launch a new round of trade negotiations at Seattle in December 1999 was not due to anti-capitalism demonstrations but, rather ironically, to the resistance on the part of *developing* countries to adopt many of the issues that they seem to be advocating, for example, in areas such as labor-organization and environmental protection.

The case for economic reform and liberalization is just too strong. Countries that have sustained economic liberalization have prospered; the ones that have not prospered generally do not have outward-oriented policies to blame but rather other economic-contextual problems, such as macroeconomic instability (e.g., Latin America) or political instability (e.g., Africa). It is hard to promote growth—let alone long-term development—in an atmosphere of hyper-inflation or civil war. China has used economic reform to transform the world's most populous country from a least-developed, autarkic economy into an outward-oriented economic powerhouse; Vietnam's reforms over the past fifteen years have cut poverty rates from one-half to one-fifth of the population.

However, the process of economic liberalization in developing countries has generally left the services sector for last. Many developing countries have been reluctant to liberalize the services area for a variety of reasons, mostly political in nature. But there is a strong sense among developing countries that services can be neglected no longer, both because of the strong spill-over effects that services have on the entire economy and the need to bring in FDI. Recognizing this, the Association of Southeast Asian Nations ("ASEAN") has agreed to a regional services framework compatible with the GATS. Vietnam, in its recent bilateral trade agreement with the United States (October 2001), has already generally committed itself to various WTO conventions, including GATS and other services-related areas, even though its services sector has remained to date almost completely closed. MERCOSUR has even proposed a plan (as noted below) for express delivery services under the WTO/GATS. The economic models focusing on economic liberalization cited above lend further credence to the potential benefits of future liberalization of the services sector in developing countries.

III. The Case for Separating Postal from Express Delivery Services in GATS

Express delivery services constitute an interesting case study in service-sector liberalization. Their importance in the day-to-day activities of firms has increased substantially over the past fifteen years, as evidenced by rapid growth in the industry. Indeed, express delivery services have now become an essential "infrastructure" to doing business for many companies, as well as being an increasingly important service for individuals. Moreover, express delivery services are particularly necessary for multinationals and, hence, easy access to markets by express delivery providers is important in attracting FDI inflows, particularly in developing countries. These services are critical in the least-developed countries and other developing countries with an under-developed infrastructure. As express delivery services operate in a very different way—and are geared to

---

[12] OECD, GATS: THE CASE FOR OPEN SERVICES MARKETS (2002).

different markets—than traditional postal services, it is important to stress their distinct nature and, indeed, their complementarity.

A. The General Problem

This is where the difficulty lies: express delivery services are often considered a competitor to postal-service providers, which are almost invariably state-owned. Hence, liberalization in this area has been tricky, constrained by competing interests from both developed and developing countries and based on a misunderstanding of the market in which basic postal services are confused with express delivery services (we argue below that they are related but distinct). It will be argued in this chapter that existing realities emphasize the need to separate express delivery services from postal activities, as this would be in the interest of all parties involved. Otherwise, successful liberalization at the GATS in this area will likely be impossible in the short- to medium-term and all countries will miss an important opportunity to improve efficiency and customer satisfaction, while at the same time preserving the basic domain of national postal services and, consequently, that of their employees.

In fact, under the GATS framework member states have tended to reserve the right to organize postal services as they see fit. However, the motivations for liberalizing express delivery services internationally are independent of the fundamental interests of the postal services sector, at least as defined under Article I(3)(c) of the GATS. Indeed, liberalization of express delivery services could actually be beneficial to national postal services; a clear separation will help the incumbent in fulfilling its universal services obligations (discussed below). Also, it would reassure postal users, who could (and should) be concerned that postal-service providers might lose their focus and efficiency in providing basic postal services. In addition, separation would reinsure postal-service employees that they will not be threatened by liberalization of express delivery services.

Thus, express delivery services need to be thoroughly differentiated from traditional postal services, both because of the clear substantive differences between the two and the defined purview of GATS. Failure to do so will lead to mixing apples and oranges to the detriment of member states, be they developed or developing countries. It could also thwart progress in Doha Agenda negotiations.

B. Current Classifications

Express delivery services are currently classified by the WTO Services Classification List (W/120), under both "postal" and "courier" services. The only distinction between postal and courier services is that the former refer to public-sector offered services, whereas the latter are private. Hence, it has to do with ownership rather than product, which is unusual in the area of international trade. This type of classification leads to a great deal of confusion of the issues, as well as complications regarding competition policy. In particular, when reforms are proposed under the current framework, the potential effects not only relate to businesses and consumers, as is usual within any economic reform framework under the WTO, but also the public sector. This renders such liberalization much more controversial, particularly in developing countries, as it brings into the formula sensitive and essential public services. Postal services are generally associated with the idea of Universal Services Obligations ("USO") and are viewed as "an element of a core of services that contribute to the cohesion and well being" of nations.[13] The concept of USO, therefore, should not be construed to include express delivery services, as it does not fit into the definition.

A typical problem in this regard is found in the EU. The European Commission has suggested that an ownership-based definition be replaced by an activity-based classification, a refinement that would help clarify issues. This move reflects the current situation in the market whereby formerly state-owned postal operators have been transformed into multi-service, privately-owned groups. These organisations offer numerous services, ranging from basic mail services to express delivery, logistics-related, and even financial services. At the same time these entities might be the universal postal service provider. A clear distinction between postal services and express services would not result in an advantage for private express companies, given the fact that the classification would no longer be ownership-based but rather activity-based. Express services provided by former national postal operators could benefit equally from such a distinction.

The EU had originally intended to complete liberalization of mail services in 2007 but now the Commission has only committed itself to study the process in 2006 to consider whether full liberalization might be feasible by 2009, or if an additional step will be necessary.[14] In any case, monopolies will continue to dominate the sector. The Commission acknowledges that the 1997 Postal Directive has not provided much, if any, competition in the market.[15] From a practical point of view, the confusion of postal services with express delivery services has led to a great deal of apprehension and hesitation among the EU's postal services employees, who number approximately 1.7 million.[16] This confusion is exacerbated by the inclusion of express delivery and postal services under one heading, in particular for the developing countries.

The US Postal Service is an independent government organization that essentially has a monopoly on delivery of letters and other activities. In the United States, like other countries, the postal service area is dominated by domestic issues rather than international ones. Hence, in the United States as well, it is important that USO services be separated from the new express-delivery market, that is, there is a clear need to separate the domestic (USO-related postal services) from the international (express delivery services in terms of international trade). Otherwise, if liberalization is thought to impinge upon USO services—and, therefore, sovereign prerogative protected by the WTO/GATS—no liberalization will take place.

But, while the United States and EU have much at stake, failure to separate clearly USO-related from express-delivery services would be even more to the disadvantage of developing countries. This is because, as noted above, infrastructure in developing countries tends to be less reliable and efficient; if a country wishes to attract FDI—and a strong majority of developing countries has placed a high priority on attracting FDI, due to its inherent benefits to the domestic economy—express delivery services are particularly important, as they reduce considerably intra-firm transaction costs in multinational corporations. By allowing for rapid and reliable means of communication and exchange both within multinational corporations and between these firms and their suppliers, express delivery services lower the costs associated with a presence in a foreign country

---

[13] Asian Development and the OECD, *Liberalization and Competition in the Service Sector: Experiences from Europe and Asia,* EIGHTH INTERNATIONAL FORUM ON ASIAN PERSPECTIVES 47 (June 2002)

[14] *Id.*

[15] *Id.*

[16] ADB/OECD, *supra* note 10

and raise the prospects for establishing and expanding foreign-affiliate operations. In other words, express delivery services have become part of the essential infrastructure of globalization; countries that fail to recognize this could be left behind. Thus, in many ways, inclusion of express delivery services liberalization as a separate item from postal services under the Doha Trade Agenda will be more important to developing than to developed countries.

Barriers affecting the express-courier services include (in no particular order)[17]:

1. Limitations on ownership, control and management;
2. Restrictions on geographic scope of operations;
3. Denial or national treatment access to essential infrastructure;
4. Lack of transparency with respect to rules and regulations;
5. Discrimination according to size, location of terminals, etc.;
6. Lack of consumer choice with respect to delivery services; and
7. Administrative delays.
8. Arbitrary levies and license fees
9. Abuse of dominant position by the incumbent operator
10. State aid provided to express activities

Hence, the express-services industry is limited by a number of non-tariff as well as tariff barriers, making it an especially attractive candidate for trade facilitation and liberalization measures under the WTO/GATS.

C. Existing Positions Regarding Liberalization

As the WTO begins its preparations for the Doha Trade Agenda, express delivery services will likely play a greater role than they ever have in the past. The industry has been growing rapidly and has become very international, even without GATS-related liberalization helping to foster it. It has grown because the world has been much more internationalized and, as noted above, express services are an important "lubricant" to this process. Many barriers to trade, such as postal taxes, licensing schemes, preferential customs treatment, and the like, need to come down in order to facilitate the industry's growth and enhance efficiency.

The inclusion of services will be important to developing countries, since: (a) services are becoming more important in most developing economies; (b) there is a growing recognition in developing countries of the key role that services play in the globalization process, that is, in making them part of the global production chain; and (c) the other two sectors that are high priorities for developing countries in the next round, textiles and agriculture, will likely make little progress.[18] Services liberalization may be one area in which some credence would be given to the sobriquet "Development Round".

While financial services and telecommunications are among the services areas that will receive the most attention in the Doha negotiations, postal/courier services, and express-delivery services in particular, will be an important area of negotiation with a

---

[17] Part of this list is found in: Ascher, Bernard, *Postal Services and Express Delivery in Trade Negotiations*, paper prepared for the World Mail and Express Americas Conference, Orlando, Florida, December 10, 2001
[18] Recent developments suggest some cause for optimism, however. As of early 2003, the United States began to demonstrate a surprising willingness to liberalize its textile sector, as well as fresh proposals to cut agricultural subsidies. While the latter proposals have been met with cool responses, especially by the EU and Japan, it appears as though the United States is increasingly dedicated to a effective, comprehensive Doha Round, which is essential for ultimate success.

great deal of potential if handled properly. At present, the situation does not lend itself to too much optimism, as a number of proposals that have been tabled thus far are conservative and will probably do little—if anything—to create a more global, barrier-free market for express delivery services. This is unfortunate, especially given the stakes to developing countries noted above. However, it is useful to evaluate existing proposals from an economic perspective to gauge which approaches offer the most potential. It is hoped that such analysis will give some light as to which direction the Doha negotiations should take; it is useful to consider what is the best-practice approach, whether or not WTO member-states decide to take advantage of it.

Thus far, there have been a number of proposals tabled in the general area of postal and courier services, made by developing (MERCOSUR, Bolivia, and Hong Kong) and developed (EU, US, New Zealand) economies. One approach[19] involves eliminating a distinction between postal services and courier services (under W/120) and substitute for them an individual heading titled, "services relating to the handling of postal items," having eight sub-items. One of these sub-items is express delivery services and its definition is relegated to a footnote. It appears to invite member-states to make specific recommendations for all eight sub-items, including express-delivery services.

Another approach defines express delivery services specifically as being separate from courier and postal services and having a single heading.[20] Under this approach, then, member-states would be able to propose liberalization of express delivery services directly. This heading could then become part of a broader range of transportation activities in the globalization of the supply-chain management.

D. Conclusions

In a nutshell, the key difference between the two approaches discussed above is that this latter approach allows negotiators to circumvent the mixing of issues pertaining to competitive delivery services issues and those affecting USO services. Under this approach, member-states would be able to avoid implicitly and explicitly infringement upon postal services provided by the public sector, but would also allow the liberalization of express delivery services. We have argued in this chapter that such a separation is essential to reform and would be in the interest of all parties.

The stakes are actually quite high for developing countries in this area. As was noted earlier, impediments to express delivery services in developing countries are especially detrimental to international competitiveness. In particular, by their very nature, multinational corporations have generally come to rely on express delivery services as part of their intra-firm production process, and inefficient postal communication (including express delivery services) serves essentially as a "tax" on globalization—a tax that multinationals are highly reluctant to pay in such a competitive global economy. Hence, they will have an incentive to go where this input "tax" is lowest, that is, developed countries. Lack of liberalization of express delivery services, therefore, at the margin could threaten FDI flows into developing countries, at a time when FDI is acknowledged to be of great important to economic development.

---

[19] Some of these positions are spelled out in the IECC Position Paper, *The Global Express Industry and the U.S. and EC Approaches to the Classification of Express Delivery Services*, 4 July 2002.

[20] These approaches are summarized in Ascher, *supra*, note 16, and are available at the WTO homepage (www.wto.org).

IV. Summary

The salient results of this study can be summarized as follows:

- Services in general and trade in services in particular have become increasingly important to developed and developing countries, both as final products and as inputs to other productive activities.
- The relationship between services and FDI (under mode 3) is extremely strong; hence, services liberalization is important as a means of attracting FDI, which has proven to be a key catalyst in the development process.
- Developing-country stakes are, therefore, particularly high in global services liberalization, as efficient services are necessary in order to help these countries compete internationally and attract foreign firms as partners in the development process. Studies have shown that approximately half of all gains that will accrue to global free trade would stem from services liberalization. Much of the gain in this area would favor developing countries.
- GATS has taken on great significance in the 21st Century, particularly for developing countries, and successful liberalization of services under the Doha Trade Agenda will be extremely important in setting the course for the future. This is especially true since the other sectors of great interest to developing countries, namely labor-intensive goods such as textiles and clothing and agricultural products, will be very difficult to liberalize under Doha, as they have been under preceding rounds.
- We have used the express delivery services case as an example of how this process plays out in the complicated political economy of services liberalization. We have stressed that it is imperative to separate postal services from express delivery services, as they are separate sectors and reform of the latter can actually help promote the former through its complementarity and general enhancement of efficiency. It is in the interest of all parties to do this. However, if a separation is not clearly made, progress in the Doha Round is unlikely, given political realities and probable misunderstandings.

BIBLIOGRAPHY

Ascher, Bernard, *Postal Services and Express Delivery in Trade Negotiations*, paper prepared for the *World Mail and Express Americas Conference*, Orlando, Florida, December 10, 2001

Asian Development and the OECD, *Liberalization and Competition in the Service Sector: Experiences from Europe and Asia*, Eighth International Forum on Asian Perspectives, June 2002 (draft monograph).

Dee, P. and K. Hanslow, *Multilateral Liberalization of Services Trade*, Canberra, Australian Productivity Commission. (as cited in OECD 2002)

OECD, *GATS: The Case for Open Services Markets* (OECD, 2002).

Robert Scollay and John Gilbert, *An Asian Trade Bloc?* (Institute of International Economics, 2001).

B.   Regional Issues

CHAPTER 46

REGULATING REGIONAL TRADE AGREEMENTS—A LEGAL ANALYSIS

Robert E. Herzstein and Joseph P. Whitlock*

TABLE OF CONTENTS

* Messrs Herzstein and Whitlock are attorneys at the law firm of Miller & Chevalier, Washington, D.C.

I. Introduction

Recent years have witnessed a remarkable increase in the number of Free Trade Agreements ("FTAs") and Customs Unions (often collectively referred to as "Regional Trade Agreements" or "RTAs") entered into by countries that are members of the World Trade Organization ("WTO").[1] The consequences of this recent and unprecedented increase in RTAs on the world trading system are likely to be significant, although they are not yet fully understood.[2] RTAs, which by their very nature discriminate against non-signatories, are a derogation from the Most-Favored Nation ("MFN") principle, one of the fundamental guides for national government behavior the world trading system was intended to establish. While RTAs have the potential to undermine the MFN principle through discriminatory application of tariffs and regulatory barriers, they also have the potential to advance trade liberalization through duty-free trade among signatories, and by allowing the participating nations to integrate their economies more thoroughly than they could through WTO agreements.

Because RTAs violate the MFN principle, WTO legal texts (specifically, GATT Article XXIV, the Enabling Clause and GATS Article V) place restrictions on the circumstances under which a WTO member may enter an RTA. The texts permit four permutations: Customs Unions, FTAs, Agreements under the Enabling Clause, and Agreements under GATS Article V. GATT Article XXIV permits WTO members to enter Customs Unions and FTAs so long as the internal preferences are applied to "substantially all" of the trade among themselves, and certain other conditions are met. Under the so-called "Enabling Clause"[3], developing country members may enter arrangements among themselves for the mutual reduction of tariffs under less stringent conditions than those imposed by Article XXIV, and may also be accorded preferential duty reductions by developed country members. Finally, under GATS Article V, WTO members may enter Economic Integration Agreements (or "Services Agreements") eliminating barriers to trade in services, provided that "substantially all" trade among the members is covered.

This basic classification of four types of regional arrangements oversimplifies the great variety of legal innovations occurring in RTAs. There are diverse reasons for entering RTAs and a wide range of forms that RTAs can take, and there is widespread disagreement about the effects of RTAs. In light of this background, a methodical examination—not only of economic effects, but also of possible institutional and legal responses—is

---

[1] Many "regional" trade agreements are not literally "regional," because they involve countries that are located great distances from each other. Although some RTAs are determined in part by geographic proximity and various related efficiencies, such as transportation and distribution costs, other RTAs are better explained by political considerations (e.g., EC FTAs with former colonies, or the U.S.-Israel and U.S.-Jordan FTAs) or considerations of cultural affinity (e.g., the British Commonwealth Preferences of the early Twentieth Century). For a range of explanations why countries enter RTAs, *see,* Sungjoon Cho, *Breaking the Barrier between Regionalism and Multilateralism: A New Perspective on Trade Regionalism,* 42 HARV. INT'L L. J. 419, 423–26 (2000) (summarizing theories advanced by political scientists and economists to explain the growth of regionalism.)

[2] There is considerable uncertainty regarding the degree to which RTAs are harmful, benign or helpful to the world trading system. *See e.g.,* THE WORLD BANK, TRADE BLOCS (2000) (remarking on the lack of evidence that RTAs either aid or impede WTO multilateral liberalization.); *See also* Committee on Regional Trade Agreements, *Note on the Meeting of 2–3 July 1996,* WT/REG/M/2, ¶ 82 (Aug. 14, 1996) ("*Second Session of CRTA*") (in which the EC warned against "partial and pre-conceived ideas about the relationship between regionalism and the multilateral trading system.").

[3] *See Differential and More Favourable Treatment, Reciprocity and Fuller Participation of Developing Countries,* Decision of November 18 1979, BISD 265/203 (1979). One-way preferential arrangements, where developed countries give preferred treatment to imports from developing countries but not *vice versa,* are discussed in Chapter 34 of this book.

urgently needed. Economic analyses[4] and initial suggestions for reform made by commentators[5] and WTO members[6] can and should be further bolstered through a discussion of how WTO institutions can most effectively channel the RTA phenomenon to ensure the maximization of global welfare. Such a discussion is important and timely in light of the generally acknowledged inadequacy of GATT and WTO supervision over the establishment of RTAs, as well as the adoption of Article 29 of the Doha Ministerial declaration, which calls for "negotiations aimed at clarifying and improving disciplines and procedures under the existing WTO provisions applying to regional trade agreements."[7]

This Chapter aims to provide an initial analysis of the adequacy of current WTO mechanisms governing RTAs, as well as some suggestions for future WTO regulation of RTAs. It bears noting that these suggestions are not intended as a detailed prescription to be carefully followed, but rather are intended to stimulate new thinking about the WTO regulation of RTAs. The proposed reforms are aimed at improving the fidelity of WTO members to the principles set forth in GATT Article XXIV and GATS Article V by improving the procedures for determining whether the limitations on discriminatory arrangements set forth in those articles have been met. We suggest (i) the creation of an independent committee of neutral experts to examine RTAs, (ii) waiting periods during which RTAs are examined before their adoption by national legislatures, and (iii) expedited access for adversely affected third parties to review by the WTO Appellate Body of the adequacy of an RTA under WTO standards.

After an initial introduction to the diversity and scope of RTAs (Part II), as well as the standard arguments made about them (Part III), the following discussion will outline the current WTO legal framework governing RTAs, as set forth in the GATT and WTO Agreements (Part IVA). We will then examine the WTO institutional response to RTAs, by reviewing the activities of the Committee on Regional Trade Agreements ("CRTA") (Part IVB), as well as Panel and Appellate Body reports (Part IVC). The Chapter will conclude by examining the adequacy of the current WTO approach, and suggesting possible modifications to enhance its effectiveness (Part V). Those readers who are familiar with the legal and institutional background may wish to focus their attention on the recommendations set forth in Section V.

II. The Recent Proliferation of RTAs

The recent proliferation of RTAs is remarkable, not only for its size and speed, but also for the diversity of participants and the variety of legal innovations adopted.

A. The Size of the Phenomenon

The number RTAs being concluded has greatly accelerated over the past decade. During the first forty-three years of the GATT's existence (until 1990) only thirty RTAs that are still in force today were notified to the GATT, of which the majority (eighteen) involved

---

[4] For an economic analysis of the RTA phenomenon, *see* Scott Baier and Jeffrey Bergstrand, ON THE ECONOMIC DETERMINANTS OF FREE TRADE AGREEMENTS (June 2001).

[5] *See infra* notes 186–7 and accompanying text.

[6] Individual WTO member governments have articulated proposals for gaining a better grasp of the RTA phenomenon and helping to ensure that it develops in a manner complementary to the multilateral trading system. *Id.*

[7] *See Doha Ministerial Declaration* (reproduced in the Appendix to this book and also available at www.wto.org), Article 29. Four WTO meetings on the subject of RTAs had been completed by mid-December 2002. Negotiations on clarifying and improving the WTO's regulation of RTAs are scheduled to be completed by January 1, 2005.

European countries.[8] By contrast, 132 RTAs that are still in force today were notified to the GATT and WTO between 1990 and 2002, with countries in all regions of the world participating.[9]

Because many RTAs have not been notified to the WTO, the true number of RTAs is greater than the number notified. Some commentators estimate that the number of RTAs currently in force that have not been notified to the WTO is as high as 119, excluding an additional 87 RTAs that are currently under negotiation and likely to be in force by 2007.[10] Additional details are provided in the following chart prepared by Jeffrey Schott of the Institute for International Economics.

Free trade agreements in effect or under negotiation (as of May 2003)

	Notified to the WTO[a]	Concluded but not notified to the WTO	Under negotiation	Grand Total	Share (%)
Total agreements	155	83	46	283	100
of which:					
USA is a partner	3	2	6	11	4
Canada is a partner	4	0	5	9	3
EU or EFTA is a partner	59	6	6	71	25
Japan is a partner	1	0	1	2	1
Intra-F.S.U./C.I.T.	41	48	6	95	34
Intra-LDCs	27	26	23	76	27

Notes: LDCs = Developing countries; FSU/CIT = Former Soviet Union and other "countries in transition".

a) Agreements are counted only once, even if they are notified to the WTO under both GATT Article 24 and GATS Article 5. However, NAFTA is counted twice, as US-NAFTA and Canada-NAFTA.

b) Current negotiations on a FTAA are counted twice as US-LDC and Canada-LDC; similarly the Canada-EFTAFTA is counted under Canada and under EFTA.

Sources: WTO (http://www.wto.org/english/tratop_e/region_e/region_e.htm) and unpublished data sheets from the WTO Secretariat.

[8] *See* Committee on Regional Trade Agreements, *Basic Information on Regional Trade Agreements: Agreements Notified to the GATT/WTO and in Force as of 31 January 2002,* WT/REG/W/44 (Feb. 7, 2002) ("*Basic Information on Regional Trade Agreements*"). Please note that this figure of twenty-five RTAs excludes five notifications of accessions by new members to the European Communities or to the European Free Trade Association.

By November 2002, there had been a total of 255 notifications (including accessions and including RTAs no longer in force) to the GATT/WTO since 1947. *See* Committee on Regional Trade Agreements, *Draft Report (2002) to the General Council,* WT/REG/W/47 (Nov. 4, 2002) ("*Draft Report (2002) to the General Council*").

[9] An initial surge in the number of RTAs entered into in the early 1990s has been attributed to European integration efforts after the collapse of the COMECON block and uncertainty over the outcome of the Uruguay Round. *See,* Clemens Boonekamp, *Regional Trade Integration under Transformation,* Seminar on Regionalism and the WTO, (Apr. 26, 2002), http://www.wto.org./English/tratop_e/region/sem_april02_e/clemens_boonekamp.doc.

With the establishment of the WTO in 1995, countries began entering into RTAs at an even faster pace. Of the 132 RTAs in force which were notified between 1990 and 2002, the overwhelming majority were notified after 1995. *See Draft Report (2002) to the General Council, supra* note 8. The United States provides a good example of the recent acceleration of interest in RTAs. Although the United States entered only three RTAs between 1947 and 1994 (the U.S.-Israel FTA in 1985, the U.S.-Canada FTA in 1988, and the NAFTA in 1994), it entered into two FTAs on January 1, 2004 (with Singapore and Chile), and—by mid-2004—had concluded negotiations on five additional FTAs (Australia, Bahrain, Dominican Republic, Morocco, and the Central American countries) and had entered into negotiations for additional FTAs (Panama, Thailand, the Andean countries and the countries of the South African Customs Union). It is also negotiating the Free Trade Area of the Americas, and has also proposed in general terms an FTA with an unspecified group of Middle Eastern Countries.

[10] *See,* Boonekamp, *supra* note 9, at ¶ 7. Jeffrey F. Schott, *Free Trade Agreements: Boon or Bane for the World Trading System*, Presentation Made at IIE Conference (May 7, 2003) (providing chart below).

In terms of trade coverage, it is estimated that regional preferential trading arrangements, which currently account for 43 percent of world trade, will account for 55 percent by 2005—assuming that all currently planned RTAs come into effect.[11]

B. Overview of RTAs by Region

The following analysis provides an overview of RTAs around the world, but does not attempt to catalogue all RTAs.[12]

1. Europe

European nations have been extremely active in pursuing RTAs. Indeed, the process began with the creation of the European Economic Community ("EEC") in 1958 (which itself was preceded by the European Coal and Steel Community), and much recent activity in the RTA arena is attributable to the efforts of European nations. In addition to the European Communities' ("EC") policy of enlarging and improving the world's largest customs union, the EC has adopted a policy of entering Free Trade Agreements with countries outside its Customs Union. There are many FTAs among neighboring Eastern European nations, and between the EC and Eastern European and Mediterranean nations.[13] This picture is further complicated by more than a dozen FTAs between the European Free Trade Association ("EFTA") and Eastern European and Mediterranean nations.[14]

2. Western Hemisphere[15]

The NAFTA[16] and the MERCOSUR[17] are the two most significant RTAs in this region, but recent years have seen an increase in the number of smaller groupings and bilateral

---

[11] *See* Ken Heydon, *Regulatory Provisions in Regional Trade Agreements: "Singapore" Issues,* WTO Seminar on Regionalism and the WTO, at 3 (Apr. 26, 2002), at http://www.wto.org./English/tratop_ e/ region/sem_ april02_ e/ken.heydon.doc.

[12] *See* World Trade Organization, *Regionalism and the World Trading System,* 29–38 (1995) (classifying major RTAs entered into until 1995 according to region.) ("*Regionalism and the World Trading System*").

[13] Prior to the accession of Eastern European countries to the EC, the EC's members were Austria, Belgium, Denmark, Finland, France, Germany, Greece, Ireland, Italy, Luxembourg, the Netherlands, Portugal, Spain, Sweden and the United Kingdom. The EC has notified the WTO of FTAs with its Overseas Countries and Territories (1971), as well as with Malta (1971), Switzerland and Liechtenstein (1971), Iceland (1973), Cyprus (1973), Norway (1973), Algeria (1976), Egypt (1977), Jordan (1977), Lebanon (1977), Syria (1977), Andorra (1991), Czech Republic (1992), Slovak Republic (1992), Hungary (1992), Poland (1992), Romania (1993), Bulgaria (1993), Lithuania (1995), Estonia (1995), Latvia (1995), Faroe Islands (1997), Slovenia (1997), the Palestinian Authority (1997), Tunisia (1998), South Africa (2000), Morocco (2000), Israel (2000), Mexico (2000) and Macedonia (2001). These agreements represent only FTAs, and do not account for other Customs Unions or Services Agreements. *See, Basic Information on Regional Trade Agreements, supra* note 8, at 2–9.

[14] The EFTA signatories are Iceland, Norway, Switzerland and Liechtenstein. The EFTA has notified the WTO of FTAs with Turkey (1992), the Czech Republic (1992), the Slovak Republic (1992), Israel (1993), Bulgaria (1993), Romania (1993), Hungary (1993), Poland (1993), Slovenia (1995), Estonia (1996), Latvia (1996), Lithuania (1996), the Palestinian Authority (1999), Morocco (1999), Macedonia (2001), Mexico (2001), Jordan (2002) and Croatia (2002). Each of the EFTA signatories has entered into an FTA with the EC. Austria, Finland and Sweden ceased to be parties to the EFTA following their withdrawal from the EFTA Convention and subsequent accession to the EC on Jan. 1, 1995. *See Basic Information on Regional Trade Agreements, supra* note 8, at 2–9.

[15] The Organization of American States has compiled a complete list of all RTAs entered into by all countries in the Western Hemisphere. *See,* SICE, Foreign Trade Information System, *Trade Agreements Sorted by Signatory Country, at* http://www.sice.oas.org/acuerdoE.ASP.

[16] The signatories to the North American Free Trade Agreement (1994) are Canada, Mexico and the United States.

[17] MERCOSUR is a Customs Union entered into pursuant to the Enabling Clause. MERCOSUR's signatories are Argentina, Brazil, Paraguay and Uruguay. MERCOSUR has reportedly been negotiating the terms of an FTA with the Andean Community, as well as the EC. *See, e.g.,* Gustavo Bizai, *Trade*

FTAs involving Western Hemisphere countries.[18] Chile and Mexico have been particularly active in entering into agreements with other American, European and Asian nations.[19] Negotiations for a Free Trade Area of the Americas ("FTAA") involving 34 countries are currently underway.[20]

Following the breakdown of multilateral negotiations at the Cancun Ministerial in September 2003, renewed attention has focused on regional initiatives, including the Free Trade Area of the Americas ("FTAA") negotiations. However, the results of the Miami Ministerial, as reflected in the November 20, 2003 Declaration, raise questions about the ability of regional initiatives to advance free trade in a vigorous and principled manner, as contemplated by GATT Article XXIV. For example, paragraph 7 of the Declaration states that,

> Taking into account and acknowledging existing mandates, Ministers recognize that countries may assume different levels of commitments. We will seek to develop a common and balanced set of rights and obligations applicable to all countries. In addition, negotiations should allow for countries that so choose, within the FTAA, to agree to additional obligations and benefits. One possible course of action would be for these countries to conduct plurilateral negotiations within the FTAA to define the obligations in the respective individual areas.

The Miami Ministerial declaration reflects a political compromise struck among competing trade interests, most prominently the United States and Brazil. Because the negotiating countries were ultimately unable to agree of a fixed agenda that would result in rights and obligations binding on all parties, the Declaration instead focuses on the right of countries to assume "different levels of commitments," and to "allow for countries that so choose . . . to agree to additional obligations and benefits." Although the ability of the countries to make real progress will not be clear until the close of negotiations (scheduled for January 2005), the Ministerial Declaration strongly suggests that countries have so far avoided committing to undertake the political and social costs that would be entailed in comprehensive trade liberalization.

In these circumstances there will be strong temptations to depart from the disciplines of Article XXIV. Will the United States, for example, refuse to eliminate barriers to

---

Liberalisation Negotiations between the European Union and MERCOSUR, 6 INT'L TRADE L. & REG. 35 (2000).

[18] The United States, for example, is a signatory to FTAs with Chile, Singapore, Jordan and Israel, in addition to the NAFTA. U.S. and Australian lawmakers approved an FTA between the countries in mid-2004. In mid-2004, U.S. lawmakers also approved an FTA with Morocco. Implementation is expected by January 1, 2005. FTA negotiations with the Dominican Republic, Bahrain and the countries of the Central American Economic Integration System (Costa Rica, El Salvador, Guatemala, Honduras and Nicaragua) were completed during 2004. Additionally, negotiations were begun in 2004 with Thailand, Panama, the Andean countries (Columbia, Peru and Equador) and the countries of the South African Customs Union (Botswana, Lesotho, Namibia, South Africa and Swaziland).

[19] Chile has either entered or is considering FTAs with Canada, Colombia, Ecuador, the EC, Japan, Mexico, Singapore, the United States, and Venezuela, among other countries.

Mexico has either entered or is considering FTAs with Bolivia, Brazil, Chile Costa Rica, the EC, the EFTA, El Salvador, Guatemala, Honduras, Israel, Nicaragua, Panama, Uruguay, Japan, Korea, Singapore and the MERCOSUR Customs Union.

See Sergio Lopez-Ayllon, *Mexico's Expanding Matrix of Trade Agreements: A Unifying Force?,* 5 NAFTA L. & BUS. REV. 241, 257 (1999) (describing intra-regional integration in Latin America, with a focus on Mexico); *see also* Website of Mexican Secretary of the Economy *available at* http://www. economia.gob.mx/?P=39 for a complete list of Mexican RTAs, either completed or under negotiation.

[20] *See generally* Rossella Brevetti, *Ambitious Schedule for Market Access Talks is Backed by FTAA Trade Ministers,* 19 INT'L TRADE REP. 1915 (2002); for a comprehensive discussion of FTAA negotiations through March 25, 2000, *see* Sherry Stephenson, *The Current State of the FTAA Negotiations at the Turn of the Millennium,* 6 NAFTA L. & BUS. REV. 317 (2000).

Brazilian orange juice if Brazil does not agree to the intellectual property protections sought by the United States? Or will U.S. unwillingness to end domestic subsidies for agricultural products mean that other countries will refuse to eliminate all their barriers to these products? In either case, the agreement would probably fall short of the Article XXIV standard.

Paragraph 3 of the Declaration states that, "[w]e also reaffirm that the FTAA will be consistent with the rules and disciplines of the World Trade Organization (WTO)." In order to achieve this goal, the FTAA parties will need to eliminate duties and other restrictive regulations on substantially all their trade in *goods,* and hope to accommodate "different levels of commitments" only with regard to subjects not covered by the Article XXIV discipline, such as intellectual property and services. Thus far there has been no detailed analysis of the consistency of the proposed FTAA with applicable international legal constraints.

3. *East Asia and the Pacific Region*

Although not RTAs in strict terms, the Asia Pacific Economic Cooperation ("APEC")[21] and the Association of South East Asian Nations ("ASEAN")[22] are the two main institutions that have encouraged regional economic integration in the Asia-Pacific region. In addition, the individual nations in this area, including Australia,[23] New Zealand,[24] Japan,[25] Korea and Singapore,[26] have actively adopted a policy of entering RTAs. Taiwan

---

[21] It should be noted that APEC cannot be considered an FTA or Customs Union within the terms of the GATT/WTO. This is because APEC—founded on a philosophy of "open regionalism"—neither covers 'substantially all the trade' among its member states, nor requires specific tariff reduction commitments from its members. Instead, APEC is a forum that tries to build economic, political and institutional ties among its members. Many of APEC's activities involve education and trade facilitation. For an overview of APEC, its history and future direction, *see* Andrew Faye, *APEC and the New Regionalism: GATT Compliance and the new WTO,* 28 L. & POL'Y INT'L BUS. 175, 184–201 (1996); Lorraine C. Cardenas and Arparon Buranakatis, *The Role of APEC in the Achievement of Regional Cooperation in Southeast Asia,* 5 ANN. SURV. OF INT'L & COMP. L. 49 (1999); For an overview of the economic implications for APEC of the recent proliferation of RTAs, S*ee* Robert Scollay and John P. Gilbert, *New Regional Trading Arrangements in the Asia Pacific ?* INST. INT'L ECON. (2001); for an overview of all FTAs either completed or under consideration among APEC members, *see* Tim Martyn, *A Complete Guide to the Regional Trade Agreements of the Asia-Pacific,* Australian APEC Study Centre (March, 2001).

[22] For background discussion regarding ASEAN, *see, e.g.,* George White, *Trying to Compete in a Global Marketplace: The ASEAN Free Trade Area,* 8 TULSA J. COMP. & INT'L L. 177 (2000); Mary Hiscock, *Changing Patterns of Regional Law Making in Southeast Asia,* 39 ST. LOUIS U. L. J. 933 (1995).

[23] New Zealand and Australia have entered into an FTA called the Australia—New Zealand Closer Economic Relations ("ANZCER"). *See* Martyn, *supra* note 21, at 17; Joan Fitzhenry and David Robinson, *Australia-New Zealand Closer Economic Relations Trade Agreement,* 7 INT'L TRADE L. & REG. 136 (2001); Australia is considering further FTAs with Asian and American nations.

[24] In addition to the ANZCER, New Zealand has also entered into an FTA with Singapore. *See Basic Information on Regional Trade Agreements, supra* note 8, at 9. Like Australia, New Zealand is considering further FTAs with Asian and American nations.

[25] Japan entered into an FTA with Singapore in 2002, and has reportedly completed negotiations on a Japan-Mexico FTA, which is to become effective in 2005. Japan has also stated its intention to enter into FTAs with Thailand, the Philippines, Malaysia, South Korea, Australia, Indonesia, Vietnam and perhaps India and China. *See* Toshio Aritake, *Japan Targets Trade, Partnership Pacts with More Than 10 Countries on PM's Trip,* BNA Daily Report for Executives (Sept. 9, 2004). Japan has also discussed the option of a trading bloc consisting of some combination of East Asian countries. *See generally,* Japanese Ministry of Foreign Affairs, *Japan Outlines Strategy Behind Push for Bilateral FTAs,* ECONOMIC AFFAIRS BUREAU, MINISTRY OF FOREIGN AFFAIRS (Oct. 2002).

[26] Singapore has entered into FTAs with New Zealand, Japan, Australia, the United States, and the European Free Trade Association. Singapore is currently negotiating or considering FTAs with Canada, Korea, Mexico, India and ASEAN and the People's Republic of China. *See, generally* Martyn, *supra* note 21, at 47–9;

has expressed interest in an FTA with the United States,[27] while the People's Republic of China has expressed interest in an FTA with Japan and South Korea,[28] has signed a framework agreement with ASEAN to create an FTA by 2012,[29] and has announced an FTA with the Customs territory of Hong Kong.

4. Mediterranean Region

Several regional arrangements already exist in this area (such as the Gulf Co-operation Council, the Arab Maghreb Union and the Arab Co-operation Council). More recently, the members of the Arab League have committed to implementation of a Greater Arab Free Trade Agreement ("GAFTA") by 2008.[30] In addition to the pre-existing FTAs that the EC and EFTA have entered in this region, Arab nations and the EC have agreed to establish an FTA by 2010.[31] The United States has either already entered or is planning to enter FTAs with individual Middle Eastern nations, and the Bush administration has also suggested the possibility of a broad-based FTA with the region as a whole.

5. Africa

The Organization of African Unity/African Economic Community has made a proposal for an Africa-wide Customs Union, the African Economic and Monetary Union, to take effect by 2028.[32] Various countries are also working toward smaller RTAs, such as the Central African Economic and Monetary Community ("CEMAC"),[33] the West African Economic and Monetary Union ("WAEMU"),[34] and the Common Market for Eastern and Southern Africa ("COMESA").[35] Members of the South African Development Community ("SADC") are working toward a goal of creating an FTA by 2004.[36] Additionally, RTAs between African nations and non-African nations are also in place or under negotiation, as in the case of the proposed FTA between the South African Customs Union and the United States.

Development Bank of Japan, *ASEAN Free Trade Area and Bilateral Free Trade Pacts: Singapore's Perspective* (2001) *at* http://www.dbj.org.sg/PDF/512e.pdf.

[27] *See generally*, Noah J. Smith and Christopher S. Rugaber, *USTR Holds Intellectual Property Talks with Taiwan, Setting Off Talk of Possible FTA*, 19 BNA INT'L TRADE REP. 41 (Oct.17, 2002).

[28] *See* Jonathan Hopfner, *China Broaches Idea of Free Trade Area with Japan and South Korea*, 19 BNA INT'L TRADE REP. 1908 (Nov. 7, 2002).

[29] *See* Jonathan Hopfner, *China, 10 ASEAN Members Sign Framework of Pact for Free Trade Area within 10 years*, 19 BNA INT'L TRADE REP. 1908 (Nov. 7, 2002).

[30] *See* Euro-Arab Management School, *Arab Commercial and Economic Co-operation: The Greater Arab Free Trade Area*, 3 (May 2001), *available at* http://www.eams.fundea.es/research/AFTArea.pdf.

[31] *See id.* at 4.

[32] For a detailed history of the negotiations and a timetable of commitments, *see* Department of Foreign Affairs of Zambia, *African Economic Community: History and Present Status* (May 28, 2001), *available at* http://www.dfa.gov.za/for-relations/multilateral/aec.htm; s*ee also* Olufemi Babarinde, *Analyzing the Proposed African Economic Community: Lessons from the Experience of the European Union*, (Sept. 1996), *available at* http://www.ecsanet.org/conferences/babarinde.htm.

[33] The membership of CEMAC is Cameroon, Central African Republic, Chad, Congo, Equatorial Guinea and Gabon. *See* USTR, *2000 National Trade Estimate Report on Foreign Trade Barriers* 25 (2000).

[34] The membership of WAEMU is Benin, Burkina Faso, Cote d-Ivoire, Guinea-Bissau, Mali, Niger, Senegal and Togo. *See* West African Economic and Monetary Union website, http://www.dfa.gov.za/for-relations/multilateral/waemu.htm.

[35] The membership of COMESA is Angola, Burundi, Comoros, Congo, Djibouti, Egypt, Eritrea, Ethiopia, Kenya, Madagascar, Malawi, Mauritius, Namibia, Rwanda, Seychelles, Sudan, Swaziland, Uganda, Zambia and Zimbabwe. *See generally* COMESA Free Trade Area website, http://www.comesa.int/trade/Ftaindx.htm.

[36] The membership of SADC is Angola, Botswana, Democratic Republic of Congo, Lesotho, Malawi, Mauritius, Mozambique, Nambia, Seychelles, South Africa, Tanzania, Zambia and Zimbabwe. *See generally* Southern African Development Community website, http://www.sadc.int/English/memberstates/index.html.

C. Innovations Found in Recent RTAs

Recent RTAs are also distinguished by the variety of legal innovations they incorporate. These innovations address new subject areas and apply a variety of innovative legal standards and trade facilitation mechanisms largely unforeseen by the WTO.[37]

These innovations can be classified into three general areas: expansion of coverage into non-traditional areas; innovations in dispute settlement procedures; and trade facilitation measures.

1. Expansion of the Scope of Coverage of RTAs

One of the most noticeable features of recent RTAs is their extension to cover substantive areas that had hitherto not been the province of RTAs. Traditionally, RTAs were concerned largely with the preferential reduction of tariffs and quantitative restrictions on trade in goods between RTA signatories. However, recent RTAs have also included financial services, investment protection, environmental protection, labor rights, government procurement, international trade regulation, and competition law issues, among other topics. This extension is a natural response to the relative greater importance—in the face of rapidly falling border restrictions—of internal laws and regulations affecting international trade and investment.

The way in which environmental and labor standards should be incorporated into RTAs has been an intensely debated topic in the United States. A politically acceptable formula appears to have emerged in the US-Jordan, US-Singapore and US-Chile FTAs. In these agreements, as in the NAFTA, an FTA signatory obligates itself to enforce its own labor and environmental laws, but does not have to adopt higher environmental protection standards than those already in place.[38]

This approach has met with approval among labor and environmental protection groups because the countries involved in these agreements had regulatory standards in place that were viewed as roughly equivalent to—and in some cases better than—those in the U.S., the only concern being effective enforcement. However, when the United States negotiates RTAs with countries that do not have legal standards of protection that are considered adequate, the formula used in U.S. RTAs to date will not be likely to satisfy U.S. legislators concerned with labor and environmental impacts.[39] The United States may well insist that such countries enact higher standards before the agreements take

[37] *See* Boonekamp, *supra* note 9, at ¶ 9 (describing a "new generation of RTAs" that "include more and more regional rules on investment, competition and standards; in a few cases, they also contain provisions on environment and labour.").

[38] The NAFTA created two side agreements outside the NAFTA: the North American Agreement on Environmental Cooperation and the North American Agreement on Labor Cooperation, which are supported by institutional mechanisms to aid in the enforcement of relevant obligations. Similar undertakings have been included directly in the Jordan, Singapore and Chile agreements, rather than in separate side agreements.

[39] *See* Sander M. Levin, *Address to Institute for International Economics ("IIE") Conference on FTAs,* May 7, 2003, p. 4:

Conditions as to labor markets are vastly different in most of Central America from those in Chile and Singapore. In Central America, unlike Chile and Singapore, domestic laws do not come close to incorporating the five ILO core labor standards, especially the right of workers to assemble and collectively bargain. According to our own State Department and ILO reports, even the highly flawed laws that exist are not enforced, but indeed flagrantly violated. The proof is in the results—in the vast garment maquila industry of the three Central American nations I visited, there is not a single collective bargaining agreement; while in Chile and Singapore, workers rights have increasingly helped grow a middle class.

effect, or within a specified time thereafter. It is also likely that some practical evidence of adequate enforcement resources will be demanded. A "capacity building" effort, with U.S. assistance, might accompany the negotiations.[40]

2. Innovations in Dispute Settlement Procedures

A number of recent RTAs have incorporated innovative dispute settlement provisions. Many RTAs contain several procedurally distinct provisions covering different substantive areas.

The NAFTA, for example, provides a broad range of dispute settlement procedures.[41] Chapter 20 provides a general procedure for settling disputes between the member countries relating to the agreement.[42] The agreement also contains six sector-based procedures, each with its own institutional and procedural characteristics. These involve investment disputes between investors and signatory states,[43] government procurement disputes,[44] antidumping and countervailing duty disputes,[45] financial sector disputes,[46] environmental disputes,[47] and labor disputes.[48]

---

[40] *See, e.g.,* United States Trade Representative, *Request for Submissions to Volunteer Trade Capacity Building Assistance,* 68 Fed. Reg. 24531 (May 7, 2003).

[41] *See generally* Denis Lemieux and Ana Stuhec, REVIEW OF ADMINISTRATIVE ACTION UNDER NAFTA, (Carswell, 1999) (examining all NAFTA dispute settlement procedures); William Merritt, *A Practical Guide to Dispute Resolution under the North American Free Trade Agreement,* 5 NAFTA L. & BUS. REV. 169 (1999) (discussing four different dispute settlement procedures); Michael Gordon, *Forms of Dispute Resolution in the NAFTA,* 13 FLA. J. INT'L L. 16 (2000) (discussing five of the dispute settlement procedures).

[42] *See generally* Vibysoun Loungnarath and Céline Stehly, *The General Dispute Settlement Mechanism in the NAFTA and the WTO System,* 34 J. WORLD TRADE 39 (2000) (introducing NAFTA Chapter 20 and criticizing its tendency to become politicized); Sidney Picker, *NAFTA Chapter 20: Reflections on Party-Party Dispute Resolution,* 14 ARIZ. J. INT'L & COMP. L. 465 (1997) (comparing main features of Chapter 20 with predecessor provisions under Chapter 18 of the Canada-U.S. Free Trade Agreement.); LEMIEUX AND STUHEC, *supra* note 41 at 99–116 (discussing procedure and precedent under NAFTA Chapter 20.).

[43] NAFTA Chapter 11, which enables investors of one member to bring cases against the government of another member, has been actively used and engendered some controversy. *See generally* JOSEPH McKINNEY, CREATED FROM NAFTA: THE STRUCTURE, FUNCTION AND SIGNIFICANCE OF THE TREATY'S RELATED INSTITUTIONS (M.E. Sharpe, 2000). (introducing key provisions and case law); David Gantz, *Potential Conflicts between Investor Rights and Environmental Regulation under Chapter 11,* 33 GEO. WASH. INT'L L. REV. 651 (2001); Joseph de Pencier, *Investment, Environment and Dispute Settlement: Arbitration under NAFTA Chapter Eleven,* 23 HASTINGS INT'L AND COMP.L. REV. 409 (2000).

[44] NAFTA Chapter 10, which deals with government procurement, also provides for dispute resolution of related disputes. *See* LEMIEUX AND STUHEC, *supra* note 41, at 59–79 (analyzing the text of Chapter 10 and practice thereunder).

[45] NAFTA Chapter 19 permits parties to antidumping and countervailing duty proceedings to appeal the decisions of the national tribunals to special binational panels instead of the domestic courts. *See generally* Patrick Macrory, *Dispute Settlement in the NAFTA* (C.D. Howe Inst. Commentary, 2002, available at www.cdhowe.org); Richard Cunningham, *NAFTA Chapter 19: How Well Does it Work?* 26 CAN-U.S. L. J. 79 (2000); Homer E. Moyer, *Chapter 19 of the NAFTA: Binational Panels as the Trade Courts of Last Resort,* 27 INT'L LAW. 707 (1993).

[46] NAFTA Chapter 14, which deals with financial services, refers relevant disputes to the dispute resolution provisions of either Chapter 11 or 20, with some procedural variations. *See* Constance Wagner, *The New WTO Agreement on Financial Services and Chapter 14 of the NAFTA,* 5 NAFTA L. & BUS. REV. 5, 75–78 (1999).

[47] *See* LEMIEUX AND STUHEC, *supra* note 41, at 121–39 (providing overview of the North American Agreement on Environmental Cooperation ("NAAEC") and its dispute resolution procedures); McKINNEY, *supra* note 43, at 90–117, 123–222 (analyzing history, institutions and procedures related to the NAAEC.).

[48] *See* Robert E. Herzstein, *The Labor Cooperation Agreement Among Mexico, Canada and the United States: Its Negotiation and Prospects,* 3 U.S.-MEX. L.J. 121 (1996). *See also* McKINNEY, *supra* note 43, at 33–89 (providing overview of the North American Agreement on Labor Cooperation, and discussing its history, institutions and procedures.).

Another innovation beyond the scope of the WTO is the payment of a monetary assessment by a party to resolve a dispute in certain circumstances, rather than the usual trade agreement remedy of compensatory tariff changes (generally referred to as "withdrawal" or "suspension" of tariff concessions).[49] This new remedy was introduced in the NAFTA Supplemental Agreements on Labor and Environment, and has subsequently been included in the labor and environment provisions of the U.S. FTAs with Jordan, Chile and Singapore.[50]

3. Innovations in the Area of Trade Facilitation and Harmonization of Domestic Regulations

Other innovations that have characterized RTAs include the harmonization by RTA signatories of a wide range of regulations, beginning with customs procedures and sometimes extending to a wide range of internal measures.[51] The RTAs have gone well beyond border measures, to harmonization of sanitary and phytosanitary ("SPS") rules and certification procedures and other technical and safety standards.[52] There is also some evidence that RTAs provide a useful forum for similarly situated countries to formulate innovative ways of harmonizing other legal measures, such as the complex and sensitive rules governing intellectual property rights and competition law.[53] The NAFTA, for example, contains provisions on intellectual property rights and competition policy. As part of its NAFTA-era reforms, Mexico completely revamped its IP laws and established a competition commission. The European Community is reportedly strengthening the IP component of its FTAs by *inter alia* requiring co-signatory nations to agree to accord protection to a long list of geographical indications. As regards competition law, Australia and New Zealand used the so-called "Australia-New Zealand Closer Economic Relations" agreement to improve binational cooperation. Although the agreement came into effect in 1983, the parties agreed in 1988 to study further cooperation in business laws. As a result of this study, both countries undertook significant legislative reforms, under which dumping laws were replaced with symmetrical competition law provisions.[54]

---

[49] Although there have been WTO dispute settlement cases in which the parties agreed upon the payment of monetary compensation instead of "retaliation" in the form of increased tariffs, such cases are not the norm. *See, e.g., United States—Section 110(5) of the Copyright Act,* Recourse to Arbitration under DSU Article 25, WT/DS160/ARB25/1 (Nov. 9, 2001).

[50] *See* McKinney, *supra* note 43, at 106–109 (discussing the procedures according to which monetary penalties may be imposed against a NAFTA party found to have engaged in a persistent pattern of failure to enforce its own environmental laws); *See also, Gary* G. Yerkey, *U.S. to Propose Use of Fines to Settle Disputes in FTA Talks with Chile, Singapore,* 19 BNA Int'l Trade Rep. 1857 (Oct. 31, 2002).

[51] Harmonization of customs and other border procedures is among the activities generally referred to as "trade facilitation." As defined by the WTO, trade facilitation consists of the simplification and harmonisation of international trade procedures, including activities, practices and formalities involved in collecting, presenting, communicating and processing data required for the movement of goods in international trade. *See* WTO website, *Overview of Trade Facilitation Work* (Dec. 11, 2002), http://www.wto.org/english/tratop_e/tradfa-e/tradefae2_e.htm

[52] *See, e.g.,* Jonathan Hopfner, *Japan, ASEAN Set Base for Future FTA, Forge 'Comprehensive Economic Partnership,'* 19 BNA Int'l Trade Rep. 1907 (Nov.7, 2002).

[53] *See* Boonekamp *supra* note 9, (noting that, "[t]here is also a general feeling that complex policy issues of commercial significance in economic relations (notably services, investment, intellectual property protection, cooperation on competition policy, technical standards and government procurement) can better be managed amongst a limited circle of 'friends'. These motivations act as an incentive to regulate on such issues through RTAs, even if it is generally recognized that RTAs are a second-best option to MFN trade liberalization.").

[54] *See, e.g.,* Brian Cassidy, *Can Australian and US Competition Policy be Harmonised?* (June 21, 2001), avail at: http://www.apec.org.au/docs/Cassidy.PDF

III. Overview of Arguments Made About RTAs

Although the economic and political implications of RTAs have been debated for many years, the arguments made have become more nuanced and complex over time. Traditionally, the debate focused on the economic welfare effects of preferential tariff reductions (balancing "trade creation" against "trade diversion"), and on political economy issues.[55] Political economy concerns included doubts regarding the wisdom of favoring certain trade partners with RTAs, thereby automatically disfavoring others, as well as fears that proliferating RTAs would quickly degenerate into antagonistic trading blocs, thus reducing international stability. The experience with a greatly increased number of RTAs has allowed for better identification of their potential costs and benefits than was possible fifteen years ago. Experience may have reduced the sense that RTAs are threatening because they could result in mutually antagonistic blocs. It has also led to an appreciation of problems and opportunities that were not part of the earlier discussion. Today, the political and economic aspects of RTAs are more likely viewed as closely intertwined issues, and not discrete matters to be regarded in isolation.

It is now widely appreciated that economic assessment of RTAs requires more than a basic analysis of tariff shifts, but also an analysis of the "dynamic effects" of the RTA, which include efficiencies of scale and scope, and efficiencies resulting from legal reforms, better understanding between the RTA signatories, and deeper integration of their economies. RTAs can also serve in the right circumstances as effective tools in strengthening international relationships, stimulating and "locking in" domestic legal reforms, providing both an impetus and a model for multilateral trade negotiations, and advancing economic and structural reform objectives in developing countries.

A. Arguments Made in Favor of RTAs

Advocates of RTAs have emphasized the following arguments, among others:

- RTAs can result in trade creation and thereby be beneficial. Trade creation occurs if overall global efficiency is enhanced through an RTA, such as when the RTA permits relatively more efficient producers to gain market share in the markets covered by the RTA at the expense of relatively less efficient producers. Global welfare is ensured through optimal allocation of global resources only if trade creation outweighs trade diversion.

- Recent arguments build upon these economic arguments, noting that RTAs are beneficial to the extent that they produce "dynamic effects,"—i.e., efficiencies gained by economic players within the larger market created by the RTA as a result of increased investment and trade. Depending on the particular RTA, such efficiencies can result from economies of scale and specialization,[56] reforms in laws governing business transactions, increased transparency in legal

---

[55] *See* Cho, *supra* note 1, at 429 (arguing that "socio-political concerns" are as important as trade-creation and trade-diversion concerns.).

[56] For an explication of the argument that RTAs engender "dynamic effects," *see, e.g.,* Colin L. McCarthy, *Regional Integration of Developing Countries at Different Levels of Economic Development: Problems and Prospects,* 4 Transnat'l L. & Contemp. Problems 1 (1994) (noting that under a dynamic effects theory, "the focus shifts from the static effects of integration to the dynamic effects found in a larger market with its opportunities for the economies of scale and specialization that do not exist in a small, low-income domestic market.")

and governmental matters, regulatory harmonization, even increased cultural rapport among business managers in the larger market. RTA advocates argue that the benefits of such reforms and harmonization of standards are enjoyed by RTA signatories and non-signatories alike.[57]

- Closely related to an appreciation of the range of RTAs' "dynamic effects" is an appreciation of their political usefulness. In some cases, such as the NAFTA, RTAs result in a more stable international environment—economically and politically—to the extent that signatory nations become increasingly aware of their common interest in a cooperative environment in which to conduct trade.[58] At least some of the impetus for the NAFTA can be explained in these terms: the U.S. Government hoped—among other things—that the NAFTA would help stabilize Mexico economically and politically, creating a more prosperous neighbor and reducing the incentive for illegal immigration, while the Mexican Government perceived NAFTA—in part—as an opportunity to advance and "lock in" its own economic reforms. Other RTAs containing a strong political motivation include the US-Jordan and US-Morocco FTAs, in which the United States may view as supporting "friendly" nations and the political and economic systems they have adopted.[59]

- As a result of recent experience, RTAs are beginning to be used as a tool for promoting economic development and political reforms in developing countries. Open markets and sound economic and democratic institutions reinforce each other, so that a developed country with a market that is attractive to a developing country can use a free trade agreement as an incentive, or a lever, for achieving institutional reform. The developed country can offer access to its large market through an RTA, as part of a package in which it receives commitments for economic and political reforms in the developing country. The promise of new markets can help business and political leaders in the developing country secure support for the reforms. And both countries can work together to secure economic assistance for the developing country (from sources such as USAID, the World Bank, and regional development banks) to help make the reforms a success. The

[57] *See, e.g.,* Heydon, *supra* note 11, at ¶¶ 53, (noting that—as a result of harmonization of standards—third parties enjoy the same rights as signatories, and adding that, "RTA provisions on trade facilitation help foster convergence of modes of operation within regional groupings. Moreover, to the extent that they draw on international agreements related to trade facilitation, regional initiatives also serve to foster moves towards wider harmonisation.").

[58] *See* Dunn and Mutti, INTERNATIONAL ECONOMICS (2000) (noting the view that RTAs result in greater international stability). The desire for peaceful international relations cannot be overemphasized as a motivating factor in many RTAs. One of the clearest articulations of this notion can be found in the Preamble to the Treaty Establishing the European Coal and Steel Community, in which the signatories state their resolve,

> to substitute for age-old rivalries the merging of their essential interests; to create, by establishing an economic community, the basis for a broader and deeper community among peoples long divided by bloody conflicts; and to lay the foundations for institutions which will give direction to a destiny henceforward shared.

See, Preamble, Treaty Establishing the European Coal and Steel Community (1951), at http://www.eurofer. org/legislation/index.htm

[59] The US-Jordan FTA and the US-Morocco FTA under negotiation, as well as the proposed FTAs with other countries in the Middle East—such as Bahrain, Egypt and other areas—are arguably less important to the United States in terms of economics and trade flows than they are politically.

combination of an open market, sound democratic institutions, and prospects for economic growth can then make the developing country an attractive destination for new private capital investment, which is a key element in economic development.

- RTAs are more attainable than multilateral trade agreements, because it is easier to reach compromises and consensus in negotiations among two or more like-minded countries than among the nearly 150 countries of the world trading system. When global negotiations are stalled or stalemated, countries wishing to move forward may do so through RTAs.

- According to the "competitive trade liberalization" view, countries independently pursuing RTA programs stimulate others to do the same, and the result is fewer trade barriers worldwide.[60] RTAs can also provide an impetus for multilateral trade negotiations, as in the case of the NAFTA, which, during 1993 and 1994 helped motivate and guide Uruguay Round negotiators in their final deliberations over the WTO agreements.

- RTAs also can provide a roadmap for the negotiation of new disciplines: Through innovative treatment of intellectual property, investment, environment and labor issues, for example, RTAs can provide a proving ground for regulatory and treaty innovations that may later be adopted on a multilateral level.[61]

- RTAs can promote multilateral trade liberalization when they facilitate the formulation of unified negotiating positions among RTA signatories. An RTA may yield improvements in relations among RTA signatories and greater appreciation of common areas of interest. The result can be closer cooperation among the RTA signatories when they enter multilateral negotiations, enabling them to unify or reduce the number of negotiating positions they present. Sometimes countries are so small that they are perceived as non-entities by other parties. By forming groupings with like-minded countries, they can help ensure that their concerns are heard, helping to produce a result that all the countries will support and implement.[62]

- RTAs allow domestic firms to adjust gradually to foreign competition, first adjusting to competition with intra-RTA companies, and becoming more prepared for competition of a worldwide scope. By permitting companies to adjust incrementally to worldwide competition, governments can effectively soften the opposition of such companies to trade liberalization.[63]

---

[60] See Fred Bergsten, *Competitive Liberalization and Global Free Trade: A Vision for the Early 21st Century*, Working Paper 96–15, Inst. Int'l Ec. (1996).

[61] See Cho, *supra* note 1, at 432–434 (noting that "one of the most powerful arguments for RTAs stems from their experimental or laboratory effect vis-à-vis multilateral trade liberalization.")

[62] The argument is that increased numbers of RTAs will aid multilateral trade negotiations because RTA members are able to present a unified negotiating position, which reduces the number of outstanding negotiating topics and results in smaller, leanly staffed negotiating teams. *See, e.g.,* Jeffrey Schott and Jayashree Watal, *Decision-making in the WTO*, INTERNATIONAL ECONOMIC POLICY BRIEFS, INSTITUTE FOR INTERNATIONAL ECONOMICS, 6 (2000) (noting that the Mercosur countries have pooled resources and shared representation in preparation for the Doha Round. According to Schott and Watal, blocs of countries with common negotiating positions will likely seek out and find other blocs with similar objectives, which will further rationalize the negotiating process. The Caribbean trading bloc, Caricom, is an example of this phenomenon.)

[63] See *Second Session of the CRTA, supra* note 2, at ¶ 85 (in which a representative of the Secretariat articulated this argument and others, such as the argument that, if RTAs create an environment in which inefficient firms are allowed to go out of business gradually, protectionist sentiment opposing multilateralism also wanes.)

B. Arguments Made Against RTAs

Opponents of RTAs have traditionally made the following arguments:

- RTAs reduce global welfare by diverting trade and investment from the world's most efficient producers to less efficient producers within the bloc. This misallocation of resources occurs when less efficient producers benefit from advantages of preferential tariffs and non-tariff barriers at the expense of producers in non-signatory countries.[64]
- RTAs reduce global welfare because their proliferation results in a complex of overlapping rules of origin. This "spaghetti bowl" of diverse and often inconsistent rules increases transaction costs and diverts resources from other uses.[65] Furthermore, the complexity of rules of origin provides a temptation for parties to create special, narrowly defined preferences for certain industries. At least in certain circumstances, the description of rules of origin as a "playground for protectionist interests" appears quite apt.[66]
- RTAs that incorporate dispute settlement provisions may undermine the WTO's dispute settlement system because the former may result in "jurisprudence conflicting with that of the WTO."[67]
- "Harmonization" of trade facilitation measures and internal regulations under RTAs can reduce global welfare if such harmonization is actually a form of "covert protectionism," designed to increase transaction costs that must be factored into

---

[64] See DUNN AND MUTTI, *supra* note 58, at 206 (noting that "discriminatory tariff cuts mean that the non-member country loses sales to less efficient producers in a member country, thus reducing world efficiency. Trade is diverted from low-cost to higher-cost sources, and world efficiency suffers.")

[65] See SCOLLAY AND GILBERT, *supra* note 21, at 13 (noting that, "the fragmentation of the regional economy may intensify if the SRTAs begin to overlap, and if they each also adopt complex, mutually inconsistent rules of origin, so that a particular product may be imported into or exported from a given country under a range of different rules, and even tariffs, depending on its origin or destination."); Jagdish Bhagwati, *Preferential Trade Agreements: The Wrong Road,* 27 LAW & POL'Y INT'L BUS. 865, 866–68 (1996) (remarking on inefficiencies created by complex rules of origin regimes required under RTAs). Rules of origin are included in RTAs in order to prevent producers in non-signatories from taking advantage of the duty-free tariff rates by exporting a nearly finished product to producers in one signatory, performing minimal processing, and thereafter shipping the product within the RTA duty-free. Bhagwati also argues that diverse RTAs, with complex and inconsistent provisions, make negotiation of a multilateral agreement more difficult.

[66] *Comments by Professor Richard Cooper,* Conference at Institute for International Economics on Regional Trade Agreements (May 7, 2003). *See* Cho, *supra* note 1, at 430–31 (explaining that, "RTAs provide abundant opportunities for local interest groups, such as producers of sensitive products, to manipulate both the design and operation of RTAs. The eventual effect of such lobbying efforts is to distort the efficient flow of interstate commerce.")

[67] *See* WTO Negotiating Group on Rules, *Compendium of Issues Related to Regional Trade Agreements,* TN/RL/W/8/Rev. 1, ¶ 120 (Aug. 01, 2002) ("*Compendium of Issues Related to Trade Agreements*") (noting that, "[t]his issue has been raised in particular with respect to RTA clauses providing that, in the event of inconsistency, RTA rules prevail over WTO rules. It has been argued that this could result in a diminution of the rights that the parties had under the WTO in relation to their trade with one another."). *See also,* David A. Gantz, *Dispute Settlement under the NAFTA and WTO: Choice of Forum Opportunities and Risks for the NAFTA Parties,* 14 AM.U.INT'L L.REV. 1025 (1999). While there is a risk that dispute settlement alternatives might result in the development of inconsistent standards, these dispute settlement alternatives may also have beneficial side effects, such as reducing the pressure on the already over-taxed WTO system. It is conceivable, for example, that at least some of the disputes being resolved under NAFTA Chapters 19 and 20 could have been brought under the WTO system.

the price of products from non-signatory nations.[68] Specifically, "streamlined procedures for RTA-originating goods" can simply mean "more burdensome procedures for third-party goods" in cases in which an RTA provides signatories—but not non-signatories—with lower customs processing fees, simplified labeling requirements or immediate recognition of SPS or TBT standards by virtue of a Mutual Recognition Agreement.[69]

- RTAs hinder multilateral trade liberalization because they create new economic stakeholders that profit from the special access an FTA gives them to a foreign market and are therefore motivated to exert political pressure against multilateral trade concessions that would confer the same access on their competitors based in other countries. In effect, each RTA creates vested interests in maintaining the RTA's discriminatory tariff and NTB regime. Similarly, member governments in a large regional trade area may lose interest in their multilateral negotiations, which would require producers in their countries to share the market with competitors based outside the region.[70]

- In the long run, the proliferation of RTAs may have a negative impact on global and regional security if regional blocs with politically and economically conflicting interests arise.[71]

The foregoing provides only a brief introduction to arguments made on both sides of the debate over RTAs. Given the range of their potential impacts, good and bad, it does not seem possible to reach a conclusion on the merits of RTAs in general. It would seem that each RTA must be evaluated in its operational setting. And in this evaluation, as recent economic research has indicated, the welfare gains or losses associated with any given RTA must be judged by looking not just at the changes in tariff levels but also at their non-tariff provisions, their "dynamic" effects and their political import.

IV. Legal and Institutional Regulation of RTAs under the WTO

A. The WTO Legal Framework for Regulation of RTAs

1. The Most Favored Nation Principle

One of the fundamental principles of the GATT/WTO system is the Most Favored Nation ("MFN") rule, enshrined in GATT Article I and GATS Article II. GATT Article I obliges WTO members to provide equal treatment to imports of products from all "other"

---

[68] *See* John McGinnis and Mark Movsesian, *The World Trade Constitution,* 114 HARV. L. REV. 550–52 (2000) (explaining that the WTO is forced to address environmental, health and safety issues because of the risk that individual nations will employ environmental, health and safety regulations in order to discriminate against outsiders—a logic that clearly can also apply to the "harmonization of standards" agreed to by countries entering an FTA.).

[69] *See* Heydon, *supra* note 11, at ¶ 61 (alleging that "[m]easures of simplification of international trade procedures undertaken at the regional level rarely have a preferential effect," while acknowledging certain exceptions to that rule).

[70] *See Second Session of the CRTA, supra* note 2, at ¶ 85 (in which a representative of the Secretariat articulated this argument against RTAs).

[71] A somewhat apocalyptic scenario is found in MICHAEL J. TREBILCOCK AND ROBERT HOWSE, THE REGULATION OF INTERNATIONAL TRADE 130 (1995), where the authors assert that regional blocs "necessarily entail playing favourites and risk reducing international relations to mutually destructive factionalism of the kind that was so dramatically evidenced in the 1930s."

members.[72] GATS Article II requires WTO members to provide equal treatment to the services and service suppliers of all other members.[73]

Although MFN clauses have existed in commercial treaties since the sixteenth century,[74] these clauses generally provided for "conditional" MFN treatment.[75] Conditional MFN clauses demand the receipt of equivalent concessions from a second country as a condition of conferring on that country the advantages already given to a third country. The use of conditional MFN clauses resulted in a complex network of trading relationships in which a given country could have negotiated an entirely unique set of concessions and obligations vis-à-vis each of its trading partners. Conditional MFN clauses also meant that countries commonly "played favorites," reserving preferential treatment to those countries deemed to be politically important, and discriminating against those countries deemed to be competitors—politically or economically. It can be argued that, in the context of widely held mercantilist trade policies, conditional MFN clauses exacerbated tensions and rivalries among trading partners.

Unconditional MFN clauses, which automatically confer on each treaty partner all the advantages already accorded to other trading partners, gained prominence around the beginning of the twentieth century.[76] In 1922 the United States adopted a policy of pursuing trade agreements incorporating unconditional MFN clauses.[77] International acceptance of the unconditional MFN principle enshrined in GATT in 1947 was closely tied to a recognition that, under the previous practice, international economic and political relations were being impaired by mercantilist trade policies that discriminated against trading partners in varying degrees.

(a) Disillusionment with Discriminatory Trading Blocs as one Major Impetus for Multilateral Trading System. Key to the development of the unconditional MFN principle

---

[72] GATT Article I provides that,

> With respect to customs duties and charges of any kind imposed on or in connection with importation or exportation . . . , and with respect to the method of levying such duties and charges, and with respect to all rules and formalities in connection with importation and exportation, and with respect to all matter referred to in paragraphs 2 and 4 of Article III, any advantage, favor, privilege or immunity grated by any contracting party to any product originating in or destined for any other country shall be accorded immediately and unconditionally to the like product originating in or destined for the territories of all other contracting parties.

See also, Trebilcock and Howse, *supra* note 70, at 114 (noting that, "[t]he MFN principle protects expectations of participants in multilateral bargaining by forbidding subsequent more favourable treatment of other participants and avoids the dead-weight loss of trade diversion, but at the cost of preventing nations from discriminating when it might be valuable to benefit certain politically powerful producer interests, and a cost of substantial incentives for participants in multilateral negotiations to attempt to free ride").

[73] GATS Article II:1 provides that: "With respect to any measure covered by this Agreement, each Member shall accord immediately and unconditionally to services and service suppliers of any other Member treatment no less favourable than that it accords to like services and service suppliers of any other country." WTO members were permitted to take exceptions to the MFN principle during the negotiation of GATS. *See* GATS Article II:2 and Annex on Article II exceptions. Such exceptions are in principle supposed to remain in effect for no more than ten years.

[74] *See Regionalism and the World Trading System, supra* note 12, at 5.

[75] *See* John H. Jackson, The Jurisprudence of the GATT and WTO: Insights on Treaty Law and Economic Relations 58 (2000).

[76] *See generally id.* at 58–59.

[77] *See* Alfred E. Eckes, Jr., Opening America's Market: U.S. Foreign Trade Policy since 1776, 90–93 (1995) (noting that U.S. State Department officials supported unconditional MFN clauses based on a view that conditional MFN clauses led to U.S. trade policies based on "special concessions to some instead of equal treatment for all," and that unconditional MFN clauses would more effectively support U.S. exports.).

and the multilateral trading system was U.S. opposition to discriminatory trading blocs not entirely dissimilar to some present-day RTAs. Examination of the pre-GATT history suggests the U.S. drive to gain international acceptance for the unconditional MFN principle[78] was based in large part on U.S. suspicion of discriminatory trading blocs, such as the Commonwealth system of trade preferences.[79] Thus, at least in part, the impetus for a multilateral trading system was a desire to scrap the discriminatory trading regimes that—in the form of unregulated RTAs—may pose a threat to the system today.

(b) Principles underlying the GATT MFN Rule.   The MFN rule quickly gained preeminence in the aftermath of World War II, and was considered by many as a key element in building a post-war architecture that minimized the risk of war.[80] By the time that the GATT was founded in 1947, the Contracting Parties agreed to put the MFN rule first and foremost among all the rules of the GATT system. The rationale underlying the GATT MFN rule is both economic and political. Among the reasons underlying MFN are the following basic notions:

- The MFN rule helps to minimize international tensions and bolsters the negotiating position of less influential nations, because it obliges "strong" nations to treat all trading partners equally. Because "strong" nations are not allowed to confer special benefits on preferred trading partners, the risk of resentment and anger on the part of otherwise disfavored nations is reduced.[81]
- The MFN rule increases global welfare by minimizing the transaction costs associated with complex and non-transparent import regulations;[82]
- The MFN rule ensures global efficiency by securing the preeminence of the most efficient producers, and by precluding the sheltering of inefficient producers through discriminatory tariff and NTB arrangements;[83]
- The MFN rule gives all trading partners the benefit of bilateral concessions, thus dramatically expanding the scope of trade liberalization.[84]

---

[78]   Along with the National Treatment principle of GATT Article III, the MFN principle should be considered a *fundamental* principle of the GATT, because the GATT system was conceived in part in reaction to the negative effects of preferential trading regimes, especially the high tariffs maintained by British Commonwealth countries against imports from non-Commonwealth countries. The Roosevelt Administration's push for lower tariffs abroad, for international acceptance of an unconditional MFN principle, and ultimately, for a multilateral trading institution was grounded in a view that trade rivalries and discriminatory trading regimes had contributed to the Great Depression and, ultimately, World War II. *See* Thomas W. Zeiler, FREE TRADE, FREE WORLD: THE ADVENT OF GATT, 8–9, 30–36 (1999); *See also,* ECKES, *supra* note 77, at 140–66 (quoting Cordell Hull: "to me, unhampered trade dovetailed with peace; high tariffs, trade barriers, and unfair economic competition, with war.").

[79]   *See* ZEILER, *supra* note 78.

[80]   For a detailed discussion of the negotiations crucial to securing worldwide support for the MFN principle, *see* ZEILER, *supra* note 77 (describing U.S. efforts during the early 1940s to persuade Great Britain to give up its trade preferences for certain trading partners, and detailing later modifications made to the MFN principle insisted on by different Contracting Parties.).

[81]   *See id.*

[82]   For a more detailed discussion, *See,* JACKSON, Davey and Sykes, INTERNATIONAL ECONOMIC RELATIONS, 436–37 (3d Ed. 1995). *See also* JACKSON, *supra* note 75, at 60–61.

[83]   *See Regionalism and the World Trading System supra* note 12, at 5 (1995) (explaining that "equal treatment of imports from different origins helps ensure that these are purchased from the lowest-cost foreign suppliers, thereby reinforcing comparative advantage in the world market and minimizing the cost of protection at home.").

[84]   *See* JACKSON, DAVEY AND SYKES , *supra* note 83, at 436–37.

2. History of GATT Article XXIV

The original drafters of the GATT contemplated only a few exceptions to the fundamental MFN rule. One of these exceptions was a provision found in GATT Article XXIV permitting the creation of Customs Unions and Free Trade Areas, so long as certain strict criteria were fulfilled.[85] Unfortunately, there is little recorded negotiating history dealing with Article XXIV. The lack of negotiating history reflects the reality that GATT drafters viewed RTAs as "a minor element in world trade relations."[86]

What little negotiating history has been recorded, however, reflects the intention of the original GATT drafters to design Article XXIV as a narrow exception to the MFN principle. The text of Article XXIV originally proposed by the United States in 1945 permitted only customs unions, and subjected them to strict conditions.[87] The inclusion of provisions on Free Trade Agreements and Interim Agreements occurred on the basis of a proposal introduced by Syria and Lebanon, and supported by other developing countries.[88] Developing countries considered that FTAs were suited to the interests of countries with relatively limited resources because negotiating a common external tariff was costly, time-consuming, and politically difficult.[89] Developed countries, in turn, supported developing country demands for an FTA provision "as a means of blunting developing-country demands for a legitimization of preferences."[90]

Another aspect of the negotiating history that reflects the GATT drafters' intention to limit the scope of the Article XXIV exception from the MFN rule was their rejection of a proposal during the Havana conference to weaken the discipline governing RTAs. The proposal would have replaced the relatively rigorous requirement that "substantially all" trade be covered by the RTA, with a less demanding requirement that only "a substantial part" of trade be covered by the RTA.[91]

3. Current WTO Disciplines Governing RTAs

(a) Overview. The disciplines governing RTAs under the WTO are largely identical to those established by the GATT drafters. The most important difference is that the original GATT rules are bolstered—procedurally and substantively—by the Understanding on GATT Article XXIV issued in 1994.[92] The WTO provides a legal framework for four different types of RTAs, namely Customs Unions, Free Trade Agreements, Services Agreements, and Agreements among Developing Nations.[93] A detailed examination of the rules governing Services Agreements and Agreements among developing nations

---

[85] John Jackson has provided a concise explanation for the practical reasons why RTAs—to be effective—need to be permitted as an exception to the GATT MFN principle: "The establishment of a customs union or free trade area requires a departure from the MFN principles. If there were no such exception to the MFN principle, the elimination of custom duties between the participants would have to be generalized to all contracting parties to GATT with no *quid pro quo.*" *See* Jackson, *supra* note 75, at 64.

[86] *See Regionalism and the World Trading System, supra* note 12, at 11.

[87] *See Regionalism and the World Trading System, supra* note 12, at 8 (noting that, despite its central desire to create a multilateral trading system based on MFN, the United States acknowledged the necessity of customs unions, based on the political importance of creating a unified Western Europe after World War II. However, the United States did not recognize the necessity of Free Trade Areas or Interim Agreements. (Interim Agreements are the legal mechanisms under which parties gradually align their economic systems in preparation for their entry into a Customs Union or Free Trade Area.).

[88] *See id.*

[89] *See id.*

[90] *Id.*

[91] *See,* General Agreement on Tariffs and Trade, GUIDE TO GATT LAW AND PRACTICE, 739 (1994).

[92] *See* discussion, *infra* at text accompanying notes 111–118.

[93] The latter agreements are governed by provisions set forth in the Enabling Clause. *See Differential and More Favourable Treatment, Reciprocity and Fuller Participation of Developing Countries,* Decision of 28 November 1979.

is beyond the scope of this chapter. For present purposes, it is sufficient to understand that the rules governing Services Agreements essentially track the provisions of GATT Article XXIV,[94] while the rules governing preferential arrangements among (or for the benefit of) developing nations are less rigorous than the provisions of GATT Article XXIV.[95] In particular, such agreements are not required to cover "substantially all" trade between the parties.

(b) Article XXIV Disciplines on Customs Unions and FTAs. To date, WTO jurisprudence has focused on Customs Unions and FTAs, both addressed in GATT Article XXIV.[96] In essence, Article XXIV permits WTO members to accord favorable tariff treatment to each other, but only when they agree to eliminate tariffs and other restrictions on substantially all trade with co-signatories of the RTA at the end of a phase-in period. Article XXIV:4 articulates the general principle that RTAs should facilitate trade between the signatories, yet not raise barriers to third parties.[97]

Three basic rules apply to both Customs Unions and FTAs. First, Article XXIV:8 requires that "substantially all trade" be covered, although it does not define "substantially all".[98] In addition, Article XXIV(5)(c) requires that both FTAs and Customs Unions be

---

[94] Article V of the General Agreement on Trade in Services provides that WTO Members may enter into agreements liberalizing trade in services, provided that such agreement (a) have substantial sectoral coverage, and (b) eliminate substantially all current and future discriminatory measures in the covered sectors. To date, twenty-two agreements have been notified under this provision. *See* Article V, General Agreement on Trade in Services, Apr. 15, 1994, art. V, Marrakesh Agreement Establishing the World Trade Organization ("*WTO Agreement*"), Annex 31, I.L.M. 44 1B, RESULTS OF THE URUGUAY ROUND MULTILATERAL TRADE NEGOTIATIONS Vol. 31 (GATT Secretariat 1994).

[95] *See* Chapter 19 and for further discussion.

[96] For an introduction to Customs Unions and RTAs under the GATT and WTO, *see,* John Jackson, *Perspectives on Regionalism in Trade Relations,* 27 LAW & POL'Y INT'L BUS. 873, 875–77 (1996) (explaining the relationship between GATT Article XXIV and the Uruguay Round's Draft Understanding on Interpreting Article XXIV).

[97] This principle is found not only in GATT Article XXIV:4, but also in the Preamble to the Understanding on the Interpretation of Article XXIV of the GATT 1994; paragraph 3(a) of the 1979 Decision on Differential and More Favourable Treatment, Reciprocity and Fuller Participation of Developing Countries; and GATS Article V:4.

GATT Article XXIV:4 provides that,

> The contracting parties recognize the desirability of increasing freedom of trade by the development, through voluntary agreements, of closer integration between the economies of the countries parties to such agreements. They also recognize that the purpose of a customs union or of a free-trade area should be to facilitate trade between the constituent territories and not to raise barriers to the trade of other contracting parties with such territories.

[98] GATT Article XXIV(8) provides that,

> (a) A customs union shall be understood to mean the substitution of a single customs territory for two or more customs territories, so that
>
>   (i) duties and other restrictive regulations of commerce (except, where necessary, those permitted under Articles XI, XII, XIII, XIV, XV and XX) are eliminated with respect to substantially all the trade between the constituent territories of the union or at least with respect to *substantially all the trade* in products originating in such territories, and,
>
>   (ii) subject to the provisions of paragraph 9, substantially the same duties and other regulations of commerce are applied by each of the members of the union to the trade of territories not included in the union;
>
> (b) A free-trade area shall be understood to mean a group of two or more customs territories in which the duties and other restrictive regulations of commerce (except, where necessary, those permitted under Articles XI, XII, XIII, XIV, XV and XX) are eliminated on *substantially all the trade* between the constituent territories in products originating in such territories. (*emphasis added*).

GATT Art. XXIV(8)(b).

completed (i.e. all duties and other restrictions on substantially all trade among the parties must be eliminated) within a "reasonable length of time," a term that as discussed below has been defined in an Uruguay Round understanding on RTAs.

Third, the rules applicable to the effect of the RTA a non-participants differ as a result of the Customs Union requirement for a common external tariff. In the case of FTAs, "duties and other regulations of commerce" applied to non-signatories must not be "higher or more restrictive" than those applied to non-signatories before the FTA came into effect.[99] A similar requirement exists in the case of Customs Unions, but because some at least of the individual tariffs of the members will inevitably rise in the conversion to a common external tariff, the requirement here is that the "duties and other regulations of commerce" applied to non-signatories are not "on the whole" higher or more restrictive than the "general incidence" of the duties that existed vis-à-vis non-signatories before the Customs Union came into effect.[100]

The exact manner in which the "general incidence" of duties in the customs territory were to be measured was oft-debated in the GATT. For example, the appropriate level of compensation to be made to the United States (which was negatively affected by the introduction of the EEC's Common External Tariff) was at issue in the so-called US-EEC "Chicken War."[101] Also, the Working Party report dealing with the 1988 accession of Portugal and Spain to the EC supported—over U.S. objections—the EC's use of a "trade coverage" methodology that took into account relative trade volumes in comparing

---

[99] *See, id.,* which provides in relevant part, [T]he provisions of this Agreement shall not prevent, as between the territories of contracting parties, the formation of a customs union or of a free-trade area or the adoption of an interim agreement . . . *Provided* that: . . .

(b) with respect to a free-trade area, or an interim agreement leading to the formation of a free-trade area, the duties and other regulations of commerce maintained in each if the constituent territories and applicable at the formation of such free-trade area or the adoption of such interim agreement to the trade of contracting parties not included in such area or not parties to such agreement shall not be higher or more restrictive than the corresponding duties and other regulations of commerce existing in the same constituent territories prior to the formation of the free-trade area, or interim agreement as the case may be.

[100] *See,* GATT Article XXIV(5),which provides that,

[T]he provisions of this Agreement shall not prevent, as between the territories of contracting parties, the formation of a customs union or of a free-trade area or the adoption of an interim agreement necessary for the formation of a customs union or of a free-trade area; *Provided* that:

(a) with respect to a customs union, or an interim agreement leading to a formation of a customs union, the duties and other regulations of commerce imposed at the institution of any such union or interim agreement in respect of trade with contracting parties not parties to such union or agreement shall not on the whole be higher or more restrictive than the general incidence of the duties and regulations of commerce applicable in the constituent territories prior to the formation of such union or the adoption of such interim agreement, as the case may be.

[101] *See US/EEC—Negotiation on Poultry,* Conciliation, 12 S/65 (Nov. 21, 1963) This dispute arose out of the withdrawal of West German tariff bindings at the time of the imposition of an EEC Common External Tariff ("CET") on poultry products. The United States not only claimed that this change resulted in a higher and more restrictive tariff level on its products than had existed before introduction of the CET, but also claimed that illegal German quantitative restrictions in force immediately before the advent of the CET had kept U.S. exports at an artificially low level, a factor that should be considered in establishing the appropriate level of compensation. The Panel agreed with the United States, and examined the level of poultry sales in a surrogate country—Switzerland—in order to estimate what U.S. exports would have been in the absence of the quantitative restrictions.

decreases in tariffs applied to some products vis-à-vis increases in tariffs applied to other products.[102] The negotiation of the 1994 Understanding of the Interpretation of Article XXIV ("1994 Understanding"), which is discussed in the following section, resolved some of the aforementioned issues. The 1994 Understanding specified—among other things—that the evaluation of the pre- and post-Customs Union general incidence of *duties* "shall . . . be based upon an overall assessment of weighted average tariff rates and of customs duties collected,"[103] while the evaluation of the general incidence of *other regulations* of commerce may require "examination of individual measures, regulations, products covered and trade flows affected."[104]

(c) 1994 Understanding on the Interpretation of Article XXIV of GATT.   The 1994 Understanding represents an attempt by the negotiating parties to the WTO to increase the rigor and consistency of the legal disciplines that govern RTAs. Although the 1994 Understanding did successfully resolve certain disputed matters, it is widely considered to have failed to address some of the most contentious issues involving RTAs.[105] An overview of the 1994 Understanding's treatment of certain substantive and procedural aspects of Article XXIV follows. The 1994 Understanding:

- Reaffirms the principle that RTAs should "facilitate trade between the constituent territories and not . . . raise barriers to the trade of other Members . . ."[106]
- Recognizes the increased significance of RTAs in light of their proliferation, and notes that RTAs will contribute the expansion of world trade if-
  - accompanied by closer integration between RTA-signatory economies;
  - duties and other restrictive regulations are eliminated on all trade; and
  - all major sectors are included within the RTA's coverage.[107]

---

[102] *See* Working Party Report, *Accession of Portugal and Spain to the European Communities,* 35 GATT BISD 295–96 (1989) (In the EC's view, "Article XXIV:5 only required an examination on the broadest possible basis. The task was general, namely to reach a view on whether the general incidence of customs duties and regulations after enlargement was on the whole more or less restrictive than before. Even if a negative incidence were shown to be the case for certain items, such as when duties were increased or replaced by variable levies, one had to consider whether these effects were not balanced by the effects of other changes in the tariff sector taken as a whole.").

[103] The 1994 Understanding further specifies that, "this assessment shall be based on import statistics for a previous representative period to be supplied by the customs union, on a tariff-line basis and in values and quantities, broken down by WTO country of origin." *See Understanding on the Interpretation of Article XXIV of the General Agreement on Tariffs and Trade 1994,* ¶ 2, Apr. 15, 1994, Marrakesh Agreement Establishing the World Trade Organization, Annex 1A, in RESULTS OF THE URUGUAY ROUND OF MULTILATERAL TRADE NEGOTIATIONS 31 (GATT Secretariat 1994) ("1994 Understanding").

[104] *Id.*

[105] *See* World Trade Organization, *Regionalism and the World Trading System,* 20 (1995)(noting that, "while the purpose of the Understanding on Article XXIV is to clarify certain of the areas where the application of Article XXIV had given rise to controversy in the past, and particularly as regards the external policy of customs unions, it fell short of addressing most of the difficult issues of interpretation . . . For example, no consensus emerged . . . concerning proposals . . . to clarify the substantially-all-trade requirement.").

[106] *See 1994 Understanding, supra* note 103, Preamble.

[107] *See 1994 Understanding,* Preamble. Commentators, the WTO Appellate Body and the WTO Secretariat have laid emphasis on the preamble's final clause, which states that RTAs contribution to the expansion of world trade is "diminished if any major sector of trade is excluded." This focus is understandable in light of the desire of some countries to exclude politically sensitive sectors—such as agriculture—from RTAs. It remains contentious today whether an RTA can exclude an entire sector, notwithstanding the 1994 Understanding's preamble. *See* discussion *infra* at 30–31. *See generally* Negotiating Group on Rules, *Compendium of Issues Related to Regional Trade Agreements,* TN/RL/W/8/Rev.1, ¶ 68 (2002).

- Defines "duties and other regulations of commerce" to be the applied rates of duty and other measures and regulations.[108]
- States that the "reasonable length of time" within which RTAs must be completed "should exceed ten years only in exceptional cases."
- Explains that, especially in the case of non-tariff barriers that are difficult to quantify, it may be necessary to examine "individual measures, regulations, products covered and trade flows affected."[109]
- Clarifies that all notified RTAs are to be examined by a working party, thus formalizing a practice that had developed during the RTA examination process in GATT[110] (this function is performed by the Committee on Regional Trade Agreements ("CRTA") today).[111]
- Requires Customs Unions and signatories of FTAs to periodically report to the Council for Trade in Goods on "the operation of the relevant agreement" and of "any significant changes and/or developments . . . as they occur."[112]
- Makes WTO dispute settlement provisions applicable with respect to any RTA-related matters arising from GATT Article XXIV.[113]

(d) Procedural Rules Governing the CRTA. The CRTA issued a special set of rules regulating the conduct of its meetings ("CRTA Rules of Procedure").[114] These are significant additions to the general oversight mechanism established in the WTO texts. For example, the CRTA Chairman's clarification (during negotiation of the CRTA Rules of Procedure) that documentation underlying a notified RTA must be circulated at least four weeks before the examination meeting[115] supports the GATT Article XXIV requirement that countries deciding to enter into RTAs shall circulate information pertinent to the RTA. Similarly, Rule of Procedure 23, which exhorts examining Members to circulate written statements to be incorporated into the examination report, provides guidance on the conduct of the RTA examination process.[116]

---

[108] *See 1994 Understanding,* ¶ 2.

[109] *See 1994 Understanding,* ¶ 2.

[110] *See 1994 Understanding,* ¶ 7 (also specifying that the working party prepare a report and submit it to the Council for Trade in Goods, which may make such recommendations to the Members as it deems appropriate.).

[111] The CRTA was not created pursuant to any of the Uruguay Round agreements. Instead, the General Council created the CRTA in a February 6, 1996 Decision. *See Committee on Regional Trade Agreements,* Decision of 6 February 1996, WT/L/127 (1996).

[112] *See 1994 Understanding,* ¶ 11. These requirements are also emphasized in the WTO's Procedures on Reporting on Regional Trade Agreements. *See,* World Trade Organization, *Procedures on Reporting on Regional Trade Agreements,* G/L/286 (Dec. 16, 1998).

[113] *See 1994 Understanding,* ¶ 12 (providing that "the provisions of Articles XXI and XXII of GATT 1994 as elaborated and applied by the Dispute Settlement Understanding may be invoked with respect to any matters arising from the application of . . . Article XXIV."). This provision of the Understanding is significant, because during the GATT era, it was disputed whether a Contracting Party that was not party to an RTA could invoke dispute settlement proceedings against an RTA signatory on the grounds that the RTA was inconsistent with Article XXIV or other relevant disciplines. For a discussion of the history and effect of the dispute over the applicability of dispute settlement provisions to RTAs, *see* Cho, *supra* note 1, at 437–38.

[114] Committee on Regional Trade Agreements, *Rules of Procedure for Meetings of the Committee on Regional Trade Agreements,* WT/REG/1 (Aug. 14, 1996) ("*CRTA Rules of Procedure*").

[115] *See* Committee on Regional Trade Agreements, *Draft Rules of Procedure for Meetings of the Committee on Regional Trade Agreements,* WT/REG/W/2, at 2 (1996).

[116] *See CRTA Rules of Procedure,* Rule 23.

4. Evaluation of WTO Legal Disciplines Governing RTAs

Even with the added detail in the 1994 Understanding and the CRTA's rules, the legal disciplines set forth in the GATT/WTO texts are widely regarded as insufficiently precise.[117] The vagueness in the legal framework is regarded as one of the main causes of the failure of the WTO system to regulate the current proliferation of RTAs in an effective manner.[118] Although there are several other provisions that have created interpretive difficulties in light of the ambiguity of the language contained therein,[119] two key legal provisions that have proved particularly contentious are:

- *Article XXIV, ¶ 4: "not to raise barriers to the trade of other contracting parties"*
  GATT Contracting Parties and WTO Members have differed on the significance of paragraph 4 generally, and this language specifically. Some argue that the provision informs other Article XXIV provisions, ultimately rendering them more rigorous than they would otherwise be;[120] others argue that the provision is merely hortatory and entirely self-contained, and thus does not modify any other Article XXIV provisions.[121]

- *Article XXIV, Paragraph 8: "substantially all the trade"*
  GATT Contracting Parties and WTO Members have differed and continue to differ on the significance of this language.[122] Some WTO members take a quantitative approach, arguing that the Article XXIV:8 obligation to remove barriers on "substantially all trade" requires only that a certain percentage of trade (e.g., eighty percent) be covered by an RTA; other WTO members insist on a qualitative

---

[117] *See e.g.,* Cho, *supra* note 1, at 436 ("Though the rationale of Article XXIV is quite understandable and idealistic in light of its legislative background, the text itself is so nebulous as to leave many important issues open to wide speculation. Consequently, actual applications of the black letter law were neither clear nor resolute, rendering Article XXIV a virtual dead letter from its inception.") JACKSON, *supra* note 74, at 64–5 ("The GATT language is unfortunately ambiguous, and the GATT has allowed some very loose preferential arrangements to exist without effective challenge in the context of GATT. Article XXIV has become, some say, the most significant loophole to the MFN obligation.").

[118] *See* Cho, *supra* note 1, at 436–43 (discussing provisions of Article XXIV that—because of their wording—have engendered controversy, specifically in regard to their application to certain allegedly trade-distorting measures.).

[119] *See* Cho, *supra* note 1, at 439–443 (discussing five Article XXIV concepts and textual provisions subject to contention during the GATT.); *Compendium of Issues Related to Regional Trade Agreements*, *supra* note 66, at ¶¶ 66–84, 85–113 (discussing contentious aspects of GATT Article XXIV and GATS Article V.); *Regionalism and the World Trading System*, *supra* note 12, at 13–15 (discussing two contentious Article XXIV provisions.). Among the other provisions which often receive attention is the provision stating that "other regulations of commerce . . . shall not on the whole be higher or more restrictive." For documents devoted specifically to discussion of this language, *see* Committee on Regional Trade Agreements, *Communication from Japan,* WT/REG/W/28 & WT/REG/W/29 (July 28, 1998); Committee on Regional Trade Agreements, *Systemic Issues Related to "Other Regulations of Commerce"* WT/REG/W/17 (Oct. 31, 1997) & WT/REG/W/17/Add.1 (Nov. 5, 1997).

[120] *See* Cho *supra* note 1, at 447 (noting that the Appellate Body and Panel in *Turkey—Restrictions on Imports of Textile and Clothing Products* (WT/DS34/AB/R & WT/DS34/R) both agreed that GATT Article XXIV obligations must be read in light of Article XXIV:4, which forms part of their context.).

[121] *See* Cho, *supra* note 1, at 439–440 (reciting the EC position during the accession of Portugal and Spain to the EC that RTA signatories "can introduce new barriers . . . if the net impact is less than what had prevailed before" the RTA's inception.). As discussed *infra* at pages 42–45, Turkey made a similar argument with regard to its Customs Union with the EU in *Turkey—Restrictions on Imports of Textile and Clothing Products, infra,* note 165.

[122] Evidence of the contentious debate of the precise meaning of this language is seen in the sheer number of WTO member submissions and CRTA official documents that have been issued in conjunction with this phrase. *See e.g.,* Committee on Regional Trade Agreements, *Systemic Issues Related to "Substantially All the Trade,"* WT/REG/W/21 (Nov. 28, 1997) and WT/REG/W/21/Add.1 (Dec. 2, 1997).

approach, arguing that the Article XXIV:8 obligation requires that no major sector be excluded from coverage. Those who insist on a qualitative approach have vigorously objected to RTAs that essentially exclude agriculture from their coverage, including the Japan-Singapore Economic Partnership Agreement or Sweden's FTAs with Baltic states.[123]

B. The WTO Institutional Framework for Regulation of RTAs

1. Examination of RTAs under the GATT System

Prior to the 1994 Understanding and the 1996 advent of the CRTA, examinations of RTAs under the GATT were performed on an *ad hoc* basis by working parties. The main features of the RTA examination process under GATT were:

- The signatories to the RTA notified the RTA to the GATT Council;
- The Council mandated a working party to examine the RTA, and invited contracting parties to issue questions;
- Once the working party collected all questions and replies, it drafted a compendium thereof;
- The working party would then meet for oral question and reply sessions, which were often accompanied by written submissions of statistical or other information;
- The working party drafted an examination report, and transmitted it to the GATT Council for adoption;
- All examinations were confidential, with the exception of circulated documents and reports;
- Each working party determined its own rules of procedure;
- Recommendations or critiques by individual contracting parties were duly recorded, sometimes briefly and sometimes at length.[124]

The GATT RTA examination process was criticized because of its inconsistency and its ineffectiveness. There was no standard format for the submission of information, each working party created its own rules for the conduct of examinations, and each working party drafted its report in a different way, with only some working parties rigorously examining the consistency of RTA provisions with GATT disciplines. Many RTAs were not notified, and Contracting Parties made no apparent efforts to amend RTA provisions criticized in examination reports, perhaps because the reports lacked legitimacy in light of their inconsistent styles. Although twenty-seven Working Party Reports on RTAs were adopted under the GATT system,[125] the reports merely articulated issues raised by the Contracting Parties without arriving at any firm conclusions.[126] Furthermore, even at the time of the GATT, there were concerns about the efficacy of the review process. For cxample, in a November 1992 General Council meeting devoted to discussion of the Canada-United States Free Trade Agreement, the Chairman noted that:

> [O]ver fifty previous working parties on individual Customs unions or free-trade areas had been unable to reach unanimous conclusions as to the GATT consistency of those agreements. On the other hand, no such agreements had been disapproved explicitly.[127]

---

[123] *See Regionalism and the World Trading System, supra* note 12.

[124] *See Compendium of Issues Relating to Regional Trade Agreements, supra* note 66, at Annex, p. 32 (2002)(comparing RTA examination under GATT and under the WTO.).

[125] *See* WTO Secretariat, *Regional Trade Agreements Notified to the GATT/WTO and in Force,* (Jan. 24, 2003) (avail. at. http://www.wto.org/english/tratop_e/region_e/status_240103_e.xls)

[126] *See* JACKSON, DAVEY & SYKES, *supra* note 82, at 471.

[127] *See* Meeting of the General Council, p. 25, C/M/253 (1992), *cited* in General Agreement on Tariffs and Trade, ANALYTICAL INDEX: GUIDE TO GATT LAW AND PRACTICE, 760 (6th ed. 1994)

The need to remedy the lack of discipline and consistency that marred GATT examinations ultimately led to the 1994 Understanding,[128] the creation of the CRTA[129] and the promulgation of various procedural rules governing the examination process[130] and related reporting requirements.[131]

2. Examinations of RTAs under the WTO System

(a) Overview. The current examination process attained its current form with the creation of the CRTA in 1996 pursuant to a General Council decision made under Article IV of the Agreement Establishing the WTO.[132] The CRTA's Terms of Reference, as determined by the General Council, are as follows:

(a) to carry out the examination of agreements in accordance with the procedures and terms of reference adopted by the Council for Trade in Goods, the Council for Trade in Services or the Committee on Trade and Development, as the case may be, and thereafter present its report to the relevant body for appropriate action;

(b) to consider how the required reporting on the operation of such agreements should be carried out and make appropriate recommendations to the relevant body;

(c) to develop, as appropriate, procedures to facilitate and improve the examination process;

(d) to consider the systemic implications of such agreements and regional initiatives for the multilateral trading system and the relationship between them, and make appropriate recommendations to the General Council; and

(e) to carry out any additional functions assigned to it by the General Council.

In practice, the first step of the examination process is the notification by the RTA signatories reporting on their agreement to the Council for Trade in Goods ("CTG"). The Council then informs the CRTA of the RTA notification. After notification and submission of information, the CRTA calls meetings at which other WTO members orally question the RTA signatories about the RTA.[133] There is also an opportunity for the exchange of written questions and replies between the examining Members and the RTA signatories. After the oral and written examinations have concluded, the WTO Secretariat drafts an examination report for circulation among WTO members. Once the draft report has been circulated, WTO members conduct several rounds of informal

---

[128] *See, infra* notes 105–113 and accompanying text. As discussed above, the 1994 Understanding clarified rules governing RTAs in several key respects.

[129] *See,* World Trade Organization, *Regionalism and the World Trading System,* 63–5 (1995)(suggesting the establishment of a single body to examine regional trade agreements.); *See also Second Session of the CRTA, supra* note 2, at ¶ 87 (discussing the decision of the WTO membership to create the CRTA.).

[130] *See, CRTA Rules of Procedure, supra* note 114.

[131] *See,* Committee on Regional Trade Agreements, *Checklist of Points on Reporting on the Operation of Regional Agreements,* WT/REG/W/3 (June 20, 1996)(acknowledging that the *ad hoc* GATT working party approach "led to a lack of consistency in the reporting procedure," which resulted—in 1971—in the Contracting Parties' adoption of a Decision to require the submission of biennial reports.). Other clarifications of the reporting process were set forth in the 1994 Understanding. *See,* discussion, *infra* footnotes 111–118 and accompanying text.

[132] The CRTA was created in February 1996 pursuant to a Decision of the General Council. *See Committee on Regional Trade Agreements,* Decision of 6 February 1996, WT/L/127 (1996).

[133] All WTO members are invited to participate in meetings of the CRTA. The CRTA's mandate is set forth in its Terms of Reference. The CRTA elects a Chairperson and a Vice-Chairperson from among the Member representatives. The Chair- and Vice-Chairpersons hold office for one-year terms. *See CRTA Rules of Procedure, supra* note 114, at Rule 12.

discussions in an effort to reach consensus on a text acceptable to all WTO members. To date, no examination reports have been adopted under the consensus rule, as required under the WTO process.

(b) Notification. Provisions of the GATT,[134] the 1994 Understanding,[135] the GATS[136] and the Enabling Clause[137] require that any WTO member deciding to enter into an RTA must promptly notify and provide relevant information to other WTO members. Technically, notification of RTAs falling under Article XXIV is made to the Council for Trade in Goods ("CTG"), which automatically issues a mandate for the examination and puts the examination on the CTG agenda.[138] Authority over the examination then passes to the CRTA.[139] Notification requirements for Services Agreements and agreements falling under the Enabling Clause are slightly different.[140]

Although the text of the RTA is usually provided at the time of notification, the RTA signatories also distribute a summary of key information in a standardized format[141] to other WTO members at least four weeks before the first meeting scheduled to discuss

---

[134] *See,* GATT Article XXIV:7, which provides that:

(a) Any contracting party deciding to enter into a customs union or free-trade area, or an interim agreement leading to the formation of such a union or area, shall promptly notify the CONTRACTING PARTIES and shall make available to them such information regarding the proposed union or area as will enable them to make such reports and recommendations to contracting parties as they may deem appropriate.

(b) If, after having studied the plan and schedule included in an interim agreement referred to in paragraph 5 in consultation with the parties to that agreement and taking due account of the information made available in accordance with the provisions of sub-paragraph (*a*), the CONTRACTING PARTIES find that such agreement is not likely to result in the formation of a customs union or of a free-trade area within the period contemplated by the parties to the agreement or that such period is not a reasonable one, the CONTRACTING PARTIES shall make recommendations to the parties to the agreement. The parties shall not maintain or put into force, as the case may be, such agreement if they are not prepared to modify it in accordance with these recommendations.

(c) Any substantial change in the plan or schedule referred to in paragraph 5(c) shall be communicated to the CONTRACTING PARTIES, which may request the contracting parties concerned to consult with them if the change seems likely to jeopardize or delay unduly the formation of the customs union or of the free-trade area.

[135] *See, 1994 Understanding,* ¶¶ 7–11 (setting forth detailed procedures for notification and provision of information.).

[136] *See,* GATS Article V:7(a).

[137] *See Differential and More Favourable Treatment, Reciprocity and Fuller Participation of Developing Countries,* Decision of 28 November 1979, ¶ 4.

[138] *See Compendium of Issues Related to Regional Trade Agreements, supra* note 66, at 32.

[139] Specifically, the following items are distributed to the WTO members at this stage: (1) an "airgram" announcing the upcoming meeting; (2) an agenda for the meeting; and (3) any necessary documentation (such as information supplied in the standard format). *See,* Committee on Regional Trade Agreements, *Draft Rules of Procedure for Meetings of the Committee on Regional Trade Agreements, Statement by the Chairman,* WT/REG/W/2 (June 13, 1996) ("*CRTA Draft Rules of Procedure*").

[140] It should be noted that RTAs falling under the Enabling Clause are notified to the Committee on Trade and Development ("CTD"), while RTAs covered by the GATS are notified to the Council for Trade in Services ("CTS"). The CTD does not generally refer RTAs falling under its purview to the CRTA for in-depth review. Similarly, it is within the discretion of the CTS to refer Services Agreements to the CRTA for review: Unlike FTAs and Customs Unions, Services Agreements are not subject to a mandatory review in the CRTA. *See Committee on Regional Trade Agreements,* Work of the Committee on Regional Trade Agreements, at www.wto.org/English/tratop_e/region_e/regcom_e.htm

[141] The CRTA has developed a standard format for the submission of information relating to trade agreements covering goods and a standard format for agreements covering services. *See,* WT/REG/W/6 and WT/REG/W/14, respectively.

the RTA.[142] The standard format requires the submission of four major categories of information: Background Information on the Agreement, Trade Provisions, General Provisions, and Other.[143]

(c) Oral and Written Examinations.   During the meetings that follow notification, WTO members pose questions orally to the RTA signatories, who either respond at that time or in writing at a later time.[144] In addition to this oral examination, WTO members may also deliver written questions to the RTA signatories, to which written answers are provided.[145] The written examination format is most appropriate for complex questions requiring extensive research and compilation of statistics by the responding parties.

The number of meetings devoted to examination of a particular RTA is determined largely by the complexity and importance of the RTA in question. A complex agreement like the Free Trade Area of the Americas is likely to require multiple and extensive meetings, while examination of a less far-reaching RTA might be concluded in a single meeting. Detailed minutes of each meeting are produced and published.[146]

(d) Issuance of the Examination Report.   Once the oral and written examination process is complete, the drafting and review process for the examination report begins. The WTO Secretariat drafts a report based on the issues covered in the oral and written examinations.[147] This draft report is then circulated among the WTO members in "open-ended informal CRTA meetings."[148] Once the WTO members have agreed on the terms of the examination report, the report is put into final form and transmitted to the Council for Trade in Goods. The Council, which "may make such recommendations to Members as it deems appropriate,"[149] must adopt the report by consensus in order to complete the RTA examination process.

(e) Further Reporting Obligations.   Even after a final examination report has been adopted, signatories remain subject to two reporting requirements: biennial reports and reports of any "significant changes and/or developments."[150]

3. Evaluation of the WTO Examination Process for RTAs
(a) Notification and Submission of Information: Timing Issues.   Confusion over the timing of notification stands out as the most troublesome issue at this stage in the examination

---

[142] *See CRTA Draft Rules of Procedure, supra* note 113, Statement by the Chairman.

[143] *See* Committee on Regional Trade Agreements, *Standard Format for Information on Regional Trade Agreements,* WT/REG/W/6 (Aug. 15, 1996)(I. Background Information includes (1) membership, dates of signature, ratification and entry into force; (2) type of agreement; (3) scope; and (4) trade data. II. Trade Provisions include (1) import and (2) export restrictions, such as duties and charges, as well as quantitative restrictions; (3) rules of origin; (4) standards; (5) safeguards; (6) anti-dumping and countervailing measures; (7) subsidies and state-aid; (8) sector-specific provisions; and other measures. III. General Provisions include (1) exceptions and reservations, (2) accession provisions; (3) dispute settlement procedures; (4) relation with other agreements; and (5) institutional framework. IV. Other is a basket provision for all other information required for the sake of transparency.).

[144] *See Compendium of Issues Related to Regional Trade Agreements, supra* note 67, at 32.

[145] *Id.*

[146] *Id.*

[147] *Id.*

[148] *Id.*

[149] *Id.*

[150] *Id.,* at 6–7.

process.[151] There is disagreement among WTO members as to when such notification must be made.[152] In light of the number of RTAs in existence that have not yet been notified, it is not even clear that all parties agree that notification should be made by the time an RTA comes into force.[153] Indeed, some parties may view the notification process as optional, or may simply be refraining from notification in the belief that they will probably not suffer any sanction for their non-compliance.

On the other hand, the establishment of the "standard format" constitutes a positive achievement of the CRTA in this area. Transmission of information in a standard format provides RTA signatories with guidelines regarding their submissions, and allows other WTO members to identify quickly potential areas of concern without first having to parse hundreds of pages of the agreement text.

(b) Oral and Written Examinations: The Only Functional Part of the RTA Examination Process.   The most important role of the CRTA is probably monitoring of reporting requirements and conduct of RTA examinations. The examinations, in particular, provide a forum in which members must explain and justify controversial features of their proposed RTAs. Under current practice, the examining members make sustained and pointed inquiries (whether orally or in writing) about all aspects of a proposed RTA, focusing in particular on any features that appear to be inconsistent with WTO disciplines.[154] The intense scrutiny characteristic of CRTA meetings may promote compliance with WTO rules in the spirit of Justice Brandeis' comment that "[s]unlight is said to be the best of disinfectants."[155] However, although exposure in CRTA meetings may serve to restrain the most egregious violations of WTO provisions, there is a danger that many trade-distorting features will nonetheless persist. The large number of RTAs that the CRTA must examine, the large amount of complex data involved, and the multitude of issues facing national delegations at the WTO make it less likely that exposure of a defect in an RTA will, in itself, result in strong pressure to correct it.

---

[151] For a discussion of other issues raised in connection with the GATT Article XXIV obligation to notify RTAs and submit information, *See Second Session of the CRTA, supra* note 2.

[152] *See,* Committee on Regional Trade Agreements, *Synopsis of "Systemic" Issues Related to Regional Trade Agreements,* WT/REG/W/37, ¶ 13 (March 2, 2000) (*"Synopsis of Systemic Issues"*) (noting that some members maintain that notification should be made "before entry into force" of the RTA. Other members respond that the imprecision regarding notification procedures "reflects the 'pragmatism' necessary to address complex negotiations for the formation of an RTA, a particularly relevant matter in the case of large agreements in which the bulk of concessions are made at the last minute.").

[153] Because of the disagreement over notifications, some WTO members have proposed that a means of gathering information on non-notified RTAs be developed. One proposal suggests a so-called "counter-notification" procedure, whereby a member having reason to believe that another member has entered into an RTA notifies the WTO of the basis for such belief; the WTO would then solicit comments and information from the members believed to have concluded an RTA. This proposal has been rejected by those WTO members who believe that it is not authorized under the WTO agreements. *See, id.,* at ¶ 16.

[154] The minutes of the examination meetings for NAFTA provide an example of a particularly sustained and thorough RTA examination. The NAFTA came into force before the advent of the WTO, and thus it was examined under the GATT RTA examination procedures. Nonetheless, the acute interest of WTO members in the NAFTA strongly influenced the examination of the NAFTA, as is reflected in the probing questions in the referenced documents. *See* World Trade Organization, *Working Party on the North American Free Trade Agreement: Questions and Replies,* WT/REG4/1 (June 25, 1995), WT/REG4/1/Add.1 (July 22, 1996) and WT/REG4/1/Add.2 (Oct. 15, 1996).

[155] Justice Brandeis emphasized the importance of transparency in his 1933 publication on the securities industry, *Other People's Money:* "Publicity is justly commended as a remedy for social and industrial diseases. Sunlight is said to be the best of disinfectants; electric light the most efficient policeman." Louis Brandeis, OTHER PEOPLE'S MONEY, 62 (1933).

(c) Examination Reports: Complete Failure of the System. The total shutdown of the examination report component deprives the WTO of a considerable measure of its sanctioning power over countries that flaunt the rules governing RTAs. Failure to adopt by consensus any examination report essentially means that the WTO is incapable of judging or making recommendations about the consistency of RTA provisions with WTO obligations.

The absence of examination reports can be attributed to several possible causes: (1) Because of the requirement that WTO members adopt the examination report by consensus, when an RTA becomes subject to serious criticism, the signatories to the RTA simply block adoption of the report; (2) because of the vigorous activity of the WTO Dispute Settlement Body, many WTO members are loathe to adopt an examination report containing statements or recommendations that could be construed by a Panel or the Appellate Body to the detriment of a WTO members' RTA; and (3) because of the controversy surrounding certain key provisions, such as "substantially all the trade," many members are unable to agree when a given RTA violates a key substantive provision of Article XXIV.[156]

(d) Further Reporting Obligations: Late Reports and Those Never Submitted. The draft 2002 CRTA Report to the General Council noted that in 2001 almost all biennial reports required by the 1994 Agreement were submitted late, and had to be considered in 2002.[157] And biennial reports were not submitted at all for six RTAs.[158] This CRTA Report also notes that other required information is generally being submitted late or not at all, as reflected in "a considerable time-lag for the first round of examination for an increasing number of RTAs" and "a gap between the number of agreements notified to the WTO and those actually in force."[159]

(e) Conclusion. It seems evident that the RTA examination system is not achieving the level of scrutiny of RTAs anticipated by GATT Article XXIV, the 1994 Understanding or the CRTA Rules of Procedure. The record of the RTA examination process is mixed at best. Although a reasonable number of notified RTAs have been subjected to some examination, systemic problems have prevented the adoption of any examination reports. Examinations either are in progress or have been completed for 118 of the 162 notified RTAs in force,[160] but not a single examination report has been adopted since the advent of the WTO.

---

[156] It should also be noted that even if WTO members were able to adopt examination reports by consensus, serious questions would remain as to whether the RTA signatories would readily comply with recommendations in the report. Domestic and international political considerations may render compliance difficult. It would be extremely difficult, if not impossible, to "rewrite" a given RTA, because the RTA represents a delicate balance of negotiating concessions, made sometimes after high-level political compromises. In some cases, a re-calibration of that balance—after the conclusion or negotiations and passage by national legislatures—could threaten to unravel the entire agreement. And since the examination reports consist of the commentary of the representatives of the various members, there may be a perception that some criticisms are partisan, designed to gain negotiating leverage, or simply impractical, unreasonable or unrealistic.

[157] *See,* Committee on Regional Trade Agreements, *Draft Report (2002) of the Committee on Regional Trade Agreements to the General Council,* WT/REG/W/47, ¶ 6 and Attachment 3 (Nov. 4, 2002); *See also,* Committee on Regional Trade Agreements, *Reporting on Regional Trade Agreements—Recommendations by the CRTA to the Council for Trade in Goods,* WT/REG/4 (March 11, 1998)(setting forth detailed reporting requirements regarding RTAs.).

[158] *See,* Committee on Regional Trade Agreements, *Draft Report (2002) of the Committee on Regional Trade Agreements to the General Council,* Attachment 3, WT/REG/W/47 (Nov. 4, 2002).

[159] *Id.,* at ¶¶ 8 and 9.

[160] *See, Basic Information on Regional Trade Agreements, supra* note 8. This information has been updated in some respects in the 2002 Draft Report to the General Council. *See,* Committee on Regional Trade Agreements, *Draft Report (2002) of the Committee on Regional Trade Agreements to the General Council,*

The non-functionality of the procedures for the adoption of examination reports does not mean that the CRTA is totally ineffectual in promoting compliance with WTO rules. The CRTA has issued reports on systemic problems that have come out in the RTA examination process,[161] and it has organized seminars analyzing the implications of the recent surge in RTAs.[162] Through those activities the CRTA serves an educational function by increasing the level of awareness about the opportunities and risks posed by RTAs.

The CRTA also serves as a forum for WTO members to discuss systemic issues and even circulate proposals for more effective regulation of RTAs. In this way, the CRTA is promoting the exchange of views, consensus building and even the diplomatic resolution of disputes. In its current form, then, the CRTA may help define the issues relating to RTAs that need to be addressed during the Doha Round.

On balance, however, it appears that the weaknesses of the current RTA examination system exceed its strengths. The absence of clear rules and strong institutions for the regulation of RTAs undermines CRTA's usefulness as a forum for information exchange, negotiation, and consensus-building, on the one hand, and as a forum for the detailed and intense review of new RTAs. Most importantly, the failure to adopt any examination reports since 1995 has robbed the CRTA of its most effective enforcement tool against RTAs with trade distorting features that weaken the multilateral system. The CRTA's effectiveness is also impaired by its inability to ensure that notification requirements are met, that complete answers are provided during the oral and written examinations, and that periodic reporting requirements are satisfied.

Because the RTA examination process has failed to require rigorous compliance with WTO disciplines, the only recourse remaining to members harmed by the trade-distorting effects of a given RTA is to invoke WTO dispute settlement procedures.[163] As discussed below, however, this is an imperfect alternative to a systematic and meaningful examination process performed at the inception of a given RTA.

C. Regulation of RTAs through WTO Dispute Settlement

1. WTO Panel and Appellate Body Rulings Involving RTAs

As of the date of writing (September 2004), five WTO dispute settlement cases have implicated RTAs, but—generally speaking—only in a tangential manner.[164] Two disputes

---

WT/REG/W/47 (Nov. 4, 2002)(recording 125 actively under examination, of which 27 are in the midst of the examination process, with the other 74 having completed the examination process, but not having resulted in the issuance of a report.).

[161] *See, e.g.,* Committee on Regional Trade Agreements, *Coverage, Liberalization Process and Transition Provisions in Regional Trade Agreements,* WT/REG/W/46 (April 5, 2002); Committee on Regional Trade Agreements, *Rules of Origin Regimes in Regional Trade Agreements,* WT/REG/W/45 (April 5, 2002).

[162] *See,* World Trade Organization, *Seminar on Regionalism and the WTO,* (April 26, 2002)(containing links to papers presented by panelists), avail. at. www.wto.org/English/tratop_e/region_e/sem_april02_e/background_obj_e.htm

[163] *See 1994 Understanding,* at ¶ 12.

[164] *See*

(1) Report of the Appellate Body, *United States—Definitive Safeguard Measures on Imports of Circular Welded Carbon Quality Line Pipe from Korea,* WT/DS202/AB/R (2002);

(2) Report of the Appellate Body, *United States—Definitive Safeguard Measures on Imports of Wheat Gluten from the E.C.,* WT/DS166/AB/R (2001);

(3) Report of the WTO Panel, *Canada—Certain Measures Affecting the Automotive Industry,* WT/DS139, 142/R (2000);

addressed the question of whether GATT violations could be justified by the existence of a Customs Union or FTA. Three disputes have involved the specific question of whether it is permissible to accord preferential treatment to a co-signatory of an FTA or Customs Union in the application of a safeguard measure.[165] Although all five disputes are discussed below, the discussions are limited to legal matters that directly impact Article XXIV disciplines.

(a) Turkey—Restrictions on Imports of Textile and Clothing Products. The most significant of all WTO cases involving GATT Article XXIV is *Turkey—Restrictions on Imports of Textile and Clothing Products* (*"Turkey—Textiles"*). In this case, the Appellate Body developed a legal formula according to which it would be determined whether derogations from WTO disciplines could be justified under Article XXIV as "necessary" to the formation of a Customs Union. The Appellate Body ultimately found that certain quantitative restrictions imposed by Turkey on textile imports could not be justified under GATT Article XXIV.

(i) Factual Background As one phase of its proposed accession to the EC, Turkey entered into the EC-Turkey Customs Union, under which Turkey committed to harmonizing its external customs tariff with that of the EC.[166] Part of this external tariff harmonization process required Turkey to adopt the EC's import regime for textiles, which included quantitative restrictions on Indian textile imports.[167] Previously, Turkey had much lower restrictions on textiles from India.

(ii) Panel Proceedings India initiated panel proceedings against Turkey claiming that the new quantitative restrictions violated *inter alia* GATT Articles XI and XIII.[168] Turkey responded that measures (adopted in connection with a Customs Union) that derogate from other GATT obligations are permitted so long as a WTO Member complies with the requirements of GATT Article XXIV. The Panel ruled against Turkey, holding that, although the Turkey-EC arrangement was a Customs Union, nothing in Article XXIV justified Turkey's adoption of quantitative restrictions that violated its various GATT obligations toward India.

(iii) Turkey's Article XXIV Arguments Upon Appeal Turkey appealed this finding to the Appellate Body. Turkey argued that the Panel had erred because—among other reasons—its analysis ignored the Chapeau of Article XXIV:5(a), which provides that GATT provisions "shall not prevent" the formation of a Customs Union so long as the conditions set out in Article XXIV:5(a) are satisfied. Turkey argued that the Panel—by ignoring this Chapeau language—came to the erroneous conclusion that Article XXIV did not authorize or permit the quantitative restrictions.

(4) Report of the Appellate Body, *Turkey—Restrictions on Imports of Textile and Clothing Products,* WT/DS34/AB/R (1999);

(5) Report of the Appellate Body, *Argentina—Safeguard Measures on Imports of Footwear,* WT/DS121/AB/R (1999).

[165] *See United States—Line Pipe, Argentina—Footwear,* and *United States—Wheat Gluten, supra* note 164.
[166] *See* Report of the WTO Panel, *Turkey—Restrictions on Imports of Textile and Clothing Products,* WT/DS139,142R, ¶¶ 2.15–2.16
[167] *See id.,* at ¶ 2.10–2.20, 2.33–2.35
[168] *See id.,* at ¶ 1.3

Turkey also argued that the Panel had incorrectly viewed Article XXIV as an "exception" to a limited set of GATT obligations, whereas in fact Article XXIV accorded WTO members an autonomous right to enter into Customs Unions, thus permitting WTO members to derogate from any GATT obligations so long as they do so consistently with the strictures of Article XXIV. Accordingly, Turkey argued that any regulations of commerce (such as the quantitative restrictions at issue) adopted in the context of the Customs Union were permissible under GATT Article XXIV:5(a) so long as such regulations were not on the whole more restrictive than previous regulations of the constituent members of the Customs Union.

Additionally, Turkey submitted that if it were unable to harmonize its textile import regulations with the EC by imposing quantitative restrictions on Indian textiles, the EC would impose those same quantitative restrictions on Turkish exports, thus excluding 40 percent of Turkey's exports from the EC-Turkey Customs Union, which would necessarily violate the GATT Article XXIV:8(a)(i) requirement that the Customs Union cover "substantially all" trade between its members.

(iv) Appellate Body Report Although the Appellate Body ultimately rejected Turkey's arguments, it criticized the Panel's reasoning on several grounds. First, it agreed with Turkey that the Chapeau to GATT Article XXIV:5 is a central provision for the analysis of the WTO-consistency of any measure that a WTO member seeks to justify under an RTA. The Appellate Body then examined the text of the Chapeau in light of its context, first examining paragraph 8 (defining "Customs Union") and the 1994 Understanding (setting standards for comparing the general incidence of duties and other regulations before and after the Customs Union), and then turning to paragraph 4 (which stresses that "the purpose of a customs union . . . should be to facilitate trade . . . and not to raise barriers to the trade of other contracting parties.") In light of this context, the Appellate Body held that Article XXIV could justify measures inconsistent with other GATT measures provided that it could make two showings:

> First, the party claiming the benefit of this defense must demonstrate that the measure at issue is introduced upon the formation of a customs union that fully meets the requirements of sub-paragraphs 8(a) and 5(a) of Article XXIV. And, second, that party must demonstrate that the formation of that customs union would be prevented if it were not allowed to introduce the measure at issue.[169]

In applying this test to Turkey's quantitative restrictions, the Appellate Body noted that other means of regulating imports than quantitative restrictions (e.g., rules of origin) were available to Turkey to the extent that it needed to act in a manner compatible with the EU textiles regime.[170] For this reason, the Appellate Body concluded that Turkey had failed to meet the burden of defending its quantitative restrictions under GATT Article XXIV, and that the restrictions violated GATT Article XI and XIII.[171]

(v) Significance of Turkey—Textiles Case The Appellate Body's discussion is significant for several reasons. Most importantly, it articulates a standard for the WTO compatibility of RTAs, pursuant to which WTO members have a clear right to enter RTAs and institute measures (even measures inconsistent with other WTO obligations), so long as such measures are (1) necessary to the formation of an RTA, and (2) the least

---

[169] *Turkey—Restrictions on Imports of Textile and Clothing Products,* WT/DS34/AB/R, ¶ 58 (1999).
[170] *See id.,* ¶ 62.
[171] *See id.,* ¶ 63.

restrictive measures available. It is also significant that the Appellate Body—in the first prong of its test—also held that Panels must establish that an RTA within the meaning of GATT Article XXIV exists before evaluating whether particular challenged measures are justified by the GATT exception set forth in Article XXIV.

This holding is significant because it indicates that the Appellate Body has sanctioned increased scrutiny of whether purported RTAs actually meet the requirements of GATT Article XXIV. As a result of this ruling, WTO members wishing to find an Article XXIV-related justification for a derogation from WTO disciplines must ensure that their Customs Unions or FTAs fully comply with GATT Article XXIV, the 1994 Understanding and applicable GATT and WTO practice. Thus, the Appellate Body has contributed—in a limited way—to establishing incentives for strict compliance with WTO rules governing RTAs.

(b) Canada—Certain Measures Affecting the Automotive Industry. Canada—Certain Measures Affecting the Automotive Industry, involved Canadian measures that gave duty preferences to a limited class of automobile imports pursuant to the Agreement Concerning Automotive Products Between the Government of Canada and the Government of the United States (the "Auto Pact"), a treaty between Canada and the United States concluded in January 1965.[172] The eligibility criteria for the exemptions effectively limited the duty-free preferences to vehicles made by General Motors, Ford and Chrysler—even if the vehicles were not produced in the United States or Mexico. The European Communities and Japan asserted that these preferences violated Canada's GATT and WTO obligations, including its MFN obligation under GATT Article I. Canada claimed, *inter alia,* that the duty exemptions accorded to U.S. and Mexican originating vehicles was justified under Article XXIV because the duty exemptions were "necessary" to the formation of the NAFTA.

(i) The E.C.'s Article XXIV Arguments   The European Communities' response to this argument had several facets. The EC claimed *inter alia* that: (1) because Canada-Mexico trade was still subject to duties, there was no FTA but rather an interim agreement between the two countries;[173] (2) even if the NAFTA qualified as an FTA, the import duty exemption was illegal because only those measures "inherent" to an FTA could be justified under Article XXIV, yet the Auto Pact and its duty exemptions were "neither part of nor required by NAFTA;"[174] (3) contrary to the requirement in Article XXIV that FTAs lead to trade liberalization, the duty exemption actually hindered trade liberalization because it *de facto* discriminated against all imported vehicles (even U.S. and Mexican-produced vehicles) other than those produced by General Motors, Ford and Chrysler, and thus prevented "NAFTA from displaying all its potential trade creating effects."[175]

(ii) Canada's Article XXIV Arguments   Canada's responses to the E.C.'s arguments were as follows: (1) NAFTA clearly constituted an FTA among Canada, Mexico and the United States, as defined by Article XXIV, because Article XXIV did not require

---

[172] *See, Canada—Certain Measures Affecting the Automobile Industry,* ¶ 2.3.

[173] *See id.,* ¶ 6.108.

[174] *See id.,* ¶ 6.109–111 (arguing that—while certain measures may be justifiable under Article XXIV if they are "necessary" to the formation of the FTA, no provision of the NAFTA "required" the duty exemptions established by the Auto Pact.).

[175] *Id.,* ¶ 6.115.

the immediate and absolute elimination of all duties among all members of an FTA; (2) It is incorrect to claim that the Auto Pact duty exemptions are not part of NAFTA as the NAFTA specifically provides for the continuation these exemptions; (3) Even if the Auto Pact was not technically "part of" the NAFTA, Article XXIV does not require duty-free treatment be "part of" or "required by" "the principal agreement establishing the [FTA]."[176]

(iii) The Panel Report   The Panel ultimately ruled that GATT Article XXIV did not provide a defense for Auto Pact duty exemptions that violated GATT Article I, because the exemptions were not guaranteed to all products of NAFTA countries, nor were they necessarily denied to products of non-NAFTA countries. As the Panel stated,

> In our view, Article XXIV clearly cannot justify a measure which grants WTO-inconsistent duty-free treatment to products originating in third countries not parties to a customs union or free trade agreement.... We further note that . . . in practice the import duty exemption does not apply to some products that would be entitled to duty-free treatment if such treatment were dependant solely on the fact that the products originated in the United States or Mexico. We thus do not believe that the import duty exemption is properly characterized as a measure which provides for duty-free treatment of imports of products of parties to a free-trade area.[177]

(c) WTO Disputes Involving the Relationship Between the WTO Agreement on Safeguards and GATT Article XXIV.   Three WTO cases involved the specific question of whether it is permissible for an FTA signatory country or Customs Union member state to <u>include</u> imports from other countries within the territory of the FTA or Customs for purposes of establishing "serious injury" in a safeguards investigation, yet <u>exclude</u> those countries from the application of the safeguard measure. In all three cases, the WTO Appellate Body held that such an approach was impermissible under the Agreement on Safeguards.

These cases are important to GATT Article XXIV jurisprudence because of the range of defenses raised under that Article. Notwithstanding variations in the arguments made by the parties in each case, the basic legal issue involved was similar in all three. For this reason, we treat only the first of these cases, *Argentina—Footwear*, in detail. The other cases are *United States—Definitive Safeguard Measures on Imports of Circular Welded Carbon Quality Pipe from Korea*[178] and *United States—Definitive Safeguard Measures on Imports of Wheat Gluten from the E.C.*[179]

The *Argentina—Footwear* case is relevant to WTO regulation of RTAs because in it the Appellate Body further clarified the relationship between Article XXIV only and

---

[176] *Id.*, ¶ 10.54.

[177] *Id.*, ¶¶ 10.55–56. The panel decision was not appealed.

[178] This is the most recent case to examine the relationship between Article XXIV and the Agreement on Safeguards. In it, the Appellate Body held that the United States had violated its obligations under the Agreement on Safeguards by including imports from Canada and Mexico in the determination regarding injury to the U.S. industry, but excluding these imports from the application of duties. *See United States— Line Pipe from Korea, supra,* note 154. This U.S. methodology resulted in application of safeguard duties to non-NAFTA countries beyond "the extent necessary to prevent or remedy serious injury and to facilitate adjustment." *Id.*, ¶ 197. The Appellate Body suggested that the non-application of duties to Canada and Mexico might have been permissible if the U.S. International Trade Commission had provided "a reasoned and adequate explanation that establishes explicitly that imports from non-NAFTA sources by themselves satisfied the conditions for the application of a safeguard measure." *Id.*, at ¶ 197.

[179] *Supra*, note 154.

the Agreement on Safeguards, while also reaffirming the principle that Article XXIV provides a defense to an otherwise WTO-inconsistent measure in very limited circumstances.

(i) Factual Background and Arguments of the Parties   In this case, the Argentine trade authorities considered imports from MERCOSUR countries in their determination of serious injury, but did not apply the safeguard measure to MERCOSUR countries. The European Communities argued that this methodology violated Article 2.2 of the Agreement on Safeguards, which requires that safeguard measures be applied "to a product being imported irrespective of its source."[180] Exclusion of MERCOSUR from application of the safeguard would only be appropriate, the European Communities argued, if Argentina had excluded MERCOSUR-origin products for purposes of the investigation as well.[181]

Among its responses, Argentina argued that GATT Article XXIV:8 prohibited it—as a member of MERCOSUR—from maintaining barriers (e.g., safeguards) to trade with the other MERCOSUR members. In support of this argument, Argentina first cited the footnote of Article 2.1 of the Safeguards Agreement, which permits Customs Unions to apply safeguard measures "as a single unit or on behalf of a Member State" yet explicitly provides that, "[n]othing in this Agreement prejudges the interpretation of the relationship between Article XIX and paragraph 8 of Article XXIV of GATT."[182] Argentina also called the Panel's attention to the fact that the MERCOSUR members had explicitly agreed not to apply safeguard measures against each other.

(ii) The Panel Report   Although the Panel acknowledged that neither the text of Article XXIV nor GATT practice were conclusive on the permissibility of safeguard measures among FTA or Customs Union signatories,[183] the Panel ultimately held that Argentina could legally apply a safeguard measure against other MERCOSUR members because (1) the MERCOSUR was in a transitional phase during which some restrictive regulations were allowed, and (2) even if the constituent member States of a Customs Union had agreed not to apply safeguard measures against each other, the footnote to Article 2.1 of the Safeguards Agreement allowed the Customs Union itself to apply a safeguard "on behalf of" its members States.[184] The Panel concluded by stating:

---

[180] *See* Report of the Panel, *Argentina—Footwear,* ¶¶ 5.67–5.76, 8.74, *supra* note 163.

[181] *See, id.*

[182] *See, id.,* ¶ 8.93. Argentina noted that the last sentence of the footnote to Article 2.1 explicitly stated there to be no consensus on the relationship between Articles XIX and XXIV of GATT. Argentina noted that although Article XXIV:8 specified some exceptions from the requirement to abolish all duties and other restrictive regulations on substantially all trade within a Customs Union, GATT Article XIX (on safeguards) was not one of those enumerated exceptions. Thus, Argentina claimed that Article XXIV:8 (not to mention MERCOSUR legislation) explicitly prohibited it from imposing safeguard measures against imports from other MERCOSUR countries.

[183] *See id.,* ¶ 8.96 (The Panel noted that Article XIX is not one of the restrictive regulations enumerated in Article XXIV:8 as one of those that must be eliminated within the territories of a Customs Union. Furthermore, the Panel found the practice of GATT Contracting Parties and WTO Members to be "inconclusive on the issue of the imposition or maintenance of safeguard measures between the constituent territories of a customs union or an [FTA]." Finally, the Panel accepted that, "[i]t is a matter of fact that many agreements establishing [FTAs]... or customs unions allow for the possibility to impose safeguard measures on intra-regional trade, while few regional integration agreements explicitly prohibit the imposition of intra-regional safeguard measures once the formation of such an integration area is completed."

[184] *See, id.,* ¶ 8.98.

we do not agree with the argument that in the case before us Argentina is prevented by Article XXIV:8 of GATT from applying safeguard measures to all sources of supply, i.e., third countries as well as other member States of MERCOSUR. . . . [I]n the light of Article 2 of the Safeguards Agreement and Article XXIV of GATT, we conclude that in the case of a customs union the imposition of a safeguard measure only on third-country sources of supply cannot be justified on the basis of a member-state-specific investigation that finds serious injury or threat thereof caused by imports from all sources of supply from within and outside a customs union.[185]

(iii) The Appellate Body Report   Although the Appellate Body agreed with the Panel's conclusion, it disagreed with the Panel's analysis. The Appellate Body first rejected the Panel's conclusion that the footnote to Safeguards Agreement Article 2.1 was applicable in this case, noting that Argentine authorities—not MERCOSUR authorities—conducted the investigation and applied the safeguard measures at issue. The Appellate Body then rejected the Panel's conclusion that Article XXIV had any application at all to this case. In support of this conclusion, the Appellate Body noted the rule it enunciated in *Turkey— Textiles* that measures derogating from WTO disciplines can be justified under Article XXIV only if "the measure at issue is introduced upon the formation o f a customs union that fully meets the requirements of sub-paragraphs 8(a) and 5(a) of Article XXIV" and only if "the formation of the customs union would be prevented if it were not allowed to introduce the measure at issue." Noting that Argentina had proffered none of these arguments in its discussion of Article XXIV, the Appellate Body concluded that Article XXIV was not relevant to the current dispute. Instead, the Appellate Body found that Argentina's decision to exempt imports from MERCOSUR countries from its safeguard measure, while applying that measure to imports from non-signatories of MERCOSUR violated certain provisions of the WTO Agreement on Safeguards.

2. Evaluation of Dispute Settlement as a Means of Regulating RTAs
The *Turkey—Textiles* Appellate Body decision raises the question whether the threat and exercise of WTO dispute settlement procedures can place sufficient discipline on the activities of members entering RTAs to ensure the WTO-consistency of those agreements. Although the Appellate Body in *Japan—Alcoholic Beverages* stated that WTO reports do not have precedential effect,[186] each report adopted by the Dispute Settlement Body adds to the corpus of *de facto* WTO precedent, as shown by the Appellate Body and Panels' continual references to prior standard-setting cases.[187] To the extent that WTO members who are also signatories to an RTA are concerned about being brought before a WTO Panel by WTO members alleging harm from "impermissible" features of an RTA, the RTA signatories are likely to craft provisions that are consistent with WTO disciplines.

However, it does not appear that the threat of being brought before a WTO panel is a sufficient deterrent to constrain RTA signatories from entering RTAs that violate GATT/WTO disciplines, for example, by failing to cover "substantially all the trade" between the signatories.

[185] Panel Report, ¶ 8.102.
[186] Report of the Appellate Body, *Japan-Taxes on Alcoholic Beverages*, WT/DS8/AB/R, WT/DS10/AB/R, WT/DS11/AB/R (1996).
[187] Raj Bhala, *The Precedent Setters: De Facto Stare Decisis in WTO Adjudication (Part Two of a Trilogy)*, 9 J. TRANS NAT'L L. & POL'Y 1, 3–4 (1999) (arguing that the Appellate Body is in the process of establishing binding principles with the effect of Stare Decisis).

Several important provisions of GATT Article XXIV contain ambiguous language, which blurs the boundary between permissible and impermissible action.[188] It is not possible to clarify these ambiguous provisions through resort to historical sources as a means of divining the intent of the drafters of the GATT, because the drafters did not foresee the vast number and far-reaching and varied provisions of RTAs being signed today. Thus, in light of the ambiguities found in GATT Article XXIV, it is possible that WTO panels and the Appellate Body would find that the text of GATT Article XXIV provides insufficient guidance to permit a ruling on some difficult issues. Should the Appellate Body draw its own conclusions about disputed language within Article XXIV, it might be accused of overstepping its mandate, which would damage its credibility and the WTO dispute settlement system.

Strong and far-reaching rulings would be necessary to bring clear and consistent standards, and a measure of discipline, to the hodge-podge of RTAs that members have entered and are negotiating. The agreements are popular and politically important to the countries that enter them—often more important for their political significance than their potential economic benefits. Thus, the Appellate Body's task of giving overall impact to the unclear standards of Article XXIV is all the more daunting.

V. Regulating RTAs in the Interest of the WTO System

Although the CRTA and Dispute Settlement Body do inject a measure of discipline into WTO member practice regarding RTAs, the two institutions seem to have only a limited ability effectively to ensure that RTAs comply with the requirements they are supposed to meet under the WTO. Some of the limits on the ability of the CRTA and the DSB to respond to the RTA phenomenon derive from ambiguities in the text of GATT Article XXIV and related provisions.[189] However, even in cases where the obligations of WTO members are clear, the CRTA and DSB have been unable to enforce compliance with them. For example, WTO members have failed to fulfill their reporting requirements in the CRTA, and consequently some examinations have been delayed and others have failed to take place altogether.[190] More importantly, WTO members have failed to adopt a single RTA examination report since the advent of the WTO, so a potentially effective enforcement tool against RTAs that violate WTO disciplines remains unused.[191]

For this reason, it is worth considering institutional reforms that would bring a greater measure of discipline to WTO member practice regarding RTAs. Over the last seven years,

---

[188] As noted by the CRTA, not only is key language in Article XXIV disputed, but the relationship between Article XXIV and other WTO provisions is also unclear. The following list of questions raises issues that WTO members consider to be unanswered by the relevant provisions of the GATT and WTO Agreements:

    — Is the introduction of new quantitative restrictions justifiable in the context of GATT Articles XXIV:5 and XXIV:8(a)(ii) in the case of a customs union?

    — How should antidumping/safeguard measures already in place within an RTA be applied by new parties to that RTA?

    — Since no multilaterally agreed methodology exists, how should individual Members' reduction commitments on domestic support and export subsidies be translated into common commitments when a customs union is established or enlarged?

Synopsis of Systemic Issues, supra note 131, at ¶ 30.

[189] *See* discussion in Part IV.A above.

[190] *See* discussion in Part IV.B.2.b above.

[191] *See* discussion in Part IV.B.2.d above.

WTO members[192] and commentators[193] have suggested a range of possible changes, some more ambitious than others. We suggest several reforms, including the creation of an independent oversight committee made up of neutral experts and the introduction of a phase-in period for RTAs during which signatory nations are encouraged to bring their RTAs into compliance with WTO and GATT obligations. It may also be useful to reform the RTA examination process to permit a more thorough and systematic inquiry into facially neutral measures that in fact discriminate against non-members of the RTA. The achievement of such a systematic examination process could pave the way for a more expedited review of RTA-related complaints by the Dispute Settlement Body than is currently possible.

A. Independent Committee made up of Neutral Experts

The CRTA could be reformed to incorporate examinations by an independent oversight committee comprising neutral experts drawn from a roster created by the WTO members. This committee would receive information submitted by parties to an RTA, would make requests for further information, and would issue a report on whether the subject RTA complied with WTO and GATT requirements. Independent committees made up of a small number of experts would be able to focus on the most significant potential WTO violations, work effectively within set timelines, and add discipline and credibility to the RTA examination process. Examinations by the independent committee need not replace, but rather could complement the current examinations performed by representatives of WTO member states in the CRTA. The current system for the issuance and adoption of examination reports by all WTO members entails a relatively lengthy timeline; the independent committee's report would have the advantage of being issued on a much more expedited basis.

The report issued by the independent committee would probably have a greater degree of credibility and respect than the reports that currently issue from the CRTA, because there would be less perception that political and economic rivalries played a role in the independent committee report. If the independent committee reports did gain a higher level of legitimacy and support from WTO member states, there would be a greater likelihood of compliance with recommendations contained within them. Although the

---

[192] See, e.g., Committee on Regional Trade Agreements, Communication from the Republic of Korea, WT/REG/W/4, ¶ 9 (June 27, 1996) ("Communication from the Republic of Korea") (proposing that, during the first WTO Ministerial Conference the General Council work:

(a) To identify elements of regionalism which may conflict with the objectives of the [multilateral trading system ("MTS")] . . . and to explore ways and means of addressing such elements;
(b) To explore creative means of capturing trade liberalizations advanced by regional initiatives and incorporating them into the MTS;
(c) To review the validity of the WTO's current legal regime on regionalism, embodied in Article XXIV of GATT 1994 and Article V of GATS, in light of its relevance in the vastly changed global trade environment;
(d) To redefine . . . RTAs' proper relationship with the MTS, and to explore ways and means by which to ensure that regionalism complements and reinforces the objectives of the MTS . . .

Over six years later, it cannot be stated unequivocally that all—or even any—of these objectives has been met. However, as countries enter RTAs at an increasing rate, it becomes increasingly urgent for WTO members to reach some agreement on appropriate rules to ensure the complementarity of the RTA phenomenon with the multilateral trading system).

[193] See e.g., Cho, supra note 1, at 430–37 (outlining several "legal solutions" to systemic problems associated with regionalism.); See also Jackson, supra note 75, at 80.

exact procedures for the panel of independent experts would have to be further elaborated, several useful models already exist, such as the panel selection procedures used in the WTO or NAFTA dispute settlement systems.

B. Phase-in Periods for RTAs Under Examination

A set of phase-in periods would address the criticism that notifications currently occur so late (i.e., after negotiations have been completed and the RTA has been passed by the national legislatures) that it is practically impossible for countries that have entered an RTA to respond to the CRTA's suggestions regarding it. Under this proposal, countries would refrain from presenting RTAs to their respective legislative bodies for a given period (perhaps nine months or a year) after completing negotiations with co-signatories. During this interim "phase-in" period, the proposed RTA would be reviewed in the CRTA by national representatives and by the independent oversight committee proposed above. The CRTA examination would proceed according to a strict timeline leading to the timely issuance of a report. This system would allow the signatories to consider the suggestions contained within the report, and take steps to bring their proposed RTA into compliance with WTO and GATT obligations.[194]

If adopted, this system of phase-in periods and strict timelines would promise considerable advantages over the current CRTA examination process, in which the few RTAs that are actually notified to the WTO are subjected to an examination process that lacks fixed timelines and very often fails to produce a report at all.

C. Systematic Investigation of Hidden Discrimination Within RTA Provisions

The advent of RTAs covering new substantive areas outside the traditional scope of RTAs is accompanied by both risks and opportunities. On the one hand, there is a chance that new agreements developed in the financial, environmental, labor and other areas, as well as measures that harmonize standards and certification procedures among RTA signatories will also yield benefits for non-signatories, leading to increased global efficiency.[195] On the other hand, there is the risk of discrimination—in aim and effect—in the proliferation of overlapping and inconsistent RTA-specific standards, not to mention RTA "trade facilitation" measures that create disadvantages and costs for non-signatories of the RTAs.

The abuse of WTO principles of non-discrimination through such measures is a threat against which the CRTA examination process should guard. In order to do so effectively, it is important that WTO members develop a checklist of the areas in which such abuses are most likely to appear, and the forms that they are most likely to take. Such a checklist could be negotiated informally among WTO Members participating in the CRTA.[196] The checklist should be subject to easy revision to account for novel forms of potential discrimination that show up in future RTAs. When the independent committee of neutral

---

[194] Although this suggestion would create some pressures on RTA signatories to reform the agreement to bring it in line with WTO disciplines, it must be acknowledged that it would remain difficult for the countries involved to re-negotiate many politically sensitive, hard-fought issues.

[195] Efficiencies created by harmonization would be generally enjoyed by all WTO members so long as the harmonization of procedures was not designed to have the "incidental" effect of increasing transaction costs for non-signatories.

[196] There is at least one precedent for negotiations of "informal guidelines" in the CRTA, namely the formulation of the Standard Format for submission of information on RTAs. This initiative, which was successful in harmonizing and streamlining information submission practices, may provide lessons for other parts of the CRTA's activities.

experts (proposed above) and national delegates review RTAs, such a checklist will provide a useful reference, and will help establish a standard for appraising RTAs.

The checklist would serve as a basic agenda for the independent committee's work in a specific case. But it should not be regarded as a limit or jurisdictional boundary on the committee's authority to prove, and appraise, problems it discovers in an RTA that are not on the checklist. The successive reports of independent committees can serve to expand and enrich the checklist so it increasingly becomes a better guidebook for parties undertaking new RTA negotiations.

Finally, it would be useful for WTO members to formulate such a checklist, because it would provide additional guidance to WTO dispute settlement panels and the Appellate Body, when these institutions are called upon to adjudicate rights and obligations in an area in which the GATT and WTO Agreements provide sparse guidance.

D. Expedited Recourse to Dispute Settlement Procedures

Another drawback of the current WTO regulatory structure governing RTAs is the extended delay in relief for non-signatory members who are adversely affected by discriminatory RTA provisions. Such a member may make objections to such a provision during the CRTA examination process. However, under the current examination process the adoption of the CRTA report takes years (if it occurs at all). Even if an examination report is adopted, an RTA signatory could simply refuse to make the changes necessary to bring the measure into conformity with WTO and GATT requirements.

The other procedure available to adversely affected parties—WTO dispute settlement procedures—also involves a protracted and costly litigation process prior to any relief. As soon as the RTA is enacted in a member's domestic legislation, an adversely affected member can request consultations, and then establishment of a panel to adjudicate the consistency of the disputed measure under the WTO and GATT Agreements. However, it can take three years or more to receive authorization to suspend concessions. Thus, in effect, a WTO member faced with a another member's RTA provision that impermissibly discriminates against products or producers of the complaining WTO member must wait for years before receiving authorization to suspend concessions in an amount equivalent to the adverse effect of the discriminatory RTA provision.

In light of the vast number of RTAs that are being negotiated and will presumably soon be notified to the WTO, and the pressure and delays that numerous complaints about these RTAs could create for the dispute settlement system, it is advisable to examine the possibility of special, expedited procedures to address allegedly discriminatory measures found in RTAs.

One possible improvement would be to dispense with the panel process in the case of complaints about RTAs that have been examined and reported upon by the CRTA and its independent committee of neutral experts. In such cases, complaints could be taken up immediately in the Appellate Body.

The Appellate Body would have the benefit of the extensive factual and legal examination set forth in the CRTA's report. Immediate recourse to the Appellate Body would not only offer expedited relief to adversely affected parties, but would also give signatories to an RTA a greater incentive to act upon the suggestions made by the national delegates and the independent committee of neutral experts in their reports. In short, making the threat of adjudication and retaliation by adversely affected parties more imminent would motivate countries negotiating RTAs to take more seriously their obligations under the GATT and WTO Agreements.

VI. Conclusion

The WTO is a community-building effort, through which nations seek to achieve a common interest in market-based commercial exchange. The instrument for building co-operation is a set of rules that help to provide security against government interference in open markets. One of the most fundamental rules is that of non-discrimination embodied in the most-favored-nation principle.

But communities exist and can be built at diverse levels of human connection—families, civic groups, towns, states, nations, regions, and across regions. And in fact the trust that underlies community building exists or can be established more readily in smaller groups than large ones. It would make no sense to limit local collaboration that goes beyond what can be achieved comprehensively.

As recognized by those who wrote the GATT, there can be economic value for all the members in allowing smaller groups of countries to liberalize their trade more rapidly and more completely than is possible for all the member countries. But, unless regulated, the preferential treatment enjoyed exclusively by countries within these sub-groups would render meaningless the overall nondiscrimination rule of Article I, which is an important part of the glue that holds the multilateral community together.

After more than half a century, the trading nations have yet to find a satisfactory way to distinguish between those regional arrangements that are beneficial to the global trading system (or are at least neutral) and those that are harmful. The current proliferation of regional arrangements makes it increasingly important to establish a practical way of making this decision.

Ideally, the WTO would have a mechanism for making an informed and scientific decision in each case as to whether a given regional agreement increases or decreases the welfare of the WTO community. But such a determination involves so many unknowns and so much complexity that the results would be subject to continuing dispute. It seems unlikely that a determination would have the clarity and legitimacy needed to maintain the respect of affected WTO members.

Alternatively, a test for determining whether an RTA fits or does not fit into the WTO system can be based on the quality of the RTA—i.e. whether it evidences a serious commitment of the parties entering into a high level of economic cooperation with each other, and within the broader open market system, or whether it evidences an opportunistic effort to gain certain trade-distorting benefits by departing from MFN requirements, at the expense of the rest of the WTO members.

Article XXIV, effectively administered, can provide such a test. By requiring that an RTA eliminate barriers to substantially all trade among the parties, it can limit the use of RTA's to countries that have or are willing to establish a high level of cooperation. The theory of Article XXIV is therefore sound: It seeks to protect the community-building effort of the WTO members by limiting divergence from the MFN rule; and it seeks to allow smaller groups of members to establish closer collaboration when they are serious about it.

The problem with Article XXIV is in its administration. There has been effectively no surveillance. Two or more WTO members can enter what they designate as a Free Trade Agreement and refer to it as justification for exclusive benefits they extend to each other. In all likelihood, no WTO official body will hold them accountable for failing to implement their FTA in accordance with the requirements of GATT Article XXIV. Neither of the usual sources of accountability—administrative oversight or judicial review—is effective.

The WTO's version of administrative oversight is found in the Committee on Regional Trade Agreements, established in 1996. It examines an RTA that has been "notified" to the WTO by the parties to it. But a significant number of countries have failed to comply with the obligation to notify their agreement. And the experience to date indicates that when an agreement is notified, the CRTA becomes bogged down in a lengthy inquiry and is unable to reach the consensus required for issuing a report on whether the agreement complies with the standards set forth in Article XXIV.

Accountability to the WTO's judicial authority is similarly weak. The handful of cases on RTAs decided by the Appellate Body have only addressed tangential issues rather than the central question whether an RTA meets the standards of Article XXIV or, failing to do so, extends trade preferences that violate Article I. Negotiating and signing an RTA normally calls for a good deal of political will on the part of national political leaders, and the results can be politically important. Since the political stakes are high, the WTO's Dispute Settlement Body might well be reluctant to rule than an RTA is not in compliance with the standards of Article XXIV—especially since the facts regarding RTAs are normally complex and there is room for argument about the precise meaning of the standards. It would not necessarily be easy for the WTO's Dispute Settlement Body to rule that an RTA is not in compliance with the rather imprecise standards of Article XXIV.

Several changes in the administrative review of RTAs and the way they are handled by the Dispute Settlement Body would improve the prospects that the limits on RTAs set forth in Article XXIV will be enforced—and therefore given greater respect by parties negotiating RTAs. Among the changes (discussed in Part V above) two are key:

- Administrative review of RTAs would be more rigorous and timely if the CRTA established an independent oversight committee of neutral experts to examine each RTA and issue a report on whether it complies with WTO requirements, and what needs to be done to bring it into compliance. Properly executed, these reports would have a good deal of credibility, and would encourage compliance with their recommendations. The reports would also provide a clear factual record that would assist the Dispute Settlement Body in reviewing whether the FTA complies with WTO requirements.

- Because administrative review of RTAs will be more thorough and systematic, review by the Dispute Settlement Body could then be improved by eliminating review by a dispute resolution panel and allowing complaints about compliance of an RTA with WTO requirements to go directly to the Appellate Body, for decision on the record established by the CRTA and its independent committee of experts.

The continuing proliferation of regional trade agreements is helping to expand the reach of open market practices and enriching the rule-based system established in the WTO. At the same time, in the absence of effective regulation, these agreements can damage the WTO system by undermining the most-favored-nation principle that is crucial for its legitimacy. The improvements in legal process suggested above offer the opportunity to regulate the regional agreements, so as to protect the foundations of the WTO system while not discouraging the energetic and creative development of regional trading arrangements.

CHAPTER 47

THE ECONOMIES IN TRANSITION, THE WTO AND REGIONALISM

Richard Pomfret[*]

TABLE OF CONTENTS

[*] University of Adelaide, Australia

I. Introduction

When the World Trade Organization ("WTO") opened its doors in 1995, its members contained just over two thirds of the world's population. The biggest challenge to becoming a truly global organization lay in incorporating the formerly centrally planned economies. China, still a Communist country, had applied for membership in 1986 but negotiations dragged on for political reasons, and more fundamentally because of the non-transparency of its still only partially market-based economy.[1] Most of the former members of the Council for Mutual Economic Assistance, which contained half a billion people (Table 1), were outside the WTO and during the 1990s had plausible regional alternatives to multilateralism, either with neighbouring established market economies or with fellow transition economies.

This chapter analyses the progress of the reintegration of the formerly centrally planned economies into the global trading system, focusing on the relationship between multilateral processes and regional integration schemes. Part II provides relevant background of the relations between centrally planned economies and the WTO's predecessor, the General Agreement on Tariffs and Trade ("GATT"). Part III analyses the various attempts by countries in transition from central planning to join or form regional trading arrangements during the 1990s. Part IV describes the progress made by formerly centrally planned economies towards joining the WTO and analyses the most important benefits to transition economies from WTO membership. Part V draws some conclusions.

II. Centrally Planned Economies and GATT

The General Agreement on Tariffs and Trade established rules for government policies which would allow a liberal international trade system to function. The GATT rules, essentially encouraging governments to use border taxes (tariffs) rather than quantitative restrictions to regulate international trade and to treat trade with all other GATT contracting partners equally when imposing such restrictions, presuppose a liberal economic order in which foreign trade decisions are made by individual buyers and sellers in response to price signals. There were, of course, exceptions both in principle and in practice, but the GATT rules were not designed to deal with economies in which resources were allocated by command rather than in response to prices.

Czechoslovakia had been a founding signatory of the GATT in 1947, and Cuba and Myanmar (then Burma) had joined in 1948, but in all three cases obligations and benefits ceased to be observed after the countries moved to planned economies. Similarly, China's GATT membership fell into abeyance after the 1949 Revolution, and neither the government in Beijing nor that in Taipei was allowed to assume the membership status.

During the late 1960s and early 1970s several eastern European states were allowed to become contracting parties to GATT under *ad hoc* conditions: Poland in 1967, Romania in 1971 and Hungary in 1973. These decisions were driven by political rather than economic considerations, as the leading market economies tried to hasten détente with favoured

---

[1] Little will be said in this chapter about China's WTO accession negotiations or their expected consequences, which are discussed in Chapter 67 of this book. There is already a huge literature; see, for example, Kym Anderson, *Complexities of China's WTO Accession*, 20(6) THE WORLD ECONOMY 749 (1997); Willem van der Geest, *Bringing China into the Concert of Nations: An Analysis of its Accession to the WTO*, 32(3) JOURNAL OF WORLD TRADE 99 (1998); Zhao Wei, *China's WTO Accession Commitments and Prospects*, 32(2) JOURNAL OF WORLD TRADE 51 (1998).

Table 1: European and Asian economies in transition (1992 and 1999)

	Population (million) mid-1992	GNP per capita (US$) 1992	Population (million) mid-1999	GNP per capita (US$) 1999
Central Europe				
Slovenia	2	6,540	2	9,890
Hungary	10	2,970	10	4,650
Estonia	2	2,760	1	3,480
Czech Rep.	10	2,450	10	5,060
Latvia	3	1,930	2	2,470
Slovak Rep.	5	1,930	5	3,590
Poland	38	1,910	39	3,960
Lithuania	4	1,910	4	2,620
German Dem. Rep.	17	LM	n.a.	n.a.
Eastern Europe				
Belarus	10	2,930	10	2,630
Russia	149	2,510	147	2,270
Ukraine	52	1,820	50	750
Balkan & Caucasus				
Bulgaria	9	1,330	8	1,380
Moldova	4	1,300	4	370
Romania	23	1,130	22	1,520
Georgia	6	850	5	620
Armenia	4	780	4	490
Azerbaijan	7	740	8	550
Albania	3	LM	3	870
Croatia	5	LM	4	4,580
Macedonia FYR	2	LM	2	1,690
Yugoslavia	11	LM	11	LM
Bosnia & Hercegovina	4	L	4	LM
Asia				
Kazakhstan	17	1,680	15	1,230
Turkmenistan	4	1,230	5	660
Uzbekistan	22	850	25	720
Kyrgyz Rep	5	820	5	300
Mongolia	2	LM	3	350
Tajikistan	6	490	6	290
Vietnam	69	L	78	370
Non-CMEA				
China	1,162	470	1,250	780
Laos	4	250	5	280
North Korea	23	LM	23	L
Afghanistan	22	L	26	L
Cambodia	9	L	12	260
Myanmar	44	L	45	L

Source: World Bank data from *World Development Report 1994*, 162–3 & 228, and *World Development Report 2000/2001*, 274–5 & 316.

Notes: n.a. = not available in the source; since 1990 the German Democratic Republic forms the eastern Länder of Germany; in 1992 lower income (L) is less than $675 and lower middle income (LM) $676 to $2,695; in 1998 L is $755 or less, LM is $756 to $2,995.

Communist countries.[2] Bulgaria and the Soviet Union, which sought similar status, were barred, and Czechoslovakia's role remained passive despite its formal membership.

The acceptance of favoured non-market economies was a low point for GATT. The new members' trade with other GATT signatories was subject to *ad hoc* arrangements which were quantity- or results-oriented rather than rules-based. The special protocols were difficult to enforce as circumstances changed, and non-fulfilment was difficult to punish. Yet, the countries were now inside GATT and the membership decision was not easily reversed. This flaw was recognized by the early 1990s and lay behind subsequent insistence that new members must adhere to GATT rules, based on principles of individual traders' freedom to act within transparent policy environments, which were only really compatible with a market-based economy. There was, of course, a grey area because in all GATT members state trading and public procurement were facts of life, but the degree mattered.

China was a crucial test case, after it lodged a formal application for accession to GATT in 1986. China had started to open up its previously closed economy in 1978, and its foreign trade was growing rapidly during the 1980s. Nevertheless, the economy remained only partially reformed, with many non-transparent features affecting its import regime. Especially after the June 1989 Tiananmen events the negotiations became highly politicized, but well-founded concerns about non-transparency were the fundamental stumbling block in the 1980s and 1990s. A request by the Soviet Union to participate in the Uruguay Round of multilateral trade negotiations which began in 1986 was turned down by the GATT contracting parties.

The situation changed dramatically in the late 1980s with the end of central planning, often dated in the USSR from the 1988 Law on State Enterprises, and the collapse of Communist regimes in Eastern Europe during the second half of 1989. The Malta summit between George Bush and Mikhail Gorbachev in December 1989 signalled the end of the Cold War, and ushered in a new era for trade relations. President Bush announced his support for the USSR being granted observer status at GATT, and this was echoed a few days later by the European Community. The USSR lodged a formal application for observer status in March 1990, which was approved in May 1990.[3]

The critical years for the emergence of economies in transition from centrally planned to market-based economies were 1989–91. All of the Communist regimes in Eastern Europe collapsed in the second half of 1989. In 1991 the Council for Mutual Economic Assistance ("CMEA"), which had managed trade between those countries and the USSR, was finally closed down. In 1991 the partition of Yugoslavia began. More surprisingly, the Soviet Union dissolved peacefully in December 1991.

This was not an auspicious time for addressing the role of the transition economies in the global trading system. The European Union was concentrating on its 1992 program for completing the internal market. In the Americas, the United States and Canada were about to extend their free trade arrangement to include Mexico in a North American Free Trade Area ("NAFTA") and the Mercosur treaty was signed in the South in 1991. In Asia pressures for regionalism were weaker, but the ASEAN Free Trade Area was about

[2] LEAH HAUS, GLOBALIZING THE GATT: THE SOVIET UNION'S SUCCESSOR STATES, EASTERN EUROPE, AND THE INTERNATIONAL TRADING SYSTEM (1992)

[3] The United States initially expressed reservations to the formal application, apparently as a consequence of inter-agency fighting, but the U.S. opposition was quickly withdrawn. Japan opposed the Soviet application due to its dispute with the USSR over the status of the Kuril Islands. The application was, however, approved, and was subject to review in April 1992. By that date, the USSR no longer existed.

to be launched and Asia-Pacific Economic Cooperation ("APEC") members discussed open regionalism. The Uruguay Round had several times come close to breaking down, and the GATT's very existence seemed in doubt as the world economy looked on some occasions poised to split into regional trading blocs.

III. The Transition Economies and Regionalism

In 1989 the CMEA included the USSR, the centrally planned economies of Eastern Europe, Mongolia, Vietnam and Cuba. The CMEA planned international trade among its members, whose economies were largely insulated from the market-driven international economy. Albania, whose membership became inoperative in 1961, and Yugoslavia as an associate member, did not participate in the planned trade.[4] None of these countries was interested in retaining membership in the CMEA after the abolition of central planning within their domestic economies. They were, however, attracted to new or alternative regional trading arrangements.

The most developed European transition economies formed their own trade bloc. Czechoslovakia, Hungary and Poland signed the Central European Free Trade Agreement ("CEFTA") in 1992. Half of intra-CEFTA trade was made tariff-free in 1994 and subsequent negotiations aimed at a full free trade area by 2002. Slovenia joined CEFTA in 1996, and Bulgaria and Romania joined later. CEFTA was, however, always viewed as a second-best alternative to integration into the European Union.

Many east Europeans welcomed the collapse of Communism as an opportunity to re-establish their position as citizens of normal democratic European countries. Poland, the Czech Republic, and Hungary, already GATT contracting parties, joined the Organization for Economic Cooperation and Development ("OECD") and the North Atlantic Treaty Organization ("NATO") during the 1990s, but most of all they aspired to membership in the European Union. The twelve EU members were initially slow to respond to these aspirations. The seventeen million people in the German Democratic Republic were automatically absorbed into the EU with German reunification in 1990, but the prospect of over a hundred million new EU citizens in the ten applicant transition countries was more difficult to digest. Moreover, in the early 1990s the EU was absorbed by the single market project, the 1992 crisis in the European Monetary System and subsequent moves towards the common currency, and expansion to include three established market economies (Austria, Finland and Sweden) as new members in 1995. Association agreements were signed with transition economies and these were transformed into so-called Europe Agreements in 1994–5 (Table 2), but they fell far short of the would-be members' aspirations.

At the June 1993 meeting of the EU Council in Copenhagen, the heads of state agreed that the associated countries could join the EU once they had achieved institutional stability (guaranteeing democracy, the rule of law, human rights, and respect for protection of minorities), a functioning market economy, and ability to take on the obligations of EU membership. Between 1994 and 1996 ten transition economies lodged formal applications for EU membership, and negotiations began in 1998 and 2000. The path is fairly clear because the EU has established that, although there may be some limited room for negotiation over transition periods to full membership, any new member must accept the already established institutions and policies (the so-called *acquis communautaire*).

---

[4] Richard Pomfret, The Economics of Regional Trading Arrangements 115–6 (1997)

Table 2: Economies in Transition and the European Union

Country	Europe agreement signed	Europe agreement came into force	Official application for EU membership
Bulgaria	March 1993	February 1995	December 1995
Czech Republic	October 1993	February 1995	January 1996
Estonia	June 1995	—	November 1995
Hungary	December 1991	February 1994	March 1994
Latvia	June 1995	—	October 1995
Lithuania	June 1995	—	December 1995
Poland	December 1991	February 1994	April 1994
Romania	February 1993	February 1995	June 1995
Slovakia	October 1993	February 1995	June 1995
Slovenia	June 1996	February 1999	June 1996

Source: From the European Union's webpage (on 22nd. September 2000) at http://europa.eu.int/comm/enlargement/intro/index.htm

The current position is that there will not necessarily be waves of enlargement and that candidates will be admitted, as they are ready, after the end of 2002.[5]

Although the EU was seen by some of the more impatient candidates, notably Poland, as dragging its collective feet during the 1990s, the decade was not wasted time because the leading candidate countries were able to implement the time-consuming measures necessary as prerequisites for accession. By 2000 the ten applicants were all WTO members or close to being so, and all ranked highly on the various liberalization or "good institutions" indices published by international organizations such as the European Bank for Reconstruction and Development (in its annual *Transition Report*) or the International Monetary Fund (in its September 2000 *World Economic Outlook*). Meanwhile the CEFTA has become more like a fifth wheel as the EU car gathers speed, although there may be some complications as some CEFTA members accede to the EU before others.

EU membership is now a matter of when rather than if for most European transition economies. Some may balk at the conditions or wish to remain independent, so that the EU's eastern border will remain in flux for some time. For those who do join, EU membership will not conflict much with integration into the global as well as the regional economy. The EU has long been accepted as a single unit for the purposes of international trade negotiations and, with the deepening of the euro arrangements, notably the withdrawal of national currencies in 2002, most EU members will operate as a common currency area. Despite some illiberal practices, the EU is generally an open trading bloc, and membership is more likely to cement liberal policies than non-membership.[6]

[5] The "first wave" of applicants with whom the EU opened negotiations in March 1998 included the Czech Republic, Estonia, Hungary, Poland and Slovenia, together with Cyprus. The second wave of EU candidates, containing Bulgaria, Latvia, Lithuania, Romania, Slovakia and Malta, began negotiations in February 2000. Developments up to 2000 are described in the IMF's September 2000 *World Economic Outlook*, Box 4.1. Heliodoro Temprano-Arroyo and Robert Feldman, *Selected Transition and Mediterranean Countries: An Institutional Primer on EMU and EU Accession,* 7(3) ECONOMICS OF TRANSITION 741 (1999) review the institutional requirements of EU membership. Since the EU's 2001 Nice summit, it is clear that for the leading candidate countries membership is now a matter of when rather than whether. The EU website http://europa.eu.int/comm/enlargement provides progress reports, including a table of specific negotiation hurdles and whether they have been overcome by each applicant.

[6] Examples of the illiberal policies emerged during WTO accession negotiations when Estonia chose to bind its tariffs on some agricultural goods above the current applied tariffs solely to allow scope for adoption of the EU common external trade policy. Nevertheless, the EU common commercial policy and EU policies

Vietnam, Laos and Cambodia have taken an ostensibly similar stance with respect to the Association of Southeast Asian Nations ("ASEAN"). The six ASEAN members were thriving market economies, whose historic economic links to the southeast Asian centrally planned economies had been broken amid the military conflicts of the 1960s and early 1970s. The ASEAN six, like the EU twelve, were preoccupied with their internal regionalism projects in the late 1980s and early 1990s when their neighbours were initiating the transition to a market economy, but the ASEAN Free Trade Area ("AFTA") which began operation in 1992 was a much weaker form of regionalism than the EU common market and ASEAN was far from accepting the political integration which underlay the EU project for many Europeans.

The looser organization meant less stringent admission criteria, with nothing like the Copenhagen Criteria to prevent non-democracies with imperfect market economies from joining ASEAN. Vietnam joined ASEAN in July 1995, and Laos and Myanmar in July 1997, when Cambodia was also scheduled to join, but Cambodia's formal accession was delayed for a year after the anti-democratic coup. Despite this gesture, none of the four new members is a democracy, and the admission of Myanmar (Burma) in the face of strong disapproval by the United States and EU provided a clear-cut signal of the lack of political prerequisites. The enlargement to ten members completed ASEAN's "natural" geographical expansion to include all Asian countries south of China and east of Bangladesh and India, but left the association as a disparate group with little prospect of pursuing common policies in the near term.[7]

Joining ASEAN has few direct policy implications, but it has been a non-trivial signal on the part of the southeast Asian transition economies. As ASEAN stands at the start of the twenty-first century, membership is not a commitment to regionalism. There is no formal commitment to introduce liberal trade policies, because ASEAN has neither a common external commercial policy nor internal free trade, let alone uniform measures in areas such as currency convertibility or capital flows. Progress on AFTA has been sporadic, and the four newest members of ASEAN are explicitly allowed to move at a slower pace than the other ASEAN members. The extent to which Vietnam, Laos, Cambodia and Myanmar reform their formerly planned economies to become open economies integrated into the global system remains a matter of domestic decision-making.[8] Nevertheless, the new members have signalled that they belong in a group of market economies, and they will be under pressure within ASEAN to liberalize their intra-regional trade. Given that the new members are unlikely to want to discriminate in favour of their ASEAN partners, such pressures if effective will lead to multilateral trade liberalization.

The successor states to the Soviet Union have made some attempts to maintain existing trade relations through regional arrangements, but these have been feeble measures with little practical impact. In 1992–3 the main concern was to retain a common currency in

in other areas such as capital flows are more liberal and far more conducive to integration into the global economy than are the more restrictive policies of some of the southeast European transition countries, not to mention those of CIS members such as Belarus or Ukraine.

[7] Richard Pomfret, *ASEAN: Always at the Crossroads?*, 1(3) JOURNAL OF THE ASIA PACIFIC ECONOMY 365 (1996); Richard Pomfret, *Enlargement to Include Formerly Centrally Planned Economies: ASEAN and the European Union Compared*, in THE EUROPEAN UNION AND ASEAN: TRADE AND INVESTMENT ISSUES 225(Roger Strange, Jim Slater and Corrado Molteni eds. 2000)

[8] An important element for Cambodia, which also applies to some of the other smaller and poorer transition economies, is that, although the government professes a desire to liberalize the economy through reduction of trade barriers, it is dependent on tariffs for some three-quarters of government revenue so that trade liberalization is connected to fiscal reform.

order to minimize payments problems, but the ruble zone had collapsed by November 1993. Since then, post-Soviet trade patterns have diversified continuously, and no serious attempt to stop this trend by introducing regional trading arrangements has been implemented.

The twelve non-Baltic successor states to the USSR formed the Commonwealth of Independent States ("CIS"), but that organization has never had any serious economic content. In September 1993 Armenia, Azerbaijan, Belarus, Kazakhstan, the Kyrgyz Republic, Moldova, Russia, Tajikistan and Uzbekistan signed an agreement to set up an economic union; Georgia signed some of the provisions, and Ukraine became an associate member.[9] Thus, eleven of the twelve non-Baltic Soviet successor states indicated commitment to some form of regional economic arrangement, but neither this nor any subsequent proposal involving a majority of CIS members made any progress.[10]

On a political level, the CIS became fractured in the second half of the 1990s. In January 1995 Belarus, Kazakhstan and Russia signed a customs union agreement, which the Kyrgyz Republic also signed in March 1996 when it became known as the Union of Four.[11] With Russia clearly the dominant partner, Russia's tariff presumably would be the putative common external tariff, but apart from preliminary steps towards a Belarus-Russia economic union nothing has been implemented. The tariff bindings in the Kyrgyz Republic's 1998 WTO accession agreement are in conflict with the would-be customs union because it is difficult to imagine Russia agreeing to such a liberal external trade policy and the Kyrgyz Republic is no longer able to raise its tariffs to the Russian level.[12]

In late 1996 and 1997, Azerbaijan, Georgia and Ukraine, later joined by Moldova, began to coordinate their strategies in security negotiations, and this became formalized in a joint communiqué in October 1997. In April 1999 Uzbekistan became the fifth member of the alignment, which became known as GUUAM. Although not having any economic content beyond coordination of infrastructure plans, the GUUAM grouping (Georgia, Ukraine, Uzbekistan, Azerbaijan and Moldova) is operating explicitly as a counter to Russian hegemony.[13] Thus, the CIS has split into two groups of five, plus two floaters (Armenia and Turkmenistan).

The five Central Asian successor states have drawn up many plans for regional cooperation among themselves. They inevitably must cooperate on some non-trade matters such as the desiccation of the Aral Sea and on developing transport and pipeline routes, but attempts to set up a regional trading agreement have had little impact. In April 1994

---

[9] Georgia and Turkmenistan only formally joined the CIS in December 1993. Turkmenistan's main foreign policy principle has been strict neutrality, which it has interpreted as allowing only limited cooperation with the CIS, even to the extent of not supplying statistics to the CIS statistical agency.

[10] Richard Sakwa and Mark Webber, *The Commonwealth of Independent States, 1991–1998; Stagnation and Survival*, 51(3) EUROPE-ASIA STUDIES 386 (1999)

[11] Tajikistan became the fifth member of the Union in February 1999. On the Union of Four, or Five, see Constantine Michalopoulos and David Tarr, *The Economics of Customs Unions in the Commonwealth of Independent States*, POLICY RESEARCH WORKING PAPER 1786, WORLD BANK (June 1997); and Vyachaslau Paznyak, *The Customs Union of Five and the Russia-Belarus Union*, in BUILDING SECURITY IN THE NEW STATES OF EURASIA: SUBREGIONAL COOPERATION IN THE FORMER SOVIET SPACE at 57 (Renata Dwan and Oleksandr Pavliuk eds. 2000)

[12] A similar conflict could arise from Kazakhstan's WTO negotiations. According to Webber (1997, 56), Kazakhstan's President Nazarbayev indicated in September 1996 that Kazakhstan would leave the customs union when it acceded to the WTO.

[13] Oleksandr Pavliuk, *GUUAM: The Maturing of Political Grouping into Economic Cooperation*, in BUILDING SECURITY IN THE NEW STATES OF EURASIA: SUBREGIONAL COOPERATION IN THE FORMER SOVIET SPACE at 33 (Renata Dwan and Oleksandr Pavliuk eds. 2000)

Kazakhstan, the Kyrgyz Republic and Uzbekistan signed a treaty for the establishment of an integrated economic space. In March 1998 Tajikistan, which had previously had observer status, became a full participant in the scheme which became known as the Central Asian Economic Community ("CAEC"). Trade within the CAEC, however, declined over the 1990s, and in most areas the members pursued independent policies without regard to intra-CAEC cooperation and at times in contradiction to stated CAEC policies and goals.[14]

The only significant attempt by CIS countries to form a regional trading arrangement with neighbouring market economies has been the accession of the Islamic former Soviet republics to the Economic Cooperation Organization ("ECO"). Plans for regional cooperation among ECO's three founding members, Iran, Pakistan and Turkey, had made little progress before 1992. The May 1991 Protocol on Preferential Tariffs covered few goods and offered small preferential margins. The dissolution of the USSR breathed new life into ECO when six former Soviet republics plus Afghanistan joined ECO in November 1992, forming a bloc of the non-Arab Islamic countries west of Bangladesh, with a combined population of over 350 million.[15]

Despite attempts to improve infrastructure and transit arrangements, ECO did little during the 1990s beyond acting as a regional talking shop In this regional confidence-building respect ECO has had some similarity to ASEAN, and like the ASEAN countries ECO's members were unwilling to match declarations of intent to have a preferential trading arrangement with actual trade liberalization measures.[16] A major reason for this failure has to do with the three founding members, who have acted more like competitors in Central Asia than cooperative partners playing a positive-sum game; all three viewed a putative customs union in terms of extending the size of the protected market for their own industries. In addition, the similarity of the ten ECO members' export mixes has limited intra-ECO trade flows (as it has done in ASEAN), and reinforced the lack of will for discriminatory trade liberalization.

There are also problems of overlapping arrangements which hinder ECO's ability to progress along the route of preferential trading arrangements. In January 1996 Turkey formed a customs union with the EU, which limits Turkey's ability to alter its tariff rates and Turkey notified the ECO Secretariat that its obligations to the EU would override any ECO commitments. Since then, Turkey's relationships with the EU have fluctuated, but the legal situation remains unchanged. Pakistan faces a potential conflict between commitments under the preferential agreements reached within the South Asian Association for Regional Cooperation ("SAARC") and any made within ECO, but in practice SAARC tariff preferences are as innocuous as those within ECO. For much progress towards an ECO regional trading arrangement, a greater obstacle is probably the Kyrgyz Republic's tariff bindings agreed to during the country's WTO accession negotiations. These tariff rates limit the Kyrgyz Republic's freedom to offer substantial tariff preferences to

[14] RICHARD POMFRET, *Trade Initiatives in Central Asia: The Economic Cooperation Organization and the Central Asian Economic Community*, in BUILDING SECURITY IN THE NEW STATES OF EURASIA: SUBREGIONAL COOPERATION IN THE FORMER SOVIET SPACE, *supra* note 13 at 11; Bakhtior Islamov, THE CENTRAL ASIAN STATES TEN YEARS AFTER: HOW TO OVERCOME TRAPS OF DEVELOPMENT, TRANSFORMATION AND GLOBALISATION? 163–89 (2001)

[15] The six countries were Azerbaijan, Kazakhstan, the Kyrgyz Republic, Tajikistan, Turkmenistan and Uzbekistan. The Turkish Muslim Community of Cyprus is not an ECO member, but its representatives often attend ECO meetings. Afghanistan has been represented by forces in opposition to the Taliban, which is a source of tension between Iran and Pakistan.

[16] RICHARD POMFRET, CENTRAL ASIA TURNS SOUTH? TRADE RELATIONS IN TRANSITION (1999)

partners in a preferential trading arrangement and, as in the Union of Five, put low limits on any common external tariffs.

The Baltic countries, which kept outside the successor organization to the Soviet Union, the Commonwealth of Independent States ("CIS"), discussed regional integration proposals but they never progressed far. More important, especially for Estonia, was the opening up of links to their Nordic neighbours, which provided them with advocates for EU membership once Finland and Sweden were inside the EU club.

In sum, the formerly centrally planned economies were not immune from the early 1990s trend towards regionalism, although they were happy enough to allow the old organization, the CMEA, to fade away after 1989 and formally dissolve in 1991. Attempts to partially reconstruct old trading patterns on a regional basis were made by the former Soviet republics and by some east European countries, but these were half-hearted and always secondary to other trade policy strategies. Much more important were attempts by the countries in transition to a market economy to link themselves to neighbouring market economies. This was especially true for the European transition economies, and to a lesser extent for the southeast Asian transition economies and for the Islamic transition economies of Central Asia and the Caucasus, but the temptations of the EU, ASEAN and ECO pose little threat to adherence to multilateralism, albeit for different reasons. Transition economies joining the EU will have discriminatory trade policies, but within a basically liberal common trade policy, while members of ASEAN and ECO are in organizations whose regional integration remains weak. The other formerly centrally planned economies have shown little interest in regionalism in their external economic relations. China is an APEC member, but its post-1978 trade policies have clearly been based on multilateralism, with WTO membership as the top priority since the mid-1980s. Since Mongolia emerged from the Soviet sphere of influence in 1990, after having become so closely integrated that it was often referred to as the sixteenth Soviet republic, it has shown no interest in preferential bilateral economic relations. The Balkan countries which are not (yet?) EU applicants have been too embroiled in regional problems to give much attention to the matter. Overall, the potential danger of regionalism proving more attractive than multilateralism has not eventuated.

IV. Transition Economies and the WTO

In 1994 the Uruguay Round was successfully concluded, and among its consequences was the superseding of GATT by a new World Trade Organization ("WTO"). All GATT contracting parties became WTO members at the start of 1995.[17] Once in place, the new organization took up outstanding and new applications for membership. For the first few years, however, it appeared difficult for countries with economies in transition from central planning to get through the admission process. Michalopoulos[18] argues

---

[17] Hungary, the Czech and Slovak republics (which had divorced in 1993), and Poland and Romania (who renegotiated the special protocols under which they had entered GATT in 1967 and 1971) were charter members of the WTO. Yugoslavia in 1992 applied to become a WTO member as successor state to the GATT-Yugoslavia, but this application was turned down because the United Nations had determined that, after Slovenia, Croatia, and Bosnia and Herzegovina declared independence and split from the Yugozlav Federation, the "new" Yugoslavia (Serbia and Montenegro) could not claim successor status. Slovenia and Bulgaria, whose GATT applications had been relatively straightforward and were far advanced, became WTO members in 1995 and 1996.

[18] Constantine Michalopoulos, *The Integration of Transition Economies into the World Trading System*, World Bank Working Paper WPS 2182 (1999).

Table 3: WTO status of former CMEA members

	WTO status
Central & Eastern Europe	
Czechoslovakia	Original GATT signatory
(Czech Rep. & Slovakia after 1993)	
Poland	Joined GATT 1967
Romania	Joined GATT 1971
Hungary	Joined GATT 1973
Slovenia	Joined WTO 1995
Bulgaria	Joined WTO 1996
Albania	Joined WTO 2000
Croatia	Joined WTO 2000
Macedonia FYR	Joined WTO 2003
Yugoslavia	negotiating
Bosnia & Herzegovina	negotiating
Former USSR	
Kyrgyz Republic	Joined WTO 1998
Latvia	Joined WTO 1999
Estonia	Joined WTO 1999
Georgia	Joined WTO 2000
Lithuania	Joined WTO 2001
Moldova	Joined WTO 2001
Armenia	Joined WTO 2003
Azerbaijan	negotiating
Belarus	negotiating
Kazakhstan	negotiating
Russia	negotiating
Tajikistan	negotiating
Ukraine	negotiating
Uzbekistan	negotiating
Turkmenistan	
Asia	
Mongolia	Joined WTO 1997
Vietnam	negotiating

Note and Source: up-to-date membership information is provided on the WTO website www.wto.org

that the procedure was too complex, and exceeded the administrative capacities of the applicants, as well as of the WTO Secretariat. Langhammer and Lücke[19] question this interpretation, and point to substantive issues which needed to be resolved before a transition economy could reasonably be admitted to the WTO. With the hindsight of just a few extra years, however, the pace of WTO accession looks more impressive, with Mongolia, the Kyrgyz Republic, Latvia, Estonia, Georgia, Albania, Croatia, Moldova and Lithuania all completing the formalities between 1998 and 2001 (Table 3), not to mention the long-awaited breakthrough in China's accession negotiations.

Why does WTO membership matter? Membership guarantees rights as well as imposing obligations. Most of the transition economies have been unilaterally granted the main right of members, MFN treatment by all other members, and in many cases they

---

[19] Rolf Langhammer and Matthias Lücke, *WTO Accession Issues*, 22(6) THE WORLD ECONOMY 837 (August 1999).

benefit from the lower Generalized System of Preferences ("GSP") tariff rate. WTO membership does, however, ensure MFN treatment as a right rather than a unilaterally granted privilege. As a GATT/WTO member China would have avoided having to face the hurdle of annual renewal of MFN status by the USA during the 1980s and 1990s, and as a WTO member Azerbaijan should gain MFN treatment from the USA, where this status has been blocked by the Armenian lobby.

More importantly, WTO membership should provide some protection against imposition of non-tariff barriers, although in the controversial area of anti-dumping formerly centrally planned economies have failed to receive full protection of their WTO rights even after becoming members. During the 1990s transition economies suffered especially from anti-dumping actions, where they faced a double penalty of not having WTO protection and being treated as non-market economies.[20] The latter actually seems to have been the more severe handicap because "surrogate" or "analogue" countries' costs and exchange rates are used, somewhat arbitrarily, in calculation of dumping margins.[21]

The WTO provides legal justification for special treatment of non-market economies under anti-dumping laws. Article 2.7 of the Anti-dumping Agreement refers to the second Supplementary Provision in paragraph 1 of Article VI in Annex 1 to GATT 1994, which permits different treatment "in the case of imports from a country which has a complete or substantially complete monopoly of its trade and where all domestic prices are fixed by the State" and which was interpreted in the original Polish and Hungarian accession negotiations to permit a surrogate country methodology.[22] It continues to be invoked even though by the late 1990s in very few countries were all prices fixed by the state and, as Palmeter stresses, "the word "all" with regard to control over domestic prices is quite specific". Although the presence of market institutions has become an important prerequisite for admission and their extent a major negotiating point, WTO membership is still not considered sufficient evidence that a country has a market economy.[23]

Nevertheless, given the obvious contrast between the legal basis and actual conditions for treating the transition countries differently in anti-dumping cases, WTO membership does offer prospects for fairer treatment and for some remedy under dispute resolution mechanisms. In other areas of non-tariff barriers without the anti-dumping history of special treatment, these benefits should be clearer. One specific area where being inside the

[20] Michalopoulos, *supra* note 18 at 20, shows that in the first three years of the WTO's operation (1995–7) both non-WTO and non-market economies were more likely to be subject of anti-dumping actions and were more likely to be the targets of definitive anti-dumping duties.

[21] The practice dates back to differential treatment of the non-market economies which joined the GATT in the 1960s and 1970s. A landmark case involved a 1975 antidumping action against Polish golf carts imported into the USA. In that case the constructed values, based on Spanish costs, led to a determination that the golf carts were not being sold below fair value, but in subsequent cases exporters complained that the surrogate was chosen after the case was opened and the choice was biased towards a ruling of unfair trade.

[22] David Palmeter, *The WTO Antidumping Agreement and the Economies in Transition*, in STATE TRADING IN THE TWENTY-FIRST CENTURY at 116 (Thomas Cottier and Petros Mavroidis eds. 1998)

[23] The EU publishes annually a list of non-market economies for the purpose of antidumping and safeguard actions, and the 1999 list included Albania, Armenia, Azerbaijan, Belarus, Georgia, Kazakhstan, the Kyrgyz Republic, Moldova, Mongolia, North Korea, Tajikistan, Turkmenistan, Ukraine, Uzbekistan and Vietnam. The United States has no formal list and proceeds on a case by case basis, but seems in practice to consider the same list of countries to be non-market economies. The Kyrgyz Republic and Mongolia were already WTO members in 1999.

WTO may make a difference is the Uruguay Round Agreement on Textiles and Clothing, by which all import quotas under the Multifibre Arrangement are to be eliminated by 2005. A new round of multilateral negotiations would benefit transition economies which have already acceded to the WTO, although in many respects these would be benefits also accruing to other middle-income members rather than specific to transition economies.

WTO membership also operates as a signalling device, or to provide a road map for reform and legally bind governments to liberal policies. For the European transition economies aspiring to EU membership, WTO membership is an essential way station, and the ten countries which have formally applied for EU membership have all completed their WTO accession negotiations. WTO membership proves intent to create a market economy and to abide by international trade law.

Elsewhere, transition economies generally show a desire for WTO membership, but have been less willing to pursue policies which will ensure an easy passage. The exceptions (Mongolia and the Kyrgyz Republic) are small countries committed to liberal policies, in part because they have been major aid recipients from donors which require such policies. Other small economies (Albania, Georgia, Croatia and Moldova) have passed through the admission process because there has been little concern over their impact on the world trading system. On the other hand, the existing WTO members have been stricter towards larger applicants, and some of the larger or more cautious transition economies may have been deterred by the hard line taken by the existing WTO members.[24] Nevertheless, even the act of negotiating signals to potential foreign investors, international financial institutions and others that a country is contemplating acceptance of WTO conditions and is committed to a market-based economy. Only Turkmenistan has shown no formal interest in WTO accession.[25]

V. Conclusions

When the Council for Mutual Economic Assistance dissolved in 1991, its member states contained half a billion people—more than either the European Union or NAFTA today—and these countries were largely insulated from the market-driven international economy. This chapter analyses the progress of the reintegration of the formerly centrally planned economies into the global trading system, focusing on the relationship between multilateral processes and regional integration schemes. Almost all the countries in transition from central planning have accepted the WTO rule-based system in principle, and the potential danger of regionalism proving more attractive than multilateralism has not eventuated.

---

[24] Existing WTO members have taken a strict position towards transition countries insisting on fulfilment of conditions that many existing members do not fulfil and on meeting all commitments before entry. It is generally believed that the transition applicants are expected to offer an average bound tariff on industrial imports of ten percent, which is double the OECD average, but well below that of many existing WTO members, eg. India's average bound rate is 34 percent (Langhammer and Lücke, *supra* note 19). The hard line may have been counterproductive in some cases, with Belarus, Russia and Ukraine stalling or even back-tracking on commitments made at a previous stage in the negotiations.

[25] Tajikistan's transition process was delayed by the 1991–6 civil war, but it applied for WTO membership in 2001. Turkmenistan has adopted a policy of positive neutrality, which the government views as inconsistent with WTO membership. Among non-CMEA countries, Myanmar, like Cuba, is a WTO member because it had been a GATT contracting party, China, Laos and Cambodia are negotiating WTO accession, and Afghanistan and North Korea have shown no interest in WTO membership.

In the 1960s and 1970s the GATT diverged from a rule-based approach and established precedents of differential treatment of some centrally planned economies. These precedents have become embodied in practices, especially with respect to antidumping actions, which discriminate against non-market economies and which continue to be applied to economies in transition from central planning even after becoming market-based economies. Nevertheless, the general picture is of the transition economies accepting WTO principles and preferring to work within rather than outside the Organization. By 2001, sixteen transition economies were WTO members, and all but one of the remainder were at some stage in the negotiating process.

Regional trading arrangements could have posed a major challenge to the multilateral trading system because the big shift from central planning to market economies in 1989–91 coincided with a surge in popularity for regionalism and of doubts about multilateralism. China led the way against regionalism by pursuing and sticking with a multilateral approach,[26] even though China's bid for accession to the World Trade Organization was an arduous process from the initial application in 1986 to the conclusion of negotiations in 2000. The other large transition economy, Russia, has adopted a similar approach, although WTO membership is further away and Russia has flirted with regional arrangements with other former Soviet republics.[27]

By contrast, most of the Central and Eastern European transition economies, including the Baltic countries, have oriented their external economic policies towards the ultimate goal of joining the EU. Vietnam, Cambodia, Laos and Myanmar have also pursued regionalism, but in practice the situation is very different from that of the European transition economies because ASEAN is a far looser organization than the EU and still effectively leaves members scope to pursue their own national trade policies, as well as independent polices in all other areas.

In sum, despite potential hurdles of reintegrating the formerly centrally planned economies into the global trading system, the process went fairly smoothly in the final decade of the twentieth century. The effects of WTO accession are difficult to quantify, because the new members are small and the turmoil of transition makes with and without comparisons particularly difficult. The important point is a systemic one; transition economies have accepted rather than challenged the existing principles of the world trading system embodied in the GATT/WTO, and have generally pursued multilateral non-discriminatory trade policies. The only serious exceptions to this last generalization are the ten EU candidates, for whom EU accession should be a guarantee of accepting WTO norms rather than a source of negative regionalism. The fairly smooth reintegration of formerly centrally planned economies is significant for people beyond these countries' borders. The global trading system should include as much of the world's population as possible, and the effective absence of China and the CMEA countries was a big gap from the 1940s until the 1980s.

---

[26] Richard Pomfret, *Regionalism in Asia and its Impact on Sino-European Trade*, in TRADE AND INVESTMENT IN CHINA: THE EUROPEAN PERSPECTIVE at 81–97 (Roger Strange, Jim Slater and Limin Wang eds. 1998) analyses the absence of regionalism in Asia, and particularly China's constancy to the non-discrimination principle.

[27] Both Russia and China, together with North Korea, have been involved in the Tumen River project which in some guises hopes to establish a sub-regional economic zone where the three countries borders meet and in other guises envisages wider economic cooperation to include Mongolia, South Korea and Japan. The Tumen scheme, however, holds out no serious prospect of discriminatory trade policies and its implications for the global economy are minimal, see Richard Pomfret, ASIAN ECONOMIES IN TRANSITION: REFORMING CENTRALLY PLANNED ECONOMIES 130–42 (1996).

BIBLIOGRAPHY

Anderson Kym, 20(6) *Complexities of China's WTO Accession*, 10(6), THE WORLD ECONOMY 749 (1997)

Haus, Leah, GLOBALIZING THE GATT: THE SOVIET UNION'S SUCCESSOR STATES, EASTERN EUROPE, AND THE INTERNATIONAL TRADING SYSTEM (1992)

Islamov, Bakhtior THE CENTRAL ASIAN STATES TEN YEARS AFTER: HOW TO OVERCOME TRAPS OF DEVELOPMENT, TRANSFORMATION AND GLOBALISATION (2001)

Langhammer, Rolf, and Matthias Lücke, *WTO Accession Issues*, 22(6) THE WORLD ECONOMY 837 (August 1999).

Michalopoulos, Constantine, *The Integration of Transition Economies into the World Trading System*, World Bank Working Paper WPS 2182, September, 1999.

Michalopoulos, Constantine, and David Tarr (1994). *Trade in the New Independent States*, Studies of Economies in Transformation 13, (World Bank 1994)

Michalopoulos, Constantine, and David Tarr, *The Economics of Customs Unions in the Commonwealth of Independent States,* World Bank Policy Research Working Paper 1786 (June 1997).

Palmeter, David, *The WTO Antidumping Agreement and the Economies in Transition,* in STATE TRADING IN THE TWENTY-FIRST CENTURY at 115 (Thomas Cottier and Petros Mavroidis eds 1998).

Pavliuk, Oleksandr (2000), *GUUAM: The Maturing of Political Grouping into Economic Cooperation* in BUILDING SECURITY IN THE NEW STATES OF EURASIA: SUBREGIONAL COOPERATION IN THE FORMER SOVIET SPACE at 33 (Renata Dwan and Oleksandr Pavliuk eds.).

Paznyak, Vyachaslau (2000): *The Customs Union of Five and the Russia-Belarus Union*, in BUILDING SECURITY IN THE NEW STATES OF EURASIA: SUBREGIONAL COOPERATION IN THE FORMER SOVIET SPACE at 57 (Renata Dwan and Oleksandr Pavliuk eds.)

Pomfret, Richard, ASIAN ECONOMIES IN TRANSITION: REFORMING CENTRALLY PLANNED ECONOMIES (1996)

Pomfret, Richard, *ASEAN: Always at the Crossroads?,* 1(3) JOURNAL OF THE ASIA PACIFIC ECONOMY 365 (1996).

Pomfret, Richard, THE ECONOMICS OF REGIONAL TRADING ARRANGEMENTS (2001).

Pomfret, Richard, *Regionalism in Asia and its Impact on Sino-European Trade*, in TRADE AND INVESTMENT IN CHINA: THE EUROPEAN PERSPECTIVE at 81 (Roger Strange, Jim Slater and Limin Wang eds. 1998).

Pomfret, Richard, CENTRAL ASIA TURNS SOUTH? TRADE RELATIONS IN TRANSITION (1999).

Pomfret, Richard, *Enlargement to Include Formerly Centrally Planned Economies: ASEAN and the European Union Compared,* in THE EUROPEAN UNION AND ASEAN: TRADE AND INVESTMENT ISSUES AT 225(Roger Strange, Jim Slater and Corrado Molteni eds. 2000)

Pomfret, Richard, *Trade Initiatives in Central Asia: The Economic Cooperation Organization and the Central Asian Economic Community,* in BUILDING SECURITY IN THE NEW STATES OF EURASIA: SUBREGIONAL COOPERATION IN THE FORMER SOVIET SPACE at 11 (Renata Dwan and Oleksandr Pavliuk eds. 2000)

Sakwa, Richard, and Mark Webber, *The Commonwealth of Independent States, 1991–1998; Stagnation and Survival,* 51(3) EUROPE-ASIA STUDIES 379 (1999).

Temprano-Arroyo, Heliodoro, and Robert Feldman, *Selected Transition and Mediterranean Countries: An Institutional Primer on EMU and EU Accession,* 7(3)ECONOMICS OF TRANSITION 741 (1999).

Willem van der Geest, *Bringing China into the Concert of Nations: An Analysis of its Accession to the WTO*, 32(3) JOURNAL OF WORLD TRADE 99 (1998).

Zhao Wei, *China's WTO Accession Commitments and Prospects*, 32(2) JOURNAL OF WORLD TRADE 51 (1998).

CHAPTER 48

RULES OF ORIGIN AND RULES OF PREFERENCE AND THE WORLD TRADE ORGANIZATION: THE CHALLENGE TO GLOBAL TRADE LIBERALIZATION

William E. James[*]

TABLE OF CONTENTS

* William E. James is Senior International Economist Growth through Investment, Agriculture and Trade (GIAT), Nathan Associates, Inc. GIAT is a USAID-funded cooperative project with the Government of Indonesia. The views expressed herein are those of author and not of USAID or the Government of Indonesia. The author acknowledges the comments and suggestions of Michael Plummer.

I. Introduction

Rules of origin are the criteria used to determine the source country or territory of an imported product. The determination of origin is important where tariffs or other trade barriers differ depending on the source of imports. This is the case in the implementation of various trade restrictions and preferences. Rules of origin, for example, are a necessary accompaniment of commercial policy instruments such as country-specific import quotas as under the Multi-Fibre Arrangement, anti-dumping measures, safeguards, government procurement and quarantine restrictions implemented for reasons of health, safety or environmental protection. Rules of origin are also used in compilation of trade statistics and in the application of labeling and marking requirements. Rules of origin are used in determining whether or not a good is eligible for preferential treatment under the generalized system of preferences and other preferential trade arrangements. In particular, rules of origin have become critically important in the implementation of discriminatory regional and cross-regional trading arrangements such as free trade agreements, customs unions and common markets.[1]

The purpose of this chapter is to provide the reader with an appreciation of the potentially serious threat of misuse that a seemingly innocuous yet necessary set of rules governing product origin may pose for the free flow of goods, services and investment, and of the complexities that face negotiators and policymakers in decisions regarding disciplines over such rules. Following this introduction, Part II provides an historical overview of how the multilateral system has gradually evolved in addressing the issue of rules of origin, the principles and agreements that have been reached, and the present work program of the World Trade Organization with regard to harmonization of non-preferential rules of origin. Part III provides a discussion of how economists and economic theory have come to view the issue of rules of origin in the context of international commercial policy, preferential trading arrangements, and the tendency towards global economic integration. Part IV reports on the available empirical studies of the economic costs of rules of origin, particularly trade diversion in the context of free trade areas but also upon firms' decisions. Part V examines the recent upsurge in notifications of regional preferential trading agreements to the WTO and the plans for even more proliferation of such agreements in the three major hubs of world trade—East Asia, the Americas and Europe. Part VI considers the problems surrounding setting rules for determination of the origin of commercial services that entail international transactions. Finally, Part VII concludes with some discussion of the WTO agenda regarding rules of origin in the context of a new round.

II. Rules of Origin in the GATT/WTO System

Under the 1947 General Agreement on Tariffs and Trade, Contracting Parties were unencumbered by any regulation governing rules of origin. The absence of any specific GATT regulation covering rules of origin is perhaps surprising as such rules are essential in implementing non-MFN tariffs, quotas and other forms of import restrictions and preferences. Reference is frequently made to the problem of determination of origin of goods entering international trade of Contracting Parties in several GATT Articles (including Articles I, II, III, VIII, IX, XI, XIX and XXIV) as well as in some side agreements of

---

[1] Indeed, Gary. N. Horlick and Michael A. Meyer, *Rules of Origin from a Policy Perspective*, in RULES OF ORIGIN IN INTERNATIONAL TRADE: A COMPARATIVE SURVEY 403 (E. Vermulst, P. Waer and J. Bourgeois eds. 1994) have referred to rules of origin as "stepchildren of other discriminatory devices."

the GATT. For example, the Agreement on Government Procurement concluded during the Tokyo Round establishes that Contracting Parties should not create rules of origin for purposes of government procurement that differ from the rules applied in the normal course of trade.

In 1953, the International Chamber of Commerce attempted to persuade the GATT to adopt a common definition of origin but no agreement resulted.[2] The inability of the Contracting Parties to reach agreement was the result of the recognition by several countries that the issue of rules of origin was not merely a technical one, but was intimately bound up with commercial policy. Hence, until the Uruguay Round negotiations, the GATT was all but silent on the issue.

A. Determination of Origin of Products by Contracting Members of the GATT: From Anarchy to First Principles

The "perfect liberty" enjoyed by Contracting Parties in setting rules of origin has resulted in a system of complex, overlapping and often conflicting rulings regarding product origin. For example, in the United States, numerous court rulings, intricate administrative decisions by the Customs and occasional Congressional interventions through legislation have resulted in a complex and confusing law on rules of origin.[3] U.S. case law on rules of origin dates back to 1907 but became increasingly important following the passage of the infamous Smoot-Hawley Tariff Act of 1930.[4] U.S. anti-dumping law has also heightened the importance and use of rules of origin, although between 1921 and 1967 of 706 anti-dumping investigations only 75 led to definitive measures.[5] By the 1980s, the number of anti-dumping investigations began to increase and a very significant proportion resulted in voluntary restrictions or in definitive measures (estimated together to be 68 percent of cases investigated[6]). Subsequently, use of restrictive rules of origin to enforce penalties or export restraint agreements rose.[7]

The EC has taken advantage of the absence of discipline over the determination of origin to design product-specific rules of origin for purposes of implementation of anti-dumping measures that can only be described as instruments of protection.[8] As in the

---

[2] A working party on the issue was formed and was supported by a majority in submitting a text that proposed use of the principle of substantial transformation in determination of the origin of a good which has resulted from materials or labor of more than one country or that undergoes specific defined processes that alter the individual character of the good (see Edurne Navarro Varona, *Rules of Origin in the GATT*, in RULES OF ORIGIN IN INTERNATIONAL TRADE: A COMPARATIVE SURVEY, *supra* note 1, at 359).

[3] N. David Palmeter, *Rules of Origin in the United States*, in RULES OF ORIGIN IN INTERNATIONAL TRADE: A COMPARATIVE SURVEY, *supra* note 1.

[4] Palmeter, *supra* note 3, at 27 cites the "marking statute" of this law noting that it requires that foreign goods have a label identifying the country they originated from either on the good itself or on the container carrying the good.

[5] J. MICHAEL FINGER (ed.), ANTIDUMPING: HOW IT WORKS AND WHO GETS HURT 26 (1993)

[6] J. Michael Finger and Tracy Murray, *Antidumping and Countervailing Duty Enforcement in the United States*, in ANTIDUMPING: HOW IT WORKS AND WHO GETS HURT, *supra* note 5, at 52.

[7] Palmeter, *supra* note 3, at 50–53, notes that regulation of steel imports in the United States has been implemented through very restrictive and complex rules of origin. Steel is the leading industry user of anti-dumping as a trade remedy in the United States but also all around the world (Jorge Miranda, Raul A. Torres and Mario Ruiz, *The International Use of Anti-Dumping*, 32(5) JOURNAL OF WORLD TRADE 5 (October 1998)).

[8] Edwin Vermulst and Paul Waer, *European Community Rules of Origin as Commercial Policy Instruments*, 24(3) JOURNAL OF WORLD TRADE (June 1990); Paul Waer, *European Community Rules of Origin*, in RULES OF ORIGIN IN INTERNATIONAL TRADE: A COMPARATIVE SURVEY, *supra* note 1, at 85.

U.S. case, the EC anti-dumping regime has become increasingly active in recent decades and has traditionally been second only to the United States in use of definitive measures.[9]

Following the establishment of the GATT, successive multilateral negotiating rounds led to the overall reduction of quantitative restrictions and tariffs. However, beginning in 1961, trade in textiles and apparel came under increasing regulation and restriction with the establishment of the Multi-Fibre Arrangement ("MFA"). The MFA quota regime was adopted at the behest of importing countries including Australia, New Zealand, Canada, Norway, the European Communities, and the United States. Implementation of the system of bilateral quotas covering trade in textiles and apparel necessitated adoption of rules of origin. Not surprisingly these rules of origin have tended to be quite restrictive and have been adapted over time to protect domestic producers in these markets. For example, U.S. rules of origin governing textiles and apparel trade under the MFA were changed by administrations seeking to afford greater protection to U.S. producers in 1984 and again in 1996, both on the occasion of elections.

The Generalized System of Preferences ("GSP"), under which preferences were to be extended from developed to developing countries on a non-reciprocal basis, provided a further boost to the global use of rules of origin beginning in the late 1960s. Criteria had to be established in order to determine which goods would be eligible for preferential tariff treatment. Japan, for example, had refrained from joining the MFA and had remained abstinent in its use of antidumping measures and so had little use for restrictive non-preferential rules of origin. However, as it decided to implement GSP, Japan was forced to adopt rules of origin for that purpose.

Similarly, the use of rules of origin has been boosted by the proliferation of reciprocal preferential trading arrangements, permitted under GATT Article XXIV as well as under the Enabling Clause in situations involving developing countries. In the European Communities not only were intra-EC rules of origin necessary to implement the common market, additional rules regarding eligibility of goods for preferential treatment had to be established with the European Free Trade Agreement and with the numerous association agreements between the EC and nearby developing countries. This increasing proliferation of overlapping and often conflicting systems of rules of origin was of course most noticeable to customs authorities and related organizations, as well as by traders and businesses engaged in international trade.[10]

The absence of regulation pertinent to rules of origin was looking increasingly less like "perfect liberty" and more like anarchy. The tendency for customs authorities to interpret and administer rules of origin in a manner favorable to particular domestic producer interests also resulted in inconsistency and uncertainty for importers. The Customs Cooperation Council ("CCC") stepped into the breach left by the failure of GATT to regulate rules of origin.[11]

B. The Kyoto Convention: Substantial Transformation

The International Convention on the Simplification and Harmonization of Customs Procedures was held in Kyoto, Japan in 1973. The Kyoto Convention dedicated part of its

---

[9] Jorge Miranda, Raul A. Torres and Mario Ruiz, *supra* note 7; William E. James, *The Rise of Anti-Dumping: Does Regionalism Promote Administered Protection?*, 14(2) ASIAN-PACIFIC ECONOMIC LITERATURE 14 (November 2000). Recently, however according to WTO statistics, India has overtaken the United States in its use of anti-dumping measures. *See* Chapter 1 of this book.

[10] Vermulst (1994) cites three factors in the rise in importance of rules of origin: 1) increased use of contingent forms of protection; 2) increased incidence of regional trading arrangements; and 3) establishment of various non-reciprocal ("positive") discriminatory measures like the Generalized System of Preferences.

[11] The CCC was formed in Brussels in 1950 and is now known as the World Customs Organization ("WCO").

Table 1: How is origin determined?

Type of tradable	Principle/Criteria
PRIMARY:	Wholly produced or Obtained within a single country
Agricultural goods	unprocessed and harvested within
Marine Fisheries	ownership of vessel and means of catch
Forestry products	unprocessed and harvested within
Mineral products	extracted within territory or seabed
Scrap/Waste products	derived from manufactured products
	Collected within and fit only for recovery of raw materials
PROCESSED or MANUFACTURED:	Last Substantial Transformation
	Change in tariff heading Test
	Specified Process Test
	Value-added or Percentage Test
	Mixed Tests
SERVICES:	Nationality of Service Provider or Owner of Service-Providing Entity
	Residency Test
	Value-added or Percentage Test
	Ownership Test
	Intellectual Input Control Test
	Mixed Tests

Source: Author's compilations.

proceedings to an effort to establish the basis of standard practices for determination of product origin and for application of rules of origin, both non-preferential and preferential. The Kyoto Convention attained general agreement on application of the rules of origin regarding goods (mainly primary products) "wholly obtained" in one country.[12] However, instead of establishing one general rule for processed primary products and manufactured goods with components or labor input from more than one country, the Convention set out the principle of substantial transformation in determining the origin of such complex products and made recommendations for three tests or criteria for satisfying this principle.[13] The three tests include: 1) a change in tariff heading; 2) a percentage or value-added test; and 3) a specified manufacturing process test. Examples of the application of these tests have been provided in detail elsewhere.[14]

The principles and criteria or tests used to verify the origin of tradable goods and services are delineated in Table 1. Examples of the application of the three types of

[12] Varona discusses Rule 2, which covers goods wholly produced in one country. In addition to primary goods, which include minerals, vegetable (including forestry) products, live animals and animal products, and fish or marine products, scrap and waste products suitable only for recovery of raw materials are included in the rule. *See* Varona, *supra* note 2, at 361n.

[13] Normally the principle of *last substantial transformation* is used, however there are cases where the origin of a complex manufactured good, such as a semi-conductor or a photocopying machine is determined by the place of *most substantial transformation* (see Waer, *supra* note 7, at 139–141 and Varona, *supra* note 2, at 376–377).

[14] *See* Chapter 15 of this book. *See also,* RULES OF ORIGIN IN INTERNATIONAL TRADE: A COMPARATIVE SURVEY, *supra,* note 1; Gary C. Hufbauer and Jeffrey J. Schott, NORTH AMERICAN FREE TRADE: ISSUES AND RECOMMENDATIONS (1992); N. David Palmeter, *Rules of Origin in Customs Unions and Free Trade Areas*, in REGIONAL INTEGRATION AND THE GLOBAL TRADING SYSTEM, (K. Anderson and R. Blackhurst eds. 1993); N. David Palmeter, *Pacific Regional Trade Liberalization and Rules of Origin*, paper presented at the PACIFIC ECONOMIC COOPERATION COUNCIL TRADE POLICY FORUM VII (June 1993)

tests governing the origin of processed and manufactured tradables are provided for clarification but also to illustrate to the reader the discretion and inconsistency with which such rules may be applied.

First, the *CTH* (*change in tariff heading*) test: canned tomato paste from Chile is imported by a Canadian catsup manufacturer. The tomato paste enters Canada under HS code 2002.90, the Canadian firm processes the paste into catsup which is exported to the United States under HS code 2103.20. Under the Canada-United States Free Trade Agreement using the CTH test, the catsup is assigned Canadian origin and is eligible to enter under the preferential tariff. However, a few years later, under the NAFTA agreement (involving Mexico, Canada and the United States) an exception (among many others) to the CTH test was inserted so that processing tomato paste into catsup was not regarded as sufficient to confer NAFTA origin. This exception was aimed at forcing catsup manufacturers to use tomato paste produced in one of the three countries rather than from Chile. Given an MFN tariff of 13.6 percent on tomato paste in the United States, one could almost certainly expect this change to result in trade diversion in tomato paste.

Second, the *specified manufacturing process* test: a product-specific rule that establishes specified manufacturing operations that do or do not confer origin upon the product. Japanese manufacturers of dynamic random access memories (DRAMs—a type of integrated circuit semiconductor) were investigated by the EEC in 1989 for alleged dumping. A ruling on product origin was necessitated by the fact that the Japanese manufacturers performed only certain operations within Japan and others in factories established within the EEC or in third countries, such as Malaysia. The EEC, using the specified process test, ruled that only the process of diffusion (performed by the manufacturers in Japan) could confer origin upon the DRAMs. This ruling disqualified DRAMs assembled and tested in Japanese-owned factories in the EEC from enjoying EC preferences and also applied antidumping tariffs to DRAMs that were assembled and tested by Japanese firms in Malaysian factories. This decision was taken even though the value-added in assembly and testing (both which are relatively labor-intensive) was thought to be higher than that of the diffusion process.[15]

Third, the *value-added* or *percentage* test is a test that requires a certain percentage of the value-added of a final good to be from within a country or region in order to obtain its origin from that country or region. The percentage test may also state that import (non-originating) content may not exceed a certain threshold or may be based upon physical criteria (minimum local components' percentage or maximum imported components' percentage). Under the Canada-United States FTA, for automobiles to qualify for preferential treatment, a fifty per cent value-added (using the net cost method) rule was adopted. Honda Civic sedans were assembled in Canada using engines produced in engine plants in Ohio that contained both U.S. and Japanese parts. Honda Canada estimated that 69 per cent of the value-added of each sedan originated in North America. However, the U.S. Customs Service used a set of rulings based on "the plain language" of the agreement to disallow most of the North American content of the engines and the labor used in assembling the sedans.[16] The Honda case revealed how a determined customs authority could turn aside logic in interpreting the value-added criteria. Add to that the uncertainty over the price of materials, exchange rate fluctuations and the lengthy and complex audits required and one can appreciate the possibilities for inconsistent and unpredictable rulings using this test.

---

[15] Waer, *supra* note 7, at 140
[16] Palmeter, *supra* note 3, at 68–73

The Kyoto Convention adopted a very flexible approach in attempting to start move-ment towards greater order and harmony in the area of rules of origin. It did not select one of the three tests as the basis for a harmonized system of rules of origin, reflecting the prevailing view that each has strengths and weaknesses and that no single test may be appropriate for all manufactured products. This is consistent with practice as countries often use mixed tests to determine product origin, particularly in the context of free trade agreements. It also left it to the discretion of national governments to select among al-ternative accepted methods used to calculate value-added for purposes of implementing the percentage test. Finally, it was recognized that the Convention was a starting point in moving towards harmonized rules of origin rather than being the last word.[17] While the Kyoto Convention was concluded in 1973, it was not until the Uruguay Round was concluded more than twenty years later that a concrete work program for harmonization of rules of origin was put in place.

The GATT Secretariat issued a note on rules of origin in 1981 and the Ministers agreed to a study of the subject. However, it was not until the Uruguay Round negotiations began in 1986 that serious attention was paid to the issue in the GATT.

C. The Uruguay Round Agreement on Rules of Origin

Article 9.2 of the Uruguay Round Agreement on Rules of Origin established the work program for harmonization of non-preferential rules of origin. Preferential rules of origin were excluded at the insistence of the EC.

A WTO Committee on Rules of Origin ("CRO") was established in 1995 with the mandate to achieve the harmonization program within three years, a fairly ambitious timetable. Technical support for the rules of origin negotiations was to be given the CRO by a Technical Committee on Rules of Origin ("TCRO") set up by the World Customs Organization ("WCO"), formerly the CCC. The TCRO was a necessity, given the com-plex issues facing the negotiators and the importance of familiarity with the intricacies of the Harmonized System ("HS") nomenclature. The coverage of non-preferential rules of origin includes those used to enforce all non-preferential commercial policy instru-ments (e.g., anti-dumping, countervailing duties and safeguards), marking and labeling requirements, discriminatory quantitative restrictions and tariff quotas, government pro-curement, and in the collection of trade statistics.

The Preamble to the Agreement on Rules of Origin states that the purposes of the Agreement include ensuring that the rules themselves "do not create unnecessary obsta-cles to trade", and that they are to be prepared and applied "in an impartial, transparent, predictable, consistent and neutral manner." The harmonization program called for by the Agreement instructs the CRO (assisted by the TCRO) to define goods "wholly obtained" from a single country as well as minimal operations or processes that do not confer origin. Rules of origin for ten categories of goods wholly obtained in one country were spelt out in the Kyoto Convention.[18]

The principle of "substantial transformation" is applicable to all other categories of goods (i.e., products that are processed or manufactured with input from more than one country). The decision to use a change in tariff classification of the product in question as the guiding criterion in determining the origin of goods produced in more than one

---

[17] The United States in its law ratifying the Kyoto Convention excluded the section on rules of origin.
[18] Varona provides a list of the ten categories of such wholly obtained goods as stated in the Kyoto Convention. Varona, *supra* note 2, at 361n.

country was a significant advance.[19] However, where the CTH or a change in tariff subheading ("CTSH") criterion was inapplicable, supplementary criteria would also be permitted. These supplementary criteria may include an *ad valorem* (percentage) test or a manufacturing operations or a specific process test. However, the Agreement requires that the percentage test be accompanied by the method of calculation and that the processing test be accompanied by a precise specification of the processing operation required to confer origin.[20]

The Agreement specifies that the TCRO will develop the harmonized definitions of goods wholly obtained in a single country in as much detail as possible as well as those of the minimal operations not conferring origin. In addition, the TCRO was directed to develop the rules of origin for goods produced in more than one country based upon the change in tariff classification test and, where necessary, supplementary criteria, and to work with the CRO in solving technical issues pertinent to non-preferential rules of origin.

Unfortunately, the negotiations of the CRO on non-preferential rules of origin have been extremely complex and progress has been exceedingly difficult,[21] to the extent that some experts have questioned the utility of the effort towards harmonization.[22] The CRO failed in any case to meet its targeted completion date in 1998 and negotiations continue to drag on several years later.[23] This is not to say that progress has not been made in the negotiations.

D. WTO Harmonization of Non-Preferential Rules of Origin

The progress of the negotiations in harmonization has been slow not only because of technical difficulties but also because rules of origin are closely connected to commercial policy in the Contracting Parties.[24] The embedded relationship between restrictive trade policies and rules of origin can be clearly seen in the implementation of antidumping measures, quota restrictions under the MFA, and in the very decision to exclude preferential rules of origin from the negotiations. The decision of the United States to change its rules of origin for textiles and apparel in 1996 in a manner that appears to

---

[19] As Sherry M. Stephenson, *Multilateralizing Harmonized Rules of Origin: Is It a Realistic Option?*, ORGANIZATION OF AMERICAN STATES 7 (July 1998) notes, this was the first time a specific method was so designated by the Contracting Parties.

[20] The Agreement permits use of rules that describe processes or operations that do *not* confer origin if they are a clarification of a positive standard or in cases where a positive determination of origin is unnecessary.

[21] *See* Chapter 15 of this book for a detailed description of the work of the CRO to date.

[22] Wim Keizer, *Negotiations on Harmonized Non-Preferential Rules of Origin: A Useless Task from a Trade Policy Perspective*, 31(4) JOURNAL OF WORLD TRADE 145 (1997) argues that the negotiation of harmonized non-preferential rules of origin is perhaps a: *"useless task from a trade policy perspective."*

[23] Philippe G. Nell, *WTO Negotiations on the Harmonization of Rules of Origin: A First Critical Appraisal*, 33(3) JOURNAL OF WORLD TRADE, 45–72 (June 1999) provides a first review of the negotiations progress. Also see the WTO homepage for updated information on the harmonization program.

[24] Stephenson, *supra* note 19; Sherry M. Stephenson and William E. James, *Rules of Origin and The Asia Pacific Economic Cooperation*, 29(2) JOURNAL OF WORLD TRADE 77 (April 1995); William E. James, *APEC and Preferential Rules of Origin: Stumbling Blocks for Liberalization of Trade?*, 31(3) JOURNAL OF WORLD TRADE 113 (1997); and Vermulst, *supra* note 10, discuss the embedded relationship between restrictive trade policies and rules of origin. For example, antidumping measures (either penalty duties or price undertakings) require very specific application of restrictive rules of origin in order to prevent circumvention of the measures through third countries. Similarly, application of country-specific quota restrictions also must be enforced by restrictive rules of origin.

contradict the purposes of the Agreement is a further demonstration of the intention of the members to retain their use as protectionist devices.[25]

The very logic of attempting to assign origin to modern manufactured goods is questionable. Hocking states:

"...it appears indisputable that the nature of the trading environment is very different from that of a century ago. The globalization of production now means that it is virtually impossible to identify in a meaningful sense the origins of a given product. Cars, computers, household electronic goods, each are sourced from components across the world and may be produced in a variety of locations." [26]

Despite the ambiguity of the actual origin of goods produced in more than one country or customs territory, governments appear to have a strong preference to retain their own discretion in conferring origin. Given the revealed preference of contracting parties to preserve the discretionary use of rules of origin as instruments of commercial policy it is not surprising that much of the provisional text in the harmonization program is in square brackets.[27]

The nature of the negotiations is that until everything is agreed upon, nothing is agreed upon. Even if the complex technical issues in determining product origin could be overcome by patient effort, there is no guarantee that at the end of the day a consensus will be achieved.

In the case of *products wholly obtained*, the CRO has been able to reach a broad consensus with two exceptions: parts and raw materials recovered from articles that can no longer serve their original purpose or otherwise be used, and products of sea-fishing. In the former case a problem arises as many spare parts may not contain origin markings and, thus, origin is conferred on the country where the parts are recovered and, further, recovery of some parts may involve environmentally hazardous or toxic waste. Some countries for reasons of environmental protection have indicated at the CRO that they wish to insert a clause that allows them to regard parts recovered that involve no such waste to be different from those that do. The CRO has resisted because of the requirement for uniform and consistent application of rules of origin. In the latter case there is general agreement that the origin of fish caught in territorial waters is based on the country concerned while for those caught in international waters origin is conferred upon the flag of registration of the ship or vessel used. There is disagreement, however, upon whether to use most or least restrictive definitions of territorial waters (twelve vs. two hundred miles) in defining a country's territorial waters and upon where to confer origin in cases where countries allow foreign vessels to fish in their territorial waters.[28]

---

[25] The U.S. decision to confer origin to where garments are cut rather than sewn was specifically intended to crack down on apparel exports of China but had adverse consequences for other trade partners. In particular, the change denied EU origin to a number of textile products that incorporated textile materials such as silk, grey cloth and cotton from China, including Italian scarfs. This meant that these products became subject to U.S. quota restrictions. The EU Commission challenged the change in the WTO (Nell, *supra* note 23). A compromise solution between the European Commission and the United States was notified to WTO in July 2000 (downloaded from: http://docsonline.wto.org).

[26] Brian Hocking, *Trade Politics: Environments, Agendas, and Processes*, in TRADE POLITICS: INTERNATIONAL, DOMESTIC AND REGIONAL PERSPECTIVES (B. Hocking and S. McGuire eds.1999) 1, 6.

[27] Stephenson, *supra* note 19; Nell, *supra* note 23

[28] Nell, *supra* note 23, elaborates on the rather significant economic issues involved in the alternative definitions. Countries with large exclusive economic zones may wish to use as broad a definition of territorial waters as possible to retain their fishing rights whereas other countries want to use a more restrictive definition in order to expand the international fishing area.

Closely related to the issues surrounding the origin of goods wholly obtained in a single country are those concerning minimal processes that do not confer origin. These are not expected to be stumbling blocks for the overall harmonization program but will not be adopted until final agreement is reached.

Nell[29] reported that the harmonized work program ("HWP") after four years of negotiations had reached significant results in approximately one-third of the HS tariff lines (35 chapters). Progress was made in agricultural goods and mineral products, both of which involve products wholly obtained in one country. However, progress was not confined to such goods. Cement, paper and printing, chemicals and pharmaceutical products are examples of processed and manufactured products for which negotiations also advanced. However, for many manufactured goods there was no consensus in the TCRO.

A sample of the so-called "big problem areas"[30] reveals once again that it is the use of rules of origin as policy instruments rather than the technical difficulties of determining product origin that has made progress most difficult. Processed agricultural items, textiles and apparel, transportation equipment, and electrical and non-electrical machinery top the list of problem sectors. Among the other types of products over which there has been disagreement are plastics, rubber, leather, footwear and iron and steel products. These sectors are among those with generally high levels of protection (processed agricultural products, textiles and clothing, leather, footwear) or that are subject to intensive use of antidumping or other safeguard measures (iron and steel, rubber and plastic products) or are regarded as "strategic industries" (transportation equipment, electrical and non-electrical machinery).

In the case of processed agricultural goods (HS Chapters 1–24), over one hundred issues were handed over to the TCRO.[31] The TCRO has provided input on substantive technical issues, indicating whether or not a manufacturing process was substantial or whether or not the character of a good obtained was substantially different from the inputs used. However, negotiators of countries resisting conferring origin have largely chosen to ignore the technical input. As of July 2000 (Committee on Rules of Origin, Minutes, June 23, 2000) no consensus was reported in ninety instances and for only eleven items was a consensus or near consensus reached for the processed agricultural goods.[32]

The TCRO has also provided input for consideration by CRO negotiators for 38 issues in chemical processes (HS Chapters 28–40) and 86 issues in machinery (HS Chapters 84–90). The input provides options for determining if certain processing or assembly activities constitute a last substantial transformation. For machinery, unassembled parts and components are found under the same chapter heading as more complete components or final products and this gives rise to the question of whether or not assembly constitutes a last substantial transformation. The TCRO provides options where the CTH test could be replaced by a CTSH test, that is a change in tariff sub-heading. The 86 issues in machinery are only the tip of the iceberg as the negotiating text is extremely long and complex. Obtaining consensus is made difficult by the absence of clear trade-offs and the fact that the interests of the thirty most active countries in the negotiations vary broadly across sectors.[33]

---

[29] Nell, *supra* note 23.

[30] *Id.*

[31] *Id.*

[32] *See* Chapter 15 of this book for a more updated account of progress.

[33] Nell, *supra* note 23, at 68–69 points out that the inconsistency of positions among the countries in these negotiations makes it nearly impossible to form alliances. Furthermore, the negotiations aim to achieve a harmonized single result applicable to all contracting parties and this makes it all but certain that residual rules will be important in finally attaining a consensus.

Other outstanding and controversial issues involve so-called "residual rules" made necessary because items undergoing a process regarded as a last substantial transformation do not meet the requirement for a change in tariff heading, or where there are one or more exceptions noted to an otherwise origin-conferring change, or when an item has minimum operations not conferring origin. These residual rules may involve a value-added or percentage test or a specified process test. The more restrictive the primary rules are, the greater the need there will be for such residual rules and the larger the stakes will be in setting such residual rules.

These complications make it very likely that the negotiations over non-preferential rules of origin will drag on for some time. The fact that every five years the HS classifications are modified, coupled with the on-going changes in technology and production processes resulting from these changes, means that the task of setting rules of origin that meet consensus may be one for Sisyphus. And even if the negotiations succeed, the large amount of preferential trade will still not be covered. Yet it is the rules of origin governing preferential trade that has attracted the most interest and concern among economists. Annex II to the Agreement on Rules of Origin contains a non-binding "Common Declaration with Regard to Preferential Rules of Origin". As Stephenson points out:

> "The distinction drawn in the WTO Agreement on Rules of Origin between non-preferential and preferential rules of origin, and the limitation of the Agreement to harmonize only those non-preferential rules, clearly indicates the importance attached by governments to their ability to design preferential rules without multilateral interference. Moreover, this distinction between non-preferential and preferential rules, and the different treatment accorded respectively, implicitly recognizes that rules of origin serve as commercial policy instruments and have trade policy objectives."[34]

The remainder of this chapter focuses on the economic analysis of rules of origin and, in particular, how rules of origin are, in the context of preferential trading arrangements, in reality rules for determining the eligibility of tradables for preferential treatment—rules of preference. The growing importance attached to preferential trading arrangements can be seen in the expansion of the European Union, the effort in the Americas to establish a hemisphere-wide free trade area, and in the new regionalism emerging in East Asia. Whether or not (and under what conditions) these arrangements will improve economic welfare for members and non-members is an important question for economic theory and empirical analysis.

III. Economic Theory and Rules of Origin

Economic analysis of preferential trade agreements involving reciprocal exchange of tariff reductions amongst members was initially focused solely on the question of a customs union ("CU").[35] Economic analysis of regional or preferential trading agreements has until recently been known as the "theory of the customs union." The dominance of the CU over other forms of preferential arrangements, including the free trade agreement ("FTA"), is a venerable tradition in economics that goes back to Viner (1950).[36]

[34] Stephenson, *supra* note 19, at 9

[35] In contrast to standard models of international trade that feature two countries and two goods, analysis of preferential arrangements requires more complex models (James, *supra* note 23). RICHARD POMFRET, THE ECONOMICS OF REGIONAL TRADING ARRANGEMENTS (1997) summarizes the theoretical literature in this regard.

[36] Jacob Viner, THE CUSTOMS UNION ISSUE (1950). *See* POMFRET, *supra* note 32 for a thorough discussion of CU dominance over the FTA. Robert Mundell, *Tariff Preferences and the Terms of Trade*, SCHOOL OF ECONOMIC AND SOCIAL STUDIES 1–13 (1964) explores how formation of a CU may influence the

Shibata's[37] seminal article drew attention to the relative neglect of forms of preferential union other than the CU, and particularly of the lack of analytical writing on free trade agreements. His focus was on the use of rules of origin in enforcing free trade agreements (as opposed to customs unions), that is, the rules used in deciding whether goods entering the member countries were eligible or ineligible for preferential treatment. In doing so, Shibata warned that such rules of preference could turn out to have protectionist effects. Why rules of origin are important in a free trade agreement is elaborated upon in the following section.

A. Customs Unions and Free Trade Agreements: Trade Deflection Prevention

The key difference between a CU and an FTA is that the CU sets a common external tariff whilst an FTA allows its members to set external tariffs independently. The central importance of rules of origin in enforcing tariff preferences and in blocking "trade deflection" in a Free Trade Area is elaborated upon in Shibata.[38] In essence, any FTA without rules of origin would in effect become a CU with the external tariff being that of lowest-tariff member. All imports from outside the FTA would initially enter through the port of the lowest-tariff member in order to evade the higher tariffs in the other members' ports. Hence, for example, without a rule of origin the ASEAN Free Trade Agreement would become a CU with Singapore's zero tariff becoming the effective external tariff.[39] Thus, rules of origin become necessary in order for member countries to set external tariffs (and non-tariff barriers) vis-à-vis non-members independently, whilst allowing goods from member countries in under preferential treatment. This enforcement function of rules of origin is referred to as "prevention of trade deflection."

One of the implications of the economic theory of Preferential Trading Arrangements is that in an FTA as opposed to a CU, members would be concerned with the implications of trade deflection for their industrial and trade policies and would, therefore, be inclined to frame rules of origin with commercial policy objectives in mind.[40] Krueger argues that a CU will always be superior to an FTA, largely because of the trade-diversion brought

---

terms of trade of member and non-member countries. Anne O. Krueger, *Free Trade Areas Versus Customs Unions*, 54 JOURNAL OF DEVELOPMENT ECONOMICS 169 (1997) continues in the tradition of finding the CU superior to the FTA. However, various authors in Jefferey J. Schott, FREE TRADE AREAS AND U.S. TRADE POLICY (1989) assert that under certain circumstances an FTA can be superior to a CU. The renewal of interest in the FTA is reflected in the most recent thorough survey of preferential trade liberalization (Arvind Panagariya, *Preferential Trade Liberalization: The Traditional Theory and New Developments*, 38 JOURNAL OF ECONOMIC LITERATURE 287 (June 2000)). He pays close attention to the FTA and its enforcement mechanism—the rules of origin.

[37] Hirofumi Shibata, *The Theory of Economic Unions: A Comparative Analysis of Customs Unions, Free Trade Areas and Tax Unions*, in FISCAL HARMONIZATION IN COMMON MARKETS, VOL. 1, THEORY (C. Shoup ed. 1967)

[38] *Id.*

[39] Various official and business interests within ASEAN have expressed concern over Singapore's tilt towards numerous free trade agreements. Prime Minister Mahathir of Malaysia expressed the fear that Singapore will become "an open backdoor" that will flood the region with duty-free imports from the various non-ASEAN FTA partner countries. For discussion of Singapore's strategy see Linda Low, *Singapore's RTA Strategy*, paper presented at the PACIFIC ECONOMIC COOPERATION COUNCIL(PECC) TRADE POLICY FORUM AND THAI MINISTRY OF COMMERCE ON REGIONAL TRADING ARRANGEMENTS: STOCKTAKE AND NEXT STEPS (June 12–13 2001).

[40] Robert Mundell, *The Theory of Tariffs and Monetary Policies*, in PROTECTIONISM AND WORLD WELFARE, 244 (1993) finds that a customs union is likely to alter the terms of trade in favor of member countries (and against the rest of the world) compared with a free trade agreement in the presence of trade deflection.

about by discriminatory tariffs and rules of origin.[41] However, as Vermulst[42] and Vermulst and Waer[43] have demonstrated, customs unions also make use of restrictive rules of origin in the context of enforcing antidumping measures.[44] Indeed, one of the problems facing the EEC as a customs union was that, while it had a common external tariff, it lacked a common commercial policy. The proliferation of non-tariff barriers within the EEC threatened an increasing segmentation of its market. Hence, the members recognized the importance of the Single Market Program and the establishment of a common market.

Rules of origin impose real costs on firms in member countries that engage in trade and seek to gain from preferential tariffs.[45] Hence, overly restrictive or complex rules of origin necessarily involve high costs and present firms with a trade-off between complying and receiving the preferential treatment or not complying and so avoiding the costs imposed (but losing the advantage of preferential tariff treatment). This trade-off is graphically analyzed in Stephenson and James[46] and James[47]. The basic point that emerges is that more restrictive and complex rules of origin reduce the expansion of intra-union trade relative to the potential, since highly restrictive rules of origin are costly for firms in member countries to comply with. Firms within the union choose to comply or not to comply based on their evaluation of the benefit they receive from preferential tariffs versus the costs they incur in meeting the rules of origin.

Article XXIV of the GATT constrains members of preferential trade arrangements ("PTAs") from raising external barriers to non-members. In this context, successive multilateral negotiation rounds have served to lower MFN tariffs and, thus, to erode the margin of preference ("MOP") that can be offered by PTAs. This lowering of the MOP offered by PTAs, coupled with increased globalization of production, may have led to efforts to impose tighter rules of origin in order to preserve preferential market access to the intended beneficiaries.[48] However, it may be the case that as multilateral liberalization occurs and MFN tariffs close in on zero, firms and other producers will have less incentive to lobby for restrictive rules of origin. The problem is that without progress at the multilateral level, where negotiations are cumbersome to say the least, there may be increasing trade discrimination as the tendency to negotiate bilateral FTA-type arrangements gains momentum.

The lowering of traditional tariff and non-tariff barriers on a most favored nation basis has led GATT Contracting Parties to substitute new forms of protection for the

---

[41] Krueger, *supra* note 34.

[42] Vermulst, *supra* note 10.

[43] Vermulst and Waer, *supra* note 7.

[44] France maintained a highly restrictive quota on autos manufactured in the U.K. by Japanese affiliates, arguing that the cars were of Japanese and not EU origin. This restriction was maintained for over a decade even though it was in violation of EU law. Ultimately, the restriction on vehicles produced by affiliates in the UK was overturned, although the quota on autos produced in Japan continued to be maintained by France (Ian Forrester, *The Economics of Rules of Origin*, in RULES OF ORIGIN IN INTERNATIONAL TRADE: A COMPARATIVE SURVEY, *supra* note 1, at 7.

[45] For example, analysis of the cost of border formalities to comply with EC-EFTA preferential tariffs is at least three percent of the value of the goods being traded (Jan Herrin, *Rules of Origin and Differences in Tariff Levels in EFTA and in the EC*, OCCASIONAL PAPER NO. 13, EUROPEAN FREE TRADE ASSOCIATION (February 1986)). Firms exporting goods from Norway to France would thus only seek to comply if the margin of preference were greater than three percent of the value of the goods exported, and would otherwise pay the MFN tariff. Hence, stringent rules of origin may vitiate the purpose of the FTA.

[46] Stephenson and James, *supra* note 24.

[47] James, *supra* note 24.

[48] This seems to underlie the development of product-specific rules of origin as instruments of commercial policy in the EU (Vermulst and Waer, *supra* note 7, and Vermulst, *supra* note 10).

old forms. For example, antidumping investigations and measures have proliferated in recent decades[49] and have become especially prevalent in seeking to restrict imports from East Asian countries.[50] As antidumping measures are inherently discriminatory in nature, they also require rules of origin to be made effective against offending exporters and to prevent "dumpers" from circumventing the measures in force by transshipment or by assembly in third countries or the country of importation.

The proliferation of free trade agreements that has occurred in recent decades has magnified the importance of rules of origin in international trade and this has rekindled the interest of economists, particularly theorists, in developing models that examine firm behavior under preferential tariffs enforced by rules of origin. Tariff revenue redistribution effects are another focus of theoretical analysis[51]. In cases where there is asymmetry in tariff levels (and, presumably, in dependence on tariff revenue) between partners (as is the case between Mexico and its NAFTA partners) it can be shown that the member with high tariffs may lose from the FTA[52].

Most analysis of PTAs has been done under the assumption of perfect competition and those that deviate from the assumption by introducing imperfect competition such as Mundell[53] and Krishna[54] do not include intermediate inputs and so exclude analysis of the impact of rules of origin.[55] An article by Krishna and Krueger[56] considers rules of origin in the presence of imperfect markets.

Consider the case with a monopolist producing a final good from components produced in two other countries. Suppose the final good producing country and one of the component-supplying countries form a free trade agreement. The monopolist producing the final good produces enough to supply all the imports demanded by the partner country once the two countries implement preferential tariffs. The reduction in the tariff on the final good in the partner country leads to lower prices and expansion of the output of the monopolist. However, if rules of origin force the foreign monopolist to purchase components from the partner and the partner is a high-cost producer, the monopolists cost function shifts upwards, and may offset the effect of the tariff reduction on the price of the final good. Once again, the result of the FTA on welfare within the FTA is ambiguous. And from the standpoint of the non-member country (the rest of the world), under imperfect competition there is even more reason to be concerned about the rules of origin and their protective impact than under perfect competition.

New applications to investment, including foreign investment, and plant location decisions are in the works as part and parcel of this effort. However, this literature is relatively new and not well developed.[57] Still, there are other pressing areas of current commercial policy interest that intimately are concerned with rules of origin and, to some of these, the chapter now turns.

---

[49] Finger, *supra* note 5; Miranda, Torres and Ruiz, *supra* note 6. *See also*, Chapter 11 of this book.

[50] James, *supra* note 8

[51] Pomfret, *supra* note 33.

[52] Panagariya, *supra* note 34.

[53] Mundel, *supra* note 34.

[54] Krishna (1988).

[55] Panagariya, *supra* note 34, reviews these models.

[56] Kala Krishna and Anne O. Krueger, IMPLEMENTING FREE TRADE AREAS: RULES OF ORIGIN AND HIDDEN PROTECTION (1994)

[57] Kingston (1994) refers to investment distortion as being one possible unintended result of restrictive rules of origin. Local content and origin requirements in protected markets may encourage otherwise uneconomic investments.

B. Rules of Origin, Antidumping and Voluntary Restraints

The increased use of antidumping in restricting international trade necessarily increases the importance of rules of origin. This is not only the case when antidumping investigations lead to definitive measures such as antidumping duties but also in cases that are resolved through "voluntary restraint agreements." Rules of origin aimed at preventing the "dumped" items being transshipped through third countries are necessary in such cases. Indeed, according to Pearson[58], both the United States and the EU have imposed antidumping duties on such third parties found to be assembling products similar to those upon which antidumping measures had previously been imposed without even investigating if the products in question were being dumped and have caused injury to domestic producers.

Voluntary restraint agreements ("VRAs") were made illegal by Article 11 of the Uruguay Round Agreement on Safeguards (but only between Members), and existing ones were required to be phased out over time. However, VRAs continue to be used as an alternative to antidumping duties in cases involving countries that are not WTO members.[59] For example, Russian steel is subject to "voluntarily" agreed-upon import quotas, negotiated in 1998 with the United States. While no exact estimate of the amount of world trade that is subject to non-preferential trade restrictions is currently available, the percentage is likely to be substantial.[60] Recent estimates of the amount of world trade subject to discriminatory preferential tariffs are as high as 42 percent, with substantial regional variations.[61] The rules of origin associated with discriminatory policies tend to be stricter than for normal trade under MFN tariffs. This is true even when the intent of the policies is positive as in promotion of trade of less-developed countries under various programs such as the Generalized System of Preferences ("GSP"), the Africa, Caribbean, and Pacific ("ACP") scheme, the Andean Pact, the Caribbean Basin Initiative ("CBI"), among others.[62] Typically, the rules of origin in such non-reciprocal preferential trading schemes include a value-added requirement which includes credit for inputs from the country giving the preference—or what Japan has called the "Preference-Giving Country Principle."[63]

C. The Problem of Rules of Origin in an Economically Integrated World

With the rise of the multinational enterprise, intra-firm and intra-industry trade has expanded and foreign direct investment has spawned international production networks

[58] Brendan Pearson, *Rules of Origin*, 7(2) ASIAN-PACIFIC ECONOMIC LITERATURE 14 (November 1993).

[59] Voluntary Export Restraint agreements could be governmental (as in the Japan-Korea Textile VER) or private (as in the Taiwan Textile VER with Japan). See Norio Komuro, *Japanese Rules of Origin*, in RULES OF ORIGIN IN INTERNATIONAL TRADE: A COMPARATIVE SURVEY, *supra*, note 1, at 313.

[60] Michel M. Kostecki, *Marketing Strategies and Voluntary Export Restraints*, 25(4) JOURNAL OF WORLD TRADE (August 1991) for example, estimated that fifteen percent of world trade was affected by "voluntary restraints" on exports.

[61] *See* Jean-Marie Grether and Marcelo Olarreaga, *Preferential and Non-Preferential Trade Flows in World Trade*, WORLD TRADE ORGANIZATION, STAFF WORKING PAPER ERAD-98-10, (September 1998), who report that in 1993–97 preferential trade as a share of total trade was seventy percent in Western Europe, twenty-five percent in the Americas, but only four percent in Asia and Oceania.

[62] See for example, Komuro, *supra* note 59, on Japan's GSP rules of origin.

[63] Also referred to as the "donor country content principle." Japan is not alone in applying this "principle." However, Japan excludes so-called sensitive finished products that are likely to be important exports of less developed countries meant to benefit from the preferences (textiles, footwear, toys and leather goods). See Komuro, *supra* note 59, at 324–5.

with specialized facilities in a variety of locations. The so-called "internationalization" of production, particularly of machinery, makes identification of a country of origin of many such products difficult or even arbitrary. In this context, the principle of "last substantial transformation" becomes relevant in assigning product origin. However, with increased use of contingent protection in the form of antidumping measures and countervailing duties, and the explosion of preferential trading agreements, there has been intensive political pressure to require more than a change in tariff heading test to satisfy the principle.[64]

In particular, the act of assembly of many products (apparel, footwear, television sets, radios, semi-conductors, etc.) is frequently referred to in "screwdriver provisions" in antidumping laws and free trade agreements as being insufficient to confer origin even in cases where there is clear economic advantage in conducting such assembly operations in countries with comparative advantage in labor-intensive activities.[65] The use of value-added requirements in rules of origin tend to make it more difficult for countries that specialize in labor-intensive activities to qualify for tariff preferences.[66] Stephenson and James[67], for example, point out that, all other things equal, for any required value-added percentage, origin and preference eligibility will be conferred more readily on a country with higher wage operations than to a country with lower wage operations. The use of a value-added rule in determining preferences in situations of divergent levels of economic development may distort investment and harm economic efficiency.

Rules of origin used to enforce preferential trading arrangements often appear to conflict with the objective of trade-creation. Waincymer states:

> "...the rules are too often designed to take back with one hand the preference given in the other. Making the rules more rigid as the level of preference diminishes in the face of overall reductions in tariff rates is surely not protected by Article XXIV."[68]

D. Local Content Protection: A Value-Added Tariff as an Alternative to Rules of Origin

There are some important economic implications of using value-added requirements in assigning product origin. A minimum value-added requirement is technically equivalent to a maximum import content rule. For example, a 55 percent value-added test is the same as a 45 percent import content test. It must noted, however, that precise definitions of numerator and denominator in calculating the import content ratio or the equivalent value-added ratio are necessary for this equivalence to hold in practice. Consistency in definitions of what constitutes originating value-added for purposes of constructing such ratios is, unfortunately, exceptional.

---

[64] A value-added rule is most often favored by politicians even though such a rule imposes costs on firms that are not present with a CTH-based rule (Horlick and Meyer, *supra* note 1).

[65] The CTH test needs to be supplemented by a change of tariff sub-heading test ("CTSH") where six-digit HS codes do not distinguish between parts and final assembled products. Instead of such a liberal rule of origin, however, politicians favor use of high value-added rules in conferring origin (see Horlick and Meyer, *supra* note 1).

[66] Horlick and Meyer, *supra* note 1.

[67] Stephenson and James, *supra* note 24, at 87.

[68] Jeffrey Waincymer, *Comment* in RULES OF ORIGIN IN INTERNATIONAL TRADE (E. Vermulst, P. Waer, and J. Bourgeois eds. 1994) at 414.

In recent preferential trade agreements definitions of originating value-added have become increasingly restrictive.[69] Moreover, discretion in selecting the formula to be used in calculating value-added has been used to exclude some products from preferential tariff treatment. Meeting the value-added requirement also implies a substantial amount of documentation and subsequent costs to firms seeking to comply with preferential rules of origin.[70] Moreover, the higher the value-added requirement to satisfy a preference in tariff treatment, the more likely is trade diversion to occur.[71]

A feature of rules of origin that emerges from the preceding analysis is their all-or-nothing nature.[72] That is, products that are imported into a member country of an FTA are either judged to be eligible for preferential treatment under the rules of origin or not. Given the internationalization of production, such judgements can easily be arbitrary in nature. For example, under NAFTA rules, an automobile with less than 62.5 percent North American content is judged to be ineligible, but footwear with 55 percent local content is eligible. For other products, only fifty percent local content is required to satisfy NAFTA's rules of origin.

Such arbitrary differences can and will introduce distortions into firms' decisions regarding purchases of production inputs. The application of local content requirements creates a bias in technological effort towards the saving on foreign or imported inputs and against saving on domestic or PTA-originating inputs.[73] Furthermore, the interpretations of customs authorities may also introduce additional uncertainty regarding application of tariff preferences.[74] Differences in accounting practices and in the definition of local content can also result in unexpected problems in compliance.

Lloyd[75] has proposed a value-added based tariff alternative to rules of origin based on a certain fixed minimum value-added or maximum import content ratio. The *ad valorem* tariff would vary inversely with the ratio of PTA-originating value added, thus eliminating the inefficiencies associated with the all-or-nothing rules of origin. The major drawback of Lloyd's proposal is the cost involved in documentation of value-added or import content ratios. Implementation of such a weighted tariff scheme would require governments to address underlying problems of inconsistent accounting practices and varying definitions of what constitutes local content. As the Honda case discussed in Part II above demonstrates, achieving agreement on actual value-added percentages is no simple matter and even the most precise calculations can be upset by fluctuating exchange rates and prices of intermediate components and materials.

[69] The NAFTA definition of value-added is more restrictive than that of the Canada-United States FTA, which, in turn is more restrictive than that of the United States-Canada Auto Pact (Horlick and Meyer, *supra* note 1).

[70] Horlick and Meyer, *supra* note 1 and Herrin, *supra* note 43, report that the potential savings from FTA tariff reductions may be completely offset by the administrative costs of complying with a value-added requirement, particularly in small and medium sized firms.

[71] William E. James and Masaru Umemoto, *NAFTA Trade with East Asia: Rules of Origin and Market Access in Textiles, Apparel, Footwear and Electrical Machinery*, 17(3) ASEAN ECONOMIC BULLETIN (June 2000).

[72] Peter Lloyd, *A Tariff Substitute for Rules of Origin in Free Trade Areas*, in THE WORLD ECONOMY (November 1993).

[73] Michael Mussa, *The Economics of Content Protection*, in PROTECTIONISM AND WORLD WELFARE 266 (D. Salvatore ed. 1993), demonstrates how protection of domestic content can bias technological effort.

[74] Honda Motors Canada experienced difficulties in this regard following the implementation of the Canada-United States FTA in 1989.

[75] Lloyd, *supra* note 72.

IV. Empirical Analyses of the Impact of Rules of Origin

In contrast to the growing theoretical analysis of rules of origin, there presently exist few empirical studies of the impact of rules of origin on trade flows or upon firms' investment and plant location decisions. This is not surprising given the computational requirements for precise empirical estimates of trade creation and trade diversion in an FTA.[76] The studies that have been conducted are indicative of the costs that rules of origin place on firms seeking to take advantage of tariff preferences and on the overall potential trade diversion that may be caused by restrictive rules of origin in the context of FTAs and various forms of contingent protection.

A. The Cost to Firms of Compliance with Rules of Origin

Surveys of companies engaged in imports and exports in the United States and the European Free Trade Area to ascertain the administrative cost burdens imposed by rules of origin applied in the European Union reveal that such costs are frequently significant. For example, the U.S. International Trade Commission reported that U.S. companies suffered from large sales volume losses and administrative costs averaging between $30,000 and $100,000 per firm as a result of complex and inconsistent rules of origin.[77] Similarly, Herrin[78] found that firms in the EFTA encountered costs of at least two to three per cent of export values in complying with the rules of origin necessary to enjoy EU tariff preferences. Both studies report that paperwork and record-keeping required for compliance was one major burden. In particular, the documentation of value-added was particularly burdensome for small and medium enterprises engaged in trade.[79]

These studies confirm that FTA rules of origin impose a trade-off between beneficial expansion of trade and costs imposed on firms through efforts by authorities to prevent trade deflection. Overly restrictive rules of origin therefore may vitiate the gains from preferential trade liberalization. As will be seen below, they may also shift the balance in such agreements away from trade creation towards trade diversion.

B. Trade Diversion and Economic Costs of Protective Rules of Origin

Trade diversion occurs when formation of a preferential trade arrangement ("PTA") results in purchases of imports by member countries shifting from a low-cost non-member producer to a higher-cost member producer. On the other hand, trade creation occurs when a member's high-cost production is substituted for by lower-cost production (imports) from the other member country. The analytical framework for evaluation of welfare effects (trade creation vs. trade diversion) of a PTA is necessarily more complex than for

[76] In contrast, quite a few simulations of the impacts of FTAs on trade and investment flows have been conducted using computable general equilibrium models. Sherman Robinson and Karen Thierfelder, *Trade Liberalization and Regional Integration: The Search for Large Numbers*, TMD DISCUSSION PAPER 34, IFPRI (January 1999) survey this literature. These models are not discussed in this chapter as they do not focus on the role of rules of origin in affecting trade and investment flows.
[77] UNITED STATES INTERNATIONAL TRADE COMMISSION, THE IMPACT OF RULES OF ORIGIN ON U.S. IMPORTS AND EXPORTS (1985).
[78] Herrin, *supra* note 43.
[79] Horlick and Meyer, *supra* note 1, at 405.

the evaluation of non-discriminatory trade policies, in that three countries rather than two must be included in the model.[80] A further distinction required for meaningful analysis of rules of origin used to enforce the PTA is that between final and intermediate goods.[81]

For example, a simple model of trade in intermediate goods under varying rules of origin is developed in order to demonstrate the potential trade diversion caused by restrictive rules of origin in a free trade agreement[82] involving trade in final and intermediate goods. Models such as these provide a theoretical justification for the assertion that restrictive rules of origin are likely to be trade-diverting in perfectly competitive markets with non-zero tariffs.

An example of the use of rules of origin in a manner that is very likely to divert trade involving intermediate and final goods is found in the NAFTA treatment of textiles and apparel. The NAFTA combines restrictive rules of origin with a high margin of preference in textiles and apparel.[83] In essence, NAFTA requires under the "yarn-forward" or "triple-transformation" rule of origin, that one hundred per cent of the content used in textile and apparel originate in North America.[84]

Empirical verification of the trade-diverting impact of rules of origin is difficult, to say the least. However, James and Umemoto[85] make an *ex post* assessment of NAFTA rules of origin and the potential impact on trade flows in textiles, apparel, footwear and electronics. Under the assumption of constant import market shares, they estimate that up to $7.4 billion (in constant 1990 prices) of textiles and apparel exports from ten East Asian developing economies may have been diverted annually from the NAFTA textiles and apparel markets.[86]

The capture of the NAFTA negotiations over rules of origin by industry lobbies has been carefully documented. Cameron and Tomlin state:

> "The reason Sorini (the US negotiator in the textiles group) was so confident that quotas could be eliminated was that the industry had already identified its price: the creation of highly restrictive rules of origin. This trade-off was repugnant to the NAFTA negotiators in the rules of origin working group, but the textile negotiators—unlike those working in autos—had won the right to negotiate their own rules of origin. The role of industry was critical in this textiles deal . . . the idea of restrictive rules of origin was discussed as a price for eliminating quotas . . . The Mexicans argued . . . it was better to lose textile jobs to a country like Mexico that imported from the United States than to low-wage Asian countries . . . "[87]

---

[80] Robert Mundell, *supra* note 34.

[81] Lloyd, *supra* note 72.

[82] James and Umemoto, *supra* note 71.

[83] *Id.*; Maxwell A. Cameron and Brian W. Tomlin, THE MAKING OF NAFTA: HOW THE DEAL WAS DONE (2000)

[84] The United States-Canada FTA did not require the yarn to be produced in member countries (Cameron and Tomlin, *supra* note 83). However, the United States insisted on a yarn-forward requirement in order for apparel to originate in NAFTA and "bribed" Mexico to accept this with an offer to eliminate quotas on apparel products produced there. *Id.*

[85] James and Umemoto, *supra* note 71.

[86] Japan, a non-quota market for textiles and apparel, is used as a control country and footwear and electronics products are used as control sectors. Import market share in NAFTA textiles and apparel for the ten East Asian economies contracts sharply after formation of NAFTA but continues to increase in Japan. In contrast, East Asia's share of NAFTA's import market of footwear remains constant, and for imports of electronics increases.

[87] Cameron and Tomlin, *supra* note 83, at 137.

C. Product-Specific Rules of Origin and Investment Distortion

Rules of origin can be used to influence investment and location of plants but, para-doxically, can also be used as instruments to prevent affiliates of non-member based multinationals from taking advantage of preferential tariffs even after they have estab-lished facilities within a member of the union.[88] Restrictive origin and anti-circumvention rules, as in the EU and U.S. decisions, have had the unintended effect of attracting in-ward investment, creating stiff competition for established local producers. In the cases of Japanese slide-fasteners and semiconductors, special product-specific rules of origin have been designed following Japanese investments in the EU to take back preferences.[89]

The NAFTA negotiations also provide some insight on the use of rules of origin to influence investment decisions. In the case of automobiles, the Big Three auto companies pressed for a highly protective value-added requirement as the rule of origin for NAFTA.[90] Negotiators from Canada were strongly opposed to changing the rule of origin from the fifty per cent content rule of the United States-Canada FTA and those from Mexico were initially also opposed, since they wanted to attract investment in auto assembly from Japan and Korea. However, following a compromise, the Big Three won a 62.5 per cent rule of origin (negotiated in the rules of origin committee rather than the auto working group). Mexico went along in order to protect its own domestic auto parts industry.[91] The NAFTA auto rules of origin also were meant to improve upon the somewhat ambiguous rules in the United States-Canada pact that contributed to the Honda impasse.[92] The "success" of NAFTA in creating very detailed rules of origin may be difficult to replicate and, in the end, may set a bad precedent if parties to future FTAs negotiate numerous sets of overlapping and inconsistent rules of origin.

V. Proliferation of Preferential Trading Arrangements

"Regionalism" in the form of preferential trading arrangements has displayed explosive growth since the early 1990s.[93] The number of agreements notified to the GATT/WTO exceeded two hundred as of March 2001 and includes 159 agreements in force. Since 1995

---

[88] Negotiators on investment in NAFTA were in an awkward position because of the opposition of labor and populist politicians such as H. Ross Perot ("the giant sucking sound"). The negotiators were tasked with getting the most open and liberal investment environment possible. Hence, the better the agreement on investment from the standpoint of achieving open investment, the worse the negotiators looked (Cameron and Tomlin, *supra* note 83, at 101).

[89] Waer, *supra* note 7, at 113, 140. In the case of semiconductors, exports from third countries such as Malaysia and Thailand were ruled to have Japanese origin since the specific process of diffusion was done in Japan. In still another case involving photocopy machines (anti-circumvention) from Japan, the EU designed a product-specific origin rule in order to find that exports of Ricoh photocopiers from an affiliate plant in California had Japanese origin, and so were subject to antidumping duties (*id.* at 140).

[90] Cameron and Tomlin, *supra* note 83, at 134.

[91] Cameron and Tomlin, *supra* note 83, at 136.

[92] This comment is based upon personal communication as to the reason NAFTA rules of origin are spelt out in detail with Matthew Rohde at the Office of the U.S. Trade Representative.

[93] For discussion see Jagdish Bhagwati and Arvind Panagariya, *Preferential Trading Areas and Multilater-alism: Strangers, Friends or Foes*, in THE ECONOMICS OF PREFERENTIAL TRADE AGREEMENTS 1 (J. Bhagwati and A. Panagariya eds. 1996); James, *supra* note 23; and Arvind Panagariya, REGIONALISM IN TRADE POLICY: ESSAYS ON PREFERENTIAL TRADING (1999). Of the 159 agreements in force in 2001, 129 were notified under GATT Article XXIV, 18 under the Enabling Clause and 12 under GATS Article V (www.wto.org). The Enabling Clause, part of the Tokyo Round agreement, permits developing countries to form preferential trade arrangements without complying with all the GATT Article XXIV requirements.

over one hundred new agreements have been notified to the WTO and presently almost all 140 WTO Contracting Parties are members of at least one PTA.[94] The overwhelming majority of agreements in force are FTAs rather than CUs, implying an important role for rules of origin or what may equivalently be referred to as the rules of preference.[95] The literature is divided on whether these agreements are "building blocks" or "stumbling blocks" for multilateral open trade.[96] The inability of the Contracting Parties to agree to the launch of a new round at the Seattle Ministerial in 1998 appears to have given new momentum to the drive towards more discriminatory preferential trade agreements.

A. Hub and Spoke Systems and Rules of Preference: the "Spaghetti Bowl" Problem

Hub and spoke systems arise when a "central" hub country or region (e.g., the EU) undertakes bilateral free trade agreements with "peripheral" spoke countries.[97] The hub country gains preferential access to all the spoke countries but the spokes do not gain such access to one another. Thus, the hub country can use its advantageous position to attract investment that might otherwise go to spoke countries. The spoke countries obtain preferential access to the large hub country market, but only firms in the hub country can import duty-free intermediate inputs and materials from the spoke countries.[98]

Rules of origin are critical in regulating preferential access between the hub and the various spokes. The hub country will have an incentive to dictate rules in a manner that protects sectors that are sensitive to competition from domestic producers in the spokes. This may result in a complex system of tariff discrimination and may lead to additional investment diversion towards the hub. The spoke countries may seek to counter this possibility through free trade agreements amongst each other. Negotiating numerous

---

[94] Panagariya (1998) states that Hong Kong and Japan are the only exceptions. Japan began negotiating a FTA with Singapore and studying similar agreements with other countries after 1998. At the time of writing Hong Kong was negotiating an agreement with New Zealand. See Low, *supra* note 37, and James, *Case Studies on RTA Developments: A U.S. Perspective*, paper presented at the PACIFIC ECONOMIC COOPERATION COUNCIL TRADE POLICY FORUM AND THAI MINISTRY OF COMMERCE ON REGIONAL TRADING ARRANGEMENTS: STOCKTAKE AND NEXT STEPS (2001).

[95] Stephenson and James, *supra* note 24. N. David Palmeter, *Rules of Origin or Rules of Restriction? A Commentary on a New Form of Protectionism*, 26 FORDHAM INTERNATIONAL LAW JOURNAL 1 (1987) goes further and refers to "rules of restriction."

[96] Panagariya, *supra* note 34, provides a survey of the theoretical literature in this regard and comes down largely for the "stumbling blocks" point of view. See Fred C. Bergsten, *Globalizing Free Trade*, FOREIGN AFFAIRS 105–20 (May/June 1996) and Lawrence Summers, *Regionalism and the World Trading System*, SYMPOSIUM ON POLICY IMPLICATIONS OF TRADE AND CURRENCY ZONES (1991) for the building blocks point of view. The literature also uses the phrase "friends or foes" of multilateral trade openness (Panagariya, *supra* note 94, at 93).

[97] Peter Lloyd, *The Changing Nature of Regional Trading Arrangements*, in REGIONAL INTEGRATION IN THE ASIA PACIFIC (B. Bora and C. Findlay eds. 1996)

[98] For in depth assessments of hub and spoke trading arrangements see Richard Snape, *Trade Discrimination-Yesturday's Problem?*, 219 THE ECONOMIC RECORD 72, 381–96 (December 1996); Paul Wonnacott, *Beyond NAFTA – The Design of the Free Trade Agreement of the Americas*, in THE ECONOMICS OF PREFERENTIAL TRADE AGREEMENTS (J. Bhagwati and A. Panagariya eds. 1996); Richard Snape, Jan Adams and D. Morgan, REGIONAL TRADE AGREEMENTS: IMPLICATIONS AND OPTIONS FOR AUSTRALIA (1993); Kym Anderson and Richard Snape, *European and American Regionalism: Effects on and Options for Asia*, 8(4) JOURNAL OF THE JAPANESE AND INTERNATIONAL ECONOMICS 454 (1994); and Christopher Findlay and Mari Pangestu, *Regional Trade Arrangements in East Asia: Where Are they Taking Us?*, paper presented at the PACIFIC ECONOMIC COOPERATION COUNCIL TRADE POLICY FORUM AND THAI MINISTRY OF COMMERCE ON REGIONAL TRADING ARRANGEMENTS: STOCKTAKE AND NEXT STEPS (2001).

agreements may be costly and may lead to the hub retaliating with more restrictive rules of origin or even with antidumping measures.[99]

Membership of new spoke countries in hub and spoke systems may have additional costs that may adversely affect the competitiveness of new member's firms in non-preferential trade. Existing spokes may also seek to limit the benefits of new member spokes, reinforcing the overlapping system of discriminatory tariffs and rules of origin.[100] One of the largest hub and spoke systems involves the EU. A developing country that chooses to integrate with the EU will need to switch input sources in textiles and apparel from low-cost Asian producers to high-cost sources within the EU and will therefore become less competitive in non-EU markets. An example of such trade diversion is found in Egyptian textiles and apparel under the rules of origin governing preferential access to the EU apparel markets.[101]

Bhagwati warned that the large and increasing number of FTAs is likely to result in a "spaghetti bowl" of varying preferential tariffs, implying varying degrees of tariff discrimination enforced by overlapping sets of rules of origin.[102] As Panagariya[103] notes, such an outcome flies in the face of global production and distribution networks that multinational enterprises are forging. The insistence on "local content" in satisfying preference-conferring rules of origin represents a backward step in this context. The prevalence of tariff discrimination and the increasing share of global trade that is preferential may ultimately undermine the fundamental WTO principle of non-discrimination. The development of preferential trade links between the EU and MERCOSUR (a CU grouping Argentina, Brazil, Paraguay and Uruguay), between the EU and Mexico, and the possibility of more cross regional FTAs is cause for concern in this context.

B. The New Asian Regionalism and Rules of Origin

After the United States opted for preferential trade beginning in 1985 (with an FTA with Israel) and then in 1989 (with Canada), Asia remained the last bastion of what might be called a "pure multilateral" approach to international trade. Japan, Korea, Hong Kong, Taiwan and mainland China are five major global trading economies that remained outside preferential trading agreements after the conclusion of the Uruguay Round Agreement. Singapore, as a member of the Association of Southeast Asian Nations ("ASEAN"), was involved in a PTA since 1977 but one that has been notified under the Enabling Clause rather than GATT Article XXIV. The ASEAN Free Trade Agreement, similarly, was notified under the Enabling Clause in 1992. Intra-ASEAN trade comprises roughly twenty per cent of ASEAN members' global trade, so the ASEAN free trade agreement ("AFTA") can hardly be viewed as having a large potential for trade diversion (or trade creation). The Asian financial and currency crisis that spread through the region in 1997,

---

[99] The members of a customs union (like the EU) do not use antidumping against one another, but this is not the case in most free trade agreements (the Australia-New Zealand FTA is an exception as the countries have managed to harmonize their competition policies).

[100] Findlay and Pangestu, *supra* note 98.

[101] Nihal El-Megharbel, THE ECONOMIC EFFECTS OF RULES OF ORIGIN: THE CASE OF THE EGYPTIAN-EU PARTNERSHIP AGREEMENT (forthcoming) reports that EU rules of origin will require Egyptian clothing exporters to purchase textile fabric that is 25 percent more costly than Asian textile fabric in order to enjoy preferential access to the EU market.

[102] Jagdish Bhagwati, *U.S. Trade Policy: The Infatuation with Free Trade Areas*, in THE DANGEROUS DRIFT TO PREFERENTIAL TRADE AGREEMENTS (J. Bhagwati and A. O. Krueger eds. 1995)

[103] Panagariya, *supra* note 94.

however, has led Singapore to reconsider its strategic position in the global economy and to opt for a more aggressive approach in seeking PTAs with major trading partners outside ASEAN. Singapore concluded its first cross-regional FTA with New Zealand in 1999 and at the time of writing was actively negotiating agreements with the United States, Japan and the EU among others.[104]

Japan's decision to enter into negotiations with Singapore marks a sharp break with its past practice of pure multilateral non-discrimination.[105] Japan has also been studying the possibility of closer economic relations with South Korea, as well as FTAs with Mexico, Chile and New Zealand. Korea has followed suit with proposals for FTAs with Singapore, New Zealand, Chile, Mexico and Japan.[106] The possibility of numerous new cross-regional FTAs in Asia has given rise to what Bergsten has called the new Asian regionalism.[107] The momentum of the trend towards preferential trade in Asia appears to be driven by the expansion of preferential trade in Europe and the Western Hemisphere. In the area of rules of origin, Asian trade agreements may be crafted so that they avoid creation of a spaghetti-bowl. Keeping rules relatively simple and general across products and services would be in keeping with the spirit of the declaration in the annex to the Uruguay Round Agreement Final Act on preferential rules of origin.

The Singapore-New Zealand FTA is a model of apparent simplicity in its rules of origin. Instead of hundreds of pages of detailed product specific rules, the agreement adopts the principle of goods wholly obtained in either country as sufficient to confer origin in the case of primary, unprocessed goods and scrap. For goods processed or manufactured in either country it uses a minimum value-added test of forty per cent. The rule allows accumulation of value-added between the two countries and also provides for partial preferential tariff treatment to the extent of local value-added if the product has undergone a last manufacturing process in either country. Goods with no local content but that undergo quality control and product testing may also qualify if expenditures on such operations are not less than fifty per cent of the ex-factory price of the product. If East Asian bilateral preferential agreements are to be compatible with broader regional initiatives for economic integration, such as a free trade area encompassing ASEAN, China, Japan and Korea, then it will be important to see that rules of origin are kept simple and consistent between bilateral agreements. Otherwise the "spaghetti bowl" phenomenon may arise.

C. The FTAA and Rules of Origin

The 34 states of the Organization of American States decided in 1995 to launch negotiations for a Free Trade Area of the Americas ("FTAA") with a target date of completion in 2005. A hemispheric free trade agreement with a single system of rules of origin would be vastly better for global trade openness than a hub and spoke system with complex

---

[104] *See* Chapter _ of this book.

[105] William E. James, *Trade Relations of Korea and Japan: Moving from Conflict to Cooperation*, in KOREA AND THE ASIAN-PACIFIC REGION (L.J. Cho, M.K. Park and C.N. Kim eds. 2001). Japan has participated in the GSP scheme since 1971. Japan's non-reciprocal tariff preferences are ostensibly in support of industrialization and economic development in the beneficiary developing countries.

[106] The possibility of a Japan-Korea FTA receded with the publication of a controversial new history textbook in Japan that fails to mention Japan's atrocities during the Second World War and the visit of Prime Minister Koizumi to the Yasukini Shrine on August 14, 2001.

[107] C. Fred Bergsten, *East Asian Regionalism: Towards a Tripartite World*, THE ECONOMIST, July 15, 2000, at 20–22.

and overlapping rules of origin centering on large countries as hubs. Such an agreement linking the entire Western Hemisphere (excluding Cuba) is a hugely ambitious negotiation and it is by no means certain that it will succeed. The difficulties currently facing Argentina and Brazil have put enormous pressure on their political leaders to increase protection and to delay or roll back MERCOSUR commitments. It is not easy to see how they could agree to a hemispheric FTA under the difficult economic conditions likely to prevail in the next few years as they struggle to restore fiscal discipline and reduce the burden of debt. Hence, it is still possible that a hub-and-spoke system will eventually emerge involving the southward expansion of NAFTA or northward expansion of MERCOSUR or of bilateral FTAs. There are also transatlantic agreements like the Mexico-EU FTA to further complicate matters.

D. The EU Expansion and Rules of Origin

The single most ambitious program for expansion of preferential trade outside of the FTAA, is in Europe. The negotiations for enlargement of the fifteen-member EU to thirteen additional countries that have already made applications were officially launched in March 1998 and are still in process.[108] The enlargement will mean a 34 percent increase in the EU area and the addition of over 105 million people to the single market. The European Commission asserts that the enlargement will benefit third parties by bringing these countries into the EU fold with a single set of trade rules, a common tariff, and uniform administrative procedures. However, the enlargement is likely to be uneven and will no doubt take some countries longer than others. In the meantime, the EU hub will gain still more spokes and more complex sets of rules of origin. In addition to the enlargement, the EU is negotiating new association agreements with nine Middle Eastern countries and with five Southeastern European countries.[109] This will also reinforce the hub-and-spoke nature of preferential trade in regions contiguous to the EU. Unless some discipline is brought to bear on preferential rules in the WTO, there is serious potential that third countries will be put at a commercial disadvantage in these markets.

VI. Rules of Origin and Services

Services trade was brought under multilateral disciplines for the first time with the coming into force of the Uruguay Round Final Act in 1995. The General Agreement on Trade in Services ("GATS") attempts to apply key GATT principles to international trade in services. For example, GATS enshrines the most favored nation principle, although permitting members to list exceptions that are to be phased out over a ten-year period.[110] Part VI of the GATS takes a very rudimentary approach to rules of origin, but it fails to elaborate upon the basic way in which to distinguish whether or not a particular service

---

[108] The thirteen countries are: Bulgaria, Cyprus, the Czech Republic, Estonia, Hungary, Latvia, Lithuania, Malta, Poland, Romania, the Slovak Republic, Slovenia, and Turkey.

[109] The EU has already concluded the negotiations with Tunisia, Israel, Morocco, the Palestinian Authority, Algeria, Syria, Egypt, Jordan and Lebanon. It is exploring association agreements (FTAs) with Bosnia-Herzegovina, Croatia, Yugoslavia, Macedonia and Albania (see the European Commission homepage: http://europa.eu.int/comm/enlargement).

[110] Michael J. Trebilcock and Robert Howse, THE REGULATION OF INTERNATIONAL TRADE (1999) and Geza Feketekuty, *Improving the Architecture of the General Agreement on Trade in Services*, in SERVICES TRADE IN THE WESTERN HEMISPHERE: LIBERALIZATION, INTEGRATION, AND REFORM (S. Stephenson ed. 2000), provide interpretations of the GATS.

is provided by a member or non-member. Article XXVII allows Contracting Parties to withhold benefits under GATS to services determined to be supplied from the territory of a non-member or by a corporate entity deemed to not be a service supplier of a member.[111] Unlike the case of goods, the test in determining the origin of a service supplier is not specified. The application of a percentage test to services is difficult given the paucity of data on services trade. Other tests of the nationality of corporate ownership might be applied but are also difficult to implement given the vagaries of determining who owns multinational enterprises that supply internationally-traded services.[112] And in cases where a service supplier is operating in a member country but is incorporated or owned by a non-member the rules are vague.

Four "modes of supply" are identified in the GATS: 1) direct cross-border transactions (as in long-distance international telephone calls); 2) consumption abroad (as in tourism services); 3) consumption at an establishment supplying the service (as in a foreign-owned bank); and 4) consumption through the presence of natural persons (as in a consultation with a foreign accountant in one's own office). Interpretation of the origin of services under these four modes of supply can be complicated. For example, if a Japanese tourist in Bali visits a Citibank branch in order to withdraw funds from his account in Citibank in Tokyo, should origin be assigned to Japan or the United States (where Citibank's headquarters is)?

Information and communications technology services also present complications in identification of origin. For example, call-back services owned by a European telecommunications company used by a customer in Australia receiving a call from the United States may route the call through operators in India or the Philippines. What then is the proper country of origin of this service?

Another problem arises because of the proliferation of preferential trading agreements that incorporate liberalization of services. Such regional integration agreements that provide for preferential liberalization of services are permitted under GATS Article V (modeled after GATT Article XXIV).[113] The "spaghetti bowl" problem discussed above for rules of origin in preferential trade in goods also applies to the case of overlapping regional agreements in the area of services. With contracting parties involved in membership in more than one such agreement, the rules for enforcing preferences in services may be difficult to administer and may raise the costs facing services suppliers. Stephenson concludes that:

> "... Article V is at present a weak and ineffective discipline. Its weaknesses may undermine the trading system in the future if it is not strengthened..."[114]

VII. Conclusion

This chapter has not argued that any one of the three criteria of last substantial transformation is preferable over the others in all circumstances, which is why we observe residual rules becoming important in the context of the harmonization work program at

---

[111] Trebilcock and Howse, *supra* note 110, at 291

[112] One might apply a formal criterion such as location of the corporate headquarters or place of incorporation but this may prove unsatisfactory.

[113] Sherry M. Stephenson, *Regional Agreements on Services in Multilateral Disciplines: Interpreting and Applying GATS Article V*, in SERVICES TRADE IN THE WESTERN HEMISPHERE: LIBERALIZATION, INTEGRATION, AND REFORM (S. Stephenson ed. 2000), elaborates upon the challenges in interpreting GATS Article V.

[114] *Id.* at 104.

the WTO. The choice of a CTH or CTSH rule however, appears to offer the broadest scope for harmonization of non-preferential rules of origin. The lack of progress in the work program is principally due to the revealed preference of governments to retain rules of origin as commercial policy instruments rather than to technical issues. Stronger political will is needed to break the logjam. In the area of preferential rules of origin there is no discipline, only a non-binding declaration.

The chancellor of the exchequer of the UK, Gordon Brown, has called for elimination of tariffs on trade in industrial products between the EU and the United States[115], a proposal that echoes that of a Transatlantic Free Trade Agreement. Such an agreement would have to cover agriculture and other sensitive areas and would not be able to gloss over the serious trade disputes that have arisen in these sectors between the United States and the EU. The proponents of a "building blocks" point of view argue that by expanding free trade agreements such as NAFTA, the EU, MERCOSUR and AFTA (each covering a significant proportion of global trade), global free trade can be gradually achieved. However, each of these agreements is enforced by different sets of rules of origin and harmonizing them would be perhaps an even more difficult task that has been the case with non-preferential rules of origin.

The presumption that Free Trade Agreements or Customs Unions necessarily reduce barriers for non-members has been challenged[116]. Moreover, there is no doubt that in particular sectors, including those of key importance to less developed countries, barriers have been raised rather than lowered (textiles and clothing) or adverse consequences have resulted for third parties in export markets (agriculture). Rules of origin have been of particular concern in textiles and clothing trade, both in the context of preferential agreements (as in NAFTA) but also in administration of MFA quotas (as shown by the fact that the EU has brought a WTO challenge to the textile rules of origin promulgated by the United States in 1996). The proliferation of antidumping measures, enforced by the application of still another set of rules of origin, further underscores the significance of discriminatory protection in global trade.

The surest and safest way to ensure that these agreements are benign is to move ahead with another WTO round that significantly reduces MFN protection, including tariffs in industrial and agricultural products, non-tariff barriers in agriculture, and that substantially opens up services.

The share of world trade that is covered by preferential trading arrangements was recently estimated to be 42 per cent.[117] Given the share of world trade affected by various forms of contingent protection, particularly antidumping, that must be enforced by rules of origin, it is plausible that one-half or more of world trade flows are now subject to varying sets of rules of origin. In the context of a new round of multilateral trade negotiations, it is recommended that efforts be made to make rules of origin more transparent and consistent. Launch of a new round might also dispel some of the posturing by Contracting Parties that has held up the harmonization program over rules of origin that are non-preferential.

In the context of the prospects for a new trade round, the following specific recommendations are offered:

---

[115] *See* Malcolm Rifkind, *Toward an Atlantic Free Trade Area*, THE ASIAN WALL STREET JOURNAL, (August 22, 2001)
[116] Panagariya, *supra* note 94
[117] Grether and Olarreaga, *supra* note 59.

First, the consistency of existing and new preferential trading arrangements with the two key conditions under Article XXIV should be rigorously assessed. The Committee on Regional Trade Agreements (CRTA) should adopt a strict interpretation of the two key conditions, that: 1) agreements must cover "substantially all trade" between constituent members; and 2) that barriers to imports facing non-members shall not be increased. In fact, it would be desirable to insist that, on average, barriers to non-members be lowered. Second, the new round must also tighten discipline over rules of origin used in prevention of circumvention in antidumping. In particular, contracting parties should not be permitted to use rules of origin to extend antidumping measures to third parties that have neither been shown to have been dumping nor of causing injury. Third, the new round should seek to strengthen international discipline over preferential trade rules of origin. In particular, turning the non-binding declaration on preferential rules of origin into a binding work program would be desirable. Fourth, new preferential trade agreements should be encouraged to adopt simple and transparent rules of origin and to avoid inconsistency in rules of origin between agreements. Fifth, agreements that incorporate services, should likewise be scrutinized under a strengthened GATS Article V. Finally, a liberal approach to rules of origin that extends benefits of reduced barriers to all modes of supply and all service providers regardless of corporate nationality would be the simplest and most comprehensive approach.

Reducing the margins of preference between preferential and non-preferential trade will render rules of origin much less harmful to global trade than would otherwise be the case. A new multilateral round is the one of the surest means to assure that preferential agreements become building blocks rather than stumbling blocks for overall global trade liberalization.

BIBLIOGRAPHY

Anderson, Kym and Richard Snape, "European and American Regionalism: Effects on and Options for Asia," 8(4) *Journal of the Japanese and International Economies*, 454 (1994).

Bergsten, C. Fred, "East Asian Regionalism: Towards a Tripartite World," *The Economist*, July 15, 2000, 20–22.

Bergsten, C. Fred, "Globalizing Free Trade," *Foreign Affairs*, May/June, 1996, 105–20.

Bhagwati, Jagdish, "U.S. Trade Policy: The Infatuation with Free Trade Areas," in J. Bhagwati and A. O. Krueger (eds.), *The Dangerous Drift to Preferential Trade Agreements* (1996) Washington, D. C.: American Enterprise Institute for Public Policy Research.

Bhagwati, Jagdish and Arvind Panagariya, "Preferential Trading Areas and Multilateralism: Strangers, Friends or Foes?" in J. Bhagwati and A. Panagariya (eds.), *The Economics of Preferential Trade Agreements*, Washington, D. C. : AEI Press: 1–78 (1996).

Cameron, Maxwell A. and Brian W. Tomlin, *The Making of NAFTA: How the Deal was Done*, Ithaca and London: Cornell University Press (2000).

El-Megharbel, Nihal, Forthcoming *The Economic Effects of Rules of Origin: The Case of the Egyptian-EU Partnership Agreement*, Ph.D. Thesis, Department of Economics and Political Science, Cairo University.

Feketekuty, Geza, "Improving the Architecture of the General Agreement on Trade in Services," in S. Stephenson (ed.), *Services Trade in the Western Hemisphere: Liberalization, Integration, and Reform*, Washington, D.C.: Brookings Institution Press and Organization of American States (2000).

Findlay, Christopher and Mari Pangestu, "Regional Trade Arrangements in East Asia: Where Are they taking us?" Paper presented at the Pacific Economic Cooperation Council Trade Policy Forum and Thai Ministry of Commerce on Regional Trading Arrangements: Stocktake and Next Steps, Bangkok, Thailand, June 12–13, 2001.

Finger, J. Michael, (ed.), *Antidumping: How it Works and Who Gets Hurt*, Ann Arbor: University of Michigan Press (1993).

Finger, J. Michael and Tracy Murray, "Antidumping and Countervailing Duty Enforcement in the United States," in J. M. Finger (ed.), *Antidumping: How it Works and Who Gets Hurt* (1993) Ann Arbor: University of Michigan Press: 241–54.

Forrester, Ian, "The Economics of Rules of Origin," in E. Vermulst, P. Waer and J. Bourgeois (eds.), *Rules of Origin in International Trade*: *A Comparative Survey* (1994) Ann Arbor: University of Michigan Press: 7–25.

Grether, Jean-Marie and Marcelo Olarreaga, "Preferential and Non-Preferential Trade Flows in World Trade," World Trade Organization, Staff Working Paper ERAD-98-10, Geneva, September 1998.

Herrin, Jan, "Rules of Origin and Differences in Tariff Levels in EFTA and in the EC," Occasional Paper No. 13, European Free Trade Association, February, 10 (1986).

Hocking, Brian, "Trade Politics: Environments, Agendas, and Processes," in B. Hocking and S. McGuire (eds.), *Trade Politics: International, Domestic and Regional Perspectives* (1999) London and New York: Routledge: 1–20.

Horlick, Gary N. and Michael A. Meyer, "Rules of Origin from a Policy Perspective," in E. Vermulst, P. Waer and J. Bourgeois (eds.), *Rules of Origin in International Trade*: *A Comparative Survey* (1994) Ann Arbor: University of Michigan Press: 403–8.

Hufbauer, Gary C. and Jeffrey J. Schott, *North American Free Trade: Issues and Recommendations* (1992) Washington, D. C.: Institute of International Economics.

James, William E., "Case Studies on RTA Developments: A U.S. Perspective," Paper presented at the Pacific Economic Cooperation Council Trade Policy Forum and Thai Ministry of Commerce on Regional Trading Arrangements: Stocktake and Next Steps, Bangkok, Thailand, June 12–13, 2001.

James, William E., "Trade Relations of Korea and Japan: Moving from Conflict to Cooperation," in L. J. Cho, M. K. Park and C. N. Kim (eds.), *Korea and the Asian-Pacific Region* (2001) Honolulu and Seoul: East-West Center and Kyung Hee University: 405–53.

James, William E., "The Rise of Anti-Dumping: Does Regionalism Promote Administered Protection?" 14(2) *Asian-Pacific Economic Literature* 14 (2000).

James, William E. and Masaru Umemoto, "NAFTA Trade with East Asia: Rules of Origin and Market Access in Textiles, Apparel, Footwear and Electrical Machinery," 17(3) *ASEAN Economic Bulletin* 293 (2000).

James, William E., "APEC and Preferential Rules of Origin: Stumbling Blocks for Liberalization of Trade?" 31(3) *Journal of World Trade*, 113 (1997).

Keizer, Wim, "Negotiations on Harmonized Non-Preferential Rules of Origin: A Useless Task from a Trade Policy Perspective?" 31(4) *Journal of World Trade*, 145 (1997).

Komuro, Norio, "Japanese Rules of Origin," in E. Vermulst, P. Waer and J. Bourgeois (eds.), *Rules of Origin in International Trade*: *A Comparative Survey* (1994) Ann Arbor: University of Michigan Press: 301–54.

Kostecki, Michel M., "Marketing Strategies and Voluntary Export Restraints," 25(4) *Journal of World Trade* (1991).

Krishna, Kala and Anne O. Krueger, *Implementing Free Trade Areas: Rules of Origin and Hidden Protection*, Centre for International Economic Studies, University of Adelaide, Seminar Paper 94-09, September, 1994.

Krueger, Anne O., "Free Trade Areas Versus Customs Unions," 54 *Journal of Development Economics*, 169 (1997).

Lloyd, Peter, "The Changing Nature of Regional Trading Arrangements," in B. Bora and C. Findlay (eds.), *Regional Integration in the Asia Pacific* (1996) Melbourne: Oxford University Press.

Lloyd, Peter, 1993. "A Tariff Substitute for Rules of Origin in Free Trade Areas," *The World Economy* 699 (November 1993).

Low, Linda, "Singapore's RTA Strategy," Paper presented at the Pacific Economic Cooperation Council (PECC) Trade Policy Forum and Thai Ministry of Commerce on Regional Trading Arrangements: Stocktake and Next Steps, June 12–13, 2001 Bangkok.

Miranda, Jorge, Raul A. Torres, and Mario Ruiz, "The International Use of Anti-Dumping," 32(5) *Journal of World Trade*, 5 (1998).

Mundell, Robert, "The Theory of Tariffs and Monetary Policies," in D. Salvatore (ed.), *Protectionism and World Welfare* (1993) Cambridge: Cambridge University Press: 244–65.

Mundell, Robert, "Tariff Preferences and the Terms of Trade," *Manchester School of Economic and Social Studies*: 1 (1964).

Mussa, Michael, "The Economics of Content Protection," in D. Salvatore (ed.), *Protectionism and World Welfare* (1993) Cambridge: Cambridge University Press: 266–89.

Nell, Philippe G., " WTO Negotiations on the Harmonization of Rules of Origin: A First Critical Appraisal," 33(3) *Journal of World Trade* 45 (1999).

Palmeter, N. David, "Rules of Origin in the United States," in E. Vermulst, P. Waer and J. Bourgeois (eds.), *Rules of Origin in International Trade*: *A Comparative Survey* (1994) Ann Arbor: University of Michigan Press: 27–84.

Palmeter, N. David, "Rules of Origin in Customs Unions and Free Trade Areas," in K. Anderson and R. Blackhurst (eds.), *Regional Integration and the Global Trading System* (1993) London: Harvester Wheatsheaf.

Palmeter, N. David, "Pacific Regional Trade Liberalization and Rules of Origin," Paper presented at the Pacific Economic Cooperation Council Trade Policy Forum VII, June, 1993.

Palmeter, N. David, "Rules of Origin or Rules of Restriction? A Commentary on a New Form of Protectionism," 1 *Fordham International Law Journal* 26 (1987).

Panagariya, Arvind, "Preferential Trade Liberalization: The Traditional Theory and New Developments," 306 *Journal of Economic Literature*, 287 (2000).

Panagariya, Arvind, *Regionalism in Trade Policy: Essays on Preferential Trading* (1999).

Pearson, Brendan, 1993. "Rules of Origin," 7(2) *Asian-Pacific Economic Literature* 14 (1993).

Pomfret, Richard, *The Economics of Regional Trading Arrangements* (1997) Oxford: Clarendon Press, Oxford University.

Rifkind, Malcolm, "Toward an Atlantic Free Trade Area," *The Asian Wall Street Journal*, August 22 (2001).

Robinson, Sherman and Karen Thierfelder, "Trade Liberalization and Regional Integration: The Search for Large Numbers," TMD Discussion Paper 34, IFPRI, Washington, D.C., January, 1999.

Schott, Jeffrey J., *Free Trade Areas and U.S. Trade Policy* (1989) Washington, D.C. : Institute of International Economics.

Shibata, Hirofumi, "The Theory of Economic Unions: A Comparative Analysis of Customs Unions, Free Trade Areas and Tax Unions," in C. Shoup (ed.), *Fiscal Harmonization in Common Markets, Vol. 1, Theory* (1967) New York: Columbia University Press.

Snape, Richard, "Trade Discrimination—Yesterday's Problem?" 72 *The Economic Record*, 381 (1996).

Snape, Richard, Jan Adams and D. Morgan, *Regional Trade Agreements: Implications and Options for Australia* (1993) Canberra: Australian Department of Foreign Affairs.

Stephenson, Sherry M. (ed.) *Services Trade in the Western Hemisphere: Liberalization, Integration, and Reform* (2000) Washington, D.C.: Brookings Institution Press and Organization of American States.

Stephenson, Sherry M., "Regional Agreements on Services in Multilateral Disciplines: Interpreting and Applying GATS Article V," in S. Stephenson (ed.) *Services Trade in the Western Hemisphere: Liberalization, Integration, and Reform* 2000 Washington, D.C.: Brookings Institution Press and Organization of American States: 86–104.

Stephenson, Sherry M., 1998. "Multilateralizing Harmonized Rules of Origin: Is It a Realistic Option?" Washington, D.C.: Organization of American States (1998).

Stephenson, Sherry M. and William E. James, "Rules of Origin and The Asia Pacific Economic Cooperation," 29(2) *Journal of World Trade*, 77 (1995).

Summers, Lawrence, "Regionalism and the World Trading System," Federal Reserve Bank of Kansas City, *Symposium on Policy Implications of Trade and Currency Zones* (1991).

Trebilcock, Michael J. and Robert Howse, *The Regulation of International Trade*, (1999) 2nd Edition, London and New York: Routledge.

United States Congress, *Congressional Record* S 8803 and 8814 (1983).

United States International Trade Commission, *The Impact of Rules of Origin on U.S. Imports and Exports*, Washington, D.C. (1985)

Varona, Edurne Navarro, " Rules of Origin in the GATT," in E. Vermulst, P. Waer and J. Bourgeois (eds.), *Rules of Origin in International Trade: A Comparative Survey* (1994) Ann Arbor: University of Michigan Press: 355–91.

Vermulst, Edwin, "Rules of Origin as Commercial Policy Instruments—Revisited," 26(6) *Journal of World Trade* (1992).

Vermulst, Edwin and Paul Waer, "European Community Rules of Origin as Commercial Policy Instruments," 24(3) *Journal of World Trade* (1990).

Viner, Jacob, *The Customs Union Issue* (1950) New York: Carnegie Endowment for International Peace.

Waer, Paul, "European Community Rules of Origin," in E. Vermulst, P. Waer and J. Bourgeois (eds.), *Rules of Origin in International Trade: A Comparative Survey* (1994) Ann Arbor: University of Michigan Press: 85–194.

Wonnacott, Paul, "Beyond NAFTA—The Design of the Free Trade Agreement of the Americas," in J. Bhagwati and A. Panagariya (eds.), *The Economics of Preferential Trade Agreements*, (1996) Washington, D. C. : AEI Press.

World Trade Organization, Committee on Rules of Origin, *Minutes of June 23, 2000, Meeting*, Geneva: downloaded from www.wto.org

World Trade Organization, Uruguay Round Final Act, *Agreement on Rules of Origin* (1995)

CHAPTER 49

SERVICES IN REGIONAL TRADING ARRANGEMENTS

Christopher Findlay, Sherry Stephenson, and Francisco Javier Prieto*

TABLE OF CONTENTS

* Christopher Findlay is Professor of Economics in the Asia Pacific School of Economics and Government at the Australian National University in Canberra; Sherry Stephenson is Deputy Director of the Trade Unit, Organization of American States, Washington DC; and Francisco Prieto is Advisor to the Ministry of Trade and Economy, Santiago, Chile. Christopher Findlay's contribution was supported in part by a grant from the Australian Research Council. The views expressed in this chapter are those of the authors alone. This version of the chapter was presented to the Australian Conference of Economists, Adelaide, October 2002.

I. Introduction

WTO members have continued to work at service sector liberalisation in regional and preferential frameworks, despite the development of the General Agreement on Trade in Services ("GATS") in the Uruguay Round, despite the negotiations since then, and despite the start of a new round of GATS negotiations in January 2000. Singapore's Minister for Trade and Industry George Yeo announcing his interest in a Free Trade Agreement with Japan, which has since been signed, said:

> As Singapore and Japan are already relatively open economies with regards to trade in goods, the focus of the FTA will likely be on investments and further integration in the services sectors. That is why we hope to go beyond a traditional FTA to a "new-age" FTA focussing on liberalisation and cooperation in the high-growth services sectors of the future, such as the transport, financial, and information and communication technology sectors. Such a forward-looking FTA will enhance and strengthen the competitiveness and capabilities of both our countries.[1]

As this remark suggests, a number of factors contribute to the interest in a regional approach to services trade liberalisation. Yet there are also significant constraints on progress. Some of these apply as well at the multilateral level and others are peculiar to regional arrangements.

While a number of motivations for a preferential approach can be identified, its long-run effects are less clear. Will it lead to a greater level of liberalisation than might otherwise be observed? Negotiating preferential arrangements with respect to services is costly, in terms of time and resources. Are they worth the effort?

We discuss these questions in this chapter. We present material on the following issues of relevance:

a) a definition of how services are traded and how this differs from the way goods are traded;

b) the dimensions of regional agreements in services: what these cover and what type of approaches members of such agreements have adopted to liberalise services;

c) opportunities and challenges in the regional approach to services liberalisation;

d) an outline of the GATS requirements for regional agreements in services (compared to the treatment of regional agreements under the GATT);

e) issues in the assessment of the economic impact of regional agreements in services on trade and welfare;

The chapter examines these issues in this order. We conclude with comments on three sets of issues involved in the question of whether regional agreements are building rather than stumbling blocks to wider liberalisation, namely incentives, architecture, and overlapping agendas.

In this chapter, we refer to regional trading arrangements on the understanding that this term refers to preferential reductions in protection that are the result of formal negotiation. In some cases currently under discussion, the members of potential agreements lie in

---

[1] From http://www.mti.gov.sg/public/FTA/frm_FTA_Default.asp?sid=28&cid=745 (accessed 14 February 2002)

different regions of the globe. However we retain the use of 'regional' in the description of the agreements of interest here.[2]

The chapter is framed in the context of viewing trade in services as inherently more complex than trade in goods, both due to the characteristics of services as well as to the numerous ways in which services can be traded. Service activities are intangible and non-storable on the whole, often require the proximity of consumers and producers in their trade, demonstrate both capital and labour mobility associated with their forms of trade, and show a high prevalence of regulatory intervention to counteract market failure and achieve non-economic social objectives.

The simultaneous nature of services transactions affects the conduct of services trade. Services can be traded in four ways, or modes of supply, as defined for the purpose of the Uruguay Round negotiations and set out in the WTO General Agreement on Trade in Services.[3] These are: cross-border trade, similar to trade in goods (mode 1); consumption abroad, where the service consumer moves to another country to purchase the services (mode 2); commercial presence, or foreign direct investment where the service activity is exchanged within one national territory between a foreign investor and a local consumer (mode 3); and movement of natural persons, where the service suppliers move to another country to supply the service (mode 4).

Barriers to trade in services take the form of regulations, laws, decrees and administrative practices, and are not usually found at the border. These measures are much less transparent than tariffs and quotas that affect trade in goods, and their impact is more difficult to assess. Moreover, there is not always a clear line between a "measure affecting trade in services" and a "barrier affecting trade in services". Some domestic regulations of a non-discriminatory nature may nonetheless have a 'de facto' restrictive impact on services trade and impede market access. For all of these reasons the liberalisation of services trade, in either a multilateral or regional context, is more challenging and complex than liberalisation of goods trade.

II. The Dimensions of Regional Agreements

In this section, we organise the various options for liberalisation regarding the structure and contents of agreements on services into the topics of coverage, liberalisation principles and approaches, and depth of commitments.

A. Coverage

The first issue that needs to be defined in any agreement on services is the coverage of the liberalising commitments—which activities are subject to the disciplines of the agreement? In the context of services trade, the term "coverage" is three-dimensional

[2] Our focus in this chapter is on negotiated regional agreements. Cooperative arrangements such as APEC are not considered here in detail. For more commentary on the contribution of APEC to the liberalisation of services trade and investment, *see* Christopher Findlay and Tony Warren, *Services Issues in APEC*, in IMPEDIMENTS TO TRADE IN SERVICES: MEASUREMENT AND POLICY IMPLICATIONS (Christopher Findlay and Tony Warren eds. 2000).
[3] *General Agreement on Trade in Services*, Article I.2 on "Scope and Definition". The first definition of services trade by four modes of supply was made by Gary Sampson and Richard Snape in *Identifying Issues in Trade in Services*, 8 (2) THE WORLD ECONOMY 171 (1985). See Chapter 19 of their book for a detected discussion of the GATS.

and comprises the four modes of supply as defined above, the number of service sectors included under the trade disciplines on the other, and the universe of the measures affecting trade in services.[4] In some cases, there may be only one option for the mode of supply so only measures affecting that mode are relevant. In other cases, the measures applying to different modes affect the substitution between them.

B. Liberalizing Principles

Liberalizing principles can be established as general obligations (as is the case of the NAFTA-type agreements) or as part of the specific negotiated commitments. In the case of GATS, some of the obligations, including MFN, are of a general nature, whereas others (such as national treatment) are part of the specific commitments.

Four principles for liberalising trade in services are usually taken into consideration in developing an agreement:

i) Most-favoured nation. This principle obliges member countries to extend the most favorable treatment that is accorded to any of their trading partners to all the other members immediately and unconditionally. Many countries accord preferential treatment to some of their commercial partners in certain sectors such as transportation, telecommunications, recognition of professional qualifications and other services. Exemptions to the MFN requirement might be included within the provisions of the agreement.

ii) No local presence requirement. Many countries frequently require a local presence (that is, an established trade presence) as a condition for foreign individuals or juridical persons wishing to provide services within their territory. This is usually the case with services that require close supervision to guarantee better consumer protection. This requirement may hinder international trade because it may impose higher costs to foreign service suppliers who are not allowed to use the other modes of supply. Thus, allowing service providers to choose their preferred mode of supply can be expected to lower their costs and stimulate trade.

iii) National treatment. This principle stipulates that services and service providers from another country be accorded treatment no less favorable than that accorded to like services and service providers of national origin. Violations to national treatment in the area of trade in services include a wide variety of situations ranging from nationality or permanent residence requirements to discriminatory practices with regard to fiscal measures, access to local credit and foreign exchange practices, limitations of the type of services which may be rendered by foreign suppliers and many others.

iv) No quantitative non-discriminatory restrictions. Technical considerations or market size may induce governments to establish quantitative non-discriminatory restrictions on the rendering of certain services. Such is the case in the allocation of radio and television frequencies, the number of banks allowed to operate in a given market, or the number of telecom companies authorized to provide cellular and basic telephony services in a given region within the country. Technology and other technical considerations

---

[4] With regard to the number of sectors included in services agreements, the approach predating the GATS was focused on individual sectors within which commitments to liberalise are limited to specific sectors or subsectors of an industry, mutually agreed upon by countries that are party to the agreement. Sectoral agreements with regard to air, land and sea transportation are typical examples of this approach. It should be noted that agreements on specific service sectors would not meet the conditions set out in Article V of the GATS, particularly with respect to the necessity for any preferential agreement to include "substantially all sectors," and thus probably would not be deemed compatible with WTO requirements. These criteria are discussed further below.

permitting, a gradual elimination of these measures is a prerequisite for full liberalisation of trade in services.

C. Liberalising Approaches

There are two mechanisms or modalities by means of which the liberalisation commitments may be met. Under a 'positive list' approach, countries subscribe to national treatment and market access commitments specifying the type of access or treatment offered to services or service suppliers in scheduled sectors. The alternative top-down approach to services trade liberalisation is based upon a 'negative list' approach, whereby all sectors and measures are to be liberalised unless otherwise specified in annexes containing reservations, or non-conforming measures. Non-conforming measures in the annexes are then usually liberalised through consultations or periodic negotiations. This is the approach adopted by the NAFTA and similar agreements and also by the Closer Economic Relations Trade Agreement ("CER") between Australia and New Zealand.[5]

Services negotiations carried out under the positive listing modality are focused on the inclusion of commitments in national schedules and on the need to determine their broad equivalency for the purpose of reciprocity. This is much more difficult to do for services than for goods, because barriers to foreign service providers are often not quantifiable border measures such as tariffs and quotas, but take the form of discriminatory elements contained in national laws, decrees, and regulations. Under the negative-listing modality, negotiations focus on the content of the lists of reservations, or non-conforming measures, to ensure that these do not excessively compromise the liberalising objective of the agreement.

In terms of the economics of the two approaches to services liberalisation, it has been argued that neither modality guarantees open markets and, under certain conditions and hypotheses, both would lead to an equivalent result. Nonetheless in the view of the authors, the negative list approach is preferable because of the transparency and legal stability that is generated under such an approach.

The quantitative and even qualitative evaluation of concessions made under a positive list approach is limited by the lack of adequate statistics on services.[6] A related disadvantage of this approach is the non-uniform and highly opaque way in which commitments by members are listed. This situation adds to the difficulty of documenting the actual liberalisation achieved under these agreements. Also, in the absence of an adequate and commonly-agreed sectoral classification list, there is rarely homogeneity in the way that commitments are recorded. Two perhaps even more detrimental limitations of positive listing are its hindrance to future liberalisation and its lack of transparency. Because the positive list approach promotes the binding of existing restrictions in the early stages of negotiation, acceleration of prompt and deep future liberalisation is unlikely. Such has

---

[5] Stephenson notes that the exceptions listed in the CER annexes have been reduced considerably over the 1990s. Sherry Stephenson, *A Comparison of Existing Services Trade Agreements within APEC*, in IMPEDIMENTS TO TRADE IN SERVICES: MEASUREMENT AND POLICY IMPLICATIONS (Christopher Findlay and Tony Warren eds. 2000) at 289. However, this outcome is rare in other agreements of the same type and the NAFTA members, for example, have not carried out significant additional liberalisation in services since the agreement has been in force (January 1994). Other variables also affect the pace of liberalisation.

[6] This is the problem being faced by WTO Members as they have tried to carry out the assessment of trade in services as it has evolved since the GATS came into force in January 1995. The lack of empirical data makes such an evaluation nearly impossible to do, particularly over time.

been the experience in the GATS, under which the majority of the specific commitments have been limited to binding the prevailing regulatory situation. Finally, lack of transparency in this approach is an impediment to international business. Information is lacking on restrictions in sectors not included in the lists of specific commitments, and even in those sectors bound by specific commitments, unrepresentative ceiling bindings may limit the accuracy of information provided.

A top-down negotiating approach under a negative listing modality offers possibilities for more complete and timely liberalisation. The initial contractual obligation incorporates the bulk of service sectors (in principle, universal coverage is targeted with limited exceptions) and binds all reservations or non-conforming measures through a 'stand-still'. Future liberalisation is then achieved through negotiations on progressive elimination of the reservations listed by each member. This approach sends clear messages to other member countries and the international community in general about the objectives and commitments of members to such services agreements. Since the core obligations enter into force at the beginning, members must make a clear commitment to both the depth of commitments and the pace of liberalisation. Considerably greater transparency is generated by the obligatory setting-out of comprehensive information on all reservations in the form of non-conforming measures. The obligation to be completed in the listing and binding of all discriminatory regulatory measures, as well as in the listing of all non-discriminatory quantitative restrictions, not only contributes to transparency but also prompts government officials and negotiators to consult with regulators in order to review the desirability of maintaining existing restrictions.

To summarise, agreements based on a negative listing provide information in a transparent form on the existing barriers to trade in services (in the reservations or non-conforming measures set out in the annexes), thus giving service providers precise knowledge of foreign markets. In agreements based on a positive listing the sectoral coverage of commitments as well as the type and comprehensiveness of information provided on the commitments may vary significantly between the members. Moreover, the type of conditions and limitations on market access and national treatment set out in national schedules are often listed as ceilings or more restrictive levels of treatment than actual regulatory practice. As a result, the level of transparency for service providers is reduced and there is less legal and economic certainty regarding market access.

Neither modality guarantees open markets. The establishment of an agreement might be easier using a positive list approach, because of the degree of flexibility and options it provides to participants in the negotiating process. But once in place, our expectation is that the negative list is the superior method for carrying out liberalisation because of the higher degree of transparency and lower level of uncertainty that it provides.

D. Depth of Commitments

The depth of the commitments undertaken in a trade agreement on services may vary substantially. An important determinant of the depth of commitments is the extent to which an agreement is binding.

Members of an agreement have at their disposal several instruments to achieve different levels of commitments. The most important of these are presented below and organized from lower to higher levels of commitments:

i) Transparency. This is normally the most basic or minimal level of commitment within a services trade agreement. It requires all members to the agreement to either directly inform the other parties of, or set up national "enquiry points" to facilitate access to, all the existing measures, at the level of the central or federal government and of state, provincial or local governments, that may affect trade in services with respect to the disciplines developed for purposes of liberalisation.

Lack of transparency in the design and enforcement of regulations constitutes one of the main impediments to services trade. Foreign investors, particularly those that are seeking to establish a commercial presence in the domestic market, are unlikely to commit resources in countries where it is unclear how the design and enforcement of regulation will affect their business activities.

ii) Ceiling Binding. A long established practice in merchandise trade agreements, the setting of a ceiling binding is also sometimes used for the adoption of commitments on trade in services. For instance, as in the GATS schedule of commitments, countries may set up or indicate conditions and limitations to market access and national treatment that are not part of the existing legal or regulatory measures within the respective country. An example of such binding could involve setting up maximum screening quotas for foreign audiovisual programs, expressed as a cap on the daily percentage of programs, where the country involved reserves the freedom to operate below the quota.

The practice of binding above the regulatory 'status quo' introduces a significant degree of uncertainty into the decisions by foreign service providers to supply a foreign market through cross-border trade or commercial presence. At the same time, governments engage in this practice because it provides them not only with the flexibility to adjust their regulatory frameworks in the event of unforeseen circumstances (e.g. financial crises), but also with significant negotiating coinage in future services negotiations.

iii) "Freeze" or "standstill" on existing non-conforming measures. This commitment involves freezing the existing regime and measures up to a given date. It involves an undertaking not to make those measures more restrictive in the future. This commitment, known as a "grandfather" clause, is used in agreements on trade in goods and in some agreements on trade in services (as in NAFTA, at federal and provincial levels, and in GATS with regard to MFN).

iv) Ratcheting. In addition to the commitment to freeze existing measures, a moving floor of commitments can also be established. Such a mechanism prevents countries from "backsliding" with respect to any preferential commitments implemented after the effective date of the freeze. If a given sector has been liberalised after the freeze date, any country party to the agreement cannot revert to a less liberal state for trade in the respective sector. This type of commitment, present in NAFTA- type agreements (at federal and provincial levels), is likely to have a positive effect on trade and investment in the economies adopting it. The reason is that it signals to eligible foreign service providers the commitment of the members not to introduce sudden regulatory changes that reverse previous liberalisation initiatives.

v) "List or Lose." This type of commitment supplements the "transparency" commitment and speeds up the process of liberalisation. In the context of a negative list or top-down approach, the parties undertake the obligation to list all non-conforming measures to the agreed provisions of the agreement. Failure to include any restrictive measure in the list is understood to eliminate the measure in question with respect to the other parties to the agreement. This is the approach adopted by NAFTA members with regard to the existing non-conforming measures at federal or national level.[7]

III. Opportunities and Challenges in the Regional Approach

A number of factors contribute to the interest in the use of a regional approach to cover services liberalisation. One is an assessment that faster progress is possible in a regional agreement if the range of issues over which negotiations take place can be extended. In other words, an agreement with greater scope and fewer members can mobilise a wider range of political interests that offset the resistance to reform in some sectors that perceive they will lose from such an agreement.[8] It pays, in other words, to have services on the negotiating table. Interest groups in favour of liberalisation of this sector may emerge for a number of reasons. For example, they may expect the efficiency of firms in the service sector to increase and the cost of their purchased services inputs to fall. The competitiveness of their sectors of the economy could therefore increase following a measure of liberalisation in the service sector.

Other interest groups in favour of including services in a regional agreement may seek to gain from the higher level of market access that the negotiations provide. Furthermore, preferential access to protected services markets may be sought in anticipation of the rents that can be captured in foreign markets in the process. In many service sectors, 'first mover' advantages are extremely important—even if others are provided access to markets later, incumbents may expect to have a stronger competitive position. Alternatively, the prospective entrants might be seeking guarantees on competition policy issues to reduce some of the risks of initiating competition with local incumbents. Meanwhile, from the importing country point of view, it might be hoped that a regional approach can provide an environment of greater predictability in which local firms can adjust, perhaps by consolidating, before they have to face global competition.

Political objectives could be paramount in seeking a regional agreement. By selecting the sequence of trading partners with whom liberalisation is organised, a greater level of control might be expected over its effects. For example, a developed country might prefer to reach agreement with another who was less threatening in terms of competitiveness or other issues. This question of sequencing might be more relevant to services than to some goods because of the variety of modes of delivery of services, including commercial establishment or foreign direct investment. Liberalisation therefore involves a higher degree of direct contact with foreign suppliers.

Finally, services transactions often raise new and complicated issues associated with liberalisation, including dealing with the impact of domestic regulation, and it might be expected that these issues could be resolved in a small group setting, whereas it may be more difficult to do so in a multilateral process.

There are also challenges in attempts to liberalise the service sector in a regional approach. The negotiation of the arrangements may seem 'easy' from the point of view of the bureaucracies involved and the preferential route seen as a quicker way of getting results. However this route is not necessarily easy for two reasons. While the number of parties involved is small, the issues under discussion retain the same degree of complexity.

---

[7] One glaring weakness in NAFTA however is that all measures applied at the level of the state governments were grandfathered.

[8] Sherry Stephenson, *Regional Versus Multilateral Liberalization of Services,* 1 (2) WORLD TRADE REVIEW (July 2002).

Much time could be spent thrashing out a solution that suits the parties involved, only to have the next set of negotiations lead to a different outcome, and for both outcomes to contradict principles established at the multilateral level. Likely areas where differences might occur include the treatment of safeguards or government procurement. We comment on this problem in more detail below.

The second difficulty is that, as some bilateral negotiations now in progress in East Asia suggest, negotiation can be easily derailed. There may be less sectoral coverage in a bilateral approach. Violent objection by one sensitive sector can stop the negotiations since the countervailing forces are insufficient. In that case, either the agreement fails to be signed, or else an exclusion of some sectors from the agreement might be accepted. But these exclusions inhibit the ability to combine the individual agreements into a more inclusive structure that is closer to achieving global free trade in services.

A number of other factors impede service sector liberalisation in all forums, including the regional one. One is the problem of the assessment of impediments and the gains from reform. Considerable time and effort is required to characterise and assess various types of impediments. As a result it is also difficult to assess the extent of change that has occurred and to associate the outcomes observed in trade, investment, and competition in the service sector with the reform that has taken place. This in turn makes it more difficult to build a constituency for policy reform.

Domestic laws and regulations represent another major challenge to successful liberalisation in all forms. The service sector is often governed by many sets of rules and regulations, and these pose limitations to the scope of commitments negotiators are able to make. The implementation of international commitments that are in contradiction with domestic laws would require new domestic legal commitments. Therefore, domestic consensus on proceeding with regulatory reform that can be adopted in the form of new or amended laws, decrees or regulations is required before any bold movements can be expected.

The complicated domestic rules and regulations that affect services trade come under the purview of many departments and ministries. Sector-specific regulations are the responsibilities of the respective ministries. With the multitude of government authorities involved, co-ordination of a national position for negotiations as well as for the implementation of negotiated agreements is indeed extremely challenging. The same challenge applies in the GATS but in that case the commitments made and arrangements adopted apply to all Members. The preferential approach, when effective, may add to the diversity in the application of regulation, unless the reforms adopted in the regional context are applied 'de facto' on an MFN basis. In such cases, the degree of preference that can be applied may also be very limited or non-existent.

Much negotiating effort is being put into many regional agreements that appear to be liberalising on paper but are not yet implemented. For example, in the Western Hemisphere, the Protocol of Montevideo covering trade in services for MERCOSUR members has not yet been ratified, though the agreement was signed in December 1997. The jury is still out on the Andean Community agreement (adopted in June 1998) and on Protocol II of the CARICOM Agreement (adopted in 1998 as well) where members have only just now begun the process of trying to lift the restrictions in place that have been identified in national inventories. A few bilateral NAFTA-type free trade agreements do not contain the annexes that provide lists of non-conforming measures or reservations. The reason is that the parties were not able to agree on this aspect at the time they completed negotiating the overall agreement, and therefore the annexes, when and if completed, appear elsewhere in local, obscure publications. This lack of fulfillment of a basic obligation contributes little to transparency of policy and its review and reform in these regional agreements.

IV. The Uruguay Round and Regionalism

It is useful to compare the requirements set out for regional agreements on services reached during the Uruguay Round to the requirements for the treatment of goods under those agreements. GATT Article XXIV specifies that members of a customs union or free trade area (or any interim agreement leading to these arrangements) should not impose 'higher or more restrictive' duties and 'other regulations of commerce' on trade with non-members. Furthermore, the article requires that 'duties and other restrictive regulations of commerce . . . are eliminated on substantially all trade'. A definite timetable for implementation is supposed to be provided and the rule of thumb adopted through an understanding of members is that the time limit is ten years. Crawford and Laird[9] provide a detailed discussion of the lack of clarity in this article. Examples of the problems, to name just a few, are:

- the interpretation of the term 'substantially all trade' (for example, does this mean relative to the share of trade or the coverage of sectors?);
- the definition of the term 'other regulations of commerce';
- the issue of special treatment of developing countries; and
- the allowance for transition periods and different time frames for implementation.

In comparison, Article V of the GATS states that groups of members can enter into an agreement to liberalise trade in services between or among themselves as long as the agreement:

- has substantial sectoral coverage; and
- provides for the absence or elimination of substantially all discrimination between or among the parties in the sectors covered through a) elimination of existing discriminatory measures and/or b) prohibition of new or more discriminatory measures.

There is also a requirement that the agreement should not raise the 'overall' level of barriers to trade in services with non-members. Developing countries that are members of an agreement are given a more flexible timetable to meet the conditions on sectoral coverage.

This Article also suffers from lack of clarity and some difficulty in interpretation. There are questions about what is meant by substantial coverage. A footnote to the article specifies that this requirement should be interpreted in terms of the number of sectors, the volume of trade affected and the modes of supply, and stresses that arrangements should not provide for the *a priori* exclusion of any mode of supply. Even if potential members are able to agree on the parameters of an agreement on services, the lack of data on trade and investment in services will make it difficult to implement. In a review of

---

[9] Jo-Ann Crawford and Sam Laird, *Regional Trade Agreements and the WTO*, 12 (2) NORTH AMERICAN JOURNAL OF ECONOMICS AND FINANCE 193 (July 2001). Paragraph 29 of the Doha Ministerial statement (reproduced in the Appendix to this book) that there should be "aimed at clarifying and improving disciplines and procedures under the existing WTO provisions applying to regional trade agreements. The negotiations shall take into account the developmental aspects of regional trade agreements." The negotiations are supposed to be completed by January 1, 2005.

Article V, Stephenson concludes that it is a "very weak and ineffective discipline".[10] Apart from the question of coverage, she notes a number of other issues. These include how to measure the elimination of substantially all discrimination, the lack of notifications (discussed further below), and the legal status of various stand-alone sectoral agreements. Another matter is the strategy of claiming regional agreements as MFN exemptions to the GATS rather than having such agreements notified to the WTO and examined under its Committee on Regional Trade Agreements.

There are two types of approaches to presenting agreements on services. For some agreements which are customs unions (for example, the Andean Community, CARICOM, MERCOSUR), the approach has been to negotiate a Protocol (latter two groupings) or a Decision (first grouping) on services which is then signed and ratified separately but is understood to form a part of the basic integration agreement. For the Andean Community these decisions, once signed by Heads of State, carry with them supranational power and override national law. For MERCOSUR and CARICOM, each separate Protocol must be ratified and incorporated into national law, as there is no effective element of supranationality. The ASEAN members also have followed this approach, in negotiating separate Agreements on issues that are then understood to form a part of the basic ASEAN agreement (such as the ASEAN Free Trade Agreement or the ASEAN Framework Agreement on Services).

In the second approach, everything is negotiated and completed at the same time. The NAFTA and all of the NAFTA-type agreements (of which there are now at least ten in the Western Hemisphere) exemplify the second type of approach to negotiating agreements on services. Here the services chapter, the investment chapter and a chapter on the temporary movement of business persons form a part of an integral agreement. The treaty is then signed as a whole and ratified by national governments in order to be incorporated into national law. In these cases, services negotiations would not proceed on a separate track but would be part of the whole outcome. This approach is also being followed in the FTAA negotiations.

Table 1 shows the regional agreements that have been notified to the WTO under GATS Article V. The notification process for regional agreements under the WTO is divided into two parts—one for goods and one for services—because of the legal structure of the WTO Agreement under which the GATT 1994, the GATS, and TRIPS Agreement are all separate parts, connected only by the Dispute Settlement Understanding. Regional agreements on goods are therefore to be notified under Article XXIV of the GATT 1994 and those on services under Article V of the GATS. This means that the notifications with respect to goods and with respect to services can be done at different points in time, even if they form a part of an integral agreement (as was done by both the EU and NAFTA). However, the practice is now to have the agreements which are notified to the WTO and cover both goods and services examined together, as a matter of convenience.

All regional agreements on services should have been notified to the WTO under GATS Article V. However, only a few agreements have been notified to date.[11] There is no legal way to oblige the parties to regional agreements to notify them and there is no currently no counter-notification procedure envisaged under the WTO. A striking feature of Table 1

---

[10] Sherry Stephenson, *Regional Agreements on Services and Multilateral Disciplines: Interpreting and Applying GATS Article V*, in THE GATS 2000 NEGOTIATIONS: NEW DIMENSIONS IN SERVICES TRADE LIBERALIZATION (Pierre Suave and Robert Stern eds. 2000)

[11] Of the fifteen regional agreements covering services and negotiated in the Western Hemisphere, only two have been notified. The ASEAN Framework Agreement on Services has not been notified.

Table 1: Notification of agreements to the WTO under GATS Article V*

Agreement	Entry into force	Notification	Stage of examination process as at September 2001
EC (Treaty of Rome)	1-Jan-58	10-Nov-95	Under factual examination
CER	1-Jan-89	22-Nov-95	Consultations on draft report
EEA	1-Jan-94	10-Oct-96	Examination not requested
EC—Hungary	1-Feb-94	27-Aug-96	Consultations on draft report
EC—Poland	1-Feb-94	27-Aug-96	Factual examination concluded
NAFTA	1-Apr-94	1-Mar-95	Consultations on draft report
EC accession of Austria, Finland and Sweden	1-Jan-95	20-Jan-95	Consultations on draft report
EC—Bulgaria	1-Feb-95	25-Apr-97	Examination not requested
EC—Czech Republic	1-Feb-95	9-Oct-96	Examination not requested
EC—Romania	1-Feb-95	9-Oct-96	Examination not requested
EC—Slovak Republic	1-Feb-95	27-Aug-96	Factual examination concluded
Canada—Chile	5-Jul-97	13-Nov-97	Examination not requested
New Zealand—Singapore	1-Jan-01	4-Sep-01	Examination not requested
EFTA—Mexico	1-Jul-01	25-Jul-01	Examination not requested

Source: WTO (downloaded from http://www.wto.org/english/tratop_e/region_e/region_e.htm)
* Membership in the various regional agreements cited above is as follows:
EC (European Communities): Austria, Belgium, Denmark, Finland, France, Germany, Greece, Ireland, Italy, Luxembourg, Netherlands, Portugal, Spain, Sweden, United Kingdom
EEA (European Economic Area): Members of the EC and the EFTA
CER (Closer Economic Relations): Australia, New Zealand
EFTA (European Free Trade Area): Iceland, Liechtenstein, Norway, and Switzerland.

is that all the agreements listed include a developed-country member. At the same time, surprisingly, the EU-Mexico agreement has not been notified but the EFTA-Mexico agreement has been. There thus appears to be no consistency in approaches to notification, and this fact considerably weakens the multilateral surveillance function of the WTO and its role of ensuring that regional agreements are compatible with multilateral rules.

V. Issues

A series of studies have been undertaken which analyze the arrangements in which services have been included. Stephenson and Prieto[12] have reviewed the experience of the regional approach in the Americas, Nikomborirak and Stephenson[13] have examined the experience in East Asia in particular within ASEAN, comparing it with that in the Americas, Stephenson has compared agreements in the Western Hemisphere and in APEC[14],

[12] Sherry Stephenson and Francisco Javier Prieto, *Evaluating Approaches to the Liberalization of Trade in Services: Insights from Regional Experience in the Americas*, in TRADE RULES IN THE MAKING (Patrick Low, Barbara Kotschwar and Miguel Rodriguez eds. 2000). *See also*, Sherry Stephenson, *Multilateral and Regional Approaches to Services Liberalization by America and the Caribbean*, OAS TRADE UNIT STUDY (March 2001)
[13] Deunden Nikomborirak and Sherry Stephenson, *Liberalisation of Trade in Services: East Asia and the Western Hemisphere*, in SERVICES TRADE LIBERALISATION AND FACILITATION (Sherry Stephenson, Christopher Finlay, and Soonhwa Yi eds. 2002)
[14] Sherry Stephenson, *Services*, in TOWARDS FREE TRADE IN THE AMERICAS (Jose Manuel Salazar and Maryse Robert eds. 2001); and Sherry Stephenson, *A Comparison of Existing Services Trade Agreements within APEC*, in IMPEDIMENTS TO TRADE IN SERVICES: MEASUREMENT AND POLICY IMPLICATIONS (Christopher Findlay and Tony Warren eds. 2000)

and a number of papers have been written on the impact of NAFTA.[15] A theme amongst these evaluations is that while the regional agreements are often consistent with the principles outlined above, their actual contribution to liberalisation over and above that already achieved in the GATS commitments is often in doubt. Some key constraints are likely to be the trade and investment diverting effects of the preferential agreements and also the difficulty of reaching consensus at the domestic level.

In the next section we summarise the various options for the use of regional approaches, based on the results of these reviews. We propose not to provide a comprehensive summary of each agreement but to note the key elements and to illustrate their application where that is advantageous.

A. Evaluating the Impact of Regional Agreements

Liberalisation of services trade must be evaluated quite differently from that of trade in goods. In the case of goods, tariff levels before and after the formation of a preferential trading arrangement can be compared. In the case of services it is the degree of application of the national treatment principle, or the extent to which discriminatory treatment has been removed among members, that must be compared with the type of treatment that is accorded service providers from non-member countries.

The problems in the assessment of agreements on services include lack of statistical data on services trade at the disaggregated or sectoral level and the nature of the regulatory barriers in place for services. One way to carry out such a comparative analysis is through the examination of the content of the commitments made at the regional level as compared with the commitments made at the multilateral level under the GATS (in the case of arrangements adopting a "positive list" approach). In the case of arrangements adopting a "negative list" approach, it is necessary to examine the content of the annexes containing the lists of reservations with commitments made in these sectors at the multilateral level under the GATS.

As noted above, it may be difficult to apply laws and regulations in a differential manner to different service suppliers. But in other cases, it is possible to apply measures in a discriminatory fashion. For example, if the form of restriction is a quantitative constraint (a rule which limits the number of entrants through a licensing system), then a preferential policy can be implemented. Eligibility for subsidies (eg, in the education sector) can also be restricted to particular firms from other members of an agreement. Even rights to appeal to local competition authorities on anti-competitive behaviour could in principle be limited to firms from member countries to a preferential agreement. The evaluation of agreements should therefore include their discriminatory impact.

Little work has been done on the assessment of regional arrangements in trade in services.[16] One exception is modeling work on a proposed amalgamation between the ASEAN Free Trade Area and the CER between Australia and New Zealand, in the context of all members' commitments to the non-discriminatory APEC process. This case is reported in Box 1, along with some comments on the value of the modeling approach.

[15] See Mary Burfisher, Sherman Robinson and Karen Thierfelder, The Impact of NAFTA on the United States, 15(1) JOURNAL OF ECONOMIC PERSPECTIVES 125-144 (Winter 2001) and other papers in the same issue on the impact of NAFTA on other members.

[16] See Arvind Panagariya, Preferential TradeLiberalization: the Traditional Theory and New Developments, 38(2) JOURNAL OF ECONOMIC LITERATURE 287 (June 2000), and Sherman Robinson and Karen Theirfelder, Trade Liberalization and Regional Integration: the Search for Large numbers, TMD DISCUSSION PAPER 34, IFPRI (January 1999) for a review of empirical work.

Box 1 The Gains From Reform: the Case of AFTA and CER

Computable general equilibrium models have the advantage over other methods of assessing preferential arrangements since they have more options for good choices of base scenarios and they can capture more of the detail of the preferential policies. The models are now able to incorporate the effects of a larger market on the scope to capture economies of scale and the effects of market opening in cases of imperfect competition. They can also capture the effects of trade agreements in flows of capital between countries and on accumulation of capital within countries. The conclusion of the review of work in this field by Srinivasan, Whalley and Wooton[17] is that the welfare effects of preferential agreements (applying to goods) have probably been positive but not necessarily very large. They suggest vigorous proponents of arguments either in favour or in opposition to preferential agreements are probably overstating the quantitative assessments in support of their case (p. 74).[18]

Krueger[19] reports larger estimates of positive effects from more recent studies that are based on models whose specifications permit the identification of more of the dynamic gains. An example of this approach is the work by Davis, McKibbin and Stoeckel[20] who simulate the effects of a free trade area involving AFTA and CER, using the APG-cubed model.[21] They allow for allocative efficiency effects, terms of trade changes, endogenous productivity effects and capital accumulation in a model of trade in goods and services. They find positive effects from a joint AFTA-CER FTA (of an extra $US25.6b GDP in net present value terms in AFTA and $US22.5b for CER[22]). These gains are nearly three times as great as those obtained in an earlier study by the same authors which excluded services liberalisation and which excluded the productivity effect. These data refer to a scenario in which there is complete liberalisation within the group by 2005 of both goods and services. An important result stressed by Davis, McKibbin and Stoeckel is that if the non-discriminatory program of liberalisation in APEC proceeds on schedule (to achieve free trade and investment by 2010 for developed economy members in the region and by 2020 for developing economy members), then the additional gains from the earlier negotiation of the AFTA-CER arrangement are relatively small. The gain to AFTA members of an FTA with CER falls to just over $US10b and those to CER members fall to just under $US2b. The reasons, as they point out, are that the AFTA-CER trade is relatively small compared to their members' trade with APEC as a whole, and because APEC is not preferential. The authors identify a number of implications of these results. One they stress is that some of the APEC gains could in fact be attributable to the AFTA-CER connection, to the extent that it encouraged further liberalisation in the larger group (p. 40). However, as discussed in the main part of this chapter, preferential arrangements could have the opposite effect. A set of preferential commitments, if they could be reached, could slow down a non-discriminatory program.

---

[17] T.N. Srinivasan, John Whalley and Ian Wooton, *Measuring the Effects of Regionalism on Trade and Welfare*, in REGIONAL INTEGRATION AND THE GLOBAL TRADING SYSTEM (Kym Anderson and Richard Blackhurst eds. 1993).

[18] Panagariya, *supra* note 16 also identifies a number of problems in the modeling approaches.

[19] Anne O. Krueger, *Are Preferential Trading Arrangements Trade-Liberalizing or Protectionist?*, JOURNAL OF ECONOMIC PERSPECTIVES, Vol. 13, No. 4, 105–25 (1999)

[20] Lee Davis, Warwick McKibbin and Andrew Stoeckel, *Economic Benefits From an AFTA-CER Free Trade Area: Year 2000 study*, CENTRE FOR INTERNATIONAL ECONOMICS (2000)

B. The Path to Global Free Trade?

1. Incentives

With respect to the effects on the world trading system, there are a number of arguments both for and against preferential arrangements. Krueger[23] reviews these arguments, finding no strong support for the view that preferential arrangements are building blocks of the multilateral system, and indeed 'grounds for concern' that they may weaken it.

Recent research[24] has identified one set of circumstances in which a preferential path might lead to global free trade. Suppose policymaking is driven solely by firm profits and consumers have no influence. There is only one service sold in oligopolistic and segmented markets in identical economies (with one firm in each economy). Global free trade emerges when there is one bloc, membership of which is considered sequentially, and where the rules of the bloc say that any country that wants to join has to be allowed to do so. In that case, outsiders will always want to join and the incumbents cannot stop them. Clearly, however, this outcome depends on the specification of the constitution of the bloc, especially the rule on accession.

In other circumstances the outcome will not be free trade. Profits per firm reach a maximum before membership is universal. So if the incumbents are given discretion, they will deny further entry to the bloc after some point. This outcome is not the end of the game. The countries excluded could then form their own arrangement. The further implication is that the first bloc would then have an incentive to increase the size of its membership. The emergence of the second bloc therefore makes the first bigger.

What incentives exist to merge the smaller blocs? Imagine a situation in which each economy forms a bloc with one neighbour. In the next stage, the members of one agreement merge with those of one other agreement. And so on. Could this process of consolidation continue until free trade is reached, or is there a circumstance in which it will stop before then? The research shows that free trade is possible but only if the inter-bloc tariff equivalents of impediments are low enough (in this case, the oligopolistic firms in the model can make greater profits with unrestricted access to all markets).

The political economy effects of the preferential route to reform are important. Export interests would normally be in favour of, or at least able to mobilised in to be in favour of, multilateral change. They do not want to give up the rents to which they now have access, and they cannot be compensated by the move to even freer trade. As a consequence, the risk is that liberalisation gets 'suspended'.

Another consideration is that the negotiation of a preferential agreement uses up scarce policy making and negotiating capacity, and diverts attention in the policy-making system. For example, in the lead-up to the Seattle WTO Ministerial meeting, some economies normally expected to be stalwarts of the multilateral process were marketing their regional initiatives, at the cost of effort that might otherwise have gone into building

---

[21] This model provides disaggregated results for six sectors and eighteen countries or regions with a focus on the Asia Pacific region. A feature is that the Asia Pacific G-Cubed Model models the links between economies in both trade and financial markets. See www.msgpl.com.au.

[22] The real consumption gain allowing for the ability to shift spending through time is 1 percent by 2005 for AFTA as a whole and 0.6 percent for CER.

[23] Krueger, *supra* note 19. See also Stephenson, *supra* note 8 and Mattoo and Fink, *Regional Agreements and Trade in Services: Policy Issues*, WORLD BANK POLICY RESEARCH WORKING PAPER 2852 (June 2002) for further discussion of preferential approaches to services sector reform.

[24] Soamiely Andriamananjara, *On the Size and Number of Regional Integration Arrangements: A Political Economy Model*, WORLD BANK POLICY RESEARCH WORKING PAPER 2117 (May 1999).

the multilateral agenda. It is important therefore to establish institutional arrangements to capture any economies of scope that arise from running preferential negotiations alongside the multilateral ones.

A regional approach provides experience in working in multilateral settings and helping participants to understand complex negotiating issues. The net benefit of starting a regional level before proceeding to the global level is a topic for further consideration, especially given the resource constraints in developing economies. Work in this environment also provides non-WTO members with a framework within which to participate in work bearing on WTO services negotiations and to help channel their reform efforts in advance of WTO membership. For example, the recent US-Vietnam bilateral free trade agreement will help Vietnam to adhere to the WTO and to the GATS in a shorter period of time than it might otherwise have taken, having already taken on some key disciplines in the services area and begun the reform process to open services markets. This has proven to be the case for several East European countries who have taken on associate membership in the EU and have adopted strict disciplines for services as well as opened key service sectors to investment and cross-border trade in the regional context. This should help them in taking on more extensive commitments under the GATS in the current negotiating round. The Central Asian countries are the next in line for EU association and will likewise benefit from being exposed to principles of services and investment liberalisation in a regional context.

2. Overlapping Fora

In making a decision to devote resources to a regional and negotiated approach, governments must also answer the question of whether it makes sense from an economic point of view to liberalise services on a preferential basis. The question of the choice of competing fora is relevant and important.

Answering this question is necessarily tied to a consideration of the nature of service activities themselves. Infrastructure or network-type services (financial, telecoms, energy, transport, and possibly distribution), to be supplied efficiently, require large amounts of capital to operate and offer significant economies of scale. The optimum level for liberalisation of such services is the largest market possible, in order to attract investment and generate output from the most efficient service operators. A preferential liberalisation of these particular activities would limit the ability of a country to draw upon the most efficient suppliers and thus maintain a higher-cost, less efficient national market for such critical services. This effect is especially important when incumbents have advantages over potential entrants in imperfectly competitive markets[25].

The world or global market is the logical forum to target for the liberalisation of infrastructure services. Regional negotiations and agreements play a role in this process as long as they both a) allow for the binding of liberalising commitments that have not yet been undertaken under the GATS and b) extend those commitments 'de facto' to other WTO members on an MFN basis. These conditions have been met in sectors of this type among the NAFTA members (with the exception of certain financial services commitments on the part of Mexico) as well as by members of the European Communities.

Commercially-oriented services include distribution, business services, professional services, tourism, construction/ engineering services, environmental services and certain categories of specialized health and educational services. Several of these sectors (tourism and business services in particular) are already quite open in most countries, and it would

---

[25] Mattoo and Flik, *supra* note 23.

make little sense to think of restricting open markets to a regional level. Discussion at a regional level might be useful for identifying commitments in these sectors which could be carried over into the GATS for subsequent application on an MFN basis.

Other sectors such as construction/engineering and professional services are subject to strictly regulated national standards. Regional agreements could have a useful role to play. It should be easier to develop a common set of criteria for the recognition of the equivalence of standards and/or the equivalence of diplomas and educational and professional training for the granting of licenses to practice various professional services when this is carried out among a small or smaller sub-set of member countries. Similar national educational and legal systems that are often found in countries of the same geographic region or those of the same legal/cultural background facilitate such recognition agreements.

Apart of the question of coverage, and the compatibility with GATS rules on regional agreements (discussed above), an important issue in this case is the additional conditions that might be applied to increase the likelihood that any agreement leads to further liberalisation. Relevant conditions[26] include the reference to existing international standards as a benchmark, plus a commitment in the agreement to permit accession by others on the same terms as the foundation members of the agreement. There should also be a mechanism for review of this process. All potential participants should have an opportunity to comment on the architecture proposed even if they do not expect to join the arrangement immediately. The definition of these principles and the implementation of the monitoring process could be a role of higher level organisations, in particular, the WTO but with support from other regional structures in which current and prospective members participate: APEC, for example, could provide this service to its members.

3. Compatibility

A key issue in achieving convergence is the compatibility of the architecture of the agreements. One important difference between existing sub-regional agreements is how their disciplines are designed to deal with investment and with other areas such as government procurement, monopolies and restrictive business practices, technical regulations, dispute settlement and temporary movement of business persons. In these areas, some agreements contain separate chapters that are pertinent not only to services but to goods (and intellectual property) as well. NAFTA and the NAFTA-type agreements thus deal with goods and services in an integral manner. Other regional arrangements have elaborated parallel agreements in these areas, separating out the disciplines for goods and for services and keeping all four modes of supply within the services chapter. This is done rather than allowing the services component of investment (mode 3), temporary movement of persons (mode 4), procurement and competition policy to be covered by the respective chapters in these areas. The resulting architecture of agreements under these two alternatives is quite different.[27]

Separate from the design of the architecture, or the structure of a regional agreement, is the choice of a liberalising modality or mechanism. A decision on the negative list

---

[26] See Richard Snape, *Which Regional Trade Agreement?*, in REGIONAL INTEGRATION AND THE ASIA PACIFIC (Bijit Bora and Christopher Findlay eds. 1996) for a discussion of these conditions in the articles on recognition in the GATS and Peter Drysdale, Andrew Elek and Hadi Soesastro, *Open Regionalism: the Nature of Asia Pacific integration*, EUROPE, EAST ASIA AND APEC: A SHARED GLOBAL AGENDA? (P. Drysdale and D. Vines eds. 1998) for further discussion of 'open clubs'.

[27] CER has no separate chapter on investment and it applies 'subject to the foreign investment policies of the Member States'.

('top down') or the positive list ('bottom up') approach will determine the liberalising modality. Although this could be viewed as a more technical question, nonetheless this choice will have serious implications, for example, with respect to the greater or lesser transparency that an agreement will provide to service providers.

The contribution of agreements on services to global free trade also depends on the nature of the origin requirements that apply. In services it is far more difficult to design complicated origin requirements than it is to design complex rules of origin for goods. The question is how to identify a services supplier who is eligible for preferential treatment. In most regional agreements, the rules are extremely liberal and allow for any foreign service supplier to benefit from the preferential agreement as long as it is a legally incorporated juridical person which shows 'substantial business activities' in one of the member countries. Some agreements also require that the activity be majority-owned and/or controlled by nationals of that member, as is often found in the GATS schedules of commitments.

VI. Policy Conclusions

In summary, we see four sets of issues related to the question of whether regional approaches lead to more wide-ranging reform. These relate to incentives, to architecture, to the appropriate forum for liberalisation, and to the economic impact of preferential agreements in services.

A regional and preferential approach runs the risk of the loss of momentum for further liberalisation. The likelihood of this problem depends on a number of conditions, one of which is the set of multilateral rules for the formation and oversight of preferential arrangements. Another determinant is the extent of remaining impediments among the member groups. Both factors point to the value of the contribution from the multilateral system, especially the rules and expectations that it creates for the formation of regional structures. The current GATS rules on regional agreements are not sufficiently demanding to ensure the liberalising content of regional agreements. There is even greater uncertainty about the application of the GATS rules than there is in the application of the respective GATT rules. The resolution of this problem and the consideration of additional requirements, related for example to accession or to commitments to schedules of MFN liberalisation, as has been proposed for merchandise trade, are both valuable.

The chapter also noted some of the architectural issues in the service sector and the challenge of ensuring that different types of agreements are compatible. The adoption of a negative or a positive list approach to scheduling commitments is one example. Our conclusion on that question was that a negative list approach is better for the pace of liberalisation, but the main hurdle is to have it taken on board in the first place. As illustrated in the chapter in the case of negotiations on standards, a solution to some architectural issues could be reference to a set of principles developed at a higher level. These principles might be negotiated in the WTO process, or developed in, and their application monitored by, other regional bodies that sit above the smaller formal agreements. The nature of the relationship between APEC and the agreements among its constituent members would support this practice.

Liberalisation with respect to the global market is the first-best option for the services sector reform. Regional agreements with similar negotiating agendas may contribute if they stimulate the awareness of participants of the value of services liberalisation and reform, and if they serve as vehicles for binding commitments on a non-discriminatory basis that have not yet been undertaken at the multilateral level. In the chapter, we divided services into three types—infrastructure services, other commercial sectors which are already relatively open, and those which are subject to regulated national standards. We saw scope for regional agreements to contribute to reform in the third area, but subject to conditions on the reference to international standards, on the process of accession and on wide participation at the establishment phase of the preferential agreement.

The economic impact of preferential agreements in services is a topic for further empirical work. The difficulty of applying some domestic regulation in a discriminatory manner and the relatively liberal origin requirements that have been adopted in most regional agreements on services contribute to wider liberalisation. Certain instruments can nonetheless be applied in a discriminatory manner. A number of key variables will most likely determine the extent of liberalisation under a preferential agreement including: a) the modality of liberalisation and the architecture of the agreement (we stressed the value of a negative list) ; b) the coverage of the agreement (in terms of sectors and modes of supply, especially with respect to the treatment of foreign investment); c) the range of policies which it is expected will be applied in a preferential fashion (mfn application is preferred); and e) the definition of the origin requirement (a less demanding rule is preferred).

BIBLIOGRAPHY

Abugattas, Luis and Sherry Stephenson, *Liberalization of Trade in Services: Options and Implications for Latin American and Caribbean Countries,* in THE PROMISE AND PROBLEMS OF TRADE NEGOTIATIONS IN LATIN AMERICA (Diana Tussie ed. 2002).

Andriamananjara, Soamiely, *On the Size and Number of Regional Integration Arrangements: A Political Economy Model,* World Bank Policy Research Working Paper 2117 (May 1999).

Burfisher, Mary, Sherman Robinson and Karen Thierfelder, *The Impact of NAFTA on the United States,* 15(1) JOURNAL OF ECONOMIC PERSPECTIVES 125 (2001).

Crawford, Jo-Ann and Sam Laird, *Regional Trade Agreements and the WTO,* 12(2) NORTH AMERICAN JOURNAL OF ECONOMICS AND FINANCE 193 (July 2001).

Davis, Lee, Warwick McKibbin and Andrew Stoeckel, *Economic Benefits from an AFTA-CER Free Trade Area: Year 2000 Study* (Centre for International Economics, Canberra and Sydney, June 2000).

Drysdale Peter, Andrew Elek and Hadi Soesastro, *Open Regionalism: the Nature of Asia Pacific Integration,* in EUROPE, EAST ASIA AND APEC: A SHARED GLOBAL AGENDA? (P. Drysdale and D. Vines eds.1998).

Findlay, Christopher and Tony Warren, *Services Issues in APEC*, in IMPEDIMENTS TO TRADE IN SERVICES: MEASUREMENT AND POLICY IMPLICATIONS (Christopher Findlay and Tony Warren eds. 2000).

Krueger, Anne O., *Are Preferential Trading Arrangements Trade-Liberalizing or Protectionist?* 13(4) JOURNAL OF ECONOMIC PERSPECTIVES 105 (1999).

Mattoo, A. and C. Fink, *Regional Agreements and Trade in Services: Policy Issues*, World Bank Policy Research Working Paper 2852, June 2002.

Nikomborirak, Deunden and Sherry Stephenson (2002*), Liberalisation of Trade in Services: East Asia and the Western Hemisphere*, in SERVICES TRADE LIBERALISATION AND FACILITATION (Sherry Stephenson and Christopher Findlay with Soonhwa Yi eds. 2002)..

Panagariya, Arvind,*Preferential Trade Liberalization: the Traditional theory and new developments*, 38(2) JOURNAL OF ECONOMIC LITERATURE 287 (June 2000)

Prieto, Francisco (2000), 'The GATS, Sub-Regional Agreements and the FTAA: How Much is Left to be Done', in Sherry Stephenson (ed.), *Services Trade in the Western Hemisphere: Liberalization, Integration and Reform,* Brookings Institution Press.

Robinson, Sherman and Karen Theirfelder, *Trade Liberalization and regional integration: the search for large numbers*, TMD DISCUSSION PAPER 34, IFPRI (January 1999)

Sampson, Gary and Richard Snape,*Identifying Issues in Trade in Services,*8 (2) THE WORLD ECONOMY171 (1985).

Snape, Richard, *Which Regional Trade Agreement?*, in REGIONAL INTEGRATION AND THE ASIA PACIFIC (Bijit Bora and Christopher Findlay eds. 1996).

Srinivasan, T.N., John Whalley and Ian Wooton, *Measuring the Effects of Regionalism on Trade and Welfare*, in REGIONAL INTEGRATION AND THE GLOBAL TRADING SYSTEM (Kym Anderson and Richard Blackhurst eds. 1993).

Stephenson, Sherry, *Regional Agreements on Services and Multilateral Disciplines: Interpreting and Applying GATS Article V*, in THE GATS 2000 NEGOTIATIONS: NEW DIMENSIONS IN SERVICES TRADE LIBERALIZATION (Pierre Suave and Robert Stern eds. 2000).

Stephenson, Sherry, *A Comparison of Existing Services Trade Agreements within APEC*, in IMPEDIMENTS TO TRADE IN SERVICES: MEASUREMENT AND POLICY IMPLICATIONS (Christopher Findlay and Tony Warren eds. 2000)

Stephenson, Sherry (2001a), 'Deepening Disciplines for Trade in Services', *OAS Trade Unit Study*, OEA/Ser.D/XXII,SG/TU/TUS-8. March. Also available at www.sice.oas.org, Trade Unit Studies.

Stephenson, Sherry, *Multilateral and Regional Approaches to Services Liberalization by America and the Caribbean*, OAS TRADE UNIT STUDY (March 2001) Also available at www.sice.oas.org.

Stephenson, Sherry, *Services*, in TOWARDS FREE TRADE IN THE AMERICAS (Jose Manuel Salazar and Maryse Robert eds. 2001)

Stephenson, Sherry, *Regional versus Multilateral Liberalization of Services,*1 (2) WORLD TRADE REVIEW (July 2002).

Stephenson, Sherry and Francisco Javier Prieto, *Evaluating Approaches to the Liberalization of Trade in Services: Insights from Regional Experience in the Americas*, in TRADE RULES IN THE MAKING (Patrick Low, Barbara Kotschwar and Miguel Rodriguez eds. 2000).

WTO (1999), *The Legal Texts: The Results of the Uruguay Round of Multilateral Trade Negotiations*, Cambridge, Cambridge University Press.

CHAPTER 50

RULES FOR FOREIGN DIRECT INVESTMENT AT THE WTO: BUILDING ON REGIONAL TRADE AGREEMENTS

Michael Gestrin* and Alan Rugman**

TABLE OF CONTENTS

* Senior Economist, Investment Division, OECD, Paris. The views expressed in this chapter are those of the authors and do not necessarily reflect those of the OECD or any of its Member States.
** L. Leslie Waters Chair in International Business, Professor of Management, Professor of Business Economics and Public Policy, Indiana University, Kelley School of Business.

I. Introduction

The purpose of this chapter is to survey investment provisions in Regional Trade Agreements ("RTAs") and to highlight how these have gone beyond World Trade Organization norms on investment. It is generally acknowledged that the Uruguay Round of GATT negotiations went further than any previous round in placing investment issues on the multilateral trade agenda. Concurrently, the pace of developments with respect to the negotiation of rules on investment at the sub-multilateral level also accelerated during the early 1990s.

This dual evolution of the international policy framework for international investment reflects the growing recognition of the role investment has come to play in international economic development and integration. Just as trade was perceived as one of the key drivers of global economic growth during the post-World War II decades, since the 1980s foreign investment has come to be perceived as an important 'new' mode of global economic linkage. Statistics indicating that flows of foreign direct investment began outstripping both global trade and GDP growth rates in the 1980s only reinforced the perception that it was time for the international policy framework to catch up with the new international economic landscape.

Investment rules can be crafted and scaled to address a range of different objectives, including;

- Promoting a more secure, predictable and transparent environment in which to plan and operate cross-border investment;
- Ensuring greater protection for investors and their investments;
- Promoting the progressive liberalisation of barriers restricting the entry and conduct of foreign firms in domestic markets;
- Reducing or eliminating measures that distort trade and investment decisions and reduce allocative efficiency; and
- Developing credible institutions and rules for solving potential disputes[1].

II. The Investment-Related Provisions in the WTO

Foreign investment issues are dealt with in several WTO Agreements. The General Agreement on Trade in Services ("GATS"), the Agreement on Trade-Related Aspects of Intellectual Property Rights ("TRIPs") and the plurilateral Agreement on Government Procurement include provisions relating to the entry and treatment of foreign enterprises and the protection of certain property rights. The Agreement on Trade-Related Investment Measures ("TRIMs") and the Agreement on Subsidies and Countervailing Measures ("ASCM") circumscribe the ability of WTO members to apply certain kinds of measures to attract investment or influence the operations of foreign investors.

A. General Agreement on Trade in Services

Of all the agreements in the WTO, the GATS deals most directly with investment issues. It does so by defining four modes of supply that are covered by the agreement, one of which, mode three, consists of the provision of services through an established presence in a foreign territory. General obligations are contained in Parts I and II of the framework.

---

[1] Pierre Sauvé, *Scaling Back Ambitions on Investment Rule-Making at the WTO*, 2(3) THE JOURNAL OF WORLD INVESTMENT 529 (2001)

The most important of these are Articles I and II. Article I, on scope and definition, stipulates that the GATS applies to measures by members affecting trade in services, defined as including any service in any sector delivered via any of the four modes, with the exception of those supplied in the exercise of governmental functions. Article II codifies the unconditional most-favoured-nation treatment principle, making it one of the agreement's core general obligations. Under the MFN rule, members of the GATS are committed to treating services and service providers from one member in the same way as services and service providers from any other member, although countries were permitted to derogate from the commitment during the GATS negotiations. Unlike the GATT, the GATS does not enshrine the right to national treatment, which is a matter for negotiated commitments.

B. Agreement on Trade-Related Investment Measures

The TRIMs Agreement recognizes that certain investment measures restrict and distort trade. It provides that no contracting party shall apply any TRIM inconsistent with Articles III (national treatment) and XI (prohibition of quantitative restrictions) of the GATT. To this end, an illustrative list of TRIMs agreed to be inconsistent with these articles is appended to the agreement. The list includes measures which require particular levels of local procurement by an enterprise ("local content requirements") or which restrict the volume or value of imports such an enterprise can purchase or use to an amount related to the level of products it exports ("trade balancing requirements").

C. Agreement on Trade-Related Aspects of Intellectual Property Rights

The TRIPs Agreement builds upon the existing framework of intellectual property conventions (i.e. the Berne Convention, 1971, the Paris Convention, 1967 and the Washington Treaty on Intellectual Property in Respect of Integrated Circuits, 1989, among others). The agreement imposes national treatment and MFN, and establishes substantive standards for the protection of specific categories of intellectual property, as well as requiring domestic enforcement procedures and providing for international dispute settlement. The importance of the agreement in the context of investment relates to the increasingly important share of multinational enterprise ("MNE") assets accounted for by intangible assets. Furthermore, virtually all modern investment agreements which lay down standards for the promotion and protection of foreign investment include intellectual property within the definition of investment.

D. Agreement on Government Procurement

The plurilateral Agreement on Government Procurement requires not only that there be no discrimination against foreign products, but also no discrimination against foreign suppliers and, in particular, no discrimination against locally-established suppliers on the basis of their degree of foreign affiliation or ownership. Another investment-related aspect of this Agreement is the provision in Article XVI that procuring entities shall not, in the qualification and selection of suppliers, products or services, or in the evaluation of tenders and award of contracts, impose, seek or consider offsets, defined as "... measures used to encourage local development or improve the balance-of-payments accounts by means of domestic content, licensing of technology, investment requirements, counter-trade or similar requirements".

E. Agreement on Subsidies and Countervailing Measures

The ASCM defines the concept of "subsidy" and establishes disciplines on the provision of subsidies. The relevance of the ASCM to investment issues is that a number of investment incentives fall under the definition of a subsidy and are either prohibited or are subject to the disciplines of the ASCM if they cause "adverse effects" to other WTO Members. Subsidies contingent upon the exportation of goods produced are prohibited. Adverse effects are defined in terms of distortions to the trade flows of subsidised goods.

III. Investment Provisions in RTAs

At the sub-multilateral level, investment issues have been addressed through RTAs, bilateral investment treaties ("BITs") and a range of plurilateral arrangements specifically aimed at dealing with investment issues. In fact, where investment protection is concerned, RTAs are not typically the main vehicle for negotiating international investment rules. Rather, BITs constitute the most popular instrument in this regard. Whereas the number of BITs is estimated to have reached 1941 in 2000, an estimated 172 RTAs are currently in force and only a small (albeit growing) minority of these deal with investment issues. Given the focus of this survey on how RTAs have dealt with investment issues, it is important to keep in perspective that these only represent one of several institutional settings at the sub-multilateral level in which investment-rule making has taken place.

Rules on investment have been linked to wider processes of trade and economic integration and cooperation in various ways. The following sub-sections deal respectively with: i) agreements that focus on the right of establishment and the free movement of capital, ii) agreements that build upon treatment and protection principles typically found in BITs, iii) agreements that distinguish between the rights accorded to local and third-party investors and iv) agreements that include provisions on the status of regional enterprises.

This classification of RTAs according to general characteristics is imperfect insofar as the complexity of many agreements means that they could be included in several categories. Indeed, the only perfectly exclusive categorisation of agreements is at the level of the individual agreements themselves since no two agreements are exactly alike. However, in order to give the discussion some structure and to avoid simply listing agreements and their investment provisions it was felt that a rough characterisation according to broad objectives would render the discussion more reader-friendly.

Finally, all of the agreements discussed below constitute examples of efforts to go beyond existing provisions on investment at the WTO, either in terms of substance or objectives. In this sense, all of the RTAs surveyed here are WTO-plus. Indeed, even the most modest rules on investment found in RTAs usually contain some sort of provisions on the right of establishment, something that does not exist in any WTO agreement.

A. Rules on Right of Establishment and Free Movement of Capital

Early efforts at introducing rules on investment at the regional level emphasised the issues of establishment and the free movement of capital. One of the most comprehensive examples of this approach was the *Treaty Establishing the European Community* (1957) (revised by the Treaty of Amsterdam which entered into force on 1 May 1999). The EC

Treaty addresses investment primarily through provisions on freedom of establishment and free movement of capital. Article 52 of the original treaty prohibits restrictions on the freedom of establishment of nationals of a member State in the territory of another member State and on the setting up of agencies, branches or subsidiaries by nationals of any member State established in the territory of any member State.[2] Freedom of establishment includes the right to take up and pursue activities as self-employed persons and to set up and manage undertakings under the conditions laid down for its nationals by the law of the country where such establishment is effected. By virtue of (original) Article 58[3], this right of establishment applies to companies or firms formed in accordance with the law of a member State and having their registered office, central administration or principal place of business within the Community.

Since the end of the transitional period on 31 December 1969, (original) Article 52[4] has been directly applicable in the sense that it can be invoked by individuals before the national courts of member States. EC Treaty rules on freedom of establishment are not only addressed to the member States but also require the adoption of measures by the Community institutions with respect to a wide range of matters specified in (original) Articles 54 and 57 in order to facilitate the implementation of the freedom of establishment.[5] Pursuant to these provisions, directives have been adopted *inter alia* with respect to standards in specific sectors, company law, government procurement, and the mutual recognition and acceptance of diplomas, certificates and other evidence of formal qualifications.

With respect to movement of capital, Article 73(b) of the EC Treaty, which was added by the 1992 Treaty on European Union, provides for the prohibition as of 1 January 1994 of restrictions on movements of capital and payments between the member States and between the member States and third countries.[6] Capital movements covered by this provision include direct investments, defined as investments of all kinds which serve to establish or to maintain lasting and direct links between the person providing the capital and the undertaking to which the capital is made available in order to carry on an economic activity. This general prohibition is subject to "grandfather" and transition clauses in respect of certain existing restrictions, exceptions (e.g. relating to taxation and prudential measures) and a safeguard clause applicable in case of difficulties for the operation of economic and monetary union caused by capital movements to or from third countries.

Agreements involving countries that have historically restricted capital movements have also tended to emphasise establishment and capital movement issues but much less comprehensively than the EC Treaties. For example, the *Europe Agreements* concluded in the early and mid-1990s between the European Community and Central and Eastern European countries, also focus primarily upon establishment issues by providing for national treatment with regard to the establishment and operation of companies and nationals. The term "establishment" is defined in each of these Agreements as meaning the right to take up and pursue economic activities by means of the setting up and management of subsidiaries, branches and agencies.

---

[2] The reference in the original text to the progressive abolition of restrictions on the right of establishment in the course of the transitional period was deleted and replaced by the concept of prohibition in amendments made by the recent Treaty of Amsterdam, Article 43. *Official Journal of the European Communities*, No. C 340, 10 November 1997, at 61.

[3] *Treaty of Amsterdam*, Article 48.

[4] *Id.*, Article 43.

[5] *Id.,* Article 48.

[6] *Id.,* Article 56.

The *Treaty Establishing the Caribbean Community* (1973)[7], as amended by a Protocol adopted in July 1997, prohibits the introduction by member States of any new restrictions relating to the right of establishment of nationals of other member States (Article 35b). Member States are also required to remove restrictions on the right of establishment of nationals of other member States, including restrictions on the setting up of agencies, branches or subsidiaries by nationals of a member State in the territory of another member State (Article 35c).

Likewise, the *Treaty Establishing the African Economic Community* (1991)[8] and the *Treaty Establishing the Common Market for Eastern and Southern Africa* ("COMESA") (1993)[9] include among their objectives the removal of obstacles to the free movement of capital and the right of residence and establishment.[10] Finally, the *Revised Treaty of the Economic Community of West African States* ("ECOWAS") (1993)[11] includes among its objectives the establishment of a common market involving, *inter alia*, the removal of obstacles to the free movement of persons, goods, services and capital and obstacles to the right of residence and establishment (Article 3(2)). *The Treaty Establishing the Economic and Monetary Union of West Africa* (1996)[12] provides for freedom of nationals of one member State to provide services in the territory of another member State and proscribes restrictions on movement of capital.

B. Rules Building on Treatment and Protection Principles of Bilateral Investment Treaties

A number of RTAs have gone beyond issues relating to establishment and the free flow of capital. For example, the *North American Free Trade Agreement* ("NAFTA") (1994) contains generic provisions on investment in Chapter 11[13]. "Investment" is defined in Article 1139 through a broad list of assets along with a negative list of certain claims to money, including claims arising from commercial transactions, which are not considered to be investments. Each Party is required to accord the better of national treatment and MFN treatment to investors of another Party, and to investments of investors of another Party, with respect to the establishment, acquisition, expansion, management, conduct, operation, and sale or other disposition of investments (Articles 1102–1104).[14]

---

[7] Member States are Antigua and Barbuda, the Bahamas, Barbados, Belize, Dominica, Grenada, Guyana, Jamaica, Montserrat, Saint Kitts and Nevis, Saint Lucia, Saint Vincent and the Grenadines, and Trinidad and Tobago.

[8] Signatories are the members of the Organization of African Unity.

[9] The signatories of the COMESA Treaty are Angola, Burundi, Congo, Democratic Republic of, Comoros, Eritrea, Ethiopia, Kenya, Lesotho, Malawi, Mauritius, Rwanda, Sudan, Swaziland, Tanzania, Uganda and Zimbabwe. The COMESA Treaty has superseded the Treaty for the Establishment of the Preferential Trade Area for Eastern and Southern Africa concluded in 1982. It entered into force in December 1994.

[10] See, respectively Article 4(2)(i) of the Treaty Establishing the African Economic Community and Article 4(4)(c) and 4(6)(e) of the COMESA Treaty.

[11] Benin, Burkina Faso, Cape Verde, Côte d'Ivoire, Gambia, Ghana, Guinea, Guinea-Bissau, Liberia, Mali, Mauritania, Niger, Nigeria, Senegal, Sierra Leone and Togo.

[12] Member States are Benin, Burkina Faso, Côte d'Ivoire, Mali, Niger, Senegal and Togo.

[13] In addition to Chapter 11, separate provisions on investment are contained in Chapter 14 on financial services, Chapter 15 on competition, monopolies and state enterprises, and Chapter 16 on temporary entry for business persons.

[14] The NAFTA adopts the negative list approach such that the actual coverage of the agreement's investment provisions is determined by the exceptions and reservations contained in the annexes to the agreement. For analysis of NAFTA's investment policies *see* Michael Gestrin and Alan M. Rugman, *The North American Free Trade Agreement and Foreign Direct Investment,* 3(1) TRANSNATIONAL CORPORATIONS 77 (1994). *See also* FOREIGN INVESTMENT AND NAFTA (Alan Rugman ed. 1994).

The provisions of the NAFTA concerning performance requirements apply to both investments of investors of a Party and investments of investors of a non-Party. Article 1106(1) proscribes the imposition or enforcement of mandatory requirements and the enforcement of any undertakings or commitments: (1) to export a given level or percentage of goods or services; (2) to achieve a given level or percentage of domestic content; (3) to purchase, use or accord a preference to goods produced or services provided in the territory of a Party or to purchase goods or services from persons in its territory; (4) to relate the volume or value of imports to the volume or value of exports or to the amount of foreign exchange inflows associated with investment; (5) to restrict sales of goods or services produced or provided by an investment in a Party's territory by relating such sales to the volume or value of exports or foreign exchange earnings of the investment; (6) to transfer technology, a production process or other proprietary knowledge; and (7) to act as the exclusive supplier of the goods produced or services provided by an investment to a specific region or world market. With the exception of the first and the last two requirements, these requirements are also prohibited if applied as conditions for the receipt of an advantage (Article 1106(2)).

NAFTA Articles 1115–1138 provide for international arbitration of disputes between a Party and an investor of another Party. An investor may submit to international arbitration a claim that another Party has breached an obligation under Chapter 11 or under certain provisions of the chapter on monopolies and state enterprises and that the investor has incurred loss or damage by reason of, or arising out of, that breach. Article 1122 contains the unconditional consent of the Parties to the submission of a claim to arbitration. The investor can elect to proceed under the International Centre for Settlement of Investment Disputes ("ICSID") Convention, the Additional Facility Rules of ICSID or the United Nations Commission of International Trade Law "(UNCITRAL") Arbitration Rules. Detailed rules are contained in these provisions on matters such as the constitution of arbitral tribunals, consolidation of claims, applicable law, nature of remedies, and finality and enforcement of arbitral awards.

A number of more recent RTAs (and proposed RTAs), especially those involving NAFTA signatories, have been broadly modelled after the NAFTA with respect to investment rules. This is the case, for example, in the *Canada-Chile Free Trade Agreement* (1997), the *Mexico-Singapore Free Trade Agreement* (2000) and in the draft text for the *Free Trade Area of the Americas*. A structure and content broadly similar to that found in the NAFTA investment provisions is also reflected in the Vaduz Convention, the revised Convention establishing the *European Free Trade Association (2001)*.[15] Likewise, the *Japan-Singapore Free Trade Agreement (2002)* contains rules on investment similar to those found in NAFTA. One interesting point to note is that some recent bilateral RTAs do not cover investment for the stated reason that a BIT already exists between the signatories. This is the case with the *US-Jordan Free Trade Agreement* (2000) and the *Canada-Costa Rica Free Trade Agreement* (2000), to mention but two examples.

Other RTAs have sought to incorporate BIT-like provisions on investment but have eschewed the strict enforcement standards (e.g. binding dispute settlement mechanisms) and the levels of protection and liberalisation found in agreements like the NAFTA. In the context of the *Asia-Pacific Economic Cooperation* ("APEC"), norms of a legally non-binding nature relating to the admission, treatment and protection of foreign investment have been adopted in the *APEC Non-Binding Investment Principles* (1994). Principles

15 The original Stockholm Convention was signed in 1960.

of a general nature state that Member economies will ensure transparency with respect to laws, regulations and policies affecting foreign investment; extend MFN treatment to investors from any economy with respect to the establishment, expansion and operation of their investments; and accord national treatment to foreign investors in relation to the establishment, expansion, operation and protection of foreign investment, with exceptions as provided for in domestic laws, regulations and policies. More specific principles provide that Member economies will not relax health, safety and environmental regulations as an incentive to encourage foreign investment; minimise the use of performance requirements that distort or limit expansion of trade and investment; and permit the temporary entry and sojourn of key personnel for the purpose of engaging in activities connected with foreign investment, subject to relevant laws and regulations.

A number of regional and plurilateral agreements exist which, instead of directly incorporating the full range of investment protection and dispute settlement provisions typically found in bilateral investment treaties, envisage the conclusion of such bilateral treaties between the parties. Although not part of the RTAs themselves, these 'side-BITs' are explicitly recognised as contributing to the wider process of liberalisation between the parties. An example of this approach is the *Fourth ACP (Lomé) Convention*. Chapter 3 of this Convention, which is part of Title III on development finance co-operation, sets forth general principles regarding the treatment of foreign investment, such as the requirement to accord fair and equitable treatment, and envisages that more specific regulation of policies on foreign investment will be dealt with through the negotiation of bilateral agreements between the Contracting Parties. With a view to facilitating the negotiation of such agreements, a Joint Declaration in Annex LIII of the Convention provides that the Contracting Parties will undertake a study of the main clauses of a model bilateral investment agreement.[16] Various recent agreements of the European Union with third countries also refer to the possible conclusion of bilateral investment treaties between member States of the European Union and the third countries in question.[17]

C. Rules that Distinguish Between Local and Third-Party Investors

Investment rules on establishment, the free flow of capital and those that build upon issues usually covered in BITs all have as their underlying purpose the promotion of a more efficient international allocation and use of capital. However, not all investment rules in RTAs have economic efficiency as their prime objective. Some agreements contain investment provisions whose aim is more developmental in nature. For example, in August 1994, Member States of MERCOSUR adopted a *Protocol on Promotion and Protection of Investments from States not Parties to MERCOSUR*. The signatories to the Protocol undertake not to accord to investments of investors of third countries more favourable treatment than that provided for in the Protocol. In respect of the treatment of established

---

[16] In this connection, a statement on Investment Protection Principles in the ACP States was adopted by the European Community in November 1992.

[17] In addition to the Europe Agreements and the Partnership and Cooperation Agreements, references to the future conclusion of bilateral investment treaties appear in, for example, the Cooperation Agreement between the European Community and the Kingdom of Nepal (1995), Article 10; the Interregional Framework Cooperation Agreement between the European Community and its Member States, of the one part, and the Southern Common Market and its Party States, of the other part (1995), Article 12, and the Framework Cooperation Agreement leading ultimately to the establishment of a political and economic association between the European Community and its Member States, of the one part, and the Republic of Chile, of the other part (1996), Article 15.

investments, the Protocol lays down general standards of treatment which are similar to those contained in the Colonia Protocol[18], except that the parties to the agreement enjoy discretion to decide whether or not to accord national treatment and MFN treatment to established investments of investors of third countries. The *Protocol on Promotion and Protection of Investments from States not Parties to MERCOSUR* contains no provisions on performance requirements.

Other agreements dealing with investments from third countries have sought to reduce restrictions traditionally aimed at these. For example, in the context of the Andean Community[19] rules aiming at the harmonisation of investment policies of member countries towards investment from third countries were first adopted in 1970. The currently applicable regime appears in *Decision 291 of the Commission of the Cartagena Agreement—Common Code for the Treatment of Foreign Capital and on Trademarks, Patents, Licences and Royalties* (1991). This Decision provides that foreign investors shall have the same rights and obligations as national investors, except as otherwise provided in the legislation of each member country, and eliminates the previously existing requirement to subject foreign investment to an authorisation procedure. It also removes restrictions contained in the previous rules on the transfer of funds by obligating member countries to permit foreign investors and sub-regional investors to remit abroad in convertible currency the verified net profits derived from foreign direct investment and the proceeds from the sale or liquidation of such investment. A third important change effected by the Decision is the removal of restrictions on access of products produced by foreign enterprises to the benefits from the trade liberalisation under the Cartagena Agreement. Prior to the adoption of this Decision, such products could benefit from this trade liberalisation only if the foreign enterprise undertook to convert into a joint or national enterprise. Aside from these provisions on rights and obligations of foreign investors, the Decision contains rules requiring the registration of contracts for imports of technology and prohibiting the inclusion of certain kinds of restrictive clauses in such contracts.

D. Rules on Regional Enterprises

Several regional agreements aim at fostering co-operation between firms of member States by establishing a special legal regime for the formation of a regional form of business enterprise. For example, the *Uniform Code on Andean Multinational Enterprises* established by Decision 292 of the Commission of the Cartagena Agreement provides for the formation of Andean Multinational Enterprises. One of the conditions for the creation of such an enterprise is that capital contributions by national investors of two or more member countries must make up more than 60 per cent of the capital of the enterprise. Among the privileges which the Decision requires member countries to grant to such enterprises are national treatment with respect to government procurement, export incentives and taxation, the right to participate in economic sectors reserved for national companies, the right to open branches in any member country, and the right of free transfer of funds related to investments. Likewise, the *Basic Agreement on the ASEAN Industrial Cooperation Scheme* (AICO Scheme) was concluded by members of ASEAN in 1996 to promote joint manufacturing industrial activities between ASEAN-based companies.

---

[18] The Colonia Protocol governs the treatment of regionally based investors and their investments.
[19] Member States are Bolivia, Colombia, Ecuador, Peru and Venezuela.

IV. Conclusions

This analysis of investment provisions in RTAs reveals that one of the attractive features of negotiating investment rules at the sub-multilateral level is the flexibility and selectivity that countries with historically similar approaches to investment issues can apply to the various goals mentioned above. This is an important point because it suggests that any negotiation of investment rules at the multilateral level (if such a negotiation ever takes place at the WTO) will have to take into account the diversity of experience with and practice of international investment policy that has evolved at the regional level.

Several themes emerge from this analysis of investment provisions in RTAs. First, the extent to which signatories to an RTA attempt to establish ambitious investment rules, with a broad definition of investment, disciplines on TRIMs that go beyond the illustrative list in the WTO agreement, and binding dispute settlement mechanisms, *inter alia*, are to be largely a function of the countries' previous experience with a liberal investment regime. Most countries that have entered into agreements containing high-standard rules on investment had either already been liberalising their investment regimes unilaterally or had experimented with investment rules in prior agreements. For example, a number of bilateral agreements recently negotiated by the NAFTA signatories (such as Canada-Chile, Mexico-E.U., United States-Jordan) contain provisions almost identical to NAFTA Chapter 11. Where countries have only recently begun to liberalise their investment regimes and where these have traditionally been highly restrictive, the preference has been for less encompassing agreements covering limited rights of establishment and the movement of capital. In other words, the negotiation of investment rules in RTAs could be characterised as taking place at the investment policy margin. Countries at similar levels on the investment liberalisation 'trajectory' can scale their investment rule-making ambitions in line with historical local norms on international investment.

A related point concerns the objectives of investment rules. In most cases these are aimed at improving economic efficiency. This is the purpose of investment rules at the WTO and in most RTAs. However, some provisions in RTAs are more oriented towards development issues, especially as concerns the promotion of local firms. This is the case in both agreements that distinguish between the rights of local and third-party investors as well as those agreements that provide incentives and preferences for regional enterprises.

Another theme to emerge from this analysis concerns the apparent convergence of investment provisions in RTAs towards what might be described as a implicit international standard. This convergence is taking place through two channels. The first channel is through 'side-bilateral investment treaties', separate agreements on investment, but nonetheless in the context of wider processes of trade and economic integration and co-operation. What this suggests is that the perceived role of BITs is shifting beyond the protection of FDI from developed to developing countries to complementing broader and deeper liberalisation initiatives.

The second channel is through RTAs that closely resemble or build upon NAFTA investment provisions. Indeed, just as most BITs are based upon model BITs, the NAFTA investment provisions have in many instances become a 'model RTA investment chapter'. The trend therefore seems to be towards a more consistent treatment of investment in RTAs, both in terms of the tendency of RTAs to include rules on investment (or side-BITs) and in terms of their content.

This apparent convergence is especially significant to the extent that most BITs and NAFTA-based RTA investment provisions do not result in the sort of preferences that RTAs give rise to with respect to trade. Third party investors typically enjoy the same rights as investors based in the RTA area. To the extent that BITs and RTA investment provisions have increasingly come to reflect similar (high) standards, the spread of such agreements results in the *de facto* plurilateralisation of investment rules—as long as these do not discriminate or create preferences vis-à-vis third party investors. Furthermore, while concerns have been raised over the potential negative effects associated with treaty congestion, there is little indication to date to suggest that the rapid proliferation of BITs and RTAs with investment provisions has given rise to such problems, at least where foreign investment is concerned. Whether this plurilateralisation through regionalism might eventually obviate the need for multilateral rules on investment or could form the basis for the eventual multilateralisation of the standards found in RTAs is an open question.

CHAPTER 51

REGIONAL TRADING ARRANGEMENTS AND DEVELOPING COUNTRIES

Maurice W. Schiff* and L. Alan Winters**

TABLE OF CONTENTS

* Maurice Schiff is Lead Economist in the Trade Section of the Development Research Group of the World Bank.
** L Alan Winters was manager of that Section and is now Director of the Development Research Group at the World Bank and Professor of Economics at the University of Sussex. The work described in the paper is based on a major World Bank project led by the authors. This project underpinned the Bank's publication WORLD BANK, TRADE BLOCS—A POLICY RESEARCH; REPORT (2000) and is presented in more detail in MAURICE W. SCHIFF AND L. ALAN WINTERS, REGIONAL INTEGRATION AND DEVELOPMENT (Oxford University Press 2003).

I. Introduction

The growth of regional trading arrangements ("RTAs") has been one of the major developments in international relations in recent years. Virtually all countries are members of a trade bloc and many belong to more than one; more than one third of world trade takes place within such agreements; and regional trade is often advanced as a route to development.

This paper discusses the main arguments that have been advanced for and against regionalism as a tool of development policy. It considers not only the 'traditional' economic issues such as trade creation and trade diversion, but also more recent economic arguments such as whether regionalism stimulates investment and growth. It also discusses a broader set of issues such as whether regional trading arrangements promote economic and political credibility, peace and stability. Since this book is about the global trading system, the chapter also includes a more extended discussion of the economic connections between regionalism and the world trading system.

The analysis is presented in two parts referring, first, to the direct implications of RTAs for their members, and, second, to their effects on the world trading system. We do not discuss directly the rules of the GATT and the GATS rules about regionalism or their application—which are the subject of chapter XX of this book—but the analysis provides a basis on which these rules might be assessed. Regionalism is highly *sui generis*, so that simple unambiguous policy recommendations are simply not feasible. However, drawing on economic theory, empirical evidence and case studies, we propose some reasonably robust rules of thumb and identify a number of questions that policy makers should ask themselves about their own and others' regional arrangements. These are not inviolable rules for economic policy but rather norms from which policy-makers should deviate only when they have established an explicit case for doing so. There is no alternative to considering regional arrangements case-by-case, for idiosyncratic elements of any arrangement can always off-set any of the more general results available. However, we hope that following the analysis offered here will help policy makers to formulate their own analyses of their own circumstances.

II. Member Countries

A. Trade Effects

The basic economic analysis of tariff preferences is fifty years old,[1] but it is central enough to be re-iterated here. Forming a regional trading arrangement by removing barriers to trade between members of the RTA but not on trade with third countries almost always increases trade between the members. The issue, however, is whether it "creates" trade by allowing cheaper products from other bloc members to substitute for more expensive domestic production, or "diverts" it by substituting intra-bloc imports for imports from outside the group. The latter can happen when 'outside' goods would be cheaper if all suppliers faced equal tariffs, but the fact that 'inside' goods no longer face tariffs gives them a competitive edge. In that case, the preference-granting country ends up paying more for the imports, the increase being financed by monies that were initially going to the government in tariff revenues now accruing to producers in the partner countries. Part of this extra cost is a simple transfer from the taxpayers in the importing partner to producers in the exporting partner, but because the real cost of imports has risen (the partner is less efficient than 'outside' producers), real resources are also wasted by the

---

[1] J. VINER, THE CUSTOMS UNIONS ISSUE (1950).

diversion. When all the commodities covered by the RTA are considered together, if trade diversion predominates, an RTA can reduce all or some of the welfare of the member countries.

Identifying and distinguishing between trade creation and trade diversion is not straightforward empirically. The greatest difficulty is deciding what trade would have looked like if no RTA had been formed—the counterfactual or what the Europeans refer to as the *anti-monde*. This is more a matter of judgement than of science, particularly when it comes to considering whether regionalism is central or incidental to the general liberalisation of trade with all countries. The evidence on the balance between trade creation and diversion in trade blocs is mixed, but recent research –shows that, contrary to what was becoming received wisdom, diversion can be quite significant.[2] Often, however, as with the recent Latin American RTAs, trade diversion has been dominated by the positive effects of the partners' reductions of barriers against imports from non-partners that have accompanied the RTA[3]. Thus, whether this multilateral liberalization is or is not part of the process of regionalism is critical to our view òf it.

The traditional analysis of trade creation and diversion is based on a view of the world in which inter-country trade is driven entirely by differences in productivity and factor endowments. In fact trade can also arise from product differentiation and economies of scale, which reduce costs as production grows. Import barriers in such worlds are additionally costly because competition between firms is weakened and consumers lose from the resulting cuts in output and increases in price. International trade offers an important means of increasing competition by allowing new suppliers to enter markets. RTAs can generate such benefits by fostering trade between members, combining larger firm sizes (which increases economies of scale) with competition between larger numbers of firms (which increases competition). This is possible because by combining several national markets, the number of producers in each country might fall, while the number of sellers with reasonable access to each market rises (because producers from partner countries now have access).

These so-called pro-competitive effects are believed to have been strong during the course of European economic integration, but the empirical evidence that developing countries will be able to reap them in large amounts is currently rather weak. Partly that reflects the latter's production structure, with fewer goods in which differentiation and economies of scale are important, and partly the fact that significant increases in competition eventually depend on far more than merely removing tariffs and import quotas. Also, of course, if the aim is large markets and buying from firms that supply large markets, no market is larger than the world as a whole. That is, pro-competitive effects will be larger from non-discriminatory trade liberalisation than from discriminatory or restricted liberalisation.

B. The Parameters of RTAs

Why is regionalism so popular if it is just a pale imitation of non-discriminatory free trade? This sub-section briefly considers the basic international trade aspects of the question, and then asks how various design features of an RTA might affect its net benefits.

---

[2] Tamim Bayoumi and Barry Eichengreen, *Is Regionalism Simply a Diversion? Evidence from the Evolution of the EC and EFTA*, in NBER EAST ASIA SEMINAR ON ECONOMICS, VOL. 6: REGIONALISM VERSUS MULTILATERAL TRADE ARRANGEMENTS (T. Ito and Anne O. Krueger eds. 1997).

[3] See for example, Isidro Soloaga and L. Alan Winters, *Regionalism in the Nineties: What Effect on Trade?*, 12(1) NORTH AMERICAN JOURNAL OF ECONOMICS AND FINANCE 1 (2001).

Among the trade reasons advanced for RTAs, are that members might:

- be better able to exploit market power against outsiders by co-ordinating their trade policies.
- place a very high value on access to partners' markets and feel that this is better assured by making access to their own conditional on reciprocation and that they prefer preferential access to non-preferential access.
- want to exploit the regional market as a basis for protected industrialisation.

These arguments are not very convincing, especially as the basis of global policy positions. The first is exploitative, the second amounts to trading inefficient market access with each other, and the third is refuted by experience.

Clearly, the benefits of regionalism are likely to depend on finding the best partners. However, the popular notion of a 'natural' trade partner is not useful in this regard. Neither large existing trade volumes nor low transportation costs are good reasons for artificially favouring a particular trade flow.[4] Amjadi and Winters show that while trade costs are high for Latin America's extra-continental trade, the conditions necessary to reap any benefits from switching to lower-cost intra-continental structure are absent.[5] Bond also neatly points out that there is no presumption that infrastructure investment in Latin America should be devoted to facilitating intra-continental trade.[6] RTAs might stimulate intra-continental flows, but because it is subject to higher policy barriers, it is extra-continental trade that offers the bigger returns to expansion. Thus reducing the cost of the latter via investment is likely to be more useful than increasing the capacity for intra-bloc trade. Besides, ports devoted to trade with the world are inherently more flexible than roads or bridges devoted to local trade.

There are, however, several reasons behind the obvious tendency for trade blocs to form between neighbouring countries (i.e. for regionalism to be regional): for example, to reduce trade costs by relaxing or abolishing border formalities or to assist in the collection of tax revenues.

Though the welfare implications of RTAs are ambiguous in general, one general result is that small countries (for which world prices are given) are likely to lose from a RTA between themselves unless they lower trade barriers with respect to excluded countries[7]. Moreover, if such trade barriers are not reduced, not only is the bloc as a whole likely to lose, but the distribution of benefits is likely to be highly asymmetric, with the more developed members gaining at the expense of the poorer, less developed, ones (because access to the latter's market for the former's manufacturing exports has become free). Examples of such problems include the East African Community in the 1960s, where Kenya gained at the expense of Uganda and Tanzania, and the Central American Common Market where El Salvador gained at the expense of Honduras.

This is essentially the reasoning behind an interesting recent result that if two countries form an RTA, the one whose pattern of factor endowments is more similar to the world

---

[4] *See* Maurice Schiff, *Will the Real 'Natural Trading Partner' Please Stand Up?*, 16(2) J. OF ECONOMIC INTEGRATION 245 (2001).

[5] Azita Amjadi and L.Alan Winters, *Transport Costs and 'Natural' Integration in Mercosur*, 14 J. ECONOMIC INTEGRATION 497 (1999).

[6] Eric Bond, *Transportation Infrastructure Investments and Regional Trade Liberalization*, POLICY RESEARCH WORKING PAPER, No. 1851, THE WORLD BANK (1998).

[7] Maurice Schiff, *'Small is Beautiful' Preferential Trade Agreements and the Impact of Country Size, Market Share, and Smuggling*, 12(3) J. OF ECONOMIC INTEGRATION, 359 (1997); MAURICE W.SCHIFF AND L.ALAN WINTERS, REGIONAL INTEGRATION AND DEVELOPMENT (2003).

average will tend to gain more than the one which is less similar[8]. If the two countries have above average incomes, this tends to lead to convergence between the two partners, but if they have below average incomes (i.e. the RTA is between developing countries), it causes divergence.

One of the recurring themes of our work in the World Bank[9] is a preference for North-South over South-South RTAs for developing countries. If a developing country is going to pursue regionalism, it will almost always do better to sign up with a rich and large country than a small and poor one. In trade terms, this is manifest in the fact that a large rich country will tend to be a more efficient supplier of most goods and a source of greater competition.

Many countries are members of several RTAs. If they are all compatible this may be beneficial—it implies free trade with more countries[10]. But there are also dangers. For example, the several RTAs may imply conflicting policies vis-à-vis third countries, they may have different regulations governing imports of the same commodity from different sources, or they may imply different technical standards. All of these increase the complexity, cost and uncertainty of trade. There is also a danger in hub and spoke arrangements, as discussed below. An important distinction is between free trade areas ("FTAs") which have free trade between members, and customs unions ("CUs") which have that plus a common external tariff or, strictly, common trade policy towards third countries. FTAs are easier to create and can be institutionally very light, whereas CUs require the negotiation of the common external tariff and co-ordination of all future trade policy changes. FTAs, however, face the danger of trade deflection—goods entering the member with the lowest tariff and transferring tax-free to other members from there. Except for the extra transportation cost, this is efficient economically because it lowers the effective tariff, but it undermines the protective effect of members' own tariff structures. Therefore, governments seek to prevent it by imposing rules of origin ("RoOs") to ensure that only locally produced goods get tariff exemption. Such rules are often cumbersome and protectionist and can greatly reduce the value of the FTA. CUs, if they avoid this problem, can induce a greater degree of integration[11].

Another important difference between FTAs and CUs lies in the incentives they create for operating a liberal (i.e. low barrier) trade policy towards non-members; it has been argued that there is a tendency for FTAs to be more liberal than CUs. They have less market power and members might compete with each other to reduce tariffs and so enlarge their share of the RTA's imports and hence tariff revenue. Once we recognise that lobbying influences tariffs, it becomes plain that it will afflict FTAs and CUs too. For both, there is a presumption that the exceptions to internal free trade negotiated as the RTA is formed will tend to reduce the degree of trade creation, and so reduce the potential benefits. Olarreaga and Soloaga, and Olarreaga, Soloaga and Winters show the importance of these political factors in the determination of the internal and external trade policies of Mercosur countries[12]. And in the case of CUs, the RTA will change

---

[8] Anthony J. Venables, *Regional Integration Agreements: A Force for Convergence or Divergence?*, PROCEEDINGS OF WORLD BANK ABCDE CONFERENCE, PARIS (1999).

[9] WORLD BANK, *supra* note 1; Schiff and Winters, *supra* note 7

[10] Glenn W. Harrison, Tom Rutherford and David T. Tarr, *Trade Policy Options for Chile: The Importance of Market Access*, 16 THE WORLD BANK ECONOMIC REVIEW 49 (2002).

[11] Anne O. Krueger, *Free Trade Agreements versus Customs Union*, 54 J. OF DEVELOPMENT ECONOMICS 169 (1997).

[12] Marcelo Olarreaga and Isidro Soloaga, *Explaining Mercosur's Tariff Structure: A Political Economy Approach*, 12(2) THE WORLD BANK ECONOMIC REVIEW 297 (1998); Marcelo Olarreaga, Isidro Soloaga and

the environment for future lobbying, although whether this will be towards or away from greater protectionism, however, is impossible to say *a priori*. Clausig discusses the trade-off between RoOs and external tariff levels in the FTA versus CU debate[13].

If countries have to use tariffs for revenue purposes, then forming a RTA may be more difficult as it will entail a loss of revenue, unless co-operation improves collection rates or member countries raise tariffs on imports from excluded countries. In the latter case, the RTA is likely to reduce welfare of its members both because of trade diversion at existing external tariffs, and because of the increased protection against excluded countries. Moreover, there are other potentially complex revenue issues to consider: e.g. how to avoid fiscal competition between members reducing taxes below optimal levels.

C. Investment

Raising investment is a prominent objective of many regional agreements. The logic is that larger markets, greater competition and improved policy credibility will increase the incentives for investment and so raise incomes. The argument applies to all investment, but is most explicitly applied to regionalism as a means of attracting foreign direct investment. Ethier composes a paean to regionalism on this basis, although expresses some serious reservations about his model[14].

Early Latin American RTAs were interventionist, co-opting regional integration into import substitution at a regional level. Such policies almost completely failed and have now been superseded by a much more market-friendly approach. Part of the latter has been a greater emphasis on policies guaranteeing the fair treatment of investment. These guarantees are often embodied in Bilateral Investment Treaties ("BITs"), or, where they exist, the investment chapters of RTA agreements. BITs typically contribute to negative integration—i.e. precluding certain policies rather than requiring policies to actively encourage investment—but they may play an important facilitating role in investment flows.

Far more positive in intent is the common argument that RTAs add credibility to government policies in general and thus help to raise investment and attract foreign direct investment ("FDI"). But contrary to the prevailing enthusiasm, South-South RTAs are unlikely to do this and may, in fact, hinder investment if they are not accompanied by trade liberalization with the rest of the world. North-South RTAs, on the other hand, can enhance a Southern country's credibility, but typically, only if the RTA is likely to enhance economic performance in its own right and if the large Northern partner is willing to enforce investment-encouraging "club rules". The latter is more likely to be true if the policies on which a developing country wants to gain credibility are specified explicitly in the agreement and if the Northern partner has an identified interest in the Southern partner's success—e.g. alleviating pressure to migrate.

Recent analysis holds that the rate of return on capital (and investment) could well rise in all members of an RTA regardless of their capital abundance[15]. For example, if tradables are more capital-intensive than non-tradables, opening up boosts the demand for capital;

L. Alan Winters, *What's behind Mercosur's Common External Tariff?*, CEPR DISCUSSION PAPER, No. 2310 (1999).

[13] Kimberly Clausig, *Customs Unions and Free Trade Areas*, 15 J. OF ECONOMIC INTEGRATION 418 (2000).

[14] Wilfred J. Ethier, *Regional Roads to Multilateralism*, in INTERNATIONAL TRADE POLICY AND THE PACIFIC RIM (John Piggott and Alan Woodland eds. 1998).

[15] Richard E. Baldwin and Elena Seghezza, *Growth and European Integration: Towards an Empirical Assessment*, CENTRE FOR ECONOMIC POLICY RESEARCH, DISCUSSION PAPER No. 1393 (1995).

lower tariffs and trading costs for capital equipment might reduce the price of investment goods; and creating a more efficient financial sector could reduce borrowing costs.

Unfortunately there are few empirical studies of the impact of RTAs on investment—most trade blocs are so new that the data are simply not there. Where we do have evidence, it tends to suggest mild positive effects on investment, but there is no evidence that this translates into higher economic growth. Firmer evidence is available that RTAs boost FDI, however, especially inflows of investment from non-member countries. In Latin America, both Mexico and Mercosur illustrate this. In Mexico, most FDI has been going to exportable sectors and seems to have generated large benefits. In Mercosur, most FDI seems to have gone to protected (and thus inefficient) import-competing sectors, and protection has even been increased to attract FDI in some sectors (e.g., automotive sector). In these cases factors of production are drained out of efficient sectors into the protected ones, with greater wastage the greater the FDI flow. Thus in the presence of protection, FDI can be harmful.

The real key to investment is the general policy stance in areas such as sound macroeconomic policies, well-defined property rights, and efficient financial and banking sectors. Regional integration may foster investment if it significantly raises policy credibility and market size, but it needs to be accompanied by good policy overall.

Investment patterns can be seriously affected by the so-called hub-and-spoke phenomenon. This occurs when a country (the hub) signs FTAs with various countries (the spokes) which do not sign FTAs among themselves. Other things equal, investors will prefer to invest in the exporting sectors of the hub than in those of the spokes, because they can reach all the spokes from the hub but cannot do so from one of the spokes. For instance, the EU has signed FTAs with Mediterranean countries (Euro-Med Agreements), Central and Eastern European countries (Europe Agreements), South Africa and Mexico, and is negotiating with MERCOSUR and Chile. These are all spokes of the EU hub. One way to minimize the potential negative FDI effect is for a spoke to sign FTAs with other countries (e.g., Mexico in NAFTA).

D. Industrial Location and Growth

While economists have long been aware that industry tends to cluster into particular locations, they have only recently learned to model the phenomenon formally and thus to start to identify precisely the combinations of conditions that must be satisfied for it to occur. The theory arose from attempts to understand the possible effects of the enlargement and deepening of the European Union and so lends itself directly to the consideration of RTAs[16]. The theory is, however, very young; the models do not yet appear to be very realistic and have not yet been accompanied by much empirical evidence. Thus they are more parables than forecasts. However, they do shed light on qualitative factors and they address such a major concern of policy makers that it is useful to explore their implications for developing countries.

Creating an RTA is likely to affect the incentives for industry to agglomerate, usually to increase them because it increases market size and allows more effective exploitation of the links between firms[17]. An RTA may attract industry into member countries at the

---

[16] Paul Krugman and Anthony J. Venables, *Integration and the Competitiveness of Peripheral Industry*, in UNITY WITH DIVERSITY IN THE EUROPEAN COMMUNITY (Christopher Bliss and Jaime De Macedo eds. 1990).
[17] *See* MASAHISA FUJITA, MASAHISA, PAUL KRUGMAN AND ANTHONY VENABLES, THE SPATIAL ECONOMY: CITIES, REGIONS, AND INTERNATIONAL TRADE (1999) for a comprehensive coverage.

expense of non-members, although if the RTA is small, such effects will also be very small. RTAs will also frequently cause industry to relocate between the members. For RTAs between poor countries this seems likely to increase inter-member inequalities because it makes it easier for firms to agglomerate in the more prosperous countries while still selling in the others. For RTAs involving richer members, on the other hand, the results are less clear-cut, and it is quite possible that poorer members will experience strong industrialization following an RTA. For developing countries, integration with richer neighbors (North-South RTAs) looks far better from an agglomeration point of view than does South-South integration.

The same preference for North–South over South-South RTAs arises from the discussion of long-run growth. Modern growth theory—the theory of endogenous growth—stresses the role of knowledge in fostering productivity and growth. It also stresses that knowledge can be effectively transferred from one country to another through international contact and trade. Rich countries are knowledge-rich and so are likely to provide far more access to technology than are poorer trading partners: RTAs that switch imports from richer to poorer sources are very likely to have a perverse effect on countries' growth rates[18]. RTAs might also help countries boost their growth rates by supporting institutional reform, and again this effect seems likely to be stronger for developing countries joining with richer partners than with poorer ones.

The direct evidence on trade and growth has been subjected to some serious methodological reservations by Francisco Rodriguez and Dani Rodrik[19]—but that on RTAs and growth is actually pretty consistent. There is little evidence that RTAs between developed countries stimulate growth, and absolutely none that RTAs between developing countries do so[20]. Given that one needs long runs of data to explore economic growth, we do not have any sound empirical evidence on North-South RTAs. Casual consideration of the recent performances of, say, Portugal and Mexico, however, suggests that serious North-South integration may foster the Southern partners' growth, reinforcing the views above about the relative merits of the two types of partners for developing countries. As discussed above, however, there are formidable problems in defining an *anti-monde* to underpin such statements.[21]

E. Domestic Policies

The discussion so far has concentrated just on trade and investment policies, the standard building blocks for analysing international intercourse. But as trade barriers have come down policy makers have started to understand the very important role that domestic regulation plays in economic integration. Cooperation on domestic policies can

---

[18] This is an implication of David T. Coe, Elhanan Helpman and Alexander. W. Hoffmaister, *North-South R&D Spillovers*, 107 ECONOMIC JOURNAL 134(1997) although not one the authors bring out. The issue is explained more fully in Emiko Fukase and L. Alan Winters, POSSIBLE DYNAMIC BENEFITS OF ASEAN/AFTA ACCESSION FOR THE NEW MEMBER COUNTRIES (1999).

[19] Francisco Rodriguez and Dani Rodrik, *Trade Policy and Economic Growth: A Skeptic's Guide to the Cross-national Evidence*, NBER MACROECONOMICS ANNUAL 2000 (2001).

[20] *See*, most tellingly, Athenasios Vamvakidis, *Regional Trade Agreements Versus Broad Liberalisation: Which Path Leads to Faster Growth? Time Series Evidence*, 46 IMF STAFF PAPERS 1 (1999).

[21] EU-Portugal and USA-Mexico are effectively North-South arrangements because of the large differences in incomes per head between the members. It is true, however, that similar sized differences could have quite different implications at much lower incomes levels for both partners—e.g. Vietnam-Malaysia in AFTA.

substantially increase the gains from forming a trade bloc. It can lift barriers that insulate national markets for similar goods and services and deliver economic benefits many times larger than those available from mere trade agreements. Inter-governmental cooperation in designing and applying domestic policies such as taxes, health and safety regulations, environmental standards—so-called policy integration—can increase competition in domestic markets by reducing transaction costs and allowing new suppliers to enter markets. Cooperation on domestic policies can also help to overcome market failures and help to ensure that trade restrictions are not re-imposed through the back door.

However, most RTAs have only "shallow" policy integration aims. Their objective is not economic union (which requires institution-building and which we would term "deep integration"), but to increase competition through inter-governmental cooperation to reduce market segmentation. The FTAA is discussing policy integration, and some existing Latin American agreements also speak of pursuing it further. However, without specific timetables for progress and further negotiation, none is likely to make great progress. Experience suggests that negotiated policy integration is very demanding both politically and technically. Moreover, RTAs are not the only game in town. Indeed, independent decisions to adopt policies used elsewhere and to pursue multilateral efforts on international technical and regulatory standards have been more common than regional efforts. Developing countries can do much to achieve the benefits of policy integration unilaterally by adopting international standards and recognizing the regulatory norms of their major markets, such as the EU and the United States.

One puzzle is 'why combine policy integration and trade integration into the same institution?' The trade component of an RTA can provide negotiating chips to help overcome opposition to institutional and domestic policy reforms, and policy integration can assist the implementation and enforcement of RTA trade policies. Of course, such linkage does not excuse selecting sub-optimal trade and domestic reforms, but if both are desirable in their own right, combining them might be politically efficient. Fundamentally, there is no technical reason why integrating domestic policies should require trade preferences. The EU and the United States have, for instance, drawn up a series of mutual recognition agreements for sectoral product standards completely outside an RTA context. To date, however, developing countries have been entirely excluded from such initiatives. Wherever possible policy integration that reduces regulatory costs should extend beyond RTA partners to non-members—so that the increase in competition is maximized and policy integration benefits all trading partners. Formal inter-governmental agreements—such as mutual recognition arrangements for product standards and testing—may be necessary for policy integration, but special efforts should be made to ensure that these do not perpetuate or increase discrimination. Discriminatory policy integration—such as including preferential rules of origin in mutual recognition agreements—should be resisted.

Competition between regulatory regimes coupled with mutual recognition is often the most efficient route to policy integration. Some element of harmonization may be called for if there are spillovers—such as a threat that the competitive relaxation of merger regulation will lead to a "race to the bottom"—or to safeguard public health or safety. These are generally best limited to minimum standards based on global norms. RTAs can serve as focal points for adopting and enforcing global minimum standards, but regional standards that diverge from global norms will be optimal only if there are region-specific characteristics.

F. Politics

Countries sometimes form trade blocs for so-called non-economic reasons, such as national security, peace, and help in developing political and social institutions. These are public goods, and so are unlikely to be efficiently provided in the absence of some form of intervention—of which creating an RTA is one. Such political objectives can be important for RTAs, sometimes overwhelmingly so, but it is still desirable that they be achieved efficiently and that policy makers pay heed to their economic cost.

Political benefits such as peace and security can sometimes swamp the simple material considerations that usually determine economic policy. Moreover, since such benefits are typically shared by only a limited number of countries—usually neighbors— they are likely to be better sought on a regional basis than multilaterally. Thus this issue forms a relatively more important part of the analysis of RTAs than of some other international issues. We have shown that under some circumstances, the formation of an RTA may be an effective way to deal with security tensions between neighbouring countries; the argument is essentially that mutual trade fosters peace between countries and regionalism fosters trade[22]. They show that for such a 'political' RTA, the optimum tariff on imports from non-members declines over time, and also as integration deepens. Mercosur may have experienced such political benefits on relations between its two major members.

Joining an RTA with large democratic countries can help a developing country to achieve or uphold democracy if the RTA imposes "club rules" such as democracy and civil rights on its members. This assistance is likely to be more effective if the other members are large economically because larger partners are generally able to impose greater costs on (withdraw greater benefits from) recalcitrants than are smaller ones. It is also likely to be more effective if the developing country in question is of a reasonable size, and if its potential partners are close by. A partner country is likely to be far more concerned about possible spillovers from events in a significantly sized and nearby developing country than elsewhere. Mexico may be one example of this sort of effect; Mercosur's role in deflecting a coup in Paraguay in 1996 is another.[23]

A concern in many RTA members is whether increased regional integration will weaken the nation-state. On the contrary, pooling sovereignty and undertaking collective action can enhance the effectiveness of the state in small or even medium-sized nations. They can assist in solving economic problems, strengthen countries against third-country security threats, and increase international influence by lowering negotiation costs and/or increasing bargaining power in dealings with the rest of the world. Caricom is the archetypal success in negotiating terms[24]. As we argued above, however, cooperation of this kind does not usually require trade preferences.

III. Non-Member Countries and The Trading System

This section considers how regionalism affects the interactions between countries within the international economy and community. Regrettably, many of the arguments are only theoretical, for we do not have enough observations of long-lived regionalism to make empirical judgements, and as we enter the twenty-first century, we are dealing with a

[22] Maurice Schiff and L. Alan Winters, *Regional Integration as Diplomacy*, 12(2) THE WORLD BANK ECONOMIC REVIEW 271 (1998).

[23] *See, e.g.,* THE ECONOMIST, October 12, 1996.

[24] See Soamiely Andriamananjara and Maurice Schiff, *Regional Groupings among Microstates*, 9(1) REVIEW OF INTERNATIONAL ECONOMICS 42–51 (2001).

completely new world of many active trade blocs as opposed to the twentieth century model of a multilateral world with a few blocs.

A. Excluded Countries

RTAs are, by nature, exclusive. After all every country in the world is excluded from nearly every RTA in the world, and every RTA excludes nearly every country. Their discrimination against excluded countries is real and, according to the latest evidence, causes significant trade diversion in some cases. Trade diversion is mainly a cost to the partners who pay more for their imports, but in two sets of circumstances, it can be costly to the excluded countries which lose exports[25].

First, if exports generate super-normal profits, losing them is costly because the income lost exceeds the value of the resources freed up by not having to produce them any more. One example would be if the exporter could charge monopoly prices. A second, more important one, is where exports are taxed, because the tax-inclusive price received for them exceeds the cost of the resources used up in production. Export taxes are rare, but trade theory teaches us that import taxes are export taxes—it is the act of trading (turning exports into imports) that is taxed and it does not matter which side of the transaction formally faces the tax. Thus, any of the many countries with significant tariffs will lose welfare if its exports fall because of others' RTAs.

The second case where trade diversion hurts exporters is if the decline in demand forces down export prices—i.e. worsens the exporter's terms of trade. Chang and Winters present new evidence that this is significant empirically for Brazil's imports of goods following the creation of Mercosur[26]. The prices of US exports **fell** so far that the USA could have lost over half a billion dollars per year in economic welfare via this route.

B. Stepping Stones, Dominoes and Open Regionalism

Possibly even more important than the static losses suffered by excluded countries is the issue of whether RTAs are stepping stones toward the long-run goal of globally freer trade, or millstones slowing progress towards it. The world of many trade blocs is still too new to allow a definitive empirical answer to this question, and economic theory is not completely clear on the matter, but our reading of the case is that there are significant dangers that regionalism could start to undermine the multilateral trading system[27]. Certainly, it hits at one of the corner stones of procedural multilateralism—the equal treatment of all.

In terms of outcomes, the majority of analyses of the effects of bloc-formation on the tariffs that non-co-operating governments would charge each other suggest that tariffs tend to increase with the spread of regionalism[28]. In some cases regionalism has been

---

[25] Won Chang and L. Alan Winters, *Preferential Trading Arrangements and Excluded Countries: Ex-Post Estimates of the Effects on Price*, 24(6) THE WORLD ECONOMY 797 (2001).

[26] Won Chang and L. Alan Winters, *How Regional Blocs Affect Excluded Countries: The Price Effects of MERCOSUR*, CENTRE FOR ECONOMIC POLICY RESEARCH, DISCUSSION PAPER SERIES, NO. 2179(1999).

[27] L. Alan Winters, *Regionalism versus Multilateralism*, in MARKET INTEGRATION, REGIONALISM AND THE GLOBAL ECONOMY (Richard E. Baldwin, Daniel Cohen, Andre Sapir and Anthony J. Venables, eds. 1999).

[28] An early proof of this proposition is in Paul Krugman, *Is Bilateralism Bad?*, in INTERNATIONAL TRADE AND TRADE POLICY (Elhanan Helpmann and Assaf Razin eds. 1991) and in Paul Krugman,, *Regionalism versus Multinationalism: Analytical Notes*, in NEW DIMENSION IN REGIONAL INTEGRATION, (Jaime De Melo and Arvind Panagariya eds. 1993). Although much of Krugman's modeling has proved fragile to small changes in assumptions his basic insight has remained untouched.

argued to bring other countries to the negotiating table to agree a new round of multilateral trade liberalisation—e.g. the formation of the EEC and the Kennedy Round—but we would argue that this is far from certain and that using such coercive tactics to get others to reduce their tariffs is extremely dangerous.

It is also possible that one act of regionalism would be met by another—giving rise to Richard Baldwin's so-called 'domino regionalism'[29] This seems to lie behind much of the spread of regionalism over the 1980s and 1990s—for example, when Canada sought access to the US-Mexican talks that eventually created NAFTA, and with several Latin American and Caribbean countries seeking accession afterwards. It is important to note, however, that under such conditions one cannot infer that, because regionalism is spreading, it is benign. If everyone is in a gang, you may want to belong to one yourself, but that does not make gangs a good thing.

One of the analytical problems with domino regionalism is that although enlarging an RTA might increase the incentives for new members to join, it does not correspondingly increase the incentives for existing members to let new ones in. Given that RTAs discriminate against excluded countries, insiders will want to stop expansion well short of the whole world—there is no point being on the inside if there is no one on the outside to exploit. For example, NAFTA has rejected overtures from many countries, and APEC had a moratorium on accession from 1993 to 1996, although in fairness, these instances were probably more to do with avoiding the strains of additional adjustment for members (especially the United States) than any exploitative intent. Whether to let more countries in or not, and how many, also depends on the entry conditions, i.e., whether it is free, whether existing members require payment for the benefits that accrue to the new member, whether they require compensation for any losses they may incur[30].

It is sometimes argued that one way around the problem of blockaded entry would be to insist on open access to all RTAs—i.e. that any country that could adhere to the rules of an RTA could join it and reap its benefits. In theory, this may be true, but in practice, given that accession has to be negotiated because the rules of nearly all RTAs entail more than just tariff reductions, there is no operational way to insist on such access. The concept of 'open regionalism', which has several definitions, is related to this[31]. We see this as more a slogan than an analytical tool, for, according to the definition, it either reduces to something else (e.g. multilateralism) or it does not separate 'good' RTAs from 'bad'.

C. Trade Negotiations

If RTAs made trade negotiations easier, perhaps they would help the world evolve toward freer trade. Co-ordinated coalitions may have greater negotiating power than their members individually, and such coalitions may facilitate progress just by reducing the number of players represented in a negotiation[32]. But the gains from having fewer players in the last stage of a negotiation are offset by the complexity of agreeing joint positions in the first phase. The difficulties of achieving a European position on agriculture and cultural protection in the Uruguay Round are well known, and formulating EEC positions in the

---

[29] Richard E. Baldwin, *A Domino Theory of Regionalism*, in EXPANDING MEMBERSHIP OF THE EUROPEAN UNION (Richard E. Baldwin, P. Haaparanta and J. Kiander eds. 1995).

[30] Andriamananjara and Schiff, *supra* note 25.

[31] Fred Bergsten, *Open Regionalism*, 20 WORLD ECONOMY 545 (1997).

[32] Paul Krugman, *Regionalism versus Multilateralism: Analytical Notes, supra,* note 29; MILES KAHLER, INTERNATIONAL INSTITUTIONS AND THE POLITICAL ECONOMY OF INTEGRATION (1995)

Tokyo Round proved complex[33]. Moreover, two-stage negotiations need not be more liberal than one-stage ones[34]. To be sure, Germany and the United Kingdom pressured France to agree to the agricultural deal in the Uruguay Round, but the liberalizers had to make potentially trade-restricting concessions on "commercial defense instruments" to clinch the deal.

The CUs that attend the next round of global trade talks will need to establish procedures for determining their negotiating positions. SACU's previous practice of delegating all responsibility to South Africa begins to look less tenable as divisions emerge between members, and Mercosur has yet to devise really robust internal decision-making capacity. Thus, at least into the foreseeable future, RTAs do not seem likely to facilitate even a traditional trade negotiation.

Moreover, as the WTO has extended its reach, it has embraced subjects in which most central CU authorities have no mandate to negotiate. Mixing national and CU responsibilities seems unlikely to simplify matters, and it is not realistic to expect member countries to surrender sovereignty on sensitive issues to regional bodies just because trade negotiations are in train.

D. Depth and Breadth in Integration

RTAs are also suggested as ways of developing blueprints for technically complex issues before they come to the global level, or as ways of tackling politically difficult issues that can not yet be agreed globally. In fact, this is not as widespread as is sometimes thought—RTAs often avoid difficult issues. Moreover, is regionalism actually more effective in liberalizing deeply than multilateralism? Has global liberalization actually been ruled out or, if RTAs were not an option, would a little more time and effort yield global progress? Having got the ball rolling, will RTAs later slow it down for the reasons discussed above? On a prescriptive note, to the extent that RTAs are justified in terms of opening up otherwise closed sectors, it is important to ensure that the subsequent switch from regionalism to the multilateral track is managed effectively. The necessity for, and the means to achieve, this switch should be written into the initial terms of RTAs.

One danger of the regional approach is that the major powers seek to use RTAs to reinforce their initial positions in future multilateral negotiations. If major players have greater politico-economic power within their own regions than in the world in general, it is easy to imagine their building up coalitions for their own policies before taking issues into a multilateral round. Sylvia Ostry has argued that the United States used approaches by potential partners in the Americas and Asia to broaden the negotiating agenda for its relations with Europe[35], while Europe did the same with the EEA and its Europe Agreements.

The benefits of developing regional blueprints depend heavily on whether they are liberalizing and whether they are otherwise well suited to developing country needs and capacities[36]. Major powers already use access to the Generalised System of Preferences

[33] GILBERT R. WINHAM, INTERNATIONAL TRADE AND THE TOKYO ROUND NEGOTIATIONS. (1986)

[34] Giorgio Basevi, Flavio Delbono and Marco Mariotti, *Bargaining with a Composite Player: An Application to the Uruguay Round of GATT Negotiations*, 3 J. OF INTERNATIONAL AND COMPARATIVE ECONOMICS 161(1994)

[35] Sylvia Ostry, *Presentation to the First Academic Colloquium of the Americas, Costa Rica* (1998)

[36] *See,* for example, Jagdish Bhagwati, *Regionalism and Multilateralism: An Overview*, in NEW DIMENSIONS IN REGIONAL INTEGRATION (Jaime De Melo and Arvind Panagariya eds. 1993).

("GSP") to impose environmental and labour conditions on developing countries; the EU looks for action in such areas and on intellectual property in the Europe Agreements, and the United States has used NAFTA as a tool for enforcing Mexican labor and environmental standards. By undermining the natural cohesion of developing countries on these topics in the WTO, RTAs could lead to very different outcomes than will straight multilateralism. It is likely that the outcome will suit developing countries less well, and may be less open and liberal as well.

Moreover, there are dangers in such tactics. First, even if the majors' aspirations are desirable in their own terms, building up rival teams can make final negotiations more, rather than less, difficult. Second, even when only one regional bloc is advocating a policy, other countries might sufficiently resent the pressure to adopt it that they pull back. Developing country *de facto* rejection of the OECD draft Multilateral Agreement on Investment in 1998 contains at least elements of this. Third, the time it takes to build regional coalitions can delay multilateral talks. Fourth, coalitions rooted in formal RTAs are here to stay, so that if multilateral processes fail, the blocs remain. This is quite different from a negotiating coalition, which dissolves if it fails to gain its objectives.

To be sure, progress is required in "new" areas such as standards, but it is frequently better pursued independently of tariff preferences. Thus, while we may as well learn from RTAs about how to tackle particular aspects of liberalization, this is not a convincing reason for pursuing regionalism per se.

C.   Developing Country Perspectives

CHAPTER 52

LDCs IN THE MULTILATERAL TRADING SYSTEM

Ratnakar Adhikari*

TABLE OF CONTENTS

* Executive Director, South Asia Watch on Trade, Economics & Environment (SAWTEE), Katmandu, Nepal

I. Background

In 1971, the poorest countries of the world were designated by the United Nations as the least developed countries ("LDCs").[1] Based on the criteria established at that time 25 countries fell into this category. However, over the period of last three decades, the number of countries falling into this category continued to grow, with only one country, Botswana, so far having been able to graduate to developing country status. At present there are 49 LDCs in the world.[2]

In its latest triennial review of the list of Least Developed Countries in 2000, the Economic and Social Council of the United Nations ("ECOSOC") used the following three criteria for determining the new list, as proposed by the Committee for Development Policy: low income, human resource weakness and economic vulnerability.[3] In the 2000 review of the list, a country qualified to be added to the list if it met the above three criteria and did not have a population greater than 75 million. Application of this rule resulted in the inclusion of Senegal.[4]

According to the UNCTAD Least Developed Countries Report for 2000 ("UNCTAD LDC Report 2000"), if the present trend of economic growth and/or recovery continues, only one country (Lesotho) will be able to graduate to developing country status by 2015.[5] At their current growth rates only four countries (Bhutan, Laos, Lesotho and Sudan) are likely to reach the threshold for graduation by 2025. At least seventeen LDCs, all from Africa, are either facing negative growth rates or are stagnant, such that they are not likely to be graduated to developing country status even after a hundred years.[6] Real GDP per capita in LDCs grew by only 0.9 percent per annum during 1990–98, and excluding Bangladesh by only 0.4 percent per annum.[7] An important feature of the performance of most LDC economies is the significant degree of income instability, with periods of slow growth followed by sharp declines in *per capita* incomes. Most of the LDCs are characterized by a low level of human development indicators. LDCs account for 32 of the 35 countries in the lowest category of the UNDP's Human Development Index.

LDCs have, for decades, been striving to find the right development strategy to enable them to reduce the economic disparities between them and more advanced economies. Over the past two decades an increasing number of LDCs have placed their hopes on

[1] UNCTAD website http://www.unctad.org/ldcs/, accessed on June 3, 2002

[2] These include 34 countries in Africa (Angola, Benin, Burkina Faso, Burundi, Cape Verde, Central African Rep., Chad, Comoros, Djibouti, Equatorial Guinea, Eritrea, Ethiopia, Gambia, Guinea, Guinea Bissau, Lesotho, Liberia, Madagascar, Malawi, Mali, Mauritania, Mozambique, Niger, Rwanda, Sao Tome & Principe, Senegal, Sierra Leone, Somalia, Sudan, Tanzania, Togo, Uganda, Zaire, Zambia); nine in Asia (Afghanistan, Bangladesh, Bhutan, Burma, Cambodia, Laos, Maldives, Nepal, Yemen), five in the Pacific (Kiribati, Samoa, Solomon Islands, Tuvalu, Vanuatu) and one in the Caribbean (Haiti).

[3] The low-income criterion is based on a three-year average estimate of the gross domestic product per capita (under $900 for inclusion, above $1,035 for graduation). The human resource weakness criterion involves a composite *Augmented Physical Quality of Life Index (APQLI)* based on indicators of: (a) nutrition; (b) health; (c) education; and (d) adult literacy. Finally the economic vulnerability criterion involves a composite *Economic Vulnerability Index (EVI)* based on indicators of: (a) the instability of agricultural production; (b) the instability of exports of goods and services; (c) the economic importance of non-traditional activities (share of manufacturing and modern services in GDP); (d) merchandise export concentration; and (e) the handicap of economic smallness (as measured through the population in logarithm). *See* UNCTAD, *supra* note 1

[4] There were 48 LDCs in the world for a long time. Inclusion of Senegal increased the number to 49.

[5] *The Least Developed Countries, 2000 Report*, at XXX (3) UNCTAD/LDC/2000 E.00.II.D.21 (December 10, 2000)

[6] *Id.*

[7] *Id.* at 3

a development strategy based on increased participation in the world economy, through exports and inward foreign investment.[8] Indeed, according to the UNCTAD LDC Report 2000, trade liberalization in the LDCs has actually proceeded further than in other developing countries. In 1999, sixty percent of the 43 LDCs for which data is available had average tariff barriers below twenty percent and non-tariff barriers that covered less than 25 percent of production and trade. Similarly, UNCTAD data on foreign investment regimes in the late 1990s shows that out of a sample of 45 LDCs, only nine maintained strict controls on the remittance of dividends and profits and capital repatriation.[9] However, their success in both increasing their trade and attracting FDI has remained marginal. It is worrisome to note that the LDCs, despite serious efforts to integrate themselves into the multilateral trading system, are being marginalized from the system.

Against this background, the objectives of this chapter are to analyze the factors responsible for the marginalization of LDCs from the multilateral trading system and to propose policies for the LDCs themselves and for the international community as a whole on how to prevent (and if possible reverse) this process. The chapter is organized as follows: Part II outlines the historical background of the participation of the LDCs in the multilateral trading system up to the second Ministerial Conference of the WTO. Part III analyzes the weaknesses plaguing the LDCs and the reasons for their persistence. Part IV presents a critical appraisal of the efforts made so far to integrate LDCs into the multilateral trading system and the reasons for their failure. Part V deals with the outcomes of the two major international conferences held in 2001 and attempts made (or lack of them) during those conferences to integrate LDCs into the multilateral trading system. Part VI provides a policy prescription for the LDCs. Finally, Part VII provides some concluding thoughts.

II. LDCs and the Multilateral Trading System: A Historical Perspective

The 49 LDCs, which collectively are home to 10.7 percent of the global population, have a 0.5 percent share in global GNP.[10] Their collective share in global trade is rapidly falling and it now stands at 0.4 percent.[11] While the decade of 1980s was dubbed the "lost decade" for developing countries in general, the 1990s became the decade of increasing marginalization, inequality, poverty and social exclusion for the LDCs.[12] If the present trend continues, the decade of the 2000s may well become a decade of rhetoric and inaction. The experience of many LDCs during the 1990s show that despite massive economic liberalization, the overall progress in increasing real incomes, combating poverty, and achieving human development has remained disappointing.[13] The efforts made at the international level to integrate these countries into the multilateral trading

---

[8] UNCTAD and Commonwealth Secretariat, DUTY AND QUOTA FREE MARKET ACCESS FOR LDCs: AN ANALYSIS OF QUAD INITIATIVE 1 (2001)

[9] *See* John Cuddy, *The State of Development in Least Developed Countries*, BRIDGES MONTHLY REVIEW, Year 5, No 4, 3 (May 2001)

[10] UNCTAD, STATISTICAL PROFILES OF THE LEAST DEVELOPED COUNTRIES 4 (2001).

[11] While the share of LDCs in global trade declined from 0.48 percent in 1990 to 0.4 percent in 1999, exports nevertheless now represent 49 percent of their gross domestic product, compared with 35.8 percent a decade ago, thus signifying increased openness to trade. *See*, International Centre for Trade and Sustainable Development ("ICTSD"), *Least-Developed Countries: No New Trade Concessions Before Doha,* in BRIDGES MONTHLY REVIEW, Year 5, No. 4, at 2 (May 2001).

[12] Cuddy, *supra* note 9 at 4.

[13] Hiramani Ghimire, *Least-Developed Countries in Search of Identity in the WTO*, in SALVAGING THE WTO'S FUTURE—DOHA AND BEYOND 350 (Amit Dasgupta and Bibek Debroy eds. 2001).

system so far have largely failed. With this background, we now discuss the history of participation of the LDCs into the multilateral trading system.

A. The Post-War Period

Prior to the Uruguay Round ("UR"), the preoccupation of the LDCs had been mainly with preserving and improving the preferential trade liberalization they received from major trading partners through various programs, paying little if any attention to the multilateral trade negotiations conducted under the auspices of the GATT, which were traditionally confined to the reduction of tariff and non-tariff barriers to trade. The perceived limited interest in the GATT trade liberalization process could partially be explained by the inability of the LDCs to supply foreign markets on a competitive basis, and thus their limited capacity to take advantage of global trade liberalization on a most-favored-nation ("MFN") basis.[14]

During the post-war period (or post-colonial period for some), it was the view of a number of prominent development economists that the quickest way for developing countries to achieve industrial status was through the adoption of import substitution policies.[15] This prescription led a number of developing countries to adopt an import substitution industrialization strategy, little realizing that this would only breed vested interest groups, requiring perpetual protection, taxing efficiency, and creating massive rents.[16] The market failure justification for infant industry protection did not work for the LDCs, despite the fact that it worked quite well in some East and South East Asian countries.[17] While developing countries in East Asia were quick to abandon such a strategy in favor of an open trade and investment regime, and were followed by countries in Latin America, the LDCs took a long time to come out of the vicious circle of protectionism, low income, low saving, low investment and limited investment in the creation of social and physical capital.

The 1960s witnessed the entry of a number of LDCs into the GATT system. Myanmar (formerly Burma), was the only LDC to be a founding member (Contracting Party) of the GATT, while Haiti was the first non-founding LDC to join the club, in 1950. This was followed by the entry of Tanzania and Sierra Leone in 1961. A large number of African LDCs entered the GATT between 1963 and 1965. Only two Asian LDCs entered the club, but much later than their African counterparts. While Bangladesh joined GATT in 1972, the Maldives did not join until 1983.[18] No other LDCs from the Asia-Pacific region are Members of the GATT/WTO. They have been unable to secure accession to the GATT/WTO, for various reasons discussed in Part III.F of this chapter.

At the insistence of the developing countries that they be provided special treatment within the GATT system, Part IV titled "Trade and Development" was added to the

---

[14] Rubens Ricupero, *Foreword* in FUTURE MULTILATERAL TRADE NEGOTIATIONS: HANDBOOK FOR TRADE NEGOTIATORS FROM LEAST DEVELOPED COUNTRIES vii (1999).

[15] Edwin Kwame Kessie, *Developing Countries and the World Trade Organization: What Has Changed*, 22 WORLD COMPETITION 2, 86 (1999)

[16] The Import Substitution Industrialization strategy, defined as "the strategy of encouraging domestic industry by limiting imports of manufactured goods", is now completely discredited and abandoned. This strategy was chosen by the developing countries and LDCs based mainly on the theories of *infant industries* and *market failure*. For further details, *see* PAUL R. KRUGMAN AND MAURICE OBSTFELD, INTERNATIONAL ECONOMICS: THEORY AND POLICY 255–261 (2000)

[17] Notable examples are South Korea and China. *See* Dani Rodrik, *Trading in Illusion,* FOREIGN POLICY, March-April 2001.

[18] The list of GATT Members which had joined the GATT by 1994 and their date of accession can be found at http://www.wto.org/english/thewto_e/gattmem_e.htm, accessed on June 3, 2002

GATT text in 1964. The next major GATT event from the perspective of developing countries was the introduction by most advanced economies of the Generalised System of Preferences ("GSP"), granting them preferential market access. The European Union and Japan introduced their GSP programs in 1971, Canada in 1974, and the United States in 1976.[19] Since these tariff preferences were inconsistent with the general most favored nation ("MFN") principle embodied in GATT Article I, the GSP programs required a GATT waiver. Initially, in 1971, a ten-year waiver was granted, but this was superseded in 1979 by the so-called Enabling Clause[20], making the GSP a permanent feature of the multilateral trading system.[21] However, the "concessions" granted to developing countries such as the inclusion in the GATT of Part IV on Trade and Development and the Tokyo Round Enabling Clause on special and differential treatment were mostly rhetorical, and others, such as the GSP, were always heavily qualified and quantitatively small. In sum, the GATT was indifferent, if not actively hostile, to the interests of the developing countries.[22]

B. The Uruguay Round

Viewed from the perspective of the developing countries in general and the LDCs in particular, the Uruguay Round was a disaster. This was mainly due to lack of preparedness on their part. However, towards the end of the Round, they managed to secure some special arrangements as well as the continuation of previous arrangements. This was possible because of their market conditions, the weakness of their institutions, and their relative lack of capacity.[23]

Acknowledgement of the difficulties which the developing countries, particularly the LDCs, are likely to encounter in fulfilling their obligations under the UR was expressed through the continuation of the special and differential ("S&D") provisions of the GATT in various WTO agreements. These provided for: (i) a lower level of obligations; (ii) more flexible implementation schedules; (iii) best endeavor commitments by developed countries; (iv) more favorable treatment for least-developed countries; and (v) technical assistance and training.[24]

Meanwhile, between 1988 and 1993, while the UR negotiations were in progress, the terms-of-trade of the LDCs fell on average by about twelve percent, although in 1994–95

[19] The GSP is defined in UNCTAD Resolution No. 21/1968. The main principles underlying the GSP programs are: i) Generality (all developing countries and beneficiaries); ii) non-reciprocity (no obligation of developing countries to reciprocate); and iii) non-discrimination among beneficiaries. *See* UNCTAD AND COMMONWEALTH SECRETARIAT, *supra* note 8, at 9.

[20] The official name of the Enabling Clause is the *Decision on Differential and More Favourable Treatment, Reciprocity and Fuller Participation of Developing Countries*, Decision of the GATT Contracting Parties of November 28, 1979.

[21] UNCTAD AND COMMONWEALTH SECRETARIAT, *supra* note 8, at 8.

[22] T.N. Srinivasan, *Developing Countries in the World Trading System: From GATT, 1947 to the Third Ministerial Meeting of WTO,* a revised version of the Keynote Speech delivered at the HIGH LEVEL SYMPOSIUM ON TRADE AND DEVELOPMENT, World Trade Organization, 10 (1999)

[23] These included the *Decision on Measures in Favour of Least-Developed Countries, the Decision on Measures Concerning the Possible Negative Effects of Reform Program on Least-Developed and Net Food-Importing* Developing Countries, and the Declaration on the Contribution of the WTO to Achieving Greater Coherence in *Global Economic Policy Making* reproduced in THE LEGAL TEXTS: THE RESULTS OF THE URUGUAY ROUND OF MULTILATERAL NEGOTIATIONS 384, 386, 392 (1999). *See* DEBAPRIYA BHATTACHARYA AND MUSTAFIZUR RAHMAN, *The Least Developed Countries in The WTO: Strengthening Participation Capacities*, paper prepared for the MEETING OF SENIOR OFFICIALS ON FUTURE WTO TRADE AGENDA AND DEVELOPING COUNTRIES, organized by U.N.-ESCAP, Bangkok, 23–25 August, 3 (1999)

[24] *Id.* at 3–4

there was an upturn that was sustained until 1997. However, there was a precipitous decline in the exports of major commodities by the LDCs during 1998 and 1999. Over the last four decades their share in world exports decreased more or less constantly from 3.06 percent in 1954 to 0.42 percent in 1998,[25] even though their volume of global trade has increased in absolute terms.

Even after the conclusion of the UR and the establishment of the WTO, the overall level of participation of the developing countries in general and the LDCs in particular remains limited. This is largely the result of their limited financial and human resources, as well as institutional weaknesses. Strengthening the capacities of the developing countries generally, and the LDCs in particular, to participate not only in the institutional structures of the WTO but also in the global market place has now been widely accepted as one of the fundamental prerequisites for the success of the WTO as a system.[26] In the case of developing countries, there has been a marginal increase in participation because they are able to make themselves heard loudly and clearly at the various international fora, including the WTO. However, in the case of the LDCs even that has not been possible (as will be explained later).

C. First WTO Ministerial Conference

The problem of marginalization of certain developing countries, in particular the LDCs, figured prominently in the First Ministerial Conference of the WTO held in Singapore in December 1996. The participating Ministers in the Declaration of the Conference acknowledged that developing country members had undertaken significant new commitments, both substantive and procedural, and recognized the range and complexity of the effort that they were making to comply with these commitments. In order to assist them in these efforts, including those with respect to notification and legislative requirements, it was decided that the WTO would improve the availability of technical assistance to the developing countries.[27]

Regarding the LDCs, the Singapore Conference agreed to:

- Develop a Plan of Action, including provisions for taking positive measures, for example duty-free access, on an autonomous basis, aimed at improving their overall capacity to respond to the opportunities offered by the trading system;
- Seek to give operational content to the Plan of Action, for example, by enhancing conditions for investment and providing predictable and favorable market access conditions for the products of LDCs, to foster the expansion and diversification of their exports to the markets of all developed countries; and in the case of relevant developing countries in the context of the Global System of Trade Preferences; and
- Organize a meeting with UNCTAD and the International Trade Center as soon as possible in 1997, with the participation of aid agencies, multilateral financial institutions and least-developed countries, to foster an integrated approach to assisting these countries in enhancing their trading opportunities.[28]

---

[25] UNCTAD AND COMMONWEALTH SECRETARIAT, *supra* note 8, at 3

[26] Bhattacharya and Rahman, *supra* note 23, at 3

[27] *Id*. at 4

[28] WTO, *Singapore Ministerial Declaration*, adopted on 13 December, WT/MIN(96)/DEC (1996), reproduced in the Appendix to this book

D. The High Level Meeting

Following up on the mandate contained in the Singapore Ministerial Declaration, a High Level Meeting on the Integrated Initiatives for Least-Developed Countries' Trade and Development ("HLM") was held at the WTO on October 27–28, 1997, with the main objective of devising a mechanism for arresting the marginalization of the LDCs from the multilateral trading system. One of the major achievements of the HLM was that it endorsed an Integrated Framework ("IF") for Trade-Related Technical Assistance, discussed in Part IV.C of this chapter. It was reported that initially forty LDCs expressed interest in the IF exercise.[29]

Offers announced or proposed to be adopted during the meeting by a group of developing countries (including Egypt, India, Korea, Mauritius, Morocco, Malaysia, Singapore, South Africa, Thailand and Turkey) and countries in transition were particularly noteworthy. Some countries such as Indonesia and Chile indicated that they were considering new initiatives, but were not yet ready to announce them at the Meeting.[30]

While there was a great deal of interest in market opening, it emerged very clearly during the HLM that market access was a necessary but not sufficient condition to guarantee more exports for the LDCs, let alone broad-based development. Improved and predictable access to the markets of both developed and developing countries would become even more crucial when actions to address supply-side constraints in least-developed countries started to bear fruit.

The LDC representatives welcomed the market access packages announced but felt that more needed to be done. They indicated that the least-developed countries were asking for a change in the legal rules as well as in discretionary actions. They believed that Part IV of the General Agreement, Articles XXXVI to XXXVIII, should commit Members to removing all of the market access problems of least-developed countries rather than leaving this to their own discretion.[31] Moreover, the Plan of Action for Least-Developed Countries, which Ministers had agreed on in Singapore, provided for WTO Members to individually open up their markets to products from least-developed countries.[32]

E. The Second Ministerial Conference

The Declaration of the *Second Ministerial Conference* of the WTO, which was held in Geneva on May 10, 1998, recommended follow-up on the decisions of the HLM on LDCs. However, the work program of the Second Ministerial was more ceremonial than substantive in nature as it was scheduled to coincide with the fiftieth anniversary of the establishment of the GATT.[33]

---

[29] These countries were: Angola, Bangladesh, Benin, Bhutan, Burkina Faso, Burundi, Cambodia, Cape Verde, Central African Republic, Chad, Comoros, Democratic Republic of Congo, Djibouti, Equatorial Guinea, Ethiopia, the Gambia, Guinea, Guinea Bissau, Haiti, Laos, Lesotho, Madagascar, Malawi, Maldives, Mali, Mauritania, Mozambique, Nepal, Niger, Rwanda, Samoa, Sao-Tome and Principe, Solomon Islands, Sudan, Tanzania, Togo, Uganda, Vanuatu and Zambia.

[30] WTO, *High Level Meeting on Integrated Initiatives for Least Developed Countries' Trade Development*, WT/LDC/HL/M/1, 26 November, 17 (1997)

[31] The GSP program, discussed earlier, was optional, not mandatory, for the developed countries, which could therefore impose any conditions they wished upon it, such as limiting the eligible products and countries. The United States, for example, excludes a number of "import-sensitive products", such as textiles and footwear, as well as countries that fail to provide internationally-recognized worker rights or engage in a variety of activities considered inimical to U.S. interests.

[32] WTO, *supra* note 30, at 18

[33] Bhattacharya and Rahman, *supra* note 23, at 5. The Declaration is reproduced in the Appendix to this book.

Other initiatives taken in various international conferences and the fourth Ministerial Conference of the WTO are discussed separately in Part V of this chapter.

III. Weaknesses Plaguing the LDCs

The LDCs continue to suffer from serious social, economic, political and structural weaknesses which are responsible for their exclusion from the global economic mainstream. Some of these are due to their specific geographical location (such as land-lockedness), some are political (such as civil strife), some are economic (such as macroeconomic instability), some are social (such as poor health and education), while some others are structural (lack of required infrastructure). However, all these factors are inextricably intertwined. A short description of the weaknesses is thus in order.

A. Competitive Ability

In the era of global competition, it is not sufficient for LDC enterprises to be locally competitive. They need to be globally competitive, for which they should possess some competitive advantage such as economies of scale, cutting-edge technology, marketing strengths, efficient production and distribution systems, and/or cheap labor.[34] The LDCs do not generally have comparative advantage in any one of these areas except for the availability of cheap labor. However, because of the low productivity of such labor, resulting mainly from lack of education and skills and poor health, even this comparative advantage of the LDCs has not been fully exploited.

The precarious socio-economic situation and structural weaknesses inherent in the economies of the LDCs relegate these countries to a weak competitive position in the current global economic setting.[35] However, unless the competitive ability of businesses in the LDCs is improved, they will not be able to achieve any significant success in integrating themselves into the multilateral trading system. As a UNCTAD LDC Report succinctly put it:

> Developing and sustaining competitiveness and productive capacities, like all other aspects of development, is a long, difficult and often frustrating process, but one which must be confronted by the Governments of LDCs and their development partners with unwavering resolve in a renewed spirit of solidarity and shared responsibility.[36]

What makes the matter more complicated is the fact that there are stark differences even among the LDCs in terms of competitive ability and resulting trade performance. For example, in the year 2000, aggregate merchandise exports from the LDCs reached a record level (US$ 34 billion), while at the same time more than one-third of the LDCs saw their exports decline.[37]

---

[34] Ratnakar Adhikari and Hiramani Ghimire, INTEGRATING LDCs INTO THE MULTILATERAL TRADING SYSTEM: RHETORIC GALORE 7 (2001).

[35] UNCTAD, *Integrating Least Developed Countries into the Global Economy: Proposal for a Comprehensive New Plan of Action in the Context of the Third WTO Ministerial Conference*, adopted at THE CHALLENGE OF INTEGRATING LDCs INTO THE MULTILATERAL TRADING SYSTEM: COORDINATING WORKSHOP FOR SENIOR ADVISORS TO MINISTERS OF TRADE IN LDCs, Sun City, South Africa (June 21–25, 1999)

[36] UNCTAD, THE LEAST DEVELOPED COUNTRIES REPORT 1999 at 4 (1999)

[37] Pradeep Mehta, *Follow-up to the Fourth Ministerial Conference in Doha: Market Access—the Major Roadblocks*, UNCTAD-CIVIL SOCIETY DIALOGUE ON SELECTED DEVELOPMENT ISSUES BEING ADDRESSED BY THE UNITED NATIONS SYSTEM, UNCTAD/ISS/Misc. 385 at 130 (2002)

B. Supply-Side Constraints

In the LDCs, lack of linkage between production facilities, service and infrastructure facilities limits their potential to specialize in crucial productive sectors and to reap the benefit of productivity gain. While poorly developed human resources have led to a paucity of managerial, entrepreneurial and technical skills, ability to conduct adaptive research is severely constrained by lack of incentive and entrepreneurial zeal. Similarly, poorly developed infrastructure (e.g., transport, power and storage facilities) and support services (e.g telecommunications, financial services and other technical support service institutions) limit their ability to supply even otherwise competitively produced goods to the international market. In the face of poor infrastructural services and administrative inefficiencies resulting from cumbersome bureaucratic procedures, many LDCs are creating specially designed export processing zones ("EPZs") and providing support services to industries. These mechanisms are worth emulating by other LDCs.

Trade facilitation services such as access to business information (particularly on rules and procedures of export markets), use of information technology, development of new products, advice on standards, packaging, quality control, marketing and distributional channels, and functioning of trade promotion organizations are virtually non-existent in the LDCs. They also lack the capacity and resources to modernize and reform customs and other government agencies participating in trade transactions and simplifying export and import procedures.[38]

Access to finance is a major problem facing exporters in the LDCs. This can, in part, be ascribed to the virtual absence of capital market in some LDCs and high interest rates on credit charged by financial institutions reflecting high risk.[39] Labour productivity is another major problem. Besides lack of skills and poor health, due to generally high degree of politicization of labour, industrial enterprises in LDCs continue to lose to their competitors from more advanced countries.[40]

C. High Export Concentration Ratio

The LDCs have not been able to diversify their domestic production structures, not only with regard to manufactured goods, but even with respect to their primary commodities. This renders them especially vulnerable to international market volatility. Of the 4,162 products exported by LDCs to thirty major trading partners in 2000, 127 accounted for ninety percent of their total export trade. On an average, the top three commodities exported by each LDC usually account for over seventy percent of its total exports.[41] The export concentration ratios (defined as the share of the principal export product in the total export value) have remained high and largely unchanged since 1980 for all LDCs. Several countries greatly depend on particular primary commodity exports, especially in sub-Saharan Africa.[42] What makes the situation even worse for many LDCs is that,

[38] See Bhattacharya and Rahman, supra note 23, at 7
[39] For example, spread (defined by the difference between the cost of credit and deposit) of financial institutions in Tanzania in 1999 was fourteen percent. See Flora Musonda, Wilfred Mbowe and Faye Sampson, The Competition Regime in Tanzania, COMPARATIVE STUDY OF COMPETITION LAW REGIMES OF SELECT DEVELOPING COUNTRIES (7-UP PROJECT), 2001
[40] See generally ADHIKARI AND GHIMIRE, supra note 34, at 9
[41] WTO Sub-Committee on Least-Developed Countries, Market Access Conditions for Least Developed Countries (WT/LDC/SWG/IF/14), (2000).
[42] For example, coffee occupies 82.7 percent, 69.4 percent and 63.6 percent of the share of total export value of Uganda, Rwanda and Ethiopia respectively. See C.P Chandrasekhar and Jayati Ghosh, WTO and Poor Countries CUTS-CITEE BRIEFING PAPER, 3. (2000).

while exports of a single product may constitute a large share of their export basket, they count for relatively little in terms of the international supply, so that they are unable to influence world prices in a way that is beneficial to them.[43]

Another analysis conducted by UNCTAD and the Commonwealth Secretariat calculates export concentration indices and the number of exported products for selected LDCs. According to this study, despite sustained efforts to diversify their export base, the number of products exported by LDCs is very small (especially for Pacific LDCs) while for others it is well below the 1998 non-LDC world average. Also, for certain LDCs, the export concentration index is close to one and much higher than the average of non-LDC countries.[44]

As discussed above, this poor trade performance of LDCs also results from domestic factors, such as structural rigidities and bottlenecks that hamper the transition to manufactured and processed products (associated with insufficient human capital, absence of capital markets, lack of infrastructure, etc.). Given the long-run tendency for relative commodity prices to deteriorate, the terms of trade of LDCs will continue to worsen if they remain locked in primary sector export production.[45]

D. Implementation Problems

For a variety of reasons, many LDCs have not been able to fully implement several WTO agreements. At the time of signing of the UR accord, it was decided that the LDCs (as well as, to a lesser extent, other developing countries) would be given certain transitional periods for implementation of some of the agreements, such as TRIPS and TRIMs. However, arguing for the need to extend the transitional periods for the LDCs, an UNCTAD report states that such "time-bound transitional periods" given to the LDCs have serious shortcomings. The report further says:

> Because of their limited duration, the transitional periods have limited impact on capacity creation for trade and production. . . . Such time-bound derogation from obligations also assumes the existence of both institutional and resource capacities in LDCs to take maximum advantage of the relevant provisions. For most LDCs these capacities do not exist.[46]

LDCs are also required to bring their trade policy regimes in line with the WTO rules. This requires new laws, new institutions, and skilled human resources. Even the administrative machinery has to undergo a significant change. In the LDCs, where the salary structure for civil servants is extremely low, these changes are difficult to implement.[47] This is particularly true in the case of Trade Related Aspects of Intellectual Property Rights ("TRIPS"). Many LDCs have very limited experience in many areas of the TRIPS Agreement. This renders the implementation of the Agreement a very costly exercise. According to Finger and Schuler,

---

[43] *Id.* at 4.

[44] Export concentration index is numbered between 0 and 1, where 0 represents the lowest concentration and 1 represents the highest. While the non-LDC world average is 0.2 for the 1990s, Kiribati had a concentration index of 0.73 and Zambia had a concentration index of 0.83 in 1995. *See* UNCTAD AND COMMONWEALTH SECRETARIAT, *supra* note 8, at 5–6

[45] UNCTAD AND COMMONWEALTH SECRETARIAT, *supra* note 8, at 4

[46] *Cf.* SUNS, *LDCs To Lose $ 3 Billion from Uruguay Round, Says UNCTAD*, in SOUTH-NORTH DEVELOPMENT MONITOR (SUNS) No. 3620, 2 (n.d)

[47] Hiramani Ghimire, *Integrating LDCs into the Multilateral Trading System: Need for a Bond Between Promise and Performance*, SAWTEE BRIEFING PAPER 5 (2000)

Least developed country institutions in these areas are weak, and would benefit from strengthening and reform. However, our analysis indicates that the WTO obligations reflect little awareness of development problems and little appreciation of the capacities of the least developed countries to carry out the functions that SPS, customs valuation, intellectual property, etc. regulations address.[48]

They estimate that the cost of implementing three of the Uruguay Round Agreements (TRIPS, SPS and Customs Valuation) for an advanced developing country like Mexico amounts to around $130 million.[49] This cost is more than the entire annual budget of many LDCs. They further warn: "The experiences we have reviewed were in the more advanced developing countries; the costs could be higher in the least developed countries who will begin further from the required standards."[50]

Non-compliance of notification obligations has been yet another obvious weakness. The WTO system puts great emphasis on transparency, which requires Members to notify the WTO about their trade policy measures. Altogether there are 215 notification obligations. The LDCs have lagged far behind other countries in meeting these obligations, with a compliance rate of less than sixteen percent.[51] These problems will be exacerbated if new areas come within the WTO ambit as a result of the Doha Round.

E. Lack of Capacity

Strengthening the capacities of developing countries in the area of international trade is of crucial importance, both for the countries themselves and for their partners, in view of the number of international trade negotiations, both ongoing and forthcoming. Developing countries in general and LDCs in particular find it increasingly difficult to cope with the commitments they have made under the WTO. An analysis of the lack of capacity reveals that three issues figure prominently. The first issue relates to the capacity to implement the WTO Agreements, which has been discussed above. A second issue relates to the capacity to understand the texts of the Agreements and their implications for the country. A third relates to the capacity to negotiate effectively in the increasingly loaded agenda items of the WTO. The latter two issues will be discussed in this part.

Most WTO Agreements reflect the tough negotiations that went on during the drafting process. Most of these negotiations took place between the developed countries, although some developing countries played a role. The final agreements are highly legalistic.[52] It takes a well-trained trade lawyer to understand these agreements and interpret them. However, most LDCs do not have such lawyers. The officials at the commerce ministries, who have in most cases received no other exposure than attending a training course on trade policy offered by the WTO Secretariat, are not likely to be able to understand some of the provisions relating to such complicated Agreements of the WTO as the Agreement on Agriculture, SPS, TBT, TRIPS or the Antidumping Agreement.

---

[48] MICHAEL FINGER AND PHILLIP SCHULER, IMPLEMENTATION OF URUGUAY ROUND: THE DEVELOPMENT CHALLENGES 1 (1999)

[49] *Id.* at 25

[50] *Id.*

[51] Ghimire, *supra* note 47, at 5

[52] This has become evident from the recent decisions of the Dispute Settlement Panel and Appellate Body, which indicate a major shift from the diplomatically-driven conciliatory dispute settlement mechanism of the GATT towards the legally-driven adjudicative system of the WTO. *See* John H Jackson, THE WORLD TRADING SYSTEM: LAW AND POLICY OF INTERNATIONAL ECONOMIC RELATIONS 109–111 (1997)

For example, interpreting some of the most convoluted provisions of the TRIPS Agreement, e.g., Article 27.3 (b)[53] is a hugely difficult task. Some members view the term "effective *sui generis*" system for the protection of plant varieties as meaning protection through any mechanism which does not impair the ability of the farmers to save, exchange or sell seeds on a non-commercial basis.[54] Other countries are of the view that the International Union for the Protection of New Varieties of Plants ("UPOV") 1991 model is the *only* effective *sui generis* model of plant variety protection (other than patents).[55] Similarly, multiple interpretations of other provisions of TRIPS Agreement such as those relating to compulsory licensing and parallel imports have generated a great deal of controversy. Thanks to the Doha Declaration on TRIPS and Public Health, this issue has been settled with respect to pharmaceuticals, at least for the time being.[56]

The capacity of the representatives of the LDCs to participate in the regular negotiation process that takes place at the various Committees of the WTO on a regular basis and to negotiate the built-in-agenda items and new issues is severely restricted for a number of reasons. The first one again relates to the lack of understanding of the issues at stake. The second one, which is more of an institutional nature, is the fact that some eleven LDCs do not have a resident mission in Geneva. Geneva Week[57] has helped to some extent in that it at least provides a platform for the LDC delegations to express themselves, but this is no substitute for having a permanent mission in Geneva, which would allow the delegates to remain in permanent touch with the issues being discussed at the WTO and to participate effectively in the negotiation process. It is quite certain that the LDCs will face serious difficulties when negotiations on a whole range of new issues like competition policy, investment, government procurement, environment and trade facilitation begin.[58] One commentator has noted that "LDCs, many of which do not have permanent missions in Geneva, will not be able to keep up with all these additional issues for negotiation and run the risk of having to make commitments at the end of the new cycle of trade negotiations, without knowing what impact they would have on their economies."[59]

---

[53] This Article in relevant part states: "However, Members shall provide for the protection of plant varieties either by patents or by an effective *sui generis* system or by any combination thereof."

[54] This is the position taken by many developing countries. India, for instance, has implemented its Plant Variety Protection and Farmers' Rights Act, 2001, with this understanding. However, lawyers are skeptical that this will survive the scrutiny of the Dispute Settlement Body, should a dispute arise.

[55] This position is advanced by the developed countries, which are the Members of the UPOV. Under this position, the rights of the farmers to save, exchange or sell proprietary seeds would be severely circumscribed.

[56] *See* WTO, *Declaration on TRIPS Agreement and Public Health*, WT/MIN(01)/DEC/2, November 20, 2001, reproduced in the Appendix to this book.

[57] Geneva week refers to the meeting organized by the WTO Secretariat every year for the trade officials of the countries not having resident missions in Geneva to help them come to grips with the issues being discussed at the WTO.

[58] These are issues to be discussed as part of the Doha Round. While some of the issues will be negotiated before the Fifth Ministerial Conference of the WTO, some will be discussed after the Conference. A least ten Agreements/issues were supposed to be negotiated (some in parts and some in full) prior to the Fifth Ministerial Conference in Canada, Mexico, in September 2003. They include the Agreement on Agriculture ("AOA"), the Agreement on Subsidies and Countervailing Measures ("ASCM"), the Agreement on Anti-dumping or Agreement on Implementation of Article VI of the GATT 1994 ("AAD"), the Agreement on Textile and Clothing ("ATC"), the Agreement on Trade Related Aspects of Intellectual Property Rights ("TRIPS") Agreement, the Agreement on Trade-Related Investment Measures ("TRIMS"), The Agreement on Safeguards ("AS"), the Agreement on Sanitary and Phytosanitary Measures ("SPS"), the Agreement on Technical Barriers to Trade ("TBT"), and Special and Differential Treatment ("S&DT"), *See* European Centre for Development Policy Management, ICTSD and Overseas Development Institute (ODI), 1 (1) TRADE NEGOTIATIONS INSIGHTS 8 (2002).

[59] Celine Charverait, *The New Cycle of WTO Negotiations as an Opportunity to Fulfill Promises Made at the U.N. LDC-III Conference: The View of Oxfam International* in UNCTAD-CIVIL SOCIETY DIALOGUE ON

F. The Tortuous Accession Process

Of the 49 LDCs, thirty are WTO members and nine are observers, of which six are in the process of accession (Cambodia, Lao Peoples Democratic Republic, Nepal, Sudan, Samoa, and Vanuatu). Thus, for as many as thirteen LDCs, the question of whether to become a member of the WTO and to begin the accession process will have to be addressed sooner or later. The first step in integrating LDCs into the global economy and the international trading system is their institutional integration into the WTO system. This should be among the first actions to be undertaken to stem and reverse the marginalization of the LDCs.[60]

The WTO accession process is governed by Article XII of the Agreement Establishing the WTO (the Marrakesh Agreement), which states: "Any State or separate customs territory possessing full autonomy in the conduct of its external commercial relations or for the other matters provided for in this Agreement and the Multilateral Trade Agreement may accede to this Agreement, on terms to be agreed between it and the WTO".

Since the WTO is a unique intergovernmental organization, having no power of its own to negotiate accession agreements with the acceding countries, it is the existing Member States that dictate the terms and conditions for such entry. The accession process to the WTO is akin to membership of a club where the existing members decide the terms and conditions. Those members who agree to comply with the requirements will be admitted to the club and those who cannot do so will never be admitted.[61]

During the accession negotiations the objectives of the existing Members will be to extract the maximum concessions from any new applicant. This is done for two reasons. First, it will help the existing members set a precedent for extracting higher concessions from other applicants in the queue. Second, it provides them benefits without their having to reciprocate. It is a harsh reality that countries applying for WTO membership *do not get what they deserve but what they negotiate.*[62] This is a single of the reasons why not one LDC has been able to enter the WTO since its inception, despite the fact that twenty new Members have been admitted to the WTO over the past six years.

The pain and suffering that Vanuatu, a small island LDC, was subjected to is a good example of this problem. During the accession process, Vanuatu was asked by the United States to join the Agreement on Government Procurement and the Agreement on Civil Aircraft, both plurilateral agreements, which it was under no obligation whatsoever to sign according to the WTO rules. Moreover, LDCs that are already members of the WTO are not required to comply with the requirements of the TRIPS Agreement before 2006. However, the United States even refused the request by Vanuatu for a two–year transitional period for the implementation of the TRIPS Agreement.[63] This means that Vanuatu would be required to comply with the requirements of TRIPS immediately upon its entry into the WTO.

Similarly, Vanuatu was asked to make an explicit commitment not to use the Special Safeguard ("SSG") Provisions despite the fact that, as per the Agreement on Agriculture,

SELECTED DEVELOPMENT ISSUES BEING ADDRESSED BY THE UNITED NATIONS SYSTEM, UNCTAD/ISS/Misc. 385, 110 (2002)

[60] UNCTAD, FUTURE MULTILATERAL TRADE NEGOTIATIONS: HANDBOOK FOR TRADE NEGOTIATORS FROM LEAST DEVELOPED COUNTRIES, 282 (1999)

[61] Ratnakar Adhikari, *Birth Defects of the WTO Accession Process,* THE KATHMANDU POST, March 27, 2002, at 4.

[62] Bhattacharya and Rahman, *supra* note 23, at 15

[63] Roman Grynberg and Roy Mickey Joy, *The Accession of Vanuatu to the WTO: Lessons for the Multilateral Trading System,* 34 (6) JOURNAL OF WORLD TRADE 116 (2000).

WTO members which have been through the "tariffication" process are allowed to maintain the same. It was also asked to commit not to use export subsidies on Agricultural products, despite the fact that the Agreement on Agriculture permits LDCs to continue to use export subsidies. Likewise, in the services area, Vanuatu was asked to make offers in eighteen areas. This is more than four times the average for LDCs that are WTO members and twice that of Solomon Islands, which is the most obvious case for comparison.[64]

These examples reinforce the notion that the developed Member Countries of the WTO, especially the powerful ones, are determined to impose so-called "WTO-plus" conditions on the new Members. Grynberg and Joy argue: "While it remains one of the enduring convenient clichés of the multilateral trading system that the WTO is a 'rule-based system', the actuality is that accession is inherently power-based and the very antithesis of the WTO's credo."[65] Therefore, it is clear that the WTO accession process has serious defects.

The most depressing aspect, however, is that these defects are not likely to be removed in the foreseeable future. The reasons are simple. First, the beneficiaries of the reforms, those who are applying for WTO access, have no voice in the WTO as they are by definition outside the multilateral trading system. Once they become members they rarely wish to discuss what is an embarrassing and highly intrusive process. Second, those who would have to pay for the reforms would be the WTO proponents, who gain nothing and have to expend scarce political capital.[66]

Developed Member Countries of the WTO justify their stand by stating that the existing rights and obligations emanating from WTO Membership are the result of hard bargaining among the existing Members during the various negotiating rounds, in which the new members did not participate. Therefore, the argument goes, newcomers should not be allowed to enter the WTO "free of charge" because they will be entitled to receive the same treatment as any other WTO Members under the MFN principle. However, countries making this argument choose to remain oblivious of the fact that LDCs have either taken autonomous liberalization measures or were subjected to the World Bank and/or International Monetary Fund's conditionalities, which included, *inter alia*, opening up their economy to foreign goods, services and investment. Therefore, they have already sufficiently liberalized their trade and investment regime. Indeed, as J. Michael Finger argues, "... trade reforms under IMF and World Bank programs liberalized more developing countries than had the Uruguay Round."[67]

Article III:5 of the Marrakesh Agreement states: "With a view to achieving greater coherence in global economic policy-making, the WTO shall cooperate, as appropriate, with the International Monetary Fund and with the International Bank for Reconstruction and Development and its affiliated agencies." However, when it comes to providing credit for trade liberalization, existing WTO Members chose not to talk about coherence. Therefore, Ahn remarks:

> [T]rade liberalization is often a high, if not top, priority for IMF stabilization programs or World Bank Development loan programs. Such political concerns for trade negotiation [holding back on unilateral trade liberalization waiting for reciprocal bargaining], however, lead a country to avoid unilateral liberalization... Therefore, a mechanism to "credit" such

---

[64] *Id.* at 166

[65] *Id.* at 159

[66] *See* Adhikari, *supra* note 61, at 4

[67] *See* Bernard Hoekman and L. Alan Winters, *A Tribute to J. Michael Finger* in DEVELOPMENT, TRADE, AND THE WTO, xiv (Bernard Hoekman, Aaditya Mattoo, and Philip English eds. 2002)

liberalization, particularly those adopted as parts of IMF or World Bank programs, in future trade negotiations should be established in the context of the WTO to facilitate trade liberalization for developing countries. In addition, in order to assure such mechanism, the trade reform and liberalization must be permanent in character and in conformity with the GATT obligations, i.e., "GATTable" in nature.[68]

Byung-il takes the same view in the context of services liberalization. According to him a provision for "crediting" countries for autonomous liberalization measures already exist in GATS Article XIX:3. However, since no modalities have been established for providing Member Countries with credit for autonomous liberalization as provided for by Article XIX:3, Members are reluctant to make commitments prior to the formal negotiations.[69]

These points were made in the context of unilateral trade liberalization measures to be taken by existing WTO Members. However, there is no reason why the same logic should not apply in the context of acceding countries.

G. Exclusion From the "Knowledge-Based Economy"

One of the major factors of production in the New Economy is knowledge. It is the only production factor that multiplies and expands when used. The level of knowledge in a given society is reflected in its technological capacity. In today's society, information technology ("IT") plays an important role in achieving one's competitive advantages.[70] In the era of globalization, the information and communication technologies ("ICTs") revolution offers genuine potential, but also presents the risk that a significant portion of the world will lose out.[71] Applied to commercial needs, IT can enhance foreign export marketing, improve the access of exporters and importers to foreign market information, establish and sustain linkages between buyers and suppliers, and facilitate access to training and technical assistance. ICTs can also strengthen trade-related development co-operation by increasing the flexibility and reach, enhancing the content and reducing the cost of many kinds of technical assistance.[72] Since LDCs are largely excluded from the digital global economy, a sharp digital divide has been created in an already divided world. As indicated in the 2001 ILO Employment Report:

> Despite the phenomenal growth of ICT in the industrialized world and its increasing penetration into developing countries, "vast swathes" of the globe remain "technologically disconnected" from the benefits of the electronic marvels that are revolutionizing life, work and communication in the digital era.[73]

The Report further highlights the very real constraints facing developing countries in their capacity to join the communications revolution. Those countries and regions that fail to make the "technological leap" not only risk missing out on the large and growing trade in ICT products, but will be unable to profit from the economic efficiency and productivity gains that derive from these industries, the Report states. Such a development

---

[68] Durken Ahn, *Linkages between International Financial and Trade Institutions: IMF, World Bank and WTO*, 34 (4) JOURNAL OF WORLD TRADE 26 (2000)

[69] Byung-il Choi, *Treatment of Autonomous Liberalization in the WTO New Service Round –To Give Credit is to Get More*, 35(2) JOURNAL OF WORLD TRADE 364 (2001)

[70] Ghimire, *supra* note 13, at 360

[71] *Cf.* UNNGLS (United Nations Non-governmental Liaison Service), GO BETWEEN 30, at 84 (January-February, 2001)

[72] OECD, THE DAC GUIDELINES: STRENGTHENING TRADE CAPACITY FOR DEVELOPMENT 50 (2001)

[73] *Cf.* UNNGLS, *supra* note 71, at 30

has created, by implication, additional barriers to the LDCs for their integration into the global economy. Access to these technologies will continue to be extremely restricted mainly because a vast majority of LDC institutions and individuals cannot afford to buy them. The following figures show how backward LDCs are in terms of harnessing the potential of ICT.

- In LDCs telephone density is 0.59 percent compared to ten percent in the developing countries.
- There is less than one Internet user per thousand people, against one user per 36 people in the developing countries.
- By April 2002, estimated number of Internet users in the world (population 6 billion) was 360 million, or six percent. In the corresponding period, the number of Internet users in the LDCs (population 680 million) was estimated at 0.58 million, or less than 0.1 percent, and representing 0.13 percent of the global Internet users.[74]

Recognizing the urgent need to harness the potential of the knowledge and technology for promoting the goals for the United Nations Millennium Declaration and to find effective and innovative ways to put this potential at the service of development for all, the Fifty-sixth Session of the United Nations General Assembly adopted a resolution on a World Summit on the Information Society. This resolution endorses the resolution adopted by the Council for the International Telecommunication Union to hold a World Summit on Information Society at the highest possible level in two phases, the first in Geneva from December 10 to 12, 2003, and the second in Tunis in 2005.[75]

Similarly, the poor performance of LDCs in stimulating research and development and developing innovations that suit their productive needs has resulted in their continued marginalization from the global economy. One measure of innovation is the number of patent applications filed in each country. Very few patent applications are filed in the LDCs. For example, only 44 patents are registered in Nepal 36 years after enactment of intellectual property legislation (the Patent, Design and Trademark Act 1965). Of these, only seventeen patents are of domestic origin, while 27 are of foreign origin.[76] Even the non-LDC developing countries are lagging far behind in terms of patent applications. For example, in 1996 a total of 401,261 patents applications were filed in Japan, 223,432 in the United States, and 114,021 in Korea. On the other hand, India only received 8,292 patent applications, and Malaysia, Indonesia and Thailand together received only 12,832 applications.[77]

This shows that developing countries in general and LDCs in particular continue to be overwhelmingly net importers of technology and new products. This puts them in an extremely disadvantageous position in the global economy where the issue of technology transfer has not moved beyond rhetoric.[78] Their distance from the knowledge-based

[74] Claudia Sarrocco, *Improving IP Connectivity in the Least-Developed Countries*, BACKGROUND STUDY, Strategy and Policy Unit, International Telecommunications Union, 12 April 2002, available at http://www.itu.int/osg/spu/ni/ipdc/workshop/presentations/Sarrocco.ppt, accessed on September 15, 2002.

[75] United Nations, *Resolution Adopted by the General Assembly,* Fifty-fifth session, A/RES/56/183, 1–2 (January 31, 2002)

[76] *See* Ratnakar Adhikari, Rajesh Khanal and Navin Verma, *National Study on TRIPS Agreement and Its Implications for Nepal*, REPORT SUBMITTED TO THE NEPAL ACCESSION TO WTO 22 (2001)

[77] *See* Keith E. Maskus, INTELLECTUAL PROPERTY RIGHTS IN THE GLOBAL ECONOMY 68 (2000)

[78] For example, Article 66:2 of TRIPS Agreement reads: "Developed country Members *shall* provide incentives to enterprises and institutions in their territories for the purpose of promoting and encouraging technology transfer to least developed country Members in order to enable them to create a sound an viable

economy is exacerbated by the fact that this segment of the economy is increasing more rapidly than others.

H. Other Weaknesses

This analysis of the weaknesses plaguing the LDCs would not be complete without addressing the problems endemic to LDCs, about which the international community can do virtually nothing. These problems are related mostly to political and governance issues in the LDCs. Some LDC economies have been marred by continued war and civil strife for decades. It would be absurd to blame globalization in general and trade liberalization in particular for the marginalization of countries like Sierra Leone, Haiti, the Democratic Republic of Congo, Somalia and Afghanistan.

Similarly, the lack of democratic culture and pluralism is the major cause of the failure to achieve sustained economic growth in many LDCs, a fact which the anti-globalization movement has chosen to ignore so far. Economic openness and democratic pluralism can and should complement each other. However, this is the major missing link in the case of LDCs.

Likewise, openness to trade and investment and leaving everything at the mercy of market mechanism do not guarantee economic growth. Institutions guaranteeing, *inter alia*, adequate protection of property rights, regulation to prevent fraud and deceptions, macroeconomic stabilization, social insurance and conflict management are necessary to fully reap the benefit of openness. As Rodrik argues, "All well-functioning market economies are 'embedded' in a set of non-market institutions without which markets cannot perform adequately."[79] However, such institutions are either non-existent or non-functional in almost all the LDCs.

Bribery and corruption in high offices, which is a recurrent phenomenon in most LDCs, has contributed significantly towards holding back the development prospects of these economies. According to the Corruption Perception Index produced by Transparency International[80], three LDCs figure among the top ten countries with massive corruption. It is no surprise that in the year 2001, Bangladesh—a longtime leader of the LDC camp in the WTO—figured on the top of this list, and Tanzania—the current leader of the LDC camp in the WTO—is the tenth on the list.[81] This problem is exacerbated by the fact that LDCs lack credible institutions to tackle corruption issues.

---

technological base" (emphasis added). Despite the use of word "shall" as opposed to "may" in this Article, developed countries have not done anything in this regard. The realization that developed countries have not done enough to facilitate transfer of technology to the LDCs led the Trade Ministers at Doha to include the following requirement on the Paragraph 11.2 of Implementation Related Issues and Concerns: "Reaffirming that provisions of Article 66.2 of the TRIPS Agreement and mandatory, it is agreed that TRIPS Council shall put in place a mechanism for ensuring the monitoring and full implementations of obligations in question. To this end developed country Members shall submit prior to the end of 2002 detailed reports of the functioning in practice of the incentives provided to their enterprises for the transfer of technology in pursuance of their commitments under Article 66.2. The submissions shall be subject to a review in TRIPS Council and information shall be updated by Members annually." At the time of writing, it seems that only Canada and New Zealand have formally submitted reports on how they implement this Article.*See* Jonathan Hepburn, *Negotiating Intellectual Property: Mandate and options in the Doha Work Programme*, OCCASIONAL PAPER 10, Friends World Committee for Consulation, Quaker United Nations Office—Geneva, 4 (2002)

[79] Dani Rodrik, *Trade Policy Reform as Institutional Reform* in DEVELOPMENT, TRADE, AND THE WTO, 4 (Bernard Hoekman, Aaditya Mattoo, and Philip English eds. 2002)

[80] A Berlin-based international anti-corruption non-governmental organization. *See* http://www.transparency.org for further details.

[81] http://www.globalcorruptionreport.org/download/data_and_research.pdf

It will be in the interest of the LDCs, saddled with corruption, to cooperate fully to conclude an Agreement on Transparency in Government Procurement ("ATGP") at the WTO[82], if not agreeing to join the Agreement of Government Procurement.[83] This will be an important step forward in controlling bribery and corruption. If the discretion of procurement officers in achieving the goals of the procurement process is structured and subject to formal rules, the opportunities for corrupt decisions, as well as the possibility of errors of judgment, would be greatly reduced.[84] This is one of the agenda items to be negotiated in accordance with the Doha mandate, and LDCs need to consider it as a part of the package they are going to negotiate under the Doha Declaration. They should also start preparing for the negotiations on this issue and use them as an opportunity to trade concessions in other areas (perhaps market access on agriculture and labour intensive products).

IV. A Brief Overview of Efforts by the International Community

The credibility of the multilateral trading system lies in its ability to ensure the full participation of the LDCs in particular and of the developing countries as a whole both in the rule-making process and in deriving an equitable share of the benefits from global trade liberalization. Integration into the trading system and preventing further marginalization of the LDCs—and indeed their continued faith in the system—mean nothing less.[85] Integration in the global economy is indeed of paramount importance to LDCs: Through international trade and foreign direct investment they can increase their access to technology and capital, learn new ways of doing business, and enhance their capacity to compete on a global basis.[86]

Recognition of the problems inherent in the LDCs and their realization of the need to integrate into the world economic system have led their development partners to make some genuine (some not so genuine) efforts to assist in this process. Such attempts have mostly failed; this chapter concentrates only upon some of the major efforts undertaken.

---

[82] As mandated by the Singapore Ministerial Conference (Paragraph 21 of the Ministerial Declaration, reproduced in the Appendix to this book) it was declared to " establish a working group to conduct a study on transparency in government procurement practices, taking into account national policies, and, based on this study, to develop elements for inclusion in an appropriate agreement." Further, Paragraph 26 of the Doha Declaration, also reproduced in the Appendix to this book, declared:

> Recognizing the case for a multilateral agreement on transparency in government procurement and the need for enhanced technical assistance and capacity building in this area, we agree that negotiations will take place after the Fifth Session of the Ministerial Conference on the basis of a decision to be taken, by explicit consensus, at that Session on modalities of negotiations....

[83] The Agreement on Government Procurement is one of the plurilateral Uruguay Round agreements, binding only on those Members who sign it. It requires signatories to open up specified areas of government procurement to competition from other signatories, as well as requiring transparent government procurement procedures. The proposed multilateral agreement, on the other hand, would only require transparency. *See* Chapter 23 of this book.

[84] Sue Arrowsmith, *National and International Perspectives on the Regulation of Public Procurement: Harmony or Conflict* in PUBLIC PROCUREMENT: GLOBAL REVOLUTION 19 (Sue Arrowsmith and Arwel Davis eds. 1998)

[85] Ricupero, *supra* note 14, at ix.

[86] Jan Pronk, *Chairman's Opening Statement at the High Level Meeting, High Level Meeting on Integrated Initiatives for Least Developed Countries Trade Development*, NOTE ON THE MEETING, WT/LDC/HL/M/1, at 25 (26 November, 1997)

A. Market Access

Improved market access is key to any effective policy to integrate least-developed countries into the world trading system and to ensure their participation in international trade and investment flows.[87] However, the experience of recent years has shown that one must get the basics right, in terms of sound domestic macro-economic policies, a good infrastructure, well-developed human and institutional capacities, and a vibrant entrepreneurial sector. Without this, no amount of market access or well-meaning technical assistance programs can make a significant long-term difference to the performance of structurally weak developing countries.[88]

The marginalization of the LDCs in world trade justifies extraordinary efforts and actions on the part of the major beneficiaries of the global trading system. Moreover, the circumstances of the LDCs warrant exceptional treatment. Existing preference schemes have not been effective because they are complex, temporary in nature, and contain numerous exclusions in areas of key interest to the LDCs. In addition, LDCs find it difficult to compete with more advanced developing countries which are also eligible for preferential treatment. In the United States, for example, only around one percent of imports entering under the Generalized System of Preferences come from the LDCs.[89]

Market access opportunities of the LDCs are not only impeded by tariff barriers, but also by non-tariff barriers. Among the tariff barriers the most pernicious one is tariff escalation, which discourages LDCs from advancing along the processing chain, where much of the added value of a product is realized. FAO studies have shown that tariff escalation even in the post-UR era has averaged seventeen percent in Europe, the United States and Japan, and in many products of interest to LDCs it has been much higher (e.g., 85 percent on second-stage fruit products entering the EU, 82 percent on first-stage sugar products entering Japan and 28 percent on second-stage sugar products entering the United States).[90] Tariff peaks are also a major problem for LDCs. The bound tariffs on certain agricultural products in the Quad countries are as follows:

Canada:	Butter (360 percent), cheese (289 percent), eggs (236.3 percent)
EU:	Beef (213 percent), wheat (167 percent), sheep meat (144 percent)
Japan:	Wheat products (388.1 percent), wheat (352.7 percent), barley products (361 percent)
United States:	Sugar(244.4 percent), peanuts (173.8 percent), milk (82.6 percent)[91]

Total LDC exports in 1999 were US$ 22.7 billion, of which US$ 17 billion went to Quad economies. More than half of the exports to the Quad countries were affected by tariff peaks—US$ 5.5 billion of LDC exports to Canada,[92] more than US$ 3 billion to

[87] WTO *High Level Meeting on Integrated Initiatives for Least Developed Countries Trade Development*, NOTE ON THE MEETING at2, WT/LDC/HL/M/1 (November 26, 1997).

[88] Rubens Ricupero, *Address to the High Level Meeting, High Level Meeting on Integrated Initiatives for Least Developed Countries Trade Development*, NOTE ON THE MEETING, WT/LDC/HL/M/1,31 (November 26, 1997)

[89] Shigemitsu Sugisaki *Trade and Development*, ADDRESS TO WTO HIGH LEVEL SYMPOSIUM ON TRADE AND DEVELOPMENT (March 17 1999)

[90] Cuddy, *supra* note 9, at 4

[92] Canada seems to be the worst offender in terms of keeping exports from the LDCs out of its market despite having a seemingly generous GSP scheme. *However*, Canada recently announced that it would provide duty-free access to products originating in 48 LDCs (excluding Myanmar) starting January 1, 2003. However, Canada, like the EU has not included three products on the list of offer. They are dairy, poultry and eggs. Canada's inclusion of textile and garments on the list of duty-free items is likely to have a positive impact on the market access of the 48 LDCs. *See* ICTSD, *Canadian LDC Initiative to Free up Entry of Goods from World's Poorest* in BRIDGES WEEKLY TRADE NEWS DIGEST, Vol. 6, No. 29 (August 6, 2002)

the United States, about US$ 500 million to Japan and about US$ 800 million to the EU.[93] It is no surprise that a study by Hoekman, Ng and Olarreaga reached the following conclusion:

> Although average tariffs in Quad markets are very low, tariff peaks and tariff escalation have a disproportional effect on exports by least developed countries (LDCs). Tariff peak products tend to be heavily concentrated in agriculture and food products and in labor intensive sectors such as apparel and footwear. Full duty and quota free access for LDCs in the Quad for tariff peak products would result in a 11 percent increase in their total exports—on the order of $2.5 billion. Exports to Quad countries of tariff peak products would expand by 30 to 60 percent. Given that LDC exports of tariff peak items account for only a small share of total developing country exports, granting LDCs duty free access has a negligible impact on other developing countries. For the same reason, Quad imports increase only marginally, suggesting that this should not be a factor constraining implementation of duty free access for the poorest countries.[94]

Quoting the US Department of Commerce, Hoekman states: "In 1999, in the US alone, imports originating in least developed countries (LDCs) generated tariff revenue of $487 million, equal to 11.6 percent of the value of their exports to the US, and 15.7 percent of dutiable imports."[95] These figures illustrate the benefits that LDCs could derive from duty-free access to the markets of the industrialized countries.

The prevalence of tariff peaks and tariff escalation on products emanating from LDCs is one of the great scandals of our time. The idea of providing zero tariff access for LDCs was conceived at UNCTAD VIII, held in Cartagena in 1992, but nothing concrete has been done so far in this direction in order to positively influence the trade performance of the LDCs. The reason for the reluctance is simple, as UNCTAD Secretary-General Ricupero explains:

> At UNCTAD VIII, the Cartagena Commitment urged exports from LDCs should be granted duty free access to major markets. This proposal was simple, entirely practical and morally unarguable. In the bigger picture, the costs of importing countries would have been miniscule, and the benefits to 600 million inhabitants of the 48 LDCs potentially enormous. But too many vested interests in particular sectors—most of them sunset industries in Western Countries—would have been hurt.[96]

As mentioned earlier, zero tariff market entry is a necessary, but not a sufficient condition for the better integration of LDCs into the multilateral trading system, but this idea has been used and abused over the years, more for political purposes than for economic reasons. The idea was reborn in the Singapore Ministerial Meeting of the WTO, when the then Director-General of the WTO made a plea to the Members of the WTO to consider the proposal seriously, but the response to his proposal was lukewarm.

During the preparation for the Third Ministerial Conference in Seattle, the European Union formally launched a proposal directed at "entering into a commitment to ensure duty-free market access not later than at the end of the new round of negotiations for essentially all products exported by the LDCs". Following the failure of the Seattle Ministerial Conference, the proposal for granting duty-free and/or quota-free access for

[93] Details can be found in Olarreaga, Marcelo and Ng., *Tariff Peaks and Preferences* in DEVELOPMENT, TRADE, AND THE WTO 109 (Bernard Hoekman, Aaditya Mattoo, and Philip English eds. 2002)
[94] Bernard Hoekman; Francis Ng; and Marcelo Olarreaga, ELIMINATING EXCESSIVE TARIFFS ON EXPORTS OF LEAST DEVELOPED COUNTRIES (2001)
[95] Bernard Hoekman, STRENGTHENING THE GLOBAL TRADE ARCHITECTURE FOR DEVELOPMENT 5 (2002)
[96] *See* http://www2.cid.harvard.edu/cidtrade/Issues/ricupero2.pdf

"essentially all" products was discussed in the context of various international forums and included in the UNCTAD X Bangkok Plan of Action.[97]

Finally, just two months before the U.N. LDC-III Conference in May 2001, the EU made its "Everything But Arms" ("EBA") proposal, which proposed duty-free treatment for all imports from LDCs except arms, and, for the time being, rice, sugar, bananas. The LDCs were jubilant, thinking of better market access opportunities, but little realizing that rules of origin requirements and non-tariff barriers could still hamper their trading prospects.[98]

A study conducted by UNCTAD and the Commonwealth Secretariat in 2001 on the possible effects of duty- and quota-free market access for LDCs should that be undertaken by all the Quad Member Countries reaches the following general conclusions:

> The result that emerged throughout the study was that duty- and quota-free market access will benefit LDCs. The sources of the benefits to LDCs are both improved terms of trade (associated with higher export prices in donor countries' markets) and improved allocation efficiency. The study also shows that the potential benefits to LDCs in terms of export diversification may be important. Taking advantage of the enhanced market access will require restructuring in beneficiary countries. This is an inevitable consequence of any trade policy initiative. As a consequence of the EU EBA, some agricultural sectors such as rice and sugar will expand significantly in LDCs. If the remaining Quad countries also grant duty- and quota-free access to LDC exports, not only will the expansion of LDC agricultural exports be broader and more diversified, but textiles and apparel exports will also be stimulated significantly. This should result in the movement of resources in LDCs out of manufactures production.[99]

However, looking at the utilization rates of the existing preferences granted by various developed countries, one finds that the LDCs still face a host of tariff barriers on exports that are supposed to be covered by the "preferential" arrangements. According to Inama:

> If one considers that a major part of current LDC exports still face MFN duties in spite of the available preferences, action should be taken to eliminate the remaining obstacles to full access by expanding product coverage and increasing utilization rates of available trade preferences.[100]

Inama further maintains that the four major factors that affect the utilization of unilateral trade preferences are:

- Lack of security of access, due to the unilateral and optional nature of preferences, which can be eliminated at the discretion of the providers.

---

[97] Stefano Inama, *Market Access for LDCs: Issues to be Addressed,* 36 (1) JOURNAL OF WORLD TRADE 85 (2002)

[98] *See id.* at 92–94 for a detailed exposition on how rules of origin and non-tariff barriers have hampered the trade prospects of the LDCs.

[99] However, this study has some limitations, which are admitted by the report itself. Firstly, the results obtained from Computable General Equilibrium ("CGE") analysis may overestimate the actual extent of sectoral reallocation in LDCs—supply rigidities and bottlenecks associated with a poor working of factor markets are relevant in these economies, which are neglected in CGE analysis. Secondly, even admitting full sectoral adjustment in LDCs, an overestimation of the sectoral effects of preferential market access may be associated with the presence of complex rules of origin. Sometimes the utilization rates of preferential schemes may be low or very low, because of problems in compliance with the rules established by the donor country—CGE modeling neglects such problems. *See* UNCTAD AND COMMONWEALTH SECRETARIAT, *supra* note 8, at 11

[100] Inama, *supra* note 97, at 114

- Insufficient product coverage, due to exclusion of certain "sensitive" sectors from the preference scheme by the providers.[101]
- Rules of origin that are excessively stringent in light of the industrial capacity of LDCs.
- Lack of understanding or awareness of the preferences available and the conditions attached thereto, leading to the application of MFN rates rather than preferential ones.[102]

B. Special and Differential Treatment

Analysts are divided on whether or not special and differential treatment is the right policy to facilitate the integration of developing countries and LDCs into the multilateral trading system. According to Srinivasan, the continued insistence of developing countries on special and differential treatment and their reluctance to take part in the GATT negotiations as equal partners was the main reason for their marginalization from the global economy.[103] However, developing countries, as a group, insisted on special and differential treatment, asserting that applying the same rules to unequal trading countries could be disastrous. It is certainly true that countries that have achieved long-term economic growth have usually combined the opportunities offered by world markets with a growth strategy that mobilizes the capabilities of domestic institutions and investors.[104] Therefore, well-designed, effective, enforceable and time-bound special and differential treatment is necessary for the successful integration of the LDCs into the multilateral trading system. Some developing economies which are now well integrated into the global economy, were major users of the preferential market access opportunities in the past and some of them (such as Thailand, South Korea and Brazil) have been reluctant to 'graduate' to a higher status.

The preamble to the WTO Agreement recognizes the special needs of developing countries for positive efforts designed to ensure that they secure a share in the growth in international trade commensurate with their economic development needs. The preambles to many of the Uruguay Round agreements contain similar language. The references to LDCs are more generous. It is stipulated that LDCs will only be required to undertake commitments and concessions to an extent consistent with their individual development, financial and trade needs or their administrative and institutional capabilities. However, there are few provisions attempting to translate these broad objectives into concrete action.[105]

The Enabling Clause of 1979 provided the basis for "special treatment of least developed countries (LDCs) in the context of any general or specific measures in favor of

---

[101] For example, the United States and Canada exclude all textile and clothing products from their GSP programs, Japan excludes some agricultural and fishery products, and until the EBA initiative came into existence, European Union granted only selected preferences under the previous Lome Convention for agricultural products covered by the Common Agriculture Policy, and even fewer under the past European GSP schemes for LDCs. Even the EU "Everything But Arms" initiative for he time being excludes rice, bananas and sugar from the tariff- and quota-free scheme offered to the LDCs.

[102] Inama, *supra* note 97, at 92–94

[103] *See* Srinivasan, *supra* note 22, at 11

[104] Rodrik, *supra* note 17

[105] South Center, *Special and Differential Treatment Under the WTO* at www.southcenter.org/publications/s&d/s&d-04.htm

developing countries".[106] The Uruguay Round Agreements contain seventeen provisions that apply specifically to LDC Members, in addition to those that are applicable to all developing Members.[107] These include provisions for more extended transitional periods than those applicable to developing countries, in the TRIPS, TRIMS, and Sanitary and Phyto-sanitary Measures agreements. The Agreement on Agriculture exempts LDCs from all reduction commitments, while the Agreement on Subsidies and Countervailing Measures places no restriction on the ability of LDCs to grant export subsidies (though it does require them phase out import substitution subsidies, but over a longer period of time than that for other developing countries). The GATS Annex on Telecommunications contains a provision seeking to encourage private suppliers to transfer technology and training to LDCs with a view to developing the telecommunications sector.[108]

The key issues that need to be addressed in the context of the special provisions for the LDCs are much the same as in the case of developing countries as a whole: are the commitments for preferential market access and treatment offered by developed countries meaningful relative to the constraints these countries face in integrating in the world trading system? Is the international technical assistance in support of these countries adequate and effective? And does the flexibility offered to these countries in meeting their WTO commitments contribute to their long-term trade and development objectives?[109]

In spite of the "special and differential" provisions contained in various WTO Agreements, the LDCs are being increasingly marginalized. The "measures" in favor of LDCs have not been of much help to them. There has been a gap between prescription and practice. There is also a strong case for extending transition periods in areas where LDCs face real difficulties in meeting the deadline for reforms called for by the Uruguay Round Agreements. In fact, a number of measures supposed to have been adopted for the LDCs have remained unimplemented. There are three main reasons for this. First, developed countries have not shown a willingness to meet their obligations because these provisions are not legally binding and are mainly "best endeavor" clauses. Second, the LDCs have remained too weak to implement their side of the program. And finally, developed countries and multilateral agencies have, by and large, failed to come together to rescue the LDCs.

Kessie analyses five sets of special and differential treatment provided to the developing countries and LDCs in the Uruguay Round and comes to the conclusion that the provisions permitting longer implementation periods and the assumption of lesser obligations are the only enforceable provisions that are being applied in practice.[110] The other provisions are nothing more than loosely drafted "best endeavor" clauses.

---

[106] Art. 2 (d), Enabling Clause, *Supra* note 20. This 1979 decision by the GATT signatories allows derogations to the most-favored nation (non-discrimination) treatment in favor of developing countries.

[107] WTO, *Background Document*, HIGH LEVEL SYMPOSIUM ON TRADE AND DEVELOPMENT, Geneva, at 39–48 (March 17–18, 1999)

[108] Constantine Michalopoulos, TRADE AND DEVELOPMENT IN THE GATT AND WTO: THE ROLE OF SPECIAL AND DIFFERENTIAL TREATMENT FOR DEVELOPING COUNTRIES 23 (2000)

[109] *Id.*, at 23

[110] The five types are: i) provisions aimed at increasing trade opportunities; ii) provisions that require WTO Members to safeguard the interests of developing countries; iii) provisions permitting developing countries to assume lesser obligations; iv) provisions relating to transitional time periods; v) provisions relating to technical assistance. *See* Edwini Kessie, *Enforceability and Legal Provisions Relating to Special and Differential Treatment under the WTO Agreements*, 3(6) THE JOURNAL OF WORLD INTELLECTUAL PROPERTY RIGHTS 965 (1999)

C. Integrated Framework

The Integrated Framework ("IF") was "endorsed" at the HLM in October 1997 essentially as the institutional mechanism for the delivery of trade-related technical assistance to LDCs by the six core participating Agencies—the International Trade Center ("ITC"), the IMF, UNCTAD, the United Nations Development Program ("UNDP"), theWorld Bank and the WTO. The IF has been in operation since October 1997.[111]

As defined in the Integrated Framework document, the IF aims to:

- Ensure that trade-related technical assistance activities are demand-driven by the least-developed countries and meet their individual needs effectively
- Enhance ownership by each least-developed country over the trade-related technical assistance activities being provided
- Enable each agency involved to increase its efficiency and effectiveness in the delivery of trade-related technical assistance activities
- Keep under review trade-related technical assistance activities in individual least-developed countries, evaluate periodically their success in meeting the country's needs, review how those needs change, and adapt the program of activities accordingly
- Provide comprehensive information about the specific needs of each least-developed country and about the trade-related technical assistance activities of the six Agencies involved to other relevant multilateral and regional intergovernmental organisations, to bilateral development partners and to the private sector.[112]

Despite the noble intentions of the IF it has not so far achieved its intended goals. Hoekman and Kostecki comment;

> The IF did little to address the underlying causes of the implementation problems of LDCs. In part this was because it did not address the disconnect between a number of the WTO agreements and the development priorities of low-income countries and in part it reflected the lack of adequate funding.[113]

The review of the Integrated Framework, pursuant to paragraph 6 of the Framework document that emerged from the 1997 High Level Meeting, was initiated in November 1999 by the six core Agencies, in consultation with LDCs and their development partners. Prior to consideration by the Agencies, an independent review team was appointed to make its own assessment. The objective of the exercise was to review the three-year operation of the IF in the light of experience that urgently required the agencies to respond to a number of issues and to improve the IF as a vehicle for delivering trade-related technical assistance.[114] The report of the independent review of the IF provided the following recommendations for the improvement of the IF, both in terms of its design and its delivery mechanism:

---

[111] WTO, *Progress Report on the Integrated Framework for Trade-Related Technical Assistance to Least-Developed Countries*, REPORT BY THE DIRECTOR-GENERAL, WT/LDC/SWG/IF/17/REV. 1, (April 17, 2001)
[112] *Id.* at 2–3
[113] Bernard M. Hoekman and Michel M. Kostecki, THE POLITICAL ECONOMY OF THE WORLD TRADING SYSTEM: THE WTO AND BEYOND 399 (2001)
[114] Problems and challenges facing the IF are well documented. *See* for example, WT/MIN(99)/7, WT/COMTD/LDC/W/18 and WT/LDC/SWG/IF/1.

1. *Clarify Policy Objectives*: Clarify the objectives of the IF by restricting it to technical assistance for trade-related development, to support, *inter alia*, policy reforms, manpower and human resources development, customs reforms, institutional change and legal environment reforms.

2. *Prioritise and Link to Overall Development Assistance Architecture*: In the future most development assistance strategy issues are likely to be developed through participatory processes, in the context of such exercises as the Poverty Reduction Strategy Papers ("PRSPs"), the Comprehensive Development Framework ("CDF") and the United Nations Development Strategy Frameworks ("UNDAF"). In all such endeavours, country strategy will define the role of trade development and related technical assistance. The IF will then be linked to the priorities established through the formulation of country development strategies.

3. *Give Ownership to the LDCs*: Make the IF process more demand-driven and country-owned by requiring LDCs to prioritise their specific needs from the list of trade-related technical assistance activities listed in the Needs Assessments.

4. *Strengthen Governance and Administration*: The review considered two options: (i) strengthening the Administrative Unit to the point that it can manage the IF while continuing to be located at the ITC in Geneva, and (ii) moving the responsibility for managing the IF to WTO (where the Administrative Unit would be integrated).

5. *Coordination Issues*: Once governance is strengthened along the lines of the foregoing recommendation, coordination can be better assured, as the WTO will be the designated clearinghouse for inter-agency coordination issues.

6. *Funding the IF*: First, the Inter-agency Working Group ("IAWG") agencies and donors will need to ensure that they budget their administrative costs related to the IF while providing whatever other incentives are needed for a better recognition of the responsibilities which they undertook when the IF was created. Second, when it comes to the financing of trade-related technical assistance projects, one approach would be for WTO, as the managing agency for the IF, to set up and manage a Trust Fund to finance such technical assistance projects. All donors, including multilateral agencies, would contribute (on a voluntary basis) to the Trust Fund as an expression of their commitment to the IF.

7. *Monitor Trade-Related Technical Assistance Performance*: As trade development activities are brought into the mainstream by including them in the overall assistance process, they will be monitored and evaluated along with the progress of other programs in the countries. However, these reviews should go beyond the review of consistency with trade rules to assess how well trade regimes and trade-related technical assistance are contributing to the integration of LDCs into the global trading environment.

8. *Enlarging the IF to Other Countries and Agencies*: This review recommends that the question of enlarging the IF be revisited in the future, after the new recommended arrangements are in place for about three years. At that time a review could be undertaken to see what progress had been made since 1997 to advance the objectives established for the IF.[115]

Based on the review report, it was decided that a pilot scheme would be initiated. The IF Steering Committee also agreed to proceed with the implementation of the IF Pilot

[115] WTO, *supra* note 111, at 7.

Scheme based on the Pilot Phase Work Program prepared by the World Bank, on behalf of the IAWG. The Work Program sets out the stages for implementing the trade integration strategy chapters, and lists the cluster of possible countries in the Pilot scheme on the basis of which the mainstreaming of trade integration analysis into PRSPs would proceed.[116] A typical pilot project begins with diagnostic trade studies that assess the external competitiveness of the LDC. The studies present recommendations for enhancing trade capacity and undertaking pro-poor reforms, and it is anticipated that these will inform the PRSP process.

To date, integration studies for three pilot LDCs (Cambodia, Madagascar and Mauritania) have been completed and submitted to respective government authorities. Diagnostic studies for Lesotho, Malawi and Senegal are now being prepared and it is expected that a total of eight such studies will be implemented during the course of 2002.[117] Based on the successful implementation of the Pilot Scheme, it will be replicated in other LDCs. However, it must be pointed out that without the commitment of the donors to commit funds for building capacity of the LDCs to enhance their trade performance, the efforts are likely to be futile.

V. Achievements of Recent International Conferences

Of late there has been a growing recognition of the need to prevent the marginalization of LDCs from the multilateral trading system, due to the untiring efforts made by United Nations bodies such as UNCTAD and UNDP, coupled with the increase in the size and influence of pro-LDC constituencies in the developed countries—mostly civil society organizations, development agencies and media. This realization is reflected in the commitment made by the global leaders at a number of international conferences. However, one needs to recognize the fact that commitments made during these conferences do not serve any useful purpose if they are not implemented in practice. To further complicate the matter, some of the commitments made during the international conferences do not have any more than moral value—they are only a reflection of the admittance of the fact that problems do exit and that they need to be corrected. However, commitments made in some of the Conferences such as the WTO Ministerial Conferences are binding to a large extent.

In the recent past, five major conferences have made some reference to the marginalization of LDCs and drawn the attention of the international communities of the need to reverse this trend.[118] However, this paper only analyzes the impacts of two of these conferences, both held in 2001, which have a direct bearing on the topic being discussed here. They are: the Third United Nations Conference on LDCs; and the Fourth Ministerial Conference of the WTO.

A. *Third United Nations Conference on LDCs*

The Third U.N. Conference on LDCs held in Brussels in May 2001 provided one more opportunity to the international community to identify ways of integrating the LDCs

---

[116] *Id.*, at 9

[117] *See* http://www1.worldbank.org/wbiep/trade/Integrated_framework.html.

[118] They are: the United Nations Millennium Summit held in New York in September 2000; the Third United Nations Conference on LDC ("UNLDC III") held in Brussels in May 2001; the Fourth Ministerial Conference of the WTO held in Doha in November 2001; the Financing for Development Conference held in Monterrey in March 2002; and the World Summit on Sustainable Development held in August-September 2002 in Johannesburg.

into the world economy. Its main focus was the *Paris Declaration* and *the Programme of Action for the Least Developed Countries for the 1990s*. In this Declaration, the international community had committed itself to urgent and effective action, based on the principle of shared responsibility and strengthened partnership, to arrest and reverse the deterioration in the socio-economic situation of the LDCs and to revitalize their growth and development.

The Conference focused on making objective assessments with regard to commitments made in the areas of Official Development Assistance ("ODA"), debt relief, investment promotion, and international trade. The Conference agreed on seven areas of commitment, in which both the international community and national governments would work together: a people-centered policy framework, good governance, capacity building, productive resources, trade and development, environmental protection, and mobilization of financial resources.[119]

The Conference recognized the need to transform trade into a powerful engine for growth and poverty alleviation in LDCs. The role of trade in generating resources for financing growth and development as a complement to ODA and FDI was fully underscored. Accordingly, the international community has undertaken to assist LDCs in capacity building in trade policy and related areas, developing human and institutional capacities for meaningful participation in multilateral trade negotiations, and removing procedural and institutional bottlenecks that increase transaction costs. Similarly, LDCs have been assured of assistance, *inter alia*, in the areas of trade diversification, infrastructure development and regional/sub-regional cooperation.

The Conference also underlined the need for improving preferential market access for LDCs, full implementation of special and differential treatment measures contemplated by the WTO system, simplified accession procedures, and due representation of LDCs in international standards organizations. In the area of market access, however, the Brussels Program of Action cautiously states that development partners will 'aim at' (rather than 'commit to') enhancing LDC participation in the multilateral trading system. In their declaration, trade, finance and development cooperation ministers resoundingly underscored their belief that increased trade was "essential for the growth and development of LDCs", but they only committed themselves "to seizing the opportunity of the fourth WTO Ministerial meeting in Doha to advance the development dimension of trade, in particular for the development of LDCs".[120] For example, paragraph 68 (h) of Commitment 5 (enhancing the role of trade in development) reads:

> "Development partners will aim at...(h) Improving preferential market access for LDCs by working towards the objective of duty-free and quota-free market access for all LDCs' products."

This contrasts with earlier draft language that would have committed the partners to aiming a little higher, i.e., "removing all trade barriers facing LDC exports in the markets of developed trade partners in the shortest possible time, and in any case no later than 2003."[121] Similarly, the aim to make technical assistance for "the implementation of multilateral trade agreements mandatory and an integral part to be undertaken in

---

[119] UNCTAD, *Programme of Action for the Least Developed Countries adopted by the Third United Nations Conference on Least Developed Countries in Brussels on 20 May*, A/CONF. 191/11 (2001)

[120] ICTSD, *Least Developed Countries: No New Trade Concessions Before Doha*, BRIDGES MONTHLY REVIEW 1 (2001)

[121] *Id.*

future trade agreements" emerged in the adopted action program as "strengthening, as required, technical assistance for the implementation of multilateral trade agreements and considering making such technical assistance an integral part of commitments to be taken in future trade agreements."[122]

Despite the use of 'soft' language, the Conference emphasises effective implementation of the Integrated Framework and encourages new and additional contributions to the Trust Fund created under the Framework. Importantly, the Conference requested developed countries and multilateral agencies to provide assistance to LDCs in their efforts to develop infrastructure for tradable services in which they have comparative advantage.[123]

The Brussels Conference outcome could still be considered as a major breakthrough in overcoming the semantic barriers. However, if past experience is any guide, at best it provides a basis for further talks on the possibility of implementing Conference decisions. As mentioned above, what is intriguing is the language in which these decisions are presented. They are expressed as being "commitments" on the part of the respective governments/agencies. However, the Program of Action adopted at the Conference uses recommendatory language. In fact, the so-called "commitments" are even weaker than recommendations. Reviewing the text of the Program, one gets the impression that participants of the Conference wanted to present to the international community an ideal situation without bothering about how this could be realized. In other words, this is again simply "best-endeavour" language, not a series of binding commitments.[124]

B. Fourth WTO Ministerial Conference (Doha)

Despite their meager achievements at the Brussels Conference, the LDCs were of the opinion that whatever little had been achieved should be reviewed in the Doha Ministerial Conference (November 2001) in order to ensure that "commitments" could be made binding. In fact, one of the purposes of the Zanzibar Meeting of the LDC Trade Ministers (July 2001) was to achieve the same objective. This Meeting did conclude with a number of concrete proposals, not only on the Brussels issues, but also on other fundamental issues, including, but not limited to, the development agenda. The Meeting called upon the Doha Ministerial Conference, among other elements, to agree upon:

- A binding commitment on duty- and quota-free market access for all the products from LDCs on a secure long-term and predictable basis, with realistic and flexible Rules of Origin to match the industrial capacity of LDCs
- A binding and full implementation of the provisions of Special and Differential Treatment, including the adoption of new Special and Differential Measures to take into account problems encountered by LDCs in implementation
- A future work program manageable in scope and size and agreed by all WTO Members by consensus and future negotiations based on an agenda that would accommodate LDC interests
- Meaningful support from development partners to provide assistance to upgrade the trade-related infrastructure of LDCs, cancel debts and strengthen UNCTAD's technical assistance and capacity-building programs on multilateral trade negotiation issues.[125]

---

[122] *Id.*
[123] Ghimire, *supra* note 13, at 355
[124] *Id.* at 356–7
[125] Charverait, *supra* note 59, at 107

However, the momentum gained during the Zanzibar Meeting could not be sustained in Doha for several reasons. First, developed countries may have considered that there were many other more pressing needs during the Doha Conference than fulfilling the demands of the LDCs. Second, LDC issues became diluted because of the fight between developed and developing countries on implementation issues versus a new round of negotiations, which also implies the possibility of inclusion of new issues. Third, LDCs, as a group, despite being generally cohesive, could not create the required impact on the Conference. Although there was some mention of the LDC concerns in the final Ministerial Declaration, the imperatives of effective participation of the LDCs in the multilateral trading system could not, and did not, receive due consideration from the ministers with many diverse interests.

The Doha outcomes do not meet even a fraction of the expectations of the LDCs, particularly in relation to the so-called "confidence-building measures", devised by WTO Director-General Mike Moore. The initiative, at least in theory, included: a) a proposal for an expanded WTO technical assistance program; b) enhanced market access for LDCs; and c) consultations between the WTO and other organisations on trade-related capacity building.[126]

The Doha Ministerial Declaration recognized the particular needs, interests and concerns of the LDCs in 21 different paragraphs. These references fall into two broad categories: first, broad, systemic issues; second, part of the negotiating mandate of particular WTO Bodies.[127] These are related to, *inter alia*, marginalization, accession, services negotiations, industrial tariff negotiations, investment, competition policy, trade facilitation, environment, debt and finance, technical cooperation and capacity building, and special and differential treatment.

The single major achievement for LDCs is probably best expressed in the following sentence in paragraph 42 of the final Doha Declaration reproduced in the Appendix to this book:

> "We commit ourselves to the objective of duty-free, quota-free market access for products originating from LDCs. In this regard, we welcome the significant market access improvements by WTO Members in advance of the Third UN Conference on LDCs (LDC-III), in Brussels, May 2001. We further commit ourselves to consider additional measures for progressive improvements in market access for LDCs."

This is a much better formulation than paragraph 68 of the Brussels Program of Action, even though the developed countries might still be reluctant to act concretely in this regard. Having realized that the prevailing attitude of both the ministers of developed Member countries as well as of the WTO secretariat was to provide "lip service", the LDC ministers insisted on a time-bound action program for use by the Sub-Committee for Least Developed Countries to design a work program concerning trade-related elements of the Brussels Declaration and Program of Action, and to report on the agreed work program to the WTO General Council at its first meeting in 2002. Similarly, the following sentence is contained in paragraph 43 of the Declaration related to the Integrated Framework:

> "We request the Director-General, following coordination with heads of the other agencies, to provide an interim report to the General Council in December 2002 and a full report to the Fifth Session of the Ministerial Conference on all issues affecting LDCs."

---

[126] *See* OECD, *supra* note 72, at 24
[127] WTO, *WTO Work Programme for the Least Developed Countries (LDCs) Adopted by the Sub-committee on Least Developed Countries*, WT/COMTD/LDC/11 (February 13, 2002)

To some extent, the Doha Conference can be considered as an attempt to bridge the gap between the developed and the developing as well as least-developed countries. However, a number of proposals made by the LDCs after the Zanzibar meeting were not included in the text. For example, the LDCs were resolutely opposed to the launching of the new WTO round—for a multiplicity of reasons, including the possibility of the expansion of the jurisdiction of the WTO into the areas in which they have no expertise, and the imperative of not diverting attention from the earlier commitments made (but as yet unimplemented) in favor of LDCs.[128] Similarly, the market access text does not cover most of the decisions of the Zanzibar meeting. Nonetheless, on the whole, the Doha Declaration can be considered as a positive step towards realizing the concerns of the LDCs.

VI. What Should the LDCs Do?

Having discussed how some of the well-meaning efforts made so far at the international level to integrate LDCs into the MTS have failed to produce noticeable impact, it is also necessary to see what LDCs have done for themselves in the past three decades or so to become a part of the system and protect their interest within it. It appears that LDCs have failed to make serious efforts towards this end. This author believes that it is also necessary for them to make some of their own endeavors in this direction, which can be complemented and supplemented by international efforts. The major initiatives have to come from the LDCs themselves, since the international assistance only fills in around the edges. The following represent a non-exhaustive list of what LDCs should be doing in this respect.

A. Striving to Become a Part of the Knowledge-Based Economy

There is no shortcut to becoming part of the knowledge-based economy. One way of doing so would be to compel the advanced economies to transfer technology at favorable terms and conditions. However, given the fate of the mandated requirement contained in Article 66:2 of TRIPS Agreement[129] resulting from the notoriously apathetic attitude of the industrialized countries, the LDCs should at least start working proactively towards promoting technologies in their own countries or obtain help from their regional trading partners to gain access to modern technologies.

It is well known that the developing countries in general and the LDCs in particular are strongly opposed to the TRIPS Agreement. However, they have no choice but to accept it as a *fait accompli* and a mechanism to spur innovation in their respective countries. In order to do so, they need to enact legislation and set up institutions to promote innovation and protect intellectual property rights. The sooner they do it, the better. Similarly, in the areas of promoting information technology some LDCs have already established information technology parks and others have incubator facilities in place to attract private sector investment. These useful initiatives can be replicated by other LDCs.

B. Mainstreaming Trade with Development Strategies and Processes

Despite the fact that there is no clear linkage between trade and growth because of the difficulty in disaggregating the impact of trade openness and other policy reforms

---

[128] Hiramani Ghimire, *The WTO at a Crossroads: Implications of Doha Meeting for LDCs*, SAWTEE NEWSLETTER 22, 9 (2001).

[129] *See supra* note 78.

undertaken by countries, more open economies have grown faster than closed economies over the last four decades or so. While this chapter makes it clear that many LDCs have done their utmost to open their economies, some of them could not produce beneficial results because of a lack of coherence between trade policies and other development policies. It is in this context that mainstreaming trade with development strategies and process is being advocated. Mainstreaming has been defined as involving the process and methods for identifying priority areas for trade and integrating them into the overall country development plan.[130]

The vehicle for mainstreaming trade into comprehensive development frameworks and for ensuring more effective implementation of the Integrated Framework, will be the World Bank/IMF Poverty Reduction Strategy Papers and the United Nations Development Assistance Framework, with the World Bank taking the lead. In order to ensure that LDCs do follow this process, the six core agencies of the IF program have made it a major requirement for eligibility for support from the IF program.

C. Building Capacity

Integration of the LDCs into the multilateral trading system has been hampered by a serious lack of capacity, whether in terms of being able to trade or to participate in the trade negotiating process or in terms of implementation of the commitments assumed by them in multilateral fora. At the domestic level, LDCs should make efforts to develop the core competencies of their trade officials and promote specialization. The frequent transfer of staff who have been well trained on trade matters to other ministries and departments should be avoided. When there is a training opportunity for the officials, it should be provided to the official handling the relevant program rather than to the official who is the favored candidate of the secretary or the minister.

While donors can help to some extent by providing resources and skills, the initiative for such capacity-building exercises must come from the concerned LDC itself. A number of international and bilateral donors have come forward to help build the trade capacity of the developing countries and LDCs. However, most of them require such technical assistance to be demand-driven—i.e., demand for such technical assistance should come from the country concerned. This effectively means that unless and until LDCs request such assistance, it is unlikely to be given. The LDCs that have not even been able to identify their needs and priorities are likely to be in a disadvantageous position. Therefore, they should at least start these processes and do their utmost to tap into the international resources for building their trade capacity.

D. Developing Human Resources

Developing skilled human resources is the key to success in seizing opportunities of market opening. The emphasis placed by East Asian countries on this aspect of social development provides an outstanding example of a success story, which is worth emulating by the LDCs. Human resources are becoming key to success in international trade. From an LDC perspective, three areas of interest could be identified. First, capacities need to be developed in product innovation. Second, promotion of marketing skills should be stressed. These qualities are needed basically in private-sector enterprises. The third area of interest could be the workforce in the public sector, especially institutions dealing

---

[130] OECD, *supra* note 72, at 29

with trade and commerce. Deficiencies in trade-related expertise, analytical skills and negotiating skills are a product of small staff, limited resources for hiring and training, inadequate experience, and high turnover. Most African LDCs, for example, have fewer than five officials assigned to work on trade policy issues on a full-time basis.[131]

There is a striking dearth in the LDCs of trade personnel ranging from trade lawyers to trade diplomats. Again here, there are two challenges. First, the general competence of personnel has to be enhanced, which is easier. The more difficult part of the job is to develop a "flair" for trade among those who are supposed to handle trade issues.[132]

Finally, LDCs have been raising the issue of a more liberal framework for the movement of natural persons in developed countries under GATS. Though negotiations have stalled on the issue, recent "invitations" in some countries to IT professionals from the developing world shows that quality labour does find markets.[133] The LDCs should not only recognize this potential, but also aim at utilizing it by investing in education, training and skill development.

E. Diversification of Export Profile

High dependence on limited export items such as commodities (agricultural and mineral) and low-value products (textiles and apparel) act as a major stumbling block in enhancing trading opportunities for the LDCs. However, few if any efforts have been made so far by the LDCs either to reduce their export concentration ratio or to develop into new areas of products or services which could be exported into the international market. Therefore, it is necessary for the LDCs, first and foremost, to recognize whatever comparative advantages they may possess.

The fact that most LDCs have been dependent on exporting primary products does not mean that they should only concentrate on exporting them. The success story of Bangladesh, which used to be an exporter of primary commodities and which has now become a major LDC exporter of valued-added products (such as apparel), provides an outstanding example.[134] Moreover, there are some service sectors in which LDCs are more competitive than in any other areas, such as tourism (Bhutan, Burma, Cambodia, Nepal and Tanzania) and hydroelectricity (Bhutan[135] and Nepal). However, these sectors cannot develop unless and until LDCs recognize their comparative advantages and devote their resources towards harnessing their potential both for the domestic as well as international market.

---

[131] OECD, *supra* note 72, at 34

[132] Ghimire, *supra* note 13, at 359

[133] In fact due to the shortage of IT manpower in the United States, high-technology companies are lobbying their government to relax visa restrictions to facilitate temporary entry of IT professional into the country. *See* World Bank, GLOBAL ECONOMIC PROSPECT AND THE DEVELOPING COUNTRIES 2002, 87 (2002)

[134] Apparel exports of Bangladesh have increased at an average rate of 19.39 percent during the period 1990–2001, starting at the comparatively modest level of US$ 866.82 million in 1990 and reaching US$ 4,860 million in 2001. *See* Bangladesh Garment Manufacturers and Exporters Association website at http://www.bgmea.com/data.htm, accessed on 9 June 2002

[135] Indeed the export profile of Bhutan has been radically altered after it started exporting hydroelectricity to its Southern neighbor, India. Power generation contributes 41.7 percent (1998–99 revenue data) of the country's total revenue generation. The power sector's contribution to GDP was about ten percent. Its contribution to the national economy will be tripled after the commissioning of the Tala Hydropower project. *See* Consumer Unity and Trust Society, CONSUMER PROTECTION IN BHUTAN: PAST, PRESENT AND FUTURE, REPORT PREPARED FOR THE ROYAL GOVERNMENT OF BHUTAN (2001)

F. Promoting Accountable Governance

Misgovernance, particularly corruption in high offices and an utter disregard for transparency norms and the rule of law are major problems in the LDCs, which the politicians of these countries often refuse to acknowledge. Corruption is a tax on the capacity of a country to trade because it creates distortion and results in cost escalation of otherwise competitive exports, rendering them uncompetitive in the global market. A predictable business environment, for example, is a precondition for attracting foreign direct investment and enhancing trade opportunities. However, frequent changes in decisions based on the whim of politicians or pressures from vested interest groups , as well as political instability, are major impediments to the growth of trade and investment.

LDCs like Bangladesh, Tanzania, Uganda being on the list of highly corrupt countries shows that they have a long way to go before uprooting corruption. Their ability to counter corruption is hampered, *inter alia*, by: a) lack of credible state commitment to rule of law; b) desire of political parties to stick to power by whatever possible means and their patronage to the corrupt officials[136]; c) lack of effective legal and institutional mechanism; d) questionable efficacy of anti-corruption agencies;[137] and e) low moral standards and social prestige associated with wealth, irrespective of the means used to generate it.

Intuitively one can argue that there is a positive correlation between openness and lack of corruption—more open economies are less corrupt than their closed counterparts. Not surprisingly, there is some empirical support for this view.[138] According to the Corruption Perception Index produced by Transparency International for the year 2001, some of the open developing economies like Singapore, Hong Kong, and Chile figure among the top twenty least corrupt countries (even ahead of some OECD countries), whereas relatively closed economies like Bangladesh, Nigeria, Russia and Ukraine are among the top twenty most corrupt countries.[139] Promoting good governance through administrative reform, reduction in discretionary authority and a sound economic system based on competition and rule of law is therefore a vital component of trade and economic growth. If LDCs themselves do not have the political will to uproot corruption from their society, no amount of international support is likely to produce positive impact in the areas of trade and investment.

G. Macro-Economic Reforms

Since the late 1980s most LDCs have initiated macro-economic reforms. In fact 33 LDCs have undertaken policy reforms under the IMF-financed Structural Adjustment Facility or Enhanced Structural Adjustment Facility program since 1988. Available evidence

---

[136] In Nepal some of the bureaucrats pay huge amounts to politicians to get transfers to "lucrative" departments such as the revenue department, and some of them promise continued streams of benefits to the politicians during their tenure.

[137] In Uganda, for example, anti-corruption agencies are often doled out large sums of money as a part of the government's patronage. They have turned into bodies managing public relations, not for combating graft. *See* Charles Obbo-Onyango, *The NRM Factor in Uganda's Corruption" in The East Africa*, available at http://www.charlesobbo.com/article134.htm, accessed on 18 September 2002

[138] A "naturally more open economy"—as determined by its size and geography—devotes more resources to building good institutions and displays less corruption. *See* Shang Jin Wei, NATURAL OPENNESS AND GOOD GOVERNMENT at http://econ.worldbank.org/docs/1166.pdf

[139] Transparency International (2001), *Corruption Perception Index* at http://www.transparency.org/cpi/2001/cpi2001.html#cpi, accessed on 9 June 2002.

suggests that LDCs have kept up with other developing countries in the process of structural reform in all areas except financial sector reform and the reform of the public enterprises sector, and they have gone further than other developing countries in the area of pricing and marketing reform.[140] However, the stability of the macro-economic environment and sending the right signal to the market players require much more than what most LDCs have been able to achieve so far.

Trivial though this may sound, economic analysis and interviews with entrepreneurs inevitably lead to the conclusion that obstacles to trade itself are dwarfed by the constraints stemming from the macro-economic environment.[141] No amount of trade liberalization, export orientation or trade capacity development could help a country enhance its trade performance if it has a wrong macro-economic policy such as an overvalued exchange rate. In fact, an overvalued exchange rate is often the root cause of protection, and the country will be unable to return to the more liberal trade policies that allow growth without exchange rate adjustment.[142] The CFA countries provide one of the most striking examples of the impact of exchange rate overvaluation on growth and the gains from improved exchange rate policies. The currencies of CFA countries (Burkina Faso, Cameroon, Central African Republic, Chad, Ivory Coast, Gabon, Mali, Niger, Senegal and Togo) are tied to the French franc, and at various times appreciation of franc, deterioration in the terms of trade, and higher inflation in CFA countries contributed to a highly appreciated currency that tended to depress export and GDP growth, the latter to 0.7 percent for 1986 to 1993. The CFA franc was devalued in 1994, and GDP growth accelerated to 4.7 percent per year during 1994–1998. Similarly, exports grew from—4.8 percent per year in 1986–93 to 7.8 percent per year in 1994–98.[143]

H. Compensating the Losers

International trade scholars have long understood that although for small countries, trade interventions are generally inefficient and wasteful, their inefficiency is usually dominated quantitatively by their re-distributive effects. Although removing interventions will generally be income enhancing overall, it is likely to generate both winners and losers.[144]

In part countries are reluctant to take trade liberalization measures because of the fear of huge adjustment costs they could impose on the economy. Protectionist lobbies in many countries are more vocal and powerful than the lobby in favor of trade liberalization. Protectionists often make the case that possible downsides such as increase in poverty is a strong reason to oppose reforms. While it is true that poverty may be accentuated in the short run, the long run impact of trade liberalization is often found to be income enhancing. What is therefore required is a transitional compensatory and adjustment mechanism to overcome the problem of temporary poverty. However, the adjustment process is glacially slow in some countries as compared to others. LDCs in particular find it impossible to make necessary adjustment without external assistance.

---

[140] UNCTAD, *supra* note 7, at 13

[141] Lecomte H.B Slignac, *Building Capacity to Trade: A Roadmap for Development Partners—Insights from Africa and the Caribbean*, European Centre for Development Policy Management, DISCUSSION PAPER 33 (2001)

[142] Harward J Shatz and David G. Tarr, *Exchange Rate Overvaluation and Trade Protection* in DEVELOPMENT, TRADE, AND THE WTO 17 (Bernard Hoekman, Aaditya Mattoo, and Philip English eds., 2002)

[143] *See* World Bank, GLOBAL ECONOMIC PROSPECTS AND DEVELOPING COUNTRIES 2001, 13 (2001)

[144] L. Alan Winters, *Trade Policies for Poverty Alleviation*, in Hoekman, Mattoo, and English, *supra* note 142, at 28.

According to Bhagawati: "We need adjustment assistance programs to take care of these adverse effects when they arise. In some poor countries, the ability to provide such adjustment assistance, which requires budgetary support, may be strictly circumscribed. In that case, it should be precisely the role of Bretton Woods agencies to provide grant funds to make possible a welfare-enhancing, poverty-reducing transition to free trade."[145] However, one must also admit that adjustment process should begin at home. Unless and until potential losers from trade reform are assured of due compensation they are likely to oppose any reform process. Therefore, it is the duty of the State to ensure that they are provided with appropriate compensation.

I. Use of Safeguards

It is well established that openness in general is preferable to protectionism. However, unfettered free trade without any checks and balances can be an open invitation to disaster, as has been made clear by the Asian crisis and the ongoing crisis in Argentina. It is therefore necessary to create space for policy manoeuvres, especially in the economically sensitive sectors. It is in this sense that safeguard arrangements are recommended. The purposes of safeguards include the promotion of self-reliance, especially in critical areas such as food security, the protection of natural resources, and the arrest of capital flight.[146]

There may be scope for retaining and utilizing domestic measures selectively and in a transparent manner that is not in contradiction with the multilateral obligations (such as WTO rules) of the countries concerned, in order to foster industries that make a strong contribution to overall export growth and competitiveness in the economy. A liberal trade regime, which provides vital access to competitive imports and is supplemented by selective and relatively moderate domestic safeguard measures is a surer way to achieve openness and reduce poverty than a complicated system of taxes and subsidies.[147]

J. Improving Communications Between Government and Non-Government Sector

Mechanisms for consultation on trade policy among governments, the private sector and civil society are weak or non-existent in most LDCs. In addition, the lack of competent enterprise sector and civil society interlocutors is an impediment to policy dialogue.[148] Involvement of private sector and civil society is crucial in three of the following four stages in the policy cycle: a) formulation of trade policy and strategy; b) preparation of negotiating positions and strategy; c) implementation of agreements; and d) monitoring and evaluation of policies and agreements. The participation of these stakeholders is of vital significance in each of these except stage (c).[149]

This is more a matter of culture and ethos in the LDCs and has nothing to do with the way the global trading system functions. No amount of market access or special and differential treatment could help LDCs improve the process of consultation. Technical assistance provided by some agencies is specifically targeted to improve communication between government on the one hand and non-governmental actors such as private sectors and civil society organizations on the other. However, the process should begin at home.

---

[145] Jagdish Bhagwati, FREE TRADE TODAY, 90 (2002)
[146] Ghimire, supra note 13, at 361
[147] OECD, *supra* note 72, at 27
[148] OECD, *supra* note 72, at 34
[149] OECD, *supra* note 72, at 42

While it is true that private sector and civil society organisations are poorly funded and do not clearly understand the issues at stake in order to be able to make informed contributions to the policy dialogue, and therefore may require some form of technical assistance and capacity building exercise, this should not preclude the LDC governments from at least initiating the process of consultation with the key stakeholders.

K. Building Credible Alliances

Forty-nine LDCs, which collectively account for 0.42 percent of the world trade, cannot produce any noticeable impact at the international fora, including the WTO, unless and until they become a part of larger alliances.[150] One of the most difficult choices for the LDCs is whether they should all form an LDC alliance or make their positions known through the regional integration agreements to which they belong.

LDCs belong to different categories of groupings with varied interests. Therefore, when it comes to preparing one position for international meetings, they have usually failed to come up with a unified position because of their inherent propensity to splinter for reasons of narrow self-interest or because they have been swayed by other interest groups. It is understandable why it is often impossible for them to make issue-based alliances, because they have different priorities. For example, the Asian LDCs may be more interested in an extension of the apparel quota system after its planned demise at the end of 2004, while African LDCs, which are primarily dependent on exports of primary agricultural products, may be more interested on lowering of trade barriers in agricultural products. However, when it comes to key policy issues such as providing zero tariff access to the OECD market, they could take a firm stand and should not be swayed by the arguments of other groups.

VII. Conclusion

Reversing the appalling trend of marginalization of the LDCs within the global trading system, despite their relative openness to international trade, will not be an easy task. Some of the genuine efforts by various multilateral, bilateral and intergovernmental agencies to achieve such a reversal have not produced desired results. Clearly, there is a need to arrest this adverse trend by moving beyond rhetoric. This is not only necessary for helping LDCs overcome the vicious circle they are faced with, but also for the very survival of the multilateral trading system. However, the LDCs are equally to be blamed for the continuation of the *status quo*.

At the same time the international community must show solidarity with the poorest of the world, guaranteeing open markets for all products exported by the LDCs. This would be in the enlightened self-interest of the developed countries as it would be creating markets for increased imports from their countries in the long run. If the marginalization of LDCs continues unabated, it would not only threaten to derail the process of trade liberalization achieved through several rounds of acrimonious multilateral trade negotiations, but also imperil the prospect of global peace and security.

As time goes by and the international community becomes increasingly aware of the need to better integrate LDCs into the multilateral trading system, things seem to be moving in the right direction. The LDCs have been gaining incremental support or commitments from their development partners. There is a growing realization that

---

[150] *See* H.B Slignac, *supra* note 141

industrial countries must open their markets for the products of the LDCs—not only in letter but also in spirit—to help the LDCs come out of the present trap they have fallen into.

Starting from the Marrakesh Ministerial Conference, and traversing through Singapore, Geneva and Brussels, the Doha Ministerial Conference too did recognize the special problems facing the LDCs. However, Doha Declaration has fallen far short of the expectation of the LDCs. Considering the attitude of the developed countries, and taking their past record of fulfillment as a guide, even the few commitments made during the Doha Conference should also be closely monitored by the LDCs to ensure that they are translated into reality. As a priority the LDCs should focus on operationalizing Paragraph 42 of Doha Declaration.

Finally, it is necessary for the LDCs to understand that they need to keep their own house in order, so as to reap the benefits of improved market openings. If they continue to blame the international community for their failure to correct the problems they have created for themselves, they will not be taken seriously.

Taking account of the lack of sincere commitment and paucity of efforts on the part of various actors and tendency of pointing fingers on one another for the lack of progress in terms of integrating LDCs into the MTS, it is necessary to set *time tables* and *targets* with the binding commitment on the part of the key actors to fulfill them. However, the exercise of setting the timetable requires further research and assessment (which is beyond the scope of this chapter) without which it would be as arbitrary as the transitional timetables agreed during the UR.

BIBLIOGRAPHY

B.L Das, THE WORLD TRADE ORGANISATION: A GUIDE TO THE FRAMEWORK FOR INTERNATIONAL TRADE, 232 (1999)

Bernard Hoekman and L. Alan Winters, *A Tribute to J. Michael Finger* in DEVELOPMENT, TRADE, AND THE WTO, xiv (Bernard Hoekman, Aaditya Mattoo, and Philip English eds. 2002)

Bernard Hoekman, Francis Ng, and Marcelo Olarreaga, ELIMINATING EXCESSIVE TARIFFS ON EXPORTS OF LEAST DEVELOPED COUNTRIES (2001)

Bernard Hoekman, STRENGTHENING THE GLOBAL TRADE ARCHITECTURE FOR DEVELOPMENT, 5 (2002)

Bernard M. Hoekman and Michel M. Kostecki, THE POLITICAL ECONOMY OF THE WORLD TRADING SYSTEM: THE WTO AND BEYOND, 380 (2001)

Byung-il Choi, *Treatment of Autonomous Liberalization in the WTO New Service Round—To Give Credit is to Get More*, 35 JOURNAL OF WORLD TRADE 2, 364 (2001)

C.P Chandrasekhar and Jayati Ghosh, *WTO and Poor Countries* CUTS-CITEE BRIEFING PAPER 3. (2000)

Celine Charverait, *The New Cycle of WTO Negotiations as an Opportunity to Fulfill Promises Made at the U.N. LDC-III Conference: The View of Oxfam International* in UNCTAD-CIVIL SOCIETY DIALOGUE ON SELECTED DEVELOPMENT ISSUES BEING ADDRESSED BY THE UNITED NATIONS SYSTEM UNCTAD/ISS/Misc. 385, 110 (2002)

Charles Obbo-Onyango, *The NRM Factor in Uganda's Corruption" in The East Africa*, available at http://www.charlesobbo.com/article134.htm

CONSTANTINE MICHALOPOULOS, TRADE AND DEVELOPMENT IN THE GATT AND WTO: THE ROLE OF SPECIAL AND DIFFERENTIAL TREATMENT FOR DEVELOPING COUNTRIES 23 (2000)

CONSUMER UNITY AND TRUST SOCIETY, CONSUMER PROTECTION IN BHUTAN: PAST, PRESENT AND FUTURE, REPORT PREPARED FOR THE ROYAL GOVERNMENT OF BHUTAN (2001)

Dani Rodrik, *Trade Policy Reform as Institutional Reform* in DEVELOPMENT, TRADE, AND THE WTO, 4 (Bernard Hoekman, Aaditya Mattoo, and Philip English eds. 2002)

Dani Rodrik, *Trading in Illusion,* FOREIGN POLICY, March-April 2001

Debapriya Bhattacharya and Mustafizur Rahman, *The Least Developed Countries in The WTO: Strengthening Participation Capacities*, paper prepared for the MEETING OF SENIOR OFFICIALS ON FUTUR WTO TRADE AGENDA AND DEVELOPING COUNTRIES, organized by U.N.-ESCAP, Bangkok, 23–25 August, 3 (1999)

Durken Ahn, *Linkages between International Financial and Trade Institutions: IMF, World Bank and WTO*, 34 JOURNAL OF WORLD TRADE 4, 26 (2000)

ECDPM, ICTSD AND ODI, TRADE NEGOTIATIONS INSIGHTS, Vol. 1, Issue No. 1, 8 (2002)

Edwin Kwame Kessie, *Developing Countries and the World Trade Organization: What Has Changed*, 22 WORLD COMPETITION 2, 86 (1999)

Edwini Kessie, *Enforceability and Legal Provisions Relating to Special and Differential Treatment under the WTO Agreements*, 3 THE JOURNAL OF WORLD INTELLECTUAL PROPERTY RIGHTS, 6, 965–74 (1999)

Flora Musonda,, Wilfred Mbowe and Faye Sampson *The Competition Regime in Tanzania*, COMPARATIVE STUDY OF COMPETITION LAW REGIMES OF SELECT DEVELOPING COUNTRIES (7-UP PROJECT), 2001

Harward J Shatz and David G. Tarr, *Exchange Rate Overvaluation and Trade Protection* DEVELOPMENT, TRADE, AND THE WTO, 17 (Bernard Hoekman, Aaditya Mattoo, and Philip English eds., 2002)

Hiramani Ghimire, *Integrating LDCs into the Multilateral Trading System: Need for a Bond Between Promise and Performance,* SAWTEE BRIEFING PAPER, 5 (2000)

Hiramani Ghimire, *Least-developed Countries in Search of Identity in the WTO*, in SALVAGING THE WTO'S FUTURE - DOHA AND BEYOND 350 (Amit Dasgupta and Bibek Debroy eds. 2001).

Hiramani Ghimire, *The WTO at a Crossroads: Implications of Doha Meeting for LDCs*, SAWTEE NEWSLETTER 22, 9 (2001).

http://www.bgmea.com/data.htm

http://www.globalcorruptionreport.org/download/data_and_research.pdf

http://www.transparency.org

http://www.unctad.org/ldcs/

http://www.wto.org/english/thewto_e/gattmem_e.htm

http://www1.worldbank.org/wbiep/trade/Integrated_framework.html

http://www2.cid.harvard.edu/cidtrade/Issues/ricupero2.pdf

ICTSD, *Canadian LDC initiative to free up entry of goods from world's poorest* in BRIDGES WEEKLY TRADE NEWS DIGEST, Vol. 6, No. 29, 6 August (2002)

ICTSD, *Least Developed Countries: No New Trade Concessions Before Doha, Bridges Monthly Review*, Year 5, No. 4, 1 (May 2001)

Jagdish Bhagwati, FREE TRADE TODAY, 90 (2002)

Jan Pronk, *Chairman's Opening Statement at the High Level Meeting, High Level Meeting on Integrated Initiatives for Least Developed Countries Trade Development*, NOTE ON THE MEETING, WT/LDC/HL/M/1, 25 (26 November 1997)

John Cuddy, The State of Development in Least Developed Countries, BRIDGES MONTHLY REVIEW, Year 5, No 4, 3 (May 2001)

John H Jackson, THE WORLD TRADING SYSTEM: LAW AND POLICY OF INTERNATIONAL ECONOMIC RELATIONS, 109–111 (1997)

Jonathan Hepburn, *Negotiating Intellectual Property: Mandate and options in the Doha Work Programme*, OCCASIONAL PAPER 10, Friends World Committee for Consulation, Quaker United Nations Office—Geneva, 4 (2002)

KEITH E MASKUS, INTELLECTUAL PROPERTY RIGHTS IN THE GLOBAL ECONOMY, 68 (2000)

L. Alan Winters, *Trade Policies for Poverty Alleviation,* DEVELOPMENT TRADE AND THE WTO, 28 (Bernard Hoekman, Aaditya Mattoo, and Philip English eds. 2002)

Least-Developed Countries: No New Trade Concessions Before Doha, in BRIDGES MONTHLY REVIEW, 2, Year 5, No. 4, 1 May 2001.

Lecomte H.B Slignac, *Building Capacity to Trade: A Roadmap for Development Partners—Insights from Africa and the Caribbean*, European Centre for Development Policy Management (ECDPM), DISCUSSION PAPER 33, (2001)

Michael Finger and Phillip Schuler, IMPLEMENTATION OF URUGUAY ROUND: THE DEVELOPMENT CHALLENGES, (1999)

OECD, THE DAC GUIDELINES: STRENGTHENING TRADE CAPACITY FOR DEVELOPMENT 50 (2001)

Olarreaga, Marcelo and Francis Ng. "Tariff Peaks and Preferences" in DEVELOPMENT, TRADE, AND THE WTO, 109 (Bernard Hoekman, Aaditya Mattoo, and Philip English eds., 2002)

PAUL R. KRUGMAN AND MAURICE OBSTFELD, INTERNATIONAL ECONOMICS: THEORY AND POLICY 255–261 (2000)

Pradeep Mehta, *Follow-up to the Fourth Ministerial Conference in Doha: Market Access—the Major Roadblocks*, UNCTAD-CIVIL SOCIETY DIALOGUE ON SELECTED DEVELOPMENT ISSUES BEING ADDRESSED BY THE UNITED NATIONS SYSTEM, UNCTAD/ISS/Misc. 385, 130 (2002)

Ratnakar Adhikari And Hiramani Ghimire, INTEGRATING LDCS INTO THE MULTILATERAL TRADING SYSTEM: RHETORIC GALORE, 7 (2001).

Ratnakar Adhikari, *Birth Defects of the WTO Accession Process*, THE KATHMANDU POST, 27 March, 4 (2002)

Ratnakar Adhikari, Rajesh Khanal and Navin Verma, *National Study on TRIPS Agreement and Its Implications for Nepal*, REPORT SUBMITTED TO THE NEPAL ACCESSION TO WTO, 22 (2001)

Roman Grynberg and Roy Mickey Joy, *The Accession of Vanuatu to the WTO: Lessons for the Multilateral Trading System*, 34 JOURNAL OF WORLD TRADE, 6, 116 (2000).

Rubens Ricupero, *Address to the High Level Meeting, High Level Meeting on Integrated Initiatives for Least Developed Countries Trade Development*, NOTE ON THE MEETING, WT/LDC/HL/M/1, 26 November, 31 (1997)

Rubens Ricupero, *Forewords* in FUTURE MULTILATERAL TRADE NEGOTIATIONS: HANDBOOK FOR TRADE NEGOTIATORS FROM LEAST DEVELOPED COUNTRIES, vii (1999).

Sarrocco, Claudia (2002). *Improving IP Connectivity in the Least-Developed Countries*, BACKGROUND STUDY, Strategy and Policy Unit, International Telecommunications Union, 12 April 2002, available at http://www.itu.int/osg/spu/ni/ipdc/workshop/presentations/Sarrocco.ppt

SHANG JIN WEI, NATURAL OPENNESS AND GOOD GOVERNMENT at http://econ.worldbank.org/docs/1166.pdf

Shigemitsu Sugisaki (1999), *Trade and Development*, ADDRESS TO WTO HIGH LEVEL SYMPOSIUM ON TRADE AND DEVELOPMENT, March 17 (1999)

SIMON J. EVENETT AND BERNARD M. HOEKMAN, GOVERNMENT PROCUREMENT DISCRIMINATION AND MULTILATERAL TRADE RULES, (2000).

South Center, Special and Differential Treatment Under the WTO at www.southcenter.org/publications/s&d/s&d-04.htm

Stefano Inama, *Market Access for LDCs: Issues to be Addressed*, 36 JOURNAL OF WORLD TRADE 1, 85 (2002)

Sue Arrowsmith, *National and International Perspectives on the Regulation of Public Procurement: Harmony or Conflict* in PUBLIC PROCUREMENT: GLOBAL REVOLUTION 19 (Sue Arrowsmith and Arwel Davis eds. 1998)

SUNS, *LDCs to lose $ 3 billion from Uruguay Round, says UNCTAD* in SOUTH-NORTH DEVELOPMENT MONITOR (SUNS) No. 3620, 2 (n.d)

T.N. Srinivasan, *Developing Countries in the World Trading System: From GATT, 1947 to the third Ministerial Meeting of WTO*, a revised version of the Keynote Speech delivered at the HIGH LEVEL SYMPOSIUM ON TRADE AND DEVELOPMENT, World Trade Organization, 10 (1999)

The Least Developed Countries, 2000 Report, XXX, UNCTAD/LDC/2000 E.00.II.D.21 (December 10, 2000)

Transparency International, *Corruption Perception Index* at http://www.transparency.org/cpi/2001/cpi2001.html#cpi

UNCTAD and Commonwealth Secretariat, DUTY AND QUOTA FREE MARKET ACCESS FOR LDCS: AN ANALYSIS OF QUAD INITIATIVE: 1 (2001)

UNCTAD, FUTURE MULTILATERAL TRADE NEGOTIATIONS: HANDBOOK FOR TRADE NEGOTIATORS FROM LEAST DEVELOPED COUNTRIES, 282 (1999)

UNCTAD, *Integrating Least Developed Countries into the Global Economy: Proposal for a Comprehensive New Plan of Action in the Context of the Third WTO Ministerial Conference*, adopted at THE CHALLENGE OF INTEGRATING LDCS INTO THE MULTILATERAL TRADING SYSTEM: COORDINATING WORKSHOP FOR SENIOR ADVISORS TO MINISTERS OF TRADE IN LDCS, Sun City, South Africa: 21–25 June, 1 (1999)

UNCTAD, *Programme of Action for the Least Developed Countries adopted by the Third United Nations Conference on Least Developed Countries in Brussels on 20 May*, A/CONF. 191/11, (2001)

UNCTAD, STATISTICAL PROFILES OF THE LEAST DEVELOPED COUNTRIES 4 (2001).

UNCTAD, THE LEAST DEVELOPED COUNTRIES REPORT 1999, 4 (1999)

United Nations, *Resolution adopted by the General Assembly, Fifty-fifth session*, 31 January, A/RES/56/183, 1–2 (2002)

UNNGLS (United Nations Non-governmental Liaison Service), GO BETWEEN 30, January-February, 84 (2001)

World Bank, GLOBAL ECONOMIC PROSPECT AND THE DEVELOPING COUNTRIES 2002, 87 (2002)

World Bank, GLOBAL ECONOMIC PROSPECTS AND DEVELOPING COUNTRIES 2001, 13 (2001)

World Trade Agenda, *Doha ministerial breaks the WTO logjam and successfully launches a new round . . . agenda . . . work programme*, November 26, No. 01/21, 8 (2001)

WT/MIN(99)/7, WT/COMTD/LDC/W/18 and WT/LDC/SWG/IF/1.

WTO (*High Level Meeting on Integrated Initiatives for Least Developed Countries Trade Development*), NOTE ON THE MEETING, WT/LDC/HL/M/1, 2 (26 November, 1997).

WTO Sub-Committee on Least-Developed Countries, *Market Access Conditions for Least Developed Countries* (WT/LDC/SWG/IF/14), (2000).

WTO, *Background Document*, HIGH LEVEL SYMPOSIUM ON TRADE AND DEVELOPMENT, Geneva, 17–18 March, 39–48 (1999)

WTO, *Declaration on TRIPS Agreement and Public Health*, WT/MIN(01)/DEC/2, 20 November 2001

WTO, *High Level Meeting on Integrated Initiatives for Least Developed Countries' Trade Development*, WT/LDC/HL/M/1, 26 November, 17 (1997)

WTO, *Progress Report on the Integrated Framework for Trade-Related Technical Assistance to Least-Developed Countries*, REPORT BY THE DIRECTOR-GENERAL, WT/LDC/SWG/IF/17/REV. 1, 17 April (2001)

WTO, *Singapore Ministerial Declaration*, adopted on 13 December (1996)

WTO, *WTO Work Programme for the Least Developed Countries (LDCs) Adopted by the Sub-committee on Least Developed Countries*, WT/COMTD/LDC/11, 13 February (2002)

CHAPTER 53

TEXTILES AND DEVELOPING COUNTRIES

Magda Shahin[*]

"The Textiles Arrangements are legitimate opportunism that avoided something worse, it would be unrealistic not to recognize the violence they have done to the GATT concepts."[1]

TABLE OF CONTENTS

[*] Magda Shahin, Assistant Minister for International Economic Relations, is a Member of the Egyptian Foreign Ministry. She served as a Deputy Head of Mission in Geneva and Egypt's Representative to the WTO during 1992–1997. She was also a member on an *ad personam* basis of the WTO's Textiles Monitoring Body ("TMB") during her posting in Geneva. As of December 2003, she was Egypt's Ambassador to Greece. The opinions expressed in this Chapter are personal.
[1] Claudia Jimenez Cortes, GATT, WTO AND THE REGULATION OF INTERNATIONAL TRADE IN TEXTILES 64 (1997) (quoting a Director General of the GATT in 1973 who participated directly in the LTA negotiations).

I. Introduction

This chapter analyses the historical development of the textiles negotiations that eventually led to the WTO Agreement on Textiles and Clothing ("ATC"), one of the Uruguay Round Agreements on Trade in Goods. It reviews prior arrangements governing the sector and illustrates how and why this sector remained outside the disciplines of the GATT multilateral trading system for so long. The paper then examines the ATC and assesses the way it has been implemented during the first three stages of the integration process. It also looks at the impact of the Agreement on exporting developing countries and discusses some of the disputes that have arisen since the Agreement was put into place. Textile and clothing disputes are examined in greater detail in another chapter in this book.[2]

A. The Importance of Textiles in International Trade

The textiles and clothing sector is one of the most important sectors of international trade. In 1997 it accounted for nine percent of world exports in manufactured products.[3] It is a significant contributor to many national economies, providing 142 million jobs (formal and informal) around the world.[4] In the European Community, it accounts for nine percent of all jobs in the manufacturing sector.[5] Textile and Apparel industries in the United States are expected to continue to provide more than 1.3 million jobs in 2005 or nearly eight percent of all projected jobs in manufacturing.[6] For developing countries, its importance is much higher. As one of the important sources of export earnings, textiles and clothing accounted for approximately twenty percent of total exports of manufactures by developing countries and 15.5 percent of their total merchandise exports.[7] Some of these countries are extremely dependent on the textiles and clothing industry for their export earnings. For example, 73 percent of Pakistan's overall merchandise exports is in textiles and clothing. The share of textiles and clothing in the export trade of many least developed countries is even larger.

The textiles and clothing sector often plays an important role in the early stages of the industrial development process, because it is labor-intensive and requires little capital. However, as industrialization takes place there has historically been an outsourcing stage in related sub-sectors, brought about by a loss of competitiveness in the face of new exporters.[8] More specifically, as industrialization takes place, the lower-level technology sectors in the textiles and clothing industries, e.g., grey fabrics (and related sub-sectors) are pushed outward, i.e., to the developing countries when the developed country industries lose in competitiveness to new developing country exporters.

What we see today is that in the developed countries it is only these so-called low-tech sub-sectors that are being discarded since much of the textiles and clothing industry

---

[2] See Chapter 9.

[3] Wenguo Cai, *Impact of the WTO Agreement on Textiles and Clothing: An International Perspective*, in CHALLENGES AND OPPORTUNITIES OF WTO FOR ESCWA MEMBER COUNTRIES IN SELECTED SECTORS 125, 4 ESCWA, UNCTAD/ITD/17 (1999)

[4] *Id.*

[5] *Id.*

[6] Mark Mittelhauser, *Employment Trends In Textiles and Apparel, 1973–2005*, Monthly Labor Review (August 1997), at 33.

[7] Submission by the International Textiles and Clothing Bureau to the CTG, *Implementation Issues and Concerns: The Agreement on Textiles and Clothing*, IC/W/251/REV.1, March 1, 2002, para. 4.

[8] Jimenez Cortes, *supra* note 1, at 21.

in the developed countries is no longer a low-tech industry. A clear division of labor has arisen in the textiles industry, with a highly developed, sophisticated and expensive design industry in the developed countries and independent production in certain low-tech sub-sectors in the developing countries. The highly automated textile industry in the developed countries is leading to increased productivity in this sector, in addition to the outsourcing of the operations involved in making apparel to take advantage of lower labor costs while continuing to control most production and distribution decisions.[9] The essence is that a large part of the textile and apparel industry continues to remain in the developed countries.

It is during this transition stage that conflicts between groups with different vested interests in protectionism and liberalization begin to emerge. These vested interests make the sector highly sensitive to change, and for this reason, trade in textiles and clothing has been particularly difficult to liberalize.

Moreover, it is difficult to draw the line between the policies of the developed countries as a group in the textiles and clothing industry. We continue to see U.S. intransigence to the opening of its market for textiles and clothing. While some European countries seem more flexible in this regard, this may soon change with the expansion of the European Union to encompass the lower-income countries of Eastern Europe. The result may be that European textiles, just like European agriculture, could become another sector in need of protection.

B. The Era of Restrictions

Trade in textiles and clothing has been subjected to a large variety of protective measures since the early 1960s. Because developing countries were not treated as full-fledged members in the GATT, they were easy targets for such measures. Developed countries chose to deal with textiles and clothing as an exception to the GATT. As a result the textiles and clothing sector was removed from the purview of GATT rules and disciplines and placed under extended special arrangements that allowed developed countries to restrict trade in textiles and clothing, and to apply a wide range of discriminatory actions, particularly against developing countries.

Initially, restrictive arrangements were instituted cautiously and were justified as short-term adjustment measures in the cotton industry. Restrictive measures gradually expanded and eventually encompassed virtually all of the textiles and clothing industry, covering nearly all types of cloth, including man-made fibers, wool, and silk blends. The result was the corruption of the original objective of these arrangements, which eventually became purely protectionist measures rather than a means of helping industries in developed countries to adjust to changing circumstances. In its last years of existence, the Multi-fiber Arrangement ("MFA") even permitted importing countries to apply import restrictions on products that they did not produce domestically.[10]

The textiles and clothing sector was essentially withdrawn from the GATT system in the early 1960s. During the Tokyo Round in the 1970s,[11] developed countries were

[9] Mittelhauser, *supra* note 6 at 26.
[10] *Agreement on Textiles and Clothing,* in UNCTAD, THE OUTCOME OF THE URUGUAY ROUND: SUPPORTING PAPERS, THE TRADE AND DEVELOPMENT REPORT: CHAPTER V, AGREEMENT ON TEXTILES AND CLOTHING 108, UNCTAD/TDR/14 (Supplement) (1994).
[11] The Tokyo Round was the sixth round of multilateral trade negotiation. It lasted from 1973–1979. Around 100 countries participated in the Tokyo Round as compared to 45 in the previous Round.

feeling increased pressure from recently independent developing countries that wanted additional market access in textiles and clothing, but it was not until the early 1980s that exporting developing countries made their first serious attempt to change the system. By this time, developing countries were becoming conscious of their strengthened status in the international arena, and they began to act more uniformly, pushing for the tabling of the textiles and clothing sector in the new round of trade negotiations.

The textile-exporting developing countries realized that the aim of developed countries in general, and the United States in particular, was to negotiate a round in which "free-riders," as they labeled developing countries, would be integrated on the basis of the reciprocity principle. In other words, the developing countries would be required to make concessions in order to obtain trade benefits. In addition, the philosophy of free trade was gaining clout among developing countries, and it became evident that developed countries could no longer afford to be exposed as countries with double standards in trade negotiations.

The developed countries knew that eventually they would have to agree to the application of the normal GATT rules to textiles and clothing. From the very beginning of the Uruguay Round, however, they managed to do so at their own pace. Developing countries used the textiles and clothing sector as one of their major bargaining chips in the Uruguay Round in return for the inclusion of two new areas—services and trade related-intellectual property rights. Newly established but strong interest groups from the services and intellectual property sectors outweighed the influence of the textiles and apparel lobby groups in the developed countries. They played a pivotal role in softening the position of the developed countries in general and the United States in particular, so ensuring that concessions would be made with respect to textile and apparel trade.

As a result, the developed countries saw their opportunity to extract a large number of concessions from the developing countries reach its zenith, in return for what was assumed by many developing countries to be the inclusion of the textiles sector. Developed countries knew that the liberalization of trade in textiles and clothing was one of the few enticements that could be offered to developing countries for their participation in a new Round and, albeit reluctantly, the developed countries agreed to pay this price—opening their textile and clothing sectors, in order to entice developing countries to enter into new commitments in other sectors, in particular intellectual property and services. The developed countries were "shamed" into making concessions with regard to this sector.[12] Developed countries nevertheless succeeded in attaching a myriad of caveats and conditions to the liberalization of this sector. Nowhere have developed countries manipulated the GATT system as in the textiles and clothing sector.

C. The Uruguay Round and Beyond

It was the promise that liberalization of textile trade would lead to greater foreign earnings and a significant increase in domestic employment that motivated many developing countries to participate in the Uruguay Round negotiation of the Agreement on Textiles and Clothing.[13] The 1998 WTO Annual Report concluded that if the Uruguay Round Agreements are fully implemented, world income would grow by up to one percent per

---

[12] Marcelo Raffaelli and Tripti Jenkins, THE DRAFTING HISTORY OF THE AGREEMENT ON TEXTILES AND CLOTHING 10 (International Textiles and Clothing Bureau 1995).

[13] *Agreement on ATC: Evaluation of Implementation,* Communication by ITCB Members to the General Council of the WTO", WTO Document WT/GC/W/283 (August 3, 1999) at 3.

year, or by U.S. $200–500 billion, and world trade would increase by 6–20 percent. More specifically, "more than one-third of the benefits were expected to derive from liberalization of textiles and clothing and another one-third from liberalization of other manufactures".[14] When one realizes that in 1996 approximately 59 percent of world textiles exports came from developing countries, while their share of clothing exports was 73 percent of the world's total,[15] it becomes clear that developing countries would gain considerably from the liberalization of this sector.

Unfortunately, although the developing countries were promised an opening of markets with an increase in trade and gains in textiles and clothing exports, nothing has materialized from these promises. This reality is lost on neither the pundits nor politicians, nor is it lost on diplomats in Geneva who debated the launch of a new round of WTO trade negotiations. It is also not lost on developing countries which feel they have been hurt the worst. Why? Because while the GATT and the WTO aim at liberalizing trade, agreements on textiles and clothing do just the opposite. The Multi-Fiber Agreement ("MFA") and the Agreement on Textiles and Clothing ("ATC") undermine the integrity of both the GATT and the WTO, and threaten the credibility of negotiations in other sectors.

The ATC undermines the GATT/WTO trading system since it grants the developed countries treatment analogous to the special and differential treatment provided to the developing countries throughout the Uruguay Round agreements, i.e., a longer time for implementation. Portions of the ATC amount to a ten-year extension of the MFA. According developed countries such privileges weakens the GATT/WTO Agreements and disadvantages many developing country Members. Assuming that the ATC is faithfully implemented, the ATC will have added another ten years of protection to a sector that has already received forty years of protection. The WTO is further undermined by the fact that the negotiation and implementation of the ATC took place behind the scenes, thus allowing special interests to protect their advantages.

In the lead up to the November 2001 Doha WTO Ministerial Meeting, there were many speeches and calls for developing countries to endorse a new round of negotiations on liberalization in new sectors. Many references were made to the benefits of reducing industrial tariffs and trade barriers in agriculture, services, finance, and telecommunications, but there was conspicuously no mention of trade in textiles or of the ATC.

This is no surprise. Textiles agreements not only inflict "violence" on the very concepts of the GATT system, they jeopardize the framework upon which trade liberalization is built. It is no exaggeration to say that what we see today in terms of mistrust and the hardening of positions of some major developing exporting countries is a backlash from a badly negotiated agreement and, even worse, a badly implemented agreement. In sum, credibility in multilateral trade negotiations has always been important, but it is now more critical than ever, because the WTO works by consensus and developing countries are likely to block an agreement that does not adequately satisfy their interests. The Seattle Ministerial failed in part due to opposition to a new Round by the developing countries.[16] The MFA and the ATC are thus not models to be used when

---

[14] *Id.* at 2, ¶ 4.

[15] WTO Secretariat, *Background Statistical Information with Respect to Trade in Textiles and Clothing,* WTO Document G/L/184 (Sept. 30, 1997) at 5, 31.

[16] The developing countries were not ready to start a new Round when so many issues of importance to them remained hanging, and when the developed countries had failed to address developing country issues adequately. Developed countries overburdened the agenda with issues of interest to them. Seattle also failed because the EU overburdened the agenda with new issues, such as investment, competition and the

considering new sectors in future trade negotiations. Indeed, textiles agreements have undermined trade liberalization and feed widening divisions in the perceptions of developed and developing countries about the benefits of participation in the multilateral trading system.

It is vital to realize that competing trade agendas drive negotiations, the outcome of which can cause political change and social upheaval, and even conflict.[17] In Europe and the United States stakeholders have formed powerful political interest groups. The stakeholders in the textiles and clothing industries in the developing countries are less organized, but the impact of changes in textile trade rules is often more important. This is especially true for developing countries that depend heavily on textiles, such as Pakistan. It has been the political strength of key stakeholders in the developed countries and not the relative economic needs of countries that has kept textiles outside the purview of the GATT-based trading system for thirty years.

When textiles and clothing are fully incorporated into the international trading system, beginning in 2005, there will be an employment shift in this sector from Canada, the United States and Europe, to Asia, Africa and Latin America. In the former countries, greater employment in services and high technology will absorb many of the lost jobs. In the latter regions, the move from basic fiber production to finished fabrics and clothing will enable skill development, assist poverty reduction, and lead to technology transfer and industrialization. For example, the successful development of textiles industries in several of the Asian Tigers has led to significant foreign investment and technology transfer. More recently, foreign aid has played a similar role. For example, in Vietnam (which is not yet a WTO Member), foreign aid has promoted textiles production as a basis for economic expansion and skills development. This has led to increased foreign investment and technology transfer.[18]

Since industrialized countries still have significant vested interests in textiles and clothing production, it should therefore come as no surprise that they have sought to avoid effective liberalization of this sector, meaning that in the post-Uruguay Round era tariffs on imported textiles and clothing will remain the highest of all major industrial products. Average tariffs in developed countries on imported textiles and clothing products will be 12.1 percent in the final stages of the ATC reduction commitments, while the average rate for all industrial products will be 3.8 percent.[19] Whereas in the Uruguay Round the average tariffs in textiles and clothing were reduced by only 22 percent (from 15.5 percent to 12.1 percent) industrial tariffs on average were reduced by 40 percent. In addition, only four percent of tariff lines of imported textile and clothing imports were duty-free in developed countries; 27 percent were in the range of 15 to 35 percent.[20] The corresponding figures for all manufactured products were 49 percent and one percent respectively.[21]

environment, and was not willing to move on agriculture. The EU, however, was shrewd enough to push the blame for the failure of Seattle on the United States (as a result of "bad organization") and present itself as the guardian of developing country interests.

[17] *See generally,* J.W. Wright, Jr., THE POLITICAL ECONOMY OF THE MIDDLE EAST: THE IMPACT OF COMPETING TRADE AGENDAS (1999).

[18] Lynn Mytelka, Dieter Ernst and Tom Ganiatsos, *Learning, Technological Capability Building and Sustainable Export Growth,* in TECHNOLOGICAL CAPABILITIES AND EXPORT SUCCESS IN ASIA 324–335 (L. Mytelka, D. Ernst and T. Ganiatsos eds. 1998).

[19] WTO SECRETARIAT, NOTES ON WTO AGREEMENTS 47–49 (1997); WTO SECRETARIAT, THE WORLD TRADE ORGANIZATION: A TRAINING PACKAGE, Table II.1, at E1-81 (December 15, 1998).

[20] *Id*. at 47–49.

[21] *Id*.

Textiles and clothing is a highly sensitive sector and remains, as shall be demonstrated throughout this chapter, full of controversies and conflicts. Although many view the meager results of more than eight years of ATC implementation with disappointment, many also view the future of this sector with a feeling of hope, and the ardent expectation that this sector will continue to be the backbone of their industrialization. For developed countries the liberalization of this sector will continue to be a measure of their sincerity regarding trade liberalization and openness.

II. Textiles and Clothing as an Exception to the GATT System

The roots of the current textiles and clothing regime date back to the 1930s and grew out of highly restrictive measures later to be known as "voluntary export restraints" ("VERs"). At that time Japanese exports were beginning to out-compete the traditional British textiles and clothing industry, as well as that of the United States. In response to complaints by the United Kingdom and the United States, in 1936 Japan agreed to limit its exports through self-imposed restraints.[22] In 1937, an agreement formalizing these constraints was signed between the United States and Japan in Osaka.[23] The United States, then in the midst of a depression, sought a transitional period during which jobs would be protected. Japan decided that agreeing to a system of voluntary restraints was preferable to stricter unilateral measures that could be invoked, such as higher duties and quantitative restrictions on textile and clothing exports.

Unlike agriculture, the GATT 1947 did not treat trade in textiles and clothing as an exception to the normal rules.[24] Yet, it became evident early in the trade liberalization process that, like agriculture, the textiles and clothing sector was prone to capture by protectionist interests. This became the basis for the exceptional protectionist treatment of this sector by the most outspoken proponents of free trade.

One of these proponents, the United States, was reluctant to request a GATT Article XXV:5 waiver with respect to textiles and clothing for fear of negatively affecting its stature as an advocate of trade liberalization, already tarnished by the waiver it obtained in 1955 with respect to trade in agricultural products.[25] As a result, although the textiles and clothing sector was seemingly included in the GATT system, it became an area prone to secretive deals between importers and exporters.

As Bagchi notes, by the end of December 1956, after protracted bilateral negotiations, an agreement was struck between Japan and the United States, where Japan agreed to restrain its exports for five years with an aggregate ceiling covering its entire cotton textile exports. The aggregate ceiling was divided into five broad groups consisting of cotton cloth, made-up goods, woven apparel, knitted goods and miscellaneous textiles. There were further specific limits for particular products, which could be increased up to ten percent by borrowing from unused quotas. This structure of restrictions, with some modifications, became the model for subsequent bilateral agreements that have continued ever since. Perhaps inspired by the Japan/United States Agreement, Britain reached agreements with three Commonwealth countries, India, Hong Kong and Pakistan, to limit their exports of cotton products for three years beginning February 1, 1959 for

---

[22] This was first known voluntary export restraint ("VER") in textiles. John H. Jackson, William Davey, Alan Sykes, Jr., LEGAL PROBLEMS OF INTERNATIONAL ECONOMIC RELATIONS 1184 (1995).

[23] Jimenez Cortes, *supra* note 1, at 21.

[24] GATT Article XI (General Elimination of Quantitative Restrictions) and Article XVI (Subsidies) contained significant exceptions with respect to agricultural products. *See* Chapter 6 of this book. By contrast there were no specific exclusions for textiles and clothing.

[25] See Chapter 6 of this book.

Hong Kong, and January 1, 1960 for India and Pakistan. However, the United States failed in its attempt to reach a bilateral agreement with Hong Kong similar to the one it had concluded with Japan, which led the United States to drop the bilateral overtures and to seek a multilateral solution (initially) in the GATT.[26] A new framework for managing trade in textiles and clothing was emerging.

Parallel negotiations on textiles and clothing began in 1960 in the Dillon Round of trade talks[27] where negotiators attempted to restructure the system of bilateral arrangements that was emerging. The eventual result was the Short-term Arrangement Regarding International Trade in Cotton Textiles ("STA") and the Long-term Arrangement Regarding International Trade in Cotton Textiles ("LTA"), which led to the Arrangement Regarding International Trade in Textiles, known as the Multi-Fiber Arrangement ("MFA").[28] These arrangements (discussed in the following section) were primarily the result of the concern of developed importing countries that the GATT Article XIX Safeguard provision was inadequate to protect their textile industries. These special arrangements, initially meant to allow industries in the United States and Europe to adjust over a one year period to market shocks, were expanded in coverage and extended in time for over thirty years.

The textile and clothing sector has always been considered as fertile ground for imaginative protectionist policies. Under the STA, LTA, and MFA it became a web of Voluntary Export Restraints ("VERs"), price undertakings, and "gray area measures", the net effect of which has been significant trade restrictions and protectionism. These measures, which found their roots in the textiles and clothing trade, started to be used in other sectors in the 1970s and 1980s, such as the automobile, iron and steel industries. They eventually posed a threat to the entire GATT system. Out of fear that they would gradually permeate the system, the elimination of gray area measures became a necessary condition for the successful conclusion of the Uruguay Round.[29]

A. The Short-Term and Long-Term Arrangements

The Kennedy Administration found itself facing a difficult predicament in its first year in office. On the one hand, the United States faced mounting criticism from developing

---

[26] Sanjoy Bagchi, INTERNATIONAL TRADE POLICY IN TEXTILES; FIFTY YEARS OF PROTECTIONISM 27–29 (2001).

[27] The Dillon Round was the fifth round of multilateral trade negotiations. It was held in Geneva from 1960–1961.

[28] See GATT, GUIDE TO GATT LAW AND PRACTICE, ANALYTICAL INDEX 320–497 (6th ed., 1994), which notes that:

> The Short-term Arrangement Regarding International Trade in Cotton Textiles (STA/10S/18) came into force on 1 October 1961 for a twelve-month period pending a long-term solution. A year later, the STA was superseded by the Long-term Arrangement Regarding International Trade in Cotton Textiles (LTA/11S/25) which came into force on 1 October 1962 for a five-year period and continued into force until 31 December 1973. The stated objectives of the LTA, as of the STA, were two-fold: to promote the economic progress of developing countries by providing larger opportunities for exchange earnings, while ensuring that cotton textiles trade developed in such a way as to avoid disruptive effects in individual markets. . . .
>
> . . . [T]he arrangement regarding international trade in textiles, commonly known as the Multi-fiber Arrangement or "MFA" (21S/3), covering textile products of man-made fiber and wool as well as cotton, entered into force on 1 January 1974 for a period of four years. . . . The MFA, as extended by various Protocols, allowed for various quantitative restrictions among participating countries but states in paragraph 6 of Article 1 that: "The provisions of this arrangement shall not affect the rights and obligations of the participating countries under the GATT."

The MFA was extended a number of times and expired on December 31, 1994.

[29] See Article 11:1(b) of the *Agreement on Safeguards*, discussed in Chapter 18 of this book.

countries, notably Korea, Taiwan, Hong Kong and Brazil, who were resisting repeated U.S. requests to restrict their textile exports. On the other hand, the Administration faced growing domestic pressure by textile lobbies that wanted additional restrictions placed on textile imports. In response to pressure from both sides, the United States orchestrated the creation of the STA, which was presented as a formal means of striking a textiles deal with the exporting countries, thereby legitimizing restrictive actions and helping to restore the image of the United States as a bastion of free trade. This interim arrangement reduced domestic pressure on the Kennedy administration, and was seen as a payback for textile industry support during the election campaign. It also helped secured the United States administration the necessary negotiating authority in the Congress prior to the Round.

The STA was signed in July 1961 at which time it had nineteen participating countries: Australia, Austria, Belgium, Chinese Taipei, Canada, France, Germany, Hong Kong, India, Italy, Japan, Korea, the Netherlands, Pakistan, Portugal, Spain, Sweden, United Kingdom and the United States. It was a short document, containing two articles based on a U.S. proposal.[30] The primary objective was the entitlement of Members to impose quotas on countries whose imports caused market disruption. Article I enabled a country to restrain imports from a source, with or without its consent, at specified levels. It also obliged countries maintaining restrictions to increase access to their markets significantly. Article II established a Cotton Textiles Committee to find a long-term solution to the problems in the trade of cotton textiles.

The STA was confined to cotton and cotton textiles, and covered 64 categories of products, subjecting them to a wide range of quantitative restrictions on exports and imports. The short-term arrangement would permit the United States to control and regulate imports of cotton textiles from sources perceived to be responsible for market disruption. It was, however, stated that this procedure would be used "sparingly"—a phrase that was to recur repeatedly in the textile agreements.[31] It shortly became clear that the transitional character of the STA was an illusion, and that the Agreement contained the seeds of a perpetual "special" system for textiles and clothing.

The key to the new system was the concept of "market disruption,"[32] defined as "instances of sharp import increases associated with low import prices not attributable to dumping or foreign subsidies".[33] This concept and the provisions that grew out of it

---

[30] *See* GATT: Basic Instruments and Selected Documents, 10S/18.

[31] Bagchi, *supra* note 26, at 41.

[32] The concept was introduced by the United States and was developed in GATT textile discussions held in 1959 and 1960.

[33] *Decision on the Avoidance of Market Disruption*, GATT Document 9S/26, 26–27, adopted November 19, 1960 (reproduced in GUIDE TO GATT LAW AND PRACTICE, *supra* note 27, at 496). The Decision recognizes that:

(a) In a number of countries situations occur or threaten to occur which have been described as 'market disruption'.

(b) These situations generally contain the following elements in combination:

    (a) a sharp and substantial increase or potential increase of imports of particular products from particular sources;

    (b) these products are offered at prices which are substantially below those prevailing for similar goods of comparable quality in the market of the importing country;

    (c) there is serious damage to domestic producers or threat thereof;

    (d) the price differentials referred to in paragraph (ii) above do not arise from governmental intervention in the fixing or formation of prices or from dumping practices. . . .

went beyond the general safeguard provision of GATT Article XIX.[34] For example, under the concept of "market disruption" there was no need to show a link between increased imports and any injury or even threat of injury being experienced by the domestic industry, and relief could be applied on a non-MFN basis. Although the original 1960 Decision[35] adopting the concept of market disruption was not limited to textiles and apparel, use of the concept did not spread to other sectors during the GATT era.[36]

The greatest benefits of the STA for the United States were that (1) the STA institutionalized restrictive actions within a multilateral setting outside the rules and procedures of the GATT, and (2) it obtained wide-ranging support from U.S. producers, as well as support from exporting countries, since it allowed regular exports without disruption from many kinds of unilateral protectionist measures. The stand-alone system for trade in textiles formalized a "special system" that both accommodated the U.S. situation and was internationally acceptable. Many, however, saw this special carve-out as the thin end of the wedge, opening the door to broad exceptions to the established trade rules. They saw the STA as a real threat to the entire GATT system, undermining the credibility of the GATT negotiating framework.

It was not long before the STA, initially negotiated for a one-year period, became the Long-term Arrangement ("LTA"). The LTA was agreed on October 1, 1962 and was renewed several times. Renewal of the LTA became a condition for the grant of negotiating authority by the U.S. Congress, and thus allowed the Administration to enter into the Kennedy Round of multilateral trade negotiations (1964–67). Like the preceding arrangements, the LTA only covered cotton textiles.

The LTA was considered to be a solution for emerging conflicts in the area of textiles and clothing. Even before the expiration of the STA and the establishment of the Cotton Textiles Committee on November 16, 1961, the LTA had emerged from the deliberations in the Committee.

The LTA started with 24 members, and expanded over the years to include all exporting and importing countries that had an interest in the cotton textile trade. At its height the members were Australia, Austria, Belgium, Brazil, Canada, China, Colombia, Denmark, Egypt, France, Finland, Germany, Greece, Hong Kong, India, Israel, Italy, Jamaica, Korea, Luxembourg, Mexico, the Netherlands, Norway, Pakistan, Portugal, Spain,

----

(c) These situations have often led governments to take a variety of exceptional measures. In some cases importing countries have taken or maintained discriminatory measures either outside the framework of the General Agreement, or contrary to the provisions of the General Agreement. In some other cases exporting countries have tried to correct the situation by taking measures to limit or control the export of the products giving rise to the situation.

(d) Such measures, taken unilaterally or through bilateral arrangement, may in some cases tend to cause difficulties in other markets and create problems for other contracting parties.

[34] GATT Article XIX (Emergency Action on Imports of Particular Products) requires that all safeguard actions should be non-discriminatory in application (i.e., applied on an MFN basis) and temporary in duration, and it provides the right to equivalent compensation for the loss of markets suffered by the affected parties, failing which the affected parties are entitled to retaliate. Article XIX is an exceptional remedy designed to allow industries time to adjust to unforeseen crises where serious harm is caused by increased imports. *See* Chapter 18 of this book.

[35] *Decision on the Avoidance of Market Disruption, supra* note 33.

[36] *See generally,* William R. Cline, *The Evolution of Protection in Textiles and Apparel,* in INTERNATIONAL ECONOMICS AND INTERNATIONAL ECONOMIC POLICY: A READER(1990). In June 1960 a working party on "Avoidance of Market Disruption" was established. In November 1960, a decision was adopted (*see supra* note 33) that provided for a work program. This work program did not lead to the elaboration of any generally applicable solutions, but indirectly to the negotiation of a special safeguard clause relating to a single industrial sector—cotton textiles. *See* GUIDE TO GATT LAW AND PRACTICE, *supra* note 28, at 535.

Sweden, Chinese Taipei, Turkey, United Kingdom, United States, and Yugoslavia. Non-member countries were under constant threat from the United States which had made clear that no country outside the new framework would benefit "... and have unlimited access to the United States market while cooperating nations were held down".[37]

The LTA was based on the above-mentioned definition of "market disruption", and its stated objective was the "reasonable and orderly" expansion of trade. The LTA was designed to permit the continuation of existing discriminatory restrictions on developing countries, and, upon insistence of the EC Member States, the introduction of new ones where none existed.[38]

It was clear from the beginning that exporting developing countries were left with little choice—if any. The importing developed countries, led by the United States, set the tone. The use of the above-mentioned definition of "market disruption" by importing countries was the centerpiece of this parallel trading system, and remained the basis for the imposition of quotas and other restrictions. Article 3 of the LTA entitled an importing country, when it "believed" it was facing a situation of market disruption to limit its imports from the exporting country in question, if agreement failed to be reached within sixty days of bilateral consultations between them.

The United States refused to grant any power of arbitration to the Cotton Textiles Committee that would "impair or diminish the right of any country to unilaterally (to) interpret and apply the agreement".[39] Thus determination of the existence of "market disruption" continued to be left solely to the discretion of the importing country.

The irony of the situation is that while Article I of the LTA stipulated that "special practical measures of international cooperation" would not affect participants' rights and obligations under the GATT, the Agreement called upon developing countries to restrain their exports, thus implicitly forcing them to curtail their GATT rights. As Sanjoy Bagchi, a long term veteran in the area of textiles and clothing, put it in his book, "with the LTA entering into force on 1 October 1962 ... [t]hus began an institutionalized form of protection that continued to provide legal cover for the GATT inconsistent restrictions up to the end of the century".[40]

After twelve years of application, the LTA was deemed inadequate by developed countries. Exporting developing countries, finding their exports of cotton and cotton textile products "restrained", had shifted production to other materials, in particular artificial fiber. The accelerated growth of non-cotton fiber exports that flooded into developed country markets produced a reaction similar to that in the 1950s with respect to cotton fiber exports.

Prior to the launch of the Tokyo Round negotiations (1973–1979), domestic political lobbies in the United States and Europe began to push for broadening the coverage of the LTA. The increased competitiveness of Japan and developing countries in synthetic fiber products outside the scope of the LTA led to the negotiation of the Multi-fiber Arrangement.

Controversies concerning the STA and the LTA created wide rifts between supporters and critics. Even today, as the so-called Doha "Development Round" commences, the protracted debates in other areas are affected by the questions and difficulties inherent in

[37] Bagchi, *supra* note 26, at 46 (*citing* Statement by George Ball, U.S. Undersecretary of State).
[38] GATT Document L/1659, December 5, 1961, para. 41.
[39] GATT Document Spec (62) 58, February 1, 1962 at 7 (*citing* Statement by W. Willard Wirtz, U.S. Undersecretary of Labor to Cotton Textiles Committee).
[40] Bagchi, *supra* note 26, at 48.

the arrangements on textiles and clothing. Have the textiles and clothing arrangements aided trade liberalization and assisted developing countries to grow? Have they assisted the textiles and clothing industries in general, and those in developing countries, in particular? Or have they better served the interests of special interest groups in the industrialized nations? Would it have been better to avoid these arrangements due to their systemic implications for the GATT-based trading system? Would it have been better for the developing countries had the most ardent proponents of the GATT-based trading system treated textiles and clothing in a fairer manner? Many of these questions do not have easy answers.

B. The Multi-Fiber Arrangement

In the Tokyo Round the United States, as the strongest trading power, manipulated the system in order to make it responsive to domestic special interest groups. The Nixon Administration had made electoral promises to the textiles and clothing lobbies, most of whom wanted to widen the coverage provided in the LTA. A new wave of protectionism had surfaced with the Nixon administration and its pre-election pledges to extend LTA-type trade restrictions to man-made fibers and wool production. The then Commerce Secretary, Maurice Stans, strived to fulfill the promise that the "Nixon Administration [would] do for synthetics and wool producers what Kennedy had done for cotton manufacturers"[41]. In 1971 the Nixon Administration forced so-called "voluntary" aggregate ceilings, and the imposition of product-specific quotas, on the export of man-made fiber and wool products from Japan, Hong Kong, Korea, and Chinese Taipei.

It was the cumbersome nature of bilateral negotiations, and the desire for equity in case other countries swiftly acted to fill the space in the U.S. market left by the restraints on Japan, Hong Kong, Korea and Chinese Taipei, that prompted the negotiation of a new multilateral framework. The result was a negotiation that led to "The Arrangement Regarding International Trade in Textiles", also known as the Multi-fiber Arrangement ("MFA"). The MFA was initially a four-year agreement. It was signed on December 20, 1973 and came into force on January 1, 1974. The MFA had 44 signatories,[42] among them approximately 31 exporting developing country members. It included China, even though China was not a GATT Contracting Party. The MFA stands in sharp contrast to the 1961 STA which only had India and Pakistan as developing country members. This is testament to the fact that developing countries felt a strong need to be a part of the MFA in order to promote their positions in the marketplace. This was not without cost. The MFA permitted importing countries to apply import restrictions on products in which there was no domestic production.[43] Also, excessive protection in developed countries, and the additional restrictions on products that were not yet produced domestically, discouraged innovation by developing country producers who were sure that any new

---

[41] Id. at 74 (quoting DAVID YOFFIE, POWER AND PROTECTIONISM 133 (1983)).

[42] These included: Argentina, Austria, Bangladesh, Brazil, Canada, China, Colombia, Costa Rica, Czech Republic, Dominican Republic, the European Community, Egypt, El Salvador, Fiji, Finland, Guatemala, Honduras, Hong Kong, Hungary, India, Indonesia, Jamaica, Japan, Lesotho, Macao, Malaysia, Mexico, Norway, Pakistan, Panama, Paraguay, Peru, Philippines, Poland, Republic of Korea, Romania, Singapore, Slovak Republic, Sri Lanka, Switzerland, Thailand, Turkey, the United States and Uruguay. GATT Document COM.TEX/75/Rev. 1, November 26, 1993.

[43] Agreement on Textiles and Clothing, in THE OUTCOME OF THE URUGUAY ROUND, supra note 10, at 107–111.

products they developed would also be refused entry by the developed countries or be subject to new restrictions.

The most significant change in the MFA was tightening the use of the concept of "market disruption" by establishing the requirement of a causal link between the disrupting imports and the existence of serious damage to the domestic industry.[44] The earlier definition referred to the simultaneous existence of an increase in low-priced imports and of serious damage to the domestic industry, without linking the two.[45] Another important change, which was due to the active participation of exporting developing countries in the negotiations, was a reference to consideration of the interests of the exporting country when taking into account the question of "market disruption".[46] This issue had previously been ignored, but its addition did not remove the biases inherent in the concept of "market disruption".

The MFA provided that when textile imports from a particular country caused "market disruption" and the exporting and importing countries could not reach an understanding with respect to export restraints, the importing country was entitled to take unilateral action for up to one year in order to prevent import surges.[47] In addition the MFA stipulated that:[48]

1) If an importing country wished to impose new quotas, the new quotas sought should be large enough to accommodate the actual trade level reached during the twelve-month period ending two or three months prior to holding consultations.[49]

2) When a restraint was renewed, the new quota should not be lower than the previous one. In the case of continuing quotas, the annual growth rate should not be less than six percent.[50]

3) The growth rate of a particular quota could exceed seven percent provided there was a corresponding reduction in another quota, referred to as the "swing provision".[51]

4) Up to ten percent of the unused portion of the previous year's quota could be "carried over" to the following year, e.g., up to five percent of the following year's quota could be combined with any carry-over in order to maintain a ten percent carry-over of the quota.[52] Annex B, para. 5 provides that:

> Where restraints are established for more years than one, the extent to which the total of the restraint level for one product or product group may, after consultation between the parties concerned, be exceeded in either year of any two subsequent years by carry forward and /or carry over is 10 percent of which carry forward shall not represent more than 5 percent.

This flexibility was introduced to partially offset the rigidities of the quota system and to increase the extent to which exporters could respond to changing market conditions. The swing provision together with the "carry overs" and "carry forwards" were additional flexibilities brought from bilateral agreements and added to the multilateral quota system.

---

[44] *See Arrangement Regarding International Trade in Textiles* ("MFA"), Annex A, para. I.

[45] Bagchi, *supra* note 26, at 81.

[46] MFA, Annex A, III.

[47] MFA, Article III.

[48] MFA, Annex B. Pursuant to Article 17, the Annexes are an integral part of this Arrangement.

[49] MFA, Article III (3); Annex B, paragraph 1(a).

[50] MFA, Annex B, para. 2. After almost twelve years of LTA implementation, the rate of increase in the renewed quotas was one percent higher than the LTA rate of five percent.)

[51] MFA, Annex B, para. 5.

[52] MFA, Annex B, para. 5.

They were not a part of the LTA. Exporting developing countries wanted to avoid or decrease the proliferation of bilateral agreements to the largest extent possible. They were unsuccessful. Bagchi notes that throughout the life of the MFA bilateral agreements were the chosen mode of restriction. All restraining countries made lavish use of such agreements.[53]

The MFA was administered by the Textiles Surveillance Body ("TSB"). The Board of the TSB was selected by MFA members and its function was to ensure the smooth functioning and implementation of the general obligations, rules, and regulations of the MFA. The MFA was supposed to provide a means to assure minimum guarantees for "orderly" market penetration, to track the products being traded, and to report on the volumes of trade to which annual growth rate restrictions would be applied. The TSB was to be notified if the terms of unilateral and bilateral measures were changed. Its working guidelines were grafted into the Agreement on Textiles and Clothing during the Uruguay Round negotiations.

The MFA was renewed three times prior to the Uruguay Round. During the Uruguay Round negotiations, it was extended four more times on a yearly basis.[54] One problem with these renewals was that they were not automatic, but were based on consultations, thereby opening the sector to debate with each renewal. New restrictions were introduced during each consultation. Product and country coverage were increased. Importing countries continued to resort to additional restrictive measures on top of quota restrictions under existing arrangements.[55]

MFA II, which entered into force in January 1978, resulted in a significant tightening of the developed countries' restrictions on imports from developing countries. The developed countries successfully pushed for a modification of the rules to make it much easier for them to avoid the requirement that quotas be increased six percent per year. The key to this change was a provision for "jointly agreed reasonable departures" from the MFA's rules, which themselves are a jointly agreed departure from the rules of the General Agreement. The Protocol of MFA III, which entered into force in January 1982 for a period of four years and seven months, involved a further tightening in the application of restrictions. Its main addition became known as the "anti-surge" provision[56] governing the use of unutilized quotas carried over from the previous year.[57] Also the unilateral one-year application of quantitative restrictions in situations of market disruption was extended to a second year to be applied unilaterally if the restricting country faced special difficulties.[58] The MFA itself was a departure from the GATT, and the renewed MFA was labeled a "departure from the departure".[59]

---

[53] Bagchi, *supra* note 26, at 87.

[54] The extensions took place in 1974, 1978, 1982, 1991, 1992, 1993, and 1994.

[55] According to the 1998 UNCTAD TRADE AND DEVELOPMENT REPORT (UN Publication, Sales No.1998, II, D.8) about one-half of the imports of textiles and clothing in developed countries are subject to non-tariff measures, both within and outside the MFA. In the textiles and clothing sector the ratio of imports into major developed countries from developing countries affected by non-tariff measures exceeds seventy percent.

[56] The anti-surge mechanism came into effect as a result of an internal EC debate between the protagonists of liberalization, led by Germany, which insisted that the quota levels for 1983 be related to the 1982 quota levels, and a protectionist group that wanted to use 1980 as the base year. As a compromise, the EC put forward an "anti-surge mechanism" that allowed for suspending flexibility in whole or in part to prevent a sharp and substantial increase of imports of highly sensitive products covered by underutilized quotas. *See* BAGCHI, *supra* note 25, at 131 (*referring* to the EC's elaboration of the anti-surge mechanism found in para. 53, COM.TEX/26, March 4, 1982).

[57] Jackson, Davey and Sykes, *supra* note 22, at 1186.

[58] 1986 Protocol of Extension, ¶ 8.

[59] Quoting from Bagchi *supra* note 26, at 118 (*citing*UNCTAD document TD/B/C2/192, International Trade in Textiles and Developing Countries, March 23, 1978, at 24).

Discriminatory treatment was directed solely at developing countries, with the exception of Japan. Only on rare occasions did developed countries take action against one another outside the MFA. Moreover, quotas and growth rate restrictions were usually determined by reference to historical import levels. This method of calculation put new textile producers at a further disadvantage, and tightened the reins on existing producers in developing countries with a history of export growth.

The MFA, unlike its sister agreements the STA and the LTA, was more closely linked with the GATT system. A peculiar and non-conventional relationship developed between the MFA and the GATT. Although the GATT Council had the role of overseeing the operation of the MFA since the Textiles Committee, an MFA body, was part of the GATT's hierarchy; the Council, did not have the power to question any of the derogations inherent in the MFA, which became GATT *acquis*. Moreover, the MFA was serviced by the GATT's Secretariat, whose Director General was at the same time the Chairman-elect of the Textiles Committee.

Developing countries continued to believe that these special measures would be limited since developed countries had asked for a dispensation from the normal GATT regime on a temporary basis to allow time for domestic industries to adjust to their declining competitiveness. They expected that foreign investment would move in their direction during the adjustment period. However, like the earlier arrangements, the MFA was repeatedly extended, thus entrenching existing investment patterns. The negotiation process institutionalized discriminatory behavior and further circumvented GATT rules and disciplines.

C. A Comparison of the GATT and the MFA

In order to provide insight into the MFA and other arrangements which served as a basis for the Agreement on Textiles and Clothing, this section compares the mechanisms and legal frameworks embodied in the GATT and the MFA. Supporters of the MFA emphasized its focus on transparency and its enforcement mechanisms. They also emphasized its multilateral framework of agreed rules and disciplines that were aimed at the orderly liberalization of trade in textiles and clothing. However, those overseeing the evolution of the MFA found it difficult to implement "orderly" market penetration, preferring instead to rely on the term "orderly" as a pretext for "restricting" access to developed country markets.

MFA critics argued that the MFA contradicted certain core aims of the GATT system, i.e., promoting consistent treatment between various goods sectors and promoting trade liberalization. These critics recognized that the MFA was antithetical to the GATT's core principles since it permitted import restrictions based on "market disruption" (a much lower standard than the "serious injury" required under Article XIX of the GATT). The MFA inhibited market penetration resulting from comparative advantage, and it developed as a stand-alone agreement. Some checks and balances were attempted in MFA Articles 1 and 4.[60] However, in the end restrictive measures far outweighed liberalization measures.[61]

[60] Article 1 stipulated that the basic objectives of the MFA were to achieve the expansion of trade, the reduction of barriers and the progressive liberalization of world trade in textiles. Article 4 allowed for bilateral agreements consistent with the basic objectives and principles of this Arrangement—reinforcing the expansion and orderly development of trade in textiles.
[61] By removing the textiles and clothing sector from the GATT, the developed countries believed, or at least argued, that they were serving the GATT system well. They saw this as a purification of the GATT

With respect to transparency, it is generally accepted that bound tariffs, which are quantifiable, controllable, and allow no backtracking, are a key element of a transparent trade system. However, there was little transparency in the MFA framework, given that the MFA tolerated exceptions based on bilateral agreements that permitted discriminatory treatment through the use of quotas and gray area measures. It is difficult to envisage complete transparency and the non-discriminatory application of customs duties within a "multilateral" system dominated by bilateral exceptions.

As already noted, discrimination in textiles and clothing came about, in part, as a result of the dissatisfaction of the importing countries with the safeguard mechanism provided by GATT Article XIX. Like safeguards, the apparent reason for the development and extension of the textiles and clothing arrangements was to allow industries to adjust to import competition. Unlike safeguards, however, "flexibility" rather than "exceptional regulations" were at the heart of the textile arrangements. The MFA remained in existence for nearly twenty-five years, which is considerably more than is necessary for adjustment purposes.[62] The net result was perennial protection rather than temporary safeguards.

D. The Objectives and Impact of the MFA

Like its predecessor arrangements, the MFA has been justified on a number of grounds. Its proponents claimed that sustainable liberalization of trade in textiles and clothing depended on the orderly growth of trade and minimal market disruption, because of the fact that developed and developing countries both had significant producer interests. This meant that success in controlling trade liberalization was a *sine qua non* for trade expansion, and minimizing market disruption a necessary condition for industrialized countries to accept the agreement. By failing to mount strong and effective opposition to it, the exporting developing countries acquiesced in the repeated extension of the MFA.

The MFA was praised for its use of consultations and its transparency provisions. But the MFA contained many caveats and reservations, and allowed for many exceptions. This meant that although bilateral consultations took place, the industrialized importing countries maintained effective control over the rules, since if consultations were ineffective the importing country could impose unilateral restraints. In this way developed countries evaded having to demonstrate the existence of market disruption. By the time the MFA expired, three of the Quad countries, Canada, the EC and the United States, had resorted to this subterfuge extensively. Their argument in the TSB was that two sovereign governments had entered into an agreement whose contents cannot be challenged by others. That the two governments were not equal and one of them had exercised its economic power to extract an irregular benefit was overlooked.[63] Moreover, because Europe and the United States did not apply the MFA to one another, it became a *de facto* arrangement for discriminating against developing countries.

system since removal of the textiles and clothing sector removed the inherent inconsistency of the MFA with basic GATT principles. They believed, or at least argued, that this treatment avoided a double standard within the GATT, when in reality removal of the textiles and clothing sector, and subjection of this sector to discriminatory treatment, created a double standard.

[62] Under Article 7 of the *Agreement on Safeguards*, safeguard action can remain in place for no more than eight years (ten years in the case of developing countries). *See* Chapter 18 of this book.

[63] Bagchi, *supra* note 26, at 167.

Although trade in textiles has increased,[64] the MFA has had a significant adverse impact on developing country exports. Without the MFA, developing country exports of textiles and clothing to developed countries would have been significantly greater. Several studies have found that the MFA reduced export opportunities for developing countries. For example, a 1989 study by the U.S. International Trade Commission showed that the value of textile and clothing exports to the U.S. market would have been 20.5 and 36.5 percent higher respectively if MFA restrictions had not been imposed.[65] Another study estimated that without MFA restrictions the United States would have increased its textile imports by ten percent and clothing imports by 26 percent.[66] The World Development Report published by the World Bank in 1987 estimated that protectionism in the textiles and clothing sector raised consumer prices by billions of dollars and cost developing countries billions of dollars in lost income.[67]

There was too little opposition to the MFA to prevent its repeated renewal. Some exporters felt that the relatively "bad rules" that guaranteed minimum market access were better than "no rules" in a global multilateral framework. Some exporter proponents also felt they would have more influence if negotiations took place in a multilateral setting and that this would lead to developed country acceptance of a gradual, although belated, liberalization process. Despite increased costs to consumers, developed importing countries, notably the European Community, favored a restrictive system, in part because they feared that without such a system the United States would unilaterally close its textiles market to imports. The result would have been devastating to EC producers. They would probably have faced a serious increase in low cost textile and clothing imports from developing countries as a result of diversion from the U.S. market.

Assessments of the effect of the MFA on textiles and clothing industries differed from one developing country, or group of countries, to another. The more competitive developing countries felt that the MFA was implemented solely to protect against imports from developing countries. Other exporting developing countries which supported the successive extensions believed that the MFA provided them with a guaranteed "niche" in developed country markets that would otherwise have been difficult to acquire. When the MFA terminated on December 31, 1994, upon entry into force of the WTO Agreement, the United States, Canada, the European Community, Norway, Finland, and Australia had a total of ninety bilateral restraint agreements with exporting countries. In addition, there were more than thirty non-MFA agreements or unilateral measures that imposed restrictions on textile imports.

There have been many empirical studies demonstrating the MFA's adverse effects on both the exporting restrained countries and importing restraining countries. As for the former, the MFA has negatively affected their exports, even if some major exporting

[64] Researchers in the IMF had estimated in 1984 that the trade of the developing countries into the main OECD markets would rise by 82 percent in textiles and 93 percent for clothing in the absence of restrictions. This estimate had been based on the assumption of infinitely elastic supply. A couple of years later, UNCTAD had estimated an increase of 78 percent in textiles and 135 percent in clothing in the exports of developing countries if complete liberalization on a non-discriminatory basis took place. N. Kirmani, *Effects of Increased Market Access on Exports of Developing Countries*, IMF Staff Papers, December 1984, at 661–684; Bagchi, *supra* note 26, at 210 (*citing* UNCTAD, "Protectionism and Structural Adjustment", TD/B/1081 (1986)).
[65] *See* generally USITC, *The Economic Effects of Significant U.S. Import Restraints*, ITC Publication 2222 (October 1989).
[66] Y. Yang, THE IMPACT OF MFA PHASING OUT ON WORLD CLOTHING AND TEXTILE MARKETS, (1993).
[67] *See generally*, WORLD BANK, WORLD DEVELOPMENT REPORT 1987.

countries were able to extract large quota rents on their sales, e.g., Hong-Kong (China). With respect to the importing restraining countries, almost all of the studies have stressed the considerable welfare losses incurred by these countries as a result of the MFA. Most such studies were conducted in the importing countries themselves[68] and by their highly renowned institutions. This leaves little doubt that the MFA is an agreement of a purely political nature, without regard to economic parameters or welfare gain. Powerful lobbies in the restricting, as well as in some of the restrained countries, pulled the strings and found common interests, which they—strangely enough—mutually defended. The MFA thus became a *modus vivendi* between different groupings, including producers and labor unions in the developed countries, and large as well as small exporters. They found their interests intertwined and stuck together to preserve the quota system.

III. The Agreement on Textiles and Clothing: Unbiased Policies or Undermining Principles

The first serious attempt by developing countries to bring the textiles and clothing sector under the umbrella of GATT disciplines was made in the early 1980s in the aftermath of the Tokyo Round. The frustration of the exporting developing countries had its origin in the belief that the MFA had (1) failed to rectify the imbalances inherent in textiles and clothing trade, and (2) had not allowed for a sufficient "orderly" expansion of such trade. Exporting countries also became increasingly aware that certain "improvements" that were negotiated during MFA renewals were detrimental to their interests. Despite strong resistance, exporting developing countries eventually had to accept two concepts, "reasonable departures" and the "anti-surge clause" that were introduced by the European Commission in the 1977 and 1981 Protocols of Extension of the MFA.[69] These two concepts were portrayed as a way of easing restrictions, but in reality they gave impetus to the continuation and even increase of restrictions. Irritated by the prevailing injustices in the system and the lack of progress, exporting developing countries made the integration of the textiles and clothing sector into the GATT regime their most important priority.

A. Punta del Este Preparations

At a meeting held in November 1980 in Bogota, a group of exporting developing countries clarified their position in a communiqué:

---

[68] Bagchi, *supra* note 26, at 199 notes that "These estimates were certainly not accurate to the last decimal or even in rounded figures. They merely showed the range and extent of the costs. There should never be any doubt, however, that the welfare costs of the MFA quotas, in their magnitude, far outweighed the possibilities of any gains for the restraining countries".

[69] As the EC industry wanted to adopt an even more restrictive position for the second and third extensions of the MFA, it bluntly conditioned its acceptance of any extension on satisfactory bilateral agreements with major suppliers. Thus, upon the EC's insistence, the protocol of MFA extension contained a provision indicating that consultations and negotiations should be conducted in a spirit of equity and flexibility with a view to reaching a mutually acceptable solution, including the possibility of jointly-agreed "reasonable departures" from particular elements in particular cases. This was a major dilution of the MFA. The changes introduced in MFA II and subsequently MFA III were considered to be "jointly agreed reasonable departures" from the MFA's rules, which themselves are a jointly agreed departure from the rules of the GATT. *See supra* note 56 on the roots of the anti-surge mechanism. The anti-surge provision was introduced in MFA III to govern the use of unutilized quotas carried over from the previous year, and was agreed that consideration should be given to the removal, upon request, of under-utilized quotas.

For more than two decades, developing countries have faced an increasingly discriminatory and restrictive regime that has derogated the normal rules and practices of the GATT. This regime has been renewed repeatedly and expanded in scope despite the original and specific understanding that it would be temporary. The perpetuation of this discriminatory and restrictive regime is unacceptable to exporting developing countries. World trade in textiles and clothing must be liberalized in real terms by means of a gradual return to free trade in conformity with normal GATT rules and practices."[70]

Following the issuance of the communiqué, the exporting countries succeeded in generating sufficient momentum to place the textiles and clothing sector on the negotiating table during the 1982 GATT Ministerial Meeting that took place in Geneva. The proposal by the developing countries, which was substantially diluted by the developed countries in the course of negotiation, was finally included in the GATT Ministerial Declaration of 1982 and in the work program that resulted.[71] As a result of the strenuous efforts of the exporting countries, the first "Working Party on Textiles and Clothing" (1984–1986) was established.

A difficult debate took place in the Working Party between exporting and importing countries about how to achieve liberalization of the textiles and clothing sector. Although the debate achieved little, its seriousness indicated that this sector would stay on the negotiating agenda. It did however not prevent developed importing countries from extending the MFA for the third time in 1986, while preparations were ongoing for the launching of the Uruguay Round of trade negotiations. In spite of this extension, it seemed beyond doubt that the textiles sector would eventually be brought under GATT rules.

Aware of divergent interests and conflicting views, the textile-exporting developing countries were determined to develop an effective common position. They succeeded in doing so within the framework of the International Textiles and Clothing Bureau ("ITCB"),[72] which was established for that purpose in 1985 in preparation for the next round of multilateral trade negotiations.

A GATT preparatory committee met from January to July of 1986 to prepare for the new round of negotiations. This committee succeeded in forcing the "restraining" countries to come into the open. A group of exporters[73] argued forcefully for a "rollback commitment" on textiles and clothing, and pushed for an ambitious three-year phase-out program, under which all restricting measures incompatible with the GATT system would be withdrawn.[74]

On the other side, the European Community argued against the integration of the sector, stating that until the conditions which had necessitated the creation of the LTA, and subsequently the MFA, were eliminated, an ill-prepared return to GATT rules would cause problems. The EC maintained that as long as the original imbalance of rights and obligations in this sector had not been corrected,[75] abandoning a regime that had enabled

[70] *Bogota Declaration* (November 1980).
[71] THE OUTCOME OF THE URUGUAY ROUND, *supra* note 10, at 111.
[72] The ITCB was established in 1985 as an independent inter-governmental organization with the aim of strengthening the process of cooperation and coordination among developing countries in the field of textiles and clothing. The Bureau acts, *inter alia*, as a forum where members exchange views in order to develop a common position in the textile negotiations. Its present members are Argentina, Bangladesh, Brazil, China, Colombia, Costa Rica, Egypt, El Salvador, Hong Kong, India, Indonesia, Jamaica, Macao, Maldives, Mexico, Pakistan, Peru, Republic of Korea, Sri Lanka, Turkey, Uruguay and former Yugoslavia.
[73] The group consisted of Argentina, Brazil, Egypt, India, Nigeria, Pakistan, Peru, and Tanzania.
[74] The GATT Preparatory Committee on Textiles and Clothing, PREP. COM (86) GATT Document W/3/Rev.1 (1986).
[75] Both the Cotton and the Multi-fiber Arrangements were based on the concept of market disruption, and not, as suggested by the EC representative in 1986, on an "imbalance of rights and obligations in this sector".

members to manage the expansion of trade, first in cotton textiles and then in all fibers, would merely lead to a recurrence of market disorder. The EC also argued that the MFA had enabled a number of exporting countries to avoid tough competition and to begin production of textile products, something they could not have accomplished without market access guarantees.[76]

After a protracted and often intense debate between the restricting and restricted countries, a joint proposal was put forward by Colombia and Switzerland to the Preparatory Committee that found its way unaltered into the Punta del Este Declaration that launched the Uruguay Round. It provided that:

> Negotiations in the area of textiles and clothing shall aim to formulate modalities that would permit the eventual integration of this sector into GATT on the basis of strengthened GATT rules and disciplines ("SGRAD"), thereby also contributing to the objective of further liberalization of trade.[77]

This same text, which unaltered became the first paragraph of the ATC's preamble, was subject to much controversy and attracted harsh criticism during the Uruguay Round negotiations. While India and Pakistan emphasized that liberalization of textiles and clothing should be pursued independently and not be contingent on other agreements, it was obvious that consensus on this very sensitive subject would only be possible if it formed part of an overall trade agreement. This was evidenced by the firm conviction of both the European Commission and the United States that a close link had to be made between the progressive elimination of quantitative restrictions on textiles and the application of strengthened GATT rules and disciplines generally, to which they gave the highest priority. In addition, it became evident that all participants, developed and developing countries alike, would be required to make contributions in other negotiating areas, particularly those concerning tariffs, non-tariff measures, balance of payments, and infant industry protection.

The result was that for the first time the textiles and clothing sector was included as a subject in the multilateral trade negotiations, in sharp contrast to earlier GATT rounds in which the textiles and clothing sector was either dealt with before the negotiations began, or handled in negotiations that ran parallel to the rounds.

B. The Uruguay Round Negotiations

The Negotiating Group on Textiles and Clothing was established in February 1987, a few months after the launch of the Uruguay Round in September 1986. It was entrusted with the task of examining the techniques and modalities for the liberalization and eventual integration of the textiles sector into the GATT/WTO system. The negotiations were cumbersome and in many instances highly politicized. It was only towards the end of 1990, after the failed mid-term review in Montreal, that the negotiations started to take shape. Four issues remained highly controversial:

1) Product coverage under the agreement,
2) The percentage for the integration of products in each stage ("staged integration"),
3) Increases in the MFA quota growth rates for products not yet integrated, and
4) The duration of the agreement.[78]

---

[76] The GATT Preparatory Committee on Textiles and Clothing, PREP. COM (86) SR/3, at 29 (1986).
[77] GATT Document MIN.DEC, September 20, 1986.
[78] GATT Document MTN.TNC/W/89/Add.1, November 7, 1991.

404TEXTILES AND DEVELOPING COUNTRIES

C. The Agreement on Textiles and Clothing

The ATC was drafted by experts who had the MFA negotiations very much in mind. These experts formed what can be viewed as an exclusive club in which everyone was cognizant of the maximum political limits of their negotiating partners. This was clearly reflected in the ATC, which came out as a highly sensitive "deal" between exporting and importing country negotiators.

The ATC calls for the integration of the textiles and clothing sector over a ten-year period that is explicitly non-renewable.[79] Some see the Agreement as a delicate compromise between the competing interests of importing developed and exporting developing countries, and as representing an essential step towards achieving trade liberalization in a sector that has served as the engine of growth for many developing countries. Others view the ATC, with all its inherent weaknesses, as asymmetrical since the overall balance of the Agreement tilts very much in favor of the developed restricting countries. This is so to the extent that the ATC allows developed countries extra time for protection and only provides "the appearance" of special and differential treatment for cotton producers, small suppliers and LDCs.

The ATC is a relatively short agreement, containing nine articles, and an Annex[80] entitled "List of Products Covered by this Agreement". The Annex lists approximately 800 HS tariff lines, including all textiles and clothing products, whether subject to existing MFA restrictions or not. The tacit purpose of the developed countries in including such an extensive list was to "inflate" the product coverage with a view to slowing down the integration process.

The Agreement operates on the basis of three essential principles. These principles are: (1) the flexibility provisions adopted from the MFA, (2) the "integration" process, and (3) the "liberalization" process. The "flexibility" provisions permit an exporting country to maintain existing rights under the MFA with respect to products under MFA quota and not yet integrated. Accordingly, an exporting country is entitled to trade off part of a quota on one product against the quota on another product, or to use part of one year's quota for a particular product in either the preceding or subsequent year.[81] The "integration" process manages the gradual removal of existing quotas and the inclusion of products into the GATT system. This process is compounded by what is known as the "liberalization" process or "growth-on-growth." "Growth-on-growth" is intended to increase the rate of integration of non-integrated quotas thereby producing additional growth in textiles and clothing trade.

Textiles and clothing is a highly politicized sector, in which manufacturers and lobbies, particularly in developed countries, have high economic stakes. As a result, WTO Members realized that bringing this sector under GATT discipline would require time. This was evident in numerous proposals from developed countries tabled during the Uruguay Round that supported integration of this sector over a long transition period. Many small developing country exporters, fearing fierce competition from larger developing countries, were also more comfortable extending the quota system. They found that they

---

[79] ATC Article 9.

[80] The Annex, which constitutes the basis for the integration of products into GATT during the transition period, includes all items defined by HS codes at the six-digit level in Chapters 50–63 of the Harmonized System, plus various textile and clothing products listed in Chapters 30–49, and 64–96.

[81] This provision is found in ATC Article 2.16. Article 2.16 provides: "Flexibility provisions, i.e. swing, carryover and carry forward, applicable to all restrictions maintained pursuant to this Article, shall be the same as those provided for in MFA bilateral agreements for the 12-month period prior to the entry into force of the WTO Agreement. No quantitative limits shall be placed or maintained on the combined use of swing, carryover and carry forward."

had certain common interests with importing developed countries. It was therefore agreed that the integration must be gradual, and must be implemented pursuant to a timetable that would avoid too much disruption in the early years of liberalization, as well as too much back-loading during the final stage of the phase-out.

The division and classification of exporting developing countries into a number of groupings, each with its specific characteristics and interests, adds to the uniqueness of the ATC. These divisions are characteristic of the textiles and clothing sector, and are rooted in the bilateral quota restrictions negotiated in the 1960s to avoid market disruptions resulting from import surges. The ATC differentiates between small suppliers, new entrants, cotton suppliers, wool producers, as well as the least-developed countries, and calls for special and differential treatment for each group with respect to the application of transitional safeguards.[82] Such a categorization implies the continuation of covert deals, even if within a multilateral setting. Nevertheless, the ATC would not have been agreed to without the acceptance of preferential treatment for these groups.

In the first major review of the ATC, which occurred in 1998, these sub-groups were highly critical of the lack of benefits accruing to them from the preferential treatment accorded by the ATC. They were successful in persuading the Council for Trade in Goods to reiterate the importance of the full implementation of the ATC's Preamble, Article 1, and Article 6(6)(a) and (c).[83]

1. The Liberalization and Integration Process

One point that distinguishes the ATC from the MFA is that the ATC was negotiated and is being implemented within the framework of the rules and disciplines of GATT 1994. The ATC also embodies a gradual, progressive, time-limited phase-out of all MFA restrictions and the integration of all textile and clothing trade into the general disciplines of GATT 1994. While the ATC focuses largely on the phase-out of MFA restrictions, it also deals with non-MFA restrictions on textiles and clothing products, including "all unilateral quantitative restrictions, bilateral arrangements, and other measures having a similar effect."[84] All GATT-inconsistent, non-MFA restrictions were to be notified and brought into conformity with GATT 1994 within one year of its entry into force, or otherwise phased out progressively before January 1, 2005 when the ATC terminates.[85] Any new restrictions must be in accordance with GATT 1994,[86] i.e., safeguards may only be imposed in accordance with Article XIX of GATT 1994 and the Agreement on Safeguards.[87] Any restrictions that were not notified were required to be terminated forthwith.[88]

---

[82] The ATC differentiates between the developing countries based on their interests and needs, as well as the special treatment they are granted. Distinctions are made between small suppliers, new entrants, cotton-producing exporting countries and wool-producing developing country members. Special and Differential Treatment is referred to in ATC Article 1.2 (small suppliers and new entrants), Article 1.4 (cotton producing exporting Members), Article 2.18 (small suppliers) and Article 6.6(a)–(d) (transitional safeguards vis-à-vis a variety of disadvantaged Members).

[83] *Major Review of the Implementation of the Agreement on Textiles and Clothing in the First Stage of the Integration Process,* Council for Trade in Goods, GATT Document G/L/224, February 19 1998, at 55 ("*ITCB First Major Review*").

[84] ATC Article 3 note 4.

[85] ATC Article 3.1–3.2.

[86] ATC Article 2.4.

[87] Pursuant to Article 6.4 of the ATC, the transitional safeguard mechanism is only applicable to products not yet integrated into the GATT.

[88] ATC Article 2.4.

This dual process of liberalization and integration, the heart of the ATC, is set forth in the 21 paragraphs that make up ATC Article 2. Article 2 incorporates the elements designed to bring this sector, progressively and in stages, under the rules and disciplines of the trading system. Article 2 provides clear procedural and substantive guidance as to how the textiles and clothing products listed in the Annex to the Agreement are to be integrated.

The integration program is the main pillar of the ATC, and has four stages.[89] Members are required to integrate products from four product groups—tops and yarns, fabrics, made-up textile products, and clothing—in each stage. Unlike the MFA, however, no prior consultations are envisaged before each stage of integration. It is left entirely to each importing country to decide upon the most suitable way to integrate each of the four groups of products, both in terms of the percentage of integration and the combination of products.

Article 2.6 required each WTO member to integrate sixteen percent by volume of its 1990 imports of the products listed in the Annex on the date the WTO Agreement entered into force (January 1, 1995). Article 2.8 covers the three additional stages of integration. It required integration of an additional seventeen percent at the end of the third year (January 1, 1998), an additional eighteen percent at the end of the seventh year (January 1, 2002), and integration of the remainder at the end of the tenth year (January 1, 2005), at which point Article 9 specifies that the textiles and clothing sector will be fully integrated into GATT 1994, and the ATC "shall stand" terminated. Article 9 explicitly provides that: "There shall be no extension of this Agreement."

The negotiators were aware of the possibility that importing developed countries would back-load ATC commitments, i.e., would integrate products not subject to MFA restrictions first, leaving integration of the restricted products until as late as possible.[90] As a result, an additional instrument for increased market access was provided in the ATC. Articles 2.13 and 2.14, providing for "integration" and "liberalization", grant increased access for restricted products throughout the transition period. Under this "growth-on-growth" principle, additional growth rates beyond those agreed in the MFA are required for restricted products. Such products are to have their quota increased by an additional 16 percent in the first stage, 25 percent in the second stage, and 27 percent in the third stage. Small suppliers are to be accorded "advancement by one stage" in the growth rates.

The interpretation of this last provision has been the subject of considerable debate. "Advancement by one stage" was generally interpreted by major importing countries to mean the substitution of the second stage growth rate for the first stage growth rate. In other words beneficiaries would see an increase in their quotas of 25 percent in the first stage compared with 16 percent for other countries, followed by a 27 percent increase in the subsequent two stages. Such a view was criticized by the beneficiaries, which understood "advancement by one stage" to mean adding the growth rates of the first and second stages to allow for a cumulative effect. This view was strengthened by the methodology used by the European Community. The European Community viewed

---

[89] ATC Articles 2.6–2.8.

[90] Despite the fact that back-loading was foreseen, many developing countries have cried foul with regard to the implementation of the ATC. Those who have objected the most are large exporters such as India, Pakistan, and Hong-Kong/China. They were hoping for a more meaningful implementation consistent with the spirit of liberalization and integration present in the ATC. In addition, they had hoped for more value-added products to be integrated in the first and second stages. This is one of the inherent weaknesses of the ATC—it maintained the balance in favor of the restraining countries for as long as possible.

"growth-on-growth" as the only way to deliver "meaningful improvement" for small suppliers in conjunction with the full and faithful implementation of Article 2.18.[91]

2. The Transitional Safeguard Mechanism

An examination of the transitional safeguard mechanism will help to better understand the various checks and balances built into the ATC. Pursuant to Article 6 of the ATC, which was agreed to after lengthy and tedious negotiations, and in response to strong protectionist pressure from producers, transitional safeguards can be invoked if an importing country can demonstrate that increased quantities of imports of a product that has not yet been integrated into the GATT system are causing serious damage to its domestic industry or threaten to cause such damage.[92] This mechanism can be viewed as an "intermediate" measure, stronger than the safeguard measure provided in GATT Article XIX, but weaker than the protection obtained through the application of the "market disruption" principle in the STA.

Aware that gray area measures outside the GATT system could no longer be used, but responsive to the concerns of their textile and clothing industries, developed countries favored this "intermediate" form of protectionism. Exporters however expressed concern with the maintenance of restrictions, and the introduction of restrictions on products that not been under restraint when the phase-out process began. Exporters feared that the transitional safeguard mechanism would delay the reintegration process, or in the worst case, replace one selective safeguard mechanism (MFA) with another.[93]

To convince exporters to accept such a mechanism, strings had to be attached. Not only does the verb "may" dominate the first two paragraphs of ATC Article 6, denoting a lack of enthusiasm for the too frequent application of the transitional safeguard mechanism, exporters were also able to include language stating that the mechanism "should be applied as sparingly as possible".[94]

Clear guidance on the use of transitional safeguards by importing countries is provided in the ATC. An importing country is first required to prove that the serious damage to its industry was caused by a sharp and substantial increase of imports from the individual country or countries concerned.[95] Furthermore, the importing country must examine the effect of the increased imports based on a number of relevant economic variables, such as "output, productivity, utilization of capacity, inventories, market share, exports, wages, employment, domestic prices, profits and investment".[96] Lastly, the specific transitional safeguard mechanism is only applicable to products not yet integrated into the GATT.[97]

---

[91] The provision for "advancement by one stage" was implemented in different ways on the two sides of the Atlantic. Canada and the United States applied the factor of 25 percent on the prevailing growth rates in stage one. The EC, on the other hand, first applied the normal factor of 16 percent and then raised it further by 25 percent. A comparison of the two methods showed that, during the first two stages, the additional access granted in North America was less than half of that in west Europe. It was 0.5 percent and 1.2 percent during the two stages respectively in North America compared with 1.7 percent and 3.5 percent in Europe. This minuscule benefit was provided by Canada to sixteen small suppliers and by the United States to 22 small suppliers. Compared with the much larger number of small suppliers restricted in North America, there were only two (Peru and Sri Lanka) restricted by the EC, based on the definition contained in ATC Article 2:18. *See* Bagchi, *supra* note 26, at 240 (*quoting Agreement on Textiles and Clothing: Evaluation of Implementation*, WTO Document WT/GC/W/283, August 3, 1999, at 3, table 1.

[92] ATC Article 6.2

[93] Raffaelli and Jenkins, *supra* note 12, at 34–40.

[94] ATC Article 6.1.

[95] ATC Article 6.4.

[96] ATC Article 6.3.

[97] ATC Article 6.4.

Cortes has stated that the difference between ATC Article 6 and the MFA is not to be found in the model chosen, but rather in the way its application is controlled.[98] Pursuant to Article 6, a showing of real harm, and not mere "market disruption", is required. In addition, the measure solicited will have to be fully justified, an aspect that will remain under the supervision of the Textiles Monitoring Body ("TMB"), which will make the recommendations that it considers appropriate.[99] Moreover, use of transitional measures is subject to WTO dispute resolution, and several such measures have in fact been successfully challenged.[100]

3. The Disputed Balance of Rights and Obligations

Although loose, a link between the integration of textile and clothing trade into the multilateral trading system, and the fulfillment of certain commitments, including commitments made by developing countries, appears to be established in ATC Article 7. This provision provides that <u>all</u> Members are required to:

1) Achieve improved market access for textiles and clothing products by tariff reductions and bindings, or through liberalization or other non-tariff measures;
2) Ensure the application of policies relating to fair and equitable trading conditions regarding textiles and clothing in such areas as anti-dumping, subsidies, and countervailing duties; and
3) Avoid discrimination against textiles and clothing imports when taking measures for general trade policy reasons.[101]

In this regard, Members are obliged to notify to the TMB actions which have a bearing on the implementation of the ATC, including the items set forth in Article 7. Members may also make "reverse notifications", thereby notifying the TMB when a Member is harmed by actions mentioned above and no notification has been made.[102] This procedure is intended to aid developing countries in making sure that the above commitments are implemented. In the event of a dispute arising from an imbalance between the integration process and the requirements of Article 7, Members may bring the dispute before the relevant WTO bodies and so inform the TMB.[103] Any subsequent findings or

---

[98] Jimenez Cortes, *supra* note 1, at 278. By this it is meant that the model for safeguard measures was more or less the same but stronger criteria governed their application under the ATC. In both the MFA and the ATC the measures are applied on a member-by-member basis in order to assist the adjustment process required by the changes in the pattern of world trade in textile products. (*Compare* ATC Article 6.4 with MFA Article 1.5.) However, as opposed to the MFA, the ATC safeguard measure has a series of requirements and conditions. The most important of these is that the harm or the risk must be genuinely demonstrable, i.e., real effective harm and not mere "disruption" is required. Also the Textiles Monitoring Body has been stricter in monitoring and controlling the application of the ATC and that has forced the United States to refrain from recourse to the transitional safeguard mechanism after its excessive use of this mechanism in the first year of its operation. Conditions and criteria for the application of safeguard measures in the MFA and the ATC are nevertheless weaker than the disciplines present in the safeguards provision of GATT Article XIX, as amplified by the *Agreement on Safeguards*.

[99] ATC Article 6.8; Jimenez Cortes, *supra* note 1, at 278.

[100] *See e.g.*, *United States—Restrictions on Imports of Cotton and Man-Made Fiber Underwear*, Report of the Panel, WT/DS24/R, and Report of the Appellate Body WT/DS24/AB/R, adopted February 25, 1997; and *United States—Measures Affecting Imports of Woven Wool Shirts and Blouses from India*, Report of the Panel WT/DS33/R, and Report of the Appellate Body WT/DS33/AB/R, adopted May 23, 1997.

[101] ATC Article 7.

[102] ATC Article 7.2.

[103] ATC Article 7.3.

conclusions by the WTO bodies shall form part of a comprehensive report to be made by the TMB.[104]

ATC Article 7 was a difficult article to negotiate and continues to be the subject of much controversy in the framework of the TMB review process, as well as in regard to the implementation of the ATC. The European Community, which basically negotiated Article 7 on its own,[105] intended to set forth the inherent balance in the Agreement. The European Community felt that exporting developing countries should be obligated to remove trade barriers on their textiles and clothing imports as a *quid pro quo* for the integration of this sector into GATT rules and disciplines and the reduction of developed country quotas on sensitive products. Developing countries were, however, not ready to pay again for concessions that they viewed as legitimately owed to them. They first argued that including textiles and clothing in the multilateral trade negotiations was part of the overall framework of the system and should be granted in return for the many concessions they were already making in the Round, e.g., on services and intellectual property rights. Moreover, as a matter of principle, the developing countries did not want to "pay" for the abolition of what was in reality a derogation from GATT principles.

During the negotiations, as a result of the insistence of the importing countries, India safeguarded its interests by linking its tariff reductions on textiles and clothing products to the ATC integration program. India's tariff schedule provides that if the integration process envisaged in ATC Article 2.6–2.8 does not materialize in full or is delayed, its duties will revert to the level prevailing on January 1, 1990. This may be the first time that a developing country has used a "snap back" clause in multilateral trade negotiations, thereby linking its tariff concessions to the commitments of developed countries.[106]

Some major importing countries have linked the integration process and increases in growth rates for MFA quotas to the further opening of developing country markets for textiles and clothing. The United States emphasized that the concessions it provided on all textiles and clothing products were based upon an understanding that the maintenance of the balance of rights and obligations, particularly as set forth in ATC Article 7, means that Members will provide effective market access to textiles and clothing entering their territory from the United States. Such reasoning, which is the thrust of Article 7 in the minds of the major importing countries, has its origins in the "strengthened GATT rules and disciplines" ("SGRAD") of the Punta del Este Declaration, where it was agreed that better import access should be provided by all Members, including developing countries. The European Community and the United States, along with other importing countries, were firm that the exporting developing countries must become fully involved in the integration process by contributing their part to SGRAD. Developing countries rejected this demand for reciprocity. They argued that since they were not responsible for keeping the textiles and clothing sector outside GATT rules for more than thirty years, and since they were not beneficiaries of the MFA, they should not be required to pay twice. However,

---

[104] ATC Article 7.3.

[105] Jimenez Cortes, *supra* note 1, at 291, note 54. The United States, which at the time was seeking to establish a system of global quotas, did not support this provision.

[106] *See* UNCTAD Secretariat, *The Implementation of the Uruguay Agreement on Textiles and Clothing: Some General Issues* in Harmon Thomas and John Whalley, Uruguay Round Results and the Emerging Trade Agenda: Quantitative-Based Analyses from the Development Perspective 291 (UNCTAD 1998).

as already noted, it would appear that developing countries did indeed pay too much for the ATC.

4. The Textiles Monitoring Body

From the outset of the Uruguay Round, it was clear to the negotiators of the ATC that a surveillance body, designed along the same lines as the MFA's Textiles Surveillance Body, needed to be established. Differences existed among the negotiators concerning the function of the Textiles Monitoring Body ("TMB"). The United States was of the view that it should operate as a mere notification entity, lending the needed transparency to the implementation of the ATC. The International Textiles and Clothing Bureau, on the other hand, as well as the European Community, favored the establishment of a body that would monitor transparency and the phase-out process, supervise the implementation of the ATC, and act as a dispute settlement body.[107]

The latter view prevailed. Article 8.1 of the ATC provides for the establishment of the TMB, consisting of a Chairman and ten members serving in their personal capacity, to supervise the implementation of the ATC and to examine the conformity of measures taken under the Agreement.

The TMB has succeeded in defusing many disputes, thus avoiding the need to take them to the Council for Trade in Goods. It has also managed to make recommendations by achieving a consensus among its members. Many view decision-making by consensus as weakening the TMB's decision-making ability. However, because the TMB is limited to issuing recommendations, majority decisions risk not being implemented by the country concerned.

As discussed below, the considerable success of the TMB has not prevented Members from invoking the Dispute Settlement Mechanism to hear certain ATC disputes. Nor has it kept Members from occasionally exposing the wide differences between the exporting developing countries and the developed importing countries before the Council for Trade in Goods. Such occurrences usually arise during the ATC review process, prior to the implementation of a new stage of commitments, or during the preparation for Ministerial Conferences.

IV. Implementation of the Agreement

Whereas the developed importing countries maintain their position that they have faithfully implemented the ATC, exporting developing countries now realize that the ATC has intrinsic deficiencies, as discussed below. The implementation of the first three stages of the ATC has led to little meaningful integration of the textiles and clothing sector into GATT rules and disciplines, because of the practice of back-loading, i.e., the delaying by the major importing countries of integration of products subject to MFA quotas for as long as possible. Although they negotiated the ATC in good faith, exporting developing countries did not fully realize that importing countries would postpone integration of more sensitive products as long as possible. Their legitimate expectation of increased access to the markets of exporting developing countries, in accordance with the progressive integration process, has failed to materialize. This has led exporting developing countries to conclude that while the letter of the ATC may have been implemented, the spirit has not.

---

[107] This idea was proposed prior to the establishment of a strong dispute settlement mechanism in the WTO.

A. Inherent Weaknesses of the Agreement

Because of the inherent weaknesses of the ATC, there has to date been no significant elimination of MFA restraints by the major importing countries. There are two problems. First, under Article 2.6 and 2.8 of the ATC, the bulk (49 percent) of imports do not have to be integrated until the final stage, on January 1, 2005. Second, although the Agreement requires the items integrated at each stage to include some products from each of the four categories of tops and yarns, fabrics, made-up textile products, and clothing, it does not specify any particular percentage of each. These two weaknesses have permitted the importing developed countries to "back-load" integration of the products subject to MFA restriction. In a statement circulated by the ITCB on November 10, 2001,[108] commending Norway for its elimination of all quota restrictions by the third stage of integration on January 1, 2002, the United States, the EU, and Canada were reproached for their inadequate implementation of the ATC. In the case of the United States, 701 out of 757 MFA quotas will remain in effect until January 1, 2005. The corresponding figures for the EU and Canada are 167 out of 219 and 239 out of 295.[109]. Moreover, most of the products integrated to date have been those with little value-added, such as tops, yarns and fabrics. Few higher value-added products, such as made-up textile products and clothing, have been integrated so far.[110] Thus, in the first two stages of integration the United States had integrated only 17.35 percent of imports by value compared with 33.24 percent by volume.

In the third stage of integration, despite the fact that all three trading entities were careful to implement the percentages agreed pursuant to the ATC, only a small degree of liberalization has resulted and it has been concentrated in low-value added products. Using the integration program of the United States as an example, eighty percent of its restrained products will remain restricted until the last day of the Agreement. By December, 2002, the United States had liberalized only 56 quotas out of a total of 757 quotas in existence at the start of the ATC. Whereas in stage one the United States technically integrated 16.21 percent of its textile imports, that did not result in the liberalization of any of its restricted imports. With respect to stage two and stage three, the United States integrated 17.03 percent and 18.11 percent respectively; this resulted in the liberalization of 2.13 percent and 9.61 percent of its restricted imports. That means that out of the required 51.35 percent integration, the effective U.S. liberalization of quotas was only 11.74 percent. Moreover, out of the 51.35 percent of products integrated, only six percent covered clothing. The rest was concentrated in low-value added products, i.e., yarns, fabrics and made-ups.[111]

Neither the EU nor Canada has done better in their implementation of the first three stages. On the contrary, the similarities in the features of their integration programs with those of the United States are striking, having only liberalized small percentages of their restricted products, leaving the bulk to the last day and concentrating on less value-added

[108] ITCB, *Statement Circulated by the ITCB*, Doha Ministerial Conference, WT/MIN(01)/ST/27 November 10, 2001.

[109] *Second Major Review of the Implementation of the Agreement on Textiles and Clothing by the Council for Trade in Goods*, Communication from Uruguay (on behalf of the members of the ITCB), (G/C/W/304), September 26, 2001, at ¶ 25 ("*ITCB Second Major Review*").

[110] "The above numbers will look even worse after quotas on China and Chinese Taipei are also taken into account. These two have joined the WTO only recently and complete notifications with respect to their quotas have not yet become available". ITCB; IC/W/251/Rev.1, March 1, 2002, at ¶ 6 (i).

[111] Statement made on September 27, 2001 by Mr. William Ehlers, Acting Chairman ITCB, at the Meeting of the Council for Trade in Goods, G/C/W/325, October 22, 2001, at 6 (Table 3 Observations).

products in the first three stages of integration, in which clothing amount to nine percent and seven percent of the products integrated for the EU and Canada respectively.

B. Analysis of the Integration Program

In expressing disappointment with the outcome of the first two stages of integration, the ITCB's Council of Representatives pointed out three major deficiencies: (1) The weaknesses in the implementation of the integration process; as discussed above; (2) The European Community's misuse of antidumping investigations and actions for protection purposes, and (3) the use by the United States of rules of origin to pursue restrictive trade objectives.[112]

The findings in WTO dispute settlement proceedings confirm that the EU has abused antidumping investigations and actions. The EU has not shied away from invoking and imposing antidumping duties even on products that have been under quota restrictions. The ITCB has also denounced repeated antidumping investigations by the EU, most of which, it said, were based on unsubstantiated claims. Despite being unsubstantiated, these investigations affected imports to the detriment of the exporting countries in question, causing losses in their market share which are difficult to recapture. The TMB acknowledges this, stating its view that "... protracted or repeated investigations (into alleged dumping), even if they do not result in the imposition of provisional or final antidumping duties, create uncertainties to the exporters of the products in question".[113]

The United States has been more cautious in invoking antidumping actions. However, in the first year it made excessive use of safeguard measures, invoking unilateral measures 24 times. It gave this up under after severe criticism from the TMB and the exporting countries. Manipulation of rule of origin requirements, and its visa requirement remain barriers that serve to restrict exports from the developing countries.

With respect to U.S. safeguard measures, invoked by the United States under Article 6 of the ATC, not only were they not justified, in most cases they were found by the TMB to be in violation of the U.S. obligations. Furthermore, the ITCB has shown that the U.S. actions on safeguard measures affected over $1 billion worth of exports from developing countries.[114] The U.S. actions reflect a pattern of providing protection to domestic industry by "exploiting" the lengthy process of the TMB, dispute settlement panels and the Appellate Body. Under the ATC, a safeguard action can be taken for a maximum of three years. The TMB process, and recourse to panels and the Appellate Body unavoidably take about two years to complete. During the period, U.S. industry benefits from unfair protection when the measures are ultimately found to be invalid.

Not only has the United States shown reluctance to make meaningful integration in the third stage, it attempted to maintain its visa requirements for the integrated products

---

[112] *See generally ITCB Second Major Review, supra* note 109.

[113] *ITCB Second Major Review, supra* 109 (referencing the review of the TMB, G/L/459). The report lists the antidumping proceedings "initiated in 1998, 1999 and 2000". The EU has had repeated recourse to antidumping investigations and/or measures on already restricted imports of bed linen, also on cotton fabrics and man-made fiber fabrics from several countries. The EC action on bed linen was against India, which took the case to the DSB. *See* note 126 *infra* and accompanying text. The antidumping measures on bed linen involved imports from Egypt and Pakistan. The action on cotton fabrics involved imports from Egypt, India, Indonesia, Pakistan, Turkey and China. The action on man-made fiber and fiber fabrics involved exports from India, Indonesia, Pakistan and Thailand. *Id.* ¶ 108.

[114] *Id.* ¶¶ 79–86.

in spite of the fact that they were challenged during the second stage.[115] The ITCB stated to the CTG during its second major review of ATC implementation,[116] that unless the United States confirmed the withdrawal of its visa arrangements, it should not be deemed to have complied with its obligation to fully integrate the relevant products.[117] In December 2001 the United States agreed to drop the requirement.[118]

The U.S. changes in rules of origin for the textiles and clothing sector, which went into effect in July 1966, have also been inconsistent with U.S. obligations under the ATC,[119] and have had a discriminatory effect on imports from developing countries. These changes were specifically undertaken for trade policy reasons, targeting only the textiles and clothing sector. The main challenges to these modifications came from the EU, which threatened to invoke the DSU procedures against the United States for violating Article 2.4 of the ATC. However, under a clandestine agreement between the two entities the United States agreed to partially reinstate the pre-ATC rules. This agreement may have satisfied the EU, but it did not nothing to facilitate exports from developing countries. On the contrary it continued to impede their access to the U.S. market, in particular for cotton products.[120]

V. Dispute Settlement in Textiles and Clothing

The bulk of textiles and clothing imports remain subject to stringent quota restrictions. In spite of this, and the fact that all commitments made under the ATC are not yet in place, importing countries have not shied away from protectionist actions. Although the disputes brought to the Dispute Settlement Body ("DSB") are few in number, they are revealing. In addition, numerous disputes dealt with in the TMB did not find their way to the DSB. These disputes were significant in their own right in rectifying actions by the major importing countries that some developing country exporters considered tantamount to trade harassment.[121]

The importance of ATC disputes brought to the DSB should not be underestimated. The dispute settlement system has given developing countries new leverage in trade negotiations involving this highly sensitive sector. Developing countries scored victories in four cases involving textiles and clothing.[122] These cases are described in detail in another chapter,[123] so will not be discussed in detail here. Instead, a few points of particular importance to developing countries will be mentioned.

---

[115] *Id.*

[116] *Id.* ¶ 78

[117] *Id.* ¶ 75. The ITCB explains that visas are a requirement additional to normal shipping documents. They were devised as an administrative arrangement to help control and monitor the exports of textiles and clothing products under quota restriction with a view to keeping these exports within the applicable quantitative limits.

[118] *Amendment of Export Visa Requirements for Textiles and Textile Products Integrated into GATT 1994 in the Third Stage,* 66 Fed. Reg. 63225 (2001).

[119] *Id.* ¶¶ 87–93.

[120] *Id.*

[121] *ITCB First Major Review, supra* note 83, at ¶ 37.

[122] *United States—Cotton Underwear, supra* note 100; *United States—Shirts and Blouses, supra* note 100; *European Communities—Antidumping on Imports of Cotton-type Bed Linen from India*, Report of the Appellate Body (WT/DS141/AB/R), adopted March 12, 2001; and *United States—Transitional Safeguard Measures on Combed Cotton Yarn from Pakistan*, Report of the Appellate Body (WT/DS192/AB/R), adopted November 5, 2001.

[123] *See* Chapter 9 of this book.

Two complaints by India, one against the United States concerning transitional safe-guard measures, and the second against the European Community concerning an antidumping measure, appear to have been filed in an attempt to demonstrate the repeated abuses of the rules in this sector by the United States and the EU. India is one of the developing countries that is most aware of its rights and obligations under the WTO and of the opportunities that the dispute settlement system offers.

A. United States—Shirts and Blouses[124]

When the TMB examined this dispute between India and the United States, it concluded that the U.S. transitional safeguard action was in conformity with the ATC, whereupon India invoked its right in the DSB to establish a panel to examine the legality of the U.S. action.

Although the United States announced its withdrawal of its transitional safeguard measure on wool shirts and blouses from India in November 1996 before the panel ruling was due, India nevertheless wanted the Panel to rule on the legality of the U.S. measure. Furthermore, in spite of a clear finding by the Panel that the United States had violated the provisions of Articles 2 and 6 of the ATC when imposing its transitional safeguard measure, India appealed certain issues of law covered in the Panel Report and certain legal interpretations developed by the Panel. Included in the appeal by India were three important issues: (a) the issue of the burden of proof, (b) the relationship between the TMB and the DSU and the legal role of the former, and lastly (c) the question of judicial economy—whether a panel must examine all claims submitted.

With respect to judicial economy, India submitted that the Panel's application of the notion of judicial economy undermined the objectives of the DSU, as set forth in Article 3.2 of the DSU and in India's view, included both dispute resolution as well as dispute prevention. India maintained that these objectives could only be achieved if panels resolved both the dispute over the particular contested measure and the issues of interpretation arising from all legal claims made in connection with that measure.[125]

The Appellate Body disagreed and upheld the application of judicial economy.[126] A lesson to be learned from the case is that one cannot expect too much "rule making" from the WTO dispute settlement system. As "adjudicatory" organs, both panels and the Appellate Body tend to exercise judicial restraint and limit their rulings to issues that are absolutely necessary for bringing the dispute to a satisfactory conclusion. While it remains important to seek clarifications of existing rules from panels and the Appellate Body, the Dispute Settlement Mechanism should not be viewed as a substitute for the role of negotiators in resolving systemic issues.[127] However, as the ATC demonstrates, developing countries must be very much on guard in the negotiation process.

---

[124] *U.S.—Shirts and Blouses, supra* note 100.

[125] *Id.* at 5–8.

[126] *Id.* at 17–20.

[127] *See generally,* The South Center, Issues Regarding The Review Of The WTO Dispute Settlement Mechanism, *Trade-Related Agenda Development and Equity* ("TRADE"), Working Paper 1, February 1999. *Cf. United States—Import Prohibition of Certain Shrimp and Shrimp Products,* Report of the Appellate Body (WT/DS58/AB/R), adopted November 6, 1998, where arguably the Appellate Body failed to exercise judicial restraint and moved into the area of rule making, which is the mandate of the WTO membership only.

B. EC—Bed Linen[128]

India's case against the European Community, involving an EC antidumping measure on bed linen from India, demonstrates that developing countries are not powerless to challenge abusive antidumping measures taken against textiles and clothing products. Antidumping measures had become a standard EC tool to protect its textiles and clothing manufacturers, even before the creation of the WTO. Counting on the relatively high cost of dispute settlement proceedings for developing countries, as well as the low probability of winning antidumping cases as a result of the restrictive standard of review established in the Antidumping Agreement,[129] the European Commission applied excessive dumping margins. The use of antidumping actions against products under quota, and repeated actions against the same products, ran counter to the objective of liberalization of this sector that the ATC was meant to achieve.[130] The findings and conclusions of the Panel, in which Egypt participated as a third party, criticize the European Commission's calculation of dumping margins. The Panel found that the method applied (the practice of "zeroing") by the European Commission was inconsistent with Article 2.4.2 of the Antidumping Agreement, and the Appellate Body affirmed the Panel's decision in this regard.[131]

An interesting feature of the case is that India was the first Member to invoke Article 15 of the Antidumping Agreement ("Developing Country Members"), insisting that as a developing country Member it was entitled to special treatment by the European Community in the application of antidumping measures. The Panel supported India's position, finding that the European Communities had acted inconsistently with its Article 15 obligations by failing to explore constructive remedies before applying antidumping duties.[132]

Another more general lesson to draw from this case is the apparent reluctance of developed countries to implement a provision designed to help developing country Members level the playing field. This reluctance raises fundamental questions of good faith. Developing countries should not have to undertake expensive dispute settlement proceedings just to procure the benefits accorded to them in the negotiations. This reticence on the part of developed countries to implement their side of the bargain compelled developing countries to bring up the issue of "Implementation,"[133] and to push for it prior to the initiation of new round of negotiations.

C. United States—Underwear[134]

Costa Rica's dispute against U.S. restrictions on imports of cotton and man-made fiber underwear was also significant for developing countries. It has become a frequently cited

---

[128] *European Community—Bed Linen, supra* note 122.

[129] *Agreement on Implementation of Article VI of the GATT.* Article 17.6 (ii) sets out the standard of review for cases arising under the this agreement.

[130] *ITCB First Major Review, supra* note 83, at 37.

[131] See *European Communities—Bed Linen, supra* note 122, ¶ 66.

[132] *European Communities—Antidumping on Imports of Cotton-type Bed Linen from India*, Report of the Panel, WT/DS141/AB/R, ¶¶ 62–64.

[133] Developing countries were inspired by UNCTAD's "Positive Agenda" Program, developed at UNCTAD IX (1996) which urged developing countries to develop their own agenda and participate actively in the framework of a new round of negotiations. As a result, developing countries decided to push for the so-called "implementation" issues. In December 1999 in Seattle, developing countries conditioned any new round of trade negotiations on a prior satisfactory response to the implementation issues, among which is to address the imbalances inherent in the Uruguay Round Agreements, a highly controversial topic.

[134] *United States—Cotton Underwear, supra* note 100.

example for the effectiveness of the WTO's Dispute Settlement Understanding ("DSU"). It was the first challenge under the DSU in the textiles and clothing sector. As a result of losing this case, and its portrayal in the TMB and the Council for Trade in Goods for using transitional safeguards to an excessive degree during the first year of the ATC, the United States began to restrain its use of the transitional safeguards mechanism.

After having unilaterally invoked the transitional safeguards 24 times in the first year of implementation, the United States, under constant criticism from developing countries, stopped its use of these actions altogether. The 24 safeguard measures taken by the United States in 1995 involved nine product groups. Of the nine, the TMB did not find any evidence of serious damage in five categories. In regard to actual threat of serious damage, the TMB's findings were positive with respect to one category and negative with respect to two categories. The TMB was unable to reach consensus in the two other categories. The excessive use of transitional safeguards by the United States prompted the exporting countries to contest the U.S. claims of serious damage, and to use the good offices of the DSB to redress their complaints. The strict requirements of Article 6 were upheld by the DSB and "this played an important role in the decline in U.S. actions".[135]

D. United States—Cotton Yarn[136]

This dispute involved a typical case of an abusive measure by a major importing country and the clear exploitation of the dispute settlement procedures.

Already in April 1999, one month after the measure became effective on March 17, 1999, the TMB ruled on the matter and asked the United States to rescind its measure. The TMB found that the United States was unable to demonstrate serious damage or any threat thereof to its industries by the imports of yarn from Pakistan. The matter was examined in June for the second time by the TMB, which did not alter its first recommendation. Refusing to heed the recommendation of the TMB, and with the failure to reach a mutually agreed solution through consultations, Pakistan had recourse to the DSU and requested the establishment of a Panel on April 3, 2000. In its Report on May 31, 2001, the Panel concluded that the transitional safeguard measure imposed by the United States on imports of yarn from Pakistan was inconsistent with the provisions of Article 6 of the ATC. Without further ado, the Panel suggested that the United States bring its safeguard measure into conformity with its obligations under the ATC and that this could best be achieved by the prompt removal of the safeguard measure.

The United States, however, decided to file an appeal and request the Appellate Body to reverse the Panel's findings, in particular with regard to Article 6.4 of the ATC, which concerns the attribution of serious damage or actual threat thereof. The Appellate Body upheld the Panel's main findings and requested the United States to bring its measure into conformity with its obligations in the Agreement.[137]

Despite the fact that both the TMB and a Panel found against the United States, the United States chose to buy more time by taking this dispute to the Appellate Body. The result was that the United States was able to impose its safeguard measure from March 17, 1999 until after the Appellate Body's ruling against the United States in October 2001.

---

[135] Bagchi, *supra* note 26, at 248 and 250 respectively (*quoting* Kenneth Reinert, *Give us Virtue, But Not Yet: Safeguard Actions Under the Agreement on Textiles and Clothing*, Paper presented at a WTO seminar (1998)).

[136] *United States—Cotton Yarn, supra* note 122.

[137] *Id.* ¶ 129.

This tactic suggests that there is a serious flaw in the dispute settlement understanding, which seems to countenance such delay. It also raises questions about the good faith of the developed countries who are willing to preserve their upper hand in this highly sensitive and vital sector through delay, and once delay is no longer possible, through the imposition of new measures, such as rules of origin and visa requirements.

VI. Conclusion

Labeling the new round of negotiations "The New Development Agenda" was an attempt to lure developing countries into the next round of trade talks. Nevertheless, the fate of textiles and clothing in the lead up to, and at Doha, remained unclear. At no stage in the Doha preparations did the sector have the potential to be a "make or break" issue. Intellectual property rights ("IPR"), agriculture and the environment were far thornier issues. Few exporting developing countries tried to table textiles and clothing in the framework of the so-called Implementation issues. In the Doha Ministerial Meeting (November 9–13, 2001) India demanded that the pace of liberalization in the textiles and clothing area be quickened, and it held up the negotiations on this issue until the eleventh hour.

Although textiles and clothing were a lower priority issue in Doha, their importance has not diminished. The next few years will see more aggressive bargaining in this vital sector. One need only remember that textiles and clothing were among the problem sectors that led to the extension of the negotiations in the Uruguay Round. With a prolonged and difficult round of trade negotiations in sight, textiles and clothing are likely to surface once again as a principal bargaining chip for an increasing number of developing countries.

In this context, the smoothing out of tariff peaks and the reduction of tariff escalation in the area of textiles and clothing will become even more important as a negotiating chip in return for developing countries agreeing to negotiate on a reduction of their industrial tariffs. Although some already speculate that the ATC will be replaced by some new form of agreement, I believe that developing exporting countries will not allow tariffs on textiles and clothing to be considered separately or governed again by a separate agreement.

My view is that the low priority given textiles and clothing could well change as negotiations proceed in the new round. The subject will be pushed forcefully not only by the traditional proponents of liberalization in this sector, such as India and Pakistan, but also by countries like Egypt, Indonesia and Malaysia, who want something in return, perhaps in the textiles and clothing sector, if they are to lower their industrial tariffs. Furthermore, my expectation is that negotiations on textiles and apparel will go beyond traditional borders and encompass negotiations among developing country exporters themselves, based on their desire:

a) To open up each other's markets in addition to the markets of the expected newcomers from Africa and the LDCs;

b) To prepare for the possible outcome of additional regional integration which, with more modern machinery and better quality products, may facilitate the relocation of industries such as textiles and clothing from the North to the South; and

c) To develop new markets in preparation for new types of restrictions in the developed importing countries, perhaps based on more stringent environmental standards.

To many, including this author, the ATC is and remains a ten year "quasi-extension" of the MFA. This is undoubtedly contrary to the perception of many others, notably among the exporting country negotiators who like to view the ATC as a full-fledged, stand-alone agreement.[138] Whichever view is correct, the ATC has failed, after more than seven years of implementation, to further the liberalization of trade in textiles and clothing, or to provide greater market access. Spinanger notes that "It was indeed a masterpiece of watering down and postponing."[139] It "watered down" the liberalization process by including a far wider range of textiles and clothing products than necessary. It "postponed" any significant liberalization until the final stage in January 1, 2005 ("back-loading"). The integration to date has concentrated on products of less export interest to developing countries, and only a few quota restrictions have been removed, leaving the bulk in place. The additional access provided through increases in quota growth rates during the transition period has not significantly lessened the restrictive nature of the quotas. Developing countries, including their small suppliers, as well as least-developed countries, have not received any "meaningful" increase in their access possibilities. It remains to be seen what will happen between now and January 1, 2005.

[138] Raffaelli and Jenkins insist that the ATC should not be considered as a mere extension of the MFA. Raffaelli and Jenkins, *supra* note 12, at 88.

[139] Dean Spinanger, *Textiles Beyond the MFA Phase Out*, paper presented at the GATT/WTO Fiftieth Anniversary Conference at the University of Warwick (July 17–18, 1998) and on file with the author.

CHAPTER 54

THE TRIPS AGREEMENT AND DEVELOPING COUNTRIES

Carlos M. Correa[*]

TABLE OF CONTENTS

* Professor, University of Buenos Aires.

I. Introduction

The WTO Agreement on Trade-Related Aspects of Intellectual Property Rights ("TRIPS") brought about a very important change in international standards relating to intellectual property rights.[1] Because of its far-reaching implications, particularly with respect to developing countries, the agreement has been one of the most controversial components of the WTO system. Strong disagreements on the scope and content of the Agreement emerged during the Uruguay Round negotiations, both between developed and developing countries and among developed countries themselves. Implementation of the Agreement and its review under the "built-in agenda" have also been contentious with regard to many aspects.

The developed countries (notably the United States) insisted upon the negotiation and adoption of standards on intellectual property rights ("IPRs") in the Uruguay Round, based on the argument that strengthened protection of IPRs would promote innovation as well foreign direct investment ("FDI") and technology transfer to developing countries.[2] Although the TRIPS Agreement only became effective in advanced developing countries on January 1, 2000, meaning that there has not been much time to assess its impact, most developing countries seem to remain unconvinced about the benefits that they will obtain from the implementation of the new IPR standards. Moreover, many of them fear that the costs to be paid may be too high, particularly in critical areas such as public health. Essentially, many developing countries feel that despite the balance sought in some provisions, the Agreement mainly benefits technology-rich countries. There are a number of reasons for these concerns.

First, higher levels of IPR protection do not appear to lead to tangible increases of FDI in or technology transfer to developing countries. The evidence on the relationship between IPR protection on the one hand and FDI and technology transfer on the other continues to be inconclusive.[3] In addition, the share of developing countries in world research and development expenditures remains very low (only four percent of the total).[4] Certainly, IPRs may promote innovative activities to the extent that they offer the promise of extraordinary benefits based on the temporal exclusion of competitors. But in order for those benefits to be realized, an adequate industrial and technological infrastructure must exist at the national level, which is not the case in most developing countries. There is also strong evidence suggesting that most of the rewards from innovation are reaped by a small minority of successful companies, while the majority of innovative efforts confer

---

[1] *See, e.g.*, United Nations Conference on Trade and Development, THE TRIPS AGREEMENT AND DEVELOPING COUNTRIES 18 (1996).

[2] The U.S. government has stated that:

> apart from stimulating innovation, however, a strong IPR regime—particularly a strong patent regime—can also produce other benefits for countries, regardless of whether the countries are developed or developing. For example, countries that have strong patent regimes are more effective in attracting investments and market entry by innovative companies. The reasons for this are fairly simple—patents provide a greater capacity for the innovator to compete based on the innovation. If the innovator cannot use the innovation to provide a market advantage, there is a disincentive to enter the market, particularly where others in that market can charge lower prices because they do not need to recover the costs of research and development, nor invest in new research and development.

TRIPS Council, *Special Discussion on Intellectual Property and Access to Medicines*, IP/C/M/31, at 35 (July 10, 2001).

[3] *See, e.g.,* Keith Maskus, INTELLECTUAL PROPERTY RIGHTS IN THE GLOBAL ECONOMY 87–141(2000).

[4] United Nations Development Program, HUMAN DEVELOPMENT REPORT 67 (1999).

only modest benefits, in addition to the fact that, because of the high cost of litigation, IPR enforcement is biased in favor of large organizations.[5]

Second, in some sectors IPRs appear to act as a powerful barrier to access to technologies and products, particularly by the poor. This is notably the case in relation to pharmaceuticals. By their very essence, patents enable pharmaceutical manufacturers to charge higher prices than those that would have existed in a competitive environment. While the high prices are said to be justified by the need to recover costly investments in R&D, the magnitude of such investment, as well as the pricing of drugs in developing countries, has been strongly contested.[6]

The AIDS crisis in Africa, and growing evidence about the negative implications of patents for access to medicines by the poor, have brought the relationship between TRIPS and health to the forefront. With more than thirty million people living with HIV, most of them in the poorest regions of the world, the need to address the problem of access to patented medicines has emerged as a global priority. While it is true, as argued by the pharmaceutical industry, that other factors such as infrastructure and professional support play an important role in determining access to drugs,[7] it is also true that the prices that result from the existence of patents ultimately determine how many will die from AIDS and other diseases in the years to come. It is important to note that the problem of access to medicines is not limited to anti-retrovirals, but involves all kinds of medicines that may fall under patent protection.

Some recent WHO-sponsored studies provide an indication of the potential effects of the TRIPS Agreement in the area of pharmaceuticals. A study undertaken in Thailand on the impact of that country's 1992 revised patent law, which essentially applies the same standards as those required by the TRIPS agreement, found that there had been no significant increase in transfer of technology or foreign direct investment, and that spending on pharmaceuticals had increased at a higher rate than overall health care spending.[8]

Another study on the implications of the new Industrial Property Code (1996) on local production and access to medicines in Brazil revealed *inter alia* that:

- Only 36 (2.6 percent) of the 1387 drug patent applications filed since 1996, when the new Brazilian Industrial Property Act was signed into law, were filed by residents of Brazil. More than five hundred of the filings were made by U.S. residents.
- While Brazil's total imports roughly doubled during the period 1982–1998, pharmaceutical imports increased over 47 times.

The study concluded that "the greatest beneficiaries of recent changes in Brazilian legislation and the implementation of the World Trade Organisation's TRIPs Agreement have not been Brazilian companies or institutions, but transnational companies...."[9]

---

[5] F.M. Scherer, *The Innovation Lottery*, in EXPANDING THE BOUNDARIES OF INTELLECTUAL PROPERTY. INNOVATION POLICY FOR THE KNOWLEDGE SOCIETY 15, 21 (Rochelle Dreyfuss, Diane Zimmerman, and Harry First eds. 2001).

[6] OXFAM, CUT THE COST—FATAL SIDE EFFECTS: MEDICINE PATENTS UNDER THE MICROSCOPE 31 (2000).

[7] International Intellectual Property Institute, PATENT PROTECTION AND ACCESS TO HIV/AIDS PHARMACEUTICALS IN SUB-SAHARAN AFRICA 23 (2001).

[8] Siripen Supakankunti, *et al.*, STUDY OF THE IMPLICATIONS OF THE WTO TRIPS AGREEMENT FOR THE PHARMACEUTICAL INDUSTRY IN THAILAND 82 (1999).

[9] Jorge Bermudez, Ruth Epsztejn, Maria Auxiliadora Oliveira and Lia Hasenclever, *The WTO TRIPS Agreement and Patent Protection in Brazil: Recent Changes and Implications for Local Production and Access to Medicines* 95 (MSF/DND Working Paper 2000), available at http://www.neglecteddiseases.org/4-4.pdf.

More generally, Maskus has noted the scarcity of data on price elasticities and market-structure parameters, and the uncertainty about the potential effects of patents on prices, profitability and innovation. However, based on available literature, he found that "the preponderance of conclusions is pessimistic about the net effects of drug patents on the economic welfare of developing countries (or, more accurately, of net importers of patented drugs)."[10]

Some of the concerns of developing countries about the implications of the TRIPS Agreement on public health were reflected in the negotiation and adoption of the "Doha Declaration on the TRIPS Agreement and Public Health"[11], at the Fourth WTO Ministerial Conference (November 9–14, 2001). WTO Members took the unprecedented step of adopting a special declaration[12] on this controversial matter. Discussion of the declaration was one of the major issues at the Conference[13], and was the first outcome of a process that started in early 2001 when, upon the request of the African Group and other developing countries, the Council for TRIPS agreed to deal specifically with the relationship between the TRIPS Agreement and public health[14].

Third, the adoption of the TRIPS Agreement as a component of the WTO system[15] means that any controversy relating to compliance with the minimum standards established by the Agreement should be resolved under the multilateral procedures of the WTO. The adoption by another Member of unilateral trade sanctions would be incompatible with the multilateral rules. Any complaint should be brought to and settled according to the rules of the Dispute Settlement Understanding ("DSU")[16].

Despite this, many developing countries have continued to be pressured by unilateral demands by some developed countries, notably the United States and the EU, in the area of IPRs, aiming not only at the implementation of the TRIPS Agreement standards, but often asking for "TRIPS-plus" protection, that is, levels of protection beyond the minimum standards required by the TRIPS Agreement. A telling case that received

[10] MASKUS, *supra* note 3, at 160.

[11] WT/MIN(01)/DEC/W/2, November 14, 2001, ("the Doha Declaration".) The text of the Declaration is reproduced in the Appendix to this book.

[12] Paragraph 17 of the general Ministerial Declaration states: "We stress the importance we attach to implementation and interpretation of the Agreement on Trade-Related Aspects of Intellectual Property Rights (TRIPS Agreement) in a manner supportive of public health, by promoting both access to existing medicines and research and development into new medicines and, in this connection, are adopting a separate Declaration".

[13] The Director General of WTO emphasized the importance of this issue on the opening day of the Conference, indicating that agreement on public health and TRIPS was the "deal breaker" of the new round. Pascal Lamy, the EU Commissioner for Trade, stated at the Conference that "... we must also find the right mix of trade and other policies—consider the passion surrounding our debate of TRIPS and Access to Medicines, which has risen so dramatically to become a clearly defining issue for us this week, and rightly so".

[14] The Council for TRIPS convened special sessions (which were held in June, August and September 2001) to deal with the relationship between health and TRIPS. *See* the submissions made by the European Communities and their Members States on *The Relationship Between the Provisions of the TRIPS Agreement and Access to Medicines*, IP/C/W/280 (June 12, 2001); the paper submitted on the same issue by the African Group, Barbados, Bolivia, Brazil, Cuba, Dominican Republic, Ecuador, Honduras, India, Indonesia, Jamaica, Pakistan, Paraguay, Philippines, Peru, Sri Lanka, Thailand and Venezuela, *TRIPS and Public Health*, IP/C/W/296 (June 29, 2001). *See also, Special Discussion on Intellectual Property and Access to Medicines*, IP/C/M/31, (July 10, 2001).

[15] The TRIPS Agreement is contained in Annex 1C to the Marrakesh Agreement Establishing the WTO.

[16] However, a WTO panel in a case initiated by the EC and their Member States that examined the consistency with WTO obligations of the authorization given to the U.S. government to retaliate under several provisions (such as "Special 301") of the U.S. Trade and Tariff Act of 1984 (19 U.S.C § 2114c(2)(A)) did not find—based on a commitment by the U.S. government not to apply sanctions without WTO authorization—a violation of WTO obligations. *See* Report of the WTO Panel, *United States—Section 301–310 of the Trade Act of 1974*, WT/DS152/R (2000). *See also* Part III.B.7 *infra*.

considerable public attention was the attempt by the U.S. government and pharmaceutical industry to block the use of parallel imports and compulsory licenses by the South African government to obtain access to cheaper HIV/AIDS drugs[17]. In other cases, developing countries were persuaded to adopt " TRIPS-plus" standards in order to benefit from other trade concessions under bilateral agreements.[18]

In addition, nothing seems to prevent WTO Members from applying unilateral pressure, for instance, by threatening the removal of trade preferences that go beyond WTO commitments or cuts in development aid, or through simple moral persuasion. As noted by Primo Braga and Fink:

> The United States has continued to put unilateral pressure on countries where it felt that weak IPR systems disadvantaged U.S. companies. The two most prominent cases in this context were the dispute with Argentina on pharmaceutical patents, which in 1997 led to the removal of 50 per cent of Argentina's benefits under the generalized system of preferences (GSP); and the dispute with South Africa, also on pharmaceutical patents, where the U.S.A reached a 'joint understanding' with South Africa in late 1999. The U.S. government did not initiate settlement proceedings under the WTO in these cases, partly because both countries were still under transition with regard to their TRIPS obligations and partly because some aspects of these disputes related to matters where the TRIPS Agreement has no specific obligation (e.g. parallel imports) or where the outcome of WTO arbitration would be highly uncertain (e.g. compulsory licenses).[19]

Fourth, Article 66.2 of the TRIPS Agreement establishes an outright obligation on developed countries "to provide incentives to enterprises and institutions" in their territories for the transfer of technology to least-developed countries. Though Article 66.2 leaves a great deal of leeway to developed countries to determine what kind of incentives to provide, it does require the establishment of a system to encourage technology transfer (including technology protected under intellectual property rights) to least-developed countries. The provision also provides a general standard to judge the appropriateness of such incentives, i.e., that they should enable least developed countries "to create a sound and viable technological base". This obligation remains unfulfilled.

In sum, developing countries generally feel that the concessions they made during the Uruguay Round with respect to IPRs are not providing them with significant benefits. Strong asymmetries in the development of and access to technologies remain or are even

---

[17] An estimated twenty percent of South Africans are infected with HIV. A very minor portion of these have access to AIDS drugs. South Africa law established provisions that were challenged by the pharmaceutical manufacturers trade association and 39 pharmaceutical companies before the South African Supreme Court. U.S. development aid to South Africa was also conditioned on the withdrawal of the provisions (see US Public Law 105–277 (105th Congress, 1999). After a global NGO campaign, in which activists from the U.S., Africa and Asia opposed the U.S. government and commercial sanctions, the legal action was withdrawn. Several pharmaceutical companies offered to provide AIDS drugs at a discounted price (60–85 percent off the price charged in the U.S. or Europe) See, e.g., Marie Byström and Peter Einarsson, *TRIPS—Consequences for Developing Countries: Implications for Swedish Development Cooperation* 38 (2000), Consultancy Report to the Swedish International Development Cooperation Agency, available at http://www.grain.org/docs/sida-trips-2001-en.PDF.

[18] For example, the bilateral agreements entered into between the EC and their Member States and South Africa (1999), Tunisia (1998) and the Palestinian Authority (1997) require the latter to ensure adequate and effective protection of intellectual property rights "in conformity with the highest international standards". *See*, e.g. Peter Drahos, *Developing Countries and International Intellectual Property Standard-Setting* 14–18 (2002), study prepared for the UK Commission on Intellectual Property Rights, available at www.iprcommission.org.

[19] Carlos Primo Braga and Carsten Fink, *Trade-related Intellectual Property Rights: From Marrakech to Seattle*, in THE WORLD TRADE ORGANIZATION MILLENNIUM ROUND 192(Klaus Günter Deutsch and Bernehard Speyer eds. 2001).

growing. Though developing countries still expect to derive some benefits from certain types of IPRs (such as geographical indications), so far they are bearing the costs of a system of reinforced IPR protection under the WTO, while enjoying few of the potential advantages.

Part II of this chapter examines some of the principles of interpretation that may be derived from TRIPS-specific WTO jurisprudence, as well as from other GATT/WTO cases, which may be relevant for the implementation and interpretation of the TRIPS Agreement. This part does not attempt to analyze the TRIPS disputes in particular, but simply tries to draw some general conclusions for the future. Part III considers some important issues for developing countries in the light of national practice and GATT/WTO jurisprudence. Such issues—exceptions to patent rights, compulsory licenses and parallel imports—are of crucial importance for the design of a pro-competitive intellectual property system and, in particular, to attain public health objectives as specifically recognized (in relation to two of such issues) by the Doha Declaration. Part IV includes a brief commentary on the latter Declaration, which is referred to in other parts of the Chapter as well. Part V provides some conclusions.

II. TRIPS Disputes

A. The Decisions

The TRIPS Agreement has been one of the most controversial components of the WTO system. It has given rise to a large number of proceedings under the Dispute Settlement Understanding, involving alleged violations by developing and developed countries, even before January 1, 2000 when the core of the obligations imposed by the Agreement entered into force in the advanced developing countries. Twenty-four complaints have dealt with the TRIPS Agreement (as of June 30, 2002), most of them initiated by the United States and the EC Communities and their Member States.

Six cases involving the TRIPS Agreement have already been decided by panels or the Appellate Body.[20] Three of these cases dealt with issues relating to transitional provisions, two concerning the implementation of Article 70.8 (the "mailbox" provision) by India.[21] The third, brought by the United States against Canada with respect to the extension of the term of patents granted before the entry into force of the Agreement (Article 70.2), found Canada to be in violation to the Agreement.[22] There were two other cases between developed countries, in which the issues of exceptions to patent rights (brought by the EC and their Member States against Canada[23] and copyright (brought by the EC and

---

[20] The Agreement was also incidentally invoked in the *Indonesia-Autos* case, in relation to the protection of trademarks. The panel, however, found that the United States had not demonstrated that Indonesia was in breach of its TRIPS obligations (Report of the WTO Panel, *Indonesia—Certain Measures Affecting The Automobile Industry,* WT/DS 54/R, WT/DS 55/R, WT/DS 59/R, WT/DS 64/R (1998), ¶¶ 11.1–11.43). It is also to be noted that in an arbitration decision (Decision by the Arbitrators, *European Communities—Regime for the Importation, Sale and Distribution of Bananas—Recourse to Arbitration by the European Communities under Article 22.6 of the DSU,* WT/DS27/ARB/ECU, March 24, 2000) Ecuador was authorized to suspend its obligations under the TRIPS Agreement as retaliation against the EC for not complying with the panel and Appellate Body rulings in the Bananas dispute (*see* Report of the Appellate Body, *European Economic Community-Regime for the Importation, Sale and Distribution of Bananas,* WT/DS27/AB/R(1997)).

[21] *See* Report of the Appellate Body, *India-Patent Protection for Pharmaceutical and Agricultural Chemical Products,* WT/DS50/AB/R (1998), and Report of the WTO Panel, *India—Patent Protection for Pharmaceutical and Agricultural Chemical Products,* WT/DS79/R (1998).

[22] *See* Report of the Appellate Body, *Canada—Term of Patent Protection,* WT/DS170/AB/R (2000), ¶ 7.1.

[23] *See* Report of the WTO Panel, *Canada—Patent Protection for Pharmaceutical Products,* WT/DS114/R (2000).

their Member States against the United States[24] were considered. The last case, brought by the EC and their Member States against the United States,[25] involved the protection of trademarks.

The issues in these cases were as follows:

1. Mailbox Cases[26]

The United States and the EC and their Member States argued in two separate complaints that India had failed to provide a mechanism for implementing the "mail box" to be established in accordance with Article 70.8 of the TRIPS Agreement.[27] India was found to have failed to comply with its obligations under this provision, since there was no legal basis—procedural or substantive—for the grant of exclusive marketing rights when a product that was the subject of a patent application under Article 70.8 became eligible for protection under Article 70.9 of the TRIPS Agreement.[28]

2. Canada—Term of Patent Protection[29]

The United States challenged Section 45 of Canada's Patent Act. It claimed that the patent protection term of seventeen years (counted from the date of grant) accorded to patent applications filed before October 1, 1989, often ended before twenty years from the date of filing. The United States argued that pursuant to Articles 33 and 70.2 of the TRIPS Agreement, Canada was obligated to make available a term of protection that lasted at least twenty years from the date of filing to all inventions which enjoyed patent protection on January 1, 1996—the date on which the TRIPS Agreement went into effect for developed countries—including those protected by the old Patents Act. Inventions enjoying protection under that Act were covered by Article 70.2 of the TRIPS Agreement (protection of "subject matter" existing on the date of application of the TRIPS Agreement). The Canadian law was found inconsistent with the Agreement in this respect.

3. Canada—Patent Protection for Pharmaceutical Products[30]

This case addressed the TRIPS-consistency of Section 55(2)(1) and (2) of the Canadian Patent Act, as revised in 1993. Section 55(2)(1), the "early working", "regulatory review" or "Bolar" exception, permitted the use of a patented invention, without the consent of the patent holder, for testing required for the submission of data to obtain marketing approval

[24] See Report of the WTO Panel, United States—Section 110(5) of the US Copyright Act, WT/DS160/R (2000).
[25] Report of the Appellate Body, United States—Section 211 Omnibus Appropriations Act of 1998, WT/DS176/AB/R (2002).
[26] Supra, note 21.
[27] Article 70.8–9 of the TRIPS Agreement required members that did not grant patent protection for pharmaceutical and agricultural chemical products as of the date of entry into force of the WTO Agreement (under Article 65.4 of the Agreement, a developing country Member could delay providing patentability to products not then patentable in the country for ten years) to provide a means of filing patent applications (the "mailbox") and up to five years of exclusive marketing rights.
[28] In order to comply with Article 70.9, the President of India, on December 31, 1994, promulgated an Ordinance (the Patents Amendment Ordinance 1994) so as to provide a means for the filing and handling of patent applications for pharmaceutical and agricultural chemical products, and for granting of exclusive marketing rights. The Ordinance was issued on the basis of the President's constitutional powers to legislate when Parliament is not in session but, without Parliament's confirmation, it lapsed on March 26, 1995. The "exclusive marketing rights "were later implemented by the Patents (Amendment) Act, 1999.
[29] Supra, note 22.
[30] Supra, note 23.

for pharmaceutical or other products. Section 55(2)(2) allowed potential competitors of the patent holder to manufacture and stockpile pharmaceutical products covered by the patent during the six months immediately prior to the expiry of the twenty-year patent term. The panel found that Section 55(2)(1) was consistent with the TRIPS Agreement but that Section 55(2)(2) was not.

4. *United States—Section 110(5) of the US Copyright Act*[31]
Upon a complaint brought by the EU, the panel found that Section 110(5)(b) of the U.S. copyright law[32]—relating to the enjoyment of nondramatic musical works by customers in business premises, such as food service and drinking establishments under a certain size limit—was inconsistent with Article 13 of the TRIPS Agreement.

5. *United States—Section 211 Omnibus Appropriations Act of 1998*
(also known as the "Havana Club" case).[33]
A panel considered the consistency of Section 211 of the U.S. Omnibus Appropriation Act of 1998 which deals with trademarks, trade names, and commercial names that are the same as or substantially similar to trademarks, trade names, or commercial names that were used in connection with businesses or assets that were confiscated by the Cuban Government on or after January 1, 1959. The panel was requested to examine the consistency of that provision with Articles 2.1, 3.1, 4, 16.1 and 42 of the TRIPS Agreement, in conjunction with the relevant provisions of the Paris Convention (Articles 2 (1), 6 *bis*, 6 *quienquies*, and 8). The panel also considered whether the Agreement was applicable to trade names (as argued by the EC), but concluded that trade names were not a category of IPR covered by the Agreement. The panel found that the EC had not proven the inconsistency of the U.S. law, except with regard to Article 42 of the TRIPS Agreement. The AB reversed several findings of the panel; in particular, it considered that trade names were covered by the TRIPS Agreement since it incorporates the obligations under the Paris Convention.

Two consultations, settled before the establishment of a panel, involved developing countries' compliance with the TRIPS Agreement. Consultations were requested by the United States (joined by the EC and Switzerland) on various aspects of the Argentine patent and confidentiality laws.[34] The issues in contention included, *inter alia,* compulsory licenses to remedy anti-competitive practices, importation of patented products, reversal of the burden of proof, preliminary injunctions, and the protection of data submitted for the approval of pharmaceutical and agrochemical products. On the latter issue, the United States and the EC and their Member States have argued that Article 39.3 of the TRIPS Agreement requires the granting of a certain period of exclusivity (the term of which is to be determined by national law) after the first commercial authorization of a pharmaceutical (or agrochemical product). No such exclusivity is granted in Argentina. The Argentine law[35] protects such data against unfair commercial

---

[31] *Supra,* note 24.

[32] *United States Copyright Act of 1976,* as amended, Pub. L. 94-553, 90 Stat.2541.

[33] *Supra,* note 25.

[34] *Argentina—Patent Protection for Pharmaceuticals and Test Data Protection for Agricultural Chemicals,* WT/DS171, May 6, 1999, and *Argentina—Certain Measures on the Protection of Patents and Test Data,* WT/DS196, May 30, 2000.

[35] *See* Argentine Law 24766, "Confidencialidad sobre información y productos que estén legítimamente bajo control de una persona y que se divulgue indebidamente de manera contraria a los usos comerciales honestos", *Boletín Oficial,* 30 December, 1996.

practices in the framework of unfair competition as regulated by Article 10 *bis* of the Paris Convention.[36]

In January 2001, the United States launched a challenge against Brazilian legislation that authorizes the granting of compulsory licenses and parallel imports in instances when patents are not worked.[37] The dispute ended several months later, when the U.S. complaint was withdrawn.[38] In a separate case Brazil asked the United States for consultations with regard to provisions of a U.S. patent law that limits the right to use or sell any federally-owned invention only to a licensee that agrees that any products embodying the invention or produced through the use of the invention will be manufactured substantially in the United States.[39]

Though with the exception of the "mail box" cases, the panel and Appellate Body decisions relate to disputes involving developed countries only, they are certainly relevant to developing countries, since they provide an indication of the interpretive patterns that panels and, particularly, the Appellate Body, have developed in relation to the TRIPS Agreement. The analysis of the principles applied and arguments made may be important for the implementation of the Agreement by developing countries in a manner that maximizes the use of the flexibilities allowed by the Agreement while ensuring consistency with its obligations. Of course, while recognized that the reports are not, strictly speaking, precedential, this analysis is also important for the defense of national interests in possible future disputes involving developing countries.

B. Interpretation of the TRIPS Agreement

The rulings in the six cases discussed above, as well as other WTO jurisprudence, allow one to draw some lessons on the interpretation of the TRIPS Agreement. Though panels and Appellate Body reports are not strictly precedential in the sense that they do not bind future opinions on the same matter,[40] they do provide guidance to both governments and the DSU bodies as to how future cases are likely to be decided.

Given that developing countries undertook the heaviest burden in terms of the modifications to their IPR laws necessary to comply with the obligations of the TRIPS Agreement, they are also most exposed to possible complaints by other members, notably industrialized countries. The analysis of GATT/WTO jurisprudence may provide developing countries with some useful elements for the design of their intellectual property laws, as well as to respond to demands of changes in legislation based on grounds of

---

[36] A mutually agreed solution was notified to the DSB on 20 June, 2002. However, the parties did not reach a common understanding on the interpretation of Article 39.3 of the TRIPS Agreement, nor on the application of Article 70.7. *See Notification of Mutually Agreed Solution According to the Conditions Set Forth in the Agreement* (IP/D/18/Add.1, IP/D/22/Add.1).

[37] *See Brazil—Measures Affecting Patent Protection*, Request for the Establishment of a Panel by the United States, January 9, 2001, WT/DS199/3. On February 1, 2001, the DSB authorized establishment of a panel, although no panel members had been appointed by the time the complaint was withdrawn. Cuba, the Dominican Republic, Honduras, India and Japan reserved third party rights.

[38] Without prejudice to their respective positions, the United States and Brazil have agreed to enter into bilateral discussions before Brazil makes use of Article 68 against a U.S. patent holder. *Brazil—Measures Affecting Patent Protection,* Notification of Mutually Agreed Solution, WT/DS199/4, G/L/454, IP/D/23/Add.1, July 19, 2001.

[39] *United States—US Patents Code*, WT/DS224/1, February 7, 2001. This case was not pursued.

[40] Decisions under the DSU only benefit or affect the parties to the dispute, and need not be followed by subsequent decisions on the same matters. John H. Jackson, THE WORLD TRADE ORGANIZATION: CONSTITUTION AND JURISPRUDENCE 83 (1998)

possible inconsistency with the Agreement. Needless to say, such analysis would be essential if a case were formally brought under the DSU.

1. *Relationship Between the TRIPS Agreement and the GATT*[41]

The panel in *India—Patent Protection for Pharmaceutical and Agricultural Chemical Products* held that the TRIPS Agreement has a "relatively self-contained, *sui generis* status within the WTO"[42]. However, it also held that the Agreement is "an integral part of the WTO system, which itself builds upon the experience of over nearly half a century under the GATT 1947."[43] In *United States—Section 110(5) of the U.S. Copyright Act*, the panel noted that caution was required when interpreting the TRIPS Agreement provisions in the light of precedents developed in GATT dispute settlement practice. It stated however that

> "given that the agreements covered by the WTO form a single, integrated legal system, we deem it appropriate to develop interpretations of the legal protection conferred on intellectual property right holders under the TRIPS Agreement which are not incompatible with the treatment conferred to products under the GATT, or in respect of services and service suppliers under the GATS, in the light of pertinent dispute settlement practice".[44]

The panels and the Appellate Body have, in practice, applied previous GATT and WTO jurisprudence extensively in cases involving the TRIPS Agreement. They have used the same method of interpretation applied to cases involving other WTO Agreements, i.e., the customary rules of treaty interpretation contained in Article 31 and Article 32 of the Vienna Convention on the Law of Treaties. No consideration has been given to the fact that while IPRs constitute private rights,[45] the other components of the WTO system deal with restrictions imposed on governments.

The clarification of the relationship between the TRIPS Agreement and the GATT/WTO may be crucial for the interpretation of several aspects of the Agreement, such as the permissibility of banning parallel imports, the extent to which exceptions can be established under Article 8.1, and, more generally, the criteria to be applied to the interpretation of exceptions provided under the TRIPS Agreement. Under GATT/WTO jurisprudence the exceptions to the obligations of states have been generally construed narrowly.[46] This also applies to the case of TRIPS as illustrated by the panel's opinion in *Canada—Patent Protection for Pharmaceutical Products* on the exceptions to exclusive patent rights conferred by Article 30 of the TRIPS Agreement.[47] However, IPRs themselves constitute exceptions in terms of the GATT—authorized by GATT Article

---

[41] This section is partially based on a paper prepared by the author for the Quakers United Nations Office, *TRIPS Disputes—Implications for the Pharmaceutical Sector* (2001), available at http://www.geneva.quno.info/main/search_publication.php?loop= 0.

[42] *Supra,* note 21, ¶ 7.19.

[43] *Id.*

[44] *Supra*, note 24, at ¶ 6.185.

[45] *See* the Preamble to the TRIPS Agreement, fourth paragraph.

[46] *See* Carlos Correa, *Implementing National Public Health Policies in the Framework of the WTO Agreements*, 34 (5) JOURNAL OF WORLD TRADE 92 (2000).

[47] "As long as the exception is confined to conduct needed to comply with the requirements of the regulatory approval process, the extent of the acts unauthorized by the right holder that are permitted by it will be small and narrowly bounded. Even though regulatory approval processes may require substantial amounts of test production to demonstrate reliable manufacturing, the patent owner's rights themselves are not impaired any further by the size of such production runs, as long as they are solely for regulatory purposes and no commercial use is made of resulting final products". *Canada—Patent Protection for Pharmaceutical Products, supra* note 23, at ¶ 7.45.

XX (d)—since by their very nature such rights restrict trade.[48] In applying the exceptions under TRIPS, therefore, panels and the Appellate Body should carefully consider the trade *restrictive* effects of IPRs and the need to ensure as much competition and free trade as possible. The purpose and effects of IPRs should be appraised in the light of the general principles and objectives of the WTO system and, in particular, the objectives of the TRIPS Agreement as stated in Article 7[49].

2. Principles of Interpretation

As mentioned above, GATT/WTO panels and the Appellate Body have interpreted the WTO Agreements in accordance with the principles contained in Articles 31 and 32 of the Vienna Convention on the Law of the Treaties. In accordance with Article 31(1) of the Convention, "a treaty is to be interpreted in good faith in accordance with the ordinary meaning to be given to the terms of the treaty in their context and in the light of its object and purpose." The Convention also admits as an element for interpretation the "subsequent practice" by the parties to a treaty,[50] as well as certain "Supplementary Means of Interpretation".[51]

A corollary of these rules of interpretation, addressed in several GATT/WTO cases,[52] is the concept of "effective interpretation" (or *"l'effet utile"*), which requires that a treaty be interpreted to give meaning and effect to all the terms of the treaty. Accordingly, whenever more than one interpretation is possible, preference should be given to the interpretation that will give full meaning and effect to other provisions of the same treaty.

The "effective interpretation" principle has been applied by the Supreme Court of Argentina in a case concerning the application of TRIPS Articles 70.7 and 70.8. The Court dismissed the plaintiff's request (which had been upheld by the lower court) of acquiring product patent rights based on a patent application originally filed in 1986 on the basis, *inter alia*, that Article 70.7 could not be interpreted in isolation from other TRIPS provisions, particularly Article 70.8 which established a regime with specific implications for pharmaceutical products (which were not patentable before the implementation of the TRIPS Agreement in Argentina)[53]

Panels and the Appellate Body have used the negotiating history of the TRIPS Agreement to confirm the literal interpretation of particular provisions. In *India—Patent*

---

[48] *See also* the Preamble of the TRIPS Agreement, first paragraph.
[49] *See* sub-section 3 below.
[50] The Appellate Body ruled in *Japan—Taxes on Alcoholic Beverages*, WT/DS8/AB/R, WT/DS 10/AB/R, and WT/DS11/AB/R 11 (1996), at p. 7: "the essence of subsequent practice in interpreting a treaty has been recognized as a 'concordant, common and consistent' sequence of acts . . . which is sufficient to establish a discernable pattern implying the agreement of the parties regarding its interpretation."
[51] Article 32 of the Vienna Convention provides that:

"Recourse may be had to supplementary means of interpretation, including the preparatory work of the treaty and the circumstances of its conclusion, in order to confirm the meaning resulting from the application of Article 31, or to determine the meaning when the interpretation according to Article 31:

(a) leaves the meaning ambiguous or obscurè; or
(b) leads to a result which is manifestly absurd or unreasonàble."

[52] *See*, e.g., Report of the Appellate Body, *Argentina—Safeguard Measures on Imports of Footwear*, WT/DS121/AB/R (2000) at ¶ 88. *See also* Paolo Mengozzi, *The World Trade Organization Law: an Analysis of its First Practice*, in INTERNATIONAL TRADE LAW ON THE 50TH ANNIVERSARY OF THE MULTILATERAL TRADE SYSTEM 26(Paolo Mengozzi ed. 1999).
[53] Corte Suprema de Justicia, *Pfizer Inc. c/ Instituto Nacional de la Propiedad Industrial s/ denegatoria de patente*, May 21, 2002.

Protection for Pharmaceutical and Agricultural Chemical Products, for example, the panel used the negotiating history of the TRIPS Agreement to confirm its interpretation of Article 70.8:

> The findings above can be confirmed by the negotiating history of the TRIPS Agreement. We note that in the negotiation of the TRIPS Agreement the question of patent protection for pharmaceutical and agricultural chemicals products was a key issue, which was negotiated as part of a complex of related issues concerning the scope of the protection to be accorded to patents and some related rights and the timing of the economic impact of such protection. A critical part of the deal struck was that developing countries that did not provide product patent protection for pharmaceutical and agricultural chemicals were permitted to delay the introduction thereof for a period of ten years from the entry into force of the WTO Agreement. However, if they chose to do so, they were required to put in place a means by which patent applications for such inventions could be filed so as to allow the preservation of their novelty and priority for the purposes of determining their eligibility for protection by a patent after the expiry of the transitional period. In addition, they were required to provide also for exclusive marketing rights in respect of the products in question if those products obtained marketing approval during the transitional period, subject to a number of conditions.[54]

One interesting feature is that the negotiating history may include not only the negotiating history of the TRIPS Agreement as such but also the history of the Conventions that are specifically referred to by the TRIPS Agreement, such as the Paris Convention and the Berne Convention. Therefore, a negotiation that took place more than one hundred years ago, such as in the case of the Paris Convention, may be used as a supplementary means of interpretation of the TRIPS Agreement.

Thus in *Canada—Patent Protection for Pharmaceutical Products,* the Panel noted that in the framework of the TRIPS Agreement, which incorporates certain provisions of the major pre-existing international instruments on intellectual property, the context to which the Panel may have recourse for purposes of interpretation of specific TRIPS provisions is not restricted to the text, Preamble and Annexes of the TRIPS Agreement itself, but also includes the provisions of the international instruments on intellectual property incorporated into the TRIPS Agreement,[55] as well as any agreement between the parties relating to these agreements within the meaning of Article 31(2) of the Vienna Convention on the Law of Treaties. Also, in *United States—Section 110(5) of the U.S. Copyright Act*, the panel supported its interpretation by reference to the negotiating history of the Berne Convention that has become part of the TRIPS Agreement.[56]

In *United States—Section 211 Omnibus Appropriations Act of 1998 (Havana Club),* the panel had used the preparatory work of the Paris Convention (1967). The EC argued that such an invocation was erroneous under Article 32 of the Vienna Convention, since none of the conditions for the application of that rule were present in this case and the history of the Paris Convention failed to provide a clear indication of the intentions of

---

[54] *India—Patent Protection for Pharmaceutical and Agricultural Chemical Products, supra* note 21, at ¶ 7.40. The panel also stated: "The observation above can be confirmed by the drafting history of the TRIPS Agreement. Exclusive marketing rights were a *quid pro quo* for the delay of the availability of product patents for pharmaceutical and agricultural chemical products until 1 January 2005, based on a careful balancing of obligations between interested parties during the Uruguay Round negotiations". *Id.* at ¶ 7.72.

[55] In that case, the panel considered the negotiating history of Article 9(2) of the Berne Convention, from which part of the text of Article 30 of the TRIPS Agreement was drawn. *See Canada—Patent Protection for Pharmaceutical Products, supra* note 23, at ¶¶ 7.70–72.

[56] *See United States—Section 110(5) of the U.S. Copyright Act, supra* note 24, at ¶ 6.18. The panel held that the "minor exceptions" doctrine—not formally incorporated either in Berne or in the TRIPS Agreement—was part of the "Berne *acquis*" (¶¶ 6.60–6.66)

the negotiators. The Appellate Body, however, relied on the negotiating history of the Paris Convention in order to confirm its own interpretation of Article 6quinquiesB of the Convention.[57]

This jurisprudence indicates a clear inclination by panels and the Appellate Body to firmly consider the obligations emanating from the IPR conventions incorporated in the TRIPS Agreement as forming part of the set of Members' obligations under the Agreement, as well as to have recourse to the negotiating history of the conventions to confirm their own interpretations. This approach may put an unexpected burden on developing countries, since many of them were not parties to the conventions at the time of the adoption of the Agreement, or were not familiar with developments with respect to the conventions. The full integration of the obligations imposed by the conventions may however in some cases support developing country claims, such as in the case of Article 5A of the Paris Convention, often quoted as a basis for permitting the granting of compulsory licenses for the lack or insufficient local working of a patented invention.[58]

There has so far been no formal recognition of state practice subsequent to the adoption of the Agreement as an element for interpretation of the TRIPS provisions. However, in *Canada—Patent Protection for Pharmaceutical Products,* the panel considered comparative law in order to determine whether the interest claimed as "legitimate" by the EC was a "widely recognized policy norm" (¶ 7.77).[59] As mentioned below (Part III.6), the panel also examined the status of the legislation at the time of the negotiation of the Agreement to determine the interpretation of one of the key concepts in Article 30. In *United States—Section 110(5) of the US Copyright Act*, the panel confirmed its conclusion with reference to examples of "state practice" of members of the Berne Union and WTO, but it warned that it "did not wish to express a view on whether these are sufficient to constitute 'subsequent practice' within the meaning of Article 31(3)(b) of the Vienna Convention"[60].

3. Object and Purpose of the Agreement

The panel report in *Canada—Patent Protection for Pharmaceutical Products* (involving the "Bolar" exception) was particularly important in clarifying the weight to be given to the "Objectives" (Article 7) and "Principles" (Article 8) of the Agreement in the interpretation of the Agreement's provisions. The panel stated that

> Article 30's very existence amounts to a recognition that the definition of patent rights contained in Article 28 would need certain adjustments. On the other hand, the three limiting conditions attached to Article 30 testify strongly that the negotiators of the Agreement did not intend Article 30 to bring about what would be equivalent to a renegotiation of the basic balance of the Agreement. Obviously, the exact scope of Article 30's authority will depend on the specific meaning given to its limiting conditions. The words of those conditions must be examined with particular care on this point. Both the goals and the limitations stated in Articles 7 and 8.1 must obviously be borne in mind when doing so as well as those of other provisions of the TRIPS Agreement which indicate its object and purposes[61].

---

[57] *See United States—Section 211 of the Omnibus Appropriations Act of 1998, supra* note 25, at ¶¶ 145–146.

[58] *See TRIPS and Public Health, supra* note 14, at ¶ 31.

[59] The panel concluded that the extension of the term of patent protection in the case of pharmaceuticals to compensate for delays in obtaining marketing approval "has not been universal". *Canada—Patent Protection for Pharmaceutical Products,* ¶ 7.79.

[60] *See United States—Section 110(5) of the U.S. Copyright Act, supra* note 24, ¶ 6.55, n. 68.

[61] *See Canada—Patent Protection for Pharmaceutical Products, supra* note 23, ¶ 7.26.

Although the literal interpretation is the necessary starting point for an interpretation exercise under Article 31 (1) of the Vienna Convention, this provision refers to the application of contextual and teleological as well as literal methods. While some reports of the Appellate Body have stressed the importance of the literal interpretation, this cannot be seen as a total rejection of teleological interpretations. It is difficult to think of judgments that are absolutely neutral in terms of policy objectives.

There is no universally accepted philosophy on the role and objectives of IPRs, and there is still much debate on their impact on welfare, economic growth and equity.[62] The "purpose" of the Agreement may be differently understood depending on the perspective from which it is examined. Thus, while the goals of developed countries are presumably to provide maximum protection against infringement and to maximize royalty payments for their technologies, developing countries are looking for an application of the TRIPS Agreement that is as pro-competitive as possible, in order to enhance the affordability of protected products and to promote local development through the dissemination and transfer of technology.[63]

Panels may be tempted to introduce their own policy views on IPRs and the TRIPS Agreement. In *Canada—Patent Protection for Pharmaceutical Products*, despite the clear reference to Articles 7 and 8.1 noted above, the panel advanced its own conception of the "policy" of patent laws, relying on its understanding of the intent and practical effect of those laws rather than on the referenced provisions of the Agreement[64]. It stated:

> The normal practice of exploitation by patent owners, as with owners of any other intellectual property right, is to exclude all forms of competition that could detract significantly from the economic returns anticipated from a patent's grant of market exclusivity... Patent laws establish a carefully defined period of market exclusivity as an inducement to innovation, and the policy of those laws cannot be achieved unless patent owners are permitted to take effective advantage of that inducement once it has been defined.[65]

Though this statement—developed in the context of a discussion of the concept of "normal exploitation" of a patent—is too simplistic and does not provide a serious discussion of the justification and objectives of the patent system, it does hint at the panel's own view of a matter that raises considerable debate—especially among economists—and on which different positions and theories have been elaborated.[66] The panel's view, while emphasizing stimulation to innovation, failed to consider other equally essential objectives of the patent grants, thereby concluding with an interpretation of Article 30 that essentially reflects the perspective of patent owners. Like other IPRs, patents are granted in the public interest, and not merely to allow the patent owners to obtain the "economic returns anticipated from a patent's grant of market exclusivity". The diffusion

[62] *See, e.g.*, Christopher May, A GLOBAL POLITICAL ECONOMY OF INTELLECTUAL PROPERTY RIGHTS—THE NEW ENCLOSURES? (2000) at 95–97.

[63] *See, e.g., Communication From India*, IP/C/W/196, July 12 2000, at 1.

[64] *See, e.g*, SARA WILLIAMS, *Developing TRIPS Jurisprudence—The First Six Years and Beyond*, 4(2) THE JOURNAL OF WORLD INTELLECTUAL PROPERTY 191(2001). For a criticism of the panel's failure to take the wording of Article 7 into account and reducing the range of regulatory diversity permitted under the TRIPS Agreement, *see also* ROBERT HOWSE, *The Canadian Medicine Panel: A Dangerous Precedent in Dangerous Times*, BRIDGES: BETWEEN TRADE AND SUSTAINABLE DEVELOPMENT, Year 4, No. 3, at 3.

[65] *Canada—Patent Protection for Pharmaceutical Products, supra* note 23, at ¶ 7.55.

[66] *See* Alan Gutterman, INNOVATION AND COMPETITION POLICY: A COMPARATIVE STUDY OF REGULATION OF PATENT LICENSING AND COLLABORATIVE RESEARCH & DEVELOPMENT IN THE UNITED STATES AND THE EUROPEAN COMMUNITY 36–70 (1999).

of knowledge and its continuous improvement are equally important objectives of the system.[67]

The interpretation of provisions affecting health-related issues, in particular, cannot be based on such a simplistic vision of the patent system as expressed by the panel, but, as required by the Doha Declaration, should be firmly grounded in the objectives and principles of the Agreement as stated in Articles 7 and 8[68]. Access to health is a major public policy concern, to the point that the right of everyone to the enjoyment of the highest attainable standard of physical and mental health is deemed to be a human right.[69] Moreover, on April 23, 2001, the United Nations Commission on Human Rights issued a resolution calling on governments to ensure the accessibility of pharmaceuticals and medical treatments used to treat pandemics such as HIV/AIDS, as well as "their affordability for all, " in accordance with international law and international agreements.[70] The resolution also calls on governments "to safeguard access to such preventive, curative or palliative pharmaceuticals or medical technologies from any limitations by third parties."[71]

If the commercial interests of the patent owner were the only ones to be considered, the interpretation of the Agreement would in practice defeat its intended objectives. Patents—like other intellectual property rights protected under the TRIPS Agreement— are means for the realization of the public interest via the "inducement to innovation" *and* access to the results thereof by those who need them. In other words, the objectives of the patent system would not be fulfilled if it served to benefit only those who control the innovations.[72]

The "purpose" of the Agreement is clearly stated in Article 7, which should be read jointly with Article 8.1. This is the guidance that panels and Appellate Body should apply. According to Article 7:

> The protection and enforcement of intellectual property rights should contribute to the promotion of technological innovation and to the transfer and dissemination of technology, to the mutual advantage of producers and users of technological knowledge and *in a manner conducive to social and economic welfare, and to a balance of rights and obligations*[73]

An important development was the Appellate Body's unambiguous rejection of the panel's opinion in the *U.S. India Mailbox* case,[74] relating to the "reasonable expectations" of the parties. The panel had concluded that the complaining party—in this case the United States—had reasonable expectations that were not fulfilled by the Indian legislation, thus relying on the doctrine applied in the few non-violation cases decided under the GATT dispute resolution system.[75] The Appellate Body correctly reversed this aspect

---

[67] *See* P. Welfens, J. Addison, D. Audretsch, T. Gries, and H. Grupp, GLOBALIZATION, ECONOMIC GROWTH AND INNOVATION DYNAMICS 138 (1999).

[68] *See* ¶ 5 (a) of the Doha Declaration, *supra* note 11.

[69] *See* Article 12 of the International Covenant on Economic, Social and Cultural Rights.

[70] Resolution 2001/33 of the 57th Session of the United Nations Commission on Human Rights.

[71] *See also* the Doha Declaration, *supra* note 11, particularly ¶¶ 1 and 5(c).

[72] *See, e.g.*, Frederick Abbott, *The TRIPS-Legality of Measures Taken to Address Public Health Crises: a Synopsis* 14 (paper presented at the MSF Working Group on IP and Access to Medicines, New Delhi, June 5–6, 2001). Abbott notes that, in relation to public health issues: "the TRIPS Agreement is not *only* about protecting pharmaceutical industry profits. It is also about the health of the global economy, and about the health of individuals ". *Id.* at 32.

[73] Emphasis supplied.

[74] *India—Patent Protection for Pharmaceutical and Agricultural Chemical Products, supra* note 21.

[75] On the application of this doctrine, *see* Note by the WTO Secretariat, *Non-violation Complaints and the TRIPS Agreement,* IP/C/W/124, January 28, 1999. *See also* Chapter 29 of this book.

of the panel report, stating that the "reasonable expectations" of the Members were
already contained in the TRIPS provisions, so that it was not the task of the panel
or the Appellate Body to find other expectations outside the text of the Agreement
itself:

> The legitimate expectations of the parties to a treaty are reflected in the language of the treaty
> itself. The duty of a treaty interpreter is to examine the words of the treaty to determine
> the intentions of the parties. This should be done in accordance with the principles of
> treaty interpretation set out in Article 31 of the Vienna Convention. But these principles of
> interpretation neither require nor condone the imputation into a treaty of words that are not
> there or the importation into a treaty of concepts that were not intended.[76]

It is important to note, finally, that Paragraph 5(a) of the Doha Declaration has unambiguously confirmed the importance of TRIPS Articles 7 and 8 in the interpretation of
the Agreement, without overlooking the fact that other provisions of the Agreement, as
well as the preambular provisions, also contribute to the determination of its object and
purpose.

4. Interpreting Domestic Law

In *India—Patent Protection for Pharmaceutical and Agricultural Chemical Products*,[77]
the panel and the Appellate Body were confronted with the issue of whether a panel
could interpret national law in order to determine whether or not it was consistent with
the TRIPS Agreement. The Appellate Body stated that there was simply no way for the
Panel to make a determination without engaging in an examination of Indian law, and
that the Panel was not interpreting Indian law "as such", but only for the purpose of
determining whether India had met its obligations under the TRIPS Agreement:

> To say that the Panel should have done otherwise would be to say that only India can assess
> whether Indian law is consistent with India's obligations under the WTO Agreement.[78]

Though the Appellate Body approach was correct, many questions arise in connection
with the interpretation, not of a particular provision as such, but of that provision in the
context of a particular legal system. For instance, what would be the situation in a case
where, according to the legal system of a particular country, the TRIPS Agreement was
deemed to be self-executing and binding on domestic courts, but the domestic law failed
to adequately incorporate certain of the standards required by the Agreement? Since
under Article 1 of the TRIPS Agreement, Members can determine for themselves the
means of implementing their obligations, any inconsistency with the Agreement in such
a situation would be *de jure* cured by the direct application of the Agreement. Therefore,
the panel or Appellate Body should decide on the basis of how the legal system effectively
operates, and not on the basis of an isolated provision. This consideration is particularly
important for many Latin American countries, where international treaties are deemed
self-executing and can be directly invoked by private parties. Thus, in cases where the
national law is silent or inconsistent with the treaty obligations, a Member may still be

[76] *India—Patent Protection for Pharmaceutical and Agricultural Chemical Products, supra* note 21 at ¶ 45.
[77] *Supra* note 21.
[78] *Id.* at ¶ 66. India was found in violation of the TRIPS Agreement because, according to the Appellate
Body, there was no legal basis—procedural or substantive—under the Indian legislation for the grant of
exclusive marketing rights when a product which is the subject of a patent application under Article 70.8
(commonly called a "mailbox" application) becomes eligible for protection under Article 70.9 of the TRIPS
Agreement.

deemed to be in compliance with the TRIPS obligations if the courts can directly apply the treaty provisions[79], as already decided by some national courts[80].

5. Deference to National States

A very important question is the degree of deference given to national states in cases in which different interpretations of particular obligations are involved. As mentioned, the TRIPS Agreement contains a number of gaps and ambiguities and these were, in most cases, deliberate.

The basic question is the extent to which a panel or the Appellate Body can make a choice when a particular provision is subject to two or more permissible interpretations.[81] For example, the TRIPS Agreement requires Members to protect inventions, but does not define what an "invention" is. This definition differs quite significantly among different jurisdictions. Under U.S. law, for example, a microorganism that has merely been isolated and whose function has been identified is patentable, i.e., it may be treated as an "invention". This concept, however, is not shared by other countries. For instance, the legislation of Brazil only allows for the patenting of a genetically modified microorganism. If merely found in nature (even if isolated) it cannot be deemed an "invention", but only a "discovery". This means that subject matter (e.g. an isolated natural gene) that may eligible for protection under U.S. law would not be protectable in Brazil. Both interpretations are reasonable under patent law and admissible under the Agreement.

It would not be within the authority of the panel or the Appellate Body to decide in a case like this which of these permissible and reasonable interpretations is the "correct" one under TRIPS. As stated in *Canada—Patent Protection for Pharmaceutical Products*, they should not "decide, through adjudication, a normative policy issue that is still obviously a matter of unresolved political debate".[82] More generally, panels and the Appellate Body may not fill in the gaps or cure the ambiguities of the Agreement. Their only competence is to "clarify the existing provisions, " and "[r]ecommendations and rulings of the DSB cannot add or diminish the rights and obligations provided in the covered agreements".[83]

6. Contemporaneity

Another question relates to the weight that may be given in future cases to changes in intellectual property law, which continues to evolve, in particular to adapt to new

---

[79] According to the doctrine of "consistent interpretation", where national law permits different interpretations, the one in accordance with the treaty obligations is to be applied. *See,* e.g, THOMAS COTTIER, *The Impact of the TRIPS Agreement on Private Practice and Litigation*, in DISPUTE RESOLUTION IN THE WORLD TRADE ORGANIZATION (James Cameron and Karen Campbell eds.1999), at 124.

[80] See, for instance, the decisions of the Argentine Supreme Court of Justice in *Unilever NV c/Instituto Nacional de la propiedad Industrial s/denegatoria de patente* of 24 October 2000, and *Dr. Karl Thomae Gesellscaht mit Beschränker Haftung c/Instituto Nacional de la propiedad Industrial s/denegatoria de patente* of 13 February 2001.

[81] The WTO Dispute Resolution Understanding does not specify a standard of review as such, but merely directs panels to "make an objective assessment of the matter before it, including an objective assessment of the facts of the case and the applicability of and conformity with the relevant covered agreements. . . ." (DSU Article 11). The only specific "standard of review" provision in a WTO agreement is Article 17.6 of the Agreement on Implementation of Article VI of the General Agreement on Tariffs and Trade 1994 (Anti-Dumping). *See* Chapter 11 of this book.

[82] *See Canada—Patent Protection for Pharmaceutical Products, supra* note 23 at ¶ 7.82.

[83] Article 3.2 of the DSU.

technological developments such as digital technology[84]. Would the panels and Appellate Body be authorized to apply an evolutionary interpretation of TRIPS rules in the light of such developments? If so, there is a risk that higher standards of protection adopted in response to demands from industries from developed countries become part of the interpretive framework for the TRIPS Agreement.

Article 71 of the TRIPS Agreement specifically provides for the TRIPS Council to review the Agreement "in the light of any relevant new developments, which might warrant modification or amendment of this Agreement". This makes clear that amendments or adaptations cannot be made via interpretation. The panels and Appellate Body should confine themselves to the meaning of the terms as understood at the time of their adoption.[85]

In *Canada—Patent Protection for Pharmaceutical Products,* the panel examined the status of the legislation *at the time of the negotiation* of the Agreement to determine the concept of "legitimate interest" as contained in Article 30. In the panel's opinion, on balance:

> the interest claimed on behalf of patent owners whose effective period of market exclusivity had been reduced by delays in marketing approval was neither so compelling nor so widely recognized that it could be regarded as a "legitimate interest" within the meaning of Article 30 of the TRIPS Agreement, notwithstanding the number of governments that had responded positively to that claims. Moreover, the Panel believed that it was significant that concerns about regulatory review exceptions in general, although well known at the time of the TRIPS negotiations, were apparently not clear enough, or compelling enough, to make their way explicitly into the recorded agenda of the TRIPS negotiation. The Panel believed that Article 30's "legitimate interests" concept should not be used to decide, through adjudication, a normative policy issue that is still obviously a matter of unresolved political debate.[86]

However, in the report in the *United States—Section 110(5) of the US Copyright Act* case, the panel stated that the WIPO Copyright Treaty of 1996 should be viewed as "relevant to seek contextual guidance ... when developing interpretations that avoid conflicts within the overall multilateral copyright framework..."[87]. Although the panel cautioned that the statement concerning WCT Article 10 adopted by the signatory parties did not fall under the Vienna Convention rules on a subsequent treaty on the same matter or subsequent practice[88], the recourse to a post-TRIPS treaty—not even in force—constitutes a troubling precedent[89] as long as it may lead to interpretations of the TRIPS Agreement well beyond its own boundaries.

---

[84] For instance, in 1996, very shortly after the adoption of the TRIPS Agreement, two new treaties were adopted by the World Intellectual Property Organization ("WIPO") relating to copyright and related rights: the WIPO Performances and Phonograms Treaty ("WPPT"), December 20, 1996 and The WIPO Copyright Treaty ("WCT"), December 20, 1996.

[85] However, the Appellate Body has held that certain terms in the WTO Agreements are not "static" but evolutionary (in relation to the term "exhaustible natural resources" as it appears in GATT Article XX(g), adopted more than fifty years ago). Report of the Appellate Body, *United States—Import Prohibition of Certain Shrimp and Shrimp Products*, WT/DS58/AB/R (1998), at ¶¶ 127, 130.

[86] *Canada—Patent Protection for Pharmaceutical Products*, supra note 23, at ¶ 7.82. This approach is consistent with the general principle of treaty interpretation requiring that the meaning of the terms of a treaty be considered at the time of its signature. On the importance of the principle of "contemporaneity" in treaty interpretation, *see* Ian Brownlie, PRINCIPLES OF PUBLIC INTERNATIONAL LAW 627(1998).

[87] *United States—Section 110(5) of the U.S. Copyright Act*, supra note 24, at ¶ 6.70.

[88] *Id.* ¶ 6.69.

[89] According to Sara Williams, this was one of the panel's "most adventurous remarks" and "an aberration from the Panel's otherwise constructionist approach", *supra* note 64, at 203.

7. Mandatory vs. Discretionary Provisions

Another important issue relating to the interpretation of the TRIPS Agreement relates to the mandatory or discretionary nature of a disputed national rule. Based on GATT/WTO jurisprudence a panel or the Appellate Body would generally conclude that a law or regulation violates a WTO provision "as such" if it *mandates* WTO-inconsistent behavior. If, instead, the government or the court has the *discretionary* power to apply such law or regulation in a TRIPS-consistent manner, no violation would be found.

This interpretive principle was invoked by the United States and applied by the panel in *United States—Section 301–310 of the Trade Act of 1974*.[90] The EC and their Member States had complained about the application of several sections of the U.S. law that authorized the U.S. Government to retaliate against countries which, *inter alia*, did not provide an adequate level of IPR protection. According to one commentator:

> Without overruling the general principle of the mandatory-discretionary distinction, the panel found that U.S. Section 301 mandated U.S.T.R. to make a critical determination as to the WTO-consistency of the acts of other WTO members prior (in some cases) to the completion of a decision by the WTO Dispute Settlement Body. Even though U.S.T.R. was not bound to make an adverse determination, the fact that the determination needed to be made was inconsistent with the terms of the WTO DSU.[91]

However, the panel did not find the United States in violation of the WTO rules based on an assurance given by the U.S. Government that the relevant provisions of Section 301 would be administered consistently with the WTO DSU. This commitment was considered by the panel as a sufficient basis on which to find that there had not been a violation of WTO rules.

III. Some Contentious Issues

The TRIPS Agreement only incorporates *minimum standards* for the protection of intellectual property; and constitutes neither a uniform law nor an exhaustive codification of IPR law. It deals with *some* issues relating to intellectual property, but leaves out many others on which it was not possible to reach consensus or which were deemed inappropriate for standardization.[92] In addition to these deliberate "gaps", there are many ambiguities in the text that were the result of difficult compromises reached during the negotiations. These gaps and ambiguities mean that Members have been left a certain amount of room for maneuver at the national level which should not be limited by interpretations that may eventually be provided by panels or the Appellate Body.[93]

Maintaining the flexibility allowed by the TRIPS Agreement is an important objective for developing countries. Thus, in relation to health issues, the African Group and other developing countries have indicated that:

> Some provisions of the TRIPS Agreement may elicit different interpretations. The room for maneuver left serves the purpose of accommodating different positions held by Members

---

[90] Report of the WTO Panel, *United States—Section 301–310 of the Trade Act of 1974*, WT/DS152/R (2000), ¶¶ 7.51–.54 and n. 675.

[91] Abbott, *supra* note 72, at 13.

[92] For example, in the area of patents, the issue of the "first to file" or "first to invent" principle was not resolved; the national treatment principle does not apply to the distribution of levies on blank tapes as applied in European and other countries; there is no protection for program-carrying satellite signals as well as for utility models (granted in some countries to protect incremental innovations, mainly in the mechanical field); and there are no specific standards for the protection of plant varieties.

[93] John H. Jackson, THE JURISPRUDENCE OF GATT AND THE WTO 184, 186 (2000).

at the time of negotiations of the Agreement. We strongly believe that nothing in the TRIPS Agreement reduces the range of options available to Governments to promote and protect public health, as well as other overarching public policy objectives.[94]

The EU and its Members States have also accepted the existence of such flexibility:

> The Agreement on Trade-Related Aspects of Intellectual Property Rights (TRIPS), which emerged from the Uruguay Round negotiations has, however, sometimes been criticized as limiting policy options in relation to public health concerns. In the view of the EC and their member States, the Agreement's objectives, principles and purpose (set out in Articles 7 and 8), special transitional arrangements and other provisions give these countries a sufficiently wide margin of discretion in implementing it. This margin enables them to set up an intellectual property regime that meets their policy needs and is capable of responding to public health concerns.[95]

The extent of the flexibility allowed by the Agreement will ultimately depend upon the interpretation given to particular provisions by panels and the Appellate Body, which are expressly prohibited by DSU Article 3.2 from adding rights and obligations when adjudicating disputes. However, "the line between interpretation and providing clearer parameters of the rights and obligations of Members under these agreements is often very fine."[96]

The following discussion examines more in detail three of the areas where such flexibility is crucial for developing countries. The Doha Declaration has confirmed that flexibility in relation to two of them (compulsory licenses and parallel imports), while it has clarified the interpretation principles to be applied in relation to other areas[97].

A. Exceptions

1. GATT Jurisprudence

The GATT 1947 provides for various circumstances under which the Members may ignore their general obligations under the GATT.[98] Article XX specifically provides for exceptions to GATT/WTO obligations, including national treatment.[99]

In *United States—Standards for Reformulated and Conventional Gasoline*[100] —the first case to be considered by the WTO Appellate Body ("AB")—the panel had accepted that a policy to reduce air pollution was consistent with measures for the protection of human, animal or plant life or health. It did not accept, however, that the measures in question were "necessary", because there were measures available to the United States— for instance a single statutory baseline covering both domestic and foreign refiners or a

---

[94] *TRIPS and Public Health, supra* note 14 at 3.

[95] *The Relationship Between the Provisions of the TRIPS Agreement and Public Medicine, supra* note 14 at 2.

[96] Gabrielle Marceau and Peter Pedersen, *Is the WTO Open and Transparent? A Discussion of the Relationship of the WTO with Non-governmental Organizations and Civil Society's Claims for more Transparency and Public Participation*, 33 (1) JOURNAL OF WORLD TRADE 33 (1999).

[97] *See* Part V below.

[98] Correa, *supra* note 41, at 91.

[99] John Jackson, THE WORLD TRADING SYSTEM—LAW AND POLICY OF INTERNATIONAL ECONOMIC RELATIONS 23 (1999)

[100] *United States—Standards for Reformulated and Conventional Gasoline*, WT/DS4, April 12, 1995. The case involved gasoline programs established by the United States under the auspices of the Clean Air Act, which provided that in specific high pollution areas as measured by ozone concentration, only "clean" reformulated gasoline could be sold, which meant that it had to be blended with ethanol. An interim standard was allowed over a five-year period, which was calculated using a formula for U.S. producers that began with

more detailed examination of the production of foreign refiners—that would be consistent (or at least less inconsistent) with the GATT, and that would have achieved the same objective.

In reviewing the panel decision, the AB stated that the exceptions listed in Article XX "relate to all of the obligations under the General Agreement", and not only the national treatment and the most-favored-nation clause[101]. The AB held that any Article XX analysis is two-tiered. The first question is whether the measure is provisionally justified under the specific exception invoked; if the answer to this question is affirmative, the same measure must be further appraised under the introductory clauses (or "chapeau") of Article XX.[102] The AB accordingly stated that:

> The purpose and object of the introductory clauses of Article XX is generally the prevention of abuse of the exceptions of (what was later to become) Article XX. This insight drawn from the drafting history of Article XX is a valuable one. The chapeau is animated by the principle that while the exceptions of Article XX may be invoked as a matter of legal right, they should not be so applied as to frustrate or defeat the legal obligations of the holder of the right under the substantive rules of the General Agreement.[103]

The AB added that the burden of demonstrating that a measure falling within one of the specific Article XX exceptions does not constitute abuse under the chapeau in its application rests on the party invoking the exception.[104]

Article XX of GATT has been interpreted narrowly[105], even in the context of public health issues. For instance, in the *Thai Cigarette case,*[106] decided under the GATT dispute resolution system, the panel applied the "less trade restrictive"[107] test and held that other measures (not simply banning the imports of cigarettes, as the Thai government had done) that were less incompatible with the GATT were available to achieve the intended public health objectives.

This extreme interpretation of exceptions has been somewhat qualified by the doctrine established in the *EC Measures Concerning Meat and Meat Products (Hormones)* case, in which the Appellate Body held that

> "merely characterizing a treaty provision as an "exception" does not by itself justify a "stricter" or "narrower" interpretation of the provisions than would be warranted by

a company-specific 1990 baseline and would reduce the amount of olefines yearly on a percentage basis. Foreign producers, however, were required to use a statutory baseline rather than their own 1990 baseline, which often imposed a stricter burden on them. Venezuela and Brazil filed complaints claiming that the regulation violated Article III of the GATT.

[101] Report of the Appellate Body, *United States—Standards for Reformulated and Conventional Gasoline*, WR/DS2/AB/R (1996) (*"United States—Gasoline")*, at p. 24.

[102] The chapeau language had received little consideration in earlier GATT cases falling under Article XX. The new significance attributed to this language may make it more difficult for a Member to justify a trade restrictive measure than under previous jurisprudence.

[103] *United States—Gasoline, supra* note 101, at p. 22.

[104] *See also,* Edwin Vermulst, Petros Mavroidis, and Paul Waer, *The Functioning of the Appellate Body after Four Years—Towards Rule Integrity*, 3(2) JOURNAL OF WORLD TRADE 22 (1999).

[105] *See, e.g.,* Ernst-Ulrich Petersmann, THE GATT/WTO DISPUTE SETTLEMENT SYSTEM—INTERNATIONAL LAW, INTERNATIONAL ORGANIZATIONS AND DISPUTE SETTLEMENT 100 (1998); Michael Trebilcock and Robert Howse, THE REGULATION OF INTERNATIONAL TRADE 135–165 (1999); Correa, *supra* note 41 at 92–96.

[106] *See* Report of the Panel (adopted), *Thailand—Restrictions on Importation of and Internal Taxes on Cigarettes* (DS 10/R), BISD 37th Supp. 200 (1990).

[107] The panel applied the interpretation of "necessary" as developed in *United States—Section 337 of the Tariff Act of 1930* (adopted), BISD 36th Supp. 393 (1989), ¶ 5.26, in relation to Article XX(d) of GATT.

examination of the ordinary meaning of the actual treaty words, viewed in context and in light of the treaty's object and purpose..."[108]

This clarification may contribute to rectify the trend towards narrow interpretation emerging from previous jurisprudence[109], thereby facilitating the adoption by Members of measures required to protect public health or the environment that do not comply with some of the basic GATT/WTO obligations.

2. The TRIPS Agreement

Article 8.1 of the TRIPS Agreement provides that:

> Members may, in formulating or amending their national laws and regulations, adopt measures necessary to protect public health and nutrition, and to promote the public interest in sectors of vital importance to their socio-economic and technological development, provided that such measures are consistent with the provisions of this Agreement.

Some developing countries, notably India, have expressed concerns about the implications of the phrase "provided that such measures are consistent with the provisions of the TRIPS Agreement", since it might be interpreted as not allowing any derogation from the obligations of the Agreement'. If this were the case, public interest factors (including human health) would receive less protection under the TRIPS Agreement than under GATT, SPS or TBT.[110] In order to be meaningful at all, the consistency test of Article 8.1 should be assessed in the light of Article 7 which defines the "Objectives" of the Agreement and of the Preamble, i.e., taking social and economic welfare into account. In particular, nothing in the TRIPS Agreement should be read as preventing Members from adopting measures to protect public health, as well as from pursuing the overarching policies defined in Article 8.[111]

The "consistency" requirement may permit, for example, patentability exclusions in cases of distinct public health emergencies as defined by the national government, and as distinct from ordinary or everyday health and nutrition measures.[112] Emergency cases could trigger the application of a different test of "inconsistency" (as provided for under Article 8.1) or qualify as a situation not "conducive to social and economic welfare" (as provided for under Article 7). In such a case, a suspension or exclusion

[108] Report of the Appellate Body, *EC Measures Concerning Meat and Meat Products (Hormones)*, WT/DS26/AB/R, WT/DS48/AB/R (1998), ¶ 104.
[109] In *European Communities-Measures Affecting Asbestos and Products Containing Asbestos*, WT/DS135/AB/R (2001), a trade restriction based on Article XX (b) was upheld, but it is debatable whether this ruling may be read as relaxing the "necessity test" as previously developed in GATT/WTO jurisprudence.
[110] In the case of the SPS Agreement, Members have the right to take measures they deem appropriate to protect human, animal or plant life or health, but must ensure that they are "not more trade restrictive than required to achieve their appropriate level of sanitary or phytosanitary protection, taking into account technical and economic feasibility" (Article 5.6). The Preamble of the TBT Agreement recognizes that "no country should be prevented from taking measures necessary . . . for the protection of human, animal or plant life or health . . .". Article 2.2 allows to authorities to consider, in assessing the risks ". . . available scientific and technical information, related processing technology or intended end-uses of products". In the case of a dispute, the complaining country may have to provide *prima facie* evidence that there is an unnecessary obstacle to trade, and the defending country may have to give evidence that the adopted standard is not more trade-restrictive than necessary to fulfill a legitimate objective, taking account of the risks that non-fulfillment would create (Article 2 of the TBT Agreement).
[111] *See, e.g.*, the position of the developing countries in *TRIPS and Public Health, supra* note 14 at 5.
[112] Carlos M. Correa, *Integrating Public Health Concerns into Patent Legislation in Developing Countries* 13 (2000), available at http://www.southcentre.org/publications/publichealth/publichealth.pdf.

from patentability[113] might be linked to and justified by a specific emergency. Once the emergency subsides, the TRIPS requirement of patentability could be restored.

The Doha Declaration established in paragraph 5 (b) that

"Each member has the right to determine what constitutes a national emergency or other circumstances of extreme urgency, it being understood that public health crises, including those relating to HIV/AIDS, tuberculosis, malaria and other epidemics, can represent a national emergency or other circumstances of extreme urgency".

This paragraph confirms what is an unquestionable right of Members States: the right to determine "what constitutes a national emergency or other circumstances of extreme urgency". Such determination may be relevant for the establishment of exceptions under Article 30, the granting of compulsory licenses, or the adoption of other measures permitted under Article 8.1 of the Agreement[114].

This provision is important for three reasons. *First*, it clarifies that "public health crises" can represent "a national emergency or other circumstances of extreme urgency", thereby allowing for the granting of compulsory licenses when provided for under national law and, pursuant to TRIPS Article 31 (b), without the obligation for prior negotiation with the patent owner.

Second, the reference to "HIV/AIDS, tuberculosis, malaria and other epidemics" indicates that an "emergency" may be not only a short-term problem, but a long lasting situation, as is the case with the epidemics specifically mentioned for illustrative purposes. This recognition may be deemed an important achievement for developing countries in the Doha Declaration, since it implies that specific measures to deal with an emergency may be adopted and maintained as long as the underlying situation persists, without temporal constraints.

Third, if a Member complains about the qualification of a specific situation by another Member as a "national emergency or other circumstances of extreme urgency", the language of paragraph 5 (c) places the burden on the complaining Member to prove that such emergency or urgency does *not* exist. This represents an important difference with respect to earlier GATT/WTO jurisprudence outside of the TRIPS context that, under the "necessity test", put the burden of proof on the Member invoking an exception to its obligations[115].

A key consideration is clearly the purpose for which any subject-matter exclusion was to be adopted and the proportionality of the adopted measure. If, for example, the same objective could be obtained by imposing permissible compulsory licenses under TRIPS

---

[113] It is debatable whether an exception to patentability may be justified under the general GATT exception to trade disciplines, when the exception is necessary to protect human health. Article XX(b) has been interpreted and applied rather narrowly in GATT/WTO case law. In addition, it is doubtful whether GATT Article XX(b) would apply in the TRIPS context, since the TRIPS Agreement constitutes the *lex specialis* in the WTO system to deal with intellectual property issues. *See India—Patent Protection for Agricultural and Chemical Products*, *supra* note 21, at ¶ 7.19.

[114] In May 2002, the Minister of Justice, Legal and Parliamentary Affairs of Zimbabwe issued a Declaration of Period of Emergency (HIV/AIDS Notice, 2002). In view of the rapid spread of HIV/AIDS among the population of Zimbabwe, the Minister declared "an emergency for a period of six months, with effect from the date of promulgation of this notice, for the purpose of enabling the State or a person authorized by the Minister under Section 34 of the Act (a) to make or use any patented drug, including any antiretroviral drug, used in the treatment of persons suffering from HIV/AIDS or HIV/AIDS related conditions; (b) to import any generic drug used in the treatment of persons suffering from HIV/AIDS or HIV/AIDS-related conditions". A Declaration of Sanitary Emergency—until 31 December 2002—was also issued by the Executive Power of Argentina (Decree 486, 12 March, 2002), but it does not make explicit reference to patent law provisions.

[115] *See* Correa, *supra* note 41, at 96.

Article 31, an exclusion of patentability could be seen as an attempt to circumvent the pre-conditions of Article 31, in contradiction with the last sentence of Article 8.1. If, instead, local situations posed such unusual problems as to merit a public interest exception, these problems might also justify overriding or limiting other Articles, such as Article 31, in favor of some non-permanent exclusion of subject matter, if that exclusion was necessary to solving the problem.

Another important issue is the extent of the exceptions to exclusive rights allowed under the TRIPS Agreement. The panel in *Canada—Patent Protection for Pharmaceutical Products*[116] took a narrow approach to this issue in relation to Article 30 (exceptions to patent exclusive rights). It made a detailed analysis of some of the elements in Article 30 and held that the exceptions must be read narrowly. It failed to adequately consider the principles and objectives of the Agreement as set forth in Articles 7 and 8, thereby arriving to an interpretation that disregarded the broad economic and social interests that patents are intended to serve. As noted by Howse, in making such analysis the panel ignored the provision of Article 7 "about balance and mutual advantage, interpreting the patent provisions of the TRIPS Agreement primarily from the perspective of intellec-tual property rights holders, largely dismissing competing social interests, and reducing considerably the range of regulatory diversity permitted under TRIPS"[117].

A similar line was followed in *United States—Section 110(5) of the US Copyright Act* case, where Article 13 of the Agreement was examined. The panel reasoned that whether a limitation or exception conflicts with the normal exploitation of a copyrighted work is to be judged for each exclusive right separately[118], that the "legitimate interests of the right holder" were not necessarily limited to the economic value of exclusive rights, and that an "unreasonable" prejudice to such interests existed when an exception caused or had the potential to cause an unreasonable loss of income to the copyright owner[119]. Again the panel missed an opportunity to introduce a more balanced approach in its reasoning as required by the terms of Article 7 of the TRIPS Agreement, and limited its superficial analysis on the "crucial question" of unreasonable prejudice to the economic impact of the exception on right-holders' profit, without any consideration to the possible impact on consumers or the society as a whole[120].

B. Compulsory Licenses for Non-Working of the Invention

Many national laws require that the compulsory licensee undertake the *production* of the patented invention in the country where the license is to be granted. However, not all de-veloping countries possess either the entrepreneurial and technical capabilities necessary to permit the local production of inventions or the markets large enough to justify it.

Nothing in the TRIPS Agreement prevents a Member from establishing that a com-pulsory license be worked through importation rather than local production. However, it may not be possible to find independent foreign sources for the importation of a protected product other than the patent owner or its voluntary licensees, meaning that a compulsory license would be *de facto* impracticable. The only alternative source of supply might be another compulsory licensee for the same patent in a foreign country, but this approach

---

[116] *Supra* note 23, at ¶ 4.37.
[117] Howse, *supra* note 64, at 3.
[118] *United States—Section 110(5) of the US Copyright Act, supra* note 24, at ¶¶ 6.173 and 6.174.
[119] *Id.* at ¶ 6.229.
[120] *Id.* and n. 205.

also has a limitation: a compulsory license must be granted, in accordance with Article 31(f) of the TRIPS Agreement, to supply "predominantly" the domestic market.

The European Commission has pointed to another possible interpretation of the Agreement that would allow a Member to issue a compulsory license to a manufacturer in another country, provided that the government of that other country recognized the license (which it would not be obliged to do under the Agreement), and provided that all the goods manufactured under the license were exported to the country granting the license.[121] It is, however, far from certain whether such a reading of the Agreement would withstand scrutiny by a panel or the Appellate Body.

This suggestion seems to ignore the basic principle of independence of patents, as enshrined in Article 4*bis* of the Paris Convention. In the ultimate case, the validity of the proposed scheme would depend on the national law of the exporting country, which may exempt under Article 30 of the Agreement the exploitation of an invention solely for export purposes. In this case, there would be no need to grant a compulsory license in the exporting country.

If exports were made under a compulsory license, the importation may also be deemed covered under the "exhaustion principle". If so, it would not be necessary to issue a compulsory license in the importing country (since "parallel imports" would be legitimate). As discussed below, however, the application of the exhaustion principle when the product has been commercialized in a foreign country without the *consent* of the patent owner is controversial, and would need to be clarified by a ruling under the DSU, or an authoritative interpretation by the TRIPS Council.

Another very controversial issue has been the extent to which a compulsory license may be granted based on the failure to work a patent. The obligation to "work" a patent—understood as the local manufacture of the patented product or use of the patented process—was established in the United Kingdom in the Sixteenth Century, and was incorporated in many national laws during the Nineteenth and Twentieth Centuries.[122]

The U.S. government and some commentators have argued that the mere importation of a patented product (or of a product made with a patented process) constitutes the "working" of a patent.[123] They have also argued that Article 27.1 of the Agreement effectively outlaws compulsory licenses based on non-working of the invention, since that would constitute discrimination between imported and locally manufactured products. This is not the view, however, that prevails among developing country Members of the WTO,[124] nor is it reflected in the national laws of many Members who have adopted local working obligations.[125] The Uruguay Round records also reveal that during the

---

[121] *The Relationship Between the Provisions of the TRIPS Agreement and Access to Medicines*, *supra* note 14, at ¶ 13.

[122] Edith Penrose, LA ECONOMÍA DEL SISTEMA INTERNACIONAL DE PATENTES 131 (1974); Carlos Correa and Salvador Bergel, PATENTES Y COMPETENCIA 59 (1996).

[123] Michael Halewood, *Regulating Patent Holders: Local Working Requirements and Compulsory Licences at International Law*, 35 (2) OSGOODE HALL LAW JOURNAL 243 (1997).

[124] *See TRIPS and Public Health*, *supra* note 14, at 7–8.

[125] A draft review of comparative law conducted by Oxfam found working obligations in the patent laws and regulations of Indonesia and Cuba (similar to Brazil); Ghana, Ireland, South Africa, Sudan and Zimbabwe (based on former United Kingdom laws); Greece and Lesotho (compulsory licensing linked to local working); Turkey, Spain and Portugal (certificate of working required); Sweden, Norway, Finland and Iceland (local working tied to reciprocity); India; Israel; Zaire; Thailand; Pakistan; Liberia. Oxfam, *Local Working Requirements and the TRIPS Agreement: Using Patent Law as a Means of Ensuring Affordable Access to Essential Medicines. A Case Study from the U.S.-Brazil Dispute (draft)* (2001), available at http://www.field.org.uk/papers/pdf/twrta.pdf.

negotiations several developing countries argued for the right to impose working re-quirements.[126] It would be an incorrect interpretation of the negotiating history of the TRIPS Agreement to consider that those countries withdrew their position when they accepted the ambiguous text adopted in Article 27.1 of the Agreement.

As mentioned in Part III.A above, the United States initiated a case against Brazil arguing that Article 68 of the Brazilian patent law[127] was inconsistent with the TRIPS Agreement. That provision authorizes the government to grant a compulsory license if the patent owner fails to work the subject matter of the patent in Brazil. A critical issue in ad-dressing the consistency or not of working obligations is whether the non-discrimination clause in TRIPS Article 27.1 governs Article 31 (conditions for the granting of compul-sory licenses). Developing countries have expressed the concern that Article 27.1 may be read in a way that restricts the use of compulsory licenses, for instance, on the grounds of non-working. The non-discrimination clause may be also used to challenge compulsory licenses specifically dealing with certain sectors, such as pharmaceuticals. Developing countries have argued in this respect that:

> As regards the relationship of the provisions related to compulsory licenses with Articles 27.1 and 28 of TRIPS, we believe that both set of provisions address different matters and circumstances. In no way do Articles 27.1 and 28 limit the right of Members to issue compulsory licenses[128].

The "patent rights" referred to in Article 27.1 are defined in Article 28.1, which only requires the granting of *negative* rights with regard to the exploitation of the invention, that is, the right to prevent third parties from using (without authorization) the patented invention. According to Article 28.1:

---

[126] *See, e.g.*, Negotiating Group on Trade-Related Aspects of Intellectual Property Rights, including Trade in Counterfeit Goods, *Meeting Of Negotiating Group Of 2, 4 and 5 April 1990,* Note by the Secretariat MTN.GNG/NG11/20, April 24, 1990, ¶ 34; Negotiating Group on Trade-Related Aspects of Intellectual Property Rights, Including Trade in Counterfeit Goods, *Existence, Scope And Form Of Generally Interna-tionally accepted And Applied Standards/Norms For The Protection Of Intellectual Property,* Note Prepared by the International Bureau of WIPO, MTN.GNG/NG11/W/24, May 5, 1988, p. 2; Negotiating Group on Trade-Related Aspects of Intellectual Property Rights, including Trade in Counterfeit Goods, *Meeting Of Negotiating Group Of 11, 12 And 14 December 1989*, Note by the Secretariat, MTN.GNG/NG11/17, Jan-uary 23, 1990, ¶ 41; Negotiating Group on Trade-Related Aspects of Intellectual Property Rights, including Trade in Counterfeit Goods, *Meeting Of Negotiating Group Of 11–12 May 1989,* Note by the Secretariat, MTN.GNG/NG11/12, June 13, 1989, ¶ 5; Negotiating Group on Trade-Related Aspects of Intellectual Prop-erty Rights, including Trade in Counterfeit Goods, Meeting *Of Negotiating Group Of 11–12 May 1989*, Note by the Secretariat, MTN.GNG/NG11/12, June 13, 1989, ¶ 36; Negotiating Group on Trade-Related Aspects of Intellectual Property Rights, including Trade in Counterfeit Goods, *Meeting Of Negotiating Group Of 30 October—2 November 1989*, Note by the Secretariat, MTN.GNG/NG11/16, December 4, 1989, ¶ 24; Negotiating Group on Trade-Related Aspects of Intellectual Property Rights, including Trade in Counterfeit Goods, *Meeting Of Negotiating Group Of 12–14 July 1989,* Note by the Secretariat, MTN.GNG/NG11/14, September 12, 1989, ¶¶ 75, 83.

[127] Article 68 (1) of the Brazilian Industrial Property Code (Law 9.279) provides as follows:

> Art. 68. A patent shall be subject to compulsory licensing if the owner exercises his rights therein in an abusive manner or if he uses it to abuse economic power under the terms of an administrative or judicial decision.

(1) The following may also be grounds for compulsory licensing:

> I. Failure to work the subject matter of a patent on the territory of Brazil, failure to manufacture or failure to completely use a patented process, except for failure to work due to the lack of economic viability, in which case importing shall be admitted; or
> II. Marketing that does not satisfy the needs of the market.

[128] *TRIPS and Public Health, supra* note 14, at 8.

A patent shall confer on its owner the following exclusive rights:

(a) where the subject matter of a patent is a product, to prevent third parties not having the owner's consent from the acts of: making, using, offering for sale, selling, or importing 6 for these purposes that product;

(b) where the subject matter of a patent is a process, to prevent third parties not having the owner's consent from the act of using the process, and from the acts of: using, offering for sale, selling, or importing for these purposes at least the product obtained directly by that process.

An interpretation of Article 27.1 read in conjunction with Article 28.1, based on the rules of the Vienna Convention, suggests that the products mentioned in Article 27.1 are *infringing* products, not the products of the patent owner itself, since patents only confer exclusionary rights in relation to the former. In other words, Article 27.1 forbids discrimination between *infringing* imported and *infringing* locally-made products, but it does not prevent the establishment of differential obligations with regard to non-infringing imported and locally-made products (i.e., products made or imported by the patent owner or with his/her consent).

The non-discrimination clause of Article 27.1 may apply, for instance, to a case in which the rights enjoyed by patent owners who import legitimate products are different (substantially or procedurally) from the rights of patent owners who domestically manufacture them. For instance, Section 337 of the U.S. Tariff Act was found inconsistent with the GATT in *United States—Section 337 of the Tariff Act of 1930*,[129] since it accorded less favorable treatment to imported products challenged as infringing U.S. patents than the treatment accorded to similarly challenged products of United States origin.[130]

It should also be noted that Article 5(A)(2) of the Paris Convention provides that each party to the Convention "shall have the right to take legislative measures providing for the grant of compulsory licenses to prevent the abuses which might result from the exercise of the exclusive rights conferred by the patent, for example, *failure to work*." (Emphasis supplied). Article 8..1 of the TRIPS Agreement expressly contemplates that Members may adopt necessary measures "consistent with" the Agreement to address "the public interest in sectors of vital importance". Would it be possible to establish specific types of compulsory licenses for, e.g., pharmaceuticals or products needed to remedy environmental damages? In *Canada—Patent Protection for Pharmaceutical Products* the panel held that Articles 30 (exceptions) and 31 (compulsory licenses) of the TRIPS Agreement were subject to Article 27.1 of the Agreement.[131] However, the factual and legal basis for this finding are unconvincing, since it would seem logical to limit certain exceptions or modalities of compulsory licenses to certain fields of technology, rather than being forced to apply them to fields where such measures are not required.

---

[129] *Supra,* note 107.

[130] The USA "hesitantly effected an amendment of Sec. 337 in 1994 in order to improve the position of foreign respondents, but left the substance of the proceedings unchanged". Maximilian Haedicke, *U.S. Imports, TRIPS and Section 337 of the Tariff Act of 1930*, 31 (7/8) INTERNATIONAL REVIEW OF INDUSTRIAL PROPERTY AND COPYRIGHT LAW 1774 (2000). Although the express maximum time limits of twelve and eighteen months were abolished, the Section 337 proceedings still needed to be concluded by the International Trade Commission (ITC) "at the earliest practicable time", and within 45 days after the initiation of the proceedings the ITC had to establish a target date for its final determination. If the complainant requested an exclusion order during the investigation, a determination with regard to that petition had to be made within the relatively short period of ninety days.

[131] *Canada—Patent Protection for Pharmaceutical Products, supra,* note 23.

The panel in fact clarified that the conduct prohibited by Article 27.1 is "discrimination" as to the field of technology, that "discrimination" is not the same as "differentiation", and that WTO members can adopt different rules for particular product areas, provided that the differences are adopted for *bona fide* purposes. The panel held that:

> Article 27 prohibits only discrimination as to the place of invention, the field of technology, and whether products are imported or produced locally. Article 27 does not prohibit *bona fide* exceptions to deal with problems that may exist only in certain product areas. Moreover, to the extent the prohibition of discrimination does limit the ability to target certain products in dealing with certain of the important national policies referred to in Articles 7 and 8.1, that fact may well constitute a deliberate limitation rather than frustration of purpose.[132]

The Doha Declaration seems to confirm that differentiation in intellectual property rules may be legitimate in the WTO system. It singles out public health and, in particular, pharmaceuticals (paragraphs 6 and 7), as an issue needing special attention in TRIPS implementation.

France provides one example of a patent law that differentiates the treatment of pharmaceutical products on public health grounds. The French patent law provides that:

> Where the interest of public health demand, patents granted for medicines or for processes for obtaining medicines, for products necessary in obtaining such medicines or for processes for manufacturing such products may be subject to *ex officio* licenses in accordance with Article L. 613–17 in the event of such medicines being made available to the public in insufficient quantity or quality or at [abnormally high prices] by order of the Minister responsible for industrial property at the request of the Minister responsible for health.[133]

Finally, it is pertinent to recall that the Preamble to the TRIPS Agreement, as well as Articles 7 and 8, make it clear that one of the important objectives of the Agreement is to promote technology transfer, which may be ensured in some circumstances by means of compulsory licenses for nonworking.

C. Parallel Imports

Parallel imports involve the importation and resale in a country, without the consent of the patent holder, of a patented product that was put on the market of the exporting country by the title holder or in another legitimate manner. The underlying principle on which parallel imports are allowed is that since the inventor has been rewarded through the first sale or distribution of the product, he has no right to control the further use or resale of goods put on the market. In other words, the inventor's rights have been "exhausted".[134]

Members choose whether or not to allow for parallel imports. Allowing for such imports permits any person in its territory to purchase products protected under IPRs in the exporting or importing country, wherever such products are cheaper. In particular cases, such as in the case of health-related products, allowing for parallel imports might be an important public health policy.

---

[132] *Id.* at ¶ 7.92.

[133] 1 Loi No. 92–597, Code de la Propriété Intellectuelle (Law No. 92–597) of 1 July, 1992, Article L. 613–16).

[134] The doctrine of "exhaustion of rights" may be applied at the national level (rights are deemed exhausted domestically and commercialization in foreign countries is not deemed to have exhausted the patentee's rights), at the regional level (exhaustion is deemed to have occurred if commercialization took place in a country member of a regional agreement), as in the case of the EC, or at the international level. The discussion in the text refers to this latter case.

Despite some dissenting views,[135] it seems clear that parallel imports, based on the principle of exhaustion of rights, are allowed under the TRIPS Agreement. According to Article 6:

> For the purposes of dispute settlement under this Agreement, subject to the provisions of Articles 3 and 4 nothing in this Agreement shall be used to address the issue of the exhaustion of intellectual property rights.

In the submission to the Council for TRIPS referred to above, a number of developing countries stated that:

> Article 6 of the TRIPS Agreement is extremely relevant for Members, especially developing countries, and particularly the least developed and smaller economies among them. Article 6 provides that Members are free to incorporate the principle of international exhaustion of rights in national legislation. Consequently, any Member can determine the extent to which the principle of exhaustion of rights is applied in its own jurisdiction, without breaching any obligation under the TRIPS Agreement.[136]

A similar interpretation was given by the Swiss Federal Supreme Court in *Kodak v. Jumbo-Markt,*[137] where the Court persuasively argued that:

> Pursuant to Art. 28 of the TRIPS Agreement, the patent holder has *inter alia* the right to prevent third parties selling patented objects and importing such for this purpose. This provision with its protection of imports merely lays down that the import of products that infringe the patent must be prohibited, without itself laying down a prohibition on parallel imports. This follows not only from Art. 6 of the TRIPS Agreement but is also clarified in a reference to Art. 6 in a footnote to Art. 28 of the Agreement (GATT Message 1, 1994 Federal Gazette IV, p. 301/2; cf. also Bollinger, Die Regelung der Parallelimporte im Recht der WTO, sic! 1998, p. 548; Alesch Staehelin, Das TRIPS-Abkommen, 2nd ed., Berne 1999, p. 57 et seq. and 148/9; Cottier & Stucki, loc. cit., p. 52; Cohen Jehoram, International Exhaustion versus Importation Right: a Murky Area of Intellectual Property Law, 1996 GRUR Int., p. 284). The claim expressed occasionally in the literature that the substantive protection of importation practically requires national exhaustion through the TRIPS Agreement is not, on the other hand, convincing (argued by Straus, Bedeutung des TRIPS für das Patentrecht, 1996 GRUR Int., p. 193/4); for the attempt to derive the exclusive application of national exhaustion from this agreement ignores and misinterprets the objectives of the agreement to establish the World Trade Organisation dated April 15, 1994, one element of which is the TRIPS Agreement, namely to eliminate all kinds of trade restrictions. On the contrary, TRIPS is intended to balance two sets of interests, namely the demand for the freedom of trade on the one hand and an increased protection of intellectual property rights on the other hand (Bronckers, The Exhaustion of Patent Rights under WTO Law, Journal of World Trade 1998, p. 144). Exhaustion, and hence the question of whether in particular parallel imports can be prohibited by the party entitled to the patent, is not, however, regulated by Art. 28 of TRIPS, but expressly reserved to national law pursuant to Art. 6 of the Agreement (cf. also Kunz-Ballstein, Zur Frage der Parallelimporte im internationalen gewerblichen Rechtsschutz, 1998 GRUR, p. 269/70).

[135] "There is no question that Article 6 denies Members the ability to avail themselves of dispute settlement in relation to questions involving parallel imports, except when those questions involve failure to provide national or most-favored-nation treatment. However, Article 6 of the TRIPS Agreement does not, in our view, authorize parallel imports. Members must remember that Article 6 does not alter the substantive obligations of the TRIPS Agreement, particularly those contained in Part II of the Agreement" (Delegation of the United States, Council for TRIPS Meeting of June 1822, 2001, JOB(01)/97/Add.5, Council for TRIPS, June 28, 2001.)
[136] *The Relationship Between the Provisions of the TRIPS Agreement and Access to Medicines, supra,* note 14, at 6.
[137] *Kodak SA v. Jumbo-Markt AG,* 4C.24/1999/rnd, December 7, 1999.

The right of any Member to allow for parallel imports has been clearly confirmed by the Doha Declaration, which includes the principle of exhaustion of rights as one of the "flexibilities" incorporated by the Agreement:

> 5. Accordingly and in the light of paragraph 4 above, while maintaining our commitments in the TRIPS Agreement, we recognize that these flexibilities include:
>
> . . . .
>
> d. The effect of the provisions in the TRIPS Agreement that are relevant to the exhaustion of intellectual property rights is to leave each member free to establish its own regime for such exhaustion without challenge, subject to the MFN and national treatment provisions of Articles 3 and 4.[138]

Though this paragraph does not add substantively to the TRIPS Agreement, it certainly reassures Members wishing to apply an international exhaustion principle that it would be legitimate and fully consistent with the Agreement to do so.

Some national laws permit parallel imports on relatively broad terms.[139] However, parallel imports are not permitted under many national laws,[140] or they are only allowed under quite restrictive conditions. Thus, parallel importation is permitted in the Andean Group countries when the product was sold by the patent owner or by another party with his/her consent or by a party economically linked to the patent owner.[141] In Brazil, parallel importation is permitted only if the products are sold with the consent of the owner and provided that the invention is not exploited locally.[142] In Argentina, only a local voluntary licensee is authorized by regulations to engage in parallel importation.[143]

In the case of South Africa, the scope for parallel importation is also quite limited, since it is subject to a Ministerial order (by the Minister of Health) and only applies to medicines if they were put on the market by the patent owner or with his consent.[144] Despite this narrow scope, the provision of the South African law was vigorously challenged by large pharmaceutical companies, as mentioned above.[145]

---

[138] *Supra,* note 11.

[139] *See, e.g.,* Article 8 of the Kenya Industrial Property Act, 2001.

[140] Many laws do not clarify whether parallel imports are permitted or not. In the absence of a specific rule allowing them, imports are likely to be subject to the patent owner's exclusive rights.

[141] Article 54, Decision 486 (*Common Industrial Property Regime*) of the Andean Community, available at www.comunidadandina.org/ingles/treaties/dec/dec.htm.

[142] Article 68.4 of the Brazilian Industrial Property Code Law 9.279, 1996, available at www.sice.oas.org

[143] Article 36 (c) of the Argentine Decree 260/96, 1996.

[144] Article 15C, Medicines Act, Section 15C of the South African Medicines and Related Substances Control Amendment Act, No. 90 of 1997, provides as follows:

Measures to Ensure Supply of More Affordable Medicines

15C. The Minister may prescribe conditions for the supply of more affordable medicines in certain circumstances so as to protect the health of the public, and in particular may—notwithstanding anything to the contrary contained in the Patents Act, 1978 (Act. No. 57 of 1978), determine that the rights with regard to any medicine under a patent granted in the Republic shall not extend to acts in respect of such medicine which has been put onto the market by the owner of the medicine, or with his or her consent; prescribe the conditions on which any medicine which is identical in composition, meets the same quality standard and is intended to have the same proprietary name as that of another medicine already registered in the Republic, but which is imported by a person other than the person who is the holder of the registration certificate of the medicine already registered and which originates from any site of the manufacture of the original manufacturer as approved by the council in the prescribed manner, may be imported; prescribe the registration procedure for, as well as the use of, the medicine referred to in paragraph (b).

[145] The pharmaceutical industry also argued that the authorization given to the Health Minister was too broadly drafted and unconstitutional. The legal action was withdrawn in April 2001.

The pharmaceutical industry's strong objection to parallel imports[146] does not seem to be supported by the current situation in the trade of pharmaceuticals. It has been argued that the export of drugs sold at low cost in developing countries to higher-priced markets would affect the industry's ability to fund future R&D.[147] This might be true if parallel trade reached a significant dimension, but there is no indication that this is likely to happen, at least in the short term.

Trade in medicines is in fact subject to quite stringent national regulations that erect effective barriers to market access. Moreover, parallel imports would only take place where significant price differentials exist. Pharmaceutical firms may reduce such differentials or sell the patented products under different trademarks or packaging in major markets, in order to make parallel importation difficult or unattractive.[148] Further, any country may adopt measures to prevent parallel imports (provided that such restrictions are not found inconsistent with WTO obligations).[149] Some countries have suggested that, in order to keep a system of tiered pricing and to prevent low-priced medicines in developing countries flowing to developed countries, the former should adopt measures to prevent their exportation.[150] Export restraints of this kind may however be inconsistent with WTO rules, especially Article XI of the GATT.

Parallel imports increase static efficiency, that is, the allocation of products at the lowest possible price. Like the availability of compulsory licenses, parallel imports provide an important device to discipline markets and to induce suppliers to commercialize their products on reasonable conditions. Parallel imports from compulsory licensees may provide in some instances (particularly after the TRIPS Agreement becomes fully operative in all countries) the only way to get access to low-priced medicines.

Some national laws and jurisprudence[151] stipulate that in order for parallel imports to be admissible, the product must have been put on the market in a foreign country by or with the *consent* of the patent owner. Therefore, the supply by a compulsory licensee,

---

[146] *See, e.g.,* Harvey Bale, *TRIPS, Pharmaceuticals and Developing Countries: Implications for Drug Access and Drug Development,* paper presented at the WHO Workshop on the TRIPS Agreement and its Impact on Pharmaceuticals, IFPMA, Jakarta, May 2–4, 2000.

[147] Another argument against parallel trade is that it will increase opportunities for "counterfeit and substandard products to enter the market" (Bale, *supra* note 146 at 18), but this is a essentially a problem of law enforcement that can be addressed under normal procedures.

[148] Jayashree Watal, P*harmaceutical Patents, Prices and Welfare Losses: a Simulation Study of Policy Options for India Under the WTO* TRIPS *Agreement,* 23(5) The World Economy 733 (2000).

[149] *See* Carlos Correa, INTELLECTUAL PROPERTY RIGHTS, THE WTO AND DEVELOPING COUNTRIES 82 (2000).

[150] The U.S. delegation stated at the Council for TRIPS Special Session of June 21, 2001, that "In our view, advocates of parallel importation overlook the fact that permitting such imports discourages patent owners from pricing their products differently in different markets based upon the level of economic development because of the likelihood that, for example, products sold for a low prices in a poor country will be bought up by middle men and sent to wealthiest country markets and sold at higher prices, for the benefit primarily of the middle men. The lack of parallel import protection can also have significant health and safety implications. Our law enforcement and regulatory agencies, especially FDA, have commented on how very difficult it is for them to keep counterfeit and unapproved drugs out of our country even with the strong parallel import protection provided in the United States. Advocating parallel imports, therefore, could work to the disadvantage of the very people on behalf of whom the advocates purport to be speaking. As Dr. Brundtland in Oslo recently noted, 'For differential pricing to work on a large scale, I think we can all agree that there must be watertight ways of preventing lower priced drugs from finding their way back into rich country markets.'" *Special Discussion on Intellectual Property and Access to Medicines, supra* note 14, at 40.

[151] *See, e.g.,* several decisions by the European Court of Justice, which has held that the application of the doctrine of exhaustion is conditional upon the existence of the right holder's consent to putting its products on the market (e.g. *Pharmon v Hoechst,* Case 19/84, 1985 ECR 2281; *Merck & Co. v Primecrown Ltd,* joined cases C-267/95 and C-268/95).

or even by a voluntary licensee who is not authorized to parallel export, would not be legitimate.[152]

In some jurisdictions, the sale of goods by an intellectual property owner carries with it an implied license that the purchaser may use the goods for reasonable contemplated purposes. Exhaustion of the exclusive rights is presumed if the owner of the IPR abstained from imposing restrictions in the sales contract with regard to the use, sale or distribution of the product by the acquirer.[153] In the United States, for instance, the doctrine of exhaustion has been accepted as a basis for parallel importation, but the patentee may impose contract limitations to avoid the effects of the doctrine. In other words, parallel importation is authorized in the absence of enforceable contractual restrictions.[154]

Under the "implied license" theory, the exhaustion of IPRs ultimately rests on the discretion of the title-holder. This is well illustrated by a case decided by the High Court of Kenya and described in Box 2.[155]

Box 2   Parallel Imports under the Implied License Theory

In *Beecham Group v. International Products Ltd*[156] the High Court of Kenya ruled against the importation of the product into Kenya by a local distributor based on territorial restrictions imposed by a U.K. patentee on a U.S. licensee from whom the local distributor bought the product. The plaintiffs (Beecham Group) licensed the Bristol-Myers Company of New York to sell a new penicillin drug, under the name Pembritim, throughout the world, except in the British Commonwealth. The defendant, a Kenyan distributor, purchased Pembritim directly from the U.S. licensee in New York. The defendant maintained that the Beecham Group's rights were exhausted when they placed the goods in the U.S. market through a licensing agreement. Therefore, although the licensee was not authorized to sell in Kenya, the goods on which a royalty had once been paid were thereafter free in the hands of the purchaser to be sold anywhere in the world.

The Court held, however, that when a patented product is sold, it is free in the hands of the purchaser only from such monopoly rights as the vendor possesses. Therefore, a sale by a patentee, in the absence of any specific reservation, frees the article from the patentee's agents anywhere in the world, and a sale by the patentee's agent confers on the purchaser the same rights as a sale by the patentee. However, in the case of a sale by licensee, the extent to which the article is released from the patentee's rights depends on the extent of the authority conferred and Bristol-Myers had no authority to sell goods in infringement of the Kenyan patent. Hence, the Kenyan distributor could not acquire any better rights than those possessed by Bristol-Myers (the U.S. licensee)[157].

---

[152] *See, e.g., Pharmon v Hoechst, supra* note 151, and INGE GOVAERE, THE USE AND ABUSE OF INTELLECTUAL PROPERTY RIGHTS IN E.C. LAW 161–162 (1966).

[153] Abdulqawi Yusuf and Moncayo Von Hase, *Intellectual Property Protection and International Trade-Exhaustion of Rights Revisited*, 16(1) WORLD COMPETITION 118 (1992).

[154] Margreth Barrett, *The United States Doctrine of Exhaustion: Parallel Imports of Patented Goods*, 27(5) NORTHERN KENTUCKY LAW REVIEW 984 (2000).

[155] This decision preceded an amendment to the Kenya patent law in 2001 which introduced a provision allowing for parallel imports in broader terms.

[156] Quoted by D. Gladwel, *The Exhaustion of Intellectual Property Rights*, 12 European Intellectual Property Review 368 (1986).

[157] Yusuf and Moncayo von Hase, *supra* note 153, at 118–119.

The requirement of the right-holder's consent is grounded on the assumption that the patent owner enjoys a *positive* right to the first sale of a protected product, as is the case under the "consent theory" developed in Europe.[158] The right of "first sale" or "first publication" is established in some countries in the copyright field, as a means of allowing authors control over their works.[159]

Under the "consent theory", exhaustion can only take place when the product was put on the foreign country market by or with the consent of the patent owner. This would exclude a compulsory licensee as the source of legitimate parallel imports. In contrast, according to the "reward theory",[160] when selling the patented product in a foreign country, the patent owner is obtaining, as part of the product's price, compensation for the protected technology[161] (when the product is sold by a licensee, either voluntary or compulsory, the patent owner receives a royalty payment). Hence, parallel importation does not deprive the patent owner of contributions to future R&D.[162]

There is no basis for considering that the "consent theory" has been incorporated into the TRIPS Agreement for all types of IPRs. Patents, in particular, according to Article 28 of the Agreement, only grant *negative* rights, that is, the legal ability to exclude competition by infringers, but no positive rights.[163] In other words, the Agreement does not assure the patent owner a positive right of first marketing, as is often the case under copyright law.[164]

In addition, TRIPS Article 31(f) allows a compulsory license to be granted "predominantly" for the domestic market, thereby permitting at least part of the production under license to be "parallel exported".[165] Such exports may take place to countries where there is or where there is no patent protection; the referred provision does not make any distinction in this regard. Excluding parallel exports from a compulsory

[158] However, some decisions by the European Court of Justice have permitted parallel imports originating from a country where no patent protection was granted. *See, e.g.*, the *Merck v. Primacrown* and *Beecham Group v. Europharm* cases, ECJ, 5 December 1996, joined cases C 267/95 and C-268/95.

[159] Jack Cline, *Moral Rights: the Long and Winding Road Toward Recognition,* 14 NOVA L. REV.121 (1990). In some countries, this right is provided for in the framework of the recognition of the "moral rights" of authors.

[160] The reward theory was first formulated by the U.S. Supreme Court which held in *Adams vs. Burke,* 84 U.S. 453 (17 Wall.) (1873) that "[W]hen the patentee, or the person having his rights, sells a machine or instrument whose sole value is in its use, he receives the consideration for its use and he parts with the right to restrict that use. The Article ... passes without the limit of the monopoly. That is to say, the patentee or his assignee having in the act of sale received all the royalty or consideration which he claims for the use of his invention in that particular machine or instrument, it is open to the use of the purchaser without further restriction on account of the monopoly of the patentee".

[161] Yusuf and Moncayo von Hase, *supra* note 153 at 117; Govaere, *supra* note 152, at 80.

[162] No economic analysis on this issue has been made. The net impact of parallel importation on contributions to R&D will depend, among other things, on the price differentials and volumes of sales, as well as on price elasticity in the importing country.

[163] See the unambiguous wording of Article 28 of the TRIPS Agreement, and the interpretation given by the WTO Secretariat in *TRIPS and Pharmaceutical Patents—Fact Sheet,* April 2001; *see also* Govaere, *supra* note 152 at 80–81.

[164] *See, e.g.,* Anthony D'Amato and Doris Long, INTERNATIONAL INTELLECTUAL PROPERTY ANTHOLOGY 113–118 (1966).

[165] A restrictive interpretation of the scope of Article 6 of the TRIPS Agreement has been suggested, according to which the patent owner's consent will be required as a condition for the legality of parallel imports. This interpretation has been grounded on the footnote to TRIPS Article 51 and on the approach adopted by the Treaty on Intellectual Property in Respect of Integrated Circuits, Washington D. C., on May 26, 1989. However, Article 51 only applies to trademarks and copyrights and the Treaty only deals with semiconductors.

licensee[166] to a country where there is patent protection would deprive Article 31 (f) of its full meaning. There is no basis to assume that Article 31 (f) would only apply when the product produced under the compulsory license is not protected in the importing country.

If parallel imports were outlawed in cases where there is remuneration of, but no consent by the patent owner (as in the case of compulsory licenses), the usefulness of parallel imports as a pro-competitive mechanism would be seriously curtailed, since in most instances the patent owner may attach sale limitations to the products that he puts on the market, or impose contractual limitations on his licensees not to export without the patent owner's authorization.

In sum, whenever the patent owner receives adequate remuneration in the country from which a product is imported, he should be deemed to have exhausted his rights over that product. The "reward theory" provides a solid basis for the application of the exhaustion principle under the TRIPS Agreement, and allows full meaning to be given to all its relevant provisions.

IV. The Doha Declaration on Public Health[167]

The Doha Declaration includes preambular provisions (paragraphs 1 to 4), a provision aimed at confirming the interpretation of certain rules of the TRIPS Agreement (paragraph 5), and two operative provisions requiring action by the Council for TRIPS in relation to countries with no or insufficient manufacturing capacity in pharmaceuticals (paragraph 6), and for the extension of the transitional period for LDCs in relation to the protection of pharmaceutical products (paragraph 7).

While some developed countries attempted to limit the scope of the Declaration to the HIV/AIDS crisis, the adopted text recognizes the "gravity" of the public health problems afflicting many developing countries and LDCs, especially those resulting from HIV/AIDS, tuberculosis, malaria and other epidemics. Access to medicines certainly was the main preoccupation that led to the Doha Declaration, but it covers not only medicines, but any health care product, method or technology.

Paragraph 4 of the Doha Declaration was one of the most controversial provisions of the document and the subject of intense negotiations during the preparations for and at the Ministerial Conference in Doha. The negotiating target of the developing countries was to obtain recognition that nothing in the TRIPS Agreement should be interpreted as preventing Members from adopting measures necessary to protect public health. After intense negotiations a compromise text was reached which apparently satisfied all parties:

> 4. We agree that the TRIPS Agreement does not and should not prevent members from taking measures to protect public health. Accordingly, while reiterating our commitment to the TRIPS Agreement, we affirm that the Agreement can and should be interpreted and implemented in a manner supportive of WTO members' right to protect public health and, in particular, to promote access to medicines for all.
>
> In this connection, we reaffirm the right of WTO members to use, to the full, the provisions in the TRIPS Agreement, which provide flexibility for this purpose.

---

[166] Any compulsory licensee will be bound—according to TRIPS Article 31(h)—to pay "adequate remuneration" to the patent holder, "taking into account the economic value of the authorization". This means that the patent holder will be rewarded whenever his/her patent is exploited.

[167] The text of the Declaration is reproduced in the Appendix to this book.

Though interpretations on this paragraph are likely to differ, it seems clear that the intention of the Members was to indicate that in cases where there is conflict between intellectual property rights and public health, the former should not be an obstacle to the realization of the latter[168]. The realization of public health becomes, with the Doha Declaration, a clearly stated *purpose* of the Agreement. In affirming that the TRIPS Agreement, "can and should be interpreted and implemented in a manner supportive of WTO Members' right to protect public health and, in particular, to promote access to medicines for all", paragraph 4 gives guidance to panels and the Appellate Body for the interpretation of the Agreement's provisions in cases involving public health issues. In doing so, Members have developed a specific *rule of interpretation* that gives content to the general interpretive provisions of the Vienna Convention on the Law of the Treaties (hereinafter "the Vienna Convention") on which GATT/WTO jurisprudence has been built up.

The confirmation that the TRIPS Agreement has left room for flexibility at the national level in certain areas, as noted above, has important political and legal implications. It indicates that the pressures to impede the use of available flexibilities run counter to the spirit and purpose of the TRIPS Agreement, especially in the light of the recognized "gravity of the problems" faced in the area of public health by developing countries and LDCs. In legal terms, such confirmation means that panels and the Appellate Body must interpret the Agreement and the laws and regulations adopted to implement it in light of the public health needs of individual Members States. Therefore, in cases of ambiguity, or where more than one interpretation is possible, panels and the Appellate Body should opt for the interpretation that is effectively "supportive of WTO Members' right to protect public health"[169].

In paragraph 6 the Doha Declaration instructed the Council for TRIPS to address a delicate issue: how can Members lacking or with insufficient manufacturing capacities make effective use of compulsory licensing. The Declaration requests the Council for TRIPS "to find an expeditious solution to this problem and to report to the General Council before the end of 2002". In order to be effective such a solution should be economically viable, and not only legally acceptable.[170]

Finally, the Doha Declaration agreed that LDCs should be granted an extension until 2016 of the transitional period provided for under Article 66.1 of the TRIPS Agreement with respect to pharmaceutical patents (TRIPS Section 5) and protection of undisclosed information relating to pharmaceuticals (TRIPS Section 7). Paragraph 7 constitutes a

---

[168] The Brazilian delegation pointed out at the Doha Ministerial Conference that "in the area of intellectual property, different readings of the TRIPS Agreement have given rise to tensions. To a certain extent, it is natural that conflicts of interests should reflect themselves in divergent interpretations of common rules. But the commercial exploitation of knowledge must not be valued more highly than human life. There are circumstances in which the conflict of interests will require that the State exercise its supreme political responsibility... Brazil promotes and upholds intellectual property rights... However, if circumstances so require it, Brazil, like many other countries, will not hesitate to make full use of the flexibility afforded by the TRIPS Agreement to legitimately safeguard the health of its citizens" (WT/MIN(01)/ST/12, November 10, 2002).

[169] *See* Carlos Correa, *Implications of the Doha Declaration on the TRIPS Agreement and Public Health 26*, World Health Organization (2002).

[170] *See id.,* at 33. Despite considerable efforts, the Council for TRIPS was unable to agree (as of 16 February 2003) on a solution on paragraph 6 of the Declaration. Consensus on a compromise text proposed by the Council's Chairman was broken due to the US insistence on limiting such a solution only to HIV/AIDS, malaria and tuberculosis. This limitation—allegedly aimed at protecting the global interests of the US pharmaceutical industry—was found inacceptable by developing countries, as it would narrow down the agreed scope of the Doha Declaration.

"duly motivated request"—in the terms of Article 66.1 of the TRIPS Agreement[171]—on the basis of which the Council for TRIPS must give effect to that extension. LDCs do not need to individually follow the procedure provided for under Article 66.1 to obtain the extension. The Declaration, however, explicitly preserves the right of LDCs to request extensions for other matters (not related to pharmaceutical patents) in accordance with the Article 66.1 procedure[172], without diminishing their right to request further extensions for pharmaceutical patents after 2016[173].

It is implicit within the Doha Declaration that differentiation in patent rules may be necessary to protect public health. The singling out of public health, and in particular pharmaceuticals (paragraphs 6 and 7), as an issue needing special attention in TRIPS implementation constitutes recognition that public health-related patents deserve to be treated differently from other patents.

A "declaration" has no specific legal status in the framework of WTO law[174]; it is not strictly an authoritative interpretation in terms of Article IX.2 of the Marrakesh Agreement Establishing the WTO. However, given the content and mode of approval of the Doha Declaration, it can be argued that it has the same *effect* as an authoritative interpretation. In particular, in providing an agreed understanding on certain aspects of the TRIPS Agreement in paragraph 5, Members have created a binding precedent for future panels and Appellate Body reports. According to the European Commission,

> "in the case of disputes (e.g. in the context of WTO dispute settlement procedures) Members can avail themselves of the comfort provided by this Declaration. Panelists are likely to take account of the provisions of the TRIPS Agreement themselves as well as of this complementary Declaration, which, although it was not meant to affect Members' rights and obligations, expresses the Members' views and intentions. Hence, the Declaration is part of the context of the TRIPS Agreement, which, according to the rules of treaty interpretation, has to be taken into account when interpreting the Agreement"[175].

[171] TRIPS Article 66.1. "In view of the special needs and requirements of least-developed country Members, their economic, financial and administrative constraints, and their need for flexibility to create a viable technological base, such Members shall not be required to apply the provisions of this Agreement, other than Articles 3, 4 and 5, for a period of 10 years from the date of application as defined under paragraph 1 of Article 65. The Council for TRIPS shall, upon duly motivated request by a least-developed country Member, accord extensions of this period".

[172] In fact, it would have seem more logical to extend the transitional period for all fields of technology since, unless individual extensions are accorded, LDCs would be required anyway to bear the costs of granting patents in other sectors.

[173] In pursuance to paragraph 7 of the Doha Declaration, on June 27, 2002, the Council for TRIPS agreed to extend the transitional period for LDCs to introduce pharmaceutical patent protection until 2016 (Decision on the Extension of the Transition Period under Article 66.1 of the TRIPS Agreement for Least-Developed Country Members for Certain Obligations with respect to Pharmaceutical Products (IP/C/25)The General Council also granted a waiver (adopted in its meeting of 8th and 31st July 2002) to such countries with regard to the granting of exclusive marketing rights (provided for under Article 70.9 of the TRIPS Agreement) during that period (available at www.wto.org)

[174] The WTO adopted several "declarations" at the Marrakesh Conference that adopted the WTO Agreement, e.g.: *Declaration on the Contribution of The World Trade Organization to Achieving Greater Coherence In Global Economic Policymaking*; *Declaration on the Relationship of the World Trade Organization with the International Monetary Fund*; *Declaration on the Dispute Settlement Pursuant to the Agreement on Implementation of Article VI of the General Agreement on Tariffs and Trade 1994 or Part V of the Agreement on Subsidies and Countervailing Measures*.

[175] European Commission, *WTO Ministerial Declaration on the TRIPS Agreement and Public Health*, Brussels, November 19, 2001, at 2.

Moreover, the Declaration can be regarded as a "subsequent agreement" between the parties regarding the interpretation of a treaty or the application of its provisions, under Article 31.3 (a) of the Vienna Convention on the Law of the Treaties.

V. Conclusion

The WTO dispute settlement system faces a very complex and delicate task in the area of the TRIPS Agreement, perhaps more difficult than with respect to other WTO agreements. The great sensitivity of the issues involved, both for developing and developed countries, suggests that opinions on the matter will be subject to very strict scrutiny and may significantly influence future developments in the area of IPRs.

An "activist" approach by panels and the Appellate Body in the interpretation of the TRIPS Agreement would be likely to imperil the dispute settlement system. The Agreement has neither addressed nor resolved all issues in IPR law. Its gaps and ambiguities were the unavoidable result of difficult negotiations. If the panels or Appellate Body try to make expansive interpretations or to make choices which the Members did not make during the negotiations, the credibility of the dispute settlement system will be seriously undermined.

If confronted with the task (in applying the rules of Article 39(1) of the Vienna Convention on the Interpretation of Treaties) of defining the "purpose" of the treaty in relation to a disputed provision, panels and the Appellate Body should be aware that the role of the TRIPS Agreement is not merely to guarantee the commercial interests of IPRs holders, but also to further the public interest.

Panels and the Appellate Body should recognize that there are fundamental differences among the WTO members in relation to the role of intellectual property and, in particular, on how it can affect the realization of basic human rights as well as the development prospects of developing countries. Decisions on TRIPS matters should be adopted having in view the objectives and principles set forth in Articles 7 and 8 of the TRIPS Agreement.

The adoption of the Doha Declaration has represented an important step in recognizing the flexibilities permitted by the TRIPS Agreement, and the right of Members to adopt measures to protect public health. The Declaration not only has political value, but legal effects, equivalent to those of an authoritative interpretation under WTO rules.

Finally, due attention should be given to the fact that one of the principal objectives of the GATT/WTO system is to expand the production of and trade in goods and services by reducing barriers to trade and ensuring the realization of competitive opportunities on a non-discriminatory basis. The TRIPS provisions should therefore be interpreted bearing in mind that it is the promotion rather than the restriction of competition that is the foundation of the international trade system.

CHAPTER 55

TRADE-RELATED TECHNICAL COOPERATION AND CAPACITY BUILDING

Esperanza Durán*

TABLE OF CONTENTS

* Executive Director of the Agency for International Trade Information and Cooperation (AITIC). The views
expressed in this article are the responsibility of the author and should not be taken as those of AITIC.

I. Introduction: The Importance of Definitions

During the last fifty or so years international trade has been a powerful engine of growth and trade has become a key component of the economic strategies of all major countries. This statement, apart from being evident, is uncontroversial. What is not so evident, and may prove contentious, is how to make it possible for all countries to share the benefits of trade and to ensure that the developing and least-developed countries do not become casualties of the globalisation process. Some may argue that trade-related capacity building is a *sine qua non* condition to achieve this end.

It is also indisputable that not all countries have participated either in international trade or in the rules-making body, the World Trade Organization ("WTO") and its predecessor, the General Agreement on Tariffs and Trade ("GATT"). The GATT, which came into force in 1948, was set up to create a stable and predictable environment for liberalising international trade and undoing the results of the tide of protectionism that had exacerbated the effects of the Great Depression and had contributed in no small part to the second global armed conflict. Subsequently, after eight rounds of multilateral trade negotiations under the GATT that had greatly advanced trade liberalisation, the WTO was established in 1995, after the completion of the Uruguay Round negotiations. The Uruguay Round was the most ambitious of all of the GATT negotiating rounds. It resulted in agreements on disciplines on issues that went far beyond cross-border trade and gave the new organisation a greatly expanded scope, not only by bringing textiles and clothing into the regime and eliminating the exceptions that applied to agricultural trade, but by broadening the coverage of the rules to other areas, including trade in services and trade-related aspects of intellectual property rights.

After the successful completion of the Uruguay Round, it was clear that membership in the WTO—which had by April 2003 had expanded to 146, compared with the 23 original Contracting Parties to the GATT—did not by itself entail full involvement in the system, either measured by contribution to global trade or involvement in the activities and negotiations of the WTO. A wide gap existed between the active participation of a select few, mostly the OECD countries, and the scant contribution of most developing countries, with a few exceptions, such as Brazil and India.

In the fifty odd years since the GATT came into being and multilateral trading rules were established, integration of developing countries into the multilateral trading system has been an important objective of the more active traders. However, despite much lip service paid to "integrating the developing countries into the multilateral trading system", the definition of what this means and the ways of achieving it have not been clearly formulated. It can be assumed that integrating countries with a low level of participation in international trade implies that they will genuinely become part of the global trading system by increasing their exports and their contribution to overall trade. Similarly, and a logical conclusion, is that their increased involvement and contribution to the global expansion of trade will lead them to a more active participation in the activities of the rules-making body, the WTO, and in the negotiations that take place under its aegis. The reverse, i.e. that a better understanding of the rules will lead them to be more active traders is not so evident. To be able to export, countries need to produce something that is exportable, quite apart from having an understanding of the trade-related multilateral rules. Those potential traders that have traditionally been inactive also need to overcome the supply-side constraints that have made it difficult for them to achieve efficient production for export.

Another basic term that is in need of an agreed definition is "trade related technical co-operation and capacity building" ("TRTCCB") for developing countries.[1] It is surprising to note that, although TRTCCB has acquired such overwhelming importance, a clear, explicit definition of what it is, and what its components are, is rarely found. A few attempts have been made to define TRTCCB, but they are usually either vague or elusive. The OECD has examined this issue and has provided a definition that focuses on differentiating trade-related capacity building today from that of the past. From the OECD viewpoint, capacity building in the past was synonymous with institution–building, whereas "today is synonymous with building systems or networks . . . often across borders to achieve common objectives. The network promotes a critical mass of human and institutional resources that can overcome the limits inherent in the old approach"[2]. At present, according to the OECD, capacity building for trade involves mobilising participatory approaches to deal with the trade agendas, thus developing expertise of policy-makers, the private sector and civil society. This expertise in turn would contribute to a number of objectives, including: formulation and implementation of a trade development strategy, firmly placed in the broader national development strategy; diversifying and increasing the value-added of exports and creating foreign investment regimes through reforming import regimes and strengthening trade policy and institutions; and participating in and benefiting from the institutions and negotiations and processes that conform national trade policy and the rules of international trade[3]. A crisper definition, adapted from the OECD Guidelines[4]. views TRTCCB as a "broad range of activities" aimed at effective participation in the global trading system and helping countries exploit their comparative advantage[5].

So, simplifying this attempt at a broad definition of TRTCCB, there are at least two distinct components of TRTCCB: one, general and systemic, views technical assistance and capacity-building in a wide sense, to consist of a "domestic" and "concrete" approach that would provide assistance to acquire the know-how to design policies conducive to including trade in overall policy-making, to reform the trade policy regime to facilitate export diversification and expansion, and although not explicitly included in the OECD definition, to provide financial and other means to overcome problems related to supply-side constraints. A second component of TRTCCB relates to an "international" and more "abstract" approach, that focuses on assisting developing country officials to participate in (and benefit from) the institutions and negotiations relating to the rules of international trade, i.e. assistance to acquire a better understanding of the WTO Agreements to ensure compliance, as well as more effective participation in WTO activities, including negotiations.

The two components of TRTCCB described above, namely assistance to trade more and assistance to understand international trade rules better are two sides of the same coin: real integration into the multilateral trading system necessitates a holistic approach that would include capacity to produce exportable goods or services and to develop

[1] For brevity's sake, in this article, the term "developing countries" refers to different groups of resource-constrained countries or customs territories that are members of or observers to the WTO, including the 49 least-developed countries ("LDCs") as designated by the UN, small island developing and land-locked countries, small and vulnerable economies and several transition economies, mostly those in Central Asia.
[2] OECD, *Trade and Development in the New Global Context: the Capacity Dimension*, in www.oecd.org.
[3] *Id.*
[4] OECD, *Strengthening Trade Capacity for Development. The DAC Guidelines* (2001).
[5] Federico Boinaglia and Kiichiro Fukasaku, *Export Diversification in Low-Income Countries: An International Challenge after Doha,* OECD Development Centre, Technical Papers 209 (2003) at 9.

adequate physical infrastructure (roads, ports, customs facilities) on the one hand, and on the other the training of government officials to enable them to understand, implement and negotiate internationally-agreed rules.

However, the attention—and resources—committed to TRTCCB is not in direct relation to the time and effort devoted to giving thought to what it consists of, what are the concrete objectives pursued through it (apart from the triteness of "closer integration into the multilateral trading system"), what are the best means to deliver it, and how best to evaluate its results. It would seem logical that more consideration should be given to these matters prior to making TRTCCB such an important constituent part of development cooperation plans in general and of the Doha Work Programme of the WTO in particular. A more systematic approach to TRTCCB seems necessary to make the most of the vast resources that have been made available for TRTCCB.

Without well-defined objectives, specific deadlines and means of assessing results, the extent of the resources available for TRTCCB is of no consequence. Several bilateral donors concerned with TRTCCB and the multilateral institutions that provide it have realised this need. Indeed there have been some noteworthy attempts to try to rationalise TRTCCB and to foster inter-agency and donor coordination. However, in view of the enormous needs, of the multiplicity of areas to be covered, and of the bilateral, multilateral, regional, official and non-governmental institutions involved, it is a tall order to instil a measure of coherence and effectiveness into TRTCCB.

The main objective of this chapter is to provide an inventory and analysis of the resources available for TRTCCB offered to developing countries, concentrating on the more restrictive interpretation, i.e. TRTCCB that refers to improving the understanding of multilateral trade rules and achieving greater participation in negotiating them. Part II of the chapter traces how and why TRTCCB has evolved to acquire the prominent place within trade and development agencies it has today. Part III sets the framework by a brief description of the "core" TRTCCB resources within the three trade-related Geneva-based organisations—the WTO, the United Nations Conference on Trade and Development ("UNCTAD") and the International Trade Centre ("ITC")—and their mandate. To complement this section, Part IV provides an overview of which Uruguay Round Agreements have TRTCCB built in, and what kind of TRTCCB is contemplated in them. An illustration of how TRTCCB as foreseen in the Uruguay Round Agreements has fared in practice is given through a couple of examples of TRTCCB: in TRIPS, which exemplifies the wide spectrum of institutions that have taken initiatives to provide TRTCCB, and Dispute Settlement, which demonstrates in practice the limitations of the WTO Secretariat in providing TRTCCB, due to its obligation to remain neutral and its frequent administrative changes regarding TRTCCB.

II. Recent Evolution of Trade-Related Capacity Building: The Basis for its Increasing Importance

The importance of TRTCCB has been growing, first gradually, then exponentially, particularly after the WTO was established in 1995. At the first Ministerial Conference of the new organisation held in Singapore in December 1996 a momentous decision was taken: a Plan of Action for the Least-Developed Countries which sought to render operational the *Decision on Measures in Favour of Least-Developed Countries* (an integral part of the results of the Uruguay Round Negotiations) through a series of "actions," such as improving their capacity to meet their notification obligations, assisting in trade-related institutional capacity building by a comprehensive approach with a division of labour between the relevant organisations: UNCTAD, ITC, the World Bank, the International Monetary Fund ("IMF"), the United Nations Development Programme ("UNDP"), and regional development banks, with the participation of the OECD's Development Assistance Committee ("DAC"), and in cooperation with the WTO. The Decision also called for improved market access through preferential access with the possibility of granting duty- free access.[6]

The implementation of this Decision took place in October 1997, with the launching of the Integrated Framework for trade-related technical assistance for Least-Developed Countries ("IF"), which was a joint programme of six agencies: the IMF, the ITC, UNCTAD, UNDP, the World Bank and the WTO. It focused attention on the importance of TRTCCB and the desirability of rationalising it. Donors and recipients, aware of the lack of coordination of inter-governmental organisations ("IGOs") that accounted for a certain inefficiency in the provision of TRTCCB, sought to create a framework that would coordinate TRTCCB activities between the concerned IGOs, avoid duplicative activities and render TRTCCB more effective.

TRTCCB thus became firmly established as a prime objective. Following the Second Ministerial Conference of the WTO held in Geneva in 1998, which was mostly a celebratory occasion marking the fiftieth anniversary of the multilateral trading system, the importance of TRTCCB began to acquire increasing visibility and political importance. Most of the speeches from developed country representatives applauded the launching of the IF at the High-Level meeting that had taken place in October 1997. Developed countries' enthusiasm is illustrated by the announcement of the UK Prime Minister, Tony Blair, at the Geneva Ministerial that Britain would contribute £6 million ($10 million) to help developing countries participate in the multilateral trading system.

Since then, the importance of TRTCCB has soared. At present, it is not a deficit of resources devoted to TRTCCB that is the problem. The difficulty at present relates more to a surplus of TRTCCB, at times uncoordinated and without a well-defined focus or goal, as well as a waning absorptive capacity on the part of TRTCCB recipients. However, little has been done to assess and evaluate what has worked and what is leading to waste resources without achieving clear results. There has been no evaluation of the modes of delivery for TRTCCB to help make it more effective.

The realisation that during the most ambitious round of multilateral trade negotiations developing country participation had been scarce, led several of the developed country members to seek to correct this imbalance. Despite the growth in the number of WTO members, mostly from the developing world, in the wake of the completion of the Uruguay Round, few developing countries had a clear idea of what were the commitments they had signed on to and what rights they had achieved in return. As the scope of international trade rules broadened to cover issues beyond cross-border trade and extended to other areas of economic activity, developed countries realised that only if developing countries received assistance to understand the new rules would they be able to comply with them.

At the same time, developing countries became aware of the gap that existed between them and the developed countries, particularly as they began to face the difficulties of implementing the Uruguay Round Agreements. This awareness became more acute as the transition periods drew to a close. To be able to take advantage of the special conditions granted to developing countries under the special and differential treatment provisions, developing countries became convinced of the need to achieve a more thorough

---

[6] WT/MIN(96)/14, *Comprehensive and Integrated WTO Plan of Action for the Least-Developed Countries*, January 7, 1997.

understanding of the WTO Agreements and international trade rules. Indeed, part of this special and differential treatment took the form of TRTCCB. Finally, if new negotiations were to take place, developing countries grasped the importance of TRTCCB as a means of improving their negotiating skills, increasing their bargaining power and ultimately defending their interests effectively. However, there was another side to this: TRTCCB could be used as a bargaining chip by developed countries to nudge developing countries into agreeing to begin negotiations on new areas that developing countries were not certain it was in their interest to negotiate.

Interestingly, in the last fifty years the position of TRTCCB in the scale of priorities has dramatically changed: in the GATT 1947 (and 1994) there is not a single article that refers to technical cooperation. In contrast, several of the Uruguay Round Agreements have not only references, but also full articles devoted to technical assistance, at times making its provision legally binding, as will be seen below. Naturally, as mentioned above, the recognition that to be able to comply with the agreements, developing countries needed technical cooperation, the Uruguay Round Agreements that include the granting of technical cooperation within their provisions relate to the more "technical" subjects or the new issues.

The Doha Ministerial Declaration moved much further ahead on the recognition of the importance of TRTCCB, recognising that "sustainably financed technical assistance and capacity-building programmes have important roles to play" in ensuring that developing countries "secure a share in the growth of world trade commensurate with the needs of their economic development".[7] There is a sharp contrast between the GATT 1947, where technical assistance is not mentioned even once in a 28,000-word document and the Doha Ministerial Declaration, a five thousand-word document, where technical assistance is mentioned nineteen times.

III. The Geneva Three-Pronged Approach

Three closely related institutions dealing with trade issues in Geneva (i.e. the WTO, UNCTAD and the ITC) have substantial programmes of trade-related technical cooperation. However, problems of overlapping, duplication and effective use of resources have become apparent. Member countries, particularly bilateral donors, have shown an interest in instilling some order in what is perceived as a somewhat anarchic web of TRTCCB programmes, whose usefulness did not always seem to match the expectations. One course of action was to call for closer integration of TRTCCB. Cases in point are the *Joint Integrated Technical Assistance Programme to Selected Least Developed and Other African Countries* ("JITAP"), jointly sponsored by the WTO, UNCTAD and the ITC, and the *Integrated Framework for Trade-Related Technical Assistance* ("IF"), in which six international organisations participate, the three Geneva-based ones plus the World Bank, the IMF, and UNDP.

Each of the Geneva-based organisations has a specific and complementary mandate, although they are not the exclusive providers of TRTCCB. Other intergovernmental organisations, whose mandate is related to the subject of a particular WTO Agreement, provide TRTCCB to WTO members (and each has important technical cooperation programmes). With the risk of oversimplification, this is in essence the mandate of the Geneva-based trade-related IGOs:

The WTO is the rules-making body. It is also a forum for negotiations for the liberalisation of trade among its member countries and for resolution of trade disputes. Its

---

[7] WT/MIN(01)/DEC/W/, November 14, 2001, ¶ 2.

technical cooperation focuses on its own areas of competence. However, given that the Secretariat cannot interpret the Agreements, a prerogative of the Members, and in view of the requirement that the Secretariat maintains its neutrality, the role of the WTO in TRTCCB is confined to assisting Members to understand the agreements or to assist in their implementation. The Secretariat is not authorised to give policy advice or to touch on the implications of the agreements for the economic and development policies of the TRTCCB recipients. These limitations, of which members receiving TRTCCB have become increasingly aware, has led some developing country members to demand a TRTCCB which is more related to their needs. They also stressed the "value of quality over quantity", and proper auditing and evaluation of the WTO's TRTCCB were signalled as indispensable elements for accountability and transparency[8].

UNCTAD is a permanent conference[9] whose aim is to promote economic development, originally through trade. It has evolved to become the focal point within the UN for the "integrated treatment of development and interrelated issues in the areas of trade, finance, technology, investment and sustainable development". Its technical cooperation covers the four areas of its work programme[10] and thus is more diffuse than in the other two institutions. UNCTAD's "portfolio" of subjects goes beyond trade matters, and on trade the number of subjects is vast. Developing countries have come to regard UNCTAD as their own forum and have counted on this institution for providing the policy advice that WTO cannot give. Indeed, UNCTAD has provided valuable inputs for developing countries on most of the trade subjects under negotiation at the WTO. It is worthwhile mentioning the *Positive Agenda and Future Trade Negotiations*[11], which emerged after the first WTO Ministerial Conference in Singapore and assisted developing countries in preparing for the Ministerial Conference at Seattle and for the negotiations that were finally agreed to at Doha. Its focus was formulating proposals and counterproposals for actions in their interest, instead of the usual opposition to including certain subjects in the multilateral negotiating agenda. Similarly its Commercial Diplomacy Project has been active in providing TRTCCB to developing countries.

The International Trade Centre ("ITC"), the "daughter" organisation of the WTO and UNCTAD, based in Geneva, is "the focal point in the UN system for technical cooperation with developing countries in trade promotion". Its mission is to support developing and transition economies, and particularly their business sectors, to develop their export potential and improve import operations. It "is responsible for implementing UNDP-financed projects in developing countries and economies in transition related to trade promotion". The ITC is the only one of the three organisations that has technical cooperation as its mandate. ITC and UNCTAD depend to a large extent on UNDP and bilateral donors (Canada, Netherlands, Norway, Germany, Switzerland, Japan, the UK, etc.) for finance to back TRTCCB activities.

A preliminary impression—although this may be corrected after acquiring more familiarity with the institutions concerned—is that the organisations in Geneva, although paying lip service to closer coordination, in fact go their own way in the design and development of their technical cooperation activities. An example of this is the fact that

---

[8] WT/COMTD/43, *High Level Briefing Meeting on Technical Co-operation and Capacity Building for Capital-Based Senior Officials*, September 20, 2002.

[9] Although it started out as a UN Conference, UNCTAD evolved into a fully-fledged organisation, with its own programmes and secretariat.

[10] (i) Globalisation and development; (ii) investment, enterprise development and technology; (iii) international trade in goods and services and commodity issues; and (iv) services infrastructure for development and trade efficiency.

[11] UNCTAD/ITCD/TSB/10, July 1, 2000.

collaboration with other organisations does not figure as a criterion for evaluation of the WTO TRTCCB activities, as illustrated in the Technical Cooperation Audit Report for 2002[12]. The advisory services and group training activities of UNCTAD's International Trade in Goods and Services and Commodities programme have greatly overlapped with those of the WTO in areas such as assisting countries to understand the multilateral trading system and the WTO; options in the post-Uruguay Round framework; accession to the WTO, etc.

At times, the TRTCCB programmes, as presented by the organisations themselves, give the impression that some TRTCCB activities are conducted randomly (often on the back of activities already being organised by national institutions), dependent on fund-availability and justified as "demand-driven". To determine the extent to which TRTCCB activities are integrated between the different entities would require finding out what is the framework for joint TRTCCB, and the mechanism devised to formulate collaborative projects and strategies, ultimately resulting in joint activities and coordinated missions. Has any effort to create such a mechanism been made? *A priori,* isolated activities with participation of the three trade-related institutions do not necessarily reflect an integrated approach, nor do missions that include staff members of the three organisations.

IV. Technical Assistance in the Uruguay Round Agreements

As has already been mentioned, the stated objective of the provision of technical assistance in the Uruguay Round Agreements is mostly to facilitate implementation and enforcement of the Agreements by developing countries. Technical assistance is also understood to mean not only training of officials, but has wider connotations, including the provision of finance (credits, donations) and know-how, as well as assistance with building up infrastructure (equipment, laboratories). Furthermore, although the WTO Secretariat is mandated explicitly in the General Agreement on Trade in Services and in the Dispute Settlement Understanding to provide assistance, the Secretariat also provides TRTCCB with respect to all of the WTO agreements.

What follows is an inventory of TRTCB measures in the various WTO Agreements. This will give an idea of the enormity and complexity of the spectrum that TRTCCB is mandated to cover. It is also worth mentioning that apart from the explicitly stipulated provision of TRTCCB, there are other areas where TRTCCB is provided, including important areas such as the "new" areas, including those of the Singapore issues: trade and investment, trade and competition, transparency in government procurement, trade facilitation, as well as trade and environment, market access, rules, etc.

Article 9 of the Agreement on **Sanitary and Phytosanitary Measures** ("SPS") specifies that the members of the WTO will provide technical assistance to developing countries to allow them to adjust and comply with the SPS measures and to achieve appropriate protection in their export markets. The areas where technical assistance would be granted include processing technologies, research, and infrastructure to enable the setting up of national regulatory bodies. This assistance would be granted either bilaterally or through the appropriate international organisation, i.e. either one of the "three sisters" referred to in the Agreement, namely the three standard-setting organisations, the FAO/WHO Codex Alimentarius Commission, the International Animal Health Organization, and the FAO's Secretariat of the International Plant Protection Convention. The form that technical cooperation takes includes advice, credits, donations and grants, training and equipment. Furthermore, in the cases significant investments would be needed for an exporting developing country to fulfil the SPS measures of an importing member, the importing member "shall consider"[13] granting technical assistance to permit the developing country to maintain and expand its exports of the product involved.

Article 11 of the **Technical Barriers to Trade** ("TBT") Agreement is comprehensive in requiring developed country members to provide technical assistance on "mutually agreed terms and conditions", if so requested, to developing country members (and others) and giving priority to the LDCs on a number of issues: on establishing the institutions and legal framework which would enable them to fulfil the obligations of membership; to advise them on the preparation of technical regulations and the establishment of national standardizing or regulatory bodies and participation in them; for facilitating their participation in technical systems for conformity assessment. Technical assistance is stipulated also for developing country producers if they wish to have access to systems for conformity assessment operated by governmental or non-governmental bodies of the member they wish to export to.

Another technical agreement that has a section devoted to technical assistance is the **Customs Valuation Agreement** (the Agreement on Implementation of Article VII of the GATT 1994), in Part III, Article 20, under special and differential treatment. It states that developed countries have the obligation to provide technical assistance to those countries that so request and, on the basis of the requests, are to design programmes of technical assistance that would cover training of personnel, assistance in preparing implementation measures, information on customs valuation methodology, and how to apply the provisions of the Agreement. The implementation of the Customs Valuation Agreement by developing countries has been a main concern of developed countries.

Article 3.3 of the **Agreement on Pre-Shipment Inspection** also contains a clause specifying that, in order to assist in the achievement of the Agreement's objectives, exporter members "shall offer to provide" technical assistance.

Through Article 67 of the **Agreement on Trade-Related Aspects of Intellectual Property Rights ("TRIPS"),** WTO Members from developed countries commit themselves to the provision of technical and financial assistance to developing countries to facilitate implementation of the Agreement, through the preparation of laws and regulations for the enforcement of intellectual property rights and to prevent their abuse. The wide scope of the TRIPS Agreement has led a number of intergovernmental organisations to join the WTO in the intellectual property technical assistance and capacity building efforts. The World Intellectual Property Organization ("WIPO") has been active in this respect, in particular in assisting countries to draft legislation on intellectual property protection. WIPO and WTO signed an agreement for legal and technical assistance to developing countries that came into force on January 1, 1996.[14]

Article XXV of the **General Agreement on Trade in Services** is devoted to technical cooperation. It covers two kinds of technical assistance: bilateral and multilateral. With respect to bilateral assistance, it states that suppliers of services of Members that are in need of assistance shall have access to "contact points" established by developed country Members within two years of the entry into force of the WTO Agreements. The purpose of these points is to facilitate access of the developing country suppliers

---

[13] The word "shall" in WTO Agreements has a legally binding connotation.
[14] WIPO/TRIPS/2001/1, *WIPO's Legal and Technical Assistance to Developing Countries For the Implementation of the TRIPS Agreement From January 1 1996 to December 31 2000*", WIPO, Geneva.

to information on the commercial and technical aspects of the supply of services; the registration, recognition and obtaining of professional qualifications; and the availability of services technology.

At the multilateral level, technical assistance is entrusted to the WTO Secretariat, upon the decision of the Council for Trade in Services. This is in contrast to the TRIPS Agreement, on which other intergovernmental organisations, although not specifically mentioned in the Agreement, have been active in the provision of technical cooperation, in particular, WIPO. Through its Cooperation for Development Program, WIPO assists in the establishment or modernisation of intellectual property systems of developing countries, in particular of LDCs. Also, a bilateral donor organisation, the UK's Department for International Development ("DFID") established a Commission on Intellectual Property Rights to investigate how intellectual property rights "might work better for poor people and developing countries"[15].

A number of non-governmental organisations are also active in undertaking research and providing technical assistance to developing countries. On TRIPS, for example, the Quaker United Nations Office ("QUNO") in Geneva organises seminars for government delegates and staff of NGOs, corporations and IGO's, including the WTO, on subjects related to intellectual property rights, including the implications of the TRIPS Agreement for developing countries. QUNO has established a programme to support developing country negotiating capacity with the objective of avoiding the requirement of full patent coverage in the WTO rules.

The **Dispute Settlement Understanding** ("DSU") is the second Agreement that specifically mandates the Secretariat to offer technical assistance. Indeed, Article 27.2 stipulates that, as developing country Members may need legal advice and assistance with respect to dispute settlement, "the Secretariat shall make available a qualified legal expert from the WTO technical cooperation services to any developing country Member which so requests."

In accordance with this mandate, the Technical Cooperation Division set up a unit on Legal Advice to Developing Countries, also in charge of coordinating four-day dispute settlement courses at the headquarters of the WTO in Geneva. These courses are open to delegations and participants from all WTO Members. The unit was staffed with one or two junior legal affairs officers. These officers were always the first contact for delegations of developing countries wishing to raise any matter related to the DSU, including general information on its functioning, technical legal advice on the feasibility of potential cases, and in the end, referral to outside legal experts for specific advice. These outside legal experts work with the WTO on a consultancy basis. Two outside senior legal experts were under contract with the Secretariat on a part-time basis (one day per week) to assist developing countries bringing cases to the DSB. In 1998, the Budget, Finance and Administration Committee of the WTO decided, in keeping with the priorities of the Director General, to include in the 1999 Budget proposals three additional professional staff for the provision of legal expertise, at a cost of almost 500,000 Swiss Francs.

However, although in 1999 senior management of the WTO considered the provision of legal assistance as a priority, two years later, the unit on Legal Advice to Developing Countries disappeared from the new Technical Cooperation Division[16], the coordination of the Dispute Settlement courses was turned over to the Training Division and the legal advice work continued on an ad hoc basis through the regional coordinators.

---

[15] http://www.iprcommission.org.
[16] *See* organisational chart adopted in June 2001.

An important point that emerges from the DSU-related technical assistance that has a bearing on the global provision of TRTCCB by the WTO is related to the question of why did the negotiators of the DSU decide to place the legal advice activity within the technical cooperation services of the Secretariat? The answer is the requirement of the "continued impartiality of the Secretariat", specified by the last sentence of Article 27.2 of the DSU. Placing the responsibility for legal advice in the Legal Division would probably have impaired this impartiality, so that a firewall had to be set up between the legal servicing responsibilities of the Legal Affairs Division to the DSU and the legal advice services provided as technical assistance to developing countries.

The illustration of how many official and non-official organisations are involved in providing TRTCCB on the specific subject of TRIPS, as seen above, can be extended to the rest of the Agreements. Thus, if each area was to be researched and the resources available for TRTCCB on each of them calculated, the figures would be staggering. This is illustrated by a WTO and the OECD report, issued in December 2002. This report provides a database of the TRTCCB activities related only to the Doha Work Programme in 2001. It indicates that there were around 4500 different activities provided by 28 multilateral donors. The baseline for 2001 reveal over 1200 commitments to activities identified with the Doha Declaration, amounting to US$466 million, and a further 1300 activities related to trade development for a total of US$1.02 billion[17].

The modes of delivery of building capacity in resource-constrained countries are also worth considering. Most trade-capacity building activities are delivered through seminars and workshops. However, although the limitations of this mode of delivery are well known, more effective alternatives are still to be implemented. Long-term training and capacity building are costly and not practical for officials who have routine responsibilities that make it impossible for them to engage in full-time training. However, other alternatives would include private sector involvement, in modalities yet to be determined. Finally, academic programmes in universities and institutions of higher education are also viable options to consider, although these would require a longer time perspective than the short- to medium term urgency imposed by the negotiating programme. In any case, further discussion on effective means of providing capacity building on trade and investment seem essential if TRTCCB are to improve the effective participation of developing countries in any future trade negotiations and assist them in implementing the Agreements and benefiting from multilaterally agreed trade rules.

V. Conclusion

The brief overview of the resources available for TRTCCB, the subjects that it covers and the actors involved in providing it, may lead to some frustration on how to begin tackling the challenging task of assessing whether or not efforts relating to TRTCCB are efficient and effective. It is extremely difficult to measure the effectiveness of something as abstract as TRTCCB. Although answers to these questions are not likely to be arrived at easily, at least donors and recipients of TRTCCB and the institutions themselves are posing the questions. The OECD's Development Assistance Committee has provided the first such answer by the way of the guidelines for TRTCCB[18]. This has been the first step, although more reflection is needed to achieve concrete results from TRTCCB. Some

---

[17] WTO/OECD, *First Joint WTO/OECD Report on Trade-Related Technical Assistance and Capacity Building*, Geneva/ Paris, November/December 2002.
[18] *Supra,* note 3.

thought should be given of the modes of delivery. Seminars and workshops that account for the lion's share of the TRTCCB's budgets are useful, but other more effective means of delivery should be found.

Coherence has been often mentioned, and it is indeed a key concept in all trade (and other) policy formulation, both at the international as well as the domestic level. The need for greater international policy coherence was among the significant results of the Uruguay Round. Coherence must surely involve not only international organisations but should also be part of the donor community's efforts regarding technical cooperation. Effective coordination amongst donors should become a permanent feature of TRTCCB.

BIBLIOGRAPHY

Bonaglia, Federico and Kiichiro Fukasaku, *Export Diversification in Low-Income Countries: An International Challenge after Doha,* OECD Development Centre, Technical Papers 209, Paris, June 2003.

DFID, *Eliminating World Poverty, Making Globalisation Work for the Poor, White Paper on International Development*, London, 2000.

Japan International Cooperation Agency, *Japanese Approach for WTO Capacity Building Cooperation—Basic Concept and Measures,* JICA, Tokyo 2003.

Luke, David, *Rethinking the Poverty Reduction Strategy Paper (PRSP) as an Instrument of Mainstreaming Trade Capacity Development,* Paper presented at the OECD Regional Workshop on Trade Capacity Building, Mombasa, Kenya, 26–27 August 2002.

OECD, *Strengthening Trade Capacity for Development. The DAC Guidelines*, Paris, OECD, 2001.

Pallangyo, Abraham, *Integrated Approaches to Trade Capacity Building Lessons from the JITAP*, Paper presented at the OECD Regional Workshop on Trade Capacity Building, Mombasa, Kenya, 26–27 August 2002.

UNCTAD, *Positive Agenda and Future Trade Negotiations*, (UNCTAD/ITCD/TSB/10), 1 July 200.

UNDP, *Making Global trade Work for People*, London, Earthscan Publications, 2003.

WTO/OECD, *First Joint WTO/OECD Report on Trade-Related Technical Assistance and Capacity Building*, Geneva/ Paris, November/December 2002.

World Intellectual Property Organization, *WIPO 's Legal and Technical Assistance to Developing Countries For the Implementation of the TRIPS Agreement From January 1 1996 to December 31 200"*, WIPO, Geneva

CHAPTER 56

TRADE AND ELECTRONIC COMMERCE

Stewart Baker and Maury Shenk*

TABLE OF CONTENTS

* Stewart Baker and Maury Shenk are partners in the Technology Group of the law firm Steptoe & Johnson LLP. Mr. Baker is based in Washington, D.C. and Mr. Shenk is based in London.

I. Introduction

Much of electronic commerce (or "e-commerce") is governed by the same basic principles of GATT, GATS, TRIPS and other WTO agreements that apply to offline commerce. For example, it should not matter for purposes of trade analysis if a physician delivers cross-border medical advice by letter, by telephone, or via the Internet. And a book that is ordered online from Amazon.com is still subject to ordinary GATT principles when it is delivered internationally. However, in important respects the WTO system must adapt to e-commerce—both through changes to existing rules and adoption of new rules. This chapter considers the new WTO issues presented by e-commerce.

II. History of Electronic Commerce at the WTO

A. Basic Telecommunications Agreement

The first significant negotiations at the WTO in which e-commerce was explicitly discussed were the 1995–1997 negotiations of the Basic Telecommunications Agreement, which involved commitments on basic telecommunications (*i.e.*, services for transmission of electronic communications without alteration of the information transmitted)—an area on which agreement had not been reached at the time GATS was initially agreed and which until the negotiations remained outside the most-favored nation obligation of GATS.[1] While basic telecommunications services are not typically considered to be "e-commerce", basic telecommunications provide the transmission infrastructure of the Internet, which was rapidly entering the global consciousness at the time that the Basic Telecommunications Agreement was being negotiated.

The Basic Telecommunications Agreement involved 69 countries representing over 95 percent of the global market for basic telecommunications services,[2] and a number of countries have made subsequent commitments on basic telecommunications through WTO accession.[3] Fifty-five of the countries joining the Basic Telecommunications Agreement (and others later joining through accession) adopted a "Reference Paper" setting out regulatory commitments for basic telecommunications.[4] There is a significant amount of variation among the scope of commitments under the Basic Telecommunications Agreement, with developed countries generally guaranteeing much more open markets than developing countries. Given the nascent nature of the Internet at the time of the Basic Telecommunications Agreement negotiations, the negotiations did not resolve any of the key issues for e-commerce—although the negotiating parties discussed some of these issues and recognised that significant questions regarding the Internet and e-commerce were left on the table. Therefore, the commitments under the agreement address e-commerce only to the limited extent discussed in Part II.C.1 below—*i.e.*, to the extent that basic telecommunications services supply the infrastructure for e-commerce.

[1] *See* GATS, *Annex on Negotiations on Basic Telecommunications*; Fourth Protocol to the General Agreement on Trade in Services, WTO Doc. S/L/20 (April 30, 1996).
[2] *See id.*; *Basic Telecom Negotiations, Statement of Ambassador Charlene Barshefsky* (Feb. 15, 1997), available at http://www.ustr.gov/releases/1997/02/barshefsky.pdf.
[3] *See, e.g.,* Republic of Estonia, Schedule of Specific Commitments, WTO Doc. GATS/SC/127 (Oct. 5, 1999); Oman, Schedule of Specific Commitments, WTO Doc. GATS/SC/132 (Dec. 22, 2000); Republic of Croatia, Schedule of Specific Commitments, WTO Doc. GATS/SC/130 (Dec. 22, 2000).
[4] *See, e.g., United States of America, Schedule of Specific Commitments*, WTO Doc. GATS/SC/90/Suppl.2 (Apr. 11, 1997).

B. Work Programme on Electronic Commerce

At the Second Ministerial Meeting held in Geneva in May 1998, the WTO adopted a Declaration on Global Electronic Commerce, which stated:

> The General Council shall, by its next meeting in special session, establish a comprehensive work programme to examine all trade-related issues relating to global electronic commerce, including those issues identified by Members. The work programme will involve the relevant World Trade Organization ("WTO") bodies, take into account the economic, financial, and development needs of developing countries, and recognize that work is also being undertaken in other international fora.[5]

The General Council formally established the Work Programme on Electronic Commerce ("Work Programme") on September 30, 1998.[6]

The most important products of the Work Programme so far are four interim reports issued in mid-1999 by the Council for Trade in Goods,[7] the Council for Trade in Services,[8] the Council for Trade-Related Aspects of Intellectual Property Rights,[9] and the Committee on Trade and Development.[10] These reports sought to identify broad issues for e-commerce and the positions of WTO Members on such issues, but did not engage in extensive substantive analysis. For example, both the Council for Trade in Goods and of the Council for Trade in Services set out the various viewpoints on the "classification debate" discussed below, without attempting to resolve the issue.[11] Likewise, the Council for Trade in Services identified the ambiguity regarding modes 1 and 2 for delivery of services (which is discussed in Part II.C.3 below), "but no conclusion was reached as to how to clarify the matter."[12] The Council for Trade-Related Aspects of Intellectual Property Rights and the Committee on Trade and Development both noted that bodies other than the WTO play a major substantive role in formulating rules for e-commerce.[13]

A striking aspect of the Work Programme, and of the four interim reports, is that in 1998 and 1999 e-commerce was clearly one of the major items on the WTO agenda. Nevertheless, other than providing a forum for discussions on trade issues for e-commerce, the Work Programme did not make significant progress in any of the relevant substantive areas—other than the agreement to maintain the moratorium on customs duties on electronic transmissions (discussed below). Therefore, although e-commerce is now lower on the WTO agenda, much work in the area remains to be done.

---

[5] *Declaration on Global Electronic Commerce,* WTO Doc. WT/MIN(98)/DEC/2 (May 20, 1998) ("*Second Ministerial E-Commerce Declaration*"), text reproduced in the Appendix to this book.

[6] *Work Programme on Electronic Commerce*, WTO Doc. WT/L/274 (Sept. 20, 1998).

[7] *Interim Review of Progress in the Implementation of the Work Programme on Electronic Commerce*, WTO Doc. WT/GC/24 (Apr. 12, 1999) ("*Work Programme Goods Report*").

[8] *Work Programme on Electronic Commerce, Progress Report to the General Council*, WTO Doc. S/L/74 (July 27, 1999) ("*Work Programme Services Report*").

[9] *Work Programme on Electronic Commerce, Progress Report to the General Council*, WTO Doc. IP/C/18 (July 30, 1999) ("*Work Programme TRIPS Report*").

[10] *Contribution by the Committee on Trade and Development to the WTO Work Programme on Electronic Commerce*, WTO Doc. WT/COMTD/19 (July 15, 1999)("*Work Programme Development Report*").

[11] *Work Programme Goods Report, supra* note 7, ¶¶ 2.3–2.11; *Work Programme Services Report, supra* note 8, ¶ 6.

[12] *Work Programme Services Report, supra* note 8, ¶ 5.

[13] *Work Programme TRIPS Report, supra* note 9, ¶¶ 6–7 (noting role of WIPO*); Work Programme Development Report, supra* note 10, ¶ 17 (noting role of UNCTAD and other organizations).

C. Seattle Ministerial

E-commerce remained high on the WTO agenda at the time of the Third Ministerial Meeting in Seattle in late 1999. Sources within the U.S. government believed that e-commerce was a leading issue on which meaningful agreement was possible in Seattle. For example, it was expected that progress could be made on the "classification debate" (discussed below) and on expansion of GATS commitments for e-commerce. However, as is well known, for a variety of reasons the Seattle Ministerial ended without agreement on these and other issues.

D. Doha Round

By the time of the November 2001 Fourth Ministerial Meeting in Doha, Qatar, e-commerce had assumed a much lower profile at the WTO—as a result of the collapse of the "dotcom" bubble, the substantial contraction in the e-commerce-based "new economy", and the emergence of other priorities in the work programme of trade negotiations initiated at the meeting (e.g., developing country issues; environment, labour and health issues; investment; government procurement). However, e-commerce remains on the agenda and received some new attention during the preparations for the Doha Round. In June 2001 and June 2002, the WTO General Council held discussions on e-commerce that addressed, among other things, the classification debate, development issues and fiscal implications of e-commerce.[14]

In Doha, the WTO has explicitly decided to continue the Work Programme. The Doha Ministerial Declaration states:

Electronic Commerce

34. We take note of the work which has been done in the General Council and other relevant bodies since the Ministerial Declaration of 20 May 1998 and agree to continue the Work Programme on Electronic Commerce. The work to date demonstrates that electronic commerce creates new challenges and opportunities for trade for Members at all stages of development, and we recognize the importance of creating and maintaining an environment which is favourable to the future development of electronic commerce. We instruct the General Council to consider the most appropriate institutional arrangements for handling the Work Programme, and to report on further progress to the Fifth Session of the Ministerial Conference. We declare that Members will maintain their current practice of not imposing customs duties on electronic transmissions until the Fifth Session.[15]

The activities of the Work Programme are continuing as the Doha Round begins.[16]

III. Current Issues at the WTO for Electronic Commerce

A. The Classification Debate—Goods vs. Services

An important background for e-commerce issues under GATT and GATS is the "classification debate" at the WTO regarding whether products sold through e-commerce should

---

[14] *Dedicated Discussion of Electronic Commerce Under the Auspices of the General Council 15 June 2001*, WTO Doc. WT/GC/W/436 (July 6, 2001) ("*2001 Discussion*"); *Second Dedicated Discussion on Electronic Commerce*, WTO Doc. WT/GC/W/475 (June 20, 2002) ("*2002 Discussion*"); *see also Communication from Switzerland*, WTO Doc. IP/C/W/286 (June 22, 2001) (addressing TRIPS issues for e-commerce).

[15] *Ministerial Declaration*, WTO Doc. WT/MIN(01)/DEC/1 (Nov. 20, 2001) ("*Fourth Ministerial Declaration*"), reproduced in the Appendix to this book.

[16] *See, e.g., Work Programme on Electronic Commerce in the Committee on Trade and Development*, WTO Doc. WT/COMTD/35 (Dec. 19, 2001) ("*2001 CTD Report*").

be treated as goods or services (or some hybrid of the two).[17] There is consensus that goods ordered electronically but delivered in physical form are subject to GATT and the other Multilateral Agreements on Trade in Goods, and that "real world" services that are delivered online (*e.g.*, medical or legal services) are subject to GATS.[18] The debate centers around content-based "digitized products", including music, books and video, that can be delivered either in physical or electronic form.

The classification debate is important because of the greater trade protections that are available under the long-established GATT rules for trade in goods than under the much newer GATS rules for trade in services.[19] The United States has been the primary advocate of the position that digitized products should be treated as goods and benefit from GATT protections:

> While some have suggested that all commerce based on electronic transmission is a service, this conclusion needs further examination.... While the <u>transmission</u> of these products can certainly be characterized as a service, the products themselves are not consumed in their transmission, but rather retain a permanence analogous to the goods world.... The United States is not arguing that intangibles should be classified as "goods" in the traditional sense. Given the broader reach of WTO disciplines accorded by the GATT (i.e. market access and national treatment are not dependent on specific commitments) there may be an advantage to a GATT versus GATS approach to such products which could provide for a more trade-liberalizing outcome for electronic commerce.[20]

The U.S. position gained some support from Japan,[21] but was at least initially a clear minority view at the WTO. However, the U.S. position has been much more seriously discussed in the beginning of the Doha Round.[22]

At the other end of the spectrum, the EU contends categorically that digitized products should be treated as services:

[17] *See, e.g.,* Council for Trade in Goods, *Work Programme on Electronic Commerce, Information Provided to the General Council,* ("wide range of opinions and questions regarding the characterization of the content of electronically transmitted digitalized data"); *Work Programme Services Report, supra* note 8, at ¶ 6. It is generally agreed that in order to avoid the need to develop an entirely new trade regime, e-products should not be classified as "something else" other than goods or services.

[18] *See, e.g.,* United Nations Conference on Trade and Development, *E-Commerce and Development Report 2001,* at 126 (Nov. 2001) ("*UNCTAD E-Commerce Report*") ("a number of commodities... traditionally have been shipped physically and been subject to border tariffs, but which today can be transformed into a digitized format and sent through the Internet").

[19] Under Articles I and III of the GATT, all goods imported from WTO Members must receive MFN and National Treatment. Under the GATS, by contrast, Members could take an exception from the MFN requirement for particular service sectors at the time of negotiation, and National Treatment is only provided for sectors with respect to which a Member has made a positive commitment. See Chapter 19 of this book.

[20] *Work Programme on Electronic Commerce,* Submission by the United States, WTO Doc. WT/GC/16, at 5 (Feb. 12, 1999) ("*U.S. Submission*").

[21] *See Preparations for the 1999 Ministerial Conference, Electronic Commerce,* Communication from Japan, WTO Doc. WT/GC/W/253, at 1 (July 14, 1999) ("With respect to the treatment of digital contents transmitted electronically, it is appropriate to examine the issue further so that the principles stipulated under GATT, namely the most-favoured-nation treatment, national treatment and the general elimination of quantitative restrictions, can be applied to such contents.").

[22] *See* 2002 Discussion, *supra* note 14 ("Many delegations highlighted the classification issue as a key element in the Work Programme, and felt that it was not desirable to try to seek a definitive determination of the classification of digital products in their entirety as either goods or services."); *see also* 2001 Discussion, *supra* note 14, at 1–2; *Discussion Paper: The Classification of Software Delivered Electronically,* Non-Paper from Canada (Apr. 29, 2002).

Electronic commerce involves two types of deliveries:

— goods delivered physically, while ordered electronically, which fall within the scope of the GATT;
— electronic deliveries, which consist of services and therefore fall within the scope of the GATS.[23]

The EU position commands fairly substantial support among WTO Members. This support appears to be due to a number of factors, including the practical considerations described in Part II.A.3 below, and the fact that a services classification offers more scope for protection of national service providers from competition by the powerful e-commerce companies of the United States.

Other WTO Member countries have taken a moderate approach, focusing on the principle that WTO rules should not discriminate between digitized products and their physical analogues. For example, Indonesia and Singapore have stated:

> The advent of digitized products however has blurred the boundary between goods and services.... Whatever the classification, the basic principles of MFN and national treatment have to apply in order to ensure fair, open and transparent market access for e-commerce.[24]

We consider the classification debate under three general frameworks: theoretical principles regarding the nature of goods and services; certain basic WTO trade principles; and practical considerations of whether trade in digitized products is best administered under GATT or GATS.

1. Theoretical Principles

It has been argued that essential characteristics of goods are that they possess value which can be owned, exist independently of their owners, and can be traded.[25] Services, by contrast, involve some desired change caused by the service provider to something owned by the consumer or to the physical or mental state of the consumer himself. The delivery of a service requires a relationship between the service provider and consumer.[26] Under this analysis, digitized products that can be owned, including books, music and video, constitute goods, even though they do not have tangible form. Increasingly however, suppliers are offering such products in forms that look more like services (*e.g.*, streaming audio, video on demand).

Another approach is that a good is tangible while a service is an intangible, a distinction that played a role in the WTO Appellate Body decision in *Canada—Certain Measures Concerning Periodicals*.[27] In that case, Canada argued that a tax on periodicals applied to advertisements and was thus subject to GATS rules. The Appellate Body found that

---

[23] *Preparations for the 1999 Ministerial Conference, Work Programme on Electronic Commerce*, Communication from the European Communities and their Member States, WTO Doc. WT/GC/W/306, at ¶ 1 (Aug. 9, 1999).

[24] *Preparations for the 1999 Ministerial Conference, Work Programme on Electronic Commerce*, Communication from Indonesia and Singapore, WTO Doc. WT/GC/W/247, at 2–3 (July 9, 1999); *see also* 2001 Discussion, *supra* note 14, at 2 ("It was suggested that certain products now categorized as goods and enjoying national treatment and duty-free access under the ITA and GATT should continue to be given similar treatment if it were agreed that they should be classified as services.").

[25] Peter Hill, *Tangibles, Intangibles and Services: A New Taxonomy for the Classification of Output*, 32 CANADIAN J. ECON. 426, 437–41 (1999).

[26] *Id.* at 441–43.

[27] Report of the Appellate Body, *Canada—Certain Measures Concerning Periodicals*, WT/DS31/AB/R, at 3–4 (1997).

while advertising and editorial content had "service attributes," they formed a "physical product" in the periodical itself.[28]

Finally, it is possible that digitized products could be treated as *both* goods and services, and that trade in digitized products could be governed by both GATT and GATS.[29] The WTO Appellate Body most recently considered this issue in the *EC Bananas* case:

> Certain measures . . . could be found to fall within the scope of both the GATT 1994 and the GATS. These are measures that involve a service relating to a particular good . . . However, while the same measure could be scrutinized under both agreements, the specific aspects of that measure examined under each agreement could be different . . . Whether a certain measure affecting the supply of a service related to a particular good is scrutinized under the GATT 1994 or the GATS, or both, is a matter that can only be determined on a case-by-case basis.[30]

While classification of digitized products as both goods and services is thus theoretically possible, such a classification would likely produce substantial confusion regarding which trade rules to apply to particular types of transactions.

In sum, there is no clear principle that establishes whether the essential nature of digitized products is that of goods or of services.

2. Basic Trade Principles

Under the basic WTO principles of national and most-favored nation treatment, imported products from one Member must be treated identically with imports of like products from other Members, and "no less favorably" than like domestic products.[31] Because digitized products demonstrably are substitutable with their physical analogues,[32] these principles appear to indicate that digitized products should be treated no less favorably than the equivalent physical products and enjoy the full protections of GATT. Although the principles of national and most-favored nation treatment generally apply only where products are "like"—and one might argue that digitalized products and their physical analogues are not "like", even if they are substitutable—the fundamental principle of non-discrimination that inheres in the principles of national and most-favored treatment militates in favour of equality of treatment.

A closely related (and newer) principle is that of technology neutrality[33]—*i.e.*, that a change in delivery technology should not change applicable trade protections.[34] Likewise,

---

[28] *Id.* at 17.

[29] *See generally* John P. Gaffney, *The GATT and the GATS: Should They Be Mutually Exclusive Agreements?*, 12 LEIDEN J. INT'L L. 135 (1999); *see also UNCTAD E-Commerce Report, supra* note 18, at 125 ("Or should there be a third category of electronic transmissions, some mixture of goods and services—but in that case, which would be the governing multilateral rules?").

[30] Report of the Appellate Body, *European Communities—Regime for the Importation, Sale and Distribution of Bananas*, WT/DS27/AB/R, at ¶ 221 (1997).

[31] *See* GATT, Articles I, III; GATS, Articles II, XVI–XVIII.

[32] *See, e.g.,* Ludger Schuknecht & Rosa Pérez-Esteve, *A Quantitative Assessment of Electronic Commerce,* WTO Economic Research and Analysis Division Staff Working Paper ERAD-99-01, at 5–6 (Sept. 1999).

[33] *See* 2001 Discussion, *supra* note 14, at 2, for a brief discussion of the interaction of like product and technology neutrality issues for e-commerce.

[34] In particular, GATS commitments apply to services "provided through any means of technology (e.g., cable, wireless, satellites)." Group on Basic Telecommunications, *Notes for Scheduling Basic Telecom Services Commitment*, WTO Doc. S/GBT/W/2/Rev.1, ¶ 1(c) (Jan. 16, 1997) ("*GBT Scheduling Note*").

under this principle, a digital book or record should not benefit less from liberalized trade than if it were delivered on paper or vinyl.

A final bedrock WTO principle is that of progressive trade liberalization. Under both GATT and GATS, withdrawal of commitments requires compensation to affected countries.[35] Giving digitized products only the lesser trade protections of GATS (rather than the GATT protections applicable to their physical analogues) would be a step backward in trade protection, and would therefore appear to contravene the principle of progressive liberalization.[36] In sum, traditional principles of trade analysis indicate that digitized products should receive the full protections available under GATT to their physical analogues.

3. Practical Considerations

Classification of digitized products as goods presents two significant practical problems. First, a line-drawing problem arises because, as even the U.S. recognizes, "[m]ost market access commitments for electronic commerce activities fall under Members' service commitments."[37] If both goods and services can be delivered online, there will be persistent and difficult questions regarding which e-commerce activities are subject to GATT and which to GATS. Second, there is an enforcement problem, because customs duties are the primary national measures affecting trade in goods; and it may be nearly impossible reliably to assess customs duties on digitized products, given the nature of the Internet.

It may ultimately be necessary for the WTO Dispute Settlement Body to resolve the classification debate. On the other hand, a possible negotiated solution would be for WTO Members to agree to treat digitized products as services in exchange for GATS commitments to give such products trade benefits reasonably equivalent to comparable physical goods. This approach was advanced in a recent WTO General Council report that "suggested that certain products now categorized as goods and enjoying national treatment and duty-free access under the ITA and GATT should continue to be given similar treatment if it were agreed that they should be classified as services."[38] However, a potential problem is that this approach is premised on substantial elimination of the disparity between GATT and GATS protections for digitized products—*i.e.*, exactly the disparity that led to the classification debate. Nevertheless, a solution along these lines may be possible in the Doha Round.

B. GATT Issues

Aside from the difficulties surrounding the classification debate, e-commerce presents relatively few difficult issues under GATT. The primary reason is that ordinary GATT rules apply to goods that are ordered or traded electronically but are delivered in physical form. However, two GATT issues that appear to be of particular relevance to e-commerce are (1) the moratorium on customs duties on e-commerce, and (2) the possibility of broadening of the Information Technology Agreement regarding customs duties on information technology goods.

---

[35] GATT, Article XXVIII; GATS, Article XXI.

[36] *See 2001 Discussion*, supra note 14, at 2 ("It was also suggested that the most favourable approach to classification would be the least trade restrictive one.").

[37] *U.S. Submission, supra* note 20, at 3.

[38] 2001 Discussion, *supra* note 14, at 2.

1. Customs Duty Moratorium

In February 1998, the United States proposed to the WTO General Council that WTO Members agree not to impose duties on electronic transmissions.[39] At the May 1998 Second (Geneva) Ministerial Meeting, the WTO decided that "[w]ithout prejudice to the outcome of the work programme or the rights and obligations of Members under the WTO Agreements,... Members will continue their current practice of not imposing customs duties on electronic transmissions."[40] Again at the November 2001 Fourth (Doha) Ministerial Meeting, the WTO "declare[d] that Members will maintain their current practice of not imposing customs duties on electronic transmissions until the Fifth [Ministerial Meeting]."[41]

However, the value of this moratorium is open to question. First, the moratorium is irrelevant if digitized products are classified exclusively as services, since services are not subject to customs duties. Second, it is not clear that any WTO Members have ever tried to assess customs duties on electronic transmissions—or that they could do so successfully if they were to try. Indeed, one might argue that in pursuit of a meaningless "photo-op" agreement, the proponents of the moratorium sowed the seeds of future discord, since the moratorium is now viewed as something that developed e-commerce countries must make concessions to maintain. As if in confirmation of this view, the United Nations Conference on Trade and Development ("UNCTAD") in late 2001 published a detailed calculation of the "tariff revenue losses" from the moratorium that would occur if digitized products both are treated as goods, and largely replace their physical analogues in international commerce.[42]

2. Information Technology Agreement

The Information Technology Agreement ("ITA")[43] was concluded at the First WTO Ministerial Conference (Singapore) and as of late 2001 covered more than 40 countries (including some that are not yet WTO Members) representing approximately 93 percent of world trade in information technology ("IT") products.[44] The ITA eliminated all customs duties on a wide variety of IT products, including computers, monitors and flat panel displays (but not televisions); computer network equipment and storage devices; telephones, wireless telephones and pagers; photocopiers; semiconductors, printed circuits and electronic components; semiconductor manufacturing equipment; capacitors; and a significant number of other products. Duties were eliminated in four steps ending on January 1, 2000, although certain developing countries are permitted to extend duty reductions through as late as 2005.

Although the ITA does not directly involve e-commerce transactions, the IT products that it covers are fundamental to e-commerce. In order to promote the continued growth of e-commerce, it will be important to expand the number of countries participating in the ITA, to add new products (including those for wireless and multimedia applications) to its coverage, and to ensure that the scope of the tariff categories covered by the ITA is clear. A Committee of Participants on the Expansion of Trade in IT Products (the "ITA

[39] *Global Electronic Commerce*, Proposal by the United States, WTO Doc. WT/GC/W/78 (Feb. 9, 1998).

[40] *Second Ministerial E-Commerce Declaration, supra* note 5.

[41] *Fourth Ministerial Declaration, supra* note 15, ¶ 34; *see also* 2002 Discussion, *supra* note 14.

[42] *See UNCTAD E-Commerce Report, supra* note 18, at 125–132.

[43] *Ministerial Declaration on Trade in Information Technology Products*, WTO Doc. WT/MIN96/16 (December 13, 1996).

[44] *See Report (2001) of the Committee of Participants on the Expansion of Trade in Information Technology Products*, WTO Doc. G/L/484 (Oct. 2, 2001) ("*ITA 2001 Report*").

Committee") during 1997 and 1998 negotiated, fairly intensively regarding expansion of the product coverage of the ITA, but these negotiations were unsuccessful.[45] Negotiations in the ITA Committee have since continued at a less intense level.[46]

Disputes related to the ITA can arise if similar IT products are subject to different customs duties. This was the case in the WTO dispute between the United States and the European Communities regarding certain computer equipment with multimedia capabilities.[47] Furthermore, the removal of tariffs under the ITA has not eliminated non-tariff barriers to trade in IT products, a problem which could be addressed in further negotiations under the GATT and the TBT Agreement, either in the Doha Round or otherwise.

C. GATS Issues

GATS is by far the most important piece of the WTO framework for e-commerce. Whatever the outcome of the classification debate discussed above, it is clear that a very substantial portion of e-commerce involves services that are subject to the GATS. This section proposes a division of the e-commerce services covered by GATS into "infrastructure services" and "end-user services", and then considers certain classification issues applicable to e-commerce services, as well as the nature of new GATS commitments that would promote the growth of e-commerce trade.

1. E-Commerce Infrastructure Services

E-commerce "infrastructure services" are the services that provide the infrastructure for delivery of e-commerce to end-users. At a minimum, these include telecommunications services, other electronic communications services, and computer services. Commitments for basic telecommunications services and computer and related services, which provide the physical infrastructure for e-commerce, are covered by Sections 2.C.a-g and 1.B of GATS schedules respectively. Commitments for value-added telecommunications services (e.g., Internet access, e-mail), which provide the platform over which e-commerce applications are delivered, are covered by Section 2.C.h of GATS schedules. And commitments for audiovisual services, which involve content transmitted over the Internet and other networks are covered by Section 2.D of GATS schedules.

U.S. submissions to the WTO in December 2000 illustrate the potential overlap of basic telecommunications services, value-added telecommunications services and audiovisual services with respect to the Internet. In a submission on telecommunications services, the United States noted:

---

[45] See ITA Expansion Talks Suspended as New Dispute Prevent Final Deal, INSIDE US TRADE (July 24, 1998); WTO Members Headed for Final Showdown on ITA Expansion Agreement, INSIDE US TRADE, (Nov. 27, 1998); US Informally Backs Off Demands for Seattle Action on ITA II, INSIDE US TRADE, (Oct. 15, 1999).

[46] See Report (1999) of the Committee of Participants on the Expansion of Trade in Information Technology Products, WTO Doc. G/L/332 (Oct. 14, 1999); Report (2000) of the Committee of Participants on the Expansion of Trade in Information Technology Products, WTO Doc. G/L/420, (Dec. 4, 2000) ("ITA 2000 Report"); ITA 2001 Report, supra note 45.

[47] See European Communities—Customs Classification of Certain Computer Equipment, WT/DS62/AB/R, WT/DS67/AB/R, WT/DS68/AB/R (June 5, 1997). See also the discussion of "classification divergences" in ITA 2001 Report, supra note 44, ¶5, and ITA 2000 Report, supra note 46, ¶6.

market access commitments for services enhanced through use of networks stimulate growth both of the underlying networks and the services that 'ride' over them. This is most obvious in value-added telecommunications services such as Internet-based services, which provide a layer of functionality above basic telecom services, and which in turn are the vehicle for delivering other services.[48]

Likewise, in a contemporaneous submission on audiovisual services, the United States included various "transmission services", including "'converged' transmission services which also transmit other forms of data, voice or other communications services" in a "Summary List of Audiovisual and Audiovisual Related Service Activities."[49]

A longer list of infrastructure services could be developed, incorporating financial services relevant to payment and certain distribution services. The EU has proposed such a list and argued that it is necessary "to facilitate the availability of the e-commerce critical services".[50] There may be a case for development of pro-competitive principles tailored to infrastructure services considered "e-commerce critical". Such a proposal has been made by a group of developing countries in respect of services, such as computer reservation services, which they consider to be essential for the development of their tourism industry.[51] Likewise, Cuba has called more generally for priority to be given to liberalisation of infrastructure and finance-related services, arguing that such services must be made available to developing country service suppliers if the so-called "digital divide" between rich and poor nations is to be reduced.[52]

2. E-Commerce End-User Services

In contrast to e-commerce "infrastructure" services, most e-commerce services that are delivered to business and consumer end-users are analogous to services that may also be delivered offline (*e.g.*, financial services, medical services, legal services, engineering services, etc.), and are covered by the same GATS commitments that apply to their offline analogues.

There is a tremendous amount of variation among WTO Members in the extent of their GATS commitments of market access and national treatment for such e-commerce services. The substantial majority of existing commitments were made when the WTO agreements were finalized in 1994, a time when the potential of e-commerce had hardly been identified. In many cases, the result is a lack of specificity of commitments, which can present a hurdle to enforcement[53]—either because the rapid development of e-commerce has meant that the relevant commitments did not anticipate the development of e-commerce (*e.g.*, where it is unclear whether a commitment for an offline service also extends to its online analogue) or because commitments are insufficiently specific in a sector in which technological specificity can be critical.

[48] *Communication from the United States, Market Access in Telecommunications and Complementary Services: the WTO's Role in Accelerating the Development of a Globally Networked Economy*, WTO Doc. S/CSS/W/30, ¶ 12 (Dec. 18, 2000).
[49] *Communication from the United States, Audiovisual and Related Services*, WTO Doc. S/CSS/W/21, Annex A (Dec. 18, 2000).
[50] *E-Commerce Work Programme*, WTO Doc. S/C/W/183 (Nov. 30, 2000).
[51] Communication from Bolivia containing a proposal for a Draft Annex on Tourism, WTO Doc. S/CSS/W/107 (Sept. 26, 2001).
[52] WTO Doc. WT/GG/W/435 (May 2001).
[53] To the extent a WTO Member has made GATS commitments for e-commerce services, the commitments may be enforced in state-to-state dispute resolution under the WTO Dispute Settlement Understanding, which is discussed in detail in Chapters 25 *et seq.* of this book.

These difficulties are somewhat mitigated by the principle of "technology neutrality", which was first recognized in the 1996–1997 negotiations of the Basic Telecommunications Agreement, under which commitments apply to services "provided through any means of technology (e.g., cable, wireless, satellites)."[54] This principle has become widely accepted at the WTO as generally-applicable to services delivered by technological means, including e-commerce services.[55] Continued careful application of this principle is critical if GATS commitments are to provide real trade protections as e-commerce continues to develop, since the technological developments of e-commerce move much faster than trade negotiations. The basic alternative to application of the principle of technology neutrality is negotiation of detailed commitments specific to e-commerce. But application of technology neutrality to existing commitments and negotiation of e-commerce-specific commitments are not mutually exclusive alternatives.

For example, in the case of financial services—which are one of the most important potential examples of e-commerce end-user services—the WTO has been actively considering the impact of e-commerce. In a detailed issues paper released after the December 1997 conclusion of the WTO Financial Services Agreement, the WTO raised a number of questions regarding the extent to which technological change affects trade rules for financial services:

> What are the implications of technological innovations on the structure of financial services industries and markets? How will such changes affect financial services trade? . . . How will developing countries be affected by the technological changes taking place in the sector? What conditions may be required for developing-country Members to be able to benefit from the opportunities provided by the new technologies?[56]

More recently, recognizing distance-selling opportunities provided by e-commerce, the financial services industry has called for financial services trade liberalization without the need for establishment.[57] As a practical matter, it is likely that many other service sectors will also require such a two-faceted approach to application of GATS commitments to e-commerce—involving both the principle of technology neutrality and the consideration of e-commerce-specific issues.

3. Classification Issues

There can be difficult line-drawing issues regarding GATS commitments for e-commerce services, in at least the three respects discussed below. Resolution of such classification ambiguities is an important issue regarding application of GATS to e-commerce services.

First, GATS schedules categorize services according to the Service Sectoral Classification List,[58] a document developed in 1991 which is largely based on the UN Central Product Classification ("CPC") and which does not include categories for most e-commerce services. The difficulty in using CPC codes to specify GATS classifications

---

[54] *GBT Scheduling Note, supra* note 34.
[55] *See Work Programme Services Report,supra*note 8, ¶ 24 ("Delegations endorsed the view that all services, whether supplied electronically or otherwise, are covered by the GATS, and that the GATS makes no distinction between services provided electronically or by other means.").
[56] *Financial Services,* Background Note by the Secretariat, WTO Doc. S/C/W/72 (Dec. 2, 1998).
[57] *Press Release by Financial Leaders Group* (Sept. 24, 2001).
[58] WTO/GATT Doc. MTN.GNS/W/120 (July 10, 1991); *see also Uniform Classification Systems,* WTO Doc. GPA/W/17 (May 15, 1996).

presented particular problems as WTO Members submitted requests for detailed bilateral negotiations under GATS in June 2002.[59]

Second, there can be ambiguity regarding what category of GATS commitments applies to particular e-commerce services.[60] For example, Internet access services appear to implicate the commitments for basic telecommunications services (*i.e.*, telecommunications circuits for delivering Internet communications to end-users), value-added telecommunications services (*i.e.*, software and related services to handle Internet content, such as web pages and e-mail), and audiovisual services[61] (*i.e.*, the content itself).

Third, GATS schedules for each service include separate commitments for four "modes" of service delivery, and commitments can be different for different modes.[62] There is substantial ambiguity whether certain e-commerce services involve mode 1 (cross-border delivery—*i.e.*, supply of a service "from the territory of one Member into the territory of any other Member") or mode 2 (consumption abroad—*i.e.*, supply of a service "in the territory of one Member to the service consumer of any other Member").[63] That is, the question becomes whether (a) the Japanese consumer is "traveling" abroad to visit a U.S.-based website (*i.e.*, Mode 2), (b) the U.S. website is providing medical advice across borders (*i.e.*, Mode 1), or (c) the two are meeting in some no-man's land called cyberspace.[64]

4. New Commitments

Because GATS is by far the most important WTO agreement governing e-commerce, WTO Members can substantially promote the growth of trade in e-commerce by expanding their GATS commitments for both e-commerce infrastructure services and e-commerce end-user services. As discussed above, it appeared not long ago that extension of commitments for e-commerce was likely to be a primary focus of the current round of trade negotiations. Although this is no longer the case, the Doha Round continues to present huge opportunities for new commitments on e-commerce. There are also many powerful interests pushing for liberalization of e-commerce trade; and compared to many other sectors, there is a relative lack of entrenched industries that seem likely to oppose trade liberalization. Accordingly, significant expansion of trade protections for e-commerce in the Doha Round remains quite likely.

D. TRIPS Issues

E-commerce is widely recognized as raising new issues for the international intellectual property system, bringing challenges for the balanced protection of creative content and commercial brands, as well as the technologies facilitating access to them, on digital networks.[65] As stated above, however, very little of substance has been accomplished

---

[59] These proposals are available at http://www.wto.org/english/tratop_e/serv_e/s_propnewnegs_e.htm.

[60] *See Classification of New Services Non-Paper*, Contribution of Japan (May 13, 2002).

[61] GATS commitments for audiovisual services are covered by Section 2.D of GATS schedules. There has been significant debate over whether and how the GATS should apply to audiovisual services, and audiovisual service commitments under the GATS are very limited.

[62] *See* Chapter 19 of this book.

[63] GATS, Art. I(2)(a), (b).

[64] Emad Tinawi & Judson O. Berkey, *E-Services and the WTO: The Adequacy of the GATS Classification Framework*, at 3 (1999) (available from OECD at http://www.oecd.org/pdf/M000014000/M00014377.pdf).

[65] *See Primer on Electronic Commerce and Intellectual Property Issues*, WIPO Doc. WIPO/OLOA/EC/Primer (May 2000).

by the WTO in this area since the Work Programme commenced in September 1998.[66] At that time, the Council for TRIPS was charged "to examine and report on the intellectual property issues arising in connection with electronic commerce," including the protection and enforcement of trademarks, copyright and related rights, and impact of new technologies and access to technology.[67] A Background Note prepared by the WTO secretariat in February 1999 observed that the question in this context "is whether the norms contained in the TRIPS Agreement provide 'effective and adequate protection of intellectual property rights' in respect of the new forms of exploitation made possible by means of interactive digital networks.[68] At the same time, however, the Note advanced the preliminary view that "given the technologically neutral language used in the TRIPS Agreement, its provisions are generally relevant also in the digital network environment."

In a July 1999 report, the TRIPS Council indicated that, given the novelty and complexity of trade-related intellectual property issues, further study was required to better understand them and the Council would continue to consider developments in this area. The Council also acknowledged the role of the World Intellectual Property Organization ("WIPO") undertaking significant work in this area. In particular, the TRIPS Council noted the adoption by WIPO in December 1996 of two new copyright treaties—the WIPO Copyright Treaty ("WCT") and the WIPO Performances and Phonograms Treaty ("WPPT")—intended to respond to the impact of the convergence of information and communication technologies on copyrighted works and performances. The Council also reviewed WIPO's work in relation to trademarks and domain names, including the WIPO Internet Domain Name Process.[69]

Leading into the Seattle Ministerial, the intellectual property aspects of e-commerce were included on the Ministerial Agenda, and there were at least some discussions in particular about the implementation of the two WIPO treaties (WCT and WPPT) either as part of the TRIPS Agreement or as additional TRIPS-related agreements (*i.e.*, with or without re-opening the TRIPS Agreement itself).[70] At the same time, however, there was an emerging concern expressed by certain industry sectors that, given new pressures particularly from developing countries to "re-balance" TRIPS in favor of developing countries, any re-opening of TRIPS could prove counterproductive.

By the time of the Doha Ministerial, the focus in the international intellectual property community was squarely on the concerns being raised by developing countries.[71] Access to medicines and the relationship to patent rights, new norms of protection for traditional knowledge and folklore, and concerns by least-developed country Members in meeting

---

[66] Indeed, Member State representatives have expressed the view that it is curious, in light of the significant developments of electronic commerce, that the TRIPS Council had been virtually silent on the substance of this issue, with the exception of a very general interim report sent to the General Council in 2000, and that it is incumbent on the TRIPS Council, under Article 71, to take account of the enormous impact of technological developments on the legal and administrative framework of intellectual property protection.

[67] *Work Programme TRIPS Report, supra* note 9, at ¶ 1.

[68] Background Note by the Secretariat, *Work Programme on Electronic Commerce*, WTO Doc. IP/C/W/128 (February 1999).

[69] *Id.; see also* WIPO's e-commerce web site at http://ecommerce.wipo.int.

[70] *See* Daniel J. Gervaise, *The TRIPS Agreement After Seattle, Implementation and Dispute Settlement Issues*, 3 J. WORLD INTELLECTUAL PROP. 509, 522–23 (2000).

[71] *See, e.g., TRIPS Council Meeting on Access to Medicines: WTO Members to Press on Following 'Rich Debate' on Medicines*, WTO Press Release 233 June 22, 2001); *Poor Countries Raise Hurdle at WTO*, FINANCIAL TIMES, November 9, 2001 (developing countries' demand a clear statement that WTO's agreement on trade-related intellectual property rights ("TRIPS") should not prevent them from importing and licensing medical supplies to meet public health needs).

existing TRIPS deadlines for implementation, were being raised with some urgency.[72] In light of this climate of views, e-commerce-related intellectual property issues no longer appeared on the radar screen—despite the fact that the WIPO Copyright Treaties were both very close to achieving the 30 ratifications each required to enter into force.[73]

It is therefore unsurprising that the Doha Ministerial Declaration does not speak directly about the intellectual property dimensions of e-commerce. Instead, the Declaration refers to intellectual property and public health issues, work on geographical indications (which was previously envisaged in TRIPS Article 23), and continuing implementation of the TRIPS Agreement, which is to include an examination of the protection of folklore and traditional knowledge, as well as the relationship between TRIPS and the Convention on Biological Diversity.[74]

As noted above, however, the Doha Declaration does reaffirm the Member countries agreement "to continue the Work Programme on Electronic Commerce".[75] Among the elements of this Work Programme is the work of the TRIPS Council in this area. In addition to the points reviewed above, the Declaration instructs the TRIPS Council to examine, *inter alia,* "other relevant developments raised by Members pursuant to Article 71.1.[76] Commentators have emphasized that this language serves as a placeholder to permit the WTO, during the next several years of negotiations, to return to issues such as e-commerce-related intellectual property issues. Others would view the incorporation of the WIPO 1996 copyright treaties as a logical and virtually inevitable element to be considered in this regard.[77]

E. Trade and Development

The role for the WTO on development issues relating to e-commerce is not yet well-defined. Many countries are uncertain where their interests lie. On the one hand, there is reason to believe that expanded e-commerce will greatly improve the competitiveness of poor countries with skilled service workers; for these workers, once forced to emigrate if they wanted to participate in the markets of the developed world, e-commerce opens new economic opportunities while allowing them to live and pay taxes at home. Despite this possibility, some spokesmen for the developing world have been hostile to open e-commerce markets. The 2001 *UNCTAD E-Commerce Report* illustrates this ambivalence: as discussed above the report identifies certain negative effects of e-commerce trade, but overall it takes a very positive view of the effect of

[72] Subsequently, the WTO Member states agreed upon a separate, political *Declaration on the TRIPS Agreement and Public Health*, which reaffirmed that "the Agreement can and should be interpreted and implemented in a manner supportive of WTO Members' right to protect public health and, in particular, to promote access to medicines for all."

[73] The WCT entered into force on March 6, 2002 and the WPPT entered into force on May 20, 2002, in each case three months after the 30th ratification was achieved.

[74] *WTO Fourth Ministerial Declaration, supra* note 15, ¶¶ 17–19.

[75] *Id.*, ¶ 34.

[76] *Id.,* ¶ 19. Article 71.1 of the TRIPS Agreement provides that the TRIPS Council may undertake reviews of the Agreement "in the light of any relevant new developments which might warrant modification or amendment of this Agreement."

[77] For example, the Swiss Government in June 2001 motioned the TRIPS Council to produce a report to ascertain how the Agreement should be amended to incorporate the 1996 WIPO treaties. *Communication from Switzerland, supra* note 15. Further, at recent meetings of the TRIPS Council concerning the impact of electronic commerce, a number of Member States and the European Union have expressed the view that work should be done to consider means to recognize the WCT and WPPT in the context of the TRIPS Agreement. *See TRIPS Council December 2000 Meeting Minutes*, WTO Doc. IP/C/M/29 (June 3, 2001).

e-commerce on the developing world:

> In the end it will be as the efficiency gains derived [e-commerce related] changes in the business processes seep into the productive tissue of the developing countries that ICT [information and communication technologies] and the Internet will contribute most to global economic growth and improved living standards. Indeed, it is because the Internet revolution is relevant not just to the high-tech, information sensitive sectors but also to the whole organization of economic life that its positive effects are spilling over more quickly into most sectors of the economy and that developing countries stand a better chance of sharing in its benefits earlier that in previous technological revolutions.[78]

The Committee on Trade and Development is one of the four primary WTO bodies that have participated in the Work Programme. In its report as part of the Work Programme, the Committee noted the potential importance of e-commerce to developing countries and focused in particular on the importance of developing physical telecommunications infrastructure in developing countries in order to promote the growth of e-commerce.[79] However, the Committee did not define a clear role for the WTO in the process. It noted that "aspects of electronic commerce are being addressed in a number of multilateral or plurilateral fora", and suggested that "it would be useful for WTO to cooperate much more closely with other international organizations working in these areas, such as UNCITRAL and UNCTAD, and to identify a particular role for the WTO.[80] Because developing country issues are high on the agenda for the Doha Round (the Doha Ministerial Declaration states that "[t]he work to date demonstrates that electronic commerce creates new challenges and opportunities for trade for Members at all stages of development"[81]) it is likely that the WTO will ultimately take on some role in trade and development issues for e-commerce. The Committee on Trade and Development took this process forward in a December 2001 report proposing that the Committee make e-commerce a regular agenda item and that the Committee sponsor a series of seminars on e-commerce and development.[82]

F. Taxation

E-commerce presents a variety of complex taxation issues, most of which are not directly related to the WTO and are therefore beyond the scope of this chapter. Furthermore, because many countries are still in the process of deciding how to apply tax rules to e-commerce, it is difficult to judge whether e-commerce taxation will ultimately present significant WTO issues.[83] The most likely context in which such issues may arise is that of tax rules that discriminate against e-commerce. In *Japan—Taxes on Alcoholic Beverages*, the WTO Appellate Body made clear that taxes that have discriminatory effect, even if not facially discriminatory, violate WTO rules.[84]

For example, the European Union recently decided to amend its value-added tax ("VAT") rules to provide that foreign-based suppliers of services (including digitzed

---

[78] *UNCTAD E-Commerce Report, supra* note 18, at xxv.

[79] *See Work Programme Development Report, supra* note 10.

[80] *Id.*, ¶¶ 17, 25.

[81] *WTO Fourth Ministerial Declaration, supra* note 15, ¶ 34.

[82] 2001 CTD Report, *supra* note 16.

[83] A good recent summary of e-commerce taxation issues is provided at pages 119–25 of the UNCTAD E-Commerce Report, *supra* note 18.

[84] Report of the Appellate Body, *Japan—Taxes on Alcoholic Beverages*, WT/DS8/AB/R, WT/DS10/AB/R, WT/DS11/AB/R (1996).

products) to the EU must charge VAT at the rate applicable in the country of consumption, while EU-based suppliers will continue to be permitted to charge VAT at the rate applicable in the country in which they are established.[85] Depending upon how these new VAT rules are implemented (likely in 2003), this differential treatment may violate the WTO national treatment requirement.[86] Similarly, if the classification debate is resolved in favor of treating certain digitized products as goods, a WTO national treatment claim could be presented by national law that applies differential tax rates to digitized products and their physical analogues (so long as it can be established that the products are "like or directly competitive")[87]

---

[85] *See Council Directive 2002/38/EC* (May 7, 2002).

[86] EU Internal Market Commissioner Frits Bolkestein has publicly recognised that there may be WTO concerns with VAT rules that place greater burdens on foreign suppliers. *See* Stewart Baker et al., *E-Products and the WTO,* 35 THE INTERNATIONAL LAWYER 5, 17 n. 62 and accompanying text.

[87] GATT, Art. III:2 and Ad Article III, paragraph 2.).

CHAPTER 57

TRADE AND COMPETITION POLICY

Merit E. Janow*

TABLE OF CONTENTS

---

* Professor in the Practice of International Economic Law & International Affairs and Director, Masters Program in International Affairs, Columbia University. From 1997–2000, Professor Janow served as Executive Director of the International Competition Policy Advisory Committee to the Attorney General and Assistant Attorney General for Antitrust, US Department of Justice.

I. Introduction

Competition policy[1] and trade policy can be mutually reinforcing policy tools, working in tandem to foster markets that are contestable and competitive to the benefit of foreign and domestic interests alike. In some ways, these two policy instruments are flip sides of a coin—competition policy addresses private restraints of trade, whereas trade policy focuses on governmental restraints of trade. In the absence of effective competition policy, private restraints of trade can nullify the benefits of negotiated trade liberalization measures, reducing the benefits of the negotiated trade bargains such as tariff reductions and perhaps even public support for liberalization of trade.

Although trade and competition policy objectives are complementary along some dimensions, they are significantly different in emphasis and application. Competition policy is enforced at the national level by domestic authorities, and the history of international and especially multilateral cooperation in competition policy is limited. Much of the international cooperation and discussion that has taken place has occurred in bilateral settings. In contrast, while nations pursue their own trade policies, a defining development in trade policy in the postwar period has been the gradual expansion of multilateral trade laws, embodied in the rules of the GATT and now the WTO. Even aside from level of application, the substantive features of trade and competition policy have both areas of overlap and divergence. Under U.S. antitrust law, for example, the legal tests for injury and the pricing standards differ greatly from those found under trade remedies.[2]

At various points since the 1940s, experts and governments have considered how competition policy could be globalized. Although international consideration of competition policy is thus not new, the spread of competition law and policy around the world is. Over the last decade many countries have shown a growing interest in using competition policies as a means of bolstering the role of market-based competition in their economies. Since 1980 many developing countries and economies in transition have enacted new antimonopoly laws or strengthened existing laws and policies to facilitate the transition from planning to markets.

Multilateral consideration of the relationship between competition and trade policy moved a significant step forward in December 1996 when the world's trade ministers agreed at the WTO's Singapore Ministerial meeting to establish a working group to study and discuss the relationship between trade and competition policies. It was agreed from the outset that the initiation of the working group did not mean that international negotiations in the area of competition policy were a foregone conclusion. The Ministerial Declaration stated plainly that the work undertaken in the competition policy arena (and other areas) "... shall not prejudge whether negotiations will be initiated in the future..."[3] Now, nearly seven years later, and particularly in the aftermath of the Doha Trade Summit

---

[1] This discussion uses the term competition policy to encompass those national laws (such as U.S. antitrust laws) and policies designed to promote competition in the marketplace and to deter and punish restrictive or abusive business practices. The main concern of competition law and policy is therefore private firm actions.

[2] The antidumping laws require a showing that the dumping contributed to material injury, which is defined as harm that is not "inconsequential, immaterial or unimportant." Section 771(7)(A) of the Tariff Act as amended, 19 U.S.C. §1677 (7)(A) (2001). US antitrust laws, however, have a higher standard of injury and causation and tend to require a showing of a substantial lessening of competition or unreasonable restraint of trade. Moreover, price discrimination in the context of the Robinson Patman Act provides certain defenses which are unavailable in the antidumping context, such as meeting competition. For an excellent comparison of antitrust and trade remedies and standards, see Harvey M. Applebaum, *The Interface of the Trade Laws and the Antitrust laws*, 6 Geo. Mason L. Rev 479 (1998).

[3] *See* PWT/MIN (96) Dec., ¶ 20.

of 2001, there is serious debate as to whether competition policy should come under WTO rules in some fashion and what such global rules or principles should encompass.

This chapter starts by examining the function of the competition and trade policy tools and some possible links and tensions. It then briefly considers the postwar efforts to expand international discussion and cooperation on competition policy matters. The chapter then examines the Uruguay Round Agreements and evaluates those features that contain some fragmentary competition policy elements as well as recent efforts by governments and private groups to consider a role for the WTO. Finally, the chapter evaluates arguments for and against formal linkage of competition policy under the aegis of the WTO.

II. Why is Competition Policy Relevant to Trade Policy?

Competition law and policy is centrally concerned with the exclusionary conduct of *corporations* that restrict the operation of markets and raise costs to consumers. Trade policy, in contrast, is centrally concerned with measures taken by *governments* that restrict foreign access to markets and discriminate against foreign market participants. The effect of these two types of problems however are the same—less competition and higher costs for consumers.

Firms, governments, or some combination of the two, can impose anticompetitive or exclusionary restraints on trade. Exclusionary practices on the part of private firms can adversely affect competition in a relevant market and raise costs not only for domestic consumers, but also for foreign firms and consumers as well. Such arrangements may be between local firms, or they may be transnational in nature, taking the form of market allocation agreements, cartels with boycott arrangements, and other restrictive business arrangements across national boundaries.

Government policies or practices can support exclusionary business practices in many ways. Governments can act *affirmatively* to distort the operation of private markets and provide advantages to local firms. Examples include discriminatory enforcement of competition policy; government-authorized exemptions to national competition laws; the use of competition laws to advance industrial policy objectives, such as national champions; or trade policy measures that directly affect cross-border sales, such as anti-dumping measures and voluntary export restraint arrangements.

Alternatively, government practices can affect competition through *acts of omission*, by tolerating anticompetitive arrangements, for example, or failing to enforce competition laws if such laws are in place. Further, markets can be formally liberalized by privatizing monopolies, but privatization might not augur any change in access for new entrants, foreign or domestic, in the absence of a functioning competition policy regime. Both of these prototypes—exclusionary or anticompetitive business practices, and government practices that affirmatively or through inaction undermine competition among firms—have been largely outside the reach of international trade or antitrust rules.

Trade and competition policies are two methods of addressing such problems. Traditionally, enforcement of competition policy has been considered primarily the responsibility of national competition authorities concerned about anticompetitive effects on markets and consumers on their soil. In addition, some jurisdictions, notably the United States, have at times applied their antitrust laws (or at least asserted their willingness to apply their law) extraterritorially in an attempt to remedy such practices.

Some nations also have provisions whereby domestic trade laws are applied extraterritorially to reach certain market access restraints. For example, U.S. trade law, under

Section 301 of the Trade Act, as amended, can apply to some offshore anticompetitive business practices that are affirmatively supported or tolerated by a national government.[4]

Trade and competition policies are designed to look at restraints that come from different sources. Nondiscrimination, transparency, most-favored-nation, and national treatment have all been central pillars of the liberal trading system and the GATT. Government actions that undermine these principles present broader and different concerns than the more technical analysis of competition in a market and market entry barriers, which are typically the focus of competition authorities. Each set of policy tools also has its limitations in the international context.

To highlight some differences in focus and application of the two sets of policy tools, consider three examples that illustrate the internationalization of competition problems.

First, international enforcement of competition policy has long presented problems. History shows that international cartels and other abuses of international markets do occur and that these can be longstanding anticompetitive arrangements, detrimental to firms and consumers in multiple markets, whether located in developed or developing countries, across many different industries.[5] The recent record of U.S. international cartel cases demonstrates that sizable volumes of commerce are affected by international cartels. Some investigations have involved more than one billion dollars a year of trade in the United States alone, and in more than half of the recent criminal investigations, the volume of affected commerce has exceeded $100 million.[6]

Uncovering such abuses is itself difficult. Additionally, enforcement or litigation of international cases often raises substantial procedural and evidentiary challenges, particularly when evidence and parties are located in multiple jurisdictions. Unilateral competition policy enforcement actions occur against a backdrop of longstanding tensions surrounding extraterritorial application of national competition (or antitrust) laws.

---

[4] In Section 2411(d)(3)(B)(i)(IV) of the Omnibus Trade and Competitiveness Act of 1988, 19 U.S. C. Section 2901(d)(3)(B)(i)(IV), Congress clarified that the "toleration by a foreign government of systematic anticompetitive activities by enterprises or among enterprises in the foreign country that have the effect of restricting, on a basis that is inconsistent with commercial considerations, access of United States goods or services to a foreign market" constitutes an "unreasonable" practice, actionable under Section 301 of the Trade Act of 1974, 19 U.S.C. §2411–2420. The Senate Finance Committee Report describes the inclusion of this "toleration" claim as stemming from the "growing conviction . . . that anti-competitive, market-restrictive behavior on the part of private firms, when coupled with the failure of a foreign government to intervene to eliminate such behavior, can act as a barrier to market access, which is as great as any formal government act, policy or practice alone." *See*, S. Report No. 167, 100th Cong., 1st Sess. 85 (1987). Section 301 of the Trade Act of 1974, as amended, is the statutory basis by which the U.S. government initiates a trade case *vis-à-vis* a foreign government for possible violation of a trade agreement (e.g., a GATT or WTO commitment) or with respect to foreign governmental practices that are deemed unreasonable or discriminatory and that burden or restrict US commerce. This provision also provides the legal framework by which private parties, such as corporations, can petition the US government to investigate, and if necessary, take trade action against such governmental practices.

[5] A recent study undertaken at the behest of the World Bank presents interesting new evidence regarding the adverse impact of international cartels on developing nations. *See* Margaret Levenstein and Valerie Suslow, *Private International Cartels and Their Effect on Developing Countries*, Background Paper for the World Bank's World Development Report 2001, January 9, 2001. *See also*, Simon J. Evenett, Margaret C. Levenstein & Valerie Sulsow, *International Cartel Enforcement: Lessons from the 1990s*, 24 (9) *World Economy* 1221 (2001).

[6] There have been a number of major international cartel cases prosecuted by the Antitrust Division, Department of Justice in the lysine, citric acid, vitamins and graphite electrodes industries. There are also numerous historical examples, such as in the heavy electrical machinery sector, For additional details see International Competition Policy Advisory Committee ("ICPAC"), FINAL REPORT, March 2000, U.S. Department of Justice, at 168. ("*ICPAC Final Report*").

U.S. actions have been especially controversial in this regard. U.S. case law at the turn of the century suggested that the reach of U.S. antitrust law extended no further than the water's edge. By the mid-1940s, however, U.S. case law had established that the Sherman Act applied to conduct occurring abroad when the participants intentionally and adversely affected U.S. commerce and the effects were deemed to be more than minor. This came to be called the "effects" test.[7]

Currently there is little dispute that U.S. antitrust laws reach foreign business practices perceived as having adverse consumer effects in the United States. What distinguishes U.S. antitrust law from competition law in many countries, however, is that it carries both civil and criminal penalties, high fines, and private rights of action, which permit the award of treble damages. In years past, several countries introduced so-called "blocking" and "claw-back" statutes, their specific *raison d'être* being to thwart U.S. discovery practices and to ameliorate the effects of treble damages. While the US was once the only OECD country to apply some form of the effects test, now most industrialized countries apply some form of effects test.[8]

More recently, the locus of controversy has been the reach and application of U.S. antitrust laws with respect to foreign private practices seen as limiting U.S. exports and hence principally harming U.S. *producers* as distinct from U.S. consumers. In such "market access" cases, the competitive harm is experienced by consumers in the foreign market as well as by the would-be entrant to the foreign market. To date, few U.S. antitrust cases have been brought under this theory.[9] Nonetheless, officials from several governments have expressed their strong objections to the application of U.S. antitrust laws to offshore competitive harm. As a result, this policy tool appears to be one that could result in political or trade friction.

A second example of the internationalization of competition issues stems from trade tensions arising from perceptions that nations are not enforcing their competition laws, are enforcing them in a discriminatory fashion, or are otherwise tolerating private, ex-clusionary practices by domestic businesses to the detriment of foreign market entrants. This type of barrier to market access is often cited as one example of the way a host government may foster private restraints of trade.[10]

Private restraints of trade that restrict market access and in which governments have been implicated have created trade and economic tensions among several countries. The suspect practices include non-enforcement of rules prohibiting vertical distribution restraints, the governmental use of industrial policies that have the effect of blocking

[7] *See United States* v. *Aluminum Co. of America*, 148 F.2d, 416, 443 (2d. Cir. 1945).

[8] *See* American Bar Association, *Report of the Special Committee on International Antitrust,* September 1, 1991.

[9] The International Competition Policy Advisory Committee, ICPAC, which this author directed, was able to find only five cases since 1978 that involved export restraint allegations. The most recent case, *United States v. Pilkington PLC* is the only case involving export restraint allegations since the Department of Justice eliminated footnote 159 of its enforcement guidelines that had suggested that the Department would not make it a priority to pursue export restraint cases. In this 1994 case, the DOJ charged the UK firm Pilkington with entering into unreasonably restrictive patent and know-how licensing agreements with its likely competitors for the manufacture of flat glass using a proprietary process. The Department alleged that the territorial and use limitations in the agreements precluded Pilkington's licensees in the United States from competing for business to design, build or operate flat glass plants in other countries. The case was settled by consent decree. *See* 1994–2 Trade Cas. (CCH) at ¶ 70,842. For additional examples and discussion of the same, *see ICPAC Final Report*, Annex 5-A.

[10] This is the type of problem that the feature of Section 301 of the 1974 Trade Act, discussed in note 4, *supra,* was designed to reach.

access, overly broad governmental exemptions or immunities from national competition laws, and discriminatory regulatory practices, among other measures.[11] Allegations of trade-restrictive private restraints have clouded U.S.-Japan trade and economic relations for much of the 1980s and 1990s. Those two governments entered into several bilateral trade accords that included some undertakings by the Government of Japan to enforce its competition laws (called the Anti-Monopoly Act) in a more vigorous fashion. Many of the challenged business practices focused on distribution (or vertical) business practices, where U.S. and other firms alleged that unilateral and joint activities of Japanese producers foreclosed foreign firms and other new entrants from using existing or developing new distribution channels.[12]

A third source of international economic tension emanates from those legal conflicts that have arisen in the context of multi-jurisdictional review of mergers. Large international mergers typically require review by competition authorities in several different countries. Disclosure requirements, timetables, and legal standards differ a great deal, depending on the jurisdiction. The proposed merger of McDonnell Douglas and Boeing in 1997 made these points in a dramatic fashion. In that case the U.S. Federal Trade Commission decided to approve Boeing's proposed acquisition of McDonnell Douglas, concluding after an investigation that the acquisition would neither substantially lessen competition nor tend to create a monopoly in either the defense or the commercial aircraft markets.[13] The European Commission took issue with the merger, raised concerns about the effect of the merger on Boeing's dominance, and threatened to reject the merger and impose large fines unless some specified adjustments were made by Boeing. Boeing made the requested adjustments.[14]

Although neither of the two merging firms had production assets within the European Union, few competition law experts took issue with the EU's assertion of authority to review the proposed merger, given the global commercial aircraft market. Instead, the issue involved the different legal conclusions reached by U.S. and European authorities. This case generated a great deal of political heat on both sides of the Atlantic, with both sides charging that the other side's competition authorities were informed, not so much by competition law, as by national champions and trade policies hiding behind competition law.

This case demonstrated that in a global economy, two or more nations can lay jurisdictional claim to the same business transaction. It also showed that major competition authorities could come to sharply different substantive legal conclusions, even when they had the same transaction before them. Moreover, the European Union demonstrated that,

[11] *See* Merit E. Janow, *Public and Private Restraints that Limit Access to Markets*, in MARKET ACCESS AFTER THE URUGUAY ROUND (OECD, 1996).

[12] For a period of time during the late 1980s and early 1990s, a particular set of problems was thought to be presented by the Japanese *keiretsu*, groups of companies with cross-ownership of shares and established patterns of doing business with other members of the group. As discussed in the section that follows, a major US-Japan trade dispute involving allegations of discriminatory access to distribution channels was the *US Film* case, often referred to as Kodak-Fuji since it was first brought to the attention of the U.S. government by Kodak Photo Film Company. *See* Report of the WTO Panel, *Japan—Measures Affecting Consumer Photographic Film and Paper,* W/DS44/R (1998) *("Japan—Film")*.

[13] *See* Statement of Chairman Robert Pitofsky and Commissioners Janet D. Steiger, Roscoe B. Starek III and Christine A. Varney *in The Matter of The Boeing Company/McDonnell Douglas Corporation*, File No. 971-0051, available at http://www.ftc.gov/opa/1997/9707/boeingsta.htm.

[14] For a more complete discussion of this case, *see* Merit E. Janow, *Unilateral and Bilateral Approaches to Competition Policy: An Analysis Drawing Lessons from the Trade Experience*, in BROOKINGS TRADE FORUM 1998 (Robert Z. Lawrence ed. 1999) at 253.

like the United States, it is fully prepared to apply its own laws when a foreign transaction is thought to affect its interests.

Some of these same lessons arose in the 2001 GE/Honeywell merger case,which was cleared by U.S. authorities but prohibited by the EU. And, unlike the Boeing/McDonnell Douglas transaction, the parties in GE/Honeywell were unable or unwilling to make the necessary adjustments in the transaction to obtain EU clearance. Hence, this transaction represents one of the few instances of direct conflict in substantive law between the United States and the EU, resulting in the termination of a major U.S. merger.[15]

Current trade and antitrust policy tools do not provide complete solutions to the international tensions that emanate from global competition problems or those problems that reflect a mix of governmental and private restraints. And no internationally agreed-upon set of competition or trade rules directly addresses business practices. For some, this situation is a call to create new multilateral rules and consultation mechanisms in the WTO. Others see the WTO as ill suited for that purpose and call instead for expanded competition initiatives outside the WTO. This chapter examines both sides of that debate. Wherever one lands on the question of the appropriate policy response for the WTO, it is certainly the case that the reduction of governmental trade barriers has brought into sharper relief the negative effects of internal practices, both public and private, on competition and access to markets. Concerns about access to markets are now almost universal—even countries with large domestic markets have come to rely on international trade sourcesas major sources of economic growth.

III. Coverage of Private Restraints and Competition Issues under International Trade Organization Regimes

Before turning to the pros and cons of possible approaches to international competition policy, let us review multilateral and other experiences with this issue.

A. The International Trade Organization and Other Early Efforts

Some of the early U.S. and U.K. architects of the International Trade Organization ("ITO") were concerned about the pernicious effects that international cartels and other private restraints of trade could have upon the world trading system. As a result, the draft Havana Charter included a chapter on restrictive business practices. Ironically, while it was U.S. negotiators that had sought to identify and proscribe certain business practices within the ITO charter, these provisions generated considerable opposition within the United States and contributed to the quiet demise of the ITO.[16] There was considerable suspicion in the United States that other countries were more tolerant of cartels and other industrial agreements and that therefore competition law and policy provisions would result

---

[15] *See* Press Release, July 3, 2001 Department of Justice, Antitrust Division. In this press release, Assistant Attorney General Charles James states that the Antitrust Division reached "a firm conclusion that the merger . . . would have been pro-competitive and beneficial to consumers. Our conclusion was based on findings, confirmed by customers worldwide, that the combined firm could offer better products and services at more attractive prices than either could offer individually . . . the EU however apparently concluded that a more diversified, and thus more competitive, GE could somehow disadvantage other market participants . . . Clear and longstanding U.S. antitrust policy holds that the antitrust laws protect competition, not competitors. Today's EU decision reflects a significant point of divergence".

[16] *See* Clair Wilcox, A CHARTER FOR WORLD TRADE 105 (1949).

in external scrutiny of U.S. practices without serious enforcement of anticompetitive practices within the home jurisdictions of the other ITO members.[17]

After the ITO charter failed, the United Nations Economic and Social Counci in 1953 endorsed a draft convention that would have established a new international agency to receive and investigate complaints of restrictive business practices.[18] The United States rejected the draft convention, arguing that differences in national policies and practices were so large that they would make the new international organization ineffective.[19] Concerns were also expressed that the one nation, one vote provision would allow nations hostile to the United States to instigate harassing complaints.

B. GATT Deliberations and Rule Coverage

The issue of multilateral coverage of private anticompetitive business practices did not die with the ITO. In the late 1950s, a group of twelve experts was convened at the GATT to take another look at this question, but was unable to reach a consensus opinion. The majority opinion recommended that business practices be left outside of dispute settlement (in particular, GATT Article XXIII) and advised that parties in competition disputes should enter into bilateral consultations. The majority contended that the absence of consensus and experience in this policy area made it unrealistic to try to arrive at any multilateral agreement concerning the control of international restrictive business practices. One way of remedying this deficiency, they argued, would be to develop a supranational body vested with broad powers of investigation, but this option was seen as unrealistic since many countries had not yet addressed the problem at the domestic level through a domestic enforcement agency.[20] In contrast, the minority view argued that Article XXIII of the GATT should be an available tool and that it was imperative that some measures be taken to counteract restrictive business practices having harmful effects upon international trade.

One consequence of this expert report was a 1960 GATT resolution calling for the GATT to provide a forum in which contracting parties could consult as to restrictive business practices, on an *ad hoc* basis and upon request. This provision was invoked only once, in 1996.[21]

In practice, litigation of disputes in the GATT/WTO centering on private business practices restricting access to markets that are supported by governments has been rare and difficult. Some experts have argued that GATT rules can apply to claims based on competition policy; however, the complaint would have to be based upon some measure applied by a government in contravention of an existing GATT obligation regarding national treatment, or a quantitative restriction. For example, if a government measure

---

[17] William Diebold, *The End of the ITO,* 16 INTERNATIONAL FINANCE 18 (1952).

[18] The draft convention included the same list of restrictive practices as the Havana Charter, with one exception relating to technology agreements. *See* Diane P. Wood, *The Impossible Dream: Real International Antitrust,* U. CHI. LEGAL F. 277, 284 (1992). For details of the draft convention, see F. M. SCHERER, COMPETITION POLICIES FOR AN INTEGRATED WORLD ECONOMY 39 (1994).

[19] Wood, *supra* note 18, at 284–85.

[20] *See* GATT BISD 7th Supp. 29 (1960).

[21] Specifically the recommendation states that "... the party addressed should accord sympathetic consideration to and should afford adequate opportunity for consultations with the requesting party, with a view to reaching mutually satisfactory consultations, and if it agrees that such harmful effects are present it should take such measures as it deems appropriate". *See,* GATT BISD 9th Supp. 28 (1961). This resolution existed in relative obscurity until it was invoked in 1996 by the United States in the context of a film dispute with Japan. See discussion later in this section.

affirmatively created conditions by which business interests discriminated against foreign goods and services, such a set of facts could give rise to a violation claim.

GATT's nonviolation provisions provide some scope for a complaint of competitive foreclosure of a market, if for example, non-application of national antitrust or competition laws were adjudged to be a "government measure".[22] Still, at least two other conditions would have to be satisfied: the measure would need to have altered the competitive conditions established by other GATT undertakings, and the government measure taken would have to be one that could not reasonably have been anticipated at the time that the tariff or other concession was made. Each of these conditions is a high hurdle that has rarely been brought to the test.

Two GATT/WTO cases have considered actions of governments that were alleged to affirmatively promote exclusionary conduct on the part of private firms.

Semiconductors: In a 1988 case involving the Japanese semiconductor industry, a GATT panel held that even nonbinding administrative guidance by the Government of Japan could constitute a "government measure" if certain criteria were met.[23] In that case, which involved restraints on exports of semiconductors by the Government of Japan,[24] the specific criteria identified by the panel included (1) that reasonable grounds exist for believing that the government measures created sufficient incentives to persuade private parties to conform their conduct to the nonmandatory measures, and (2) that the effectiveness of the private conduct was "essentially dependent" on the nonmandatory actions taken by the government.

Film: In 1995 Eastman Kodak Company filed a Section 301 petition with the United States Trade Representative ("USTR") alleging private and government barriers to the sale and distribution of consumer photographic film in the Japanese market. It based an important part of its initial legal argument on the provision of Section 301 prohibiting governments from tolerating private restraints of trade.[25] This was the first petition accepted by the USTR that was based primarily on the "toleration of systematic anticompetitive practices "feature of Section 301.[26] In summary, it was argued in the original petition that as formal barriers to imports and investment were gradually removed, the Government of Japan implemented "liberalization countermeasures" that were designed to and did create a market structure in Japan that blocked Kodak's sales and market

[22] The GATT provided legal remedies for government actions that had the effect of nullifying and impairing the benefits that another GATT member received as part of the market access it was promised in its *quid pro quo* for the market access that it provided. The GATT also recognized there could be measures or developments that were not a direct violation of agreed-upon commitments but which nevertheless had the effect of nullifying or impairing the intended benefits of the liberalization measures. For additional discussion of this subject *see* Bernard M. Hoeckman and Petros C. Mavroidis, *Competition Policy and the GATT*, 17 THE WORLD ECONOMY 141 (1994).

[23] *See* Report of the GATT Panel (adopted), *Japan-Trade in Semiconductors*, BISD 35th Supp. 116, at 155 (1988).

[24] The Japanese Government had restrained exports of semiconductors at below-cost prices in order to settle a trade dispute with the United States.

[25] *See* Dewey Ballantine for Eastman Kodak Company, *Privatizing Protection: Japanese Market Barriers in Consumer Photographic Film and Consumer Photographic Paper* (May 1995). The facts in this case are well known and exhaustively documented. For purposes of this discussion, I shall highlight some of the policy and procedural consequences of the case. Relevant background writings include: James Durling, ANATOMY OF A TRADE DISPUTE: A DOCUMENTARY HISTORY OF THE KODAK-FUJI FILM DISPUTE (2001) ; John Linarelli, *The Role of Dispute Settlement in World Trade Law: Some Lessons from the Kodak-Fuji Dispute*, 31 LAW AND POLICY IN INT. BUSINESS 2 (2000); Sara Dillon, *Fuji-Kodak, the World Trade Organization and the Death of Domestic Political Constituencies,* 8(2) MINNESOTA JOURNAL OF GLOBAL TRADE 197 (1999).

[26] *See supra,* note 4. One earlier petition, which involved amorphous metal transformers, had focused on this provision but was ultimately withdrawn and negotiated bilaterally without invoking Section 301.

presence and whose structure continues to act as an effective barrier to Kodak's access to that market.[27] The Japanese Government refused an U.S. request to hold formal bilateral trade consultations, even after a finding of unfairness by the USTR. Instead, the Japanese Government insisted that the proper forum in which to air the governmental aspects of the complaint was the WTO and that the issue of allegedly anticompetitive business practices fell solely within the jurisdiction of Japan's Fair Trade Commission (JFTC). For its part, the JFTC surveyed conditions in the consumer photographic film sector and found no violations of domestic law.[28]

The United States took the case to the WTO, focusing on those aspects of the complaint that implicated Japanese government policies, and argued that Japan's actions violated GATT provisions regarding nullification and impairment (Article XXIII), national treatment (Article III), and transparency (Article X), as well as the General Agreement on Trade in Services (GATS). In addition, the United States called for consultations on restrictive business practices under the little-used 1960 GATT decision, but these never got off the ground.[29] The WTO panel held against the United States on the facts of that case, both with respect to the non-violation and violation claims.[30] On the general question of actionable government measures, however, the panel built upon the semiconductor case to argue that analysis of alleged "measures" must "proceed in a manner that is sensitive to the context in which these governmental actions are taken and the effect they have on private actors."[31] The Panel looked also to the semiconductor report for the proposition that, "where administrative guidance creates incentives or disincentives largely dependent upon government action for private parties to act in a particular manner, it may be considered a government measure".[32]

Whatever the legal possibility of such mixed public-private claims under GATT rules, the record shows that the GATT did not serve as a forum either for the negotiation of

---

[27] *See* Dewey Ballantine, *supra* note 25. This paper also argues that an anticompetitive market structure operated in Japan in violation of Japan's Antimonopoly Act, and that the Japan Fair Trade Commission had acted indirectly to support it, allegedly by suppressing promotional activity in the consumer photographic film and paper industry through the Government of Japan's laws against premiums and other marketing restraints.

[28] Japan Fair Trade Commission (JFTC), *Survey of Transactions Among Firms Regarding Photographic Color Film for General Use*, July 23, 1997. Available at http://www.ftc.go.jp/e-page/press/1997/film1/film1.htm

[29] The reasons for this are not entirely clear, but it appears that the Japanese Government insisted that if the United States was intending to focus on Japanese government practices that it believed were responsible for facilitating private anticompetitive conduct, the Japanese Government should be at liberty to raise issues regarding U.S. Government practice.

[30] The US argued that certain distribution-related measures, restrictions on large stores and promotional measures resulted in a GATT Article XXIII:1(b) non-violation nullification or impairment of benefits accruing to the United States based on tariff concessions made by Japan in the Kennedy, Tokyo and Uruguay Rounds. The Panel rejected these claims, relying in part on the fact that many of the challenged measures were relatively old, and that the causality between the measure and the distribution system was not well established. The Panel also rejected the U.S. violation claims, which included an argument that the JFTC and certain fair trade council's failure to publish certain enforcement actions were a violation of GATT Article X: 1. *See Japan—Film, supra* note 12, ¶¶ 10.390–393.

[31] *Id.* at ¶ 10.389. The Panel found that "government policy or action need not necessarily have a substantially binding or compulsory nature for it to entail a likelihood of compliance by private actors in a way so as to nullify or impair legitimately expected benefits within the purview of Article XXII:1(b). Indeed, it is clear that non-binding actions, which include sufficient incentives or disincentives for private parties to act in a particular manner can potentially have adverse effects on competitive conditions of market access." *Id.* at ¶¶ 10.389–90.

[32] *Id.* at ¶¶ 10.43–46

common rules pertaining to business practices or for the resolution of disputes that arose out of some mix of private and governmental practices. In other words, the GATT was used neither as a sword to reach private anticompetitive business practices, nor as a shield to protect private restraints from the unilateral reach of foreign competition laws.[33]

C. UNCTAD

In 1973, at the instigation of the developing nations, negotiations on restrictive business practices were initiated in the United Nations Conference on Trade and Development (UNCTAD). In 1980 the U.N. General Assembly adopted UNCTAD's Set of Multilaterally Agreed Principles and Rules for the Control of Restrictive Business Practices.[34] The rules are nonbinding, however, and they have not become a source of international law.[35] Although UNCTAD has an extremely broad membership base, it has not evolved into a dynamic organization for the consideration of competition policy issues.

D. OECD

Although no binding multilateral agreements on competition policy have been adopted, a variety of consultative mechanisms have been established, most notably at the Organization for Economic Cooperation and Development ("OECD"). At the forefront of efforts to consider the international dimensions of competition policy, the OECD has served as an important consultative body for countries with competition regimes as well as a source of technical assistance to many jurisdictions introducing competition laws and policies. Two different OECD bodies have engaged in serious work on competition policy: the Competition Law and Policy Committee ("CLP"); and the Joint Group on Trade and Competition. The CLP is a venue where enforcers can meet and discuss competition issues, and its work has encouraged greater substantive and procedural convergence among participating countries. More formally, the OECD has produced non-binding recommendations, including a 1998 recommendation condemning hard-core cartels and a 1995 recommendation on international cooperation among competition authorities. The OECD's Joint Group on Trade and Competition has also pursued a work program to increase members' understanding of issues relevant to the interface of trade and competition policy. The OECD has established a new series of international conferences on competition policy in a global economy, called the Global Competition Forum, which includes representatives from both developed and developing nations.

E. Bilateral Cooperation Arrangements and Experiences

International cooperation in competition policy, to the extent that it has occurred and been formalized, has tended to occur mostly on a bilateral basis. Over more than two

---

[33] For a more complete discussion of this potential application of GATT rules, *see also* Merit E. Janow, *Competition Policy and the WTO,* in The Uruguay Round and Beyond (Jagdish Bhagwati and Mathias Hirsch eds. 1998).

[34] This voluntary code contained several provisions calling for special concern to the problems facing developing nations. The code's substantive provisions condemn collusive anticompetitive actions such as price-fixing, collusive tendering, market or customer allocations, sales, or production quotas and various kinds of concerted refusals to deal. The Code also condemns abuses of dominant position such as predatory behavior, discriminatory commercial terms and anticompetitive mergers. Wood, *supra* note 18, at 286.

[35] Wood, *supra* note 18, at 28. *See also*, Global Forum on Competition and Trade Policy, Harmonization of International Competition Law Enforcement 15, n. 73 (1995).

decades, the United States has developed and entered into several generations of international antitrust arrangements. The early competition undertakings were contained within bilateral Friendship, Commerce and Navigation treaties. Later, the United States entered into several types of bilateral antitrust cooperation agreements. These agreements have become more detailed and comprehensive over time.

The first generation of cooperation agreements essentially provided that each party notify the other of a pending enforcement action that could impact upon important interests of the other party; the notification procedure implied a willingness to take the views of the other party into account. The 1995 Canadian-U.S. mutual legal assistance treaty ("MLAT") goes substantially further, in that it permits the use of formal investigative powers in criminal matters if requested by the MLAT partner.

In 1991, the United States and the European Union entered into an agreement that facilitates discovery and implements the notion of "positive comity."[36] In competition cases where both parties believe themselves to have an interest in pursuing enforcement actions, the agreement identifies comity factors to be considered in any effort to accommodate the claims of rival interests. The notion of positive comity not only seeks to ease or at least to manage tensions with respect to extraterritorial enforcement efforts, but also raises cooperation to a new level. A main contribution of the U.S.-E.U. agreement is the identification of a set of positive and negative comity principles that can guide both parties as they decide whether or not to exercise or to forgo jurisdiction over a case.[37]

Another milestone in international cooperation occurred in 1994 when the U.S. Congress passed a statute authorizing U.S. antitrust enforcement agencies to share confidential information and evidence, on a reciprocal basis, with foreign enforcement authorities[38] In 1997 the United States concluded its first comprehensive bilateral accord under this statute with Australia; the accord covers both civil and criminal matters.[39]

In sum, the United States and a number of other competition agencies (e.g., the EC and some member states, Canada, Australia, Japan, Mexico, Israel, Brazil, among others) are developing closer working relations and a measure of mutual confidence that appears to be yielding more cooperation on actual cases. Although still at an early stage, recent bilateral accords represent a further step toward making the compulsory process of one jurisdiction available for use by another requesting jurisdiction. These accords do not seek to achieve substantive legal harmonization, nor do they contain binding dispute settlement mechanisms. As a result, policy conflicts stemming from differing legal standards and national competition policy priorities are not necessarily resolved by virtue of such accords. This reality was demonstrated by the 2001 proposed GE/Honeywell merger,

---

[36] *See Agreement between the Government of the United States of America and the Commission of the European Communities Regarding the Application of the Competition Laws*, September 23, 1991, available at: http://www.usdoj.gov/atr/public/international/docs.

[37] This agreement contained six comity principles that would be considered by the parties in seeking an appropriate accommodation of the competing interests. These include factors such as the relative importance of the activities involved within the enforcing party's territory; the presence or absence of a purpose to affect consumers, suppliers or competitors within the enforcing Party's territory; the relative significant of the effects of the anticompetitive activities on the enforcing jurisdiction; the existence or absence of expectations that would be furthered or defeated; the degree of conflict or consistency between the enforcement activities and the other party's laws; and the extent to which the enforcement activities of one party would impact the other jurisdiction. For additional detail *see*, Agreement, *supra* note 36, Article VI.

[38] Pub. L. No. 103-438, 108 Stat. 4597, 15 U.S.C. §§6200–6212.

[39] *Agreement between the Government of the United States of America and the Government of Australia, A Mutual Legal Antitrust Enforcement Assistance Agreement*, available at: http:www.usdoj.gov/atr/public/international

which the United States cleared but the EU did not.[40] The contribution of bilateral accords in structuring communication and to some degree managing tension is also limited by the fact that only a small number of countries have such bilateral arrangements in place.[41]

F. Regional Arrangements

Over the past two decades, regional organizations have become actively engaged on issues of competition law and policy. The resulting arrangements range from formal cooperation agreements, such as that introduced between Australia and New Zealand as part of its treaty to establish closer economic relations; to more informal and *ad hoc* consultative mechanisms, such as those efforts undertaken by the organization for Asia-Pacific Economic Cooperation ("APEC"). Cooperation in competition policy is now under active consideration in the context of the Free Trade Agreement of the Americas involving the United States and the nations of Latin America. And indeed, many of the bilateral free trade agreements now under negotiation by Japan, the United States and the European Union include some consultation mechanism on competition policy matters.[42]

IV. The Uruguay Round Agreements and the WTO

As noted above, very few cases in the GATT/WTO dispute settlement system have considered whether and to what degree governments should be held accountable for fostering or tolerating anticompetitive private restraints of trade. This did not change fundamentally with the expansion of commitments that came as part of the Uruguay Round, and which led to the establishment of GATT's successor organization, the World Trade Organization, in 1995. However, in a limited fashion, a few provisions of the WTO agreements implicate private practices that are seen as trade-restricting and hold governments responsible to some degree for those practices. And, quite apart from coverage in specific agreements, core GATT provisions are supportive of an effective competition policy regime. A few examples are illustrative:

- The WTO's *basic nondiscrimination principles* of national treatment, most-favored-nation treatment, and transparency, which form the foundation of the WTO, are also essential features of an impartial competition policy regime. The national treatment requirement of Article III of the GATT has long been used to

---

[40] *See* discussion of the matter in Part II *supra*.

[41] For a more detailed assessment of bilateral antitrust cooperation agreements, *see* Janow, *supra* note 14 and *Transatlantic Cooperation on Competition Policy* in ANTITRUST GOES GLOBAL (Simon J. Evenett, Alexander Lehman and Benn Steil eds. 2000).

[42] A brief elaboration of several examples may be helpful. Australia and New Zealand entered into a comprehensive cooperation agreement in 1994 that requires the two competition agencies to exchange and provide information in relation to investigations and research; speeches, compliance education programs; amendments to relevant legislation; and human resources. The agreement allows information in the files of one agency to be requested by another agency. It also provides for the coordination of enforcement activities when the Agencies agree that this would be beneficial in a particular case. A far more limited instrument is Chapter Fifteen of the North American Free Trade Agreement, which establishes a Working Party and contains certain general undertakings. The provisions do not attempt to harmonize procedural or substantive rules, to provide for the exchange of confidential information, or to articulate general standards. Work on competition policy in the APEC context has taken the form of a series of annual workshops on competition policy and deregulation issues held under the aegis of the Committee on Trade and Investment. At their meeting in September 1999, APEC Leaders endorsed a set of nonbinding principles developed by this workshop that are intended to act as "benchmarks" for member economies in their efforts to design and implement competitive markets.

challenge not only border barriers but internal practices as well—indeed one of the first GATT cases of *de jure* discrimination involved a domestic credit scheme that applied only to purchasers of domestically produced tractors.[43] Determining whether a measure is discriminatory can turn on whether the affected products are "like," and analytically, the question of determining "likeness" of products can resemble the product and geographic market definition that is central to a competition analysis. Moreover, there is a tendency now in some WTO Article III:2 national treatment/nondiscrimination cases to consider whether products are directly competitive or substitutable.[44] This approach also reflects the influence of economic analysis, which has had an even greater influence on competition policy analysis, especially in the United States.

- The WTO *Basic Telecommunications Services Agreement*, officially known as the "Fourth Protocol to the General Agreement on Services", requires countries to liberalize market access and national treatment restrictions and to implement regulatory principles intended to guide domestic regulatory practices.[45] These principles are not intended to serve as a comprehensive competition policy code for the telecommunications sector. They are selective, yet bespeak a recognition that telecommunications remains a heavily regulated sector and that in many jurisdictions regulatory authorities are not independent of telecom providers. Domestic suppliers usually are dominant suppliers, whether they are private or public entities, and if left free to make decisions about how to treat other suppliers, these suppliers would be capable of thwarting the market access and national treatment commitments made by governments. The principles seek to support competition in the telecommunications sector by means of competitive safeguards designed to prevent major suppliers from engaging in anticompetitive practices.

- The *General Agreement on Trade in Services* also contains several provisions that implicate anticompetitive practices as exercised by domestic service providers. For example, the GATS provides that monopoly service suppliers must not act in a fashion inconsistent with the most-favored-nation obligation under the agreement or with their scheduled commitments.[46] Further, the GATS requires WTO member governments to ensure that domestic monopolists do not abuse their monopoly positions.[47] The accord requires mandatory consultation on alleged restrictive business practices, if requested by another WTO member.[48]

- Competition policy arises indirectly in Article 9 of the *Agreement on Trade-Related Investment Measures,* which requires the Council for Trade in Goods to review the operation of the agreement and to propose necessary amendments to it by the end of 1999.[49] The Council was directed in Article 9 to consider whether those amendments should include provisions on competition policy.

---

[43] *See* Report of the GATT Panel (adopted), *Italian Discrimination Against Imported Agricultural Machinery* BISD 7th Supp. 60 (1958).

[44] *See*, for example, the discussion of these concepts in Report of the WTO Panel, *Korea-Taxes on Alcoholic Beverages,* W/DS75/R and W/DS84/R (1998), ¶¶ 10.95–10.97 and 10.44–10.45. The Appellate Body upheld the Panel's decision. Report of the Appellate Body, *Korea-Taxes on Alcoholic Beverages,* W/DS75/AB/R and W/DS84/AB/R (1999).

[45] *See Fourth Protocol to the General Agreement on Services* (April 30, 1996) S/L 20, available at http:www.wto.org/services

[46] *See* Article VIII:1 of the GATS.

[47] *See* Article VIII:2 of the GATS.

[48] *See* Article IX(2) of the GATS.

[49] As of this writing, no comprehensive set of recommendations has been released.

An additional WTO agreement—the TRIPS accord—is notable in that it probably offers the closest existing model for competition rules and suggests an alternative "architecture" for competition policy provisions under the WTO. Historically, the GATT focused on limiting distortions introduced by governments; these limits informed governments what they *could not do* rather that setting out a set of affirmative obligations that they *were* required to undertake. The TRIPS accord introduced an entirely different construct by obliging countries to introduce intellectual property laws that contained specified minimum levels of protection to intellectual property rights. The TRIPS agreement requires nondiscriminatory treatment, and it also requires member countries to introduce effective national enforcement systems, the precise structure and design of which are left in the hands of national authorities but which must provide effective measures for both private and governmental enforcement.

The WTO has also attempted to develop various "framework" agreements that serve as non-binding guidance to members on matters of domestic regulation or oversight. These too, could offer an architecture or template for linking competition policy to the WTO. For example, in December 1998 the WTO Council on Trade in Services adopted the WTO Disciplines on Domestic Regulation in the Accountancy Sector. These are nonbinding principles that WTO members are exhorted to follow.[50]

Finally, the Singapore Ministerial Meeting in 1996 set up the WTO Working Group on the Interaction of Trade and Competition Policies. This Working Group has considered a very broad set of issues, such as the relationships among the objectives, principles, scope, and instruments of trade and competition policy; the types and effectiveness of existing instruments, standards, and activities used or undertaken by trade and competition policy; the relationship between competition policies and industrial policies; and the interaction between trade and competition policy.[51] It has held numerous formal meetings and received hundreds of written contributions from a multitude of sources, including developing and transition countries and international organizations. The Working Group has issued detailed reports that chronicle not only a very broad range of issues examined, but many areas where WTO members disagreed.

V. Competition Policy and the Next Round of Multilateral Trade Negotiations

Little, if any, substantive discussion of competition policy occurred among WTO ministers at the failed December 1999 Trade Summit in Seattle.[52] The issue was actively considered at the Doha Ministerial in Qatar on November 9–14, 2001, and WTO members agreed that "negotiations will take place after the Fifth Session of the Ministerial Conference . . . on the basis of a decision to be taken, by explicit consensus, at that Session on modalities of negotiations." The Doha Declaration states that in the period before the Fifth Session (due to be held in Cancun, Mexico, in September 2003), the Working Group on the Interaction between Trade and Competition Policy "will focus on the clarification of: core principles, including transparency, non-discrimination and procedural fairness, and provisions on hardcore cartels; modalities for voluntary cooperation; and

---

[50] *See* WTO, *Report to the Council for Trade in Services on the Development of Disciplines on Domestic Regulation in the Accountancy Sector*, S/WPPS/4 (December 10, 1998).

[51] *See Report (1998) of the Working Group on the Interaction Between Trade and Competition Policy to the General Council,* WT/WGTCP/2 (December 8, 1998).

[52] Former U.S. Trade Representative Charlene Barshefsky suggested that the EU was virtually alone in its interest in global negotiations on competition policy. *See* 17 INSIDE U.S. TRADE, No. 51, at 3 (December 24, 1999). This appears to be less the case today than when that statement was made.

support for progressive reinforcement of competition institutions in developing countries through capacity building. Full account shall be taken of the needs of developing and least-developed country participants and appropriate flexibility provided to address them."[53] There appears to have been some controversy as to whether this language in the Ministerial Declaration reflects an expectation that negotiations will commence following the Fifth Session of the Ministerial Conference, or whether that is the point in time when WTO members will decide whether or not to commence negotiations. This was clarified, to some degree, by the Chairman of the Conference, in a statement that the requirement for explicit consensus on the modalities for negotiations "gave each Member the right to take a position on modalities that would prevent negotiations from proceeding after the Fifth Session of the Ministerial Conference until that Member is prepared to join an explicit consensus."[54]

While this fundamental issue of whether a formal negotiation will commence remained unsettled until July 2004, the Working Group continued in its consultations, seminars and other preparatory activities on the specific procedural and substantive areas outlined in the Declaration.

The most intensive debate at the government level about the role of the WTO in the area of competition policy has taken place between U.S. and EU officials. Let us briefly outline the main arguments that each government has advanced, recognizing that even official positions continue to evolve and change.

A. European Union

EU officials have been forceful advocates of expanded multilateral rules on competition policy, including at the WTO. While stressing the importance of effective bilateral cooperation as a foundation, the last two Commissioners for the Competition Directorate, Sir Leon Brittan and Karel Van Miert, along with the current Commissioner Mario Monti, have each called for expanded WTO rules on competition policy.

The EU proposal has gone through some modifications from that first advanced by Sir Leon Brittan in the mid-1990s. Initially, the EU seemed to support the negotiation of substantive competition rules and suggested it was willing to have actual domestic competition or antitrust cases subject to review and challenge under the rules of the Dispute Settlement Body of the WTO.[55] Since then the EU appears to have scaled back its expectations on coverage and on panel review. At one point, for example, the Commission argued that negotiated rules should be subject to dispute settlement only for alleged "patterns of failure to enforce competition law in cases affecting the trade and investment of other WTO members". Individual cases would not be examined, according to this position.[56]

The EU argued in support of a multilateral framework on competition policy in the WTO that would include core principles comprising transparency, non-discrimination and procedural fairness in the application of competition law and/or policy, and the taking of measures against hardcore cartels; the development of modalities for cooperation;

[53] World Trade Organization, *Ministerial Declaration* (Fourth Session of the Ministerial Conference, Doha), WT/MIN(01)/DEC/1, November 9–14, 2001, ¶¶ 23–25.
[54] Robert D. Anderson and Frederic Jenny, *Current Developments on Competition Policy in the World Trade Organization*, ANTITRUST MAGAZINE, Fall 2001.
[55] This would not be unique. Individual domestic antidumping, countervailing duty, and safeguard decisions can be challenged in the WTO dispute settlement system if they violate the relevant agreements.
[56] *See* K. Mehta, The *Role of Competition in a Globalized Trade Environment*, Speech to the Third WTO Symposium on Competition Policy and the Multilateral System, Geneva, (April 7, 1999).

and enhanced support for technical assistance and institution building,[57] over time the EC retained some ambiguity as to whether the framework must be part of the WTO and a requirement of all of its members, or a separate plurilateral agreement signed by interested nations.[58]

At various times, the EU position appears to have some support from several other governments including the governments of Canada, Japan, Korea and several of the Latin American countries.

B. The U.S. Government

The U.S. Government, while actively supporting the deliberations of the WTO Working Group, has generally taken a cautious tone regarding the WTO's role as a forum for the negotiation of rules governing competition policy. This was particularly the case during the Clinton Administration. Former Assistant Attorney-General for Antitrust Joel Klein often argued that he saw greater practical value in bilateral cooperation arrangements, such as those the United States has entered with Australia, Canada, and the European Union, than in negotiating general competition rules at the WTO. This network of bilateral arrangements, coupled with technical assistance to new regimes and dialogue at the OECD, WTO, regional groupings, and other international forums, have been the core policy elements of U.S. international antitrust policy.[59]

In the Bush Administration, U.S. Trade Representative Robert Zoellick has indicated somewhat greater receptivity to some WTO treatment of competition policy than his predecessor.[60]

U.S. antitrust officials routinely raise several different types of concerns about the WTO venturing into the terrain of competition policy.[61] WTO oversight of antitrust actions taken by governments could, in Joel Klein's words, "involve the WTO in second-guessing prosecutorial decision-making in complex evidentiary contexts in which the WTO has no experience and for which it is not suited," and would inevitably politicize international antitrust enforcement in ways that are not likely to improve either the economic rationality or the legal neutrality of antitrust decision making. He further argues that the global community does not yet fully know what key trade and competition questions may benefit from binding international agreements, let alone whether there is any possibility of developing a consensus on these issues.[62]

---

[57] *See Communication from the European Community and its Member States,* WT/WGTCP/W/152.

[58] At a regional WTO workshop in Capetown, South Africa, an EU official clarified that the EU thought there was significant interest around the world in entering into a multilateral agreement at the WTO. However, if at the conclusion of negotiations, there were still developing countries that were hesitant and not convinced that such an agreement was in their interest, they should have the possibility to opt out of it. *See Informal Report on Workshop Proceedings*, WTO Regional Workshop on Competition Policy, Economic Development and the Multilateral Trading System, organized by the WTO Secretariat in Cooperation with the Governments of South Africa and the United Kingdom (February 22–24, 2001).

[59] *See,* e.g., Joel Klein, *A Note of Caution with Respect to a WTO Agenda on Competition Policy* (Remarks to the Royal Institute of International Affairs, Chatham House, November 1996).

[60] *See* "USTR Zoellick outlines US efforts to promote growth and development by launching new trade round; US-EU effort directed at expanding and strengthening global trading system", http:www.ustr.gov/releases/2001/07/01-54.pdf. This statement contains the following language, "The United States can see merit in adherence to core principles of transparency, non-discrimination and procedural fairness. We can also support consultative and capacity building efforts to help countries develop modern competition policy that promotes efficient, effective and dynamic markets."

[61] *See* Joel Klein, *A Reality Check on Antitrust Rules in the World Trade Organization, And a Practical Way Forward on International Antitrust,* Address before the OECD Conference on Trade and Competition. (Paris, June 30, 1999).

[62] *Id.*

C. Other Views

There is no unified position on competition policy among developing countries although several developing countries expressed repeated doubts about the value of negotiations on competition policy. For example, Kenya, on behalf of the African Group, has noted that only a limited number of African countries have domestic legislation on competition policy and even fewer African countries have effective enforcement agencies. At one point in 1999, the African Group advocated continuation of the educational, exploratory, and analytical work of the Working Group on the Interaction between Trade and Competition Policy with increased technical assistance to developing countries.[63] At one point, South Africa proposed a thorough educational process that would take place before any negotiations commence and would span several years and take into account the huge analytical demands on developing countries related to the preparation of the next round.[64]

Apart from official governmental discussion, the debate in the private sector and among experts on what role the WTO should have with respect to competition policy is robust and diverse. Let us mention several different approaches that have surfaced.

The most ambitious proposal, which appears to have a very limited following, calls for the establishment of some kind of supranational antitrust authority with agreed-upon substantive rules. In 1993 a private group of twelve scholars and other experts meeting in Munich (the so-called "Munich Group") proposed an International Antitrust Code, which would set out minimum standards to be incorporated into the WTO. It proposed that those standards in turn would be enforceable in domestic jurisdictions by national enforcement agencies. Disputes would be adjudicated by a permanent international antitrust panel, operating as part of the WTO's dispute settlement regime.[65]

A second approach is the call to develop a set of competition principles. For example, a former Deputy Secretary-General of the OECD, Joanna Shelton, suggested that the WTO could develop a set of core principles, both procedural and substantive, upon which there could be broad agreement. Parties would bind themselves to abide by the core principles, but the specific rules that they adopt for doing so would not be subject to dispute settlement. The multilateral approach should provide some non-binding suggestions about possible common approaches to aid nations in designing and enforcing substantive criteria, such as the tests to assess the legality of core competition problems such as horizontal agreements, vertical restraints, abuse of dominance and proposed mergers. This second approach has more of a following and there are a variety of proposals under debate with different specific principles included in the mix. Structurally, this approach attempts to integrate antitrust into a larger market access framework rather than trying to maintain a strict boundary between private and public restraints.

There have also been two influential reports, one in Europe and one in the United States, that have served to underpin the respective official approaches of their nations on the subject. A group of leading European experts issued an influential report in 1995 supporting the EU approach and called for movement on two fronts: first, a further

---

[63] See *The Interaction Between Trade and Competition Policy,* Communication from Kenya on behalf of the African Group, Preparations for the 1999 Ministerial Conference, WT/GC/W/300, August 6, 1999.

[64] See *Communication from the Republic of South Africa*, WT/WGTCP/W/138, October 11, 1999, pp. 2, 4. In recent years, South Africa has introduced an active competition law and policy regime. Perhaps as a result, South African trade and competition officials have indicated a certain receptivity to some WTO rules in this policy area.

[65] For a reprint of the Code developed by the Munich Group, *see:* 64 Antitrust & Trade Reg. Rep (BNA), August 19, 1993.

deepening of existing forms of bilateral cooperation; and second, the gradual construction of a plurilateral agreement that includes a dispute settlement procedure based on a set of jointly determined competition rules.[66]

The group argued in favor of establishing minimum rules and then gradually expanding the number of countries signing on to those rules. It suggested using common principles in some instances, such as the prohibition of cartels (building from the OECD recommendation in this area), and the rule of reason in other instances (such as vertical restraints). The report argued for harmonization of procedures in the merger field to give authorities sufficient time to consult each other. It also recommended that state trading enterprises be subject to the same competition rules as commercial enterprises. At the international level, the group suggested that the WTO serve as a forum or analyzing and possibly extending the principles, registering anticompetitive practices, and providing for dispute settlement procedures.

In the United States, the International Competition Policy Advisory Committee (ICPAC) to the Attorney-General and Assistant-Attorney General for Antitrust undertook an extensive outreach effort over a two-year period to solicit private sector and official views on international competition law and policy matters and issued a major report of its findings and recommendations in March, 2000. ICPAC was charged with focusing on global competition policy matters generally—including multi-jurisdictional merger review, international enforcement cooperation vis-a-vis cartels, and the interface of competition and trade policy. As part of that effort, it sought views on the possible future role for the WTO as a forum for the negotiation of global competition rules subject to dispute settlement.[67]

The majority of ICPAC members recommended in the Final Report that the primary focus of the WTO and its area of core competence remain as an intergovernmental trade forum focusing on governmental restraints. The report argued that the WTO had a constructive role to play regarding competition policy, but that this role should be to support capacity building and cooperation between authorities, rather than the negotiation of procedural or substantive rules.

The ICPAC Final Report identified no influential U.S. business group that was in favor of WTO rules on competition policy. For example, the Business Roundtable has consistently held that competition policy negotiations at the WTO are both "unnecessary and potentially counterproductive." The Roundtable has argued that negotiations should not proceed in the absence of an international consensus on competition policy, uncertainty about the WTO's institutional competence on competition policy matters, and the possibility that developing countries might use the negotiations to "disturb the carefully crafted multilateral balance embodied in the WTO Antidumping Code."[68] Similarly, both the U.S. Council for International Business (U.S.CIB) and the International Chamber of Commerce believe that a basis has not yet been established for international agreement in the WTO on competition principles or rules.[69]

VI. Is There a Need for a New Global Competition Forum?

Quite apart from a role for the WTO, the last several years have also seen active consideration of the merits of establishing an altogether new forum to consider global competition

---

[66] *See* Report of the Group of Experts, *Competition Policy in the New Trade Order: Strengthening International Cooperation and Rules* (July 1995)

[67] *See ICPAC Final Report, supra* note 6.

[68] *Id.* at 268

[69] *Id.*

matters. The concept of establishing a new forum, initially dubbed the Global Competition Initiative, was proposed by ICPAC in its Final Report. The rationale for establishing a separate forum devoted to international competition matters hinged on the view that in a world of expanding global markets, a widening array of competition policy problems are unlikely to be resolved through national legal responses alone. Addressing international competition policy problems requires more cooperation between competition authorities, more international discussion of problems with trans-border consequences, and new and expanded international arrangements. Competition policy problems with a global or transnational nature were not limited to matters implicating access to markets and international trade. For this reason, ICPAC urged that a new inclusive forum be established that would routinely include representatives from developed and developing economies, government officials, and other experts.

The concept received a first boost when Former Assistant Attorney General Klein said in September 2000 that he thought that the Global Competition Initiative warranted serious consideration whatever happens on antitrust at the WTO. Subsequently, the EC Competition Commissioner Mario Monti has repeatedly indicated his strong support for such an initiative and advanced a number of specific details for organizing such a forum. This idea was bolstered when in February 2001, at a meeting organized by the International Bar Association, a group of 43 senior competition law officials and professionals gathered at Ditchley Park in England to discuss the possible design and activities for the proposed Initiative or Forum.[70] This was the first "brainstorming" session on this proposed global forum among leading figures in the competition law and policy community worldwide.

Several months later, in the fall of 2001, the formation of the International Competition Network ("ICN") was officially announced. Now, more than 75 jurisdictions have joined this informal network. The ICN is designed as an informal, project oriented network of antitrust agencies from developed and developing countries. The purpose of the network is to consider antitrust enforcement and policy issues of common interest and to "formulate proposals for procedural and substantive convergence through a results-oriented agenda and structure".[71] The ICN distinguishes itself from the WTO by virtue of its project-orientation, diverse membership (including the participation of experts and non-governmental representatives), specific work program and governance structure. At this early stage, the ICN has established working groups on multi-jurisdictional merger review and competition advocacy.[72]

VII. Summary and Perspective of Key Issues for the WTO

This last part considers most directly the pros and cons of linking competition policy to the WTO: What would it mean to have competition policy integrated, in some fashion, into the World Trade Organization? What are the principal arguments in support of and in opposition to moving in this direction?

Let us start with arguments in favor of an expanded international arrangement at the WTO. As outlined at the start of this chapter, private restraints of trade can impose strains on the international trading system and frictions between nations and firms. So

---

[70] *See* Merit E. Janow, *The Initiative for a Global Competition Forum: A Report on a Meeting Convened and Hosted by the IBA and Held at Ditchley Park,* BUSINESS LAW INTERNATIONAL, Issue 2 (2001).

[71] *See About the ICN,* available at: http://www.internationalcompetitionnetwork.org.

[72] *Id.*

far, disputes have been handled in an *ad hoc* fashion. Many nations do not have effective remedies to address impediments to offshore market access or more traditional competition problems under national laws. Moreover, there are no meaningful international rules or institutions that deal with these problems. This lack of an international context for resolving international competition problems with market access implications can fall disproportionately on developing nations that do not have the expertise, resources, and established forms of bilateral cooperation to address competition problems that are occurring offshore. But such transborder enforcement problems are felt by many nations across the development spectrum.

As formal governmental barriers to trade and investment have been reduced or eliminated, policymakers around the world have begun to focus their attention and concern on internal practices of nations that impact global trade and investment. And, since many more countries now have a degree of experience with competition policy, the time has come to develop ways of addressing internal business practices that thwart the free flow of commerce. Failure to address such underlying restraints of trade and investment could erode public confidence in the international trading system. And, in this period where there is considerable antipathy to globalization, every effort should be made to instill greater confidence in the world trading system.

Why turn to the WTO? The core nondiscrimination principles of the GATT and now the WTO are compatible with competition policy objectives, and the development of principles or rules at the WTO holds at least the potential of containing the intergovernmental and commercial frictions that result from the absence, ineffectiveness, and perhaps heterogeneity of national competition rules with adverse transnational consequences. Moreover, for some countries, international rules can help to support the development of domestic policy systems. Developing countries and economies in transition are increasingly interested in establishing more open and contestable markets. Competition policy can help in this pursuit, and international agreements can sometimes be used to complement or reinforce domestic policies.

Further, the WTO has shown itself capable of addressing trade-restricting and discriminatory government practices and of serving as a forum for negotiating the reduction and elimination of such trade distortions. With its wide membership, including both developed and developing economies, enhanced dispute settlement capabilities since the creation of the WTO itself, and broad coverage of issues, the WTO is becoming a credible institution for considering and solving difficult problems in international commerce.

The precise architecture within the WTO is, of course, another important consideration. The TRIPS agreement is probably the most directly analogous model, in that it sets forth a set of affirmative core requirements (countries must have a domestic intellectual property protection scheme, it must be enforced, etc.) This model could be adapted for competition policy, with room for varying degrees of generality or specificity, depending on where consensus can be reached. Of course, the WTO members could also chose to develop a looser less binding "framework" agreement of some kind or establish an ongoing deliberative committee on competition issues.

These positive arguments notwithstanding, the integration of competition policy into the WTO gives rise to certain questions. While the benefits of formal harmonization of competition laws have long been debated, neither the need for that step nor the requisite trust to undertake that step has shown itself to be evident. The reasons for this are various: competition laws and policies are not uniform across countries and embed different analytical approaches, values and procedural characteristics. If such harmonization is unlikely, one must ask whether it is possible (or desirable) to have general rules or principles in the absence of agreement on underlying law? The considerable variation that exists among even facially similar national competition laws is likely to mean that a new overarching set of binding rules might have to be drafted at such a level of generality as to make the effort of questionable value. For example, there may be broad agreement in many OECD jurisdictions regarding the impermissibility of horizontal agreements among competitors to fix prices, engage in group boycotts, and allocate markets. And yet, once outside the narrow area of hardcore offenses, differences in national standards as to permissible business practices become substantial. As recent merger disputes have illustrated, in some key areas of law (such as abuse of dominance and monopolization matters) U.S. and EU laws diverge. Hence, although some degree of "soft harmonization" is occurring as a result of increased interaction between firms and legal regimes, formal harmonization, especially by means of a set of international rules, seems problematic and unlikely to be productive.

The case for an international body reviewing international merger cases under binding dispute settlement procedures raises other problems. The concerns raised by the majority opinion in the 1960 GATT expert study group remain alive today: there is likely to be considerable objection in some countries to the idea of an international body attempting to sit in judgement of the fact-specific decisions rendered by national competition authorities and courts.

If competition policy disputes were to become subject to WTO dispute settlement, what standard of review would be applied by a dispute settlement panel? Some argue that a WTO panel could apply the law of the jurisdictions whose practices are at issue. This step, while logical, goes far beyond current WTO practice, which limits panels to simply reviewing the consistency of national measures with established WTO rules. Surely, a number of areas that could potentially be integrated into the WTO's agenda would involve an expansion of international rules into areas of national policy. Hence, although this question of standard of review is not confined to competition policy, it is particularly critical for competition policy given the evolving legal doctrine in the field. In the competition policy context, this bespeaks a need to accord a high degree of deference to the decisions of national authorities. (This point of view has been stressed in the EU expert report and emphasized in the earlier 1960 GATT expert committee report).

Furthermore, the WTO itself as an institution has some obvious limitations when applied to competition law and policy matters. As noted earlier, the goals of competition and trade policy are not identical, and it is not clear whether the negotiation of competition rules within the context of a multilateral trade negotiation will result in the codification of the most politically feasible as opposed to the economically most efficient or the most consumer welfare-enhancing outcomes.[73] It is possible that multilateral negotiations could, over time, ratchet up an improved appreciation for competition policy and its enforcement, but this is uncertain.

VIII. Final Observations

This complex landscape suggests to this author the following: first, that the next steps at the WTO are likely to be fairly modest. The more general and less binding the framework, the more support there appears to be for it. Indeed, in this sense the discussion of

---

[73] *See* Remarks by Assistant Attorney-General Joel I. Klein, Antitrust Division, Department of Justice, Presented at Fordham Law Institute, 24th Annual Conference on International Antitrust Law and Policy (New York, October 16, 1997).

competition policy and the WTO is somewhat akin to the curious paradox occurring in other areas of domestic economic regulation. For example, countries around the world have unilaterally liberalized their investment regimes to attract foreign capital and much of the antipathy to foreign investment that characterized the 1960s and 1970s appears to have vanished. At the same time, many countries have been willing to do far more by way of liberalization of their domestic investment regimes than they have been willing to commit to in binding international agreements. Similarly, many countries have introduced competition laws in the last decade. Both mature systems, such as the United States, and some new systems are worried about the potentially intrusive consequences of WTO rules in this policy area. For a number of developing countries, there appears to be concern that the introduction of WTO competition principles or rules will constrain developing countries in their ability to utilize infant industry policies, social policies, or other development tools. This anxiety also translates into a call for long-phase ins or other ways of giving developing countries the equivalent of special and differential treatment should some new rules or principles be developed.

Second, if this first somewhat cautious assessment of the next steps proves accurate, it may suggest that the more general the framework, the less useful it is likely to prove with respect to particular disputes between nations. For example, transparency and nondiscrimination are useful and important underpinnings to a competition policy regime, but one is still left asking whether embedding procedural screens of that sort at the WTO are likely to be truly useful in the competition policy context? Do market access tensions stem from facially discriminatory competition policies? One suspects the numbers are limited. Moreover, there are situations where the legal and institutional competition policy infrastructure is in place, largely transparent, and reasonably well funded, but the end result is not a well-functioning or effective enforcement regime. Is this a problem that could be challenged effectively at the WTO? Importantly, are WTO members prepared to take additional steps, in the form of supporting capacity building in this policy area, and use the WTO as a forum for supporting the development of sound competition policy regimes around the world? If so, then the consequences of general undertakings on competition policy could, over time, prove useful.

Currently, there is no agreement that the WTO should become an instrument for full market integration. Instead, the WTO is only tugging gently, and with no shortage of opposition, in that direction. Its main focus remains on trade-distorting governmental practice—which in the competition policy context would be a narrow slice of global competition policy challenges.

How issues are linked will also prove important. For example, some may favor the inclusion of competition policy into the WTO as a way of limiting, over time, the scope for antidumping measures. But in this author's view, the linkage of competition policy commitments to antidumping reform has only served to chill and further politicize multilateral discussion of competition policy.

Third, and more positively, even if one has some skepticism about the practical utility of WTO rules on competition policy, for the foreseeable future there is both a need and apparently some international interest in further developing effective competition laws, policies, and enforcement capabilities at the national level. For some countries, bilateral cooperation agreements are realistic next steps, and an expanding web of these arrangements seems to hold few, if any, dangers to the international trading system. Additional bilateral or even regional cooperation agreements may be constructive incremental steps for addressing practical enforcement problems and building a degree of trust across agencies.

Fourth, a host of global competition issues are not trade issues, but are perceived as costly and burdensome to firms involved with international commerce. It seems unlikely that the WTO can do much to advance procedural harmonization of merger practices, but these soft convergence and best practices efforts are now underway in multiple fora such as the ICN and the OECD. A soft convergence framework does not necessarily mean talk without progress.

As the recent record suggests, an active and public dialogue about the general internationalization of competition law and policy is now well under way. This degree of international engagement on the subject is both new and in my view, constructive. Yet, improvements in competition rules and their enforcement may be a necessary but insufficient condition for effective market access; many areas will require additional initiatives in terms of trade liberalization and regulatory reform. Some experts argue that it is important for the WTO to create new rules and institutional frameworks that allow for democratic experimentalism at the domestic level with new institutional structures and approaches at the international level. This viewpoint suggests that any resulting arrangements at the WTO may not be rules-based but could, for example, be an analytical exercise, plurilateral in membership, subject to opt-in provisions, and so forth.[74] This conceptualization of a possible architecture for integrating competition policy into the WTO is in fact a systemic question for the WTO itself, and it will surely be an important part of the post-Doha Agenda.

It is now obvious that all roads do not lead to the World Trade Organization as the forum for settlement of competition-related disputes or negotiation of rules. Indeed, at the Cancun Ministerial Conference in September 2003, the majority of developing countries objected to the launching of formal negotiations on a multilateral framework on competition as proposed by the European Union. The reasons appeared to be various but included concerns about capacity constraints in the developing world, uncertainty about the benefits of multilateral rules, and concerns that negotiated rules might impose constraints on other economic policies that developing countries might pursue. These concerns then translated into an agreement among the WTO Members in the summer of 2004 that no work towards negotiations on competition policy will take place within the WTO during the Doha Round. Thus, current conditions suggest that substantial public and private engagement on competition law and policy matters is well underway in various international settings but multilateral negotiations at the WTO are unlikely for the foreseeable future.

---

[74] *See* Robert Howse *From Politics to Technology—and Back Again: The Fate of the Multilateral Trading Regime,* 96 AMERICAN JOURNAL OF INTERNATIONAL LAW 94 (2002).

CHAPTER 58

TRADE AND THE ENVIRONMENT

Matthew Stilwell and Jan Bohanes*

TABLE OF CONTENTS

* Matthew Stilwell serves as Managing Director of the Program on Governance for Sustainable Development at the Bren School of Environmental Science and Management, University of California, Santa Barbara, and as Legal Counsel to the UN Environment Program's Economics and Trade Branch in Geneva, Switzerland. Jan Bohanes is Legal Affairs Officer at the World Trade Organization. The views expressed in this article are strictly personal and do not bind or necessarily reflect the views of their respective organizations. The cut-off date for this article is September 1, 2002. We are grateful to Arthur E. Appleton, James Bacchus, Valerie Hughes, Gabrielle Marceau, and Alice Palmer for their comments, advice and assistance. All errors, or course, remain our own.

I. Introduction

This chapter provides an overview of a broad range of issues that arise at the interface of trade and the environment. After this introduction, Section II considers trade and environment in the context of the WTO, by examining relevant WTO agreements, recent trade disputes with environmental implications, the WTO's Committee on Trade and Environment ("CTE"), and relevant mandates resulting from the recent WTO Fourth Ministerial in Doha, Qatar. Section III then seeks to place the traditional issues of trade and environment in the broader context of sustainable development, a concept that connotes a development path that optimizes human activities within economic, social and environmental spheres, and that meets the needs of present generations without compromising the ability of future generations to meet their own needs. This is followed in subsequent sections by a thematic discussion of the main trade and environment issues, organized according to three main categories: 1) issues arising from *material linkages* between trade and other facets of the world we live in (Section IV); 2) *legal and policy-related issues* arising between trade and other fields of law and policy (Section V); and 3) *organizational issues* arising between the WTO and other institutional arrangements (Section VI). Section VII concludes with some thoughts on the future development of international economic law and policy as it applies to the environment and sustainable development. The scope, diversity and complexity of this field prevent a single chapter from covering the subject in detail; this chapter, consequently, is designed to provide a sketch of some of the main issues of trade and environment and to complement the discussion of related issues as they are addressed in other chapters of this work.

II. The WTO, Environment and Sustainable Development

A. Relevant WTO Agreements

The WTO legal system does not address the relationship between trade, environment and sustainable development in one comprehensive document. Rather, issues relating to the environment are scattered through many of the agreements annexed to the Marrakesh Agreement Establishing the World Trade Organization. The main ones are described below, with an emphasis on those obligations and exceptions that are especially relevant in the field of trade and environment.

1. The Marrakesh Agreement Establishing the World Trade Organization ("WTO Agreement")

The WTO Agreement establishes the WTO as the preeminent international institution governing international trade. It encompasses the original GATT 1947, augmented by the amendments of the past fifty years, as well as the other agreements negotiated during the Uruguay Round of trade talks. Its preamble includes reference to the objective of sustainable development and the need to protect and preserve the environment. It states in the relevant part:

> *Recognizing* that their relations in the field of trade and economic endeavor should be conducted with a view to raising standards of living, ensuring full employment and a large and steadily growing volume of real income and effective demand, and expanding the production of and trade in goods and services, *while allowing for the optimal use of the world's resources in accordance with the objective of sustainable development, seeking both to protect and preserve the environment and to enhance the means for doing so in a*

manner consistent with their respective needs and concerns at different levels of economic development.[1] (emphasis added)

To achieve these objectives, WTO rules are directed at the "substantial reduction of tariffs and other barriers to trade and to the elimination of discriminatory treatment in international trade relations."[2] In addition, the WTO Agreement recognizes the "need for positive efforts designed to ensure that developing countries, and especially the least developed among them, secure a share in the growth in international trade commensurate with the needs of their economic development."[3]

2. The General Agreement on Tariffs and Trade ("GATT")

The GATT sets down the original framework for the liberalization of trade in goods, a framework that has been augmented by subsequent agreements such as the Agreement on the Application of Sanitary and Phytosanitary Measures ("SPS Agreement")[4] and the Agreement on Technical Barriers to Trade ("TBT Agreement").[5] Through its two most fundamental principles, the GATT seeks to reduce trade protectionism and liberalize trade by obliging its signatories to avoid discrimination between "like" foreign products ("most favored nation" obligation or "MFN", contained in Article I), and between "like" foreign and domestic products ("national treatment obligation", contained in Article III). These and other GATT obligations are qualified by an exception in Article XX, which allows WTO Members to derogate under certain conditions from their obligations for certain non-trade policy reasons. Measures covered by Article XX include those "necessary for the protection of human, animal or plant life or health" (Article XX(b)) or "relating to the conservation of exhaustible natural resources" (Article XX(g)). The chapeau to Article XX provides that these measures may not, however, be applied in a manner that causes "arbitrary or unjustifiable discrimination between countries where the same conditions prevail" or "disguised restrictions on international trade." The GATT formed the backbone of the multilateral trading system for over half a century, and these provisions have been interpreted and applied in a number of GATT/WTO disputes, some of which are discussed below.

3. The Agreement on Technical Barriers to Trade ("TBT Agreement")

The TBT Agreement is among the most important WTO agreements from an environmental perspective. It augments the GATT by providing more specific disciplines

---

[1] *Agreement Establishing the World Trade Organization, Preamble*, Reprinted in WORLD TRADE ORGANIZATION, THE LEGAL TEXTS—THE RESULTS OF THE URUGUAY ROUND OF MULTILATERAL TRADE NEGOTIATIONS 3-14 (1999), ("WTO AGREEMENT"). The WTO Appellate Body has referred to the Preamble of the WTO Agreement in several disputes. In the Report of the Appellate Body, *United States—Standards for Reformulated and Conventional Gasoline*, WT/DS2/AB/R (1997), at 28, the Appellate Body emphasized the importance of the objective of environmental protection, as contained in the preamble; in *United States— Import Prohibition of Certain Shrimp and Shrimp Products*, WT/DS58/AB/R, ¶ 159, the Appellate Body referred to the Preamble as support for its evolutionary interpretation of the term "exhaustible natural resources", stating that in view of the current state of ecological management, the term could not be understood as comprising only non-living natural resources. The Preamble to the WTO Agreement also reflects the extent to which the GATT/WTO system has developed to encompass environmental objectives in addition to its originally exclusively economic purpose. The Preamble to the GATT 1947 did not refer to the protection of the environment; rather it recommended the "full use of the resources of the world".

[2] WTO AGREEMENT, Preamble, *supra* note 1.

[3] *Id.*

[4] *Reprinted in* WTO AGREEMENT, *supra* note 1, at 59–72.

[5] *Id.*, at 121–142.

regarding two categories of national rules: *technical regulations*, which are mandatory rules establishing the characteristics that products or their related processes and production methods must have; and *standards*, which are non-mandatory rules, guidelines or characteristics for products or related processes and production methods.[6] These include a range of national measures designed to protect the environment, such as certain efficiency standards, eco-labeling schemes, laws for waste management, energy conservation, and natural resource preservation, as well as a variety of measures designed to implement multilateral environmental agreements ("MEA"s). The TBT Agreement requires Members to ensure that these standards and regulations are non-discriminatory, and are not more trade restrictive than necessary to achieve a legitimate objective, such as protection of human health or safety, animal or plant life or health, or the environment.[7] The TBT Agreement also seeks to improve market access by encouraging harmonization of the regulations used by different countries. Members must use international standards "as a basis for their technical regulations" unless they can demonstrate that the relevant international standard "would be an ineffective or inappropriate means for the fulfillment of a legitimate objective".[8]

4. The Agreement on the Application of Sanitary and Phytosanitary Measures ("SPS Agreement")

The SPS Agreement applies to a variety of national measures that are designed to protect human, animal and plant life or health within a WTO Member's territory. It covers measures that are designed to ensure that food is free of risks due to contaminants, additives, toxins or disease-causing organisms; to prevent the spread of animal, plant and other disease-causing organisms; and to control pests. The SPS Agreement requires Members to ensure that their SPS measures are "based on scientific principles . . . [and] sufficient scientific evidence" and are applied "only to the extent necessary to protect human, animal or plant life or health".[9] As a further requirement, SPS measures are not to be "applied in a manner which would constitute a disguised restriction on international trade"[10] and must display a certain degree of consistency in the stipulated levels of protection in comparable situations.[11] The principle that SPS measures must be consistent with ("based on") scientific evidence permeates the entire SPS Agreement; measures which "conform to international standards, guidelines or recommendations shall be . . . presumed to be consistent with the relevant provisions of this Agreement and of the GATT 1994",[12] while the scientific basis of SPS measures which do not conform to international standards must be established in every individual case. However, in cases where "relevant scientific evidence is insufficient", the Agreement allows Members to "provisionally adopt measures on the basis of available pertinent information, including that from the relevant international organizations as well as from measures applied by other Members".[13] The SPS Agreement is important from both environmental and health perspectives. While the Agreement covers measures designed to protect human, plant and animal *life and health*, these measures will often be broad enough to acquire general

---

[6] *See TBT Agreement*, Annex 1.

[7] *TBT Agreement*, Articles 2.1 and 2.2

[8] *Id.*, Article 2.4.

[9] *SPS Agreement*, Article 2.2.

[10] *Id.*, Article 2.3.

[11] *Id.*, Article 5.5.

[12] *Id.*, Article 3.2.

[13] *Id.*, Article 5.7.

environmental significance. The SPS Agreement, for example, covers measures to control invasive species and could also cover measures regulating certain aspects of trade in genetically modified organisms. At a general and systemic level, the SPS Agreement is an attempt to balance Members' rights to set and effectively enforce their own levels of protection, including in situations of scientific uncertainty, and the need to ensure that measures are not used as disguised protectionist restrictions by ensuring, among other things, that SPS measures are supported by scientific evidence.

5. The Agreement on Subsidies and Countervailing Measures ("SCM Agreement")

The SCM Agreement[14] imposes disciplines both on trade distorting subsidies, and on the countervailing measures that may be taken by individual countries in response to them. As subsidies can cause over-production and environmental degradation, their removal can bring both trade and environmental benefits. At the same time, some environmental subsidies are necessary to address market failures and to protect the environment. The SCM Agreement divides subsidies into three main categories along a spectrum according to their effect on trade. At one end of the spectrum are *prohibited ("red light") subsidies,* which are the most problematic from a trade perspective and so are subject to special dispute settlement procedures, and must be withdrawn immediately if identified. At the other end of the spectrum are *non-actionable ("green light") subsidies* (i.e., subsidies that are non-specific and certain defined specific subsidies), which were protected from challenge through 2000 and included certain subsidies to encourage environmental improvement. These provisions were not extended by WTO Members upon their expiry in 1999. Between these extremes are *actionable ("yellow light") subsidies* (i.e., those that are neither prohibited nor non-actionable), which are permissible, but may be challenged in WTO dispute settlement if they cause adverse effects to the interests of other WTO Members.

6. The Agreement on Agriculture

The Agreement on Agriculture[15] embodies a move towards increased market orientation in agricultural trade. It seeks to liberalize trade in agricultural products and to reform certain domestic agricultural policies. In relation to trade liberalization and market access, the Agreement requires Members to replace non-tariff border measures with tariffs ("tariffication"), and to reduce these tariffs over time. It also requires Members to reduce export subsidies. In relation to domestic agricultural policies, it provides for a reduction of so-called Aggregate Measures of Support ("AMS"), a matrix embodying a large part of domestic support granted to the agricultural sector. The Agreement on Agriculture contains several references to environmental protection: the preamble states that the commitments made under the Agreement should have regard for the environment, and Article 20 links the continued negotiations toward further agricultural reform to non-trade concerns, including the environment. These references, however, merely hint at the complex set of ecological implications arising from agricultural liberalization. Broadly speaking, there are concerns, on one hand, that liberalization of agricultural trade may have implications for food security and increase pressure on traditional farming practices, leading to a loss of agricultural biodiversity. In other cases, however, extensive subsidization of the agriculture sector contributes to agricultural overproduction and excessive use of soil, water and other natural resources. Consequently, a reduction of

[14] *Reprinted in* WTO AGREEMENT, *supra* note 1, at 231–274.
[15] *Reprinted in* WTO AGREEMENT, *supra* note 1, at 33–58.

certain agricultural subsidies may have positive environmental effects. The Agreement on Agriculture aims to reduce domestic agricultural subsidies substantially, but seeks to provide for environmentally beneficial support by including within the so-called "green box" subsidies for research, infrastructure and food security, making them exempt from the reductions commitments.[16]

7. The General Agreement on Trade in Services ("GATS")

The GATS[17] establishes binding rules to liberalize international trade in services. While not always immediately apparent, the ecological implications of services liberalization are potentially significant. On one hand, liberalization of environmental services such as sewage, refuse and sanitation services may reduce environmental pressures (e.g., due to efficiency or knowledge gains); on the other hand, liberalization of transportation, mining or energy services, in the absence of adequate regulation, may increase environmental pressures (e.g., it may increase the level or intensity of such activities).

Services are covered by a series of GATS disciplines and commitments designed to liberalize their trade. These services are, according to the GATS, traded through four "modes of delivery": cross-border delivery, consumption abroad, foreign direct investment, and movement of natural persons supplying the service. The GATS includes basic principles of national treatment, most favored nation treatment, market access, and transparency. Most favored nation treatment and transparency apply "horizontally" to all services sectors except those specifically exempted at the time the Agreement was negotiated. National treatment and market access, by contrast, apply only to the specific services sub-sectors as well as modes of supply that a Member agrees to liberalize. The GATS includes a general exception to these and other GATS obligations in Article XIV, which is similar to Article XX of the GATT (except that it includes no provision explicitly protecting exhaustible natural resources similar to GATT Article XX(g)). The GATS also includes provisions requiring an assessment of the application of the agreement, which some WTO Members have proposed should include an assessment of the agreement's economic, social, and environmental implications.[18]

8. The Agreement on Trade-Related Aspects of Intellectual Property ("TRIPS Agreement")

The TRIPS Agreement[19] establishes uniform minimum standards for the protection and enforcement of intellectual property rights by all WTO Members. According to its preamble, it is designed to "promote effective and adequate protection of intellectual property rights" and to "reduce distortions and impediments to international trade" that result from the enforcement of intellectual property rights. The TRIPS Agreement's stated objectives include "the promotion of technological innovation and . . . the transfer and dissemination

---

[16] The "green-box" subsidies are set out under Annex 2 of the Agreement on Agriculture. Article 13 of the Agreement stipulates that such subsidies cannot be challenged in the WTO dispute settlement system and that they are non-countervailable. It may be noted that the term "green-light" subsidy does not refer to the ecologically friendly nature of the subsidies; rather, it signals, according to the "traffic-light" approach adopted also by the SCM Agreement, that these subsidies can be used freely, as long as they qualify for the "green box". The common link between the various types of green box subsidies is that they are "decoupled" from production decisions. In addition to the "green box", so called "blue box" payments are exempt from reduction commitments. This category comprises direct payments to agricultural producers under production limiting programs. These payments are only partially decoupled.

[17] *Reprinted in* WTO AGREEMENT, *supra* note 1, at 284–319.

[18] GATS, Article XIX:3.

[19] *Reprinted in* WTO AGREEMENT, *supra* note 1, at 321–353.

of technology, to the mutual advantage of the producers and users of technological knowl-edge. . . "[20] The TRIPS Agreement covers a broad range of intellectual property rights, such as copyright, trademarks, geographical indications, trade secrets, and patents. A number of these forms of intellectual property rights have implications for environmental management. For instance, Article 27.3(b) requires WTO Members to offer patents on certain elements of life (e.g., micro-organisms), and to protect plant varieties through either patents or *sui-generis* systems. The TRIPS Agreement's provisions on technology transfer are also relevant to efforts to transfer and disseminate environmental technology, including in the context of MEAs.[21] The TRIPS Agreement allows Members to exclude inventions from patentability where such exclusions are necessary to protect human, animal or plant life or health. However, unlike WTO agreements governing trade in goods and services, the TRIPS Agreement includes no general exception for the protection of health and the environment.

9. The Understanding on Rules and Procedures Governing the Settlement of Disputes ("DSU")

The DSU[22] sets out detailed procedures for the settlement of disputes arising out of the implementation of WTO agreements. As it provides the framework within which WTO adjudication bodies balance trade and non-trade issues, including environmental matters, it is important in the context of trade and environment discussions. In addition to setting forth the rules governing the conduct of adversarial inter-governmental dispute resolution at the WTO, the DSU includes provisions for a minimum period of pre-litigation consultations and for good offices, mediation, and/or conciliation, which may be used to prevent tensions—including those relating to trade and the environment—from escalating into full trade disputes. The DSU establishes a two-tiered dispute settlement system to address issues that are not resolved through consultations. The first tier is comprised of panels, which have the responsibility of fact-finding, determining the applicability of and conformity with relevant WTO agreements, and making findings to assist WTO Members acting collectively as the Dispute Settlement Body ("DSB"). If a disputing party is not satisfied with the legal interpretation of the panel, it may appeal to the Appellate Body, which, however, is limited to making findings of law. An Appellate Body or panel report will be adopted by the DSB, the political organ of the dispute settlement system, unless all WTO Members agree by consensus to reject it.[23]

At the panel level, the DSU also empowers panels to seek information and technical advice from any individual or body, and to establish expert review groups to offer advisory opinions on specific issues (this latter possibility may be relevant in environmental-related WTO disputes as a means of obtaining information from scientists and relevant environmental organizations). As discussed in Section IV below, provisions of the DSU

---

[20] *TRIPS Agreement*, Article 7.

[21] For a general discussion of MEAs and their relation to WTO law, *see* section V(J).

[22] *Reprinted in* WTO AGREEMENT, *supra* note 1, at 354–379.

[23] DSU, Art. 17.14. Once the Appellate Body has rendered its decision, it "shall be adopted by the DSB and unconditionally accepted by the parties to the dispute unless the DSB decides by consensus not to adopt the Appellate Body report within 30 days following its circulation to the Members". If a Member fails to bring into compliance a measure found to be inconsistent with a covered agreement, then the complaining Member may seek to negotiate mutually acceptable compensation, failing which the DSB may authorize the complaining Member to suspend concessions or other obligations to the Member that is contravening WTO rules. (DSU, Art. 22.2).

have recently been interpreted by the Appellate Body to allow both panels and the Appellate Body to accept non-requested information such as *amicus curiae* (or friend of the court) briefs from non-governmental sources.

In addition to the WTO agreements discussed above, a number of other WTO agreements may have important implications for environment and sustainable development, including the Agreement on Government Procurement,[24] and the Agreement on Trade-Related Investment Measures.[25]

B. *Relevant WTO Disputes*

Since its inception, the WTO's dispute settlement system has adjudicated a number of disputes that touch directly on issues of trade and environment. The principal cases are considered below.

1. *United States—Gasoline*

United States—Gasoline[26] involved a challenge by Venezuela and Brazil to a U.S. regulation designed to address air quality problems in urban areas by reducing emissions of toxic and smog-causing agents from motor vehicles. Among other things, the regulation required domestic and foreign petroleum refiners to establish baselines against which the "cleanliness" of fuels could be measured. These baselines treated domestic and foreign refiners differently. Domestic refiners were permitted to set their baselines against either a statutory level, or against actual 1990 gasoline quality. Foreign refiners, due to perceived difficulties in monitoring and enforcing rules abroad, were permitted only to use the more onerous statutory baselines. These regulations were challenged by Venezuela and Brazil, who argued that the rules discriminated against gasoline from their refineries, were inconsistent with GATT provisions, and were not justified in the light of Article XX. Their complaint was ultimately upheld by the Appellate Body, which agreed that while the U.S. measure satisfied Article XX(g), it failed to satisfy Article XX's introductory paragraph or "chapeau".[27]

The Appellate Body commenced by examining Article XX(g)'s requirement that measures must "relat[e] to the conservation of exhaustible natural resources". The U.S. measure satisfied this requirement as clean air was identified by the Appellate Body as a "natural resource" that could be depleted, there was a "substantial relationship" between the baseline establishment rules and the conservation of clean air in the United States, and, finally, the measure was not merely "incidentally or inadvertently" aimed at that end.[28] In examining this requirement, the Appellate Body established a number of important propositions. One is that WTO agreements are "not to be read in clinical isolation from public international law" recognizing the importance of coherence between WTO and

---

[24] Available at http://www.wto.org/english/docs_e/legal_e/gpr-94_e.pdf (last visited February 28, 2003).

[25] *Reprinted in* WTO AGREEMENT, *supra* note 1, at 143–146.

[26] *United States—Standards for Reformulated and Conventional Gasoline, supra* note 1.

[27] The U.S. regulations could also have been challenged on the grounds of the so-called product-process distinction, a subject-area of great interest for the trade-environment agenda. *See* section V(A) dealing with process and production methods ("PPMs"). For a more detailed discussion of the product-process doctrine in the context of *United States—Standards for Reformulated and Conventional Gasoline, see* Robert E. Hudec, *The Product-Process Doctrine in GATT/WTO Jurisprudence*, in NEW DIRECTIONS IN INTERNATIONAL ECONOMIC LAW 187, 207–211 (Bronckers and Quick eds. 2000).

[28] *United States—Standards for Reformulated and Conventional Gasoline, supra* note 1, at 19.

certain other sources of international law.[29] The Appellate Body also identified the need to read GATT provisions in their context, and to strike a careful balance between rights and obligations. Consequently, "the phrase 'relating to the conservation of exhaustible natural resources' may not be read so expansively as seriously to subvert the purpose and object of Article III:4. Nor may Article III:4 be given so broad a reach as effectively to emasculate Article XX(g) and the policies and interests it embodies."[30] The Appellate Body also established that Article XX paragraphs (a) to (j) were not intended to establish the same kind or degree of connection between the measure and the policy sought to be realized, and consequently that Article XX(g)'s "relating to" test sets a different threshold than does the "necessary" test elsewhere in Article XX.[31]

After determining that the U.S. measure was one "relating to" the conservation of exhaustible natural resources, the Appellate Body examined the U.S. measure in light of Article XX(g)'s requirement that measures are "made effective in conjunction with restrictions on domestic production or consumption", which it characterized as a "requirement of *even-handedness* in the imposition of restrictions, in the name of conservation, upon the production or consumption of exhaustible natural resources."[32] The U.S. measure satisfied this requirement as it affected both domestic and imported gasoline, and restrictions on the consumption or depletion of clean air by regulating the domestic production of "dirty" gasoline were established jointly with corresponding restrictions with respect to imported gasoline.[33]

Following its examination of Article XX(g), the Appellate Body examined the U.S. measure in light of Article XX's "chapeau", which requires measures not to be "applied in a manner which would constitute a means of arbitrary or unjustifiable discrimination between countries where the same conditions prevail, or a disguised restriction on international trade". The Appellate Body noted that the "chapeau by its express terms addresses, not so much the questioned measure or its specific contents as such, but rather the manner in which that measure is applied",[34] and that "measures falling within the particular exceptions must be applied reasonably, with due regard both to the legal duties of the party claiming the exception and the legal rights of the other parties concerned."[35] In applying the chapeau, the Appellate Body "located two omissions on the part of the United States: to explore adequately means, including in particular cooperation with the governments of Venezuela and Brazil, of mitigating the administrative problems relied on as justification by the United States for rejecting individual baselines for foreign refiners; and to count the costs for foreign refiners that would result from the imposition of statutory baselines."[36] Accordingly, the "resulting discrimination must have been foreseen, and was not merely inadvertent or unavoidable" and constituted "unjustifiable discrimination" and a "disguised restriction on international trade."[37] In its consideration of the U.S. measure, the Appellate Body emphasized the importance of international

---

[29] *United States—Standards for Reformulated and Conventional Gasoline, supra* note 1, at 17. For an excellent discussion of the relationship between WTO law and other sources of international law, *see* Gabrielle Marceau, *Conflicts of Norms and Conflicts of Jurisdictions. The Relationship between the WTO Agreement and MEAs and Other Treaties,* 35 JOURNAL OF WORLD TRADE 6, 1081–1131 (2001).

[30] *United States—Standards for Reformulated and Conventional Gasoline, supra* note 1, at 19.

[31] *Id.*

[32] *Id.,* at 20.

[33] *Id.,* at 22.

[34] *Id.*

[35] *Id.*

[36] *Id.,* at 29.

[37] *Id.*

cooperation in resolving environmental problems, without foreclosing the possibility that in some cases unilateral measures may find justification under Article XX.

2. *United States–Shrimp and United States-Shrimp 21.5* (implementation decision)

The second WTO decision to consider the provisions of Article XX was *United States–Shrimp*.[38] This case involved a challenge by India, Pakistan, Malaysia and Thailand (the Complainants) to a ban by the United States on imports of shrimp harvested with equipment that kills sea turtles, an endangered marine species. The ban was imposed pursuant to a 1989 amendment to its Endangered Species Act (known as "Section 609"), which requires exporting countries, as a prerequisite for access to the U.S. market, to certify that their shrimp fisheries do not threaten endangered sea turtles. In practice the law required foreign fishing fleets to equip their trawling gear with "turtle excluder devices", a mechanism allowing turtles to escape from shrimp nets without any significant loss of shrimp.

The Complainants successfully challenged the U.S. measure arguing that it was inconsistent with GATT obligations. The Appellate Body commenced by examining and upholding the U.S. measure under the three main elements of Article XX(g). First, it agreed that endangered sea turtles are "exhaustible natural resources". According to the Appellate Body, sea turtles constitute "natural resources" which are threatened with extinction and therefore "exhaustible".[39] Notably, the Appellate Body determined that the term "natural resources" should be read in an "evolutionary" manner (i.e., it is a term that cannot remain unaffected by the subsequent development of law) and so should be interpreted in light of the term's use in other international conventions and declarations such as the Convention on Biological Diversity.[40] The Appellate Body did not rule on the jurisdictional application of Article XX, and thus upon whether the United States was permitted to use trade measures to protect natural resources located outside its territorial limits. It stated:

> We do not pass upon the question of whether there is an implied jurisdictional limitation in Article XX(g), and if so, the nature or extent of that limitation. We note only that in the specific circumstances of the case before us, there is a sufficient nexus between the migratory and endangered marine populations involved and the United States for purposes of Article XX(g).[41]

Second, the Appellate Body determined that the U.S. measure was one "relating to the conservation of" exhaustible natural resources. It stated that:

> In its general design and structure, therefore, Section 609 is not a simple, blanket prohibition of the importation of shrimp imposed without regard to the consequences (or lack thereof) of the mode of harvesting employed upon the incidental capture and mortality of sea turtles. Focusing on the design of the measure here at stake, it appears to us that Section 609 . . . is not disproportionately wide in its scope and reach in relation to the policy objective of protection and conservation of sea turtle species. The means are, in principle, reasonably related to the ends. The means and ends relationship between Section 609 and the legitimate policy of conserving an exhaustible, and, in fact, endangered species, is observably a close and real one, a relationship that is every bit as substantial as that which we found in *United States—Gasoline* between the EPA baseline establishment rules and the conservation of clean air in the United States.[42]

---

[38] *United States—Import Prohibition of Certain Shrimp and Shrimp Products, supra* note 1, ¶ 159.

[39] *Id.,* ¶ 132.

[40] *Id.,* ¶ 109.

[41] *Id.,* ¶ 133.

[42] *Id.,* ¶ 141.

Third, the Appellate Body agreed that the U.S. measures "were made effective in conjunction with restrictions on domestic production or consumption". The Appellate Body determined that this requirement of "even handedness" was satisfied as the U.S. requirements on imported shrimp were also imposed in respect of shrimp caught by U.S. shrimp trawl vessels.[43]

After determining that the U.S. measure satisfied each of Article XX(g)'s requirements, and that it was therefore eligible for provisional protection under Article XX(g), the Appellate Body went on to examine the measure under Article XX's chapeau. According to the Appellate Body, the chapeau:

> ... embodies the recognition on the part of WTO Members of the need to maintain a balance of rights and obligations between the right of a Member to invoke one or another of the exceptions of Article XX, specified in paragraphs (a) to (j), on the one hand, and the substantive rights of the other Members under the GATT 1994, on the other hand.[44]

The U.S. measure failed, according to the Appellate Body, to meet the chapeau requirements. Among other things, the measure's "intended and actual coercive effect on the policies of other governments",[45] the U.S. failure to "have prior consistent recourse to diplomacy as an instrument of environmental protection policy",[46] and the absence of predictable procedures (including opportunities for hearing, written reasons for decisions, and opportunities for review and appeal)[47] were identified by the Appellate Body as reasons the U.S. measure constituted "arbitrary and unjustifiable discrimination" for the purposes of Article XX. Additionally, the United States had negotiated seriously with some, but not with other WTO Members that export shrimp to the United States—a discriminatory practice the Appellate body determined was "unjustifiable", as it resulted in a unilateral rather than a negotiated solution, in shorter time for "phase in" of the requirements, and in reduced efforts by the United States to transfer TED technology.[48]

In addition to the above findings, the Appellate Body made a number of comments that are relevant when considering the relationship between trade, the environment and sustainable development. First, it established that the WTO Agreements' preambular reference to *sustainable development* "must add colour, texture and shading" to the interpretation of the WTO agreements.[49] This statement, in conjunction with its statement in *United States-Gasoline* that the agreements cannot be read in "clinical isolation", may provide the basis for a coherent interpretation and application of WTO rules and other international rules that seek to promote sustainable development. Second, the Appellate Body considered whether panels could receive non-requested *amicus curiae* ("friend of the court") briefs from non-WTO Members. Finally, the Appellate Body's decision seems to retain room for the use of measures based on the process and production methods used in an exporting country (in this case turtle excluder devices); a conclusion bolstered by the Appellate Body's subsequent implementation decision in *United States-Shrimp 21.5*. The extent to which such measures are permissible remains to be developed in future cases. A number of these issues are considered further in Sections IV and V.

---

[43] *Id.*, ¶ 145.

[44] *Id.*, ¶ 156.

[45] *Id.*, ¶ 161.

[46] *Id.*, ¶ 167.

[47] *Id.*, ¶ 180.

[48] *Id.*, ¶¶ 172–176.

[49] *Id.*, ¶ 153.

In *United States-Shrimp 21.5*, Malaysia challenged the implementation of the Appellate Body decision in *United States-Shrimp* by the United States. This case was brought under Article 21.5 of the DSU, on the basis that the United States had failed to bring its measures into conformity with WTO rules as recommended by the Appellate Body. Malaysia argued that the United States had failed to satisfy the requirements of the Article XX chapeau, including its obligation to pursue international cooperation for the protection of sea turtles. The Appellate Body considered the nature and extent of the U.S. duty to pursue international cooperation, and found that, in view of the "serious, good faith efforts made by the United States to negotiate an international agreement, Section 609 is now applied in a manner that no longer constitutes a means of unjustifiable or arbitrary discrimination".[50] Consequently, the U.S. measure "as applied so far" is justified under Article XX "as long as the conditions stated in the findings of this Report, in particular the ongoing serious good faith efforts to reach a multilateral agreement, remain satisfied."[51]

3. The SPS "Trilogy"—European Communities-Hormones, Australia-Salmon, and Japan-Varietals

Since the SPS Agreement establishes disciplines for national measures taken to protect human, animal, and plant life and health, its interpretation and application may have implications for certain measures designed to protect the environment. At the time of writing, the Appellate Body has considered three cases that directly apply the SPS Agreement: *European Communities-Hormones*,[52] *Australia-Salmon*,[53] and *Japan-Varietals*.[54]

(a) European Communities—Hormones ("EC-Hormones"). The first case to consider the SPS Agreement, *EC—Hormones,* involved challenges by the United States and Canada to the European Union's ban on the import of meat from cattle to which bovine growth hormones ("BGH") had been administered for the purpose of promoting the animals' growth. The import ban was an integral part of an EC directive that also prohibited the use of hormones for domestic growth promotion and the domestic sale of any meat products from animals so treated.

The Appellate Body found that the EC's measure was inconsistent with WTO law as it was not sufficiently "based on" a risk assessment, as required by Article 5.1 of the SPS Agreement. In the course of its ruling, the Appellate Body made several important interpretations of key provisions of the SPS Agreement and began to define the equilibrium of rights and obligations established in the SPS Agreement, the role of international standards, and the degree of flexibility that WTO Members retain when defining their national SPS measures. First, the Appellate Body confirmed that the burden of proof under both Articles 3.1 and 3.3 is on the Member challenging another Member's SPS measure.[55] Thus, even if a Member establishes a level of (health or environmental) protection that is higher than that contained in an international standard, another Member

---

[50] *See United States—Import Prohibition of Certain Shrimp and Shrimp Products*, Recourse to Article 21.5 by Malaysia, WT/DS58/AB/RW (2001), ¶ 152.

[51] *Id.,* ¶ 153.

[52] Appellate Body Report, *European Communities—Measures Concerning Meat and Meat Products (Hormones)*, WT/DS26/AB/R, WT/DS48/AB/R (1998).

[53] Appellate Body Report, *Australia—Measures Affecting Importation of Salmon*, WT/DS18/AB/R (1998).

[54] Appellate Body Report, *Japan—Measures Affecting Agricultural Products*, WT/DS76/AB/R (1999).

[55] *European Communities—Measures Concerning Meat and Meat Products (Hormones), supra* note 52, ¶¶ 102, 104, and 108.

challenging this measure must still make a *prima facie* demonstration of inconsistency with the SPS Agreement.[56]

Second, the Appellate Body held that Members are not obliged by Article 3.1 to conform their domestic regulations to standards enacted by international standard setting bodies.[57] The view of the Appellate Body is that, although the SPS Agreement seeks to *promote* international harmonization, it does not create an *obligation* for Members to abide by such international standards.

Third, as a consequence and corollary of the previous finding, the Appellate Body held that Members have a right under Article 3.3 to depart from levels of protection established by international standards and to establish their own levels of protection, in accordance with their societal preferences and usage.[58] The SPS Agreement recognizes the prerogative of Members to establish levels of protection higher than those reflected in relevant international standards.[59]

Fourth, the Appellate Body stressed the obligation of Members to base their SPS measures on a risk assessment, and interpreted Articles 5.1 and 5.2 as an obligation of Members to demonstrate a "rational relationship" between (scientific) risk assessment and the SPS measures.[60] The Appellate Body described this requirement as a "counterbalancing element" to Member's freedom to establish their own levels of protection under Article 3.3.[61] Nevertheless, the Appellate Body stated that where scientific opinion is not unanimous and where diverging risk assessments exist, Members have significant discretion as to which risk assessment should be the basis of their regulation, and may rely on "a divergent opinion coming from qualified and respected sources".[62]

Fifth, the Appellate Body also provided useful clarification of Articles 5.5 and 5.6. According to these provisions, Members may not establish arbitrarily different levels of protection in situations involving the same or similar types of risk so as to create disguised restrictions to international trade. While setting an appropriate level of protection under Article 3.3 remains a fundamental sovereign prerogative, the SPS Agreement requires Members to maintain a degree of consistency in the choice of levels of protection across comparable situations. Nevertheless, arbitrarily different levels of protection across comparable situations do not *automatically* imply a disguised restriction on trade.[63]

Finally, although the EC had not explicitly relied on Article 5.7, the Appellate Body discussed the relationship of the precautionary principle and the SPS Agreement in the context of Article 5.7. It recognized that Article 5.7 was a reflection of the precautionary principle, but held that the principle could not override other explicit provisions of the SPS Agreement, in particular Article 5.1's requirements that a Member's SPS measures

---

[56] This seemingly technical finding is of significant importance. Although standards for a *prima facie* case may vary from one international tribunal to another, in international law a not insignificant number of cases are essentially decided by the allocation of the burden of proof.

[57] *European Communities—Measures Concerning Meat and Meat Products (Hormones)*, *supra* note 52, ¶ 166.

[58] *Id.*, ¶ 177.

[59] This is in line with an economic approach that regulatory diversity at the national level, in light of diverse preferences, can be an important tool of overall welfare maximization.

[60] *Id.*, ¶ 193.

[61] *Id.*, ¶ 177.

[62] *Id.*, ¶ 194. The Appellate Body added that this is true "... especially where the risk involved is life-threatening in character and is perceived to constitute a clear and imminent threat to public health and safety." *Id.*

[63] *European Communities—Measures Concerning Meat and Meat Products (Hormones)*, *supra* note 52, ¶¶ 239–246.

be based on a risk assessment.[64] Consequently, WTO Members must comply with the risk assessment requirement contained in Article 5.1 of the SPS Agreement, an interpretation that was largely the basis for the ultimate finding that the EC's measure was inconsistent with the SPS Agreement.

(b) Australia—Salmon. In *Australia—Salmon*,[65] the second case under the SPS Agreement, Canada challenged Australia's prohibition on the importation of uncooked salmon. The Australian measure was based on studies of several fish disease agents that were found in uncooked salmon of Canadian (and U.S.) origin, and that were considered a risk to Australian salmon populations.

The central issue of this case was whether the Australian measure was "based on a risk assessment" as required by Article 5.1 of the SPS Agreement. The Appellate Body first determined that risk assessment in relation to animal life or health consists of three elements: 1) identification of the diseases a Member seeks to prevent within its territory as well as the potential biological and economic consequences of their entry of the pests or diseases; 2) evaluation of the likelihood of entry and of the consequences of entry in the absence of the SPS measure; and 3) evaluation of the likelihood of entry if the SPS measure were applied.[66] The Appellate Body then held that Australia's import ban failed to meet the second and third of these elements.[67] In essence, the Appellate Body interpreted "risk assessment" as a quantitative (and to some extent also qualitative) statement of probability, resulting from the application of scientific methodology, and added that the "risk" evaluated in a risk assessment must be an ascertainable risk and must be sufficiently specific to the subject matter at hand. The Appellate Body reiterated its finding in *EC—Hormones* that theoretical uncertainty is "not the kind of risk which, under Article 5.1, is to be assessed."[68] The systemic implication of this finding is that Members must follow strictly scientific criteria and methodology in the context of a risk assessment.[69] The Appellate Body stated that Members have the right to choose the level of protection they consider appropriate and stated that Members may legitimately follow a policy of zero risk. Nevertheless, balancing this discretion is the requirement that Member's health measures must be based on sufficient scientific evidence. In *Australia–Salmon*, the Appellate Body tightened the methodological requirements for risk assessments necessary to satisfy the SPS Agreement.

Next, the Appellate Body found that Australia violated Article 5.5 of the SPS Agreement, because it applied a different, higher level of protection to imports of salmon than to imports of other fish species; this difference was arbitrary and unjustifiable; and it resulted in a disguised restriction on international trade. The Appellate Body's decision confirms the approach adopted under *EC—Hormones* that an arbitrarily different level of protection applicable in similar or comparable situations does not of itself violate Article 5.5. While the Appellate Body in *EC—Hormones* had not found a violation of Article 5.5, in *Australia-Salmon* it held that Australia's measure resulted in a disguised restriction on international trade based on: (1) the extent of the differential treatment,

[64] *Id.,* ¶¶ 124–125.
[65] *Australia—Measures Affecting Importation of Salmon, supra* note 53.
[66] *Id.,* ¶ 121.
[67] *Id.,* ¶¶ 126–35.
[68] *Id.,* ¶ 125.
[69] Although risk assessment will have to fulfill different criteria based on whether the national measure in question is designed to protect plant or animal life or health on the one hand and human life or health on the other, it is clear that a risk must always be scientifically ascertainable and quantifiable.

(2) the fact that the measure was not based on a risk assessment, and (3) the significant difference between the draft and the final version of the Report which served as the basis for the Australian measure. The Appellate Body reasoned that the third factor might have been "inspired by domestic pressures to protect the Australian salmon industry".[70]

The findings in the *Australia—Salmon* case suggest that the Appellate Body is likely to follow a case-by-case balancing approach when applying Article 5.5 of the SPS Agreement. If applied flexibly, this approach would appear to leave room (albeit with respect to Article 5.5 only) for *bona fide* health protection measures. This approach also provides room for the upward revision of protection, reflecting the reality that national policy-makers often cannot address uniformly all similar situations at one time, and so different levels of protection in comparable situations may provide evidence of piecemeal, upward revision of protection, rather than evidence of protectionist behavior. To avoid creating a chilling effect on environmental and health standards, Article 5.5 should arguably continue to be read flexibly to retain the right of Members to harmonize their health protection measures upwards over a period of time.

(c) Japan—Varietals. In the *Japan—Varietals*[71] case, the United States challenged a Japanese prohibition on the import of apples, cherries, and six other orchard crops, which was established on the ground that the imports could carry pests (codling moths) that could damage Japanese fruit crops. The Japanese law allowed the importation of fumigated products if exporters demonstrated that fumigation is effective to eliminate the risk of carrying the pest; however, this demonstration had to be effectuated on a variety-by-variety basis for each crop. The United States argued that it was sufficient to demonstrate the effectiveness of the fumigation for one variety per crop.

The Appellate Body first determined that the Japanese measure violated Article 2.2's requirement that SPS measures not be maintained without "sufficient scientific evidence".[72] The Appellate Body interpreted this requirement to mean that there must be a rational and objective relationship between the SPS measure and scientific evidence, and found no such relationship between scientific evidence and the Japanese measure. As the scientific underpinnings of the Japanese measure were indeed limited, it is unclear what the Appellate Body would consider to be a "rational and objective relationship" in more complex and nuanced cases. Guidance might be obtained from the Appellate Body's Article 5.1 finding in *EC—Hormones* that responsible governments may reasonably base decisions on minority scientific opinion.

Next, the Appellate Body found that Japan failed to satisfy the requirements of Article 5.7 which, as already noted, sets forth the precautionary approach under the SPS Agreement.[73] The Appellate Body identified four cumulative requirements under Article 5.7.[74] First, provisional measures must be imposed in respect of a situation where "relevant scientific information is insufficient." Second, provisional measures must be adopted "on the basis of available pertinent information." Third, provisional measures may not be maintained unless Members "seek to obtain the additional information necessary for a more objective assessment of risk". Finally, the Member invoking Article 5.7 must demonstrate that it has reviewed the measure within a reasonable period of time.

---

[70] *Australia—Measures Affecting Importation of Salmon, supra* note 53, ¶ 170.
[71] *Japan—Measures Affecting Agricultural Products, supra* note 54.
[72] *Id.,* ¶ 85.
[73] *Id.,* ¶ 94.
[74] *Id.,* ¶ 89.

The Appellate Body's analysis focused only on the third and fourth requirements and concluded that Japan had failed to fulfill both of these requirements.

The Appellate Body's report in *Japan-Varietals* is the first to examine in detail the elements of Article 5.7, and thus provides important guidance from the Appellate Body on the types of provisional or "precautionary" measures that are permitted under the SPS Agreement. The Appellate Body focused on the requirements of Article 5.7 relating to the concept of a "reasonable period of time" (which in this case was approximately four years, but will likely vary on a case-by-case basis). It was not asked, however, to provide a detailed analysis of the first two elements of Article 5.7, which determine the circumstances under which precautionary action is permissible under the SPS Agreement. The questions associated with these two requirements—namely, the situation in which scientific information can be regarded as "insufficient", and the precise nature of the "available pertinent information" upon which precautionary measure are to be adopted— have yet to be examined by the Appellate Body.

4. EC—Asbestos

The *EC—Asbestos* case[75] involved a challenge by Canada to a French ban on the manufacture, sale, and import of asbestos fibers and any product containing asbestos fibers. The statutorily stated purpose of this ban was the protection of the health of workers and consumers, in the light of the carcinogenicity of asbestos fibers. The decree provided for certain limited exceptions to the ban on chrysotile asbestos fibers (also called white asbestos). Canada claimed that the French measure was discriminatory, in that it accorded less favorable treatment to imported (Canadian) asbestos and asbestos-containing products than to domestic (French) "like" products, namely substitute fibers and products containing these fibers, thereby violating GATT Article III:4's non-discrimination requirement.

The Appellate Body first examined whether the French decree at issue fell within the purview of the TBT Agreement. For this purpose, the Appellate Body examined the definition of "technical regulation" under Annex 1.1 of the TBT Agreement, and noted that a technical regulation must lay down, on a mandatory basis, "product characteristics" of an identifiable product or a group of products. The Appellate Body noted that the French decree prescribed certain characteristics of all products, in the sense that it required that "all products" not contain asbestos fibers.[76] Consequently, the French measure fell within the definition of a technical regulation. The Appellate Body therefore reversed the panel's finding that the TBT Agreement did not cover the French measure. Nevertheless, given the specifics of the case, the Appellate Body felt that it did not have an "adequate basis" to complete the analysis and to examine Canada's substantive claims under the TBT Agreement.[77]

Subsequently, the Appellate Body examined whether asbestos fibers and certain less hazardous substitute fibers are "like products" for the purposes of Article III:4 of the GATT 1994 (a question which the panel had answered in the affirmative). The Appellate Body found that "like products" are products in a competitive relationship, since imported products which are in a competitive relationship with domestic products can conceivably

---

[75] Appellate Body Report, *European Communities—Measures Affecting Asbestos and Asbestos-Containing Products*, WT/DS135/AB/R (2001).

[76] *Id.*, ¶ 72.

[77] *Id.*, ¶ 84.

be subject to "less favorable" treatment.[78] The Appellate Body referred extensively to GATT/WTO precedents and noted that in the past, four broad criteria had been used to determine "likeness": (1) physical properties of the products, (2) their end-uses, (3) consumers' tastes and habits, their perceptions and behavior, and (4) tariff classification. However, the Appellate Body stated that these four categories are not the only criteria that could be relevant. Contrary to the panel, the Appellate Body found that the health "risk" associated with a product (in the specific case, the carcinogenicity of asbestos fibers) is a relevant physical property to be taken into consideration under the analysis of "likeness".[79] The Appellate Body also critiqued other aspects of the panel's findings and repeatedly referred to the focus of Article III:4 as one of "competitive relationships in the marketplace". After considering the evidence on record, the Appellate Body concluded that Canada had not demonstrated that the two sets of products were "like" and therefore had not proven that the measure was inconsistent with Article III:4.[80]

The Appellate Body also examined whether the French ban was justified by Article XX(b) as a measure "necessary" for the protection of human life or health. Canada argued that the panel had erred in finding that "controlled use" was not a reasonably available alternative to the outright ban imposed by the French decree. The Appellate Body referred to its report in *Korea—Beef*[81] and the GATT *Thailand—Cigarettes*[82] case and recalled the "necessary test" under Article XX(b) involves an examination of whether there is an alternative measure consistent with the GATT (or less inconsistent with it) that a Member could be reasonably expected to employ to achieve its objectives. In this context, the Appellate Body stated that the more important the policy question at issue, the easier it will be for a Member to demonstrate that a measure is indeed necessary to achieve these objectives. The Appellate Body then stated that the preservation of human life and health is a value that is important "to the highest degree".[83] With these statements in mind, the Appellate Body determined that "controlled use" had not been demonstrated to be a reasonably available, less trade-restrictive alternative measure able to achieve the same result as the measure at issue.[84]

The significance of the *Asbestos* case in the fields of environmental and health protection lies in the Appellate Body's confirmation that toxicity and other risks associated with a product are relevant when considering its likeness to other products.[85] Another important result is the consideration of reasonably available alternatives under Article XX(b). The Appellate Body noted that the more important the policy objective pursued,

---

[78] *Id.,* ¶ 99.

[79] *Id.,* ¶¶ 114–116.

[80] It is important to note that the Appellate Body did *not* state that the two sets of products at issue were "not like". In a "concurring statement", one Member of the Appellate Body stated that the Appellate Body rather should have found expressly that the sets of products at issue were not like and expressed his reservation towards the "'fundamentally' economic interpretation" of the term "like products" under Article III:4.

[81] *Appellate Body Report, Korea—Measures Affecting Imports of Fresh, Chilled and Frozen Beef,* WT/DS161/AB/R, WT/DS169/AB/R (2000).

[82] GATT Report, *Thailand—Restrictions on Importation of and Internal Taxes on Cigarettes,* DS10/R, BISD 37th Supp. 200 (1990).

[83] *European Communities—Measures Affecting Asbestos and Asbestos-Containing Products, supra* note 75, ¶ 172.

[84] *Id.,* ¶ 174.

[85] Whether health risk is considered for the purpose of "likeness" under Article III:4 or under Article XX(b) is of potentially great significance to the Member whose measure is under challenge. Whereas under the affirmative defense of Article XX(b), the burden of proof is on the defending Member, under Article III:4 the burden of proof for establishing "likeness" and less favorable treatment rests upon the complaining Member.

the easier it will be to prove that a measure is "necessary" to meet those objectives and that alternatives are not reasonably available. Specifically, the Appellate Body stated that the preservation of human life or health by eliminating a known and grave risk is a value that is "vital and important" to the "highest degree".[86] Finally, the Appellate Body may have broadened the "like products" test under Article III:4 by moving an additional step towards determining "likeness" from the perspective of the market place and the consumer.[87] The implications of the Appellate Body's views on "like products" for certain environmental measures are discussed in Section V(A).

C. Committee on Trade and Environment

The traditional trade and environment debate is largely reflected in the agenda of the WTO's Committee on Trade and Environment ("CTE"). The CTE was established under the Marrakesh Ministerial Declaration with a broad mandate to examine the relationship between trade and environment in all areas of the multilateral trading system, including goods, services and intellectual property. Pursuant to the Decision on Trade and Environment, the CTE has the twofold responsibility to:

(a) to identify the relationship between trade measures and environmental measures, in order to promote sustainable development;

(b) to make appropriate recommendations on whether any modifications of the provisions of the multilateral trading system are required, compatible with the open, equitable and non-discriminatory nature of the system, as regards, in particular:

— the need for *rules to enhance positive interaction between trade and environmental measures*, for the promotion of sustainable development, with special consideration to the needs of developing countries, in particular those of the least developed among them; and

— the *avoidance of protectionist trade measures*, and the adherence to effective multilateral disciplines to ensure responsiveness of the multilateral trading system to environmental objectives set forth in Agenda 21 and the Rio Declaration, in particular Principle 12; and

— *surveillance of trade measures used for environmental purposes*, of trade-related aspects of environmental measures which have significant trade effects, and of effective implementation of the multilateral disciplines governing those measures....[88]

As set forth in the Decision on Trade and Environment, the CTE's agenda comprises the following ten items:

---

[86] *European Communities—Measures Concerning Meat and Meat Products (Hormones), supra* note 52, ¶¶ 169–172.

[87] Robert Howse and Elisabeth Tuerk, *The WTO Impact on Internal Regulations: A Case-study of the Canada-EC Asbestos Dispute,* in THE EU AND THE WTO: CONSTITUTIONAL AND LEGAL ASPECTS (BÚRCA AND SCOTT eds., 2001). This is significant for the so-called PPM issue (*see infra* Section V(A)). Conceptually, determining "likeness" through substitutability in the market place—as opposed to the physical characteristics of a product—would make it easier for national regulation based on non-product related PPMs to survive a challenge under Article III:4. However, it has to be noted that the Appellate Body did not consider PPM issues in the *EC—Asbestos* case.

[88] *Decision on Trade and Environment, reprinted in* WTO AGREEMENT, *supra* note 1 (emphasis added).

— [1] The relationship between trade provisions of the multilateral trading system and trade measures for environmental purposes, including those pursuant to multilateral environmental agreements;

— [2] the relationship between environmental policies that are relevant to trade and environmental measures and that have significant trade effects, and the provisions of the multilateral trading system;

— [3] the relationship between the provisions of the multilateral trading system and:

(a) charges and taxes for environmental purposes;

(b) requirements for environmental purposes relating to products, including standards and technical regulations, packaging, labeling and recycling;

— [4] the provisions of the multilateral trading system with respect to the transparency of trade measures used for environmental purposes and requirements that have significant trade effects;

— [5] the relationship between the dispute settlement mechanisms in the multilateral trading system and those found in multilateral environmental agreements;

— [6] the effect of environmental measures on market access, especially in relation to developing countries, in particular to the least developed among them, and the environmental benefits of removing trade restrictions and distortions;

— [7] the issue of the exports of domestically prohibited goods;

— [8] that the Committee on Trade and Environment will consider the work program envisaged in the Decision on Trade in Services and the Environment and the relevant provisions of the Agreement on Trade-Related Aspects of Intellectual Property Rights as an integral part of its work, within the above terms of reference;

— [9] that, pending the first meeting of the General Council of the WTO, the work of the Committee on Trade and Environment should be carried out by a Sub-Committee of the Preparatory Committee of the World Trade Organization (PCWTO), open to all members of the PCWTO;

— [10] to invite the Sub-Committee of the Preparatory Committee, and the Committee on Trade and Environment when it is established, to provide input to the relevant bodies in respect of appropriate arrangements for relations with intergovernmental and non-governmental organizations referred to in Article V of the WTO.

The CTE's work on these agenda items is to be given careful consideration when exploring the field of trade and environment. At the same time, this work does not delimit the scope of future discussions of trade and environment, and the field will continue to develop and evolve as new issues arise and old ones are resolved. While the documents issued by the CTE are not binding, they nevertheless constitute an important contribution to the on-going debate on the relationship between trade and environment.

The CTE and the parallel committee for development, the Committee on Trade and Development, were given a mandate by WTO Members at the Fourth WTO Ministerial Meeting (held in Qatar from November 9–14, 2001) to act as fora to identify and debate environmental and developmental aspects of upcoming WTO negotiations, in order to help achieve the objective of having sustainable development appropriately reflected in those negotiations.

D. The WTO's Fourth Ministerial Mandate on Trade and Environment

In addition to these specific mandates for the Committee on Trade and Environment and the Committee on Trade and Development, WTO Members agreed at the Fourth Ministerial (Doha) to a range of elements and mandates relating to trade, environment and sustainable development. The Ministerial Declaration includes:

- "Negotiations on the relationship between existing WTO rules and specific trade obligations set out in multilateral environmental agreements (MEAs);"[89]
- Negotiations on "procedures for regular information exchange between MEA Secretariats and the relevant WTO committees, and the criteria for granting observer status;"[90]
- Negotiations on "the reduction or, as appropriate, elimination of tariff and non-tariff barriers to environmental goods and services;"[91]
- Negotiations on subsidies which "aim to clarify and improve WTO disciplines on fisheries subsidies, taking into account the importance of this sector to developing countries;"[92]
- Establishment of "a Working Group under the auspices of the General Council to examine the relationship between trade and transfer of technology, and of any possible recommendations on steps that may be taken within the mandate of the WTO to increase flows of technology to developing countries;"[93]
- Instruction to the TRIPS Council to examine "the relationship between the TRIPS Agreement and the Convention on Biological Diversity, the protection of traditional knowledge, and other relevant new developments...";[94]
- Encouragement "that expertise and experience be shared with Members wishing to perform environmental reviews and assessments at the national level;"[95] and
- Recognition of "the importance of technical assistance and capacity building in the field of trade and environment to developing countries, in particular to the least developed among them."[96]

In addition to these elements, the CTE was instructed in paragraph 32 of the Ministerial Declaration to give particular attention in pursuing its work to "the effect of environmental measures on market access, especially in relation to developing countries", "the relevant provisions of the Agreement on Trade-Related Aspects of Intellectual Property Rights" and "labelling requirements for environmental purposes". Finally, the WTO's mandate on trade and investment may have significant implications for environment and sustainable development.[97]

These references in the Ministerial Declaration reflect the belief by a number of WTO Members that more can be done within the context of the WTO to promote a mutually supportive relationship between trade and the environment. While celebrated by some NGOs and governments, the addition of new negotiating mandates on trade and environment mandates has not been universally welcomed. Some developing countries,

[89] *WTO Fourth Ministerial Declaration*, WTO Doc. WT/MIN(01)/DEC/1 (November 20, 2001), ¶ 31(i).
[90] *Id.,* ¶ 31(ii).
[91] *Id.,* ¶ 31 (iii).
[92] *Id.,* ¶ 28.
[93] *Id.,* ¶ 37.
[94] *WTO Fourth Ministerial Declaration, supra* note 89, ¶ 19.
[95] *Id.,* ¶¶ 6 and 33.
[96] *Id.,* ¶ 33.
[97] *Id.,* ¶¶ 20–22.

for example, have expressed concern that new negotiations will increase the burden on their already limited resources. Whatever view is adopted of these aspects of the Ministerial Declaration, the implications of these elements are significant and are thus examined in further detail as appropriate in Sections V and VI.

III. Placing the Trade and Environment Debate in Context

The relationship between international trade and the environment raises a complex and interrelated web of issues that cut across the various WTO agreements, as well as the work of the committees and councils responsible for administering them. Before examining the principal trade and environment issues, this section offers some comments to place the trade and environment debate in the broader context of sustainable development, a concept that connotes identifying development paths (at all levels, from the local to the global) that balance and optimize the economic, social and environmental aspects of human behavior, and that meet the needs of present generations without compromising the ability of future generations to meet their own needs.

First, issues of trade and environment are part of and should be considered together with the broader economic, social and environmental challenges facing humanity. The last few decades have seen a significant expansion in international economic activity. This expansion has been driven, at least in part, by the removal of barriers to the trans-border movement of goods, services and capital, and has contributed to a significant increase in the wealth and well-being of many, but not all, segments of human society. The same period, however, has seen rapidly growing pressure on the life-support system that sustains human activity—the environment. Human behavior is heralding a wave of mass extinctions; by some estimates the world is losing 27,000 species a year (i.e., 27 a day, three every hour) at a rate more than a thousand times faster than the natural rate as determined through the fossil record.[98] Eighty percent of the forests that originally covered the Earth have been cleared, fragmented or otherwise degraded, and of the remaining twenty percent, about two fifths are threatened by logging, mining and other large-scale development projects.[99] Approximately sixty percent of the Earth's fisheries are depleted, and many local communities have suffered catastrophic reductions in annual harvests.[100] Human behavior is changing the global climate with potentially profound implications for weather systems, ecosystems and human well-being.[101] In the last seventy years, the world's population has tripled, and is projected to peak at around 9 billion people in 2050.[102] At the dawn of a new century, humanity is faced with an unparalleled challenge: How to continue to raise the material well-being of a growing population while respecting the constraints of the Earth's biosphere? The lessons of the previous century include the

---

[98] Edward O. Wilson, THE DIVERSITY OF LIFE 280 (1992). In 1996, 25 percent of mammal species and 11 percent of bird species were assessed as at significant risk of total extinction, and countless other species now exist in reduced numbers and fragmented populations. *See also*, UNEP, GLOBAL ENVIRONMENT OUTLOOK 39 (2000).

[99] UNEP, GLOBAL ENVIRONMENT OUTLOOK 38 (2000).

[100] *Id.,* at 45.

[101] The Intergovernmental Panel on Climate Change ("IPCC") has concluded that "recent regional climate changes, particularly temperature increases, have already affected many physical and biological systems", for example, by causing shrinkage of glaciers, thawing of permafrost, delayed freezing of ice on rivers and lakes, pole-ward shifts in plants and animal ranges, a decline of some plant and animal populations, and earlier flowering of trees, emergence of insects and egg-laying birds. The Intergovernmental Panel on Climate Change, *Summary for Policymakers of the Third Assessment Report of Working Group 1 of the IPCC* (Climate Change 2001: The Scientific Basis 1–8 (2001)).

[102] *See* UN Population Fund, *State of the World Population* (2001).

realization that the various spheres of our activity—economic, social, environmental and others—are intimately related. Achieving a minimum level of well-being for all humans in a 2050 world, and avoiding serious environmental and social dislocation, will require a highly sophisticated and integrated approach that is implemented through a coherent and balanced architecture of laws, policies and other institutional arrangements across different jurisdictions and levels of governance. The laws, policies and institutions governing international trade, and environmental management, form an essential part of this coherent architecture.

Second, the trade and environment debate should be considered in light of its historical context. Historically, the contours of the trade and environment debate were influenced by a number of factors that defined the positions of its parties, and the lines of their disagreement. Among these factors were two disputes between Mexico and the United States, known as the *Tuna-Dolphin* disputes,[103] which polarized discussions and helped to establish the commonly held perception that the trade and environment debate is a North-South battle, pitching Southern economic development against the protection of Northern environmental concerns. In reality, however, the debate is more complex. In some cases developed rather than developing countries have collectively promoted a strong environmental agenda in trade. Developing countries have, for example, championed the cause of the Convention on Biological Diversity at the TRIPS Council. In other cases, mixed North-South coalitions promote or oppose environmental issues. In the debate about trade in genetically modified organisms and biosafety, for instance, the coalitions of developed and developing countries that promote (or oppose) strong biosafety rules, are similar to those that oppose (or promote) strong proposals to liberalize agricultural trade at the WTO. Agricultural importing countries want the security of international rules on biosafety, whereas agricultural exporting countries want a laissez-faire system for their agricultural exports that does not have to contend with biosafety rules. The relative positions of developed and developing countries should thus be examined carefully, on a case-by-case basis, for each trade and environment issue, including those addressed below.

Third, as the number of economic sectors covered by the multilateral trading system has expanded during the last decade, so too has the number and diversity of non-economic, social, environmental, and other issues that must be considered by the trading community. Trade liberalization is no longer confined to the relatively technical task of removing tariffs and ensuring non-discrimination between goods, as it was in the early days of the GATT. Rather, the trading system has expanded to reach deep into the territory of national governance to promote economic liberalization, with the potential to affect many national policy areas. Indeed, the term "trade" seems no longer adequate to describe the breadth of issues covered by the multilateral trading system, which includes not only rules regarding trade in goods, but also address the areas of intellectual property, services, investment, government procurement, and so on. Similarly, the term "environment" does not seem broad enough to cover the diversity of non-economic issues often considered in the context of the WTO under the trade and environment banner. Some of these issues—such as scientific uncertainty and precaution—span the environmental field and other fields, leaving the "trade and environment" rubric as an insufficiently broad framework within which to examine the issues holistically. And other issues arise that are closely linked to, but are not primarily, environmental issues, including food safety, consumer's right to know, human rights, and the protection of traditional knowledge. As yet many of these

---

[103] Report of the GATT Panel, *United States—Restrictions on Imports of Tuna*, Complaint by Mexico, BISD, 39th Supp. 155 (1993) (unadopted).

issues—which would be better subsumed under a broader "sustainable development" banner—do not have a formal institutional home within the WTO.

Fourth, the role of key players in the debate is changing. One source of change is the increasing congruence in the interests of developing countries and many civil society organizations, illustrated by common calls by developing countries and NGO coalitions to reform the TRIPS Agreement to promote access to drugs and protect biodiversity, to comprehensively assess the impact of the Services agreement, and to delay consideration by the WTO of additional issues such as investment, competition and government procurement. The importance of this shift in alliances, evident particularly since the WTO's Third Ministerial Meeting in Seattle, remains to be seen, but could prove significant in future discussions about trade, environment and sustainable development.

Finally, the linkages between trade and the environment are complex, and should be examined carefully on a case-by-case basis. These relationships can also be explored in a variety of ways and from a variety of perspectives. In the following sections of this chapter, we explore some of the principal issues in the context of three main categories: 1) material; 2) legal and policy-related; and 3) organizational.[104] We emphasize that this is not the only or even necessarily the best approach to these issues. Nevertheless, we consider it one useful framework by which the issues can be examined. As these categories provide the organizing framework for discussions in the remainder of this chapter, we explain them briefly here before elaborating on them in Sections IV–VI.

At the level of the material or physical world, international trade can have both positive and negative economic, social and environmental effects. These effects arise because the economic and social systems, and the ecosystems upon which they rely, are linked in the material world through a complex web of inter-relationships. As a result of these *material linkages*, trade liberalization may change the pattern or nature of activity in one sphere, with resulting implications for the pattern or nature of activity in another sphere.

Responding to these material linkages and regulating human activity accordingly to maximize long-term welfare is one of the key roles of law and policy. Just as linkages exist in the material world, linkages arise among the different systems of law and policy that are responsible for promoting trade and managing the environment across different levels of governance—local, national, regional and international. These relationships between different fields of law and policy give rise to a range of *legal and policy issues* discussed below. Some of these arise between rules at the international and national level (for example, between international trade rules and domestic environmental policies), and others arise at the international level among different trade rules and rules for environmental management (such as multilateral environmental agreements or MEAs).

Legal and policy issues are for the most part created and ultimately resolved by institutions. *Organizational issues* arise between the different bodies responsible for developing, interpreting and executing law and policy at the trade and environment interface. The institutions responsible for economic, social and environmental policy are related, giving rise to a complex web of organizational linkages. In the following three sections, respectively, we examine a selection of issues arising from relationships in the

---

[104] These categories—material, legal/policy, and organizational—are not mutually exclusive, and many trade and environment issues will exhibit a mixed character; they will arise in the material world, raise questions of law and policy, and/or require action by organizations or other institutional arrangements for their resolution. Here we use the framework to offer generic comments on the nature of trade and environment issues, and to structure discussions by organizing issues according to their primary character, with an emphasis on the legal and policy aspects of trade and environment issues. A similar framework was adopted in the United Nations Environment Programme/International Institute for Sustainable Development, ENVIRONMENT AND TRADE—A HANDBOOK 50 (2000).

material world, from relevant laws and policies, and between the institutions responsible for trade, environment and sustainable development.

IV. Material Linkages—Economic, Social and Environmental

We live in a highly interdependent world. Trade and trade liberalization are closely tied to numerous other economic and social aspects of human behavior. These, in turn, are intimately connected to each other, and to the natural environment. As a result of these material linkages between the economy, society and the environment, changes in trade and or trade policy may have significant economic, social and environmental effects. The goal of policy-makers should be to understand these linkages and to act in a manner that maximizes positive impacts and minimizes negative impacts by adjusting both proposed trade policy and other associated policies as part of an integrated package of measures to maximize the net gains from trade liberalization.

A. Nature of Material Linkages

As with any set of complex systems, the material linkages between trade liberalization (and associated economic activity), society and the environment are not easily reducible to a set of simple categories or relationships. While a number of analytic frameworks are available, a frequently used framework suggests that trade may affect society and the environment by introducing new *products*; disseminating new *technologies*; affecting the *structure of economic activity*; or increasing the *scale* of impacts on the environment.[105] *Product effects* are related to the flow of products or services between countries, and will depend both on the nature of products (which may be environmentally benign or environmentally risky) and on the volume of trade.[106] *Technology effects*, which are closely related to product effects, arise from the transfer and dissemination of environmentally sound or hazardous production technologies between countries.[107] *Structural effects* arise as trade liberalization often affects the underlying composition of economic activity both within and between countries—for example, between primary secondary or tertiary production—with associated implications for the environment.[108] *Scale effects* arise as trade liberalization may spur an increase in the volume of goods and services consumed, with resulting implications for the amount of material and energy required by the economy.[109] By increasing aggregate consumption it may increase pressure on environmental "sources" (e.g., natural resources that provide an input into the human economy) and/or "sinks" (e.g., the assimilative capacity of air, land or water to absorb the outputs and waste of the human economy).

B. Positive and Negative Linkages

Across each of these categories, trade liberalization may have positive or negative (or neutral) effects. In many cases, both positive and negative effects of some kind and degree will occur simultaneously. Positive effects will arise when trade liberalization causes changes in economic activity that, in turn, reduces pressure on the environment.

[105] *See* OECD, METHODOLOGIES FOR ENVIRONMENT AND TRADE REVIEWS, OECD/GD(94) 103 (1994). *See also* UNEP, REFERENCE MANUAL FOR THE INTEGRATED ASSESSMENT OF TRADE-RELATED POLICIES (2001).
[106] *Id.*
[107] *Id.*
[108] *Id.*
[109] *Id.*

Positive *product effects*, for example, may arise where environmentally benign substitutes replace more harmful products (such as polluting automobiles, inefficient electric goods, or high-sulfur coal). Positive *technology effects* arise from the transfer of more efficient or environmentally sound technologies. *Structural effects* may be positive where trade provides opportunities for countries to re-orient their economic activity towards less resource-intensive or polluting industries (for example, away from certain primary industries into services sectors). Finally, positive *scale effects* may arise from three main sources: allocative efficiency may arise as a country specializes according to its comparative advantage; competitive efficiency may arise as competition forces firms to become more efficient and innovative; and production efficiency may arise as firms benefit from economies of scale.[110] In addition, in some cases, an increased scale of economic activity may be accompanied by rising incomes and an associated higher level of demand for environmental protection.

While trade liberalization may in some cases strengthen environmental protection, it may also have significant negative impacts, especially when national regulatory frameworks are inadequately developed or enforced. Negative *product effects* might include the damage associated with transboundary movement of dangerous products such as hazardous wastes or chemicals. Negative *technology effects* may arise where obsolete or inappropriate technology is transferred through international trade. Negative *structural effects* may include shifts into resource intensive sectors or highly polluting sectors. And negative *scale effects* will often accompany an increase in the volume of traded goods, although these may be at least partially offset by the potential positive scale effects mentioned above.

C. Direct and Indirect Linkages

These positive and negative material linkages may also be more or less direct. In some cases, small changes in trade policy may have major implications for social and environmental welfare. In other cases, the positive or negative impacts of trade liberalization may be less direct, or may take longer to materialize. In designing policy, it is important for policy-makers to understand not only the nature of linkages, but also their degree. The degree of interdependence will depend in many cases on the particular sector being liberalized. Liberalization of some services sectors, for example, may have only indirect implications for the environment. But the liberalization of energy or mining services is likely to have greater environmental implications than the liberalization of accountancy services. Liberalization of trade involving environmentally sensitive sectors (such as agriculture, fisheries, forestry and mining) is likely to have considerable implications for environmental protection. Ensuring that trade liberalization maximizes its contribution to human welfare and to national development objectives requires a careful evaluation of the complex linkages between trade, the economy, society and the environment, on a sector-by-sector basis, before liberalization takes place.

V. Legal and Policy Issues

Addressing the material linkages between trade, the economy, society and the environment, and regulating human activity accordingly in order to maximize long-term welfare,

---

[110] *See* UNEP, *supra* note 105, at 26. Under this classification, the categories of structural and scale effects are not mutually exclusive; allocative efficiency leading to positive scale effects, for example, may arise through structural changes in an economy.

is a key role of law and policy. Laws and policies play an important role in shaping the nature and pattern of economic activity, and consequently on a range of important factors including employment, social standards, resource use, and environmental protection. Just as linkages exist in the material world, linkages arise among different systems of law and policy, across different jurisdictions, and between different levels of governance—local, national, regional and international—giving rise to a range of legal and policy issues at the interface of trade and environment.

Many trade and environment debates center on legal and policy linkages. One set of linkages arises "horizontally" across the international level between WTO rules and the rules established in other fields of international law, such as those embodied in multilateral environmental agreements. In many cases legal and policy issues arise because the same underlying issues or activities are addressed by more than one field of international law. For example, transboundary movement of certain hazardous waste has both trade and environmental effects, giving rise to efforts to ensure its coverage by international rules in the fields both of trade and the environment. Linkages between MEAs and the WTO also arise in areas as diverse as depletion of the ozone layer, biodiversity conservation and intellectual property rights, trade and trade-related measures in MEAs, and approaches to scientific uncertainty and precaution.

Another important set of linkages arises "vertically" between international trade law and the national laws and policies to which it applies. International trade rules often seek to promote trade and to reduce protectionism by delimiting the kinds of rules national regulators may use to protect social and environmental assets. In certain cases, the "liberalizing tendency" of trade rules operates in tension with the need to ensure that governments retain regulatory authority to protect health, safety and the environment; policy areas whose management presupposes the existence of effective regulation. Trade rules, unless carefully defined, interpreted and applied, may operate in tension with national rules designed to protect health or environment, affecting the scope of government discretion to adopt regulations tailored to existing social preferences.

WTO rules thus seek to define a careful line of equilibrium that, on one hand, promotes trade and, on the other, preserves the ability of governments to protect health, safety and the environment through rules at the national and international level. This balance is inherent in the substantive rules of the WTO agreements, and in the exceptions to these rules. As noted by the WTO Appellate Body in relation to the GATT Article XX(g) exception, the appropriate balance will depend on the measure under consideration and the circumstances of the case.[111] Such a case-by-case approach may ensure the needed flexibility in a particular dispute, but it does vest WTO adjudication bodies with significant discretion.

Ensuring a coherent and balanced architecture of rules to realize the benefits of trade liberalization while protecting social and environmental capital—at each level of governance and between levels of governance—remains a major challenge; one that will likely increase as the economic, social, environmental and other interdependencies between

---

[111] *See United States—Import Prohibition of Certain Shrimp and Shrimp Products, supra* note 1, ¶¶ 119–120. The Appellate Body, discussing the introductory paragraph of the Article XX exceptions to the GATT 1994, stated: "The task of interpreting and applying the chapeau is, hence, essentially the delicate one of locating and marking out a line of equilibrium between the right of a Member to invoke an exception under Article XX and the rights of the other Members under varying substantive provisions (e.g., Article XI) of the GATT 1994, so that neither of the competing rights will cancel out the other and thereby distort and nullify or impair the balance of rights and obligations constructed by the Members themselves in that Agreement. The location of the line of equilibrium, as expressed in the chapeau, is not fixed and unchanging; the line moves as the kind and the shape of the measures at stake vary and as the facts making up specific cases differ" (¶ 159).

States increase. In this section, we provide a brief overview of the legal and policy aspects of ten of the most prominent trade and environment issues, as they are presently defined, with a focus on discussions that have taken place within the WTO's formal institutions such as the Committee on Trade and Environment. Where appropriate, we also offer some preliminary thoughts on areas where the debate about trade, environment and sustainable development could be advanced.

A. Process and Production Methods

Among the first and most fundamental issues is whether importing countries should be entitled to ban or regulate products based on how they are produced in an exporting country. This issue—known as the *process and production methods* or the *"PPM"* issue—has been at the forefront of the trade and environment debate. In many ways, it epitomizes the challenge of striking a balance between the right of governments to regulate in order to protect health and the environment, and the need for international trade law and policy to ensure that such regulations are not used for protectionist purposes.

From a trade perspective, allowing importing countries to treat products differently because of how they are produced in an exporting county threatens to allow the former to impose their environmental and social standards on the latter, and/or to use such standards as a pretext for protectionism. From the perspective of many environmentalists, by contrast, regulators should encourage the consumption of environmentally- and socially-friendly products by distinguishing between products according to their impact over a product's life cycle—its production, use and disposal—including certain transboundary impacts, and impacts in exporting countries.

This debate has played out in discussions of the term "like product" included in WTO non-discrimination obligations (Notably Article III GATT). The term "like products" was interpreted restrictively by GATT panels, which generally required likeness to be determined not by reference to the *processes* by which products were made, but by reference to other factors, including their *physical* characteristics. Under this approach, products were "like products" if they were physically similar, even though they were produced using more or less environmentally friendly processes or production methods.[112] While these decisions provided a bright line for the trading community, for some environmentalists they lacked the flexibility required to strike an appropriate balance between economic, social and environmental factors in different cases.

The PPM distinction has not been directly addressed by the WTO's Appellate Body. Although three cases since 1995 have touched on the issue,[113] the Appellate Body has

---

[112] *See* Report of the GATT Panel *United States—Restrictions on Imports of Tuna*, Complaint by Mexico, BISD, 39th Supp. 155 (1993) (unadopted). The PPM distinction was first formulated in the *Tuna/Dolphin* case in the context of GATT Article III and *Ad* Note to Article III. Although the precise legal basis for the PPM distinction was not spelled out clearly in this report, it rested on several suppositions; that the *Ad* Note to Article III and Article III did not cover regulations which did not apply to "products as such" and that the "like product" distinction under Article III does not permit distinction based on non-product related characteristics, i.e., on process-related matters. Upon closer analysis, the latter argument seemed to be the most convincing as the basis for the PPM theory and was confirmed in subsequent GATT jurisprudence. *See* Report of the GATT Panel, *United States—Measures Affecting Alcoholic and Malt Beverages*, Complaint by Canada, BISD, 39th Supp. 208 (1993). (adopted June 19, 1992). *See also* Report of the GATT Panel, *United States—Taxes on Automobiles*, Complaint by the European Community, DS31/R (1994). The question therefore became whether otherwise similar products are rendered "unlike" because of how they were produced and processed, and therefore can be the subject of different treatment. For a comprehensive critique of the legal basis of the PPM doctrine, *see* Hudec, *supra* note 27, at 193–200.

[113] *United States—Standards for Reformulated and Conventional Gasoline, supra* note 1; Report of the WTO Panel, *Canada—Certain Measures Concerning Periodicals*, (WT/DS31/R (1997) and Appellate Body

not definitively expressed its agreement with the distinction. A leading scholar has questioned whether the distinction was actually being adopted by the Appellate Body.[114] While not addressing the PPM distinction as such, recent Appellate Body decisions have clarified the scope and content of key WTO obligations including GATT Articles III and XX, both of which are likely to be considered when determining whether and how WTO Members can ban or regulate products based on their process and production methods.

In *EC-Asbestos*, the Appellate Body acknowledged the value of the traditional "like product" test established by the Report of the Working Party on *Border Tax Adjustments*, which consists of "employing four general criteria in analyzing 'likeness': (i) the properties, nature and quality of the products; (ii) the end-uses of the products; (iii) consumers' tastes and habits—more comprehensively termed consumers' perceptions and behavior—in respect of the products; and (iv) the tariff classification of the products...".[115]

According to the Appellate Body, however, these general criteria are neither treaty-mandated nor are they a closed list of criteria, and their use "does not dissolve the duty or the need to examine, in each case, *all* of the pertinent evidence."[116] The Appellate Body stated:

> ...the kind of evidence to be examined in assessing the "likeness" of products will, necessarily, depend upon the particular products and the legal provision at issue. When all the relevant evidence has been examined, panels must determine whether that evidence, as a whole, indicates that the products in question are "like" in terms of the legal provision at issue. We have noted that, under Article III:4 of the GATT 1994, the term "like products" is concerned with competitive relationships between and among products. Accordingly... it is important under Article III:4 to take account of evidence which indicates whether, and to what extent, the products involved are—or could be—in a competitive relationship in the marketplace.[117]

While the *EC-Asbestos* case did not directly address PPM-based measures, the Appellate Body's approach to "like product" requires consideration of "all the relevant evidence". In a future case it is at least conceivable that this may comprise non-product-related or non-trade concerns (including those arising out of a product's process or production methods), at least to the extent they relate to elements of the traditional test—such as consumer's perceptions and behavior—or to the nature and extent of a competitive relationship between and among products.[118]

Report, *Canada—Certain Measures Concerning Periodicals*, WT/DS31/AB/R (1997); Report of the WTO Panel, *Indonesia—Certain Measures Affecting the Automobile Industry*, WT/DS54, DS55, DS59, DS64/R (1998).

[114] Hudec, *supra* note 27, at 207.
[115] *European Communities—Measures Affecting Asbestos and Asbestos-Containing Products, supra* note 75, ¶ 85.
[116] *Id.,* ¶ 102.
[117] *Id.,* ¶¶ 101–103.
[118] From an economic standpoint, if PPMs issues are significant in consumers' perceptions such that they reduce the substitutability and thus the cross-price elasticity between products, then such products are clearly less "like". Thus, an economic, market-oriented approach to the "like product" question, taking into account consumers' perceptions, could arguably—at least in theory—accommodate very well a differentiation between products based on PPMs. However, it could be argued that there is an in-built limit to this "marketization" or "economization" of the "like product" concept—GATT Article III:2 clearly differentiates between "like" and "directly competitive" products, such that a more "market competition-based" approach to the "like products" issue could arguably not cross a conceptual line which would blur the distinction between "like" and "directly competitive" products—this would largely deprive Article III:2 of meaningful legal effect.

Even in the event that a PPM-based measure is struck down under Article III's "like product" test, it may still be allowed under the more permissive standard embodied in the GATT Article XX exception. The Appellate Body has established that Article XX addresses a higher degree of discrimination between domestic and imported products than does Article III:4.[119] A question nevertheless arises regarding the conditions under which a Member may be permitted to condition market access based on PPM requirements. The recent decisions in *United States—Shrimp* and *United States—Shrimp 21.5* suggest that PPM-based measures may, under certain circumstances, be permissible under Article XX. In those cases, the U.S. measure effectively required exporting countries to use a production method involving "turtle excluder devices" as a precondition to market entry for their shrimp products. Effectively, the Appellate Body's decision in *United States—Shrimp 21.5* permits the United States to retain its PPM-based measure as long as it continues to satisfy the requirements set out by the Appellate Body, including the requirement to seek a negotiated solution.[120]

It is important to note that a distinction has been made between two kinds of PPMs. Those discussed above are PPMs that do not affect the physical properties of the final product (for instance, where paper is produced from timber which is managed in accordance with sustainable forestry policies). Because they do not affect the product, these PPMs are known as non-product-related PPMs or "NPR-PPMs". In contrast, some PPMs do affect the physical characteristics of the product (and so are known as product-related PPMs). Product-related PPMs do not raise significant concerns under the GATT, and have traditionally been considered as a possible basis for distinguishing between otherwise "like products". This distinction has been important in some WTO discussions, including those about labeling.

B. Labeling

Labeling, including labeling for environmental purposes, has featured prominently in trade law.[121] Labeling for environmental purposes (also referred to as "eco-labeling") may be defined as product labeling that provides consumers with ecological information about a product's characteristics or life-cycle.[122] Eco-labeling is an important

[119] *United States—Standards for Reformulated and Conventional Gasoline, supra* note 1, at 22, *stating*: "The provisions of the chapeau cannot logically refer to the same standard(s) by which a violation of a substantive rule has been determined to have occurred. To proceed down that path would be both to empty the chapeau of its contents and to deprive the exceptions in paragraphs (a) to (j) of meaning. Such recourse would also confuse the question of whether inconsistency with a substantive rule existed, with the further and separate question arising under the chapeau of Article XX as to whether that inconsistency was nevertheless justified".

[120] Although it flows from the obligation to avoid "arbitrary and unjustifiable discrimination between countries where the same conditions prevail", the Appellate Body has not yet offered a clear and textually-based rationale for the implied obligation to seek a negotiated solution.

[121] The relationship between labeling requirements and free trade is somewhat ambiguous. Labeling has traditionally been regarded as a less restrictive alternative to many other types of regulatory measures. *See* for instance GATT Report, *Thailand—Restrictions on Importation of and Internal Taxes on Cigarettes, supra* note 82. On the other hand, far-reaching and varying labeling requirements can impose high compliance costs upon a producer and prevent market access. Even if market access is not foreclosed, labeling requirements varying from jurisdiction to jurisdiction can, like all other technical regulations, prevent a producer from taking advantage of economies of scale.

[122] *See* Arthur E. Appleton, Environmental Labeling Programmes: International Trade Law Implications 1 (1997). Some studies refer to "environmental labeling" as labeling of any type pertaining to environmental concerns, while taking the term "eco-labeling" to refer to labels awarded on the basis of a life-cycle analysis. *See* for instance GATT Document No. TRE/W/12 (June 14, 1993), at 1.

tool of sustainable development policy, providing an effective market-based instrument to assist consumers to make environmentally sound purchasing decisions, and to create an incentive for the production of environmentally sound products and production technologies.

Labeling has potential implications for consumer demand, market access and thus trade. For some WTO Members, particularly developing countries, eco-labeling schemes have raised trade concerns. They note the potential for labeling schemes to create multiple, different requirements for their producers and distributors that limit their effective market access. Many labeling schemes are based on PPM considerations[123] or other criteria that reflect the environmental conditions, preferences and priorities of importing countries, but not necessarily those of exporting countries.[124] Some developing countries are also concerned about the potential for labeling to be used as a form of green protectionism and trade discrimination.[125]

These concerns have stimulated discussion about a number of related issues at the WTO, such as which of the WTO agreements apply to labeling schemes, how these agreements apply to mandatory and voluntary labeling schemes, and how they apply to labels based on product characteristics or their related process and production methods (PPMs) (e.g., labels referring to food content), and to labels based on non-product related PPMs (e.g., labels referring to whether a product is produced sustainably or humanely where that production process has no effect on the final product).

First, a question arises about how the various WTO agreements apply to labeling. The main WTO agreement to cover labeling is the TBT Agreement, which applies disciplines to both mandatory "technical regulations" and to non-binding "standards" (both of which are defined to include "packaging, marking or labeling requirements as they apply to a product, process or production method").[126] The SPS Agreement, similarly, applies to "packaging and labeling requirements directly related to food safety".[127] Accordingly such schemes must comply with the SPS Agreement's rules regarding risk assessment and sufficient scientific evidence. The precise relationship between the SPS and TBT disciplines on labeling remains unclear, and has not been the subject of a WTO dispute at the time of writing. Consequently, it is unclear whether some labels (for example those relating to levels of fat, or cholesterol, or genetically modified content) would fall under the SPS Agreement as labels "directly related to food safety" or under the

---

[123] *See supra* section V(A) for a discussion of PPMs. In practice, the distinction between PPM regulations and purely product-related regulations may not always be clear. For example, when comparing a certain quantity of organically produced vegetables with conventionally-produced vegetables, the first category will, on the average, contain a lower concentration of, say, pesticide residues. An eco-label attached to each individual organically-grown vegetable in this situation would signal physical differences with respect to the conventionally produced vegetable. However, *each single* piece of organically-grown vegetable does not necessarily contain a lower concentration of such substances; in this situation, an eco-label attached to *each single* product would seem to refer, at least partially, also to a production method. *See* WTO Docs. No. WT/CTE/W192 and G/TBT/W/162 (June 19, 2001).

[124] *See Trade and Environment in the GATT/WTO*, Background Note by the Secretariat (1999), WTO Special Studies No. 4, Annex I, ¶ 58; WT/CTE/W/101, *Technical Barriers to the Market Access of Developing Countries*, Background Note by the Secretariat (January 25, 1999), ¶¶ 4–15.

[125] *See, e.g.,* Marwa J. Kisiri, *International Trade and Environment: An Additional Non-Tariff Barrier Against the Developing Countries' Trade?* 15 WORLD COMPETITION 75 (1992); C. Ford Runge, *Trade Protectionism and Environmental Regulations: The New Nontariff Barriers,* 11 NORTHWESTERN JOURNAL OF INTERNATIONAL LAW AND BUSINESS 47 (1990).

[126] *TBT Agreement*, Annex 1.

[127] *SPS Agreement*, Annex A.

TBT Agreement as relating to a "product, process or production method".[128] Based on discussions in WTO Committees and notifications pursuant to both agreements, however, it is very probable that most labeling issues will fall under the TBT Agreement. Finally, the GATT, in particular Articles III:4 and XX, will also apply to labeling to the extent that its provisions do not conflict with those of the SPS and TBT Agreements.

Second, to the extent they are covered by the TBT Agreement, eco-labeling schemes may be classified as either mandatory technical regulations or voluntary standards. Labeling schemes that fall under the definition of technical regulations will be covered by requirements relating to, among other things, non-discrimination,[129] least trade restrictive measure,[130] preferential use of international standards,[131] notification requirements,[132] transparency,[133] technical assistance,[134] and special and differential treatment.[135] In practice, however, most eco-labeling schemes are the result of voluntary programs enacted by governmental standardizing bodies or private institutions. Voluntary schemes that fall within the Agreement's definition of "standards" will be considered under the Code of Good Practice for the Preparation, Adoption and Enforcement of Standards. The Code largely mirrors the Agreement's requirements for technical regulations, and may be adopted by governmental and non-governmental bodies enacting voluntary standards.[136] Member States are required to take "such reasonable measures as may be available to them" to ensure that their local- and non-governmental bodies do in fact adopt the Code.

Third, broadly speaking, both mandatory and voluntary eco-labeling schemes based on product characteristics or product-related PPMs are covered by the TBT Agreement.[137] In the case of voluntary programs, the applicability of the TBT Agreement would additionally depend on whether the body administering such program has adopted the Code of Good Practice. While Members must ensure that central government standardizing bodies adopt the Code, it is not entirely clear how much due diligence Members would have to exercise with respect to local and non-governmental standardizing bodies. Furthermore, apart from the non-discriminatory character of the criteria set forth for the granting of a label, questions may arise about the implementation and management of eco-labeling programs, for example, issues of transparency and technical support for developing countries.

Finally, with respect to measures based on non-product related PPMs (such as labeling schemes relating to child labor or to sustainable forest management, where these practices do not affect the physical characteristics of the final product), it is unclear from the

[128] The TBT Agreement states in Article 1.5 that its provisions "do not apply to sanitary and phytosanitary measures as defined in Annex A of the [SPS Agreement]". The SPS Agreement provides in Article 1.4 that "[n]othing in this Agreement shall affect the rights of Members under the [TBT Agreement] with respect to measures not within the scope of this Agreement".
[129] *TBT Agreement*, Article 2.1.
[130] *Id.,* Article 2.2.
[131] *Id.,* Article 2.4.
[132] *TBT Agreement*, Article 2.9.
[133] *Id.,* Article 10.
[134] *Id.,* Article 11.
[135] *Id.,* Article 12.
[136] The difference between mandatory regulations and voluntary standards may of course become largely theoretical in a context where compliance with a standard (e.g., qualifying for an eco-label) becomes such an important competitive factor in the market-place that from a business perspective the voluntary standard in fact becomes binding.
[137] *See* Appleton, *supra* note 122, at 94–132.

language of the TBT Agreement whether such regulations and standards fall under the scope of the TBT Agreement.

Some WTO Members and some scholars are of the view that measures based on non-product related PPMs do *not* fall within the purview of the TBT Agreement, emphasizing the definition of the term "technical regulation" in Annex 1 to the TBT Agreement and the expression "product characteristics or *their related* processes and production methods" (emphasis added).[138] Some other WTO Members, by contrast, have expressed the contrary view that such measures are covered on the basis that the definition of technical regulations in the second sentence of Annex 1 paragraph 1 does not contain the word "related" and merely speaks about "requirements as they apply to a product, process or production method".[139]

It is unclear from this controversy what consequence the exclusion of such PPM-based measures from the purview of the TBT Agreement would have for their permissibility under other provisions of WTO law. In other words, if the TBT Agreement does not apply, then which other covered agreement, if any, would govern non-product related PPMs and would such PPMs be permissible under that agreement?

In this regard, it has been claimed by some developing countries that non-product related PPMs fall outside the scope of coverage of WTO law *altogether*.[140] Others Members are of the view that PPMs falling outside the scope of the TBT Agreement *are* covered by the GATT 1994, a view also shared by some commentators.[141] If the GATT 1994 should be found to apply, would non-product related PPMs be consistent with its provisions? Certain WTO Members are of the view that non-product related PPMs are inconsistent with Articles I and III of the GATT 1994.[142] However, the issue remains open, as neither a WTO panel nor the Appellate Body have ruled on this question.

If Articles III:1 and III:4 of the GATT 1994 do apply, then an examination of eco-labeling schemes would necessitate the examination of the "like product" and "no less favorable treatment" criteria. It also remains unclear whether Article III:4 can apply to *voluntary* labeling schemes because they are voluntary and may conceivably fall outside the definition of "laws, regulations and requirements" contained in Article III:4, and which WTO agreement should apply where an eco-labeling scheme falls partly within the ambit of the TBT Agreement and partly outside.[143] Eco-labeling schemes found to be in violation of Article III:4 would have to be justified under the affirmative defense of Article XX, most likely under paragraph (g). Under the Article XX chapeau, a key question would be whether an eco-labeling scheme was applied in a manner that constitutes arbitrary or unjustifiable discrimination or a disguised restriction on international trade.

---

[138] *Id.,* at 52, with further references. This view is also shared by most developing country Members of the WTO; *See, e.g.,* Statement by India, contained in WTO Doc. G/TBT/M/5 (September 19, 1996), ¶ 78; and Statement by Egypt, *id.,* ¶ 79.

[139] *See, e.g.,* Statement of the EC, contained in WTO Doc. WT/CTE/M/26 (March 30, 2001), ¶ 104; Statement by Switzerland, contained in WTO Doc. G/TBT/M/5, (September 19, 1996), ¶ 84.

[140] *See, e.g.* , Statement of Korea, contained in WTO Doc. G/TBT/M/4 (June 10, 1996), ¶¶ 102 and 104; and Statement of Egypt, *id.,* ¶ 117. Among developed country Members, *see* the Statement of Norway, *id.,* ¶ 112.

[141] *See, e.g.,* Statement of Canada, *id.,* ¶ 80; *see also* Statement by ASEAN, *id.,* ¶ 107. *See also* APPLETON, *supra* note 122, 147–158; *see also* the discussion of Article III of GATT 1947 and environmental regulations by Ernst-Ulrich Petersmann, *International Trade Law and International Environmental Law: Prevention and Settlement of International Environmental Disputes in GATT,* 27 JOURNAL OF WORLD TRADE 43 (1993).

[142] *See, e.g.,* Statement of Canada, WTO Doc. G/TBT/M/4 (June 10, 1996), ¶ 80; *see also* Statement by ASEAN, *id.,* ¶ 107.

[143] *See* Appleton, *supra* note 122, at 124, 153. *See also* WTO Doc. G/TBT/M/4, ¶ 91 (June 10, 1996).

C. Scientific Uncertainty and Precaution

Scientific uncertainty is endemic. In many cases, threats to health and environment are too complex to be resolved scientifically in time to take effective policy action, yet their potential consequences may be too great to defer policy action until clear scientific evidence emerges. Consequently, policymakers are regularly required to make important policy decisions in the absence of clear scientific evidence. At the same time, governments may abuse the existence of scientific uncertainty to justify unwarranted restrictions on their trading partners' market access. Consequently, requiring a sound scientific basis for national measures offers an important safeguard against protectionism. Balancing these two priorities—making decisions under conditions of scientific uncertainty, and preventing protectionist abuse by requiring measures to be based on science—is a complex and often controversial task.

The need to make decisions under conditions of scientific uncertainty is addressed by the precautionary principle. The principle's most commonly cited formulation is found in the Rio Declaration, which states:

> Where there are threats of serious or irreversible damage, lack of full scientific certainty shall not be used as a reason for postponing cost-effective measures to prevent environmental degradation.[144]

The precautionary principle addresses the relationship between the quest to reduce scientific uncertainty and the need to make policies in light of incomplete scientific information. The principle has a scientific basis—to the extent that scientific data on a given subject does exist, such data should be taken into account, and further efforts should be made to improve scientific knowledge. Nevertheless, the principle acknowledges that consideration of the soundest science currently available does not obviate the need for decision-makers to make decisions under conditions of uncertainty. While the concept of precaution appeals to common sense and is present in many policy areas, its operational requirements and implications are difficult to state in the abstract, and will depend on the specific circumstances. Like other principles, precaution is designed to provide a guide to policy-makers. Consequently, the precise threshold level of scientific knowledge or evidence of harm necessary to invoke the principle, as well as the specific steps that should be undertaken once the principle has been identified as relevant, must be identified by policy makers in view of the particular risks and possible responses.[145] While the precautionary principle appears to be a well-accepted tool in the field of environmental management, its application to issue of food safety has proven more controversial due generally to its potential implications for trade in agricultural products, and due in particular to its potential impact for trade in genetically modified food products.

Notions of precaution give rise to a number of interrelated issues in the context of the multilateral trading system. First, to what extent is the precautionary principle reflected in existing WTO rules? According to the Appellate Body in *Hormones* "the precautionary principle has been incorporated in, *inter alia*, Article 5.7 of the *SPS Agreement*",[146] which addresses the right to take provisional SPS measures where "relevant scientific information is insufficient", and "in the sixth paragraph of the preamble and in

[144] *Rio Declaration on Environment and Development*, Principle 15 (June 14, 1992), UN Doc. A/Conf. 151/5/Rev. 1 (1992), *reprinted in* 31 I.L.M. 876 (1992).
[145] Jan Bohanes, *Risk Regulation in WTO Law: A Procedure-based Approach to the Precautionary Principle*, 40 Col. J. Trans. L 323, 333 (2002); Steve Charnovitz, *The Supervision of Health and Biosafety Regulation of World Trade Rules*, 13 Tul. Envtl. L. J. 271, 291 (2000).
[146] *EC-Measures Concerning Meat and Meat Products (Hormones)*, *supra* note 52, ¶¶ 124 and 253.

Article 3.3".[147] The Appellate Body stated that:

> ...a panel charged with determining, for instance, whether "sufficient scientific evidence" exists to warrant the maintenance by a Member of a particular SPS measure may, of course, and should, bear in mind that responsible, representative governments commonly act from perspectives of prudence and precaution where risks of irreversible, e.g. life-terminating, damage to human health are concerned.[148]

The Appellate Body noted that the precautionary principle "does not, by itself, and without a clear textual directive to that effect, relieve a panel from the duty of applying the normal (i.e., customary international law) principles of treaty interpretation in reading the provisions of the *SPS Agreement*."[149] The Appellate Body has not been requested to explore the extent to which precaution is reflected in other WTO agreements.

A second and closely related issue is how WTO rules (including those that "reflect" precaution and others) apply to national measures that are based on notions of precaution. A brief discussion of the SPS Agreement's provisions requiring measures to be based on scientific principles and not maintained without sufficient scientific evidence, for example, are included in Section II above, and in more detail in the SPS chapter of this work.[150] How these rules apply to individual measures will require a case-by-case analysis, and will have important implications for the balance between national discretion to take measures under conditions of scientific uncertainty, and oversight by the multilateral trading system to prevent protectionist abuse of such measures. In this context we merely note that the precautionary principle now provides the basis for many domestic measures that are covered by WTO rules. References to precaution are now found in the laws of both developed and developing countries, and in countries representing the major legal systems and the major regions of the world.

A third issue is whether the precautionary principle can itself influence how WTO rules are interpreted and applied. The role of this principle will depend, in part, on its status in international law. In dispute settlement, some WTO Members have argued that the principle has fully crystallized as a principle of customary international law and therefore constitutes a relevant "rule of international law applicable in the relations between the parties" that must be used to interpret WTO agreements.[151] Other Members,

---

[147] Similar provisions are found in the TBT Agreement's preamble, which provides that:

> ...no country should be prevented from taking measures...for the protection of human, animal or plant life or health [or] of the environment,...at the levels it considers appropriate, subject to the requirement that they are not applied in a manner which would constitute a means of arbitrary or unjustifiable discrimination between countries where the same conditions prevail or a disguised restriction on international trade, and are otherwise in accordance with the provisions of this Agreement.

[148] *See EC-Measures Concerning Meat and Meat Products (Hormones)*, *supra* note 52, ¶ 124.

[149] *Id.*, ¶ 124.

[150] *See* Chapter 7.

[151] *See EC-Measures Concerning Meat and Meat Products (Hormones)*, *supra* note 52, ¶ 16, where the Appellate Body notes that "[t]he precautionary principle is already, in the view of the European Communities, a general customary rule of international law or at least a general principle of law, the essence of which is that it applies not only in the management of a risk, but also in the assessment thereof." *See also Japan—Measures Affecting Agricultural Products*, *supra* note 54, ¶ 10, where the Appellate Body notes that "[i]n Japan's view, the Panel failed to give due regard to the precautionary principle, which was recognized in both *European Communities—Measures Concerning Meat and Meat Products (Hormones)* and *Australia—Measures Affecting Importation of Salmon.* Having lawfully established a prohibition on the importation of host plants of codling moth, Japan submits that it is in a position which warrants a precautionary approach and that Japan's varietal testing requirement, therefore, needs to be understood in the context of the precautionary principle, a principle which is echoed by the practice of Member States and reflected in the *Codex Alimentarius* and the *FAO Guidelines for Pest Risk Analysis*." (citations omitted).

by contrast, have argued that the precautionary principle is not a customary rule of law, and is thus not relevant to the interpretation of WTO provisions.[152] The Appellate Body has not offered a definitive ruling on this issue.[153] In *EC-Hormones*, under the heading "*The Relevance of the Precautionary Principle in the Interpretation of the SPS Agreement,*" the Appellate Body referred to the question of whether the precautionary principle constitutes a principle of customary international law that should be taken into account in the interpretation of WTO agreements, but felt that it was unnecessary to take a position on this question.[154]

Finally, issues of precaution also arise in the relationship between the trading system and MEAs. Many obligations in MEAs—including those that directly affect international trade—are based on the precautionary principle. The principle is embodied explicitly in preambular language and provides the basis for a range of substantive obligations that address issues as diverse as biodiversity conservation, climate change, management of hazardous waste and chemicals, protection of the seas, management of fisheries, and prevention of air and water pollution. The recently concluded Cartagena Protocol on Biosafety goes further and includes explicit reference to precaution in its operative text. In the event of a trade dispute regarding trade in genetically modified agricultural products, the meaning of the Protocol's provisions permitting precautionary trade restrictions, and

---

[152] *See EC-Measures Concerning Meat and Meat Products (Hormones)*, *supra* note 52, ¶ 43, where the Appellate Body notes: "In the view of the United States, the claim of the European Communities that there is a generally-accepted principle of international law which may be referred to as the 'precautionary principle' is erroneous as a matter of international law. The United States does not consider that the 'precautionary principle' represents a principle of customary international law; rather, it may be characterized as an 'approach'—the content of which may vary from context to context. The *SPS Agreement* does recognize a precautionary approach; indeed, Article 5.7 permits the provisional adoption of SPS measures even where the relevant scientific evidence is insufficient. Thus, the United States believes that there is no need to invoke a 'precautionary principle' in order to be risk-averse since the *SPS Agreement*, by its terms, recognizes the discretion of Members to determine their own level of sanitary protection." *See also id.*, ¶ 122, where the Appellate Body notes that "Canada, too, takes the view that the precautionary principle has not yet been incorporated into the corpus of public international law; however, it concedes that the 'precautionary approach' or 'concept' is 'an *emerging* principle of law' which may in the future crystallize into one of the 'general principles of law recognized by civilized nations' within the meaning of Article 38(1)(c) of the *Statute of the International Court of Justice.*"

[153] *Id.*, ¶ 123: "The precautionary principle is regarded by some as having crystallized into a general principle of customary international *environmental* law. Whether it has been widely accepted by Members as a principle of *general* or *customary international law* appears less than clear. We consider, however, that it is unnecessary, and probably imprudent, for the Appellate Body in this appeal to take a position on this important, but abstract, question." (citations omitted).

[154] The Appellate Body seems to have defined two points on a continuum. On one hand, it has stated that the precautionary principle "finds reflection" in certain *existing* WTO provisions (*European Communities—Measures Concerning Meat and Meat Products (Hormones)*), *supra* note 52, ¶ 124). On the other hand, it has stated "the precautionary principle does not, by itself, and without a clear textual directive to that effect, relieve a panel from the duty of applying the normal (i.e., customary international law) principles of treaty interpretation". *Id.* Thus, according to the Appellate Body "the precautionary principle does not override" specific WTO provisions. Whereas the Appellate Body has stated that the principle may find reflection in, but may not override, specific provisions, it seems to have left open the question of whether, and, if so, to what extent, the principle may be used to *interpret* specific WTO rights and obligations in order to clarify how they should be applied on a case-by-case basis. *See also Japan—Measures Affecting Agricultural Products*, *supra* note 54, ¶ 81. "We note Japan's argument that the requirement in Article 2.2 not to maintain an SPS measure without sufficient scientific evidence should be interpreted in light of the precautionary principle. In our Report in *EC—Hormones*, we stated that the precautionary principle finds reflection in the preamble, Article 3.3 and Article 5.7 of the *SPS Agreement* and that this principle:

> . . . has not been written into the *SPS Agreement* as a ground for justifying SPS measures that are otherwise inconsistent with the obligations of Members set out in particular provisions of that Agreement.

their relationship to the provisions of relevant WTO agreements, would probably require clarification.

In each of these cases, science and precaution play a role in determining both when and how policy-makers should act, and the distribution of the benefits and burdens of action and inaction among different interests, both within and between countries. Faced with uncertainty, those who benefit most from the status quo will generally prefer inaction by policy-makers, thereby avoiding immediate and known costs, and imposing unknown future costs on others. By contrast, those who benefit most from change will generally prefer action by policy-makers, thereby avoiding unknown future costs, and imposing immediate known costs on others. Caught between these different interests, science and uncertainty regularly become tools of political influence. The challenge for policy-makers is to identify specific principles and criteria upon which national laws and policies can be evaluated, and to identify mechanisms to reduce scientific uncertainty more rapidly. In an integrated international economy, where the benefits and burdens of risk and uncertainty and of regulatory action and inaction are distributed across national borders, it is likely that issues of science and precaution will remain hotly contested for the foreseeable future.

D. Market Access

Improving market access through the reduction of both tariff and non-tariff trade barriers (such as tariff peaks, tariff escalation, export restrictions and subsidies) has the potential to yield economic, environmental and other benefits. At a general level, secure and predictable market access can provide WTO Members with the trading opportunities that allow them to generate income, reduce poverty, and obtain resources to implement and enforce effective environmental policies.[155] In the long-run, improved market access has the potential to foster economic development and growth in developing countries, and may provide increased resources to address environmental and social concerns.

The environmental benefits of enhancing market access are particularly clear where products, technologies or services are themselves environmentally friendly. In these cases, market access may improve the state of the environment in both importing and exporting countries. Importing countries may benefit from new products and technologies whose use and disposal require fewer environmental resources (e.g., energy, other inputs, and sinks to absorb pollution and waste). Exporting countries may benefit by exporting products whose production involves lower environmental costs (e.g., organic products that avoid extensive fertilizer use and/or maintain soil quality).

Improving market access may also have benefits in specific sectors. In the agriculture sector, for example, improving market access opportunities for developing countries may have trade and environment benefits due to the small initial size of environmental niche markets, and limited use of harmful chemicals in many developing countries. Similarly, environmentally friendly services, such as eco-tourism, carbon sequestration and, biodiversity protection also hold promise for some developing countries. The benefits of liberalizing market access for "environmental goods and services" were recognized in the Fourth Ministerial Declaration, which provides for negotiations for the "reduction or, as appropriate, elimination of tariff and non-tariff barriers to environmental goods and

---

[155] See, e.g., James Andreoni and Arik Levinson, The Simple Analytics of the Environmental Kuznets Curve, NBER Working Paper No. W6739 (1998). Elisabetta Magnani, The Environmental Kuznets Curve, Environmental Protection Policy and Income Distribution, XXXII ECOLOGICAL ECONOMICS 431 (2000).

services". The Ministerial Declaration does not define the term "environmental goods and services", and at the time of writing no definition has been agreed by WTO Members. The precise scope of the negotiation therefore remains largely undefined.

Improving market access is, of course, not necessarily consistent with strengthening environmental protection (see Section IVB above). Many legitimate environmental measures may themselves limit market access, and increasing market access for environmentally harmful products may have serious adverse effects. Legal and policy tensions between environmental protection and market access may also arise where regulations—for example those applying to eco-labeling or to conservation of water resources—may restrict trade in certain products.[156]

The net effect of these environmental measures is often difficult to ascertain as the lost benefits of market access for less environmentally-friendly products (e.g., income and related demand for environmental protection) may, at least in part, be compensated for by the creation of new niche markets for environmental goods. In empirical terms, the extent to which domestic environmental requirements will act as market entry barriers for overseas goods will vary from sector to sector. Trade-related environmental requirements in developed countries are often sector-specific, affecting products from specific industries such as fisheries and forestry.[157] Several studies argue that existing environmental policies of developed countries on the whole do not have widespread negative effects on market access for developing countries.[158] To minimize the potential negative impact of environmental measures on market access, a cooperative and transparent approach, coupled with technical support for developing countries to enable them to maintain market access while complying with non-protectionist environmental regulations, appears essential.

E. Subsidies

Subsidies are broadly-speaking state-sponsored benefits to businesses. They have mixed blessings, both economic and environmental. Economically, subsidies can distort otherwise efficient markets, or they can correct existing market failures to enhance efficiency. Environmentally, subsidies can encourage overuse of scarce environmental resources, or they can provide incentives for environmentally sound behavior.

Inspired by neo-liberal economics, trade law generally views subsidies with suspicion on the grounds that they distort product prices, production costs, and the allocation of resources and, by creating an artificial comparative advantage, distort trade flows. The regulation of subsidies under international trade rules is contained in the SCM Agreement and in Articles VI and XVI of GATT 1994.[159] From the standpoint of the SCM Agreement, the fact that a particular state action is classified as a subsidy does not *per se* imply anything about its compatibility with international trade law.[160] The SCM

---

[156] *See, e.g.,* the study on Colombian-grown flowers, WTO Doc. G/TBT/W/60 (March 9, 1998).

[157] Veena Jha, Anil Markandya & René Vossenaar, RECONCILING TRADE AND ENVIRONMENT (1999).

[158] *See* references in WTO Doc. WT/CTE/W/101, *Technical Barriers to the Market Access of Developing Countries*, Background Note by the Secretariat (January 25, 1999), ¶¶ 19–23. This Note also states that studies suggesting the contrary exist, but concludes that the overall effect is not negative.

[159] The provisions of the GATT and the SCM Agreement apply cumulatively. *See* Appellate Body Report, *Brazil—Measures Affecting Desiccated Coconut*, WT/DS22/AB/R (1997), at 17–20.

[160] The Appellate Body has expressly stated in Appellate Body Report, *Canada—Measures Affecting the Export of Civilian Aircraft* (Recourse by Brazil to Article 21.5 of the DSU), WT/DS70/AB/RW (2000), ¶ 47, that "[t]he universe of subsidies is vast. Not all of them are incompatible with the SCM Agreement."

Agreement prohibits two types of subsidies: those contingent upon export performance or on the use of domestic over foreign products ("import-substitution" subsidies), and those which are granted specifically to certain firms or industries and which have an adverse effect on another Member State.[161]

From the standpoint of environmental management, subsidies are widely considered to have the potential for both good and bad outcomes. On one hand, subsidies may be required to address insufficient incentives to protect the environment due to market failures arising from externalities, the treatment of resources as public goods, or other spill-over effects. On the other hand, certain domestic subsidies—including some provided to fishing, fossil fuel and agricultural industries—can promote environmental harm (often referred to as "perverse subsidies"). Due to this complex relationship between subsidies and environmental management, the application of trade rules to remove subsidies may produce both ecologically desirable and deleterious results.

Desirable results—from both a trade and environmental perspective—arise from the removal of "perverse subsidies". For instance, if subsidies to fishing industries are held incompatible with WTO law or reduced in the framework of negotiations, ecologically harmful over-fishing is likely to be reduced. The importance of tackling environmentally and economically perverse fishing subsidies was emphasized in the WTO's Fourth Ministerial Declaration. Similarly, if trade law were to limit the extent to which WTO Members subsidized their coal industries, then alternative renewable energy generation may become more competitive and, as a result, carbon dioxide emissions may be reduced. Nevertheless, the ability of trade law to regulate such harmful subsidies is limited. For instance, where harmful subsidies are not contingent on export, or on the use of domestic goods (under Article 3 of the SCM Agreement), or are not granted "specifically" to an export-oriented industry (within the meaning of Article 2 of the SCM Agreement), WTO law would not apply to prevent a Member State from granting such subsidies.[162]

Deleterious environmental effects may arise where trade law stands in the way of subsidies that provide an efficient and effective environmental policy tool. For instance, a State may decide to grant subsidies to firms that invest in "cleaner" production technologies, or to subsidize the production of renewable energy. If such subsidies are held to be specific within the meaning of the SCM Agreement, they could violate WTO law.[163] Prior to 2000, the SCM Agreement established an automatic exemption for limited government subsidies to industries for the purpose of adapting existing facilities to new environmental requirements.[164] However, the exemption for these and the other categories of

[161] The latter group are so-called actionable subsidies. Unlike export and import-substitution subsidies, the harmful effect of such domestic subsidies on international trade flows is not immediately discernable. As a result, the SCM Agreement requires evidence of harmful effects is required before such subsidies can be found to be inconsistent with the Agreement. This is in contrast to export subsidies, where such a trade-distorting effect is assumed.

[162] This can happen for instance if energy itself is not traded and the subsidization of one particular type of energy occurs across the board in the domestic economy. In these circumstances, the lack of specificity of this energy subsidy excludes the application of the SCM Agreement. Even if a subsidy is specific, it still has to be shown that it has adverse effects, i.e., causes injury to a trading partner within the meaning of Article 5 of the SCM Agreement.

[163] Again, however, this would be contingent on finding that such subsidies cause adverse effects within the meaning of Article 5 of the SCM Agreement. On the link between subsidies and differential taxation, *see* Ole Kristian Fauchald, ENVIRONMENTAL TAXES AND TRADE DISCRIMINATION (1998).

[164] *SCM Agreement*, Article 8. Other green-light subsidies were subsidies granted for research purposes and for regional development.

"green-light" subsidies had an initial duration of five years and was not extended.[165] Furthermore, the SCM Agreement does not have a provision on subsidies designed to offset positive externalities. For instance, a State may want to promote programs in order to increase "carbon sequestration" (i.e., the removal of carbon dioxide from the atmosphere).[166] Carbon sinks and other measures to promote carbon sequestration are endorsed in the UN Convention on Climate Change and its Kyoto Protocol.[167]

So far disputes under the SCM Agreement have involved only export subsidies and subsidies contingent upon the use of domestic over imported goods. At the time of writing, no environmentally motivated domestic subsidy has been challenged under the WTO Dispute Settlement Understanding. The absence of disputes, however, does not necessarily mean that further clarification of the Agreement's application would not help to increase certainty and protect subsidies granted for sound environmental purposes. At the same time, the lack of disputes may mean that, among other things, WTO Members consider environmental subsidies as legitimate, or are aware of the legal and political difficulties such challenges might cause.

F. Biosafety

Considerable controversy exists among WTO Members on the subject of biotechnology, biosafety and trade in genetically modified organisms ("GMO"). Some Members have voiced concerns about the risks associated with the introduction of genetically modified organisms into the food chain and the environment. Other Members, by contrast, have emphasized the potential benefits of the production of and trade in genetically modified organisms. This debate has raised a range of issues, and is likely to remain among the most controversial questions in international trade law and policy for the foreseeable future.

Issues of biosafety and trade in genetically modified organisms reach across various areas of the WTO's work-program. They may arise under the SPS Agreement, which covers certain national measures protecting human, animal or plant life or health from risks relating to genetically modified organisms. They may arise under the TBT Agreement, which covers national technical regulations and standards, including those requiring the labeling of genetically modified organisms. They may arise under the TRIPS Agreement, which requires WTO Members to offer intellectual property protection over certain plant genetic resources. They may arise under the Agreement on Agriculture, which addresses both market access and non-trade concerns arising from trade in agricultural products. And issues of biosafety may arise under the GATT, which will govern trade in genetically modified organisms to the extent that its obligations do not conflict with those in other WTO agreements.[168]

---

[165] See SCM Agreement, Article 31. The green-light exemption was not extended due to the uncertainty surrounding the period prior and subsequent to the failed Seattle Ministerial Conference, as well as opposition by many but not all developing countries. See Minutes of the November 1–2, 1999, Meeting of the Committee on Subsidies and Countervailing Measures, WTO Doc. G/SCM/M/24.

[166] See, e.g., the 1992 European Commission Proposal for a Council Directive, Introducing a Tax on Carbon Dioxide Emissions and Energy, COM (92) 226 final, at 21 (1992), noting that forests are CO_2 sinks since they absorb CO_2 via photosynthesis and thus decrease the greenhouse effect.

[167] See Framework Convention on Climate Change, Art. 4(2)(a), U.N. Doc. FCCC/1992 (1992), reprinted in 31 I.L.M. 854 (1992) (entered into force Mar. 21, 1994); Kyoto Protocol, Art. 2(1)(a)(ii), UN Doc. FCCC/CP/1997/L.7/Add.1 (1997), reprinted in 37 I.L.M. 22 (1998). For a discussion, see Hyung-Jin Kim, Reflections on the Green Light Subsidy for Environmental Purposes, 33 JOURNAL OF WORLD TRADE 167–175 (1999).

[168] See Interpretative Note to Annex 1A of the WTO Agreement.

Biosafety has also proved an important issue in other international forums, including the UN Food and Agriculture Organization, the Codex Alimentarius Commission, the Organization for Economic Cooperation and Development ("OECD"), and the UN Conference on Trade and Development ("UNCTAD"). Among the most comprehensive frameworks to address issues arising from trade in certain types of genetically modified organisms is a protocol to the Convention on Biological Diversity, the Cartagena Protocol on Biosafety.[169]

The Cartagena Protocol on Biosafety seeks to protect biological diversity from the potential risks posed by certain genetically modified organisms resulting from modern biotechnology (defined in the Protocol as "living modified organisms" or "LMOs"). It establishes an "advanced informed agreement" ("AIA") procedure to ensure that countries are provided with the information necessary to make informed decisions before agreeing to the import of such organisms into their territory. In both its preamble and its operative provisions, the Protocol refers to a precautionary approach and reaffirms the language of Principle 15 of the Rio Declaration. The Protocol also establishes a Biosafety Clearing-house to facilitate the exchange of information on living modified organisms and to assist countries to implement the Protocol.

Potential for tension between the Protocol and the WTO regime (particularly the SPS Agreement) arises from a number of sources. First, the Protocol and the SPS Agreement adopt somewhat different approaches to risk assessment: whereas the Protocol explicitly permits importing countries to require exporters to carry out risk assessments,[170] the SPS Agreement makes no such explicit provision. Second, the Protocol and the SPS Agreement use different language regarding decisions under conditions of scientific uncertainty: whereas the Protocol explicitly states that countries may decide to prohibit the import of certain LMOs,[171] the SPS Agreement in Article 5.7 only allows Members to "provisionally adopt sanitary or phytosanitary measures", and requires them to "review the sanitary or phytosanitary measure accordingly within a reasonable period of time". Third, issues may arise over measures regarding a specific category of LMOs (known as LMOs "intended for direct use as food or feed, or for processing"): the Protocol does not explicitly note the right of countries to prohibit the import of such LMOs, but rather states that they may make "a final decision regarding domestic use, including placing on the market, of a living modified organism".[172] In the event of a trade ban, an exporting Member may conceivably challenge the measure under the SPS Agreement's requirements, which would require an examination of the provisions of, and relationship between, the two agreements. Finally, in the event of a dispute regarding trade in LMOs, a question may arise about whether the Convention on Biological Diversity or the WTO is the appropriate forum for addressing the dispute.

There are a number of possible approaches to reducing these potential tensions. Could, for example, the Protocol be considered as an international standard for the purposes of WTO agreements? The SPS Agreement in Article 3.1 states that Members are generally to base their sanitary or phytosanitary measures on international standards, in order "to harmonize sanitary and phytosanitary measures on as wide a basis as possible."[173]

---

[169] The Cartagena Protocol on Biosafety (adopted January 29, 2000), is available on the website of the Convention on Biological Diversity http://www.biodiv.org/biosafety/protocol.asp.

[170] *Id.,* Article 15.

[171] *Id.,* Article 10.3.

[172] *Id.,* Article 11.1.

[173] Use of the Biosafety Protocol as an international standard for the purposes of the SPS Agreement would require it to fall within the definition of "international standards, guidelines and recommendations" included in Annex A of the SPS Agreement.

A second approach might be for each agreement to be interpreted in light of the other, in accordance with the international law presumption against conflicts.[174] In *United States—Shrimp*, for example, the Appellate Body interpreted the term "natural resources" in light of obligations imposed by international environmental law. Third, "fact-finding" under the Protocol could be used by panels if called upon to determine whether scientific evidence is insufficient within the meaning of Article 5.7 of the SPS Agreement.[175] Finally, one author has suggested that if both parties to a WTO dispute are signatories of the Protocol, the theory could be followed according to which an "*inter se*" agreement between WTO Members would supersede, in their mutual relationship, their WTO obligations.[176]

G. Agriculture

Agriculture is intimately related to many aspects of the human and natural world. In many countries it affords income and livelihoods, provides food and sustenance, supports social values and culture, and is deeply linked to environmental resources such as the earth, water, air and ecosystems. Consequently, liberalizing trade in agricultural products, and moving to a more market-based international agricultural system, raises a constellation of non-trade issues for many WTO Members, including poverty alleviation, rural development, food security, food safety, consumer protection, animal welfare, and conservation of the environment.

Reducing barriers to trade in agricultural products is one of the goals of the WTO's Agreement on Agriculture. The international trade system gives trade in agricultural products a special status, allowing protection of domestic agricultural producers and export subsidization to a greater extent than in other domains.[177] The Agreement on Agriculture initiates a process of successive reductions of protection and subsidization, and provides a framework for future commitments.[178] The three main areas of commitments are market access (import limitations and high tariffs), domestic support, and export subsidies.

The Agreement on Agriculture includes reference to the importance of non-trade concerns including the environment. The preamble states that commitments made under the reform program should have regard for the environment,[179] and Article 20 requires negotiations for further liberalization commitments to take account of non-trade concerns. Non-trade concerns, including protection of the environment, ensured that agriculture was a contentious element of the Fourth Ministerial Declaration, which calls for a phasing out of export subsidies for agricultural products.

---

[174] *See* Barbara Eggers and Ruth MacKenzie, *The Cartagena Protocol on Biosafety*, 3 JOURNAL OF INTERNATIONAL ENVIRONMENTAL LAW, 525, 541 (2000) for an excellent discussion of the relationship between the two agreements.

[175] *Id.* at 542.

[176] *See* Joost Pauwelyn, *The Role of Public International Law in the WTO: How Far Can We Go?*, 95 AMERICAN JOURNAL OF INTERNATIONAL LAW 535, 547–550 (2001).

[177] *See* Chapter 6 of this work addressing the Agreement on Agriculture. For an overview of the history of protection of agriculture under GATT, *see* William J. Davey, *The Rules for Agricultural Trade in GATT*, in GATT AND TRADE LIBERALIZATION IN AGRICULTURE 4–55 (Masayosi Homna, Ako Shimizu & Hideki Funatsu eds., 1993).

[178] In some areas, the Agreement establishes a more stringent regime for agricultural products than is applied by other WTO agreements to non-agricultural products; the agreement requires Members to bind *all* tariffs, and requires quantitative commitments on the reduction of domestic as well as export subsidies. *See* BHAGIRATH LAL DAS. THE WORLD TRADE ORGANIZATION—A GUIDE TO THE FRAMEWORK FOR INTERNATIONAL TRADE 227 (1999).

[179] *Agreement on Agriculture*, ¶ 6 of the Preamble.

Improving market access for agricultural products requires the reduction of the unusually high tariffs in this sector, as well as the reduction of tariff escalation. SPS measures are also important: while food safety concerns are high on the political agenda in many developed countries, many developing country producers are finding it difficult and costly to comply with the high SPS standards imposed by developed countries. However, as the three cases so far decided under the SPS Agreement have demonstrated, market access issues linked to SPS measures are very contentious even among developed countries.[180] Reconciling improved market access with robust national food safety policies and environmental management will require increased transparency in the promulgation of health standards, a reasonable degree of harmonization of international standards (which must, nevertheless, leave enough space for countries to establish the risk management policies they deem most appropriate), and financial and technical assistance to developing countries.

Another element of the Agreement on Agriculture is the removal of production subsidies and other forms of support linked to production. In some cases, subsidies encourage overproduction and thus exacerbate many of the ecological problems linked to agricultural production, such as excessive use of water resources for irrigation and of inputs like pesticides and fertilizers.[181] Their reduction is thus a shared area of interest for trade and sustainable development advocates. By contrast, subsidies not related to production (known as "decoupled support" to agricultural producers) are afforded some protection under WTO law, as are certain payments linked to research and structural adjustment programs (green box)[182] and, in a less privileged manner, payments for production limiting programs (blue box).[183]

An emerging concept in the subsidies debate is "multifunctionality"—the notion that agriculture not only produces food, but fulfills a variety of other purposes, such as protecting biodiversity, conserving soil, ensuring self-sufficiency and national food security and preserving landscapes.[184] Some countries would like to see these benefits paid for by the State and be exempted from international trade rules by placing such payments in the "green box" (which would make these subsidies non-countervailable); other countries reject these considerations as another form of protectionism.

The environmental implications from a reduction of export subsidies are likely to follow the same pattern as the elimination of domestic support. A reduction in export

---

[180] For a summary of the SPS cases, *see supra* Part II(B)(3).

[181] *Trade and Environment in the GATT/WTO*, Background Note by the Secretariat (1999), WTO Special Studies No. 4, Annex I, ¶ 99.

[182] Annex 2 of the Agreement on Agriculture provides a very detailed set of criteria for determining which subsidies are exempt from the requirements of the Agreement. One of the fundamental requirements common to all green-box subsidies, however, is that they may not have any, or at most minimal, trade distortion effects or effects on production. Article 13 of the Agreement stipulates that such subsidies are non-countervailable and may not be challenged under WTO dispute settlement procedures.

[183] Unlike measures falling into the "green box", these measures are not completely exempt from challenge in the WTO dispute resolution system, nor are they exempt from countervailing measures, however, WTO Members are enjoined to exercise "due restraint" in the initiation of countervailing investigations against blue box subsidies, which fall under Article 6.5 of the Agreement on Agriculture. *See Agreement on Agriculture*, Article 13.

[184] Yet another claimed benefit is the preservation of a traditional way of life, an aspect particularly difficult to capture in economic terms. For a summary of these and related claims, *see* B. Wilson and Peter Finkle, *Is Agriculture Different? Another Round in the Battle Between Theory and Practice*, in AGRICULTURAL TRADE: DOMESTIC PRESSURES AND INTERNATIONAL TENSIONS 17 (Grace Skogstad and Andrew F. Cooper eds., 1990). For a useful clarification of the terms "multifunctionality" and "non-trade concerns" and their relation, *see* Fiona Smith, *"Multifunctionality" and "Non-trade Concerns" in the Agriculture Negotiations*, 3 JOURNAL OF INTERNATIONAL ENVIRONMENTAL LAW 707–713 (2000).

subsidies has the potential to decrease the incentives for overproduction and decrease the concomitant strain on the environment. Moreover, by reducing the dumping of agricultural products on world markets and artificial price wars, the reduction of export subsidies may contribute to ensuring viable agricultural markets in developing countries and to avoiding some of the social and ecological problems associated with the decline of rural communities in these countries.

H. Services

Many services are linked closely to environmental resources. Some services—such as waste treatment, sewage, and sanitation services—play an important role in mitigating humanity's impact on the environment. Other services—such as mining, transportation and energy services—can have negative consequences for the environment, and must be carefully regulated to ensure a balance between environmental and other objectives.

The relationship between services and the environment has been on the WTO agenda since the conclusion of the Uruguay Round, and discussed in the negotiations carried out under the General Agreement on Trade in Services ("GATS"). During the Uruguay Round, a number of governments expressed concern about whether the general exceptions contained in Article XIV of the GATS are sufficient to address the agreement's environmental implications. At the first meeting of the Council for Trade in Services, a Ministerial Declaration on Trade in Services was adopted acknowledging that "measures necessary to protect the environment may conflict with the provisions of the Agreement" and noting that "since measures necessary to protect the environment typically have as their objective the protection of human, animal or plant life or health, it is not clear that there is a need to provide for more than is contained in paragraph (b) of Article XIV."[185]

WTO Members also agreed that the Committee on Trade and Environment should examine the relationship between services trade and the environment in two main areas. The first area for examination is whether any modification of Article XIV is required to protect the environment. The CTE was required to "report, with recommendations if any, on the relationship between services trade and the environment including the issue of sustainable development".[186] The second area for examination is the "relevance of inter-governmental agreements on the environment and their relationship to the Agreement..."[187]

Progress at the CTE on the issue of services trade and the environment has been relatively slow. The 1996 CTE Singapore Report stated that the GATS is a new agreement which is still evolving and includes concepts which are not contained in the GATT. It stated that preliminary discussions have not led to the identification of environmental protection measures that would not be adequately covered by Article XIV. However, it acknowledged that further work by the CTE on this item "is necessary before it could be in a position to draw any conclusions on the relationship between services trade and the environment, or on the relevance of inter-governmental agreements on the environment and their relationship to the GATS in the context of sustainable development."[188]

Since the Singapore meeting WTO Members have discussed the potential environmental benefits of liberalizing trade in environmental services, but little emphasis has been given to the potential environmental effects of liberalizing trade in other services

---

[185] S/L/4 (April 4, 1995).

[186] Council for Trade in Services, *Decision on Trade in Services and the Environment*, WTO Doc. S/L/4 (adopted March 1, 1995).

[187] *Id.*

[188] Committee on Trade and Environment, *Report (1996) of the Committee on Trade and Environment*, WTO Doc. WT/CTE/1 (adopted November 12, 1996).

sectors such as mining, transportation or tourism. Recently, some WTO Members have called for a more comprehensive assessment of the GATS to examine the potential impacts of liberalization on the standards of services provided, especially to populations that are poor, vulnerable or socially disadvantaged.[189] It is hoped that such an assessment if undertaken would also consider the potential environmental impacts of the GATS, both positive and negative.

In such an assessment, at least two areas of law and policy stand out as requiring further examination. One is the possible environmental implications of future negotiations under Article VI. Article VI(4) includes a mandate to negotiate additional disciplines on certain national regulations to ensure they do not "constitute unnecessary barriers to trade in services" and are "not more burdensome than necessary to ensure the quality of the service". At the time of writing the scope and content of these proposed future obligations remain undefined. What, in practice, would be considered "more burdensome than necessary"? Is the "quality of services" the only legitimate objective of such measures, and should other non-trade justifications be considered? If so, how could this be achieved?

A second area for further inquiry is the relationship between GATS and MEA rules. Although these linkages remain largely unexplored, it is possible that both services liberalization and GATS disciplines may influence the successful implementation of MEAs. For example, liberalization of waste management services may affect the transboundary movement and disposal of hazardous waste covered by the Basel Convention; liberalization of tourism or mining services may affect the conservation of biodiversity as required by the Convention on Biological Diversity; and liberalization of energy or transport services may affect global warming, the subject of the UN Framework Convention on Climate Change and its Kyoto Protocol. Similarly, GATS disciplines—including those negotiated under Article VI—may define and delimit the domestic legal and policy measures available to implement MEAs. To ensure that MEAs and the GATS are mutually supportive, WTO Members may wish to examine these and other areas of overlap as part of the mandated assessment of the GATS, with input from national environmental policy-makers and Secretariats of the MEAs.[190]

I. Intellectual Property

Intellectual property protection affects the process of innovation, the development and use of technology, and the patterns of economic development, and as a result may have significant implications for environment and sustainable development. Forms of intellectual property protection, such as patents, may influence the development of new environmentally friendly (or harmful) technologies; and intellectual property protection over plant varieties may influence the development of crops, with implications for agriculture, food security and biodiversity. The importance of the relationship between intellectual property rights and the environment is reflected in Item 8 of the CTE's agenda (see above).

Among the main international agreements establishing minimum standards for the protection and enforcement of intellectual property rights is the WTO TRIPS Agreement. Arising from the TRIPS Agreement is a range of issues concerning the relationship

---

[189] *See Communication of Cuba, Dominican Republic, Haiti, India, Kenya, Pakistan, Peru, Uganda, Venezuela and Zimbabwe*, WTO Doc. S/CSS/W/114 (October 9, 2001).

[190] Discussion on these issues is also underway in the CTE, where under Agenda Item 9, the WTO Secretariat has been asked to conduct a literature survey on the environmental impacts of services liberalization with a focus on tourism, transport, energy and the environmental services sector. While these efforts are to be welcomed, it is crucial to conduct a comprehensive assessment of trade in services and its liberalization in the Council on Trade in Services ("CTS"), the main services negotiating body, to ensure that any results are adequately fed into the negotiating process.

between intellectual property rights and the environment. Prominent among these environmental issues are the development, transfer and dissemination of new technologies and products; and the relationship between the TRIPS Agreement and the Convention on Biological Diversity.

The development, transfer and dissemination of technology is widely recognized as a critical determinant of sustainable development. Agenda 21 affirms that "... access to and transfer of environmentally-sound technology are essential requirements for sustainable development".[191] Technology transfer is an important aspect of the TRIPS Agreement. Article 7, entitled *Objectives,* states that "the protection and enforcement of intellectual property rights should contribute to the ... transfer and dissemination of technology, to the mutual advantage of producers and users of technological knowledge and in a manner conducive to social and economic welfare, and to a balance of rights and obligations". Article 8, entitled *Principles,* notes that abuse of intellectual property rights may adversely affect the international transfer of technology.

These general provisions are complemented by specific obligations to assist least-developed countries. Article 66.2 requires developed country Members to "provide incentives to enterprises and institutions in their territories for the purpose of promoting and encouraging technology transfer to least-developed country Members in order to enable them to create a sound and viable technological base". This article reflects that, unless the price of the technology can be brought within manageable limits, the cost of technology may impose a burden on the development of least-developed countries.

Despite these references, many developing countries remain unconvinced that the Agreement's substantive provisions in fact promote technology transfer.[192] Empirically the relationship between intellectual property rights and technology transfer remains unclear.[193] To explore the relationship between technology transfer and other aspects of the WTO's mandate, WTO Members have established a Working Group under the auspices of the General Council to examine the relationship between trade and transfer of technology, and of "any possible recommendations that might be taken within the mandate of the WTO to increase flows of technology to developing countries."[194]

Ensuring a positive relationship between intellectual property and technology transfer would be helped by more targeted analyses of the relationship between trade rules and technology transfer in specific sectors and regions. One such area that WTO Members may wish to consider is the relationship between relevant WTO processes (including the TRIPS Council, CTE and the Working Group on Technology Transfer), and discussions in the international environmental system. Recent UNEP-sponsored meetings, for example, have noted the potential for synergies in the implementation of the TRIPS Agreement's technology transfer obligations, and the technology transfer provisions in selected MEAs.[195] Similarly, technology transfer is likely to remain an important issue in

---

[191] *Agenda 21,* ¶ 34.7. Agenda 21 is available on the website of the United Nations Division for Sustainable Development http://www.un.org/esa/sustdev/documents/agenda21/english/agenda21toc.htm. It was adopted at the United Nations Conference on Environment and Development, held in Rio de Janeiro from June 3–14, 1993.

[192] *See, e.g., Communication from India*, WT/GC/W/147 (February 18, 1999).

[193] *See, generally, UNCTAD, The TRIPS Agreement and Developing Countries,* UNCTAD/ITE/1 (1996); and UNCTAD, WORLD INVESTMENT REPORT 1997: TRANSNATIONAL CORPORATIONS, MARKET STRUCTURE AND COMPETITION POLICY(1997).

[194] *WTO Fourth Ministerial Declaration, supra* note 89, ¶ 37.

[195] *See Chairman's Summary,* UNEP Meeting on Enhancing Synergies and Mutual Supportiveness of Multilateral Environmental Agreements and the World Trade Organization, October 23, 2001, www.unep.ch, *stating,* in relation to technology transfer, that "there are significant synergies to be realized in the implementation of these measures in MEAs and the WTO, including in relation to technology transfer."

the implementation of Agenda 21, and at future meetings in the Rio process. To maximize their benefits from future negotiations, WTO Members wishing to promote technology transfer may consider exploring the linkages between technology transfer issues as they arise on the WTO's agenda, and in international environmental forums.

A second area of law and policy where intellectual property rights and the environment intersect is the relationship between the TRIPS Agreement and the Convention on Biological Diversity. The importance of this relationship was highlighted in the WTO's Fourth Ministerial Declaration, which called on the TRIPS Council to "examine, *inter alia*, the relationship between the TRIPS Agreement and the Convention on Biological Diversity" ("CBD").[196] The TRIPS Agreement includes a number of forms of intellectual property protection of relevance to the conservation of biodiversity. Patents and *sui generis systems* for plant variety protection are relevant to the implementation of the CBD because they play a key role in defining what technologies are developed and transferred, how genetic resources are conserved and used, and how the benefits of use are shared (including with traditional communities).

The conservation and use of genetic resources may be affected by intellectual property rights in a number of ways. On one hand, intellectual property rights may provide an incentive for the conservation of certain kinds of genetic resources. For example, patents or geographical indications may provide a financial incentive to conserve commercially valuable plant or animal species. On the other hand, there is concern that intellectual property rights may also operate in tension with attempts to conserve biodiversity. For example, some governments and non-governmental organizations are concerned about the patenting by Northern companies of genetic resources taken from countries of the South. In the TRIPS Council, a number of developing countries have raised concern that intellectual property rights may affect the objectives of the CBD. Brazil, for example, has stated that "... patents over a Member's genetic resource, but granted outside its territory raises the issue of potential conflict with the principle of the sovereignty of the Contracting Parties of the CBD over their own genetic resources" and that "amending Article 27.3(b) of TRIPs to accommodate principles of the CBD will be a necessary outcome of the review of that Article. Failure to clarify this relationship may turn out to be detrimental to both instruments."[197] Other WTO Members, by contrast, have argued that changing patent procedures is unnecessary, and that a more effective system of contracts between the users and custodians of genetic resources would address the concerns of developing countries.[198] The need for international cooperation to resolve issues of this type is recognized in the Convention on Biological Diversity, which states that:

> The Contracting Parties, recognizing that patents and other intellectual property rights may have an influence on the implementation of this Convention, shall cooperate in this regard subject to national legislation and international law in order to ensure that such rights are supportive of and do not run counter to its objectives.[199]

---

[196] *See WTO Fourth Ministerial Declaration, supra* note 89, ¶ 19. *See also*, www.wipo.org for an overview of the work of the World Intellectual Property Organization's ("WIPO") Intergovernmental Committee on Genetic Resources, Traditional Knowledge and Folklore, which is discussing models for intellectual property-related provisions in access contracts, the possibility of a requirement for the disclosure of origin of biological resources in patent applications, and methods for defensive and positive *sui generis* protection of traditional knowledge.

[197] *See Communication from Brazil*, WTO Doc. IP/C/W/228, ¶¶ 21–22 (November 24, 2000).

[198] *See Communication from the United States*, WTO Doc. IP/C/W/209, at 5–6 (October 3, 2000).

[199] Article 16.5, *Convention on Biological Diversity*, June 5, 1992, UNEP/Bio.Div./N7-INC5/4; 31 I.L.M. 818 (1992).

Closely related to issues of biodiversity protection are questions concerning the relationship between intellectual property rights and the protection of traditional knowledge. Article 8(j) of the CBD requires Parties to "respect, preserve and maintain knowledge, innovations and practices of indigenous and local communities embodying traditional lifestyles relevant for the conservation and sustainable use of biological diversity". Again, the relationship between intellectual property rights and the protection of traditional knowledge is complex. On one hand, IPRs may provide some local and traditional communities with a tool to protect their traditional knowledge. On the other hand, western-style intellectual property systems may prove too expensive for poor communities, and fail to recognize community rights, as opposed to individual rights. There is also the additional concern of free riding on, and misappropriation of, knowledge across national borders. Some developing countries have noted in the TRIPS Council that innovations based on the traditional knowledge of communities in the South are patented in the North without any effort to share the benefits with the source communities or countries.[200] The importance of addressing these issues was emphasized in the Doha Ministerial Declaration, which called on the CTE to "examine, *inter alia*, the relationship between the TRIPS Agreement and the Convention on Biological Diversity, the protection of traditional knowledge and folklore".[201]

These issues are likely to remain a subject of controversy in the WTO's discussions of intellectual property. Making progress will require a well-defined agenda and a clear division of competence between the relevant reviews of the TRIPS Agreement (including the Article 27.3(b) and Article 71.1 reviews), among relevant WTO bodies (including the TRIPS Council, CTE, and Working Group on Technology Transfer), and between the WTO other international bodies such as the CBD, the World Intellectual Property Organization and UNCTAD.

J. Multilateral Environmental Agreements ("MEAs")

MEAs are agreements among states to address shared environmental problems. The importance and scope of MEAs has increased dramatically as the international community struggles to address growing global environmental problems. They provide the preferred way to deal with transboundary and global environmental problems such as climate change, biodiversity loss and ozone depletion. From an economic perspective, MEAs may also help reduce unnecessary economic and trade effects by harmonizing measures and preventing a proliferation of different national rules. Compared to unilateral measures, they also embody cooperative approaches that reflect an equitable sharing of the benefits and burdens of environmental protection.

The policies and rules embodied in MEAs and the WTO Agreement intersect in a number of ways. They apply to many of the same issues, products and parties, albeit from different perspectives. Individual MEAs and WTO agreements may simultaneously touch on issues of scientific uncertainty and precaution, intellectual property protection, biodiversity protection, and the transboundary movement of living modified organisms, endangered species, invasive species, and hazardous waste, to name a few issues. In some cases, these linkages may give rise to unrealized synergies and in others to unresolved tensions. Identifying ways to realize synergies, resolve tensions and maximize the supportiveness of these rapidly evolving regimes would make an important contribution to a

[200] *See, e.g., Communication from Brazil, supra* note 197.
[201] *Ministerial Declaration, supra* note 89, ¶ 19.

coherent intellectual architecture for sustainable development. One of the primary sets of linkages—those arising out of the relationship between trade-related measures in MEAs and WTO rules—is addressed in this section.

Trade-related measures are used in over twenty MEAs including those addressing the transboundary movement of hazardous waste (Basel Convention on Transboundary Movements of Hazardous Wastes and their Disposal),[202] genetically modified organisms (Cartagena Protocol on Biosafety),[203] ozone depleting substances (Montreal Protocol on Substances that Deplete the Ozone Layer),[204] persistent organic pollutants (Stockholm Convention on Persistent Organic Pollutants),[205] and endangered species (Convention on International Trade in Endangered Species of Wild Flora and Fauna (CITES)).[206] Among other things, trade-related measures serve to regulate trade in environmentally harmful products, remove the economic incentives that encourage environmental destruction, ensure compliance with an MEA's provisions, and encourage broad country participation, thereby reducing the potential for non-parties to undermine a treaty's objectives. (See Box 1).

Box 1   Trade-related measures serve a variety of purposes. They may:

- *Ban transboundary movement*: Where the threat posed by a product or substance to the environment is significant, trade-related measures may prohibit trade in the product altogether. The Basel Convention, for example, bans trade under conditions where the importing country lacks the capacity to manage the waste in an environmentally sound manner;

- *Remove market incentives that promote environmental harm:* In some cases, access to foreign markets through trade provides an incentive for environmentally harmful activity. Trade-related measures may reduce or remove these incentives. CITES, for example, bans trade in endangered species thereby removing the economic incentive to kill them;

- *Encourage compliance:* As is the case with the non-compliance with WTO obligations, some MEAs permit targeted trade-related measures as a response to non-compliance. The Montreal Protocol, for example, allows the meeting of the parties to use trade-related measures to address non-compliance by a party to the Protocol; and

- *Promote broad participation:* In relation to global environmental problems, broad membership may be critical to the success of an MEA. Trade-related measures may be used to create incentives for non-parties to join the agreement, or to establish a comparable bilateral, multilateral or regional agreement. Bans on trade with non-parties remove incentives to remain outside the Montreal Protocol and have increased its coverage, and prevented its goals from being undermined by the actions of non-parties.

---

[202] *Reprinted in* 28 I.L.M. 657 (1989), entered into force May 5, 1992.

[203] *Reprinted in* 39 I.L.M. 1027 (2000), not yet in force.

[204] *Reprinted in* 26 I.L.M. 1550 (1987), entered into force January 1, 1989.

[205] *Reprinted in* 40 I.L.M. 531 (2001). The Convention has not yet entered into force but is being applied on a voluntary basis in the meantime.

[206] *Convention on Trade in Endangered Species of Flora and Fauna* ("CITES"), March 3, 1973, 993 U.N.T.S. 243, 12 I.L.M. 1085 (1973), in force since July 1, 1975.

The relationship between MEA trade-related measures and WTO rules was identified by WTO Members at the end of the Uruguay Round in Items 1 and 5 of the CTE's mandate.[207] This mandate was augmented at the WTO's Fourth Ministerial where Members agreed to negotiations on the "relationship between existing WTO rules and specific trade obligations set out in multilateral environmental agreements (MEAs)".[208]

Although there has been no formal WTO dispute directly involving an MEA, the potential for a WTO dispute has arguably increased as a result of the decision by some States not to join key conventions such as the Convention on Biological Diversity, the Cartagena Protocol on Biosafety, the UN Convention on the Law of the Sea, and the Kyoto Protocol. While the WTO has stated a preference for multilateral solutions to environmental problems, it remains unclear whether trade-related measures involving non-parties to an MEA are consistent with the WTO.[209] Particularly at risk are trade-related measures that apply to non-parties to an MEA, as these are more likely to contravene the WTO's non-discrimination requirements, and would likely fall within the ambit of the WTO's (rather than an MEA's) dispute settlement system.

Clarifying the relationship between trade-related measures in MEAs and WTO rules is an important step towards promoting a coherent framework of international rules and institutions. WTO negotiations under paragraph 31(i) of the Doha Ministerial Declaration will likely raise some complex issues regarding what constitutes "specific trade obligations" and an "MEA" for the purposes of the negotiating mandate. Developing countries may seek to keep the mandate narrow by limiting the scope of these terms; while the proponents of the negotiations seem likely to seek to broaden the mandate to protect not only the trade-related provisions embodied in the MEAs, but also national measures taken pursuant to them. Both the *form* of any outcome to the negotiations (e.g., ranging from a simple political declaration to a legally binding amendment of WTO rules) as well its *content* will likely be hotly debated by WTO Members. As they continue discussions in the CTE, WTO Members can take note of and build on past statements by relevant WTO bodies, including the Ministerial Council and relevant Committees. Among other things, they could conceivably seek to build on the CTE's 1996 joint statement that "if a dispute arises between WTO members, Parties to an MEA, over the use of trade measures they are applying between themselves pursuant to the MEA, they should consider trying to resolve it through the dispute settlement mechanisms available under the MEA."[210]

[207] *See Decision on Trade and Environment, supra* note 88 and accompanying text.
[208] WTO *Fourth Ministerial Declaration, supra* note 89, ¶ 31(i).
[209] Non-parties to an MEA may file a complaint in the WTO. In such a case, the WTO would be required to hear the dispute and to apply the WTO rules. Recent WTO cases have interpreted Article XX—especially its chapeau—as restricting the extent to which countries may use trade measures to pressure other countries to change their environmental policies. The Appellate Body in *United States—Shrimp, supra* note 1, stated that, "the policy goal of a measure at issue cannot provide its rationale or justification under the standards of the chapeau of Article XX." (¶ 149). In *United States—Shrimp 21.5*, the panel stated:

> The Appellate Body Report [in the *Shrimp* case] found that, while a WTO Member may not impose on exporting Members to apply the same standards of environmental protection as those it applies itself, this Member may legitimately require, as a condition of access of certain products to its market, that exporting countries commit themselves to a regulatory program deemed comparable to its own....

While these statements may go some way in creating policy space for certain MEA measures that are aimed at non-Parties, the situation remains unclear.
[210] Committee on Trade and Environment, *supra* note 188, ¶ 178.

VI. Organizational Issues

Many of the legal and policy issues such as those discussed above are created and ultimately resolved by organizations, and other institutional arrangements. Organizations perform the function of developing, interpreting and executing rules to achieve agreed objectives. Where more than one body is responsible for defining objectives and related laws and policies in a particular arena—such as trade and the environment—then an examination of organizational or institutional linkages and issues is required.

Organizational linkages exist at a number of levels. At the national level, relationships exist among trade and non-trade ministries. At the international level, relationships exist among formal bodies of trade and non-trade international organizations. They also exist among the secretariats of international organizations. This section examines a selection of these institutional relationships, focusing on those that are particularly important for ensuring that the multilateral trading system is able to maximize its contribution to sustainable development.

A. Assessment

Integrated sustainability assessments provide a powerful tool for examining the material effects of trade liberalization on economic, social and environmental systems; for exploring the legal and policy implications of trade rules for other sub-systems of law and policy at the local, national, regional and international level; and for identifying opportunities to increase the cooperation of institutions at and between all levels. According to UNEP, "an integrated assessment considers the economic, environmental and social impacts of trade measures, the linkages between these effects, and aims to build upon this analysis by identifying ways in which the negative consequences can be avoided or mitigated, and ways in which positive effects can be enhanced."[211]

Integrated assessments may be conducted prior to, concurrently with, or subsequent to trade negotiations. They can focus on implications for a particular sector (such as agriculture, forestry, fisheries or mining), across a particular country or geographic region, or for a particular social or environmental structure or system. The ultimate goal of integrated assessments is to maximize the net benefits of trade and trade liberalization, by enabling countries to design and implement integrated policies that minimize associated social and environmental problems.

The importance of assessing the impacts of trade rules and liberalization was recognized in the WTO's Fourth Ministerial Declaration, which notes the role of technical assistance and capacity building in the field of trade and the environment, and encourages "expertise and experience [to] be shared with Members wishing to perform environmental reviews at the national level".[212] Such expertise and experience has been gained through recent national level assessments conducted in a number of countries. These studies, conducted with the assistance of UNEP's methodology for integrated assessment of trade-related policies, took place in countries including Argentina, China, Ecuador, Nigeria, Senegal and Tanzania, and in relation to sectors including agriculture, fisheries and forestry. According to UNEP's summary report, the studies revealed significant positive and negative linkages between trade liberalization, society and the environment, and underpin the importance of integrated policy-making.[213]

---

[211] *See* UNEP, *supra* note 105, at iii.

[212] WTO *Fourth Ministerial Declaration, supra* note 89, ¶ 33.

[213] UNEP, *Integrated Assessment of Trade and Trade-Related Policies: UNEP Country Projects-Round II, A Synthesis Report* (2002).

Just as there is value in assessment at the national level, so there is also value in the collective assessment of trade rules and policies at the multilateral level. Assessments, of one form or another, are mandated in the provisions of a number of WTO agreements. GATS Article XIX, for example, calls on future negotiation of specific commitments to be guided by negotiation guidelines which themselves are prepared in light of "an assessment of trade in services in overall terms and on a sectoral basis with references to the objectives of this Agreement." WTO Members have subsequently agreed that the "Council for Trade in Services in Special Sessions shall continue to carry out an assessment of trade in services in overall terms and on a sectoral basis . . . and negotiations shall be adjusted in the light of the results of the assessment."[214] Similarly, in relation to the Agreement on Agriculture, WTO Members agreed to continue negotiations, taking into account "the experience . . . from implementing reduction commitments; the effects of the reduction commitments on world trade in agriculture; non-trade concerns, special and differential treatment to developing country Members, and the objective to establish a fair and market-oriented agricultural trading system . . . ".[215] These assessments provide WTO Members with a valuable opportunity to examine the effects of existing policies, and to design future trade policies to maximize the welfare of WTO Member countries and their citizens.

As with assessment of the existing agreements, assessment of proposed negotiations (for example, on investment, government procurement and market access for non-agricultural products) could help to refine negotiating positions and to ensure that future negotiations maximize their contribution to WTO Members' sustainable development objectives. In the longer term, WTO Members may wish to consider ways to institutionalize procedures for assessment, in order to examine more systematically the impacts of past liberalization, and to ensure that proposed future liberalization supports the WTO preamble's commitment to ensuring that trade occurs in "accordance with the objective of sustainable development".

B. Transparency and Public Participation

The CTE is mandated under Item 10 of its agenda to "provide input to the relevant bodies in respect of appropriate arrangements for relations with inter-governmental and non-governmental organizations referred to in Article V of the WTO".[216]

To what extent should the public have access to and participate in WTO processes? On one hand, it is clear that the WTO is an intergovernmental organization and so its decisions should be made by Member governments on behalf of their citizens. On the other hand, WTO processes increasingly reach beyond traditional trade issues (such as reduction of tariff barriers) into the domestic policymaking territory of national parliaments. Many NGOs, and some governments, have therefore argued that greater openness and transparency is required to ensure that WTO decision-making is legitimate and accountable, and reflects an appropriate balance between trade and other goals, including the need to protect the environment. Indeed, NGOs representing many different perspectives—environment, development, consumer, gender, indigenous and others—have claimed that

---

[214] *See, Guidelines and Procedures for the Negotiation on Trade in Services*, adopted by the Special Session of the Council for Trade in Services on March 28, 2001, paragraph 14, (S/L/93). *See also* Communication from Cuba, Dominican Republic, Haiti, India, Kenya, Pakistan, Peru, Uganda, Venezuela and Zimbabwe to the Council for Trade in Services, *supra* note 189, calling for assessment of the economic and social impacts of the GATS.

[215] *See Agreement on Agriculture*, Article 20.

[216] WTO *Decision on Trade and Environment, supra* note 88.

the interests of citizens could be better reflected in WTO decision-making procedures, and have thus demanded greater opportunities for "public participation".

The WTO has taken some steps towards improving transparency and public participation. The WTO's General Council is empowered by Article V of the WTO Agreement to make arrangements with other organizations.[217] In 1996, the General Council adopted Guidelines for Arrangements on Relations with Non-Governmental Organizations, which recognized the role of NGOs in the relationship between the WTO and the broader public, and agreed to improve transparency and develop better communications with NGOs.[218] One practical implication has been that WTO documents are now derestricted earlier than in the past.[219] At the same time, however, the guidelines state "there is currently a broadly held view that it would not be possible for NGOs to be directly involved in the work of the WTO or its meetings"[220] and note that "the primary responsibility for closer consultation and cooperation [lies] at the national level."[221]

This view is repeated in the Doha Ministerial Declaration, which stresses the "intergovernmental character of the organization", while reaffirming the Members' commitment "to making the WTO's operations more transparent, including through more effective and prompt dissemination of information, and to improve dialogue with the public."[222] Despite the formal view of WTO Members, some non-state actors already participate indirectly in WTO dispute settlement proceedings. For example, governments often initiate disputes in close collaboration with—and frequently at the initiative of—private firms,[223] and NGOs participate in WTO-organized symposia and meetings.

Some observers claim that the real question is not whether public participation should occur, but rather in which way it should be formalized and institutionalized.[224] Calls for strengthened participation by NGOs are based on the view that NGOs can provide new perspectives, know-how and values that national governments do not adequately supply.[225] Discussions of enhanced public participation can be divided into two main

---

[217] Article V of the WTO Agreement, entitled "*Relations with Other Organizations*", stipulates in paragraph 1: "The General Council shall make appropriate arrangements for effective cooperation with other intergovernmental organizations that have responsibilities related to those of the WTO." Paragraph 2 authorizes the General Council to "make appropriate arrangements for consultation and cooperation with non-governmental organizations concerned with matters related to those of the WTO."

[218] *Guidelines for Arrangements on Relations with Non-Governmental Organizations*, WTO Doc. WT/L/162 (July 23, 1996).

[219] Decision adopted by the General Council, *Procedures for the Circulation and Derestriction of WTO Documents*, WT/L/160 (July 18, 1996).

[220] *Guidelines for Arrangements on Relations with Non-Governmental Organizations, supra* note 218, ¶ 6.

[221] *Id. See also Trade and Environment in the GATT/WTO*, Background Note by the Secretariat (1999), WTO Special Studies No. 4, Annex I, ¶ 69. In the scholarly debate, an expression of this argument is that NGOs should not have "two bites at the apple", signifying that private parties should (as they already do) participate in policy-making at the national level and should not get an opportunity to intervene again at the international level. *See, e.g.,* Jeffrey Dunoff, *The Misguided Debate Over NGO Participation at the WTO*, 1 JOURNAL OF INTERNATIONAL ENVIRONMENTAL LAW 433, 434 (1998).

[222] WTO *Fourth Ministerial Declaration, supra note 89, ¶ 10.*

[223] *See, e.g.,* the Report of the WTO Panel, *Japan—Measures Affecting Consumer Photographic Film and Paper*, WT/DS44/R (1996), involving a dispute between Kodak and Fuji, and *United States—Standards for Reformulated and Conventional Gasoline, supra* note 1, which involved major U.S. and Venezuelan oil corporations.

[224] *See Dunoff, supra note 221, at 433–456.*

[225] *See, e.g.,* Daniel C. Esty, *Non-Governmental Organizations at the World Trade Organization: Cooperation, Competition, or Exclusion*, 1 JOURNAL OF INTERNATIONAL ENVIRONMENTAL LAW 123–147 (1998). FOR AN ALTERNATIVE VIEW, *see* ANDREA KUPPER SCHNEIDER, *Unfriendly Actions: The Amicus Brief Battle at the WTO*, 7 WIDENER LAW SYMPOSIUM JOURNAL 88, 93 (2001); *see also* GREGORY C. SHAFFER, *The World Trade Organization Under Challenge: Democracy and the Law and Politics of the WTO's Treatment of Trade and Environment Matters*, 25 HARV. ENVTL. L. REV. 1 (2001).

areas, which give rise to distinct but related issues: participation in WTO meetings and decision-making processes; and participation in dispute settlement.[226]

Should WTO Members decide to enhance public participation in WTO meetings, this could occur in a variety of ways. A minimal level of participation could involve passive observer status in selected WTO meetings (such as the CTE). The public could also be offered limited rights to comment after governments have made statements, as is the case in some international environmental negotiations. Whereas some other international bodies, such as the International Labor Organization, include direct participation by non-governmental actors, it seems unlikely that the WTO can or would adopt such an approach.

Participation in WTO dispute settlement raises an additional set of issues. The expansion in the coverage of trade policy culminating with the conclusion of the Uruguay Round has increased the number and scope of disputes involving trade and other policy considerations, notably health and environmental protection.[227] In these disputes, participation by affected NGOs, if desired, could provide factual information and know-how ensuring that WTO adjudication bodies have access to all relevant facts and arguments (including those not put forward by governments).[228] It could also enhance the persuasive authority of the WTO by making dispute settlement proceedings more transparent and dispelling their aura of secrecy.

The debate about public participation in dispute settlement has focused on the issue of *amicus curiae* (or friend of the court) briefs.[229] The Appellate Body has stated that both panels and the Appellate Body have the right to consider unsolicited *amicus* briefs. The Appellate Body in *United States—Shrimp* stated that "[a] panel has the discretionary authority either to accept and consider or to reject information and advice submitted to it, whether requested by a panel or not".[230] In relation to *amicus* briefs submitted to the Appellate Body, the Appellate Body has stated that Article 17.9 of the DSU gives it "legal authority . . . to accept and consider *amicus curiae* briefs in an appeal in which we find it pertinent and useful to do so."[231] It is equally within the discretion of adjudicating bodies to adopt procedures governing the submission of such briefs.[232]

Amicus briefs have met with protest from many WTO Members, who feel that participation by non-state actors changes the inter-governmental character of the organization.[233] Some developing countries have expressed concern that commercial interests from developed countries may gain an additional avenue through which to influence WTO

---

[226] *See* Schneider, *supra* note 225, 93–95. A third possible area related to the "public participation issue" would be to give private actors legal standing, e.g., to bring claims under the WTO Dispute Settlement. *See, e.g.,* Steve Charnovitz, *Participation of Nongovernmental Organizations in the World Trade Organization*, 17 U. Pa. J. Intl. Econ. L. 331 (1996).

[227] Esty, *supra* note 225, at 127. *See also* Jan Bohanes, *supra* note 145. Jeffrey L. Dunoff, *Institutional Misfits: The GATT, the ICJ and Trade-Environment Disputes*, 15 Mich. J. Intl Law 1043 (1994). Gabrielle Marceau and Matthew Stilwell, *Practical Suggestions for Amicus Curiae Briefs Before WTO Adjudicating Bodies*, 4 Journal of International Economic Law (2001).

[228] *See, e.g.,* Rule 37.1. of the United States Supreme Court, which states that "[a]n *amicus curiae* brief that brings to the attention of the Court relevant matter not already brought to its attention by the parties may be of considerable help to the Court."

[229] Marceau and Stilwell, *supra* note 227, footnote 4.

[230] *United States—Import Prohibition of Certain Shrimp and Shrimp Products, supra* note 1, ¶¶ 108–110.

[231] Appellate Body Report, *United States—Imposition of Countervailing Duties on Certain Hot-rolled Lead and Bismuth Carbon Steel Products Originating in the United Kingdom*, WT/DS138/AB/R (2000), ¶ 42.

[232] *See* the Additional Procedures adopted by the Appellate Body in *European Communities—Measures Affecting Asbestos and Asbestos-Containing Products, supra* note 75, ¶ 52.

[233] *See* Minutes of the DSB Meeting held on November 6, 1998, WT/DSB/M/50, 1–13.

processes.[234] Some others have noted that, while WTO Members must fulfill procedural conditions to participate as third parties (e.g., time limits, involvement at the panel stage to be eligible as participant at the Appellate level, etc), no such requirements exist for the filing of *amicus* briefs.[235] A few other WTO Members, by contrast, support the Appellate Body's approach to *amicus* briefs. Regardless, it seems from the decision of the Appellate Body that both panels and the Appellate Body itself may accept and consider *amicus* briefs. In the absence of explicit guidance by WTO Members (for example, in the form of criteria or other procedures) it will be left to WTO adjudicating bodies to develop procedures for the use of *amicus* briefs on an *ad hoc* basis.

C. Information Exchange and Observer Status

To promote cooperation, the WTO Secretariat is regularly invited to attend the meetings of UNEP and MEA Secretariats. UNEP and MEA Secretariats may, in turn, participate as observers in selected WTO forums such as the Committee on Trade and Environment. An interest in streamlining observer status for environmental organizations in WTO bodies, as well as delays in the granting of some requests, however, gave rise at the Doha Ministerial to a mandate for negotiations on "procedures for regular information exchange between MEA Secretariats and the relevant WTO committees, and the criteria for observer status".[236]

In future negotiations, procedures for regular information exchange between MEA Secretariats and relevant WTO Committees could be developed to build on existing informal practices. WTO Members may wish to consider discussing ways to encourage the two regimes to notify each other about any work programs and projects of mutual interest; to exchange technical documents; to share draft documents for comment; to provide national legislation notified to the WTO or an MEA Secretariat upon request; to give access to relevant computerized databases; and to exchange information concerning scientific and technical experts. Criteria for observer status could also build from a baseline of existing practice by examining the membership and geographical coverage of existing observer organizations, the nature and scope of their interests and activities, and the degree of connection between these interests and activities and those of the WTO. Given the acknowledged need to improve cooperation among trade and environment institutions, criteria for observer status should presumably be negotiated with the goal of expediting requests for observer status, and providing new opportunities for environmental organizations to participate as observers in relevant WTO Committees and Councils.

When exploring ways to expand institutional cooperation between the WTO and MEA Secretariats, trade and environmental policy-makers may wish to draw on the models of cooperation developed between the WTO and other international organizations. The most informal of these are the memoranda of understanding signed between the WTO and other international agencies to promote their mutual work on technical cooperation. These agreements are often developed by individual WTO Divisions, and describe areas of intended cooperation and a framework for carrying out joint activities.

Another model of inter-institutional cooperation is the agreement between the WTO and the United Nations. This agreement involves an exchange of letters among chief

[234] *Id.*
[235] *See* Daniel Pruzin, *Key WTO Members Score Appellate Body for its Decision to Accept Amicus Briefs*, 17 INT'L TRADE REP. (BNA), No. 24, at 924 (June 15, 2000).
[236] *WTO Ministerial Declaration, supra* note 89, ¶ 31(ii).

executive officers, and reflects the pre-existing relationship of cooperation between the GATT and the United Nations. While it is still relatively informal, this model has provided a useful basis for cooperation between the WTO and UN organizations, especially UNCTAD. Cooperation with UNCTAD has included exchange of information, reciprocal representation in accordance with decisions of competent bodies of both organizations, participation by the WTO in various UNCTAD Committees, and cooperation among secretariats. Paralleling the exchange of letters between the UN and the WTO is an exchange of letters between the WTO and UNEP. [237] This sets out a number of areas of mutual cooperation, and could be augmented and strengthened as part of an effort to improve cooperation among MEAs (many of which are UNEP-administered) and the WTO.

More detailed than the letters between UN organizations and the WTO is the formal agreement between the World Bank and the World Trade Organization, which establishes a High Level Working Group on Coherence to oversee cooperation between the three organizations and prepare joint reports.[238] This agreement promotes a range of cooperative activities, including the participation at meetings, information sharing, and contacts between staff on specific projects. The WTO also has formal agreements with the World Intellectual Property Organization, and the International Telecommunications Union,[239] which may provide useful models for future frameworks for cooperation between environment and trade institutions.

D. Compliance, Enforcement and Dispute Settlement

Another set of linkages among institutions arises out of the provisions for compliance, enforcement and dispute settlement included in MEAs and the WTO. Generally, *compliance* refers to measures designed to assist parties to honor their treaty obligations, and would include technical cooperation and technology transfer. *Enforcement* may be used to refer to multilateral measures designed to respond to a party's failure to comply, and would include suspension of certain rights and privileges or trade-related measures. And *dispute settlement* may be used to refer to procedures designed to address bilateral (or plurilateral) disputes between parties, and would include provisions for consultation, good offices, mediation, arbitration or judicial settlement. In each of these areas there are overlaps between the institutional mechanisms in MEAs and the WTO, giving rise to the potential for synergies and conflicts. Joint technical cooperation, for example, has been identified at recent meetings as an area of mutually supportive cooperation between MEAs and the WTO.[240]

The area most likely to give rise to challenges to institutional coherence, however, is dispute settlement. The provisions of MEAs and the WTO may apply simultaneously

[237] *See* WTO Press Release 154 (1999), available at www.wto.org/english/news_e/pres99_e/pr154_e.htm, (last visited March 2, 2003).
[238] *Agreement between the International Bank for Reconstruction and Development, the International Development Association and the World Trade Organization*; and the Agreed Commentary thereto, WT/GC/W/43 (28 April 1997).
[239] *Agreements between WTO and WIPO*, WIPO Publication No. 223(E), (January 1, 1996); Agreement between WTO and ITU, on file with the authors (October 10, 2000).
[240] *See Chairman's Summary*, UNEP Meeting on Enhancing Synergies and Mutual Supportiveness of Multilateral Environmental Agreements and the World Trade Organization, October 23, 2000, www.unep.ch, *stating* "Technical cooperation and capacity building were identified as areas requiring the enhanced and concerted efforts of UNEP, MEAs and the WTO. The UNEP-UNCTAD Capacity Building Task Force on Trade, Environment and Development was identified as being able to make an important contribution in this context."

to the same countries and activities. In the event a dispute arises—over, for example, transboundary movement of genetically modified organisms or hazardous chemicals— different parties may seek to have the dispute resolved in different fora, according to different rules, with potentially different results. A lack of clarity about the relationship between dispute settlement systems gives rise to the risk of forum shopping, and for the potential for uncoordinated, inconsistent or conflicting outcomes.

The importance of coherence between MEA and WTO dispute settlement systems was recognized by WTO Members in Item 5 of the CTE's agenda, which empowers the Committee to examine and make recommendations on the "relationship between the dispute settlement mechanisms in the multilateral trading system and those found in multilateral environmental agreements". A joint UNEP-WTO paper on compliance and dispute settlement mechanisms in MEAs and the WTO notes "the two regimes emphasize different approaches to securing compliance with their respective agreements":

> The WTO system, while encouraging Members to resolve their disputes through consulta-tion, focuses on a legalistic approach to resolving conflicts. MEAs, on the other hand, have concentrated on developing measures to promote compliance ... and rely on a process of facilitation, not adjudication.[241]

While the two regimes emphasize different approaches, the potential for overlapping jurisdiction does arise. For example, in a trade/fisheries dispute between the European Union and Chile over swordfish, a last-minute settlement narrowly averted parallel pro-ceedings at the WTO and the International Tribunal on the Law of the Sea. The potential for overlapping jurisdiction raises a series of interesting legal and practical issues, in-cluding which forum should be primarily responsible for resolving a dispute.[242]

Determining which forum should decide which matter requires an examination of a number of factors. Explicit treaty language on dispute settlement may help to clarify the relationship between dispute settlement forums. The SPS Agreement, for exam-ple, provides that "nothing in this Agreement shall impair the rights of Members under other international agreements, including the right to resort to the good offices or dis-pute settlement mechanisms of other international organization or established under any other international agreement."[243] More general treaty language on the relationship be-tween treaties may also exercise some influence on choice of forum. The Convention on Biological Diversity, for example, provides that "the provisions of this Convention shall not affect the rights and obligations of any Contracting Party deriving from any existing international agreement, except where the exercise of those rights and obligations would cause a serious damage or threat to biological diversity."[244] Finally, general principles of law, such as the duty of good faith and *res judicata* (the principle that the same matter cannot be decided twice), might require consideration in a case of overlapping jurisdic-tion. In the absence of explicit guidance by governments, dispute settlement bodies will be required to answer these questions on an *ad hoc* basis. How these different factors play out in a particular dispute will require an analysis of all relevant rules and evidence.

---

[241] *See* Joint Paper by WTO and UNEP Secretariats, entitled *Compliance and Dispute Settlement Provisions in the WTO and in Multilateral Environmental Agreements*, WTO Doc. WT/CTE/W/191 (June 6, 2001), ¶ 140.

[242] Different dispute settlement bodies may be responsible for addressing different aspects of a dispute. Nevertheless, the resolution of one overarching dispute by two dispute settlement bodies, in the absence of some coordination mechanism, raises considerable challenges.

[243] DSU, Article 11.3.

[244] DSU, Article 22.1.

While explicit guidance by governments is preferable, there are less direct approaches to reducing the potential for conflict. According to the joint UNEP-WTO paper strengthening compliance mechanisms in MEAs would "enhance the effective implementation of MEAs, and... prevent MEA-related disputes from arising in the WTO dispute settlement system".[245] Additionally, the WTO could "put less focus on judicial settlement of disputes, and more on mediation and conciliation combined with technical assistance and capacity building for implementation."[246]

In the event an MEA-related dispute does arise at the WTO, the DSU also includes a number of mechanisms that allow the dispute settlement system to consider environmental factors. These include the use of procedures for good offices, mediation and consultation (Article 5) to encourage dispute avoidance and to ensure participation by MEA Secretariats and other experts; use of experts on an *ad hoc* basis under Article 13(1); establishment of Expert Review Groups under Article 13(2) and Appendix 4 to provide non-binding advisory opinions; and increased use of environmental experts as panelists.

VII. Looking Forward

This chapter has examined a range of issues arising at the interface of trade and the environment. It has sketched the WTO agreements, disputes, institutional forums and new negotiating mandates that we believe are most relevant to trade and environment discussions, and it has examined a range of issues that arise from the relationships between trade and environment at the levels of the real or material world, laws and policies, and institutions.

The linkages within and across each of these areas are complex. An understanding of them, however, is central to any effort to ensure trade liberalization maximizes its contribution to the well-being of individuals and communities, and to the economic and social development of any nation. We believe that, until now, too little attention has been paid to the real-world intersection between trade and other areas of human activity. Indeed, despite years of successive rounds of liberalization the impact of past liberalization has not been comprehensively assessed by many WTO Members. The increasing emphasis given by some countries and international organizations to assess the impacts of both current and proposed future trade liberalization and trade policies is therefore to be welcomed.

Trade liberalization is potentially a powerful tool. Yet, the goal of the WTO as set out in its preamble is not merely the liberalization of trade. Liberalization is not an end in itself. As recent studies have shown, inappropriate liberalization may lead to economic de-industrialization, social dislocation and/or environmental damage.[247] On the other hand, conducted under the right conditions, at the right pace, and accompanied by the right policy measures, liberalization may yield significant economic, social and environmental benefits. A major challenge facing all WTO Members is thus to encourage trade that promotes their national developmental goals; to increase the *quality* of trade, and not merely its volume.

---

[245] Joint Paper by WTO and UNEP Secretariats, *supra* note 241, ¶ 141.

[246] *Id.*

[247] *See, e.g.,* UNEP country study entitled "Integrated Assessment of Trade Liberalization and Trade-Related Policies: A Country Study on the Fisheries Sector in Argentina", available at http://www.unep.ch/etu/publications/CSII_Argentina.pdf, which documents that unchecked trade expansion in Argentina, combined with an absence of appropriate fisheries policies in the 1990s had a *net economic cost* of about US$ 500 million for one fish species (hake).

Institutions grow and change over time. We believe that in the longer term the goal of the WTO must be explicitly one of promoting a human-centered development process that meets the needs of current generations—especially the poorest individuals, communities and countries—without compromising the capacity of future generations to meet their needs. Such an approach is at least partially reflected in the WTO's preamble, which identifies trade liberalization as a means to the end of "raising standards of living . . . in accordance with the objective of sustainable development, seeking both to protect and preserve the environment" with "positive efforts designed to ensure that developing countries, and especially the least developed among them, secure a share in the growth in international trade commensurate with the needs of their economic development."

Truly achieving these goals—and realizing the benefits for all people and countries rather than for a privileged few—will require a deeper effort to understand the linkages between the social, environmental and economic aspects of human life on a sector-by-sector, country-by-country, region-by-region basis across countries at vastly different levels of development, and with different social, cultural and environmental attributes. As WTO Members adopt policies and rules that more deeply affect the lives and aspirations of people and communities around the world, they must also assume the responsibility to measure the performance of the multilateral trading system against the standard established in the WTO Agreement's preamble.

CHAPTER 59

TRADE AND LABOR I

Friedl Weiss*

TABLE OF CONTENTS

* Professor of International Economic Law and International Organizations at the University of Amsterdam; Visiting Professor, International Law Department, Catholic University of Louvain-la-Neuve; former Consultant, Legal Affairs Division, GATT Secretariat.

I. Introduction and Background

A. *Preliminary Remarks*

During the closing stages of the Uruguay Round of multilateral trade negotiations, the question was raised as to whether the rules governing international trade should include provisions in the social field. The ensuing debate has not been limited to trade ministers and scholars, but has spilled onto the streets in sometimes-violent protests, first at the 1999 Third World Trade Organization Ministerial Conference in Seattle, and later at subsequent international conferences covering a variety of topics all over the world. While such protests may have sharpened police crowd control methods and made the prospect of hosting international conferences a double-edged sword for municipal officials hungry for international prestige, the World Trade Organization ("WTO") position on social issues, especially those related to international labor standards, has remained the *status quo* established at the First WTO Ministerial conference at Singapore in 1996. The challenge to labor leaders and others who hope to bring the social field into the trade regime is to reinvigorate the debate to create some movement on the trade-labor front. Those who wish to keep trade rules free of environmental and labor concerns need to demonstrate that increased trade will improve overall social welfare leading to improved regulation and enforcement of environmental and labor standards.[1]

B. *Themes and Issues*

Some have referred to the trade connection of both environmental and labor standards as "social issues".[2] This term, undoubtedly, has a certain evocative resonance. But by attempting to map out an area for discourse that appears separate from, if not antagonistic to that of trade, the term risks further polarizing these mono-dimensional constituencies and obscuring the need for their reconciliation. Defining labor standards as a social issue may frame the debate in a perspective favorable to those trade purists who eschew any connection between trade rules and labor standards. Labor advocates may be well advised to focus their efforts on reconnecting labor with trade the same way that capital is connected with trade. Given the centrality of low labor costs to the workings of comparative advantage, one could argue that labor standards are more relevant to trade than intellectual property rights, which the United States successfully brought into the trade regime through the Agreement on Trade-Related Aspects of Intellectual Property Rights ("TRIPS").[3] Placing labor standards within the framework of comparative advantage has the advantage of framing the debate in a context already envisioned by the International Labor Organization's ("ILO") Declaration on Fundamental Principles and Rights at Work, which "[s]tresses that labor standards should not be used for protectionist

---

[1] The author would like to thank James Chalker for his research assistance. Portions of this essay are drawn from a chapter by the author entitled *International Recognized Labor Standards and Trade*, INTERNATIONAL ECONOMIC LAW WITH A HUMAN FACE 79–115 (Friedl Weiss, Erik M.G. Denters and Paul J.I.M. de Waart eds., 1998).

[2] S. Charnovitz, *The World Trade Organization and Social Issues*, 28(5) JOURNAL OF WORLD TRADE 17–33 (1994); S. Charnovitz, *Fair Labor Standards and International Trade*, 20(1) JOURNAL OF WORLD TRADE 61 (1986).

[3] For an argument as to why both labor standards and TRIPS do not belong in the WTO, *see* Jagdish Bhagwati, *Afterword: The Question of Linkage*, 96 AMERICAN JOURNAL OF INTERNATIONAL LAW 126 (2002) (stating that, "[b]y putting TRIPS into the WTO, in essence we legitimated the use of the WTO to extract royalty payments").

trade purposes, and that nothing in this Declaration and its follow-up shall be invoked or otherwise used for such purposes; in addition, the comparative advantage of any country should in no way be called into question by this Declaration and its follow-up."[4] Can advocates of the trade-labor link define comparative advantage in such a way as to legitimate the role of labor standards in assessing the relevant advantage, or does comparative advantage hold such an esteemed place in the international trade regime that discussion of labor standards is foreclosed? By affirming its support for the notion of comparative advantage in almost the same breath as it warns against the use of labor standards for protectionism is the ILO signaling a reluctance to see comparative advantage connected with labor standards?[5]

Since the relevant substantive standards involved are not in question, whether for the conduct of multilateral trade or the protection of fundamental human rights pertaining to working conditions, the central issue revolves around the suitability of using trade measures as a means of enforcing international labor standards. This, then, is primarily an institutional and procedural matter. However, while the case for global environmental protection can be based to some extent on the survival of humanity at large, backed up to a degree by objective scientific evidence, it has been far more difficult to strike a balance between the trade and labor standards constituencies. There is little common ground between countries which advocate the effective enforcement of recognized international labor standards and those countries that see such concerns as merely a facade for protectionism.

C. International v. Fair Labor Standards

Confusingly, the proximate yet distinct concepts of "international labor standards" and "fair labor standards" have often been used interchangeably. The former concept refers to international agreements and instruments based on values widely shared in the international community. All countries, whether bound by these instruments or not, are encouraged to accept and respect them. In dealing with countries unable or unwilling to incorporate such international standards in their own social legislation, the ILO's distinctive tripartism has relied on consensus and persuasion rather than on sanctions or penalties.[6] This much criticized "lack of teeth" is exactly the reason why the United States previously sought the inclusion of a social clause in the WTO framework, "policed" by the WTO Understanding on Rules and Procedures Governing the Settlement of Disputes ("DSU"). However, no concerted efforts were made by the United States to introduce a "social clause" in the Doha Negotiations. By contrast, labor standards are only considered fair by particular countries which seek to use their own "fair" standards as the socially correct yardstick for unilateral coercive action in an attempt to raise their competitors' production costs.[7] It is pursuant to such a "domestic" perspective that the United States has persistently attempted to internationalize its own national "fair labor standards" and to justify economic or trade sanctions in case of their breach. More recently, the United

[4] International Labor Organization, *Declaration on Fundamental Principles and Rights at Work*, ¶ 5 (1998), http://www.ilo.org/public/english/standards/decl/declaration/text/index.htm (visited November 14, 2003).
[5] My thanks to Janelle M. Diller, the author of another chapter on labor issues in this book, for drawing my attention to the Declaration's comments in this regard and for other helpful comments on this essay.
[6] The International Labour Conference, one of the principal organs of the ILO, as well as committees established by it, are tripartite in composition. That is to say, two delegates from each member state represent the government, and one each employers and workers.
[7] B. Streil, *Social Correctness is the New Protectionism*, 73 FOREIGN AFFAIRS 19 (1994).

States has pursued the inclusion of core international labor standards into its bilateral and multilateral trade agreements.[8]

D. From Marrakesh to Singapore

At the Ministerial Conference held at Marrakesh on April 15, 1994, the United States, supported by France and a few other countries, requested that a reference be made to internationally recognized workers' rights in the Final Ministerial Declaration.[9] The United States also requested the establishment of a WTO Committee on Labor Standards similar to the Committee on Trade and Environment. Both requests were rejected, but it was agreed that the issue of the "social clause" or "trade-labor link", *i.e.*, that of "the relationship between the trading system and internationally recognized labor standards" should be made a new agenda item for future consideration by the WTO.[10] Similarly, the issue of a social clause appeared dormant in the ILO after inconclusive debates on the constitutionality of a "trade-labor link" during the 1994 International Labor Conference and in its Governing Body.[11] Since then, however, there was a remarkable resurgence of interest in international labor standards and in their role in an open trading system, as reflected in a considerable amount of academic writing on the subject.[12] The Final Declaration of the First WTO Ministerial Conference held in Singapore in December 1996 signaled the reemergence of this issue when it devoted a paragraph to the subject. It stated:

> We renew our commitment to the observance of internationally recognized core labor standards. The International Labor Organization (ILO) is the competent body to set and deal with these standards, and we affirm our support for its work in promoting them. We believe that economic growth and development fostered by increased trade and further trade liberalization contribute to the promotion of these standards. We reject the use of labor standards for protectionist purposes, and agree that the comparative advantage of countries, particularly low-wage developing countries, must in no way be put into question. In this regard, we note that the WTO and ILO Secretariats will continue their existing collaboration.[13]

Those who wanted the WTO to stay out of labor standards found this provision's acknowledgment of the primacy of comparative advantage supportive of their position.

---

[8] 19 U.S.C.A. § 3813 (6).

[9] *Marrakesh Ministerial Declaration of April 15, 1994*, 33 ILM 1263 (1994).

[10] *See* ¶ 8(c)(iii) of the Decision on the Establishment of the Preparatory Committee for the WTO.

[11] In 1994 the Governing Body established a Working Party on the Social Dimension of the Liberalization of International Trade.

[12] *See* J.M. Diller and D.A. Levy, *Child Labor, Trade and Investment: Toward the Harmonization of International Law*, 91 AMERICAN JOURNAL OF INTERNATIONAL LAW 663 (1997); B.A. Langille, *General Reflections on the Relationship of Trade and Labor (or: Fair Trade is Trade's Destiny?*, in FAIR TRADE AND HARMONIZATION-PREREQUISITES FOR FREE TRADE 231 (J. Bhagwati and R.E. Hudec eds., 1996); P. de Waart, *Minimum Labor Standards in International Trade*, in CHALLENGES TO THE NEW WORLD TRADE ORGANIZATION 245 (P. van Dijck and G. Faber eds., 1996); J. de Castro, *Trade and Labor Standards*, 34 UNCTAD BULLETIN 9 (Nov.–Dec. 1995); V.A. Leary, *The WTO and the Social Clause,* 1 EUROPEAN JOURNAL OF INTERNATIONAL LAW 118–122 (1997); J.A. Canela-Cacho, The *Social Dimensions of the Liberalization of World Trade and Trade and Labor Standards: Can Common Rules be Agreed?: The View from the ILO*, in REGIONALISM AND MULTILATERISM AFTER THE URUGUAY ROUND (Bellis Demaret and Garcia Jiménez eds., 1998); John W. Head, *Throwing Eggs at Windows: Legal and Institutional Globalization in the 21st Century Economy*, 50 UNIVERSITY OF KANSAS LAW REVIEW 731 (2002); Ajit Singh and Ann Zammit, THE GLOBAL LABOR STANDARDS CONTROVERSY: CRITICAL ISSUES FOR DEVELOPING COUNTRIES (2000); José E. Alvarez and David W. Leebron, *Linkages*, 96 AMERICAN JOURNAL OF INTERNATIONAL LAW 5 (2002).

[13] Singapore Ministerial Declaration, Article 4 (December 13, 1996), http://www.wto.org/english/thewto_Pe/minist_e/min96_e/wtodec_e.htm (visited November 14, 2003), reproduced in the Appendix to this book.

Others, however, considered it an important first step towards such standards. To date, the interpretation of the former has prevailed; leaving those who wondered what form WTO support for the ILO might take, still wondering.

II. Evolution of the Link Between Trade and Labor Rights

A. From Integrated to Segregated Standards and Back?

Human welfare derives from peace as well as socio-economic and cultural well-being.[14] As a complex, pluri-dimensional concept it also encompasses labor standards and a range of human rights, including the right to development. This matrix of complex issues was recognized after the Second World War, when international economic and social co-operation tackled unemployment and trade barriers simultaneously.[15] Thus, the abortive Havana Charter, once described as "the high watermark in the post-1945 world of liberal and social democratic thinking in the field of international economic relations,"[16] was a multilateral agreement on trade and employment. It was a comprehensive instrument designed for the implementation of one of the objectives of the United Nations, the attainment of higher standards of living, full employment, and conditions of economic and social progress and development.[17] Since then, various regulatory regimes governing trade, human rights and labor standards co-existed in "splendid isolation", supposedly as self-contained regimes, without being attuned to one another. In the free-wheeling debate over globalization, however, attempts are being made to integrate these separate but related concerns by such methods as bringing labor rights within the competence of the trade regime, matched by equally determined forces committed to keeping such concerns segregated.

B. The Impact of Globalization

Under the neoliberal model, which has been in the ascendancy since the collapse of the Soviet Union, it is common to speak of the "global market place" and the "global economy". Neoliberals argue, *inter alia*, that the globalization of markets, the internationalization of investment, production and distribution is the key to economic dynamism and growth, competitiveness and wealth. Integral to the globalization of markets is the removal

---

[14] *Preamble to the Charter of the United Nations*; Article 2(1)(iii) European Bank for Reconstruction and Development: "(...) raising (...) the standard of living and conditions of labor"; the objective of the NAFTA Side Agreement on Labor Cooperation: improving working conditions and living standards, promoting compliance with and effective enforcement of labor laws.

[15] Article 1 of the Havana Charter for an International Trade Organization; Preamble and Article 1 of the Charter of the United Nations; preamble to OEEC Convention, of April 16, 1948; Convention on the Organization of European Economic Cooperation and Development ("OECD") of 1960, 888 UNITED NATIONS TREATY SERIES 179–199 (1973). For a summary of these antecedent debates, *see* F. Weiss, *The GATT 1994: Environmental Sustainability of Trade or Environmental Protection Sustainable by Trade?*, in SUSTAINABLE DEVELOPMENT AND GOOD GOVERNANCE 382, 391–393 (K. Ginther, E. Denters & P.J.I.M. de Waart eds., 1995).

[16] G. Schwarzenberger, *The Principles and Standards of International Economic Law*, 89 RECUEIL DES COURS 89 (1966).

[17] Article 55(a) UN Charter; discussion of the Interim Report of the second session of the Preparatory Committee of the United Nations Conference on Trade and Employment (doc. E/469), Official Records of the Economic and Social Council, Second year, Fifth session, 96th Meeting, at 78–79. *See also* W.M. Scammell, *International Economic Co-operation and the Problem of Full Employment*, 6 YEARBOOK OF WORLD AFFAIRS 222–245 (1952).

of barriers to the transnational movement of capital and goods. The internationalization and free movement of labor is not on the neoliberal agenda, however.[18] Globalization's detractors warn of economic dislocation, unemployment, and environmental degradation and of the risk of friction or conflict between states due to the divergence of their regulatory systems and standards and to competition between them.[19] This is because economic and trade policy-making are no longer matters self-contained within a "national jurisdiction", but are part of the "global economy" where developments in major economies are significantly reflected in others. Yet national governments and international institutions continue to work mostly within traditional, fragmented jurisdictional frameworks and, as a result, have to deal with difficulties arising from such fragmentation. For example, unemployment is often seen as a trade problem caused by import competition from low wage economies with little or no social regulation affecting the price of labor. At the height of protectionism in the 1930s, Keynes saw the trade link clearly and offered a prescription which would make a neoliberal blanch:

> If nations can learn to provide themselves with full employment by their domestic policy (. . .) there need be no important economic forces calculated to set the interest of one country against that of its neighbors. There would still be room for international division of labor (. . .). International trade would cease to be what it is, namely, a desperate expedient to maintain employment at home (. . .), but a willing and unimpeded exchange of goods and services in conditions of mutual advantage.[20]

European and U.S. trade barriers against *e.g.*, Japanese imports constitute governmental action against trade-induced unemployment.[21] While economists admit that the pursuit of private interests in the market does not lead automatically to a socially acceptable outcome,[22] some doubt that trade policy is the right way to create jobs.[23]

C. The Link: ILO, GATT and Unilateral State Practice

A link between labor rights and trade is certainly not a recent issue, neither in the ILO nor even the GATT itself. From its inception, the ILO promoted international labor legislation—a certain equalization of levels of social protection between countries—so

---

[18] For two different perspectives on the neoliberal recipe for Latin America, *see* Paul Craig Roberts and Karen LaFollette Araujo, THE ECONOMIC DEVELOPMENT OF LATIN AMERICA AND ITS PRINCIPAL PROBLEMS (1997); and María Eugenia Padua, *Mexico's Part in the Neoliberal Project*, 8 UNIVERSITY OF CALIFORNIA DAVIS JOURNAL OF INTERNATIONAL LAW & POLICY 1 (2002).

[19] D. Charney, *Competition Among Jurisdictions in Formulating Corporate Law Rules: An American Perspective on the "Race to the Bottom" in the European Communities*, 32 HARVARD INTERNATIONAL LAW JOURNAL 423, 430–431 (1991).

[20] John Maynard Keynes, THE GENERAL THEORY OF EMPLOYMENT, INTEREST, AND MONEY 382 (1936), cited by Arthur Smithies, *Effective Demand and Employment*, in THE NEW ECONOMICS, KEYNES' INFLUENCE ON THEORY AND PUBLIC POLICY 558, 567 (1948); for critical discussions of labor market developments and protectionism to save jobs, *see also*, R. Blackhurst, N. Marin and J. Tumlir, *Adjustment, Trade and Growth in Developed and Developing Countries*, 6 GATT STUDIES IN INTERNATIONAL TRADE (1978); and GATT, TRADE POLICIES FOR A BETTER FUTURE, PROPOSALS FOR ACTION (1985) (the "Leutwiler Report").

[21] M. Hudson, *Trade, Development and Foreign Debt*, I INTERNATIONAL TRADE 143 (1992).

[22] *See, e.g.*, E. Matzner, *Policies, Institutions and Employment Performance*, in BEYOND KEYNESIANISM. THE SOCIO-ECONOMICS OF PRODUCTION AND FULL EMPLOYMENT 231, 252 (E. Matzner, and W. Streeck eds., 1991).

[23] A.K. Dixit, *Trade Policy: An Agenda for Research*, in STRATEGIC TRADE POLICY AND THE NEW INTERNATIONAL ECONOMICS 283, 295 (P.R. Krugman ed. 1993).

as to provide a remedy for what became later known as "social dumping", *i.e.*, the risk of unfair competition based on the exploitation of workers.[24]

In the GATT, which unlike the Havana Charter made no reference to workers' rights,[25] the issue was discussed under labels such as "social dumping",[26] "social clause" and "workers or labor rights". Such debates past and present reflect a common fear that wages in developed countries are being forced down in a "race to the bottom" by unfair competition from countries with much lower labor costs. In the developed countries of the "North", the issue has normally manifested itself in the form of pressure by interest groups, often trade unions, on their governments to use market access as a lever for improving labor conditions in developing countries in the "South". Hitherto, a variety of strategies, including penalties and incentives, have been used to that end. Thus, unilateral trade measures resorted to in the past included antidumping duties[27] and countervailing duties.[28] More recently, import prohibitions were sought under unfair competition legislation[29] and under suspension of the MFN clause,[30] and preferences accorded under the Generalized System of Preferences ("GSP"), and other preferences made conditional upon the recognition by beneficiary countries of internationally-recognized workers rights. Thus, under the U.S. Trade Promotion Authority Act 2002 ("TPA")[31] it is envisaged that future TPA agreements should ensure that trading partners do not systematically fail to enforce their labor laws in a manner that affects their trade with the United States. It also includes provisions designed to promote the ability of trading partners to enforce, and raise their labor standards. Likewise, under the Andean Trade Preference Act ("ATPA") as amended by the US Andean Trade Promotion and Drug Eradication Act ("ATPDEA")[32] benefits for beneficiary countries depend, *inter alia*, on the extent to which the country provides internationally recognized workers rights, including whether it has implemented its commitments to eliminate the worst forms of child labor. Similarly

---

[24] F. Maupain, *Trade and Core Labor Standards*, 44, 6 WIRTSCHAFTSPOLITISCHE BLÄTTER 582 (1997); Jackson sees in "social dumping" the exploitation of prison or "sweated labor" (forms of forced labor including child labor), JACKSON, WORLD TRADE AND THE LAW OF GATT § 16.02 (1969).

[25] The GATT preamble merely mentions "raising standards of living" and "ensuring full employment"; Article XX (general exceptions) permits restrictive measures relating to the production of prison labor.

[26] The problem was considered as early as 1927 at the League of Nations World Economic Conference. It is based on the idea that lower wages paid to poorer workers in developing countries means that firms are able to compete unfairly against employers in more advanced countries, who must provide more benefits for their workers; the underlying reasoning is flawed because it undermines the very foundation and essence of free trade based on competition according to comparative advantage and because it tends to make things worse for poorer countries.

[27] For example, in 1924 Austria authorized penalty duties of up to 1/3 of the statutory rate on goods produced by labor working excessive hours. *See* ¶ 4(c) of the Federal Law of September 5, 1924 (Tariff Act, BGBl. No. 4 as amended), cited in Annex 4 to GATT Study on "Anti-Dumping and Countervailing Duties", Study of the GATT Secretariat, GATT July 1958, at 153.

[28] In 1926 the CSSR authorized countervailing duties on goods produced under "unfavorable social conditions of labor" that threatened domestic production.

[29] A 1980 action by a German asbestos producer under the German Unfair Competition Act for an import prohibition of Korean asbestos and a mandatory information of potential buyers failed because the court considered that unethical conditions of production even if in breach of an ILO Occupational Cancer Convention was not of essential importance to buyers.

[30] Uruguay, Colombia and Mexico unsuccessfully proposed amendments to the Havana Charter so as to permit "reasonable and equitable measures to protect its industry from the competition of like products produced under substandard conditions of labor and pay". The United States suspended Poland from MFN treatment in 1982 *inter alia* because of the outlawing of the independent trade union Solidarity.

[31] The Trade Act of 2002 (Pub.L.107210) was enacted on August 6, 2002.

[32] 19 U.S.C.3201, *et seq.*

the U.S. African Growth and Opportunity Act, as amended by the Trade Act of 2002 ("AGOA II"),[33] includes these conditions as best practice criteria. More recently, the bilateral Textiles Agreement between the Governments of the United States of America and the Socialist Republic of Vietnam stipulated that the Parties:

> reaffirm their commitments as members of the International Labour Organization (ILO), and agree to further cooperation with the ILO . . . [to] support the implementation of codes of corporate social responsibility by enterprises on a voluntary basis and in compliance with domestic laws and regulations, as a means to improve working conditions in the textiles sector.[34]

Reference is also made to a November 2000 Memorandum of Understanding between their respective Labor Ministries in accordance with which they are mandated to consider a cooperative program to improve working conditions in the textiles sector in Vietnam.[35]

Occasionally, boycotts were used to keep imports out.[36] Such international coercive reactions are spasmodic and, above all, primarily unilateral. Besides, it only provides temporary relief from import competition. Sadly, it is true that internationally recognized labor standards are disregarded, that children perform hazardous jobs, that labor laws are not enforced and, that trade union activists are harassed, jailed, disappear and are murdered.

Discussions of a "social clause" have been protracted, fraught with controversy and are replete with economic and political complexity and conflicting value systems. However, social issues are accepted as part of the global agenda which must be addressed by means of international cooperation, as was made clear, most recently, at the Johannesburg World Summit on Sustainable Development.[37] It is also clear that so called "social dumping" cannot be assessed on the basis of national "fair labor standards" of particular countries, but only with reference to international labor standards.

III. The Changing Framework

A. Integrating Separate Concerns

Globalization and related "one-world" views signal a new intellectual climate that appears to favor integrating the interdependent sectoral world orders of economic, trade and monetary relations.[38]

The WTO is mandated to "provide the common institutional framework for the conduct of trade relations among its Members (. . .)."[39] But it is also deemed well suited for wider economic, legal and political cooperation and for the development of "an integrated, more

---

[33] *See Section* 3108 of the Trade Act of 2002 on trade benefits under the African Growth and Opportunity Act, www.sice.oas.org/Trade/tradeact/act10.asp#SEC.%203108 visited November 25 2003).

[34] Article17(A) of the Agreement Relating to Trade in Cotton, Wool, Man-Made Fibre, Non-Cotton Vegetable Fiber and Silk Blend Textiles and Textile Products Between the Governments of the United States of America and the Socialist Republic of Vietnam of July 17, 2003, *see* http://web.ita.doc.gov/Otexa/OTEXAGRE.NSF/ 5b1ca13778763be98525647400649053/ac51417721ec6b3885256d6b00481c00! OpenDocument   (visited November 16, 2003).

[35] *Id.* Article17(B).

[36] In 1976 Scandinavian transport unions objected to practices of ships flying "flags of convenience". In 1985 violent incidents in South Africa triggered boycotts of Royal Dutch Shell which maintained coal and oil investments in South Africa.

[37] *The Johannesburg Statement on Sustainable Development* (September 4, 2002), http://www.johannesburg summit.org/html/documents/summit_docs/1009wssd_pol_declaration.doc (visited November 14, 2003).

[38] The three guiding principles are: freedom, equality and reciprocity and values derived from principles of market economies, in particular private ownership, competitive enterprise and free trade.

[39] Article II(1) of the Agreement Establishing the WTO.

viable and durable multilateral trading system."[40] Some have argued that, as a matter of law, such integration must take place in harmony with peremptory norms and fundamental human rights and labor standards.[41] There is also the view that full respect for a minimum core content of universal and inalienable human rights for every person is essential for the implementation and enforcement of economic, social and cultural rights.[42] These views point to the relatively new concepts of "sustainable development"[43] and "good governance"[44] which evidently seek to reconcile civil and political human rights with economic, social and cultural rights.

However, governments will probably continue to use protectionist measures when these are deemed necessary, fair and reasonable, *e.g.*, for environmental reasons, or to uphold fair labor standards as originally envisaged in the Havana Charter.[45] The question then arises whether these measures will be employed unilaterally or in accordance with WTO disciplines interpreted in the light of their "social dimension".[46] Realistically, unilateral action is only within the arsenal of economically powerful nations and its use by such nations at the expense of economically vulnerable developing countries, even when deemed necessary, fair and reasonable by the former, will be perceived as protectionist by the latter. Turning to the multilateral approach, the critical issue is not primarily a formal but improbable link between the respective complaint procedures of the ILO and the WTO, it is instead the emerging consensus on the necessity of introducing "social aspects" into the multilateral trade regime or "economic aspects" into the setting and the supervision of international labor standards, as was clearly identified by the ILO in 1994.[47] Three options remain, leaving aside the punitive element inherent in the intermittent use or threat of unilateral trade restrictions to sanction or "enforce" certain labor standards.[48] One somewhat haphazard and slow approach could be based on case law from relevant domestic and international litigation, especially the GATT/WTO mechanism of dispute settlement.[49] A second approach could involve the insertion of references to relevant labor standards into various trade agreements. The third approach could involve the obverse inclusion of a "trade liberalization dimension" into the ILO's multilateral labor standards.

B. Historical Antecedents

1. From Linkage to Social Policy Conditionality

A linkage between labor rights and standards and multilateral trade rules has been proposed repeatedly in multilateral GATT negotiation rounds, but was consistently opposed

---

[40] ¶ 4 of the preamble to the WTO Agreement.

[41] Diller and Levy, *supra* note 12, at 664.

[42] De Waart, *supra* note 12, at 247; Article 28 of the Universal Declaration of Human Rights; ¶¶ 8 and 10 of the 1993 Vienna Declaration and Programme of Action, adopted on June 25, 1993 at the Vienna World Conference on Human Rights, June 14–25, 1993, 32 ILM 1661 (1993).

[43] *See* ¶ 1 of the preamble to the WTO Agreement.

[44] ¶ 11 of the 1993 Vienna Declaration and ¶¶ 66–67 of the Programme of Action, adopted at the Vienna World Conference on Human Rights; M.J. Kane, *Promoting Political Rights to Protect the Environment*, 18, YALE JOURNAL OF INTERNATIONAL LAW 389 (1993).

[45] Article 7 of the Havana Charter.

[46] On this *see further*, Weiss, *supra* note 15, at 382–401.

[47] ILO Governing Body, *Social Dimensions of the Liberalization of World Trade*, GB. 261/WP/SLD/1, of November 1994.

[48] Charnovitz analyzed four tracks: multilateral rules, unilateral action, bilateral conditionality and regional agreements, S. Charnovitz, *Environmental and Labor Standards in Trade*, 15 THE WORLD ECONOMY 335, 348 (1992).

[49] *Understanding on Rules and Procedures Governing the Settlement of Disputes* ("DSU"), 33 ILM 1226 (1994).

by developing countries suspecting a protectionist ploy. The regular rejection of such a linkage prompted U.S. statutory actions in the 1980s,[50] some of which link trade and investment policies to performance with respect to U.S. labor standards,[51] some providing for unilateral trade sanctions against countries that violate basic workers' rights.[52]

More recently, various trade agreements contain provisions on "social policy conditionality". For instance, some refer to the improvement of living standards or employment or working conditions,[53] or even full employment[54] or generally to the need to uphold labor standards.[55] Some agreements require labor cooperation in a broad range of areas,[56] and others explicitly require coordination of policies on labor relations in accordance with ILO conventions and recommendations.[57] Such "linkage" discussions are therefore not new. To date, however, they have yet to result in the integration of carefully selected minimum international labor standards into the multilateral trading system, using the WTO as a permanent negotiating forum.

2. The ITO Connection

Member states of the League of Nations agreed to "endeavor to secure and maintain fair and humane conditions of labor for men, women and children, both in their own countries

---

[50] Five U.S. laws explicitly link worker rights and trade: the GSP, 19 U.S.C. §§ 2461–2467; the Overseas Private Investment Corporation(OPIC) Act, 22 U.S.C. §§ 2191–2200; the Caribbean Basin Economic Recovery Act, 19 U.S.C. §§ 2701–2706; the Agency for International Development (AID) Program, 22 U.S.C.§ 2151 *et seq.*; section 301 of the Omnibus Trade and Competitiveness Act 1988, 19 U.S.C. §§ 2411–2420. *See also*, the Acts referred to *supra* notes 31 and 32.

[51] On issues of extraterritoriality of jurisdiction and on the inconsistency of U.S. standards with the principle of equal treatment in U.S. bilateral FCN treaties, *see* J.M. Zimmerman, *International Dimension of U.S. Fair Employment Laws: Protection or Interference?,* 131(2) INTERNATIONAL LABOR REVIEW 217, 225 *et seq.* (1992); on the 1984 re-authorization of GSP which turned its use into a bargaining chip, *see* R.E. Hudec, *Developing Countries in the GATT Legal System*", 50 THAMES ESSAY 115 (1987).

[52] For an overview *see* L. Compa, *Labor Rights and Labor Standards in International Trade,* 25 LAW & POLICY INTERNATIONAL BUSINESS 165, 182 (1993); Section 304(a)(2) and (3) of the U.S. Omnibus Trade and Competitiveness Act of 1988 vests discretionary authority in the U.S.T.R. to "suspend, withdraw, or prevent the application of, benefits of trade concessions (. . .)" to retaliate against "unreasonable", not necessarily unlawful, foreign trade practices including denial of foreign workers' right of association, and of the right to organize and bargain collectively; forced or compulsory labor; failure to provide minimum age for the employment of children; or failure to provide standards for minimum wages, hours of work, and occupational health or safety of workers. *U.S. Omnibus Trade and Competitiveness Act of* 1988, 28 ILM 15 (1989).

[53] Article 1(2)(a), *Central European Free Trade Agreement* ("CEFTA") 1992; Articles 3(b), 143(1)(a) *Treaty Establishing the Common Market for Eastern and Southern Africa 1993.*

[54] *Preamble to the GATT*; Article 2, *Stockholm Convention Establishing the European Free Trade Association 1960.*

[55] *See, e.g.,* the International Commodity Agreements on Natural Rubber (1987), Article 53; and successive International Sugar Agreements, Article 63; Article 64 of the 1986 Cocoa Agreement, J.-M. Servais, *The Social Clause in Trade Agreements: Wishful Thinking or an Instrument of Social Progress?,* 128(4) INTERNATIONAL LABOR REVIEW 423 (1989).

[56] *Annex 1 on Labor Principles to the North American Agreement on Labor Cooperation* ("*NAFTA Labor Side Agreement*") between the United States, Canada and Mexico of 1993 contains a list of eleven such principles, 32 ILM 1499, 1515 (1993); *NAFTA Comes into Force-with a Glimmer of a Social Clause,* 133 INTERNATIONAL LABOR REVIEW 113 *et seq.* (1–1994); *see also,* the *Maastricht Protocol on Social Policy* of 1992 which expanded the European Union's legislative capacity by stipulating majority voting on a number of legislative issues; B. Bercusson, *The European Community's Charter of Fundamental Social Rights of Workers,* 53 MONTHLY LABOR REVIEW 624 (1990); for a comparative study of the NAFTA and the EU approaches, *see* K. van Wezel Stone, *Labor and the Global Economy: Four Approaches to Transnational Labor Regulation,* 16 MICHIGAN JOURNAL OF INTERNATIONAL LAW 987, 997 *et seq.* (1995).

[57] Article 20 of the *Treaty on the Creation of Economic Union of the Commonwealth of Independent States,* 1993, 34 ILM 1298 (1995).

and in all countries to which their commercial and industrial relations extend (. . .)."[58] After the Second World War, the ITO—which of course failed to come into being—was mandated to curtail unemployment and eliminate trade barriers, thereby implementing one of the objectives of the United Nations.[59]

The Havana Charter, the ITO's constituent treaty, would have revolutionized international trade relations by prohibiting, restricting or controlling the right of governments to interfere with the free flow of private trade, thereby curbing potential misuse or arbitrary use by states of their monopoly of regulation.[60] However, developing countries pointed out at that time "the apparent equality of the procedure can involve the most tremendous and unjust inequalities"[61] and that "free trade means free competition" which "implies the elimination of those who find themselves in less favorable conditions." Consequently, "a policy of trade freedom should be developed in harmony with the peculiar conditions prevailing in industrially backward countries."[62] In the end, Article 7(1) of the Havana Charter on "Fair Labor Standards" required Members to recognize that all countries have a common interest in the achievement and maintenance of fair labor standards related to productivity, and thus in the improvement of wages and working conditions as productivity may permit, and that unfair labor conditions, particularly in production for export, create difficulties in international trade. Such conditions had to be eliminated by appropriate action within the territory of each Member.[63] In cases of dispute settlement regarding complaints relating to labor standards, the ITO was required to consult and cooperate with the ILO.[64] Such implicit hedging of free trade ideology reflected the views of Keynes and Robbins on the eve of the creation of the Bretton Woods institutions.[65]

C. Labor in GATT Practice

1. Proposals by Contracting Parties

Already in 1953 the United States unsuccessfully proposed a provision declaring that unfair labor standards "create difficulties in international trade which nullify or impair benefits under this Agreement".[66] Unfair standards were defined broadly, and vaguely, as the "maintenance of labor conditions below which the productivity of the industry and the economy at large would justify". The United States also contended that trade problems attributable to unfair labor standards were actionable under Article XXIII GATT. A 1955 Working Party rejected New Zealand's proposal for a GATT article on full employment,

---

[58] Article 23(a), *Covenant of the League of Nations.*

[59] Article 55(a) *UN Charter, see also, supra* note 14.

[60] K.W. Dam sees in the Charter a "codification" reflecting the U.S. view that its provisions constitute legally enforceable rules, but not that they amount to customary international law, *see* K.W. Dam, THE GATT: LAW AND INTERNATIONAL ECONOMIC ORGANIZATION 10 (1970).

[61] Colombian representative at first session of the ECOSOC, Church House, Westminster, London, (Doc.E/4, Annex 1a), at 74.

[62] *Id.* at 75.

[63] Havana Charter for an International Trade Organization, March 24, 1948, U.N.Doc.E/Conf.2/78.

[64] Article 7(2) Havana Charter.

[65] *See also* P.R. Krugman, *Introduction: New Thinking about Trade Policy*, in STRATEGIC TRADE POLICY AND THE NEW INTERNATIONAL ECONOMICS 15 (P.R. Krugman ed. 1993); for an analytical framework on a measurable correlation, if not causality between economic freedom and prosperity, *see* J. Gwartney, R. Lawson, W. Block, ECONOMIC FREEDOM AND WORLD: 1975–1995 (1995).

[66] P.S. Watson, *The Framework for the New Trade Agenda*, 25(4) LAW & POLICY OF INTERNATIONAL BUSINESS 1237, 1253 (1994).

inter alia, on the ground that "the interest of every member-country to seek to maintain the highest possible level of productive employment and growing demand in its own territory was so obvious that an international commitment on this point would add little if anything to this already compelling incentive."[67] Likewise, during the mid-fifties the British Government was urged by the British Trade Union Congress to press for a fair labor clause in GATT and to use Article XXIII GATT "to impose sanctions on countries which did not take steps to eradicate unfair labor standards". Suggestions of that kind were probably made in contemplation of the possibility of a non-violation complaint[68] claiming "nullification or impairment" of tariff concessions in cases where the competitive position of an imported product had been upset by a subsequent domestic measure, which could not have reasonably been anticipated by the complaining party at the time it negotiated the tariff concessions on the imported product. Similar suggestions were made by other bodies from time to time.[69]

2. The Request of the United States for a Working Party

In June 1986 the issue was raised again in GATT when the United States attempted to inscribe "workers' rights" on GATT's agenda, a term later changed to "labor standards". In April 1987 the U.S. House of Representatives defined as one of the U.S. Uruguay Round negotiating objectives the adoption "as a principle of GATT, that the denial of worker rights should not be a means for a country or its industries to gain competitive advantage in international trade."[70] In July 1987, the United States formally requested the establishment of a Working Party to discuss the issue of the relationship of internationally recognized worker rights to international trade.[71] This led to some polarization amongst GATT contracting parties, some giving cautious support (Nordic countries, the European Communities, Japan and Israel), others, mainly the developing countries, either doubting GATT's competence in the matter, or reserving their position[72] or considering the ILO to be the proper forum for the issue.[73]

In support of their formal request, the United States invoked Article XXIX GATT according to which the contracting parties undertake to observe the general principles of certain chapters of the Havana Charter (I to VI & IX), including Article 7(1) of Chapter II relating to "Fair Labor Standards".[74] In requesting a Working Party the U.S. government attempted to prevent the adoption of protectionist U.S. legislation after the ILO's

---

[67] BISD 3S/231, at 240–241, ¶ 28.

[68] Article XXIII:1(b) GATT. *See* Chapter _ of this book.

[69] For more detail see F. Weiss, *Internationally-recognized Labor Standards and Trade*, 1 LEGAL ISSUES OF ECONOMIC INTEGRATION 161–178 (1996).

[70] S. Charnovitz, *The Influence of International Labor Standards on the World Trading Regime: A Historical Overview*, 126 INTERNATIONAL LABOR REVIEW 565 (October 1987).

[71] C/M/212, 6.8.1987, at 32. The five basic international labor standards—freedom of association, freedom to organize and bargain collectively, freedom from forced or compulsory labor, a minimum age for the employment of children, and minimum standards in respect of conditions of work—were essentially those contained in the U.S. Generalized System of Preferences Renewal Act of 1984.

[72] *Id.* Mexico, Brazil, Colombia, Cuba, Yugoslavia, Tanzania, Malaysia, Chile, Singapore, Philippines, Indonesia, Hong Kong, Nigeria, Thailand and Czechoslovakia.

[73] Nicaragua, Mexico and Cuba.

[74] When, in September 1948, Article XXIX GATT on the relation of this Agreement to the Havana Charter was redrafted by a Working Party on Modifications to the General Agreement it stated that "by virtue of the Final Act signed at Havana, the contracting parties must regard themselves *morally bound* not to go back on the principles evolved at Havana" (emphasis added), Analytical Index, 2 GUIDE TO GATT LAW AND PRACTICE 996 (1995); see also WTO Analytical Index, 1st edition (2003).

refusal to consider the matter on the ground that it belonged to the GATT.[75] The United States also indicated that it was ready to exclude from discussion in GATT any issues related to *comparative advantage*. This stance shows awareness beyond tactical calculation that comparative advantage crucially reflects differences of economic development, including "cheaper" labor which does not necessarily mean ill-treated or oppressed labor. Nonetheless, its request for a Working Party was repeatedly rejected. Lastly, it should be noted that pursuant to the 1988 U.S. Omnibus Trade and Competitiveness Act, worker rights became a principal U.S. objective for the Uruguay Round negotiations.[76]

3. Deliberations in GATT Councils

Informal consultations in search of a consensus on the Working Party continued.[77] In seeking to win broader support, the United States stressed that the purpose of the Working Party would be to examine the "possible relationship" of internationally recognized labor standards to trade, without prejudice to the position of any country as to whether such a relationship would be found to exist. The United States also offered other reassurances: it was not seeking to impose its own labor standards on the world, nor to negotiate an international minimum wage. It also recalled that workers' rights were not a new issue in GATT, making reference to its Preamble,[78] as well as to Articles XX(e),[79] and XXIX.[80] However, Mexico and many other contracting parties, considered internationally-recognized labor standards to be those found in numerous ILO Conventions, rather than in legislation or domestic practices of some countries. These countries also argued that the GATT and the ILO should not get involved in matters of each other's competence.[81] Pakistan, echoing the anxieties of others, thought the request for a Working Party motivated by protectionist considerations and ultimately designed to neutralize whatever comparative advantage developing countries had. In that context, it recalled the bitter experience of developing countries with the establishment of the Working Party on Market Disruption in the 1950s, which had culminated in the imposition on developing countries of the Multifibre Arrangement.[82]

In re-submitting to the GATT Council of October 3, 1990 its request in slightly amended form, the United States sought to dispel two types of concerns: the issue of GATT relevance, and the possible misuse of GATT discussions of this matter toward protectionist ends. Once again the United States stressed that the very issue of GATT relevance was without prejudice to any delegation's view of the matter and that, like other

---

[75] The proposed terms of reference were: "to examine the possible relationship of internationally-recognized labor standards to international trade and to the attainment of the objectives of the GATT". *See* GATT/CP.2/22/Rev.1, BISD II/39 adopted on September 1 and 2, 1948.

[76] Section 1101(b)(14); the Act also envisages a review of their relationship to GATT articles, objectives, and related instruments with a view to ensuring that the benefits of the trading system are available to all workers as well as the adoption as a principle of the GATT that the denial of worker rights should not be a means for a country or its industries to gain competitive advantage in international trade.

[77] *See, e.g.*, C/M/217, 8.3.1988, at 32.

[78] ¶ 1 of the preamble requires trade and economic relations to be conducted with a view to raising "standards of living".

[79] Article XX(e) GATT permits contracting parties to prohibit imports of "products of prison labor".

[80] Article XXIX(1) GATT stipulates: "The contracting parties undertake to observe to the fullest extent of their executive authority the general principles of Chapters I to VI inclusive and of Chapter IX of the Havana Charter pending their acceptance of it in accordance with their constitutional procedures." This incorporation by reference includes the Havana Charter's provisions on internationally-recognized labor standards; C/M/220, 8.6.1988, at 26.

[81] *Id.* at 27.

[82] *Id.* at 30; *see also*, C/M/234, July 31, 1989, at 74–76.

delegations, it was determined to prevent misuse of the discussion of internationally recognized labor standards as a justification for protectionist measures. Therefore, the proposed Working Party should not put into question *legitimate* comparative advantage or limit the range of internationally-recognized labor standards to only a select few.[83]

IV. GATT Panel Practice

A. Adjudication Without Law?

As mentioned above, one of several approaches to the integration of separate concerns extrinsic to the WTO into the WTO framework might consist of WTO panel adjudication as between competing regulatory standards of WTO Members. However, in the absence of a "social clause" in the WTO framework and of an express general exception in the GATT, on what legal basis could a WTO panel seek to reconcile protecting "free trade" with trade restrictions? For instance, could a panel condone restrictions on the basis that they are used against products supposedly made in breach of international labor standards?

   As to the approach itself, it might be instructive to consider relevant WTO practice with proximate "trade and environment" issues. It is noteworthy that while these issues have been discussed extensively in the WTO Committee on Trade and Environment, considerably more progress was made in the Dispute Settlement Body ("DSB") administering the DSU and the panel process, than at the political level. This is not surprising. On the contrary, there would seem to be an emerging pattern according to which WTO panels, by default of WTO Members, have virtually exercised law-making power delegated by WTO Members unable or unwilling to take decisions on new standards. For the time being, interests and positions of WTO Members engaged in the debate on a social clause in trade agreements are simply too far apart for such an agreement to be reached. On the other hand, while the panel process might in certain instances yield "markers" for the ongoing debate, it is, nonetheless, restricted to preserving the rights and obligations of Members and to clarifying the existing provisions of covered agreements in accordance with customary rules of interpretation of public international law. It should be recalled that "recommendations and rulings of the DSB cannot add to or diminish the rights and obligations provided in the covered agreements."[84]

B. Protection of Domestic Labor

A 1960 GATT Report of Experts on "Anti-Dumping and Countervailing Duties"[85] discussed "labor" as a factor of production in connection with dumping and noted "(. . .) that the term "production costs" covered all those items involved, directly or indirectly, in the cost of producing an article" including labor. However, measures seeking to improve domestic labor or employment conditions, directly or indirectly, have not been accepted as justifying exemptions from the prohibition of import restrictions. A 1958 Panel Report examined the alleged inconsistency with GATT Article III:4 of an Italian law which provided special credit facilities to some categories of farmers for the purchase of

---

[83] Relevant but not exhaustive standards included the freedoms of association, organization and collective bargaining, and from forced or compulsory labor nor should it attempt to interject the GATT into the process of establishing labor norms. C/M/245, November 1, 1990.
[84] Article 3.2 DSU.
[85] L/1141, BISD 9S/194, adopted on May 27, 1960.

agricultural machinery produced in Italy. Italy's defense was that the law only concerned the improvement in the employment of labor and was not, therefore, related to the matters covered by Article III:4, namely the sale, purchase or transportation of imported and domestically produced products. The Panel, however, rejected this defense, and observed that while the GATT does not limit the right of contracting parties to adopt measures for improving the conditions of employment, or to protect a domestic industry, it will not condone discriminatory measures which might adversely modify the conditions of competition between the domestic and imported products on the internal market.[86]

Similarly, a Working Party was not swayed by Italy's argument that it needed import restrictions against potassium sulphate imported from Israel because it wanted to establish a domestic industry in areas of high unemployment and, consequently, urged Italy to dismantle them.[87]

Another Panel held Japanese import restrictions, quotas and import licenses on leather products, to be contrary to Article XI:1 GATT, even though Japan had claimed that they operated for the benefit of a distinct underprivileged population, the Dowa people. That Panel narrowly adhered to its terms of reference under which it was required to examine the matter "in the light of the relevant GATT provisions." It pointed out that Japan had failed to invoke any provision of the GATT to justify the import restrictions, and therefore declined to take the special historical, cultural and socioeconomic circumstances into account, deciding that it was not for the Panel to establish whether the present measures would be justified under any of the GATT provisions.[88]

Similarly, the European Community failed to persuade another Panel that Article XI GATT did not constitute an absolute prohibition of quantitative import restrictions and that it should not, therefore, be applied in an absolute and legalistic manner. Again the Panel rejected both the EC's defense that the relevant import restrictions were necessary to deal with economic and social problems, and its contention that historical and general factors must be taken into account, as well as the specific economic and social situation in each sector, such as the threat of serious injury to domestic production and employment through increases in imports and competition with lowpriced foreign products. As the European Community did not claim any GATT justification for these arguments, the Panel considered such matters to be outside the purview of Articles XI and XIII of the GATT and, therefore, outside its consideration.[89]

In the course of the proceedings of the *First Tuna Panel*, Venezuela as an interested third party submitted that the U.S. import prohibition was inconsistent with Article XI:1 of the GATT and not covered by any of the exceptions in Article XI:2. It also observed that to allow a country to impose a non-discriminatory ban on the sale of both domestic and imported goods because their production causes harm would potentially allow any nation to justify unilaterally imposing its own social, economic or employment standards as a criterion for accepting imports. If that were accepted, it would mean that influential contracting parties could effectively regulate the internal environment of others simply by

[86] Report of the GATT Panel, *Italian Discrimination against Imported Agricultural Machinery*, BISD 7S/60, adopted on October 23, 1958.

[87] Report of the GATT Working Party, *Italian Restrictions Affecting Imports from Israel*, BISD 10S/130, adopted on December 9, 1961.

[88] Report of the GATT Panel, *Japanese Measures on Imports of Leather*, BISD 31S/94, adopted on May 15/16, 1984.

[89] Report of the GATT Panel, *EEC—Quantitative Restrictions Against Imports of Certain Products from Hong Kong*, BISD 30S/129, adopted on July 12, 1983.

erecting trade barriers based on unilateral environmental policies which was, of course, contrary to the fundamental premises of the GATT.[90]

The Panel Report also determined that while contracting parties are free to adopt environmental policies to any standard of their own choice, they must not in so doing either prohibit imports from countries with lower standards nor expect that their unilateral higher standards will be accepted as being higher to and exempted from their GATT obligations by virtue of the general exemptions laid down in Article XX GATT. The Panel further concluded that the concerns of the drafters of Article XX(b) GATT had focused on the use of sanitary measures to safeguard life or health of humans, animals or plants within the jurisdiction of the importing country.[91] It also indicated ways in which the Contracting Parties could establish trade restrictions considered desirable beyond those limited by Article XX GATT, namely either by amending that article, or by waiving GATT obligations, or indeed by developing standards on a case-by-case basis or through multilateral standard setting for instance under the auspices of the United Nations.

In the *Second Tuna Panel* case[92] the EC and the Netherlands contended, contrary to the view of the United States, that when interpreted contextually, the provisions of paragraphs (b) and (g) of Article XX GATT, as indeed those of other paragraphs of Article XX GATT, were subject to a jurisdictional limitation. Consequently, the exception in paragraph (e) in respect of the products of prison labor was not intended to eliminate prison labor practices in other contracting parties, because paragraph (e) was not conceived as a humanitarian provision. Virtually all contracting parties operated systems of prison labor, not necessarily forced or hard labor. Contracting parties simply wanted to be able, if necessary, to protect themselves against the "unfair competition" resulting from the low cost labor employed in the production of products of prison labor. Nevertheless, the Panel observed that the example of Article XX(e) GATT relating to products of prison labor showed that the GATT did not proscribe in an absolute manner measures that related to things or actions outside the territorial jurisdiction of the party taking the measure.[93]

Another Panel found Canada's export restrictions of unprocessed herring and salmon contrary to Article XI:1 GATT and neither justified by Article XI:2(b) nor by Article XX(g) GATT.[94] However, the Panel did not directly endorse the U.S. argument that the purpose and effect of the export restrictions was not the conservation of resources but the protection of Canadian processors and the maintenance of employment for Canadians in British Columbia.

All the aforementioned Panel Reports clearly show that GATT Panels have not condoned trade restrictions as a means of enforcing domestic legislative or regulatory standards, unless these can be justified under specific provisions of the GATT.

While panels under the WTO DSU have not abandoned the requirement that trade restrictions be justified under specific provisions of the GATT, they have signaled a

---

[90] Report of the GATT Panel, *United States—Restrictions on Imports of Tuna,* BISD 39S/155, ¶ 4.27, circulated September 3, 1991 (unadopted); note that Venezuela was more sympathetic to an exception to Article XI for agreed compliance measures taken under an international environmental treaty regime.

[91] *Id.* ¶ 5.26.

[92] *United States—Restrictions on Imports of Tuna: Reports of the Panel,* DS29/R, dated June 16, 1994 (unadopted).

[93] For a discussion of this Panel, *see* F. Weiss, *The Second Tuna GATT Panel Report,* 8(1) LEIDEN JOURNAL OF INTERNATIONAL LAW 135–150 (1995).

[94] *Canada—Measures Affecting Exports of Unprocessed Herring and Salmon,* BISD 35S/98, ¶¶ 3.11 and 5.1, adopted on March 22, 1988.

willingness to allow such restrictions if they are implemented in a non-discriminatory manner. The Appellate Body in *US—Shrimp*, held that U.S. trade restrictions on the importation of shrimp fell within the exception offered by Article XX(g) GATT, but they were "applied by the United States in a manner which constitutes arbitrary and unjustifiable discrimination between Members of the WTO, contrary to the requirements of the chapeau of Article XX."[95] Confirming the suitability of unilateral trade restrictions that meet the requirements of both the chapeau and a specific provision of Article XX GATT, a later Appellate Body ruling found that the United States had brought its application of its shrimp regulations into compliance with its GATT/WTO obligations.[96] The original Appellate Body *US—Shrimp* decision did not decide the question of whether there was any implied territorial limitation to jurisdiction under Article XX(g) GATT, deciding that since all five species of sea turtles protected by the U.S. regulation passed through U.S. territorial waters, there was a sufficient "nexus" between the United States and the sea turtles.[97] The issue of an implied territorial limitation to jurisdiction under Article XX GATT may prove of primary importance should a Member implement trade restrictions to protect the life or health of workers in other Members under Article XX(b) GATT.

C. Protection of Foreign Labor

1. Potential Legal Bases in GATT/WTO Law

In view of the apparent readiness of WTO panels to address the growing interface between trade and other issues within the existing GATT/WTO legal framework, it might be interesting to survey GATT provisions that could serve potentially as a legal basis for trade restrictions against imports produced in violation of workers' rights or other international human rights standards. Not surprisingly, a recent study concluded that "little support exists for interpretations permitting such restrictions on imports" based on rules governing antidumping, subsidies, safeguards and general exceptions for restrictions relating to the products of prison labor.[98]

Last but certainly not least, there is Article XX(b) GATT under which measures restrictive of trade could be adopted or enforced provided they can be shown to be "necessary to protect human, animal or plant life or health." The critical question is whether it can be interpreted in such a way that domestic regulations adopted pursuant to international standards protecting workers rights may be relied upon to restrict imports of products made under conditions of production which fall short of those international standards. Panel case law to date holds little promise in that respect.

2. The Implications of United States—Reformulated Gasoline

The Panel Report on *United States—Standards for Reformulated and Conventional Gasoline* of 1996 ruled that regulations of the U.S. Environmental Protection Agency adopted

---

[95] *United States—Import Prohibition of Certain Shrimp and Shrimp Products*, Report of the Appellate Body, WT/DS58/AB/R (1998), ¶ 186

[96] Report of the Appellate Body, *United States—Import Prohibitions of Certain Shrimp & Shrimp Products; Recourse to Article 21.5 of the DSU by Malaysia*, WT/DS58/AB/RW (Oct. 22, 2001), ¶ 154.

[97] *United States—Import Prohibition of Certain Shrimp and Shrimp Products*, Report of the Appellate Body, WT/DS58/AB/R (1998), ¶ 133.

[98] Diller and Levy, *supra* note 12, at 695–96; Article VI GATT and Agreement on Implementation of Article VI GATT 1994; Agreement on Subsidies and Countervailing Measures; Article XIX and Agreement on Safeguards; Article XX(e) GATT.

under the 1990 Clean Air Act Amendments (P.L.101–549 §219) unlawfully assigned different methods for measuring emission standards for "reformulated" and "conventional" gasoline to domestic and foreign refiners respectively. The Panel found that the U.S. regulations "are not consistent with Article III:4 of the GATT, and cannot be justified under paragraphs (b), (d) and (g) of Article XX of the GATT."[99] The Panel rejected the general exemption invoked by the United States under Article XX(b) GATT, taking the view that the contested measure was not necessary for the protection of human life or health as required by that Article because alternative measures "less inconsistent" with the GATT were "reasonably available".

The Appellate Body partly upheld the appeal of the United States by reversing the Panel's main legal conclusion.[100] However, the Appellate Body also examined a question that was not addressed by the first-instance panel: whether the regulations also meet the requirements of the introductory provisions of Article XX GATT, its head note or "chapeau". According to that "chapeau", all exceptions under Article XX GATT are only available on condition that the qualifying measure is not applied "in a manner which would constitute a means of arbitrary or unjustifiable discrimination between countries where the same conditions prevail or [be] a disguised restriction on international trade."

The Appellate Body found that provision to be aimed at preventing abuse or misuse of the exceptions contained in Article XX GATT in the sense that "the measures falling within the particular exceptions must be applied reasonably, with due regard both to the legal duties of the party claiming the exception and the legal rights of the other parties concerned." But the Appellate Body neither clarified the notion of "legal rights of the other parties concerned", a notion which may well hold the key to future interpretations of Article XX GATT, nor whether due regard for those rights would have to involve some balancing of interests. The Appellate Body also criticized the United States for its failure to pursue the possibility of cooperative arrangements with the governments of the complainants, Venezuela and Brazil. Again, the Appellate Body failed to indicate whether by describing the non-pursuance of cooperative arrangements as an omission, it meant to establish a legal requirement that negotiations be sought as a condition for invoking Article XX GATT. Picking up this thread, the *United States—Shrimp* Appellate Body report found that the United States' unilateral attempts to protect sea turtles via trade restrictions amounted to unjustifiable discrimination under the chapeau.[101] More pertinently, the Appellate Body in the *Gasoline* report also censured the failure of the United States "to count the costs for "foreign refiners" resulting from the use of a different method",[102] but again did not explain why regulators have a legal obligation to take foreign costs into account, nor how this should be done. Could these reasons, placed in the context of labor standards, justify resort to the exception of Article XX(b) GATT, at least *vis-à-vis* a defendant Member who has accepted relevant international labor standards, but has failed to implement them effectively? Would prior cooperative arrangements need to involve assistance toward such implementation? Could it be argued that governments must henceforth weigh the regulatory impact of their measures on foreigners, and if so

---

[99] *United States—Standards for Reformulated and Conventional Gasoline*, Report of the Panel, WT/DS2/R (1996), ¶ 8.1.

[100] Report of the Appellate Body, *United States—Standards for Reformulated and Conventional Gasoline*, WT/DS2/AB/R (1996).

[101] Report of the Appellate Body, *United States—Import Prohibition of Certain Shrimp and Shrimp Products*, WT/DS58/AB/R (October 12, 1998), ¶ 172.

[102] *United States—Standards for Reformulated and Conventional Gasoline*, *supra* note 101.

could a ban on products made for instance with child labor ever succeed,[103] considering that throughout WTO panel proceedings special consideration is to be given to the interests of developing countries?[104] How are these interests defined? Even in the face of mounting evidence of the long-term damage done to developing countries by the use of child labor, the interests of developing countries may continue to be defined by trade ministers in such a way that any restriction on their trade may be viewed with hostility.

However, despite present doubts about the suitability of the WTO's case-by-case approach for the reconciliation of trade rules and labor standards, there are also more hopeful developments. Although leaving many of the questions raised by the Appellate Body in *United States—Reformulated Gasoline* unanswered, subsequent Appellate Body decisions have addressed the necessity requirement of XX(b) GATT. In a case involving France's prohibition of the import of certain asbestos containing products, the Appellate Body held that the restrictions were "necessary to protect human life or health within the meaning of Article XX(b) of the GATT."[105] Drawing from the *Korea—Beef* case, the Appellate Body reasoned that a trade restrictive measure cannot be deemed "necessary" if there is "an alternative measure which it could reasonably be expected to employ and which is not inconsistent with other GATT provisions is available to it." If such a measure is not available, a Member "is bound to use, among the measures reasonably available to it, that which entails the least degree of inconsistency with other GATT provisions."[106] Such an interpretation of Article XX(b) GATT offers the possibility that a trade restrictive measure designed to combat child labor would be tenable if it were shown that alternative measures, not inconsistent with GATT had failed and no reasonable alternative remained. In determining the appropriateness of trade restrictive measures the record of U.S. actions to promote the abolition of child labor, within the ILO and elsewhere would no doubt be integral.

Another hopeful sign is that panels increasingly invoke general principles of international law and have always extensively used the Vienna Convention on the Law of Treaties, at least for purposes of textual interpretation.[107] Such relatively greater openness to international law has been confirmed by the Appellate Report in *United States—Standards for Reformulated and Conventional Gasoline*. In that case, the Appellate Body not only observed that the "GATT is not to be read in clinical isolation from public international law", but also cited decisions of the International Court of Justice, the European Court of Human Rights and of the Inter-American Court of Human Rights.[108] In *United States—Shrimp*, the Appellate Body looked to the United Nations Convention on the Law of the Sea and other international agreements to determine that sea turtles constituted an exhaustible natural resource.[109] Such efforts to interpret GATT provisions in light of other principles of international law may bode well for those who advocate the use of unilateral trade restrictions to promote respect for international labor standards, which are highly codified within international law.

---

[103] S. Charnovitz rhetorically raised the question whether future panels might require this for a ban on elephant ivory or a pesticide residue restriction, S. Charnovitz, *New WTO Adjudication and its Implications for the Environment,* 19 INTERNATIONAL ENVIRONMENT REPORTER 851–856 (September 18, 1996).

[104] *See* Articles 3.2, 4.10, 8.10, 12.10, 12.11, 21.2, 21.7, 21.8 and 27.2 of the DSU.

[105] Report of the Appellate Body, *European Communities—Measures Affecting Asbestos and Asbestos-Containing Products,* WT/DS 135/AB/R (2001), ¶ 175.

[106] *Id*. at para 171.

[107] *See* Article 3.1 of the DSU which recognizes that panels may wish "to clarify (...) provisions of (...) agreements in accordance with customary rules of interpretation of public international law".

[108] *United States—Standards for Reformulated and Conventional Gasoline, supra* note 101, at p. 17.

[109] Report of the Appellate Body, *United States—Import Prohibition of Certain Shrimp and Shrimp Products,* WT/DS58/AB/R (1998), ¶¶ 130–134.

V. Standard Setting

A. Merits and Demerits of the Incorporation of Standards

In view of the restrictive interpretation of Article XX GATT in GATT panel practice, and of the limited scope within the dispute settlement mechanism for integrating some kind of social clause in the multilateral trading system, it is necessary to consider alternative approaches. Based on the integrative objective of "sustainable development" laid down in the preamble to the Agreement Establishing the World Trade Organization,[110] such an alternative approach might consist of introducing labor standards either by reference to the ILO or other conventions, or by the insertion of appropriate language in the WTO Agreement. The terms of the preamble are wide enough to permit action pursuant to a social clause in the sense of a "floor" governing working conditions everywhere. But should there be such a clause in the multilateral trading system? The supporters of a social clause have argued, *inter alia*, that it would promote fair competition between exporters of developing countries while ensuring that those respecting minimum labor standards are not penalized for their efforts to promote social development; that it would prevent increased international competition from leading to a destructive "race to the bottom" in the conditions of work and life of workers worldwide; that it would prevent industrialized countries from collaborating in the exploitation of workers in developing countries if they failed to press for the adoption of universal minimum labor standards; and above all that it would strengthen the resolve to resist pressures for increased protectionism.

Developing countries on the other hand oppose such a clause because they view it as disguised protectionism potentially obstructing their industrial development and depriving them of their key comparative advantage which is the productive use of low-cost labor; and because they resent interference in their domestic affairs as well as being asked for reciprocity in social obligations in return for trade concessions.

Whatever the merits of any of these points of view, much will depend on agreement being reached as to the standards to be included in a social clause.

B. Selection of Standards for a Social Clause

The first question is whether ILO Conventions should be used; secondly, whether all or most of them should be selected; and thirdly, on what basis such a selection should be made?

If ILO Conventions are to be chosen, the standards concerned would have to be both fairly precise to be enforceable and reasonably flexible to secure worldwide acceptance by countries with different social structures, climates and cultures at different stages of economic development.[111] Thus, reference could be made in the WTO Agreement to certain ILO minimum standards which command widespread respect, do not appreciably impact on developing countries competitive position in world trade, and are subject to monitoring and enforcement by appropriate machinery. The approach would be reminiscent of the

---

[110] The Parties recognize, *inter alia*, that "their relations in the field of trade and economic endeavour should be conducted with a view to raising standards of living, ensuring full employment (. . .) and expanding the production and trade in goods and services, while allowing for the optimal use of the world's resources in accordance with the objective of sustainable development (. . .)"; see N. Schrijver and I. Weiss, INTERNATIONAL LAW AND SUSTAINABLE DEVELOPMENT, PRINCIPLES AND PRACTICE (2004).

[111] For a review of different proposals see, G. van Liemt, *Minimum Labor Standards and International Trade: Would a Social Clause Work?*, 128 (4) INTERNATIONAL LABOR REVIEW 433, 436 *et seq.* (1989).

debate concerning TRIPS which originated in a desire, mostly on the part of the United States, to use the "teeth" of the GATT dispute settlement system to enforce existing standards of intellectual property rights.[112]

Relevant minimum labor standards would have to include the Freedom of Association and Protection of the Right to Organize Convention 1948 (Nr.87),[113] the Right to Organize and Collective Bargaining Convention 1949 (Nr.98), the Convention concerning Forced or Compulsory Labor 1930 (Nr.29), the Convention concerning the Abolition of Forced Labor 1957 (Nr.105), the Discrimination (Employment and Occupation) Convention and Recommendation 1958 (Nr.111), which promotes equality of opportunity and treatment in respect of employment and occupation.[114] To these must be added the Worst Forms of Child Labor Convention (Nr.182). At present, however, it must be doubted that the WTO could become an enforcement agency in respect of social standards evolved by the tripartite ILO and under its supervisory machinery. The WTO obviously lacks competence and experience in the matter, not to mention a tripartite structure. Moreover, developing countries might feel that rich countries police poor countries, using trade restrictions to penalize them for falling below certain human rights standards. Such an approach would also involve the risk of being extremely divisive and contrary to the spirit of Article 14 of the Charter of Economic Rights and Duties of States.[115] For these reasons, institutional collaboration between the ILO and the WTO, if any, should be established on "ILO turf", for instance by introducing some kind of trade liberalization component. On the other hand, existing flexibilities built into the WTO's system of dispute settlement which benefit developing countries might yet induce them to accept the enforcement of agreed standards in accordance with the provisions of the DSU.

C. Supervision of Compliance

The United States pushed TRIPS into the Uruguay Round of multilateral trade negotiations, *inter alia*, so as to secure compliance with a future TRIPS Agreement in accordance with the planned WTO dispute settlement mechanism. For the same reason the United States and other developed WTO Members prefer the WTO forum.

A broad approach to "enforcement" of labor standards would grant a large number of people and institutions some supervisory role, as is the case, for instance, in the United States where organizations and individuals have standing to request the President each year to review the status of labor rights within the GSP, or the system of written communications by individuals to the UN Human Rights Committee under the Optional Protocol to the International Covenant on Civil and Political Rights. A narrow approach to "enforcement" would restrict complaints to those brought against governments, as is

---

[112] *See* F. Weiss, *Trade Related Intellectual Property Rights and the Uruguay Round Negotiations*, in Liber-ALIZATION OF SERVICES AND INTELLECTUAL PROPERTY IN THE URUGUAY ROUND OF GATT 87–113 (Georgio Sacerdoti ed. 1990).

[113] *See also, The Universal Declaration of Human Rights; The International Covenants on Economic, Social and Cultural Rights and on Civil and Political Rights; The American Convention on Human Rights ("Pact of San Jose"); The Banjul Charter on Human Rights and Peoples' Rights of the Organization of African Unity; The European Convention for the Protection of Human Rights and Fundamental Freedoms and the European Social Charter.*

[114] International Labor Organization, 1 INTERNATIONAL LABOR CONVENTIONS AND RECOMMENDATIONS 1919–1991 (1992); Van Liemt, *supra* note 112; *see also* H.K. Nielsen, *The Concept of Discrimination in ILO Convention No. 111,* 43 *ICLQ* 827 *et seq.* (1994); for a survey of these standards, *see* Compa, *supra* note 52, at 169 *et seq.*

[115] *UN General Assembly Resolution 3281* (XXIX).

currently the case under the ILO and WTO regimes which exclude complaints against individual companies. However, states are notoriously reluctant to act against each other in the labor field as this is seen as an unfriendly act involving risks of counter-claims, and small economies feel particularly vulnerable to retaliation.[116] Techniques such as consultation, negotiation and conciliation should be given priority. The withdrawal of trade advantages—always amounting to some contraction of free trade—should only be used as a last resort.

VI. Beyond Singapore?

A. WTO Ministerial Meetings

Since Singapore there have been four WTO ministerial meetings, but there has been no progress on labor standards. Although the 1999 Seattle Ministerial sparked street protests, there was little movement inside the ministerial itself. The United States and the European Union came to Seattle armed with trade-labor working group proposals, but the divisions and tensions between developed and developing country delegates were as deep as those between protestors and police out on the streets. The ministers left Seattle with no declaration. Two years later, the WTO ministers sidestepped the issue, suggesting that those who interpreted the Singapore Declaration as removing labor issues from the competence of the WTO may have been correct. The Doha Declaration states, "[w]e reaffirm our declaration made at the Singapore Ministerial Conference regarding internationally recognized core labor standards. We take note of work under way in the International Labor Organization on the social dimension of globalization." Reference to the ILO's ongoing investigative work into the social dimension of globalization doubly reaffirms the interpretation of the Singapore Declaration that the ILO, not the WTO is the correct arena for international labor standards. For its part, it is doubtful that the ILO is going to advocate that states be granted the weapon of unilateral trade sanctions to further workers' rights.[117] One wonders how long the WTO can keep pushing the trade-labor debate onto the ILO.

B. Using Multilateral and Bilateral Agreements as a Model for WTO Action

The lack of progress since Singapore has not dampened U.S. support for bringing labor standards into the WTO, but the United States has adopted a new approach to further the attainment of this goal. In recently enacted legislation granting the U.S. President "trade promotion authority", which limits Congress' ability to consider trade agreements piecemeal, the Congress reiterated its support for the inclusion of labor standards in trade agreements.[118] This legislation requires U.S. trade negotiators to pursue as "principal negotiating objectives" assurances that trade agreement partners enforce their labor laws, strengthen their respect for core labor standards, and that labor "policies and practices of the parties to trade agreements with the United States do not arbitrarily or unjustifiably discriminate against [U.S.] exports or serve as disguised trade barriers." Core labor standards are identified as, "the right of association[,] the right to organize and bargain collectively[,] a prohibition on the use of forced or compulsory labor[,] a minimum age

---

[116] See S. Leckie, *The Inter-state Complaint Procedure in International Human Rights Law: Hopeful Prospects or Wishful Thinking?*, 10 HUMAN RIGHTS QUARTERLY 249 (May 1988).
[117] International Labor Office, *ILO Activities on the Social Dimension of Globalization: Synthesis Report*, (July 12, 2002) http://www.ilo.org/public/english/wcsdg/docs/synthesis.pdf (visited November 16, 2003).
[118] 19 U.S.C.A. § 3802 (b) (11) *et seq.*

for the employment of children[,] and acceptable conditions of work with respect to minimum wages, hours of work, and occupational safety and health."[119]

The United States has shifted its focus from bringing workers' rights into the WTO to reaching bilateral and multilateral trade agreements that incorporate core labor standards into their regimes. Washington hopes that such agreements can serve as models for the WTO and "contribute to the WTO system by introducing innovation and strengthened disciplines."[120] Among the regional trade agreements that the United States is trumpeting with regard to promoting labor rights is the North American Agreement on Labor Co-operation ("NAALC"), a side agreement accompanying the North American Free Trade Agreement ("NAFTA"). The United States is negotiating similar multilateral agreements and bilateral trade pacts throughout the globe. One such bilateral agreement with Jordan includes an article on labor standards. Each nation pledges to enforce its labor laws and offers a set of core labor standards, which are the same five standards enunciated in the aforementioned trade promotion authority legislation.[121] The agreement also sets up a dispute resolution process which, after a panel and conciliation process, allows for an aggrieved party "to take any appropriate and commensurate measure."[122]

Although it remains to be seen how bilateral arrangements like that with Jordan will play out and if they will have a didactic effect on the WTO, it is questionable if many labor rights advocates would join the U.S. government in offering the NAALC as a possible model for the WTO. A recent Human Rights Watch report found the NAALC's protections of workers rights somewhat wanting.[123] Labor organizations have even embarked on inter-American cooperation as a new range of trade agreements are negotiated. The AFL-CIO and the Central Unitaria de Trabajo ("CUT"), a Chilean labor organization, have issued joint declarations regarding trade negotiations between their respective countries calling for the inclusion of labor protection in any final agreement.[124] There have also been specific campaigns targeting countries for their failure to live up to their obligations to respect international labor standards. For example, a recent Human Rights Watch Report on child labor in the Ecuadorian banana industry called upon international trade agreements to include fundamental workers' rights provisions and recommended that "failure to effectively enforce or progressively implement such standards should trigger the same dispute settlement, enforcement procedures, or penalties available to other issues covered by these agreements."[125] Perhaps the most aggressive campaign is that of the International Confederation of Free Trade Unions ("ICFTU"), which is endeavoring to hold WTO Members accountable for their statements made in Singapore and reiterated at Doha regarding their "commitment to the observance of internationally recognized core labor standards." To date the ICFTU has issued over seventy country reports in which it examines a WTO Member's respect for and enforcement of international core labor

[119] 19 U.S.C.A. § 3813 (6).
[120] WTO, *Trade Policy Review*, Report of the United States Government to the Trade Policy Review Body, WT/TPR/G/88 (August 20, 2001).
[121] WTO, *Free Trade Area Between the United States and Jordan*, WT/REG134/1 (March 13, 2002), Article 6.
[122] *Id.* at Article 17 (2)(b).
[123] Human Rights Watch, *Trading Rights Away: The Unfulfilled Promise of NAFTA's Labor Side Agreement* (April 2001) http://www.hrw.org/reports/2001/nafta.
[124] *The Declaration of the CUT/Chile and the AFL-CIO Concerning the Proposed Free Trade Agreement Between Chile and the United States*, (August 26, 2002), www.union-network.org/uniflashes.nsf/2c8c0184e55e3d98c1256872003e613e/173a99c02ce845edc1256c2100584054?OpenDocument (visited November 28, 2003).
[125] Human Rights Watch, *Tainted Harvest: Child Labor and Obstacles to Organizing Ecuador's Banana Plantations*, (April 2002) http://hrw.org/reports/2002/ecuador/ (visted November 16, 2003).

standards.[126] The reports are issued at the same time as the WTO General Counsel's review of the trade policies of the subject country, which is not to suggest that the reports are part of the WTO trade policy review process. Not surprisingly the reports often demonstrate the links between trade and workers' rights violations. For example, the ICFTU report on India highlights the direct link between trade and poor working conditions, such as the absence of trade union rights in special export processing zones.[127]

The efforts of human rights and labor groups are going to have to be sustained and imaginative if they are going to bring the protection of labor rights into the competence of the WTO. The AFL-CIO/CUT joint campaign may signal the increase of meaningful collaboration between trade organizations in the developed and developing worlds, which could go a long way toward easing the criticism of poor countries that talk of labor standards is really just disguised protectionism. NGO reporting processes like that being used by the ICFTU could provide weighty evidence to trade ministers, if not WTO panels, that WTO compliant measures like those offered by the ILO are not solving the worst problems of labor rights violations and that WTO Members are not meeting their oft-stated commitments to observe internationally recognized core labor standards. Such and similarly inspired campaigns could ultimately prod a WTO Member into instituting unilateral trade restrictions against another WTO Member as "a measures necessary to protect human life or health", under Article XX(b) GATT. However, it remains questionable whether such an attempt would survive the WTO panel process. In addition to the previously discussed potential pitfalls under Article XX(b) GATT, there is the remaining difficulty of getting evidence from NGOs, like that gathered by the ICFTU, before a WTO panel.[128]

---

[126] *See* http://www.icftu.org/list.asp?Language=EN&Order=Date&Type=WTOReports&Subject=ILS& start=0&finish=19 where these reports are available (visited November 16, 2003).

[127] International Confederation of Free Trade Unions, *Internationally Recognized Core Labor Standards in India*, Report for the WTO General Council Review of Trade Policies of India (June 2002).

[128] There are a variety of initiatives attacking the labor-trade issue from outside the multilateral and bilateral trade frameworks. One, the social labeling movement seeks to empower consumers to make informed choices about the products they buy, but at least some critics have found such initiatives ineffectual. *See* Alakh N. Sharma, Rajeev Sharma and Nikhil Raj, *The Impact of Social Labelling on Child Labor in India's Carpet Industry*, 78 ILO/IPEC Working Paper, (2000) at http://www.ilo.org/public/english/standards/ ipec/publ/policy/papers/india/india.pdf (visited November 14, 2003). Another tactic used of late by numerous human rights groups to try to hold multinational corporations liable for human rights abuses, including workers' rights violations, which occur in their operations in developing countries, is the United States Alien Tort Claims Act. In one such case a U.S. Federal Circuit Court of Appeals held that plaintiffs, villagers who were subjected to forced labor in Myanmar (a/k/a Burma), could proceed with their claims against multinational energy corporation Unocal. Although the court split as to the grounds on which Unocal could be held liable for the forced labor practices of the Myanmar military units providing security and construction services for the pipeline project of a Unocal joint venture, all three judges agreed that Unocal could be held liable either under international law or under federal common law. *John Doe I v. Unocal Corp.* 2002 WL 31063976. *See also, John Doe etc., et al. v. Unocal Corp.,* 110 F.Supp.2d 1294 (C.D. Cal. 2000); *John Doe etc., et al. v. Unocal Corp.,* 963 F.Supp. 880 (C.D. Cal. 1997). Reader may also wish to consult an excellent overview of the legal analysis in the BNA OVERVIEW, DAILY LABOR REPORT NO. 187, at A-1, *International Labor Ninth Circuit Lets Burmese Citizens Bring ATCA Suit Against Unocal for Forced Labor,* at A-1 (September 26, 2002); *see also,* Tam, *Myanmar Human-Rights Suit Against Unocal Is Reinstated,* WALL STREET JOURNAL, September 19, 2002; Girion, *U.S. Ruling Says Firms Liable for Abuse Abroad,* LOS ANGELES TIMES, September 19, 2002; Kravets, *Court Reinstates Suit Against Unocal,* WASHINGTON POST, September 19, 2002. It remains to be seen what role, if any, such initiatives may play in prompting WTO action on labor standards. On February 14, 2003, the Ninth Circuit granted the motion for rehearing en banc and ordered that the panel decision could not be cited as precedent within the Circuit. (*Doe v. Unocal Corp.,* Nos. 00-56603, 00-57197 (9th Cir. February 14, 2003); Girion, *U.S. Court Will Rehear Case Against Unocal,* LOS ANGELES TIMES, February 15, 2003; Tam, Appeals Court Will Revisit Ruling in Suit Against Unocal, WALL STREET JOURNAL, February 14, 2003.)", *see* www1.umn.edu/humanrts/intlhr/supp-chapter14.html (visited November 28, 2003).

VII. Concluding Remarks

The Uruguay Round Ministerial Declaration on the contribution of the WTO to achieve greater coherence in global economic policymaking recognized that the globalization of the world economy has led to ever-growing interactions between the economic policies pursued by individual countries, including interactions between the structural, macroeconomic, trade, financial and development aspects of economic policymaking.[129] Labor standards are necessarily part of this panoply of economic policies.

Since the end of the process of decolonization there has been a remarkable and somewhat paradoxical shift in international standard setting. For a period of time after the influx of developing countries into the United Nations, it was the diversity of the (largely developing country) UN membership, rather than the globalization of markets and economic processes that demanded additional standard setting. At first it was the developing countries who fought, *inter alia*, for the replacement of "international standards" governing the adequacy of amounts of compensation to be paid in cases of nationalization.[130] At present it is overwhelmingly developed industrialized countries which display regulatory zeal in respect of globalized markets, whether for trade, services, intellectual property, investment, environmental protection or labor standards.

There is growing concern about the appalling conditions of work in many places in the world. However, before a multilateral social clause can be established, several issues need to be addressed.

In the first place, to operate fairly such a clause would have to reflect a balance of principles and interests and of degrees of trade dependence and hence vulnerability to sanctions. Secondly, a social clause would need to give special consideration to the interests of small and weak economies and, where poor labor conditions are attributable to a low level of development additional financial, economic and technical assistance should be provided. Thirdly, if surveillance of worldwide labor standards is to be linked to sanctions, it would be necessary to assess case-by-case whether sanctions (loss of trade preferences) are appropriate at all, given that poor working conditions may also be attributable to factors such as high levels of indebtedness, low world market prices for primary commodities or difficulties in securing market access for developing countries' exports.

The ILO and the WTO share a common interest in eliminating unfair labor conditions, the former by vocation, the latter in the interest of free trade based on common labor standards rather than on the parochial standards of certain countries. The WTO to some extent embraces policies and goals that reflect the internationalization of production. The unreformed ILO on the other hand has become a constraint upon social change rather than an accelerator of it because it is still steeped in the ideology of tripartism rooted in industrial organization that pre-dates that internationalization.[131] At its core, the idea of international fair labor standards is not protectionist. On the contrary, agreed minimum standards, establishing a floor for workers' rights, potentially remove one of the chief justifications for import restrictions. In the final analysis, of course, the best way to disprove the charge of protectionism would be to couple a social clause with reduced trade barriers for complying countries. It seems probable that the issue of a social clause in multilateral trade will remain on the agenda for the foreseeable future. However, as a highly complex and controversial issue it is unlikely to be resolved anytime soon.

---

[129] 33 ILM 1249 (1994).

[130] Article 2, ¶ 2(c) of the Charter of Economic Rights and Duties of States, UNGAOR 3281 (XXIX) of 1974.

[131] R.W. Cox, *Labor and Employment in the Late Twentieth Century*, in THE INTERNATIONAL LAW AND POLICY OF HUMAN WELFARE 525, 542 (R. St. John Macdonald, D.M. Johnston and G.L. Morris eds., 1978).

CHAPTER 60

TRADE AND LABOR II

Janelle M. Diller*

TABLE OF CONTENTS

* International Labour Office, Geneva, Switzerland. This chapter was written while on leave at the University of St. Thomas School of Law (Minneapolis), and the author is grateful to the law school and Caitlin Firer, in particular, for their valuable research support. Any opinions herein are solely attributable to the author and do not represent the views or endorsement of the ILO.

I. Introduction: Trade and Labor in a Broader Context

We live in times that challenge multilateral approaches to resolving persistent global problems like poverty and conflict. The unilateral exercise of economic and military power threatens the international system of co-operation as we know it. However, notwithstanding their sharp divergence in method, proponents of both unilateral and multilateral approaches often invoke similar ultimate aims as their motivation. Their common aims reflect values[1] that are shared at a very fundamental level—values such as peace, justice, and human dignity and security. The means for achieving these basic objectives are collectively valued as well; these include poverty reduction, economic development, and conflict resolution. Progress toward these common goals necessarily involves the markets and workplaces of the world, and the rules and relationships that govern economic and social transactions within and across borders.

For most people, a sustainable job is the only secure way out of poverty. In principle, economic growth and enterprise development, fueled by trade and market access, bring more jobs.[2] Multiplied many fold, decent jobs raise standards of living and contribute to a universal and lasting peace based on social justice.[3] Yet, the evident interaction between promoting jobs and freer trade has failed to diminish the labor-trade debate at international level. Many questions remain on how application of the principles of "decent work"[4] and "free trade"[5] could be better coordinated to more effectively bring

[1] In this chapter, the term "values" connotes the beliefs and perspectives of individuals, groups or communities that certain goals and ways of behaving are important. For further detail, *see infra* notes 38, 42 and accompanying text.

[2] See *infra* Part B discussing trade, growth and poverty.

[3] *International Labor Organization Constitution*, June 28, 1919, preamble, 49 Stat. 2712, 15 U.N.T.S. 35 ("ILO Constitution").

[4] The International Labor Organization's ("ILO") mission, defined as "decent work" in modern terms, is to find sustainable opportunities for women and men to obtain decent and productive work, in conditions of freedom, equity, security and human dignity. *See, e.g., Report of the Director General, Decent Work: International Labor Conference,* ILO, 87th Session, 3ff (1999). Four pillars support the objective of decent work according to the ILO and are informed by international labor standards: rights at work; employment protection; security and social protection; and representation and dialogue. The interconnected dimensions of decent work are central to whether that work meets social goals, including peoples' needs for livelihood, dignity and poverty elimination. The term "rights at work" refers to four categories of core labor standards: freedom of association and effective recognition of the right to collective bargaining, elimination of discrimination in employment and occupation, elimination of all forms of forced or compulsory labor, and effective abolition of child labor. *Id.* at 14. These enabling rights have achieved global scope through the acceptance at the 1995 United Nations ("UN") Copenhagen Social Summit, *Copenhagen Declaration on Social Development*, U.N. Doc. A/CONF/.166/9 (1995), (adopted by the World Summit for Social Development, March 6–12, 1995) ("*Copenhagen Declaration*") and subsequently the ILO Declaration of Fundamental Principles and Rights at Work, June 18, 1998, 37 I.L.M. 1233 (1998) ("*ILO Fundamental Principles*").

[5] The principle of "free trade" or "liberal trade" motivates the international trading rules though the terms themselves are not explicitly used in the WTO Agreement itself. See *generally Marrakesh Agreement Establishing the World Trade Organization*, April 15, 1994, *Final Act Embodying the Results of the Uruguay Round of Multilateral Trade Negotiations*, 33 I.L.M. 1125, 1146 (1994) ("*Uruguay/WTO Agreement*"). Trade flows between countries with a minimal amount of restrictions by governments are often described by reference to their benefits to individual economies and the society of nations. As stated by the leading economist Paul Samuelson, "there is essentially only one argument for free trade or freer trade, but it is an exceedingly powerful one, namely: Free trade promotes a mutually profitable division of labor, greatly enhances the potential real national product of all nations, and makes possible higher standards of living all over the globe." Paul Samuelson, Economics 651 (11th ed., 1980). Given a fixed stock of productive resources, free trade in principle permits the consumption possibilities available to the economy to expand beyond the economy's production possibilities; in contrast, in an isolated economy without trade, domestic consumption is limited to production. Melvyn Kraus, The New Protectionism: The Welfare State And International Trade, 2–4, 6 (1978).

economic growth, jobs, and development as well as decreased poverty and ultimately justice, peace, and dignity.

This chapter examines the quest for coherence in the global governance of work and trade.[6] I use the term "global governance" to refer to the system of international institutions, rules, and processes that guide the conduct and relations of states and non-state actors across borders.[7] I first review the origins and effects of the current deficit of coherence within the global governance system. I consider the extent to which the growing cohesion among universally-accepted values offers a means for building normative and institutional coherence between the WTO and the ILO in the context of other international institutions and actors. In pointing out the resulting sense of "shared responsibility" among those concerned, I propose that such values should continue to inform the development of governance and accountability mechanisms to guide international organizations, States, and non-state actors in more effectively co-ordinating their policies and practices in the market and the workplace.

A. The Apartheid of Labor and Trade

For more than half a century, the institutions mandated to facilitate international relations and cooperation in trade and labor have operated largely in isolation from each other. The International Labor Organization ("ILO") and World Trade Organization ("WTO") and its predecessor Secretariat for the General Agreement on Tariffs and Trade ("GATT"),[8] have functioned in large part like two productive units side by side, with chimneys pumping outputs into a common space yet leaving the air-quality effects unmeasured. No inter-institutional agreement governs their relationship, and ad hoc consultations, while increasing in frequency, remain irregular.[9]

---

[6] Coherence does not mean harmonization or standardization; it contemplates a sufficient coordination of effective governance which, *inter a lia*, is marked by plurality of participation and an appropriate balance of national and international levels of jurisdiction. See, e.g., *infra* note 101 and accompanying text. Applying the principle of subsidiarity in allocating jurisdiction helps ensure effective governance and the achievement of common ultimate goals. *Cf.* Katharina Pistor, *The Standardization of Law and Its Effect on Developing Countries*, 50 AM. J. COMP. L. 97 (2002).

[7] The term "state actors" includes national and local governments and inter-governmental organizations. The term "non-state actors" encompasses multinational and local enterprises, trade unions and business associations, consumer, investor and other civic organizations, religious and ethnic groups, and the media, among others; and in the private sector.

[8] The ILO was created in 1919 with functions defined in its Constitution, *supra* note 3. The General Agreement on Tariffs and Trade (GATT) 1947, 55 U.N.T.S. 194, as amended and in force as the General Agreement on Tariffs and Trade 1994, Annex 1A to the WTO Agreement, was a provisional agreement designed to cover the period prior to entry into force of the Havana Charter, *infra* note 10. Upon the latter's stillbirth, the GATT, serviced by a Secretariat, remained in force as the forum for multilateral trade negotiations until the vacuum was filled by the WTO Agreement, *supra* note 5, and the World Trade Organization formally came into being on January 1, 1995.

[9] The World Trade Organization ("WTO") General Council is to make appropriate arrangements for cooperation with international organizations that have "responsibilities related to those of the WTO." *Uruguay/WTO Agreement, supra* note 5, Article V(1). According to guidelines on observer status of international governmental organizations, participation in WTO proceedings can be obtained by request or by invitation. However, the ILO has no observer status permitting participation at WTO General Council meetings. The WTO, for its turn, has participated in public meetings of the ILO Governing Body and other ILO bodies. In a discussion held with the Governing Body Working Party on the Social Dimension of Globalization, the then Director-General of the WTO, Mr. Mike Moore, emphasized the role of values such as universalism and solidarity in putting into place redistributive mechanisms to assist workers displaced by trade-related shifts in labor demand. *E.g., Report of the Working Party on the Social Dimension of Globalization*, ILO Doc. GB.283/15, at ¶ 2 (March 2002). The ILO Director-General further reported that the Director-General

The current deficit in coherence developed following the demise of the integrated vision expressed in the Havana Charter for an International Trade Organization of 1947.[10] In the Havana Charter, fifty-three States devised an interdependent approach to international cooperation in fields including employment, development and trade.[11] Their purpose was to realize the aims envisaged in Article 55 of the UN Charter, notably higher standards of living, full employment, and conditions of economic and social progress and development.[12] In pledging national and international action, individually and collectively, to realize these aims, Havana Charter aspirants sought to "foster and assist industrial and general economic development," and "further the enjoyment by all countries, on equal terms, of access to markets, products and productive facilities which are needed for their economic prosperity and development."[13] Chapter II stressed the centrality of employment to the achievement of these general purposes and objectives and the need for concerted action within the UN, in collaboration with the appropriate inter-governmental organization, to supplement domestic measures to avoid unemployment.[14] The parties recognized that fair labor standards were a matter of common interest among all countries and that "unfair labor conditions, particularly in production for export, create difficulties in international trade."[15]

Since its failure to enter into force, no institutional project to integrate the global governance of trade, labor, and development as ambitious as the Havana Charter has been attempted.[16] The ILO, which was created several decades before the United Nations and the attempted Havana Charter,[17] supervises a singular remnant of the quest for coherence from that era. The 1944 Declaration of Philadelphia, incorporated as an annex to the ILO Constitution, calls for prioritizing the pursuit of the conditions necessary for social justice as a central policy objective, both in national and international policies and measures, and in particular those of an economic and financial character.[18] Along

of the WTO, Mr. Supachai Panitchpakdi, had held discussions with the ILO-convened World Commission on the Social Dimension of Globalization. *E.g., Report of the Working Party on the Social Dimension of Globalization*, ILO Doc. GB.285/16, at ¶ 34 (March 2003). The World Commission is an independent body with a mandate to review the implications of globalization for economic and social progress, and to recommend innovative ways to respond to the needs of people ; a final report is to be released in early 2004. http://www.ilo.org/public/english/wcsdg/index.htm, accessed on May 9, 2003.

[10] *UN Conference on Trade and Employment: Final Act and Related Documents*, March 24, 1948, U.N. Doc. E/CONF 2/78, U.N. Sales No. 1948.II.D.4 (1948) ("*Havana Charter*"), never entered into force.

[11] *See, e.g., id*, Chs. II (employment), III (development), IV (tariffs, quotas, subsidies, etc.),

[12] *Id.*, Chapter I, Article 1. The first two aims are re-articulated in the preamble to the WTO Agreement, *supra* note 5.

[13] *Id.* Chapter I, arts. 2 (economic development) and (3) (equal access). These goals do not appear in the preambular principles and objectives of the WTO Agreement, which recognizes in pertinent part "the need for positive efforts designed to ensure that developing countries . . . secure a share in the growth in international trade commensurate with the needs of their economic development". *WTO Agreement, supra* note 7, preamb. ¶. 2.

[14] *Id.* Chapter II, Article 2(1) and (2).

[15] *Id.* Chapter II, Article 7.

[16] The Havana Charter never entered into force, a development precipitated by the failure of the U.S.Senate to ratify. John Jackson, The World Trading System: Law And Policy Of International Economic Relations 38 (2002).

[17] The ILO was created in 1919. ILO Constitution, *supra* note 3.

[18] *Declaration Concerning the Aims and Purposes of the International Labor Organization* (May 10, 1944), ILO Constitution, *supra* note 3, at Annex, Article II (revised 2001) ("*Declaration of Philadelphia*"): "Believing that experience has fully demonstrated the truth of the [1919 constitutional premise] that lasting peace can be established only if it is based on social justice, the International Labour Conference affirms that (a) all human beings, irrespective of race, creed or sex, have the right to pursue both their material well-being and their spiritual development in conditions of freedom and dignity, of economic security and

with national level commitments, the governmental and social partner representatives of the ILO Member States conferred upon the Organization itself the responsibility "to examine and consider all international economic and financial policies and measures" in the light of "the fundamental objective" of achieving lasting peace based on social justice, and to "include in its decisions and recommendations any provisions which it considers appropriate".[19] They further pledged "the full cooperation of the ILO with such international bodies as may be entrusted with a share of the responsibility" in the fields of international trade, development, and financial stability.[20] While no direct constitutional mechanism for implementation of the entire Philadelphia Declaration exists,[21] its call for coherence is reflected in ILO instruments and mechanisms relating to employment policy[22] and fundamental principles and rights at work,[23] and in a complaints mechanism relating to freedom of association.[24]

B. The Unfulfilled Promise of Liberalized Trade

The growing disparity in ownership of the gains of trade, both within and between countries, demonstrates the gaps in fulfillment of the promise of a better life for all through liberalized trading rules, both in principle and practice. As a system based on and designed to exploit inequalities among states, international trade, in theory, promises to benefit a particular country when its "peculiar powers bestowed by nature" are put to the

---

equal opportunity; (b) the attainment of the conditions in which this shall be possible must constitute the central aim of national and international policy; (c) all national and international policies and measures, in particular those of an economic and financial character, should be judged in this light and accepted only in so far as they may be held to promote and not to hinder the achievement of this fundamental objective . . . "

[19] *Id*, Article II (d), (e).

[20] *Id.*, Article IV.

[21] ILO constitutional principles have inspired the development of follow-up reporting involving fundamental principles and rights at work, *infra* notes 37, 100–101, and complaints procedures on freedom of association, *infra* note 24.

[22] States parties to the Employment Policy Convention assume an obligation to promote full and free employment "within the framework of a co-ordinated economic and social policy". *Employment Policy Convention*, ILO Convention No. 122 (1964), arts. 1, 2. The preamble to the Convention recalls the relevant provisions of the Philadelphia Declaration. Two non-binding recommendations further instruct ILO Members on how to co-ordinate the social objectives of employment policy with other measures of economic and social policy, including fiscal, monetary, and trade policies, at both national and international levels. *Employment Policy (Supplementary Provisions) Recommendation*, ILO Recommendation No. 169 (1984), Article IX; *Annex to Employment Policy Recommendation*, ILO Recommendation No. 122 (1964), Article I(2).

[23] All ILO member states share a commitment to a minimum social floor of fundamental principles and rights at work by virtue of obligations arising from the ILO constitution, including the Declaration of Philadelphia. The four categories of fundamental principles and rights are recognized in the 1998 Declaration of Fundamental Principles and Rights at Work, *supra* note 4.

[24] Two mechanisms permit complaints concerning infringement of constitutionally-based freedom of association principles in respect of countries which have ratified the freedom of association Conventions and, contingent upon consent of the country concerned, those which have not. In 1950, the Philadelphia Declaration's emphasis on freedom of expression and of association as a fundamental principle provided constitutional inspiration for creating an independent Fact-Finding and Conciliation Commission on Freedom of Association (FFCC), created by agreement with ECOSOC. Composed of nine independent members, the body examines complaints of infringement of trade union rights. In 1951, a tripartite Committee on Freedom of Association of the ILO Governing Body was established which has examined nearly 2000 cases to date. See http://www.ilo.org/public/english/standards/norm/enforced/foa/index.htm, visited May 13, 2003. The relevant fundamental conventions on freedom of association and collective bargaining are *Freedom of Association and Protection of Right to Organize Convention*, ILO Convention No. 87 (1948), 68 U.N.T.S. 17 and *Right to Organize and Collective Bargaining Convention*, ILO Convention No. 98 (1949), 96 U.N.T.S. 257.

most efficacious use.[25] Moreover, economic growth supported by trade is recognized, in theory, as a key determinant of levels of employment and working conditions, including enhanced wage equality, income distribution, and poverty reduction.[26]

Yet, in practice, the application of the principle of comparative advantage is complicated by a number of intervening variables, including levels of development and technological capacity, foreign direct investment, skills and adaptability of work forces, and multinational enterprise global strategies.[27] Trade liberalization in some developing countries, especially those less advantaged, appears to be producing exactly the opposite of the promised gains: marginalization, de-industrialization, and increasing wage inequality and poverty within and between countries.[28] Developing countries, civil society organizations, trade unions, and local businesses adversely affected by export competition have expressed growing discontent with the effects of a liberalized trading regime. Empirical studies on the impact of trade on real income, poverty reduction and development have sought positive correlations but the conclusions have faced challenges on grounds of limited evidence and methodological shortcomings.[29] Developing countries

---

[25] The theory of comparative advantage is based on the presumption that, under a system of perfectly free commerce, each country naturally devotes its capital and labor to such employments as are most beneficial to each, admirably connecting the pursuit of individual advantage with the universal good of the whole. David Ricardo, *On Foreign Trade*, in ON THE PRINCIPLES OF POLITICAL ECONOMY AND TAXATION, *reprinted in* George T. Crane and Abla Amawi, THE THEORETICAL EVOLUTION OF INTERNATIONAL POLITICAL ECONOMY, 74–75 (1991).

[26] Under the Heckscher-Ohlin model, in a two-factor world comprising capital and labor as the only factors of production, comparative advantage would turn on either capital or labor abundance; the Stolper-Samuelson theorem extended this model to predict that free trade would increase the demand for unskilled labor in labor-abundant countries and raise wages once any labor surplus is eliminated. *See, e.g., Trade Liberalization and Employment*, ILO Doc. GB.282/WP/SDG/2, ¶¶ 15–19 (Nov. 2001). Global systems encouraging liberalization of trade and, in many applications, development policy reflect similar presuppositions. *Cf.* J. Jackson, THE WORLD TRADING SYSTEM 11–25 (2000).

[27] The economic vulnerability of developing countries in the context of a trading system dominated by industrialized states intensified during colonization and post-war decolonization periods, even as developing countries sought U.N. alternatives to post-Havana GATT frameworks. *See, e.g.,* Frank Garcia, *Trade and Inequality: Economic Justice and the Developing World*, 21 MICH. J. INT'L. L. 981–985 (2000). Deterioration associated with trade imbalances may be attributable to a confluence of factors, including the marginalization of low-income countries due to debt burdens, commodity price fluctuation, lower skills levels of work forces, and environmental degradation. Some observers have noted that trading between unequal size economies creates heightened vulnerability for less dominant trading partners due to such factors as the relative openness of small economies to external transactions in relation to total economic activity, and the relatively undiversifed economic base and heavy reliance on primary product exports of small economies *See, e.g. id.* at 987.

[28] Observers have blamed trade liberalization for employment ills within advanced and developing countries alike, although empirical research has cast doubt on some such views. *See generally,* ILO Doc. GB.282/WP/SDG/2, *supra* note 20. In advanced economies, rising unemployment and wage inequality have been linked to the perceived exodus of low-skilled jobs due to the lifting of import barriers, resulting in increasing imports from low-wage economies, together with the relocation of labor-intensive industries to those countries. *Id.* ¶ 9. In developing economies, the liberalization of trade has been perceived as stimulating a "race to the bottom" in exercising a low-wage comparative advantage, and at the root of increased exploitation of workers in developing countries, deteriorating working conditions and labor standards. For a review of such perceptions, see Kimberley Elliott and Richard Freeman, CAN LABOR STANDARDS IMPROVE UNDER GLOBALIZATION?, 17–22 (2003).

[29] *See, e.g.,* P. Agenor and J. Aizenman, *Trade Liberalization and Unemployment*, 5 J. INT'L TRADE & ECON. DEV., 265 (1996); D. Greenaway, *Liberalizing Foreign Trade Through Rose-Tinted Glasses*, 103 ECON. J. 208 (1993). *questioning* D. Papageorgiou et al., *Liberalization of Foreign Trade in Developing Countries: The Lessons of Experience* (World Bank, 1990). See also *Coherence in Global Economic Policymaking and Cooperation between the WTO, the IMF and the World Bank*, WTO Doc. WT/TF/COH/S/7, 29 April 2003 (*Coherence Note*), ¶ 36 ("the links between trade liberalization and poverty reduction are complex, and

confront inequitable trade-offs in allocation of fiscal and administrative resources to local needs, on the one hand, or international institutional requirements, on the other hand.[30]

Left unmoored from an integrated social and economic framework, the system of international trade cooperation is being challenged as unfair in outcome and process.[31] Limited resources and know-how hinder developing countries in making effective use of dispute settlement mechanisms and of trade policy tools designed to provide preferential access and special protection to their markets.[32] In principle, the legal right to retaliation provides recourse in the face of inadequate compliance but, in practice, economic inability significantly reduces the value of this right for those with less economic "staying power".[33]

Experience illustrates that the rules for integration within the world economy do not present economically sustainable propositions for all, even when trade openness is coupled with institutional reforms like social safety nets and labor market adjustments.[34] While "the mutually profitable division of labor" plays a central role in trade theory,[35] the interaction between trade undertakings and working conditions, wages, and levels of employment is left largely unaddressed in international policy and practice. In 1997, the WTO Ministerial Conference expressed a desire to maintain "existing collaboration" at Secretariat level between WTO and ILO.[36] Within the ILO, the 1998 Declaration of

in some respects controversial. While it is well-established that trade openness and growth are mutually supportive, and that poverty reduction requires economic growth, the direct impact of trade liberalization on different groups among the poor can vary").

[30] Trade-offs have been noted in the area of legal reforms, public health, industrial strategy, economic policy transparency. In each area, reforms may serve more the interests of foreign investors and markets rather htan building capacity to meet local needs. *See* Dani Rodrik, *The Global Governance of Trade as if Development Really Mattered*, 30 (UN Development Programme, 2001); Ben Thirkell-White, *The IMF, Good Governance and Middle-Income Countries*, 15 EUR. J. OF DEV. RSCH. 99, 118–19 (2003).

[31] Critics have claimed that issues in trade negotiating rounds are set for discussion without transparency or consensus and conclusions arrived at without the effective participation of all. *E.g.*, Deepak Nayyar, *The Existing Systems and the Missing Institutions*, in GOVERNING GLOBALIZATION 377–78 (Deepak Nayyar ed. 2002). The greatest fissure in the multilateral trading system has been identified as that between developed and developing countries. Raj Bhala, *Assessing the Modern Era of International Trade*, 21 FORDHAM INT'L L. J. 1647, 1658 (1998). The inconclusive results of the fifth WTO Ministerial Conference, particularly the lack of consensus on "Singapore" issues (investment, competition policy, transparency in government procurement), reflect a new filibustering power on the part of developing countries. Ministerial Conference, Fifth Sess. (cancan) *Ministerial Statement*, WT/MIN(03)/20, Sept. 23, 2003, reproduced in the Appendix to this book.

[32] *See, e.g.*, Gerry Helleiner, *Global Economic Governance*, in Nayyar, *supra* note 31, at 323–26.

[33] For the use of retaliatory measures for lack of full compliance, *see generally* the *Understanding on Rules and Procedures Governing the Settlement of Disputes* ("*DSU*"), Article 22.

[34] *See, e.g.*, Rodrik, *supra* note 30, at 31. "WTO rules on anti-dumping, subsidies and countervailing measures, agriculture, textiles, TRIMS, and TRIPs are utterly devoid of any economic rationale beyond the mercantilist interests of a narrow set of powerful groups in the advanced industrial countries." Id. *See also* Thirkell-White, *supra* note 30. Critics claims that the so-called "enlightened standard view", which augmented the Washington Consensus by espousing the need for more than simply removal of trade and investment barriers, further burdened developing countries by requiring a full complement of other institutional reforms to ensure favorable economic outcomes. Those included tax reforms, policies to enhance labor mobility across industries, technological assistance to upgrade domestic firms affected by import competition, training programs to ensure skilled labor market for export-oriented firms, etc. *See, e.g.*, Rodrik, *supra* note 30, at 29.

[35] See *supra* notes 5 and 25.

[36] The relationship of labor to trade was addressed in brief at the Singapore Ministerial Conference of WTO: "We renew our commitment to the observance of internationally recognized core labor standards. The International Labor Organization ("ILO") is the competent body to set and deal with these standards, and we affirm our support for its work in promoting them. We believe economic growth and development fostered

Fundamental Principles and Rights at Work committed all Member States to a minimum social floor of fundamental principles and rights at work reinforced by a follow-up
procedure that combines reporting and technical cooperation, and affirming the premise
that adherence by all to this floor will preclude any principle effect on comparative
advantage.[37]

II. Values in Markets and the Workplace

Values play an important role in markets and at work that offers an opportunity for
bridging the current gaps in the governance of trade and labor to seek higher standards of
living for all. At local and national levels, values shared across society[38] serve to shape
the social institutions and customs which, to a large extent, organize work and trading
activities. By nature, markets and workplaces are embedded in society and operate on the
basis of social expectations. How well they function depends in part on the level of shared
attitudes and expectations that build trust between people.[39] The greater the coherence of
moral norms or values, the more common interests generate the confidence that facilitates
market transactions and approaches to negotiating and resolving differences.[40] This sort
of dynamic in the workplace, fostered by commonly agreed expectations, is at the heart
of industrial relations systems based on social dialogue and freedom of association for
workers and employers.[41]

---

by increased trade and further trade liberalization contribute to the promotion of these standards. We reject
the use of labor standards for protectionist purposes, and agree that the comparative advantage of countries,
particularly low-wage developing countries, must in no way be put into question. In this regard, we note that
the WTO and ILO Secretariats will continue their existing collaboration." Ministerial Conference, *Singapore
Declaration*, WTO Doc WT/MIN/96/DEC, Dec. 13, 1996, ¶¶ 4, 13 I.L.M. 220, 221 (1997), reproduced in
the Appendix to this book.

[37] See discussion *infra* at notes 96–97, 100–101 and accompanying text. While not directly addressing the
Declaration's premise, empirical and economic analyses on the interaction of trade, labor, and globalization
have informed policy-level discussions in the ILO Governing Body. *E.g., Country Studies on the Social
Impact of Globalization: Final report*, ILO Doc. No. GB.276/WP/SDL/1 and Add.1; GB.283/15, ¶¶ 10–15
(2002) (panel discussion of paper: *Trade Liberalization and Employment*, ILO Doc. GB.283/WP/SDG/1
(2002)). The results of a recently-convened independent World Commission on the Social Dimension of
Globalization, mandated by the ILO to prepare a Report on related issues, are pending at date of writing.
See supra note 9.

[38] For a working definition of values, *see supra* note 1. Values common to a society may be reflected
in social contracts or customs, or expressed through behavioral patterns at individual or societal level.
Philip Nichols, *Trade Without Values,* 90 NW. U. L. REV. 658 (1996). Values theory distinguishes various
perspectives on values: contractarian (social contracts embodying behavioral norms which derive from shared
perspectives); utilitarian (promoting self or societal interest), skeptic individualism (matter of personal taste)
and universalism (values founded on universal truth). *Id.* at note 72 and accompanying text.

[39] *See, e..g.*, Hazel Henderson, BEYOND GLOBALIZATION: SHAPING A SUSTAINABLE GLOBAL ECONOMY (1999).

[40] Shared values breed predictability of expectation and, in optimal situations, trust. *See, e.g.,* F. Fukuyama,
TRUST, THE SOCIAL VIRTUES AND CREATION OF PROSPERITY (1995). According to some analysts, it is possible
to economize substantially on transaction costs in a modern market-oriented economic system if market
institutions are supplemented by social capital and trust. In this view, trust is understood to be the expectation
that arises within a community from regular behavior based on commonly shared moral norms or values. *Id.*
at 26; K. A. Elliott, *The Role of Incentives, Trust, and Institutions in Sustainable Single Markets*, prepared
for "Lessons for a Globalizing World? Historical Experiences of Europe and the United States in Market
Integration", sponsored by the European Union Center, Maxwell School, Syracuse University, N.Y. (2002)
(unpublished manuscript on file with author).

[41] *See, e.g., Your Voice at Work: Global Report on Freedom of Association and Effective Recognition of the
Right to Collective Bargaining,* ILO (2000). Social dialogue is defined by the ILO to include all types of
negotiation, consultation or simply exchange of information between, or among, representatives of governments, employers and workers, on issues of common interest relating to economic and social policy. The

At international level, the expanded reach of communications networks has increasingly linked the global and the local, raising public awareness of the imbalance in resources and power between haves and have-nots within and across countries, businesses, and communities. The emerging conscience is building a consensus on core values and commitments to common goals. Expectations and goals common both to open markets and to decent work and life are converging from a wide range of State and non-state actors across different cultures, beliefs, and economic contexts.[42] At the heart of this advance is a conviction that solidarity must accompany individual gain; the world's markets must incorporate morals to sustain themselves and to function effectively in the workplace and in society.[43] There is a recognition that market forces alone cannot guarantee equity, freedom, or human dignity and diversity, nor can they alone produce the enabling conditions for development like sustainable and decent work.[44] Rather, the co-ordinated commitments of public, market and social actors signal a new process for implementing common goals through the sharing of responsibility in respective spheres of competence.[45] In a manner akin to local interactions, the sharing of universal values is critical to building trust and allocating responsibility for achieving common goals

definition and concept of social dialogue varies from country to country and from region to region and it is still evolving. http://www.ilo.org/public/english/dialogue/ifpdial/sd/index.htm, visited January 24, 2004. Respect for freedom of association rights is considered by the ILO as essential to social dialogue, which in turn is a vital component of "decent work", *See supra* note 3. For economic analyses of such systems, *see, e.g.*, Toke Aidt and Zafiris Tzannatos, UNIONS AND COLLECTIVE BARGAINING: ECONOMIC EFFECTS IN A GLOBAL ENVIRONMENT, 14–16 (World Bk., 2002); David Kucera, *Core Labour Standards and Foreign Direct Investment*, 141 INT'L LABOUR REV. 1–2, 31 (2002).

[42] Values that are shared at some fundamental level, across cultures and peoples, provide a common threshold for identifying commitments to certain objectives and expectations of certain conduct. As in the context of individual societies, values shared across societies may result in widespread customs or expectations that, over time, create a mutual trust strengthening economic, social and cultural exchanges across the groups involved. Between countries, some of these values may find official expression in treaties or other agreements, or even trading and security alliances. When values are shared on a widespread, or global scale, their strength or primacy in guiding the conduct and objectives of multinational relations may be embodied in multilateral treaties, declarations and other sources of international law or political commitments.

[43] For an approach to understanding the causal links between institutional market arrangements and the realization of fundamental social values of well-being, freedom, and justice, *see* Amartya Sen, *The Moral Standing of the Market*, in ETHICS AND ECONOMICS (Ellen Frankel Paul *et al.*, eds. 1985). A more recent political effort within the United Nations itself, the Global Compact, seeks to promote universal values for global markets through learning, policy, and active partnerships among business, labor, civil society, and the public sector. *See* www.unglobalcompact.org. The three categories of universal values consists of human rights, the environment, and labor; the labor category is comprised of the fundamental principles and rights at work found in the ILO Declaration of the same name. *See* ILO Fundamental Principles, *supra* note 4 and accompanying text. Among relevant international organization initiatives, the Multilateral Investment Guaranty Agency of the World Bank Group excludes support for projects that use forced labor or harmful child labor. *See* Multilateral Investment Guarantee Agency: *Operational Regulations*, June 22, 1988, ¶ 3.08, 27 I.L.M. 1227 (1988); *Standard Contract of Guarantee and General Conditions of Guarantee for Equity Investments*, Jan. 27, 1989, at Schedule A, Articles 10.1, 32, 28 I.L.M. 1233 (1989).

[44] *See, e.g.*, *Universal Declaration on Cultural Diversity*, United Nations Educational, Scientific and Cultural Organization ("UNESCO"), Article 11 (2002), (market forces need public policy and partnership with private sector and civil society to ensure diversity). *Prague Declaration*, approved by the Fifth Forum 2000 Conference, at Section 2, Prague, Czech Republic, 17 Oct. 2001, available at www.forum2000.cz/2001/declaration, ("effective policies for the global economy have to be addressed by social and political institutions . . . [to increase] social capital and develop human capacities and opportunities").

[45] *See, e.g.*, *UN Millennium Declaration*, GA Resolution 55/2, UN Doc. A/RES/55/2, Sept. 18, 2000 ("*Millennium Declaration*"), Article I(6) (shared responsibility is a fundamental value essential to international relations in the 21st century); *Copenhagen Declaration*, *supra* note 4, ¶¶. 26, 27 (while States have primary responsibility of social development, we acknowledge the interdependence of public and private spheres of activity).

through agreed methods. Through this dynamic, a growing framework of globally-shared values essential to a balanced operation of trade and labor offers a platform for coherent governance at international level.

III. Discovering Shared Values

Examining the values common to trade and labor requires looking at the surrounding context of international cooperation. Trade and work function in markets and society together with other international efforts to achieve global public goods, including social and economic development, monetary stabilization, democratic governance, and public health.[46] Because the various regimes governing international cooperation operate inter-dependently, the relationship between trade and labor is only effectively addressed within this larger "community" of global actors which includes states, international organizations, business and worker associations, and civil society organizations. Shared values, discernible across these public and private spheres, are the starting point for a system to manage trade and labor at global level.

A. Values Instruments

At local and national levels, shared values may be expressed through unwritten customs in socio-economic relationships and structures, or in written texts like popular manifestos and official laws and regulations.[47] At international level, values shared across borders may find expression in international customary or conventional law, in general principles of international law or in political resolutions of international and regional organizations.[48] Such "values channels" vary in their binding or authoritative character. Internationalized values are also found in influential popular declarations and collective statements of business and civil society groups, scholars, and global commissions. While these commitments may have no direct legal force, they sometimes lead to the adoption or more effective recognition of officially-endorsed values.[49]

A common core of shared values connects official and popular declarations at international level.[50] One key element is the call to balance the pursuit of private gain

---

[46] Relevant institutions that manage international cooperation in these areas include the World Bank Group, the International Monetary Fund, World Health Organization, and a number of UN bodies and agencies.

[47] In the case of official instruments, fuller meaning may be given the underlying values by structures and people that interpret or apply the legal regimes. Nichols, *supra* note 38, at note 72 and accompanying text. Law's relationship to values may be in serving as a "tool for arranging today's social relations and expressing today's social values." Alex Aleinikoff, cited in *id.* note 70.

[48] *See Statute of the International Court of Justice*, June 26, 1945, 1977 UN Yearbook 1190, Article 38.

[49] In the context of global commissions of eminent persons, the principles annexed to the report of the Brundtland Commission on Environment and Development laid the foundation for the Rio Declaration on Environment and Development, UN Doc. A/CONF.151/26 (Vol. 1) (1992). Summary of Proposed Legal Principles for Environmental Protection and Sustainable Developed adopted by the WCED Experts Group on Environmental Law, OUR COMMON FUTURE, REPORT OF THE WORLD COMMISSION ON ENVIRONMENT AND DEVELOPMENT, Annexe I (1987). One example of the influence of non-governmental scholars is found in the Siracusa Principles on the Limitation and Derogation of Provisions in the International Covenant on Civil and Political Rights, *infra* note 52, initially adopted by a group of legal scholars, which has grown in authoritative recognition within UN bodies themselves. *Siracusa Principles on the Limitation and Derogation of Provisions in the International Covenant on Civil and Political Rights*, UN Doc E/CN.4/1985/4, Annex (1985).

[50] The "essential values" proclaimed by the UN Millennium General Assembly, and the resulting Millennium Development Goals derived from it, provide an authoritative model for building a universally-recognized

with collective effort to enhance the common good.[51] This general directive embodies a fledgling mandate for governing the markets and workplaces of a globalizing world. The balance sought is reflected in three types of common values: over-arching objectives, and applied through normative principles and instrumental rules for working, trading, and living together. The following sections examine these three types of common values that help to build the framework for international governance in the fields of work and trade.

B. Values as Over-Arching Objectives

The specialized frameworks governing labor and trade, along with other regimes, are based upon ultimate objectives that guide international cooperation. These overarching *objectives* of the world community echo the intrinsic desires of humanity that reflect our longings for freedom, dignity, equity and peace.[52]

The objectives underlying the international labor regime encompass such aims in striving for conditions of decent work[53] that are essential to achieving social justice, or equity. The ILO Constitution recognizes social justice as the foundation for universal

---

values framework that encompasses public and non-state actors in trade and labor. *See Millennium Declaration, supra* note 45, Sec. 6..For other declarations on point, see *infra* note 52.

[51] A wide range of texts reflect consensus in calling for balance, including treaties that use the language of obligation, and political or civil declarations and statements of public and private actors that employ the language of commitment. These articulations have originated in the course of dialogue within multilateral forums, UN-led world conferences, independent global commissions, and gatherings of civil society, labor, business, and religious leaders. While the values-based expressions may not yet be fully put into practice, the various sources do reflect a solemn and consistently-expressed commitment to achieve ultimate objectives through the use of agreed principles and means.

[52] *See, e.g., Charter of the United Nations*, June 26, 1945, 59 Stat. 1031 (1945); *Universal Declaration on Human Rights*, Dec. 10, 1945, UN GA Resolution 217 (A)III, GAOR, 3d. Session, UN Doc. A/810 (1948) *("UDHR"); International Covenant on Civil and Political Rights ("ICCPR")*, Dec. 16, 1966, 999 U.N.T.S. 171 (1966); *International Covenant on Economic, Social and Cultural Rights*, Dec. 16, 1966, 993 U.N.T.S. 3 (1966); *Copenhagen Declaration supra* note 3; *Vienna Declaration and Programme of Action for Human Rights*, UN Doc. A/CONF.157/23, as adopted by the World Conference on Human Rights (1993); *Cairo Report of the International Conference on Population and Development*, UN Doc. A/CONF.171/13 (1994); *Beijing Declaration and Plan of Action on the Advancement of Women*, A/CONF.177/20 (1995); *Final Outcome of the International Conference on Financing for Development*, A/CONF.198/3 (2002) *("Monterrey Consensus"); Report of the World Summit for Social Development, Johannesburg Plan of Implementation*, A/CONF.199/20 (2002) *("Johannesburg Declaration"); Global Compact, supra* note 43. The charters of various specialized agencies, including the WTO, *supra* note 5, and ILO, *supra* note 3, reflect the determination of the global community to cooperate together in advancing progress and resolving challenges in trade, labor and other international spheres of activity. For popular declarations reaffirming the fundamental principles of the global constitutional order and echoing the calls of the UN Charter, International Bill of Rights, Millennium Declaration, and cooperative treaty systems, *see, e.g., Our Global Neighborhood*, The Report of Commission on Global Governance (1995); *The Earth Charter*, www.earthcharter.org/earthcharter/charter.htm, ("Earth Charter"); *Prague Declaration, supra* note 44; *Private Sector Declaration*, The World Economic Forum available on-line at www.weforum.org/pdf/Latin_America/Private_Sector_Declaration.pdf; *World Social Forum Charter of Principles*, approved and adopted by the World Social Forum Organizing Committee in Sao Paulo on April 9, 2001, as modified by the World Social Forum International Council on June 10, 2001; *The Principles for Business*: Caux Round Table (1994) at www.cauxroundtable.org; OUR COMMON FUTURE, *supra* note 49; OUR CREATIVE DIVERSITY, World Commission on Culture and Development (1995). While the ethical framework of the emerging global community is not yet fully put in practice, the values and principles do reflect a solemn commitment, repeatedly expressed by states, public organizations, and non-state actors, to adhere to a core of ultimate objectives, and principles and means for achieving them.

[53] *Id.*, preamb. ¶ 2. "Decent work", a term adopted by the ILO to refer to work performed under standards, terms and conditions that affirm respect for the dignity of the human being, *See also supra* note 4 defining "decent work".

and lasting peace.[54] Freedom is vital to improving conditions of labor and establishing peace, particularly freedom of association.[55] In the family and society, the opportunity for a decent job represents a source of human dignity and identity as well as livelihood; for the individual, decent jobs contribute to material well being, fulfill human rights, and enable spiritual development.[56] At a macro level, decent work promotes a more equitable distribution of resources and opportunities within and among countries and people.[57]

Ultimate objectives of like nature underlie the multilateral trade regime. The act of trading itself is an exercise in freedom—freedom of commerce within and between countries.[58] While such freedom is itself beneficial, the purpose of the multilateral trading system is deeper: the system is to serve as a means for a better life, developing the conditions necessary for people and countries to improve their livelihoods and live in dignity. Parties to the WTO Agreement recognize that their relations in the multilateral trading system are to be conducted with a view to raising standards of living, ensuring full employment and growth of real income and effective demand, and expanding the production of and trade in goods and services while allowing for use of the world's resources in accordance with the objective of sustainable development.[59] Security and predictability are acknowledged pre-requisites for the durable and viable functioning of the trading system, and they account for the centrality of the dispute settlement mechanism in the system.[60] Trade rules designed to secure for developing countries a share in the growth in international trade commensurate with their economic development needs reflect the value of equity between nations, at least in principle, though not always in outcome.[61]

---

[54] *ILO Constitution, supra* note 3, at preamb. ¶ 1. Conditions of work involving injustice, hardship and privation to large numbers of people produce unrest so great that the peace and harmony of the world are imperiled; for this reason, improvement of those conditions is urgently required through regulation of working terms and conditions, and provision for old age and injury, as well as recognition of fundamental principles and rights at work. See ILO Constitution, *supra* note 3, preamble.

[55] *ILO Convention 87, supra* note 24, at preamble.

[56] *See, e.g., ILO Declaration of Philadelphia, supra* note 18, Articles II and III; *ILO Fundamental Principles, supra* note 4, Article 2(b); *UDHR, supra* note 52, Articles 22 and 23.

[57] The guarantee of fundamental principles and rights at work links social justice with economic growth, ILO Fundamental Principles *supra* note 4, at preamble, and informs the proportional balance of rights and freedoms with other common goods. *See, e.g.,* ICCPR, *supra* note 52, Article 19(3), ICESCR, *supra* note 52, Article 4, and *Limburg Principles on the Implementation of the International Covenant on Economic, Social and Cultural Rights,* UN Doc. E/CN.4/1987/17, ¶¶ 46–69 (1987).

[58] Freedom of commerce is a general principle of international economic law recognizing "the right—in principle unrestricted—to engage in any commercial activity, whether it be concerned with trading properly so-called, that is the purchase and sale goods, or whether it be concerned with industry, and in particular the transport of business; or, finally whether it is carried on inside the country or, by the exchange of imports and exports, with other countries." *Oscar Chinn Case,* P.C.I.J. (Ser. A/B) No. 63 (1934). *See also* Georg Schwarzenberger, I Recueil De Cours 47–48 (1966). The related principle of freedom of contract is of paramount importance in the context of international trade. International Institute for Unification of Private Law ("UNIDROIT"), *Principles of International Commercial Contracts,* Article 1.1 Commentary, ¶ 1, 33 I.L.M. 1395 (1994). On the interdependence of economic, political and social freedoms and capacities, *see* generally Amartya Sen, Development As Freedom. 35–41 (1999).

[59] *WTO Agreement, supra* note 5, at preamb. ¶ 1. With several notable exceptions, the goals specified in the WTO preamble parallel those of the original GATT 1947, *supra* note 8. New provisions within the preambular framework include the referenced proviso regarding sustainable development, and a paragraph addressing the need for positive efforts to ensure that developing countries secure a share in the growth in international trade commensurate with their needs for economic development. For a development-oriented perspective on trade, see Rodrik, *supra* note 30.

[60] *DSU, supra* note 33, Article 3(2). See also *WTO Agreement, supra* note 5, preamb. ¶ 4.

[61] *WTO Agreement, supra* note 5, at preamb. ¶ 2. Part IV of the GATT on "Trade and Development" (Articles XXXVI, XXXVII and XXXVIII) establishes the principle of non-reciprocity in trade negotiations between developed and developing countries, and provides for developed countries to adopt special measures to

C. Values as Normative Principles

Normative principles are essential building blocks in reaching the over-arching objectives grounding international cooperation. They include human rights; equality among states and among individuals; full, productive and freely-chosen employment; higher standards of living and economic development; and respect for the environment. Treaties and political declarations across general and specialized fields of international law, including in trade and labor, reflect a broad consensus on this level of values.[62]

International labor law is built upon values-based normative principles. The ILO is founded on the development-oriented premise that decent work must be made available in every nation because "poverty anywhere is a threat to prosperity everywhere."[63] Core international labor standards focus on fundamental human rights and equality as enabling pre-requisites to claiming one's fairshare of the fruits of labor.[64] The promotion

promote the expansion of imports from developing countries. Various provisions, including the special and differential treatment provisions, exempt developing countries from aspects of such basic trading principles as Most-Favored-Nation treatment for all (GATT, Article I), tariff bindings (Article II), national treatment (Article III), and non-tariff barriers (Articles X and XI). A waiver from Article I(1) for example was granted the members of the African, Caribbean, and Pacific States-European Economic Community under the now-expired ACP-EEC Convention of Lomé, Dec. 15, 1989, 29 I.L.M. 783 (1990), to permit preferential treatment for products originating in ACP states as required by that Convention, noting that the parties to the convention consider that it is compatible with obligations under Article XXIV in view of Part IV. For a critique of the results of the "special treatment" principle, see Peter Lichtenbaum, *Special Treatment vs. Equal Participation: Striking a Balance in the Doha Negotiations*, 17 AM. U. INT'L L. REV. 1003 (2002). Action on the mandate to review the S&D provisions agreed in the Doha Ministerial Declaration (¶ 44) and its Decision on Implementation-related Issues and Concerns (¶ 12) remained pending as of date of writing. For an analysis of the impact of other GATT rules on "late industrializing countries" *see* Alice H. Amsden, *Industrialization under New WTO Law*, UN Doc. No. TD(X)/RT.1/7, paper presented at UNCTAD X, High-level Round Table on Trade and Development, Directions for the Twenty-first Century, Bangkok, Feb. 12, 2000, available on-line at http://www.unctad-10.org/pdfs/ux_tdxrt1d7.en.pdf.

[62] For human rights, *see generally UN Charter, supra* note 52, Articles 1(3), 55(c); *UN Millennium Dec., supra* note 45, Article I(4); UDHR, *supra* note 52; *ICCPR, supra* note 52; ICESCR, *supra* note 52; *Earth Charter, supra* note 52. For equality among states, *see, e.g., UN Charter, supra* note 52, at Article 2(1); *Declaration on Principles of International Law Friendly Relations and Cooperation Among States in Accordance with the UN Charter*, UN GA Resolution 2625, UN Doc. A/55/L.56/Rev.1 (1970); *Millennium Dec., supra* note 45, Article I(6). Equality among individuals is a fundamental value essential to international relations in the 21st century. Millennium Dec., *id.*, Article I(6). It is recognized within the UN Charter, *supra* note 52, Article 1(2) and in a number of general and specific human rights treaties and declarations as well as labor law conventions. *E.g.*, ICCPR, *supra* note 52, Article 2; ICESCR, *supra* note 52, Article 2(2), and *generally International Convention on the Elimination of All Forms of Racial Discrimination ("ICERD")*, March 7, 1966, 660 U.N.T.S. 195, I.L.M. 352 (1966); *Convention on the Elimination of All Forms of Discrimination Against Women ("CEDAW")*, Dec. 18, 1979, 1249 U.N.T.S. 13, 19 I.L.M. 33 (1980). Special measures to ensure equality are called for in various contexts. *E.g.*, ICERD, *id.*, Article 1(4), 2(2); *CEDAW*, at Article 4. Democracy involves a comprehensive set of rights to government by the will of the people. *E.g.*, *UDHR*, *supra* note 52, Article 21; *Respect for the principles of national sovereignty and non-interference in the internal affairs of States in electoral processes as an important element for the promotion and protection of human rights, UNGA Resolution 56/154*, UN Doc. A/RES/56/154 (2001), preamble; *ICCPR, supra* note 52, Article 25. The principle of development entitles individuals and peoples to the process and results of States' efforts, individually and collectively, to promote economic and social progress and solve related problems. *E.g., Vienna Dec., supra* note 52, Article I(10); *Declaration on the Right to Development*, UNGA Resolution 41/128, UN Doc. A/RES/41/28 (1986), Article 1. Environmental respect is an essential value leading to the sustainability of healthy and productive human life and economic and social activity in harmony with nature and the environment. *E.g., UN Millennium Dec., supra* note 45, Article I(6), *Johannesburg Declaration, supra* note 52, Chapter IV. For labor, *see infra* notes 63–65; for trade, *see infra* notes 66–71.

[63] *Philadelphia Declaration, supra* note 18, Article I(c).

[64] *See ILO Fundamental Principles, supra* note 3, Article 2; *Equal Remuneration Convention*, ILO Convention No. 100 (1951); *Discrimination in Employment and Occupation Convention*, ILO Convention No. 111 (1958); *Workers with Family Responsibilities Convention*, ILO Convention No. 156 (1981). Special measures

of full employment, decent working terms and conditions, and income security are all rights-based development objectives of the ILO.[65]

International trade rules correspondingly reflect normative principles common to the international system. The principle of equality in principle among states underlies the obligation of non-discrimination in most-favored nation ("MFN") and national treatment principles,[66] and in the right to take sanitary and phyto-sanitary measures necessary to protect human, animal or plant life or health.[67] In turn, the pursuit of equality in effect can be seen in the commitment to reciprocity *subject to mutuality of advantage*, and in special clauses for more favorable treatment of developing countries with a view to their fuller participation in international trade.[68] The principle of development has become increasingly recognized at political level in calls for positive efforts to ensure that developing countries secure a share in the growth of world trade and to improve effective participation of least-developed countries in the multilateral trading system.[69] The value of preserving the world's resources is reflected in the WTO Agreement preamble; this pledge was not part of the earlier GATT framework.[70] Various exceptions to protect "legitimate objectives" in the areas of human life, health, and safety, and environmental resources, also implicate WTO Members' commitments to human rights and the environment.[71]

D. Values as Instrumental Tools

The means by which countries put shared values into practice differ depending upon circumstances and local preferences. While maintaining the necessary freedom of choice for differing situations, certain common approaches are evolving that form patterns of consultation, negotiation, and the settlement of disputes at both national and international levels. These *instrumental values* guide the way actors in the international community relate, individually and collectively. They address methods of conduct like

---

to ensure equality are called for in the Indigenous and Tribal Peoples Convention, ILO Convention No. 169 (1989).

[65] *ILO Constitution, supra* note 3, preamble. *See, e.g., Employment Policy Convention, supra* note 22; *Protection of Wages Convention*, ILO Convention No. 95 (1949); *Minimum Wage Fixing Convention*, ILO Convention No. 131 (1970); *Occupational Safety and Health Convention*, ILO Convention No. 155 (1981); *Vocational Rehabilitation and Employment (Disabled Persons) Convention*, ILO Convention No. 159 (1983).

[66] E.g., *GATT, supra* note 8, Articles I and III.

[67] E.g., *Agreement on the Application of Sanitary and Phytosanitary Measures (SPS)*, Article 2.1.

[68] E.g., *DSU, supra* note 33, Articles 3.2 and 19.2 (rights and obligations); Differential and More Favorable Treatment, Reciprocity and Fuller Participation of Developing Countries, GATT, BISD (1980).

[69] *Doha Ministerial Declaration*, WT/MIN(01)/DEC/1, Nov. 20, 2001, ¶¶ 2, 3, *passim* reproduced in the Appendix to this book); *see also* Monterrey Consensus, *supra* note 52. Concrete steps include duty-free and quota-free access for LDC exports; conducting a work program and negotiating process with a view to development needs including on agriculture, trade in services, intellectual property rights, and a review of all S&D treatment provisions; and supporting technical cooperation and capacity building in coordination with other agencies as core elements of the development dimension of the multilateral trading system. *See also Johannesburg Declaration, supra* note 52, Chapters V, IX (supporting Doha and Monterrey work programs for action to address needs and interests of developing countries).

[70] *See, e.g., WTO Agreement supra* note 5, preamble (expanding the production of and trade in goods and services while allowing for use of the world's resources in accordance with the objective of sustainable development).

[71] E.g., *GATT, supra* note 8, Article XX; *Agreement on Technical Barriers to Trade (TBT Agreement)*, Article 2.2. See also *Decision on Trade and Environment*, Ministerial Decision adopted by Ministers at the Meeting of the Trade Negotiations Committee in Marrakesh (14 April 1994) (establishing Committee on Trade and Environment); *United States—Import Prohibition of Certain Shrimp and Shrimp Products*, Report of the Appellate Body, WT/DS58/AB (1998) ("*Shrimp*"), ¶¶ 129–31, 152–53.

transparency, participatory decision-making, and accountability.[72] Such "process values" underlie international relations in various fields, including the labor and trade regimes.

In the labor sphere, consultative decision-making is at the heart of the way decent work is promoted and sustained, and underlies central ILO standards.[73] At the international level, by constitutional mandate, the Organization's decision-making is shared by representatives of governments, employers and workers organizations.[74] Other members of the international community, such as non-governmental international organizations and official international organizations, when accredited as observers, have the right to participate and take the floor under certain circumstances.[75] Documents for discussion at the ILO Governing Body are, as a rule, made public in advance, a transparency which aids meaningful consultation.[76]

In the multilateral trade regime, transparency operates as a motivating principle in a number of contexts. The Trade Policy Review Mechanism is mandated to use greater transparency in WTO Members' trade policies and practices as the primary means to contribute to improved adherence to WTO rules, disciplines, and commitments.[77] Transparency is at the heart of public notice and comment rules for national level decision making on technical regulations with trade effects.[78] Recent steps have been taken to achieve more participation as well as transparency in trade negotiations[79] and in dispute settlement procedures.[80]

IV. Normative Implications of a Values Framework for Trade and Labor

A. Toward the Internationalization of Values

The drive for a values-based mandate to balance the power of trading with the pursuit of public good resembles in some ways the movement toward internationalization of human

---

[72] The responsibility for implementing good governance rests with states. UN Commission on Human Rights, *The Role of Good Governance in the Promotion of Human Rights*, UN Doc. E/CN.4/RES/2002/76, CHR Resolution 2002/76 (2002). Attributes of good governance are a "transparent, responsible, accountable and participatory government, responsive to the needs and aspirations of the people" *Id.* at ¶ 1; see also ILO Governing Body, *Policies and Social Partnerships for Good Governance*, ILO Doc. GB.288/WPSDG/2 (Nov. 2003). Good governance also rests on the rule of law and democracy. *Copenhagen Declaration, supra* note 4, at Commitment 18(f) and Copenhagen Programme of Action, ¶ 14(b); *Johannesburg Declaration, supra* note 52, ¶ 31. Economic systems are "based on the principles of ... democracy ... participation, transparency, accountability and inclusion. *Monterrey Consensus, supra* note 52, Article I(9). Therefore, both trade and labor have intersecting interests in the enabling conditions of good governance: the rule of law and democracy, transparency, accountability, and participation in the government, promoting universal values and open markets. *See UN Global Compact, supra* note 43. Important in the concept of good governance and accountability is the right of redress for personal and economic injury. *See, e.g., UDHR, supra* note 52, Article 12, *ICCPR, supra* note 52, Article 2.

[73] *ILO Tripartite Consultation (International Labour Standards) Convention* No. 144 (1976).

[74] *ILO Const., supra* note 3, Article 3 (General Conference), Article 7 (Governing Body). Established procedures permit examination of the credentials of delegates and their advisers to the International Labour Conference and of any objection thereto. *Standing Orders of the International Labour Conference LC*, adopted by ILC, 1st Sess. (1919) ("*ILC Standing Orders*") (as amended), Articles 5, 26.

[75] *ILO Const., supra* note 3, Article 12; *ILC Standing Orders*, Articles 14, 56.

[76] *Standing Orders of the Governing Body* (adopted 1920, as amended), Article 14.

[77] *WTO Agreement, supra* note 5, Annex 3 (Trade Policy Review Mechanism), § A(i).

[78] *E.g.,, TBT Agreement, supra* note 71, Article 2.9.

[79] At the Doha Ministerial Conference in 2001, a Trade Negotiations Committee was established to supervise trade negotiations under the authority of the General Council. *Doha Declaration, supra* note 69, ¶ 46, reproduced in the Appendix to this book. Explicit directives that negotiations shall be open to all WTO members and "shall be conducted in a transparent manner among participants in order to facilitate the effective participation of all." *Id.*, ¶¶ 48–49.

[80] *Shrimp, supra* note 71, ¶¶ 79–91.

rights of the past century. Like its earlier counterpart, this modern-day movement seeks to empower the weak and vulnerable.[81] However, the human rights movement grew in response to the abuse of public power, while the values movement of today seeks to address imbalances in economic power associated with the globalization of markets and workplaces. Today's movement seeks to ensure that needy individuals, peoples, and countries are not only protected from market abuses, but affirmatively benefit from market gains.

The normative framework of the new movement builds upon human rights law yet differs in its orientation and effect. Human rights law has traditionally focused upon State obligation, in both negative and positive terms, with relatively recent attention to the roles of non-state actors.[82] In contrast, the emerging framework of values for governing trade and labor activities stresses shared responsibility among public and private actors for the processes and outcomes of globalization in markets and society. While the primary responsibility of States, and state actors, is still recognized, the new system calls for commitment and effort by the entire international community. This community, which is voluntarily coming together on the basis of common values, includes a wide variety of actors, from international and regional public organizations and local authorities to businesses, unions, the media, and religious and other civil society groups.

The shared responsibility of all actors that marks today's movement reflects the distinctive premise that everyone in society and the market stand to benefit from a values-based governance of economic activity. In this respect, the focus on intended beneficiaries of the human rights system and the modern approach differs. While both systems seek to benefit individuals and peoples, today's quest for values in globalization aims at strengthening the governance of States themselves as well as the effective functioning of markets. This approach draws upon emerging norms of accountability in international law in aiming to transform the relationships, rules and systems that dominate the worlds of work and trade.

B. Ordering Priorities

The emerging values-based foundation for international cooperation encourages interdependence and coherence among trade, work and other economic and social activities

---

[81] Responding to unprecedented abuses of public power in World War II, the human rights movement recognized and applied the basic values of humanity in establishing a universal, rules-based framework to protect individuals and peoples from the State, and from each other. *See, e.g.*, P.H. Kooijmans, *Human Rights—Universal Panacea?* 37 NETHERLANDS INT'L L. REV. 315 (1990).

[82] State obligations in human rights law are commonly understood as a multi-faceted commitment to respect, protect and fulfill human rights. Asbjorn Eide, *Economic, Social and Cultural Rights as a Human Right* in ECONOMIC, SOCIAL, AND CULTURAL RIGHTS: A TEXTBOOK 21–40 (A. Eide, Catarina Kraus, and Allan Rosas eds., 1995). Human rights theory has expanded the focus on the role and responsibility of non-state actors in a duties-based approach. UDHR, *supra* note 52, Article 29. *See also* Erica Daes, *Status of the Individual and Contemporary International Law*, UN Doc. E/CN.4/Sub.2/1989/40; Andrew Clapham, HUMAN RIGHTS IN THE PRIVATE SPHERE 343–56 (Ian Brownlie, ed., 1993); *Duties sans Frontiéres: Human Rights and Global Social Justice* (Int'l. Council on Human Rights Policy, 2003) available on-line at www.ichrp.org/ac/excerpts/137.pdf Nonetheless, enforcement mechanisms for holding non-state actors directly accountable for commission of human rights abuses are found primarily in international criminal law. "Since the latter half of the nineteenth century it has been generally recognized that there are acts or omissions for which international law imposes criminal responsibility on individuals and for which punishment may be imposed, either by properly empowered international tribunals or by national courts and military tribunals." Ian Brownlie, PRINCIPLES OF PUBLIC INTERNATIONAL LAW 565 (1998). A recent effort within the UN human rights system to broaden enforcement to civil responsibility remains controversial and, to date, inconclusive. *See Draft Norms on the Responsibilities of Transnational Corporations and Other Business Enterprises with Regard to Human Rights*, UN Doc. E/CN.4/Sub.2/2003/12 (2003).

of a globalizing world. In cases of conflict or trade-off, a balancing of the competing priorities based on universally-recognized social expectations and needs leads to greater synergy between international requirements and local needs. Applying a shared values framework contributes to resolving conflicts over social values in trade negotiations, international economic policy making, and the trade disputes.

The mandate for coherence finds support in a growing presumption that there need be no policy contradiction between an open, non-discriminatory and equitable multilateral trading system, on the one hand, and contemporary non-trade-specific concerns of the international community on the other. At the WTO policy level, the importance and legitimacy of strategies of development and poverty reduction beyond trade openness have been explicitly acknowledged. Ministerial Decisions and Appellate Body rulings have highlighted the social values enshrined in the WTO Agreement Preamble relating to the environment and sustainable development.[83]

Further support for the use of a values framework is found in the interpretation of trading rules. Obligations under the international trade regime are to be clarified "in accordance with the customary rules of interpretation of public international law".[84] The modern international conventions and declarations giving expression to international social values are thus considered a relevant part of the broader legal context for inter-pretation of the treaty rules which embody these concepts.[85] Indeed, application of a framework of shared values has proved dispositive in some cases and has encouraged predictability and fairness in determining when a State may autonomously pursue a pol-icy choice subject to challenge as inconsistent with trade rules. In the *Asbestos* case, for example, a challenged measure was considered, in purpose and application, to be consistent with commonly agreed values that informed trade rules, and the measure at issue was considered sustainable.[86] However, as demonstrated in the *Shrimp* case, if a

---

[83] E.g., *Shrimp, supra* note 71, ¶ 129. A similar presumption is reflected in the mandate of the Committee on Trade and the Environment. Decision on Trade and Environment, supra note 71, preamble, also noting *Rio Declaration, supra* note 49, *cited in Shrimp, supra* note 71, ¶ 151, note 146 ("'[c]onsidering that there should not be, nor need be, any policy contradiction between upholding and safeguarding an open, non-discriminatory and equitable multilateral trading system on the one hand, and acting for the protection of the environemtn, and the promotion of sustainable development on the other").

[84] *DSU, supra* note 33, Article 3(2). That provision is seen as a measure of recognition that the General Agreement on Tariffs and Trade is not to be read in clinical isolation from public international law. For an application of the mandate, *see, e.g., United States—Standards for Reformulated and Conventional Gasoline ("Gasoline")*, Report of the Appellate Body (WT/DS2) (1996), at 15–16 (turning to a basic principle of treaty interpretation based in customary and treaty law to analyze Article XX in context and the meaning of specific provisions of Article XX (g)). *See* also *Shrimp, supra* note 71, ¶¶ 158, 131, applying the principle of good faith and effectiveness in treaty interpretation, respectively.

[85] Where concepts embodied in a treaty are "by definition, evolutionary" their interpretation requires resort to modern international conventions and declarations. *Shrimp, supra* note 71, ¶ 130, applying the principle to interpret GATT, The reference in Article XX(g) to "natural resources", *quoting Namibia (Legal Conse-quences) Advisory Opinion* (1971), I.C.J. Rep., at 31: "An international instrument has to be interpreted and applied within the framework of the entire legal system prevailing at the time of the interpretation".

[86] This type of result occurred in the Asbestos case, which reviewed a challenge against France's public health measure which targeted an objective that was higher than relevant international requirements. *European Communities—Measures Affecting Asbestos and Asbestos-Containing Products*, Report of the Appellate Body, WT/DS135/AB/R (2001) ("Asbestos"). The measure was deemed, in relevant part, to not be a disguised protectionist measure since it had been taken at the insistence of the public in democratic fashion. *E.g., id.,* ¶ 8.238. Critical to the analysis was the panel's decision that it could not question France's autonomy in setting this objective by democratic process. See *id.,* note 176 and accompanying ¶ 8.210 (XX(b) of GATT does not impose same constraints as Article 3.3 of SPS Agreement on Members wishing to apply measures that involve a level of protection higher than that obtained by basis on relevant international standards).

measure conforms with commonly agreed values in one respect but not another, it may still be found objectionable.[87]

While environmental and social values have been the subject of dispute settlement, no disputes have squarely turned specifically on labor or employment values. None has invoked the only explicit reference to labor found in the Article XX exceptions.[88] Yet the approach that has been adopted, one in which evolving concepts embodied in trading obligations are interpreted consistently within the broader legal context, logically lends itself to giving priority to internationally-agreed goals of decent work when conflicts arise.[89] The major planks of the social floor of decent work qualify for such prioritization as they reflect commonly-agreed ethical values of widespread application[90] as may even be said to contribute to the evolution of obligations *erga omnes*[91] Other pillars of decent work, such as promoting full employment and raising standards of living through social protection, are recognized as explicit policy objectives in the WTO Agreement itself.[92] While these objectives have not been the subject of dispute settlement to date, there is no evident reason to treat them differently than those objectives involving protection of the environment and sustainable development.

[87] In *Shrimp*, a measure was found consistent with universal values in purpose, but not in application. Shrimp, *supra* note 71, ¶¶ 166–72. The U.S. measure at issue in *Shrimp* was consistent on its face with the international community's value expressed in a number of international instruments calling for environmental respect and conservation of nature, yet its application was found inconsistent with the value placed by the international community on bilateral or multilateral cooperation in achieving the substantive objective. The Appellate Body reasoned in part that, although the measure itself fell within the exception of Article XX(g), the highly selective pursuit by the United States of negotiations to establish consensual means of protecting and conserving the marine resources at issue constituted unjustifiable discrimination against excluded WTO members that exported shrimp to the United States.

[88] *See GATT, supra* note 8, Article XX(e) (measure relating to the products of prison labor).

[89] For a discussion of decent work, see *supra* note 4.

[90] The fundamental principles and rights at work apply at constitutional level across all ILO member states, *see supra* note 2, and share common ground with human rights imperatives of the UN chapter, *supra* note 52, at Arts. 55 and 56, This broad-based consensus within and across countries offers additional weight to a challenged State measure that is consistent with the Declaration's expression of the international community's values.

[91] Obligations *erga omnes* arise from fundamental principles necessary for humanity and concern the universal enforceability of norms of international law, the violation of which is deemed to be an offence not only against the state directly affected by the breach, but also against all members of the international community. P. Malanczuk, Akehurst's MODERN INTRODUCTION TO INTERNATIONAL LAW 58–59 (1997), noting that the ICJ has so far not addressed the legal consequences of breach of such obligations. *Erga omnes* obligations, such as those bearing on human rights, have been viewed as more compelling for multilateral enforcement than those that would involve responsibility to other states seeking to espouse commercial rights, for example, of foreign investors. *See, e.g.*, C. Wilfred Jenks, *The General Welfare as a Legal Interest* in JUS ET SOCIETAS: ESSAYS IN TRIBUTE TO WOLFGANG FRIEDMANN 151–58 (1979). For ICJ dictum on the subject, *see Barcelona Traction. Light and Power Co., Ltd.*, (Belgium v. Spain), Judgment, I.C.J. Reports, 1970, at 3. Such rules rest upon general principles of international law calling for the primacy of *erga omnes* obligations in cases of conflict. For example, peremptory norms of international law prevail over conflicting treaty provisions. *Vienna Convention on the Law of Treaties*, May 23, 1969, Article 53, 1155 U.N.T.S. 331, U.N.Doc. A/CONF.39/27 (1969) (a treaty is void if, at time of conclusion, it conflicts with peremptory norm; such norms are accepted and recognized by the international community of States as a whole as a norm from which no derogation is permitted). *See* IV ENCYC. OF PUBLIC INTERNATIONAL LAW 938 (1999); *UNIDROIT Principles, supra* note 49, at Article 1.1, Comment, ¶¶ 2, 3 (both public and private law rules of mandatory character enacted by States may prevail over contracting principles).

[92] *WTO Agreement, supra* note 5, at preamb. ¶ 1 ("with a view to raising standards of living and ensuring full employment"). See *supra* notes 71, 86 and accompanying text, discussing *Asbestos* and *Shrimp* cases.

V. Institutional Implications of a Cohesive Framework

In practice as well as principle, placing the goal of decent work in a central position in international economic policy making will serve to discipline and guide the growth that trade generates in the direction of more and better jobs as well as other conditions necessary to eliminate poverty. It also expands the openings for policy space at local levels to democratically pursue domestic economic and social strategies with the public good in mind.[93] Doing so requires normative innovations toward greater coherence in the governance and accountability of the three main types of actors: international organizations, states and non-state actors.

A. Coherence among National Policies in Trade and elsewhere

The structure of the multilateral trading regime presupposes a world in which trading activities are one part of a larger set of national policies in which, under certain safeguards, social or other policies may take priority over the fundamental principles governing trading obligations.[94] Yet the various interpretations applying these provisions are as yet unpredictable, reflecting the fact that few agreed standards exist at global level to govern the processes by which States exercise discretion in setting and applying the non-trade related objectives of Article XX.[95] Similarly, little guidance exists on how to apply

---

[93] *See generally* John Jackson, *Sovereignty, Subsidiarity, and Separation of Powers* in THE POLITICAL ECONOMY OF INTERNATIONAL TRADE LAW, 13–31 (Daniel L. M. Kennedy and James D. Southwick eds. 2002); Rodrik, *supra* note 30. Recently debate has arisen regarding trade rights and the rights of WTO Members to refuse genetically modified organisms ("GMOs"). For example, the Cartagena Protocol to the Convention on Biological Diversity allows for countries to refuse genetically altered food for a variety of reasons, including safety and the value of biological diversity to indigenous and local communities. *Cartagena Protocol on Biosafety to the Convention on Biological Diversity*, Jan. 29, 2000, Articles 1, 2, and 26, 39 I.L.M. 1027 (2000). Another important aspect of the debate centers on intellectual property rights and the obligations of states to respect, preserve and maintain collective knowledge of indigenous peoples and developing countries. *See, e.g., International Treaty on Plant and Genetic Resources for Food and Agriculture and the Convention on Biological Diversity*, Nov. 3, 2001, Article 1.1, <www.fao.org/Legal/TREATIES/033s-e.htm> (not yet entered into force); *Convention on Biological Diversity*, June 5, 1992, Article 8(j), 31 I.L.M. 818 (1992). Autonomy over matters in the public interest is also important for developed countries who have worked to pass stricter food safety and public health rules. *See generally* SPS Agreement, *supra* note 67.

[94] Consider, for example, the balance between trade and non-trade related policies in Article XX of the GATT, *supra* note 8. *See, e.g., Asbestos, supra* note 86 (asbestos-related prohibitions qualified under Article XX(b) as exception). *Accord, United States—Import Prohibition of Certain Shrimp and Shrimp Products—Recourse to Article 21.5 of the DSU by Malaysia*, Report of the Appellate Body, WT/DS58/AB/RW (2001), ¶ 153 (compliance merited exception for measure, particularly on-going serious good faith efforts to reach a multilateral agreement). *Cf. United States—Restrictions on Imports of Tuna (Tuna II)*, DS 29/R, June 10, 1994 (not adopted), ¶ 5.42 (sustainable development, though a widely recognized goal shared among parties, was insufficient to qualify trade embargo as an exception under Article XX. *See* Article XX cases discussed generally in Raj Bhala, *The Jurisprudence of GATT Article XX: (B) and (G)*, in INTERNATIONAL TRADE LAW: THEORY AND PRACTICE 2091 (2001); *Paul de Waart, Quality of Life at the Mercy of WTO Panels: GATT's Article XX an Empty Shell?* in INTERNATIONAL ECONOMIC LAW WITH A HUMAN FACE, 109–30 (Friedl Weiss, Erik M.G. Denters, Paul J.I.M. de Waart eds. 1998) ("HUMAN FACE").

[95] A number of decisions demonstrate that at the heart of the matter is the Organization's concern with the governance of State discretion over non-trade related objectives that may have trading effects. This concern for the scope and conditions under which governmental discretion is exercised underlies the analytical emphasis restricting the application of the "necessary to" or "relating to" prongs of the Article XX tests. *E.g., Thailand—Restrictions on Importation of and International Taxes on Cigarettes*, BISD 37 S/200–228, November 7, 1990 ("*Thai Cigarettes*") ("necessary to" requirement is only met if no other reasonable alternative is available). Similar concerns underlie analyses under Article XX chapeau provisions. In these cases, the Dispute Settlement Body has sought to avert measures that are applied in a manner constituting arbitrary or

or interpret the provision in the ILO Fundamental Principles and Rights Declaration, which states that "labor standards should not be used for protectionist trade purposes, and . . . nothing in this Declaration and its follow-up shall be invoked or otherwise used for such purposes; in addition the comparative advantage of any country should in no way be called into question by this Declaration and its follow-up."[96] Read *in pari materia*, the references would appear to underscore the coherence between principles in trade and labor regimes. The first reference affirms the general principle against protectionism in the context of labor standards, as reflected in the WTO Singapore Declaration, while the second reference could be interpreted as emphasizing the fact that the commitments of the Declaration, which arise from the constitutional obligations of each Member State, represent a global social floor which is not to be subject to cross-border competition inherent in comparative advantage.[97]

The experiences above illustrate the need for clarifying international expectations on State responsibility for national policymaking in areas that are likely to have cross-border effects within the nexus between labor and trade. Responsible exercise of this type of autonomy depends largely upon effective governance structures within each Member State and extends beyond any one international organization's mandate.[98] While the outcomes of effective governance differ across national contexts, generally-established principles of State responsibility and effective governance help to enable participatory and accountable systems for using public resources, including labor, fiscal, and trading policies.[99]

unjustifiable discrimination between countries where the same conditions prevail, or to prevent a disguised restriction on international trade. *Shrimp, supra* at ¶ 145 ("close and real" relationship between means and ends found to satisfy "relating to" prong of Article XX (g)). Reflecting similar concerns, applications of the Article XX chapeau provisions have sought to "maintain a balance of rights and obligations between the right of a Member to invoke one . . . of the exceptions of Article XX . . . and the substantive rights of the other Members under [the trading system]." *Shrimp, supra* note 71, at ¶ 160. In seeking this balance, the standards of the chapeau are considered to be "*necessarily broad in scope and reach*" and, "when applied in a particular case, the actual contours and contents of [the chapeau] standards will vary as the kind of measure under examination varies." *Shrimp, supra* note 71, at ¶ 123 (emphasis supplied) (explaining *e.g.*, that the standard of arbitrary discrimination could be different for a measure involving public morals than for one involving products of prison labor). Several cases have involved the definitional boundaries of the objectives themselves, *e.g., Shrimp, supra* note 71 (clarifying meaning of "exhaustive natural resources" under Article XX(g)). Formally, no challenges have been filed involving measures relating to products of prison labor under Article XX(e).

[96] See Article 5, *ILO Fundamental Principles, supra* note 4. While no mechanism for formal challenges under Article 5 exists, perceived risks to comparative advantage may influence, in certain cases, governmental decisions concerning relevant law and practice, and negotiation of bilateral and other economic treaties.

[97] *WTO Singapore Declaration supra* note 36, reproduced in the Appendix to this book. The Fundamental Principles Declaration "[d]eclares that all Members, even if they have not ratified the Conventions in questions, have an obligation arising from the very fact of membership in the Organization to respect, to promote and realize, in good faith and in accordance with the Constitution, the principles concerning the fundamental rights which are the subject of those Conventions." *Id.* at Article 3.

[98] A cohesive framework for sharing responsibility based on universal values incorporates expectations for such governance among State actors, built upon mechanisms for transparency, participation and accountability. See *supra* note 72.

[99] Effective governance of states is a process based on transparent, responsible, accountable and participatory government operating under the rule of law. *E.g., CHR Resolution* 2002/76, *supra* note 72; *Copenhagen Dec., supra* note 3, at ¶ 26(n), and *Programme of Action,* ¶ 14(b). *See also* OUR COMMON FUTURE, *supra* note 49, at Annexe, Principle 6; *The Earth Charter, supra* note 52, at Principle 13. Institutions of effective governance include, but are not limited to, electoral systems for periodic and genuine elections, an independent judiciary, a transparent and accessible legislature, and participatory systems for effective management of public resources. *See, e.g., Monterrey Consensus, supra* note 52, at I (9); II (15) *Vienna Dec., supra* note 52, at I (27); and *UDHR, supra* note 52, at preamb. ¶ 3.

B. Coordination of Mandates among International Organizations

Rarely is coordination with other specialized regimes mandated expressly within an international organization's charter.[100] In this regard, WTO and ILO are no exception. As international organizations, their governance, based on the rule of law, comprises interconnected domains including relationships with Member States, third/external parties, and each other. While the charters of the two organizations bear no express mandates for coordination with each other, such mandates can arguably be implied, particularly in the context of relationships with other international economic institutions. WTO has the duty to pursue consistent and mutually supportive policies with other international institutions responsible for monetary and financial matters through cooperation with them.[101] While follow-up of this mandate delivered at Marrakesh has focused primarily on WTO's relationship with IMF and the World Bank,[102] the coherence mandate more broadly targets the need for complementary and supportive policies to strengthen the relationship between trade liberalization as an engine for growth, and other economic policies affecting growth and development.[103] The development dividends of national and international economic policies that promote employment, transferable skills and other conditions for decent work are vital to making market access meaningful as well as distributing market gains more broadly.

In turn, the ILO possesses a mandate to examine and consider all international economic and financial policies and measures in light of the fundamental objective of attaining conditions necessary for social justice.[104] As with WTO's coherence mandate, ILO responsibility is presumably exercised in accordance with the subsidiarity principle

---

[100] International organizations exercise authority effectively when they operate within the powers and responsibilities granted to them. The functions and powers, express or implied, of international organizations are limited; they are defined by constituent instruments, decisions and resolutions adopted in accordance with them, and established practices. The Organization has an obligation to carry out its functions and exercise its powers in accordance with the rules set down under this authority. *E.g., Vienna Convention on the Law of Treaties between States and International Organizations or Between International Organizations*, March 21, 1986, Article 1(j), 25 I.L.M. 543; *Reparation for Injuries Suffered in the Service of the United Nations*, 1949 I.C.J. 174 (Advisory Opinion) ("*Reparations Case*"); *International Status of Southwest Africa*, 1950 I.C.J. 128 (Advisory opinion); *Certain Expenses of the United Nations*,1962 I.C.J. 151 (Advisory Opinion) ("*Certain Expenses*"). *See also* International Law Association, Committee on Accountability of International Organizations, Third Report Consolidated, Revised and Enlarged Version of Recommended Rules and Practices (New Delhi Conference, 2002), Section I, available on-line at http://www.ila-hq.org/pdf/Accountability/Accountability%20Of%20International%20Organisations%202002.pdf ("*Accountability of Int'l Orgs. Third Report*").

[101] *Declaration of the World Trade Organisation to Achieving Greater Coherence in Global Economic Policymaking*, Ministerial Decisions and Declarations adopted by the Trade Negotiations Committee on 15 December 1993, reprinted in THE LEGAL TEXTS: THE RESULTS OF THE URUGUAY ROUND OF MULTILATERAL TRADE NEGOTIATIONS 386 (WTO, 1999) ("*WTO Coherence Declaration*"), ¶ 5. The Declaration recognizes that international coherence is subsidiary to national-level pursuit of harmony between economic policies. *Id.*, ¶¶ 1–4. This coherence is to be achieved under the subsidiarity principle with deference to national jurisdiction: "While the task of achieving harmony between these policies is seen to fall primarily on governments at the national level, their coherence internationally is an important and valuable element in increasing the effectiveness of these policies at national level." *Id.*, ¶ 1.

[102] See *Coherence Note, supra* note 29 (cooperation in policy, research, and technical assistance).

[103] Punta del Este Mandate, Preamble and Part A (Objectives) (20 September 1986), cited in *Coherence Note, supra* note 29, at Annex 1, ¶ 4.

[104] *Declaration of Philadelphia, supra* note 18, Article II. The ILO is mandated to cooperate fully with international bodies entrusted with a share of the responsibility for international and national action to secure fuller use of the world's productive resources necessary to achieve social justice and peace, including measures to expand production and consumption, avoid severe economic fluctuations, and assure greater stability in world prices of primary products and promote international trade. *Id.* at Article IV.

granting to national jurisdiction a primary role in achieving harmony in economic and social policymaking.[105] Follow-up to this mandate within ILO has involved research cooperation,[106] participation in the World Bank process of Poverty Reduction Strategy Papers,[107] and development of the follow-up to the Declaration on Fundamental Principles and Rights at Work.[108] The terms of reference of the ILO-convened World Commission on the Social Dimension of Globalization further this mandate to seek ways to make economic and social policies and goals mutually reinforcing.[109]

In addition to implied mandates for coherence, general rules of international law also support a level of policy and operational consistency between WTO and ILO. As subjects of international law,[110] both organizations operate under general rules of international law that recognize the principle of internal coherence within public international law, and the particular priority to be given to obligations involving fundamental human and workers' rights.[111]

C. Beyond Coherence to Accountability

Beyond coherence in principle, mechanisms are needed in practice to ensure the accountability of international organizations, including WTO and ILO, to each other, their Member States, and third parties to operate consistently with common underlying global values. Evolving recommended rules and practices for the effective governance of international organizations contemplate transparent, participatory and rules-based decision making, procedural attributes which help to secure participation by Member States on

---

[105] *Compare, e.g., WTO Coherence Declaration, supra* note 101, with *Employment Policy Convention, supra* note 22, Article 2(a). Article 2 of the Employment Policy Convention directs States Parties to adopt measures to promote full, productive and freely chosen employment "within the framework of a co-ordinated economic and social policy".

[106] *See, e.g., Country Studies on the Social Dimension of Globalization: Final Report*, ILO Doc. No. GB.276/WP/SDL/1 (Nov. 1999); *Overview of Global Developments and Office Activities Concerning Codes of Conduct, Social Labelling and Other Private Sector Initiatives Addressing Labour Issues*, ILO Doc. No. GB.273/WP/SDL/1 (Nov. 1998).

[107] *E.g., Poverty Reduction Strategy Papers (PRSPs), An Assessment of the ILO's Experience*, ILO Doc. No. GB.283/ESP/3 (March 2002).

[108] See *supra* notes 9, 37, 100–101.

[109] The objectives of the Commission are to identify policies for globalization which reduce poverty, foster growth, employment and development in open economies, and widen opportunities for Decent Work; to identify policies which can make globalization more inclusive, in ways which are acceptable and seen to be fair to all, both between and within countries; and to assist the international community forge greater policy coherence in order to advance both economic and social goals in the global economy. See *Enhancing the Action of the Working Party on the Social Dimension of Globalization: Next Steps*, ILO Doc. No. GB.282/WP/SDG/1 (Nov. 2001), ¶¶ 9–11; *Report of the Working Party on the Social Dimension of Globalization: Report by the Chairperson of the Working Party, Ambassador Jean-Jacques Elmiger of Switzerland*, GB.282/12 (Nov. 2001), ¶¶ 11, 13.

[110] The legal personality of an international organization depends upon its constituent treaty, and exists with the limits of the Organization's purpose and functions. Once international legal personality is conferred, the Organization enjoys specific rights and exercises certain obligations. *E.g., Reparations Case, supra* note 67. *See also* II ENCYCL. PUBLIC INT'L LAW, *supra* note 61, at 1299.

[111] Authoritative expert declarations have confirmed the priority of human rights in the conduct of international organizations. *Maastricht Guidelines on Economic, Social and Cultural Rights*, 15 NETH. QUARTERLY OF H. RTS., 244–52 (1997); 20 H. RTS. QUARTERLY 3, ¶ 19 (1998) (crucial for international organizations to correct their policies and practices so that they do not result in deprivation of ESC rights). *See also UDHR, supra* note 52, at Article 28 (everyone is entitled to a social and internal order in which the rights and freedoms set forth in this Declaration can be fully realized).

the basis of functional equality and, as possible, participation by non-state actors.[112] Sound governance procedures encourage meaningful access and participation by both state and private actors within the international community. They help to guide the policies and practices of international organizations such as ILO and WTO consistently with the emerging framework of common values developed by the international community, even in areas of accountability beyond legal responsibility.[113]

The accountability of the ILO and WTO directly to the people whom their mandates are intended to serve is essential to coordinating labor and trade with other economic policies and practices at global and local levels. International organizations with international legal personality exercise certain rights and responsibilities that are reasonably well-settled in the contexts of internal accountability and responsibility for binding acts.[114] However, the responsibility of international organizations to third parties is not subject to judicial review in national or international courts absent consent to be sued, as in treaties or arbitral clauses of agreements, or in keeping with the rules of international law for internationally wrongful acts.[115] In practice, certain international institutions are developing self-governance mechanisms that permit claims by people directly and adversely affected by the organization's operations. The most long-standing practice in this regard—still only a decade old—involves the operation of independent inspection mechanisms by the World Bank and several regional multilateral development banks.[116] In some instances, these types of mechanisms have encouraged greater public participation in decision-making and administration, and greater respect for human and peoples' rights.[117]

A further frontier for ensuring accountability among global actors involves the responsibility of member States to protect the rights of third parties in situations where the States act collectively through international organizations. Whether States have concurrent or

---

[112] *Accountability of Int'l Orgs. Third Report, supra* note 100. *See also* Christian Dominicé, *Organisations Internationales et Démocratie* in THE INTERNATIONAL LEGAL SYSTEM IN QUEST OF EQUITY AND UNIVERSALITY / L'ORDRE JURIDIQUE INTERNATIONAL, UN SYSTÈME EN QUETE D'ÉQUITÉ ET D'UNIVERSALITÉ, LIBER AMICORUM GEORGES ABI-SAAB 731–743 (L. Boisson de Chazournes and V. Gowlland-Debbas eds. 2001).

[113] *See discussion infra* notes 114–117 and accompanying text.

[114] The legal responsibility of an international organization with international legal personality encompasses internal accountability and judicial review for binding acts. On internal accountability to its staff and member states, *see generally Certain Expenses, supra* note 67. On judicial review, *see, e.g.*, Elihu Lauterpacht, *Judicial Review of the Acts of International Organizations* in INTERNATIONAL LAW, THE INTERNATIONAL COURT OF JUSTICE AND NUCLEAR WEAPONS 92–102 (L. Boisson de Chazournes and Philippe Sands eds. 1999).

[115] Legal responsibility to third parties for internationally wrongful acts is based upon the fact that international organizations are, by their very nature, subjects of international law. II ENCY. OF PUBLIC INT'L LAW, *supra* note 90, at 1318 ff. Legal responsibility to external third parties to ensure compliance with principles and rules, and in cases of liability for damage caused by its own acts, is commonly accepted to be governed as agreed by treaty and without prejudice to the rules of international law. *See, e.g., Treaty on the Principles Governing the Activities of States in the Exploration and Use of Outer Space, Including the Moon and Other Celestial Bodies*, Jan. 27, 1967, Article VI, 610 U.N.T.S. 205 ("*Outer Space Treaty*"); *United Nations Convention on the Law of the Sea*, December 10, 1982, Article 139, 1833 U.N.T.S. 3 (responsibility to ensure that the activities of international organizations are conducted in conformity with the treaty is on the organization and member states).

[116] In the World Bank Inspection Panel, complaints are received from one or more persons who claim to be directly and adversely affected by Bank-supported projects on grounds of the Bank's failure to abide by its own binding policies and procedures in design appraisal and implementation of projects it finances. Resolution 93–10 IBRD and Resolution 93–6 IDA, The World Bank Inspection Panel, Sept. 22, 1993.

[117] *See, e.g., Annual Report*: August 1, 2001 to June 30, 2002, Vol. I (Inspection Panel, IBRD and IDA, 2002).

subsidiary liability for fulfillment of international organization's obligations due solely to their membership is a matter of international law, to be determined by reference to rules of the Organization.[118] States' accountability for their own actions through international organizations is limited by the presumption against derivative liability of member States for the actions of the organization, members of an organization may be liable for its obligations in accordance with a relevant general principle of international law, such as acquiescence, or abuse of rights.[119] Practice in organizations administering common spaces may lend relevant analogies for the WTO and ILO. Expressly agreed by treaty in those instances, the organization and member States share collective responsibility to ensure compliance with governing principles and rules for cooperation in managing the resources of common spaces, and liability under certain conditions for damages due to non-compliance.[120] While neither WTO nor ILO operate within such frameworks of collective responsibility, these types of cooperative arrangements could ultimately offer a way to share responsibility with accountability across international organizations and States in managing the practical effects on growth, employment, income equity, and poverty related to the implementation of their mandates.

The theory of shared responsibility focuses not only on accountability of international organizations and States but also on the duties of non-state actors. Non-state actors bear duties to respect the rule of law and deal in good faith in a manner that facilitates market and workplace environments based on freedom and dignity.[121] These duties reflect the starting point for pursuit of new horizons in developing effective means for non-state actor accountability to shared global value systems. Dialogue among States, international organizations and market and workplace actors represents a first step toward the effective functioning of internationally-accepted social values in a trading world.

---

[118] The responsibility of an international organization is exercised separately from that of its Member States in the absence of express or implied consent to collective responsibility. *See* Brownlie, *supra* note 82, at 686–88.

[119] ANNUAIRE DE L' INSTITUT DE DROIT INTERNATIONAL, *The Legal Consequences for Member States of the Non-fulfilment by International Organizations of their Obligations toward Third Parties* 449, Vol. 66-II, Article 5 (1996).

[120] The collective responsibility extends to liability for damage caused by non-compliant activities, provided that the organization has declared that it accepts the rights and obligations of the relevant Liability Convention and that the majority of its members are parties to both the liability Convention and the underlying treaty. *See Convention on International Liability for Damage Caused by Space Objects*, March 29, 1972, Article XXII, 961 U.N.T.S. 187, referencing responsibility for activities under *Moon Treaty and Outer Space Treaty, supra* note 115.

[121] Well-functioning markets depend for success on respect for the rule of law, good faith dealings, absence of corruption and presence of transparency and accountability, and a culture of decent work. On respect for law, *see Copenhagen Programme of Action, supra* note 4, ¶ 14(b); *Johannesburg Declaration,* ¶ 29 and *Organization for Economic Cooperation and Development Declaration on International Investment and Multi-National Enterprises* ("OECD Guidelines on MNEs"), June 21, 1976 ¶ II(5), DAFFE/IME(200) 20; ILO *Tripartite Declaration of Principles Concerning MNEs and Social Policy* (adopted 1977 and amended November 17, 2000), ¶ 8, 41 I.L.M. 186 (2000). On good faith dealings, *see, e.g., UN Sales Convention*, A/CONF.97/19, Article 8 (1980); *UNIDROIT Principles of International Commercial Contracts, supra* note 58, at Article 1.3; II ENCYCL. OF PUBLIC INT'L LAW 1995, *supra* note 90, at 599. On corrupt practices, *see* prohibitions in OECD Convention on Combating Bribery of Foreign Public Officials in International Business Transaction, Nov. 21, 1997, OECD/IME/BR(97)20; *OECD Guidelines on MNEs*, Chapter VI, OECD/GD(97)40 (1997); *UN Convention Against Transnational Organized Crime*, Jan. 8, 2001, Articles 7, 9, A/RES/55/25. Supportive rules-based relationships, built on public law and policy and on partnerships across public and private sectors, help markets operate for public good and achieve fairer distribution of resources and benefits. *See also* Oscar Schacter, *The Erosion of State Authority and its Implications for Equitable Development*, in HUMAN FACE, *supra* note 94, at 36–38.

VI. CONCLUSION

The long-standing deficit in coherent governance of international economic activities has provoked calls for improved coordination across international trade, financial, development and labor regimes, as envisioned at the outset of the modern multilateral system. The dislocation has left unfulfilled, particularly in developing countries, the promise that liberalized trading systems will lead to more productive employment and higher standards of living. Social values contribute to cohesion by building common expectations and priorities in markets and the workplace, both nationally and increasingly at global level. International instruments reflect a broadening consensus that markets must incorporate shared values that enable progress toward fundamental objectives like freedom, dignity, equity and peace.

The emerging values-based foundation for international cooperation offers a means for developing interdependence and coherence among labor, trade and other economic and social priorities of a globalizing world. A growing presumption that trade and non-trade related aims need not be contradictory is evident in specific instances of policy making and dispute settlement. While environmental, health and development-based values have led the way, the prioritization of labor rights and decent work policies is likewise merited in cases where globally-shared values are implicated. In practice, giving equal priority to labor and employment values will help guide the growth that trade generates in the direction of more and better jobs, and contribute to eliminating poverty. Recent trends in policy negotiation and dispute settlement have invoked shared values in opening necessary policy spaces at national level for the democratic pursuit of economic and social strategies with particular local needs in mind.

While coordination of national policies and international organization mandates appears feasible in principle, more and better accountability mechanisms are required to bring the international system, including labor and trade regimes, into harmony with the globally-declared values that the system is intended to serve. Market and social actors, along with public authorities, will need to be held accountable for their influence and conduct among each other and with States and international organizations. While a coherent system of global governance is still evolving, the time for interdependence is approaching as widely-shared social values inform policy making, dispute settlement, and private transactions within markets, workplaces and society.

CHAPTER 61

TRADE AND HUMAN RIGHTS I

Ernst-Ulrich Petersmann*

TABLE OF CONTENTS

* Joint Chair Professor for Public Law and Policy at the European University Institute and its Robert
Schuman Center in Florence, Italy. Former Professor at the University of Geneva and its Graduate Institute
of International Studies, and former legal advisor in the German Ministry of Economic Affairs, GATT and
the WTO.

I. Introduction: A "Human Rights Approach" to International Trade?

From the 1648 peace treaties of Westphalia to the 1945 U.N. Charter, public international law has evolved as a system of reciprocal rights and obligations among states based on sovereign equality and non-intervention into the internal affairs of states.[1] The state-centered U.N. Charter, and its collective security system established by the victorious powers of World War II,[2] assert legal priority over other conflicting international treaties.[3] The one-sided focus of the traditional "international law of states" on the freedom and power of governments, rather than on the human rights of their citizens is, however, increasingly challenged by national parliaments and civil society groups as being incompatible with the universal recognition of inalienable human rights and with the need for democratic legislation protecting human rights and "democratic peace".[4]

From the perspective of human rights and constitutional democracies, the validity of inalienable human rights no longer depends on the consent of the rulers; democratic legitimacy of all governments and of intergovernmental organizations derives from the consent of their citizens and from respecting and promoting their "constitutional contracts" and universally recognized, inalienable human rights. In case of conflicts, the inalienable core of human rights—especially in so far as they have become recognized as *ius cogens*—must be given priority over intergovernmental power politics, as acknowledged in Article 53 of the Vienna Convention on the Law of Treaties ("VCLT"). Citizens and civil society groups increasingly claim that, similar to the regional integration law in Europe and North America, the democratic legitimacy and effectiveness of the global integration law of the World Trade Organization ("WTO") could be enhanced by interpreting WTO rules as part of a democratic "international law of peoples",[5] and of a cosmopolitan "integration law of citizens",[6] rather than only as "international law among states".

The Agreement establishing the WTO establishes rights and obligations for states and other "members" (like the EC) to liberalize market access barriers and market distortions "with a view to raising standards of living, ensuring full employment, and a large and steadily growing volume of real income and effective demand, and expanding the production of and trade in goods and services, while allowing for the optimal use of the world's resources in accordance with the objective of sustainable development" (Preamble). As goods and services are produced and consumed by individuals, WTO dispute settlement panels have emphasized that "one of the primary objects of the GATT/WTO . . . is to produce certain market conditions which would allow . . . individual activity to flourish" by protecting the international division of labor against discriminatory

---

[1] Article 2 U.N. Charter.

[2] Chapter VII, U.N. Charter.

[3] Article 103 U.N. Charter.

[4] On the emerging "human right to democratic governance" *see, e.g.,* T.M. Franck, *The Emerging Right to Democratic Governance*, 86 AMERICAN JOURNAL OF INTERNATIONAL LAW ("AJIL") 46–91 (1992); E. Stein, *International Integration and Democracy: No Love at First Sight*, 95 AMERICAN JOURNAL OF INTERNATIONAL LAW 489–532 (2001). On empirical evidence that democracies very seldom fight each other, and on the reasons why constitutional democracy and accountability tend to limit abuses of foreign and military policies, *see, e.g.,* P.K. Huth and T.L. Allee, THE DEMOCRATIC PEACE AND TERRITORIAL CONFLICT IN THE 20th CENTURY (2002).

[5] *Cf., e.g.,* J. Rawls, THE LAW OF PEOPLES (1999).

[6] *Cf., e.g.,* E.U. Petersmann, *Human Rights in European and Global Integration Law: Principles for Constitutionalizing the World Economy*, in FESTSCHRIFT FÜR C.D. EHLERMANN 383–402 (A. Bogdandy, P. Mavroidis and Y. Mény eds. 2002).

trade restrictions and other distortions.[7] Yet, the same dispute settlement panel also emphasized that "(n)either the GATT nor the WTO has so far been interpreted by GATT/WTO institutions as a legal order producing direct effect", *i.e.*, creating rights and obligations not only for WTO members but also direct individual rights for traders, producers and consumers.[8] In accordance with these intergovernmental structures and functionally limited economic objectives of GATT and the WTO, the words "human rights" are nowhere mentioned in the text of GATT 1947 and in the WTO Agreement. WTO obligations have been recognized as an "integral part of the Community legal order" inside the EC and have been incorporated into the domestic laws of many WTO members. But the EC Court of Justice—like the domestic courts of some other WTO members—has concluded from the intergovernmental structures and reciprocity principles of WTO law that the "purpose of the WTO agreements is to govern relations between States or regional organizations for economic integration and not to protect individuals" which, as a consequence, "cannot rely on them before the courts and . . . any infringement of them will not give rise to non-contractual liability on the part of the Community."[9]

All 146 WTO Members have accepted obligations to respect, protect and fulfill human rights under international law as well as under their respective domestic laws. All WTO Members have also recognized, for instance in various U.N. resolutions like the 1948 Universal Declaration of Human Rights ("UDHR"), that "[e]veryone is entitled to a social and international order in which the rights and freedoms set forth in this Declaration can be fully realized".[10] If, as universally recognized in Principle 1 of the "Stockholm Declaration" of the U.N. Conference on the Human Environment of 1972, "(m)an has the fundamental right to freedom, equality and adequate conditions of life, in an environment of a quality that permits a life of dignity and well-being", such rights and "sustainable development" must be protected in international relations no less than inside states.[11] Hence, the U.N. resolutions on the "right to development" define development in terms of fulfillment of basic needs and of human rights.[12] U.N. human rights bodies increasingly insist that all WTO Members should adopt a "human rights approach to trade" which:

    (i) sets the promotion and protection of human rights as objectives of trade liberalization, not exceptions;

    (ii) examines the effect of trade liberalization on individuals and seeks to devise trade law and policy to take into account the rights of all individuals, in particular vulnerable individuals and groups;

---

[7] *See United States—Sections 301–310 of the Trade Act of 1974*, Report of the Panel, WT/DS152/R, (2000), ¶¶ 7.73 *et seq.*

[8] *Id.* ¶ 7.72. The Panel makes the following important reservation: "The fact that WTO institutions have not to date construed any obligations as producing direct effect does not necessarily preclude that in the legal system of any given Member, following internal constitutional principles, some obligations will be found to give rights to individuals. Our statement of fact does not prejudge any decisions by national courts on this issue."

[9] According to the same judgment, "it is only where the Community intended to implement a particular obligation assumed in the context of the WTO, or where the Community measure refers expressly to the precise provisions in the WTO agreements, that it is for the Community judicature to review the legality of the Community measure in question in the light of the WTO rules", *cf. Etablissement Biret SA v. EU Council*, EC Court of Justice, Case T-210/00, 31 COMMON MARKET LAW REPORTS, 787 808 (2002), (¶¶ 71–73).

[10] Article 28 UDHR.

[11] *Cf.* M. Pallemaerts, *The Human Right to a Healthy Environment as a Substantive Right*, in HUMAN RIGHTS AND THE ENVIRONMENT 11–21 (M. Déjeant-Pons and M. Pallemaerts eds., 2002).

[12] *See, e.g.*, U.N. General Assembly Declaration 41/128 of December 4, 1986 on the "Right to Development".

(iii) emphasizes the role of states in the process of liberalization—not only as negotiators of trade law and setters of trade policy, but also as the primary duty bearers of human rights;

(iv) seeks consistency between the progressive liberalization of trade and the progressive realization of human rights;

(v) requires a constant examination of the impact of trade liberalization on the enjoyment of human rights;

(vi) promotes international cooperation for the realization of human rights and freedoms in the context of trade liberalization.[13]

This chapter shows that—as a result of the universal recognition of human rights in international treaty law and in general international law—human rights are relevant for the interpretation and application of WTO rules, especially for WTO guarantees of freedom, non-discrimination, rule of law, private property, access to courts, due process of law, and for the numerous WTO exceptions that permit restrictions of freedom of trade so as to protect human, animal or plant life or health, public morals and other "human rights values". Just as human rights law recognizes the need for protecting and mutually balancing human rights through non-discriminatory democratic legislation, international trade law, e.g., in the WTO Agreements Preamble, acknowledges its instrumental function for the promotion of non-economic policy goals, such as "raising standards of living", promoting "sustainable development" and "preserv(ing) the environment". The "balancing principles" in the "exception clauses" in international trade law—such as non-discrimination, necessity and proportionality of restrictions of individual freedom,[14] and rights of individual access to courts,[15] are similar to the "balancing principles" in the "exception clauses" in human rights treaties;[16] from a human rights perspective, both serve complementary functions for protecting individual freedom, non-discrimination and rule of law. Human rights and the corresponding obligations accepted by all WTO members require to interpret and design national and international trade rules—like other democratic legislation—as instruments for the promotion and protection of human rights, with due respect for the broad regulatory discretion of democratic legislatures and governments regarding the domestic implementation and balancing of human rights and of related WTO rules for the protection of freedom and non-discrimination in the international division of labor among producers, traders and consumers.

This contribution focuses on *international* human rights rather than on *domestic* human rights guarantees that may provide for additional obligations and legal requirements to take into account human rights in the domestic interpretation and application of WTO rules. Even though parliaments in constitutional democracies, such as the U.S. Congress, and civil society groups increasingly insist that WTO decision-making processes must become more transparent and, as expressed in the U.S. Trade Act of 2002, must respect the legislative intent of parliaments when they ratify WTO agreements, this chapter does not discuss the legal and political implications of the emerging "human right to democracy"

---

[13] Report of the High Commissioner for Human Rights on *Liberalization of Trade in Services and Human Rights*, document E/CN.4/Sub.2/2002/9, p. 2.

[14] *Cf.* Articles XX GATT, XIV GATS.

[15] *Cf., e.g.*, GATT Article X.

[16] *Cf., e.g.*, the indirect references to the principles of non-discrimination, necessity and proportionality in Article 4 of the 1966 International Covenant on Economic, Social and Cultural Rights ("ICESCR"): "The States Parties to the present Covenant recognize that, in the enjoyment of those rights provided by the State in conformity with the present Covenant, the State may subject such rights only to such limitations as are determined by law only in so far as this may be compatible with the nature of these rights and solely for the purpose of promoting the general welfare in a democratic society."

for the WTO, such as the need to promote transparent discussion and decision-making, more effective parliamentary control and democratic participation in WTO matters.[17]

II. Human Rights Obligations of WTO Members as Part of the Context for the Interpretation of WTO Rules

A. Human Rights Obligations of WTO Members

There exist today more than one hundred multilateral and bilateral international treaties on the protection of human rights.[18] For instance, as of 2002, 112 WTO member states had ratified the 1966 U.N. Covenant on Economic, Social and Cultural Human Rights ("ICESCR"), and all but the United States had ratified the 1989 U.N. Convention on the Rights of the Child. There are also hundreds of unanimous U.N. Resolutions, such as the Universal Declaration on Human Rights ("UDHR") and the 1993 Vienna Declaration on Human Rights, in which all U.N. member states have committed themselves to protect inalienable human rights as part of *general international law*. In addition, most states and some international organizations[19] recognize human rights in their respective constitutional laws as constitutional restraints on government powers, sometimes with explicit references to human rights as legal restraints also on the collective exercise of government powers in international organizations.[20]

The International Court of Justice ("ICJ") has recognized that all U.N. member states have legal obligations to respect human rights under the U.N. Charter and under general international law, and that at least some human rights constitute not only *individual rights* but also, in the case of universally recognized human rights, *erga omnes* obligations of governments.[21] The quasi-universal ratification of some human rights treaties, such as the U.N. Convention on the Rights of the Child ratified by 190 states, and the recognition in these treaties "of the equal and inalienable rights of all members of the human family" as set out in the UDHR,[22] reflects a worldwide *opinio iuris* on the *inalienable erga omnes* character of certain core human rights.

This *opinio iuris* on essential and inalienable core human rights is not contradicted by the diversity of views on the precise scope, meaning and *ius cogens* nature of many specific human rights whose legal definition in domestic constitutions, and implementation through democratic legislation and international agreements may legitimately differ from country to country and from treaty to treaty. In contrast to the EC Court of Justice which construed the common human rights guarantees of EC member states as constituting general constitutional principles limiting the regulatory powers also of the EC,[23]

---

[17] *Cf.* E.U. Petersmann, *European and International Constitutional Law: Time for Promoting Cosmopolitan Democracy in the WTO*, in THE EU AND THE WTO 81–110 (G. de Burca and J. Scott eds., 2001); S. Charnovitz, *WTO Cosmopolitics*, 34 NEW YORK UNIVERSITY JOURNAL OF INTERNATIONAL LAW AND POLITICS 299–354 (2002).

[18] *See, e.g.,* Council of Europe, HUMAN RIGHTS IN INTERNATIONAL LAW (2000).

[19] *Cf.* Article 6 of the EU Treaty.

[20] *See, e.g.,* Article 23 of the German Basic Law and Article 11 EU Treaty.

[21] *See, e.g., The Barcelona Traction* judgment, ICJ REPORTS 32 (1970), and the *Nicaragua* judgment, ICJ REPORTS 114 (1986).

[22] The quoted words are from the preamble to the 1989 U.N. Convention on the Right of the Child and, arguably, confirm the universal recognition of rights set out in the UDHR. *See* HUMAN RIGHTS IN INTERNATIONAL LAW, *supra* note 18, at 169.

[23] In *Internationale Handelsgesellschaft* (Case 11/70, ECR 1970, 1125,1134), the ECJ held that respect for human rights forms an integral part of the general principles of Community law: "the protection of such rights, whilst inspired by the constitutional traditions common to the Member States, must be ensured within the framework of the structure and objectives of the Community" (¶¶ 3–4).

the ICJ has not yet specified to what extent human rights entail constitutional limits also on the U.N., *e.g.*, the Security Council, and on Specialized U.N. Agencies. Likewise, the WTO jurisprudence has not yet clarified the impact of human rights, including the right to human health and food, on the interpretation of, for example, the intellectual property rights guaranteed in the WTO Agreement on Trade-Related Intellectual Property Rights ("TRIPS"), or on the numerous WTO exceptions protecting national policy autonomy for non-trade concerns. Closer cooperation between the WTO and U.N. Specialized Agencies could facilitate clarification of the extent to which human rights recognized in the law of the International Labor Organization ("ILO") and of the World Health Organization, and other international organizations, are relevant also for the interpretation and application of WTO rules.

As a result of the universal recognition of human rights, international law is increasingly confronted with the "constitutional problems" addressed in the human rights jurisprudence of the EC Court of Justice: What is the essential core of human rights that must be recognized today as *erga omnes* obligations and *ius cogens*? Can governments evade their human rights obligations by exercising government powers collectively in specialized international organizations? Can the legal supremacy of international law over national law remain effective and be judicially enforced if human rights are not effectively protected in all fields of international law? Can international courts ignore the worldwide experience of states that seems to demonstrate that the protection of human rights risks to remain ineffective without respect for complementary due process guarantees and other "constitutional principles" of rule of law, democratic governance and judicial review? How are we to interpret and, in case of conflict, reconcile "state sovereignty", "popular sovereignty" and "individual sovereignty" in a manner respecting the constitutional primacy of "inalienable" human rights?[24]

B. Limited WTO Jurisdiction and Customary International Law Rules for the Interpretation of WTO Law

Articles II and III of the WTO Agreement emphasize the limited jurisdiction of the WTO. Article II:1 provides:

> The WTO shall provide the common institutional framework for the conduct of trade relations among Members in matters related to the agreements and associated legal instruments included in the Annexes to this Agreement.

Article III:1 provides:

> The WTO shall facilitate the implementation, administration and operation, and further the objectives, of this Agreement and of the Multilateral Trade Agreements, and shall also provide the framework for the implementation, administration and operation of the Plurilateral Trade Agreements.

Article III:2 authorizes the WTO to "provide the forum for negotiations among its Members concerning their multilateral trade negotiations", and Article III:5 authorizes the WTO to "cooperate, as appropriate, with the International Monetary Fund and with the International Bank for Reconstruction and Development and its affiliated agencies". Article V:1 further requires "the General Council [to] make appropriate arrangements for effective cooperation with other intergovernmental organizations that have responsibilities related to those of the WTO". Yet, notwithstanding the few explicit references in

---

[24] *Cf.* E.U. Petersmann, *From State Sovereignty toward "Popular Sovereignty" and "Individual Sovereignty" in the International Relations Law of the EU?* in SOVEREIGNTY IN TRANSITION (N. Walker ed., 2003).

WTO provisions to other international organizations and international agreements concluded outside of the WTO, the jurisdiction of WTO bodies is essentially limited to the application and implementation of WTO rules. This is confirmed by Article 3.2 of the WTO Dispute Settlement Understanding ("DSU") which "serves to preserve the rights and obligations of Members under the covered agreements", and Article 7.1 DSU which limits the jurisdiction ("terms of reference") of dispute settlement panels to the examination "of the relevant provisions in . . . the covered agreement(s) cited by the parties to the dispute".

Government representatives in specialized international organizations sometimes appear to believe that governments retain sovereign powers to exclude human rights from the law of specialized agencies, for example from the interpretation of the "covered agreements" of WTO law. Despite the *lex posterior* and *lex specialis* rules for the relationships between successive international treaties[25] states cannot derogate from the *ius cogens* nature of the obligation of all national and international governments to respect the "inalienable" core of human rights.[26] The U.N. Charter likewise prescribes human rights obligations for all 197 U.N. member states, for example in Articles 55 and 56 which, in case of conflict, assert legal primacy over other international treaties.[27] The precise scope of the "inalienable" core of universally recognized human rights obligations remains controversial. U.N. human rights law,[28] and the jurisprudence of the EC Court of Justice and the European Court of Human Rights,[29] explicitly recognize that human rights entail obligations also for intergovernmental organizations. From a human rights perspective, all national and international rules—including economic agreements like the International Monetary Fund ("IMF") and WTO agreements that protect liberty, non-discrimination, property rights and other "human rights values" in transnational economic relations—derive their democratic legitimacy from protecting human rights which today constitutionally restrain all governmental and intergovernmental powers. Arguably, universally recognized "inalienable" human rights limit the powers not only of WTO members but also of intergovernmental WTO bodies.

General international law, as codified in Article 31.3 of the VCLT, requires interpreting international treaties "in their context", including "any relevant rules of international law applicable in the relations between the parties" such as universal human rights. Article 3 of the DSU imposes the requirement "to clarify the existing provisions of those agreements in accordance with customary rules of interpretation of public international law". Universally recognized human rights can be applied by WTO dispute settlement bodies as a relevant context for the interpretation and application of WTO rules, yet not as separate legal claims independent from applicable WTO rules.[30] They may be important for interpreting not only "general exceptions" such

---

[25] As laid down in Articles 30, 41 and 58 of the 1969 VCLT.

[26] *See* Article 53 VCLT.

[27] *Cf.* Article 103.

[28] *See, e.g.*, Article 28 of the UDHR, quoted in the introduction above.

[29] *Cf.* E.U. Petersmann, *Time for Integrating Human Rights into the Law of Worldwide Organizations*, Jean Monnet Working Paper 7/2001 (Harvard Law School), at 24–25.

[30] This follows from the limited terms of reference of WTO dispute settlement panels as stipulated in the DSU (*e.g.*, Article 7). *Cf.* G. Marceau, *The WTO Dispute Settlement System and Human Rights*, 13 EUROPEAN JOURNAL OF INTERNATIONAL LAW 753–814 (2002), who rightly emphasizes that human rights and WTO rights and obligations are cumulatively binding on states, but are enforceable under different and complementary rules and procedures. Mainstream human rights specialists often overlook the limited scope of jurisdiction of WTO dispute settlement panels and misinterpret calls for interpreting WTO rules with due respect for

as GATT Article XX, but also the "objective of sustainable development" found in the WTO Agreement's Preamble, the basic guarantees of freedom found in GATT Articles I-XI, the WTO rules on non-discrimination, property rights, and individual access to courts, and the WTO's "necessity" requirements for safeguard measures restricting individual freedom of trade so as to protect "public interests" such as the respect for human rights.

The text of the WTO Agreement offers no indication of an intention of WTO Members to deviate from their human rights obligations. A good faith interpretation of WTO rules leads to a legal presumption that all WTO rules must be legally interpreted and applied consistent with the human rights obligations of WTO members. This is in line with the welfare-creating function of WTO rules, *i.e.*, to prohibit welfare-reducing trade restrictions and discrimination, subject to broad discretionary WTO exceptions designed to safeguard the sovereign rights of WTO members to "protect human, animal or plant life or health" and adopt other "measures necessary to protect public morals" or other public interests.[31] Both the welfare-increasing function of WTO rules and the numerous WTO exceptions suggest that, just as GATT dispute settlement practice has never identified a conflict between GATT rules and the human rights obligations of GATT contracting parties, conflicts between WTO obligations and human rights can and must be avoided by interpreting WTO rules and WTO decisions in conformity with the human rights obligations of WTO Members. The Doha Declaration on the TRIPS Agreement and Public Health of November 2001 illustrates the commitment of all WTO members to ensuring that the rules-based trading system remains compatible with public health interests and universally recognized human rights.[32]

The generously drafted "exceptions" in global and regional integration law, and the usually deferential jurisprudence of international dispute settlement bodies vis-à-vis national restrictions necessary for protecting public interests—such as import restrictions on asbestos and other products endangering human health,[33] confirm that, in cases of conflict, the essential core of human rights must prevail. As in EC law, the obligations of states to respect, promote and fulfill human rights must be recognized as extending also to their participation in worldwide organizations like the WTO. Neither the "progressive realization" commitment in Article 2 of the ICESCR,[34] nor the proviso in its Article 24 that "[n]othing in the present Covenant shall be interpreted as *impairing* the provisions of the Charter of the United Nations and of the constitutions of the specialized

---

universally recognized human rights as a "proposal for the enforcement of human rights through the WTO", *e.g.*, P. Alston, *Resisting the Merger and Acquisition of Human Rights by Trade Law*, 13 EUROPEAN JOURNAL OF INTERNATIONAL LAW 815 (2002).

[31] *See* Article XX GATT and Article XIV GATS.

[32] For the text and a discussion of the Doha Ministerial Declaration on the TRIPS Agreement and Public Health *see, e.g.,* WHO and WTO Secretariat, WTO AGREEMENTS AND PUBLIC HEALTH (2002), reproduced in the Appendix to this book.

[33] *See, e.g., EC—Import Restrictions Affecting Asbestos and Asbestos-Containing Products*, Report of the Appellate Body, WT/DS135/AB/R (2001).

[34] *Cf. General Comment No.3 on The Nature of States Parties Obligations (Art.2, ¶ 1 of the Covenant)*, adopted by the U.N. Committee on Economic, Social and Cultural Rights in 1990 and reproduced *e.g.*, in ECONOMIC, SOCIAL AND CULTURAL RIGHTS 442–445 (A. Eide, C. Krause and A. Rosas eds., 1995). The fact that the ICESCR formulates some rights in terms of *principles* rather than precise *rules* only indicates that some economic and social human rights, like certain civil and political rights (such as the right to vote), need to be concretized through implementing legislation and administrative or judicial decisions. On the distinction between *principles* and *rights see, e.g.,* R. DWORKIN, TAKING RIGHTS SERIOUSLY 23 *et seq.* (1977).

agencies" (emphasis supplied), can serve as pretexts for non-compliance by governments and international organizations with their human rights obligations.

C. Diversity of National and International Implementation of Human Rights

Human rights protect individual and democratic diversity, such as human dignity in the sense of the moral, rational and legal autonomy of individuals. This diversity of individual preferences, of "constitutional contracts" and human rights traditions at the national and international level, and of national forms of democracy, confirm that democratic legislatures must enjoy a broad "margin of appreciation" in regulating and mutually balancing human rights. International human rights jurisprudence, including that of the European Court of Human Rights, emphasizes the need to respect the regulatory discretion of domestic democratic institutions.[35]

The scarcity and uneven distribution of resources entail that protection of individual liberty, property and of other human rights inevitably gives rise to competition among utility-maximizing individuals (e.g., producers and consumers in economic markets, politicians and citizens in political markets), as well as among groups (e.g., competition among "rent-seeking" interest groups, "regulatory competition" among states so as to attract mobile international financial and other resources). The resulting conflicts of interests require a "limiting constitution" to limit abuses of power so as to protect human rights, as well as an "enabling constitution" to enable the individual and collective supply of private and public goods and services, in the economy no less than in the polity. Effective protection of human rights in, and of democratic control over, bi-level rule-making and policy-making at national and international levels requires constitutional limitations on abuses of private and public power not only inside states but also in international organizations.[36]

At the international level, the human rights guarantees in the six major worldwide U.N. human rights treaties,[37] and in the regional human rights treaties in Europe, Africa and in the Americas, differ from treaty to treaty. Each human rights treaty has set up its own institutions and its separate monitoring and implementation procedures, with at present inadequate coordination among these treaty systems.[38] The EC Treaty provides for comprehensive legal and judicial protection of fundamental individual "market freedoms", non-discrimination and social rights. Other regional integration agreements, such as NAFTA, and worldwide economic agreements, including the WTO Agreement, do not link their legal protection of market access and economic freedom to protection of human rights. Yet, as explained in Part III, the international guarantees in NAFTA and

---

[35] On the "margin of appreciation" doctrine in the case-law of the European Court of Human Rights *see* H.C. Yourow, THE MARGIN OF APPRECIATION DOCTRINE IN THE DYNAMICS OF EUROPEAN HUMAN RIGHTS JURISPRUDENCE (1996).

[36] This dependence of effective protection of human rights on national as well as "international constitutionalism" tends to be ignored by many human rights specialists, *e.g.*, Alston, *supra* note 30, and is explained in Petersmann, *Human Rights and International Economic Law in the 21ˢᵗ Century*, 4 (3) JOURNAL OF INTERNATIONAL ECONOMIC LAW 39 (2001).

[37] The 1966 Covenants on Civil and Political Rights ("ICCPR"), Economic, Social and Cultural Rights ("ICESCR") and on Elimination of all Forms of Racial Discrimination ("ICERD"), the 1980 Convention on the Elimination of all Forms of Discrimination against Women ("ICEDAW"), the 1984 Convention against Torture ("ICAT"), and the 1989 Convention on the Rights of the Child ("ICRC").

[38] *Cf.* C. Scott, *Institutional Integration of the Core Human Rights Treaties*, in GIVING MEANING TO ECONOMIC SOCIAL AND CULTURAL RIGHTS (I. Merali and V. Osterveld eds., 2001).

WTO rules of freedom of trade across frontiers, non-discrimination and rule of law can serve "human rights functions" by protecting individual freedom, non-discrimination, legal security and social welfare across frontiers. Economics demonstrates that "individual rights are a cause of prosperity";[39] economic welfare can be increased by the "successful struggle for rights of which the right to property is the most fundamental";[40] and "almost all of the countries that have enjoyed good economic performance across generations are countries that have stable democratic governments".[41] The U.N. Development Program[42] likewise emphasizes that national human rights and international legal protection of individual rights establish incentives for people to become not only "better democrats" but also to save, invest and become "better economic actors".

As long as so many areas of human rights, such as the nature and contents of economic and social human rights, and their interrelationships with other fields of international law which historically evolved without reference to human rights, remain controversial, any examination of the legal relevance of human rights for the law of the WTO risks being influenced by the particular human rights perspectives and "constitutional premises" of the interpreter (*e.g.*, as regards the "inalienable character" of core human rights). This entails legal uncertainty and suggests that WTO dispute settlement bodies must respect the diversity of human rights traditions and interpret the relevance of trade-related human rights with due deference to agreed U.N. human rights practice and to the margin of discretion of democratic legislatures.

D. Constitutional Primacy of Human Rights in International Law?

Numerous regional and worldwide human rights treaties and other human rights instruments, like the December 2000 Charter of Fundamental Rights of the EU,[43] commit states to "recognition of the inherent dignity and of the equal and inalienable human rights of all members of the human family [as] the foundation of freedom, justice and peace in the world".[44] Most national human rights instruments likewise recognize inalienable "birth rights" of every human being which precede and constitutionally limit government powers. Human dignity, in the sense of respect for the moral, rational, personal and legal autonomy of each individual to decide on one's personal goals in life, has become the common value premise of national and international human rights law.[45]

Human rights need to be legally specified, mutually balanced and implemented by democratic legislation which tends to vary from country to country. Their inalienable core, however, is "acknowledged" rather than "granted" by governments, as recognized

---

[39] M. Olson, POWER AND PROSPERITY 43 (2000).

[40] *See* R. PIPES, PROPERTY AND FREEDOM 291 (1999).

[41] Olson, *supra* note 39, at 187. *See, e.g.,* the annual reports on "Economic Freedom in the World" published by the Fraser Institute in Vancouver, which emphasize the empirical correlation between economic freedom, economic welfare, relatively higher average income of poor people and, with a few exceptions (such as Hong Kong), political freedom. Already Adam Smith's inquiry into the NATURE AND CAUSES OF THE WEALTH OF NATIONS (1776) concluded that the economic welfare of England was essentially due to its legal guarantees of economic freedom, property rights and legal security for investors, producers, traders and consumers.

[42] *Cf.* UNDP, HUMAN DEVELOPMENT REPORT 2000: HUMAN RIGHTS AND HUMAN DEVELOPMENT (2000).

[43] Reproduced in OFFICIAL JOURNAL OF THE EC, C 364/1 of December 18, 2000.

[44] Preamble of the UDHR.

[45] *See, e.g.,* Council of Europe, THE PRINCIPLE OF RESPECT FOR HUMAN DIGNITY (1999); HUMAN DIGNITY: THE INTERNATIONALIZATION OF HUMAN RIGHTS (A. Henkin ed., 1979).

in national as well as international legal practice: "Human dignity is inviolable. It must be respected and protected".[46] U.N. human rights conventions are explicitly based on "recognition of the inherent dignity and of the equal and inalienable rights of all members of the human family [as a] foundation of freedom, justice and peace in the world", and emphasize—like many national constitutions—that human rights "derive from the inherent dignity of the human person."[47] In U.N. practice, the "right to development" and the corresponding government obligations are defined in terms of the realization of all human rights.[48]

The legal consequences of the universal recognition of an "inalienable core" of human rights as, arguably, part of international *ius cogens* remain to be clarified. International legal practice, such as the 1998 ILO Declaration on Fundamental Principles and Rights at Work, confirms an increasing *opinio iuris* that membership in the U.N. and ILO entails a legal obligation to respect core human rights.[49] Dictatorial governments can no longer freely "contract out" of their human rights obligations by withdrawing from U.N. human rights covenants or ILO conventions.[50] Legal practice suggests that not only the prohibitions of genocide, slavery and apartheid, but also the core of other human rights must be respected even "in time of public emergency"[51] and have become *erga omnes* obligations of a *ius cogens* nature.[52]

E. Indivisibility and Incomplete Enumeration of Specific Human Rights?

Human rights instruments recognize an ever larger number of specific "civil", "political", "economic", "social" and "cultural" human rights in response to changing civil society demands and human rights problems. How can this dynamic evolution and diversity of human rights law be reconciled with the "inalienable" character of human rights? For instance, does the non-ratification by the United States of the ICESCR mean that economic and social human rights cannot be part of the legal context relevant for the interpretation of the WTO obligations of the United States? Does the non-ratification of the ICCPR by China have similar consequences for the interpretation of its WTO

---

[46] Article 1 of the Charter of Fundamental Rights of the European Union. Similar statements are to be found in many U.N. human rights instruments (*e.g.*, Article 1 of the UDHR: "All human beings are born free and equal in dignity and rights") as well as in national constitutions (*e.g.*, Article 1 of the German Basic Law: "Human dignity is inviolable. To respect and protect it shall be the duty of all state authority").

[47] The quotations are from the preambles of the ICCPR and of the ICESCR of 1966. Article 1 of the German Basic Law of 1949 states in a similar manner: "The German people therefore acknowledge inviolable and inalienable human rights as the basis of every community, of peace and of justice in the world" which "shall bind the legislature, the executive and the judiciary as directly applicable law".

[48] *See* U.N. General Assembly Declaration 41/128 of December 4, 1986 on the "Right to Development".

[49] ILO, The ILO Declaration on Fundamental Principles and Rights at Work (1998) at 7, adopted by the International Labour Conference on June 18, 1998, recognizes in ¶ 2 "that all Members, even if they have not ratified the Conventions in question, have an obligation, arising from the very fact of membership in the Organization, to respect, to promote and to realize, in good faith and in accordance with the Constitution, the principles concerning the fundamental rights which are subject of those Conventions, namely: (a) freedom of association and the effective recognition of the right to collective bargaining; (b) the elimination of all forms of forced or compulsory labour; (c) the effective abolition of child labour; and (d) the elimination of discrimination in respect of employment and occupation".

[50] *See* General Comment 5 on Article 4 of the U.N. Covenant on Civil and Political Rights, adopted by the Human Rights Committee on July 31, 1981 and recently revised. *Cf.* D. GOLDRICK, THE HUMAN RIGHTS COMMITTEE 315 (1994).

[51] *Cf.* Article 4 of the ICCPR, Article 15 of the European Convention on Human Rights ("ECHR").

[52] For detailed references to state practice *see* I. SEIDERMAN, HIERARCHY IN INTERNATIONAL LAW (2001).

obligations? Are only universally recognized human rights part of the "relevant context" for the interpretation of WTO rules? Or can regional human rights treaties be part of the relevant context for the interpretation of WTO rules among WTO members that are parties to the human rights treaty concerned?

Several human rights treaties recognize that "[t]here shall be no restriction upon or derogation from any of the fundamental human rights recognized or existing in any State Party to the present Covenant pursuant to law, conventions, regulations or custom on the pretext that the present Covenant does not recognize such rights or that it recognizes them to a lesser extent".[53] The enumeration of specific human rights in international legal instruments is thus recognized as incomplete and without prejudice to more comprehensive human rights guarantees in domestic laws. All U.N. member states have also acknowledged in numerous U.N. resolutions that "all human rights are universal, indivisible and interdependent and interrelated."[54]

Just as Article 6 of the EU Treaty, and the Charter of Fundamental Rights of the EU, recognize human rights as general constitutional principles limiting the powers of the EU and of all EU member states, the universal recognition of the "inalienable nature" and "indivisibility" of human rights can be interpreted to imply that international human rights treaties recognize the existence of "inalienable human rights" as general principles of national and international law.[55] Recognition of core human rights as general "constitutional principles" reduces the dangers of a "positivist" reliance on separate "civil", "political", "economic", "social" and "cultural" human rights that were acknowledged by governments at particular times in particular human rights instruments, such as the risk of leaving non-enumerated "inalienable" human rights without legal protection. Treating separate human rights treaties as mutually agreed codifications of how inalienable core human rights should be understood in relations between the contracting states better protects the diversity and holistic nature of human personality and helps to overcome partial human rights perspectives, such as the widespread resistance to protecting human rights in "economic markets" no less than in "political markets." Human liberty rights, property rights, non-discrimination rights, social rights, and procedural and democratic rights can be protected more effectively if they are understood as part of national and international constitutional law that dynamically evolves in particular national and international contexts, in response to new human rights preferences and challenges, for example those formulated in the December 2000 EU Charter of Fundamental Rights.

The universal recognition of the indivisibility of civil, political, economic, social and cultural human rights has contributed to increasing jurisprudence by national and international courts that economic and social rights, such as the EC Treaty guarantees of

---

[53] *See, e.g.*, Article 5.2 ICCPR.

[54] Vienna Declaration of the U.N. World Conference on Human Rights (1993), section I.5, *cf.* U.N., THE UNITED NATIONS AND HUMAN RIGHTS 1945–1995 450 (1995). On the interdependence, indivisibility and "justiciability" of economic and social "core human rights" and "core obligations", such as the rights to food and to education, *see, e.g.,* K. Arambulo, STRENGTHENING THE SUPERVISION OF THE INTERNATIONAL COVENANT ON ECONOMIC, SOCIAL AND CULTURAL HUMAN RIGHTS—THEORETICAL AND PROCEDURAL ASPECTS (1999), Chapter IV.

[55] *Cf.* E.U. Petersmann, *Taking Human Dignity, Poverty and Empowerment of Individuals More Seriously*, in 13 EUROPEAN JOURNAL OF INTERNATIONAL LAW 845, 851 (2002). *See also* C. Scott, *supra* note 38, at 7, 8, who argues for a "radical breaking down of the normative boundaries among the categories framed by each of the human rights treaties", and recommends to the six U.N. human rights committees to "consider their six treaties as interconnected parts of a single human rights constitution and thereby consider themselves as partner chambers within a consolidating supervisory institution".

freedom of trade and non-discrimination against women, may be no less justiciable than civil and political rights.[56]

F. Obligations by Governments and Intergovernmental Organizations to Respect, Protect and Promote Human Rights

U.N. human rights practice, such as the "General Comments" and "Concluding Observations" adopted by U.N. human rights treaty bodies, emphasizes that human rights entail obligations to *respect* human rights (*e.g.*, by not interfering with human rights), to *protect* human rights (*e.g.*, by means of implementing legislation, administrative and judicial protection), and to *fulfill* human rights (*e.g.*, by making available essential goods and services necessary for the survival and personal development of human beings).[57] The U.N. High Commissioner for Human Rights[58] and the U.N. Committee on Economic, Social and Cultural Human Rights[59] have endorsed calls for developing human rights approaches to the interpretation and application of WTO rules,[60] taking into account the human rights obligations of all WTO members to respect, protect and fulfill human rights at home and abroad. Some U.N. Specialized Agencies, such as the U.N. Educational, Scientific and Cultural Organization ("UNESCO") and the ILO, explicitly commit themselves to the promotion of human rights, such as the right to education and to core labor standards. Other U.N. Specialized Agencies, like the IMF and the World Bank, have so far avoided explicitly recognizing that international organizations are legally bound by universally recognized international human rights.[61] A few organizations— like the World Bank, the Organization for Economic Cooperation and Development ("OECD") and the EU Commission—have committed themselves to "principles of good governance", including transparency, participation, accountability, effectiveness and coherence, so as to legitimize their "international governance" and "integration law".[62] But such commitments to often vague "good governance principles", without clarification of

---

[56] European jurisprudence, by the EC Court of Justice and the European Court on Human Rights, has long since recognized that obligations to respect, protect and fulfill economic and social human rights may be "justiciable" even if they entail not only "negative" but also "positive" obligations (*e.g.*, to promote non-discriminatory access to education). On the particular problems of "welfare rights" (such as indeterminacy of redistributive rights, their dependence on personal responsibility), the distinction between social rights in welfare states and social human rights, and the need for constitutional safeguards against abuses of welfare institutions, *see, e.g.*, K. ARAMBULO, *supra* note 54. Many civil and political human rights (like the right to vote) also imply not only "negative" but also "positive obligations" (*e.g.*, to render the right effective through legislation and administrative procedures).

[57] *Cf., e.g., Compilation of General Comments and General Recommendations adopted by Human Rights Treaty Bodies*, U.N. Document HRI/GEN/1/Rev.5 of April 26, 2001. *See also e.g.*, K. Arambulo, *supra* note 54, Chapter IV, and B.C.A. Toebes, THE RIGHT TO HEALTH AS A HUMAN RIGHT IN INTERNATIONAL LAW (1999), Chapters III, IV and VI.

[58] *See, e.g.*, the report submitted by the High Commissioner for Human Rights to the U.N. Commission on Human Rights on *Globalization and its Impact on the Full Enjoyment of Human Rights* (E/CN.4/2002/54 of January 15, 2002), ¶¶ 9–17, 40–54.

[59] *See, e.g.*, the Statement by the Committee on Economic, Social and Cultural Human Rights on *Human Rights and Intellectual Property* (E/C.12/2001/15 of December 14, 2001).

[60] *See, e.g.*, E.U. Petersmann, *Constitutionalism and WTO Law—From a State-Centered Approach Towards a Human Rights Approach in International Economic Law*, in THE POLITICAL ECONOMY OF INTERNATIONAL TRADE LAW—*LIBER AMICORUM* ROBERT E. HUDEC 32–67 (D.L.M. Kennedy and J.D. Southwick eds, 2001).

[61] *Cf.* S.I. Skogly, THE HUMAN RIGHTS OBLIGATIONS OF THE WORLD BANK AND THE IMF (2001).

[62] *See, e.g.*, World Bank, GOVERNANCE AND HUMAN RIGHTS (1995); OECD, PARTICIPATORY DEVELOPMENT AND GOOD GOVERNANCE (1995); EUROPEAN COMMISSION, GOVERNANCE IN EUROPE—A WHITE BOOK (2001).

their human rights implications, offer no effective legal and judicial protection of human rights and constitutional democracy.

G. Principles for the Mutual Balancing of Human Rights: Non-Discrimination, Rule of Law and Necessity Principles

Human rights treaties and the jurisprudence of human rights bodies emphasize that governmental limitations on human rights are subject to requirements of non-discrimination, necessity and proportionality. Non-discrimination requirements are to be found in all human rights instruments.[63] The numerous provisions on restrictions and limitations of human rights often state that such limitations must be "prescribed by law",[64] and must be "necessary" or "proportionate" to the legitimate aim pursued.[65] Article 29:2 of the UDHR, for instance, states:

> In the exercise of his rights and freedoms, everyone shall be subject only to such limitations as are determined by law solely for the purpose of securing due recognition and respect for the rights and freedoms of others and of meeting the just requirements of morality, public order and the general welfare in a democratic society.

In Article 4 of the ICESCR, for instance, the:

> States Parties to the present Covenant recognize that, in the enjoyment of those rights provided by the Sate in conformity with the present Covenant, the State may subject such rights only to such limitations as are determined by law only in so far as this may be compatible with the nature of these rights and solely for the purpose of promoting the general welfare in a democratic society.

1. Are the Balancing Principles of Human Rights Law Relevant for the Interpretation of WTO Rules?

The "exception clauses" in regional and worldwide economic integration agreements[66] often provide for similar "balancing principles" limiting the right to restrict imports or exports for non-economic public policy purposes. The non-discrimination, "necessity" and "proportionality" requirements in the "general exceptions" of WTO law[67] may raise legal questions similar to those that arise from the corresponding requirements of non-discrimination, necessity and proportionality in human rights treaties. WTO law gives clear priority to the sovereign right to restrict trade if this is necessary for the protection of life, health and other human rights objectives. The WTO panel and Appellate Body reports in *United States—Import Restrictions of Shrimps* confirmed that import restrictions may be justifiable under WTO law for protecting non-economic values, not only inside the importing country but also in other countries and on the High Seas.[68] WTO jurisprudence has progressively relaxed the traditionally strict interpretation of some of the "necessity"

---

[63] For a list of such non-discrimination requirements, *see, e.g.*, P. SIEGHART, THE INTERNATIONAL LAW OF HUMAN RIGHTS (1983), Chapter 7.

[64] *Cf.* Articles 9–11 ECHR.

[65] For a list of such limitations clauses, and of the pertinent jurisprudence, see SIEGHART, *supra* note 63, Chapter 8.

[66] *See, e.g.*, GATT Article XX and GATS Article XIV.

[67] *See, e.g.*, in GATT Article XX and GATS Article XIV.

[68] *See United States—Import Prohibition of Certain Shrimp and Shrimp Products, Recourse to Article 21.5 by Malaysia,* Report of the Appellate Body, DS58/AB/RW (2001), with references to the earlier WTO panel and Appellate Body reports. The restrictions at issue were aimed at protecting endangered species of sea turtles.

requirements in WTO law (*e.g.*, in the sense of requiring the "least-trade restrictive measure") so as to permit more policy discretion in balancing legitimate trade and non-trade concerns.[69] For example, in the *Korea Beef case*, the Appellate Body bifurcated the necessity test by distinguishing (1) situations where the claim may be that a measure is indispensable, *i.e.* where the measure is the only available; and (2) situations where a Member may be able to justify its measure as "necessary" within the meaning of Article XX, even if there would be other measures available. For the second situation, the Appellate Body adopted the following approach:

> A measure with a relatively slight impact upon imported products might more easily be considered as "necessary" than a measure with intense or broader restrictive effects.[70]

> [...] [D]etermination of whether a measure, which is not "indispensable", may nevertheless be "necessary" within the contemplation of Article XX(d), involves in every case *a process of weighing and balancing a series of factors* which prominently include the contribution made by the compliance measure to the enforcement of the law or regulation at issue, the importance of the common interests or values protected by that law or regulation, and the accompanying impact of the law or regulation on imports or exports.[71]

If human rights, the customary international law rules on treaty interpretation, and WTO law[72] require interpreting WTO rules "in their context", with due regard to the human rights obligations of WTO members which may be applicable "in the relations between the parties" in the sense set forth in Article 31:3(c) of the VCLT, does this imply that the general principles for the balancing of the rights and obligations under human rights law may be legally relevant also for the interpretation of the corresponding "balancing principles" when reconciling rights and obligations under WTO law? For instance, does the universal recognition of the right to liberty and of other human rights, such as the protection of human health, call for an interpretation of the numerous public interest clauses in WTO law in conformity with the human rights requirement that personal freedom and other human rights "shall not be subject to any restrictions except those which are provided by law, are necessary to protect national security, public order, public health or morals or the rights and freedoms of others, and are consistent with the other rights recognized in the present Covenant" (*e.g.*, Article 12:3 ICCPR)? How are we to construe human rights concepts, such as "the right to liberty", non-discriminatory treatment, "necessity", the "right of everyone to the enjoyment of the highest attainable standard of physical and mental health", and similar WTO concepts, for instance those regarding non-discrimination, "necessity" and protection of "public health" in GATT Article XX, in a mutually consistent manner?

2. *Legal Consequences of a "Human Rights Approach to International Trade"*

From a state-centered perspective, the traditional "international law of states" serves the "sovereign equality" of states and of their governments. In view of the intergovernmental structures of GATT and WTO law, it is hardly surprising that in GATT and WTO practice

---

[69] The quotations are from the Appellate Body report on *Korea—Various Measures on Beef*, WT/DS161/AB/R (2002), ¶ 164. For a survey of the WTO jurisprudence, *see* GATT/WTO Note by the WTO Secretariat, *Dispute Settlement Practice Relating to GATT Article XX*, of March 8, 2002 (WT/CTE/), at 14–16, which concludes from the evolution in the judicial interpretation of the necessity requirement of GATT Article XX (b) and (d) "that there might be differing levels of scrutiny applicable to the analysis of the necessity text, depending on the importance of the 'interests or values' it served".

[70] *Korea Beef, supra* note 69, ¶ 163.

[71] *Id.* ¶ 164.

[72] *See, e.g.*, Article 3:2 of the DSU.

governments have only very rarely referred to human rights in their invocations of the "general exceptions"[73] and other safeguard clauses in GATT and WTO law so as to justify measures "necessary to protect human, animal or plant life or health."[74] There appears to be no evidence, however, that past GATT practice under Article XX has been inconsistent with human rights. GATT dispute settlement jurisprudence, for instance, has never challenged the legality of non-discriminatory and "necessary" safeguard measures under GATT Article XX. Also WTO practice seems to be consistent so far in interpreting the "general exceptions" in WTO law[75] in conformity with human rights.[76]

The "human rights approach to international trade" advocated by U.N. human rights bodies "sets the promotion and protection of human rights as objectives of trade liberalization, not exceptions."[77] Human rights instruments emphasize that protection of "human dignity" and of inalienable rights to liberty and to other human rights are the ultimate objective and source of legitimacy of national and international law. Legal respect for "human dignity" requires legal protection of moral, rational, and personal liberty and individual responsibility,[78] with due regard to the scarcity and uneven distribution of the economic and other resources necessary for the enjoyment of human rights. Especially in England where liberty of the person has been constitutionally guaranteed since the Magna Carta of 1215,[79] the right to liberty is often construed narrowly as protecting the physical liberty and freedom from arrest and detention. In the constitutional democracies that emerged from anti-colonial struggles, like the United States and India, Supreme Courts have interpreted and protected rights to liberty in a much broader manner to encompass

[73] *See, e.g.*, GATT Articles XX and XXV. The recent "waiver" granted by the WTO Council for Trade in Goods for the "Kimberley Process Certification Scheme for Rough Diamonds" justifies the need for regulating trade in "conflict diamonds" by, *inter alia*, "recognizing the extraordinary humanitarian nature of this issue and the devastating impact of conflicts fuelled by the trade in conflict diamonds on the peace, safety and security of people in affected countries and the systematic and gross human rights violations that have been perpetrated in such conflicts". *Cf.* WTO document G/C/W/432/Rev.1 of February 24, 2003.

[74] For an exception, *see* the submission from Mauritius in WTO document G/AG/NG/W/36/Rev.1 of November 9, 2000, which claims that Article 20 of the Agreement on Agriculture (regarding the taking into account of "non-trade concerns") should be read in conjunction with Article 11 of the ICESCR recognizing the right of everyone to adequate food.

[75] *See, e.g.* , Article XIV GATS and Article 8 TRIPS Agreement.

[76] A computer search of references to human rights in WTO panel and Appellate Body reports indicates ten reports between 1996 and 2001 where parties, third parties, experts, panelists or the Appellate Body referred to human rights. In the negotiations for the WTO Ministerial Declaration of November 2001 on access to medicines and review of Article 27.3(b) of the TRIPS Agreement, the "Africa Group", for instance, referred explicitly to human rights as criteria for interpreting the TRIPS Agreement. The WTO Secretariat actively contributed to the discussions leading to the report of the U.N. High Commissioner for Human Rights on *The Impact of the TRIPS Agreement on Human Rights* (UN document E/CN.4/Sub.2/2001/13 of June 27, 2001) and to Resolution 2001/21 by the U.N. Sub-Commission on Human Rights on "Intellectual Property and Human Rights" (E/CN.4/Sub.2/RES/2001/21 of August 16, 2001).

[77] *Cf. supra* note 13 and the accompanying text.

[78] Whereas most courts have avoided legal definitions of the concept of "human dignity", such as whether "human dignity" should be understood as an "intrinsic value" inherent to personhood or as an "extrinsic value" dependent on merit or achievement, the German Federal Constitutional Court has determined human dignity not only in negative terms (*i.e.*, by deciding case-by-case on infringements) but also by adopting the "object formula": "it contradicts human dignity to turn man into an object within the state". 27 BUNDESVERFASSUNGSGERICHT ENTSCHEIDUNGSSAMMLUNG 1, at 6: "The maxim 'man must always be an end in itself' applies without limitation for all areas of law; for the dignity of a human being as a person, which cannot be lost, exists precisely in the fact that he continues to be recognized as an autonomous personality." *Cf.* D. Ullrich, *Concurring Visions: Human Dignity in the Canadian Charter of Rights and Freedoms and the Basic Law of the Federal Republic of Germany*, in 3 GLOBAL JURIST FRONTIERS 1–103 (2003).

[79] "[N]o freeman shall be taken or imprisoned . . . but . . . by the law of the land".

additional rights and liberties that are essential to the orderly pursuit of happiness by free men, including freedom of contract, liberty to pursue any livelihood or lawful vocation, and the right to travel abroad.[80] German constitutional law and European Community law have reacted to the historical experiences of abuses of economic and regulatory powers, such as the cartelization of German industries under the Hitler dictatorship, by extending constitutional protection of liberty rights[81] to professional and economic liberties across frontiers, subject to democratic legislation.[82]

If constitutional protection of "personal liberty" is extended to mutually beneficial private cooperation across frontiers, then international government obligations in, for example, EC, GATT and WTO law, to protect freedom and non-discrimination among citizens across frontiers can serve "constitutional functions" for limiting welfare-reducing abuses of government powers and for reinforcing judicial protection of individual rights.[83] Legal and judicial protection of the rights to equality of liberty and of non-discriminatory treatment across frontiers enables a higher degree of legal autonomy, empowerment and responsibility of individuals, without unduly limiting the regulatory discretion of democratic legislatures and governments, than does a state-centered reliance on foreign policy discretion of governments without legal and judicial protection of individual freedom and non-discrimination across frontiers (as in many foreign policy areas).[84] For example, the GATT and WTO prohibitions of discriminatory and protectionist abuses of trade policy powers offer precise legal criteria for reconciling freedom of trade with the "human rights functions" of the various GATT and WTO exceptions for the protection of human rights and social security in the importing country. In such legal and judicial balancing processes, human rights may be relevant for interpreting not only the WTO's "exceptions" and safeguard clauses; they may also be relevant for the interpretation of the basic WTO guarantees of freedom, non-discrimination, property rights and rule of law which protect the corresponding human rights guarantees of individual liberty, non-discrimination, private property and access to courts. For instance, the recent statement by the U.N. Committee on Economic, Social and Cultural Rights on "Human Rights and Intellectual Property"[85] has been criticized for interpreting the TRIPS obligations too one-sidedly in the light of social human rights without recognizing that property rights, including the "moral and material interests" of the holders of intellectual property rights, are protected as human rights themselves.[86] The rights and obligations of the importing country to protect the human rights of its citizens

[80] *See* the texts and jurisprudence referred to in SIEGHART, *supra* note 63, Chapter 14.2.

[81] *See, e.g.,* the individual right to general freedom of action and free development of a person's personality in Article 2.1 of the German Basic Law which has been recognized by the courts to protect also individual rights *e.g.,* to import and export goods and services subject to democratic legislation. On the legal and procedural advantages and problems of such a broad constitutional guarantee of general individual freedom *see, e.g.,* Robert Alexy, THEORIE DER GRUNDRECHTE (1994), Chapter 7.

[82] For a comparative analysis of protection of economic liberties in federal states and in the EC, *see* E.U. PETERSMANN, CONSTITUTIONAL FUNCTIONS AND CONSTITUTIONAL PROBLEMS OF INTERNATIONAL ECONOMIC LAW (1991), Chapters VIII and IX.

[83] For an explanation of these "constitutional functions" *see id.* Chapter VII.

[84] *Cf.* Petersmann, *supra* note 55, at 850.

[85] *See supra* note 59, notably ¶ 12: "The Committee wishes to emphasize that any intellectual property regime that makes it more difficult for a State party to comply with its core obligations in relation to health, food, education, especially, or any other right set out in the Covenant, is inconsistent with the legally binding obligations of the State party."

[86] *Cf., e.g.,* Article 17 of the UDHR ("Everyone has the right to own property") and Article 15 UNCESCR, together with Article 27 of the UDHR, requiring "the protection of the moral and material interests resulting from any scientific, literary or artistic production" of authors.

also need to be balanced with the corresponding rights and obligations of the exporting country, as well as with the economic insight that trade restrictions are only rarely an efficient instrument for correcting "market failures" and supplying "public goods."[87]

An explicit recognition of universally recognized human rights as part of the legally relevant context for the interpretation of WTO rules could enhance the legitimacy of WTO decision-making processes and WTO law. Yet, in view of the numerous WTO exceptions and safeguard clauses and the regulatory discretion of WTO Members regarding their legislative implementation and administrative protection of international human rights obligations, WTO decisions and dispute settlement rulings explicitly referring to human rights would presumably remain rare. It is illustrative in this respect that, even though the EC has insisted on including explicit "human rights clauses" into its international economic agreements with more than one hundred countries, such human rights provisions have been used only rarely as a legal justification for the adoption of trade restrictions in response to foreign human rights violations.[88] Although European Community law explicitly commits the EC institutions to respect for human rights,[89] there appears to have been not a single judgment by the EC Court invalidating an EC measure on human rights grounds.

H. Human Rights as Institutional and Constitutional Guarantees: The Example of the Human Right to Health

U.N. human rights law and practice emphasize that human rights need to be protected and mutually balanced through legislation, administrative and judicial protection. For example, General Comment No.14 (2000) by the U.N. Committee on Economic, Social and Cultural Rights on the right to the highest attainable standard of health states that "the right to health must be understood as a right to the enjoyment of a variety of facilities, goods, services and conditions necessary for the realization of the highest attainable standard of health"; the obligations to protect and fulfill this human right should be implemented "preferably by way of legislative implementation, and . . . a national

---

[87] In its Resolution 1999/30 of August 26, 1999 on *Trade Liberalization and its Impact on Human Rights*, the Sub-Commission (of the U.N. Commission on Human Rights) on the Promotion and Protection of Human Rights declared "that sanctions and negative conditionalities which directly or indirectly affect trade are not appropriate ways of promoting the integration of human rights in international economic policy and practice." *See also* Resolution 1998/12 on *Human rights as the Primary Objective of Trade, Investment and Financial Policy* adopted by the U.N. Sub-Commission on the Promotion and Protection of Human Rights, and Resolution 1999/30 *Trade Liberalization and its Impact on Human Rights* adopted by the same U.N. Sub-Commission in 1999.

[88] The EC's suspension of trade preferences for Yugoslavia in November 1991, for instance, was initially motivated by the military hostilities in the former Yugoslavia rather than by human rights violations. In the context of the Lomé Convention, the EC reacted to human rights violations (*e.g.*, in Rwanda) by suspension of financial and technical assistance rather than trade restrictions. The EC's Generalized System of Tariff Preferences ("GSP") offers additional preferences to developing countries which respect basic ILO guarantees (such as freedom of association and minimum age for admission to employment); temporary withdrawal of GSP benefits by the EC in response to violations of human rights have been rare (*e.g.*, in the case of Myanmar). It is difficult to find an empirical basis for the criticism (*e.g.*, by P. Prove, *Human Rights at the WTO* ? in HUMAN RIGHTS AND ECONOMIC GLOBALISATION 32 (M. Mehra ed., 1999) of an alleged "bias of the WTO" because "the primary entry point for human rights concerns would be as justifications for sanctions and trade conditionalities".

[89] *Cf.* Article 6 EU Treaty.

health policy with a detailed plan for realizing the right to health."[90] General Comment No.14 further recognizes that "any person or group victim of a violation of the right to health should have access to effective judicial or other appropriate remedies at both national and international levels."[91] "Depending on the availability of resources, States should facilitate access to essential health facilities, goods and services in other countries, wherever possible and provide the necessary aid when required."[92] As the essential medicines, food (including drinking water) and health services are tradable, the U.N. Commission on Human Rights has emphasized that WTO rules on access to such goods and services may be of direct relevance for the protection and fulfillment of the human right to health.[93]

International human rights instruments provide for numerous specific obligations to protect human rights through implementing legislation and through judicial or other effective remedies.[94] Some of these rights include institutional guarantees, for example to "periodic and genuine elections ... by universal and equal suffrage and ... held by secret vote",[95] and to representative legislatures and independent judicial institutions. Such human rights obligations may be of relevance for the interpretation of corresponding WTO obligations, for instance the obligation in Article X:3 GATT to "administer in a uniform, impartial and reasonable manner all its laws, regulations, decisions and rulings" and "maintain, or institute ... judicial, arbitral or administrative tribunals or procedures".

III. Human Rights as Constitutional Restraints on the Powers of WTO Bodies?

In Europe, human rights have become recognized as "constitutional restraints" on government powers, not only at the national level but also at the level of international organizations which exercise government powers collectively through intergovernmental, parliamentary or judicial organs.[96] The European Court of Human Rights has likewise held:

> Where States establish international organizations, or mutatis mutandis international agreements, to pursue cooperation in certain fields of activities, there may be implications for the protection of fundamental rights. It would be incompatible with the purpose and object of the (European Convention on Human Rights) if Contracting States were thereby absolved from their responsibility under the Convention in relation to the field of activity covered by such attribution.[97]

---

[90] *See General Comment No.14*, ¶¶ 9, 36, in COMPILATION OF GENERAL COMMENTS, *supra* note 57, at 90.

[91] *Id.*

[92] *Id.* ¶ 39.

[93] *See* Resolution 2002/32, ¶ 1 of the U.N. Commission on Human Rights and the Report by its Special Rapporteur on *The Right of Everyone to the Enjoyment of the Highest Attainable Standard of Physical and Mental Health*, document E/CN.4/2003/58 of February 13, 2003. For a comprehensive survey and discussion of health-related WTO provisions see the joint study by the WHO and WTO on WTO AGREEMENTS AND PUBLIC HEALTH, *supra* note 32.

[94] *See, e.g.*, Article 2 ICCPR, and C. Harlow, *Access to Justice as a Human Right: The European Convention and the European Union*, in THE EU AND HUMAN RIGHTS 187–214 (P. Alston, M. Bustelo and J. Heenan eds., 1999).

[95] Article 21 UDHR.

[96] *See supra* note 20 and accompanying text.

[97] European Court of Human Rights, Application No. 43844/98, *T.I. vs. United Kingdom*, Admissibility Decision of March 7, 2000, 4 EUROPEAN HUMAN RIGHTS LAW REVIEW 429–430 (2000). In *Matthews v. UK*, the European Court of Human Rights found the United Kingdom in violation of the human right to participate in free elections of the legislature even though the law which denied voting rights in Gibraltar implemented a treaty concluded among EC member states on the election of the European Parliament: "there is no difference

Other international courts, like the ICJ, and quasi-judicial bodies, like the WTO Appellate Body, might follow the example of the EC Court of Justice and of the European Court of Human Rights and recognize that human rights, such as due process of law and judicial protection, bind not only *national governments* but also collective rule-making and decision-making in international organizations. The U.N. Commission on Human Rights has called upon all states parties to the ICESCR to "ensure that the Covenant is taken into account in all of their relevant national and international policy-making processes."[98]

A. Due Process of Law in the WTO: The Controversy over Amicus Curiae Briefs

According to Article 3:2 of the DSU, the "dispute settlement system of the WTO is a central element in providing security and predictability to the multilateral trading system", and "serves to preserve the rights and obligations of Members under the covered agreements, and to clarify the existing provisions of those agreements in accordance with customary rules of interpretation of public international law." Article 31 of the VCLT gives priority to the "ordinary meaning" of the terms of the treaty "in their context and in the light of its object and purpose". The ICJ has, however, made clear that "... an international instrument has to be interpreted and applied within the framework of the entire legal system prevailing at the time of the interpretation"[99]. The universal recognition of human rights, including procedural guarantees of access to courts and due process of law, may therefore be part of the relevant "context" for the interpretation and progressive development of the dispute settlement procedures set out in the DSU. The differences of view regarding the WTO Appellate Body findings on admissibility of *amicus curiae* (friend-of-the-court) briefs in panel and appellate proceedings illustrate the potential legal relevance of human rights considerations for the interpretation of DSU rules.

The DSU contains no provision on the admissibility of *amicus curiae* briefs. In *United States—Shrimp*, the Appellate Body decided that panels have the right to accept *amicus* briefs based on a broad interpretation of the panels' right in Article 13 of the DSU to seek information.[100] As for the three briefs that had been attached to the appellant's submission of the United States, the Appellate Body found that they had become part of the U.S. submission and were therefore no longer *amicus curiae* briefs.[101] This interpretation of Article 13 of the DSU, and the acceptance by the Appellate Body itself of an unsolicited *amicus curiae* brief by the Center for International Environmental Law ("CIEL") without providing any reasons, were criticized by several WTO Members. In

---

between European and domestic legislation, and no reason why the United Kingdom should not be required to 'secure' the rights (under the ECHR) in respect of European legislation in the same way as those rights are required to be 'secured' in respect of purely domestic legislation". *Cf.* European Court of Human Rights, judgment of February 18, 1999 on complaint No. 24833/94, *see* EUROPÄISCHE GRUNDRECHTSZEITSCHRIFT ("EUGRZ") 200 (1999).

[98] Resolution 2002/24, ¶ 7, quoted by the Special Rapporteur on *The Right of Everyone to the Enjoyment of the Highest Attainable Standard of Physical and Mental Health* whose report likewise emphasizes "the fundamental principle that international human rights law, including the right to health, should be consistently and coherently applied across all relevant national and international policy-making processes" (*supra* note 93, ¶ 8).

[99] *Legal Consequences for States of the Continued Presence of South Africa in Namibia (South West Africa) Notwithstanding Security Council Resolution 276 (1970)*, ICJ Reports 1971, at 31, ¶ 53.

[100] *United States—Shrimp, supra* note 68, ¶¶ 100–110.

[101] *Id.* ¶ 89.

United States—British Steel,[102] the Appellate Body confirmed its own right, without any duty, to consider *amicus* briefs based on Article 17.9 of the DSU.[103] This provision gives the Appellate Body the authority to adopt procedural rules, which do not conflict with any rules and procedures in the DSU or the covered agreements. The Appellate Body also held that Rule 16(1) of the Working Procedures allows it to fill gaps in the Working Procedures by adopting new rules.[104]

In the Appellate Body decision in *EC—Asbestos,*[105] the Appellate Body established special rules applicable to *amicus* briefs based on Rule 16(1) of the Working Procedures.[106] In these rules the Appellate Body stated specific requirements that *amicus* briefs were expected to meet and posted them on the WTO website. At an extraordinary meeting of the General Council, many WTO member countries expressed their concern about these legal interpretations and activities of the Appellate Body. The additional rules were criticized as a legislative act that exceeded the Appellate Body's competence and granted non-governmental third parties access to the intergovernmental dispute settlement process. As most NGOs come from developed countries, and the "friends of the court" might turn out to be no friends of the governments concerned, less-developed WTO members, in particular, expressed concern that *amicus curiae* briefs might render their complaints and defenses in WTO dispute settlement proceedings more burdensome. The General Council meeting ended with the chairman asking the Appellate Body to approach the issue of the admissibility of *amicus* briefs with "*extreme caution*" in the future. In addition, it was agreed that the chairman would lead informal discussions with the member countries on formulating rules for the consideration of *amicus curiae* briefs.

The text of Articles 13 and 17.9 of the DSU does not mention *amicus curiae* briefs. The national legal and judicial systems of most WTO member countries do not appear to recognize a right of domestic courts to accept such briefs. The different interpretations of the "ordinary meaning" of the terms of Articles 13 and 17.9 DSU—by the Appellate Body *in favor* of the admissibility of *amicus curiae* briefs, and by most WTO Members *against* their legal admissibility—are to be explained in terms of divergent interpretations of "their context" and of the "object and purpose" of these WTO provisions. Human rights considerations were neither mentioned in the extremely scant reasoning by the Appellate Body, nor in the debates among WTO Members in the General Council. Yet, human rights considerations—such as the human rights guarantees of due process of law,[107] and the universal commitment[108] to incorporate human rights into the policies of international organizations[109] so as to promote participation of individuals and civil society organizations in the work of international organizations[110]—could offer legal arguments to dispute

---

[102] *United States—Imposition of Countervailing Duties on Certain Hot-Rolled Lead and Bismuth Carbon Steel Products Originating in the United Kingdom,* Report of the Appellate Body, WT/DS138/AB/R (2000), ¶¶ 36–42.

[103] *Id.* ¶ 39.

[104] For a more detailed discussion, *see* Gabrielle Marceau and Matthew Stilwell, *Practical Suggestions for Amicus Curiae Briefs before WTO Adjudicating Bodies,* 4 JOURNAL OF INTERNATIONAL ECONOMIC LAW 155 162–163 (2001).

[105] *European Communities—Asbestos, supra* note 33.

[106] *European Communities—Measures Affecting Asbestos and Asbestos-Containing Products,* Communication from the Appellate Body (Additional Procedures), WT/DS135/9 (November 8, 2000).

[107] *Cf., e.g.,* C. Harlow, *Access to Justice as a Human Right, supra* note 94.

[108] *See, e.g.,* in the U.N. resolutions on the right to development.

[109] *Cf.* in this context the commitment to "sustainable development" in the Preamble to the WTO Agreement.

[110] *See e.g., Report of the Intergovernmental Group of Experts on the Right to Development,* U.N. Doc. E/CN.4/1998/29 of November 7, 1997.

settlement bodies to construe WTO rules, including the due process guarantees of the DSU, in favor of the admissibility of *amicus curiae* briefs by those private citizens who are affected by the administration, judicial application and implementation of WTO rules.

It is characteristic in this respect that the common law concept of *amicus curiae* briefs has become accepted only in international dispute settlement proceedings directly affecting individuals, notably in international human rights courts, international criminal courts, WTO and NAFTA dispute settlement bodies, but neither in the ICJ nor in intergovernmental arbitration. In the *Asbestos Case*, the conditions imposed by the Appellate Body for application for leave to file *amicus curiae* briefs made it clear that the Appellate Body was prepared to authorize the submission of *amicus curiae* briefs only if the brief was likely to promote due process of law and proper administration of justice in the dispute at hand. Unfortunately, the Appellate Body did not adequately explain how admission of *amicus curiae* briefs with new legal arguments could be reconciled with protection of the rights of the parties to the dispute (*e.g.*, rights to control the "legal claims", rights to defend themselves against legal arguments in *amicus curiae* briefs within the strict time-limits) and of third WTO Members intervening in the dispute (*e.g.*, their interest in being treated no less favorably than *amici curiae*).

B. Substantive Restraints: The Example of the Human Right to Health and Access to Medicines

According to the Constitution of the World Health Organization ("WHO"), "(t)he enjoyment of the highest attainable standard of health is one of the fundamental rights of every human being without distinction of race, religion, political belief, economic or social condition." In Article 12.1 of the ICESCR, the so far 146 ratifying "States Parties to the present Covenant recognize the right of everyone to the enjoyment of the highest attainable standard of physical and mental health." Article 12:2 adds:

The steps to be taken by the State Parties to the present Covenant to achieve the full realization of this right shall include those necessary for:

  (a) The provision for the reduction of the stillbirth-rate and of infant mortality and for the healthy development of the child.
  (b) The improvement of all aspects of environmental and industrial hygiene.
  (c) The prevention, treatment and control of epidemic, endemic, occupational and other diseases.
  (d) The creation of conditions which would assure to all medical service and medical attention in the event of sickness.

1. Trade-Related Aspects of the Right to Health: General Comment No. 14

In its General Comment No. 14 (2000), the U.N. Committee on Economic, Social and Cultural Rights has emphasized that the human right to health is recognized in numerous worldwide, regional and national human rights instruments and "includes certain components which are legally enforceable."[111] Moreover, the "right to health is closely related to and dependent upon the realization of other human rights..., including the rights to food, housing, work, education, human dignity, life, non-discrimination, equality, the prohibition against torture, privacy, access to information, and the freedoms of association, assembly and movement. These and other rights and freedoms address integral

---

[111] *See* General Comment No. 14, *supra* note 90, ¶ 1.

components of the right to health."[112] "The right to health contains both freedoms and entitlement", such as "the right to a system of health protection which provides equality of opportunity for people to enjoy the highest attainable level of health",[113] and the "right to the enjoyment of a variety of facilities, goods,services and conditions necessary for the realization of the highest attainable standard of health."[114] The right to health is thus interpreted as:

> an inclusive right extending not only to timely and appropriate health care but also to the underlying determinants of health, such as access to safe and potable water and adequate sanitation, an adequate supply of safe food, nutrition and housing, healthy occupational and environmental conditions, and access to health-related education and information, including on sexual and reproductive health. A further important aspect is the participation of the population in all health-related decision-making at the community, national and international levels.[115]

The right to health thus depends upon the availability, acceptability, quality and non-discriminatory, physical as well as economic accessibility of health goods and health services which are tradable and subject to legal regulation and liberalization in WTO law. General Comment No. 14 confirms this potentially transnational legal effect of the human right to health: "States parties have to respect the enjoyment of the right to health in other countries"; depending on the availability of resources, "States should facilitate access to essential health facilities, goods and services in other countries, wherever possible and provide the necessary aid when required."[116] More generally:

> [t]he right to health, like all human rights, imposes three types or levels of obligations on States parties: the obligations to *respect, protect* and *fulfill*. In turn, the obligation to fulfill contains obligations to facilitate, provide and promote. The obligation to *respect* requires States to refrain from interfering directly or indirectly with the enjoyment of the right to health. The obligation to *protect* requires States to take measures that prevent third parties from interfering with Article 12 guarantees. Finally, the obligation to *fulfill* requires States to adopt appropriate legislative, administrative, budgetary, judicial, promotional and other measures towards the full realization of the right to health.[117]

While Article 2 of the ICESCR provides for progressive realization and acknowledges the constraints due to limits of available resources, General Comment No. 14 recalls that the Covenant:

> imposes on States parties various obligations which are of immediate effect. States parties have immediate obligations in relation to the right to health, such as the guarantee that the right will be exercised without discrimination of any kind (Art.2:2) and the obligation to take steps (Art.2.1) towards the full realization of Article 12. Such steps must be deliberate, concrete and targeted towards the full realization of the right to health.[118]

As regards governmental limitations of human rights, General Comment No. 14 infers from the limitation clauses in Articles 4 and 5 of ICESCR that:

---

[112] *Id.* ¶ 3. On national and international jurisprudence relating to the right to health, *see also* TOEBES, *supra* note 57.

[113] *See* General Comment No. 14, *supra* note 90, ¶ 8.

[114] *Id.* ¶ 9.

[115] *Id.* ¶ 11.

[116] *Id.* ¶ 39.

[117] *Id.* ¶ 33.

[118] *Id.* ¶ 30.

such limitations must be proportional, *i.e.* the least restrictive alternative must be adopted where several types of limitations are available. Even where such limitations on grounds of protecting public health are basically permitted, they should be of limited duration and subject to review.[119]

States parties should refrain at all times from imposing embargoes or similar measures restricting the supply of another State with adequate medicines and medical equipment. Restrictions on such goods should never be used as an instrument of political and economic pressure.[120]

2. WTO Practice on Access to Medicines

The expanding subject matters and "universalization" of both human rights and intellectual property law have prompted negotiations in various U.N. bodies, and also in the WTO, on the clarification of the complex interrelationship between the TRIPS Agreement and human rights. The advantages of intellectual property as both a reward and an incentive for research and development, for example in the area of new pharmaceuticals products, are no longer contested.[121] However, the proper balancing between the social objectives of the TRIPS Agreement,[122] its "regulatory exceptions",[123] and the appropriate scope of intellectual property protection, for example for genetic and other living materials, or the protection of rights of indigenous peoples, raise numerous controversial questions.[124]

There seems to be broad agreement so far that the TRIPS provisions are flexible enough to permit necessary health protection measures so as to ensure access to affordable medicines to treat AIDS and other pandemics.[125] In the WTO Ministerial Declaration on "The TRIPS Agreement and Public Health" of November 2001, all WTO Members "affirm that the Agreement can and should be interpreted and implemented in a manner supportive of WTO Members' right to protect public health and, in particular, to promote access to medicines for all". WTO Members also "reaffirm the right of WTO Members to use, to the full, the provisions in the TRIPS Agreement, which provide flexibility for this purpose."[126] Rather than granting a general waiver from WTO law in favor of the human right to health, WTO members preferred to specify those TRIPS provisions which they understand to grant sufficient flexibility for promoting public health and access to medicines for all. This approach seems consistent with the general principle that human rights must be legally implemented through legislative measures taking into account all other human rights.

Paragraph 6 of the Doha Ministerial Declaration on TRIPS and Public Health reads:

We recognize that WTO Members with insufficient or no manufacturing capacities in the pharmaceutical sector could face difficulties in making effective use of compulsory licensing

---

[119] *Id.* ¶ 29.

[120] *Id.* ¶ 41. In this regard, the Committee recalls its position, stated in General Comment No. 8, on the relationship between economic sanctions and respect for economic, social and cultural rights.

[121] *Cf.* WTO AGREEMENTS AND PUBLIC HEALTH, *supra* note 32, at 91–93.

[122] *See* Articles 7 and 8 TRIPS.

[123] *See, e.g.*, Article 6 TRIPS regarding "parallel imports", Article 31 TRIPS regarding "compulsory licensing", and Article 40 concerning abuses of intellectual property rights.

[124] *See, e.g.*, G. DUTFIELD, INTELLECTUAL PROPERTY RIGHTS, TRADE AND BIODIVERSITY (2000).

[125] *See also* the Report of the Joint WHO/WTO Workshop on Differential Pricing and Financing of Essential Drugs of April 8–11, 2001 (which notes that about 95 percent of the WHO list of "essential drugs" are not or no longer patented, and differential pricing and international financing of essential drugs are consistent with the TRIPS Agreement).

[126] *See* WTO document WT/MIN (01)/DEC/W/2 of November 14, 2001, ¶ 4.

under the TRIPS Agreement. We instruct the Council for TRIPS to find an expeditious solution to this problem and to report to the General Council before the end of 2002.[127]

Similar technological, financial and trade problems may exist in case of exports of healthcare technologies, lack of know-how or trade secrets necessary for manufacturing medicines or other medical devices, or if a compulsory license for the production of an expensive drug for one single market would not justify the production costs without authorization of exports to third markets. For example, while countries may authorize, pursuant to Article 31 of the TRIPS Agreement, non-voluntary and non-exclusive uses of inventions, Article 31(f) stipulates that "any such use shall be authorized predominantly for the supply of the domestic market of the Member authorizing such use", subject to certain exceptions.[128] Some controversial Canadian practices designed to speed up introduction of generic drugs following the expiration of patents were reviewed in the WTO dispute settlement ruling on the EC's complaint against Canada's use of Article 30 of the TRIPS Agreement to permit "pre-expiration testing" and warehousing of generic drugs before the expiry of the patent.[129] Various proposals to permit the use of Article 30 of TRIPS for exports of medicines needed to address public health emergencies and necessary for achieving economies of scale continue to be under negotiation in the WTO.

As of April 2003, the United States and the U.S. pharmaceutical industry continued to block consensus on a WTO decision clarifying the rights of WTO Members (*e.g.*, under Articles 30 or 31 of the TRIPS Agreement) to authorize exportation of the predominant part of medicines produced under compulsory license to other WTO member countries that lack sufficient pharmaceutical manufacturing capacities. In view of paragraph 4 of the Doha Ministerial Declaration ("the TRIPS Agreement does not and should not prevent Members from taking measures to protect public health") and the necessity (recognized in paragraph 6 of the Doha Declaration) to address the health problems of WTO Members without adequate domestic manufacturing capacities, the human right to health may be invoked as relevant legal context for interpreting the TRIPS Agreement (*e.g.*, Articles 30 or 31) in a manner also enabling less-developed countries to address public health emergencies effectively.

C. Judicial Deference vis-à-vis Democratic Legislation: The Example of the Hormone Beef Dispute

The European Court of Human Rights and other international human rights bodies have emphasized the "margin of appreciation" which democratic governments enjoy in implementing and mutually balancing different human rights. In the U.S. complaint in *EC—Import Restrictions on Meat and Meat Products*, involving restrictions that the EC adopted under the Council Directive Prohibiting the Use in Livestock Farming of Certain Substances Having a Hormonal Action,[130] the panel report found that the EC ban on

---

[127] *See note* 90, ¶ 6. At a Ministerial Meeting of 25 WTO members at Sydney in November 2002, agreement was reached on further relaxing TRIPS rules for poor countries' access to patented drugs and to cheap generic copies so as to address public health emergencies (*cf.* FINANCIAL TIMES, November 16–17, 2002). Yet, neither the TRIPS Council nor the WTO's General Council could reach agreement, by the end of 2002, on additional WTO rules as envisaged in paragraph 6 of the Doha Declaration.

[128] *See, e.g.*, Article 31(k) TRIPS.

[129] Report of the WTO Panel, *Canada—Patent Protection of Pharmaceutical Products*, WT/DS114/R (2000).

[130] EC Council Directives 81/602, 88/146 and 88/299 were replaced by Council Directive 96/22 of April 29, 1996, Official Journal of the EC, No. L 125, May 23, 1996, p. 3.

imports of meat and meat products from cattle treated with any of six specific hormones for growth promotion purposes was inconsistent with Articles 3.1, 3.3, 5.1 and 5.5 of the WTO Agreement on Sanitary and Phytosanitary Measures ("SPS"). The Appellate Body upheld the Panel's finding that the EC import prohibition was inconsistent with Articles 3.3 and 5.1 of the SPS Agreement, but reversed the Panel's finding that the EC import prohibition was inconsistent with Articles 3.1 and 5.5.[131]

Article 3.1 of the SPS Agreement provides:

> To harmonize sanitary and phytosanitary measures on as wide a basis as possible, Members shall base their sanitary or phytosanitary measures on international standards, guidelines or recommendations, wherever they exist, except as otherwise provided for in this Agreement, and in particular paragraph 3.

The Appellate Body disagreed with the Panel's interpretation that "based on" should be construed in the sense of "conform to":

> The Panel's interpretation of Article 3.1 would...transform those standards, guidelines and recommendations into binding *norms*. But...the SPS Agreement itself sets out no indication of any intent on the part of the Members to do so. We cannot lightly assume that sovereign states intended to impose upon themselves the more onerous, rather than the less burdensome, obligation by mandating *conformity* or *compliance* with such standards, guidelines and recommendations. To sustain such an assumption and to warrant such a far-reaching interpretation, treaty language far more specific and compelling than that found in Article 3 of the SPS Agreement would be necessary.[132]

The Appellate Body referred, in this context, to the interpretative principle of interpreting treaties in deference to the sovereignty of states (*"in dubio mitius"*). This objective of protecting domestic sovereignty is similar to the objective of the "margin of appreciation doctrine" to protect the legitimate discretion of democratic legislatures. The Appellate Body emphasized that the right of a WTO Member to determine its own appropriate level of sanitary protection pursuant to Article 3.3 of the SPS Agreement is an important "autonomous right and not an 'exception' from a 'general obligation' under Article 3.1".[133] "The object and purpose of Article 3 is to promote the harmonization of SPS measures of Members on as wide a basis as possible, while recognizing and safeguarding, at the same time, the right and duty of Members to protect the life and health of their people."[134]

The concern to take into account "not only risk ascertainable in a science laboratory operating under strictly controlled conditions, but also the risk in human societies as they actually exist, in other words, the actual potential for adverse effects on human health in the real world where people live and work and die",[135] permeates numerous findings of the Appellate Body in favor of domestic regulatory discretion to protect "the ordinary lives of people."[136] This functional interpretation of WTO rules coincides with the objective of a "human rights approach" according to which all national and international law must be designed and applied so as to promote human rights (*e.g.*, to

---

[131] *See* Report of the Appellate Body, *EC—Import Restrictions on Meat and Meat Products*, WT/DS26/AB/R (1997).
[132] *Id.* ¶ 165.
[133] *Id.* ¶ 172.
[134] *Id.* ¶ 177.
[135] *Id.* ¶ 187.
[136] *Id.* ¶ 221.

life, food and health), including the human right to democratic legislation implementing and mutually balancing human rights.[137]

IV. "Human Rights Functions" of WTO Rules: Promotion of Human Rights in Domestic Legal Systems by Means of WTO-Consistent Interpretations of Domestic Law

Most national legal systems and domestic courts recognize a legal obligation to construe domestic law in conformity with the international legal obligations of the country concerned. The WTO guarantees of freedom of trade, non-discrimination, rule of law and access to courts can thereby reinforce corresponding legal guarantees in the domestic laws of WTO member countries and protect individual freedom of choice (*e.g.*, of traded goods, services, related professions and investments), non-discrimination and the rule of law for the benefit of individual traders, producers, investors and consumers. For instance, many national constitutions,[138] the EU Charter of Fundamental Rights,[139] and human rights instruments[140] guarantee "everyone... the right to liberty" subject "only to such limitations as are determined by law solely for the purpose of securing due recognition and respect for the rights and freedoms of others and of meeting the just requirements of morality, public order and the general welfare in a democratic society".[141] Especially in the increasing number of countries where such personal liberty rights are construed as protecting not only physical liberty (*e.g.*, in the sense of freedom from arbitrary arrest and detention) but personal liberty in a wide sense covering also economic and social dimensions of personal self-development (*e.g.*, freedom of contract, freedom of movement, freedom of occupation), the WTO guarantees of freedom, non-discrimination and rule of law may reinforce the corresponding guarantees in constitutional law and human rights law.

A. WTO Guarantees of Freedom, Non-Discriminatory Conditions of Competition, Necessity and Proportionality

The WTO prohibitions of tariffs, non-tariff trade barriers, trade discrimination and trade distortions protect freedom (*e.g.*, market access) and non-discriminatory conditions of competition in international trade for the benefit of traders, producers, investors and consumers. In EC law, the EC Treaty prohibitions of tariffs, non-tariff trade barriers and trade discrimination—notwithstanding their formulation in terms of rights and obligations of governments—have long been construed by the EC Court as directly applicable *individual freedoms* of trade that must be protected by national and EC courts in conformity with "freedom of trade as a fundamental right"[142] and "freedom to conduct a

---

[137] On the gradual emancipation of the individual, and the emergence of a human right to democracy in national and international law see above note 4 and *e.g.*, T.M. Franck, THE EMPOWERED SELF: LAW AND SOCIETY IN THE AGE OF INDIVIDUALISM (1999).

[138] *See, e.g.*, Article 2 of the German Basic Law.

[139] *See id.*, Article 6.

[140] *E.g.*, Article 3 UDHR, Article 9 ICCPR.

[141] Article 29 UDHR, Article 4 ICESCR.

[142] *See, e.g.*, Case 240/83, *ADBHU*, ECR 1985 531, ¶ 9: "the principles of free movement of goods and freedom of competition, together with freedom of trade as a fundamental right, are general principles of Community law of which the Court ensures observance." Especially the freedom of movements of workers and other persons, access to employment and the right of establishment have been described by the EC Court as "fundamental freedoms" (Case C-55/94, *Gebhard*, ECR 1995, I 4165, ¶ 37) or "a fundamental

business in accordance with Community law and national laws".[143] By contrast, the corresponding GATT and WTO prohibitions of tariffs, non-tariff trade barriers and trade discrimination continue to be construed by most WTO Members as rights and obligations of governments without corresponding rights and obligations of their citizens.

In spite of the intergovernmental legal structure of many WTO rules, the parallels between WTO guarantees and corresponding national and international constitutional guarantees of liberty, non-discrimination, "necessity", and "proportionality" of government restrictions remain evident. This is particularly so in national and international legal systems which—like German and European constitutional law and U.N. human rights law—recognize that all legislative, executive and judicial government measures must aim at promoting "human dignity" by empowering individuals and protecting their human rights.[144] Similar to domestic legislation implementing human rights obligations, WTO rules and their domestic implementation can serve mutually reinforcing "human rights functions" for the benefit of individual freedom, non-discrimination and the welfare-increasing division of labor among citizens across frontiers. This can be illustrated by the numerous general and specific exceptions in WTO law, for example in GATT Articles XX and XXI, that recognize the comprehensive right of governments to restrict trade so as to protect non-economic values considered by WTO Members to be more important than access to foreign markets.

1. WTO Dispute Settlement Practice Relating to Protection of Health and Environment and to the Necessity, Proportionality and Non-Discrimination Principles in GATT Article XX

The increasing number of national and international laws and agreements establishing individual rights to a clean environment, often formulated in terms of human rights,[145] are not referred to in WTO law. Yet, the WTO Agreement contains an explicit commitment to "the optimal use of the world's resources in accordance with the objective of sustainable development, seeking both to protect and preserve the environment and to enhance the means for doing so".[146] Prior to April 1, 2003, there have been six GATT panel proceedings, and three WTO panel and appellate proceedings, involving an examination of environmental measures or human health-related measures under GATT Article XX (b), (d) or (g). They have made it clear that, in the words of the Appellate Body, "WTO Members have a large measure of autonomy to determine their own policies

---

right which the Treaty confers individually on each worker in the Community". *Heylens*, Case 22/86, ECR 1987, 4097, ¶ 14. The ECJ avoids "human rights language" for the "market freedoms", the right to property and the freedom to pursue a trade or business in EC law, and some of these "market freedoms" (*e.g.*, for free movement of persons) are limited to EC citizens. Yet, such "fundamental rights" and "citizen rights" remain functionally linked to broader human rights.

[143] *See* Article 16 EU Charter of Fundamental Rights.

[144] For references to the relevant guarantees of human dignity and human rights in German, EU and U.N. law, *see supra* notes 45–47 and 78 and accompanying text. This author's long-standing arguments, *cf.* E.U. Petersmann, *Application of GATT by the Court of Justice of the EC*, 20 Common Market Law Review 397–437 (1983), in favor of "direct application" by domestic governments and courts of precise and unconditional GATT/WTO guarantees of freedom, non-discrimination, "due process" and rule of law for the benefit of traders, producers, investors and consumers have always been primarily motivated by the human rights objective of empowering individuals and treating citizens as legal subjects rather than mere objects of public law, *cf. supra* note 78, on the "object formula" used by the German Constitutional Court for defining and protecting "human dignity".

[145] *Cf., e.g.,* M. Déjeant-Pons and M. Pallemaerts, *supra* note 11; Human Rights Approaches to Environmental Protection (A. Boyle and M. Anderson eds., 1998).

[146] *Preamble to the WTO Agreement.*

on the environment (including its relationship with trade), their environmental objectives and the environmental legislation they enact and implement."[147] None of the panel and Appellate Body reports questioned the environmental or health policy choices made by the government parties. Already in the 1990 *Thailand—Cigarettes* case, the "Panel noted that this provision [Article XX] clearly allowed contracting parties to give priority to human health over trade liberalization."[148] In the *EC—Asbestos* case, the Appellate Body likewise confirmed each WTO Member's "right to determine the level of protection of health that [it] considers appropriate in a given situation."[149]

According to WTO jurisprudence, GATT Article XX requires a two-tiered test: the defending party has the burden of proving that the measure (i) falls under at least one of the ten exceptions listed under Article XX paragraphs (a) to (j), and (ii) satisfies the requirements imposed by the opening clause of Article XX, *i.e.*, is not applied in a manner which would constitute "a means of arbitrary or unjustifiable discrimination between countries where the same conditions prevail", and is not "a disguised restriction on international trade." The provisional justification of the measure as falling under one of the exceptions must precede examination of the conditions of the introductory clause which, according to the Appellate Body, is "but one expression of the principle of good faith"[150] aimed at prevention of "abuse of the exceptions of Article XX".[151]

The judicial interpretation of the necessity requirement of Article XX(b) and (d) has evolved from a "least-trade restrictive" to a "less-trade restrictive" standard, supplemented by a proportionality test:

> determination of whether a measure, which is not 'indispensable', may nevertheless be 'necessary' within the contemplation of Article XX(d), involves in every case a *process of weighing and balancing a series of factors* which prominently include the contribution made by the compliance measure to the enforcement of the law or regulation at issue, the importance of the common interests or values protected by that law or regulation, and the accompanying impact of the law or regulation on imports or exports.[152]

In the *Asbestos* case, the Appellate Body observed that "the more vital or important [the] common interests or values" pursued (as the preservation of human life and health through import restrictions on asbestos), the easier it would be to accept the measures designed to achieve those ends as "necessary".[153] Again, this balancing among competing values recognized in WTO law is similar to, and influenced by, the mutual balancing of human rights principles.

Another important evolution in the judicial application of Article XX has been the justification of import restrictions to protect non-economic values, not only inside the importing country, but also on the High Seas and inside the exporting countries through measures differentiating among countries. In *United States—Tuna (Mexico)*, a GATT panel found that Article XX(b) did not justify unilateral import restrictions designed to protect human, animal or plant life or health outside of the jurisdiction of the country taking the measure; even if Article XX(b) were interpreted to apply "extrajurisdictionally", the United States had failed to demonstrate that it had exhausted all options reasonably

[147] *United States—Gasoline*, Report of the Appellate Body, WT/DS2/AB/R, in WTO DISPUTE SETTLEMENT REPORTS 1996 (1998), at 28.
[148] *Thailand—Restrictions on Importation of and Internal Taxes on Cigarettes*, BISD 37S/200 (1990), ¶ 73.
[149] *EC—Asbestos, supra* note 33, ¶ 168.
[150] *United States—Shrimp, supra* note 68, ¶ 158.
[151] *United States—Gasoline, supra* note 147, at 21.
[152] *Korea—Various Measures on Beef*, Report of the Appellate Body, WT/DS/161/AB/R (2001), ¶ 164.
[153] *EC—Asbestos, supra* note 33, ¶ 162.

available to it to pursue its dolphin protection objectives through measures consistent with the GATT, such as the negotiation of an international cooperative agreement which seemed desirable in view of the fact that dolphins roam the waters of many states and the High Seas.[154] This narrow interpretation of Article XX was partly corrected in *United States—Tuna (EEC)* where the GATT panel held that Article XX(b) and (g), and the jurisdiction over nationals and national vessels, could also justify policies related to the protection of human, animal or plant life, or health or to the conservation of natural resources, located outside the territory of the contracting party.[155] In *United States—Shrimp*, the Appellate Body confirmed that the U.S. measures for the protection of sea turtles in U.S. territorial waters and on the High Sea qualified for provisional justification under Article XX(g); however, the import restrictions were found to discriminate, in violation of the chapeau of Article XX, among WTO Members exporting shrimp to the United States.[156] In *United States—Shrimp (Article 21.5)*, the Appellate Body upheld the panel's finding that, in order to implement the dispute settlement rulings, the United States had made serious good faith efforts to negotiate an international agreement on the protection and conservation of sea turtles and was entitled under Article XX to condition market access on the adoption by the exporting country of a program comparable in effectiveness to the sea turtle protection measures of the importing country.[157]

WTO dispute settlement practice thus seems to confirm that import restrictions may be inconsistent with WTO law if they do not take into account legitimate rights of exporting countries (*e.g.*, their regulatory sovereignty over production methods in their own country, rights to market access and to non-discriminatory treatment), and that protection of human rights may be an important criterion in the process of balancing the respective rights of exporting and importing WTO member countries.

2. Balancing of Economic and Non-Economic Values in WTO Dispute Settlement Practice Relating to GATT Article III

The *Asbestos* case illustrates that human rights considerations may be legally relevant for the interpretation not only of the exception clauses in WTO law, but also of the basic WTO guarantees of freedom and non-discrimination in the economic area. Even though the Appellate Body did not refer to the human right to health, it emphasized the relevance of health risks associated with the physical properties of products in the examination of "like products" and regulatory distinctions made under Article III GATT.

The Panel had found that chrysotile asbestos fibers and synthetic fibers that can be substituted for them, as well as asbestos-cement products and fibro-cement products, were "like products" within the meaning of GATT Article III:4, and that the health and safety objectives leading to the regulatory distinction among like products could only be taken into account in the analysis under Article XX, *not* in the analysis under Article III:4 where the "likeness" of products had to be determined solely on the basis of commercial factors.[158]

The Appellate Body rightly disagreed and concluded "that, given the textual difference between Articles III:2 and III:4, the 'accordion' of 'likeness' stretches in a different way in

---

[154] *United States—Restrictions on Imports of Tuna*, DS 21/R, (1991), (unadopted), ¶¶ 5.26–5.28.

[155] *United States—Restrictions on Imports of Tuna* (EEC), DS 29/R (1994), (unadopted), ¶¶ 5.16–5.33.

[156] *United States—Shrimp, supra* note 68, ¶¶ 165–166.

[157] *United States—Import Prohibition of Certain Shrimp and Shrimp Products*, Recourse to Article 21.5 by Malaysia, WT/DS58/AB/RW (2001), ¶ 144.

[158] *EC—Import Restrictions Affecting Asbestos and Asbestos-Containing Products*, Report of the Panel, WT/DS135, (2001), ¶¶ 8.132, 9.1.

Article III:4.... ."[159] A "determination of 'likeness' under Article III:4 is, fundamentally, a determination about the nature and extent of a competitive relationship between and among products", and "evidence relating to the health risks associated with a product may be pertinent in an examination of 'likeness' under Article III:4 of the GATT 1994".[160] As "carcinogenicity, or toxicity, constitutes ... a defining aspect of the physical properties of chrysotile asbestos fibers", the Appellate Body could "not see how this highly significant physical difference *cannot* be a consideration in examining the physical properties of a product as part of a determination of 'likeness' under Article III:4 of the GATT 1994."[161] As the Appellate Body could "not agree with the Panel that considering evidence relating to the health risks associated with a product, under Article III:4, nullifies the effect of Article XX(b) of the GATT 1994", it found "that the Panel erred ... in excluding the health risks associated with chrysotile asbestos fibers from its examination of the physical properties of that product."[162] The Appellate Body reversed the "like product" findings of the panel and concluded that—in view of their different properties and end-uses—the products concerned were not "like products" for the purposes of Article III:4 of GATT 1994 and, hence, the different regulatory treatment applied to these products was not in violation of Article III:4.

The *Asbestos* case illustrates the potential relevance of the human right to health for the interpretation of apparently "technical" trade law concepts such as "like products". Even though the Appellate Body did not refer to human rights as part of the relevant legal context for determining the treatment of toxic products, trade law must be construed in a manner consistent with effective protection of universally recognized human rights. The *Asbestos* case further demonstrates the legal relevance of trade law for non-economic human rights objectives: Division of labor through trade and trade law not only enable each trading country to increase resources necessary for the enjoyment of human rights, they may also require trade regulations restricting dangerous products and protecting human rights in exporting and importing countries.

3. Primacy of Non-Economic Values in WTO Dispute Settlement Practice Relating to the WTO Agreement on Sanitary and Phyto-Sanitary Measures ("SPS")

GATT Articles II and III imply a large degree of national sovereignty to decide on the level of tariff protection for domestic import-competing producers, on national taxes, product and production regulations, consumer protection, and other domestic laws, provided they do not treat imported products less favorably than competing domestic products. The border adjustment rules in GATT Articles II, III and VI likewise protect broad government discretion on how to respond to "regulatory competition", for example by exempting exported products from domestic taxes and regulations, or by applying domestic taxes and regulations to imported products. By contrast, the WTO rules on technical barriers to trade, phytosanitary standards, services and trade-related intellectual property rights have introduced far-reaching new obligations on the "necessity", mutual recognition and harmonization of domestic regulations. WTO jurisprudence has so far interpreted these rules in favor of national policy autonomy to decide, *e.g.*, on the national level of health protection measures and to deviate from

---

[159] *EC—Asbestos*, Report of the Appellate Body, *supra* note 33, ¶ 96.
[160] *Id.* ¶¶ 99, 113.
[161] *Id.* ¶ 114.
[162] *Id.* ¶ 116.

relevant international standards in favor of stricter domestic health, environmental, security and other standards.

In the disputes over the complaints by the United States and Canada against the EC's import restrictions on meat and meat products (the *Hormones* cases), the two panel reports reached the same conclusion that, *inter alia*, the EC, "by maintaining sanitary measures which are not based on existing international standards without justification under Article 3.3 of the Agreement on the Application of Sanitary and Phytosanitary Measures, has acted inconsistently with the requirements of Article 3.1 of that Agreement."[163] The Panel noted that "Article 3.2 . . . equates measures *based on* international standards with measures which *conform to* such standards", and concluded that "based on" and "conform to" are identical in meaning also in Article 3.1. As already mentioned above,[164] the Appellate Body disagreed that "based on" could be equated with "conform to". It found instead that a measure "based on" an existing relevant international standard could "adopt some, not necessarily all, of the elements of the international standard", and that the "right of a Member to establish its own level of sanitary protection under Article 3.3 of the SPS Agreement is an autonomous right and *not* an "exception" from a "general obligation" under Article 3.1."[165] Moreover, to:

> the extent that the Panel purported to require a risk assessment to establish a minimum magnitude of risk, we must note that imposition of such a quantitative requirement finds no basis in the SPS Agreement . . . the risk that is to be evaluated in a risk assessment under Article 5.1 is not only risk ascertainable in a science laboratory operating under strictly controlled conditions, but also risk in human societies as they actually exist, in other words, the actual potential for adverse effects on human health in the real world where people live and work and die. [166]

As regards the SPS requirement that "Members shall ensure that their sanitary or phytosanitary measures are based on an assessment . . . of the risks to human, animal or plant life or health",[167] the Appellate Body found that "'based on' a risk assessment is a substantive requirement that there be a rational relationship between the measure and the risk assessment."[168]

The Appellate Body jurisprudence so far suggests that, in the interpretation of WTO rules, WTO dispute settlement bodies will respect the broad discretion of governments to restrict trade by means of non-discriminatory domestic rules necessary for the protection of human health and other human rights values. As human health can be perceived as a "primary good"[169] that is a condition of "dignity" (in terms of the philosopher Immanuel Kant) rather than a matter of "price", the Appellate Body's reasoning could also have been supported by human rights arguments to the effect that the rights and obligations of WTO Members to protect human health must rank higher than their sovereign rights to regulate merchandise trade and "instrumental freedoms" (*e.g.*, to buy and sell commercial goods).

---

[163] *EC—Import Restrictions on Meat and Meat Products*, Report of the Panel, WT/DS26/R/USA and WT/DS26/R/Canada (1997), ¶ 9.1.

[164] *See* Part II(C) of this chapter.

[165] *EC—Import Restrictions on Meat and Meat Products*, Report of the Appellate Body, WT/DS26,48/AB/R (1998), ¶¶ 171,172.

[166] *Id.* ¶¶ 186–187.

[167] Article 5.1. of the SPS Agreement.

[168] *Id.* ¶ 193.

[169] As defined by JOHN RAWLS, A THEORY OF JUSTICE 62 (1973).

B. WTO Guarantees of Property Rights: WTO Disputes over TRIMS and TRIPS

The WTO rules on pre-shipment inspection, government procurement, services trade, intellectual property rights and trade-related investment measures reflect an increasing trend to go beyond the traditional scope of GATT rules by protecting, albeit in an indirect manner, also private rights, for instance rights of "service suppliers",[170] holders of intellectual property rights, exporters subject to pre-shipment inspection, bidders in government procurement proceedings, or foreign investors subjected to purchase and sales "requirements" in terms of GATT Article III:4. The frequent characterization of intergovernmental WTO disputes by referring to the names of the company interests involved (*Kodak/Fuji, Bacardi/Pernod-Ricard*) illustrates that, notwithstanding the intergovernmental structures of WTO dispute settlement proceedings, the underlying conflicts often relate to private operators and to their private rights (*e.g.*, Pernod-Ricard's rights in the trademark *Havana Club*). The proposals to negotiate, in the Doha Development Round, additional WTO rules on the protection of international competition and investment are likely to lead to further WTO rules protecting the private rights of traders and investors, for example "due process rights" during the investigations of domestic competition authorities and in the proceedings of domestic investment authorities screening the admission of foreign direct investments.

The 1999 complaint by the EC against Section 110(5) of the U.S. Copyright Act illustrates that WTO dispute settlement proceedings can be used as a basis for WTO arbitration proceedings leading to financial compensation of private holders of intellectual property rights. The Panel report, adopted on July 27, 2000, found that the "business exemption" provided for in Section 110(5)—which allows the amplification of music broadcasts, without authorization and a payment of a fee, by certain food service and drinking establishments—did not meet the requirements of Article 13 of the TRIPS Agreement and was thus inconsistent with Articles 11 and 11*bis* of the Bern Convention on Copyright (1971).[171] In July 2001, the United States and EC pursued arbitration pursuant to Article 25 of the DSU that led to an award in November 2001 which determined the level of EC benefits being nullified or impaired as a result of Section 110(5) to be Euro 1,219,900 per year.[172] The U.S. administration subsequently requested Congressional approval to set up a compensation fund for adversely affected holders of property rights until the U.S. legislation can be brought into conformity with WTO law.

Most WTO Members recognize the domestic legal right of private actors to invoke WTO rules as a means to demonstrate the relevant legal context for interpreting domestic laws and regulations in conformity with the international legal obligations of the country concerned. Yet, in most WTO member countries, domestic courts deny private rights to invoke WTO rules to override subsequent domestic laws; they also deny granting individuals direct rights to challenge domestic laws that are inconsistent with WTO obligations in domestic courts. Under both Section 301 of the U.S. Trade Act as well as under the EC Trade Barriers Regulation, however, private economic operators can request domestic governments to introduce GATT and WTO dispute settlement proceedings against perceived violations of GATT and WTO rules by other WTO Members.[173] There

---

[170] *Cf.* Article XXVIII GATS.

[171] *United States—Section 110(5) of the U.S. Copyright Act*, Report of the Panel, WT/DS160/R (2000).

[172] *United States—Section 110(5) of the U.S. Copyright Act*, Report of the Appellate Body, WT/DS160/ARB/25/1 (2001).

[173] *Cf.* C.T. Garcia Molyneux, Domestic Structures and International Trade: The Unfair Trade Instruments of the United States and the EU (2001). Out of nineteen private complaints submitted under

are numerous GATT and WTO dispute settlement proceedings that were initiated at the request of private exporting industries or foreign investors and resulted in dispute settlement findings protecting private rights.

For example, the 1984 GATT panel proceeding in *Canada—Administration of the Foreign Investment Review Act of Canada* was initiated at the request of U.S. investors in Canada and, following a GATT dispute settlement ruling that "requirements to purchase from Canadian suppliers . . . are contrary to Article III:4" of GATT,[174] led to the cancellation of these discriminatory purchase requirements adversely affecting the property rights of the U.S. investors concerned. Similarly, the panel report, adopted in July 1998, examining the complaints by the EC, Japan and the United States in *Indonesia—Certain Measures Affecting the Automobile Industry* upheld prior complaints by automobile producers that Indonesia granted discriminatory benefits to "national vehicles" and components thereof in violation of, *inter alia*, its national treatment obligations under Article 2 of the WTO Agreement on Trade-Related Investment Measures ("TRIMS").[175] In a communication dated July 15, 1999, Indonesia informed the WTO that its new automotive policy had effectively implemented the dispute settlement rulings and recommendations.

As explained by economic theory, trade and investments, and their legal protection through national and international guarantees of freedom of trade and property rights, are preconditions for creating the resources necessary for realizing human rights and democratic self-government. Human rights, trade law and investment law condition each other: Human rights protect individual demand for, and supply of, scarce goods and services and, at the same time, require legal limitations on "market failure" as well as on "government failure".[176] In order to maximize the benefits from trade and investments for the enjoyment of human rights, and minimize the potential risks of unregulated market competition for human rights, trade and investment law, including WTO law, must be interpreted and applied in conformity with human rights law. For example, intellectual property rights and other trade and investment rules (*e.g.*, for the private supply of drinking water and essential health services) must be legally protected as well as limited by human rights law. What is expressed as a right to regulate under WTO law may be a duty to regulate under human rights law. The less effective international legal and judicial remedies in U.N. human rights conventions than those existing in WTO law illustrate that the needed "balancing" and mutual coherence between trade law and human rights law continue to be inadequate in many ways.

C. WTO Legal Restraints on Discrimination and Trade Sanctions for Political Ends

The WTO rules on non-discriminatory conditions of trade and competition (*e.g.*, the prohibitions of discrimination among "like products", "like service suppliers" and among

the EC's Trade Barriers Regulation (until summer 2002), eight led to the initiation of WTO dispute settlement proceedings by the EC.

[174] *Canada—Administration of the Foreign Investment Review Act of Canada,* BISD 30S/140, 159–161, ¶ 5.11.

[175] *See Indonesia—Certain Measures Affecting the Automobile Industry,* Report of the Panel, WT/DS54,55,59,64/R (1998). In the three other WTO dispute settlement proceedings in which the complainants claimed violations of the TRIMS Agreement (*EC-Bananas III*, WT/DS27/R; *Canada-Auto Pact*, WT/DS139 and 142/R; *India-Autos,* WT/DS146 and 175/R), the panels did not consider it necessary to examine the consistency of the contested measures with the TRIMS Agreement after having found violations of GATT Article III:4.

[176] *Cf.* E.U. Petersmann, *Constitutional Economics, Human Rights and the Future of the WTO*, 58 AUSSENWIRTSCHAFT 49–91 (2003).

WTO Members) act as legal constraints on the use of trade restrictions as instruments for discrimination among WTO member countries for political ends (*e.g.*, so as to impose the labor, environmental or human rights standards of the importing country as preconditions for the admission of "like products" from exporting countries with different production standards). Yet, WTO law[177] admits production and consumption subsidies that may prove necessary for fulfilling the non-discrimination requirements of human rights law as well as other social human rights (*e.g.*, so as to ensure non-discriminatory individual access to drinking water and to essential health services if their deregulation and privatization entail commercial prices that are not affordable for poor people). The GATT and the WTO Agreement also include numerous "general exceptions"[178] and "security exceptions"[179] that grant WTO members broad governmental discretion to restrict trade and introduce "justifiable discrimination" for non-economic reasons.

According to GATT Article XXI(c) and GATS Article XIV *bis*:1(c), "[n]othing in this Agreement shall be construed . . . (c) to prevent any contracting party from taking any action in pursuance of its obligations under the United Nations Charter for the maintenance of international peace and security." As, "(i)n the event of a conflict between the obligations of the Members of the United Nations under the present Charter and their obligations under any other international agreement, their obligations under the present Charter shall prevail",[180] economic sanctions based upon Chapter VII of the U.N. Charter have never been challenged in GATT and WTO dispute settlement proceedings.[181] The very broad formulation, in paragraph (b) of these "security exceptions", that "[n]othing in this Agreement shall be construed . . . (b) to prevent any contracting party from taking any action which it considers necessary for the protection of its essential security interests". . . , has prompted most GATT and WTO members to take the view that, as expressed many times in GATT practice, "every country must be the judge in the last resort on questions relating to its own security."[182] Thus, the human rights obligations to protect the life and security of domestic citizens clearly prevail over conflicting WTO obligations to promote non-discriminatory conditions of trade and competition.

In the dispute between the EC and the United States over the economic sanctions applied by the United States against Cuba pursuant to the "Cuban Liberty and Democratic Solidarity Act",[183] the DSB established a dispute settlement panel in November 1996 so as to examine the EC claims that the U.S. trade restrictions on goods of Cuban origin, as well as the refusal of visas and the exclusion of non-U.S. nationals from U.S. territory, were inconsistent with U.S. obligations under the WTO Agreement.[184] Following the invocation by the United States of the security exceptions in GATT Article XXI and GATS Article XIV *bis* and a bilateral EC-U.S. agreement on the settlement of this dispute, the panel suspended its work at the request of the EC in April 1997 without deciding on the U.S. claim that the United States alone had the right to decide on

---

[177] *See, e.g.*, GATT Articles III:8, XVI and the WTO Agreement on Subsidies.

[178] *See, e.g.*, GATT Article XX and GATS Article XIV.

[179] *See, e.g.*, GATT Article XXI and GATS Article XIV *bis*.

[180] Article 103 U.N. Charter.

[181] For example, sanctions imposed by U.N. members against Rhodesia, South Africa and Yugoslavia.

[182] For an overview of GATT practice relating to GATT Article XXI *see*: I WTO, ANALYTICAL INDEX: GUIDE TO GATT LAW AND PRACTICE 600–608 (1995). On the various kinds of trade sanctions in response to foreign human rights violations, and on their respective GATT consistency, *see* S.H. Cleveland, *Human Rights Sanctions and International Trade: A Theory of Compatibility*, 5 JIEL 133–189 (2002).

[183] Pub. L. No. 104–114, 110 Stat. 785 (1996), *reprinted in* 35 INTERNATIONAL LEGAL MATERIALS 357 (1996).

[184] *United States—The Cuban Liberty and Democratic Solidarity Act*, WT/DS38 (1996).

U.S. security interests.[185] Similarly, the joint WTO panel established in October 1998 to examine complaints by the EC and Japan that an act adopted by Massachusetts restricting state contracts with companies doing business with Burma (Myanmar) violated U.S. obligations under Articles III, VIII(b), XIII:4(b) and XXII.2 of the WTO Agreement on Government Procurement, suspended its work at the request of the complainants after the dispute had been settled based on a U.S. Supreme Court decision finding the legislation by Massachusetts to be in violation of the U.S. Constitution.[186] Due to the scarcity of GATT and WTO jurisprudence in this field, it remains controversial whether it is legally consistent with WTO law, more specifically the Government Procurement Agreement of 1994, to limit government contracts with companies that deal with non-democratic governments engaged in human rights violations, or to impose other trade sanctions as a means to promote respect for human rights and ILO labor standards abroad.[187]

V. The Future of the WTO Constitution: Explicit Recognition of Human Rights so as to Better Protect Social Welfare and Democratic Governance in the WTO?

The WTO Agreement and the related implementing legislation of WTO Members include formal as well as substantive "constitutional principles" limiting welfare-reducing abuses of policy powers to tax and restrict producers, traders and consumers.

A. Formal and Substantive "Multi-Level Constitutionalism" in WTO Law

The WTO Agreement asserts legal priority over the multilateral trade agreements listed in its Annexes,[188] and over certain domestic "laws, regulations and administrative procedures" of WTO Members.[189] It establishes intergovernmental, administrative and quasi-judicial organs with limited legislative, administrative and quasi-judicial powers to adopt amendments to WTO rules, authoritative interpretations, "waivers" from WTO obligations, and dispute settlement rulings binding on WTO members. The intergovernmental rule-making by WTO Members, regular review of domestic legislation and trade policies in WTO bodies, *ad hoc* decisions on matters such as "waivers", panel and Appellate Body reports, and their review and adoption by the Dispute Settlement Body have evolved into a dynamic system of mutual "checks and balances" where, for instance, the legal interpretations by the "judicial branch" (for example on the admissibility of *amicus curiae* briefs in panel and Appellate Body proceedings) have been criticized and challenged by the "administrative branch"—*e.g.*, the chairman of the WTO General Council, and

---

[185] WTO Document, WT/DS/OV/9 (October 2002), at 151.

[186] *Id.* at 152. The U.S. Supreme Court judgment in *Crosby v. National Foreign Trade Council* of June 19, 2000 is reproduced in 39 INTERNATIONAL LEGAL MATERIALS 1234 (2000).

[187] *Cf., e.g.*, C. McCrudden, *International Economic Law and the Pursuit of Human Rights: A Framework for Discussion of the Legality of 'Selective Purchasing' Laws under the WTO Government Procurement Agreement*, in: 2 JIEL 3–48 (1999); S. Griller, *International Economic Law as a Means to Further Human Rights: The WTO Agreement on Government Procurement*, in INTERNATIONAL ECONOMIC GOVERNANCE AND NON-ECONOMIC CONCERNS (S. Griller ed. 2003). As Article VI of the Government Procurement Agreement permits technical specifications of the contract based on process and production methods, and the "public order exceptions" in WTO law may justify safeguard measures to prevent human rights violations, non-discriminatory human rights considerations may be lawful criteria also under the Government Procurement Agreement, especially if human rights clauses are included into the procurement documentation.

[188] *Cf.* Article XVI:3.

[189] *Cf.* Article XVI:4.

have prompted suggestions for new authoritative interpretations or formal amendments of WTO rules by the WTO's "legislative branch" pursuant to Articles IX or X of the WTO Agreement.

As illustrated by the U.S. "fast track legislation" of 2002, granting a limited mandate to the U.S. government for multilateral negotiations in the Doha Development Round, the intergovernmental decision-making processes in the WTO are subject to parliamentary and political control in WTO Members. This results in interrelated "bi-level negotiations" at national and international levels, and in additional constitutional constraints on national and international trade policy-making. For instance, the periodic WTO "rounds" of multilateral rule-making depend on prior mandates by domestic legislatures and on subsequent domestic legislation approving and implementing newly agreed WTO rules in domestic legal systems. By committing WTO member governments to international legal obligations to protect freedom of trade, non-discrimination and the rule of law among producers, traders and consumers across frontiers, the legal and judicial guarantees of the WTO Agreement serve "constitutional functions" by limiting abuses of foreign policy powers and by protecting individual freedom of choice and the welfare-increasing division of labor across frontiers for the benefit of domestic citizens.

The legal obligations of all WTO member states, under general and conventional human rights law, to respect and promote human rights in all national and intergovernmental activities form part of the legal context of the "WTO constitution."[190] As subjects of international law, international organizations have obligations under international human rights law and have no mandate for undermining the human rights obligations of their member states. The comprehensive agenda of the Doha Development Round reflects the increasing agreement among WTO Members that further liberalization of international trade needs to be supplemented by multilateral regulation of trade and by multilateral adjustment assistance for less-developed WTO member countries. Future WTO negotiations risk failure unless their legitimacy and respect for human rights are recognized by civil society and by parliaments through democratic deliberation and parliamentary ratification of future WTO agreements.

B. Explicit Recognition of Human Rights in WTO Law so as to Promote Social Welfare and Democratic Governance in the Trade Policy Area?

In the process of European integration, the institutions of the EC committed themselves to respect for human rights long before the incorporation of explicit human rights clauses into the EC Treaty.[191] A similar commitment by WTO bodies—for instance in a WTO Ministerial Declaration—could enhance the democratic legitimacy of WTO law and the WTO decision-making process. By acknowledging the constitutional limits of WTO law and of WTO bodies, such a WTO declaration could make it more evident that the WTO objective of promoting "sustainable development" through non-discriminatory trade liberalization and trade regulation, and WTO law in general, must be construed with due regard to the universal human rights obligations of WTO members. Although such a declaration would neither change the existing legal rights and obligations of WTO Members nor enlarge the powers of WTO bodies, it could enhance public understanding of the WTO and facilitate the successful conclusion and parliamentary ratification of future WTO agreements.

---

[190] On these "multi-level constitutional constraints" on trade policy-making *see, e.g.*, E.U. Petersmann, *The WTO Constitution and Human Rights*, 3 JOURNAL OF INTERNATIONAL ECONOMIC LAW 19–25 (2000).

[191] *Cf., e.g.*, L. BETTEN AND N. GRIEF, EU LAW AND HUMAN RIGHTS LAW (1998).

In contrast to the anti-market bias of earlier U.N. reports that condemned the world trading system as a "nightmare" for less-developed countries,[192] the recent reports by the U.N. High Commissioner on the human rights dimensions of WTO rules acknowledge the constitutional significance of a rules-based trading system for producing and supplying the goods and services demanded by consumers.[193] The reports rightly emphasize that poverty, in the sense of deprivation of human capacities resulting from "transformation of a person into a being incapable of satisfying his minimum needs for survival", is often due to inadequate local, regional, national and international rules, governance systems and policies.[194] Human rights offer legal incentives for the personal self-development of individuals, and for private savings, investment, and the division of labor among free citizens, by empowering individuals, limiting abuses of powers, and by defining the welfare objectives of governments in a non-discriminatory manner that promotes the general interests of citizens and consumer welfare.[195] Explicit recognition of the human rights dimensions of WTO law could reinforce rights-based struggles against unnecessary poverty, and strengthen legal incentives for creating the economic goods and services needed for the enjoyment of human rights and for the satisfaction of consumer demand.[196]

Mainstream human rights specialists often perceive creation of welfare as a legislative and administrative task of "benevolent governments" and neglect the constitutive function of human rights for empowering individuals and for protecting their dignity, self-development, private division of labor and common social interests in economic markets no less than in "political markets."[197] As in European integration law, the protection of human rights in WTO law can make citizens not only "better democrats" but also "better economic producers and consumers", and more vigilant guardians against the abuse of government power at national and international levels, such as the centuries-old practice of "rent-seeking" rulers to discriminate, tax and restrict foreign goods, foreign services, foreign traders and foreign producers in a manner that reduces the welfare of domestic consumers.

---

[192] *Cf. Globalization and its Impact on the Full Enjoyment of Human Rights* (E/CN.4/Sub.2/2000/13 of June 15, 2000), ¶ 15: "for certain sectors of humanity—particularly the developing countries of the South— he WTO is a veritable nightmare."

[193] In addition to the reports mentioned *supra* notes 13, 58, and 76, *see also* the report by the High Commissioner on the WTO Agreement on Agriculture and Human Rights (E/CN.4/2002/54).

[194] *Cf. Poverty and Human Rights* (E/CN.4/Sub.2/2002/15 of June 25, 2002), *e.g.,* ¶¶ 9 and 14.

[195] *Cf.* also Petersmann, *Constitutional Economics, Human Rights and the Future of the WTO, supra* note 176.

[196] On the contribution of the international division of labor and trade to poverty reduction, *see, e.g.,* D. BEN-DAVID, H. NORDSTRÖM AND I.A. WINTERS, TRADE, INCOME DISPARITY AND POVERTY (2000). The report on *Poverty and Human Rights, supra* note 194, at 2 states: "While it can be said that poverty in general violates the enjoyment of economic, social and cultural rights in many ways, extreme poverty is a gross violation of the right to life and human dignity and thus strikes at the heart of the human rights system, which is the foundation of world peace, security and human society."

[197] See the careless accusations invented by Alston, *supra* note 30, and refuted by Petersmann, *supra* note 55. The "Alston/Petersmann debate" in 13 EJIL 815 and 845 (2002) illustrates the difficulties that some human rights specialists have in understanding and discussing the need for protecting human rights, "normative individualism" and "constitutional democracy" in economic markets no less than in political markets.

CHAPTER 62

TRADE AND HUMAN RIGHTS II

Sheldon Leader*

* Professor, Dept of Law and Centre for Human Rights, University of Essex. My thanks to Paul Hunt, Director of the Essex Centre for Human Rights for valuable assistance with sources, and to Alexis Kontos, Sabine Michalowski, Steve Peers, and the editors for their careful review of and insightful comments on drafts of this chapter.

I. Introduction

What difference do human rights potentially make to the logic and practice of international trade; and—running in the opposite direction—what difference does trade make to the way in which human rights are understood and deployed? The importance of these questions is highlighted by the fact that, as one authority has recently observed, the relationship between these two domains "... is one of the central issues confronting international lawyers at the beginning of the twenty-first century."[1] The challenge, of course, reaches well beyond lawyers to all of those individuals and institutions ultimately responsible for pulling these two domains into a viable relationship.

There is mutual suspicion on both sides of the divide between the practices of trade and human rights, manifested both by the heat of recent academic debate and by confrontations on the street. Each side worries that the other might sabotage its best-laid plans. Yet the international community has less and less tolerance for this standoff. It demands an effective and workable synthesis, allowing the two disciplines to widen and to coordinate their agendas. This chapter is concerned with this prospect. It raises two broad issues: which, if any, human rights have a relevant role to play in shaping the rules of trade; and how should we understand the relative priority among, and balances between, rights in trading relations? If analysis can provide an appropriate map for working out the problem of priorities and balances, then it might be possible to see respect for human rights as being—as the United Nations puts it—the objective of international trade, while at the same time preserving the ability of a robust system of trade to pursue, within that framework, many of its traditional goals as well.[2]

The focus here is on the existing framework of WTO rules. It does not follow existing interpretations of the rules that make up this framework, but looks closely at alternative ways of construing them. There is, in these constructions, potential for including a wide range of human rights within the work of the WTO, extending from entitlements that run with the grain of widening trading relationships, through to those that cut across and limit the reach of such trading relationships. The prospect for such a wide inclusion depends on a choice from among foundation principles that are at once political and legal.

The chapter proceeds by first setting out fundamentals. It aims to show how the different ways of understanding the WTO's mandate have an effect on deciding which human rights should be linked to the work of the institution. It also sketches some features of the integration of markets, both within the developed world and between it and the developing world, that affect the exercise of human rights. With these pieces of the picture in place, the chapter then considers some of the problems of priority and balance among rights and other interests in the global trading system.

II. The Challenge

If it is to be successful, this enquiry will have to follow certain background principles.

---

[1] P. Alston, *Resisting the Merger and Acquisition of Human Rights by Trade Law: A Reply to Petersmann*, 13(4) EUROPEAN JOURNAL OF INTERNATIONAL LAW 815 (2002).

[2] J. Oloka-Onyango and Deepika Udagama, *Human Rights as the Primary Objective of International Trade, Investment and Finance Policy and Practice*, a paper submitted in accordance with U.N. Sub-Commission Resolution 1998/12 E/CN.4/Sub.2/1999/11; U.N. Sub-Commission on the Promotion and Protection of Human Rights, *Liberalization of Trade in Services and Human Rights*, E/CN.4/Sub.2/2002/9, June 25, 2002, ¶ 7; *cf.* U.N. Commission On Human Rights, Fifty-Ninth Session, *The Fundamental Principle of Non-discrimination in the Context of Globalization*, E/CN.4/2003/50, December 2002.

A. Navigating Among Rival Political Philosophies

The international trading system should be able to plausibly link regimes animated by different and sometimes incompatible foundation principles. Even were all Members to subscribe to the same set of international human rights instruments, they are often deeply divided over the way these instruments integrate social values and economic relations. How should international norms regulate a world in which some societies assign priority to market-oriented liberty and property rights, with a relatively lower rank given to any human rights that would limit market freedom; while others arrange their priorities in the opposite way—along with many other different solutions located in between? Can a trading system bring these actors together in an impartial way? The system aspires to bridge these differences while avoiding, in principle, a structure in which the values of the strong Members dominate those of the weak. It may well fall far short of this ideal as things stand, but that criticism tacitly endorses the benchmark of political impartiality as one way of measuring progress by the system. It is this benchmark that is our concern here, for there is more to it than meets the eye.

In part, one can achieve the objective of impartiality in the regulation of trade by seeing where the traps lie. For example, the advocates and skeptics of free trade argue about whether or not the practice benefits the poorest parts of the world's population. The WTO has published work aimed at showing that the opening of markets in goods and services to international competition serves the interests of more than the richer parts of the world, also having a good deal to offer the least well-off.[3] Critics of the WTO look at the same opening of markets and find damage rather than gains for the poorest.[4] In part, this is a difference over the facts and in part a difference over principles: the latter guiding views about what *counts* as benefiting the least well-off. It pits advocates of competitive individualism against those who favor various species of communitarian position; or those who believe that political liberalism requires market liberalism against those who believe the latter works against the former. The result, in this portion of the confrontation, appears to be an intense disagreement over the relationship between trade and human rights, but it is not at bottom a disagreement about that at all. It is instead a conflict between visions of society and of social justice. As such, this ought ideally to be the province of Member states, each with their local mandate to further one or another of these social ideals.

We can properly focus on the relationship between trade and human rights only if we try to follow the approach taken by the U.N. Committee charged with interpreting the International Covenant on Economic, Social and Cultural Rights. In deciding whether or not one of the rights has been violated, the Committee insists that the Covenant "... cannot accurately be described as being predicated exclusively upon the need for, or the desirability of a socialist or a capitalist system, or a mixed, centrally planned, or laissez-faire economy, or upon any other particular approach."[5] This does not mean that we can shelve the politically divisive issues in working out the proper relationship between international trade and human rights. Some such issues have to be confronted. However, as this chapter will try to illustrate, we can be optimistic about reaching consensus on them only if we can build on a platform that gives all participants—the weak as well

---

[3] *See e.g.* DAN BEN-DAVID, HAKEN NORDSTROM, AND LALAN WINTERS, TRADE, INCOME DISPARITY AND POVERTY (WTO Special Studies 2001).

[4] *See e.g.* MICHEL CHOSSUDOVSKY, THE GLOBALIZATION OF POVERTY 35 ff. (1997).

[5] Committee on Economic, Social and Cultural Rights, *General Comment 3, Concerning the Nature of States Parties' Obligations Under Art.* 2, ¶ *1 of the Covenant.* ¶ 8, U.N. Doc. HRI\GEN\1\Rev.1 at 45 (1994).

as the strong—the conviction that their priorities have the chance of making an impact on trading rules. There is a difference between forcing a compromise onto a trading partner, and forcing that partner to abandon a set of priorities among values it thinks are fundamentally important to its social health. The trading system must navigate in this terrain. It is here that new strategies for assigning priorities to and adjusting conflicts between basic rights can make a difference.

B. Institutional Identity

We must not blur the line between the WTO and a state. The trading body has a specific and distinct role in international society. When it is called on to conform to international human rights requirements, this does not mean that it must do so in the same way that its Members do. The rights must be fitted to its distinct and defining purpose, which is set out in the preamble to its constitution. However, although the WTO is different in kind from a state, it pools the power of states into rules and policies of greater impact than most states can wield singly. In turn, these impacts have the potential to affect the ability of any one of its Members to pursue policies that their own human rights obligations might call for. If the WTO is asked to move away from what it sees as its core mission, easing the pressure it exerts on some of its members because of its respect for human rights standards, then there is a problem of translation. How is it possible to take rights standards fitted to the work of states and transfer them to a non-state actor with a specialized mission that seems at first glance to have nothing to do with human rights?

III. A Closer Look at Human Rights

Before we go any further, it is important to fix some fundamental points about the nature of human rights. As a working definition we shall say that "human" rights are those entitlements that people have, anywhere in the world, by virtue of their being human beings. That starting point is in turn built on the perception that certain basic human needs are the same, whatever the society is in which one is located. There are also sets of needs that are more variable, being dependent on the culture in which one is located. However, traversing all cultures is this set of common requirements. They are divided into two categories. First, there are needs to be protected from the wrongful use of coercive power, underpinning the civil and political rights to freedom of expression; the right to a fair trial; the right not to be tortured; the right to freedom of association; and others. A second category of rights is labeled economic and social. They have to do with the basic needs for fair access to all to the basic goods that society produces. Here we find the rights to an adequate education; health protection, and others.

The initial source to which those linking global trade and rights often make reference is the Universal Declaration of Human Rights.[6] In turn, we find the two categories of rights just mentioned in two legal instruments: the International Covenant on Civil and Political Rights ("ICCPR")[7] and the International Covenant on Economic, Social and Cultural Rights ("ICESCR").[8] This second set of rights has an evolutionary side to it: parties to the Covenant are obligated not simply to refrain from reducing the provision

---

[6] U.N. Doc A/810 at 71 (1948).

[7] *International Covenant on Civil and Political Rights*, U.N. Doc A/6316 (1966)

[8] *International Covenant on Economic, Social and Cultural Rights*, U.N. Doc A/6316 (1966)

of basic goods and services that they guarantee, but are also required progressively to improve on their provision insofar as their resources permit.[9]

The WTO is not a party to either of the international covenants (nor, indeed, to any other), although most of the states that are its Members adhere to them. Nevertheless, there are two ways in which these rights could affect the organization's work. First, there are some basic rights that are considered to be so firmly established that they do not need to be formally placed in any treaty. They occupy a place as part of what is known as customary international law, and arguably bind both states and non-state actors such as the WTO. The list of these rights is not firmly established, but a core of understanding covers matters such as the right not to suffer discrimination on grounds of race.[10] Secondly, as has been mentioned, WTO rules and their interpretation have the potential for placing Member states in the position of not satisfying human rights requirements themselves.[11] To the extent that this is so, the way is open to the WTO to decide to give direct attention to these standards as it goes about its work. While the WTO is not in a position to force Members to obey human rights norms, it is in a position to interpret its own rules in a way that gives different degrees of room for Members to satisfy those norms themselves.

A. Selecting and Balancing the Basic Rights

It is tempting to resolve different views about the proper relation between trade and human rights by filtering out the particular rights to be taken into account. Some authors argue, for example, that the rights associated with freedom to trade do not fall within the range of recognized human rights.[12] Others are firmly of the view that the rights do have this quality.[13] There is something to be said for both positions, but there is also a trap for those who put too much store in ultimately deciding who is right. For it is tempting to allow an answer to the question of whether or not a given right exists tacitly to decide the question of what priority that right should have. Even if the exercise of the right to freedom of trade qualifies as fundamental in the international system, it does not follow that the WTO should give it systematic priority over other rights. In this chapter, we want to focus on the issue of priorities, and so will be relatively accommodating on the issue of whether or not a given candidate for consideration qualifies as a human right *per se*. This will allow us to concentrate on the next steps: working out the basis on which the list

---

[9] This is a feature, *inter alia*, of ICESCR Article 11, the "... right to an adequate standards of living ... including adequate food, clothing and housing, and to the *continuous improvement* of living conditions." For the implications of this principle as it might or might not apply to the IMF and World Bank, *See* S. SKOGLY, THE HUMAN RIGHTS OBLIGATIONS OF THE WORLD BANK AND INTERNATIONAL MONETARY FUND (2001); and the review by Leader, KINGS COLLEGE LAW JOURNAL forthcoming (2003).

[10] On human rights as part of customary international law *see* RESTATEMENT (THIRD) OF FOREIGN RELATIONS LAW OF THE UNITED STATES, ¶ 102 (1986) cited in R. HOWSE, AND M. MUTUA, *Protecting Human Rights in the Global Economy: Challenges for the WTO*, RIGHTS AND DEMOCRACY (www.ichrdd.ca) (2000). For an argument linking human rights to trade *see* Ernst-Ulrich Petersmann, *Time for Integrating Human Rights into the Law of Worldwide Organizations*, WORKING PAPER 7/01 Jean Monnet Program, Harvard Law School (2001)

[11] Examples are to be found in several UN reports on trade and human rights, considered in various places in the text to follow, and cited *supra*, note 2

[12] See e.g. Alston, supra note 1.

[13] *See e.g.* Petersmann, *supra* note 10. Recent support for such a right can be found in *Biret International SA and Etablissements Biret et Cie. SA v Council of the European Union* Cases C-93/02 P and C-94/02 P, Opinion of Advocate General Siegbert Alber, 15 May 2003

of human rights is properly brought within the ring of WTO concerns; and then looking at the priorities among those rights that are included.

Consequently, the important question for us is not whether human rights *per se* are to be linked to the global trading regime, but rather how extensive that linkage is to be. The real choice is between alternative clusters, or sets, of rights, and between alternative weightings of elements within a cluster. We will examine a position that draws the WTO into the terrain of norms about human health, education, and environment, and we will contrast this with a position in favor of a narrow range of commitments, keeping the organization on the more familiar ground of human rights focused on secure and stable commercial relations and the protection of property.

When we come to the principles governing priorities within the group of rights that a trading system should respect, we are forced to deal with a problem that occupies human rights lawyers whatever the context is in which they work. Few, if any, human rights have absolute priority, such that they should not be partly compromised in order to satisfy another right. Some highly abstract rights might have this absolute status, such as the right of one person to be treated as the equal of another.[14] However, when they are brought down to concrete inclusion in human rights law and policy, they often enter into mutual conflict, making it impossible to completely satisfy the demands of one without limiting the satisfaction of another. Some of these conflicts are between individuals or groups holding the same right, as when two or more vie, in the name of freedom of expression, for the chance to speak at a public meeting; or two or more vie for scarce resources in the name of the right of access to adequate protection of health. There may also be conflict between holders of different rights, as when the right to freedom of expression for demonstrators competes with the right to freedom of movement by normal users of the highway; or the right to adequate protection of health is in competition with the right to respect for one's intellectual property.[15] Since these fundamental competitions for priority take place in all human rights regimes, there is no reason to think that the conflicts would be less acute when these regimes are linked to trading relations. Does this mean that even if their place was made secure within the working of the WTO, we must nevertheless expect to see the promise of human rights diluted or diverted as the disputes mechanism and policy makers administering trade go about the work of balancing one right against another? That depends on how the objectives of the organization are located within a wider set of basic principles, which is investigated in the following discussion.

IV. Linking the WTO's Objectives to Human Rights

The stated goals of the WTO can be found in its preamble, which provides a useful source for both lawyers and non-lawyers wanting to see what the Members of the organization have committed themselves to achieve. There is room for debate over the best way to interpret these paragraphs, and this difference of view can affect the potential entry points for, and character of, the human rights that can be recognized by the institution. There are seven overlapping goals within the preamble. While they are run together in the text, it is useful to separate them as commitments to:

---

[14] This was made famous in the work of the legal philosopher Ronald Dworkin as the "right to equal concern and respect". *See* R. DWORKIN, SOVEREIGN VIRTUE 1 ff (2000).
[15] The right to intellectual property is recognized in Article 15(1)(c) of the International Covenant on Economic, Social and Cultural Rights (1966). For this distinction between types of conflict among basic rights, *See* Jeremy Waldron, *Rights in Conflict* 99 (3) ETHICS 503, 509–512; 516–18 (1989); and S. Leader, *Integration, Federation, and Rights* in MORALE ET POLITIQUE DES DROITS DE L'HOMME (Monique Costillo ed. 2003) at 63.

1) Raising standards of living,

2) Ensuring full employment,

3) Ensuring a large and steadily growing volume of income and effective demand,

4) Expanding the production of, and trade in, goods and services,

5) Allowing the optimal use of the world's resources in accordance with the objective of sustainable development,

6) Seeking both to protect and preserve the environment, consistent with the contracting parties respective needs and concerns at different levels of economic development, and

7) Assure developing countries, especially the least developed, a share in the growth in international trade commensurate with the needs of their economic development.

In addition, the preamble describes a particular objective, which serves the others.

8) The Members aim at "contributing to these objectives by reciprocal and mutually advantageous arrangements directed to substantial reduction of tariffs." It will do this by developing "... an integrated, more viable and durable multilateral trading system...".

The first thing to note about these objectives is that they can and often do complement one another, and are sometimes furthered by the kind of market integration addressed in the preamble. The U.N. Commission on Human Rights has published a series of recent reports on the impact of international trade on intellectual property rights,[16] agriculture,[17] and the provision of services.[18] In each of these reports, which are considered later, the beneficial effects of free trade for some parts of the population are described. However, the reports then go on to indicate areas in which trade can damage other parts of the population. At this point, a tension arises between the latter's entitlement under human rights standards, and the central mission of the WTO to sustain and encourage trade.

A. Embedded and Imported Rights

Human rights are not explicitly mentioned in the preamble of the WTO Agreement. However, they can be linked to the text, depending on how it is read. Some of the rights are embedded in some of the objectives, as necessary for their attainment. Take, as an example, the commitment to "sustainable development". As a report from the United Nations Development Program argues:

> Development is unsustainable where the rule of law and equity do not exist; where ethnic, religious or sexual discrimination are rampant; where there are restrictions on free speech, free association and the media; or where large numbers of people live in abject and degrading poverty.[19]

That is, societies must be in a position to remove internal obstacles to their ability to renew themselves. If the least well-off are provided with these rights, then the U.N. argues

---

[16] U.N. Commission on Human Rights, *Agreement on Trade-Related Aspects of Intellectual Property Rights*, E/CN.4/Sub.2/2001/13.

[17] U.N. Commission on Human Rights, *Globalization and its Impact on the Full Enjoyment of Human Rights*, E/CN.4/2002/54.

[18] *See* E/CN.4/Sub.2/2002/9, *supra* note 2.

[19] UNDP, HUMAN RIGHTS AND SUSTAINABLE DEVELOPMENT Section C (Nov. 1997), http://magnet.undp.org/e-list/hr.htm#N1C.

that they will be less likely to deplete their own key resources such as land, water, or human capital, in the effort to survive.[20] Certain rights are therefore embedded in the goal of sustainable development.

While important, this way of picking out certain rights that the WTO must respect has its limits. It treats human rights as means to ends rather than as goals worth of pursuit in their own right. To continue with our example, if a commitment to give effect to certain human rights is grounded on and flows from a particular feature of development—its sustainability—then before the WTO was to take seriously any given right it would have to be convinced that it plays a demonstrable role in helping a society to renew its basic resources, both material and non-material. That does not fully cover the wider goals of a human rights agenda, such as that of the ICESCR, which is aimed at progressively improving access to certain basic social goods because of their intrinsic worth, quite apart from their ability to contribute to a society's ability to husband and renew its resources.[21]

For several other objectives announced in the preamble, it is not possible to find human rights embedded in them. Any connection to such rights therefore has to come from importing the relevant guarantees into the text. For example, the institution can pursue the first item on the list, raising aggregate or even average standards of living, without necessarily satisfying the right of *all* relevant portions of society to an adequate standard as would be called for by the ICESCR.[22] It is notoriously possible to increase the average standard while allowing the level enjoyed by the least well-off to fall. Any concern for the least well-off engages entitlements to distributive justice. *Prima facie,* this falls within the province of Members' domestic policy, and is not the business of the WTO. However, the trade treaties draw a balance between objective of furthering trade and various permissions given to member states to refuse to trade. In the latter case, the member might be motivated by a concern that the terms on which a good or service are entering the country might damage the well being of the least well-off. The question that then arises is, to what extent do the trade treaties have to be sensitive to the demands of social and economic rights as part of the legitimate reason that Members can have for the refusal to trade? That is, to what extent is it appropriate to take the rights standards that bind Members and import them into the legitimate concerns of the WTO as it interprets the relevant treaties? Is it possible to go further and call on the WTO itself to formulate policies with the avowed intention of actually facilitating (rather than simply not obstructing) the task of Members in meeting their required social and economic targets?

Would it be necessary to amend the organization's Articles in order to open up these possibilities? That depends on how the Articles are interpreted.[23]

[20] E. Barbier, *The Concept of Sustainable Economic Development,* 14 Environmental Conservation 101 (2–1987) ("...the primary objective is reducing the absolute poverty of the world's poor through providing lasting and secure livelihoods that minimize resource depletion, environmental degradation, cultural disruption and social instability"); R. Goodland and G. Ledoc, *Neoclassical Economics and Principles of Sustainable Development,* 38 ECOLOGICAL MODELLING. 38 (1987) ("Sustainable development is a policy which optimizes the economic and societal benefits available in the present, without jeopardizing the likely potential for similar benefits in the future.") All citations drawn from *Definitions of Sustainable Development,* collected by Jennifer DuBose, http://www.srl.gatech.edu/education/ME4804/definitions.html. *See also* United Nations Development Programme, *Integrating Human Rights with Sustainable Human Development: A UNDP Policy Document* (1998).
[21] This freestanding quality of the right can be seen in ICESCR Article 11.
[22] *Id.* Art 11.
[23] For an excellent consideration of the interpretive options, *see* Gabrielle Marceau, *WTO Dispute Settlement and Human Rights,* 13(4) EUROPEAN JOURNAL OF INTERNATIONAL LAW 753, 814 (2002)

B. Techniques of Interpretation: (I) Institutional Purpose and Founders' Intentions

The U.N. Sub-Commission on the Prevention of Discrimination and the Protection of Minorities, has declared that "the full and indivisible range of human rights should be the 'primary objective' of trade, investment, and financial policy."[24] As attractive as this might sound in general terms, it is an opening that will make sense to a lawyer—and to others interpreting WTO rules—only if certain fundamental options are chosen when it comes to working with the Articles.[25] The first involves an approach whereby an international organization is understood to have not only those powers and competence which are explicitly conferred upon it but also those powers and competences which may reasonably be inferred from inspection of the purposes and functions of the organization.[26] One is not bound by the literal words in the body of the instrument if they are manifestly inadequate to achieve the relevant purposes and functions.[27]

How should content be given to these purposes and functions? When lawyers answer this question, they sometimes add what they call a teleological element to this principle of interpretation.[28] According to this element, the significance to be attached to the organization's statement of its goals is not limited by what its founders happen to intend at the time they set up the institution. It is instead also to be interpreted in the light of wider understandings of those purposes held by the community on whose behalf the institution acts—be that community global or local. The content of this wider understanding can be seen in other basic commitments that the community has made, such as those found in its formulation of human rights norms. As one legal philosopher put it, one does not look at what the founders of the institution said, but at what they did.[29] What they did is properly subject to changing interpretations, and properly brought into line with the evolution of the wider community's basic understanding of what makes any exercise of institutional power legitimate. Human rights norms therefore form a central part of this wider foundation, even if their inclusion was not intended by the founders of the WTO. On this approach, they should be read into the existing preamble, without needing to amend it, and in turn should inform a reading of all of the detailed provisions in the remainder of the Articles.

This view of interpretation can be contrasted with one which is not necessarily hostile to incorporating human rights norms into the WTO mandate, but admits them on a more restrictive basis. It takes as its point of departure a quite different protocol, according

---

[24] Resolution of September 4, 1998 (http://www.pdhre.org/involved/uncommission.html) See also the seminal work of Ernst-Ulrich Petersmann, *Time for Integrating Human Rights into the Law of Worldwide Organizations*, WORKING PAPER 7/01 Jean Monnet Program, Harvard Law School (2001); R. Howse, and M. Mutua, *Protecting Human Rights in the Global Economy: Challenges for the WTO*, Rights and Democracy (www.ichrdd.ca) (2000); J. Oloka-Onyango and Deepika Udagama, *supra* note 2; *cf.* Caroline Dommen, *Raising Rights Concerns in the WTO*, 24 HUMAN RIGHTS QUARTERLY 1 (February 1, 2002).

[25] For the particular principles applicable to the interpreting of constituent instruments, *see* P. Sands and P. Klein, BOWETT'S LAW OF INTERNATIONAL INSTITUTIONS ¶ 14–023 (2001).

[26] H. G. Schermers & N. M. Blokker, INTERNATIONAL INSTITUTIONAL LAW (3rd ed) 141–2, (1997), Kelsen, PRINCIPLES OF INTERNATIONAL LAW 284–5, 833–4 (1966). For similar possibilities in the interpretation of the powers of the World Bank and IMF, *see* Skogly, *supra* note 9, at 72.

[27] Sands and Klein, *supra* note 25, ¶ 14–023. This approach "...looks to the object and purpose of the organization, rather than adopt a literal (and therefore restrictive) approach to what the constituent instrument does or does not say". It is an approach that takes "...into account the object pursued by the organization rather than the text of its constituent instrument".

[28] *Id.* ¶ 14–021. "There is some authority for the proposition that a treaty of a constitutional character should...allows for the 'intrinsically evolutionary nature of a constitution'".

[29] Ronald Dworkin, LAW'S EMPIRE, Chapter 10 *passim* (1986).

to which an international organization may only perform such acts as are expressly laid down in the statutes of the organization, and any acts that are not mentioned there will be outside the scope of the organization's range of maneuver. On this basis, the only human rights the WTO is bound to respect are those that the contracting parties agreed to respect when they came together and formulated the objectives of the organization in the Articles.[30]

The difference between the teleological approach and that rooted in the intentions of the contracting parties is fundamental in any project connecting the WTO and human rights. Both approaches are open to such rights, but in very different ways. The latter starts from within the organization, and looks to the moment of its foundation. The former starts from outside the organization, and looks to the way in which it fits into wider and evolving understandings of what makes power—both of states and of organizations transcending states—legitimate.

C. Techniques of Interpretation (II): Functional versus Civic Inclusion

A teleological approach to the interpretation of WTO treaties, with its eye on the evolution of standards, can itself develop in two distinct directions. One of these takes a functional view of power, and another takes what can be called a civic view.[31] The difference can best be appreciated by going back to the eight objectives in the WTO Agreement's preamble. The first seven are general goals: they are shared by a number of other national and international organizations along with the WTO. The eighth is a special objective. That is, it specifies the particular way in which the WTO is meant to pursue its general objectives: its commitment to achieve a "substantial reduction of tariffs" and "an integrated, more viable, and durable multilateral trading system". Now, according to the functional approach, it is the special and not the general objectives of the institution that fix the appropriate scope of its responsibilities. Its duties are, for the functionalist, to the actors who are directly involved in the process of this movement to integrated trade, and no further. Thus, even if it could be shown that opening markets to certain goods and services damages the prospects of certain local populations, the functionalist claims that this is not enough to attach the responsibility for those effects to the WTO. The proper concern of the organization, from this perspective, is not to achieve *comprehensive* fairness, but only to achieve the limited sorts of fairness that its commitment to non-discrimination among goods and service providers involves. Debra P. Steger, former Director of the WTO Appellate Body Secretariat, has recently articulated this view. She refuses to include concerns about users of services or of goods within the scope of WTO responsibility, confining herself to their producers. "The WTO's mandate," she says:

> is to promote freer trade and market access through the application of the principles of non-discrimination. Although I would equate the principle of non-discrimination with the fight against protectionism, nowhere in the GATT is the term "fairness" used. That does not mean that the GATT is "unfair"; it simply means that "fairness" in trading relations is not a GATT principle or norm—non-discrimination is.[32]

[30] Sands and Klein, *supra* note 25, at 450 (2001).
[31] The functional outlook described here is different from functionalism as it normally figures in the literature on trade. See e.g. Ernst-Ulrich Petersmann, *supra* note 24, text associated with his footnote 6. Compare this with the distinction between civic and functional approaches in S. Leader, *Three Faces of Justice and the Management of Change*, 63 MODERN LAW REVIEW 55–83 (January 2000) passim.
[32] Debra P. Steger, *The "Trade and . . . ." Conundrum—A Commentary*, 28 AMERICAN JOURNAL OF INTERNATIONAL LAW 135, 139 (2002)

This is a position standing in sharp contrast with that which embraces users; producers; as well as potential beneficiaries and victims of both. Several recent reports by the U.N. take this wider view, as do commentators such as Steve Charnovitz and Ernst- Ulrich Petersmann.[33] They implicitly endorse what can be called a civic approach. This does not tie the WTO's responsibility to its special objectives, but roots these objectives within wider concerns. To illustrate this difference, consider the WTO rules that affect access to education or health, or affect the full range of labor rights. Based on the civic approach, if those effects are significant then the organization is responsible for them. Based on the functional approach, the organization might not be responsible for these same effects. For the functionalist, there is an additional issue of institutional identity at stake: the special mission of the WTO distinguishes it from a state, and in turn from the International Labor Organization, the World Health Organization, etc. A *Member* may well be responsible for implementing policies that violate its own commitments to basic rights, but it does not follow for the functionalist that the WTO is therefore also responsible.[34]

Even if the Members, working collectively as the WTO, make demands on one of their number to open its markets, the way in which the latter then copes with any negative effects of such an opening is, for the functionalist, not the proper concern of that organization. It is an issue that calls on the state's particular range of responsibilities that are wider than those of the trading body. It may, for example, be appropriate that the Member seek the international assistance to which the ICESCR refers so as to obtain the technical advice, and possibly the resources necessary, to protect any human right that would be jeopardized as a by-product of opening its markets.[35] This would call, *inter alia*, for contributions from specialized agencies of the U.N. to provide the requisite assistance—to fill the gap that might be opened up by market integration. The civic approach is fundamentally different. It is not primarily concerned with the distinct or special *roles* of states and other institutions, but instead focuses on their overlapping *power*. If the policies of a given Member, and those of all Members working as the WTO, have equivalent effects on a population, then on applying the civic view the responsibility of each member singly, and their responsibility collectively could well be similar.

This is one of the fundamental points of division in the free trade / fair trade debate. The parties to that confrontation are not, whatever the appearances, divided about whether "fairness" as a value does or should form part of the WTO's existing principles. This is true despite the way in which Steger has expressed her point. For the principle of non-discrimination to which she refers is itself a species of fairness—and as Brian Languille

---

[33] *See* Steve Charnovitz, *Triangulating the World Trade Organization*, 28 AMERICAN JOURNAL OF INTERNATIONAL LAW 28, 41 (2002): "The capacity of horrendous working conditions to render trade unfair was acknowledged by the parties to the Covenant of the League of Nations . . . Whether the addition to the WTO Agreements of a provision on workers' rights would enhance fairness or erode it depends upon what that provision would require. Yet it can hardly be doubted that the labor issue fits the trade fairness frame." Petersmann, *supra* note 24, text associated with his fn 16.

[34] For this approach in international economic law, *see* FRANCOIS GIANVITI, *Economic, Social and Cultural Rights and the International Monetary Fund* WORKING PAPER FOR THE U.N. COMMITTEE ON ECONOMIC AND SOCIAL AND CULTURAL RIGHTS, E/C 12/2001/WP.5, para 6 ff. (2001). *See also* the discussion of functionalists in Charnovitz, *supra* note 33 at 48.

[35] ICESCR, *supra* note 9, Article 2, ¶ 1: "Each state party to the present Covenant undertakes to take steps, individually and *through international assistance and cooperation* . . . with a view to achieving progressively the full realization of the rights recognized in the present Covenant . . . ." For an example of such damage as a by-product, consider the U.N.'s analysis of the possible effects of trade policy on the ability of the least well off to gain access to education and health facilities. See *Liberalization of Trade in Services*, *supra* note 3, ¶ 60

has pointed out, some degree of concern for fairness is therefore built into the very fabric of free trade.[36] The real clash between the fair trade and free trade advocates is over the *scope* of the demand for fairness.

Telling against the civic view of appropriate scope is the fact that the WTO is clearly not a state, and therefore would not seem to have the same range of responsibilities as a state. But telling against the functional alternative is the possibility that Member states may be caught between the twin pressures of market integration and human rights concerns, each sometimes pointing in opposite directions. It does not seem right, or realistic, to offload the negative affects of trade onto other international organizations meant to assure respect for labor, health or environmental standards. That creates tension and rivalry among international organizations that should be complementing the work of one another. A clash of international demands becomes particularly aggravated when a state finds that the steps it takes to satisfy a requirement of one of the trade treaties places it in possible violation of one of the human rights treaties. While all sides—within and outside the WTO—would deplore this situation, the devil lies in the detail: as will be explored in Part V.

D. Two Types of Market Integration

These legal concerns have to be placed alongside the concrete work of the WTO as it gives daily effect to the development of an integrated trading system. Here, it is important to note the difference between "positive" and "negative" integration of markets, and the potential effect of each on a human rights policy.[37] A negative strategy requires that a Member of a trading system not use domestic policy to erect undue barriers to trade. Market integration in this mode happens via a series of prohibitions of such obstacles. Examples include the prohibitions against discrimination among sources of imports; against discrimination in favor of domestic producers; and against unjustified non-tariff barriers to trade. A positive strategy takes the demand for market integration a step further, requiring that the terms on which goods, services, or people are allowed to penetrate the borders of another country should be based on common standards fashioned through a policy set by the institution administering trade. The distinction is between the different degrees of centralization required to implement the integration sought. Speaking of the European Community, for example, Nicholas Bernard says that:

> Negative integration leaves instruments of policy, such as regulatory powers or fiscal powers, at the national level, although the use of those instruments is prohibited when it creates or maintains impediments to trade between Member states. On the other hand, positive integration entails the centralization of policy instruments at Community level.[38]

E. Human Rights from the Center: Positive Integration

When they are linked to positive market integration, human rights are a potentially critical tool deployed at the center. At the moment they play no such role, and exploring their

---

[36] A point ably demonstrated in Brian A. Languille, *Labour Standards in the Globalised Economy and the Free Trade/Fair Trade Debate*, in INTERNATIONAL LABOUR STANDARDS AND ECONOMIC INTERDEPENDENCE 329–339 (W. Sengenberger and D. Campbell eds, 1994).

[37] *See* the seminal work of Prof. Petersmann on this point, Petersmann, *From Negative to Positive Integration in the WTO: Time for Mainstreaming Human Rights into WTO Law?*, 37 COMMON MARKET LAW REVIEW 1363 (2000).

[38] Nicolas Bernard, *The Future of European Economic Law in the Light of the Principle of Subsidiarity*, 33 COMMON MKT. L. REV. 633, 636 (1996)

potential takes us into an area of possible reform. The changes could come at several levels of strength. One could imagine making the WTO a party to the several international human rights covenants, including the ICCPR and ICESCR. This would require it to make and to interpret the agreements it administers such that they have no effects that violate such rights. Less radically, the WTO could, without becoming a party to the covenants, voluntarily incorporate their standards into its own internal order. A further mode of linking human rights to a positive integration strategy would involve not simply looking at the internal order of the WTO, but outwards to the Members themselves. One could imagine a fresh agreement demanding that each Member adopt adequate human rights standards as a condition of it engaging in international trade. Here, we have a partial analogy in the Agreement on Trade-Related Aspects of Intellectual Property Rights ("TRIPS"). TRIPS takes a step towards a human rights demand: that the contracting parties implement adequate protection for intellectual property entitlements.[39] The right to this species of property has also acquired a place in the ICESCR's declaration that everyone is entitled "to benefit from the protection of the moral and material interests resulting from any scientific, literary or artistic production of which he is the author."[40]

Is this overlap between the demand made by TRIPS and the demand made by the Covenant enough for us to say that the former is requiring Member states to respect a human right? If so, we already have an example of the WTO including respect for human rights as part of its mission. But TRIPS is not making a human rights demand, and the reasons for reaching this conclusion are instructive. It is certainly calling for the protection of an interest that overlaps with the interest that the ICESCR is protecting. However, more is needed for this to overlap to turn into a human rights approach. The difference lies in the gap between a functional and a civic outlook. The functionalist approach, which is popular in interpretations of the agreement, focuses on one of what we have called the special objectives in the preamble of the WTO: the aim of developing an integrated, more viable, and durable multilateral trading system. It ties TRIPS to this objective. The agreement is thereby predominantly focused on the need to create an integrated system by protecting a producer's intellectual property. Those applying the agreement do not consider it appropriate to *demand* that Member states provide a fair balance between those producer needs and the needs of local populations for e.g. the adequate provision of health protection. That is, the TRIPS agreement does not require that other interests be protected alongside the protection given to producer interests. True, Member states are given a certain margin of *liberty* to protect the latter. But this margin is seen as derogation from a core requirement of the agreement, with a presumption against it. It is a presumption that can be rebutted, but the protection of non-producer interests has to swim against the tide: it faces a burden of justification, as going against the spirit of the agreement.

A civic approach to the interpretation of TRIPS comes closer to capturing what is characteristic of a human rights approach. It would focus on the terms of Article 7 of TRIPS, which provides that:

> The protection and enforcement of intellectual property rights should contribute to … the mutual advantage of producers and users of technological knowledge, and in a manner conducive to social and economic welfare, and to a balance of rights and obligations.

---

[39] On the ability of this portion of the TRIPS Agreement to fit human rights criteria, see the discussion in the text accompanying notes 41 to 43 *infra*

[40] ICESCR, *supra* note 8, Article 15.

Article 7 could be taken as establishing a wider objective for the protection of intellectual property than that which would be established by the functionalists. The TRIPS agreement can be understood, on this approach, as inducing countries to adopt an intellectual property regime that provides both protection of intellectual property and room for overriding that protection, where both are on an equal footing.[41]

In both its strengths and its weaknesses, the TRIPS example provides several lessons. The TRIPS regime has spawned confrontation on its own terrain: having taken the step to demand a property right on behalf of one set of actors in the trade relationship, what about other actors wanting to enjoy potentially competing basic rights, such as the right to adequate protection of health? A human rights approach demands that any instrument that starts by focusing on one right, must tacitly make room for other basic rights and allow them to be brought into a fair balance.

But there is something more: the balances sought by Article 7 of TRIPS open further questions about what it is for the agreement to operate in the spirit of human rights protection. Does the concern for users' rights extend to contributing to the progressively greater levels of welfare that the ICESCR calls for, or is the system at most required to refrain from pulling the least well-off further down? When we observe the decision by the TRIPS Committee to extend to the least developed countries ("LDC's") an additional period of time before they will be required to comply, it is useful to consider what the benchmarks for their progress should be.

Should their obligations arise once it becomes clear that no significant part of their populations will be made substantially worse off by adhesion; or is it appropriate to apply the more ambitious principle that application of the TRIPS will actually give them enough control over their domestic policy so as to progressively improve basic social, economic, and cultural goods? In considering these questions, it is important to note the dual emphasis in the Doha Declaration on the TRIPS agreement. In part the Declaration highlights the importance of interpreting the agreement so as not to *prevent* Members from taking measures to protect public health, and it also emphasizes the more dynamic need to *assist* them in their effort to promote greater access to medicines for all. This could be interpreted as incorporating the positive obligation to gradually improve certain health protection standards as required by the ICESCR, Arts 2(1) and 12.[42]

F. Human Rights, Refusals to Trade, and the Discipline of Negative Integration

In this portion of the chapter we enter a different domain, one in which there is a greater prospect for seeing human rights brought to bear within the existing trade rules, because they can be initiated by one particular WTO Member rather than depending on achieving

---

[41] This is a central point about TRIPS made by the U.N. Sub-Commission on the Promotion and Protection of Human Rights. It argues that as presently implemented (not as presently formulated) the agreement "does not adequately reflect the fundamental nature and indivisibility of all human rights, including the right of everyone to enjoy the benefits of scientific progress ... (and) the right to health..." *Intellectual Property Rights and Human Rights,* Sub-Commission Resolution 2000/7, ¶ 2. August 16, 2001

[42] WTO, *Ministerial Declaration on the TRIPS Agreement and Public Health,* 2001 WT/MIN(01)/DEC/2, ¶ 4, reproduced in the Appendix to this book. On the extra time given for compliance to LDCs the Declaration says, "We also agree that the least-developed country Members will not be obliged, with respect to pharmaceutical products, to implement or apply Sections 5 and 7 of Part II of the TRIPS Agreement or to enforce rights provided for under these Sections until January 1, 2016, without prejudice to the right of least-developed country Members to seek other extensions of the transition periods as provided for in Article 66.1 of the TRIPS Agreement." *Id.* ¶ 7.

a new consensus among all.[43] The GATT, GATS and TRIPS all create space within which a Member can refuse to accept a given good or service, or can override a claim of intellectual property, because of the demands of its domestic policy.[44] Depending on how the existing rules are read, human rights can figure as acceptable reasons for such a refusal to accept market integration.

There are two possible scenarios, which we shall illustrate by focusing on the GATT. In one, prompted by what can be called outwardly-directed concerns, country X refuses to import goods or services from country Y because it is concerned that Y is violating the human rights of its own population. In another, prompted by inwardly-directed concerns, X refuses to import from Y because it is concerned about the effect that the entry of such goods and services might have on the human rights of its, X's, population.

As an example of the outwardly-directed concern, Y might have acted so abusively that it is considered by the U.N. Security Council to be a threat to international peace and security, as South Africa was when it practiced apartheid. If so, Article 41 of the U.N. Charter provides for the legitimate use of economic sanctions. Article XXI(c) of the GATT in turn permits Members to refuse to import goods from that country for reasons of international peace and security. Similarly, objections to the importing of products that have been made by prison labor might overlap with human rights concerns, and this refusal is permitted under Article XX(e).[45] What about objections that X might raise to Y's non-respect of the basic trade union rights of its labor force? What about its objections to abuses of other human rights?[46] While these fall outside the explicit grounds mentioned in the treaties, there is potential room within their more general terms. For example, Article XX(a) of GATT permits refusals to trade when this is "necessary to protect public morals." Steve Charnovitz has suggested that, under suitable constraints, this clause could accommodate refusals to trade based on human rights violations, given the centrality of such standards at the core of the moral standards of many societies.[47]

There is a danger in this outwardly-directed strategy, however. One country, particularly if it is powerful, might be able to unilaterally impose its own understanding of human rights requirements on another. It might do this for protectionist reasons, or for reasons that arise from a good faith interpretation of the importance of a given right with which its trading partner disagrees. Given free reign, refusals to trade for such reasons would cause the system to fragment. The WTO decisions show some sensitivity to this possibility. While, as was said, human rights issues have not yet been directly raised in past cases, decisions have made it clear that WTO will allow a Member to refuse to import from another because of outwardly—directed concerns about issues such as the protection of

[43] Note that decisions reached by panels or the Appellate Body no longer need a consensus for adoption. Instead a consensus is required to block a decision. The losing party therefore no longer has the power to block the adoption of a decision of the Dispute Settlement Body, as was the case under the GATT dispute settlement system. DSU Article 17 ¶ 14

[44] *See inter alia* GATT, Article XX; GATS, Article XIV; and TRIPS, Article VIII.

[45] Concerns about prison labor and about human rights potentially overlap. Note, however, that other chapters in the book make it clear that the original purpose of this provision was protection, not respect for human rights. Many countries which take human rights seriously, including the United States, produce prison goods

[46] An example is the abuse of human rights in Myanmar, and the reaction of Massachusetts with the "Burma" law. The law restricts the authority of the Commonwealth to buy goods and services from companies that do business with Burma/Myanmar. Mass. Gen. Laws Ann. Ch. 7, §§ 22G–22M (West 1998 Supp.). The matter was not dealt with by a panel, but it is not difficult to imagine circumstances in which an issue like this would reach that stage.

[47] *See* Steve Charnovitz, *The Moral Exception in Trade Policy*, 38 VIRGINIA JOURNAL OF INTERNATIONAL LAW 689 (1998).

endangered species, and not simply because of concerns about its own domestic situation. However, the Appellate Body in the famous *Shrimp-Turtle* litigation has also made it clear that before a country can refuse to trade on such Article XX grounds, it must have made good faith efforts to negotiate with other countries a common understanding of the content of any such standard. The negotiation need not be with all interested parties, and indeed it might not result in an agreement before the embargo is imposed, but the coverage of parties must be substantial enough to be convincingly multilateral, and the efforts to reach agreement must be made in good faith.[48]

Turning to inwardly-directed concerns, the Member refusing to accept a WTO demand for entry into its market, or a demand for shaping its intellectual property rights, can also rely on the same provision in the GATT and its equivalent in GATS and TRIPS. It is worth noting in particular the scope for inwardly-directed human rights concerns potentially available in Article 8 of TRIPS. As they give effect to the agreement's core provisions, Members may adopt measures "... necessary to protect public health and nutrition, and to promote the public interest in sectors of vital importance to their socio-economic ... development.... Provided that such measures are consistent with the provisions of this Agreement."[49] The Doha Declaration on TRIPS and Public Health gave added emphasis to the need to interpret the Agreement such that it gives scope to Members' "... right to protect public health and ... to promote access to medicines for all".[50] If there is room for a Member's *right* to protect public health, then there must equally be room for a Member's *obligation* to protect public health—an obligation arising, *inter alia*, from the ICESCR.[51]

At this stage, we can see why the trading system is likely to have a built-in resistance to a human rights claim, when these claims prompt Members to refuse to accept goods, services, or the recognition of intellectual property rights. As was true of the earlier example of derogations from TRIPS, they are all claims to carve out an exception to demands that a trading partner go along with market integration.[52] As a result, the system looks at human rights much as it does other non-tariff barriers. It may reluctantly admit them but on condition that, like other barriers, they do "least damage" to the core objective to free trade from among alternatives available. In other words, when they prompt refusals to trade, human rights demands face the rigors of a policy of negative integration. Quite apart from any views trade officials or adjudicators might have about the proper place for such rights in a trading system, this is an institutional influence on the way in which they see the problem. The result might radically shrink the force of any

---

[48] For a statement of these principles, see the views of the Appellate Body in *United States—Import Prohibition of Certain Shrimp and Shrimp Products* ("*Shrimp-Turtles I*"), WT/DS58/AB/R (1998), followed by *United States—Import Prohibition of Certain Shrimp and Shrimp Products—Recourse to Article 21.5 of the DSU by Malaysia* ("*Shrimp-Turtles II*") WT/DS58/AB/RW (2001). *See also* Joanne Scott, *On Kith and Kine (and Crustaceans)*, in THE EU, THE WTO AND THE NAFTA 162 ff (J. Weiler ed. 2000).

[49] In the same spirit, though with different detail, are Article XX(b) of the GATT and Article IV (b) of GATS.

[50] *WTO Ministerial Declaration on the TRIPS Agreement and Public Health*, *supra* note 42.

[51] *Id.*

[52] When a refusal to import a good is accompanied by local production of the same or a similar good, then there is *prima facie* a violation of the ban by Article III:4 on according domestic goods better treatment than is given to imported goods. This can happen in the situations we are considering, since the country refusing an import because of the policies or conditions surrounding the production of a good in another country, or because of its impact on the basic rights of its own citizens, might not have the same objections to similar goods produced in its own borders. At that point, while the Member might look benignly on local producers, there is a case to answer under Article III: 4. The Member will only be able to overcome the presumption against such differential treatment by relying on one of the Article XX or XXI exceptions.

given human right—taking it well below the promise it offers in other quarters, where it does not have to be provided in a version that is the least trade restrictive. This is one factor that fuels the feeling of many skeptics that international trade is inherently corrosive of social standards. It is a product of a functionalist vision of the mission and responsibility of the WTO. We shall explore more of the civic alternative in a moment.

G. Human Rights and Trade with Developing Countries: A Special Case?

This is a further part of our map, raising some of the most politically-charged issues about the place of human rights in a trade regime. Some developing country Members have been called on to respect certain human rights demands as a condition of their enjoying certain special trading advantages. The demands concerning the rights do not come from the WTO itself but from certain countries that are developed country Members.[53] In return for preferential access to their markets—that is, a degree of access that is not granted to other WTO Members—these richer partners demand in return that the recipients of the preference accept certain conditions. The European Community, for example, splits its preferential treatment into several tiers, and offers what it calls "special incentive arrangements" if the recipient country incorporates into its national legislation the substance of the standards laid down in key ILO conventions, including those on forced labor and on freedom of association, and the right to collective bargaining.[54] The special inducements take the form of additional tariff reductions at twice the level of the basic preferences accorded.[55] It offers similar incentives for measures to protect the environment and to control drug trafficking.[56] Under the U.S. Generalized System of Preferences ("GSP") scheme, all eligible items are duty-free. The main conditions attached to granting this eligibility to particular countries relate to protection of intellectual property, the respect of labor rights (including the elimination of the worst forms of child labor), and the resolution of investment disputes. No specific mention is made of ILO Conventions or TRIPS, but these standards have been referred to in decisions about non-compliance.[57]

These arrangements have been the subject of a debate that raises many of the headline items in the politics of trade, about which feelings run strongly. It is a debate that is fundamental to the future role for human rights in this portion of the trading regime. On one side, there are those who argue that the conditions attached to preference are objectionable because they are often prompted by protectionist motives; are impositions by the powerful on the sovereignty and distinct values of weaker countries; and that some of the conditions erect obstacles to developing countries' ability to pursue economic growth.[58] On the other side, defenders of the system deny each of these points, and they sometimes add the argument that the GSP scheme is entirely voluntary. Developing

---

[53] Or groups of countries, such as those belonging to the European Union.

[54] *Council Regulation Applying a Scheme of Generalized Tariff Preferences for the Period January 1, 2002 to December 31, 2004* [12732/4/01 REV 4] Preamble, ¶ 19; and Title III.

[55] *Id. Preamble*, ¶ 16.

[56] *Id. Section* IV

[57] *A Preliminary Analysis of the GSP Schemes in the Quad,* Note by the Secretariat, WT/COMTD/W/93. For a reference to ILO standards in US decisions, see the report on Indonesia's worker rights laws in 1992 *GSP Annual Review*, Case 007-CP-92, July 1993. The original authority for the U.S. GSP scheme is Title V of the Trade Act of 1974 (19 USC 2461 et seq.). The scheme was originally introduced in January 1976 for a ten-year period and has since been renewed at various times.

[58] *See e.g.* the complaint brought by Brazil in 1987, *U.S. Actions On GSP Assailed In GATT,* discussed in http://www.sunsonline.org/trade/process/during/uruguay/gsp/05160087.htm. The dispute never reached the hearing stage.

countries, they say, make the choice to opt for the extra margin of reduced tariff that carries the conditions to which they object. If they are unhappy, they could simply decide to choose the basic amount of reduction in the core of the EC's preferential scheme and forego the additional special incentive of doubling the tariff reduction that is offered. In the case of the U.S. system, they could give up any preference at all.[59]

This series of disputes expresses some classic stand-offs in political economy. One side is claiming that labor rights impede wealth creation, while the other side denies that; one side claims that there is an imbalance of power that vitiates developing countries' free consent to conditions attached to preferences, while the other side insists that the consent is freely given. However, and this is of central importance in drawing our map, the clash also raises a fundamental structural issue. Alongside the question about which strings are legitimately attached to the grant of preferences, runs the fundamental question about power: who is, and who should be, entitled to affix the strings in the first place? Core WTO law, as we have seen, does allow Members to attach conditions to their willingness to trade, but at the same time does not allow those Members a free hand in deciding the exact nature of those conditions, even when these are prompted by their strong convictions on matters of social or environmental ethics. They have to meet the requirement that the conditions be negotiated with a significant number of affected partners[60], and that they satisfy other elements of the requirement of "necessity" in e.g., Articles XX of the GATT and Article IV of the GATS, examined more fully below.

The programs set up under GSP, for the moment, contain none of these restraints. Trading partners granting preferential terms of access to developing countries do so at their own initiative, and are entitled to pick and choose the terms on which the grant will be made or withheld. True, the international benchmark of ILO standards for labor rights is contained in the EC scheme, and is also followed by others, but this reference is the free choice of those setting the standards, and in all cases it is for the trading partners granting the preference to decide unilaterally whether or not those standards have been violated.[61] It is therefore not surprising that GSP schemes are often political tools. That is, the grant and refusal to trade on the terms contained in a particular GSP scheme are linked to a calculation that takes into account which developing countries a particular Member can or cannot afford to alienate; which local industries a Member wants to protect; and so on.[62] Indeed, the European Court of Justice has recently acknowledged this role for politics in the EC scheme.[63]

Whatever the bill of health this structure might have received from certain WTO Members, the political confrontation that it engenders continues to smolder. Those who

---

[59] For example, the United States responded to the Brazilian complaint with the claim that it was fully entitled to do what it had done under its "autonomous" GSP scheme. *See*.

[60] *See*, for example, the requirement of good faith attempts to reach agreement on shared standards with a significant number of potentially affected trading partners in *United States—Import Prohibition of Certain Shrimp and Shrimp Products—Recourse to Article 21.5 of the DSU by Malaysia ("Shrimp-Turtles II")* WT/DS58/AB/RW (2001). ¶ 123 ff.

[61] Compliance is determined by committees designed to monitor compliance established by each of the GSP grantors.

[62] For the political factors influencing GSP decisions, *see* J. H. JACKSON ET AL, LEGAL PROBLEMS OF INTERNATIONAL ECONOMIC RELATIONS § 24.3 (1995).

[63] *See DuPont Teijin Films Luxembourg SA v. Commission of the European Communities* ECJ, Court of First Instance, September 12, 2002, Case T-113/00, ¶ 85, "...the decision to withdraw the benefit of the preferential arrangements is pre-eminently a political issue concerning the Community and the beneficiary countries." This is the view taken by the ECJ in administering its scheme within the terms of its own GSP regulation. A WTO panel could well take a view that gives less discretion in a decision to withdraw preference, as discussed *infra*.

defend the imposition of conditions, as a *quid pro quo* for preferences accorded, consider GSP essentially to be an autonomous set of arrangements, lying outside the purview of WTO regulation.[64] On this view, two types of decisions might be thought to be voluntary, and therefore to be left alone: that of the developed country to offer preference, and that of the developing country to accept the offer. These voluntary choices should, on this view, seal off these arrangements from regulation by the rest of the trading world.

Developing countries are not convinced. India has taken steps toward a legal challenge of the EC GSP scheme before the WTO and, if it is successful, such schemes could become less of a discretionary political tool in the hands of the developed world.[65] The challenge is based on the terms of the agreement between GATT contracting parties that authorizes these schemes to be set up, known informally as the "Enabling Clause".[66] This instrument states that if one of their Members decides to offer certain developing countries special and more favorable access to their markets than other trading partners enjoy, then the grantor will not be in violation of the most favored nation requirement of Article I of the GATT, which would otherwise apply. The Clause also makes it clear that any conditions attached to the grant of preferential access must be focused on the development needs of the recipient.[67] India's complaint is that this latter demand is not met by the EU. The conditions attached to the preference granted which require protection of labor rights; protection of the environment; and the elimination of drug trafficking are, it is argued, either unrelated to or actually damage those development needs. If this claim were ever to be successful, then the EU scheme could fall outside the terms of the special permission given by the Enabling Clause. In turn, when the EU uses such conditions to differentiate among those developing countries that receive preferential treatment and those that do not, then those who lose out would have grounds for a complaint of discrimination based on Article I of the GATT.

It remains to be seen whether the Enabling Clause is to be given a status that raises issues for a WTO panel of such a fundamental and politically divisive nature. However, the legal terms in which the challenge is framed express the political issue with which the organization will have to grapple in any event, and which is central to our concerns in this chapter. India's claim is that the permission to engage in preferential treatment given by the WTO is not a blank check, but a partial opening: any conditions attached to trade preferences must be focused on the development needs of the recipients. Any given condition must, on this view, be matched against the requirements of the Clause. There could be two consequences if this argument were to succeed, either as a matter of legal or of political principle: one would be that the trading partners would not be able to use GSP schemes with as free a hand as they have hitherto. Conditions attached to preferential access to markets would still be possible, but they would need policing to see if in any given case they satisfy development needs. The second consequence takes us back to the divisive issue of voluntary choice. What looks to powerful countries like voluntary acceptance of their offer of preference with conditions attached, looks to some Members in the developing world like forced imposition. However, looked at through the lens of

[64] *Cf* the U.S. response to Brazil's 1987 complaint *supra* note 59.
[65] *India Seeks WTO Talks With EU Over Labor, Drugs Clauses in GSP Program*, 19 INTERNATIONAL TRADE REPORTER 456, (Number 11, March 14, 2002). As of the time of going to press, it has been announced on 28 October 2003 that a WTO panel has upheld India's complaint. See BRIDGES: WEEKLY TRADE NEWS DIGEST—Vol. 7, Number 37, 5th. The panel report will be released in early December, 2003
[66] *Differential and More Favorable Treatment, Reciprocity and Fuller Participation of Developing Countries*, GATT No. L/4903, Decision of November 28, 1979.
[67] *Id.* ¶ 3(c)

the Enabling Clause, the question of voluntary choice is *irrelevant*. If any given condition attached to preferential access does not fall within the opening for differential treatment of trading partners allowed by the Clause, then it does not matter that the condition was freely accepted. The Member setting the condition had no power to make that demand in the first place.[68] The Clause grants a special permission to a developed country to do something that would otherwise be illegal: to give a degree of special access to certain less developed trading partners. If country X grants less developed country Y preferred access to its markets which it denies to similarly situated country Z, because the former is willing but the latter is not to comply with a given condition, then Z can complain of a violation of the requirements of GATT Article I *if* that condition does not fall within the limited permission given by the Clause. Once it is clear that the boundaries set by the Clause have been exceeded by a particular condition attached to market access, then it is not relevant to Z's complaint that the condition is voluntarily accepted.

The scope for attaching conditions to the granting of GSP might therefore shrink. However, that does not mean that a Member could not impose a larger set of human rights concerns on those countries wanting access to its markets. Now, however, its refusal would fall within the principles governing what was earlier called 'outwardly directed' refusals to trade, as permitted *inter alia* by GATT Article XX.

H. Taking Stock

Before moving on, it is useful to stand back and briefly summarize the points made in Parts III and IV, since they will figure in what follows. We have been primarily concerned to see which pieces belong in the puzzle. This involved a look at the candidates for the group of human rights that the global trading system should respect and further. We then explored different possible linkages: prospects for linking trade to different sets of rights are affected by ideas about the WTO's institutional responsibility. We sketched two possible foundations for such responsibility: functional and civic principles. In turn, these distinct notions of the basis of the WTO's responsibility affect the approach to positive and negative integration of markets, as well as relations with the developing world. In Part V we will move from a static to a dynamic picture. We now look more closely at the priorities and balance between competing rights. This is a set of issues faced both by the WTO and by Member states. As the national and international systems interact, we will investigate the reasons for which free trade is condemned for wrongly imposing on national priorities, and where it has the potential to be—and be seen to be—impartial between the rival visions of the good society and of social justice held by trading partners.

V. Putting the System to Work in a Cosmopolitan Democracy[69]

As we watch the trading system relate to national priorities—moving in the same direction of some and upsetting others—it is important to see where this influence fits. Does the system of trade law stand a chance of being seen as an extension of the mandates of all of

---

[68] It is also irrelevant, from this perspective, that a system of preferences is left to developed countries to institute or not, as they see fit. It is *once* they decide to extend this benefit that they should then be required not to discriminate in its implementation. The requirement is similar to the one most national systems place on employers, who freely choose whether or not to create a type of employment, but once they do are required to offer it on a basis that does not discriminate on grounds of gender, race, etc.

[69] See S. Leader, *The Reach of Democracy and Global Enterprise*, 8 (4) CONSTELLATIONS 538 (2001).

its Members towards their citizens, or are there in-built features that risk pulling it away from that democratic ideal as a benchmark for measuring progress?

The political theorist David Held argues that the promise and challenge that globalization presents lies in its potential for bringing forth what he calls "cosmopolitan democracy". This he defines as an order in which there is "... the increasing diffusion of responsibility for the maintenance of human rights, or the defense of cosmopolitan rights and duties, across different agencies at different levels of governance."[70] It is democracy protected by supra-national human rights organs which are also sensitive to layers of power and authority, both state and non-state, aiming to move in the direction of global standards of social justice.[71] If the general idea of cosmopolitan democracy is to assist us, we need to face up to a fundamental threat to it. Alongside questions about unilateralism and multilateralism in the worlds of trade and of human rights, there is what can be called the issue of "collateralism".

A. The Problem of Collateralism

If and when the protection of human rights becomes a concern of bodies such as the WTO, the form of protection offered to them risks undergoing change of focus. Whereas many states aim to hold the whole range of such rights in an equitable balance with one another—limiting the exercise of some so as to make room for others—this balance can lose a central place in the work of certain international organizations: organizations that have the most power to influence the domestic policies of those same states. In place of the sort of equilibrium among rights that democratic states seek, we find that some rights receive automatic preference over others in some international organizations: the latter becoming collateral concerns of the organization, while the former are deemed to lie at the core of its objectives.

If the WTO is thought to draw its legitimacy from its particular mandate to promote an integrated trading system—what was identified earlier as item 8 in the preamble—then it can seem reasonable to conclude that this core function should generate the basic rights that deserve its prior attention. Others will become collateral concerns. However seriously human rights are taken by an organization such as the WTO, they are easily prone to being filtered through this perspective. Thus, those who make and interpret the norms of the organization might fully accept that they should respect the obligations on member states arising from social, economic and cultural rights. However, they might also insist that while these ICESCR rights constrain what the WTO does, they cannot constrain it in the way they would constrain a state. When a hard choice has to be made between the objectives of market integration and concerns to protect those who might lose out from such integration, then on this view the WTO must stick by its special function and shape the rights involved so as to impede as little as possible its central mission.

True, the rules of the various agreements managed by the WTO do build in room for allowing its Members to assign ultimate priority to certain non-trade concerns, as we have seen. However, this deference to national priorities is sometimes accorded at a price. The Member might be required to compromise on their preferred content and method of achieving those non-trade objectives more than it would in other settings. This downward pressure on certain human rights standards may well occur even if one were

---

[70] Interview with Montserrat Guibernau, 8 (4) CONSTELLATIONS 427, 432 (2001).
[71] *Id.*

to place the objectives of the WTO on a human rights foundation. This link does not alter the fact that, as was seen at the outset, the particular means by which the WTO is committed to achieving those objectives is via the instruments of the mutual reduction of tariffs, and the development of an integrated multilateral trading system. This is a way of reaching its fundamental goals that distinguishes the WTO from the ILO, WHO, World Bank, and other international bodies that share many of the same general objectives such as the promotion of sustainable development and the raising of standards of living.

The result of this reasoning is not that human rights are compromised *per se*, but that particular priorities within the cluster of relevant rights will be established in advance of any given situation to which trading rules are applied. Those human rights that complement the goal of market integration will be given priority over those human rights that cut across the aim of such integration. As a result, when hard choices have to be made between the protection of economic freedoms that animate the goals of free trade, as against the protection of other welfare rights involving health, labor standards, and the environment—where the latter cause a Member to derogate from free trade principles—then, from the perspective offered by what we are calling collateralism, the WTO must shape the welfare rights so as to do least damage to economic liberties. The social and economic rights in the ICESCR are seen as incapable of rising to more than a secondary concern in a body that defines its tasks in what was earlier called functionalist terms.

The result is what we are familiar with: the perceived bias towards market liberalism in WTO policies. This priority flows as much from the institutional constraints faced by the organization as it does from deeper convictions on matters of political economy in the hearts of those running it. The price paid is a high one, since the system loses its ability to show Members that, while it might put pressure on their domestic agenda, it does so in a politically impartial way, and in doing so truly respects their other international human rights commitments. Things could conceivably be different.

B. From Collateralism Towards an Impartial Order for Trade Relations

It is possible to frame the work of the WTO in a way that reduces the damage done by collateralism. States are certainly not forbidden by their entry into the organization to pursue a strong domestic human rights agenda. Yet, this is a permission that is more formal than real for many weaker states and economies. It can be turned into a live option by appropriate balances within the trade treaties. These balances would carve out greater space for human rights in the pursuits of both positive and negative integration explored in Part IV. That is, the treaties could give greater priority to human rights in framing the demands for engaging in trade; and also in framing the terms on which trade can be refused or diminished so as to protect other non-trading interests.

In order to explore these possibilities, we can draw on our earlier distinction between civic and functional principles.[72] These, we saw, provide fundamentally different starting points in deciding on the standards that should guide the formulation and interpretation of trading rules. Those different starting points in turn lead to two distinct ranges of human rights that the organization might respect. A civic order incorporates a wide range, since it looks for continuity in regulating principles across a large spectrum of different institutions, from the nation state through to international bodies. A functional order—which

---

[72] For these distinctions, *see* S. Leader, *supra* note 69, at 538–553; S. Leader, *Three Faces of Justice and the Management of Change*, 63 MODERN LAW REVIEW 55–83 (January 2000); S. Leader, *Integration, Federation, and the Ethics of Rights* in MORALE ET POLITIQUE DES DROITS DE L'HOMME (Monique Costillo, ed., Zurich: Olms Verlag, 2003).

underpins collateralism—is different in that it divides up the terrain, looking for unique matches between particular organizations and their particular domains of responsibility. We can now go further with this distinction, using it to see the different ways of balancing disparate concerns in a trading regime.

C. Approaching the Balance between Trade and Non-Trade Interests

As indicated in Part III of this chapter, we will assume that respect for *some* human rights calls for the opening up of markets to trading relations, while respect for *other* human rights calls for closing or limiting access to those markets. Everything turns on the balance between the two sets of considerations. How does a civic order approach such a balance? Whereas in a functional order the special, defining objectives of an organization fix priorities among rights, in a civic order human rights are assigned priorities for reasons that are independent of the specific functions assigned to the organization. Even if the WTO has the special objective of promoting free trade this does not, on civic principles, dictate the relative weight of rights that the organization must respect. There is no reason for trading rules to give priority to a service provider's claim for market access over a state's claim to close its markets to such a service in order to protect a competing and fundamentally important priority. Instead, a civic order calls—in a distinctive way—for mutual adjustment between the rights.

We can see what is distinctive in a civic approach by comparing it with the functional approach to the well-known "necessity" requirement in the balance between trade and non-trade interests. When systems are confronted by competing rights, calling for their impartial adjustment, they often resort to the device of saying that one right may be limited if doing so is necessary for the fair exercise of the other. For example, the International Covenant on Civil and Political Rights ("ICCPR") requires respect for the right to freedom of expression, and then permits the right to be restricted if doing so is necessary for achieving, *inter alia*, respect of the rights of others and the protection of public morals.[73] Similar phrases also figure in the structure of the GATT, the GATS and TRIPS, as a qualification to their ability to protect public health, public morality, and other fundamental interests. In all such treaties, "necessary" does not mean what it seems to. That is, one does not have to show that any given measure is indispensable to the protection of the countervailing objective, such that there is no alternative measure that would protect it. There are usually several such routes available to protecting something like public morality, each sufficient to yield the result while none is literally the only way to go about it. Instead, the notion of necessity points at something quite different: it identifies the core objectives of the treaty in question, and then asks whether a Member state's overriding of those objectives by its domestic policy does the least damage to that treaty commitment, as compared with alternative possible domestic measures. The implicit question is not, "do you need to protect e.g., your public morality?", but rather "is this the way of protecting public morality that imposes the least cost on the ability of the treaty to do what it is designed to do?" We can call this the "least impact" feature of necessity.

Along with the requirement of least impact, there is sometimes a requirement of proportionality. Even if a particular policy has the least impact on a core value advanced by a trading system, that may not be enough to justify the policy since its impact on the core value may be deemed disproportionate. For example, a state might begin with a particular

---

[73] ICCPR, *supra* note 8, Article 19(2) and (3).

level of commitment to consumer protection, or a level of commitment to access by the least well-off to health or education. The state might have adopted means to achieve these ends that have the least impact on trade, from among reasonably available alternatives. Nevertheless—to take the example of consumer protection—its decision to pursue a particular *level* of commitment to such protection in the first place might be considered as imposing a disproportionately heavy burden on trade. As an example of this thinking in the analogous setting of the European Community, there is the *Danish Bottles* case. Here, the European Commission challenged a Danish environmental protection regulation that restricted the use of certain drink containers by imposing two requirements: a deposit and return scheme, and a ceiling on the total number of containers each firm could use. The European Court of Justice found this second element to be an illegal quantitative restriction.[74] It said that the deposit and return scheme would be enough by itself to render the containers environmentally friendly. The Court was aware that the full set of Danish restrictions achieved a higher level of protection for the environment than would the pared-down set, but was tacitly prepared to sacrifice this extra margin in order to allow an extra margin of access to markets for foreign goods. In the name of proportionality, the Court was willing to frustrate the country in question in its choice of level of commitment to a non-trade objective.[75]

In a functional order, these two parts of the necessity requirement—least impact and proportionality—receive an interpretation that is familiar, but of which many are suspicious. It demands that domestic priorities protecting public morals, and human, animal, plant life or health, all be pursued in a way that does least damage to international trade. There is clear room in the trade agreements for domestic priorities to prevail, but this is a potential that is largely lost—say the critics—when the Member state is forced to select that version of its priorities that is most friendly to the commercial interests of international providers of goods and services.[76] As Esty puts it, "... a policy approach that intrudes less on trade is almost always conceivable and therefore in some sense 'available'." As a result the non-trade exception is eviscerated.[77] In considering this critique, we should notice that the "least trade restrictive" demand does not necessarily flow from the fact that these agreements place the intrinsic merits of free trade above the protection of morals or human life. Instead, this priority is a result of a functional reading of the agreements. As was indicated in the earlier discussion of functional interpretation in Part IV, it is the special and not the shared general objectives of WTO that set the priorities among the interests the organization is to satisfy. That is, the market integration goals that give the institution its particular role among international organizations are primary, and any other interests that are contained in the shared, general objectives—which the WTO pursues along with many other organizations—are to be given a place that does least to upset the special objectives. It follows, based on this approach, that the shared, general aim of promoting, say, sustainable development, to which the WTO is committed along with other international bodies, should be interpreted so as to least trouble the special objective of market integration via free trade. Shared, general objectives are to be adjusted in favor of special ones and not vice versa, says the functionalist.

[74] *Commission of the European Communities v Denmark* Case 302/86 [1988 E.C.R. 4607]. It was held to be inconsistent with Article 28 (ex Article 30) of the Treaty Establishing the European Community. *See especially* ¶¶ 17 ff.
[75] *See* M. J. Trebilcock, and R. Howse, THE REGULATION OF INTERNATIONAL TRADE 153 (2001).
[76] *See e.g.* Michael Albert, *A Q&A on the WTO, IMF and World Bank and Activism* (2000) (www.zmag.org/Zmag/articles/jan2000albert.htm.
[77] D. Esty, GREENING THE GATT 48 (1994) *cited* by M. J. Trebilcock, and R. Howse *supra* note 75, at 140.

Before looking further into the civic alternative, notice that the direction in which functional adjustment moves can cut quite deeply into domestic priorities. This is because functional alternatives do not just put pressure on the means selected to achieve certain policy goals; they can—as in *Danish Bottles*—also affect the content of those goals. We can see this by contrasting two WTO cases, *Thai Cigarettes*[78] and *Asbestos*[79].

In the *Thai Cigarettes* case, Thailand limited imports of tobacco while permitting their domestic manufacture and sale. The limitation partly took the form of a refusal to grant licenses to import, raising a complaint under GATT Article XI(1); and partly a tax regime favoring local manufacturers, raising complaints of a violation of the national treatment provisions of GATT Article III:4. Thailand sought to defend the measures, *inter alia*, as necessary for the protection of human health within the terms of GATT article XX(b). It claimed to be concerned to keep domestic demand from growing beyond its present level.[80] The entry of foreign producers would, it argued, lead to expertly targeted marketing that would increase consumption among parts of the population who smoked far less than their foreign counterparts.[81] This result, it said, would damage the GATT's own objectives as set out in its preamble. For, smoking "...lowered the standard of living, increased sickness and thereby led to billions of dollars being spent every year on medical costs, which reduced real income and prevented an efficient use being made of resources, human and natural."[82] The Thai Government also claimed to be concerned about harmful ingredients in the imported cigarettes. The United States countered that these reasons were a thinly disguised attempt to carve out special protection for Thai producers.[83] It also argued—and this is central for our purposes—that Thailand would be able to protect public health by less trade restrictive methods: there were other ways of limiting consumption, and regulations could require requiring that the potentially harmful ingredients in different sorts of cigarettes, domestic or foreign, be clearly indicated to the consumer.[84] The panel decided in favor of the US. It found that labeling and ingredient disclosure regulations, as well as price rises induced by non-discriminatory taxation strategies, were less trade restrictive methods of reducing domestic demand.[85] Thailand's measures were therefore not necessary for the protection of public health.[86]

Of interest here is the *character* of the non-trade objective that a member state can pursue, such as the protection of public health or the environment. Objectives such as these do not stand on their own. The level at which they are pursued domestically is tied up with other social values demanding satisfaction. One society, placing a high value on consumer sovereignty, will also accept the greater risks to public health that go with allowing people to make up their own minds about a product. Another society will aim at a higher level of health protection because it feels less constrained by the value placed on informed consumer choice. The second was true of Thailand. Assuming for these purposes their bona fides when they denied protectionist motives, they did not trust the

---

[78] Report of the GATT Panel, *Thailand—Restrictions on Importation of and Internal Taxes on Cigarettes*, GATT No. DS10/R, BISD 37S/200, adopted on November 7, 1990.
[79] *European Communities—Measures Affecting Asbestos and Asbestos—Containing Products* Appellate Body WT/DS135/11
[80] *Id.* ¶ 28.
[81] *Id.* ¶ 54
[82] *Id.* ¶ 21.
[83] Id ¶ 23
[84] Id ¶ 23
[85] Id. ¶ 77, 78
[86] Id. ¶ 75—setting the issue in terms of 'necessity'

average consumer to react appropriately to warning labels on cigarette packages, nor to price increases. In short, they took a paternalist approach to the proper balance between achieving certain health objectives and respecting freedom of consumer choice.

The GATT panel did not reject this paternalist approach as a matter of ethical principle. That would not be within its brief. It rejected the approach because of the need to find the solution with least impact on trade. The effect—if not in intention—substituted a different weighting for the value of free consumer choice, and this in turn yielded a different level of health protection that would probably be attained. Labeling requirements place public health objectives more in the hands of individuals deciding the level of risk they will run. Within a population, the pattern of choice is likely to result in more smoking related illness than would an outright ban on imports. It is a lesser level of protection, but one that gives greater place to other important values in keeping with what was identified earlier as the proportionality element, rather than the 'least impact' element, in the requirement that a measure must be necessary for the promotion of a non-trade objective.

From a functionalist perspective, this decision makes sense. If one's point of departure is that the WTO's distinctive mission is to bring about "... an integrated, more viable and durable multilateral trading system...", then this is the dominant concern, and the panel should require Members to arrange their local values so as to do least damage to that objective.

A different approach can be seen in the more recent *Asbestos* case.[87] There, the Appellate Body was willing to allow France to ban imports of asbestos and products containing asbestos. It found, *inter alia*, that the prohibition was 'necessary' to protect human life or health within the terms of GATT Article XX(b). It specifically said, "WTO members have the right to determine the *level* of protection of health that they consider appropriate in a given situation."[88] [SL's emphasis] Canada had argued that the French could not unilaterally fix the level of risk to health to be avoided, but this was precisely what the Appellate Body said did fall within the prerogative of a WTO member.[89]

The approach to levels of health protection in *Asbestos* certainly gives more room to domestic priorities than does the approach taken in *Thai Cigarettes*. However, this result might be thought to have gone too far in the opposite direction. For if, as Prof. Petersmann argues,[90] the objective of free trade is thought to be underpinned by a fundamental 'right to freedom of economic activity', then it is not clear that a member state should be able to pitch the level of protection it seeks at just the level it desires. That would fly in the face of other fundamental rights jurisprudence. By way of analogy, the international human rights system sets itself to protect freedom of expression, and the system allows that right to be balanced against a member state's need to protect national security.[91] If the state were allowed to unilaterally set the level of national security it wanted, and then to fix restrictions on speech that were necessary to attain *that level*, the result of fixing the ultimate objective so high could easily shrink freedom of expression to a vanishing point.

An impasse threatens here. Too little deference to the priorities of WTO Members risks unduly shrinking the room for them to make basic value choices; and too great a deference to those priorities risks unduly shrinking the place of the right to freedom of

---

[87] Report of the Appellate Body, *European Communities—Measures Affecting Asbestos and Asbestos—Containing Products* WT/DS135/11 (2001)

[88] Id ¶ 165, 168

[89] Id. ¶ 168

[90] Petersmann supra note 24

[91] ICCPR, Arts 19(2) and (3)

economic activity, insofar as this is considered to be a fundamental right. Both of these are routes that this chapter has set itself to avoid, for the sake of an approach that is not a hostage to the sometimes deep political cleavages among trading partners. An impartial solution might lie in looking more closely at the proper adjustments between trade and non-trade interests.

D. Rethinking the Directions of Adjustment between Trade and Non-Trade Interests

Elements of a different approach can be borrowed from the constitutional traditions of modern democracies, though they do require some alteration in this context, since we need to keep in mind the fundamental differences between an organization like the WTO on the one hand, and the state on the other. On a functional approach to the balance between trade and non-trade interests, as has been seen, the basic rights located in the shared, general objectives of the WTO—such as those embedded in the promotion of sustainable development—must always be adjusted so as to have least impact on the rights furthered by its unique, special objective: the promotion of free trade. In a civic order, the adjustment runs in the opposite direction. It is the general objectives that are primary, even if they are widely shared with other institutions, and the special objectives that must be read so as to do least damage to them. Respect for the human rights furthered by free trade, as well as for those potentially damaged by free trade, are all to be shaped in the light of the general objectives, with no automatic priority for one set over the other. Instead, any one of the basic rights can be adjusted in favor of any of the others. This is so even if, once mutual adjustment is accomplished, one of the rights does take ultimate priority.

To draw an analogy from another constitutional domain, the preservation of life is ultimately more important than is the interest in freedom of movement along the highway. But it is not true that each and every level of risk of death is more important to prevent than is any given level of freedom of movement. Evidence shows that the death rate on highways is reduced by a significant but decreasing number for every mile per hour of reduction in permitted speed. Assume that the reduction in a given country is 10,000 deaths in a given population for every mile of reduction between 100 and 90 mph; 1000 from 50 to 40 mph; and 100 from 40 to 20, and 10 between 20 and 10. Even though the preservation of life is more important than is freedom of movement along the highway, it does not follow that the right to freedom of movement must always be adjusted downwards so as to have the least impact on the death rate. At a certain point a polity may, and sometimes must, *reverse the direction of compromise*, limiting the attention paid to the risk of death in favor of the right to freedom of movement, however clearly a certain number of deaths is linked to a further reduction in speed.[92]

Looking at the same point in a trade setting, consider the example of a country that wants to ban imports of a certain product on grounds of risk to health, but allows local producers to manufacture and market a like product. Assume that it wishes to exclude the imports because their pricing and packaging will substantially increase their consumption per person. Now consider two such products: the higher *per capita* consumption of one carries a marginally higher risk of threat to life-threatening illness, and another that carries a substantially higher risk of a life threatening illness. An example of the former could be a food that, beyond a certain level of consumption, tends to cause obesity which in turn can marginally increase the incidence of certain diseases such as cancer;

---

[92] This argument builds on some points made by Waldron, *supra* note 15, at 503, 509–512, 516–18 (3-1989)

and an example of the latter could be another food which, beyond a certain level of consumption, radically increases the incidence of that cancer. Assume finally that, as in *Thai Cigarettes*, it is not practical or desirable for a country to totally ban the domestic consumption of these products, the local variety of which is much less attractive to the population.

In the first situation, if the local production and sale of such food is allowed then it seems appropriate for the WTO to demand that all regulations aimed at controlling level of its consumption be effected in the least trade-restrictive way: such as by non-discriminatory labeling requirements that carry appropriate warnings. Leaving the choice of the imported product up to the consumer—where it and its domestic cousin carry the appropriate warning label—would be likely to yield a greater number of cases of obesity, than would an outright ban of the import. Nevertheless, it would be an equitable way of balancing the two competing concerns of sustaining non-discriminatory access to markets and protecting this domain of public health. There would be compromise on the level at which the non-trade objective could be pursued.

In the second situation, if the state allows increased consumption of a product which leads to a substantial threat to life, it might be in violation of relevant international conventions for a failure to act.[93] How should the trading system approach the options in front of it? Once again, the options range from labeling requirements through to outright bans on imports. Here, it is submitted, the state should be allowed to choose the import-reducing measure that will do most to reduce the risk to life which it is obliged by other international conventions to pursue. The direction of adjustment is reversed: rather than finding a method of protecting human life that has the least negative impact on trade; the state would be allowed here to adjust the flow of trade in a way that has the least impact on human life.

It is, of course, not easy to draw lines between degrees of risk of harm arising from the import of different sorts of goods and services, and hence to know when it would be appropriate to alter the direction of adjustment between trading and non-trading interests in the light of human rights requirements. However, the bodies charged with the primary duty of interpreting the meaning of these basic rights do provide us with guidelines: either in the form of guidelines coming from organizations that specialize in a particular domain, such as the ILO or WHO; or from bodies with a more general mandate, such as the Committee on Economic Social and Cultural Rights, General Comments and Statements on the meaning of provisions in the ICESCR. These can be drawn upon by WTO panels in order to see when a Member should be given the scope by the trading treaties to adjust the requirements of trade so as to do least damage to a non-trading interest, and when it should be required to adjust the non-trading interest to the requirements of trade.

The important thing is to move away from a *blanket* commitment to a 'least trade restrictive' reading of the 'necessity' requirement. There are indeed principles established in some WTO cases that take us in this direction, acknowledging the right of a state to restrict imports in order to meet its international obligations, and allowing the level at which that commitment is to be fixed to flow from that undertaking rather than be

---

[93] For a recent example in which the failure by the state to secure individuals against a reasonably apprehend danger to health and safety that was so grave as to amount to a violation of the right to life under Article 2 of the European Convention on Human Rights, *see Oneryildiz v Turkey* No 48939/99 Judgement of 18 June 2002

compromised by the 'least trade restrictive' demand. [94] Unless this is done, a commitment to the least tradé restrictive solution can sit like a lid on top of a wide range of states' engagements to their subjects. The result is something we are familiar with: the world wide complaint that the WTO weakens the ability of Member states to pursue policies that are valuable in themselves, but which when pursued might make the promotion of free trade more difficult. The approach considered here aims to keep an equitable balance of the full range of basic rights at stake in trading relations. This is the approach called for by civic principles of interpretation.

E. Factoring in Trading Interests

It is important that we not lose sight of our initial willingness to place human rights on both sides of the divide between trade and non-trade interests, as indicated in Part III. Those offering goods and services, as well as those potentially damaged by the terms on which those offers are made, have fundamental rights potentially at stake. This means that when a WTO panel is considering, for example, whether or not a Member state has violated TRIPS by refusing to grant a local patent to the inventor of an important drug, as is normally required by Article 27 of the TRIPS Agreement, then the panel should take into account the inventor's fundamental property rights as provided for by Article 15 (1) (c) of the ICESCR. However, as was argued earlier, the inventor's property right under TRIPS will also count as a property right in the human rights instrument only if it is brought within the full set of other relevant rights, and adjusted against them. Sometimes, as was argued above, the direction of adjustment must be from the dominant objective of the treaty towards having least impact on an objective lying outside the treaty. If these balances are made part of the approach, then the U.N. Sub-Commission on the Promotion and Protection of Human Rights is likely to conclude that all facets of the applicable intellectual property rights have been respected. [95]

This cannot be adequately done in the functionalist mode, requiring as it does that those who might suffer from an abuse of intellectual property rights should have their own rights regularly adjusted so as to do least damage to the interests of those who claim their property rights under TRIPS. The Member is allowed by the WTO administered treaties to give ultimate priority to certain non-trade interests, including the space provided by Article 8 of TRIPS. Mutual compromise among rights, along the lines sketched in the previous section, would be the better route.

F. Cosmopolitan Democracy, Political Impartiality, and the WTO

Recall the element of global democracy that can be potentially enriched by world trade. These are what David Held calls the "... the increasing diffusion of responsibility for the maintenance of human rights ... across different agencies at different levels of governance."[96] We have seen how the WTO has a role to play as one of these levels of governance. It can be one of a handful of international bodies that have the power to

[94] See the "*Shrimp/Turtle*" litigation, supra note 48.
[95] The Sub-Commission's report "... affirms that the right to protection of the moral and material interests resulting from any scientific, literary or artistic production of which one is the author is a human right, subject to limitations in the public interest, in accordance with Article 27, ¶ 2, of the Universal Declaration of Human Rights and Article 15, ¶ 1 (c), of the International Covenant on Economic, Social and Cultural Rights", *Sub-Commission on Human Rights Resolution 2000/7* ¶ 1.
[96] See 8(4) *Constellations, supra* note 70, at 432.

make human rights meaningful. However, the "diffusion" of responsibility for human rights can lead international society in one of two directions. It will either move towards a fragmented set of interpretations of the meaning and force of these rights, with the nation state giving one result; the WTO another; and specialist international human rights bodies yet another—or there can be an attempt towards greater coherence and integrity in the system. If the former is the course taken, then the WTO is likely to collide with its Members, as well as with bodies such as the U.N. commission on Human Rights—not because it ignores human rights, but because it interprets them in its own way. It is this suspicion that has led Philip Alston to want to prevent what he calls the "merger and acquisition" of human rights by trade law.[97] He does not want to see the cluster of values around market liberalism being considered the only appropriate way of spelling out the impact of human rights on trade relations, leading to pressure on nation states to adopt such values at the core of their policies.

This facet of the problem emerges most clearly from a clash of political philosophies that often divides national policy makers: individualist, choice-based approaches on the one hand, and strategies of social solidarity on the other. Some authors seem to think international trade carries within it an inevitable bias in favor of the former. For example, writing about labor rights, Christopher McCrudden and Anne Davies argue that some, but only some, of the core labor rights "... are not only theoretically consistent with the ideology of free trade, but [are] also required by it." These are, they say, those rights that serve to increase individual freedom of choice and freedom of contract.[98] If this is correct, then those who are concerned that national political will is undermined when their country signs up to a free trade regime would indeed have reason to worry. For individualist values are by no means the necessarily dominant ones in the core of fundamental labor rights. Many rights related to trade union organization and collective bargaining are based precisely on a rejection of individualist solutions. The ILO provides a large menu of such rights, and states configure them in a variety of ways, reflecting their different commitments to values of individual choice, social solidarity, or a particular mixture of the two.[99] At certain crucial points, the international trading system overreaches itself when it delves so deeply into domestic political preferences that it effectively bars one or another of these options. This is a particular problem when a human right protecting a non-trading interest is at stake, as has been seen. If an interpretation of the WTO administered treaties forces on a Member one route rather than another in trying to satisfy that right, then the WTO is moving beyond the boundary of impartiality that we saw the Committee on Economic, Social and Cultural Rights fix itself as it interprets the relevant human rights.[100]

This danger of unintentional bias is vivid when we turn to national policies that favor cross-subsidies. A recent U.N. report highlights the importance of these strategies, as well as their vulnerability to certain incursions of trade policy. It points out that:

> ... cross-subsidization, such as government schemes ensuring that wealthy people subsidize access to health care for the poor or maintaining lower interest rates for loans in rural as

[97] Alston, *supra* note 1, at 815 ff

[98] C. McCrudden and A. Davies, *A Perspective on Trade and Labor Rights,* in F. FRANCIONI (ED.), ENVIRONMENT, HUMAN RIGHTS AND INTERNATIONAL TRADE 187 (2001).

[99] Thus the ILO Committee on Freedom of Association says that Member states are allowed to make their own adjustments between free choice of union Membership and the demands unions make that Membership be a condition of having a job. *See* DIGEST OF DECISIONS, Number 323. *Cf* S. L. Leader, FREEDOM OF ASSOCIATION (1992)

[100] *Supra* note 8.

compared to urban areas, can be a means of reducing poverty, assisting the development of local infant service suppliers, increasing universal access to essential services and thus promoting human rights.[101]

Cross-subsidization can also operate within the group of the least well-off: it does not only run from rich to poor. Sometimes such subsidies involve a transfer from the young and healthy to the old and vulnerable or from the old to children needing health care that will help their access to education. It sometimes reaches across the various institutions providing for the distinct human rights needs of these groups, and demands that there be compromises, or trade-offs among them. When this course is taken, some of those previously high in order of priority of need might then legitimately find themselves lowered on the scale in order to account for a cross-cutting set of needs that come from the right to a decent education. In such situations, institutions vary their priorities in order better to serve a basic right that does not fall strictly within their purview.

What exactly is it about the push towards free trade that can cause such policies of cross-subsidy to break apart? The Report considers the point in the framework of the provision of services, and points out that:

> GATS subjects the grant of subsidies to the trade principle of non-discrimination. According to the non-discrimination (national treatment) principle, where a Government has made commitments in a particular service sector in its schedule under national treatment, GATS requires subsidies to national service suppliers or services to be available to like foreign service providers and services, unless an exception is specifically made in the national schedule. Thus, for example, where commitments were made in the education sector, the Government that provides a subsidy to a domestic not-for-profit education service provider might have to provide the same subsidy to foreign for-profit service providers.[102]

The result, says the Report, is that governments might withdraw their subsidies to this sector altogether, due to lack of resources, with consequent damage to universal access.[103] Apart from this, we can add the observation that when for-profit providers are brought in, they will avoid a strategy of cross-subsidy within a given population, since it costs more. As explained by the World Bank:

> ... rural borrowers may pay lower interest rates than urban borrowers, and prices of local telephone calls and public transport may be kept lower than the cost of provision. This structure of prices is often sustained through cross-subsidization within public monopolies, or through government financial support. Liberalization threatens these arrangements.[104]

---

[101] *Liberalization of Trade in Services and Human Right, supra* note 2, ¶¶ 60 ff. For further criticisms of current WTO policy, arguing that because of it "The long tradition of European welfare states based on solidarity through community risk-pooling . . . is being dismantled." *See* Albert *supra* note 76, in section entitled 'When and why is trade harmful?'

[102] *Liberalization of Trade in Services, supra* note 2, ¶ 60.

[103] *Id.*

[104] *Id.* ¶ 61 n.66 *quoting* World Bank, GLOBAL ECONOMIC PROSPECTS 80 (2001). *See also* Perrine Lhuillier, *The Impact Of The Privatization Of Water And Sanitation Services On The Implementation Of The Child's Rights To Drinking Water And Sanitation*, (Master's Thesis, University of Essex 2002) at 22, drawing on oral evidence presented to the Committee on the Rights of the Child, Sept 20, 2002 "Governments . . . tend to promote an integrated approach of service delivery that is lost when the service is privatized. It has been pointed out, for instance, that the privatization of the healthy system in the UK resulted in the breaking up of service delivery, resulting in the abolition of risk sharing strategies such as cross-subsidization and in the collapse of the planning system. (S)tates being legally accountable with respect to human rights results in children's rights being more likely to figure among the items of the agenda when the delivery of public services is envisaged."

As with earlier examples, this impact on local policy does not simply emerge from enthusiasm about the virtues of market liberalism among those setting trading rules. Whatever the inherent merits or demerits of such a set of values, it is more likely that alternative positions will take hold because of something quite distinct: it arises from the functional way in which an international organization such as the WTO structures its priorities. Where a civic order integrates institutional responsibilities in civil society, a functional order tends to separate them. Each institution, based on the latter view, has its specialized role and must remain faithful to its organizing objective. A civic perspective widens the scope of interests that should be within the WTO's mandate. It places providers alongside users of services, and the two are often in tension: the more a system aims at fairness towards providers, putting the for-profit and not-for-profit service providers on a par, the less it may be possible to achieve fairness towards users, yielding a distribution of the service that skews access towards the better off. If domestic priorities of a Member state are aimed at giving priority to fairness to users over fairness to providers, in those situations where it is impossible to achieve both, then a politically impartial WTO should avoid forcing the Member into the opposite position: making it give fairness to providers systematic priority over fairness to users. It can do this if it abandons a functionalist outlook.

VI. Conclusion

What has been discussed in this chapter is the need to give concrete meaning to the U.N.'s claim that human rights should be the "primary objective" of trade, investment, and financial policy.[105] In doing so, we have tried to navigate between two poles of a dilemma. On the one hand, it is essential to respect the fact that the WTO is qualitatively different from a state: it has a mandate to promote free trade that is stronger and more narrowly focused than are the agendas of its constituent Members, while its Members have an obligation to further values such as the right to freedom of expression that the WTO as an organization does not have. On the other hand, if the WTO is encouraged to focus too narrowly on its particular mandate, this can disrupt the wider domestic agendas of its Members, so pulling them away from their attempt to achieve a fair balance of all relevant human rights. We have tried to reconcile these two elements by insisting that there is one thing that the trading body and Member states have in common: they must both respect the *relationships of equitable balance* among human rights in the same way. This need for a fair balance means several concrete things. It means that the Members of the organization should consider a wider range of rights than allowed by a functional understanding of the WTO's powers. It also means that none of these rights, including trade-related rights, is to be given systematic priority over other rights. Instead, the priorities to be achieved are more varied, depending on the rights concerned and on the circumstances surrounding their realization—a variety of solutions that a civic outlook encourages.

The civic approach might also permit the trading system to respond to the criticism that it is only willing to take account of non trade interests as exceptions to its core objectives.[106] The argument here is designed to move the system beyond this occasional

---

[105] U.N. Human Rights Commission, *Resolution of September 4, 1998.* (http://www.pdhre.org/involved/uncommission.html

[106] "The fundamental nature of these entitlements as rights requires an approach that sets the promotion and protection of human rights as objectives of trade liberalization, not as exceptions." *Liberalization of Trade in Services, supra* note 2, para 7

and exceptional status for such values. It calls for two possible directions of adjustment—shaping trading rules to be least restrictive of non-trading interests in some cases, and shaping the protection of non-trading interests to be least trade restrictive in others.

The civic rather than the functional approach to human rights can make a concrete difference to the possible inclusion of concern for these rights in the positive and negative integration of markets; in working out the place of conditions on preferential market access for developing countries; and in understanding the necessity and proportionality principles by which trade and non-trade interests are brought into balance. This might make it possible to move beyond some of the traditional rhetoric in debates. There is, for example, the fear that linking human rights to trade is a protectionist ploy designed by strong Members to filter out inconvenient demands from weaker Members. In response, we have seen how it might be possible to be attentive to this worry while also preserving a major role for rights as conditions attached to trade: by removing the ability of richer countries to unilaterally dictate the terms of GSP schemes and placing the schemes under the jurisdiction of the WTO's disputes settlements mechanism.

There is also the fear that linking trade to a human rights agenda will wrongly mix politics and economics. For some, this translates into a worry that the economic agenda at the centre of the WTO will dominate the domestic political agendas of Member states. We have considered how it might be possible to avoid this result, while preserving a distinct and robust role for the WTO as a trade body. There are also those who fear that linking trade and human rights draws the WTO into politics, and that this is to be avoided. However, there is no such thing as a free trade agenda that does not carry within it some priorities with political significance. Whichever way the WTO turns, its decisions will have an affect on available political options. The same is true for international human rights: however they are interpreted, they will also have an impact on political choices. What we need in both cases is a way of setting an international benchmark for what is minimally acceptable in the relationship between the two domains. We can no longer allow the standards set by international trade and those set by international human rights to function separately. Human rights can frame world trade, so that trade can in turn be a motor for bringing about what these rights promise.

BIBLIOGRAPHY

Note: In addition to the works cited in the text, the following books and articles are useful. Where they do not directly mention human right, they are nevertheless important for a background understanding of various facets of the linkage between rights and trade.

Books

Francesco Francioni (ed) Environment, Human Rights, and International Trade (Hart Publishing, 2001)

Lance Compa and Stephen Diamond (eds) Human Rights, Labor Rights, and International Trade (U Penn Press, 1996)

W. Sengenberger and D. Campbell (eds) International Labour Standards and Economic Interdependence, (Geneva: International Institute for Labour Studies, 1994)

R. Siegel, Employment and Human Rights: The International Dimension (U Penn Press, 1994)

Jean-Louis Bianco et Jean-Michel Severino, Une Politique Economique Globale Pour Les Defis Mondiaux: Un Autre Monde Est Possible (Paris: Notes De La Fondation Jean-Jaures n° 20, 2001)

Articles

Democratising International Trade Decision-Making, Robert F. Housman, Symposium on *'Greening the GATT* 27 Cornell International Law Journal 699 (1994)

"Trade and . . . .": Recent Developments in Trade Policy and Scholarship—and Their Surprising Political Implications.' Jeffrey L. Dunoff, 17 Northwestern Journal of International Law and Business 759 (Winter-Spring 1996–1997)

Trade and Justice: Linking the Trade Linkage Debates, Frank J. Garcia, Symposium: *Linkage as Phenomenon: An Interdisciplinary Approach*, 19 University of Pennsylvania Journal of International Economic Law 391 Summer (1998)

The Global Market and Human Rights: Trading Away the Human Rights Principle Frank J. Garcia, 25 Brooklyn Journal of International Law 51 (April, 1999)

Globalization and the Convergence of Values, Alex Y. Seita 30 Cornell International Law Journal 429 (1997)

Adjudicating Copyright Claims Under the TRIPS Agreement: The Case for a European Human Rights Analogy, Laurence R. Helfer 39 Harvard International Law Journal 357 (Spring 1998)

Trade Without Values, Philip M. Nichols, 90 Northwestern University Law Review 658 (Winter, 1996)

Protecting Human Rights in a Globalized World, Dinah Shelton, *Symposium: Globalization & the Erosion of Sovereignt*, 25 Boston College International and Comparative Law Review 273 (Spring, 2002)

The World Trade Organization under Challenge: Democracy and the Law and Politics of the WTO's Treatment of Trade and Environment Matters, Gregory C. Shaffer, 25 Harvard Environmental Law Review 1 (2001)

Trade Legalism and International Relations Theory: An Analysis of the World Trade Organization, G. Richard Shell, 44 Duke Law Journal 829 (March, 1995)

CHAPTER 63

TRADE AND GENDER

Eugenia McGill

TABLE OF CONTENTS

Overall, globalization to date has done too little to minimize gender inequalities. While in some circumstances it may have decreased them (particularly in countries where it [has] led to an unprecedented employment of female labour), in other cases it has intensified them.[1]

Men and women are affected differently by globalization because of their different social positions and command over resources. An assessment of these issues is needed, in order to identify ways of promoting gender equality in the process of globalization.[2]

Trade falls in the intersection between economics and law, both of which are very mysterious fields . . . that claim to be gender-neutral.[3]

---

[1] RUBENS RICUPERO, SECRETARY GENERAL OF THE UNITED NATIONS CONFERENCE ON TRADE AND DEVELOPMENT, Foreword to TRADE, SUSTAINABLE DEVELOPMENT AND GENDER, Papers Prepared for Pre-UNCTAD Expert Workshop on Trade, Sustainable Development and Gender, Geneva, July 12–13, 1999, U.N. Doc. UNCTAD/EDM/Misc. 78 (1999) ("UNCTAD").

[2] World Commission on the Social Dimensions of Globalization, *Cross-Cutting Themes*, *at* http://www.ilo.org/public/english/wcsdg/policy/topic7.htm.

[3] International Gender and Trade Network, *Summary of Workshop from International Forum on Re-inventing Globalization*, organized by the Association for Women's Rights in Development, Guadalajara, Oct. 3–6, 2002, *at* http://www.awid.org/article.pl?sid=02/12/12/2038259&mode=nocomment.

I. Introduction

The gender dimensions of international trade and investment, and the related fields of trade economics and international trade law, are attracting increasing attention from academic and policy researchers, policymakers and civil society groups. While these issues are now on the agendas of United Nations bodies, some international financial institutions and development organizations, they are still at the periphery of international trade negotiations and World Trade Organization ("WTO") operations. However, the gender-differentiated effects of trade liberalization and other trade-related processes are extremely relevant to the mandate and operations of the WTO, particularly in the context of the Doha Development Agenda.[4] This chapter provides an overview of current research, policy analysis and advocacy on gender, trade and investment issues; preliminary gender analysis of selected WTO agreements and processes; and suggestions for integrating a gender perspective in future trade negotiations and implementation of trade commitments.

Part II of the chapter includes an introduction to gender concepts and their relevance to international trade and investment; activities of international organizations, regional bodies, bilateral agencies and civil society groups related to gender, trade and investment; and gender-aware empirical research, economic modeling and legal analysis related to trade and investment. Part III highlights gender issues in trade and investment agreements related to key economic sectors and trade-related areas, and in WTO processes such as trade negotiations, dispute settlement, trade policy review and trade-related capacity building. Part IV includes recommendations for integrating a gender perspective in trade policy formulation, trade negotiations and implementation of trade commitments within the WTO and other trade fora.

II. Relevance of Gender to International Trade and Investment

A. Gender Concepts and Terms

Gender as an analytical concept originated in the social sciences and quickly crossed over into other fields, including law, and into national, regional and international policy. The Development Assistance Committee of the Organization for Economic Cooperation and Development ("OECD"), for example, defines gender as

> The economic, social, political and cultural attributes and opportunities associated with being male and female. In most societies, men and women differ in the activities they undertake, in access and control of resources, and in participation in decision-making. In most societies, women as a group have less access than men to resources, opportunities and decision-making. These inequalities are a constraint to development because they limit the ability of women to develop and exercise their full capabilities, for their own

---

[4] The Doha Development Agenda refers to the agenda outlined in outcome documents of the Fourth WTO Ministerial Conference held in Doha, Qatar in November 2001. This chapter also refers to "developed," "developing" and "least-developed" countries, mindful that these terms are contested, and that countries' self-categorization in terms of "development" can vary from one context to another. *See, e.g.*, ARTURO ESCOBAR, ENCOUNTERING DEVELOPMENT: THE MAKING AND UNMAKING OF THE THIRD WORLD (1995) (critiques "development" as an "historically produced discourse" rooted in particular Western concepts of tradition, modernity and progress); WTO, *Who Are the Developing Countries in the WTO?*, at http://www.wto.org/english/tratop_e/devel_e/d1who_e.htm (WTO agreements do not define "developed" and "developing" countries; a new member's status depends on the outcome of accession negotiations with existing members; however, WTO recognition of "least-developed" countries is based on designation as such within the United Nations system).

benefit and for that of society as a whole. The nature of gender definitions (what it means to be male and female) and patterns of inequality vary among cultures and change over time.[5]

As the OECD definition implies, the concept of gender is closely related to normative goals such as *gender equity* or *gender equality*.[6] As the definition also suggests, gender is an extremely fluid and dynamic concept. In any gender analysis, attention needs to be paid to differences and disparities among groups of women and men, even within the same country or community, which may be related to age, race or ethnicity, citizenship, class, religion, marital status, geographic location, individual characteristics, or other factors.[7] Gender roles and relations are also subject to change, most noticeably in times of rapid social change, economic growth, or economic or political crisis.

In this regard, economists have noted a two-way interaction between gender and economics: on the one hand, economic change can affect groups of women and men differently, for example, because of their different access to employment and resources; on the other hand, because gender assumptions and relations influence the division of labor, distribution of work, income, wealth, education levels, access to public goods and services, and other aspects of economic life, these gender differences can influence the outcome of economic policy changes, such as agriculture reform or the promotion of particular industries.[8] The interactions between gender and economics, including trade economics, are discussed further in Part II.D of this chapter.

[5] Organization for Economic Cooperation and Development ("OECD"), *DAC Guidelines for Gender Equality and Women's Empowerment in Development Co-operation* (1998), at 10, *available at* http://www.oecd.org; *see also* INTERNATIONAL BANK FOR RECONSTRUCTION AND DEVELOPMENT ("WORLD BANK"), ENGENDERING DEVELOPMENT THROUGH GENDER EQUALITY IN RIGHTS, RESOURCES AND VOICE, World Bank Policy Research Report (2001), at 34–35; CANDIDA MARCH ET AL., A GUIDE TO GENDER-ANALYSIS FRAMEWORKS, Oxfam GB Publication (1999), at 18.

[6] Although these terms are sometimes used interchangeably, they can be distinguished. For example, the United Kingdom Department for International Development ("DFID")makes a distinction between *equality of opportunity* and *equity of outcomes*: "equality of opportunity . . . means that women should have equal rights and entitlements to human, social, economic and cultural development, and an equal voice in civic and political life; equity of outcomes . . . means that the exercise of these rights and entitlements leads to outcomes which are fair and just." DFID, *Gender Manual: A Practical Guide for Development Policy Makers and Practitioners* (2002), at 7, *available at* http://www.dfid.gov.uk. Similarly, the World Bank defines *gender equality* in terms of "equality under the law, equality of opportunity—including equality in access to human capital and other productive resources and equality of rewards for work—and equality of voice." WORLD BANK, *supra* note 5, at 35. The World Bank stops short of defining gender equality in terms of outcomes for several reasons, including the possibility that different societies may pursue gender equality through different means, and the need to allow for women's and men's individual preferences and goals, which may lead to different outcomes. *Id.* In international law, the concept of *equity* has been used to justify positive measures to overcome structural inequalities or to achieve *substantive* (rather than *formal*) *equality*, for example, between women and men, or between differently situated women. However, it has been argued that the term *gender equity* can also be misused to dilute the principle of *gender equality* and thereby diminish women's status and possibilities. *See* Dianne Otto, *Holding Up Half the Sky, But for Whose Benefit?: A Critical Analysis of the Fourth World Conference on Women*, 6 AUSTL. FEMINIST LAW J. 7, 14–15 (1996).

[7] In the context of international development, for example, Chandra Mohanty has cautioned against generalizations about "women" or "gender relations" in "the Third World", or even within a particular country. Chandra Talpade Mohanty, *Under Western Eyes: Feminist Scholarship and Colonial Discourses*, in THE WOMEN, GENDER AND DEVELOPMENT READER (N. Visvanathan ed. 1997).

[8] *See, e.g.*, NILÜFER ÇAĞATAY, TRADE, GENDER AND POVERTY, United Nations Development Programme ("UNDP") Background Paper (2001), at 14; LORRAINE CORNER, WOMEN, MEN AND ECONOMICS: THE GENDER-DIFFERENTIATED IMPACT OF MACROECONOMICS, United Nations Development Fund for Women ("UNIFEM") Publication (1996).

In international policy, attention to "gender issues" can be traced to the 1970s, when the United Nations ("UN") General Assembly made the integration of women into development efforts an objective of its International Development Strategy for the Second United Nations Development Decade (1971–1980), and the First World Conference on Women was held in Mexico City in 1975, launching the UN Decade for the Advancement of Women.[9] In the area of human rights, the Convention on the Elimination of All Forms of Discrimination Against Women ("CEDAW") was adopted by the UN General Assembly in 1979 and entered into force in 1981.[10] The focus of early "women in development" programs was on increasing women's participation in economic activities in developing countries. However, many of these initiatives were structured as small, stand-alone "women's projects", and were evaluated to have had only marginal impact on women's lives. Moreover, it became apparent that an "add women and stir" approach did not address structural barriers to women's fuller involvement in social, economic and political life.

By the time of the Fourth World Conference on Women in Beijing in 1995, most international and bilateral development agencies and national machineries for women's affairs had shifted from a "women in development" to a "gender and development" approach. In principle, this policy change signaled a greater attention to differences in power relations between women and men (and among groups of women and men based on other social factors), and also to ways that gender assumptions influence social, political and economic institutions and policies.[11] The shift to a "gender and development" approach was accompanied by the introduction of various methodologies for gender analysis—geared originally to the planning, implementation and evaluation of externally-funded development projects in sectors such as agriculture, education and health.[12] These methodologies reflected a number of goals, including improved welfare, efficiency, equity and empowerment. Some of these methodologies also lent themselves to the "mainstreaming" of gender concerns in planning, budgeting and other institutional processes. "Gender mainstreaming," which was promoted at the Fourth World Conference on Women in 1995, was adopted by the UN Economic and Social Council ("ECOSOC") in 1997 as an operative goal for the entire UN system.[13] It was subsequently endorsed by the UN General Assembly in 2000,[14] and is being implemented by a large number of international and bilateral development agencies and national governments. Within the UN system,

[9] UNITED NATIONS "UN"), 1999 WORLD SURVEY ON THE ROLE OF WOMEN IN DEVELOPMENT: GLOBALIZATION, GENDER AND WORK (1999), at viii. By the end of this decade, 127 countries had established national institutions to promote women's advancement and participation in development, and UNIFEM and the International Research and Training Institute for the Advancement of Women had been established within the UN system. *Id.* During the same period, "women in development" units were established in a number of UN and bilateral development agencies, and several international networks of women's organizations were formed.
[10] *Convention on the Elimination of All Forms of Discrimination Against Women* ("CEDAW"), Dec. 18, 1979, 1249 U.N.T.S. 13.
[11] UN, *supra* note 9, at viii–ix. In practice, however, many development agencies and national women's machineries continue to follow more of a "women in development" approach.
[12] *See, e.g.,* CANDIDA MARCH ET AL., *supra* note 5; CAROLINE MOSER, GENDER PLANNING AND DEVELOPMENT: THEORY, PRACTICE AND TRAINING (1993); Carol Miller and Shahra Razavi, *Gender Analysis: Alternative Paradigms* (1998), *available at* http://www.undp.org/gender/resources/mono6.html.
[13] UN, *supra* note 9, at ix.
[14] G.A. Res. S-23/2, U.N. GAOR, 23rd Special Sess., Agenda Item 10, Annex, para. 8, U.N. Doc. A/RES/S-23/2 (2000).

Mainstreaming a gender perspective is the process of assessing the implications for women and men of any planned action, including legislation, policies or programmes, in all areas and at all levels. It is a strategy for making women's as well as men's concerns and experiences an integral dimension of the design, implementation, monitoring and evaluation of policies and programmes in all political, economic and societal spheres so that women and men benefit equally and inequality is not perpetuated. The ultimate goal is to achieve gender equality.[15]

B. Gender Differences and Trends in Global Economic Activity

In 1999, the UN Secretariat published an analysis of statistics on women's participation in the global economy. This analysis confirmed a number of trends that highlight some of the "gendered" aspects of international trade and investment:

- In newly industrializing countries, the share of women workers in export manufacturing—including labor-intensive industries located in export-processing zones established to attract foreign investors—has increased substantially, although the demand for women's labor in some middle-income countries weakened starting in the late 1980s as export production became more capital- and skill-intensive;

- The rapidly expanding international services sector—including tourism, finance and information processing—also employs a high proportion of women;

- In some regions, export crop expansion has displaced women from permanent, subsistence agriculture to seasonal work on export crops, including non-traditional agricultural exports;

- For every formal sector job created by trade and foreign direct investment, it is believed that several jobs are created in the informal sector (for example, through subcontracting chains), where workers are predominantly women;

- On the other hand, there is evidence that the expansion of certain *imports* under trade liberalization has had a *negative* multiplier effect on women's employment in the informal sector, as local producers lose market share to cheaper imports;

- Despite the global increase in women's paid employment, labor markets continue to be segregated by sex; women continue to be employed in a narrower range of occupations than men; and in general "women's jobs" pay less, and have lower status and opportunities for advancement;

- Women's employment in export industries in developing countries tends to be concentrated in lower-paying, labor-intensive work involving little or no training, poor working conditions and high turnover;

- Evidence is mixed as to whether female-male pay differentials (the "gender wage gap") are diminishing as more women enter the paid workforce;

- Full-time formal sector employment in both developed and developing countries is giving way to more irregular types of employment, including part-time work, home-based work and other informal sector activity. While these "flexible" jobs can allow women to juggle paid work with childcare and other responsibilities, many of these jobs are also characterized by low pay, few or no benefits, little training, insecurity and few opportunities for advancement; and

---

[15] U.N. ESCOR, 1997 Sess., 33rd mtg, Agreed Conclusions 1997/2, in *Official Records of the General Assembly, Fifty-second Session, Supplement No. 3*, ch. IV, para. 4, U.N. Doc. A/52/3.

- Women comprise an increasing proportion of migrants, particularly in the categories of temporary and irregular migrants.[16]

Based on these trends, the UN Secretariat found that "[g]lobalization has given rise to ambiguous and at times contradictory effects on gender equality."[17] It concluded that "[t]rade policy initiatives need to identify their likely social impact beyond producer interests and to include broadly conceived welfare support measures."[18]

More recently, the UN reported that women now represent nearly half of the total number of people infected with the HIV virus. However, in Sub-Saharan Africa, close to 60 percent of HIV-positive adults are women and about twice as many young women as men are infected.[19] Women's risk of HIV infection from heterosexual contact is estimated to be two to four times that of men, with girls and young women at the highest risk. Research has also found that gender roles and relations affect exposure to (and infection from) a number of tropical diseases, as well as influencing access to prevention and treatment programs.[20] These facts underscore the gender dimension of current debates about the impact of the Agreement on Trade-Related Aspects of Intellectual Property Rights and similar agreements on access to patented, life-saving drugs in developing countries.

C. International Attention to Gender and Trade Liberalization

Reflecting growing concern about potential negative aspects of trade liberalization for women, particularly in developing countries, a number of commitments have been made at international and regional levels to address these concerns. The Beijing Platform for Action, which was adopted unanimously at the Fourth World Conference on Women in 1995, called on governments to "ensure that national policies related to international and regional trade agreements do not have an adverse impact on women's new and traditional economic activities," and called on the UN General Assembly to "give consideration to inviting the World Trade Organization to consider how it might contribute to the implementation of the Platform for Action, including activities in cooperation with the United Nations system."[21] In its review of progress in implementing the Beijing Platform in 2000, the UN General Assembly found that

---

[16] UN, *supra* note 9, at 8–36; *see also* UN, THE WORLD'S WOMEN 2000: TRENDS AND STATISTICS (2000) ("UN 2000"), at 109–50; UN INTERAGENCY TASK FORCE ON GENDER AND TRADE, TRADE AND GENDER: OPPORTUNITIES AND CHALLENGES FOR DEVELOPING COUNTRIES (Ang-Nga Tran-Nguyen and Americo Beviglia Zampetti, eds., 2004), U.N. Doc. UNCTAD/EDM/2004/2 ("G&T Task Force"), pp. 1–37. Marzia Fontana et al., *Global Trade Expansion and Liberalisation: Gender Issues and Impacts*, BRIDGE Report No. 42 (1998), *available at* http://www.ids.ac.uk/bridge; Martha Chen et al., *Counting the Invisible Workforce: The Case of Homebased Workers*, 27 WORLD DEV. 603 (1999); Susan Horton, *Marginalization Revisited: Women's Market Work and Pay, and Economic Development*, 27 WORLD DEV. 571 (1999); Rekha Mehra and Sarah Gammage, *Trends, Countertrends, and Gaps in Women's Employment*, 27 WORLD DEV. 533 (1999); Guy Standing, *Global Feminization Through Flexible Labor: A Theme Revisited*, 27 WORLD DEV. 583 (1999); Zafiris Tzannatos, *Women and Labor Market Changes in the Global Economy: Growth Helps, Inequalities Hurt and Public Policy Matters*, 27 WORLD DEV. 551 (1999).

[17] UN, *supra* note 9, at 58.

[18] *Id.* at 61.

[19] Joint United Nations Programme on HIV/AIDS, United Nations Population Fund and United Nations Development Fund for Women, *Women and HIV/AIDS: confronting the crisis* (2004).

[20] UN 2000, *supra* note 16, at 68–69 & 74.

[21] *Report of the Fourth World Conference on Women, Beijing, Sept. 4–15, 1995*, Annex II (Beijing Platform for Action), U.N. Doc. A/CONF.177/20 (1995), ¶¶ 165(k) & 343.

Globalization has presented new challenges for the fulfillment of the commitments and realization of the goals of the Fourth World Conference on Women.... Although in many countries the level of participation of women in the labour force has risen, in other cases the application of certain economic policies has had such a negative impact that increases in women's employment often have not been matched by improvements in wages, promotions and working conditions.[22]

The General Assembly followed the recommendation of the Fourth World Conference on Women and called on the WTO, as well as the Bretton Woods institutions, UN organizations, and other international and regional intergovernmental bodies, to "support government efforts and, where appropriate, develop complementary programmes of their own to achieve full and effective implementation of the Platform for Action."[23]

The UN Commission on the Status of Women ("CSW") and the CEDAW expert committee have also addressed gender issues related to increased global trade and investment. In considering the challenges of reducing poverty and empowering women in a globalizing world, the CSW has urged governments, international organizations and other stakeholders to mainstream a gender perspective in development, trade and financial institutions; to enhance market access for developing countries and transitional economies, particularly in sectors that provide greater employment opportunities for women; and to help women-owned businesses benefit from international trade and investment.[24] In its concluding comments on the reports submitted by state parties to CEDAW, the CEDAW expert committee has also expressed concern about some of the negative aspects of increased integration in global markets. Recently, for example, the committee noted the poor working conditions of women in export-processing zones in Fiji, Guatamala, Mexico and Sri Lanka, and urged governments to more effectively enforce their labor laws and to require foreign investors to adhere to codes of conduct. The committee also expressed concern about the increased incidence of trafficking of women and girls related to the expansion of tourism in Barbados and Saint Kitts and Nevis.[25]

Other UN bodies have also identified gender issues in their work on trade and investment. For example, in 1999 the UN Conference on Trade and Development ("UNCTAD") organized an expert workshop on trade, sustainable development and gender, which made a number of recommendations for mainstreaming the consideration of gender issues in its activities and publications.[26] A subsequent expert meeting made further recommendations to UNCTAD and governments for mainstreaming gender concerns in the areas of commodities, trade in services, foreign direct investment policy, enterprise development,

[22] G.A. Res. S–23/3, U.N. GAOR, 23rd Special Sess., Agenda Item 10, Annex, para. 35, U.N. Doc. A/RES/S-23/2 (2000).

[23] *Id.*, ¶ 49.

[24] Commission on the Status of Women, Report on the Forty-Sixth Session, Ch. I.A., Draft Resolution III.A, para.5, in *Economic and Social Council Official Records 2002, Supp. No. 7*, U.N. Doc. E/2002/27-E/CN.6/2002/13.

[25] Committee on the Elimination of Discrimination against Women, Reports of the Twenty-Sixth, Twenty-Seventh and Exceptional Sessions, in *Official Records of the General Assembly, Fifth-seventh Session, Supplement No. 38, Parts I–III*, U.N. Doc. A/57/38. Other UN human rights bodies, such as the Committee on Economic, Social and Cultural Rights ("CESCR") and the Sub-Commission on the Promotion and Protection of Human Rights ("Sub-Commission"), have raised similar concerns. *See* Beth Lyon, *A Post-Colonial "Agenda" for the United Nations Committee on Economic, Social and Cultural Rights Through the Post-Colonial Lens*, 10 AM. U.J. GENDER SOC. POL'Y & L. 535, 566–67 (2002) (cites CESCR comments on country reports related to NAFTA and WTO trade commitments); Dinah Shelton, *Protecting Human Rights in a Globalized World*, 25 B.C. INT'L & COMP. L. REV. 273, 294–315 (2002) (surveys comments, resolutions and commissioned studies of the CESCR, Sub-Commission and other UN bodies related to trade, operation of multinational companies and globalization generally).

[26] UNCTAD, *supra* note 1, at 445–451.

and information and communication technologies. Based on the outcomes of this expert meeting, UNCTAD's Commission on Enterprise, Business Facilitation and Development recommended a number of actions by governments, the international community and UNCTAD, including that UNCTAD should appoint focal points on gender in each of its divisions to integrate a gender dimension in all substantive areas.[27] In 2003, a UN inter-agency task force on gender and trade was created, headed by UNCTAD, to coordinate research, capacity building and advocacy activities within the UN system. Gender and trade was also a cross-cutting issue considered at UNCTAD XI, which took place in Sao Paolo, Brazil in 2004.[28]

Regional trade bodies have also taken steps to mainstream gender concerns in trade policy. In 1997, the Southern Common Market ("Mercosur") initiated broad consultations to decide on a mechanism for integrating a gender perspective in its activities, resulting in the establishment of a gender advisory unit within Mercosur.[29] In 1999, members of the Asia-Pacific Economic Cooperation ("APEC") forum endorsed a Framework for the Integration of Women in APEC.[30] APEC's Second Ministerial Meeting on Women, held in September 2002 in Guadalajara, recommended that APEC and the APEC economies intensify their work on gender analysis, collection of sex-disaggregated data and inclusion of more women in all APEC activities. APEC ministers also recommended that APEC economies take account of the gender-differentiated impacts of trade liberalization in the design of trade policies, and address the negative impact on women workers of industry restructuring resulting from trade liberalization. The ministers also endorsed the establishment of an APEC Gender Focal Point Network, which began activities in 2003.[31] Other regional bodies that have taken steps to mainstream gender concerns in their trade-related work include the Caribbean Community (CARICOM), the Pacific Islands Forum and the Southern African Development Community (SADC).[32] The Commonwealth Secretariat is also promoting gender mainstreaming more generally in trade and industry.[33]

---

[27] *Report of the Expert Meeting on Mainstreaming Gender in Order to Promote Opportunities, Geneva, Nov. 14–16, 2001,* U.N. Docs. TD/B/COM.3/40, TD/B/COM.3/EM.14/3 (2001); Commission on Enterprise, Business Facilitation and Development, 6th Sess., Agenda Item 5, *Mainstreaming Gender in Order to Promote Opportunities: Agreed Recommendations,* U.N. Doc. TD/B/COM.3/L.22 (2002).

[28] UNCTAD, *Meeting of the UN Inter-Agency Task Force on Gender and Trade,* Geneva, July 17–18, 2003 ("G&T Task Force Meeting"), *available at* http://www.unctad.org/Templates/Meeting.asp?m=7308&intItemID=1942&lang=1; UNCTAD, *First Session of the Preparatory Committee for UNCTAD XI,* Trade and Development Board, Geneva, Oct. 15, 2003, *available at* http://www.unctad.org/Templates/Webflyer.asp?docID=4214&intItemID=2068&lang=1.

[29] Maria Alma Espino, *Women and MERCOSUR: The Gendered Dimension of Economic Integration,* in WOMEN'S EMPOWERMENT AND ECONOMIC JUSTICE: REFLECTING ON EXPERIENCE IN LATIN AMERICA AND THE CARIBBEAN, UNIFEM Publication, at 21–22 (Liliana De Pauli ed. 2000); *but see* KAMAL MALHOTRA ET AL., MAKING GLOBAL TRADE WORK FOR PEOPLE (2003), at 95–96 (some believe gender unit has had limited impact on negotiations within Mercosur).

[30] Ad Hoc Advisory Group on Gender Integration, *Report to the Ministers on the Implementation of the Framework for the Integration of Women in APEC* (2002), at 1, *available at* http://www.apecsec.org.sg/apec/documents_reports/ministerial_meeting_on_women/2002.html.

[31] *Joint Ministerial Statement,* APEC Second Ministerial Meeting on Women, Guadalajara, Sept. 28–20, 2002, *available at* http://www.apecsec.org.sg/apec/documents_reports/ministerial_meeting_on_women/2002.html; APEC, *Gender Focal Point Network, available at* http://www.apecsec.org.sg/apec_groups/other_apec_groups/gender_focal_point_network.html.

[32] MARIAMA WILLIAMS, GENDER MAINSTREAMING IN THE MULTILATERAL TRADING SYSTEM: A HANDBOOK FOR POLICY-MAKERS AND OTHER STAKEHOLDERS, Commonwealth Secretariat New Gender Mainstreaming Series on Development Issues (2003), App. 3.

[33] LOUISE O'REGAN-TARDU, GENDER MAINSTREAMING IN TRADE AND INDUSTRY: A REFERENCE MANUAL FOR GOVERNMENTS AND OTHER STAKEHOLDERS, Commonwealth Secretariat Gender Management System Series (1999); WILLIAMS, *supra* note 32.

Several international agencies have commissioned research and policy analysis on gender and trade issues. Even before the establishment of the WTO, the United Nations Fund for Women ("UNIFEM") commissioned a background paper on the implications of the WTO and other trade initiatives for women.[34] More recently, the United Nations Development Programme ("UNDP") commissioned a background study on gender, trade and poverty for a publication on trade and human development.[35] The International Monetary Fund ("IMF") and World Bank are also beginning to consider gender implications of trade liberalization through their poverty and social impact analyses of macroeconomic policy changes in certain countries.[36] A World Bank research project currently under way is also examining the gender dimensions of trade liberalization through cross-country analysis and country-level studies in Latin America and Asia.[37] Similar studies and policy briefs have also been prepared for bilateral development agencies.[38]

Civil society organizations and networks have also been extremely active in raising gender concerns related to trade liberalization and foreign direct investment at international and regional levels, and with national governments. Women's organizations from several regions organized a Women's Caucus at the First Ministerial Conference of the WTO in Singapore in 1996, where they issued a press statement calling on the new WTO to adopt gender-aware policies and procedures. The Women's Caucus evolved into an Informal Working Group on Gender and Trade ("IWGGT"), which met with WTO officials in 1997 to discuss opportunities for addressing gender issues within the WTO, for example, through the work of the Trade Policy Review Body. IWGGT members subsequently produced briefing papers on gender and trade and participated in civil society activities around the Second Ministerial Conference in Geneva in 1998 and the Third Ministerial Conference in Seattle in 1999.[39] A second network, the International Gender and Trade Network (IGTN) was formed in early 2000, and includes seven regional networks of women involved in research, economic literacy and advocacy on trade and investment issues. IGTN members participated in civil society activities around the Ministerial Conferences in Doha and Cancún, and are also engaged in regional and bilateral trade developments.[40] Many members of the IWGGT are also active in the IGTN.

---

[34] SUSAN JOEKES AND ANN WESTON, WOMEN AND THE NEW TRADE AGENDA, UNIFEM Publication (1994). UNIFEM has continued to support a variety of research and capacity-building activities related to gender and trade. See http://www.unifem.org/economic_security/gender_trade.html.

[35] ÇAGATAY, supra note 8; MALHOTRA ET AL., supra note 29.

[36] See Caroline M. Robb, Poverty and Social Analysis—Linking Macroeconomic Policies to Poverty Outcomes: Summary of Early Experiences, IMF Working Paper, WP/03/43 (2003), at 27–30.

[37] Telephone interviews with Andrew Mason (Sept. 20, 2002), Susan Razzaz (Sept. 25, 2002) and Nayantara Mukerji (Oct. 23, 2003); see, e.g., Günseli Berik et al., International Trade and Wage Discrimination: Evidence from East Asia, World Bank Policy Research Working Paper 3111 (2003), and Alessandro Nicita and Susan Razzaz, Who Benefits and How Much? How Gender Affects Welfare Impacts of a Booming Textile Industry, World Bank Policy Research Working Paper 3029 (2003), available at http://econ.worldbank.org.

[38] See, e.g., Canadian International Development Agency ("CIDA"), Gender Equality and Trade-Related Capacity Building: A Resource Tool for Practitioners (2003), and Angela Keller-Herzog, Globalisation and Gender—Development Perspectives and Interventions, CIDA Discussion Paper (1996), available at http://www.acdi-cida.gc.ca; see also Cathy Blacklock, Women and Trade in Canada: An Overview of Key Issues (2000), and Soraya Hassanali, International Trade: Putting Gender into the Process: Initiatives and Lessons Learned (2000), Status of Women Canada Discussion Papers, excerpts available at http://www.swc-cfc.gc.ca.

[39] Jo Brew, WTO, European Union Trade Policy and Women's Rights—A Review, in GENDER, TRADE AND RIGHTS: MOVING FORWARD (Benedicte Allaert and Nicole Forman eds. 1999), at 3; Janice Goodson Foerde, Current Concerns on the Interrelationship Between Trade, Sustainable Development and Gender, in UNCTAD, supra note 1, at 61.

[40] See International Gender and Trade Network website, at http://www.igtn.org.

Several of these organizations have also participated in civil society activities related to other international conferences, where they have raised trade-related concerns.[41] Geneva Women in International Trade, a professional association, also organized programs on women as economic players in sustainable development and international trade as part of the June 2003 and 2004 public symposia hosted by the WTO in Geneva.[42]

The IWGGT originally called on governments and WTO officials to collect sex-disaggregated data and undertake gender impact assessments of trade policies, and to develop in-house capacity to undertake gender analysis in all trade sectors and trade-related areas.[43] Several women's organizations and researchers are now working to develop gender-and-trade indicators and other tools for carrying out gender assessments of existing or proposed trade commitments.[44] Women's organizations are also calling for greater attention to gender issues in the sustainability impact assessments of trade that are being carried out, for example, within the European Union.[45] Recommendations have also been made to establish "gender desks" within national trade ministries;[46] and to establish an independent focal point to monitor the coherence between policies and practices of the WTO and international financial institutions and the operations of UN programs and specialized agencies, as well as coherence between WTO agreements and other international instruments such as the Universal Declaration of Human Rights, CEDAW and the Convention on Biological Diversity.[47] The IGTN's current advocacy

[41] *See, e.g.*, WOMEN'S ENVIRONMENT AND DEVELOPMENT ORGANIZATION ("WEDO") AND UNIFEM, WOMEN CHALLENGING GLOBALIZATION: A GENDER PERSPECTIVE ON THE UNITED NATIONS INTERNATIONAL CONFERENCE ON FINANCING FOR DEVELOPMENT, MARCH 18–22, 2002, MONTERREY, MEXICO (2002); WEDO, Rede de Desenvolvimiento Humano and UNIFEM, *Women's Action Agenda for a Healthy and Peaceful Planet 2015: A Decade of Women's Advocacy for Sustainable Development* (agenda presented by international coalition of women's organizations at the World Conference on Sustainable Development, held in Durban in August–September 2002), *available at* http://www.wedo.org.

[42] *See* WTO, *Symposium Program: "Challenges Ahead on the Road to Cancún,"* at http://www.wto.org/english/tratop_e/dda_e/symp_devagenda_prog_03_e.htm; WTO, *Symposium Program:* "Multilateralism at a Crossroads," at http://www.wto.org/english/tratop_e/dda_e/symp_devagenda_prog_04_e.htm

[43] Brew, *supra* note 39.

[44] *See, e.g.*, SARAH GAMMAGE, HELENE JORGENSEN, EUGENIA MCGILL AND MARCELINE WHITE, FRAMEWORK FOR GENDER ASSESSMENTS OF TRADE AND INVESTMENT AGREEMENTS (2002); GENDER, TRADE AND RIGHTS: MOVING FORWARD, Women in Development Europe Publication (Benedicte Allaert and Nicole Forman eds. 1999), at 43–46 (includes checklists for gender and trade analysis); WILLIAMS, *supra* note 32 (includes situation analysis of women and trade policy and identifies key sectoral issues); Pamela Sparr, *Basic Building Blocks for a Gender and Trade Analysis* (2002), *available at* http://www.igtn.org/EconoLit/Literacy.html; Irene van Staveren, *Gender and Trade Indicators: A Contribution to a Sustainability Impact Analysis for EU Trade* (2001), *available at* http://www.eurosur.org/wide/Globalisation/Gender_indicators.htm. *See also infra* text accompanying notes 63–66.

[45] *See, e.g.,* Maria Karadenizli, Meeting on Sustainability Impact Assessments (SIAs) with DG Trade (2001), *at* http://www.eurosur.org/wide/PROJECTS.htm#ALter%20Eco. The importance of including gender considerations in the development of trade policy and in trade impact assessments was also raised at the fourth informal consultation between the OECD Trade Committee and civil society organizations. *See Summary of the 4th Informal Consultation between the OECD Trade Committee and Civil Society Organisations, Oct. 28, 2002,* at http://www.oecd.org/EN/document/0,, EN-document-24-nodirectorate-no-20-37454-24,00.html. Some sex-disaggregated indicators are included in the guidelines prepared by the United Nations Environment Programme ("UNEP") for carrying out "integrated assessments" of trade-related policies, which are intended to consider economic, environmental and social effects. *See* UNEP, REFERENCE MANUAL FOR THE INTEGRATED ASSESSMENT OF TRADE-RELATED POLICIES, U.N. Doc. UNEP/01/4 (2001), at 20 & 55–57.

[46] Maria S. Floro, *Gender Audit of the Facilitator's Draft Outcome Document of the International Conference on Financing for Development* (2001), at 5, *available at* http://www.undp.org.unifem.

[47] Mariama Williams, *Globalisation of the World Economy: Challenges and Responses*, Statement to the Enquete/Commission of the German Parliament, Feb. 18, 2002, at 11, *available at* http://www.igtn.org/Research/GenderTrade.htm.

position is that thé comprehensiveness of the Uruguay Round agreements interferes with governments' responsibilities to ensure food security, protect public health and determine their own development agendas. The IGTN therefore has opposed the introduction of new issues into the WTO agenda, and believes that the scope of WTO rules should be scaled back essentially to the regulation of trade in goods.[48]

D. Socioeconomic Approaches to Gender, Trade and Investment

A growing number of economists are now studying international trade and foreign direct investment from a gender perspective. Their work, which includes empirical research, economic modeling and policy analysis, draws on several related areas of study: the gender biases in economic development programs; the gender dimensions of the international division of labor; gender-differentiated impacts of structural adjustment programs; and gender analysis of macroeconomic policies.

Since the early 1970s, economists and other social scientists have documented the ways in which development programs financed by external agencies have ignored the important economic activities of women in developing countries, and even undermined their position, for example, through the introduction of land-titling systems that ignored women's traditional land use rights.[49] Research since the 1980s has also documented the evolution of an "international division of labor", as manufacturing firms in industrialized countries have relocated or subcontracted more labor-intensive production processes to countries with lower labor and other costs, and developing countries have established duty-free zones to attract more of these firms. This research also has highlighted the preference of many firms operating in duty-free zones to employ young women workers for labor-intensive tasks—arguably on the grounds of their greater "manual dexterity," but also implicitly based on assumptions about their "docility" and willingness to accept lower wages than men.[50] As a consequence, the "international division of labor" has been observed to be highly "gendered," with significant job segregation on the basis of sex and age.[51]

The macroeconomic stabilization and structural adjustment policies promoted by the IMF and World Bank for developing countries have also attracted considerable attention from economists, social scientists and policy analysts. A collection of studies commissioned by the United Nations Children's Fund ("UNICEF") was among the first to highlight the social costs of adjustment.[52] A large number of studies followed which highlighted the adverse impacts of adjustment policies on poor households, and particularly

---

[48] See International Gender and Trade Network ("IGTN"), *IGTN at Doha*, Position Paper on the WTO (2001), and *IGTN at Cancún and Beyond*, Advocacy Document (2003), *available at* http://www.igtn.org/WTO/WTOResources.htm.

[49] See, e.g., ESTER BOSERUP, WOMEN'S ROLE IN ECONOMIC DEVELOPMENT (1970); MALE BIAS IN THE DEVELOPMENT PROCESS (Diane Elson ed. 1991).

[50] See, e.g., SUSAN P. JOEKES, WOMEN IN THE GLOBAL ECONOMY—AN INSTRAW STUDY (1987); WOMEN, MEN AND THE INTERNATIONAL DIVISION OF LABOR (June Nash and Maria Patricia Fernandez-Kelly eds., 1983); Diane Elson and Ruth Pearson, *Nimble Fingers Make Cheap Workers: An Analysis of Women's Employment in Third World Export Manufacturing*, 7 FEMINIST REV. 87 (1981); Linda Y.C. Lim, *Women's Work in Export-Oriented Industries: The Politics of a Cause*, in PERSISTENT INEQUALITIES: WOMEN AND WORLD DEVELOPMENT (Irene Tinker ed. 1990); Guy Standing, *Global Feminization Through Flexible Labor*, 17 WORLD DEV. 1077 (1989).

[51] This research has been updated more recently to take account of gender differences and trends in employment in export agriculture and cross-border services, as well as manufacturing. *See supra* note 16; *see also* UNIFEM, PROGRESS OF THE WORLD'S WOMEN 2002, VOL. 2 (2002), at 30–39.

[52] ADJUSTMENT WITH A HUMAN FACE, UNICEF Publication (Giovanni Andrea Cornia et al., eds., 1987).

on women and girls. Among the impacts noted were the layoffs of women from formal sector jobs due to industry restructuring and public sector downsizing; women's increased employment in the informal sector; and women's and girls' reduced access to education and health services due to cutbacks in social services and the imposition of "cost recovery" measures in schooling and health services.[53] Gender-differentiated impacts have also been identified in countries in transition from planned to market economies[54] and in countries affected by financial crises.[55]

In the field of economics, a gender perspective was first introduced at the micro and meso levels, to explain the allocation of roles, income and resources within households and the pervasive segregation and wage discrimination between women and men in labor markets.[56] However, the stabilization and adjustment policies of the IMF and World Bank prompted a number of economists in the 1990s to begin examining macroeconomics as well from a gender perspective. At a conceptual level, these economists identified several levels of "gender blindness" in mainstream macroeconomic theory and modeling. First, they noted that assessments of macroeconomic performance based on conventional indicators such as Gross Domestic Product ("GDP") are incomplete because the national accounts on which GDP measures are based generally ignore or undercount home-based production carried out primarily by women.[57] Second, they pointed out that the macroeconomic models used to formulate stabilization and adjustment policies ignore women's unpaid labor in reproductive and care-giving activities, and therefore fail to recognize that reductions in basic services, such as health care, effectively shift the related costs from the public sector to the "reproductive" or "care" sector. Third, they noted that mainstream macroeconomics fails to recognize that labor markets are dependent on the "reproductive" or "care" sector, and therefore that cutbacks in basic services such as education and health care can have a negative effect on the welfare of the future labor force, and thus on future economic performance.[58]

---

[53] *See, e.g.*, COMMONWEALTH SECRETARIAT, ENGENDERING ADJUSTMENT FOR THE 1990S (1989); GITA SEN AND CAREN GROWN, DEVELOPMENT, CRISES AND ALTERNATIVE VISIONS: THIRD WORLD WOMEN'S PERSPECTIVES (1987); MORTGAGING WOMEN'S LIVES: FEMINIST CRITIQUES OF STRUCTURAL ADJUSTMENT (Pamela Sparr, ed., 1994); UNEQUAL BURDEN: ECONOMIC CRISES, PERSISTENT POVERTY AND WOMEN'S WORK (Lourdes Beneria and S. Feldman eds. 1992); *see also Special Issue on Gender, Adjustment and Macroeconomics* (Nilüfer Çağatay et al. eds.), 23 WORLD DEV. 1825 (1995); WORLD BANK, *supra* note 5, at 211–215 (summarizing the literature on the costs and benefits of adjustment for gender equality).

[54] *See, e.g.*, WORLD BANK, *supra* note 5, at 219–222.

[55] *See, e.g.*, Maria Floro and Gary Dymski, *Financial Crisis, Gender, and Power: An Analytical Framework*, 28 WORLD DEV. 1269 (2000); Joseph Y. Lim, *The Effects of the East Asian Crisis on the Employment of Women and Men: the Philippine Case*, 28 WORLD DEV. 1285 (2000); Ajit Singh and Ann Zammit, *International Capital Flows: Identifying the Gender Dimension*, 28 WORLD DEV. 1249 (2000).

[56] *See, e.g.*, JOYCE P. JACOBSEN, THE ECONOMICS OF GENDER (1998).

[57] Established by the United Nations in 1953, the System of National Accounts ("SNA") is intended to provide a consistent basis for calculating national income. In its earliest formulations, the SNA excluded most forms of subsistence production and other household activities such as cooking, cleaning and care of children and elders—tasks carried out primarily by women in most societies. However, statisticians who advised developing countries such as Papua New Guinea and Jamaica on setting up their SNAs did make adjustments to include subsistence production and other unpaid work performed (or assumed to be performed) by men. MARILYN WARING, IF WOMEN COUNTED: A NEW FEMINIST ECONOMICS (1988), at 103–111. The most recent version of the SNA methodology now recommends counting a variety of tasks related to subsistence production. However, these tasks are still "undercounted" because of weaknesses in data-gathering. Unpaid work such as cooking, cleaning and childcare is still considered outside the "production boundary" of the SNA. UNIFEM, PROGRESS OF THE WORLD'S WOMEN 2000 (2000), at 22–24.

[58] Nilüfer Çağatay et al., *Introduction to Special Issue on Gender, Adjustment and Macroeconomics*, 23 WORLD DEV. 1827, 1828–29 (1995); *see also* CORNER, *supra* note 8; THE STRATEGIC SILENCE: GENDER AND ECONOMIC POLICY (Isabel Bakker ed. 1994); Ingrid Palmer, *Social and Gender Issues in Macro-Economic Policy Advice*, GTZ Social Policy Series No. 13 (1994).

Based on these insights, several economists began developing approaches to integrate gender in macroeconomic modeling. Initial approaches included the disaggregation of key variables by gender; the introduction of gender as an additional variable; the use of a two-sector or two-system approach, for example, to model interactions between the "paid" and "unpaid" economies; and combinations of these methods.[59] More recently, economists have begun applying these methods to topics in international economics, including the relation between gender inequality and trade liberalization in manufacturing and agriculture, and the gender-differentiated impacts of financial liberalization and financial crises.[60] They are also integrating gender in a wider range of economic models, including computable general equilibrium models.[61]

One of the key insights from this work is that there is a two-way interaction between gender and macroeconomic or trade policy: on the one hand, macroeconomic and trade policies are likely to have different impacts on women and men (and within groups of women and men) because of different access to resources, different household responsibilities, gender segregation and discrimination in labor markets, and other gender-related factors; on the other hand, these gender differences can influence the outcome of macroeconomic and trade policies, for example, by affecting the "supply response" to the liberalization of a particular sector.[62] Stated differently, to the extent women and men in a particular country or locality face different opportunities and constraints, this may influence their ability to benefit from trade liberalization and also to adjust to any adverse changes that result from it.

Nilüfer Çağatay, one of the leading economists working on the gender dimensions of trade and trade policy, has suggested that a comprehensive assessment of the gender-related impacts of a particular trade reform should consider

- changing patterns and conditions of work, including paid and unpaid work;
- changes in gender gaps in wages, earnings, patterns of ownership and control over assets;

---

[59] Çağatay et al., *supra* note 58, at 1830–31. While these economists believe it is important to introduce gender into formal economic modeling, they also emphasize the limitations of economic models and their underlying assumptions. Therefore, they stress the importance of seeing models as complements—not substitutes—for other types of analysis. *Id*. at 1829.

[60] Caren Grown et al., *Introduction to Special Issue on Growth, Trade, Finance, and Gender Inequality*, 28 WORLD DEV. 1145, 1149–1153 (summarizing articles included in the special issue). For information on current research in these areas, see the website of the International Working Group on Gender, Macroeconomics and International Economics (http://www.genderandmacro.org). The extension of gender analysis from macroeconomic policy to international trade and investment was a logical one, particularly since the stabilization and structural adjustment policies that first attracted the attention of gender-aware economists frequently included measures to liberalize trade and attract foreign direct investment. *See* Anne O. Krueger and Sarath Rajapatirana, *The World Bank Policies Towards Trade and Trade Policy Reform*, 22 WORLD ECON. 717, 718–20 (1999); World Bank, *World Bank Support for Developing Countries on International Trade Issues*, DC/99–19 (Sept. 14, 1999) (between 1990 and 1998, 68 percent of World Bank adjustment loans included support for trade and exchange rate policy reforms).

[61] *See, e.g.*, Channing Arndt and Finn Tarp, *Agricultural Technology, Risk and Gender: A CGE Analysis of Mozambique*, 28 WORLD DEV. 1307 (2000); Marzia Fontana and Adrian Wood, *Modeling the Effects of Trade on Women, at Work and at Home*, 28 WORLD DEV. 1173 (2000) (using gendered social accounting matrix for Bangladesh, model covers all market sectors plus social reproduction and leisure activities); Marzia Fontana, *Modeling the Effects of Trade on Women, at Work and at Home: A Comparative Perspective*, International Food Policy Research Institute TMD Discussion Paper No. 110 (2003) (compares gendered computable general equilibrium simulations for Bangladesh and Zambia with econometric and qualitative approaches), *available at* http://www.ifpri.org/divs/tmd/dp/tmdp110.htm.

[62] ÇAĞATAY, *supra* note 8, at 15.

- changes in consumption patterns and use of technology by men and women;
- changes in public provisioning of services and their gendered impacts; [and]
- the gender-differentiated empowerment implications of trade flows.[63]

Other "transmission channels" that could be examined include the impact on the government budget of lost tariff revenues (in the case of tariff liberalization) and the implementation costs of the trade reform;[64] the social and economic impact of changes in migration patterns attributable to the trade reform;[65] and the impact of the trade reform on existing laws and regulations.[66] The scope of such a gender assessment depends on the availability of relevant statistics, disaggregated by sex, age, ethnicity and other relevant categories, and including baseline data against which to measure changes. It may also be difficult methodologically to distinguish the effects of a particular trade reform from the effects of other economic policies and global or regional events and trends.

To date, most of the research and analysis related to gender, trade and investment has focused on the positive employment and income effects of export promotion. Much less work has been done on the displacement effects of trade liberalization in import-competing sectors, and on the impact of trade liberalization on consumption patterns. In terms of sectors, most of the research thus far has focused on export manufacturing, including in particular duty-free zones, and traditional export crops. Relatively less work has been done on non-traditional agricultural exports (such as specialty vegetables and flowers) and services. Because of the difficulty of obtaining relevant data, little research has been done on trade links with the informal and reproductive sectors.[67] New areas covered by international trade rules, such as intellectual property protection, are also just beginning to be analyzed.

E. Legal Analysis of Gender, Trade and Investment

As trade agreements expand into new sectors such as services and into "trade-related" areas such as intellectual property rights, and as greater attention is paid to "behind-the-border" issues, "the central domain of 'trade' policy is increasingly domestic regulation and legal systems."[68] However, domestic laws and regulations are also critical tools for redressing discrimination and structural disadvantages experienced by women and other groups (including indigenous people and ethnic minorities), and many countries have enacted laws to fulfill international obligations under treaties such as CEDAW and

[63] *Id.* at 19. *See also* GAMMAGE ET AL., *supra* note 44 (gender assessments of trade agreements should consider likely effects on prices, employment, wages, consumption, access to public goods and services, laws and regulations important to women and other disadvantaged groups, unpaid household and community work, and migration trends, as well as implementation costs); Fontana et al., *supra* note 16 (effects of trade policy reform on income distribution are typically analyzed in terms of effects on employment, relative prices and government expenditure); Sparr, *supra* note 44 (gender analysis of trade or investment policy could start with study of gender-differentiated impacts on "reproductive" and "productive" work at the family/household and community levels; or gender differences in employment and consumption patterns within a tradeable sector).
[64] *See infra* text accompanying notes 100–104.
[65] *See infra* text accompanying notes 83 and 84.
[66] Legal and regulatory impacts are discussed in Part II.E of this chapter.
[67] *See* ÇAĞATAY, *supra* note 8, at 20–27; UN, *supra* note 9; Fontana et al., *supra* note 16; Susan Joekes, *A Gender-Analytical Perspective on Trade and Sustainable Development*, in UNCTAD, *supra* note 1, at 33.
[68] Jeffrey L. Dunoff, *The WTO in Transition: Of Constituents, Competence and Coherence*, 33 GEO. WASH. INT'L L. REV. 979, 1004 (2001).

other international commitments such as the Beijing Platform for Action.[69] Therefore, policymakers, academics, practicing lawyers and activists interested in gender equality and women's rights have become increasingly concerned about the implications of trade liberalization and specific trade and investment agreements for national and subnational laws that benefit women and other historically disadvantaged groups. A number of critical approaches to international economic law have also pointed to ways in which specific trade and investment agreements, and related institutions and processes, may themselves be "gender-biased," or at least "gender-blind."

In recent years, a number of "new approaches" to international law have been extended to international economic law, and specifically trade law.[70] Several of these new approaches are multidisciplinary, including international law and international relations[71] and law and economics.[72] The new approaches also include a variety of critical perspectives on legal norms, rules and institutions, sometimes described as "critical jurisprudence."[73] The earliest of these perspectives, referred to as "Third World," "Southern" or "postcolonial" critiques of international law, emerged in the 1970s and highlighted the Western origins and biases in international legal principles, as well as the dominance of European and North American countries in the international law-making processes and international institutions.[74] Other critical perspectives—sometimes referred to as "new-stream" approaches—challenge the neutrality, objectivity and coherence of international law rules, and emphasize the extent to which they are grounded in substantive political values.[75] A third set of critical approaches to international law has emerged from the

[69] UNIFEM, Bringing Equality Home: Implementing the Convention on the Elimination of All Forms of Discrimination Against Women (Ilana Landsberg-Lewis ed. 1998); UNIFEM, *supra* note 57, at 38–60; WEDO, Mapping Progress: A WEDO Report Assessing Implementation of the Beijing Platform (1998) (survey found that over 130 governments have drafted national action plans to address women's needs and priorities, and 64 countries have enacted laws and adopted policy measures to address the 12 critical areas of concern identified in the Beijing Platform for Action); World Bank, *supra* note 5, at 107–146.

[70] Joel R. Paul, *The New Movements in International Economic Law*, 10 Am. U.J. Int'l L. & Pol'y 607, 609 (1995); *see also* David Kennedy and Chris Tennant, *New Approaches to International law: A Bibliography*, 35 Harv. Int'l L.J. 417, 417–20 (1994); Steven R. Ratner and Anne-Marie Slaughter, *Appraising the Methods of International Law: A Prospectus for Readers*, 93 Am. J. Int'l L. 291, 293–95 (1999).

[71] *See, e.g.,* Anne-Marie Slaughter et al., *International Law and International Relations Theory: A New Generation of Interdisciplinary Scholarship*, 92 Am. J. Int'l L. 367 (1998).

[72] *See, e.g.,* Jeffrey L. Dunoff and Joel P. Trachtman, *Economic Analysis of International Law*, 24 Yale J. Int'l L. 1 (1999).

[73] William J. Aceves, *Critical Jurisprudence and International Legal Scholarship: A Study of Equitable Distribution*, 39 Colum. J. Transnat'l L. 299, 304 (2001).

[74] *See, e.g.,* R.P. Anand, International Law and the Developing Countries: Confrontation or Cooperation (1987); Mohammed Bedjaoui, Towards a New International Economic Order (1979); Third World Attitudes Toward International Law: An Introduction (Frederick E. Snyder and Suraklart Sathirathai, eds., 1987); Aceves, *supra* note 72, at 302–303; Antony Anghie, *Finding the Peripheries: Sovereignty and Colonialism in Nineteenth Century International Law*, 40 Harv. Int'l L.J. 1 (1999); Maxwell O. Chibundu, *Globalizing the Rule of Law: Some Thoughts at and on the Periphery*, 7 Ind. J. Global Legal Stud. 79 (1999); James Thuo Gathii, *Alternative and Critical: The Contribution of Research and Scholarship on Developing Countries to International Legal Theory*, 41 Harv. Int'l L.J. 263 (2000) (notes evolution of Third World scholarship and interaction with other critical discourses); James Thuo Gatthi, *International Law and Eurocentricity*, 9 Eur. J. Int'l L. 184 (1998); Beth Lyon, *supra* note 25; Karin Mickelson, *Rhetoric and Rage: Third World Voices in International Legal Discourse*, 16 Wis. Int'l L.J. 353 (1998); Makau Mutua, *Savages, Victims, and Saviors: The Metaphor of Human Rights*, 42 Harv. Int'l L.J. 201 (2001); Balakrishnan Rajagopal, *From Resistance to Renewal: The Third World, Social Movements, and the Expansion of International Institutions*, 41 Harv. Int'l L.J. 529 (2000); Amr A. Shalakany, *Arbitration and the Third World: A Plea for Reassessing Bias Under the Specter of Neoliberalism*, 41 Harv. Int'l L.J. 419 (2000).

[75] *See, e.g.,* Martti Koskenniemi, From Apology to Utopia: The Structure of International Legal Argument (1989); Anthony Carty, *Critical International Law: Recent Trends in the Theory of International Law*, 2 Eur. J. Int'l L. 66 (1991); David Kennedy, *A New Stream of International Law Scholarship*, 7 Wis.

various strands of feminist theory.[76] While reflecting diverse viewpoints and drawing on a variety of disciplines, feminist and other gender-aware approaches to international law highlight the ways in which international legal norms, rules and institutions tend to reflect predominantly Western "male" perspectives and experiences, and ignore or stereotype the roles and experiences of women.

Gender-aware approaches to international law have increasingly focused on international economic law and institutions, including the policies and practices of the IMF and World Bank,[77] the WTO[78] and regional trade agreements,[79] and international commercial

INT'L L.J. 1 (1988); Nigel Purvis, *Critical Legal Studies in Public International Law*, 32 HARV. INT'L L.J. 81 (1991); Phillip Trimble, *International Law, World Order and Critical Legal Studies*, 42 STAN. L. REV. 811 (1990).

[76] HILARY CHARLESWORTH AND CHRISTINE CHINKIN, THE BOUNDARIES OF INTERNATIONAL LAW: A FEMINIST ANALYSIS (2000), at 38–48; *see also, e.g.,* RECONCEIVING REALITY: WOMEN AND INTERNATIONAL LAW (Dorinda Dallmeyer, ed., 1993); THIRD WORLD WOMEN AND THE POLITICS OF FEMINISM (Chandra Talpad Mohanty et al., eds., 1991); Penelope E. Andrews, *Globalization, Human Rights and Critical Race Feminism*, 3 J. GENDER, RACE & JUS. 373 (2000); Penelope E. Andrews, *Making Room for Critical Race Theory in International Law: Some Practical Pointers*, 45 VILL. L. REV. 855 (2000); Hilary Charlesworth, *Feminist Methods in International Law*, 93 AM. J. INT'L L. 379 (1999); Hilary Charlesworth et al., *Feminist Approaches to International Law*, 85 AM. J. INT'L L. 613 (1991); Claire Moore Dickerson, *Feminism and Human Rights*, 22 WOMEN'S RIGHTS L. REP. 139 (2001) (discussing critical feminist perspectives on business law, including international business law); Ratna Kapur, *The Tragedy of Victimization Rhetoric: Resurrecting the "Native" Subject in International/Post-Colonial Feminist Legal Politics*, 15 HARV. HUM. RTS. J. 1 (2002); Celestine Nyamu, *How Should Human Rights and Development Respond to Cultural Legitimation of Gender Hierarchy in Developing Countries?*, 41 HARV. INT'L L.J. 381 (2000); Anne Orford, *Contesting Globalization: A Feminist Perspective on the Future of Human Rights*, in THE FUTURE OF INTERNATIONAL HUMAN RIGHTS (Burns H. Weston and Stephen P. Marks, eds., 1999) ("Orford 1999"); Anne Orford, *Feminism, Imperialism and the Mission of International Law*, 71 NORDIC J. INT'L L. 275 (2002) ("Orford 2002"); Sundhya Pahuja, *Trading Spaces: Locating Sites for Challenge Within International Trade Law*, 14 AUSTL. FEMINIST LAW J. 38 (2000); Saskia Sassen, *Toward a Feminist Analytics of the Global Economy*, 4 IND. J. GLOBAL LEGAL STUD. 7 (1996) ("Sassen 1996"); Saskia Sassen, *Women's Burden: Counter-Geographies of Globalization and the Feminization of Survival*, 71 NORDIC. J. INT'L L. 255 (2002); Barbara Stark, *Women and Globalization: The Failure and Postmodern Possibilities of International Law*, 33 VAND. J. TRANSNAT'L L. 503 (2000); Shelley Wright, *Women and the Global Economic Order: A Feminist Perspective*, 10 AM. U.J. INT'L L. & POL'Y 861 (1995).

[77] *See, e.g.,* Orford 1999, *supra* note 76, at 165–68; Anne Orford and Jennifer Beard, *Making the State Safe for the Market: The World Bank's World Development Report 1997*, 22 MELBOURNE U. L. REV. 195 (1998); Nandini Gunewardena, *Reinscribing Subalternity: International Financial Institutions, Development and Women's Marginality*, 7 UCLA J. INT'L L. & FOREIGN AFF. 201 (2003); Sundhya Pahuja, *Technologies of Empire: IMF Conditionality and the Reinscription of the North/South Divide*, 13 LEIDEN J. INT'L L. 749 (2000); Wright, *supra* note 76, at 876–83.

[78] *See, e.g.,* Liane M. Jarvis, *Women's Rights and the Public Morals Exception of GATT Article XX*, 22 MICH. J. INT'L L. 219 (2000); Orford 1999, *supra* note 76, at 168–75; Pahuja, *supra* note 76.

[79] *See, e.g.,* Kate E. Andrias, *Gender, Work and the NAFTA Labor Side Agreement*, 37 U.S.F. L. REV. 521 (2003); Catherine Barbieri, *Women Workers in Transition: The Potential Impact of the NAFTA Labor Side Agreements on Women Workers in Argentina and Chile*, 17 COMP. LAB. L.J. 526 (1996); Laurie Bremer, *Pregnancy Discrimination in Mexico's Maquiladora System: Mexico's Violation of its Obligations under NAFTA and the NAALC*, 4 NAFTA L. & BUS. REV. AM. 567 (1999); Joshua Briones, *Paying the Price for NAFTA: NAFTA's Effect on Women and Children Laborers in Mexico*, 9 UCLA WOMEN'S L.J. 301 (1999); Ruth Buchanan, *Border Crossings: NAFTA, Regulatory Restructuring, and the Politics of Place*, 2 IND. J. GLOBAL LEGAL STUD. 371 (1995); Nicole L. Grimm, *The North American Agreement on Labor Cooperation and Its Effects on Women Working in Mexican Maquiladoras*, 48 AM. U. L. REV. 179 (1998); A. Maria Plumtree, *Maquiladoras and Women Workers: The Marginalization of Women in Mexico as a Means to Economic Development*, 6 SW. J. OF L. & TRADE AM. 177 (1999); Renee G. Scherlen and Ruth Ann Strickland, *The NAFTA(ization) of Sexual Harassment: The Experience of Canada, Mexico, and the United States*, 3 NAFTA L. & BUS. REV. AM. 96 (1997); Michelle Smith, *Potential Solutions to the Problem of Pregnancy Discrimination in Maquiladoras Operated by U.S. Employers in Mexico*, 13 BERKELEY WOMEN'S L.J. 195 (1998); Griselda Vega, *Maquiladora's Lost Women: The Killing Fields of Mexico—Are NAFTA and NAALC Providing the Needed Protection?*, 4 J. GENDER RACE & JUST. 137 (2000).

arbitration.[80] Jurists have also examined the impact of globalization on women, and the inadequacy of state-centered human rights law to address the conduct of non-state actors such as the IMF, World Bank, WTO and multinational companies.[81] In the areas of trade liberalization and foreign direct investment, gender-aware scrutiny has been applied to the conditions of women workers (particularly those working in duty-free zones),[82] the precarious circumstances of women migrants[83] and the increased trafficking of women and girls (linked to regional economic integration, improved transport systems and expansion of tourism).[84] Gender analysis has also been applied to specific aspects of WTO agreements, including the Agreement on the Application of Sanitary and Phytosanitary Measures[85] and the Agreement on Subsidies and Countervailing Measures.[86]

Hilary Charlesworth and Christine Chinkin, two of the first international jurists to apply feminist analysis to international law, have suggested several possible levels of analysis to uncover gender biases or "silences" in particular areas of international law. These include inquiries about the relative presence of women and men in international legal institutions; the vocabulary used in international law instruments (such as the use of the term "security" to refer to military security, rather than food, health, livelihood or other forms of "human" security); and underlying concepts of international law (including the use of dichotomies such as public/private, economic/political, and binding/non-binding).[87] In the area of trade law, commentators have also noted how the links made to the "neutral science" of

[80] *See, e.g.*, Ruth Buchanan, *Constructing Virtual Justice in the Global Arena*, 31 LAW & SOC'Y REV. 363 (1997).

[81] *See, e.g.*, CHARLESWORTH AND CHINKIN, *supra* note 76, at 243–45; Alfred C. Aman, Jr., *Introduction to Symposium Issue on Feminism and Globalization: The Impact of the Global Economy on Women and Feminist Theory*, 4 IND. J. GLOBAL LEGAL STUD. 1 (1996) (overview of other symposium articles); Andrews, *supra* note 76; Lucy B. Bednarek, *The Gender Wage Gap: Searching for Equality in a Global Economy*, 6 IND. J. GLOBAL LEGAL STUD. 213 (1998); Orford 2002, *supra* note 76; Orford 1999, *supra* note 76; Sassen, *supra* note 76; Stark, *supra* note 76; Wright, *supra* note 76.

[82] *See, e.g.,* Theresa A. Amato, *Overview of Symposium on Women at Work, Rights at Risk—Toward the Empowerment of Working Women*, 17 YALE J. INT'L L. 139 (1992); Barbieri, *supra* note 79; Jennifer Bol, *Using the Inter-American System to Pursue International Labour Rights: A Case Study of the Guatemalan Maquiladoras*, 55 U. TORONTO FAC. L. REV. 351 (1997); Bremer, *supra* note 79; Briones, *supra* note 79; Lance Compa, *International Labor Standards and Instruments of Recourse for Working Women*, 17 YALE J. INT'L L. 151 (1992); Grimm, *supra* note 79; Plumtree, *supra* note 79; Sherrie L. Russell-Brown, *Labor Rights as Human Rights: the Situation of Women Workers in Jamaica's Export Free Zones*, 1 BERKELEY J. EMP. & LAB. L. 179 (2003); Scherlen and Strickland, *supra* note 79; Smith, *supra* note 79; Karen F. Travis, *Women in Global Production and Worker Rights Provisions in U.S. Trade Laws*, 17 YALE J. INT'L L. 173 (1992); Vega, *supra* note 79; Donna E. Young, *Working Across Borders: Global Restructuring and Women's Work*, 2001 UTAH L. REV. 1 (2001).

[83] *See, e.g.*, Joan Fitzpatrick and Katrina R. Kelly, *Gendered Aspects of Migration: Law and the Female Migrant*, 22 HASTINGS INT'L & COMP. L. REV. 47 (1998); Donna Maeda, *Agencies of Filipina Migrants in Globalized Economies: Transforming International Human Rights Discourse*, 13 LA RAZA L.J. 317 (2002); Young, *supra* note 82.

[84] *See, e.g.*, Nancy Beyer, *The Sex Tourism Industry Spreads to Costa Rica and Honduras*, 29 GA. J. INT'L & COMP. L. 301 (2001); Katrin Corrigan, *Putting the Brakes on the Global Trafficking of Women for the Sex Trade: An Analysis of Existing Regulatory Schemes to Stop the Flow of Traffic*, 25 FORDHAM INT'L L.J. 151 (2001); Fitzpatrick and Kelly, *supra* note 83; Emma Goldman, *The Traffic in Women*, 13 HASTINGS WOMEN'S L.J. 9 (2002); Aiko Joshi, *The Face of Human Trafficking*, 13 HASTINGS WOMEN'S L.J. 31 (2002); Kathryn E. Nelson, *Sex Trafficking and Forced Prostitution: Comprehensive New Legal Approaches*, 24 HOUS. J. INT'L L. 551 (2002); *but see* Kapur, *supra* note 76 (critiquing "victim" images in anti-trafficking discourse);

[85] Orford 1999, *supra* note 76, at 169–75.

[86] Pahuja, *supra* note 76, at 48–51.

[87] CHARLESWORTH AND CHINKIN, *supra* note 76, at 49–50; Charlesworth, *supra* note 76, at 381–85.

economics and the increasingly technical nature of trade discourse both contribute to the appearance of trade rules as neutral and objective.[88]

One way to analyze particular trade or investment agreements from a gender perspective would involve consideration of (1) the text of the agreement; (2) related implementation and enforcement mechanisms; and (3) possible interactions with the various laws and norms that influence gender roles and women's opportunities and constraints within a particular country.[89] This analysis should also be informed by an understanding of the social, economic and political context in which the relevant trade or investment activity is taking place, including the opportunities and constraints facing women and other disadvantaged groups.

Under this approach, a trade or investment agreement would first be examined to identify any overtly "gender-biased" provisions, or apparently "gender-neutral" provisions that might have a disparate effect on women and men (or on groups of women or men) in light of their different social and economic circumstances. Second, the related implementation and enforcement mechanisms would be considered, including the gender composition and gender awareness of the decision-making bodies involved. Finally, the agreement would be analyzed in terms of its possible interactions with domestic laws and regulations, taking into account the range of laws and norms that influence women's and men's status and rights in a particular country, the different circumstances of women within the same country (which could be related to age, ethnicity, religion or other factors), and institutional and practical constraints on the enforcement of laws and access to justice.[90]

More specifically, a trade or investment commitment could be examined to determine whether it supports or conflicts with any of the following:

(1) The country's international commitments relevant to gender equality and human rights;[91]

---

[88] Sara Dillon, *A Farewell to "Linkage": International Trade Law and Global Sustainability Indicators*, 55 RUTGERS L. REV. 87, 110–12 (2002); Pahuja, *supra* note 76, at 44–47. As discussed in Section II.D, there is a growing body of literature that identifies and addresses gender biases in economic concepts, indicators, research and models. *See supra* text accompanying notes 56–61.

[89] This approach to legal/regulatory analysis is based on GAMMAGE ET AL., *supra* note 44, at 23–27.

[90] The legal framework shaping gender relations and women's rights in a particular country includes the country's international treaty commitments, such as CEDAW and International Labour Organization ("ILO") conventions, international consensus documents such as the Beijing Declaration and Platform for Action, and its national constitution, statutes, regulations and judicial rulings. WORLD BANK, *supra* note 5, at 113. In federal systems, state or provincial laws, regulations and judicial decisions may also need to be considered. In many countries, religious, traditional or customary laws—which may be interpreted and enforced by a separate system of courts—will also be relevant. Taken together, this web of laws and norms may either support or undermine a country's international commitments to gender equality and rights. CHRISTINE CHINKIN, GENDER MAINSTREAMING IN LEGAL AND CONSTITUTIONAL AFFAIRS: A REFERENCE MANUAL FOR GOVERNMENTS AND OTHER STAKEHOLDERS, Commonwealth Secretariat Gender Management System Series (2001), at 14–15. Institutional, cultural and practical factors can also influence the rights and opportunities of women and other disadvantaged groups. For example, beneficial laws may not be vigorously enforced because regulatory agencies are underfunded and understaffed. Judges and government officials may be insensitive or biased toward women (or other groups) in their interpretation and enforcement of laws. In many countries, women also are not aware of their rights, or may be reluctant or unable to assert them for financial or other reasons. GAMMAGE ET AL., *supra* note 44, at 24–26.

[91] These could include CEDAW, the Convention on the Rights of the Child and other human rights treaties; ILO conventions related to discrimination and equal pay, child labor, freedom of association and the right to organize, part-time and home work, and occupational health and safety; environmental treaties such as the Convention on Biological Diversity; regional human rights conventions; and international undertakings such as the Beijing Declaration and Platform for Action.

(2) The country's constitution;[92]
(3) National and subnational laws and regulations that benefit women and other disadvantaged groups, in particular:
   (a) non-discrimination and equal treatment laws;[93]
   (b) affirmative action and other laws providing special treatment;[94] and
   (c) gender-neutral laws such as those pertaining to fair wages, food labeling, and health and safety;[95]
(4) Gaps or biases in the application or enforcement of laws that benefit women and other vulnerable groups, such as labor laws;[96] and
(5) Religious, traditional or customary laws and practices, especially those relating to land and other assets.[97]

This approach to gender-aware legal analysis is used in the following Part to analyze selected WTO agreements and processes from a gender perspective.

III. Gender Analysis of Selected Trade Agreements and WTO Processes

This section is intended to provide an overview of gender issues in trade and investment agreements related to key economic sectors and trade-related areas, as well as gender issues in trade-related processes such as trade negotiations, dispute settlement, trade policy review and trade-related capacity building. The main focus of discussion is on the Uruguay Round agreements, although some reference is made to regional and bilateral agreements. The approach is multidisciplinary, and draws on social, economic and legal/regulatory research and analysis. The approach also considers a range of gender-related impacts, including direct and indirect effects of changes in cross-border trade and investment, government spending and other activities influenced by trade and investment agreements; direct or indirect effects of specific provisions in trade or investment agreements; and gender biases in trade-related processes. This discussion is selective and reflects current limitations in data-gathering and gaps in research and analysis. The

---

[92] Many countries' constitutions include broad protections of civil, political, economic, social and cultural rights, and may include specific commitments to gender equality. *See* CHINKIN, *supra* note 90, at 48–49.
[93] These include laws that prohibit discrimination against women or other social groups in education, employment, ownership of assets and other activities, or that mandate equal payment and equal treatment.
[94] These include laws and programs that address serious gender disparities by setting targets or quotas for women's or girls' participation (including small business assistance and government procurement set-asides), or by providing subsidies or other benefits (such as reduced fees, lower borrowing rates or training) to encourage their participation. Such "special measures aimed at accelerating de facto equality between men and women" are expressly authorized under CEDAW. *See* CEDAW, *supra* note 10, art. 4.1. Also included in this category are laws that directly address women's reproductive role, such as maternity leave legislation.
[95] These could also include gender-neutral laws granting parental leave, or mandating or subsidizing childcare in the workplace.
[96] For example, the labor laws and regulations in most countries extend primarily to formal sector workers in defined "workplaces", and therefore generally do not protect domestic, home-based or agricultural workers. Gaps in legal protections can also be created when national or local governments grant exemptions—e.g., from applicable labor or workplace safety regulations—to firms operating in duty-free zones. Facially neutral laws can also be applied in a discriminatory manner (e.g., land titling, tax and social security laws that assign all rights to the "head of household", usually presumed to be a male household member). Facially neutral laws can also disadvantage women because of their more limited access to assets and employment opportunities (e.g., banking regulations that require loans to be secured by land or other traditional forms of collateral). Laws can also be overtly discriminatory (e.g., laws requiring a spouse or male guardian to countersign contracts and other loan documents). *See generally* CHINKIN, *supra* note 90, at 14–19, 34–36 and 50–60; WORLD BANK, *supra* note 5, at 107–146.
[97] GAMMAGE ET AL., *supra* note 44, at 26.

treatment of particular agreements and issue areas is not exhaustive, but is intended to complement the fuller discussion of these topics in other chapters.

A. Manufacturing and Trade in Goods

1. General Agreement on Tariffs and Trade 1994

A growing body of research indicates that liberalization of trade in goods has had a number of gender-differentiated effects within trading countries, including effects on employment. In particular, the growth of export industries in many newly industrializing countries has increased wage employment opportunities for women, although women's employment has been concentrated in labor-intensive industries characterized by low wages and poor working conditions compared to more capital-intensive industries.[98] Most of the research to date has focused on positive employment effects (i.e. "job gains") in export sectors. Less data are available on displacement effects (i.e. "job losses") in import-competing sectors, although there is some evidence of gender-differentiated effects, for example, in labor-intensive industries in African countries that have been hurt by increased imports of lower-cost products from Asia.[99] Trade theory suggests that trade liberalization would also have an effect on consumption of traded goods (and domestically-produced substitutes), through changes in relative prices, and principles of gender analysis suggest that these consumption effects are likely to be "gendered," for example, because of women's and men's different household responsibilities and access to cash income. However, relatively little research has been done in this area.

Another recognized impact of liberalized trade in goods is the reduction of government revenue resulting from progressively lower tariffs. This impact is felt most strongly by developing countries, which historically have relied on tariffs to provide a substantial portion of their revenues.[100] Indeed, recent research has found that developing countries since 1970 have suffered declining tax revenues due to tariff reductions, which have not been adequately offset by increases in income and other taxes.[101] Recent work on gender analysis of government budgets suggests that the "government revenue" effects of tariff reductions also are likely to have a gender dimension.[102] For example, if tariff

---

[98] Mehra and Gammage, *supra* note 16, at 540–41; UN, *supra* note 9, at 9–20.

[99] UN, *supra* note 9, at 9–13.

[100] Developing countries' dependence on tariff revenues is acknowledged in the General Agreement on Tariffs and Trade, as amended ("GATT"). *See* GATT, Art. XXVIII bis. 3(b). One recent study found that tariff revenue represents 35 percent of low-income countries' total revenue, compared to one percent for high-income countries. Barsha Khattry and J. Mohan Rao, *Fiscal Faux Pas?: An Analysis of the Revenue Implications of Trade Liberalization*, 30 WORLD DEV. 1431, 1437 (2002).

[101] Kattry and Rao, *supra* note 100. The authors note that tariffs are considerably easier to assess and collect than other taxes, particularly for countries with limited capacity to administer taxes and where corruption and tax evasion are common. Other commentators have noted that the economic models used to project impacts of trade liberalization typically make the unrealistic assumption that tariff revenues will be replaced by non-distortionary lump sum taxes; in fact, any domestic tax introduced to offset lost tariff revenue would lead to some economic distortion. *See* Mark Weisbrot and Dean Baker, *The Relative Impact of Trade Liberalization on Developing Countries* (2002), *available at* http://www.cepr.net/relative_impact_of_trade_liberal.htm.

[102] *See, e.g.*, UNIFEM, GENDER BUDGET INITIATIVES: STRATEGIES, CONCEPTS AND EXPERIENCES (2002); Debbie Budlender, *The Political Economy of Women's Budgets in the South*, 28 WORLD DEV. 1365 (2000); Helena Hofbauer Balmori, *Gender and Budgets: Overview Report*, BRIDGE Publication (2003), *available at* http://www.ids.ac.uk/bridge. Although most work to date has focused on public expenditures, new tools are being developed to analyze the gender dimensions of revenue collection and other economic policies. Kathleen Barnett and Caren Grown, *Gender Impacts of Government Revenue Collection: The Case of Taxation*, Commonwealth Secretariat Publication (2004); *See also* MALHOTRA ET AL., *supra* note 29, at 164, Box 7.4 (trade taxes and spending policies can have significant impact on human development and poverty reduction efforts).

reductions are not offset by increases in government revenue from other sources, government expenditures are likely to be cut. Research on the impact of reduced social spending under structural adjustment programs in many developing countries, for example, has found a disproportionate negative impact on poor women. There could also be a gender-differentiated impact depending on the taxes or other charges that are introduced to make up for lost tariff revenue. For example, consumption-based taxes such as sales taxes, and user charges on basic services, are regressive and would disproportionately affect lower-income households, and particularly women who are responsible for basic household expenditures.

There is also increasing recognition that the General Agreement on Tariffs and Trade ("GATT") and other trade agreements entail substantial implementation costs, particularly for developing countries. For example, a widely-circulated study by World Bank economists estimated that implementation of only three of the Uruguay Round agreements had cost more advanced developing countries on average about $150 million, and that the costs for least-developed countries could be greater.[103] Notification procedures alone can impose a financial and administrative burden, particularly on least-developed countries. One commentator, for example, estimates that the Uruguay Round agreements impose a total of 215 different notification requirements on WTO members.[104] These implementation costs can have gender implications for developing country governments, if they absorb a substantial portion of the national budget and reduce the amounts available for social and other developmental expenditures.

The text of the GATT also includes provisions that reflect a "gender-blind" approach to development and other domestic policy goals on the part of the original GATT contracting parties. For example, Article XVIII addresses the issue of government assistance for development in terms of "programmes and policies of economic development designed to raise the *general* standard of living," and therefore permits flexibility "to grant tariff protection required for the establishment of a particular *industry*."[105] Similarly, Part IV on trade and development emphasizes developing countries' need to expand export earnings as a means to achieve economic development. These provisions reflect an understanding of development as essentially an economic process to be pursued through promotion of particular industries, especially export industries. This concept of development is far narrower than the approaches more recently followed by international and bilateral development agencies and reflected in many countries' national development plans, which also emphasize the importance of human development, poverty reduction, gender equality and other social goals.[106]

---

[103] J. Michael Finger and Philip Schuler, *Implementation of Uruguay Round Commitments: The Development Challenge*, 23 WORLD ECON. 511 (2000) (study examined implementation costs of the Agreements on Implementation of Article VII of the GATT 1994 [Customs Valuation], the Application of Sanitary and Phytosanitary Measures, and Trade-Related Aspects of Intellectual Property Rights).

[104] Yash Tandon, *Evaluation of WTO and Other Forms of Technical Assistance to Developing Countries in the Context of the Uruguay Round of Agreements* (2002), at 2, *available at* http://www.ileapinitiative.com/pages/events.htm.

[105] GATT, Art. XVIII.2 (emphasis added).

[106] *See, e.g.*, UNDP, Development Policy, *at* http://www.undp.org/policy (UNDP supports countries' development agendas in the areas of democratic governance, poverty reduction, crisis prevention and recovery, energy and environment, information and communications technology and HIV/AIDS, and promotes gender equality in all activities); World Bank, About Us: What Is the World Bank?: At a Glance, *at* http://www.worldbank.org (World Bank supports investment in basic health and education; social development, inclusion, governance and institution building for poverty reduction; strengthening governments' ability to deliver quality services; protection of environment; private business development; and reforms for a stable macroeconomic environment). .

Article XX of the GATT, which sets out the non-trade policy areas that may provide a basis for exceptions from GATT disciplines, is also "gender-blind." The article recognizes the legitimacy of certain measures taken to protect "public morals", "human, animal or plant life or health," "protection of national treasures," "conservation of exhaustible natural resources," and laws and regulations in a variety of areas such as customs enforcement, intellectual property protection and prevention of deceptive practices.[107] However, Article XX does not refer to government measures taken to ensure equal treatment and non-discrimination, to promote gender equality or to redress historical disadvantages suffered by women and other social groups.[108] While one commentator has argued that the "public morals" exception in Article XX might be construed to cover measures to promote women's rights, she acknowledges that this argument is novel and untested.[109] The exception for "human, animal or plant life or health" could arguably apply to a variety of laws and regulations that are beneficial to women, including health regulations. However, as discussed extensively elsewhere, GATT and WTO dispute panels and the WTO Appellate Body have interpreted this and other Article XX exceptions quite narrowly.[110]

2. Agreement on Textiles and Clothing

Textile and clothing manufacturers in many countries employ predominantly women, at least in the more labor-intensive processes,[111] and therefore trade arrangements relating to textiles and clothing ("T&C") have a strong gender dimension. While the discussion here relates primarily to the Uruguay Round Agreement on Textiles and Clothing ("ATC"), similar issues can arise in the context of regional and bilateral agreements on T&C trade.

As discussed elsewhere in this book, the ATC provides for the staged phase-out of bilateral quotas on T&C imports and exports that had been in place since 1974 under the Multi-Fibre Agreement.[112] Over a five-year period, T&C that were previously subject to import quotas were to be "integrated" into the GATT in four phases. While the ATC was expected to result in a significant increase in T&C exports from developing countries, where T&C manufacturing operations are increasingly located, these benefits

---

[107] GATT, Art. XX(a)–(g).

[108] The absence of such provisions in the original text of Article XX is not surprising, since gender equality and women's rights became prominent international and national policy goals only in the 1970s (although the principles of equality and non-discrimination were already embedded in the United Nations Charter signed in 1945 and the Universal Declaration of Human Rights adopted in late 1948). Moreover, even general principles of human rights and labor rights were not included in the original Article XX text, although the ILO predated the GATT by several decades and the Universal Declaration of Human Rights was drafted concurrently with the GATT.

[109] *See* Jarvis, *supra* note 78. This proposal is limited to "outwardly-directed" trade measures, such as measures to restrict imports from countries where discriminatory or abusive practices against women are sanctioned. The proposal does not consider measures that a government might take to promote gender equality domestically, such as assistance programs for businesses owned by women, which might have effects on trade. *See infra* text accompanying notes 213–18. A number of other commentators have debated the possible use of the "public morals" exception as a basis for imposing trading sanctions on countries that violate fundamental human rights, for example, by permitting or promoting the use of slave labor. *See, e.g.*, Salman Bal, *International Free Trade Agreements and Human Rights: Reinterpreting Article XX of the GATT*, 10 Minn. J. Global Trade 62 (2001); Adelle Blackett, *Whither Social Clause? Human Rights, Trade Theory and Treaty Interpretation*, 31 Colum. Hum. Rts. L. Rev. 1 (1999); Steve Charnovitz, *The Moral Exception in Trade Policy*, 38 Va. J. Int'l L. 689 (1998); Frank J. Garcia, *The Global Market and Human Rights: Trading Away the Human Rights Principles*, 25 Brook. J. Int'l L. 1 (1999).

[110] *See, e.g.*, Bal, *supra* note 109; Blackett, *supra* note 109 (finds evidence of more flexible interpretation in recent Appellate Body decisions); Garcia, *supra* note 109.

[111] Mehra and Gammage, *supra* note 16, at 540.

[112] *See* Chapters 9 and 53 of this book.

have generally not been realized for several reasons. Observers have noted two major loopholes in the ATC text itself. First, since the phase-out schedule for import quotas is "back-loaded," a large proportion of the expected increases in market access may not be realized until the end of the implementation period.[113] Second, the phase-out schedule is structured in terms of percentages of total T&C imports, and therefore importing countries have had considerable leeway in selecting goods to be freed from quotas. As a result, many key categories of T&C exports from developing countries have not yet been released from quotas by the major importing countries.[114] Importing countries have also made heavy use of the transitional safeguard provision of the ATC, as well as antidumping procedures, to restrict T&C imports.[115]

Trends in global T&C trade have had several gender-specific effects. First, the relocation of T&C manufacturing operations from industrialized to developing countries effectively moved a large number of manufacturing jobs employing women from industrialized to developing countries.[116] Second, the slow implementation of the ATC, together with the recent global economic slowdown, have resulted in the creation of fewer new T&C manufacturing jobs—most of which would likely have been filled by women—in developing countries than would have been expected. Third, the lifting of country-specific import quotas is leading to greater competition among developing countries in the T&C sector, with gains and losses for women workers in different developing countries. Full implementation of the ATC, for example, is expected to benefit larger exporting countries such as China at the expense of smaller countries such as Bangladesh, where the garment industry employs about 1.4 million, mostly female, workers. Finally, the expansion of the T&C sector in developing countries will not necessarily narrow existing gender wage gaps if women are hired primarily for low-skilled factory work with little opportunity for training or advancement.[117]

3. Agreement on Subsidies and Countervailing Measures

The Uruguay Round Agreement on Subsidies and Countervailing Measures ("SCM Agreement"), which strengthened the disciplines on subsidies contained in the Tokyo Round Subsidies Code, has been critiqued from a variety of perspectives. While disciplines on subsidies have been justified as necessary to minimize "distortions" in trade flows, the treatment of subsidies in the SCM Agreement has been criticized by one prominent economist as "utterly devoid of any economic rationale beyond the mercantilist interests of a narrow set of powerful groups in the advanced industrial countries."[118]

---

[113] *See* WORLD BANK, GLOBAL ECONOMIC PROSPECTS IN THE DEVELOPING COUNTRIES 2002 (2001), at 51; WTO, ANNUAL REPORT 2002 (2002), at 31 ("notification of products to be integrated under the third stage of the [ATC] suggests that a significant number of quantitative restrictions . . . may not be removed until the end of 2004").

[114] WORLD BANK, *supra* note 113, at 52.

[115] Kenneth A. Reinert, *Give Us Virtue, But Not Yet: Safeguard Actions Under the Agreement on Textiles and Clothing*, 23 WORLD ECON. 25 (2000); WTO, *supra* note 113, at 31.

[116] However, the evidence is mixed as to whether this trend led to an overall decline in the female share of manufacturing jobs in industrialized countries. *See* UN, *supra* note 9, at 12.

[117] GAMMAGE ET AL., *supra* note 44, at 41; *see also* MALHOTRA ET AL., *supra* note 29, at 169–82; G & T Task Force, *supra* note 16, at 141–74; C.A.F. Dowlah, *The Future of the Readymade Clothing Industry of Bangladesh in the Post-Uruguay Round World*, 22 WORLD ECON. 933, 934 (1999); Razzaz, *supra* note 37 (analysis of Madagascar's expanding T&C sector estimated that male workers would benefit substantially more than female workers because of gender discrimination in the sector).

[118] DANI RODRIK, THE GLOBAL GOVERNANCE OF TRADE: AS IF DEVELOPMENT MATTERED, UNDP Background Paper (2001), at 27.

Another prominent economist has noted that, notwithstanding the "disciplines" of the SCM Agreement, "developed countries make use of a whole variety of other, hidden subsidies under the rubric of 'defence'."[119] In a similar vein, some commentators have found a strong bias toward industrialized countries in the hierarchy of subsidies outlined in the SCM Agreement: while the agreement treats subsidies that are more likely to be used by industrialized countries (such as those for research and development, and environmental upgrades of facilities) as "non-actionable," it categorizes export subsidies that developing countries are more likely to use as "prohibited."[120]

Commentators have also critiqued the general concept of "subsidy" reflected in the SCM Agreement. While the SCM Agreement is intended to restrict forms of government assistance that "have the effect of distorting world trade and depriving other countries of legitimate trade opportunities,"[121] one commentator notes that "[e]ven economically speaking, [some] subsidies can be rationalized not only as socially imperative deviations from principles of economic efficiency but also as correctives for distortions from other sources." She concludes that "the absence of international consensus on the use of subsidies is nothing less than a reflection of the varying views on the proper role of government in economic affairs."[122] Critical commentators have also noted various types of assistance that are *not* recognized as "subsidies" in the SCM Agreement. For example, the deregulation of labor markets could be viewed as providing a benefit to exporting firms akin to a negative subsidy.[123] Other unrecognized "subsidies" include the financial benefits provided to households by unpaid workers in family businesses and unpaid caregivers, who are usually women.[124]

A gender-aware reading of the SCM Agreement suggests a more specific way in which the agreement is "gender-blind." The "non-actionable" subsidies listed in Article 8—which lapsed in January 2000—included, among others, "assistance to disadvantaged regions . . . given pursuant to a general framework of regional development."[125] However, Article 8 did not provide similar treatment for "assistance to disadvantaged groups," such as women and ethnic minorities. Thus, a government program to assist women or minority entrepreneurs in a particular manufacturing industry—for example, through low-interest loans, tax credits or training—could conceivably be challenged under the SCM Agreement. More specifically, it might be characterized as a "prohibited" subsidy if the program were tied to export goals or domestic content requirements, or as an "actionable" subsidy if the scheme could be shown to injure a domestic industry in another

[119] Joseph E. Stiglitz, *Two Principles for the Next Round or, How to Bring Developing Countries in from the Cold*, 23 WORLD ECON. 437, 451 (2000).

[120] *See, e.g.*, THIRD WORLD NETWORK, THE MULTILATERAL TRADING SYSTEM: A DEVELOPMENT PERSPECTIVE, UNDP Background Paper (2001), at 41–42; Michael H. Davis and Dana Neacsu, *Legitimacy, Globally: The Incoherence of Free Trade Practice, Global Economics and Their Governing Principles of Political Economy*, 69 U. MO. K.C. L. REV. 733, 767–771 (2001). However, Article 8 of the SCM Agreement, relating to non-actionable subsidies, lapsed on January 1, 2000 because of a lack of consensus in the Committee on SCM to extend these provisions, as provided in Article 31. WTO, *supra* note 113, at 67 n.10. In addition, Article 27 of the SCM Agreement provides special and differential treatment for least-developed and developing countries, including a complete exemption from the prohibition on export subsidies for least-developed countries.

[121] Paul C. Rosenthal and Robert T.C. Vermylen, *The WTO Antidumping and Subsidies Agreements: Did the United States Achieve Its Objectives During the Uruguay Round?*, 31 LAW & POL'Y INT'L BUS. 871, 891 (2000) (quoting from the report of the GATT Director-General on the Tokyo Round).

[122] Pahuja, *supra* note 76, at 50.

[123] *See, e.g.*, Blackett, *supra* note 109, at 52–53; Pahuja, *supra* note 76, at 50.

[124] Blackett, *supra* note 109, at 23–24.

[125] *Agreement on Subsidies and Countervailing Measures*, Art. 8.2(b).

WTO member country, or to otherwise cause "nullification or impairment of benefits" or "serious prejudice" to that country.[126] It would be more difficult to challenge such a program if it were sponsored by a least-developed or developing country government, in light of the special and differential treatment accorded to them under Article 27 of the agreement. Nonetheless, the failure to acknowledge this type of government assistance program in Article 8 suggests a lack of awareness on the part of trade negotiators about the existence of these programs (which are not limited to developing countries), or perhaps a conclusion that since these programs generally apply to small and medium-sized businesses, they are unlikely to cause sufficient harm to competing businesses in other countries so as to trigger provisions of the SCM Agreement.

At the Fourth Ministerial Conference in Doha, developing countries proposed to treat a number of development-related measures as non-actionable subsidies under the SCM Agreement. The Ministerial Conference agreed that this proposal would be considered further within the WTO.[127] In this regard, the Committee on SCM could also consider an exemption for government assistance to enterprises owned by women and other historically disadvantaged groups. This would complement CEDAW's provision on "special measures aimed at accelerating de facto equality between men and women."[128] It would also further the recommendations of UNCTAD's Commission on Enterprise, Business Facilitation and Development and of the Commonwealth Secretariat to governments to address the needs of women entrepreneurs, for example, through special credit lines.[129]

The disciplines on subsidies contained in the SCM Agreement are closely related to the treatment of countervailing measures in the same agreement and anti-dumping rules contained in the Uruguay Round Agreement on Implementation of Article VI of GATT 1994 (Antidumping). The use of subsidies, as well as the imposition of countervailing duties and the institution of antidumping proceedings, can have indirect, gender-differentiated effects on workers in the affected industries. For example, in the T&C sector, government assistance to manufacturers in small exporting countries to upgrade their facilities could stem the layoffs of predominantly female workers that have already taken place—for example, in Bangladesh[130]—due to increased competition from other countries and other factors. The use of countervailing duties and antidumping proceedings, while intended to protect domestic firms and their workers from the competition of cheaper imports, restricts imports and therefore could lead to hiring freezes, wage cuts and layoffs in the T&C sectors of exporting countries, with a disproportionate impact on women workers. Similar effects could also be expected as a result of "safeguard" actions taken by importing countries in compliance with the Uruguay Round Agreement on Safeguards. However, the gender dimensions of subsidies, countervailing duties, antidumping and safeguard actions have not been systematically studied, due in part to the lack of sex-disaggregated data on employment in the relevant industries.

---

[126] *Id.*, Part II (prohibited subsidies) & Part III (actionable subsidies). *See* GAMMAGE ET AL., *supra* note 44, at 51.

[127] WTO, *Implementation-Related Issues and Concerns*, Decision of Nov. 14, 2001, Ministerial Conference, Fourth Session, Doha, Nov. 9–14, 2001, WT/MIN(01)/17 (Nov. 20, 2001) (reproduced in the Appendix to this book), ¶ 10.2.

[128] CEDAW, *supra* note 10, art. 4.1

[129] UNCTAD, *Mainstreaming Gender in Order to Promote Opportunities: Agreed Recommendations*, Trade and Development Board, Commission on Enterprise, Business Facilitation and Development, 6th Sess., Agenda Item 5, U.N. Doc. TD/B/COM.3/L.22 (2002); O'REGAN-TARDU, *supra* note 33, at 6–9.

[130] ASIAN DEVELOPMENT BANK, ASIAN DEVELOPMENT OUTLOOK 2002 (2002), at 85 ("Between July and December 2001, about 1,200 garment factories closed and an estimated 350,000 workers in the garment industry lost their jobs").

4. Agreement on Trade-Related Investment Measures

The gender-differentiated effects of foreign direct investment ("FDI") have not been extensively studied to date. However, some economists have used theoretical and computable general equilibrium models to examine the possible gendered effects of increases in foreign capital inflows on a country's manufacturing sector.[131] While global FDI flows expanded rapidly beginning the 1970s, they have been heavily concentrated in a small number of industrialized and developing countries. In addition, research on duty-free zones, where foreign-owned firms predominate, shows strong gender segregation in employment, with concentrations of male workers in capital-intensive processes and female workers in more labor-intensive processes.[132] Therefore, the gendered effects of FDI could be expected to vary widely across countries, industries and even stages of production.

The gender-differentiated impacts of the Uruguay Round Agreement on Trade-Related Investment Measures ("TRIMs Agreement"), and investment agreements at the regional and bilateral levels, are also not well understood. The TRIMs Agreement and other investment agreements could lead to increased foreign investment and the creation of new jobs for women. On the other hand, the elimination of domestic-content requirements as mandated under the TRIMs Agreement[133] could negatively affect particular groups of women, for example, if they own or work for local input suppliers. As workers, women can also be directly affected by investment incentives that a host government may offer to foreign investors, such as exemptions from local labor laws, health and safety standards, and environmental regulations.[134]

In addition, where an investment agreement permits the arbitration of disputes between foreign investors and the host country, as under the North American Free Trade Agreement ("NAFTA") and a large number of bilateral investment treaties, claims brought by foreign investors against the host state can raise gender issues. In one NAFTA investor-state dispute, for example, a U.S. corporation, Crompton Corp., challenged a decision of the Canadian government to phase out the use of lindane, a pesticide manufactured by Crompton, which has been linked to breast cancer.[135]

B. Agriculture Trade and the Agreement on Agriculture

A majority of the female labor force in developing countries is engaged in agriculture—62 percent in 1990.[136] As in manufacturing, researchers have identified gender divisions of

---

[131] *See, e.g.*, Elissa Braunstein, *Engendering Foreign Direct Investment: Family Structure, Labor Markets and International Capital Mobility*, 28 WORLD DEV. 1157 (2000); Fontana and Wood, *supra* note 59.
[132] WORLD BANK, GLOBAL ECONOMIC PROSPECTS AND THE DEVELOPING COUNTRIES 2003 (2002), at 46–49; Mehra and Gammage, *supra* note 16, at 540–41.
[133] *Agreement on Trade-Related Investment Measures*, Annex, para. 1(a).
[134] These and other concerns have been raised by the UN High Commissioner for Human Rights (UNHCHR). *See generally* UNHCR, *Economic, Social and Cultural Rights: Human Rights, Trade and Investment*, Report of the High Commissioner for Human Rights, U.N. Doc. E/CN.4/sub.2/2003/9 (2003). Mariama Williams has also noted possible indirect impacts of FDI on gender equality, including effects on tax revenue (and related implications for social expenditures), availability of various types of infrastructure and social services, exchange rates and balance of payments, and local finance markets. WILLIAMS, *supra* note 32, at 128.
[135] International Centre for Trade and Sustainable Development, *Latest NAFTA Investor-State Claim Launched*, BRIDGES WEEKLY TRADE NEWS DIGEST, Dec. 20, 2001, *available at* http://www.ictsd.org; *see also* GAMMAGE ET AL., *supra* note 44, at 52.
[136] Mehra and Gammage, *supra* note 16, at 538.

labor in agriculture, with men and women assuming responsibility for growing different crops, or carrying out different cropping tasks.[137] Although women are involved in production of both cash and subsistence crops, research indicates that they are primarily responsible for household food production in several regions—70 to 80 percent in Sub-Saharan Africa and 65 percent in Asia.[138] However, extensive literature documents the constraints that women farmers face due to limited access to and rights over land, limited access to credit and other inputs, and neglect by agricultural extension services.[139]

Market liberalization and promotion of export crops have had ambiguous employment effects on women farmers. For example, in some regions, women's representation in the agricultural labor force has increased as more men migrate to jobs in manufacturing or other off-farm work.[140] However, expansion of export crops has also displaced women farmers from land they had used for subsistence farming, and many of these displaced women have taken seasonal jobs as a agricultural workers. In Africa and Latin America, women make up the large majority of the workforce in non-traditional agricultural exports, such as flowers and specialty vegetables. While these jobs provide cash income, they are also characterized by low wages, health hazards and seasonality.[141] Market liberalization has also created new opportunities for women involved in food processing and trading, although they tend to be concentrated in small-scale operations. In general, the liberalization of agriculture markets has benefited mainly medium and large-scale commercial producers and traders. Women farmers and traders, who generally operate on a smaller scale, have been found less likely to benefit. It is especially difficult for small farmers, including women, to compete with heavily subsidized agricultural imports.[142]

Gender-aware economists are examining ways in which gender roles and disparities in access to resources can affect household and sector-wide responses to changes in agriculture policy.[143] For example, James Warner and D.A. Campbell have constructed a model to explain the weak "supply response" to liberalization of agriculture markets that has been observed in several countries, particularly in Africa. This analysis notes that, where women are primarily responsible for household food production but also help with cash crop production as unpaid family laborers, they are likely to realize little or no direct benefit from programs to increase production of cash crops for export. In many cases, they may be required by male family members to give up part of their subsistence farmland for cash crop production, which further weakens their property rights and may also threaten their family's food security if they are no longer able to grow subsistence

[137] See, e.g., Cheryl R. Doss, Designing Agricultural Technology for African Women Farmers: Lessons from 25 Years of Experience, 29 WORLD DEV. 2075, 2077–78 (2001). Doss emphasizes, however, that gender roles in agriculture are dynamic and context-specific.

[138] Lynn R. Brown et al., Generating Food Security in the Year 2020: Women as Producers, Gatekeepers, and Shock Absorbers, International Food Policy Research Institute 2020 Vision Brief 17 (1995), available at http://www.ifpri.org/2020/briefs/number17.htm.

[139] See, e.g., Mehra and Gammage, supra note 16, at 539; Doss, supra note 137; WORLD BANK, supra note 5, at 51–52 and 120–22.

[140] Mehra and Gammage, supra note 16, at 539.

[141] UN, supra note 9, at 11–121.

[142] Sally Baden, Gender Issues in Agricultural Liberalization, BRIDGE Report No. 41 (1998), at ii, available at http://www.ids.ac.uk/bridge; see also MALHOTRA ET AL., supra note 29, at 133–35; G&T Task Force, supra note 16, at 77–140; WILLIAMS, supra note 32, at 62–68.

[143] See, e.g., Arndt and Tarp, supra note 61; Baden, supra note 142; William Darity, Jr., The Formal Structure of a Gender-Segregated Low-Income Economy, 23 WORLD DEV. 1963 (1995); James M. Warner and D.A. Campbell, Supply Response in an Agrarian Economy with Non-Symmetric Gender Relations, 28 WORLD DEV. 1327 (2000).

crops. Women farmers may therefore resist or undermine male family members' efforts to expand production of export crops.[144]

On its face, the Uruguay Round Agreement on Agriculture does not display overt gender bias. The agreement extends "special and differential treatment" to developing countries in several respects. Moreover, a number of its "green box" exemptions from aggregate limits on domestic supports—for example, for extension services, food security stocks, domestic food aid and disaster relief—would seem likely to benefit women farmers in developing countries.[145] However, the underlying objective of the agreement is to facilitate agricultural exports. As noted above, women farmers in many developing countries are primarily responsible for household food production, and therefore household food security and sufficiency are high priorities.[146] The Agreement on Agriculture does include a domestic support exemption for "food security" stocks. However, the agreement treats food security in terms of government (or international) support rather than household self-sufficiency.[147]

At the Fourth Ministerial Conference in Doha, one of the proposals put forward by developing countries, with the support of civil society groups, was for the creation of a "development box." Among other things, this proposal would allow developing countries to exclude certain staple crops from their tariff reduction commitments and also allow governments to provide greater support to poor farmers. Similar proposals were floated at the Fifth Ministerial Conference in Cancún for a "special products" category and a "special safeguard mechanism" to address the food security and rural development needs of developing countries.[148] These proposals address the general bias of the Agreement

[144] *See* Warner and Campbell, *supra* note 143; *see also* Baden, *supra* note 142. A recent assessment of Uganda's Strategic Export Initiative also concluded that insufficient attention had been paid to the gender aspects of micro-level supply constraints in the coffee and fish sectors. Based on Ugandan case studies, the researchers warned that "women may withhold their labour or sabotage cash crops in several subtle ways because they know they will not benefit from the income earned." David Booth et al., *The Strategic Exports Initiative in Uganda: Poverty and Social Impact Analysis* (2003), at 25–26, *available at* http://lnweb18.worldbank.org/ESSD/sdvext.nsf/81ByDocName/CountryExperienceUgandaexportpromotionprogram. The researchers also observed that, because of men's spending priorities, "improvements in incomes controlled by men . . . might not significantly enhance welfare for other household members, especially women and children." *Id*. at 26. For example, in the export fishing sector, increased cash income to many fishermen appeared to be "fuelling greater recreational expenditure by men, with reported increases in alcoholism and prostitution, rather than income sharing that might moderate the negative impacts on women and children." *Id*. at 27. *See also* Robb, *supra* note 36.

[145] *Agreement on Agriculture*, Annex 2 (bases for exemptions from commitments to reduce domestic supports).

[146] Food security is not only a fundamental public policy concern, but a fundamental human right, reflected in Article 25 of the Universal Declaration of Human Rights, Article 11 of the International Covenant on Economic, Social and Cultural Rights, and Article 14 of CEDAW (which addresses the situation of rural women). UNHCHR recently analyzed the liberalization of agriculture trade and the Agreement on Agriculture from a human rights perspective, taking into account the right to food and the right to development. *See* UNHCHR, *Globalization and Its Impact on the Full Enjoyment of Human Rights*, Report of the High Commissioner for Human Rights submitted in accordance with Commission on Human Rights resolution 2001/32, U.N. Doc. E/CN.4/2002/54 (2002).

[147] *See Agreement on Agriculture*, Annex 2, para. 3 (exemption from domestic support commitments for accumulation of public food stocks).

[148] *See, e.g., ACP Declaration on the Fourth Ministerial Conference, Communication from Kenya*, WT/L/439 (Nov. 9, 2001) ("*ACP Declaration*"), para. 20; *Declaration of the Group of 77 and China on the Fourth WTO Ministerial Conference at Doha, Communication from Cuba*, WT/L/424 (Oct. 24, 2001) ("*Group of 77 Declaration*"), para. 9; FAO, *Some Issues Relating to Food Security in the Context of the WTO Negotiations on Agriculture* (2001), *available at* http://www.fao.org/trade/docs/; Duncan Green and Shishir Priyadarshi, *Proposal for a "Development Box" in the WTO Agreement on Agriculture*, CAFOD Policy

on Agriculture toward agricultural exports. They would need to be complemented by gender-sensitive agricultural policies and targeted resources in order to benefit women farmers, who have historically been excluded from agricultural extension services, credit programs and other support.[149]

C. Services Trade and the General Agreement on Trade in Services

Over the past decade, services were the fastest growing sector in the global economy,[150] and significant proportions of services jobs are now occupied by women in both industrialized and developing countries. However, patterns of gender segregation are found here as in manufacturing. In developing countries, for example, women tend to be concentrated in lower-paying jobs in trade, restaurants and hotels and community, social and personal services, with only a small percentage employed in higher-paying subsectors such as finance, insurance and business services. Women are well-represented in professional and technical jobs, but are heavily concentrated in teaching, nursing and other traditional "women's" occupations.[151] While the public service sector historically provided more skill-intensive, waged jobs for women in many countries, public sector downsizing in connection with structural adjustment programs in many developing and transitional countries has eliminated or outsourced many of these jobs.[152]

It is difficult to generalize about the gender-differentiated impacts of services trade agreements, given the wide range of subsectors covered and the potential application of services trade agreements to public/private service providers as well as "pure" private providers. Moreover, women as well as men participate in services not only as consumers, but also as employees and owners of service providers. However, a number of gender-related concerns have been raised about the Uruguay Round General Agreement on Trade in Services ("GATS"). Some of these concerns relate to the potential impact on women of liberalizing particular services subsectors. For example, in connection with tourism, evidence indicates that the vast majority of jobs filled by women are in less stable and lower-paying areas such as housekeeping, food preparation, reception and petty trading, as well as sex work.[153] In connection with financial sector liberalization, it is not clear that liberalization has had direct, positive effects on small-scale borrowers and savers, including particularly women.[154] Moreover, financial sector liberalization frequently accompanies capital account liberalization; as demonstrated in the Asian

---

Paper (2001), *available at* http://www.cafod.org.uk/policy/devbox.htm; International Centre for Trade and Sustainable Development, *Agriculture Negotiations at the WTO: Post-Cancún Outlook Report* (2003), *available at* http://www.ictsd.org; Oxfam International, *Harnessing Trade for Development* (2001), *available at* http://www.oxfam.org/eng/policy_pape.htm; *see also* MALHOTRA ET AL., *supra* note 29, at 138–41; American Lands Alliance et al., Collective Comments re: Doha Ministerial Declaration (Oct. 25, 2002), *available at* http://www.ciel.org; Tim Ruffer and Paolo Vergano, *An Agriculture Safeguard Mechanism for Developing Countries* (2002), *available at* http://www.dfid.gov.uk.

[149] GAMMAGE ET AL., *supra* note 44, at 39; *see also* WILLIAMS, *supra* note 32, at 68–74. Although the Doha Ministerial Declaration did not endorse the "development box" proposal, it did include a commitment "to enable developing countries to effectively take account of their development needs, including food security and rural development." WTO, *Ministerial Declaration*, Adopted on Nov. 14, 2001, Ministerial Conference, Fourth Session, Doha, Nov. 9–14, 2001, WT/MIN(01)/DEC/1 (Nov. 20, 2001), para. 13.

[150] WORLD BANK, *supra* note 113, at 69.

[151] Mehra and Gammage, *supra* note 16, at 543.

[152] GAMMAGE ET AL., *supra* note 44, at 61–63.

[153] *See* WILLIAMS, *supra* note 32, at 110–15.

[154] *See* Sally Baden, *Gender Issues in Financial Liberalisation and Financial Sector Reform*, BRIDGE Report No. 39 (1996), at iv–v, *available at* http://www.ids.ac.uk/bridge.

financial crisis, these combined liberalizations can increase an economy's vulnerability to external shocks, which in turn can disproportionately affect women.[155]

Since WTO members' commitments under the GATS can extend to basic services such as education, health care and water supply, the GATS touches on a number of human rights and related development priorities, which also have gender dimensions.[156] For example, in a recent report, the UN High Commissioner for Human Rights noted the possibility that liberalization of basic services such as health could lead to a two-tiered supply of health services, with private providers (including foreign providers) catering to the "healthy and wealthy" and underfinanced public health care providers treating the "poor and sick."[157] Poor women who depend on public health services for reproductive care and medical care of children would be particularly affected under this scenario.

Even within the same services subsector, different gender issues may arise depending on the "mode" of services involved. In the health sector, for example, potential gender-related impacts have been identified under each of the four modes of supply specified in the GATS: cross-border supply, consumption abroad, commercial presence and movement of natural persons.[158] In each of these cases, impacts may vary depending on the country's level of development, health care policies, health insurance schemes and other factors. The issues related to Mode 3 (commercial presence), for example, are similar to those raised with regard to the TRIMs Agreement.[159] In the case of Mode 3 supply of basic services such as health care, there are also the concerns noted above about the implications of a two-tier system for health service delivery to poor and vulnerable groups, including women.[160]

The issues related to Mode 4 (movement of natural persons) are complex, especially in relation to critical services such as health care. On the one hand, liberalization of this mode (much of which predates the GATS) has opened up opportunities for many nurses and other health care providers, particularly from developing countries, to take better paying jobs in other countries. On the other hand, there is the risk of a "brain drain" of health care professionals from developing countries, leaving fewer qualified health care providers in the "services-exporting" country. Nevertheless, developing countries have called for further liberalization of Mode 4, particularly by industrialized countries, to expand opportunities for workers to migrate legally to those countries.[161] This could have beneficial gender impacts if Mode 4 liberalization takes place in subsectors were women are active. Increased opportunities for regular migration would also help to stem some of

---

[155] *See, e.g.*, Floro and Dymski, *supra* note 55; Singh and Zammit, *supra* note 55; G&T TASK FORCE, *supra* note 16, at 175–213.

[156] *See, e.g.*, *Universal Declaration of Human Rights*, Art. 25 (right to health) and Art. 26 (right to education); International Covenant on Economic, Social and Cultural Rights, Art. 12 (right to health) & Art. 13 (right to education); CEDAW, Art. 10 (equal access to education), Art. 12 (equal access to health care services) and Art. 14.2(h) (equal enjoyment of adequate living conditions, including water supply). *See also* WILLIAMS, *supra* note 32, at 87–109; Lyla Mehta and Birgit La Cour Madsen, *Is the WTO After Your Water?: The GATS and the Basic Right to Water*, Paper for Globalisation and Poverty Research Programme, Institute of Development Studies, University of Sussex (2003), *available at* http://www.gapresearch.org/about/index.htm; Alexandra Spieldoch, *GATS and Healthcare—Why Do Women Care?* (2001), *available at* http://www.igtn.org.

[157] UNHCHR, *Economic, Social and Cultural Rights: Liberalization of Trade in Services and Human Rights*, Report of the High Commissioner for Human Rights, at 3, U.N. Doc. E/CN.4/Sub.2/2002/9 (2002).

[158] WILLIAMS, *supra* note 32, at 90–106; Spieldoch, *supra* note 156; *see also* UNHCHR, *supra* note 157 (raising more general human rights concerns related to the GATS' four modes of services supply).

[159] *See supra* Section III.A.4.

[160] *See supra* note 157 and accompanying text.

[161] *See, e.g., ACP Declaration, supra* note 148, para. 21.

the flow of irregular migrants from developing countries. Since undocumented female workers are particularly subject to abuse by agents and employers, increased opportunities to migrate legally—even under temporary work visas—would be beneficial.[162]

There are a number of uncertainties relating to the GATS that also have gender implications. These include the prospect of new, stringent disciplines on subsidies, domestic regulations and government procurement. Regarding subsidies, for example, WTO members already must disclose the subsidies they provide on services in their commitment schedules for the relevant services subsectors.[163] This imposes a burden on countries, especially developing countries, to make sure they list every conceivable subsidy or other "preference." It may also discourage countries from introducing new programs—such as small business assistance to women and minority entrepreneurs in a particular subsector, such as travel services—which might be characterized as new subsidies under the GATS. Article XV, which provides for negotiations to develop "disciplines" on subsidies in the services sector, poses a risk of further restricting governments' latitude to introduce assistance programs to domestic service providers that are owned by women or other historically disadvantaged groups.[164]

Another concern relates to the possibility of stricter disciplines on domestic regulation of services, based on Article VI of the GATS, which calls for the development of rules to ensure that qualification and licensing requirements, and technical standards, are "not more burdensome than necessary to ensure the quality of the services."[165] In particular, questions have been raised about the potential application of this "necessity" test. For example, would consumer protection, worker safety or environmental regulations qualify as "necessary to ensure the quality of services"?[166] Responding to these concerns, the Fourth Ministerial Conference in Doha reaffirmed the right of WTO members under GATS to "regulate, and introduce new regulations on, the supply of services."[167] However, a country could still be required to make a "compensatory adjustment" under Article XXI of the agreement if a new regulation of services effectively modified the country's market access commitments under the GATS. This compensation requirement could impose a serious financial burden on developing countries, and therefore would effectively discourage developing countries from making certain regulatory changes in sectors that they have committed to liberalize under the GATS.

Article XIII of the GATS, which provides for future multilateral negotiations on government procurement of services, has also raised concerns from a gender perspective. Specifically, there is a worry that the application of most-favored-nation and national treatment principles to government procurement could conflict with governments' pursuit of social and environmental goals through their procurement policies, such as "green procurement" requirements and programs designed to help women, ethnic minorities, and other groups to obtain an equitable share of government contracts. This concern is based

---

[162] At the same time, it should be noted that even workers with visas may be subject to abuse. *See, e.g.*, Human Rights Watch, *Hidden in the Home: Abuse of Domestic Workers with Special Visas in the United States* (2001).

[163] *See General Agreement on Trade in Services* ("GATS"), Art. XVII (WTO members must accord national treatment to services and service providers of any other member in the sectors for which specific commitments have been made, subject only to the conditions and qualifications set out in the specific commitment schedule).

[164] *Cf. supra* text accompanying notes 125–29 (gender analysis of SCM Agreement, applicable to subsidies related to trade in goods).

[165] *Id.*, Article VI.4(b).

[166] *Cf. infra* text accompanying notes 185–96 (gender analysis of Agreements on the Application of Sanitary and Phytosanitary Measures and Technical Barriers to Trade, applicable to food safety and health regulations on traded goods); *see* GAMMAGE ET AL., *supra* note 44, at 61.

[167] WTO, *supra* note 149, ¶ 7.

on a critical reading of the plurilateral Agreement on Government Procurement ("AGP") and comparable provisions in other trade agreements such as NAFTA. Article XXIII of the AGP, for example, includes a blanket exception for products and services of handicapped persons and philanthropic institutions. However, procurement preferences for businesses owned by women, ethnic minorities and other marginalized groups are not generally protected under the AGP. Parties to the AGP have claimed exemptions for such programs in their annexes to the agreement.[168] However this "bottom-up" approach of claiming exemptions for preferential procurement schemes in countries' commitment schedules rather than including general exemptions in the text of the trade agreement can inhibit countries from introducing new programs to assist women and minority business owners in the future (unless the scheduled exemptions are sufficiently broad), for fear of inviting claims from other countries for compensatory adjustment, on the basis that the procurement preferences discriminate against foreign bidders or create unnecessary obstacles to international trade.[169]

D. Trade-Related Areas

1. Investment

The gender dimensions of international agreements related to FDI are discussed elsewhere in this chapter, in relation to the TRIMs Agreement for FDI in manufacturing,[170] and in relation to the GATS for FDI in commercial services.[171]

2. Intellectual Property

Perhaps the most controversial trade-related area in which international trade rules have been introduced is intellectual property protection ("IPP"). Much of the current debate revolves around the Uruguay Round Agreement on Trade-Related Aspects of Intellectual Property Rights ("TRIPs Agreement"),[172] although similar concerns have also been raised with regard to regional and bilateral agreements on IPP. As discussed extensively elsewhere, the TRIPs Agreement has been roundly criticized on economic,[173] human rights[174] and development[175] grounds. These critical perspectives—in particular,

---

[168] For example, in the "General Notes" included in its annex, the United States asserts that its commitments do not apply to "set asides on behalf of small and minority businesses." Women-owned businesses are not specifically mentioned in these notes, but they are expressly excluded from the commitments of state governments listed elsewhere in the annex.

[169] See GAMMAGE ET AL., *supra* note 44, at 63–65.

[170] See supra Section III.A.4.

[171] See supra text accompanying notes 159 and 160.

[172] For a detailed analysis of the Agreement, *see* Chapters 22 and 54 of this book.

[173] See, e.g., COMMISSION ON INTELLECTUAL PROPERTY RIGHTS ("CIPR"), INTEGRATING INTELLECTUAL PROPERTY RIGHTS AND DEVELOPMENT POLICY (2002), at 15 (summarizing economists' critiques of IPP regimes in terms of economic costs of monopoly privileges and high implementation costs of IPP regimes); Finger and Schuler, *supra* note 103 (analyzing survey results on implementation costs of TRIPs Agreement and two other Uruguay Round agreements); Rodrik, *supra* note 118, at 27 (TRIPs Agreement is "utterly devoid of any economic rationale . . . "); WORLD BANK, *supra* note 113, at 129–39 (summarizing econometric and other studies of impact of TRIPs Agreement and IPP regimes on trade, FDI, administrative costs, rent transfers from technology importers to technology developers, prices of patent drugs, agricultural inputs and use of plant genetic materials).

[174] See, e.g., UNHCHR, *Economic, Social and Cultural Rights: The Impact of the Agreement on Trade-Related Aspects of Intellectual Property Rights on Human Rights*, Report of the High Commissioner, U.N. Doc. E/CN.4/Sub.2/2001/13 (2001).

[175] See, e.g., CIPR, *supra* note 173 (extensive critical analysis of TRIPs Agreement from development perspective, and recommendations for reform, in relation to health, agricultural and genetic resources, traditional knowledge, computer software and Internet use, and IPP policy and implementation); MALHOTRA

those raising human rights and development concerns—have both explicit and implicit gender dimensions. The objective of this section is to highlight some of the more specific gender issues raised by the TRIPs Agreement and similar regional and bilateral agreements.

A gender-aware analysis of the TRIPs Agreement recognizes that women, as well as men, are both producers and users of intellectual property. For example, female subsistence farmers both use seeds and contribute to the development of new plant varieties. Women are the primary consumers of reproductive health services and related medicines, and in most societies, women are primarily responsible for the health care of children and other dependents within households. In many societies, including indigenous communities, women also serve as traditional health care providers and are primary sources of knowledge on the use of medicinal plants. These multiple roles point to the gender dimensions of the TRIPs Agreement's provisions on patents (particularly relating to pharmaceutical drugs and plant varieties), and its relation to other international instruments such as the Convention on Biological Diversity, the International Convention for the Protection of New Varieties of Plants ("UPOV Convention"), and the International Treaty on Plant Genetic Resources for Food and Agriculture.

Some general observations can be made about the gender-differentiated effects of the TRIPs Agreement. First, IPP generally results in income transfers from consumers of protected goods to the owners of the intellectual property content in those goods (usually through licensing fees or royalty payments from the manufacturer to the intellectual property owner). Because women are predominantly consumers rather than licensed producers, they are likely to be net "losers" in economic terms under the TRIPs Agreement, which requires WTO members to significantly expand and strengthen their IPP regimes. As producers of intellectual property—including artists, craftspeople, scientists, farmers and indigenous experts on plant varieties—women in theory have an equal opportunity to seek protection of their creations, inventions and specialized knowledge under the IPP regimes required under the TRIPs Agreement. However, for various reasons, many women are unlikely to benefit from conventional IPP regimes.

First, women often have limited access to resources, and therefore may not have the financial means to apply for and defend a copyright, trademark or patent. Second, in societies where women have limited property rights, they may be unable to assert their rights over an innovation or artistic work, which might instead be claimed by other family members or community leaders. Third, much of the technical knowledge and artistic or cultural work developed by women, particularly as small farmers and members of indigenous communities, is collectively owned and accumulated over time. This sort of knowledge therefore does not lend itself easily to protection under conventional intellectual property rules. Therefore, the standards for IPP set out in the TRIPs Agreement provide few benefits to these innovators.[176]

As noted earlier, women represent half of the total number of people worldwide who are infected with the HIV virus, and the percentage is much higher in Sub-Saharan Africa, particularly among young women.[177] These statistics have caused the UN Secretary

ET AL., *supra* note 29, at 205–23; THIRD WORLD NETWORK, *supra* note 120, at 43–44; WORLD BANK, *supra* note 113, at 139–49 (recommendations for reform of TRIPs Agreement and other initiatives to ensure that IPP regimes benefit developing countries).

[176] GAMMAGE ET AL., *supra* note 44, at 77; MALHOTRA ET AL., *supra* note 29, at 217; G&T TASK FORCE, *supra* note 16, at 251–85; WILLIAMS, *supra* note 32, at 139–46.

[177] *See supra* text accompanying note 19.

General to observe that "in Africa, AIDS has a woman's face."[178] Therefore, the *Declaration on the TRIPs Agreement and Public Health* adopted at the Fourth Ministerial Conference in Doha—specifically its directives on the use of compulsory licenses by developing countries and extension of least-developed countries' exemption from the requirement to provide patent protection for pharmaceutical drugs—and subsequent decision of the WTO General Council on compulsory licenses, are directly relevant to women, particularly women in Sub-Saharan Africa and other regions with increasing HIV/AIDS infections.[179] However, it has been pointed out that the emphasis placed on increasing governments' flexibility to issue compulsory licenses in cases of "national emergency," including "public health crises . . . related to HIV/AIDS, tuberculosis, malaria and other epidemics,"[180] excludes consideration of life-threatening, gender-specific medical conditions and life-threatening illnesses prevalent in specific ethnic groups. Thus, if patented drugs were available to treat any of these conditions, but were prohibitively expensive for a developing country subject to the TRIPs Agreement, it could be more difficult for the country to use the full flexibility of Article 31 of the agreement on compulsory licenses because these conditions are not a health risk to the entire population and therefore would not be considered "epidemics" or "national emergencies".[181]

The UN Food and Agriculture Organization has observed that

> In many areas, the majority of smallholder farmers are women. They are largely responsible for the selection, improvement and adaptation of plant varieties. In many regions, women are also responsible for the management of small livestock, including their reproduction, and they often have a more highly specialized knowledge of wild plants used for food, fodder and medicine than men.[182]

Women in many countries therefore play critical roles not only in ensuring food security for their households and communities, but in preserving biological diversity. However, the TRIPs Agreement does not include any provisions on the protection of traditional knowledge. Moreover, to the extent that WTO members choose to protect plant varieties—as required by Article 27 of the TRIPs Agreement—by extending patent protection or adopting the most recent version of the UPOV Convention, and patented or UPOV-protected varieties of staple crops are introduced in developing countries, small farmers' traditional practice of saving seeds may be challenged. This would have a disproportionate impact on women farmers in these countries, since they have relatively less access to credit to purchase seeds and other inputs.

At the Fourth Ministerial Conference in Doha, WTO members directed the Council for TRIPs "to examine, inter alia, the relationship between the TRIPs Agreement and the Convention on Biological Diversity, the protection of traditional knowledge and folklore, and other relevant new developments raised by the Members . . ."[183] In reviewing

---

[178] Kofi Annan, UN Secretary General, *In Africa, AIDS Has a Woman's Face*, N.Y. TIMES and INT'L HERALD TRIBUNE, Dec. 29, 2002, at Op-Ed Pages, *available at* http://www.un.org/News/ossg/sg/stories/sg-29dec-2002.htm.

[179] *See* WTO, *Declaration on the TRIPs Agreement and Public Health*, Adopted on Nov. 14, 2001, Ministerial Conference, Fourth Session, Doha, Nov. 9–14, 2001, WT/MIN(01)/DEC/2 (Nov. 20, 2001) ("Doha Public Health Declaration"); WTO, Implementation of Paragraph 6 of the Doha Declaration on the TRIPS Agreement and Public Health, Decision of the General Council of Aug. 30, 2003, WT/L/540 (Sept. 1, 2003).

[180] Doha Public Health Declaration, *supra* note 179, ¶ 5.

[181] *See* WILLIAMS, *supra* note 32, at 142–44.

[182] Food and Agriculture Organization ("FAO"), *FAO Gender and Development Plan of Action (2002–2007)*, para. 41, *available at* http://www.fao.org/docrep/meeting/003/Y1521e.htm.

[183] WTO, *supra* note 127, ¶ 19.

these areas, the TRIPs Council was further instructed to "take fully into account the development dimension."[184] The gender issues noted above, which are especially relevant to developing countries, could be taken into account in the TRIPs Council's ongoing work program.

3. Domestic Regulation

With the increasing focus on "behind-the-border" issues affecting international trade, there is a general trend in WTO and other trade agreements to "discipline" domestic regulations that affect trade. As noted earlier, the GATS provides for the negotiation of rules on qualification and licensing requirements and technical standards in the services sector.[185] The trend is reflected most prominently in the Uruguay Round Agreements on the Application of Sanitary and Phytosanitary Measures ("SPS Agreement") and Technical Barriers to Trade ("TBT Agreement"), both of which apply to regulations on traded goods.

Several concerns have been raised by developing country governments, civil society groups and academic commentators about the growing impact of trade rules on the regulatory function of governments. Some commentators have argued, for example, that the standard for review of technical regulations in the TBT Agreement—"not more trade-restrictive than necessary to fulfill a legitimate objective"[186]—tips the balance of factors to be considered by government regulators too heavily in favor of trade, and away from other legitimate goals such as public health, consumer protection, and protection of the environment.[187] The requirement in the SPS Agreement that SPS measures be "based on scientific principles and ... not maintained without sufficient scientific evidence"[188] has also been critiqued as inherently biased against regulation, since data on the health risks of a particular substance may not become available for a considerable period of time and, in any case, scientific research sets a higher standard to prove that a particular substance has harmful effects than that it does not.[189]

On the other hand, many developing countries have become extremely concerned about the cost of complying with the SPS Agreement, since they view SPS measures imposed by importing countries as a major impediment to their agricultural and food exports.[190] Both developing countries and civil society groups have also been critical of the presumptions created in both the SPS and TBT Agreements in favor of standards set by international bodies such as the Codex Alimentarius Commission ("Codex"), in which they argue that their interests are not adequately represented. In response to these concerns, the Fourth Ministerial Conference in Doha urged WTO members to provide

---

[184] *Id.*

[185] *See supra* text accompanying notes 166 and 167.

[186] *Agreement on Technical Barriers to Trade*, Art. 2.2

[187] *See, e.g.,* Carlos M. Correa, *Implementing National Public Health Policies in the Framework of WTO Agreements,* 34 J. WORLD TRADE 89 *(2000); see also* Bal, *supra* note 109; Garcia, *supra* note 109.

[188] *Agreement on the Application of Sanitary and Phytosanitary Measures,* Art. 2.

[189] Some commentators have noted that "[s]cientific research begins with the premise that there is no effect, referred to as the 'null hypothesis.' The task of statistical analysis is to examine, based on available data, whether the null hypothesis can be rejected with a certain level of confidence. However, because of small sample size, measurement problems and model specification issues, the scientific research may not be able to reject the null hypothesis, even where a true relationship exists between variables." GAMMAGE ET AL., *supra* note 44, at 89.

[190] S. Henson and R. Louder, *Barriers to Agricultural Exports from Developing Countries: The Role of Sanitary and Phytosanitary Requirements,* 29 WORLD DEV. 85 (2001) (results of survey conducted by researchers at University of Leeds).

technical assistance to help least-developed countries respond to new SPS and TBT measures imposed by importing countries, and called on the WTO Director General to facilitate greater participation of developing countries in international standard-setting organizations.[191]

These concerns also have gender dimensions. For example, as noted above, some international standard-setting bodies referred to in the SPS and TBT Agreements, such as Codex, have longstanding ties to industry members and associations, and have not historically been open to consumer and other citizens' groups.[192] It is therefore possible that the standards set by these bodies may not reflect the concerns of women, particularly from developing countries. In addition, until recently, less medical research was devoted to women's health issues, and therefore less data may be available on the long-term effects on women of exposure to certain pollutants or other harmful substances.[193] Thus, should a country choose to regulate a particular substance more stringently than the applicable international standard in order to address health risks to women, it could be more difficult to establish a sufficient scientific basis for the regulation under the SPS Agreement.

Finally, concerns have also been raised about the sensitivity of GATT/WTO panels and the WTO Appellate Body to women's health issues in their reviews of particular health-based regulations. Both the WTO Appellate Body and the roster of panelists available to consider disputes under WTO agreements include primarily international law experts, and more specifically, experts in international trade law. WTO dispute panels also have considerable flexibility to engage experts to advise on scientific and other technical matters.[194] There is no assurance that these experts will be aware of the gender-differentiated health effects of particular substances as they review regulations intended to restrict their use. Commentators have noted, for example, that arguments regarding gender-specific health hazards were not received favorably by the GATT panel in the *Thailand-Cigarettes* case brought by the United States in the late 1980s to challenge the Thai government's import ban on cigarettes,[195] or in the WTO Appellate Body's more recent review of the panel report in the *European Community-Hormones* case challenging the European Union's ban on the sale of beef from cattle treated with artificial growth hormones.[196]

[191] WTO, *supra* note 127, ¶ 3.5–3.6 and 5.3–5.4.

[192] *See* D.G. Victor, *The Sanitary and Phytosanitary Agreement of the World Trade Organization: An Assessment After Five Years*, 32 N.Y.U. J. INT'L L. & POL. 865 (2000).

[193] GAMMAGE ET AL., *supra* note 44, at 93; World Health Organization ("WHO"), *Gender and Health*, WHO Technical Paper, WHO/FRH/WHD/98.16 (1998), *available at* http://www.who.int/reproductive-health/publications; *see also* Olga Ohanjanyan, *Persistent Organic Pollutants and Reproductive Health*, WECF Background Document (1999), *available at* http://www.earthsummit2002.org; Pamela Ransom, *Women, Pesticides and Sustainable Agriculture*, CSD NGO Women's Caucus Position Paper (2001), *available at* http://www.earthsummit2002.org.

[194] *See* C. Thorn and M. Carlson, *The Agreement on the Application of Sanitary and Phytosanitary Measures and the Agreement on Technical Barriers to Trade*, 31 L. & POL. INT'L BUS. 841 (2000).

[195] *See* Padideh Ala'i, *Free Trade or Sustainable Development? An Analysis of the WTO Appellate Body's Shift to a More Balanced Approach to Trade Liberalization*, 14 AM. U. INT'L L. REV. 1129, 1141–45 and n. 54 (1999) (GATT panel rejected evidence put forward by the WHO that American cigarettes presented a public health risk for Thai women because they were perceived as safer and more socially acceptable than locally-made cigarettes, and that some American brands were specifically packaged and marketed to Thai women); *see also* Correa, *supra* note 187.

[196] *See* Steve Charnovitz, *The Supervision of Health and Biosafety Regulation by World Trade Rules*, 13 TULANE ENV'T L.J. 271 (2000) (WTO Appellate Body dismissed testimony from an expert from the U.S. National Institute of Environmental Health Sciences regarding the increased risk of breast cancer from eating meat produced with growth hormones); *see also* Orford 1999, *supra* note 76.

4. Labor Standards

As discussed elsewhere,[197] the only express reference to labor issues in the GATT is the exception included for goods and services made with prison labor.[198] The Fourth Ministerial Conference in Doha confirmed that a majority of WTO members continue to believe the ILO rather than the WTO is the appropriate international forum in which to address labor issues related to the trade in goods and services.[199] However, labor issues in the global economy are being addressed in a number of other settings, including regional and bilateral trade agreements, the ILO and the World Commission on the Social Dimensions of Globalization for which it acts as secretariat, various UN bodies, and private sector initiatives to develop corporate codes of conduct. This section is intended to identify some of the gender issues that can arise in the application of labor standards to the trade in goods and services.

Much of the current debate about the impact of trade liberalization on conditions of work has focused on industries in which women are widely employed, typically in low-skilled, low-wage jobs or under subcontracting arrangements, such as textile and clothing manufacturing and menial work in hotels and other "hospitality" businesses. Historically, international labor standards and national labor laws have been framed to protect full-time workers in formal business establishments. Therefore, they have provided little benefit to the women in many countries who work in agriculture or are involved in part-time work, home-based work and small-scale trading. Over time, however, the ILO and some national governments have begun to address the needs of part-time and informal sector workers, as reflected in new labor standards and laws developed to protect these workers. The ILO, for example, has adopted the Part-Time Work Convention, 1994; the Home Work Convention, 1996; and the Safety and Health in Agriculture Convention, 2001, which includes provisions on women workers and temporary and seasonal agricultural workers.

Another gender issue arises from the definition of "core" or "fundamental" labor standards. Among the core standards included in the ILO's Declaration on Fundamental Principles and Rights at Work are the elimination of discrimination in employment and equal pay for equivalent work, which are particularly important for women workers.[200] These standards are reflected in two fundamental ILO conventions: the Discrimination (Employment and Occupation) Convention, 1958, and the Equal Remuneration Convention, 1951. However, the core principles of non-discrimination and equal pay have secondary status, or are excluded altogether, from the labor provisions in some trade agreements. For example, under the North American Free Trade Agreement ("NAFTA"), these principles are included in the North American Agreement on Labor Cooperation ("NAALC"). However, they are "second-tier" rights that can be the subject of country consultations and study by an expert committee, but cannot be the basis for convening an arbitration panel or withdrawing trade benefits.[201] These labor principles are also excluded from the

[197] *See* Chapters 59 and 60 of this book.
[198] GATT, Art. XX(e); *see also Agreement on Government Procurement*, Art. XXIII(2).
[199] *See* WTO, *supra* note 149, ¶ 8.
[200] International Labour Organization ("ILO"), *ILO Declaration on Fundamental Principles and Rights at Work* (1998), *available at* http://www.ilo.org/public/english/standards/relm/ilc/ilc86/con-dtxt.htm; *see also* ILO, *Time for Equality at Work: Global Report Under the Follow-up to the ILO Declaration on Fundamental Principles and Rights at Work* (2003).
[201] *See North American Agreement on Labor Cooperation,* signed on Sept. 13, 1993 and entered into force on Jan. 1, 1994, *available at* http://www.naalc.org/english/infocentre/NAALC.htm; HUMAN RIGHTS WATCH, TRADING AWAY RIGHTS: THE UNFULFILLED PROMISE OF NAFTA'S LABOR SIDE AGREEMENT (2001).

definition of "internationally recognized labor rights" in the labor provisions of recent US trade agreements with Chile, Jordan and Singapore, as well as from the definition of "international worker rights" that forms a basis for granting preferential trade status to developing countries under the U.S. Generalized System of Preferences ("GSP") and other preferential trade arrangements between the United States and developing countries.[202] In contrast, the ILO conventions on non-discrimination and equal pay are specifically included in the special incentive arrangements for the protection of labor rights under the European Community's current GSP scheme.[203]

Although non-discrimination and equal pay principles have "second-tier" status under NAFTA, the NAALC has provided a vehicle for addressing some gender issues in employment. For example, the Secretariat of the Commission for Labor Cooperation produced a comprehensive report on women's employment in the NAFTA countries between 1984 and 1996, including a comparative study of the legal rights of women workers in the three countries.[204] As contemplated in the NAALC, the national administrative offices ("NAOs") of the three countries have also processed a number of submissions from labor and civil society groups relating to alleged violations of labor laws and regulations in workplaces that employ large numbers of women.

These submissions include one filed in 1996 by Human Rights Watch and two Mexican nongovernmental organizations, alleging that *maquiladora* employers in Mexico regularly discriminated against pregnant job applicants and employees. Following a review that included consultation with a Mexican labor law expert and a public hearing, the U.S. NAO reported that the submission raised serious issues regarding the treatment of women workers in Mexico's *maquiladora* sector, and recommended consultations between the U.S. and Mexican Secretaries of Labor.[205] The consultations resulted in the holding of workshops and conferences, and some companies with assembly factories in Mexico have since changed their policies on pregnancy-testing of job applicants. However, much of the academic commentary on the case has been critical of the outcome as not going far enough to address the practice.[206]

[202] *Agreement between the United States of America and the Hashemite Kingdom of Jordan on the Establishment of a Free Trade Area*, signed on Oct. 24, 2000, Art. 6.6; *United States—Chile Free Trade Agreement*, signed on June 6, 2003, Art. 18.8; *United States—Singapore Free Trade Agreement*, signed on May 6, 2003, Art. 17.7; Office of the United States Trade Representative, *U.S. Generalized System of Preferences Guidebook* (1999), at 24, *available at* http://www.ustr.gov. The labor cooperation mechanisms established under the US trade agreements with Chile and Singapore do mention the possibility of cooperative activities to eliminate employment discrimination, but the dispute settlement procedures of the agreements apply only to allegations that a state party has failed to effectively enforce its labor laws directly related to "internationally recognized labor rights," which are defined in the agreements to exclude non-discrimination and equal pay. *See also* Travis, *supra* note 82; *see generally* Blackett, *supra* note 109, at 22.

[203] *Activities of the European Union: Scheme of Generalised Tariff Preferences from 2002 to 2004, at* http://europa.eu.int/scadplus/leg/en/lvb/r11015.htm.

[204] Commission for Labor Cooperation Secretariat, *The Employment of Women in North America* (1998), *available at* http://www.naalc.org/english/publications/ewna.htm.

[205] United States National Administrative Office, North American Agreement on Labor Cooperation ("NAALC"), *Public Report of Review of NAO Submission No. 9701*, Jan. 12, 1998, *available at* http://www.dol.gov/dol/ilab/public/media/reports/nao/public-reports-of-review.html. The report concluded that, while pregnancy discrimination against *existing* employees clearly violates Mexican law, there were differing views within the Mexican government on the legality of pregnancy screening of *prospective* employees. (Mexico's Human Rights Commission took the view that pregnancy testing violates the Mexican Constitution, but the Mexican NAO under the NAALC took a different view.)

[206] *See, e.g.*, Andrias, *supra* note 79; Bremer, *supra* note 79; Briones, *supra* note 79; Grimm, *supra* note 79; Plumtree, *supra* note 79; Scherlen and Strickland, *supra* note 79; Smith, *supra* note 79; Vega, *supra* note 79; *see also* Human Rights Watch, *supra* note 201.

Finally, it should be noted that women's organizations have advocated strongly for adherence by governments and private sector firms to the ILO's core labor standards, and for attention to the particular needs of women workers, including maternity leave and childcare arrangements. However, they have mixed views about the appropriateness of using trade sanctions to address violations of labor standards in particular countries. The IGTN and its members, for example, share the concerns of other civil society groups in developing countries and developing country governments about the potential abuse of a "labor" or "social clause" by importing countries. They are also concerned about further expansion of the mandate of the WTO or other trade bodies into areas beyond their expertise.[207]

5. Human Rights

Since the conclusion of the Uruguay Round, there has been increasing concern about the implications of liberalized trade and investment and specific trade agreements for the promotion and protection of human rights.[208] This is reflected, for example, in reports of the UN High Commissioner for Human Rights regarding the Agreement on Agriculture, the GATS, the TRIPs Agreement, trade and investment, and non-discrimination principles in human rights and trade law,[209] and in statements of UN human rights treaty bodies.[210] As noted in previous sections, these human rights concerns have strong gender dimensions.[211] In addition, the expert CEDAW committee has raised specific human rights concerns related to women working in export-processing zones and in tourism in its concluding comments to country reports submitted by state parties to CEDAW.[212]

The human rights concerns raised within the UN system and by many civil society groups have related mainly to the potential impact of liberalized trade and compliance with particular trade agreements on the ability of countries to fulfill their commitments under human rights treaties, such as the International Covenant on Economic, Social and Cultural Rights and CEDAW, through legislation and other domestic measures. Much of the general academic debate surrounding trade and human rights, however, has concerned the potential use of trade rules as sanctions to protest violations of the human rights of people in other trading countries. In this respect, the discussion dovetails closely with the trade-labor debate, since the human rights that are typically at issue are labor rights. One focus has been on the feasibility and desirability of interpreting Article

---

[207] *See IGTN at Doha, supra* note 48; *see also* WILLIAMS, *supra* note 32, at 35–36 and 171–72. Mariama Williams notes that the problem often is not so much the lack of labor standards as the lack of effective enforcement, and that the areas most in need of improvement in a particular country may not be export manufacturing industries.

[208] *See* Gabrielle Marceau, *WTO Dispute Settlement and Human Rights*, 13 EUR. J. INT'L L. 753 (2002), n. 1–6 and accompanying text (concise overview of current trade/human rights debates).

[209] *See supra* note 134 (UNHCHR report on human rights issues in investment liberalization), note 146 (UNHCHR report on human rights implications of the Agreement on Agriculture); note 157 (UNHCHR report on human rights aspects of trade in services, specifically under the GATS); note 174 (UNHCHR report on the TRIPs Agreement and human rights).

[210] *See* Shelton, *supra* note 25 (surveys comments and resolutions of the CESCR and Sub-Commission related to trade and human rights). *see also* UNHCHR, *Economic, Social and Cultural Rights: Analytical Study of the High Commissioner for Human Rights on the Fundamental Principle of Non-discrimination in the Context of Globalization*, Report of the High Commissioner for Human Rights, U.N. Doc. E/CN.4/2004/40 (2004); Paul Hunt, *Economic Social and Cultural Rights: the Right of Everyone to the Enjoyment of the Highest State of Physical and Mental Health–Mission to the World Trade Organization*, Report of the Special Rapporteur, Addendum, U.N. Doc. E/CN.4/2004/49/Add.1 (2004) (analysis of the right to health and selected trade issues including gender and trade).

[211] *See supra* notes 145–47, 156–57 and 172–84 and accompanying text.

[212] *See supra* note 25 and accompanying text.

XX(a) of the GATT—the "public morals" exception—to sanction trading countries that violate fundamental human rights.[213] Another approach has been to restrict government procurement of goods and services from companies doing business in countries where there are widespread human rights violations.[214] At another level, there is vigorous ongoing debate about the appropriate role of the WTO in taking into account the human rights concerns and treaty commitments of member countries.[215]

As noted earlier in the chapter, there has been some discussion of the possibility of interpreting Article XX(a) of the GATT to justify trade sanctions against countries where discriminatory or abusive practices against women are permitted.[216] However, most of the academic commentary on gender, trade and human rights has focused on the impacts of liberalized trade, specific trade agreements and international economic institutions such as the IMF, World Bank and WTO on women's human rights, particularly in developing countries.[217] In general, many of the commentators view international trade rules, not as tools for promoting women's rights, but as potential obstacles to their realization. Another theme in much of their writing is the inadequacy of state-centered human rights law to address the conduct of non-state actors, including both international economic institutions and multinational companies.[218] These concerns are also shared by many women's organizations. As in the case of labor standards, however, there is concern about the use of trade sanctions to protest human rights violations—including violations of women's rights—in other countries, because of the fear of protectionist motivations in the sanctioning country and the potential negative impact of trade sanctions on women and other vulnerable groups in the targeted country.

6. Environment

Although often underestimated, women play a critical role in the sustainable use of natural resources, particularly in rural societies, where they are generally responsible for providing water, food, fuel, clothing and health care for their households. As noted earlier, women contribute substantially to the preservation of biodiversity as subsistence farmers and users of medicinal plants and other forest products.[219] The degradation and depletion of environmental resources therefore can disproportionately affect women in many countries. Moreover, research indicates that exposure to pesticides and other pollutants can have a variety of negative impacts on reproductive health.[220] Women and women's

---

[213] *See supra* note 109 and accompanying text.

[214] *See, e.g.,* Robert Stumberg, *Preemption and Human Rights: Local Options After Crosby v. NFTC*, 32 L. & POL'Y INT'L BUS. 109 (2000).

[215] *See, e.g.,* Ernst-Ulrich Petersmann, *Time for a United Nations "Global Compact" for Integrating Human Rights into the Law of Worldwide Organizations: Lessons from European Integration*, 13 EUR. J. INT'L L. 621 (2002); Robert Howse, *Human Rights in the WTO: Whose Rights? What Humanity? Comment on Petersmann*, 13 EUR. J. INT'L L. 651 (2002); Philip Alston, *Resisting the Merger and Acquisition of Human Rights by Trade Law: A Reply to Petersmann*, 13 EUR. J. INT'L L. 815 (2002); Ernst-Ulrich Petersmann, *Taking Human Dignity, Poverty and Empowerment of Individuals More Seriously: Rejoinder to Alston*, 13 EUR. J. INT'L L. 845 (2002).

[216] *See* Jarvis, *supra* note 78; *see also supra* text accompanying note 109.

[217] *See supra* notes 77–84 and accompanying text.

[218] *See supra* note 81 and accompanying text.

[219] *See supra* text accompanying note 182; *see also* Janet N. Abramovitz, *Biodiversity and Gender Issues: Recognizing Common Ground*, in FEMINIST PERSPECTIVES ON SUSTAINABLE DEVELOPMENT (Wendy Harcourt ed. 1994), at 201–02; Vandana Shiva, *Women's Indigenous Knowledge and Biodiversity*, in ECOFEMINISM (Maria Mies and Vandana Shiva eds. 1993), at 164–69.

[220] *See, e.g.,* Ohanjanyan, *supra* note 193; Ransom, *supra* note 193; *see also* MALHOTRA ET AL., *supra* note 29, at 320.

organizations therefore have been active in national movements on environmental issues,[221] as well as at international environmental conferences such as the UN Conference
on Environment and Development held in Rio de Janiero in 1992, and the recent World
Summit on Sustainable Development held in Johannesburg in 2002.[222]

Some of the gender dimensions of environmental issues related to the Agreement on
Agriculture, and the TRIPs, SPS and TBT Agreements have been discussed in previous
sections.[223] Consideration of gender roles in natural resource management and biodiversity conservation, and the gender-differentiated impacts of environmental degradation
and pollution, are also relevant to the ongoing work of the WTO Committee on Trade and
Environment. This includes, in particular, the directive from the Ministerial Conference
in Doha to examine the relationship between WTO rules and trade-related provisions of
multilateral environmental agreements such as the Convention on Biological Diversity,
as well as environmental labeling.[224]

E. WTO Processes

The governance structure of the WTO, although in place for less than ten years, has been
scrutinized extensively by academic commentators, policy analysts and civil society
groups.[225] In particular, commentators have noted that, despite the WTO's one-country,
one-vote system, the GATT legacy of informal, "green room" negotiations and decision-
making works to the disadvantage of smaller, developing country members, many of
which do not have the resources to maintain permanent WTO missions in Geneva. Parlia-
mentarians and civil society groups have also sought to participate more directly in trade
negotiations, dispute settlement, trade policy review and trade-related capacity building.
This section highlights some of the gender issues related to these key WTO processes.

1. Trade Negotiations

The gender composition of professional staff in the WTO secretariat is more balanced in
the aggregate than that of the IMF, World Bank or United Nations.[226] However, as in those
other international organizations, the representation of women at senior levels is quite
low.[227] Moreover, unlike the World Bank, regional development banks and the United
Nations system, the WTO secretariat staff does not include gender specialists. The WTO
secretariat therefore has little capacity to identify and analyze the gender dimensions of
current WTO rules and proposals for new negotiations.

Issues of gender balance and gender awareness are also relevant to the work of country
delegations to the WTO in Geneva and trade ministries and negotiating teams more
generally. While information is not readily available on the gender composition of country

---

[221] *See, e.g.*, Maria Mies and Vandana Shiva, *Introduction* to ECOFEMINISM, *supra* note 219, at 3–5; Vandana
Shiva, *The Chipko Women's Concept of Freedom*, in ECOFEMINISM, *supra* note 219, at 246–50.

[222] *See, e.g.*, WEDO et al., *supra* note 41.

[223] *See supra* text accompanying notes 143–47 (Agreement on Agriculture), notes 182–84 (TRIPs Agreement), and notes 192–96 (SPS and TBT Agreements).

[224] WTO, *supra* note 149, paras. 31–32.

[225] *See, e.g.*, MALHOTRA ET AL., *supra* note 29, at 82–90; THIRD WORLD NETWORK, *supra* note 120, at 77–78;
UNDP, HUMAN DEVELOPMENT REPORT 2002: DEEPENING DEMOCRACY IN A FRAGMENTED WORLD (2002), at
112 & 118; Sabrina Varma, *Improving Global Economic Governance*, South Centre T.R.A.D.E. Occasional
Paper No. 8 (2002).

[226] WEDO, *The Numbers Speak for Themselves*, Fact Sheet No. 1 (2002), *available at* http://www.wedo.org
(women represent over fifty percent of all professional WTO staff, compared with less than forty percent at
the IMF and World Bank, and 31 percent at UNCTAD).

[227] *Id.*

missions to the WTO, it has been reported that less than ten percent of the country representatives at the Fourth Ministerial Conference in Doha were women.[228] Only three of twenty-one chairpersons of WTO bodies in 2004 are women.[229]

Serious gender imbalances also exist in many national trade ministries and offices, where clerical and administrative employees are usually women, and senior trade officials are predominantly men. Moreover, there is little evidence of training in gender awareness or gender mainstreaming within trade ministries and offices. While business associations often play an important role in shaping national trade policy, most of the participants in these associations are men, and gender issues are not central to their trade agendas.[230] In many countries, labor unions and civil society organizations are increasingly active in national debates about trade policy, but women are not always well represented in these organizations, and gender concerns are not raised consistently in these debates. It is not surprising, then, that the gender dimensions of trade and trade policy are rarely reflected in the negotiating positions of national trade representatives.

As noted earlier, UNCTAD and other UN bodies, the Commonwealth Secretariat, and several regional bodies have taken steps to integrate gender awareness and gender analysis in their trade-related activities.[231] Similar steps that could be taken by the WTO and WTO members are discussed further in Part IV.

2. Dispute Settlement

There are also significant gender imbalances within the WTO dispute settlement mechanism. In November 2003, the first woman was appointed to the WTO Appellate Body.[232] Of the individuals appointed to the indicative list of panelists to hear WTO trade disputes in the first instance, there has been some improvement in the gender composition, from about seven percent women in the original list approved in 1995, and about 8.5 percent women in the updated list approved in 2000, to around eleven percent women in the cumulative list approved in early 2003.[233]

The qualifications for both Appellate Body and dispute panel members emphasize expertise in trade law and trade policy,[234] and therefore there is no assurance that these

---

[228] WEDO, *supra* note 226.

[229] WTO, Press Release No. 371 (Feb. 11, 2004).

[230] O'REGAN-TARDU, *supra* note 33, at 21–23. However, there are a growing number of women's business associations in many countries. *Id.* at 23. The Organization of Women in International Trade ("OWIT"), with local affiliates in several countries, also provides networking and educational opportunities for women and men working in international trade and investment. *See* OWIT website (http://www.owit.org).

[231] *See supra* text accompanying notes 26–33.

[232] WTO, Press Release No. 364 (Nov. 7, 2003) (announcing appointment of Ms. Merit Janow to the Appellate Body); *see also* WTO, Press Release No. 32 (Nov. 29, 1995) (announcing appointment of seven original Appellate Body members); WTO, Press Release No. 179 (May 25, 2000) (announcing appointment of three replacement members of Appellate Body); WTO, Press Release No. 246 (Sept. 25, 2001) (announcing appointment of additional three replacement members of Appellate Body), *available at* http://www.wto.org.

[233] WTO, *Indicative List of Governmental and Non-Governmental Panelists,* WT/DSB/2 (Oct. 6, 1995) (8 of 115 individuals in list approved by the Dispute Settlement Body on September 27, 1995 were women); WTO, Indicative List of Governmental and Non-Governmental Panelists, WT/DSB/19 (March 29, 2000) (19 of 224 individuals on updated list approved through March 20, 2000 were women); WTO, Indicative List of Governmental and Non-Governmental Panelists, WT/DSB/33 (March 6, 2003) (33 of 293 individuals on updated list approved through February 19, 2003 were women).

[234] *See Understanding on Rules and Procedures Governing the Settlement of Disputes* ("DSU"), Art. 17.3 ("Appellate Body shall comprise persons of recognized authority, with demonstrated expertise in law, international trade and the subject matter of the covered agreements generally); DSU, Art. 8.1 ("Panels shall be composed of well-qualified governmental and/or non-governmental individuals, including persons who have served on or presented a case to a panel, served as a representative of a [WTO] Member or of a contracting party to GATT 1947 or as a representative to the Council or Committee of any covered agreement or its

individuals will be aware of, or sensitive to, gender issues related to WTO rules and the subject matter of trade disputes. As noted earlier, GATT and WTO panels have not responded favorably to gender-related concerns that have been raised in some specific trade disputes.[235] However, some individuals appointed to the Appellate Body and indicative list of panelists have broad backgrounds in international law and international development, which would suggest greater awareness of the social dimensions of trade and trade rules, including gender concerns.[236] More formal steps to ensure that gender issues are considered in WTO dispute settlement processes are discussed in Part IV of this chapter.

3. Trade Policy Review

The Trade Policy Review Mechanism ("TPRM"), which was established provisionally in 1989 and was made permanent in the Uruguay Round, is intended to "examine the impact of a Member's trade policies and practices on the multilateral trading system" through periodic assessments carried out jointly by the relevant WTO member and the WTO secretariat.[237] Notably, the TPRM exercise focuses on the impact of a WTO member's trade policies and practices on the multilateral trading system, but not the impact of multilateral trade rules, and the policies and practices of other WTO members, on that country. However, the TPRM does authorize consideration "to the extent relevant, . . . of the wider economic and development needs, policies and objectives of the Member concerned, as well as of its external environment."[238]

There is growing recognition of the need to expand the scope of trade policy assessments, particularly in the case of least-developed countries, for example, to give greater consideration to their needs for trade-related technical assistance.[239] Recently, Germany has provided trust funds to better adapt the TPRM to the situation of developing countries.[240] The WTO Secretariat's report to the Trade Policy Review Body ("TPRB") on Zambia, for example, which was prepared with German trust fund support, includes discussion of Zambia's Poverty Reduction Strategy, government programs to support micro and small enterprises, the application of labor laws to export processing zones, and various implementation concerns.[241] However, the report does not include any sex-disaggregated data—for example, on employment in export industries—or gender analysis. Nonetheless, gender issues have been raised in some country reports to

---

predecessor agreement, or in the [WTO] Secretariat, taught or published on international trade law or policy, or served as a senior trade policy official of a Member").

[235] See supra text accompanying notes 194–96.

[236] For example, on the Appellate Body, Georges Michel Abi-Saab, a professor of international law, has consulted for the United Nations on human rights issues in armed conflict, and served in the Appeals Chamber of the International Criminal Tribunals for the former Yugoslavia and Rwanda; John Lockhart, another Appellate Body member, served previously as an executive director of the Asian Development Bank. See WTO, Press Release No. 179 (May 25, 2000); WTO, Press Release No. 246 (Sept. 25, 2001), available at http://www.wto.org.

[237] Marrakesh Agreement Establishing the World Trade Organization, Annex 3, ¶ A(ii).

[238] Id.

[239] See WTO, Appraisal of the Operation of the Trade Policy Review Mechanism, WT/MIN(99)/2 (Oct. 8, 1999), ¶ 6.

[240] WTO, Report of the Trade Policy Review Body for 2002, WT/TPR/122 (Oct. 11, 2002), ¶ 5. The German trust fund also supported the WTO Secretariat's 2003 reviews of Niger and Seuegal. WTO, Report of the Trade Policy Review Body for 2003, WT/TPR/140 (oct. 31, 2003), ¶ 5.

[241] See WTO, Trade Policy Review: Zambia—Report by the Secretariat, WT/TPR/S/106 (Sept. 25, 2002), at 26–29 (human and financial resource limitations, and other implementation concerns), 45 (regulation of export processing zones), 47 (government support to micro and small enterprises), and 59 (agriculture as leading sector under Poverty Reduction Strategy).

the TPRB,[242] and in comments of TPRB members on the trade policy reviews of other members.[243]

Civil society groups, commentators and UN bodies have called for gender assessments to be included systematically in the TPRM.[244] Specific recommendations have been made to expand the scope of both the WTO Secretariat reports and country reports to include sex-disaggregated data and findings from gender-aware case studies and other research, with assistance from international institutions, national women's ministries, researchers and women's organizations.[245] National governments could also advance the "domestic transparency" goals of the TPRM by initiating "domestically oriented" trade policy reviews, which could focus on the impacts of WTO rules on women, poor households, and other constituencies.[246]

4. Trade-Related Capacity Building

Since the 1970s, international, regional and bilateral agencies have provided various types of trade-related support to developing countries, in the areas of export marketing, trade liberalization, trade facilitation and "trade capacity development," which the OECD defines as "building capacity by facilitating a country-driven participatory trade policy process as part of a comprehensive approach to overall development goals and poverty reduction strategies."[247] Trade-related capacity building took on heightened importance at the Fourth Ministerial Conference in Doha, where WTO members confirmed that "technical cooperation and capacity building are core elements of the development dimension of the multilateral trading system" and they called for "effective coordinated delivery of technical assistance" to developing countries, involving international and

[242] *See, e.g.*, WTO, Trade Policy Review Body ("TPRB") Press Release No. 89 (Nov. 13, 1998) (Burkina Faso's report to the TPRB notes that one of the government's principal policy objectives for 1998–2000 is to strengthen the role of women in development); WTO, TPRB Press Release No. 170 (July 20, 2001) (Cameroon's report to the TPRB states that the government's Strategic Framework for Poverty Reduction aims to "create conditions for strong, sustainable growth with the potential to curb the poverty currently affecting over 50 percent of the population, predominantly women").

[243] *See, e.g.*, WTO, TPRB Press Release No. 4 (Feb. 17, 1995) (in review of Pakistan's trade policies and practices, TPRB members drew attention to the low participation rate of women in the economy; Pakistan's representative acknowledged that women had historically lagged behind men in the country's development, and reported that current government policies and programs aimed to remove discrimination against women in education and employment); WTO, TPRB Press Release No. 16 (Oct. 23, 1995) (during review of Mauritius' trade policies and practices, in response to questions from TPRB members regarding women's rights, the representative of Mauritius noted that new legislation had been introduced to ensure equal treatment and employment opportunities for women); WTO TPRB Press Release No. 54 (April 10, 1997) (in reviewing Fiji's trade policies and practices, TPRB members raised issues concerning the gender and ethnic composition of employment).

[244] *See supra* text accompanying note 39; *see also* WILLIAMS, *supra* note 32, at 172–74; Barbara Evers, *Linking Trade and Poverty: Reinventing the Trade Policy Review Mechanism*, Paper for Globalisation and Poverty Research Programme, Institute for Development Studies, University of Sussex (2003), *available at* http://www.gapresearch.org/about/index.htm; UN Interagency Meeting on Women and Gender Equality— Taskforce on Financing for Development, *Mainstreaming Gender Perspectives in Issues Addressed in the Preparations for the International Conference on Financing for Development: An Initial Analysis*, Issue III: Trade (2001) (recommends incorporation of social development perspectives, including gender perspectives, in the TPRM, especially related to key development indicators such as impacts on employment patterns and income generation), *available at* http://www.wedo.org/ffd/kitmain3.htm.

[245] WILLIAMS, *supra* note 32, at 172–74.

[246] Evers, *supra* note 244.

[247] OECD, *DAC Guidelines: Strengthening Trade Capacity for Development* (2001), at 23, *available at* http://www.oecd.org.

regional institutions and bilateral donors.[248] This mandate resulted in the creation of a new technical assistance fund, the Doha Development Agenda Global Trust Fund, and expanded use of two existing funds, the Joint Integrated Technical Assistance Programme and the Integrated Framework for Trade-Related Technical Assistance to Least Developed Countries, as well as increased commitments by international and bilateral development agencies to support trade-related capacity building through their own assistance programs.[249]

A survey of the Doha Development Agenda Trade Capacity Building Database maintained by the OECD and WTO shows that some trade-related capacity building activities already address gender issues, particularly the needs of women entrepreneurs in developing countries.[250] Other gender-related activities include analysis and advice to government planners on gender and social issues posed by accession to the WTO, and pilot-testing of training and social protection measures to deal with potential layoffs of female garment workers in smaller developing countries resulting from the lifting of country-specific quotas under the ATC.[251]

The new UN inter-agency task force on gender and trade, the OECD and bilateral donors have recognized the benefits of incorporating a gender perspective more broadly and systematically in trade-related capacity building programs, particularly in light of concerns about the social and poverty impacts of trade liberalization.[252] The OECD has outlined several areas for support:

- Expanding assessments of proposed trade programs to include their impact on social development indicators;
- Removing gender-biased barriers to growth, including absence of property rights and disparities in education;
- Strengthening capacity to collect gender-related data at national and regional levels; and
- Including gender impacts in monitoring and evaluating the effects of trade policies.[253]

Training in gender analysis would also be useful in programs to strengthen the capacities of government agencies and civil society groups to undertake poverty and social impact assessments of trade and other macroeconomic policy changes.[254]

---

[248] WTO, *supra* note 149, paras. 38–39.

[249] WTO and OECD, *Second Joint WTO/OECD Report on Trade-Related Technical Assistance and Capacity Building* (2003), *available at* http://www.wto.org/english/tratop_e/devel_e/teccop_e/tct_e.htm.

[250] WTO and OECD, *Doha Development Agenda Trade Capacity Building Database*, *at* http://tcbdb.wto.org/index.asp?lang=ENG. *See also* G&T TASK FORCE, *supra* note 16, at 455–88 (survey of International Trade Centre, UNCTAD and United Nations Industrial Development Organization programs to assist women entrepreneurs.)

[251] *See, e.g.*, UNDP and UNIFEM, *China's Accession to WTO: Challenges for Women in Agriculture and Industry*, CPR/01/409, *at* http://tcbdb.wto.org/trta_project.asp?ctry=135&prjcd=CPR/01/409 (WTO/OECD database entry); Asian Development Bank, *Technical Assistance to Cambodia for Preventing Poverty and Empowering Female Garment Workers Affected by the Changing International Trade Environment*, R121–03 (July 1, 2003), *available at* http://www.adb.org.

[252] *See* G&T Task Force Meeting, *supra* note 28; OECD, *supra* note 247, at 26; CIDA, *supra* note 38.

[253] OECD, *supra* note 247, at 26.

[254] *See* WORLD BANK, A USER'S GUIDE TO POVERTY AND SOCIAL IMPACT ANALYSIS (2003). *See also* Eugenia McGill, *Poverty and Social Analysis of Trade Agreements: A More Coherent Approach?*, 27 B.C. INT'L & COMP. L REV. 371 (2004).

IV. Conclusions and Recommendations

There is increasing recognition that liberalized trade and trade agreements can affect women and men differently, and that gender differences in access to resources and employment, household responsibilities and other factors in turn can influence the outcome of trade policies. The gender-differentiated effects of increased trade and cross-border investment vary between countries, and within countries based on other social factors such as age, race or ethnicity, citizenship, class, religion, marital status and geographic location. However, gender-aware research is still needed in a number of areas, including the impact of liberalized trade in non-traditional agricultural exports and services, the impact of trade on the informal and reproductive sectors, and the gender implications of international rules governing trade-related areas such as intellectual property protection and investment.

A growing number of international and regional bodies are taking steps to address gender issues more systematically in their trade-related activities, and these efforts will be reinforced by the new UN inter-agency task force on gender and trade. Similarly, the WTO and its members could take steps to integrate gender considerations in the negotiation, implementation and review of multilateral trade rules. These include:

- Systematic collection and analysis of sex-disaggregated data, and monitoring of gender-related indicators, relevant to trade (which could include use of data and analysis generated by other international and regional organizations);
- Provision of staff training in gender analysis, establishment of a gender unit, and designation of gender focal points in each department of the WTO secretariat and national trade ministries;
- Affirmative steps to increase the number of women in senior positions in the WTO secretariat and national trade ministries;
- Inclusion of women in national trade negotiating teams and trade advisory panels, and inclusion of women's organizations in national consultations on trade policy;
- Gender analysis of proposed trade commitments, periodic gender impact assessments of existing trade obligations, and inclusion of gender assessments in WTO trade policy reviews;
- Affirmative steps to include women and men with expertise in gender and human development on the WTO Appellate Body and the indicative list of experts for WTO dispute settlement panels;
- Establishment of an expert panel on gender, human development and trade, which could serve as a resource for the WTO secretariat, WTO bodies (including the Appellate Body and the TPRB), and individual dispute settlement panels; and
- Inclusion of training in gender analysis and gender impact assessments in trade-related capacity building programs for developing and least-developed countries.

As discussed earlier, gender considerations could also be integrated in the current work programs of WTO bodies, in particular the mandates from the Doha Ministerial Conference relating to food security concerns under the Agreement on Agriculture; development-related measures under the SCM Agreement; health, environmental and traditional knowledge issues under the TRIPs Agreement; and further services liberalization and consideration of disciplines on regulations, subsidies and government procurement under the GATS. Consideration could also be given to establishing an expert group, with links to both the WTO Committee on Trade and Development and the UN inter-agency task force on gender and trade, to examine the coherence between

WTO rules and international commitments to gender equality, such as CEDAW, the Beijing Platform for Action and the Millennium Declaration and Millennium Development Goals.[255]

Increased gender awareness within the WTO, particularly relating to the gender dimensions of trade and investment in developing countries, would enhance the credibility of the Doha Development Agenda. Measures to increase the representation of women in WTO processes would also further the collective goal of WTO members to see that "all our peoples . . . benefit from the increased opportunities and welfare gains that the multilateral trading system generates."[256]

BIBLIOGRAPHY

Allaert, Benedicte, and Nicole Forman, eds. 1999. *Gender, Trade and Rights: Moving Forward*. Brussels: Women in Development Europe.

Baden, Sally. 1996. *Gender Issues in Financial Liberalisation and Financial Sector Reform*. BRIDGE Report No. 39. (http://www.ids.ac.uk/bridge)

———. 1998. *Gender Issues in Agricultural Liberalisation*. BRIDGE Report No. 41. (http://www.ids.ac.uk/bridge)

Blackett, Adelle. 1999. "Whither Social Clause? Human Rights, Trade Theory and Treaty Interpretation." *Columbia Human Rights Law Review* 31: 1.

Çağatay, Nilüfer. 2001. *Trade, Gender and Poverty*. Background Paper for Trade and Sustainable Human Development Project. New York: United Nations Development Programme.

Çağatay, Nilüfer, Diane Elson and Caren Grown, eds. 1995. *World Development* 23 (11). Special Issue on Gender, Adjustment and Macroeconomics.

Charlesworth, Hilary, and Christine Chinkin. 2000. *The Boundaries of International Law: A Feminist Analysis*. Manchester, U.K.: Manchester University Press.

Canadian International Development Agency. 2003. *Gender Equality and Trade-Related Capacity Building: A Resource Tool for Practitioners*. Gatineau, Quebec: CIDA.

Durano, Marina Fe B. *Gender Issues in International Trade*. (http://www.igtn.org/Research/GenderTrade.htm)

Fontana, Marzia, Susan Joekes and Rachel Masika. 1998. *Global Trade Expansion and Liberalisation: Gender Issues and Impacts*. BRIDGE Report No. 42. (http://www.ids.ac.uk/bridge)

Gammage, Sarah, Helene Jorgensen, Eugenia McGill and Marceline White. 2002. *Framework for Gender Assessments of Trade and Investment Agreements*. Washington, D.C.: Coalition for Women's Economic Development and Global Equality, Inc. (http://www.womensedge.org)

Grown, Caren, Diane Elson and Nilüfer Çağatay, eds. 2000. *World Development* 28 (7). Special Issue on Growth, Trade, Finance and Gender Inequality.

International Bank for Reconstruction and Development. 2001. *Engendering Development Through Equality in Rights, Resources and Voice*. World Bank Policy Research Report. New York and Oxford, U.K.: Oxford University Press.

International Gender and Trade Network. 2001. *International Gender and Trade Network at Doha*. Position Paper on the WTO. (http://www.igtn.org/WTO/WTOResources.htm)

———. 2003. *International Gender and Trade Network at Cancún and Beyond*. Advocacy Paper. (http://www.igtn.org/WTO/WTOResources.htm)

Joekes, Susan and Ann Weston. 1994. *Women and the New Trade Agenda*. New York: United Nations Development Fund for Women.

Malhotra, Kamal, Chandrika Bahadur, Selim Jahan and Mumtaz Keklik. 2003. *Making Global Trade Work for People*. London and Sterling, Virginia: Earthscan Publications, Ltd.

---

[255] United Nations Millennium Declaration, G.A. Res. 55/2, U.N. GAOR, 55th Sess., 8th plen. mtg., Agenda Item 60(b), U.N. Doc. A/RES/55/2 (2000).

[256] WTO, *supra* note 149, ¶ 2.

Mehra, Rekha, and Sarah Gammage, eds. 1999. *World Development* 27 (3). Special Section on Women Workers in a Globalizing Economy.

O'Regan-Tardu, Louise. 1999. *Gender Mainstreaming in Trade and Industry: A Reference Manual for Governments and Other Stakeholders*. Gender Management System Series. London: Commonwealth Secretariat.

Orford, Anne. 1999. "Contesting Globalization: A Feminist Perspective on the Future of Human Rights." In *The Future of International Human Rights*, Burns H. Weston and Stephen P. Marks, eds. Ardsley, New York: Transnational Publishers, Inc.

Pahuja, Sundhya. 2000. "Trading Spaces: Locating Sites for Challenge Within International Trade Law." *Australian Feminist Law Journal* 14: 38.

Tran-Nguyen, Anh-Nga and Americo Beviglia Zambetti, eds. 2004. *Trade and Gender: Opportunities and Challenges for Developing Countries*. United Nations Inter-Agency Network on Women and Gender Equality – Task Force on Gender and Trade Publications. U.N. Doc. UNCTAD/EDM/2004/2. New York and Geneva: United Nations.

United Nations. 1999. *World Survey on the Role of Women in Development: Globalization, Gender and Work*. New York.

———. 2000. *The World's Women 2000: Trends and Statistics*. New York.

United Nations Conference on Trade and Development. 1999. *Trade, Sustainable Development and Gender*. Papers Prepared for Pre-UNCTAD X Expert Workshop on Trade, Sustainable Development and Gender, Geneva, July 12–13, 1999. U.N. Doc. UNCTAD/EDM/Misc. 78.

United Nations Development Fund for Women. 2000. *Progress of the World's Women 2000*. UNIFEM Biennial Report. New York.

———. 2002. *Progress of the World's Women 2002, Volume 2*. UNIFEM Biennial Report. New York.

Williams, Mariama. 2003. *Gender Mainstreaming in the Multilateral Trading System: A Handbook for Policy-Makers and Other Stakeholders*. Commonwealth Secretariat New Gender Mainstreaming Series on Development Issues. London: Commonwealth Secretariat.

Wright, Shelley. 1995. "Women and the Global Economic Order: A Feminist Perspective." *American University Journal of International Law and Policy* 10: 861.

CHAPTER 64

TRADE AND CULTURE

Ivan Bernier[*]

[*] Professor of International Law, Laval University, since 1969; Dean of the Faculty of Law from 1981 to 1985; Director of the Quebec Centre of International Relations 1986 to 1993.

I. Introduction: A Brief History of the Trade and Culture Debate

Although the relationship between trade and culture has been described as one of those new issues that pose "serious practical and theoretical challenges...to present understanding of the trade regime,"[1] trade conflicts concerning cultural goods and services are not in fact a new phenomenon. Such conflicts go back to the 1920's when European countries, following the First World War, began resorting to screen quotas in order to protect their film industry from a sudden influx of American films that was perceived as a threat to their cultural expression.[2] The American motion picture industry responded by developing closer relations with the U.S. government. After the Second World War, through governmental arrangements such as the Blum-Byrnes agreement of 1946 which granted generous import quotas to American films as part of the settlement of the French war debt, or arrangements negotiated directly between the Motion Picture Export Association of America and various governments, it succeeded in reversing the tide.[3] In 1947, a compromise solution appeared to have been reached with the inclusion of Article IV in the *General Agreement on Tariffs and Trade* (GATT) which recognized the specificity of cultural products, at least in the case of films, without removing them from the disciplines of the agreement.[4] However, in the early 1960s, the dispute resumed when the United States asked the GATT to investigate the restrictions imposed on its television programs by a number of countries, including Canada. A special group was constituted to look at the matter but was unable to reach an agreement.[5]

Again in the early 1970s, the United States complained in the Tokyo Round catalogue of non-tariff barriers about the subsidies employed by not less than twenty countries in order to protect their cinema and television industries.[6] A new conflict arose between the United States and Europe towards the end of the 1980s concerning the EC directive "Television Without Frontiers," which stipulates in its Article 4 that "Members States shall ensure, where practicable and by appropriate means, that broadcasters reserve for European works...a majority proportion of their transmission time".[7] The United States requested GATT consultations with the European Community. After a lively exchange of views in the consultations, the matter was later dropped to

---

[1] Jeffrey L. Dunoff, *The Death of the Trade Regime*, 10 EUROPEAN JOURNAL OF INTERNATIONAL LAW 733 (1998)

[2] Film quotas were adopted by Austria, Czechoslovakia, Denmark, France, Germany, Hungary, Italy and the United Kingdom.

[3] On this development between the two wars, *see* FILM EUROPE AND FILM AMERICA: CINEMA, COMMERCE AND CULTURAL EXCHANGE 1920–1939, 346–385 (eds: Andrew Higson and Richard Maltby, 1999); see also T. Guback, *Non Market Factors in the International Distribution of American Films*, in 1 *Current Research in Films: Audiences, Economics and Law* 111, 114–115 (1985); LAURENT BURIN DES ROZIERS, *Du cinema au multimedia. Une brève histoire de l'exception culturelle*, Institut français des relations internationales, Notes de l'IFRI No 5, (1998).

[4] Article IV of GATT, as explained below, specifically authorizes screen quotas but also makes them subject to negotiations.

[5] GATT Doc. L/1741 (1962).

[6] GATT, Doc. MTN/3B1. The countries in question were Germany, Argentina, Austria, Belgium, Brazil, Canada, Chile, Denmark, Egypt, France, Greece, Indonesia, Israel, Italy, Japan, the Netherlands, Norway, Pakistan, Portugal and the United Kingdom.

[7] Council Directive 89/552/EEC of 3 October 1989 on the coordination of certain provisions laid down by law, regulation or administrative action in Member States concerning the pursuit of television broadcasting activities, *Official Journal* L 298, 17/10/1989, 0023–0030.

become part of a wider debate in the context of the Uruguay Round negotiations on services.[8]

In 1990, a working group was set up in the context of the negotiations on services to consider the feasibility of having a specific annex on audiovisual services.[9] Two conflicting views characterized the discussions, that of the United States and some other countries completely opposed to any kind of exception for audiovisual services, and that of the EEC, willing to make a commitment itself in that area only if a cultural exemption clause, more or less along the lines of what Canada had obtained in the FTA, was included.[10] After a few sessions, the group discontinued its activities for lack of agreement on the content of the proposed annex.

The question of audiovisual services was then largely ignored until 1993, when it took a new turn, with a much greater degree of visibility, with the involvement of artists from all over Europe which culminated in the simultaneous publication, on September 29, of a declaration in favour of a cultural exception in five of Europe's most prominent newspapers.[11] In the early autumn, the issue had reached such proportions that the then Director- General of the GATT, Peter Sutherland, felt obliged to respond publicly, arguing in essence that even if a general cultural exception had been considered in the negotiations and rejected, nothing in the services agreement required the deregulation of any services sector and nothing prevented governments from funding audio-visual projects.[12] The question remained unresolved until the very end of the Uruguay Round negotiations when the EC, after unsuccessfully proposing a cultural specificity clause that would have (a) accommodated exemptions from the most-favoured-nation treatment beyond the ten-year limit established in the GATS Annex on Article II Exemptions, (b) permitted the continuance and extension of public aid and operational subsidies, (c) allowed screen time to be reserved for indigenous production of films and TV programmes, and (d) permitted the regulation of existing and future broadcasting technologies and transmission techniques, finally announced that it would make no specific commitments with regard to the audiovisual sector.[13] The question having been put on the back burner, the debate remained completely open.

Unexpectedly, the debate, far from subsiding following the entry into force of the World Trade Organization in 1995, rapidly reached a new level of intensity. One only has

---

[8] For a detailed analysis of this exchange of views, *see* Jon Filipek, *'Culture Quotas': The Trade Controversy over the European Community's Broadcasting Directive*, 28 STANFORD JOURNAL OF INTERNATIONAL LAW 323, 340–342 (1992). *See also* Laurence G.C. Kaplan, *The European Community's Television Without Frontiers Directive: Stimulating Europe to Regulate Culture,* 8 EMORY INTERNATIONAL LAW REVIEW 225, 311–318 (1994).

[9] *GATT Focus*, No. 73 (1990), p. 10–11.

[10] John Peterson, *International Trade in Services: The Uruguay Round and Cultural and Information Services,* NATIONAL WESTMINSTER BANK QUARTERLY REVIEW 62 (August 1989). Under the first paragraph of Article 2005 of the Canada-U.S. Free Trade Agreement, "cultural industries are exempt from the provisions of this Agreement except as specifically provided...."; however, the second paragraph adds that "a Party may take measures of equivalent commercial effect in response to actions that would have been inconsistent with this Agreement but for paragraph 1".

[11] The declaration in question, signed by a large number of authors, actors and producers, appeared in Le Monde (September 29, 1993, 12–13), as well as in The Independent, El País, Die Frankfurter Algemeine Zeitung and Le Soir.

[12] *Peter Sutherland Responds to Debate on Audiovisual Sector*, NEWS OF THE URUGUAY ROUND, NUR 069, October 14, 1993, available on the WTO website: Documents on line, symbol NUR 069.

[13] *See Audiovisual Services,* Background Note by the Secretariat, June 15, 1998, Doc. S/C/W/40, note 27: http://www.wto.org/english/tratop_e/serv_e/w40.doc. See also INSIDE U.S. TRADE, Nov. 19, 1993, at 1.

to consider the number of conflicts about cultural industries that have arisen since 1995, the growing number of articles published on the subject, and the numerous conferences organized around that theme, to realize that we are now faced with what a 1998 book described as a "culture/trade quandary"[14]. At the end of that same year, former Under Secretary for Commerce and Dean of the Yale School of Management Jeffrey Garten, in an Article entitled "Cultural Imperialism is no Joke" went as far as to suggest that the United States should be "more sensitive to fears abroad that U.S. exports of movies, music, software, and broadcasting are harmful".[15] By then, however, the debate had taken a new direction: from a discussion strictly about the treatment of cultural goods and services in trade agreements, it had become one about the impact of trade liberalization on cultural identity and cultural diversity.

The importance of this new development did not escape the attention of the Director-General of the new WTO, Mr. Renato Ruggiero. In June 1997, in a speech that may be considered as the first public expression of concern within the new World Trade Organization regarding the cultural impact of trade liberalization, he declared before the Common Market Council of the MERCOSUR that "[m]anaging a world of converging economies, peoples and civilizations, each one preserving its own identity and culture, represents the great challenge and the great promise of our age".[16] Less than a year later, in May 1998, he warned the Member States that they "should not underestimate the growing pressure on the multilateral system to give answers to issues which are very real public concerns, but whose solution cannot rely on the trading system alone"; among such issues, he expressly mentioned that of cultural diversity.[17] As if to confirm his warning, 1998 witnessed the failure of the OECD to conclude a multilateral agreement on investment for reasons not unrelated to the question of cultural diversity.[18] In April 1999, in his last public speech as WTO Director-General, Renato Ruggiero came back to the subject, declaring:

> More and more, we are facing issues and concerns which go beyond the parameters of trade. More and more, globalization is raising a whole new set of questions about how to manage interdependence. Can we have an open world economy without a stable financial system? How to protect endangered species and promote sustainable development? Should trade be linked to labour standards and human rights? Can we preserve cultural identities in an age of borderless communications?[19]

Subsequent events have confirmed the validity of his analysis regarding the issue of cultural identity. Although the failure of the 1999 WTO ministerial meeting in Seattle cannot be related in any way to the issue of culture as such, the noisy protests that disrupted

[14] *See* Ivan Bernier, *Cultural Goods and Services in International Trade Law,*in THE CULTURE/TRADE QUANDARY: CANADA'S POLICY OPTIONS 108 (ed.: Dennis Browne, 1998).

[15] Jeffrey Garten, *Cultural Imperialism is no Joke,* BUSINESS WEEK, November 30, 1998

[16] WTO, Press/74, 19 June, 1997

[17] Opening statement by the Director-General, Mr. Renato Ruggiero, Ministerial Conference, Geneva, May 18, 1998: http://www.wto.org/english/thewto_e/minist_e/min98_e/anniv_e/dg_e.htm

[18] France, in the context of the MAI negotiations, had proposed a clause preserving the competence of the state to intervene in favour of cultural and linguistic diversity. Canada has even been accused of having sabotaged the MAI negotiations with its cultural network by creating "a cultural exchange blockade, a front for trade barriers that constitute a form of trade protectionism". *See Cultural Protectionism and the Multilateral Trade Agreement on Investment,* INTERNATIONAL ECONOMIC REVIEW, June-July 1998, Pub. 3128 1 (Office of Economics, United States International Trade Commission).

[19] *Beyond the Multilateral Trading System,* Address by Renato Ruggiero, Director-General of the WTO, 20th Seminar on International Security, Politics and Economics, Institut pour les hautes études internationales, Geneva, April 12, 1999

the meeting have been interpreted by a number of commentators as the expression of a cultural reaction to globalization, the explanations given in that respect ranging from growing insecurity about a loss of cultural references[20] to alarm about a more standardized culture[21]. In a speech given before the Trilateral Commission in Tokyo on May 9, 2000, Fred Bergsten, former U.S. Assistant Secretary of the Treasury for International Affairs, referring to the demonstrations in Seattle, Davos, Bangkok and Washington which he considered as the superficial signs of a very real issue, remarked: "The world economy today faces a more fundamental set of challenges because the backlash against globalization is much more than economics. . . . [T]here is also a huge cultural dimension which raises a mass of contentious and difficult issues of its own".[22]

More recently, Jeremy Rifkin, in a commentary published in the Los Angeles Times in anticipation of the G-8 Summit of July 2001 in Genoa, Italy, wrote:

> Protests are becoming a familiar part of world political and economic forums. But, although the attention often goes to the relatively few violent protesters, there is a bigger message worth listening to. The fact is we are witnessing the first stirrings of a cultural backlash against globalization whose effects are likely to be significant and far-reaching.[23]

The G-8 Tokyo Summit of July 2000 itself acknowledged, in its final communiqué, the importance of preserving cultural diversity "as a source of social and economic dynamism which has the potential to enrich human life in the 21st century, as it inspires creativity and stimulates innovation."[24]

The concern regarding the impact of globalization on culture has also attracted the attention of international cultural organizations such as UNESCO, the Council of Europe, and the Organisation Internationale de la Francophonie, which have all adopted declarations on cultural diversity[25]. The texts in question share the same perception regarding the need to adopt measures to respond to global market influences on culture and cultural exchange. For example, the preamble of the Council of Europe Declaration on Cultural Diversity, adopted by the Committee of Ministers on 7 December 2000, recognizes "that the development of new information technologies, globalisation and evolving multilateral trade policies have an impact on cultural diversity".[26]

Within the WTO itself, cultural identity and cultural diversity concerns are now being voiced and discussed more and more in the context of the present GATS negotiations, in effect resuming the cultural exception debate from the Uruguay Round. Although these negotiations are far from over, at least four distinct positions have been expressed on the subject so far.

---

[20] *See* David Postman and Lynda V. Mapes, *Why WTO United so Many Foes*, SEATTLE TIMES, December 6, 1999.

[21] *See* Paul Van Slambrouck, *There is More Diversity but Less . . . Diversity,* THE CHRISTIAN SCIENCE MONITOR, February 8, 2000.

[22] Institute for International Economics, http://www.iie.com/papers/bergsten0500.htm, accessed July 12, 2001

[23] Jeremy Rifkin, *World Culture Resists Bowing to Commerce*, LOS ANGELES TIMES, July 2, 2001, reproduced in the MONTREAL GAZETTE under the title *Cultural Backlash against Globalization*, July 4, 2001.

[24] For the text of the communiqué, *see*: http:// usembassy.state.gov/Tokyo/ wwwhg8ko.html

[25] UNESCO's "Universal Declaration on Cultural Diversity " was adopted by the General Assembly on December 2nd, 2001 ; see UNESCOPRESS 02/11/2001. The Council of Europe adopted its own "Declaration on Cultural Diversity" on December 7, 2000 ; for the text of the declaration, see http:// culture.coe.fr/Infocentre/txt/eng/edecldiv.htm. The Organisation Internationale de la Francophonie also adopted a declaration on cultural diversity (Déclaration de Cotonou) in June 2001 ; for the text, see http://www.francophonie.org/oif/publications/evenements/declaration_Cotonou.doc

[26] Council of Europe, DECLARATION ON CULTURAL DIVERSITY, 2000: http://culture.coe.fr/Infocentre/txt/eng/edecldiv.htm

- Canada has stated in its initial negotiating proposals that it would not make any commitment that restricts its ability to achieve its cultural policy objectives "until a new international instrument, designed specifically to safeguard the right of countries to promote and preserve their cultural diversity, can be established".[27]
- Switzerland considers that the audio-visual sector represents both an important field of commercial activity and a vector of cultural identity, and therefore identifies the challenge for trade policy as being to reconcile these two views within a balanced solution that satisfies both sensibilities. Such a solution, in the Swiss view, could take the form of an Annex to the GATS or of any other suitable instrument, but the work to be undertaken would have to take into account any relevant development outside the WTO framework on the issue of audio-visual regulation, in particular developments relating to cultural diversity.[28]
- Brazil, whose position is close to that of Switzerland, first rejects the radically conflicting views that characterized the discussions in the audiovisual sector during the Uruguay Round; on the one hand the view that the sector should be completely excluded from trade rules because of the role of audiovisual services in the promotion and preservation of cultural identity and cultural diversity, and on the other the view that rejects any special treatment of the sector because of the entertainment and commercial nature of audiovisual products and services. Instead, Brazil affirms, the question that should be considered is "how to promote the progressive liberalization of the sector in a way that creates opportunities of effective market access for the exports of developing countries in this sector without affecting the margin of flexibility of governments to achieve their cultural policy objectives as they find appropriate".[29]
- The United States argues that existing trade rules are sufficient to take into account the special cultural qualities of the sector and goes on to say that "[t]he choices are not, nor have they ever been, a choice between promoting and preserving a nation's cultural identity and liberalizing trade in audiovisual services. Especially in light of the quantum increase in exhibition possibilities available in today's digital environment, it is quite possible to enhance one's cultural identity and to make trade in audiovisual service more transparent, predictable, and open".[30]

As can be seen from this brief historical review of the policy debate about trade and culture, the issue has taken a new dimension in recent years. From an issue that until 1995 revolved almost exclusively around the treatment of cultural goods and services in international trade agreements, it has now become one that is more generally concerned with the preservation of cultural identity and cultural diversity. This last development, however, raises problems whose solution, to borrow again the words of Renato Ruggiero, "cannot rely on the trading system alone". The fact is that the WTO is poorly equipped to assess what is required to insure the preservation of cultural identity and cultural diversity: culture is simply not one of its fields of competence. As a trade organization, on the other hand, it remains competent to determine the treatment to be granted to

[27] WTO Council on Trade in Services, Communication from Canada, *Initial Canadian Negotiating Proposals*, ¶ 9, 14 March 2001: Doc. S/CSS/W/46.

[28] WTO, Council for Trade in Services, Communication from Switzerland, *GATS 2000 Audiovisual Services*, ¶ 9, 04 May 2001: Doc. S/CSS/W/74

[29] WTO, Council for Trade in Services, Communication from Brazil, *Audiovisual Services*, ¶ 7, 09 July 2001: Doc. S/CSS/W/99.

[30] WTO, Council for Trade in Services, Communication from the United States, *Audiovisual and Related Services*, ¶ 9, 18 December 2000: Doc. S/CSS/W/21.

cultural goods and services from a trade perspective. It is precisely at the intersection of these two concerns that the new issue of trade and culture arises. A prerequisite for its solution, therefore, is that both concerns be clearly articulated. Only then does it become possible to understand the exact nature of the issue and to envisage possible solutions.

The first part of this paper attempts to provide a global picture of the way in which cultural goods and services are presently dealt with under the WTO and of the types of problems that they raise or might raise. To do so, the paper looks successively at the treatment of cultural goods under the multilateral agreements on trade in goods, cultural services under the *General Agreement on Trade in Services* (GATS), and finally cultural goods and services under the *Agreement on Trade-Related Aspects of Intellectual Property Rights* (TRIPS). The second part of the paper will focus on the basic elements of the trade and culture issue and on the solutions that have been proposed to resolve that issue.

II. Cultural Goods and Services in the WTO

A. Trade in Cultural Goods

In examining the treatment of cultural goods under the WTO multilateral agreements on trade in goods, we will proceed under the assumption that such goods are covered except as otherwise provided. For each of the agreements to be examined, therefore, we shall first consider whether there are indications that cultural goods warrant specific treatment, then look at the basic rights and obligations of the parties under the agreement, and finally, with respect to such rights and obligations, consider the problems that may have arisen in relation to cultural goods. The question of whether one is dealing with a good or a service and the significance of that distinction for the choice of the applicable instrument will be examined as a separate issue in the second part of this paper.

Not all the agreements included in Annex I A (Multilateral Agreements on Trade in Goods) of the WTO Agreement apply in practice to trade in cultural goods. Some deal with specific sectors of economic activity that have nothing to do with culture, such as textiles and clothing, agriculture, and sanitary and phytosanitary measures; others deal with problems that are not normally associated with culture, such as technical barriers to trade, licensing procedures and pre-shipment inspection. The agreements that are of interest, either because they clearly apply or could apply to cultural goods, or because they have been invoked in relation to cultural goods, are first and foremost the *GATT 1994*, followed by the *Agreement on Subsidies and Countervailing Measures*, the *Agreement on the Implementation of Article VI of GATT 1994* (Anti-dumping Agreement), and the *Agreement on Safeguards*.

1. GATT 1994
(a) Article IV—Cinematographic Films. Two Articles in the *GATT 1994* specifically refer to cultural goods. The first one is Article IV which is made an exception to the requirement of national treatment through Article III:10. It provides that a member may maintain or establish screen quotas requiring the exhibition of films of national origin during a specified minimum portion of the total screen time in the commercial exhibition of all films of whatever origin; such screen quotas, however, are subject to negotiations for their limitation, liberalization or elimination.[31]

---

[31] In the Torquay Round of negotiations of 1951, Germany did include in its list of concessions a commitment regarding screen quotas which provided among other things that if it decided to establish a screen quota for the exhibition of films of foreign origin, this would not exceed 27 percent ; but this concession was later withdrawn pursuant to negotiations under Article XXVII in 1956. *See* GATT, GUIDE TO GATT LAW AND PRACTICE (1994) 192.

Article IV reproduces in essence Article 19 of the Havana Charter which was inserted, according to Clair Wilcox,

> upon a recognition of the fact that motion picture production is as much entitled to protection against foreign competition as any other industry and that such protection, in this case, cannot be provided effectively by imposing duties on imported rolls of films. The screen quota, therefore, has been accepted as the counterpart of a tariff and every other method of protection (except tariff duties) has been banned.[32]

In the summary analysis of the Havana Charter provided by the U.S. Department of State in 1950, however, the explanation given by the U.S government differs substantially; it says that movies are distinguishable because "their value is not in the film itself, but in its earning power".[33]

During the negotiation of the General Agreement on Tariffs and Trade itself, yet another explanation for the insertion of what was to become Article IV was put forward by the United Kingdom, Norway and Czechoslovakia, which particularly advocated the film exception; in their view, in the case of films, important cultural considerations entered into consideration, which was not the case for other goods.[34] This explanation was adopted by John Jackson who wrote, in his seminal 1969 work entitled *World Trade and the Law of GATT*, that the cinema exception was accepted because it was "more related to domestic cultural policies than to economics and trade".[35] It is also the interpretation that prevails in the historical review of Article IV prepared by the GATT Secretariat in 1990 for the Uruguay Round Working Group on Audiovisual Services.[36]

Recently, the United States has come up again with a new explanation for Article IV of GATT. In its communication on Audiovisual and Related Services of December 18, 2000, to the WTO Council for Trade in Services, it stated:

> GATT Article IV provides a special, and unique, exception for cinematographic films to GATT national treatment rules. In 1947, in recognition of the difficulty that domestic film producers faced in finding adequate screen time to exhibit their films in the immediate post-World War II period, GATT founders authorized continuation of existing screen-time quotas.[37]

There is no further evidence of such negotiations taking place in the context of multilateral trade negotiations. However, pressures to have screen quotas eliminated in the context of bilateral negotiations are not unheard of. In 1998–1999, a vigorous debate emerged in Korea following the decision of the government to gradually phase out the local screen quota which the U.S. government, in the context of ongoing Seoul-Washington investment negotiations, had described as a protectionist policy. See "Korean Film industry's plea for screen quota turns emotional", *Korea Herald*, June 18, 1999. The debate was still going on in early 2002 as evidenced by an article published in the *Korea Herald* entitled "Film industry leaders protest gov't bid to ease screen quota regulations" on January 29, 2002. It is interesting to contrast the attitude of the U.S. government in this instance with the position taken in its communication of December 2000 to the Council on Trade on Services regarding audiovisual and related services, where it presents Article IV of GATT as an example of the flexibility of the WTO regime in cultural matters: see supra, note 30.

[32] Clair A. Wilcox, CHARTER FOR WORLD TRADE 77 (1949). Clair Wilcox represented the United States during the Havana Charter and GATT negotiations.

[33] See U.N. Doc. EPCT/C.II/W.5, at p. 3.4: see JOHN H. JACKSON, WORLD TRADE AND THE LAW OF GATT 293, n. 1 (1969).

[34] Second Session of the Preparatory Committee of the United Nations Conference on Trade and Development (Geneva 1947), Doc. EPCT/TAC/SR/10

[35] Jackson, *supra* note 33, at 293. *See also*, to the same effect, Robin L. Van Harpen, *Mamas, Don't Let Your Babies Grow Up to Be Cowboys: Reconciling Trade and Cultural Independence,* 4 MINNESOTA JOURNAL OF GLOBAL TRADE 167 (1995)

[36] GATT, Doc. MTN.GNS/AUD/W/1 October 4, 1990.

[37] *See supra*, note 30.

It is interesting to note how from the outset and right up to today Europe has insisted that Article IV was based on cultural grounds, whereas the United States claims that it was founded on economic principles.

An important question that arises in connection with Article IV is whether its language, which refers exclusively to cinematographic films, can be extended to cover television programs recorded in video format. This is the specific issue that was raised by the United States before the GATT in 1961.[38] It stated then that "restrictions against the showing of television programs were technically a violation of the principles of Article III: 4, but that some of the principles of Article IV might apply to them."[39] Canada for its part took the position that Article IV covered the issue, even though the article did not mention television programs as such, because this was a development that could not have been foreseen in 1947. Unfortunately, the working group set up to examine the question was unable to reach a consensus on the subject.[40] In 1991, during consultations concerning restrictions on the showing of non-European films on television, the United States, while recognizing the existence of the Article IV exception, pointed out that it applied exclusively to cinematographic films.[41] Certain authors, such as Chi Carmody, have suggested that the restricted nature of the exception "should not imply that the exclusion of cinematographic film necessarily meant GATT coverage for other media" because "the form of Article IV was shaped by the awareness of its time".[42] For the moment, however, the most that can be said is that the scope of Article IV has not yet been settled.

To conclude on Article IV, it is interesting to note that one of the most common restrictions appearing in the schedules of the WTO members that have undertaken commitments in the audiovisual sector during the Uruguay Round GATS negotiations concerned restrictions on the share of screening time allotted to foreign film and television productions.[43] The preoccupation that justified the insertion of Article IV seems to still be very much present.

(b) Article XX(f)—Exception for National Treasures.   The other provision of GATT 1994 that specifically refers to cultural products is Article XX(f), which includes among the general exceptions measures which are imposed for the protection of national treasures of artistic, historic or archeological value, provided they are not applied in a manner which would constitute a means of arbitrary or unjustifiable discrimination between countries or a disguised restriction on international trade, as specified in the first paragraph (or chapeau) of Article XX. Article XX (f) is interesting in that it clearly recognizes the relationship between culture and national identity. It no doubt facilitated the conclusion of the 1970 *UNESCO Convention on the Means of Prohibiting and Preventing the Illicit Import, Export and Transfer of Ownership of Cultural Property,*[44] many signatories of

[38] *See supra*, note 5.
[39] *See GATT Analytical Index 1994*, at 192.
[40] Id.
[41] *Id.*
[42] Chi Carmody, *When 'Cultural Identity Was not at Issue': Thinking About Canada—Certain Measures Concerning Periodicals*, 30 LAW AND POLICY IN INTERNATIONAL BUSINESS 231, 255 (1999). *See also* Michael Brown and Leigh Parker, *Trade in Culture: Consumable Product or Cherished Articulation of a Nation's Soul*, 22 DENVER JOURNAL OF INTERNATIONAL LAW AND POLICY 155, 170 (1993).
[43] WTO, Council on Services, *Audiovisual Services*, Background Note by the Secretariat, ¶ 29, Doc. S/C/W/40, 15 June 1998: http://www.wto.org/english/tratop_e/serv_e/w40.doc
[44] *See* for the text of the convention: http://www.unesco.org/culture/laws/1970/html_eng/page1.shtml

which have effectively adopted legislation authorizing controls on the import and export of heritage products.

Leaving aside Article IV and Article XX(f), cultural goods are subject to all the usual GATT disciplines, the most important of which are the MFN treatment required by Article I, the national treatment requirement of Article III, the anti-dumping and countervailing duties provisions of Article VI, the prohibition against quantitative restrictions of Article XI, and the safeguards provisions of Article XIX. We will consider the Article I, III, and XI provisions in this section. The anti-dumping and countervailing duties provisions of Article VI will be examined in the context of the Anti-dumping Agreement and the Subsidies and Countervailing Duties Agreement, and the safeguards provisions of Article XIX will be examined in the context of the Agreement on Safeguards.

(c) Article I.1—Most Favored Nation. Under Article I:1 of the GATT 1994 "... any advantage, favour, privilege or immunity granted by any contracting party [now Member] to any product originating in or destined for any other country shall be accorded immediately and unconditionally to the like product originating in or destined for the territories of all other contracting parties". Cultural goods, although subject to this most favoured nation clause like any other goods, do raise a particular problem with respect to the like product requirement: they are difficult to compare because they are characterized less by their material components than by their intellectual content.[45] This issue, which has never been examined by a panel in the context of Article I, will be discussed more fully in the context of GATT Article III where the question was explicitly raised in the case of *Canada—Certain Measures Concerning Periodicals.*[46] The fact that it has never been raised in the context of Article I, however, does not mean that the problem is purely theoretical. An example of a situation where it could be raised is that of measures that provide an advantage to cultural goods that are produced in a given language, such as a subsidy program for the acquisition of books and magazines in French by public libraries. To the extent that they provide a *de facto* advantage to those States that share the same language, they could be seen as a violation of Article I. In such a situation, far from uncommon, the question of whether cultural goods produced in a given language are "like" cultural goods produced in a different language would undoubtedly be raised. The answer to that question, as will be seen now in the context of Article III, is far from obvious.

(d) Article III—National Treatment. The most relevant provisions of Article III of GATT 1994 are Paragraph 2, which deals with discriminatory taxes, Paragraph 4, which concerns laws, regulations and requirements affecting the internal sale, offering for sale, purchase, transportation, distribution or use of goods, and Paragraph 8 (b) which exempts from the application of Article III "the payment to subsidies exclusively to domestic producers". To the extent that most States intervene in the cultural sector and do this through a variety of means such as tax measures, domestic content requirements and regulatory requirements, the opportunities for conflict with the provision of Article III are numerous. The WTO decision in *Canada—Certain Measures Concerning Periodicals*, referred to

---

[45] In an article entitled *Mamas, Don't Let Your Babies Grow to Be Cowboys: Reconciling Trade and Cultural Independence*, Robin Van Harpen writes: "For the purpose of this Note, it is assumed that cultural products of the same type, such as movies, but which are from different countries are 'like' products", but then immediately adds "the accuracy of this assumption is debatable". *See* 4 MINNESOTA JOURNAL OF GLOBAL TRADE 165 n. 130 (1995).

[46] *See* the discussion in Subsection (d) below concerning "like products" in the case of *Canada—Certain Measures Concerning Periodicals.*

above, is particularly instructive with regard to the application of these provisions to cultural goods.[47]

The facts of the case are as follows. In 1965, Canada adopted Tariff Code 9958 which prohibited the importation into Canada of split-run magazines (defined as Canadian editions of foreign magazines that contain advertising directed at the Canadian market and include little or no Canadian editorial content), the objective of the measure being to reserve to Canadian periodicals the Canadian advertising market considered essential to their survival. Nearly thirty years later, in 1993, *Sports Illustrated*, owned by Time Warner, found a way to circumvent Tariff Code 9958 by electronically transmitting the content of its magazine to a printer in Canada. Canada reacted by imposing an eighty percent excise tax on the value of all advertisements in split-run magazines. As a result, *Sports Illustrated* withdrew its split-run edition and the U.S. government launched a challenge before the WTO regarding not only the new tax but also Tariff Code 9958 and two other measures affecting periodicals, one concerning the imposition of higher postal rates on imported magazines, the other concerning a postal subsidy programme for Canadian magazines.

In response to the US argument that the new provision of the *Excise Tax Act* introduced by Canada in support of its periodical industry was a discriminatory tax applying to "like" products contrary to Article III: 2, first sentence, Canada had submitted that this provision could not apply because imported split-run periodicals containing foreign content and Canadian magazines developed specifically for a Canadian readership were not "like" products:

> Content for the Canadian market will include Canadian events, topics, people and perspectives. The content may not be exclusively Canadian, but the balance will be recognizably and even dramatically different from that which is found in foreign publications which merely reproduce editorial content developed for and aimed at a non-Canadian market.[48]

Unfortunately, the Panel completely skirted the issue by using a hypothetical example where it compared two editions of the same magazine, both imported products, which could not have been on the Canadian market at the same time. On the basis of that mistaken example, it considered it most likely that periodicals would have been designed for the same readership with the same tastes and habits and concluded therefore that split-run periodicals and domestic non-split run periodicals could be like products. Although the Panel recognized that a determination of "like product" for the purposes of Article III:2, first sentence, had to be construed narrowly, on a case-by-case basis, by examining relevant factors including the product's end-uses in a given market, consumers' tastes and habits and the product's properties, nature and quality,[49] it failed to analyse these criteria in relation to imported split-run periodicals and domestic non-split-run periodicals. Having found a violation under the first sentence, it abstained from considering the matter under the second sentence.

---

[47] For the Panel decision, *see* WT/DS/31/R, March 14, 1997; for the Appellate Body decision, see WT/DS31/AB/R, June 30, 1997.

[48] WT/DS31/AB/R, June 30, 1997, Sec. II.A.2.

[49] As explained in *Japan—Alcoholic Beverages*, WT/DS8/AB/R, WT/DS10/AB/R, WT/DS11/AB/R (1996), Sec. H. Article III:2 of the GATT reads as follows: "The products of the territory of any contracting party imported into the territory of any other contracting party shall not be subject, directly or indirectly, to internal taxes or other internal charges of any kind in excess of those applied, directly or indirectly, to like domestic products. Moreover, no contracting party shall otherwise apply internal taxes or other internal charges to imported or domestic products to imported or domestic products in a manner contrary to the principles set forth in paragraph 1."

The Appellate Body did not accept the Panel's finding that imported split-run magazines and Canadian magazines were "like products". It found that "as a result of the lack of proper legal reasoning based on inadequate factual analysis...the Panel could not logically arrive at the conclusion that imported split-run periodicals and domestic non-split-run periodicals can be 'like'".[50] Lacking an adequate factual analysis to review the decision on the basis of Article III: 2, first sentence, it decided to proceed on its own to examine whether these two products could be considered as "directly competitive or substitutable products" under the second sentence of Article III:2. As a result, the "like product" issue was never resolved. This is particularly unfortunate because the factors to be taken into consideration under the first sentence of paragraph 2 (end uses, consumers' tastes and habits and product's properties, nature and quality) arguably provided the basis for Canada's best arguments.[51]

Essentially on the basis of an admission by Canada that English-language consumer magazines faced significant competition from U.S. magazines in Canada, the Appellate Body found that imported split-run periodicals and domestic non-split-run periodicals were directly competitive or substitutable products in so far as they were part of the same segment of the Canadian market for periodicals.[52] Having established that, it went on to answer the question of whether periodicals could be distinguished on the basis of their intellectual content, as argued by Canada. The answer was as follows:

> Our conclusion that imported split-run periodicals and domestic non-split-run periodicals are 'directly competitive or substitutable' does not mean that all periodicals belong to the same relevant market. A periodical containing mainly current news is not directly competitive or substitutable with a periodical dedicated to gardening, chess, sports, music or cuisine. But newsmagazines, like *Time, Time Canada* and *Maclean's*, are directly competitive or substitutable in spite of the 'Canadian' content of *Maclean's*.[53]

However, the Appellate Body did not explain why domestic as opposed to foreign content in the particular case was not a distinguishing factor. Was this because it considered that domestic content in general was not a significant factor in the choice of a newsmagazine, so that Canadian consumers, or for that matter Italian or Japanese consumers would not mind substituting an American or a German newsmagazine for one of their own country? Would the Appellate Body have similarly found that American newspapers and Canadian newspapers are "directly competitive or substitutable products"? Was it because of the admission by Canada that American and Canadian news magazines were in competition on the Canadian market? Using the same type of reasoning, one would be justified in concluding that foreign films and American films are not "directly competitive or substitutable products" on the American market, because it is widely recognized that there is no real competition between the two on that market, but are "directly competitive or substitutable" on the French market, on the German market etc., because they are in competition on those markets. The truth of the matter is that the Appellate Body, instead of addressing squarely the issue of the specificity of cultural products as vehicles of information, has simply applied to news periodicals the same type of reasoning as was applied in the Japanese Alcohols case to foreign vodka and Japanese vodka.[54]

[50] WT/DS31/AB/R, sec. VI.B.1.

[51] *See* Richard L. Matheny III, *In the Wake of the Flood: 'Like Products' and Cultural Products after the World Trade Organization's Decision in Canada—Certain Measures Concerning Periodicals*, 147 UNIVERSITY OF PENNSYLVANIA LAW REVIEW, 245, 264 (1998).

[52] WT/DS31/AB//R, Sec. VI.B.1.

[53] *Id.*

[54] *Japan—Taxes on Alcoholic Beverages*, WT/DS8R, WT/DS10/R, WT/DS11/R, 11 July 1996 (Panel), WT/DS8/AB/R, WT/DS10/AB/R, WT/DS11/AB/R, 4 October 1996 (Appellate Body).

The second question of particular interest with regard to the interpretation of Article III had to do with the use of funded postal rates to support domestic periodicals. The Appellate Body, reversing the decision of the Panel in favour of Canada, held that the "funded postal rates" maintained by Canada could not be justified by Article III: 8(b) of GATT 1994, which provides that the provisions of Article III "shall not prevent the payment of subsidies exclusively to domestic producers". Relying on a textual as well as a contextual interpretation of that provision, and taking into account its object and purpose as confirmed by its drafting history, the Appellate Body found that Article III:8(b) was "intended to exempt from the obligations of Article III only the payment of subsidies which involves the expenditure of revenue by a government".[55] And it went on to extract with approval the following comments of the Panel in *United States—Measures Affecting Alcoholic and Malt Beverages*:

> Article III:8(b) limits, therefore, the permissible producers subsidies to "payments" after taxes have been collected or payments otherwise consistent with Article III. This separation of tax rules, e.g. on tax exemptions or reductions, and subsidy rules makes sense economically and politically. Even if the proceeds from non-discriminatory product taxes may be used for subsequent subsidies, the domestic producer, like his foreign competitors, must pay the taxes due. The separation of tax and subsidy rules contributes to greater transparency.[56]

Seeing no reason to distinguish a reduction of tax on a product from a reduction in transportation or postal rates, the Appellate Body finally concluded that the postal subsidy was incompatible with Canada's obligations under Article III of GATT 1994.

It is difficult to quarrel with this decision from a purely legal point of view.[57] However, the interpretation of Article III does mark the triumph of form over substance.[58] The view that virtually any form of subsidy that is not granted directly in the form of payments to domestic producers is not compatible with GATT Article III: 8 (b) means that a serious look will have to be taken at the way financial help is granted to producers of cultural goods. Tax remittance and similar programs are frequently used as a means of subsidizing cultural producers not only in Canada[59] but elsewhere. According to a OECD publication made public in 1998, "OECD governments are increasingly relying upon policies aimed at indirectly stimulating domestic content creation through tax breaks or increased contributions from the private sector or non-profit organizations, rather than direct funding measures"[60]. No matter how the program operates, if it entails some form of discrimination against foreign cultural goods and it is not paid directly in the form of payments to domestic producers, it runs the risk of being challenged on the basis of Article III of GATT 1994.

[55] *Canada—Certain Measures Concerning Periodicals*, *supra* note 50, sec. VII.

[56] DS/23/R, BISD, 39S/206, ¶ 5.10, (June 1992).

[57] This is also the view expressed in Trevor Knight, *The Dual Nature of Cultural Products: An Analysis of the World Trade Organization's Decisions Regarding Canadian Periodicals*, 57 UNIVERSITY OF TORONTO FACULTY OF LAW REVIEW 165, 179–80 (1999).

[58] For a similar assessment, *see* Aaron Scow, *The Sports Illustrated Canadian Controversy: Canada 'Strikes Out' in Its Bid to Protect Its Periodical Industry from U.S. Split-Run Periodicals*, 7 MINNESOTA JOURNAL OF GLOBAL TRADE 245, 277 (1998), who writes: "It is clear that the Panel and not the Appellate Body rendered the more viable solution to the postal rate subsidy issue. Allowing the postal rate subsidy makes sense from both a cost-effectiveness standpoint and a policy-based standpoint".

[59] *See* for instance, for a Canadian program, *Income Tax Act*, Chap. 1, (5th Supp.) RSC 1985, as amended, Art. 125.4 and *Income Tax Regulations*, 1978, C. 945 as modified; for a provincial program, see Income Tax Act, Lois refondues du Québec, C. I-3, Art. 1029.8.34 to 1029.8.36

[60] OECD, *Policy and Regulatory Issues for Network-Based Content Services*, Doc. DSTI/ICCP/IE(96)9/FINAL, p. 16

Article III of GATT 1994 was at the root of another complaint in the cultural sector brought before the WTO by the United States in June 1996. The complaint concerned Turkey's imposition of a tax on the showing of foreign films that was not imposed on the showing of domestic films.[61] Following unsuccessful consultations, a panel was constituted in February 1997 to hear the case. Canada reserved its third-party rights to the dispute. However, on July 14, 1997, both parties notified the DSB of a mutually agreed solution,[62] the United States having decided to drop the matter after Turkey agreed to equalize any box office tax on the showing of domestic and foreign films. On December 16, 1997, the Turkish Council of Ministers published a regulation which lowered the tax on foreign films from twenty-five per cent to ten per cent, while raising the tax on domestic films from zero to ten per cent.[63] This mutually agreed solution is not without interest. It gives support to closely-related schemes used by a number of European countries whereby a non-discriminatory tax is raised at the point of exhibition and is paid into the budget of a national public funding agency for the development of cinema production.[64] The French version of that type of policy was the subject of discussion until the very end of the Uruguay Round negotiations.[65]

(e) Article XI—Quotas. With regard to Article XI of GATT 1994, the Split-Run Periodicals Panel found that a prohibition on the importation of special edition periodicals, including split-run or regional editions, that contain advertisements primarily directed to a Canadian market was a clear violation of Article XI:1 that could not be justified under any of the general exceptions of Article XX. Canada had argued that the import prohibition under Tariff Code 9958 could be justified under Article XX (d) of the GATT, which concerns measures "necessary to secure compliance with laws or regulations which are not inconsistent with the provisions of this Agreement", as a measure intended to secure the attainment of the objectives of Section 19 of the Income Tax Act, which allows for the deduction of expenses for advertising directed to the Canadian market on condition that the advertisements appear in Canadian editions of Canadian periodicals. But the Panel found that the measure was not necessary to secure compliance with the Act in question because the two pursued different objectives.[66] This finding was not appealed by Canada.

2. The Agreement on Subsidies and Countervailing Measures
Even if a subsidy is compatible with Article III of GATT 1994, it remains subject to the provisions of the *Agreement on Subsidies and Countervailing Duties* ("SCM Agreement") which supplements Articles VI and XVI of GATT 1994 by providing more

[61] *WTO Focus*, no. 16, February 1997, p. 6.

[62] *Turkey—Taxation of Foreign Film Revenues*, complaint by the United States, (WT/DS43), June 1996: *Overview of the State-of-Play of WTO Disputes, Settled or Inactive Cases*: http://www.wto.org/english/tratop_e/dispu_e/stplay_e.doc

[63] *See* Office of the United States Trade Representative, *Press Release 97–108*, December 19, 1997: "U.S. Trade Representative Charlene Barshefsky Announces Resolution of WTO Dispute with Turkey on Film Taxes".

[64] *See* European Audiovisual Observatory, *Public Aid Mechanisms for the Film and the Audiovisual Industries in Europe*, section 1.2.2: http://www.obs.coe.int/oea_publ/funding/00002095.html. The countries in question are Norway, Sweden, Finland, France, Germany, Greece and Italy.

[65] The United States had asked that some of the revenues coming from France's eleven percent box-office tax should go to American film makers. This request was rejected. *See*: THE NEW YORK TIMES, *Europeans Reject U.S. Movie Compromise* (Roger Cohen), p. 1, December 14, 1993.

[66] WT/DS31/R, ¶¶ 5.4 to 5.11.

detailed rules and procedures. Article 1.1 of the Agreement contains a detailed definition of the term "subsidy" that leaves very few financial contributions by a government or public body outside of the scope of the Agreement, provided that they are, in law or in fact, specific.[67] Subsidies subject to the Agreement fall into one of three categories, that is prohibited subsidies (export subsidies and subsidies contingent upon the use of domestic over imported goods), non-actionable subsidies (subsidies that are not specific or relate to research, regional development and environmental requirements and meet certain criterion specified in the Agreement),[68] and actionable subsidies, which are not prohibited but can be challenged in the WTO dispute settlement system if they have an adverse effect on the interests of another Member (basically all other subsidies).

Three types of adverse effect are envisaged in the category of actionable subsidies. First, injury to a domestic industry caused by subsidized imports in the territory of the complaining Member. Second, serious prejudice, which usually arises as a result of adverse effects (e.g., export displacement) in the market of the subsidizing Member or in a third country market. Finally, nullification or impairment of benefits accruing under the GATT 1994, which arises most typically where the improved market access presumed to flow from a bound tariff reduction is undercut by subsidization.

Part V of the SCM Agreement deals with countervailing measures. It sets forth substantive requirements that must be fulfilled in order to impose a countervailing measure, as well as detailed procedural requirements regarding the conduct of a countervailing investigation and the imposition and maintenance in place of countervailing measures.

It is quite possible that subsidies on cultural goods could be challenged under this Agreement. The fact is that in many countries cultural goods in general benefit from a wide variety of subsidy programs. In many instances, however, the programs in question would be considered as non-specific or, if specific, not important enough to create serious prejudice to the domestic industry, which minimizes the risk of a challenge. But this might not be true in the case of the book industry, and above all in the case of the film industry where the amounts given are often quite large and benefit a limited number of producers.[69] It will be remembered in that respect that the United States complained in the 1970 GATT Catalogue of Non-Tariff Barriers about the subsidies granted by various States to their national film industries.[70] More recently, in December 2001, the Film and Television Action Committee, the Screen Actors Guild and a number of other American film and television unions filed a petition with the U.S. Department of Commerce and the International Trade Commission asking that they investigate whether Canada was subsidizing U.S. film production in Canada through tax credit and other incentives and, in the affirmative, asking that they consider imposing countervailing tariffs on such U.S.

[67] The term "specificity" is defined in Article 2 of the SCM Agreement, and essentially means that the subsidy is restricted, in law or in fact, to a limited number of enterprises or to a particular region of the country. For more detail, *see* Chapter 16 of this book.
[68] The category of non-actionable subsidies no longer exists, since the relevant provision in the Agreement had a five-year term and was not renewed. *See id.*
[69] It would not be true also in the case of export subsidies since they are presumed specific and are totally prohibited without regard for their importance: *see* Articles 2.3 and 3 of the SCM Agreement. There is disagreement regarding the extent to which trade in films should be treated as trade in goods as opposed to trade in services. This makes it all the more important to determine whether the subsidy program in question concerns goods or services since, as we shall see, there are no constraints yet on subsidies in the General Agreement on Trade in Services, save if a national treatment commitment has been given in the cultural sector, in which case subsidies will have to respect the national treatment obligation: *see* the discussion of GATS in Part B.1 below.
[70] *See supra*, note 6.

films produced in Canada [71]. Despite the opposition of the major producers, of independent producers, and of the Motion Picture Association of America to the initiative[72], the petitioners went ahead claiming to represent the majority of the approximately 270 000 people employed in the television and film production industry in the United States and asked the U.S. Department of Commerce and the U.S. International Trade Commission to investigate whether Canadian federal and provincial governments were subsidizing film production in Canada through tax credits and other incentives. However, establishing that a sufficient proportion of the industry supports a countervailing duty enquiry proved more difficult than expected and on January 11, 2002, the petition was temporarily withdrawn in order to strengthen it[73]. In June 2002, the Film and Television Action Committee released a legal memo prepared by a leading law firm which outlined the various international trade remedy actions that members of the U.S. industry could take in response to film and television subsidies provided by the Canadian federal and provincial governments and announced by the same occasion its intention to launch a Section 301 petition with the U.S. Trade Representative in the very near future.[74] Whether the petition on countervailing duties will be filed again in light of that development remains to be seen. But if countervailing duties were to be imposed on American films produced in Canada, it could have considerable implications in view of the fact that many States (Australia, South Africa, Ireland, Great Britain among others) offer similar incentives and that a large number of State governments within the United States equally offer a broad range of incentives to the film production industry[75]. More importantly, it would tend to support the view that trade in cinematographic films comes under trade in goods, a view that a number of countries are not ready to accept.

A challenge to a cultural subsidy program could be mounted in the WTO under Part III (actionable subsidies) of the SCM Agreement, or under a domestic countervailing law (which must comply with Part V (countervailing measures) of the SCM Agreement). In both instances, it would be necessary to demonstrate that the subsidized products and the affected products are "like products", which is not particularly obvious in the case of cultural products.[76] According to Article 15.1, footnote 46, the expression "like

---

[71] The petition was filed on December 4, 2001. *See Petition on 'Runaway' Productions Filed*, LOS ANGELES TIMES, December 5, 2001; for the text of the petition, see the site of the International Trade Commission: http://www.usitc.gov/, Dockets, no 701-TA-427 (prelim)

[72] The Motion Picture Association, through its President and CEO Jack Valenti, even claimed that the petition on countervailing duties was a "direct incentive to a trade war": see Jack Valenti Press Releases, December 4, 2001, http://www.mpaa.org/jack/

[73] *Runaway Productions Petition to be Withdrawn*, LOS ANGELES TIMES, January 11, 2002.

[74] For the content of that memo, see the site of the FTAC: < http://www.ftac.net/html/2-ftacstewart.html>. In essence, the memo describes the three basic remedies available to the FTAC which are a Section 301(a) investigation by filing a petition with the Office of the United States Trade Representative ("USTR"), a Section 301(b) investigation by filing a similar petition with the Office of the USTR and finally a petition with the U.S. Department of Commerce and the U.S. International Trade Commission under U.S. domestic law, requesting the initiation of an investigation that could lead to the imposition of offsetting tariffs on imports of Canadian film and television productions. Regarding this last remedy, the memo recognized that that the difficulties encountered in defining the industry for "standing" purposes were not trivial but could be overcome. As for the petitions with the USTR, it expressed a preference for a Section 301 (a) investigation rather that a Section 301 (b) investigation.

[75] See Martha Jones, *Motion Picture Production in California,* California State Library, California Research Bureau, CRB 02–001 (2002) (http://www.library.ca.gov/html/statseg2a.cfm). See also *The Migration of U.S. Film and Television Production,* United States Department of Commerce, International Trade Administration, January 2001, 89.

[76] *See* Article 6.3 and 15.1 of the SCM Agreement.

product" is to be interpreted throughout the Agreement to mean "a product that is identical, i.e. alike in all respects to the product under consideration, or in the absence of such a product, another product which, although not alike in all respects, has characteristics closely resembling those of the product under consideration". The notion of "like product" in the context of the SCM Agreement was examined in the report of the panel in *Indonesia—Certain Measures Affecting the Automobile Industry* where it was found to be quite narrow: "It is not enough that the products have characteristics which resemble the [domestic product]; rather they must have characteristics which "closely" resemble [it]".[77] The Panel added:

> Although we are required in this dispute to interpret the term "like product" in conformity with the specific definition provided in the SCM Agreement, we believe that useful guidance can nevertheless be derived from prior analysis of "like product" issues under other provisions of the WTO Agreement. Thus, we note the statement of the Appellate Body in Alcoholic Beverages (1996)731 that, in this context as in any other, the issue of "like product" must be considered on a case-by-case basis, that in applying relevant criteria panels can only use their best judgement regarding whether in fact products are like, and that this will always involve an unavoidable element of individual, discretionary judgement.[78]

The Panel relied on the physical characteristics of the different types of cars, on the industry-recognized system of market segmentation and on its own analysis of the facts to conclude that certain cars were like products and others were not. Although the Panel made only passing references to substitutability as a test, Edmond McGovern considers that de facto it placed most emphasis on the competitiveness and substitutability of products in its analysis.[79]

In the case of cultural goods, an analysis such as that made by the Panel would raise particular difficulties. Because they are characterized not so much by their physical characteristics than by their artistic and intellectual content, they cannot easily be compared one to another. In *Canada—Certain Measures Relating to Periodicals*, the Appellate Body found that "a periodical containing mainly current news is not directly competitive or substitutable with a periodical dedicated to gardening, chess, sports, music or cuisine".[80] A similar process of distinguishing between categories of cultural goods appears even more warranted in a situation where a "like products" test applies, considering that "like products" should be viewed as a subset of "directly competitive or substitutable" products and interpreted as a consequence more narrowly.[81] Thus, in the case of books, using the industry-recognized system of market segmentation, distinctions might have to be made according to the form of expression (poetry, theatre, essays, novels, criticism), according to the subject matter (history, biographies, arts, architecture and photography, children, home and garden, cooking, mystery and thrillers, reference, religion, romance, science and nature, science fiction, fantasy and horror, self improvement and inspiration, sports and adventure, travels, etc.). Even within a given category, further distinctions might have to be made according to the language of the book (French, Swedish, Japanese, Spanish, Arab, etc.)[82] or to the nationally defined content of the book

[77] WT/DS54/R, WT/DS55/R, WT/DS59/R, WT/DS64/R, 1998, ¶ 14.172

[78] *Id.*

[79] Edmond McGovern, *International Trade Regulation*, §12.42–1 (1995)

[80] *See supra*, note 47.

[81] As established in *Japan—Taxes on Alcoholic Beverages*: *see supra* note 54, ¶ 14.175

[82] In *Canada- Certain Measures Concerning Periodicals*, the Appellate Body decided that imported American split-run periodicals and Canadian periodicals were 'directly competitive or substitutable' essentially on the basis of a Canadian admission that English-language consumer magazines faced significant

(American history books, Canadian history books, etc.). Sorting out which categories of books could be considered as like products, as can be seen, might well entail some delicate decision-making on the part of the Panel.

3. The Anti-Dumping Agreement

Paradoxically, whereas most types of goods can be the object of an anti-dumping proceeding, it appears to be difficult to challenge cultural goods on this basis. The fact is that accusations of dumping in the cultural sector have been made on a number of occasions in the past but none have lead to an inquiry. Thus, one of the arguments put forward by the Canadian Magazine Publishers Association in support of the Canadian prohibition on the importation of split-run editions of foreign magazines was precisely that American publishers could engage in editorial "dumping" of content whose costs had already been recovered in the United States, providing them with an unfair advantage over Canadian magazines competing in the same market.[83] The same argument has also been made regarding American film producers who are often accused of dumping their films in foreign markets.[84]

Whether such situations can really be described as dumping has been questioned by many commentators. Hoskins, Finn, and McFadyen, for instance, argue from an economic point of view that in matters of dumping, "the relevant reference cost is not the production cost of the original but the incremental cost of supplying the additional market, but having said that, they immediately add: "For most traded products, this is not an important distinction, but for audiovisual products, it is crucial. The production cost extractd is always for the first copy, but the relevant cost is the low replication cost…plus the distribution cost"[85] Another author, W. Ming Shao, equally questions to what extent, "if at all, conventional notions of dumping apply to goods like films and television programs that possess strong public good characteristics."[86] Whatever the explanation given for the peculiar nature of audiovisual products (and of cultural goods in general), be it their public good characteristics or what has been called the "cultural discount"[87] that characterizes trade in such products, the fact remains that cultural goods appear to be different from other goods in this context.

---

competition for sales from imported U.S. consumer magazine: *supra,* note 52. But it did not examine the question whether French language periodicals in Canada where "directly competitive or substitutable" with American split-run periodicals.

[83] *See* Canadian Magazine Publishers Association, *Split-Run Editions: The Danger to the Canadian Magazine Industry and the Implications of Tariff Item 99* 58, September 19, 1992, p. 3. *See also* Val Ross, *Sports Illustrated Tackles Canada: Time Warner Plan Assailed as 'Dumping',* THE GLOBE AND MAIL, January 13, 1993, pp. C1–C2.

[84] *See* W. Ming Shao, "*Is There No Business Like Show Business? Free Trade and Cultural Protectionism*", 20 Yale Journal of International Law, 105, 121–122 (1995).

[85] Colin Hoskins, Adam Finn, and Stuart McFadyen, *Television and Film in a Freer International Trade Environment: US Dominance and Canadian Responses*, in MASS MEDIA AND FREE TRADE—NAFTA AND THE CULTURAL INDUSTRIES 63, 70 (eds. Emile G. McAnany and Kenton T. Wilkinson 1996). But it must be pointed out that under U.S. law, dumping analysis is based on fully-allocated costs and that Article 2.2.1 of the Anti-dumping Agreement itself refers to "all costs".

[86] W. Ming Shao, *supra* note 84, 123, (1995).

[87] The notion of cultural discount "captures the notion that a particular program (or feature film) rooted in one culture and thus attractive in that environment, will have diminished appeal elsewhere as viewers find it difficult to identify with the styles, values, beliefs, institutions and behaviour patterns being portrayed": Colin Hoskins and Stuart McFadyen, *Guest Editors' Introduction*, 16 CANADIAN JOURNAL OF COMMUNICATION 186 (1991).The notion was originally developed in Colin Hoskins and Rolf Mirus, *Reasons for the US Dominance of the International Trade in Television Programmes*, 10 MEDIA, CULTURE AND SOCIETY 499–515 (1988).

If an antidumping investigation involving cultural goods was nevertheless launched, it would be necessary to establish first that dumping is effectively taking place and second to what extent dumped products are causing injury to domestic products. The basic definition of dumping in the WTO Anti-Dumping Agreement is the sale for export at a price lower than the comparable price, in the ordinary course of trade, of the like product when destined for consumption in the exporting country.[88] In the case of films, it would not be difficult to establish that they are often sold abroad at a price substantially lower than the comparable price in the exporting country since this is a common practice. What significance must be attributed to such differences in prices, however, needs to be considered in light of the previous remarks of Ming Shao. Once dumping is established, it must be shown that the dumped imports are, through the effects of dumping, causing injury to the domestic production of like products.[89] As in the SCM Agreement, the notion of "like products" is defined to mean "a product which is identical, i.e. alike in all respects to the product under consideration, or in the absence of such a product another product which, although not alike in all respects, has characteristics closely resembling of those of the product under consideration."[90] It would not be surprising therefore to see the same type of difficulties as discussed in connection with the application of the SCM Agreement to cultural goods arise in the case of the AD Agreement.

4. The Agreement on Safeguards
The notion of adapting the safeguards clause of Article XIX of GATT 1947 to fit the particular case of cultural goods is not new. In a protocol annexed to the UNESCO's *Convention on the Importation of Educational, Scientific and Cultural Goods* (Florence Agreement), the United States, as a condition of its signature, effectively obtained for itself a safeguard clause that was in essence a reproduction of article XIX of GATT, but without any explicit reference to compensation.[91]

The *Agreement on Safeguards* does not treat cultural goods differently from other goods, and should not be overlooked as a means of helping cultural industries seriously

---

[88] *Agreement on the Implementation of Article VI of the General Agreement on Tariffs and Trade*, Article 2.1

[89] *Id.*, Article 3.5 and 3.6.

[90] *Id., Article 2.6*

[91] UNESCO, *Protocol annexed to the Convention on the Importation of Educational, Scientific and Cultural Goods,* 1950. The first paragraphs read as follows: "The contracting States, in the interest of facilitating the participation of the United States of America in the Agreement on the Importation of Educational, Scientific and Cultural Materials, have agreed to the following: 1. The United States of America shall have the option of ratifying this Agreement, under Article IX, or of accepting it, under Article X, with the inclusion of the reservation hereunder. 2. In the event of the United States of America becoming Party to this Agreement with the reservation provided for in the preceding paragraph 1, the provisions of that reservation may be invoked by the Government of the United States of America with regard to any of the contracting States to this Agreement, or by any contracting State with regard to the United States of America, provided that any measure imposed pursuant to such reservation shall be applied on a non-discriminatory basis". The reservation itself reads in part as follows:

"(a) If, as a result of the obligations incurred by a contracting State under this Agreement, any product covered by this Agreement is being imported into the territory of a contracting State in such relatively increased quantities and under such conditions as to cause or threaten serious injury to the domestic industry in that territory producing like or directly competitive products, the contracting State, under the conditions provided for by paragraph 2 above, shall be free, in respect of such product and to the extent and for such time as may be necessary to prevent or remedy such injury to suspend, in whole or in part, any obligation under this Agreement with respect to such product".

injured by the importation of like or directly competitive products.[92] It is the new vehicle through which measures may be applied pursuant to Article XIX of GATT 1994 and the basic conditions for its applications are essentially those of that Article (an increase of imports of any product which is causing, or which is likely to cause, serious injury to the industry), except for requirements that the injury should occur "as a result of unforeseen developments and of the effect of the obligation incurred . . . under this agreement" which has not been repeated in Article 2.1 of the Safeguards Agreement. But the Appellate Body, in *Korea—Definitive Safeguard Measure on Imports of Certain Dairy Products*, ruled that Article XIX had to be read together with the Agreement so that the requirements in question remain effective.

To see how the Safeguards Agreement would apply in the case of cultural goods, let us assume that as a result of the WTO decision in *Canada—Certain Measures Concerning Periodicals*, serious injury, understood in the sense of Article 4.1 (a) of the Agreement as "a significant impairment in the position of the domestic industry", is caused to the Canadian periodical industry. Canada, arguably, could consider that such injury occurs as a result of an unforeseen development and of the effect of an obligation incurred under the Agreement and consider that it is justified under the Safeguards Agreement in suspending a GATT obligation in whole or in part for such time as may be necessary to prevent or remedy such injury. Before doing so, however, Canada would have to demonstrate that the injury is the result of an increase in quantities of imports, absolute or relative to domestic production, as prescribed in Article 2.1. Unfortunately, it is sometimes impossible to prove such increase in view of the fact that the intellectual content of magazines (and of most cultural goods for that matter) can easily be separated from their material support for the purpose of import. In the actual facts at the origin of the Periodicals case, the intellectual content of *Sports Illustrated* was imported electronically into Canada and printed there with the result that there was no imports of goods actually taking place. As we shall see later in discussing the distinct treatment of cultural goods and services, this particular problem has taken a new dimension with the transmission of "digitized products such as music, films, software or 'books' on the internet.

Even if it was possible to have recourse to the Agreement because evidence of an actual increase of imported split-run periodicals exists, Canada would still have to offer adequate trade compensation to the United States in the form of reduced tariffs on other products, as it would have a duty to maintain a substantially equivalent level of concessions and other obligations; in the absence of an agreement, the United States could suspend substantially equivalent restrictions.[93] But if the safeguard measure conforms to the Agreement and results from an absolute increase in imports, the compensation requirement does not apply for the first three years.[94] Whether Canada would be interested in following such a course of action remains to be seen in view of the limited protection offered by the Safeguards Agreement and of the relative complexity of the procedure regarding compensation; but the possibility is there.

---

[92] Stacie I. Strong makes this suggestion in *Banning the Cultural Exclusion: Free Trade and Copyrighted Goods*, 4 DUKE JOURNAL OF COMPARATIVE AND INTERNATIONAL *Law* 93, 105 (1993). Laurence G.C. Kaplan, discussing the possible use of Article XIX by the European Community to justify the *Television Without Frontiers* directive, mentions that this possibility was examined by Hollywood lobbyists at the end of the 1980s. *See The European Community's 'Television Without Frontiers' Directive: Stimulating Europe to Regulate Culture*, 8 EMORY INTERNATIONAL LAW REVIEW 255, 314 (1994).

[93] *Agreement on Safeguards*, Article 8.1, .2.

[94] *Id*, Article 8.3.

B. Trade in Cultural Services

Apart from the European Union with its rules regarding the free movement of services dating back to the Treaty of Rome of 1958, trade in services has only recently become the object of compulsory agreements. The OECD does have a *Code on Current Invisible Transactions*, but it is not compulsory.[95] The *Canada–US Free Trade Agreement*, concluded in 1988, was in effect the first international trade agreement to include specific, fairly detailed and compulsory provisions concerning trade in services. The two governments agreed in essence to extend the principle of national treatment to the providers of a list of commercial services established in an annex to the Chapter on services ; this obligation was prospective in this sense that it did not required either government to change anything to existing laws and practices.[96] These were further developed in the *North American Free Trade Agreement* of 1992, which draws, for its Chapter 12 on services, on the experience of the Uruguay Round negotiations on services. Chapter 12 of NAFTA establishes a set of basic rules and obligations (national treatment, most-favoured-nation treatment, prohibition to impose a local residency requirement) aimed at facilitating trade in services between the Parties. It applies to all measures affecting cross-border trade in services not otherwise excluded from coverage; furthermore, each Party can lodge reservations aimed at maintaining non-conforming measures or preserving the ability to enact new non-conforming measures in specific sectors.

1. The General Agreement on Trade in Services ("GATS")

Contrary to what was suggested in Europe and even in Canada immediately after the conclusion of the Uruguay Round negotiations, GATS does not contain a cultural exception clause.[97] Early in the negotiations, Canada argued in favour of the inclusion of such a general clause that would have covered all cultural services, but dropped the idea for lack of support. The proposal made by the EC in the last days of the negotiations concerned only audiovisual services and did not fare better. The proposal in question, described during the negotiations as a "cultural specificity clause" instead of a "cultural exception clause," envisaged three different modifications or additions to the text of the agreement. The first would have specified that in future negotiations on services, the specific needs of the member States concerning the preservation of their national culture would be fully recognized. The second would have amended GATS Article XV to provide explicitly that the negotiations to be undertaken on subsidies following the entry into force of the Agreement would take into consideration the flexibility necessary for the member States to pursue their national goals with respect to culture. Finally, an interpretative note added to the Annex to Article II of the GATS would have specified that co-production agreements could be maintained beyond the maximum period of ten years envisaged in the Annex. None of these suggestions was discussed in detail, and the proposal was quickly dropped.[98] In the end, the EC simply decided not to include audiovisual services in its list

[95] For the text of the Code, *see*: http://www1.oecd.org/daf/investment/legal-instruments/invisibe.pdf. The OECD codes are implemented through policy reviews and country examinations, relying on "peer pressure" to encourage liberalisation.

[96] *Canada—U.S. Free Trade Agreement*, Chapter 14.

[97] *See* R. Conlogue, *Taking a Stand for the Cinematic National Soul,* THE GLOBE AND MAIL (Toronto), 21 December 1993, p. A-12, where the author writes: "There is a general rejoicing among European and Canadian Film Makers about the French triumph at the GATT negotiations last week".

[98] *See* Ivan Bernier, *Commerce international et cultures nationales: le débat sur la clause d'exception culturelle dans les négociations de l'Uruguay Round*, in Mario Beaulac and Francois Colbert, INDUSTRIES CULTURELLES NATIONALES ET MONDIALISATION DES MARCHES, 45, 60–61 (1994).

of specific commitments, and Canada did the same for cultural services in general. At first sight, therefore, no distinction is made between cultural services and other services in the GATS. However, looking at the fundamental obligations contained in the Agreement, one immediately realizes that enough room was left for those members willing to limit their undertakings in the cultural sector to allow them to do so; and in the end, a good many did exactly that.

The first basic obligation of Members of the GATS is that of Article II, paragraph 1, which provides for the granting of most-favoured-nation treatment to all services and service suppliers of all Members, whether specific commitments have been made or not. The pertinence of this provision in the field of culture is well illustrated by the 1998 EU complaint against Canada concerning film distribution services which was based to a large extent on GATS Article II:1.[99] However, under paragraph 2 of that same Article, a "Member may maintain a measure inconsistent with paragraph 1 provided that such measure is listed in, and meets the conditions of, the Annex on Article II Exemptions." The conditions in question provide that all exemptions granted for a period of more than five years should be reviewed and that in principle exemptions should not exceed a period of ten years. A large number of MFN exemptions have been taken in regard to audiovisual services. Counting the European Community as a single entity, a total of 33 MFN exemptions[100] specifically applying to the audiovisual sector are in place, most of which concern cinema and television co-production agreements and regional funding arrangements inscribed in the Annex on Article II, for reasons having to do essentially with national and regional cultural identity.[101]

An interesting question that arises with regard to co-production agreements exemptions is whether they cover only the agreements in force before January 1, 1995, or whether they cover all co-productions agreements including those concluded after January 1, 1995. According to Article 2 of the Annex on Article II Exemptions, " [a]ny new exemption applied for after the date of entry into force of the WTO Agreement shall be dealt with under paragraph 3 of Article IX of that Agreement". Depending on the interpretation given to the term "exemption", one might be justified in considering, in light of that provision, that post-January 1, 1995, co-production agreements constitute new exemptions. But in practice, quite a number of such agreements have been concluded since January 1, 1995. In some instances, the exemptions covering those agreements are described in a language which explicitly indicates that they apply to existing as well as to future co-production agreements ; in other instances, the language of the exemption

---

[99] *Canada—Measures Affecting Film Distribution Services*, WT/DS117/1 (1998). The complaint was dropped a few months later when the company at the origin of the case, Polygram, was bought by a Canadian company.

[100] The 33 exemptions covering audiovisual services are by: Australia, Austria, Bolivia, Brazil, Brunei Darussalam, Bulgaria, Canada, Chile, Columbia, Cuba, Cyprus, Czech Republic, Ecuador, Egypt, European Community, Finland, Hungary, Iceland, India, Israel, Liechtenstein, New Zealand, Norway, Panama, Poland, Singapore, the Slovak Republic, Slovenia, Sweden, Switzerland, Tunisia, United States and Venezuela. The eight general MFN exemptions potentially impacting audiovisual services are by: El Salvador, Malaysia, Peru, Philippines, Sierra Leone, Thailand, Turkey and the United Arab Emirates. WTO, Council on Services, Audiovisual Services, *supra*, note 43, ¶ 31.

[101] For examples of specific exemptions see GATS/EL/82 and GATS/EL/33 for Sweden and Finland, and GATS/EL/92 for Venezuela. The member states of the EC are also covered by the broader exemptions taken by the EC which include not only co-production agreements and financial support programs (such as the Media and Eurimages programmes and the Nordic Film and TV fund) but also the EC Television Broadcasting directive (Television Without Frontiers) and which specify that the exemptions in question cover existing and future measures of that type. *See* GATS/EL/31.

is less clear and only a mention that the exemption applies to all countries suggests that it covers new agreements.[102]

But the most important provisions of GATS are to be found in Part III of the Agreement which deals with the specific commitments of members. Following the pattern originally developed in the GATT for trade in goods, GATS provides that its members, beyond the general commitment of Part II (MFN treatment, transparency, etc.) should negotiate with other members specific commitments in sectors of their choice concerning national treatment and market access. In practice, few states have made such commitments in the cultural sector. A WTO document mentions in this respect that only nineteen members (thirteen at the conclusion of the Uruguay Round negotiations, six more as a result of accession) have made market-opening commitments in the audiovisual sector, including four developed countries (the United States, Japan, New Zealand and Israel) and fifteen developing countries, and that many of these commitments include various types of limitations.[103] India, for instance, included motion picture and video tape distribution services, but only one hundred titles could be imported per year, and the designated authority had to certify that the motion pictures in question had either won an award in an international film festival, participated in any of the official sections of the specified film festivals, or received favourable reviews in prestigious film journals.[104] Canada, as mentioned above, made no market-access or national-treatment commitments on any cultural services. It even went to the extent of excluding musical scores, audio and video recordings, books, magazines, newspapers, journals, and periodicals from its commitments in the sector of wholesale trade services.[105] Clearly there is some reluctance on the part of GATS members to undertake obligations in this area.[106] The fact is that once a Member has made a commitment with regard to a particular category of services, it cannot easily withdraw the commitment.[107] New Zealand, which had committed in 1993 not to have recourse to quantitative restrictions in the audiovisual sector, was reminded of this fact in no uncertain terms following its Government's pledge in 2001 to introduce format-specific quotas for local content for radio and broadcast television.[108] The Office

---

[102] The EC (GATS/EL/31), Chile (GATS/EL/18) and the Czech Republic (GATS/EL/26) are examples of Members whose exemption explicitly refers to existing and future agreements. Canada, who has signed no less than 21 co-production agreements since January 1, 1995, provides an example of a Member whose exemption does not refer to future agreements but is described as being applicable to all countries (GATS/EL/16). For the text of those agreements, *see* http://www.telefilm.gc.ca/04/43.asp. A situation less than clear is that of those nineteen states that have signed and ratified the European Convention on Cinematographic Co-production (under the auspices of the Council of Europe) after January 1, 1995 (see Convention 147: http://conventions.coe.int/Treaty/EN/cadreprincipal.htm). The Convention provides in its Article 4 that: "European cinematographic works made as multilateral co-productions and falling within the scope of this Convention shall be entitled to the benefits granted to national films by the legislative and regulatory provisions in force in each of the Parties to this Convention participating in the co-production concerned".

[103] *See supra*, note 43, ¶¶ 24–26 and Table 9.

[104] GATS/SC/42, p. 8. Most of these limitations, however, have subsequently been dropped by India.

[105] GATS/SC/16, p. 47

[106] Christopher Arup, in *The New World Trade Organization Agreements: Globalizing Law Through Services and Intellectual Property*, 2000, writes in this regard: "The GATS has added to the pressure on those national measures which were designed to ensure that less powerful and mainstream voices, particularly local ones, enjoyed access to distribution channels. Nevertheless, for the time being, many countries have availed themselves of the opportunities inherent in the GATS itself to maintain limitations on their exposure to the open-trade and free-market norms of the WTO" (p. 301).

[107] Article XXI admittedly provides for modification or withdrawal of any commitment in a member's schedule but subject to compensation.

[108] New Zealand, Ministry for Culture and Heritage, Department Forecast Report 2001, p. 9: http://www.mch.govt.nz/publications/dfr2001/MCH 2001 DFR.pdf. A study conducted in New Zealand

of the United States Trade Representative, in its *National Trade Estimate Report on Foreign Trade Barriers 2001*, pointed out that such an action would violate New Zealand's commitments under the GATS.[109]

With respect to subsidies, Article XV of the GATS simply recognises that, in certain circumstances, subsidies may have distortive effects on trade in services, and asks that members enter into negotiations with a view to developing the necessary multilateral disciplines to avoid such distortive effects. According to Dr. Mario Kakabadse of the WTO Secretariat, "[t]here is no presupposition as to what [the disciplines] will contain or how different they will be from rules on subsidies in the goods area. Like all GATT/WTO negotiations, they will take place on the basis of consensus and it would seem unlikely that governments would abandon their explicit right to support film production."[110] In view of the substantial financial support given by many governments to their cultural industries, these negotiations should obviously be followed with care.[111] However, because of the inherent complexity of developing guidelines in this area, the negotiations in question have progressed very slowly since their beginning, in 1995, in the context of the Working Party on GATS Rules.[112] it remains unclear for the moment to what extent there is a real consensus on the need for such guidelines.

Even though there are currently no multilateral disciplines on subsidies as such in the GATS, subsidies are not totally beyond the reach of the Agreement. The Agreement does apply, for instance, in a situation where access to domestic subsidies is granted to certain States and not to others. A concrete example of this in the cultural sector is that of cinema and television co-production agreements and regional support arrangements which provide preferential access to funding: but for the exemption regime of Article II, paragraph 2, of GATS, as we have seen, those agreements would clearly have been in violation of the MFN obligation of Article II, paragraph 1. The Agreement also applies to subsidies when members list a sector in their Schedule of commitments without any limitation concerning national treatment. National treatment then requires governments providing subsidies to domestic services suppliers to make equivalent subsidies available to foreign services providers operating in the country. This explains why the United States,

---

had shown in that respect that the proportion of local content relative to total schedule time had diminished since 1995 and that when compared with ten other countries, New Zealand stood at the bottom end of the spectrum with only 24 percent. New Zealand On Air, *Broadcasting And Cultural Issues At The Start Of The New Millennium*: http://www.nzonair.govt.nz/media/policyandresearch/otherpublications/issues.pdf

[109] Office of the United States Trade Representative, NATIONAL TRADE ESTIMATE REPORT ON FOREIGN TRADE BARRIERS 2001, under New Zealand. Had New Zealand abstained from taking market access commitments in the audiovisual sector during the Uruguay Round negotiations and put in place quotas, as envisaged in 2001, they could have benefited from the position adopted by the United States in its July 1, 2002, Proposals for Liberalizing Trade in Services, where it simply "requests countries to schedule commitments that reflect current levels of market access in areas such as motion picture and home video entertainment production and distribution services, radio and television production services, and sound recording services". *See* United States Mission—Geneva, Press-2002: http://www.us-mission.ch/press2002/0702liberalizingtrade.html.

[110] Mario A. Kakabadse, *The WTO and the Commodification of Cultural Products: Implications for Asia*, 22(2) MEDIA ASIA 71–77 (1995).

[111] In a 1998 background note prepared by the Secretariat for the Working Party on GATS Rules which analyzes, on the basis of information provided in the Trade Policy Reviews, subsidies for services sectors, aids to the audiovisual industries are the most frequently mentioned type of subsidies: see doc. S/WPGR/W/25 (26/01/98).

[112] *See* the note on conceptual issues relating to subsidies prepared by the Secretariat: Doc. S/WPGR/W9. For the most recent report of the Working Party on GATS Rules, dated October 4, 2001, *see* doc. S/WPGR/6. *See also* Gilles Gauthier, with Erin O'Brien and Susan Spencer, *Déjà Vu or New Beginning for Safeguards and Subsidies Rules in Services Trade*, in *GATS 2000*: NEW DIRECTIONS IN SERVICES TRADE LIBERALIZATION, 165, 176–181(eds. Pierre Sauvé and Robert M. Stern 2000).

in one of its few limitations on specific commitments in audiovisual services, explicitly mentioned grants from the National Endowment for the Arts that are only available for individuals with US citizenship or permanent resident alien status, a clear indication that in its view such grants, in the absence of a limitation, would be incompatible with national treatment.[113] New Zealand has similarly indicated in its list that assistance to the film industry through the New Zealand Film Commission is limited to New Zealand films as defined in Section 18 of the *New Zealand Film Commission Act 1978*.[114] In practice, the majority of members have included limitations to their national treatment commitments that apply to all subsidy practices.[115]

With regard to emergency safeguard measures, Article X of the GATS calls for negotiations on the subject based on the principle of non-discrimination. It is more explicit than Article XV as to the time frame for such negotiations, declaring that the results "shall enter into effect on a date not later from three years from the date of entry into force of the WTO Agreement," i.e. January 1, 1998. However, negotiations on safeguards proved more complex than expected, and on December 1, 2000, the Council for Trade in Services adopted a decision stipulating that such negotiations were to be completed by March 12, 2002.[116] This deadline unfortunately could not be met and on July 25, 2002, the Working Party on GATS Rules decided to postpone to March 15, 2004, the finalization of the negotiations under Article X of the GATS.[117] The problems encountered includes such questions as the significance of the concept of imports in a context where services can be delivered in four different modes (cross-border trade, commercial presence, consumption abroad, and presence of natural persons), and the question of what constitutes the domestic industry providing like or directly competitive services, necessary to establish a causal link between the imported service and the injury suffered by the domestic industry.[118] This last question is particularly important for cultural services, which, as we have seen in the case of cultural goods, are inherently difficult to compare. It remains to be seen therefore whether the new emergency safeguard measures that are envisaged for services will truly be helpful in answering the problems of cultural industries in difficulty as a result of the obligations assumed under the Agreement.

2. Basic Telecommunications

This survey of the cultural impact of the GATS would not be complete without a word about the GATS Annex on Telecommunications, the Ministerial Decision on Basic Telecommunications, and the Fourth Protocol to the GATS with its commitments in basic telecommunications. Under the GATS Annex on Telecommunications, host governments undertake to provide foreign companies with access to, and the use of, public telecommunications networks and services on reasonable and non-discriminatory terms for the provision of scheduled services such as banking services, computer services, and enhanced telecommunications. Most telecommunications commitments contained in the 1994 Schedule covered "value-added" services rather than "basic" services, as

[113] GATS/SC/90, p. 46.
[114] GATS/SC/62, under audiovisual services
[115] *See* Gauthier, O'brien and Spencer, *supra*, note 112, p. 177
[116] WTO News, Press 217, 2 April 2001: *WTO Services Talks Press Ahead*. For an overall view of the evolution of these negotiations, *see* the Reports of the Working Party on GATS Rules. In the Report dated October 4, 2001, differing views continued to be expressed regarding the desirability and feasibility of an emergency safeguard mechanism (ESM) in services; see Doc. S/WPGR/6.
[117] GATS, Doc. S/WPGR/7, 25/07/2002
[118] For a detailed discussion of these problems, *see* Gauthier *et al., supra* note 112, at 166–176.

negotiations on the latter, according to the *Decision on Negotiations on Basic Telecommunications* of December 15, 1993, were to continue up to April 1996.[119] Interestingly, measures affecting the cable or broadcast distribution of radio or television programming were excluded under Paragraph 2(b) of the Annex.

The negotiations on basic telecommunications, after an extension of the deadline of April 1996 in the hope of reaching a "critical mass" of sufficient offers from the key telecom markets, eventually led to the tabling, in February 1997, of 55 offers covering 69 governments, with enough substance in the eyes of the U.S. Government to constitute an agreement. These commitments are annexed to a one-page Protocol to the General Agreement on Trade in Services, the Fourth Protocol on basic telecommunications. The formal entry into force of the commitments was scheduled for January 1, 1998,[120] but where a participant's commitments for particular services are to be phased in, the actual implementation would take place on the date specified in the schedule. Generally speaking, participant governments have made commitments to allow competitive supply (defined as permitting two or more suppliers) on voice telephone service, on data transmission services, in leased circuit services, have granted access for cellular/mobile telephone markets, and included various other commitments in areas such as satellite-related communications or regulatory disciplines.

What kind of impact could the Annex on Telecommunications and the Fourth Protocol on basic telecommunications have on trade in cultural goods and services? Two consequences are immediately apparent, one concerning content requirements, the other investment controls. Though the question of content requirements was not on the agenda of the negotiations that led to the Annex on Telecommunications and the Fourth Protocol, it is clear that in the U.S. view, the next step in the gradual opening of national markets to foreign telecom service suppliers will touch directly upon that question. The *US–Mexico DBS Protocol* of November 1996, annexed to the *US–Mexico Satellite Agreement*[121] signed earlier in April 1996, as well as the *U.S.–Argentina Framework Agreement and Protocol for Direct-to-Home Satellite Services and Fixed-Satellite Services*[122] of June 5, 1998, can be seen from that point of view as a prototype of things to come. Significantly, the two Protocols limit domestic content restrictions either side can place on satellite programming to only a "modicum" of total programming, "thereby increasing opportunities for U.S. program content producers".[123] More importantly, the new U.S. approach regarding the treatment of electronic commerce in bilateral and multilateral trade negotiations, as it emerges concretely from its free trade agreements with Chile and Singapore, establishes a clear link between a pro-competitive and fully liberalized telecommunications sector and the development of electronic commerce. It asserts, as one of its basic

[119] *Decision on Negotiations on Basic Telecommunications*, December 15, 1993, Article 5. For the text of the decision, *see*: http://www.wto.org/english/docs_e/legal_e/50-dstel.pdf

[120] *See WTO Focus*, no. 16, February 1997, p. 1–2 for an account of what is described as a "historical agreement."

[121] *Agreement between the Government of the United States of America and the Government of the United Mexican States Concerning the Transmission and Reception of Signals from Satellites for the Provision of Satellite Services to Service Users in the United States of America and the United Mexican States*, signed April 28, 1996, and *Protocol Concerning the Transmission and Reception from Satellites for the provision of Direct-to-Home Satellites Services in the United States of America and the United Mexican States*, signed November 8, 1996.

[122] Federal Communications Commission (FCC), Report No. IN 98–27, *International Bureau Announces Conclusion of U.S.–Argentina Framework Agreement and Protocol for Direct-to-Home Satellite Services and Fixed-Satellite Services,* June 5, 1998.

[123] *Id.*

principles, that trade barriers to the free flow of content in digital products do not exist today and should not be created in the future. These two agreements are the first ones to be signed by the United States to include chapters on electronic commerce, which is described as "a breakthrough in achieving certainty and predictability in ensuring access for products such as computer programs, video images, sound recordings and other products that are digitally encoded".[124] Similarly, with regards to investment controls, the pressure exerted by the United States during the basic telecommunications negotiations for the elimination of investment controls in the telecommunications sector, although it did not lead to a result that was entirely to the its satisfaction, has nevertheless forced a country such as Canada to increase substantially the level of foreign investment allowed into Canada in that sector. That in turn will make it definitely more difficult to maintain the existing controls over foreign investment in the communications sector, particularly in a situation where a domestic telecommunication concern is itself involved in the area of communications. It is noteworthy from that point of view that in its July 1, 2001 proposals for liberalizing trade in services, the United States, in addition to the sectoral requests, has made selective requests that countries remove unclear, discriminatory, or market-restricting procedures and investment barriers.[125]

The pressure to eliminate content restrictions and investment control restrictions is not however tied exclusively to actions undertaken by the United States and various other countries at the international level. Technological development, convergence, and the globalization of the economy, more than anything else, are at the root of this movement towards the opening of national telecommunication and communication markets and, as shown by the incredible development of the Internet, it will be difficult to stop that movement. This has led certain Canadian observers to declare, perhaps a little prematurely, that the notion of "Canadian content" is something of the past.[126] In the US–Mexico DBS Protocol and the U.S.–Argentina DBS Protocol, there is still room left for domestic program content requirement; and in Europe, the quotas of the "Television Without Frontiers" directive, notwithstanding some acrimonious debates on the subject, are still in place. Even the recently concluded *Chile–U.S. Free Trade Agreement* (2002) and the *U.S.–Singapore Free Trade Agreement* (2003) include reservations that make room for content requirements in broadcasting services.[127] What could happen, however, is a gradual switch, over a period of time and taking into account the particular situation of each State, from the content requirement approach to an approach making use of a variety of

---

[124] United States Trade Representative, Summary of U.S.-Chile FTA Electronic Commerce Chapter: [http://www.ustr.gov/new/fta/Chile/summaries/Chile%20Ecommerce%20Summary.PDF]. For the text of the *Chile–U.S. Free Trade Agreement*, see [http://www.chileusafta.com/] or [http://www.ustr.gov/new/fta/Chile/text/index.htm] and for the text of the *U.S.–Singapore Free Trade Agreement*, see [http://www.ustr.gov/new/fta/Singapore/consolidated_texts.htm] or [http://www.mti.gov.sg/public/FTA/frm_FTA_Default.asp?sid=36]. In their chapters on electronic commerce, these two agreements provide in essence (1) that the supply of a service using electronic means (defined as means using computer processing) benefit from the obligations in the service chapter (MFN treatment, national treatment and market access) subject to reservations; (2) that the Parties do not apply customs duties on digital products transmitted electronically (digital products being defined as "computer programs, text, videos, sound recordings and other products that are digitally encoded and transmitted electronically, regardless of whether a Party treats such products as a good or a service under its domestic law"); (3) and that trade in such digital products benefit from MFN treatment and national treatment.

[125] United States Mission—Geneva, Press Releases 2002, *U.S. Proposals for Liberalizing Trade in Services"*, under *"Commercial presence"*.

[126] *See* for instance Jonathan Bestinger, *The Electronic Highway, A Survey of Domestic and International Law Issues*, 29 UNIVERSITY OF BRITISH COLUMBIA LAW REVIEW 199 (1995).

[127] *See supra,* note 124

financial and regulatory incentives in order to preserve a national presence in the cultural field.

C. Investment

The Uruguay Round did not yield a genuine agreement on investment. There is, to be sure, the *Agreement on Trade-Related Investment Measures ("TRIMs")*, but it is limited strictly to a narrow range of trade-related investment measures affecting goods only, in effect clarifying Articles III and XI of the GATT. Furthermore, in the context of GATS, a number of countries have undertaken commitments that affect foreign investment in services.

A number of important States, including the United States, maintain various forms of controls over investment in the cultural sector (mostly in relation to ownership of radio and television stations). One only has to look at the compendium of bilateral investment treaties concluded by Western Hemisphere countries that was prepared by the Organization of American States (OAS) Trade Unit,[128] or at the similar instrument prepared for the members of APEC,[129] to realize the extent of the practice. But there is growing pressure, particularly on the part of the United States, to have such controls abolished. For example, the *Investment Canada Act* and the *Canadian Broadcasting Act* have been identified by the United States as barriers to U.S. exports.[130]

Following the failure of the OECD negotiations on a multilateral agreement on investments ("MAI"), a number of States suggested that the negotiations in question should be transferred to the WTO for inclusion in the Millenium Round agenda. Whether it would have become part of the Seattle agenda considering the lack of consensus on the subject and the outright opposition of the United States is a moot question. The Doha Ministerial Conference, as we know, has decided that it could become part of the agenda of the new round of negotiations after the Fifth Session of the Ministerial Conference on the basis of a decision to be taken, by explicit consensus, at that Session on modalities of negotiations.[131] Meanwhile, however, the possibility that new commitments regarding investment will be made in the context of the GATS negotiations is not to be discarded, which, if it happens, could interfere with the negotiations of the new instrument on investment.[132]

1. The WTO Agreement on Trade-Related Investment Measures (TRIMS)

Notwithstanding its limited scope, the WTO *Agreement on Trade-Related Investment Measures* could be used to challenge investment measures related to trade in cultural goods that are inconsistent with the national treatment obligation of Article III:4 of GATT 1994, or with the Article XI:1 requirement to eliminate quantitative restrictions. An illustrative list of such measures, annexed to the TRIMS Agreement, includes

---

[128] Organization of American States, Trade Unit, *Bilateral Investment Treaties in the Western Hemisphere*, A Compendium prepared for the Free Trade Area of the Americas Working Group on Investment (1996).

[129] APEC, *Survey of Impediments to Trade and Investment in the APEC Region*, A Report by the Pacific Economic Cooperation Council for APEC (1995).

[130] Office of the United States Trade Representative, 2001 NATIONAL ESTIMATE OF FOREIGN BARRIERS, Canada, Investment.

[131] WT/MIN(01)/DEC/W/1, 14 November 2001: http://www-chil.wto-ministerial.org/english/thewto_e/minist_e/min01_e/mindecl_e.pdf

[132] This possibility is discussed by Pierre Sauve in an article entitled *Scaling Back Ambitions on Investment Rule-Making at the WTO*, 2 JOURNAL OF WORLD INVESTMENT 529 (2001).

1 [...] those which are mandatory or enforceable under domestic law or under
   administrative rulings, or compliance with which is necessary to obtain an advantage, and which require:
   (a) the purchase or use by an enterprise of products of domestic origin or from
       any other domestic source, whether specified in terms of particular products,
       in terms of volume or value of products or in terms of a proportion of volume
       or value of its local production [...]
2 [...] those which are mandatory or enforceable under domestic law or under
   administrative rulings, or compliance with which is necessary to obtain an advantage, and which restrict:
   (a) the importation by an enterprise of products used in or related to its local
       production, generally or to an amount related to the volume or value of local
       production that it exports [...]

An investment measure concerning cultural goods that incorporated performance requirements would be particularly vulnerable to an attack under the TRIMS agreement.
Such requirements are to be found, for instance, in the *Investment Canada Act* and the
Investment Canada Regulations. An investment subject to review under the *Investment
Canada Act* may not be implemented unless the Minister responsible advises the applicant that the investment is likely to be of net benefit to Canada. Among the factors to be
taken into consideration for that purpose are "the effect of the investment on the level
and nature of economic activity in Canada, including the effect on employment, on the
utilization of parts, components and services in Canada and exports from Canada."[133] Requirements of this type that affect trade in cultural goods could potentially be challenged
under TRIMS.

2. Investment Liberalization Through GATS

A large number of WTO members have made commitments with regard to investment
in the context of the GATS. This has been done through the liberalization commitments
of members under mode 3 of the supply of services, that is, the supply of a service
through commercial presence. The majority of the 29 States that have made commitments
concerning market access in the audiovisual sector indicated that they had no restrictions
with regard to the supply of services through commercial presence; however, for those
which had made their commitments subject to restrictions, one of the most common
restrictions appearing in their schedules of commitments, other than those concerning
natural persons, concerned limits on foreign shareholdings.[134]

The process of investment liberalization through the GATS was successful enough
to suggest to Pierre Sauvé and Christopher Wilkie that for the time being, "GATS may
well offer the only serious vehicle to strengthen the WTO's existing investment-related
rules and achieve a greater number of bound liberalization commitments."[135] Through
a pragmatic and incremental approach, they suggest, "there are useful things to be done
within the multilateral system to improve and sustain investment as a force of integration
among nations."[136] Among other possibilities, they mention clarifying the definition of

---

[133] *Revised Statutes of Canada*, Chap. 28 (1st Supp.), Art.20

[134] WTO, Doc. S/C/W/40, ¶ 29.

[135] Pierre Sauve and Christopher Wilkie, *Investment Liberalization* in SAUVE and STERN, *supra* note 86, at
346

[136] *Id.*

commercial presence so as to expand the scope of covered investments, strengthening the investment protection features of GATS, and promoting greater transparency on investment incentives. But can such an approach be applied in the case of cultural services? Interestingly, Pierre Sauvé and Karsten Steinfatt, in a recent paper, suggest in that regard that

> [. . .] the time may be near when members of the international community have to contemplate more seriously the scope for, and the content of, a WTO-anchored set of disciplines aimed at striking a balance between the potentially competing logics of trade and investment liberalisation on the one hand, and of cultural diversity on the other.[137]

The lessons from the MAI negotiations from that point of view are interesting. Views diverged on how to address cultural matters in the MAI. Two distinct approaches had been proposed, the first one through a general exception for cultural measures, and the second through country-specific reservations. France had proposed a text arguing in favour of an exception clause and provided a draft that read as follows:

> Nothing in this agreement shall be construed to prevent any Contracting Party to take any measure to regulate investment of foreign companies and the conditions of activities of these companies, in the framework of policies designed to preserve and promote cultural and linguistic diversity.[138]

A number of other countries, including Australia, Belgium, Canada, Ireland, Italy, Portugal and Spain, indicated some degree of support for the idea of a cultural exception clause. However, in view of the strong opposition of the United States and some other countries to any form of cultural exception, the chances of success of the French proposal would have been slim had the MAI negotiations continued.

Another way of dealing with cultural products would have been to permit existing non-conforming measures to be maintained, or certain types of activities to be excluded, provided that they were covered by country-specific reservations. This approach, used in the GATS and NAFTA, appeared to have a greater chance of success, although it remained to be seen whether the United States would have accepted country-specific reservations that excluded cultural services altogether. All delegations involved in the OECD negotiations had already submitted a preliminary list of specific reservations. Although a majority had not submitted reservations which directly affected culture, most of them, including the United States, Italy, Turkey, the United Kingdom and the Netherlands, did reserve the right to maintain foreign investment restrictions in the media and broadcasting sectors, and four countries had submitted substantial lists of culture-related reservations. Canada, as well as Australia and Korea, stated that they had prepared their list on the assumption that there would be a general exemption for culture.

What this suggests is that further investment liberalization through GATS could prove a difficult task in the cultural sector to the extent that Members who were not ready to make concessions in that regard in the MAI negotiations retain in the GATS negotiations both the possibility of excluding the sector in question altogether, or, if they make commitments, make them subject to reservations.

---

[137] *See* Pierre Sauve and Karsten Steinfatt, *Towards Multilateral Rules on Trade and Culture: Protective Regulation or Efficient Protection?*, in PRODUCTIVITY COMMISSION AND AUSTRALIAN NATIONAL UNIVERSITY 2000, ACHIEVING BETTER REGULATION OF SERVICES, AusInfo, Canberra, 2000.
[138] OECD, Doc. DAFFE/MAI/NM(98) 126

D. Intellectual Property Rights

Intellectual property rights and cultural products are closely associated, so much so that cultural products have sometimes been described as essentially copyrighted goods.[139] The fact is that the remuneration of cultural creators and producers depends largely on the recognition of intellectual property rights and that a lack of implementation of those rights will immediately affect them. Both the Universal Declaration of Human Rights and the International Covenant on Economic, Social and Cultural Rights explicitly recognize the close relationship between the protection of copyright and culture. Article 27 of the Universal Declaration of Human Rights reads for example as follows:

1) Everyone has the right freely to participate in the cultural life of the community, to enjoy the arts and to share in scientific advancement and its benefits.
2) Everyone has the right to the protection of the moral and material interests resulting from any scientific, literary or artistic production of which he is the author

It does not come entirely as a surprise therefore to find that national copyright protection measures are covered by an express mention in GATT Article XX (d). Notwithstanding the fact that such measures act as a restraint on trade, they are specifically included within the reference to measures "necessary to secure compliance with laws or regulations which are not inconsistent with the provision of this Agreement".

Until recently, most of the attention in the intellectual property rights field was devoted to the search for common approaches and to the adaptation of basic principles to new situations. Such concerns were mostly addressed in the context of organizations such as the World Intellectual Property Organization (WIPO) and UNESCO. But a growing concern over an apparently uncontrollable flood of illegal copies has prompted the intervention of other international organizations in the field of intellectual property rights, a concern centred on the implementation of property rights. The Uruguay Round *Agreement on Trade-Related Aspects of Intellectual Property Rights* addresses in particular this concern.

The *Agreement on Trade-Related Aspects of Intellectual Property Rights* ("TRIPs") consolidates the disciplines of the *Berne Convention* (literary and artistic works), the *Geneva Convention* (phonograms) and the *Rome Convention* (neighbouring or related rights), the Paris Convention (industrial property) into a single undertaking, backed up by enforceable dispute settlement measures. Members are free to determine the appropriate method of implementing the TRIPs agreement within their own legal system, but they must give to the nationals of other members the national treatment required in the Paris, Berne and Rome conventions, subject to the national treatment exceptions contained in these same treaties. Article 9 of the TRIPS agreement is of particular interest because while it requires compliance with the substantive obligations of the Berne Convention, it makes an exception for moral rights, which are not recognized by the United States.

As far as concerns neighbouring or related rights, they are subject to the conditions, exceptions and limitations authorized by the Rome Convention.[140] If this raises no particular problems for most States in so far as concerns the rights that are explicitly recognized, it does seem to raise a difficulty, at least in the eyes of the United States, in the case of

---

[139] *See* Stacie I. Strong, *supra* note 92. For a recent study of the place of copyright industries in the U.S. economy prepared for the International Intellectual Property Alliance, *see* STEPHEN E. SIWEK, COPYRIGHT INDUSTRIES IN THE U.S. ECONOMY—THE 2002 REPORT (2002)

[140] Article 14 of the Convention.

copying. The U.S. Government has repeatedly asserted its right under the national treatment obligation to share in the benefits of programs (usually taking the form of a levy on blank audio cassettes) put in place by various governments to compensate for private copying, even though nothing similar is offered in the United States.[141] Whether such programs could effectively be challenged under TRIPS remains to be seen, as the Rome Convention explicitly authorizes reciprocity,[142] and as Article 4 (b) of TRIPS authorizes reciprocity in the case of privileges or immunities granted by a Member in accordance with the provisions of the Bern or Rome conventions.

The importance of TRIPS as an instrument to protect intellectual property rights in the cultural sector is evidenced by the number of complaints brought before the WTO in that regard. As of September 2002, no fewer than nine complaints had been formally notified to the Dispute Settlement Body, seven of them by the United States,[143] and two by the EC.[144] Most of them have been settled at the consultation level, the only exception being the complaint of the EC against the United States. In most cases, the basis for the complaint was failure to grant the required copyright and neighbouring rights protection under domestic law.[145]

III. The Trade and Culture Debate: Basic Issues and Solutions

A. The Basic Issues

1. The Dual Nature of Cultural Products: Entertainment Products or Vectors of Cultural Identity?

Two radically opposed views regarding cultural products underpin the culture and trade debate.[146] One approach sees cultural products as entertainment products that are similar, in commercial terms, to any other product and therefore completely subject to the rules of international trade. The other view is that cultural products are essential instruments of social communication which convey values, ideas, and meaning, and thus contribute to fashioning the cultural identity of a given community. As such, they should be excluded from the reach of international trade agreements. Neither extreme is satisfactory.

When considered as commercial goods, cultural products are difficult to exclude from the scope of trade agreements, although this is probably more true in the case of multilateral agreements than in the case of bilateral agreements.[147] To the extent that cultural products are exchanged with financial gain in mind, they bring into question

---

[141] *See* Office of the United States Trade Representative, NATIONAL TRADE ESTIMATE REPORT ON FOREIGN TRADE BARRIERS, 2001, http://www.ustr.gov/html/2001_eu.pdf

[142] Article 15(1) of the Convention.

[143] The complaints in question concerned Japan (WT/DS28/1), Ireland (WT/DS82/1), the EC (WT/DS124/1, WT/DS115/1) Denmark (WT/DS83/1), Sweden (WT/DS86/1) and Greece (WT/DS/125/1).

[144] One complaint was against the United States (WT/DS160/1) and one against Japan (WT/DS42/1)

[145] The exception being the complaint of the EC against the United States which concerned the interpretation of the TRIP's Agreement.

[146] *See,* e.g., Judith Beth Prowda, *U.S. Dominance in the 'Market Place of Culture' and the French Cultural Exception,* 29 JOURNAL OF INTERNATIONAL LAW AND POLITICS (1996–1997) 193,198; Knight, *supra* note 58, at 167–169; Glen M. Secor, *"Cultural Industries in United States-Canada Free Trade: The Canadian Book Publishing Industry as a Case Study",* 11 BOSTON UNIVERSITY INTERNATIONAL LAW JOURNAL 299, 302 (1993)

[147] The free trade agreements between Canada and Chile, between Canada and Israel and between Canada and Costa Rica for example, are not applicable to measures adopted or maintained with respect to cultural industries. The Free Trade Agreement between the European Union and Mexico and between the European Union and Chile totally exclude for their part audiovisual services from the Services Chapter: see below notes 176 and 177.

various and competing interests which can only be reconciled within an appropriate legal framework. Not only would leading exporters of cultural products be opposed to any exclusion of the latter from the legal framework of international trade (among the countries that have made commitments in the audiovisual sector in GATS, one predictably finds the United States, India, Japan, Mexico and Hong Kong), but also countries that are beginning to develop or want to develop a presence on that market could be concerned at such a trend. Totally excluded from the multilateral trade regime, cultural products would be left without protection in the face of discriminatory or retaliatory measures from foreign countries.[148]

If, however, exclusion of cultural products from multilateral trade agreements does not constitute a realistic solution, it does not necessarily mean that they should be considered like any other product. To the contrary, it seems that refusal to recognize the particular nature of cultural products and their special role in adapting cultures to change will only lead to increased tension within the trade regime itself and give rise to a growing number of disputes in the cultural sector. As we have seen before, the lack of success of the European Community with its proposal for a cultural specificity clause at the end of the Uruguay Round did not put an end to the trade and culture debate. Quite the contrary: cultural conflicts increased in the following years, and the trade and culture debate itself took a new dimension.[149]

Not surprisingly, there is a growing tendency now to consider that this debate on the nature of cultural products needs to be concluded. As Switzerland stated in its communication to the Council for Trade in Services in the context of the present GATS negotiations:

> In fact, none of these two positions reflects the whole reality. For Switzerland, the audiovisual sector represents both an important field of commercial activity as well as a vector of cultural identity. The challenge for the trade policy consists therefore in reconciling these two views within a balanced solution that satisfies both sensibilities.[150]

Brazil, as we have seen previously, has expressed a similar view.[151] Even the United States accepts that the "all-or-nothing" approach to the audiovisual sector in the WTO should be rejected, but in its view the trade rules are flexible enough to take into account the special cultural qualities of the sector.[152] Within the European Union, the new Article 151, paragraph 4, of the consolidated text of the *Treaty Instituting the European Community*, which provides that "[t]he Community shall take cultural aspects into account in its action under other provisions of this Treaty, in particular in order to respect and to promote the diversity of its cultures", has opened the door to the recognition of the dual nature of cultural products. Not only has it become part of the official discourse but it has also been applied to the solution of concrete problems. Thus, in its *Resolution of 12 February 2001* on the application of national fixed book-price systems, the Council, after "recognizing the dual character of books as the bearers of cultural values and as merchandise and the need for a balanced assessment of the cultural and economics aspects of books", invites the Commission

[148] *See* Franklin Dehouse and Françoise Havelange, *Aspects Audiovisuels des Accords du GATT. Exception ou Spécificité Culturelle?* in Carine Doutrelepont, L'EUROPE ET LES ENJEUX DU GATT DANS LE DOMAINE DE L'AUDIOVISUEL 117 (1994).
[149] *See* Part I above.
[150] *See supra*, note 28
[151] *See supra*, note 29
[152] *See supra,* note 30

...when applying competition rules and rules on the free movement of goods, to take account of the specific value of the book as a cultural object and the importance of books in promoting cultural diversity, and of the cross-border dimension of the book market.[153]

International organisations with an explicit cultural mandate such as UNESCO and the Francophonie have also acknowledged in recent years the dual nature of cultural products.[154]

The apparent consensus on the subject seems to justify at first sight the conclusion that recognition of the dual nature of cultural goods is no longer an issue. The problem is that there is no agreement on the concrete implications of such a recognition. Between the "do nothing" approach and the cultural exemption approach, as we shall see below, the full range of options remains open. This is where a better understanding of the exact nature of the WTO's concern with regard to culture becomes important.

2. The Nature of the Concern: From the Treatment of Cultural Goods and Services to the Preservation of Cultural Diversity

As pointed out previously,[155] in the last five years there has been a significant change of perception within the WTO concerning the trade and culture debate. From an issue that revolved almost exclusively around the treatment of cultural goods and services in international trade agreements, it has now become one that is more broadly framed in terms of the preservation of cultural identities and cultural diversity. This development in a sense was predictable. Trade liberalization effectively fosters new forms of social organization that call into question existing values, lifestyles, and ways of doing things or, to put it differently, cultural identity. When these changes upset people, trade liberalization itself comes under pressure.[156] In this sense, it was inevitable that the further development of trade liberalization would raise the question of the impact of such a process on cultural identity and cultural diversity. What is less clear is whether this new concern displaces the previous concern with the treatment of cultural goods and services in trade agreements.

The fact that trade liberalisation has an impact on national cultures does not mean that any trade initiative that might influence these cultures in one way or another should be rejected. To assert the contrary would be to attempt to freeze culture and national identity and lend them a meaning that would only benefit those people who hope to turn them into instruments of political control. Any national culture that is to remain vibrant and alive must adapt over time to a variety of changes, both internal and external. The real issue that trade liberalization poses for national cultures is whether the changes that it brings about in values, lifestyles, and ways of doing things detract from the opportunity to "promote and maintain a pluralistic public space where citizens can access and participate in cultural life, which is itself necessary for public life".[157] In other words, it is not so much a question of whether the liberalization of trade, with its underlying commercial concerns, affects values and traditional lifestyles, but whether this liberalization is understood and accepted and whether it leaves enough space beyond the simple producer-consumer

---

[153] *Official Journal* no C 073 of 06/03/2001, p. 0005–0005

[154] *See supra*, note 25.

[155] *See* Part I, *supra*.

[156] *See* Mary E. Footer and Christoph Beat Graber, *Trade Liberalization and Cultural Policy*, 3 JOURNAL OF INTERNATIONAL ECONOMIC LAW 115, 134–135 (2000).

[157] *See* Marc Raboy, Ivan Bernier, Floran Savageau, and Dave Atkinson, DEVELOPPEMENT CULTUREL ET MONDIALISATION DE L'ECONOMIE 77(1994).

relationship for the cultural expression of citizens, itself an essential element of the democratic process.[158]

Unfortunately, it is not clear whether trade liberalization is having on balance a positive effect on the maintenance of a public space for the cultural expression of citizens when the issue is considered from the standpoint of the national production of cultural goods and services. There are at least three reasons for concern. The first, somewhat older but still very present concern is related to the influx of foreign cultural products (films, television programs, compact discs, books etc.), which in certain circumstances may stifle domestic cultural production, thereby depriving the affected communities of the symbolic discourse essential for their own development. The second concern has to do with the concentration of production and the marketing of cultural products by large industrial groups, and the consequent standardization of cultural expression under the influence of basically commercial imperatives. Independent production is often put at risk in such a context. The third, more recent concern, is with exclusion from the international cultural space as it is currently being constructed with the new information technologies (the Internet, etc.). Despite all the opportunities that these new technologies provide to express the diversity of cultures, there is a very real danger of a deep digital divide between those countries that have access to these technologies and those that do not. In all three cases, it is the basic right to cultural expression that is at stake. This is all the more alarming in that the creators of culture and cultural intermediaries play a key role in adapting cultures to change since they create a space where national values and foreign values can confront one another, as can the values and behaviours of the past and those of the future.

So in the end, the new concern of the WTO with the preservation of cultural diversity does not displace the previous concern with the treatment of cultural goods and services. On the contrary, it places it in a broader context where the issue of the treatment of cultural goods and services is considered in its relationship to the goal of preserving cultural identities and cultural diversity. What has changed is the perspective from which the issue is considered. Whereas the former perspective was essentially negative in the sense that its main concern was to find ways of excluding cultural goods and services from trade agreements, the new perspective puts the emphasis on a positive goal which is that of preserving cultural diversity, with the understanding that cultural diversity entails, on the one hand, the preservation of existing cultures and, on the other, the greatest possible openness to other cultures. This new perspective excludes *a priori* any solution to the trade and culture debate that is based either on the total exclusion of cultural goods and services from the scope of trade agreements or their total assimilation to other goods and services.

3. *The Diversity of Treatment: the Cultural Goods and Cultural Services Dilemma*
Another issue that has considerably gained in importance in recent years is that of the distinct treatment of cultural goods and services in the WTO. To say that certain agreements are applicable to cultural goods as opposed to cultural services implies that there is a clear distinction between cultural goods and cultural services. Unfortunately, that

---

[158] Footer and Graber, *supra*, note 156, write in this respect : "In our view, certain forms of media like art films and public service television programs have a key role to play in the fight against political fragmentation, as identified by Habermas, or in developing adequate responses to nondivisible conflicts, as identified by Hirschman" *See also* Jeffrey L. Dunoff, *The Death of the Trade Regime*, 10 EUROPEAN JOURNAL OF INTERNATIONAL LAW 733 (1998).

is not always the case. Thus, although films are specifically mentioned in Articles III and IV of GATT 1994 and duty concessions have been made in relation to films, the fact is that cinema has been considered as a service in the General Agreement in Trade in Services ("GATS"), in the OECD *Code on Invisible Current Transactions* and in *the United Nations Central Products Classification*.[159] The same ambivalence is reflected in dispute settlement procedures. In *Turkey—Taxation of Foreign Film Revenues*,[160] the U.S. complaint against Turkey was based on Article III of the GATT, but in *Canada—Measures Affecting Film Distribution Services*,[161] the EC complaint against Canada was based on Article II and III of GATS.

The possibility of conflict in the application of GATT and GATS raises a fundamental problem that was first examined in the WTO decision of June 1997 in *Canada—Certain Measures Relating to Periodicals*. The finding of the Panel that "[t]he ordinary meaning of the texts of GATT 1994 and GATS as well as Article II:2 of the WTO Agreement, taken together, indicates that the obligations under GATT 1994 and GATS can co-exist and that one does not override the other" was supported by the Appellate Body.[162] Specifically with respect to periodicals, the Appellate Body went as far as to say that "a periodical is a good comprised of two components: editorial content and advertising content. Both components can be viewed as having services attributes, but they combine to form a physical product—the periodical itself."[163]

Barely two months later, in *European Communities—Regime for the Importation, Sale and Distribution of Bananas*, the Appellate Body attempted to explain more fully its view on the subject of potential conflicts between trade agreements. It wrote:

> Given the respective scope of the two agreements, they may or may not overlap, depending on the measure at issue. Certain measures could be found to fall exclusively within the scope of GATT 1994, when they affect trade in goods as goods. Certain measures could be found to fall exclusively within the scope of GATS, when they affect the supply of services as services. There is yet a third category of measures that could be found to fall within the scope of both the GATT 1994 and the GATS. These are measures that involve a service relating to a particular good or service supplied in conjunction with a particular good. In all such cases in this third category, the measure in question could be scrutinized under both the GATT 1994 and the GATS. However, while the same measure could be scrutinized under both agreements, the specific aspects of that measure examined under each agreement could be different. Under the GATT 1994, the focus is on how the measure affects the goods involved. Under the GATS, the focus is on how the measure affects the supply of the service or of the service suppliers involved. Whether a certain measure affecting the supply of a service related to a particular good is scrutinized under the GATT 1994 or the GATS, or both, is a matter that can only be determined on a case-by-case basis.[164]

---

[159] *United Nations Central Products Classification Version 1.0, Code 96* (Doc. ST/ESA/STAT/Ser.M/77/Ver. 1.0)

[160] Doc. WT/DS43 (1996)

[161] *See supra*, note 99.

[162] Doc. WT/DS31/AB/R, June 30, 1997 Sec. 4. Canada was arguing in that case that the provision of the *Excise Tax Act* challenged by the United States was not a measure regulating trade in goods but rather a measure regulating trade in services (access to the advertising market).

[163] *Id.*

[164] Report of the Appellate Body, *European Communities—Regime for the Importation, Distribution and Sale of Bananas*, AB-1997-3, WT/DS27/AB/R (1997), ¶¶ 221–222. In 1998, by the Panel in *Indonesia—Certain Measures Affecting the Automobile Industry*, the same reasoning was extended by the panel to a situation which involved an apparent conflict between the Agreement on Subsidies and Countervailing Measures and the Agreement on Trade-Related Investment Measures. WT/DS54/R, WT/DS55/R, WTDS59/R, WT/DS64/r, 2July 1998, ¶¶ 14.52–14.53.

But this still leaves open the possibility that the exercise of a right under one agreement becomes the negation of a right under the other. This is what would have happened, for example, if India's limitations on film distribution in its specific commitments under GATS, although in full conformity with the agreement and accepted by all the parties to it, had been successfully challenged under GATT as a restriction on the import of a good.[165] Unless a line is traced somewhere between what pertains to trade in services and what pertains to trade in goods, conflicts of this nature appear inevitable.

The possibility that measures which involve a service supplied in conjunction with a particular good (or conversely a good supplied through a service[166]) might be scrutinized under both the GATS and the GATT 1994 is still questioned by many Members in view of the difference of obligations between the two agreements. In a 1999 document entitled "Digital Products: the Case for Services," which was prepared in anticipation of the GATS negotiations of 2000, the European Commission explained its position on digital products as follows:

> The legal nature of 'digitised products' (music, films, software or 'books' on the internet) is still under discussion in the WTO. We argue that all electronic deliveries—including digitised products'—are services and therefore the GATS applies. This is also the view of most other WTO Members and the WTO Secretariat. On the contrary, the US and to a certain extent Japan argue that while the transmission of those 'products' is a service, the 'products' themselves are analogue to goods and therefore fall under the GATT.[167]

The document replies to the U.S. argument that "there may be an advantage to a GATT versus GATS approach, since the former may provide for a more trade-liberalising outcome for electronic commerce," with the assertion that this remains a matter for discussion and that it is simply too early to decide whether members prefer GATT or GATS.[168] This document of the European Commission illustrates perfectly well the difficulty of using a criteria such as the good or service nature of a product in order to resolve a difference of views regarding the legal treatment of the product in question. In the field of culture, where many products have both goods and services components, the temptation to rely on the difference in the treatment of goods and services to solve immediate problems could be great. If such a development was to happen, it could, as we shall see now, complicate singularly the search for a long term solution to the trade and culture debate.

B. Possible Solutions

The possible solutions can be grouped in three distinct categories that can be described as the "Do Nothing" approach, the "Cultural Exception" approach, and the "New International Instrument" approach.

1. The "Do Nothing" Approach

This is the solution traditionally defended by the United States but it also has the support of some other WTO Members including Japan. It is based on the view that cultural goods and services are essentially entertainment products and as such should be treated just like any other products. It has been reiterated most recently in the communication of the United States concerning Audiovisual and Related Services in the context of the GATS

---

[165] Concerning the Indian exceptions in the film distribution sector, *see supra*, note 104.
[166] For example, a magazine provided through customers via Internet. *See* SCOW, note 58, *supra*, at 278.
[167] *See*: http://europa.eu.int/comm/trade/services/ecommerce/digi.htm at 1. *See also* Chapter 57 of this book.
[168] *Id.*, at 3.

2000 negotiations.[169] In the section of that document which deals with "Trade Rules and the Audiovisual Sector", the U.S. Government observes first that the debate over the audiovisual sector in the WTO

> has sometimes been framed as an "all-or-nothing" game. Some argue as if the only available options were to exclude culture from the WTO or to liberalize completely all aspects of audiovisual and related services. Presenting such stark options obscures a number of relevant facts.[170]

It goes on to assert that "[t]he all-or-nothing approach to the audiovisual sector in the WTO implies that trade rules are somehow too rigid to take into account the special cultural qualities of the sector. This is not the case."[171] To illustrate the flexibility of the system, reference is made to Article IV of GATT 1994, to the possibility of making full or partial commitments in the context of GATS, to the general exceptions of Article XIV of GATS and Article XX of GATT 1994 concerning measures necessary to protect public morals, and finally to the fact that GATS does not presently prevent governments from funding audiovisual services[172]. The obvious message behind these remarks is that the special cultural qualities of the audiovisual sector are adequately taken care of in the existing WTO regime. But interestingly, the U.S. Government for the first time also opens the door to some form of recognition of the need of each nation to foster its cultural identity:

> In conjunction with negotiated commitments for audiovisual services, Members may also want to consider developing an understanding on subsidies that will respect each nation's need to foster its cultural identity by creating an environment to nurture local culture. To this end, many Members subsidize theatrical film production. There is a precedent in the WTO for devising rules which recognize the use of carefully circumscribed subsidies for specifically defined purposes, all the while ensuring that the potential for trade distortive effects is effectively contained or significantly neutralized.[173]

Whether one can speak of a change of mind on the part of the United States on the sole basis of this proposal appears doubtful considering the well-entrenched position of the U.S. Government on the subject and the very restrictive terms used to describe the proposal itself. What it seems to indicate, however, is that the U.S. Government now recognises the existence of a problem.

A variant of this "do nothing" approach is the strategy that was adopted by a surprising number of countries during the GATS negotiations of not making any commitments in the audiovisual sector. This kind of passive resistance to the opening up of national audiovisual markets beyond the general disciplines and obligations of the GATS may at first glance appear to offer a simple solution. Indeed, it can be claimed that it is the only solution that remains realistically available in the context of the WTO for those States which consider that cultural services should not be treated as other services. To this day it remains the basic strategy of the European Union as well as of a number of other Members in the audiovisual sector[174]. But it is essentially a passive strategy that can be

---

[169] *See* note 30 *supra*.

[170] *Id*. at 2

[171] *Id*.

[172] *Id*. at 2–3.

[173] *Id*. at 3.

[174] *See* Commission of the European Communities, Communication from the Commission to the Council, the European Parliament, the Economic and Social Committee and the Committee of the Regions, *Principles and Guidelines for the Community's Audiovisual Policy in the Digital Age*, Doc. COM(1999) 657 final.

rapidly overtaken by events as the number of members willing to make liberalization commitments in the field of culture increases and with the development of horizontally-applicable disciplines in areas such as those of domestic regulation and subsidies.[175] Pressure along these lines will only mount with each passing negotiation. Already in the service negotiations currently underway, Switzerland has suggested that "possible solutions to the audio-visual issue could take the form of an Annex to the GATS on audio-visual services, or of any other suitable instrument, depending of the nature of the solutions to be elaborated."[176]

The "do nothing" approach does not really offer a long term solution to the trade and culture issue. In both variants, the refusal to take specific actions amounts in practice to a denial of the dual nature of cultural goods and services. In the first variant, it is their cultural nature that is denied, whereas in the second variant, it is their commercial nature.

2. The Cultural Exception Approach

The second type of approach raises at the outset a conceptual problem that needs to be clarified. In the trade and culture debate, reference is often made to cultural exceptions as a generic expression encompassing not only cultural exceptions as such but also cultural exemptions, cultural reservations and cultural waivers, as if these expressions were more or less synonymous. In fact, while they each convey the same basic idea that cultural goods and services should receive distinct treatment, they differ in the way in which they operate. Exemption clauses exclude purely and simply the goods and services covered from the scope of the agreement; exception clauses provide that certain goods and services will be exempted from the obligations and disciplines of the agreement provided they meet certain conditions; reservation clauses allow a member to maintain in existence clearly identified measures in force at the date of entry into force of an agreement notwithstanding the fact that that they do not conform to the obligations and disciplines of that agreement; waivers are granted in exceptional circumstances and usually for a limited period of time in order to except certain activities from an obligation imposed on a member.

(a) Cultural Exceptions. The only examples of cultural exceptions that are operational in the WTO context are Article IV and XX (f) of GATT 1994, both of which have been discussed previously. During the Uruguay Round, the European Commission did consider the possibility of having a cultural exception included in the general exceptions of Article XIV of GATS, which would have automatically made it subject to the requirements of paragraph (1) "that such measures are not applied in a manner which would constitute a means of arbitrary or unjustifiable discrimination between countries where like conditions prevail, or a disguised restriction on trade in services". But the idea was abandoned for lack of sufficient support within the European Community itself. At the end of the negotiations, the refusal of the European Community to make commitments in the audiovisual sector was erroneously described as a cultural exception by a number of

Within the framework of the preparations for the WTO Millennium Round, the principle of cultural diversity was consecrated in the Council of Ministers Conclusion of 26 October 1999, stating that "the European Union will ensure, that as in the Uruguay Round, that the Community and its Member States maintain the possibility to preserve and develop their capacity to define and implement their cultural audiovisual polices for the purpose of preserving their cultural diversity."

[175] For the last report of the Working Party on Domestic Regulation and the minutes of the last meeting, see WTO, Doc. S/WPDR/3 (2001-10-04) and S/WPDR/M8 (2001-10–02).

[176] *See supra*, note 28.

commentators in Europe, but the truth of the matter is that there is no cultural exception in the GATS.[177] There are also very few examples of cultural exceptions in regional trade agreements. It is definitely not a formula that has met with success.

(b) Cultural Exemptions. The best-known example of a cultural exemption is the one contained in the North American Free Trade Agreement ("NAFTA").[178] This clause stipulates that cultural industries are exempt from the provisions of the Agreement, except for certain limited exceptions. However, this exemption is only a partial one in that resorting to it opens the doors to retaliatory measures of equivalent commercial effect. As drafted, in fact, it does not constitute a true cultural exemption clause: all it says is that a party can, if it is willing to pay the price, maintain provisions on cultural industries that are inconsistent with its commitments. Examples of true cultural exemption clauses can be found in Canada's free trade agreements with Israel, Chile and Costa Rica, as well as in the bilateral investment agreements Canada has signed since 1995.[179] These clauses simply stipulate that the provisions of these agreements do not apply to either party's measures respecting cultural industries. Other examples are the *EU-Mexico Free Trade Agreement*, entered into force on July 1, 2000 (according to a decision of the EC/Mexico Joint Council dated February 27, 2001, the provisions of the agreement dealing with services do not cover audiovisual services) and Article 95 of the *Agreement establishing an association between the European Community and its Member States, of the one part, and the Republic of Chile, of the other part* (which explicitly excludes audiovisual services from the scope of the Chapter dealing with services).[180] The concrete impact of these examples remains limited, however, in the sense that these clauses have been negotiated within an exclusively bilateral context. There is nothing to indicate that they could easily be transposed, as is, into a multilateral context like the WTO. To the contrary, there is every reason to consider that a complete exemption of cultural products within such a context would be virtually impossible to achieve in view of the clearly expressed opposition of the United States.[181]

(c) Cultural Reservations. Cultural reservations, strictly defined, are not frequent in trade agreements.[182] A rare example is Canada's reservation concerning films in the OECD *Code of Liberalisation of Current Invisible Transactions*: as explained under item

---

[177] Dehousse and Havelange, *supra*, note 148 at 125.

[178] Article 2106 and Annex 2106 of the *North American Free Trade Agreement*.

[179] *Free Trade Agreement Between Canada and Chile* (entered into force July 5, 1997), Article O-06 and Annex O–06; *Free Trade Agreement between Canada and Israel* (entered into force January 1, 1997) Article 10.5; *Canada-Costa Rica Free Trade Agreement* (entered into force November 1, 2002), Article XIV.6. For the texts of those agreements and the list and the main elements of the bilateral investment agreements, see: http://www.dfait-maeci.gc.ca/tna-nac/reg-e.asp

[180] *See* for the agreement with Mexico: http://europa.eu.int/comm/trade/bilateral/mexico/fta.htm, and for the agreement with Chile: http://europa.eu.int/comm/external_relations/chile/assoc_agr/agrment.pdf

[181] In a study released in January 2001 by the International Trade Administration under the title *Impact of the Migration of U.S. Film and Television Production,* one can read the following assertion which clearly reveals the U.S. viewpoint on the subject: "At the same time, at UNESCO headquarters in Paris, efforts by France and Canada to create support for a proposal to remove cultural issues from the WTO and place them in a 'new instrument,' possibly UNESCO, found little support. The United States, although not a UNESCO member, made an intervention strongly opposing this idea".

[182] Under Article 21 of the Vienna Convention on the Law of Treaties, a reservation that is established with regard to another party "(a) modifies for the reserving State in its relations with that other party the provisions of the treaty to which the reservation relates to the extent of the reservation; and (b) modifies those provisions to the same extent for that other party in its relations with the reserving State".

H of Annex A of the Code, which mentions films among the covered transactions, "the provisions of this item do not apply to Canada, which, accordingly, has neither obligations nor rights thereunder".[183] But cultural reservations, understood in the sense of specific exceptions, are more frequent. In the *North American Free Trade Agreement*, for instance, Mexico has listed 3 cultural reservations in Annex I and II of the Agreement and Canada has lodged 1. In the *Chile–U.S. Free Trade Agreement* concluded on December 11, 2002, Chile lists five cultural reservations in Annex I and II of the Agreement and in the *U.S.–Singapore Free Trade Agreement* concluded in substance on January 16, 2003, Singapore lists two cultural reservations in Annex II of the Agreement.[184] In the OECD *Code of Liberalisation of Capital Movements*, not less than 15 members have lodged reservations concerning direct foreign investment in the cultural sector (audiovisual sector in particular) and in the *Code of Liberalisation of Current Invisible Transactions*, 7 members have lodged reservations concerning films.

(d) Cultural Waiver. Notwithstanding the possibility offered by Article XXV: 5 of the *GATT 1947*, and since 1995 by Article IX, paragraphs 3 and 4, of the *World Trade Organization Agreement*, no waiver for cultural products has ever been asked for to this day. However, in an article published in 1999, the suggestion has been made that recourse to the waiver provisions of Article IX, paragraphs 3 and 4, of the World Trade Organization Agreement, supplemented by the Understanding in Respect of Waivers of Obligations under the General Agreement on Tariffs and Trade 1994, could prove a more workable proposition than a cultural exception to resolve the trade and culture issue.[185] According to the author, Chi Carmody, "[e]xceptions, being difficult to implement and interpreted restrictively, appear to be inadequate tools to safeguard culture in a living, expansive manner."[186] In the scheme that she proposes, the waiver would be of a general application, somewhat along the lines of the Enabling Clause for developing countries. Members would be entitled to invoke the waiver to derogate from certain key WTO Agreement obligations (national treatment and general elimination of quantitative restrictions) with respect to cultural industries, with the proviso that the measures be taken only after a risk assessment conducted by an objective and impartial body and notification[187]. Whether such a scheme is realistic, however, remains to be seen. A serious obstacle as the author itself recognizes, is obviously the formal voting requirement of three-quarters of the entire WTO membership for a waiver, higher than the two-thirds majority now needed to add an exception to the WTO. Furthermore, the waiver in question, if adopted, would be for a fixed period of time and subject to revision not later than one year after it is granted and then reviewed annually until the waiver terminates.

3. The New International Instrument Approach

A last approach that is gaining support internationally is that of a new international instrument on cultural diversity. This solution was initially proposed by an advisory group set up by Canada's Department of Foreign Affairs and International Trade and composed of representatives of Canada's cultural industries. This group publicly released a report in February 1999, which recommended that Canada should pursue a New International

---

[183] OECD/C(61)89 of 12th December 1961 and C(63)154/FINAL of 3rd March 1964
[184] For the text of these two agreements, including the reservations, *see supra,* note 124
[185] *See* Chi Carmody, note 42, supra at. 309–320
[186] *Id.,* at 309–310.
[187] *Id.,* at 312–313

Instrument on Cultural Diversity (NIICD).[188] The recommendation was based in part on an assessment that a set of clear rules on measures that could and could not be used to promote cultural diversity was preferable to a policy of exempting culture from trade rules, because technological change and the "convergence" of industries in the cultural sector were creating uncertainty. The proposal has since then become the object of extensive discussion in various forums including non-governmental and governmental organizations. The hypothesis of an international instrument on cultural diversity is now mentioned as a legitimate objective and as a solution to be further explored in the Declaration on Cultural Diversity adopted by the Third Ministerial Conference on Culture held under the auspices of the Organisation Internationale de la Francophonie in Cotonou on June 15, 2001[189] and in the Action Plan attached to the Universal Declaration on Cultural Diversity adopted by the General Conference of UNESCO on November 2, 2001.[190]

At the close of its 166th session on April 11, 2003, the UNESCO Executive Board unanimously decided, at the request of some of its members[191], to add the question of "a preliminary study on the technical and legal aspects relating to the desirability of a standard-setting instrument on cultural diversity" to the agenda of the 32nd session of UNESCO's General Conference, set to begin on September 29, 2003.[192] On October 16, 2003, the General Conference unanimously requested that UNESCO prepare an international standard-setting instrument on cultural diversity. At the end of a long debate on the subject, delegates agreed that "cultural diversity, as regards the protection of the diversity of cultural contents and artistic expressions shall be the subject of an international convention." They asked the Director-General to undertake consultations on the subject with the World Trade Organization, the United Nations Conference on Trade and Development and the World Intellectual Property Organization. The resolution invites the Director-General to submit a first draft convention on the protection of the diversity of cultural content and artistic expression to the next session of the General Conference.[193]

The exact nature and content of the proposed convention are still a matter of discussion. However, on the basis of the work already done by the International Network on cultural Policy, some basic characteristics of that convention are beginning to emerge. Thus,

---

[188] NEW STRATEGIES FOR CULTURE AND TRADE, Canada, Department of Foreign Affairs and International Trade, Cultural Industries Sectoral Advisory Group on International Trade—Cultural Industries, Ottawa, February 1999, p. 33.

[189] International Organisation of the Francophonie, Declaration of Cotonou, III Ministerial Conference on Culture, Cotonou, June 15, 2001: http://www.france.diplomatie.fr/francophonie/actualite/decla_cotonou. pdf. The pertinent text reads as follows (author's translation): "We also agree that the Francophonie must support the principle of an international regulatory framework of a universal character for the promotion of cultural diversity. This international instrument would establish the legitimacy of governmental intervention in favour of the maintenance, establishment and development of cultural diversity."

[190] UNESCO, Press Release no 2001–120–6, *General Conference Adopts Universal Declaration on Cultural Diversity*, November 2, 2001. Article 1 of the Action Plan attached to the Declaration mentions among other objectives to be pursued by the Members: "Deepening the international debate on questions relating to cultural diversity, particularly in respect of its links with development and its impact on policy-making, at both national and international level; taking forward notably consideration of the opportunity of an international legal instrument on cultural diversity".

[191] Germany, Canada, France, Greece, Morocco, Mexico, Monaco and Senegal. See: http://www.unesco.org/exboard/fr/166ex1provf.pdf

[192] UNESCO—Executive Board, 166th session, Paris, April 4–16, 2003. Decisions Adopted by the Executive Board, item 3.4.3: "Preliminary study on the technical and legal aspects relating to the desirability of a standard-setting instrument on cultural diversity," doc. 166 EX/SR.10 (May 14, 2003).

[193] UNESCO, General Conference, 32nd Session, Press Release No. 2003–83, Paris, October 17.

although the possibility that it could take the form of an annex to the GATS on audiovisual services has been invoked[194], the prevailing view seems to be that the new international instrument should be negotiated outside of the WTO so as to provide a much-needed cultural viewpoint on the trade and culture issue. There also appears to be a consensus that the new instrument should be legally binding. It is symptomatic from that point of view that both the Cotonou Declaration on Cultural Diversity and the Action Plan annexed to the UNESCO Universal Declaration on Cultural Diversity, which do not constitute themselves legally binding instruments, refer to the opportunity of "an international legal instrument on cultural diversity". Regarding the normative content of the instrument, there is a widely held view that it should establish as a fundamental principle the right of States and governments to promote and preserve cultural diversity while maintaining an access as large as possible to other cultures[195]. This principle would itself be made explicit in rules dealing with various aspects of governmental intervention in the cultural sector. The instrument from that point of view, would provide a framework of reference for all those States that are concerned about the preservation of cultural identities and cultural diversity.

It is obviously difficult to evaluate at this stage the chances of success of the new international instrument approach as an answer to the trade and culture issue: too much remains uncertain about it. One thing that is unclear is how the new instrument might relate to the WTO legal regime. Nevertheless, the very idea of having an instrument on cultural diversity negotiated outside of the WTO could contribute to alleviating the concerns of former Director General Renato Ruggiero that the WTO might be called upon "to give answers to issues which are very real public concerns, but whose solution cannot rely on the trading system alone"[196] The fact is that in the absence of a clearly articulated cultural perspective on the subject, it is hard to see how the WTO could by itself come up with an adequate answer to the trade and culture issue.

IV. Conclusion

This survey of the treatment of cultural goods and services in international trade law has shown that there is still a good deal of ambivalence concerning the way they should be treated. The texts themselves, except for Article IV and Article XX (f) of GATT 1994, have little to say on the subject: cultural goods and services, apparently, are to be treated exactly like any other goods and services. But the actual practice within the WTO tells a different story. Upon closer examination, it appears that cultural goods do not always benefit from the same treatment as other goods. For instance, it is not easy to apply Agreements such as the Subsidies and Countervailing Measures Agreement, the Antidumping Agreement and the Safeguards Agreement to cultural goods because the value of such goods lies in their intellectual content rather than in their material content. More importantly, the WTO practice, as we have seen, provides ample evidence

---

[194] *See* for instance the Swiss communication to the Council on Trade in Services, supra, note 28, at ¶ 19. The Swiss suggestion, it should be pointed out, does not exclude the possibility of a distinct instrument that would be negotiated outside of the WTO.

[195] As was made explicit in the Cape Town meeting of the International Network on Cultural Policy. *See* Canadian Heritage, News Release, *Sheila Copps Participates in the Fifth Meeting of the International Network on Cultural Policy in South Africa,* Capetown, October 15, 2002: (http://www.canadianheritage. gc.ca/newsroom/news_e.cfm). For the text of the proposed convention that was adopted at the Sixth meeting, *see* the site of the International Network on Cultural Policy: http://206.191.7.19/meetings/2003/index_e.shtml

[196] *Supra*, note 17.

of a resistance to the assimilation of cultural goods and services to other goods and services.

Behind this ambivalence lies a fundamental question which is that of the specificity of cultural products. For some countries, cultural products do not differ from other products and therefore should receive exactly the same treatment. But other countries consider that they are fundamentally distinct and therefore should not be treated as other products. Recent developments, particularly in the context of the GATS negotiations on audiovisual services, suggest that this "all-or-nothing" approach to the problem is no longer acceptable. What is needed is a more balanced approach that would take into consideration the double nature of cultural products and contribute thereby to the preservation of distinct cultural expressions and identities

The search for an answer to the trade and culture issue has taken a new dimension in recent years with the realization that the development of new information technologies, globalization and evolving multilateral trade policies could have a damaging impact on cultural identities. As pointed out by Faouzia Zouari, "[translation] the precedence that economic imperatives take over social and political values, backed by the prodigious expansion of the information highway, is challenging national identities, sometimes driving them into retreat and even into aggressively asserting counter-models."[197] Since Seattle, it has become obvious that the cultural and social dimension of trade liberalization had to taken into account. Creators of culture and cultural intermediaries, from that point of view, play a key role in adapting cultures to change. That is why preserving diverse cultural expressions and cultural diversity more generally can be seen as an essential component of further trade liberalization.

Unfortunately, up until now the search for a balanced solution to the trade and culture quandary has centred for the most part around various forms of cultural exceptions designed to accommodate particular cultural concerns. This approach, to the extent that it gives priority to trade over culture, cannot be considered as a satisfactory solution. To address the question of the relationship between culture and trade exclusively from the standpoint of trade is to subject culture to commercial imperatives and thereby prevent it from playing its role. A satisfactory solution requires recognition of the fact that the multilateral trade regime cannot on its own provide answers to non-trade concerns. There is a growing literature nowadays that criticizes the tendency of the multilateral trade regime to get involved in non-trade matters and various ways of approaching that problem have been proposed, using concepts such as those of "subsidiarity" and "coherence", that suggest in general greater deference to outside expertise, whether national or international[198].

---

[197] Agence intergouvernementale de la Francophonie, Conférence des ministres de la culture de Cotonou, Travaux préparatoires, *Synthèse des travaux et des contributions*, by Fawzia Zouari, 2001, 7: http://confculture.francophonie.org/TrvxPrep/pdf/Synthese.pdf.

[198] *See* Gabrielle Marceau, "*A Call for Coherence in International Law. Praises for the Prohibition Against 'clinical isolation' in WTO Dispute Settlement*", 33(5) JOURNAL OF WORLD TRADE 87 (1999); Jeffrey L Dunoff, *The Death of the Trade Regime*, 10 EUROPEAN JOURNAL OF INTERNATIONAL LAW 733 (1998); Robert Howse and Kalypso Nicolaïdis, "*Legitimacy and Global Governance: Why Constituonalising the WTO is a Step Too Far*", in EFFICIENCY, EQUITY, LEGITIMACY THE MULTILATERAL TRADING SYSTEM AT THE MILLENIUM 227 (R.B. Porter, P. Sauvé, A. Subramanian and A. B. Zampetti eds. 2001); Stephan Ohlhoff and Hannes L. Schloemann, *Rarional Allocation of Disputes and 'Constitutionalisation: Forum Choice as an Issue of Competenc*e, in DISPUTE RESOLUTION IN THE WORLD TRADE ORGANISATION 302–329 (James Cameron & Karen Campbell eds. 1998); P. Sauvé and A. B. Zampetti, "*Subsidiarity Perspectives on the New Trade Agenda*", 3JOURNAL OF INTERNATIONAL ECONOMIC LAW 83 (2000); AMERICAN JOURNAL OF INTERNATIONAL LAW, *Symposium: The Boundaries of the WTO*, Volume 96 (1), 2002

If the solution to the cultural diversity issue cannot come from the trading system alone, then obviously a contribution coming from outside that system is essential. The declarations on cultural diversity that have been adopted in the last few years may be considered as a first step in the right direction but they are not sufficient. What is needed is an international legal instrument that would articulate from a cultural perspective the basic requirements for the preservation and promotion of cultural identities and cultural diversity. As Howse and Nicolaïdis put it, "instead of looking primarily within the WTO for the relevant structural principles", consideration could then be given to the "importance of non-WTO institutions and norms in treaty interpretation that represent values other than free or freer trade."[199] But until the principles and norms in question are clearly expressed in a multilateral cultural agreement, the risk remains that cultural considerations will continue to be addressed within the WTO from a strictly trade perspective and on a piecemeal basis, which will amplify the existing problems rather than help to solve them.

BIBLIOGRAPHY

Acheson, Keith, Maule, Christopher J., *Canada's Cultural Exemption—Insulator or Lightning Road ?* 20 World Competition (1996)

Atkinson, Dave, Mondialisation culturelle et accords commerciaux internationaux: un enjeux démocratique, in Bellavance, Guy, ed., Démocratisation de la culture ou démocratie culturelle?, Institut québécois de recherche sur la culture, Québec, 113 (1999)

Baker, Edwin, C., *An Economic Critique of Free Trade in Media Products*, 78 North Carolina Law Review 1358 (2000)

Bernier, Ivan, Lamoureux, Jean-François, *Les politiques du Canada et du Québec, l'Organisation mondiale du commerce (OMC) et l'Accord de libre-échange nord-américain (ALENA),* in Sauvageau, Florian, ed., Les politiques culturelles à l'épreuve. La culture entre l'État et le marché, Institut québécois de recherche sur la culture, Presse de l'Université Laval, 1996, p. 13

Bishop, Thomas, *France and the Need for Cultural Exception*, 29 Journal of International Law and Politics 187 (1997

Browne, Dennis, ed., *The Culture/Trade Quandary: Canada's Policy Options* (1998).

Carmody, Chi, *When 'Cultural Identity Was not at Issue': Thinking About Canada—Certain Measures Concerning Periodicals*, 30 Law and Policy in International Business 231, 255 (1999).

Carlson, Andrew M., *The Country Music Television Dispute: An Illustration of the Tensions Between Canadian Cultural Protectionism and American Entertainment Exports*, 30 Law and Policy in International Business 585 (1997).

Cone, Sidney, *The Appellate Body and Harrowsmith Country Life*, 32 (2) Journal of World Trade 103 (1998)

Eberschlag, Robert, *Culture Clash: Canadian periodical Policies and the World trade Organization*, 26 Manitoba Law Journal 65 (1998)

Ezetah, Chinedu R., *Canadian Periodicals: Certain Measures Concerning Periodicals II. Review of the Case*, 9 European Journal of International Law (1998)

Filipek, Jon, *Culture Quotas: The Trade Controversy over the European Community's Broadcasting Directive*, 28 STANFORD JOURNAL OF INTERNATIONAL LAW 323, 340–342 (1992).

Gottselig Glen A., *Canada and Culture: Can Current Cultural Policies be Sustained in the Current Trade Regime?*, 5 International Journal of Communications Law and Policy 1 (2000)

Graber, Chistoph Beat, *Handel und Kultur im Audiovisionsrecht der WTO.* Völkerrechtliche, ökonomische und kulturpolitische Grundlagen einer globalen Medienordnung, Stämpfli Verlag, Bern, 2003.

[199] *Supra*, note 198, at 219.

Grant, Peter and Wood, Chris, *Blockbusters and Trade Wars, Popular Culture in a Globalized World*, Douglas & McIntyre, Vancouver, 2004.

Kakabadse, Mario A., *The WTO and the Commodification of Cultural Products: Implications for Asia*, 22(2) MEDIA ASIA 71–77 (1995)

Hahn, Michael J., *Eine kulturelle Bereichausnahme im Recht der WTO?*, 56 Zeitschrift für ausländisches und öffentliches Recht und Volkerrecht 315 (1996)

Higson, Andrew and Maltby, Richard, eds. "FILM EUROPE" AND "FILM AMERICA": "CINEMA, COMMERCE AND CULTURAL EXCHANGE 1920–1939" (1999)

Hyun-Kyung, Carolyn Kim, *Building the Korean Film Industry's Competitiveness: Abolish the Screen Quota and Subsidize the Film Industry*, 9 Pacific Rim Law and Policy Journal 71 (2000).

Hubin, Cécile, *Politique culturelle et GATT. À propos des mesures canadiennes en faveur de l'industrie des périodiques*, 2 Revue de droit des affaires internationales 245 (1998)

Kaplan, Laurence G.C., *The European Community's Television Without Frontiers Directive: Stimulating Europe to Regulate Culture,* 8 EMORY INTERNATIONAL LAW REVIEW 225, 311–318 (1994).

Knight, Trevor, *The Dual Nature of Cultural Products: An Analysis of the World Trade Organization's Decisions Regarding Canadian Periodicals*, 57 UNIVERSITY OF TORONTO FACULTY OF LAW REVIEW 165, 179–80 (1999).

Landsman, Michael L., *Restricting Foreign Television Programming in Europe: The European Community's Television Quota Reappraised*, 8 Media Law and Policy 29 (1999).

Lehman, Amy E., *The Canadian Cultural Exception Clause and the Fight to Maintain an Identity,* 23 Syracuse Journal of International Law and Commerce (1997)

MacMillan, Joanne, *Trade and Culture: Conflicting Domestic Policies and International Trade Obligations*, 9 Windsor Review of Legal and Social Issues 5 (1999)

Matheny III, Richard L., *In the Wake of the Flood: 'Like Products' and Cultural Products after the World Trade Organization's Decision in Canada—Certain Measures Concerning Periodicals*, 147 UNIVERSITY OF PENNSYLVANIA LAW REVIEW, 245, 264 (1998).

Ming Shao, W. "*Is There No Business Like Show Business? Free Trade and Cultural Protectionism*", 20 Yale Journal of International Law, 105, 121–122 (1995)

Murray, Thomas M., *The U.S. French Dispute Over GATT Treatment of Audiovisual Products and the Limits of Public Choice Theory: How an Efficient Market Solution was "Rent-Seeking"*, 21 Maryland Journal of International Law and Trade 203 (1997).

O'Keefe, R., *The Right "to Take Part in the Cultural Life" under Article 15 of the ICESCR*, 47 International and Comparative Law Quarterly 904 (1998)

Paul, J.R., *Cultural Resistance to Global Governance*, 22 Michigan Journal of International Law 82 (2000–2001)

Polka, S.E., *Canada's Cultural Industries, the United States and Trade Law: tensions, conflicts and possibilities*, 10 Windsor Review of Legal and Social Issues 105 (2000)

Prowda, Judith Beth, *U.S. Dominance in the "Market Place of Culture" and the French "Cultural Exception*", 29 New York University Journal of International Law and Politics 193 (1997)

Puentes, A.T., The Politics of Music and Film: the Validity of a Local Government Embargo on Cuba, 31 Miami Inter-American Law Review 253 (2000)

Ragosta, John, *The Information Revolution—Culture and Sovereignty—A U.S. Perspective*, 24 Canada–U.S. Law Journal 155 (1998)

Raboy, Marc, Bernier, Ivan, Sauvageau, Florian and Atkinson, Dave, *Cultural Development and the Open Economy: A Democratic Issue and a Challenge to Public policy*, 19 Canadian Journal of Communication 291 (1994)

Rothkopf, David, *In Praise of Cultural Imperialism*, 107 Foreign Policy 38 (Summer 1997)

Sauvé, Pierre and Steinfatt, Karsten, *Towards multilateral rules on trade and culture: protective regulation or efficient protection?,* in Productivity Commission and Australian National University, Conference on Achieving Better Regulation of Services, Canberra, 2000: http://www.pc.gov.au/research/confproc/abros/paper13.pdf

Schwanen, Daniel, *A Room of Our Own: Cultural Policies and Trade Agreements*, 7(4) Choices IRPP, Institute for Research on Public Policy, Montreal, 2001

Scow, Aaron, *The Sports Illustrated Canadian Controversy: Canada 'Strikes Out' in Its Bid to Protect Its Periodical Industry from U.S. Split-Run Periodicals*, 7 MINNESOTA JOURNAL OF GLOBAL TRADE 245, 277 (1998)

Sinclair, John, *Culture and Trade: Some Theoretical and Practical Considerations*, in McAnany, Emile G. and Wilkinson, Kenton T., Mass Media and Free Trade—NAFTA and the Cultural Industries, University of Texas Press, 30 (1996)

Van Harpen, Robin L., *Mamas, Don't Let Your Babies Grow Up to Be Cowboys: Reconciling Trade and Cultural Independence,* 4 MINNESOTA JOURNAL OF GLOBAL TRADE 167 (1995).

Venturelli, Shalini, *FROM THE INFORMATION ECONOMY TO THE CREATIVE ECONOMY; Moving Culture to the Centre of International Public Policy,* Washington DC, Centre for Arts and Culture, 2001, 40 p.

Warnier, Jean-Paul, *La mondialisation de la culture*, Éditions La Découverte, Paris, 1999.

WTO (World Trade Organization) 'Audiovisual services, Background note by the Secretariat', Sectoral Paper S/C/W/40, Council for Trade in Services, WTO, Geneva, 1998.

Author Biographies

Ratnakar Adhikari is the Executive Director of South Asia Watch on Trade, Economics and Environment (SAWTEE), Kathmandu, an organization he co-founded in 1994. Prior to joining this organization full time in 1999, he was working with Nepal Indosuez Bank Ltd. (a Member of the Credit Agricole Group) as Credit Manager. He served as a lecturer of Marketing Management and Managerial Economics at Tribhuvan University, Kathmandu. He is also the Vice-president of Forum for Protection of Public Interest (Pro Public), a public interest research and advocacy organization based in Kathmandu, which was co-founded by him in 1991. He served on the Program Advisory Board of the International Center for Trade and Sustainable Development (ICTSD), Geneva between 1997 and 2000. Mr. Adhikai has written extensively on trade policy, food security, consumer protection, competition policy, environment and sustainable development and livelihood issues. He has edited and written numerous trade-related publications and is currently co-editing a volume on the protection of farmers' rights in the Himalayas. He has represented his organization and presented papers at various national, regional and International seminars and conferences. Mr. Adhikari holds a Master of Commerce (M.Com) degree from Delhi School of Economics, and a Master in International Law and Economics (MILE) from the World Trade Institute, Bern.

Kym Anderson is Professor of Economics and Associate Dean (Research) in the School of Economics and foundation Executive Director of the Centre for International Economic Studies at the University of Adelaide, where he has been affiliated since 1984. From mid-2004 he has been an extended leave at the Development Research Group of the World Bank in Washington DC, as Lead Economist (Trade Policy). Previously he was a Research Fellow in Economics at ANU's Research School of Pacific and Asian Studies (1977–83), following undergraduate studies at the University of New England in Armidale (1967–70), part-time Masters studies at the University of Adelaide (1971–74) and doctoral studies at the University of Chicago and Stanford University (1974–77). During periods of leave he has spent time in Korea (1980–81), Stockholm (1988) and at the GATT (now WTO) Secretariat in Geneva (1990–92). His research interests and publications are in the areas of international trade and development, agricultural economics, and environmental and resource economics in addition to the economics of wine. He has published twenty books and about two hundred articles in journals and other books. He has been a Research Fellow of Europe's London-based Centre for Economic Policy Research since 1992, a Fellow of the Academy of Social Sciences in Australia since 1994, a Fellow of the American Agricultural Economics Association since 2004, and a Distinguished Fellow of the Australian Agricultural and Resource Economics Society since 2002. He was the first economist to serve on a series of dispute settlement panels at the World Trade Organization (concerning the EU's banana import regime), 1996–2000. In 1996–97 he served on a panel advising the Ministers for Foreign Affairs and Trade in their preparation of Australia's first White Paper on Foreign and Trade Policy. Since the late 1970s he has been a consultant with all the major international economic agencies including the World Bank, OECD, UN and ADB.

Stewart A. Baker is a partner with the Washington, D.C., law firm of Steptoe & Johnson. His practice includes issues relating to privacy, national security, computer security, electronic surveillance, encryption, digital commerce, and export controls. He has advised hardware and software companies on U.S. export controls and on foreign import controls on encryption. He also represents major telecommunications equipment manufacturers and carriers in connection with the Communications Assistance for Law Enforcement Act (CALEA) and law enforcement intercept requirements. Mr. Baker is the former

General Counsel of the National Security Agency (1992–1994) and the author of a book and several publications and articles on electronic commerce and international trade. Mr. Baker has been named to numerous US government and international bodies dealing with electronic commerce and related topics, including: Defense Science Board's Task Force on Information Warfare (1995–1996; and 1999–2001); Federal Trade Commission's Advisory Committee on Online Access and Security (2000); President's Export Council Subcommittee on Encryption (1998–2001); Free Trade of the Americas Experts Committee on Electronic Commerce (1998-present); UNCITRAL Group of Experts on Digital Signatures (1997–2001); OECD Group of Experts on Cryptography Policy (1995–1997); International Telecommunication Union Experts Group on Authentication (1999); American Bar Association Task Force on International Notarial Issues (1996–1998); International Chamber of Commerce Working Party on Digital Authentication.

Ivan Bernier is a Professor at the Faculty of Law, Laval University, Quebec City. Ph.D. in Law, London School of Economics, 1969. Dean of the Law Faculty, Laval University, 1981–1985. Director, Quebec Centre for International Relations, 1986–1993. Since 1998, he is a member of a Sectoral advisory group on cultural industries which reports to the Canadian Department of Foreign Affairs and International Trade. He has taught and done research on GATT/WTO, NAFTA and international cultural relations. On the roster of panelists for dispute settlement under NAFTA and the WTO, he has sat on two FTA cases. He is the author and co-author of a number of books and articles dealing with the topic of trade and culture. More recently, he has acted as consultant for the Working Group on Cultural Diversity of the International Network on Cultural Policy, the Department of Canadian Heritage and the Quebec Department of Culture and Communications.

Jan Bohanes holds a Master of Laws and a Doctor of Laws degree from the Law Faculty of the University of Vienna, as well as a Master's degree in International Relations from the Fletcher School of Law and Diplomacy. He is currently Legal Affairs Officer in the Appellate Body Secretariat of the World Trade Organization in Geneva. Formerly, he has held positions of researcher with the Trade Law Center for Southern Africa (TRALAC) in Stellenbosch, South Africa and legal clerk in the Austrian judiciary. His areas of interest include WTO dispute settlement, trade and environment as well as the concerns of developing countries in the global trading system.

Chad P. Bown is an Assistant Professor in the Department of Economics and International Business School at Brandeis University. Professor Bown received his PhD in economics from the University of Wisconsin-Madison, and he has been a Visiting Fellow at the Center for European Integration Studies (ZEI) in Bonn (Germany). Dr. Bown has had his research funded by grants from the Mellon and Schulhof Foundations, and has published extensively on trade-related issues.

Drusilla K. Brown is an Associate Professor of Economics at Tufts University. She was first appointed as a lecturer in 1983, was promoted to Assistant Professor in 1985 and Associate Professor in 1991. She received her Ph.D. in Economics from the University of Michigan in 1984, under the direction of Alan V. Deardorff and Robert M. Stern. Her research focuses primarily on the use of Applied General Equilibrium Models to evaluate preferential trade agreements. In addition, Professor Brown has worked on the theoretical issues concerning international labor standards and child labor. Recent publications include, "International Labor Standards: Where do they belong on the International Trade Agenda?" JOURNAL OF ECONOMIC PERSPECTIVES," Summer 2001, "Child Labor In Latin America: Policy And Evidence," 24(6) WORLD ECONOMY (2001), and "Measurement and

Modeling of the Economic Effects of Trade and Investment Barriers in Services," with R. Stern, 9(2) REVIEW OF INTERNATIONAL ECONOMICS (2001).

Carlos M. Correa is a Professor and the Director of the Center for Interdisciplinary Studies of Industrial Property Law and Economics, University of Buenos Aires as well as of the Post-graduate Courses on Intellectual Property and of the Masters Program on Science and Technology Policy and Management of the same University. He has been a visiting professor in post-graduate courses of the Universidad Carlos III (Madrid, Spain), Tulane University (New Orleans, U.S.A.), Universidad del Externado (Colombia), UNAM (Mexico), Universidad Nacional de Ingeniería (Peru), among others. He has also taught international trade law at the University of Toronto. He has been a consultant to UNCTAD, UNIDO, WHO, FAO, Inter American Development Bank, INTAL, World Bank, SELA, ECLA, UNDP and other regional and international organizations in different areas of law and economics, including investment, science and technology and intellectual property. He has advised several governments on those issues and has been a consultant to the Rockefeller Foundation. He was a member of the UK International Commission on Intellectual Property, established in 2001. He is the author of several books and numerous articles on law and economics, particularly on investment, technology and intellectual property. His recent publications include works on intellectual property and international trade; integrating public health concerns into patent legislation; policy options for intellectual property legislation on genetic resources; international investment regimes; and competition law and development policies.

Meredith Crowley is an economist in the research department at the Federal Reserve Bank of Chicago. Ms. Crowley provides research and analysis on the international economy. Her research interests include theoretical and empirical models of international trade, political economy, special forms of import protection, and technology adoption. Ms. Crowley received a bachelor's degrees in Asian Studies and chemistry from Bowdoin College (Brunswick, ME), a master of public policy degree in international trade and finance from Harvard University, and a master's and doctorate degrees in economics from the University of Wisconsin-Madison.

Alan V. Deardorff is John W. Sweetland Professor of International Economics and Professor of Economics and Public Policy at the University of Michigan. He received his Ph.D. in economics from Cornell University in 1971 and, since 1970, has been on the faculty at the University of Michigan where he served as Chair of the Economics Department from 1991 to 1995. He is co-author, with Robert M. Stern, of *The Michigan Model of World Production and Trade* and *Computational Analysis of Global Trading Arrangements* and has published numcrous articles on aspects of international trade theory and policy. His work on international trade theory has dealt primarily with theories of the patterns and effects of trade. With Professor Stern and with Professor Drusilla K. Brown he has developed a series of computable general equilibrium models of world production, trade, and employment that have been used to analyze the effects of both multilateral and regional initiatives for trade liberalization. Professor Deardorff's current research interests include: the role of trade costs in determining patterns of international trade, the causes and effects of fragmentation, and the appropriate use of trade policies for issues of economic inequality, including labor standards and child labor.

Janelle M. Diller is Policy Adviser in the Employment Sector of the International Labour Office, with a focus on integrating international labor standards into technical and advisory activities. Ms. Diller has worked with the ILO since 1998, as director of the ILO Multinationals Enterprises Programme, legal officer in the Office of the Legal Adviser, and adviser to the Secretariat for the World Commission on the Social Dimension of Globalization. On leave in 2002–03, she was Associate Professor of international law at the University of St. Thomas School of Law (Minneapolis). Prior to ILO, she taught as adjunct professor at Georgetown University Law Center and the University of Virginia School of Law. From 1990–1995, Ms. Diller was Legal Director/Advisor with the International Human Rights Law Group in Washington, D.C. Her previous work included U.S. federal appellate law practice and a judicial clerkship in the US District Court for the District of Puerto Rico. She completed the Bachelor of Arts in Religious Studies (magna cum laude) at Wheaton College, an M.A. (Journalism) at Syracuse University, and the J.D. degree (cum laude) at Georgetown University.

Esperanza Durán is the founding Director of the Agency for International Trade Information and Cooperation (Geneva, Switzerland). She has wide experience in the field of international trade and development and has numerous publications on international economics, particularly on trade and development. In addition to her research and teaching in institutions on both sides of the Atlantic (in particular at the Colegio de México, the Royal Institute of International Affairs (Chatham House) in London and the London School of Economics; at the Johns Hopkins School of Advanced International Studies (SAIS), in Washington, D.C) she has held posts of responsibility in intergovernmental organizations, such as Senior Economist at the International Monetary Fund and the World Gold Council and economist, and country officer at the World Bank. She holds an M.A. from Stanford University and a D. Phil. from St. Antony's College, Oxford.

Christopher Findlay is a Professor of Economics in the Asia Pacific School of Economics and Government at the Australian National University. Prior to that he was Associate Professor of Economics at the University of Adelaide. Professor Findlay is a principal researcher in a major research program on impediments to services trade and investment. Professor Findlay is the Chair (from April 1998) of the Pacific Economic Cooperation Council's Coordinating Group (CG). From September 1998 to December 2003, Professor Findlay was responsible for the Secretariat services provided to the Australian members of the APEC Business Advisory Council (ABAC). Professor Findlay has a Ph.D. and M.Ec. from the ANU and an Honors degree in economics from the University of Adelaide.

Michael Gestrin is currently a Senior Economist at the Investment Division of the OECD in Paris where the focus of his work is on international investment in developing countries. He is currently responsible for a project to develop a Policy Framework for Investment, a voluntary guide to help countries attract more investment and a key element of the OECD Initiative on Investment for Development. Previously he worked as an economist for the Trade Directorate of the OECD, as a research associate at Templeton College, University of Oxford, and as an economist at UNCTAD in Geneva. He has a DPhil from the University of Oxford, the focus of which was the profitability of FDI, and an MA in economics from the University of Toronto.

Robert Herzstein was lead counsel to Mexico in negotiating and implementing the NAFTA, and previously served as counsel to Israel and to Canada as they negotiated free trade agreements with the U.S. He was the first Under Secretary for International Trade, U.S. Department of Commerce and head of the International Trade Administration. He has taught at Harvard Law School on "NAFTA and Lawmaking in the Global Economy." He has practiced law in Washington regarding international trade, investment, and regulatory issues for over 30 years, and is currently with Miller & Chevalier.

William E. James is presently Senior International Economist, International Trade Group, Nathan Associates, Inc. and is serving as an advisor to the government of Indonesia, under the USAID-funded Growth through Investment, Agriculture and Trade (GIAT) Project. He has also served as advisor to the Ministry of Industry and Trade, and the central bank, Bank Indonesia, government of Indonesia. Dr. James has held positions as a member of the graduate faculty of the University of Hawaii and Kyushu University in Fukuoka, Japan. He has been Chief, Research Division of the International Centre for the Study of East Asian Development in Kitakyushu, Japan. He has also been a Senior Fellow and Assistant Director of the Institute for Economic Development and Policy at the East-West Center, Honolulu, Hawaii. Dr. James has published numerous books, book chapters and scientific papers on Asian Economic problems. His published works include: Indonesia: Deregulation and Development (2002); Public Policies in East Asian Development (1999) and Asian Development (1989).

Merit E. Janow is Professor in the Practice of International Trade at Columbia University's School of International and Public Affairs (SIPA). Professor Janow is also Director of the International Economic Policy concentration at SIPA and Co-Director of Columbia's APEC Study Center. Professor Janow teaches graduate courses in international economic and trade policy at SIPA and international trade law and comparative/international antitrust at Columbia Law School. For two years, ending in March 2000, Professor Janow served as Executive Director of a new International Competition Policy Advisory Committee to the Attorney General and Assistant Attorney General for Antitrust at the Department of Justice, Washington D.C. Before joining Columbia University from 1990–1993, Professor Janow served as a Deputy Assistant U.S. Trade Representative for Japan and China at the Office of the U.S. Trade Representative, Executive Office of the President in Washington D.C. At USTR, she negotiated over a dozen trade agreements with Japan and several with the PRC. Prior to her tenure in government, she was an Associate at Skadden, Arps, Slate, Meagher & Flom, specializing in international corporate mergers and acquisitions. She is the author of numerous articles and several books on international economic law and policy matters and on US-Japan/China trade and economic issues. Professor Janow has served as a panelist in a dispute before the WTO and serves on the board of directors of several global mutual funds. She received a B.A. in Asian Studies from the University of Michigan and a J.D. from Columbia Law School.

Mordechai Kreinin is a University Distinguished Professor of Economics at Michigan State University and past President of the International Trade and Finance Association. He is the author of about two hundred articles and nine books in economics, including the widely used text, INTERNATIONAL ECONOMICS, now in its ninth edition. Professor Kreinin has been a consultant to numerous international and national (U.S.) organizations in both the public and private sectors. He is the recipient of numerous awards. Professor Kreinin has been visiting professor at ten universities in the United States, Canada, Europe and Australia, and has also lectured to both professional economists and lay audiences (business, government and other groups) in the United States and many foreign countries, including fifteen around-the-world or regional lecture tours. He works extensively with both the print and electronic media. He has also been very active in University governance, and in the 1980s developed University-wide plans to deal with financial exigencies that were adopted at Michigan State and several other universities throughout the U.S.

Sheldon Leader is a graduate of Yale and Oxford Universities, and is a member of the UK Bar. He is Professor, Department of Law and Centre for Human Rights, University of Essex. He works on developing practical links between trade, investment and human rights as a legal advisor to Amnesty International's Business and Human Rights section, and has recently helped formulate a legally binding human rights undertaking for the Baku-Ceyhan pipeline. Leader teaches a course on international trade and human rights; as well as jurisprudence; corporate law; and labor/employment law. His current research is into the extension of fundamental rights as constraints on, and guarantees to, non-state actors. Some relevant publications are; *Human Rights on the Line: the Baku-Ceyhan Pipeline*, Amnesty International UK, 2003 (with A. Shemberg); "*The Reach of Democracy and Global Enterprise*" in *Constellations*, Vol. 8, No. 4 (2001) pp. 538–553; "*Three Faces of Justice and the Management of Change*": 63 *Modern Law Review* (2000) *p.* 55–83; "*Integration, Federation, and the Ethics of Rights*" in *Morale et politique des Droits de l'homme* ed. Monique Costillo (Georg Olms Verlag: 2003).

Peter John Lloyd is an Emeritus Professor of Economics at the University of Melbourne. His main areas of specialization are international economics and microeconomics. He is an author or an editor of ten books and has written nine monographs and over one hundred articles in refereed journals or chapters in books. He has been a consultant to the OECD, the GATT, WTO, UNCTAD, the World Bank and a number of government departments and authorities in Australia and New Zealand. He was the joint editor of the Journal of the Economic Society of Australia, *The Economic Record*, for five years and has served on numerous committees for the Economic Society, the International Economic Association, the Academy of the Social Sciences of Australia and other bodies. He is a Life member of the Victorian Branch of the Economic society. He was Dean of the Faculty of Economics and Commerce at the University of Melbourne from 1988 to 1993.

Rachel McCulloch is the Rosen Family Professor of International Finance at Brandeis University. Prior to joining the Brandeis faculty in 1987, she taught at the University of Chicago, Harvard University, and the University of Wisconsin-Madison. Dr. McCulloch serves on the Academic Advisory Council of the Federal Reserve Bank of Boston and the Advisory Committee of the Institute for International Economics, Washington, D.C. She was also a member of the Technology Assessment Advisory Council of the U.S. Congressional Office of Technology Assessment (1979–87), the President's Commission on Industrial Competitiveness (1984–85), and the Committee on International Relations Studies with the Peoples Republic of China (1984–92). Dr. McCulloch has published extensively on economic issues.

Eugenia McGill is an international lawyer and gender specialist, and consults with international and nongovernmental organizations on law and human development issues. In the area of international trade and investment, she recently collaborated with two economists on a framework for assessing trade and investment agreements from a gender perspective, commissioned by the Coalition for Women's Economic Development and Global Equality (Women's EDGE) with support from the Rockefeller Foundation. She worked previously as counsel and senior administrative/policy officer for the Asian Development Bank, based in Manila, and as an international finance lawyer with Cleary, Gottlieb, Steen and Hamilton in New York City and Hong Kong. She has a law degree from the University of Pennsylvania (1984), a masters in international affairs from Columbia University (2000) and an undergraduate degree from Williams College.

Charles Pearson is Professor and Director of the International Economics Program at the School of International Studies at the Johns Hopkins University. His areas of expertise include international economics, economic development, energy and environment, and multinational corporations. He served as a senior staff economist for the Commission on International Trade and Investment Policy and as a consultant to the World Bank, the U.S. Department of Commerce and other organizations; and has been an adjunct senior associate at the World Resources Institute and at the East-West Center. He received his Ph.D. in economics from Cornell University. Publications include: ECONOMICS AND THE GLOBAL ENVIRONMENT (2000); FREE TRADE, FAIR TRADE? THE REAGAN RECORD (1989); DOWN TO BUSINESS: MULTINATIONAL CORPORATIONS, THE ENVIRONMENT AND DEVELOPMENT (1985); and ENVIRONMENT: NORTH AND SOUTH (1978).

Ernst-Ulrich Petersmann is Professor of International and European Law at the European University Institute (EUI) at Florence and Academic Director of the EUI's Transatlantic Program at the Robert Schuman Centre for Advanced Studies. He previously taught at the Universities of Geneva, Lausanne, Fribourg, St. Gallen (Switzerland), Saarland, Heidelberg and Hamburg (Germany), as well as visiting professor in the Americas, Africa and Asia. He worked as legal adviser in the World Trade Organization, GATT and the German Ministry of Economic Affairs, as German representative in numerous international organizations, and as secretary, member or chairman of numerous GATT and WTO dispute settlement panels. His publications include twenty books and more than two hundred articles and book contributions.

Michael G. Plummer is Professor of International Economics, Johns Hopkins University SAIS-Bologna. He was previously Associate Professor of Economics with tenure (1998–2001) and Assistant Professor of Economics (1993–1998), Brandeis University; and Reseach Fellow, East-West Center (1988–1993). His main fields of interest are international economic integration and Asian economic development. He received his Ph.D. and M.A. in Economics from Michigan State University and holds a BA in Economics and French from the University of Michigan. Academic honors and positions include: Fulbright Chair in Economics, Viterbo (2000); Pew Fellow in International Affairs, Harvard University (1994–95); research professor, Kobe University (1996–97); Editorial Board, *World Development* and *Journal of Asian Economics*; visiting scholar, International Center for Study of South East Asian Development (2002), University of Auckland (1999), and Institute of Southeast Asian Studies (1997); and faculty member, Summer Macroeconomic Policy Program, Harvard Institute of International Development (1995–1997). He is consultant to numerous international and official organizations, and has published extensively in the general areas of international economics and Asian economic development. He is a Co-editor of this book.

Richard Pomfret is Professor of Economics at Adclaide University. Before coming to Adelaide in 1992, he was Professor of Economics at the Johns Hopkins University School of Advanced International Studies in Washington DC, Bologna (Italy) and Nanjing (China). In 1993 he was seconded to the United Nations for a year, acting as adviser on macroeconomic policy to the Asian republics of the former Soviet Union, and he has since then been a consultant to the World Bank, UNDP and Asian Development bank on Central Asian issues. He has written seventeen books, including books on China, Central Asia, Regional Trading Arrangements, as well as textbooks on Canadian economic development, international trade theory and policy, and development economics.

Francisco Javier Prieto is former chair of the Free Trade Area of the Americas (FTAA) Working Group on Services and a consultant on services to the Ministry of Foreign Affairs, Chile. Previous positions include work with the UNCTAD Secretariat in Geneva,

Switzerland and with the ECLAC Secretariat in Santiago de Chile. He was responsible for negotiating services for the Chilean Government in the US-Chile Free Trade Agreement, concluded in 2002.

Alan M. Rugman has published widely, appearing in leading refereed journals that deal with economic, managerial and strategic aspects of multinational enterprises, and with trade and investment policy. His recent books include: *Multinationals as Flagship Firms* (co-author) (Oxford University Press 2000); *International Business* (FT/Prentice Hall 2003); *The End of Globalization* (Random House 2000; 2001); (co-ed) *The Oxford Handbook of International Business* (Oxford University Press 2001) and, forthcoming, *The Regional Multinationals* (Cambridge University Press 2005).

Professor Rugman is one of the world's leading researchers in multinational business. An International expert on free trade among nations, he has served as a consultant to major private sector companies, research institutes, government agencies, and served as an outside advisor on free trade, foreign investment, and international competitiveness to two Canadian Prime Ministers.

Professor Rugman was Thames Water Fellow in Strategic Management at Templeton College, University of Oxford, where he remains an Associate Fellow. Dr. Rugman previously served as Vice-President of the Academy of International Business is now President-Elect, and beginning August 2004 will serve as President until 2006.

Maurice Schiff is a Lead Economist in the International Trade Unit, Development Research Group, World Bank. He obtained a B.A. and M.A. from the Hebrew University and a Ph.D. from the University of Chicago in 1983. Before joining the World Bank, he was Research Director in the Faculty of Economics and Management at the University of Concepcion, Chile. He is currently doing research on regional integration and on trade and technology transfers. He has published some ten books and a large number of articles in the areas of agriculture and the macroeconomy, regionalism, trade and migration, social capital, international knowledge diffusion, nutrition, and commodity trade policy. His work has included policy analysis and advice in Sub-Saharan Africa, Latin America, the Middle East, North Africa and Central Asia.

Magda Shahin, who holds a Ph.D. in Economics from Cairo University, is Ambassador of Egypt to Greece (2001). She served previously as Assistant Minister of Foreign Affairs for International Economic Relations. Parallel to her diplomatic function, Dr. Shahin was Professor of Economics at the American University in Cairo (AUC) teaching on selected topics, notably the Multilateral Trading System (GATT/WTO) and the Developing countries (1997–2001). She was a Counselor at the Egyptian Mission to the United Nations in New York (1984–1989), as well as Deputy Chief of Mission at the Egyptian Mission to the United Nations – Geneva (1992–1997). She has served as a member of the WTO Textiles Monitoring Body during her tenure in Geneva and is on the WTO's Indicative List of Panelists. Mrs. Shahin has also served as a Consultant and an expert in various seminars, symposiums and workshops organized by UNCTAD/UNDP, ESCWA, and the Islamic Development Bank (IDB). She has written and published numerous articles in Arabic and English.

Maury Shenk is managing partner of the London office of Steptoe & Johnson. His practice focuses on the international aspects of electronic commerce and telecommunications. Mr. Shenk advises frequently on the WTO issues facing e-commerce and telecommunications companies, and was actively involved as a representative of US industry in the negotiations of the WTO Basic Telecommunications Agreement.

Sherry M. Stephenson is Deputy Director of the Trade Unit of the Organization of American States. Her responsibility includes overseeing the role of the OAS in providing analytical support to the majority of the negotiating groups in the Free Trade Area of the Americas (FTAA) negotiations as well as providing direct support to the FTAA Negotiating Group on Services and technical assistance to the countries participating in the FTAA process. She received a Ph.D. in International Economics from the Graduate Institute of International Studies, University of Geneva, Switzerland in 1986, and an M.A. in Economics from New York University. Prior to her position with the OAS, Dr. Stephenson was an Advisor to the Ministry of Trade, Government of Indonesia, Jakarta, for three years. Previous positions have been with the GATT and UNCTAD Secretariats in Geneva and with the Trade Directorate of the OECD in Paris. She has also done consulting work. Dr. Stephenson has taught within the Masters of Arts Program in International Commerce and Policy at George Mason University, Virginia. She is a member of the International Trade Policy Forum of the Pacific Economic Cooperation Council (PECC) and of the Inter-American Dialogue. Dr. Stephenson has written extensively on trade policy issues, particularly in the area of services and standards.

Robert M. Stern is Professor of Economics and Public Policy (Emeritus) in the Department of Economics and the Gerald R. Ford School of Public Policy at the University of Michigan and is also a Faculty Associate of the William Davidson Institute at the University of Michigan Business School. He received his PhD in Economics from Columbia University. He has published numerous papers and books on a variety of topics including international commodity issues, the determinants of comparative advantage, price behavior in international trade, balance-of-payments policies, the computer modeling of international trade and trade policies, trade and labor standards, and services liberalization. His current research interests include applications of the Michigan Model of World Production and Trade for the computational modeling and analysis of multilateral trade negotiations and regional trading blocs (jointly with Professor Deardorff and Professor Drusilla Brown of Tufts University), issues in U.S.-Japan international economic relations, international labor standards, and the political economy of U.S. trade policy.

Matthew Stilwell serves as a Senior Attorney at the Center for International Environmental Law's (CIEL) European Office and as Managing Director of the Program on Governance for Sustainable Development at the Bren School of Environmental Science and Management, University of California, Santa Barbara. Based in Geneva, he supports a range of governments, intergovernmental and non-governmental organizations on issues of international economic and environmental law. He teaches a Summer Program entitled *Institutions for Sustainable Development Governance* in Geneva and Paris on behalf of the American University and CIEL, and serves on UNEP's Working Group on Economic Instruments, and Working Group on Integrated Assessment. He holds a Masters Degree in Law from Columbia University's School of Law, and a Bachelor of Economics and Bachelor of Laws with Honors from the University of Tasmania.

Alan Sykes is the Frank & Bernice Greenberg Professor of Law at the University of Chicago. He received his J.D. from Yale in 1982 and a Ph.D., in economics from Yale in 1987. From 1982–1986, he was in private practice in Washington, D.C. at the firm of Arnold & Porter, specializing in international trade cases. He joined the Chicago faculty in 1986, and has served as Visiting Professor at New York University and Harvard Law Schools. He was editor of the Journal of Law and Economics from 1990–2000, and currently serves as editor of the Journal of Legal Studies, as an associate editor of the Journal of International Economic Law, and as a reporter for the American Law Institute project on Principles of Trade Law.

Friedl Weiss studied law at the Universities of Vienna, Brussels and Cambridge and is Professor for International Economic Law and International Organizations at the University of Amsterdam and Visiting Professor at the University of Louvain-la-Neuve. Friedl Weiss is member and rapporteur for trade and investment of the International Trade Law Committee and of the Committee on the Law of Foreign Investment of the International Law Association, as well as a member of the American, Austrian, German, Dutch and French Societies of International Law. He has worked as legal adviser in the EFTA Secretariat and as a legal consultant in the GATT. His research interests encompass public international law, especially international economic law, international organizations, including those of international economic governance (trade and monetary relations) and European Community law. His Recent Publications include: INTERNATIONAL LAW OF SUSTAINABLE DEVELOPMENT: PRINCIPLE AND PRACTICE (ed. with N. Schrijver) (2004); Free Movement of Persons Within the European Community, 30 EUROPEAN MONOGRAPHS (with Frank Wooldridge, 2001); IMPROVING WTO DISPUTE SETTLEMENT PROCEDURES. ISSUES AND LESSONS FROM THE PRACTICE OF OTHER INTERNATIONAL COURTS AND TRIBUNALS (ed.), (2000); and INTERNATIONAL ECONOMIC LAW WITH A HUMAN FACE, (with Paul de Waart and Eric Denters, eds., 1998).

Joseph P. Whitlock is an associate attorney at Miller & Chevalier Chartered. He focuses his practice on trade policy, Customs and intellectual property issues. In the trade policy area, he advises foreign Governments and private parties on trade negotiations, WTO and NAFTA disputes, and the interrelationship of national and multilateral trading rules. He also advises clients on a wide range of Customs issues, including classification and valuation matters, ruling requests, administrative settlements and Customs security programs. Finally, he helps clients enforce their intellectual property rights at the border through the U.S. Customs Service and advises clients on the TRIPs Agreement and Section 337 of the Tariff Act of 1930. Mr. Whitlock is a frequent contributor to U.S. and foreign trade-related publications.

L. Alan Winters is Professor of Economics at the University of Sussex. He is a Research Fellow of the Centre for Economic Policy Research (CEPR, London), and a Senior Visiting Fellow of the Centre for Economic Performance, at the London School of Economics. He was formerly Research Manager for International Trade in the World Bank and has worked at the Universities of Cambridge, Bristol, Wales and Birmingham. In addition he has advised, *inter alia*, the World Bank, OECD, the European Commission, the European Parliament, UNCTAD, the WTO, DfID and the Inter-American Development Bank. L. Alan Winters specializes on empirical and policy analysis of international trade. His one hundred and seventy published books and articles cover areas such as regional trading arrangements, non-tariff barriers, European Integration, East-West trade, global warming, agricultural protection, trade and poverty, and the world trading system.

INDEX

internal regulations affecting imports
  Article III:4, I:122–5
  Article III:5, I:125
  national treatment exceptions, I:125–7
  Article III:8(a), I:125
  Article III:8(b), I:126
  Article III:10, I:127
NATO. *See* North Atlantic Treaty Organization
natural economic bloc (NEB), II:13–14, 15. *See also*
    preferential trading arrangements
natural resources conservation, I:162
Negotiating Group on Basic Telecommunications
    (NGBT), I:926
Net Food-Importing Developing Countries, I:215–7
New Partnership for Africa's Development (NEPAD),
    III:363
New Zealand, III:270
  multilateral liberalization (Doha Round), III:280
    agriculture, III:280–82
    non-agricultural products, III:282
    rules, III:283–5
    services, III:283
    sustainable development, III:285–6
  trade liberalization, III:274
    bilateral liberalization (FTAs), III:277
    competitive liberalization, III:278–80
    regional liberalization (APEC), III:275–7
  trade policy, III:271
  Uruguay Round participation, III:272–4
NFIDC Decision. *See* Decision on Measures Concerning
    the Possible Negative Effects of the Reform
    Program on Least-Developed and Net
    Food-Importing Developing Countries
NGBT. *See* Negotiating Group on Basic
    Telecommunications
NGO. *See* non-governmental organizations
NIP. *See* Notice of Intended Procurement
non-automatic import licensing. *See also* Agreement on
    Import Licensing Procedures; automatic
    licensing system
  defined, I:592
  under AILP (Article 3), I:597
non-discrimination
  global free trade and, III:451–3
  principle under TBT Agreement, I:388
  under API (Article 2.1), I:576
  WTO and, I:40–41
non government bodies, under TBT Agreement
    (Article 8), I:387
non-governmental organizations (NGOs)
  external transparency issues, I:86
  global integration and, III:463–9
  Indonesia and, III:155
  Mexico, III:242–3
  panel process participation of, I:1239
  relations with WTO, I:72
  role in WTO, I:86–7
  trade policy development and, I:31
  WTO democratic roots and, I:47
non-market economies, I:77
  under ADA, I:508
non-preferential rules of origin, I:604; II:270–3.
        See also harmonized non-preferential rules
        of origin architecture; preferential rules of
        origin

non-product-related processes and production methods
    (NPR-PPM), I:238
  TBT Agreement and, I:392
  TBT Agreement inapplicability to, I:382
non-tariff barriers to trade (NTB), I:93. *See also*
    Agreement on Technical Barriers to Trade
  in MTN rounds, I:93
  in Tokyo Round, I:94
  under GATT
    Article V [Freedom of Transit], I:140
    Article VI [Antidumping and Countervailing Duties],
        I:140
    Article VII [Valuation for Customs Purposes], I:142
    Article VIII [Fees and Formalities Connected with
        Importation], I:143
    Article IX [Marks of Origin], I:144
    Article XV [Exchange Controls and Exchange
        Arrangements], I:146
    Article XVI [Subsidies], I:148
    Article XVII [State Trading Enterprises], I:148
    Article XIX [Emergency Action on Imports of
        Particular Products], I:151
non-violation complaints, I:1237. *See also* situation
    complaints; violation complaints
  under GATT, I:170–71
  re-appraisal, I:1372
    complaints origins, I:1373
    EC-Asbestos case, I:1379–82
    GATT 1947, complaints experience under, I:1374–7
    Korea-Government Procurement case, I:1377–9
    non-violation remedy and TRIPs Agreement,
        I:1384–7
    reflections on non-violation remedy, I:1382–4
    WTO Agreement (GATT 1994 and GPA), complaints
        experience under, I:1377
  under GATS (Article XXIII), I:868
  under TRIPs Agreement, I:1112
non-WTO rules application. *See under* dispute settlement
non-WTO treaties. *See under* World Trade Organization
    law
normative principles, II:609–10. *See also* values in trade
    and labor
North American Agreement on Labor Cooperation
    (NAALC), II:174, 175, 593
  gender analysis of, II:735
North American Free Trade Area (NAFTA), I:175; II:10,
    281. *See also* free trade areas
  Canada, III:40
  CUSFTA and, I:809, 810
  dispute settlement procedures innovations, II:213
  double density measures of trade intensity, II:20t
  EC and, I:807
  gender analysis of, II:735
  labor standards and, II:174, 175
  Mexico and, III:236
  RTAs and, II:297
    compatibility issues, II:309
    investment provisions and, II:318, 319
  rules of origin, II:279, 282
  trade facilitation and harmonization of domestic
      regulations, II:214
  Uruguay Round and regionalism, II:303
North Atlantic Treaty Organization (NATO), II:251
Notice of Intended Procurement (NIP), I:1149–50
Notice Of Planned Procurement (NPP), I:1150